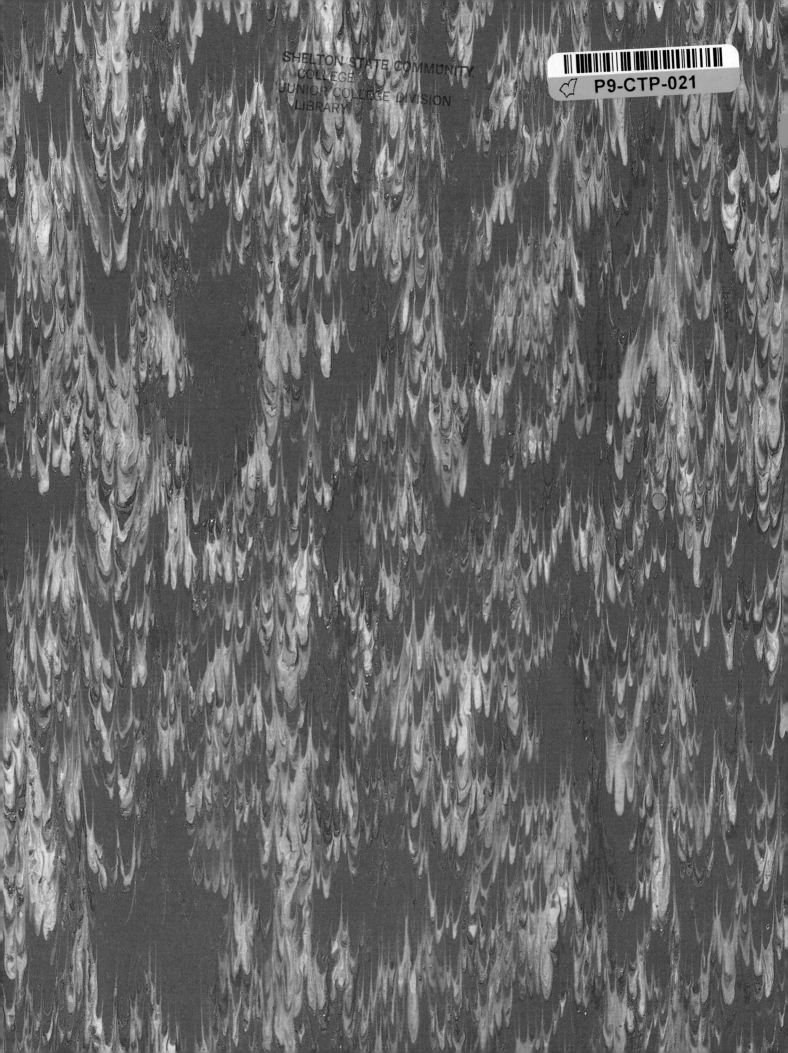

International
Encyclopedia of
Communications

THE UNIVERSITY OF PENNSYLVANIA

The *International Encyclopedia of Communications*
was conceived, developed, and edited at
The Annenberg School of Communications,
University of Pennsylvania.

International Encyclopedia of Communications

ERIK BARNOUW
Editor in Chief

GEORGE GERBNER
Chair, Editorial Board

WILBUR SCHRAMM
Consulting Editor

TOBIA L. WORTH
Editorial Director

LARRY GROSS
Associate Editor

Volume 2

Published jointly with
THE ANNENBERG SCHOOL OF COMMUNICATIONS,
University of Pennsylvania

OXFORD UNIVERSITY PRESS
New York   Oxford

Oxford University Press

Oxford   New York   Toronto
Delhi   Bombay   Calcutta   Madras   Karachi
Petaling Jaya   Singapore   Hong Kong   Tokyo
Nairobi   Dar es Salaam   Cape Town
Melbourne   Auckland

and associated companies in
Berlin   Ibadan

Published jointly by
The Annenberg School of Communications,
University of Pennsylvania,
and Oxford University Press, Inc.,
200 Madison Avenue, New York, New York 10016

Oxford is a registered trademark of Oxford University Press

Library of Congress Cataloging-in-Publication Data

International encyclopedia of communications / Erik Barnouw, editor-in-chief . . . [et al.].
p.   cm.
Bibliography: p.
Includes index.
1. Communication—Dictionaries.   I. Barnouw, Erik, 1908–   .
P87.5.I5   1989   001.51′0321—dc19   88-18132   CIP
ISBN 0-19-504994-2 (set)
ISBN 0-19-505802-X (vol. 1)
ISBN 0-19-505803-8 (vol. 2)
ISBN 0-19-505804-6 (vol. 3)
ISBN 0-19-505805-4 (vol. 4)

2 4 6 8 9 7 5 3 1

Printed in the United States of America
on acid-free paper

Editorial Board

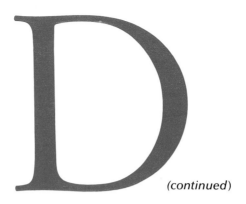

(continued)

DEMONSTRATION

Public manifestation of grievances and opinions, usually by way of processions or mass meetings. The right to dissent is generally regarded as fundamental to democracy, but the expression of that right and its portrayal by the media present serious problems in democratic societies. Demonstrations represent one form of the expression of dissent.

Demonstrations are not a new form of protest. Historically this form of collective behavior has always been part of the political processes of Western societies. Demonstrations have been used both as signaling and collective BARGAINING devices and have played a part in facilitating social and political change. Demonstrations differ in both purpose and form. They may be peaceful or violent or both. What starts out as peaceful may become violent and even develop into a riot.

The Role of Violence

Throughout history, collective VIOLENCE has been more normal, central, and historically rooted than is often thought. Rioting and violent demonstrations by the poor—both "respectable" and otherwise—in eighteenth- and nineteenth-century Europe have been well documented by historians. Those seeking to seize, hold, or realign the levers of power often have turned to collective violence as part of their struggles.

Terms such as violence are used and applied selectively in different political contexts. During the course of a demonstration, specific actions may be regarded as violent when coming from one group but as the legitimate use of force when carried out by another group. Much of what we now accept is the legitimated outcome of what was once regarded as violent. Official violence is frequently overlooked and the horrific outcomes of institutionalized violence conveniently forgotten.

No matter how demonstrations are portrayed, the evidence suggests that most of them are nonviolent and that when violence does occur it often stems from the frustration brought about by a lack of positive response to years of peaceful protest about deeply felt grievances. Some people join in demonstrations with violence in mind, but there are also examples of violent provocation by the forces of law and order that show both sides to be equally violent. Violence can be a cause as well as a symptom.

The media not only cover demonstrations as they occur; they also attempt to account for them and to advocate courses of action. In doing this they draw on conventional wisdom about the nature of collective behavior, the roots of social problems, the notion of law and order, and the relationships among these. Many people believe that the collective behavior associated with demonstrations marks off the unruly crowd from the respectable public. In this context, collective behavior, violent or peaceful, may be seen as disruptive, degenerate, deviant, irrational, meaningless, and provoked by external forces. Although some social scientists such as the French sociologist Gustave Le Bon offer support for this view, the available evidence does not. *See also* CROWD BEHAVIOR.

Nevertheless, this thinking has been used as an excuse for ignoring the basic causes of the problems that provoke demonstrations, so that attention has been focused on the demonstration or disruption rather than on the problem itself. When this happens, the official response has emphasized control and law and order rather than amelioration and social reform, notwithstanding the escalation of the problem that may ensue from such policies.

Media Coverage of Demonstrations

Despite national differences, media coverage of demonstrations is influenced by such climates of opinion.

1

Figure 1. *(Demonstration)* Women's suffrage parade in support of U.S. president Woodrow Wilson's campaign for women's votes, 1916. The Bettmann Archive, Inc.

The media are also influenced by other considerations that are internal to their structure and organization.

One of these internal considerations is the fact that the media operate within a system in which readers and viewers have to be won and kept. For the daily news media, persons, events, and happenings (particularly negative ones) are the basic units of news. One reason for the concentration on events is the *publication frequency* of the media. Events are more likely to be reported by the media working within a daily publication cycle if they occur within the space of one day. Thus a demonstration is a news event; the development of a political movement is not, as it lacks the correct "frequency." *See also* TELEVISION NEWS.

The concentration on events makes some aspects of a story more likely to become news than others. Violence may be directly related to the visible forms of events in the streets, but the focus on violence tends to exclude background, explanations, and context.

Research on the media coverage of one political demonstration in England pointed to similarities in presentation of fundamental issues right across the media. Viewers and readers were not presented with various interpretations focusing on different aspects of the same event but with basically the same interpretation of the same limited aspect, namely, violence. Yet in reality violence was not central. The "set" of violence was used because, together with the other implications of underpinning news values, it was the logical outcome of the existing organiza-tion of the news process and of the assumptions on which this rested.

This form of presentation could lead to labeling and stereotyping, to the association—perhaps unjustifiable—of certain groups with violent behavior, and possibly to the acceptance of violence as a legitimate way of dealing with problems or as a necessary form of retaliation (*see also* TERRORISM). Perceptions derived from these presentations may influence attitudes and behavior, so that they come to match the stereotype, and all sides behave as "expected."

In the aforementioned case, and given the climate of opinion at the time, the largely negative presentation by the media tended to devalue the case of the protesters. In the long run such practices might increase rather than reduce the risk of violence, because a minority group may have to do something violent before its case is presented to the general public.

There are also indications that, irrespective of the theme of the demonstration, the news story will center on violence and confrontation if there is any opportunity to do so. The account most likely will not mention antecedent conditions and will convey little understanding of either root causes or aims. Foreground prevails over background, and the whole presentation is fragmented and oversimplified. Moreover, this decontextualization tends to reinforce the tendency to put control before reform. Another consequence of this type of presentation is that alternative conceptions of social order are minimized or not considered at all; the status quo of power and control is maintained, with conflict and dissent being managed in the interest of whoever is in charge.

Figure 2. *(Demonstration)* A ban-the-bomb rally held during a special session of the UN General Assembly's conference on world disarmament, New York, 1978. UPI/Bettmann Newsphotos.

It is said, particularly by those who favor a law-and-order stance, that the media, especially television, offer support for the demonstrators by providing publicity, and that at times they may encourage disruptive behavior by their very presence and mode of reporting. Copycat behavior cannot be ruled out entirely, but there is no convincing evidence from research to support general claims for its inevitable occurrence. The presence of cameras may even reduce the likelihood of violence.

Staged incidents have occurred, but the relationships among the media (camera crews in particular), the demonstrators, and the police vary. The media have been seen as the enemy of the police, particularly when photographing police violence. But they have also been criticized by the demonstrators for being part of the establishment and for facilitating police identification of demonstrators. In the direct reporting of demonstrations, the position of the camera—more often than not behind police lines—is very important in determining what perspective is created.

Media portrayals of demonstrations have led to the increased visibility of a problem and perhaps to its amelioration in some cases. However, the degree to which a demonstration is an effective method of communication depends on factors other than the media; the media may simply reinforce the contending positions.

The views and criticisms of media coverage from both the right and the left are probably too crude to account for a complex situation adequately. For example, nonnews programs, including nonfiction, are not subject to the restrictions surrounding the news process. The news and some other programs are relatively closed to any but the "official" perspective, but other programs may be more open, so that alternative and even oppositional views are presented. Consequently, meanings can be negotiated from what is made available at any given time. *See also* FACT AND FICTION.

But this diversity is strictly limited in terms of what is available (quality and quantity) and the restricted use that is made of it. Consequently, although media presentation is not quite as closed as some would claim, the negotiations, the giving of meanings, are inevitably confined within the frameworks determined by available definitions of events and newsworthiness. Currently this tends to focus on the crowd/public approach to collective behavior.

The likelihood is, then, that even allowing for national differences and some degree of openness, the media (television in particular) in most Western societies will reinforce the prevailing simplistic analyses of complex situations in their portrayal of demonstrations. This might lead to an exacerbation of the situation, but it will certainly not lead to an increased understanding of the social conditions that give rise to demonstrations.

See also MASS MEDIA EFFECTS; POLITICAL COMMUNICATION—IMPACT OF NEW MEDIA.

Bibliography. James D. Halloran, Philip Elliot, and Graham Murdock, *Demonstrations and Communication*, London and Baltimore, Md., 1970; Philip Schlesinger, *Putting*

"Reality" Together: BBC News, London and Beverly Hills, Calif., 1978; Philip Schlesinger, Graham Murdock, and Philip Elliot, *Televising "Terrorism": Political Violence in Popular Culture*, London, 1983; Jerome H. Skolnick, *The Politics of Protest*, New York, 1969; John Stevenson and Roland Quinault, eds., *Popular Protest and Public Order*, London, 1974; Howard Tumber, *Television and the Riots*, London, 1982; Daniel Walker, ed., *Rights in Conflict*, New York, 1968.

JAMES D. HALLORAN

DESIGN

Design has two meanings: as a verb, it describes the activity of preparing instructions for the production of any physical ARTIFACT; as a noun, it may describe either those instructions or the general form or appearance of the finished article. It is in this latter, looser sense that most attention to design as communication has been directed, though of course the practice of design is itself a means of communication, with its own specific techniques and conventions.

History. The activity of design arose out of the division of labor between those who conceived the form of objects and those who made them. In craftwork this distinction does not arise. Since the object is generally both conceived and made by the same person or group of people, no preliminary set of instructions is required for them to follow, and design is not distinguished from the work of production. The first instances of design as a specialized practice occurred in the fifteenth-century Italian RENAISSANCE, when artists were employed to produce architectural designs for buildings to be executed by others (*see* ARCHITECTURE). This development also made it possible for buildings to be constructed in the absence of the architect, whose instructions might be conveyed in writing, by word of mouth, or through models or drawings. Drawings were used increasingly to communicate designs, and this development gave rise to special graphic techniques, particularly orthogonal projection, for conveying instructions to workers (*see* GRAPHICS).

The introduction of design into the production of artifacts occurred somewhat later than in architecture. In successive industries during the eighteenth and nineteenth centuries craftwork was replaced by workshop production, in which manufacture was broken down into separate processes carried out by individuals, and an additional, design stage of production was required to prepare instructions or patterns for workers to follow in their various tasks. Designers were known differently in different industries—in the English pottery industry as modelers, in printed textiles as pattern drawers. The eighteenth-century English pottery manufacturer Josiah Wedgwood relied heavily on modelers and employed artists

from outside the industry to introduce nontraditional forms that would be attractive to fashionable markets.

Mechanization and mass production did not alter the basic nature of design but made it infinitely more valuable, as substantial investment in tools and plant made the variety found in craft industries uneconomical. The more articles produced to a single design, the more valuable that design becomes. Recognition of this fact in the nineteenth century stimulated the introduction of COPYRIGHT to protect ownership of designs. Recognition of the importance of design in commercial competition also led to the establishment of organized (and, in some countries, government-backed) training for designers.

The establishment of design as an activity separate from the rest of production stimulated innovation in product form. Appearance previously had been determined largely by the traditions of the craft, but the freedom to employ designers with different training, from different geographical areas, and often with their own contact with fashionable markets, created

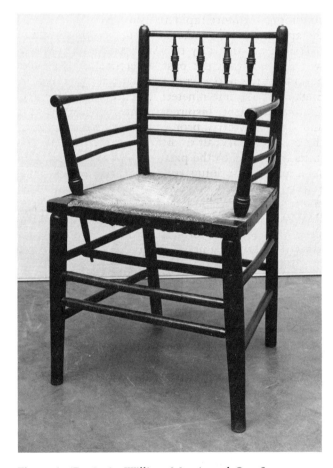

Figure 1. *(Design)* William Morris and Co., Sussex chair, ca. 1865. Ebonized beech with rush seat. Courtesy of the Board of Trustees of the Victoria and Albert, London.

Figure 2. *(Design)* The Model T Ford. Courtesy of Ford Motor Company.

conditions for more rapid and substantial changes in the appearance of goods. *See* ARTIST AND SOCIETY.

Style. Until the early twentieth century most style was derived from the past, reference to particular periods of the past carrying specific associations. In England in the late nineteenth century the Arts and Crafts movement, inspired mainly by John Ruskin and William Morris, promoted a style deriving from the continuity of craft traditions that was nonspecific in its references to the past (*see* TYPOGRAPHY). This style exalted the intuitive, tradition-derived knowledge of the artisan above that of the trained designer and in this way attempted to subvert the entire post-Renaissance development of the specialization of design. Traditional or vernacular forms continue to be used, usually to signify opposition to the dominant CULTURE.

In the early twentieth century a new style that referred neither to the past nor to tradition was developed in Europe, especially in Germany. This kind of design aimed to express efficiency, scientific rationalism, and social utopia (*see* UTOPIAS). Often known as functionalism (from the aphorism "form follows function"), it was claimed to derive from the logic of the manufacturing process and was often presented as a language of design so perfectly rational as to be styleless. The success of Henry Ford's standardized automobile, the Model T, was widely cited as an example. Functionalism was associated particularly with the Bauhaus, a German school of design operating between 1918 and 1933, but similar ideas were held in other countries and formed a basic premise of modernism in design. Although a historical critique of functionalism was not offered until 1960, by Reyner Banham, its practical weaknesses had been exposed in the late 1920s when Ford's main rival, General Motors, began to produce automobiles in various different styles and succeeded in capturing a significant share of the market. Ford was forced to abandon the standard design and in 1927 introduced the Model A, which had styled bodywork. From that time on, the U.S. automobile industry was committed to styling, creating in the process a specific automobile imagery that was to be highly influential and was used for many other, quite unrelated products.

Design and communication. To some people design conveys quite specific things, like the technical expertise of the manufacturer or the aesthetic ideas of the designer; others regard it as an ideological practice that casts into physical, tangible form general and unstated ideas about the social order and social relations, ideas designers themselves may not be conscious of in their work. The construction of MEANING in design arises out of the conjunction of the processes of production, mediation (e.g., ADVERTISING), and reception or consumption. Here again there is disagreement about the relative importance that should be ascribed to each of these processes in the interpretation of design.

Until the early nineteenth century most architecture signified either political power or religious SYMBOLISM. During the nineteenth century growing commercial and industrial concerns, such as banks, stores, and railway companies, started to use architecture as a means of self-advertisement. In the early

Figure 3. *(Design)* Mass-produced chairs by Charles and Ray Eames. (*a*) Molded plywood chair, revised design, 1946. Wood, metal, and rubber. (*b*) Stacking shell chair, 1955. Fiberglass-reinforced polyester, metal, and rubber. Courtesy of Herman Miller, Inc., Archives.

twentieth century, following the revolutions at the end of World War I in Germany, Russia, and Austria-Hungary, a new architecture based on functionalism was developed to signify the new political order and was used for buildings serving welfare functions (housing, schools, and hospitals) that had not previously received much architectural attention. The style was subsequently extended to a variety of buildings to signify progress and modernity. The study of architectural meanings originated in ICONOGRAPHY, which was concerned mainly with the interpretation of motifs and symbols used in medieval and Renaissance architecture, and focused on the intentions of clients and architects. The development of semiotic criticism in the 1950s and 1960s stimulated a new interest in the communicative aspects of architecture, especially in its reception, which had largely been ignored in iconography (*see* SEMIOTICS).

Another important difference between architecture and consumer goods is that buildings are usually commissioned by their future owners and are not designed for immediate exchange, but with consumer goods the process of exchange is central to their existence and is the principal means through which meaning is constructed. Design plays an important part in selling and marketing; its value was recognized early by entrepreneurs such as Wedgwood, who commented that in his trade "fashion is infinitely superior to merit." Marketing strategy requires the differentiation of consumers into categories and the production of designs appropriate to each category. When successful, this identifies particular designs with particular groups and gives those designs a social meaning. In the early period of industrial production, in the eighteenth and nineteenth centuries, principal market segmentation was between exports and domestic consumption, but with the development of domestic markets in Britain, the United States, and Germany, manufacturers looked for differentiation within those markets in terms of factors such as region, social class, GENDER, and age. Mail-order catalogs from the late nineteenth century show an enormous proliferation of designs for many products, as entrepreneurs attempted to produce designs for every conceivable subsection of the market. For example, the Vespa motor scooter was introduced in Italy in the late 1940s for sale to women and teenagers, neither group part of the traditionally male market for larger motorcycles.

Mediation of consumer-goods design occurs mainly through advertising, which usually reinforces the meaning intended by the manufacturer, although it may also create additional ones. Sometimes the desire

to advertise a product has been a reason for attending to its design or its packaging, so as to give it a brand identity distinct from its competitors. For example, soaps and cigarettes depend on brand design to be advertised effectively.

It is in reception and consumption that interpretation becomes most difficult, for often designs are not understood in the way manufacturers or advertisers intend. There have been many notable failures of this kind. Ford's Edsel, an automobile launched in 1958, was designed on the basis of exhaustive market research, but there turned out to be no demand from the projected market. Moreover, designs are often reinterpreted by the market. The Italian motor scooter was adopted in the 1960s by a British youth subculture known as "mods" and became a symbol of youth rebellion, displacing the original

Figure 4. *(Design)* Advertisement for Hille office desk range, designed by Robin Day, 1961. The problem of office management in the 1960s was to preserve an illusion of equality while preserving hierarchies. By permission of Hille Ergonom plc., London.

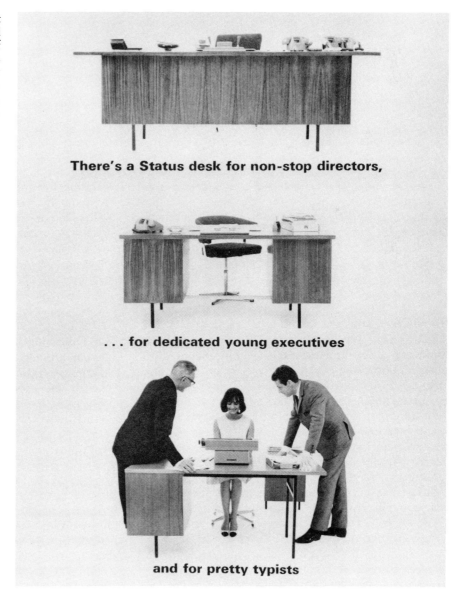

There's a Status desk for non-stop directors,

... for dedicated young executives

and for pretty typists

Figure 5. *(Design)* Vespa motor scooter, Chicago, 1979. UPI/Bettmann Newsphotos.

meaning intended by the manufacturers. Such changes in meaning occur through fashion, a process manipulated partly by consumers and partly by manufacturers themselves (particularly of automobiles and CLOTHING), who change designs in order to create obsolescence and stimulate new demand.

Consumer behavior and the formation of taste have been approached from a variety of perspectives (*see* CONSUMER RESEARCH; TASTE CULTURES). Thorstein Veblen saw consumption as related to class identity, and taste as a means by which dominant classes maintained their ascendancy. Similarly, Pierre Bourdieu discussed consumption as behavior predicated on existing patterns of social difference. Following Bourdieu, some authors attach considerable importance to consumption within the process of exchange in the construction of meanings; an opposing theoretical view regards consumers as relatively passive and meanings as created primarily through the process of production.

Exchange is not the only context in which design can be understood. Many goods shape or affect other kinds of experience. For example, ideas about the nature of work in offices have been mediated through the design of office furniture and equipment. Similarly, large commercial organizations often attempt to communicate their corporate identity to employees and to the public through design strategies that unify company buildings, capital equipment, products, and services.

Design is particularly labile; the meanings intended by designers are often interpreted differently by recipients, while designs can change their meanings substantially over time. In certain categories of design, notably clothing, such changes can occur very rapidly. However, design's ambiguous nature has often been used to advantage, for it lends itself to the communication of contradictory or opposing sets of ideas or ideologies.

See also AESTHETICS; ART.

Bibliography. Reyner Banham, *Theory and Design in the First Machine Age,* 2d ed., New York, 1967, reprint 1981; Pierre Bourdieu, *Distinction: A Social Critique of the Judgement of Taste* (Le distinction: Critique sociale du jugement), trans. by Richard Nice, London and Cambridge, Mass., 1984; Adrian Forty, *Objects of Desire: Design and Society from Wedgwood to IBM,* London and New York, 1986; Siegfried Giedion, *Mechanization Takes Command,* New York, 1948, reprint 1969; Wolfgang Fritz Haug, *Critique of Commodity Aesthetics,* Minneapolis, Minn., and Cambridge, 1986; Dick Hebdige, *Subculture: The Meaning of Style,* London, 1979; John Heskett, *Industrial Design,* New York and London, 1980; Thorstein

Veblen, *The Theory of the Leisure Class,* New York, 1899, reprint 1965.

ADRIAN FORTY

DETECTIVE FICTION. *See* MYSTERY AND DETECTIVE FICTION.

DEVELOPMENT COMMUNICATION

This entry includes three articles, each dealing with a different aspect of the subject:
1. **History and Theories**
2. **Alternative Systems**
3. **Projects**

The first and third cover predominantly the Western (especially the U.S.) approach; the second raises some criticisms directed at both the theoretical and the practical limitations of the Western perspective and presents alternative views.

1. HISTORY AND THEORIES

A common way to discuss development is as purposive changes undertaken in a society to achieve what may be regarded generally as a different ("improved") state of social and economic affairs. The concept has been used to describe Western (particularly European) economic growth since the MIDDLE AGES, as well as to explain the process through which all societies are expected to achieve certain economic, political, social, cultural, and other goals. Thus the notion of development is often seen as a derivation of the much older idea of progress, which has roots going back to ancient Greece.

Change in human society is widely considered inevitable. Whether it is (or should be) slow and gradual (evolutionary) or fast and radical (revolutionary) is a matter of dispute. Throughout much of its history humanity did not seem to be overly concerned with the direction of progress, for the most part assuming that all change—and therefore progress—was good. In the Western world the Industrial Revolution, along with major political events that introduced important changes in social organization and life-style (e.g., the French and American revolutions), supported the view that secular development and not just progress (as guaranteed by religious ideas on the perfectibility of humankind) was not only possible but desirable and achievable as well.

The emergence of Europe since the fifteenth century as the major force in the EXPLORATION and COLONIZATION of the globe established patterns of economic relations among nations, or between nations and their colonies, that have had an enduring impact. Economic "development" was seen as emanating from the benefits of trade and the possession of colonies that provided abundant raw materials, cheap labor, and outlets for the manufacturing industries of the metropolis. Throughout the nineteenth and early twentieth centuries European powers attached great importance to the possession of colonies and the advantages derived from them. Nations without such colonies felt they were at a disadvantage (e.g., by not being able to trade in their own currency) and defined themselves as the "have-nots" in opposition to the "have" countries with colonies. It would not be until well into the twentieth century that Europe would come to realize that the true "have-nots" were the colonies themselves.

The Twentieth Century

If the United States emerged from World War I as the preeminent economic power, the outcome of World War II established the United States as the foremost political power as well. The reconstruction of Europe and the establishment of a functioning world economy became the principal objectives of U.S. foreign policy. At a political level the increasing differences with the Soviet Union, its wartime ally, and the perceived threat to U.S. national security from Soviet intentions toward Europe and the rest of the world led U.S. President Harry S. Truman to redefine his country's foreign policy from an isolationist stance to one of active leadership. Rather than "sit back and do nothing" or respond militarily to the postwar situation, the United States decided on a program of financial and economic assistance to Europe. And rather than implement this program through heavy-handed intervention in the affairs of the recipient countries or channel aid through newly created multilateral organizations—mainly the United Nations and the International Bank for Reconstruction and Development—the United States offered the Marshall Plan, which extended financial and economic assistance in a multilateral framework of consultation and cooperation between donor and recipient countries. *See* INTERNATIONAL ORGANIZATIONS.

The Marshall Plan was successful both in rebuilding the economies of the participating European countries and in achieving its major political goal: the "containment" of the spread of communism. This goal was first advanced with the declaration of the Truman Doctrine in March 1947 and was reaffirmed in the Point Four Program of 1949, in which Truman offered the world "the benefits of our [U.S.] scientific advance and industrial progress . . . for the improvement and growth of underdeveloped areas."

Whether one chooses to interpret U.S. actions as derived from humanitarian concerns, economic self-interest, or larger political considerations (i.e., confrontation with the Soviets), the offer of technical assistance and economic and financial aid was unprecedented and raised a series of formidable problems, not the least of which was how to approach the whole enterprise. Because of its very limited experience in (government-sponsored) foreign aid and development administration the U.S. government turned to the academic establishment for help. Contemporary historians and social scientists tried to distill the lessons of Western "development" into a model appropriate to different states and regions. Around the late 1950s the model that began to emerge might be summarized as follows:

- Industry is the prime mover of the economy. Therefore, a major part of investment must go into industry and what is necessary to fuel it, including raw materials, transportation, and training.
- Modern society requires more specialists rather than generalists, with each sector (e.g., industry, health) expected to have its own special skills and responsibilities.
- Public EDUCATION is needed to raise the abilities of the entire work force and of the proportion able to participate in government. Health care and family planning are needed to increase the well-being of the population and curtail demand for jobs, housing, and the like.
- In situations in which rapid development is desired, necessary information can be diffused and PERSUASION can occur through the mass media with the aid of an extension service (see DIFFUSION; INTERPERSONAL COMMUNICATION). Adoption of promising innovations should be encouraged, along with increases in productivity.
- The profits from centrally owned and managed industry, trade, and sale of manufactured goods would be expected to "trickle down" from the center of the system to the periphery, from the industries and central markets to the farms, from the cities to the villages.

This outline represents the core ideas of "development planning." More specific theories focusing on economic, political, psychological, sociological, and other factors were also advanced.

Economic theories. During the 1950s economic analysts rejected wealth distribution from rich to poor countries as the source of economic progress in favor of the notion of *growth.* Walt Rostow's *The Stages of Economic Growth* (1960) was very influential through the early 1960s. His approach described development as consisting of five successive stages: (1) traditional society, (2) preconditions for "takeoff," (3) "takeoff," (4) "drive toward maturity," and (5) self-sustained growth, in which it is possible for the country to move on without further help from the outside. Rostow claimed to have derived his scheme from the experience of the West, and he provided guidelines about the time periods involved in each stage as well as several specific economic measures associated with each (e.g., Gross National Product per capita, rate of savings and investment). Rostow's scheme provided for the classification of countries according to the stage of development they were judged to be in, thus allowing certain decisions concerning the type and amount of aid to be made on a more "rational" basis.

Rostow's and other stage theories faced substantial criticisms almost from the start. The traditional/modern dichotomy was challenged on the grounds that "traditional" was only defined negatively as what is not "modern," the latter taken to be self-evident. Whether the West had actually "developed" by passing through the five stages was also questioned: when had the West (particularly western Europe) been a "traditional" society? The mechanisms or factors moving societies from one stage to the next were not explicit, and the assumption that *all* countries were going to develop as the Western ones had or not develop at all raised many eyebrows. Yet many of these problems were overlooked by people who found the imagery of the theory compelling.

Other economic theories of development were less ambitious and concentrated on purely economic factors, usually to their detriment. Frederick Frey, in a comprehensive review published in 1973, argued that economic theories had paid little or no attention to communication factors even though several were clearly implicit in their assumptions and formulations for action. By emphasizing organization and economies of scale, for example, these theories ignored relevant social, political, cultural, and other noneconomic factors that influence development. However flawed, Rostow's theory included a recognition of those noneconomic elements that can promote or derail efforts at social change. Development was acknowledged to mean more than just economic growth, opening the field to other social sciences.

Psychological theories. Although economists commonly interpreted development to mean broad changes in the social and economic structure of a country, psychologists approached the problem at the level of the individual, taking development to be a problem of "modernization" of the people and not just of abstract macrosocial or macroeconomic structures. The work of two U.S. scholars was very influential in the early 1960s: David C. McClelland's *The Achieving Society* (1961) and Everett E. Hagen's *On the Theory of Social Change* (1962). Both emphasized individual characteristics as determinants of social structure and change. Hagen argued that social structure is a function of personality, and he paired traditional society with a "traditional personality" and modern society with a creative, innovative personality. The predominant features of the traditional personality were defined as low self-esteem, authoritarianism, resistance to innovation, and little or no inclination to perceive the world as subject to human manipulation—characteristics opposite to those of the modern personality. Hagen argued that only fundamental changes in the home environment, tied to wider social changes such as increased urbanization, LITERACY, and modern communication media, are capable of producing enduring changes in the personality of individuals.

McClelland's view elaborated MAX WEBER's treatment of the Protestant ethic. His argument was that Protestantism promotes the need for achievement among its followers, which in turn encourages individual entrepreneurship and socioeconomic development. He described the "need for achievement" as fostering an individual's desire to meet demanding challenges, to surmount tests, and to succeed in the face of difficulties. A society full of such persons is likely to be an achieving—and consequently a "developing"—society.

For both authors contact with the West and the creation and evolution of Western-style social institutions were crucial features of the development process. Although both theories claimed to be supported by empirical evidence, from historical analyses as well as from contemporary survey studies, their conceptual soundness (because of their reliance on the traditional/modern view of societies) and their applicability and usefulness were questioned. Few could deny the importance for development of individual-level changes, but experience was showing that in many cases social structures were much more difficult to change than at first had been imagined, and even willing and able individuals or groups could often make little or no significant changes in their social environment.

Political theories. Political scientists took a different approach, emphasizing the importance of the country's political system as a determinant of the social and economic domains. Because many of the "underdeveloped" countries were, in fact, new nations that had attained their independence after World War II, analysts in the West hypothesized that a major, immediate need was the integration of those countries as viable political and economic entities. Some of these countries could draw on offers of assistance from their former colonial rulers, but others could not or did not want to do so. Whereas many of the new countries were more or less homogeneous with respect to ancestry, LANGUAGE, RELIGION, and so on, many others faced formidable problems trying to integrate into a unified country peoples from different ethnic, linguistic, cultural, religious, and social backgrounds. "Nation-building" was defined as a problem amenable to study by Western scholars, including noted political scientist Karl Deutsch. Throughout the 1950s and 1960s a common assumption (often based on correlational studies) was that economic and political development were closely related, and this led to suggestions that the "developing" countries should try to establish Western-style political institutions and practices (mainly, a democratic form of government and a free-market economic system). Thus the need to promote national identity was tied to ways of adding legitimacy to existing political institutions and power structures in charge of creating a broad consensus behind a nation's development goals.

Even though political theories of development paid substantial attention to communication issues, they were still mainly political, that is, mostly concerned with the ways in which communication processes and the mass media in particular could affect a nation's process of political development (e.g., instill democratic values in a population or act as tools for social mobilization).

Communication theories of development. Another group of social scientists addressed development from a different perspective. Rather than considering communication as one factor affecting a central process deemed to be social, psychological, political, or of any other nature, they took communication to be at the center of the development process, incorporating all other aspects in one form or another.

Sociologists, anthropologists, communication researchers, and other specialists working from this perspective in the early 1960s also assumed the problem to be one of transforming "traditional" societies and peoples into "modern" ones. Those taking an anthropological view looked at the problem as one of *individual modernization,* a consequence of cultural and social factors and the specific characteristics of the innovations being promoted. Power relations between "donor" and "recipient" cultures, the content of the "message" implicit in the innovations, and the resistance to change at both the cultural and the individual level were analyzed. The common stages of the innovation-adoption process were identified, but it would be up to sociologists to provide a more complete picture.

The details that sociologists filled in identified adopter and nonadopter groups, the patterns of social communication within each (*see* NETWORK ANALYSIS), and elaboration of the "stages" of the adoption process to include the following five: awareness, interest, evaluation of the innovation, trial, and acceptance (or rejection). Groups studied included farmers (e.g., adoption of new attitudes, seed types, or farming practices), women of childbearing age (e.g., adoption of family planning), and doctors (e.g., adoption of new drugs). Many valuable lessons on the ways in which social groups assimilate (or reject) innovations were learned, but the theoretical and practical limitations of the approach also became evident, among them a tendency to rely on survey methods even when they were inadequate for the cultural and historical context or for the specific problem under study.

At a more general level, one of the most influential theories that assigned a very important role to communication was proposed by U.S. scholar Daniel Lerner. In *The Passing of Traditional Society* (1958) Lerner identified four critical variables that he said summarized the development process: *urbanization*, leading to increased *literacy*, which in turn affects *mass media exposure*, resulting in greater economic and political *participation* in society. This simple, linear scheme was initially modified by Lerner himself to allow for reciprocal influences between literacy and mass media exposure. Several other researchers tested many other models, using the same four variables on different data sets and later including other variables to create more complex models. At the individual level, Lerner's most important hypothesis has to do with the nature of the "modern individual," characterized by an ability to accommodate to change plus a high degree of empathy—the ability to imagine oneself in the role or with the responsibilities of someone else. Lerner argued that the primary step toward individual modernization was the acquisition of this capacity for empathy as well as the willingness to hold opinions on a wide variety of issues and questions not usually familiar to "traditional" peoples (who may not even have knowledge of those issues owing to lack of access to mass media sources of information). Frey synthesized into two variables, which he labeled "exposure to change" and "cognitive flexibility," what he considered to be the most important features required for the process of individual modernization.

By the mid-1970s the ideas embodied in the "dominant paradigm" of the previous two or three decades were called into question. The role of communication as the central "mover" in the development process was acknowledged to be substantially limited by political, economic, cultural, and other factors, leading practitioners to the recognition that communication was perhaps best conceptualized as a *complement* to development.

This overview has dealt with only a few of the multitude of development theories advanced since the 1950s, namely, those that most often provided the conceptual background for the impressively large number of development assistance projects carried out or sponsored by Western governments and scientists. Some of the projects having to do explicitly with communications are covered in section 3, below; section 2 presents an assessment of that experience from a Third World perspective.

Bibliography. Everett E. Hagen, *On the Theory of Social Change*, Homewood, Ill., 1962; Bert F. Hoselitz and Wilbert E. Moore, eds., *Industrialization and Society* (North American Conference on the Social Implications of Industrialization and Technological Change), Paris, 1963, reprint The Hague, 1968; Daniel Lerner, *The Passing of Traditional Society: Modernizing the Middle East*, New York, 1958; David McClelland, *The Achieving Society*, Princeton, N.J., 1961; Robert Nisbet, *History of the Idea of Progress*, New York, 1980; P. W. Preston, *Theories of Development*, London and Boston, 1982; Lucien W. Pye, ed., *Communications and Political Development*, Princeton, N.J., 1963; Everett M. Rogers, *Modernization among Peasants*, New York, 1968; Walt W. Rostow, *The Stages of Economic Growth: A Non-Communist Manifesto*, Cambridge, 1960; Wilbur L. Schramm, *Mass Media and National Development*, Stanford, Calif., 1964.

PEDRO F. HERNÁNDEZ-RAMOS
AND WILBUR SCHRAMM

2. ALTERNATIVE SYSTEMS

The record of economic and social development has been disappointing. In the years since World War II ended and the United Nations (UN) was established, assistance began to flow from developed countries to less developed ones. Thousands of millions of dollars have been spent in support of development, resulting in significant economic growth and material advancement in some underdeveloped countries. But the dreams of widespread economic development have not materialized, and communication in the service of development has hardly accomplished what was expected of it.

Some Results of Two Development Decades

By 1980, after two UN "Development Decades," the developing countries had accumulated a foreign debt of nearly $440 billion, up from only about $68 billion in 1971. Between 1971 and 1980 interest rates had increased by more than 800 percent. Three-fourths of the world's population, some 3.2 billion people in 140 developing countries, accounted in 1980 for only 20 percent of the world's gross product. Some 30 of these countries, the least developed, had a yearly per capita income of less than $300—about eighty cents per day. The annual figure for Bangladesh was $100, whereas that of some of the developed countries was above $10,000. Not even the most basic of human needs, food for survival, has been completely satisfied. It is estimated that more than 800 million persons still suffer from malnutrition, and as the 1985 crisis in Ethiopia illustrated, thousands or millions are wiped off the earth by famine. Yet Asia, Latin America, and Africa were all net exporters of grains before World War II.

The recession that struck the industrial nations between 1981 and 1983 was devastating to the economies of developing countries, particularly in Latin America. The (average) growth rate of its gross internal product collapsed from 5.5 percent during the 1950–1980 period to *minus* 0.9 percent in 1982. This part of the world saw its development aspirations virtually halted. At the beginning of that year Mexico had to commit as much as 85 percent of its export earnings to interest payments and, along with several other countries in a similar situation, was trying to renegotiate the debt itself. In 1985 Peru declared its intention to apply no more than 10 percent of export earnings to servicing the debt. "Banks can wait, hunger cannot," said its president, Alan García. The Colombian delegate to a general assembly of the UN's Food and Agriculture Organization (FAO) charged that "the developed countries have unleashed a commercial war against the Third World," and the World Bank estimated that "dozens of countries have lost ten or more years of development." *See* INTERNATIONAL ORGANIZATIONS.

A divided world. The northern ("developed") and southern ("developing") nations see their relationship differently. Through northern eyes explosive population growth rates, lack of entrepreneurship, poor planning, poor management, technological incompetence, bureaucratic corruption, and inability to apply foreign aid, among other factors, effectively explain the economic woes. Through southern eyes the central explanation is unfair economic relations between industrial and nonindustrial states. At the end of World War II developing countries were assigned a primitive role in the world economy: to produce raw materials and consume imported manufactured goods. Because the developed nations are able to determine the prices for these transactions, the developing countries have to sell cheap and buy dear. The results are chronic trade imbalances, ever-growing budgetary deficits, and increasing debts to the industrial nations (which charge increasingly higher interest rates). To compound these problems, developed countries have even begun to produce synthetically some of the raw materials exported by the developing countries. Southern countries feel that no amount of aid can compensate for this kind of trade.

At the 1955 Bandung Conference that gave rise to the "Non-Aligned Movement," the concept of a "Third World" searching for a pattern of development independent of either capitalist or socialist industrialized powers was proposed. The establishment of the UN Conference on Trade and Development (UNCTAD) was urged as a neutral forum for north-south discussion. UNCTAD met for the first time in 1964 and argued for a new international economic order (NIEO) that was eventually embraced by the UN General Assembly in 1974. Third World countries said they wanted "justice, not charity," and the NIEO was intended to seek a fair balance in north-south trade relations and put an end to exploitative "neo-colonial" practices.

Not all injustice, however, is external to the developing countries. In a situation that Mexican sociologist Pablo González Casanova calls "internal colonialism," elite minorities in many developing countries concentrate economic, political, and cultural power in their hands at the expense of deprivation and often oppression of the majorities. Showing at times greater ideological affinity and coincidence of interest with the developed world than with their own people, native oligarchies are also the main beneficiaries of their countries' development-oriented activities, including those supported from abroad. Just as on the international scene, the abyss between rich and poor is expanding dangerously instead of being bridged. National income is concentrated in the hands of a few rather than being redistributed more evenly. Popular reform-minded movements of social democratic leanings are usually discouraged and often forcibly repressed. In some countries rural guerrilla warfare and urban TERRORISM introduce violent strategies to the struggle for social transformation in search of national (and sometimes international) justice.

A statement by the former prime minister of Jamaica, Michael Manley, perhaps provides the best summary (and the ideal) of what Third World countries desire:

I wish to make clear that we do not speak of the New World International Economic Order as an excuse for shortcomings in our own development process. . . . Nor do we believe that the developed world owes its former colonies a living. Equally, I accept, indeed assert, the obligation of the Third World countries to pursue unflinchingly the objectives of equity and social justice within their own systems.

Western Development Models Revisited

Experiences like these have led to challenges to many of the tenets of "classic" development theory. Latin American economists and social scientists, such as Argentina's Raúl Prebisch and Brazil's Celso Furtado, were among the earliest critics. With other scholars they shared a structural view of underdevelopment and contributed to dependency theory, which effectively contends that genuinely democratic development can occur only if crippling intranational and international power relations (political, economic, and cultural) are restructured in the direction of justice and liberation for the majorities.

In the early 1970s a number of meetings in different parts of the world began to take note of the shortcomings of existing development programs and the models behind them. Among these were the Stockholm Conference on Human Environment, the Bucharest World Population Conference, the Rome Food Conference, and the 1974 meeting of the UN General Assembly that approved the proposal for the

NIEO. Academic conferences during the same period argued that existing development models sacrificed human dignity, justice, and freedom in favor of "abundance and prosperity at any price . . . for the privileged minorities." Such noted researchers as Juan Jamías (the Philippines), Andreas Fugelsang (Sweden), Peter Golding (Great Britain), and Juan Díaz Bordenave and José Marques de Melo (Brazil) coincided in their assessment of the classic development models as ethnocentric, unidimensional, deterministic, and lacking a historical perspective.

By the mid-1970s Western scholars, especially in the United States, were aware of the limitations of the models applied so far. WILBUR SCHRAMM and Daniel Lerner acknowledged that much, and other leading figures provided their own assessments. One of the most striking was that of Everett Rogers, who had worked extensively in the area of DIFFUSION of innovations. In 1976 Rogers argued that we were witnessing "the passing of the dominant paradigm" and summarized the errors in the old paradigm as follows:

1. It posits that persons are rational economic actors, and assumes that the profit motive is enough to bring about behavioral changes.
2. It measures development in terms of Gross National Product (GNP) or per capita income, ignoring the need to distribute development benefits equally.
3. It assumes infinite economic growth, ignores problems like population growth, pollution, etc., and does not take into account the "quality of life."
4. It assumes the need for central economic planning, and fails to account for the possibilities of autonomous development, as exemplified by China.
5. It emphasizes technology and capital rather than labor, thus encouraging economic dependence on advanced countries. Low priority is given to agriculture.
6. It blames the developing countries for their failings, ignoring external factors beyond their control.
7. It takes an ethnocentric (Western) bias by emphasizing the modernization of "traditional" individuals.
8. It equates poverty with underdevelopment.

Along the same lines, a 1977 gathering of U.S. and foreign scholars in Houston, Texas, noted other elements in classic development models that lacked validity for developing nations. These included the notion of stages (from Walt Rostow's theory), the "trickle-down" effect for the rewards of development, the priority on heavy industrialization, and the import-substitution strategy to promote the growth of domestic industry. In summary, classic development theories were seen more as hypothetical reconstructions of the material advancement in industrial societies and no longer as valid universal formulations or blueprints for development in the Third World.

Communication and Third World Development

Does the failure of development imply a failure of communication as a factor to encourage development in the Third World? One important difference between developed and developing countries is that in most Third World countries the availability of press, RADIO, film, and television is one more privilege enjoyed principally by urban minorities. Even radio, the most widespread medium, falls short of reaching every potential audience member.

Very significant increases in the availability of mass media have taken place in recent decades. In the "Decade of the Transistor," between 1963 and 1973, the number of radio receivers in the Third World grew by 100 million units, more than quadrupling the figures for Asia, tripling them for Africa, and doubling them for Latin America. Reviewing those years, Schramm warned:

But let us not forget how far behind the rich countries these poorer countries are. Even the rather spectacular growth in radios must be interpreted in light of the fact that two-thirds of the world's people still have no more than one-fifth of all the world's radios, less than one-fifth of the newspaper circulation, less than one-tenth of the world's television receivers, one-sixteenth of the world's telephones.

Thus the lack of economic resources ran parallel to shortfalls in the availability—and actual control—of media. Beyond this, the content of media programming troubles many observers. Private mass media typically favor SPORTS and ENTERTAINMENT fare and tend not to regard such functions as fostering national unity or teaching the principles, values, and skills of development as a part of their responsibility. They attribute such social duties to the state, but in general the state does not fulfill them either. The most common explanations for these omissions are a failure to perceive the importance of communication for development, lack of funds, and preference for political indoctrination. Another is that public media are few and weak, and government attempts to bolster them are often inhibited by strong opposition from the private (commercial) sector. By the mid-1970s it had become apparent that the mass media have no special power to accelerate changes in society and that communication cannot alter an unfair social and economic structure on its own.

The imbalance seen in intranational mass communication is also typical of international media. It occurs, for example, in such areas as television programs (see TELEVISION HISTORY—WORLD MARKET STRUGGLES), foreign news (see NEWS AGENCIES), and ADVERTISING, in which the predominance of the developed nations, and of the United States in particular, has become overwhelming. U.S. predominance in the transnational information industry involving satellites, computers, and other highly advanced communications technologies appears to be even more formidable (see COMPUTER: IMPACT—IMPACT ON THE WORLD ECONOMY; SATELLITE; TELECOMMUNICA-

TIONS NETWORKS). This situation causes concern in the Third World because many countries feel that their cultural integrity and even their national sovereignty is threatened by such mighty alien influence through technologies that are rapidly widening the gap between developed and developing countries. *See also* MARXIST THEORIES OF COMMUNICATION—THIRD WORLD APPROACHES.

The concern turned combustible in 1976 after the Non-Aligned Movement proclaimed the need for a NEW INTERNATIONAL INFORMATION ORDER and UNESCO sponsored the Intergovernmental Conference on Communication Policies in Latin America and the Caribbean, in San José, Costa Rica. International controversy erupted, not only between north and south but also between those in developed and developing countries who felt that such a change is essential to achieving development and those who resisted it. Among the latter were the inter-American associations of mass media owners who argued that the establishment of national communication policies would be a threat, for example, to freedom of information. Nevertheless, through the *Declaration of San José* and thirty accompanying recommendations, the meeting did suggest steps toward the implementation of pluralistic national communication policies, improving the use of communication for development, ways to achieve better-balanced circulation of information at both the national and international levels, and the strengthening of community media. Coming from political decision makers, these conclusions broadened the scope of the debate considerably. The debate intensified during discussions concerning a UNESCO "Mass Media Declaration," initially advanced by the Soviet Union and finally approved by consensus in 1978, and around the work of the MacBride Commission, a consultative body of experts representing many nations and ideologies who delivered to UNESCO's General Conference in 1980 the report *Many Voices, One World*. By the mid-1980s the withdrawal of the United States from UNESCO (later followed by Great Britain), brought about mainly by concern over these issues, made the confrontation a serious international episode.

A New Approach?

Old development models and ideas about the role of communication in them could be dismissed as inappropriate, but was there anything to substitute for them? New proposals called for "another development" and "alternative communication." Not surprisingly most of them were based on the premise that structural changes toward more equitable relationships within and between nations are necessary preconditions. Some sought to learn from distinct experiences such as those of China, Tanzania, and Yugoslavia. However, contrary to what is often assumed in developed nations, a movement like this one for democratic communication in the Third World is not the product of Communist revolutionary inspiration. Many proponents of these changes are nonpartisan reformers of social democratic leanings who tend to condemn authoritarianism whether it comes from the right or the left. They know that communication in most Communist countries, dominated by one-party regimes, is no less undemocratic than transnational capitalist communication. Furthermore, the main supporter of these kinds of justice-seeking concerns in Latin America has often been, since the late 1960s, the Catholic church.

A report by the Hammarskjöld Foundation on the movement toward "another development" says that "it is not the absolute scarcity of resources which explains poverty in the Third World, but rather their distribution." Domestic democratization is only one element of the structural modifications required to solve the problem of distribution, the report states firmly. The other is changing the pattern of exploitative economic, political, and cultural relationships between developed and developing nations in terms of both trade and aid so that fairness and balance are attained.

An ambitious study by Argentina's Fundación Bariloche (Bariloche Foundation), supported by Canada's International Development Research Center, published its report in 1976 under the title *Catastrophe or New Society?* It challenged the Club of Rome's conclusion that the main problem facing the world is population growth in the Third World and that, if universal disaster is to be avoided, it is essential that such growth be contained. In opposition the Bariloche study argues that the main problems are not physical but sociopolitical,

based on the uneven distribution of power between nations and within nations. The result is oppression and alienation, largely founded on exploitation. The deterioration of the physical environment is not an inevitable consequence of human progress, but the result of social organizations based on destructive values.

What is proposed is a shift toward a society rooted in equity and widespread participation of the people in decision making, and this is deemed viable "only through radical changes in the world's social and international organization." The study suggested a different measure of development (life expectancy at birth) that truly reflects the general living conditions of a population. A new society instead of catastrophe will not be easy to achieve "because to change the organization and values of society, as history has shown, is much more difficult than overcoming physical limitations."

Satisfying the need for communication—considered basic by several writers—in this kind of changing environment is a major problem. Chilean economist Juan Somavía has argued:

Satisfying the need for communication is as important for a nation and its citizens as ensuring health, food, housing, and employment, together with all the social needs that make it possible for its members to develop fully in justice and autonomy. The social need to inform and be informed is one of the fundamental human rights, since it is an essential component in the improvement of mankind and in society's capacity for development.

Critical questions about commonly accepted notions of communication, chiefly as applied to adult EDUCATION, were raised in the 1960s and 1970s by Paulo Freire. Working among the downtrodden peasants in northeastern Brazil, he conceived and tested a "pedagogy of the oppressed." He condemned traditional LITERACY training as authoritarian "banking education," in which teachers "deposit" the set of values of the rich in the minds of the poor, who can later "cash in" on those "deposits" for material goods given to them as rewards for submission and passivity. Traditional teachers, Freire charged, really never communicate with the people. Genuine communication, he said, is free dialogue aimed at actively sharing experiences and jointly reconstructing experience. Education "as the practice of freedom," he contended, is creative discovery of the world, not transmission of knowledge from the powerful to the powerless.

Freire proposed "conscientization" (*conscientização* in Portuguese) as a democratic method for people to gain collective awareness of natural and social realities so as to overcome oppression. This method is based on nondirected discussion of individual and cultural problems in small "cultural circles," stimulated only by "generative words" selected from the people's "minimum thematic universe." This process of autonomous education will show the exploited and dominated minorities that nature is controllable and society changeable, and it should ultimately lead them to liberation.

The relation of Freire's ideas to the process of development education is evident. For example, he had little or no use for the agricultural extension format transplanted from the United States, which he regarded as opposite to true educational practice because it wrongly assumed that something could be transplanted "from the seat of wisdom to the seat of ignorance" (see section 3, below).

The first attempt at employing in a development communication context the provocative postulates of Freire, along with other related and pioneering ideas, was conducted in Bolivia in the early 1970s by two Catholic communication practitioners—a North American, Frank Gerace, and a Latin American, Hernando Lázaro. Their conclusions were published in 1973 in *Comunicación horizontal* (Horizontal Communication). A study by Francisco Gutiérrez, *Lenguaje total* (Total Language), joined this line by also

arguing that *dialogic* interaction is crucial to democratic communication.

In the early 1970s Belgian Marxist scholar Armand Mattelart wrote, in collaboration with the Chileans Biedma and Funes, a book on mass communication and socialist revolution that also contributed to the rethinking of the nature of development communication and made Mattelart perhaps the best-known critic of communication used for domination.

With Swedish and U.S. support, a Latin American institute for transnational studies (Instituto Latinoamericano de Estudios Transnacionales, ILET) was established in Mexico City in 1976. Headed by Somavía, who became one of the two Latin American members of the MacBride Commission, ILET emphasized communication and rapidly established itself as a leading institution in the campaign for a new international economic order and a new world information and communication order, directed toward building "another development" and "alternative communication." Somavía has argued that information is a *social good,* not a commodity, and therefore cannot be regarded as a business governed by profit motives. Inasmuch as owning, using, and controlling media afford power, in truly democratic societies power should be accountable to the community, and thus media behavior should no longer be left exclusively in the hands of private merchants or public bureaucrats. In order to democratize communication, Somavía said, an evolution must take place "from private social monopoly to majority social representation," perhaps requiring the creation of "social property" (i.e., communal, popular, collective) different from state or private media ownership.

At the end of the 1970s Luis Ramiro Beltrán made an initial attempt at integrating most of the new concepts into a framework for international communication. He took access as a precondition, dialogue as the axis of the process, and participation as the culminating result. This was his summary:

Communication is the process of democratic social interaction, based upon exchange of symbols, by which human beings share experiences under conditions of free and egalitarian access, dialogue, and participation. Everyone has the right to communicate in order to satisfy communication needs by enjoying communication resources. Human beings communicate with multiple purposes. The exertion of influence on the behavior of others is not the main one.

Lively activity has been under way along this line during the 1980s in developing countries. A diversity of approaches has given rise to the use of a great variety of adjectives, among them *dialogic, group, marginal, interactive, horizontal, liberating, popular, participatory,* and *alternative.*

Alternative seems to be the most pervasive, despite

some doubts. Proponents consider it the option most nearly opposite the prevailing undemocratic national and transnational systems of communication. Fernando Reyes Matta of ILET points out three crucial tasks in building alternative communication: attaining participation in the process of creating new ways and means, generating the alternative language through popular creativity and egalitarian dialogue, and organizing the communication institutions and processes through direct ties with the social and political system supporting them. The final realization of alternative communication should occur, Reyes Matta concludes, when structural changes make possible "another development."

Overview

More than forty years of development efforts have failed to resolve the major problems they were designed to solve: poverty, hunger, malnutrition, illiteracy, low crop yields, and so on. The dominant paradigm guiding communication for development eventually gave way to alternative views coming from both developed and developing countries. Although some superficial similarities persisted (e.g., in the use of terms like *participation* as a goal for development programs), the distance between old and new views remains substantial. New views have not become entirely prevalent, for the old ideas still have considerable economic and political appeal (especially in some developed countries) and have evolved conceptually as well, with key concepts being redefined and new models proposed. The criticisms exchanged by proponents of old and new have helped each camp to address areas of weakness in its theories, and this process is still unfolding.

The role that communication can or should play in society has also been intensely debated, ranging from how media institutions should be organized (e.g., ownership) to issues of content and cultural impact. As in the larger debate on how "underdeveloped" societies should develop and what form such "development" should take, questions of how media should be incorporated into society and what they can do to promote a certain type of "development" are far from settled. Everyone agrees that much was learned from the myriad projects that either succeeded or failed. What these lessons tell us about how to proceed in the future is another matter.

See also AFRICA, TWENTIETH CENTURY; ASIA, TWENTIETH CENTURY; COMMUNICATIONS, STUDY OF; COMMUNICATIONS RESEARCH: ORIGINS AND DEVELOPMENT; LATIN AMERICA, TWENTIETH CENTURY; TELEVISION HISTORY—GLOBAL DEVELOPMENT.

Bibliography. Luis Ramiro Beltrán, *Farewell to Aristotle: Horizontal Communication*, Paris, 1979; Fernando H. Cardoso and Enzo Faletto, *Dependência e desenvolvimento na América Latina* (Dependency and Development in Latin America, trans. by Marjory M. Urquidi, 1979), Rio de Janeiro, 1969; Dag Hammarskjöld Foundation, *What Now? The 1975 Dag Hammarskjöld Report*, Uppsala, Sweden, 1975; Guy F. Erb and Valerina Kallab, eds., *Beyond Dependency: The Developing World Speaks Out*, New York, 1975; Elizabeth Fox de Cardona and Héctor Schmucler, eds., *Comunicación y democracia en América Latina*, Lima, Peru, 1982; Paulo Freire, *Pedagogy of the Oppressed* (Pedagogía del oprimido), trans. by Myra Bergman Ramos, New York, 1970; Celso Furtado, *Dialética do desenvolvimento*, Rio de Janeiro, 1964; Albert O. Hirschman et al., *Toward a New Strategy for Development* (A Rothko Chapel Colloquium), New York, 1979; International Commission for the Study of Communication Problems (UNESCO), *Many Voices, One World: Communication and Society, Today and Tomorrow*, Paris and New York, 1980; Marc Nerfin, ed., *Another Development: Approaches and Strategies*, Uppsala, Sweden, 1977; Antonio Pasquali, *Comunicación y cultura de masas*, Caracas, 1972; Fernando Reyes Matta, ed., *Comunicación alternativa y búsquedas democráticas*, Mexico, D.F., 1983; Everett M. Rogers, ed., *Communication and Development: Critical Perspectives*, Beverly Hills, Calif., 1976; Karl P. Sauvant and Hajo Hasenpflug, eds., *The New International Economic Order: Confrontation or Cooperation between North and South?* Boulder, Colo., 1977; Vickie A. Sigman, ed., *Development Communications in the Third World*, Urbana-Champaign, Ill., 1984.

LUIS RAMIRO BELTRÁN S.

3. PROJECTS

Advocacy of purposive use of communication, and of the mass media in particular, for national development reflected intellectual currents of the post–World War II years. Some scholars (e.g., David McClelland, Daniel Lerner, Everett Hagen) focused on the supposed deficits in the people who live in poor countries as one explanation for their countries' failure to develop rapidly and along Western lines. To the extent that these personal deficits accounted for slow development rates, they called for solutions stressing more formal EDUCATION, more training for adults, and more information DIFFUSION. However, implementing such solutions in poor countries was difficult because the conventional strategies associated with educational activities in North America and Europe for doing such tasks through face-to-face instruction foundered on the thin supply of teachers and trained field agents and on inadequate budgets to support their work.

Projects through the Mid–1970s

Practical limitations of the sort mentioned above led many to argue for the use of mass media, with their potential for reaching audiences that were otherwise unreachable, either as a substitute for unavailable teachers and field agents or as a complement to inadequately trained personnel. Enthusiasm for the perceived "power" of mass media resulted in the creation of hundreds of mass media–based projects worldwide.

Formal education. Early uses of RADIO and television (*see* TELEVISION HISTORY) in the classrooms of developing countries were derived from approaches current in more developed countries. Most often they featured radio as an enrichment to existing CLASSROOM instruction; for example, weekly broadcasts might include a dramatic presentation of some event in the nation's history to enrich the standard social sciences curriculum. This "schools broadcasting" approach, though it made sense in the SCHOOL systems of more developed countries in which teachers were well trained and students were attending and learning, solved none of the major problems typical of school systems in developing countries, such as lack of adequate facilities and resources and high dropout rates. If mass media were to be justified in those educational systems as anything other than a luxury, they would have to address more fundamental problems.

Core instructional uses of mass media designed to address basic problems of schooling quality did emerge starting in the 1960s. The incorporation of television in Colombia, the Ivory Coast, American Samoa, El Salvador, and other places was central to major changes in their school systems. The core instructional model has been successful in achieving short-term pedagogic outcomes. In El Salvador the school system quadrupled its enrollment, increased class size, and, although employing teachers with lesser qualifications, nonetheless produced learning gains superior to the conventional system at a lower cost per student. Most other evaluations of core instructional uses report either improved learning or learning comparable to that in conventional systems, as well as reaching otherwise underserved populations. Three main reasons for their success have been identified. First, they improve the quality of instructional content in subjects in which classroom teachers are weakest. Second, they may serve as catalysts to other needed changes. And third, they are able to build the communication system on an existing schooling infrastructure.

The core instructional model has been less successful as an innovation that has rapidly diffused. In most major school systems that used it, it has been reduced in size or (as in the Ivory Coast) ended, and few new comparable projects have been implemented. The use of television—still too expensive for many countries—and dependence on foreign financial and technical assistance were common features,

so that when assistance agencies shifted their attention the projects languished. The lack of qualified teachers, the problem that mass media were best able to address, was perceived as less urgent as teacher-training levels were raised. Of greater moment, media-based schooling has rarely established a constituency, as William Smith has argued. The enhancement of quality that it promised and often achieved is difficult to rally around: teachers feared loss of their jobs, parents feared its use as a substitute for teachers, and administrators realized that it did not solve their day-to-day problems of system management. Despite its pedagogic successes, core instructional use of media has remained a political orphan.

Basic skills: out-of-school. Only a small portion of those who were seen to need schooling-related skills, like LITERACY and numeric skill, were to be found in school buildings. Consistent with human deficit explanations for slow development, many governments and private organizations considered literacy for adolescents and adults a prerequisite to individual modernization. Mass media instruction was often attractive to sponsors of literacy programs because they could not afford the training and salaries of a rural teaching staff, and the teaching skills of local volunteers were limited. In the church-run radio schools of Latin America—the best known of them is Acción Cultural Popular (ACPO, Popular Cultural Action) of Colombia—radio courses were and are broadcast to rural adults in their homes, and the coursework is reinforced by regular group meetings with local volunteer monitors. In West Africa, notably Senegal, roughly equivalent programs combined a local group leader (the *animateur*) with radio broadcasts to reach rural adults and provide literacy and other types of training. *See* AUDIOVISUAL EDUCATION.

Other countries, often with UNESCO technical assistance, used mass media as part of national literacy campaigns, conducting instruction by radio and television, providing textual materials through commercially distributed texts or newspaper supplements, sometimes incorporating local volunteer instructors. Some short-term and intensive campaigns, like those in Cuba and Nicaragua, have produced substantial effects and important political outcomes, although skepticism remains about the long-term functionality of the skills thus acquired. By contrast, long-term programs have proved to be difficult operationally. Despite some exceptions, local groups are difficult to organize, volunteer leaders are difficult to recruit and train, and both, once started and recruited, tend to lose momentum. Isolated media learners may lack the incentive to keep going on their own all the way to functional literacy, and available evidence suggests that relatively few nonliterates actually become functionally literate in such programs.

Distance education. For some people basic skills instruction out of school may be sufficient, but others bypassed by conventional schooling have a need for more extended school-equivalent education and credentials. Distance education programs satisfy both the need for substance and the credentials of in-classroom schooling. They typically combine mass media instruction with self-teaching texts, correspondence, and brief periods of face-to-face instruction. Scarce resources for education in the developing world, the increasing demand for secondary and postsecondary education, and the success of the British Open University made distance education attractive. It promised an acceptable quality of schooling at lower costs to governments, which did not have to (or could not) pay for buildings, and to students who could still work while "attending" school.

Distance education programs have been used for adult education from primary to UNIVERSITY levels and for teacher education (*see* TEACHING). As might be expected, some of these projects produced the promised quality and cost reduction, and others did not. Quality depends on the development of excellent instructional materials and the effective coordination of multiple channels of communication with the target audience. This may entail lower capital costs than for conventional schooling only when substantial student enrollment is achieved. In addition, all distance education programs depend on motivation among learners. Factors such as the longer time period required to complete studies, the common need both to work and to study, and personal isolation tend to limit enrollment and to increase drop-out rates.

Agriculture

Intellectual skills and academic credentials were not the only targets for deficit theories of development. A simple (and often misleading) comparison between crop yields in poor and wealthy countries suggested how high a price developing countries were paying because of the inefficiencies of their farmers. The task then became the transfer of agricultural technology, and a large literature grew up tracing the diffusion of innovations in agriculture.

One view of U.S. agricultural history credited the extension system and its associated institutions as the key to its success. That argument served as the basis for the implementation of similar systems in much of the developing world. With few exceptions, such systems reached a small proportion of farmers. As a response, many countries used radio as a complement to extension systems. The most common approach was an "open broadcast" strategy, particularly important examples being the "Farm and Home" broadcasts produced by most regional units

of All India Radio. In them, local producers depend on printed agricultural guides and local expert sources for the preparation of daily broadcasts encouraging new practices and presenting other useful information.

A second model, derived from a Canadian service called Farm Forums, was eventually adapted in India, in many African countries, and in Indonesia. Farm forums linked weekly radio broadcasts with meetings of local farmer groups, who would discuss broadcast recommendations and decide whether or not they were locally relevant. Some versions encouraged written questions from listeners that were then answered on the air.

Both major broadcast models and the extension model assumed that there was an available supply of innovations that farmers ought to adopt but that lack of knowledge and a tendency to be closed to change (a feature of the "traditional" personality) kept them from adopting. The remedy was to get information out to farmers and to provide, if possible, a social support structure that would stimulate change. However, hard looks at the range of both extension and broadcast farmer information programs led to questioning these assumptions. With only a few exceptions, such systems reached only a limited portion of target farmers and were particularly likely to miss subsistence farmers. Agricultural technology closely adapted to local growing and soil conditions was often unavailable, and even when it was, there often were capital requirements and risks that were beyond what subsistence farmers could accept. Evidence mounted that farmers were not reluctant innovators, as the first studies had portrayed them, but rational ones, changing practices when the incentives were economically correct. In contrast, information programs including broadcast ones had few mechanisms for ensuring that what they recommended was what farmers needed.

Health, Nutrition, and Family Planning

Curative medical systems reach only part of the population of most developing countries. To overcome system limitations, improvements in health status then had to come from preventive efforts or curative actions that people might take for themselves. Health and nutrition education were possible paths to that end. Person-to-person education, as in agriculture, remained the primary mode although the shortfall in outreach was evident to many observers. Media-based strategies were slowly incorporated into educational programs, and three major models of use evolved. The first was the open broadcast approach, which featured a physician or other "expert" source who talked with audiences about health problems. A second model was the intensive campaign; for example, Tanzania used ten- to twelve-week mobilizations, like one entitled "Man is Health," that combined weekly radio broadcasts and printed materials directed to locally organized groups recommending a small set of health practices (e.g., latrine building, malarial underbrush clearing). The third model was borrowed directly from commercial ADVERTISING. Sometimes called "social marketing," it used brief, frequently broadcast advertising spots focused on a small set of health practices or on a single one.

Like agriculture programs, health communication programs have been sporadically successful, more often as pilot programs than in full-scale operation, and for similar reasons. Notions that poor health could be explained by health practices within the control of individuals were too often untrue. The quality of education and communication programming was typically quite low, reflecting trivial investment in educational activities on the part of health systems.

Political Mobilization and Socialization

Along with assumptions of deficits in basic skills and in agricultural and health practices, many scholars and national leaders of all political stripes perceived substantial political deficits in their citizens. African leaders sought to unify ethnically and culturally diverse people around nation-states whose boundaries suited only the needs of former colonial empires. China and other countries encouraged their citizens to sacrifice current consumption in order to accumulate savings crucial to development plans. All political leaders running for ELECTION (or seeking popular support without benefit of votes) required acceptance and legitimation for their policies and actions.

There are striking examples of political education using communication technology. Efforts to raise the consciousness of Latin American peasants were linked to some of the literacy programs of the radio school movement previously described. In Brazil and Honduras major programs were based on the consciousness-raising theories of Brazilian educator Paulo Freire, described in one of his early books, *The Pedagogy of the Oppressed* (1970). Cuba and Nicaragua, among other countries, are examples of revolutionary governments that forged mass mobilization efforts to improve national literacy levels. At the same time, by galvanizing popular support and action in favor of one socially desirable policy, they expected broader legitimation.

Although mass mobilization campaigns with political objectives so close to the surface are less frequent in nonsocialist countries, mass communication for political legitimation is just as common. Control over news programming, extensive coverage of government leaders, and the intense use of media during political campaigns are nearly universal examples of POLITICAL COMMUNICATION. *See also* POLITICAL SYMBOLS.

Some mobilization programs work, and some do not. Ethnic, linguistic, religious, and other differences in African nations, in India, and elsewhere, when associated with inequalities in power, clearly cannot be counteracted solely by nation-affirming media-based campaigns. In contrast, short-term mobilizations that incorporate communication campaigns as one element of broader structural change can lead to dramatic social transformations, China offering perhaps the most striking example.

The Mid-1970s Assessment

In the late 1960s and early 1970s the "roll up your sleeves and do" development optimism of the post–World War II period faded. The realization of substantial changes in the quality of life in many countries was less than had been hoped for. Along with increasing skepticism about development models in general came doubts about communication for development; most of the projects had not brought about the expected outcomes.

Two explanations for this state of affairs were most persuasive. First, the "human deficit" model that underpinned so much of communication for development was no longer credible to many. Too often information was being thrown at problems defined by lack of *resources,* not lack of knowledge. Assumptions that if only people knew more they could readily improve their situation were judged by some as a cruel deception. Poverty, it was argued, was not only the result of failures by the poor to change but a reflection of their powerlessness to alter political and economic structures that limited their progress. The image of benevolent national and international elites sharing their progress with the less fortunate to make up their deficits (the "trickle down" notion) was replaced for many by an image of substantial conflict between those parties. Hospital beds, universities, and food subsidies for a nation's urban residents meant fewer resources for rural populations. Determinations that were made in wealthier nations concerning the price of commodities (e.g., oil, coffee), export/import limitations, technology transfer costs, and interest on loans had profound implications for the development of poorer countries but were beyond their control. This explanation has led some to move away from purposive uses of communication altogether, except as a means of political organizing.

An alternative explanation suggested that communication for development often failed because it was badly done, not because it lacked the potential to affect development outcomes. The problem, it was argued, was not in the theory but in its implementation, and a pattern of difficulties emerged. First, projects too often operated on assumption rather than evidence. It may have been possible to choose practice changes consistent with what people could and would do, but programmers lacked the detailed knowledge of their audiences required to make those choices. There was no money or staff to do research before the initiation of programs or to maintain contact with audiences as programs progressed. Second, inadequate attention was paid to the content of the development process. Governments and private programs that used the mass media for their sheer reach frequently lacked the necessary commitment to the production of effective, high-quality messages.

A third problem was that the isolation of broadcasters from other agencies and from their audiences led to what became usually an ineffectual solution: the incorporation of face-to-face outreach networks to complement broadcasts. However, the funds to pay for such a system, the logistical capacity to manage it, or the skilled agents to serve as part of it were not regularly available on the scale required for its success. As a result, the bland statement that media programs had to have as complement an expert face-to-face network served only to relieve broadcasters of the need to be pedagogically effective since they could claim that the real responsibility for change was in the hands of the field agents.

A fourth problem some media-based projects faced was their anomalous institutional status. If they were placed in a broadcasting bureaucracy (e.g., the national radio system, the ministry of information or communication) they were isolated from the sectoral bureaucracy (e.g., health, education, agriculture) they were meant to serve, with an almost inevitable coordination problem. On the other hand, when they were incorporated directly into a sectoral ministry they often found it difficult to gain a permanent foothold.

A final common problem is derived from the nature of political support that media-based projects may attract. Intense media campaigns appeal to politicians because they are not only doing good but can be *seen* to be doing good. However, the political value is in the public nature of the broadcast, not in its effectiveness at achieving change, and that can skew the way program resources are spent.

Gradually, recognition of these common problems produced a new generation of projects of two contrasting sorts: one addressing political failures, the other technical failures.

The political view. One set of program developers argued that previous projects rarely benefited the poor and explained this failure in political terms: a program controlled by central authorities and not by its beneficiaries would inevitably serve the needs of the central authorities. As long as the "targets" of development efforts had to depend on the elite's willingness to spend resources for the benefit of the powerless, little good would be done. The answer was to be found in small-scale efforts, called participatory programs, run for and by the intended beneficiaries. These grass-roots programs were initiated in many development sectors. One application in communication for development involved support of local media production capacity and distribution mechanisms. The materials would sometimes have a pedagogic element, addressing health, agriculture, or literacy, for example, and always included a "popular promotion" function—an attempt to raise political awareness in poor communities. Reviewers of such programs in Latin America generally have praised both the ideology and the courage of their creators but have admitted that in practice their successes were limited.

Like many other development projects, participatory efforts have been initiated mostly by outsiders to the local or specific community and have relied on outside funding. When the external funding ends the projects are incorporated into conventional institutions—often government-controlled—and often lose their participatory character. In addition such participatory programs may enhance community organization, but they do not directly affect material inequalities or the social and political constraints that motivated the participatory efforts. Social organization, if it does not complement or is not allowed a clear path for action, may lead to frustration. In a sense participatory communication programs, although rejecting individual human deficits as an explanation for failure to develop, implicitly pose a parallel community deficit explanation: the poor are poor because their communities lack organization and political consciousness. Just as the failure of the individual deficit assumption is one explanation for the irregular success of an earlier generation of development projects, the short lives and minimal success of participatory projects may reflect the questionable status of the community deficit assumption.

The technical view. The other set of second-generation projects focuses on using communication for development *better*. Whether addressing health, agriculture, or formal education, all these projects share certain characteristics. They invest heavily in the message-development process, they are informed about and responsive to their audiences, and they link media messages to material and educational actions of other institutions.

One group of projects concerned with in-school education is called interactive radio programs. In the pioneer program, teaching mathematics in Nicaragua by radio in early primary grades, fourteen professionals spent one year producing the materials for a single grade. Meticulous and artful planning of the substance and style of presentations, lessons that actively involved students, and extensive classroom observation all were brought together to produce learning substantially better than that achieved in nonradio classrooms. *See* EVALUATION RESEARCH.

A second group of projects, common in the health sector, is often called "social marketing." These projects encourage specific changes in behavior, whether in the use of a product (e.g., oral rehydration salts for the treatment of diarrheal disease) or in the adoption of new practices (e.g., increased use of weaning foods). The projects link extensive analyses of current audience ATTITUDES, beliefs, and behavior to study of the capacities of health and communication institutions (*see* CONSUMER RESEARCH). Together they guide the selection of a target health practice and a program strategy associating communication activities with complementary actions by other institutions. Extensive pretesting and evaluation of materials allow for readjustments of strategy as the project progresses. Egypt, Honduras, and Indonesia, among other countries, have implemented projects of this type, with the Egyptian program claiming a sharp drop in child mortality.

Both the interactive radio education projects and the health social marketing programs have resolved some of the central problems limiting the success of earlier communication for development efforts. In a technical sense the evidence suggests that they do communication for development "better." What they have not done is breach the political boundaries constraining them. In the case of the interactive radio projects, national adoption and continuation have proved elusive. Successful limited programs have not been extended because—perhaps like their predecessor in-school education projects—their success in improving learning did not satisfy the most urgent needs perceived by the constituencies involved in education. The health programs have had some success in achieving national scope, but their long-term continuation—especially after foreign funds are withdrawn—is not yet proved. Social marketing is not a common activity for ministries of health, so regardless of the short-term success of such programs, they must compete successfully with conventional activities that have an established call on sectoral budgets.

Overall Assessment

The history of communication for development contains broad swings in theory and practice. Early programs, with some exceptions, assumed that development was to be readily accelerated by investment in human knowledge and skills and that the use of mass media would, in turn, speed the building of such knowledge and skills. The rare success of these programs testified sometimes to theory failure—a failure to recognize the limits that economic and political constraints placed on knowledge and skills as the explanation for levels of development—and sometimes to technical failure—the confusion of mass media broadcasts with doing communication for development well.

The second-generation projects recognize these failures and attempt to remedy them. The participatory projects choose the political constraints as their primary target, albeit with limited success. The technically sophisticated programs (like the health social marketing programs) address political and economic constraints by lowering their sights and choosing targets achievable within those limits and then by focusing on reaching those targets with as much skill as can be mustered.

Bibliography. Robert Hornik, *Development Communication: Information, Agriculture, and Nutrition in the Third World*, New York, 1987; Jeremiah O'Sullivan and Mario Kaplun, *Communication Methods to Promote Grass Roots Participation*, Paris, 1978; Hilary Perraton, ed., *Alternative Routes to Formal Education*, Baltimore, Md., 1982; Everett M. Rogers, *Diffusion of Innovations* (1962), 3d ed., New York, 1983; Wilbur L. Schramm, *Big Media, Little Media*, Beverly Hills, Calif., 1977.

ROBERT C. HORNIK

DEWEY, JOHN (1859–1952)

U.S. philosopher, educational reformer, and social critic. During a career spanning seven decades, John Dewey made substantial contributions to nearly every branch of philosophical inquiry, grappling with such issues as the genesis of human society, the emergence of LANGUAGE, and theories of ethics, AESTHETICS, EDUCATION, and government. In all of these the concept of communication played a central role for Dewey. Its centrality in his thinking is implicit in the famous passage from his *Democracy and Education* (1916):

Society not only continues to exist by transmission, by communication, but it may fairly be said to exist in transmission, in communication. Men live in a community in virtue of the things they have in common; and communication is the way in which they come to possess things in common.

For Dewey the communicative process seemed to involve far-reaching moral and metaphysical meanings. In *Experience and Nature* (1925) he claimed that "of all affairs communication is the most wonderful. . . . [T]hat the fruit of communication should be participation, sharing, is a wonder by the side of which transubstantiation pales."

Born on a farm near Burlington, Vermont, Dewey was raised in a small-town milieu. He taught school for several years after graduating from the University of Vermont. His philosophical career began with doctoral studies at Johns Hopkins, which led to periods of teaching at the Universities of Michigan and Chicago, followed by a forty-seven-year stint at Columbia University. Throughout these periods he wrote voluminously, traveled widely, and gained worldwide influence. The changes he witnessed in the United States, which transformed it from an agrarian into an industrial nation, formed a backdrop to much of his thinking. His vision of a society fused and enriched by communication—one in which communication was indeed a communal experience, a sharing and not an imparting—reflected the small-town life of his youth, in which communication and democracy had a very natural linkage.

Dewey saw communication above all as "an activity in which there are partners, and in which the activity of each is modified and regulated by the partnership." Through symbolic communication an aggregate of individuals becomes something far more, a society with multiple threads of interconnection.

The communication media evolving in the modernization process were seen by Dewey as instruments of potential and danger. He was enthusiastic about the possibility of creating a more "organized intelligence"—combining new media, social science techniques, and ways of artistic presentation to provide a continuous, systematic, and effective exposition of social and political movements. Toward this end Dewey even became involved in an aborted attempt at publishing a new kind of newspaper, to be called "Thought News." The fullest treatment of these issues came in *The Public and Its Problems* (1927), which was Dewey's most ambitious statement on the relations among political affairs, modern mass media, and methods of social inquiry. His basic concern, lending a special tension to these discussions, was whether media spanning a nation could fuse it into a "great community" or whether the communal values would be eroded by depersonalized systems under remote and faceless control. He noted that the new media, hypnotizing nationwide audiences, seemed to divert them from political interests, even if not setting out to do so. Here Dewey saw great danger to democracy, an issue he never quite resolved. Yet he clung to a faith that these same media could be used to create the great community he envisioned.

See also COMMUNICATION, PHILOSOPHIES OF.

DANIEL J. CZITROM

DIARY

In common usage "to keep a diary" means to maintain a private record of day-to-day life in a series of dated installments, chiefly for one's own use and satisfaction. In this general sense diary keeping has been adopted by many millions of people over a period of at least four centuries, and many thousands of the resulting texts have been published or preserved in public ARCHIVES. These documents display the wide range of uses that have been made of the diary-keeping practice and, correspondingly, the variety of conventions and forms of expression evident in the development of this MODE of communication. As firsthand accounts of every kind of human situation, often replete with the kind of detail that more formal history and AUTOBIOGRAPHY would omit, diaries are an invaluable source for historians and in some cases have achieved the eloquence and density of literature.

The diary form. The term *diary* has been applied quite loosely to a broad array of texts. As the word itself implies, the diary—or journal or *Tagebuch* — is strictly to be conceived of as a BOOK composed of daily entries, and for many diarists this is indeed the governing code of practice. Even when the entries are not in fact composed one day at a time, the text will continue to be structured as a series of daily installments. In this way the diary medium retains its peculiar property of registering the contents, however selected, of a single day as the basic unit of significance. For other diarists, however, the primary characteristic of the medium is not the dated regularity of its record but rather its availability as a vehicle for unpremeditated, informal utterance. Given this emphasis, the diary may become an accumulation of irregular notes and reflections composing, more or less haphazardly, an imprint of the diarist's life.

A further distinction should be made between the public and the private diary. Although the word tends to suggest a personal or even secret document—the *journal intime*—a diary may well be kept as a public record, conscientiously preserving matters of fact or meditation for future generations of family, community, or nation. In English the choice of the term *journal* sometimes signifies a relatively impersonal record of events or public transactions. Between the private diary and the proceedings of a public body there is also an intermediate species of diary that records an individual's experience but that is nonetheless intended for eventual publication. Thus, for example, people in public life, witnesses of historic scenes, travelers, scientists, or artists have often recorded their perceptions and insights for posterity in the day-to-day format of the diary.

Most diaries, from the most mundane jottings about the weather to the most intimate searchings of the soul, have not been written with the idea of being published or even read. Yet the very act of writing intelligibly implies a communication of some sort. Many diarists undoubtedly write only for their own

Figure 1. *(Diary)* Jules and Edmond Goncourt. Photograph by Nadar, 1850s. The Bettmann Archive, Inc.

subsequent perusal or for the sheer satisfaction of registering ideas and impressions in words. But many others discover that their mode of expression is conditioned by the relationship with an imagined reader, for whose interest or judgment or sympathy the diary is being maintained. Thus the diary becomes a species of endless LETTER, a form of utterance that can play an important part in the writer's emotional life. For many diarists, communicating their feelings to a silent companion is felt to be an indispensable relief, and the diary text itself becomes a treasured possession, representing the repository of the writer's essential being.

Two other features of the diary mode are the commitment to truthfulness and the informality of style. Not all diarists are scrupulously honest, even with themselves, and many have distorted or suppressed portions of their record. But on the whole it is a convention of diary writing, public and private, that the writer should be as unguarded and as truthful as possible, both in the selection of matter to be reported and in the manner of reporting. For some diarists, indeed, the pursuit of utter truthfulness becomes a major motive for writing and prompts deliberate exercises of style designed to elicit the greatest candor. Although diaries have naturally been written in a wide variety of styles, reflecting the class, culture,

education, and historical epoch of the writer, a frequent feature of the diary text is a deliberately careless and elliptical style, contracting standard syntax and resorting to abbreviations and note forms. Such a stylistic feature stands as a sign that the utterance is unstudied and uncorrected, hence more authentic than a polished text. *See* STYLE, LITERARY.

History of the form. The origins of the diary may be traced back to a number of unrelated sources. As a conventional practice, diary writing apparently became common in Europe in the seventeenth century. Prior to this time, however, several habits of regular recordkeeping were in use that both contributed to the emergence of the diary proper and have continued in use to the present. First of all, there was the custom of maintaining detailed accounts of the transactions of public bodies—government, church, trading ventures, and so on—and of keeping such registers of events as ships' logs and campaign annals. Private persons, too, have made notes of public happenings. From as early as the fifteenth century, anonymous citizens of Paris can be seen to have recorded over many years items relating to the communal life of the city. Another component of the diary habit was the keeping of travel journals, frequently the raw material for published narratives. Among many other early practitioners, Albrecht Dürer, the German painter, kept a journal of a visit to the Low Countries (1520–1521), and French essayist Michel de Montaigne documented a tour in Italy (1580–1581). Specifically recommended by the seventeenth-century English essayist Francis Bacon ("Of Travel"), the travel journal has never lost its popularity. Another precursor of the personal diary was the practice of making notes of one's reading or of preserving selected passages in a commonplace book. Artists and experimenters likewise kept notebooks of their insights and discoveries. The *Notebooks* of Leonardo da Vinci are an early and prime example; the notebooks of writers such as Fyodor Dostoyevsky, Franz Kafka, Henry James, and Albert Camus show the continuity of the custom. And in the wake of the Protestant Reformation, devout persons sometimes made memorandums of sermons, while English and American Puritans were urged to make a daily examination of their spiritual state—a motive for diary keeping that persisted for centuries in a more secular guise.

Emerging from these various proto-diary forms is the personal chronicle of everyday life, blending NARRATIVE with reflection, kept essentially for its own sake as the document of a person's existence. For English readers *The Diary of Samuel Pepys* is the great original and paradigm of this kind of diary. Kept between 1660 and 1669 by an ambitious public servant in the admiralty, it gives the impression of registering every night just about everything Pepys

Figure 2. *(Diary)* Photograph of Anne Frank. The inscription reads, "This is a photo as I would wish myself to look all the time. Then I would maybe have a chance to come to Hollywood. Anne Frank, 10 Oct. 1942." The Bettmann Archive, Inc.

could remember and find words for, in a tone of simple and sometimes touching candor. In fact the diary was composed with some care from notes accumulated over several days. Its distinction as a human document is that it combines intimate detail with matters of historic interest, while being neither too self-absorbed nor too external. As an element in his psychic economy, Pepys's diary habit seems not only to exhibit but actually to have promoted an exemplary mode of awareness.

In the centuries that followed, as diary writing became a more widespread practice it also became increasingly self-conscious as a quasi-literary activity. As well as recording their doings or confiding their thoughts and feelings, diarists were increasingly conscious of composing a book. James Boswell, for example, the biographer of SAMUEL JOHNSON, set out in 1762 to make his diary the colorful saga of a young man's adventures, and he proudly showed the growing volumes to his friends. Among romantic artists and writers of the early nineteenth century the *journal intime* became a fashionable vehicle for luxuriating in the convolutions of the soul (*see* ROMANTICISM). French novelists Benjamin Constant and George Sand may be cited as examples. At the same time, the diary habit as literary exercise became widespread among persons of culture. Whereas some nineteenth-century diaries, such as those of the Danish theologian Søren Kierkegaard, were passionately private expressions of spiritual anguish, many others were written by travelers and intellectuals, monarchs and ladies of leisure, as a kind of civilized accomplishment or duty. If not printed in the writers'

lifetimes, they were often edited for publication by a biographer (*see* BIOGRAPHY).

In the twentieth century people have continued to write, or in recent years to tape-record, diaries of all kinds, from conventional daily narratives to intense autobiographical quests, as well as experimental exercises in self-documentation. As more diaries have been published, more diarists have written with publication in view. For writers such as W. N. P. Barbellion, Arthur Inman, and the novelist Anaïs Nin it is no exaggeration to say that the diary constituted their literary magnum opus. Less obsessively, many people in public life, or in situations of dramatic interest such as war, REVOLUTION, or a hijacking, have embarked upon journals deliberately for what may be called their journalistic potential. Whether for immediate or delayed publication, the diary format has provided them with the one-day-at-a-time perspective on unfolding events that preserves the immediacy of actual experience. For the same reason, the diary mode has been subtly employed as a vehicle for FICTION and blatantly exploited for forgeries such as the briefly notorious "secret diaries" of Adolf Hitler (1983). At the same time, however, the diary composed unselfconsciously, in response to a personal need to record and communicate everyday experience, continues to be kept by all sorts of people, purely for its own sake.

A number of variables combine to make some diaries stand out from the great mass that have survived. To be historical documents of more than archival value they need to afford a perceptive and advantageous view of intrinsically interesting events and personalities, whether local or national. Diaries as different as those of John Quincy Adams, with a unique view of U.S. politics in the early nineteenth century, of the Goncourt brothers, observing the Parisian literary scene in the late nineteenth century, and of Harold Nicolson, in the thick of British politics before and during World War II, fulfill this criterion abundantly. The creation of arresting autobiographical documents requires that the diarists be people of some complexity, engaged in an active process of self-encounter. Boswell's mammoth diaries may stand for an example of this type, as may those of the French novelists Stendahl and André Gide and the English novelist Virginia Woolf. And for both types the interest is enhanced by an expressive energy that exploits the available resources of language. Many published diaries derive their primary interest from their illumination of the lives of already celebrated figures—politicians, writers, artists, and the like. In such cases the intrinsic literary qualities of the text may be secondary to its documentary value. On the other hand, some rare diaries are autobiographical masterpieces by people otherwise totally unknown, such as the English curate Francis Kilvert, writing in the 1870s, or the young German-born Jewish victim of Nazism, Anne Frank, writing in hiding in Amsterdam.

See also AUTHORSHIP.

Bibliography. Porter H. Abbott, *Diary Fiction*, Ithaca, N.Y., 1984; Robert A. Fothergill, *Private Chronicles: A Study of English Diaries*, London and New York, 1974; Alain Girard, *Le journal intime*, Paris, 1963; Gustav Hocke, *Das europäische Tagebuch*, Wiesbaden, 1963; Thomas Mallon, *A Book of One's Own: People and Their Diaries*, New York, 1984.

ROBERT A. FOTHERGILL

DIASPORA

The Diaspora (from the Greek, meaning "dispersion"), which has been the characteristic mode of existence of the Jewish people for more than two and a half millennia, has been a pivotal theme in the development of global communications (*see* MIGRATION). It came into being with the forcible deportation of the Israelites from their Northern Hebrew kingdom in 597 B.C.E. by the Assyrians and of the Judahites from the Southern Hebrew kingdom in 586 B.C.E. by the Babylonians. These two exiles resulted in the establishment of the first Diaspora in Mesopotamia. Also in 586 B.C.E. began the voluntary settlement of Jews from Judah in Egypt. It was from these two primary Diaspora centers that Jewish contingents moved on to the east, to Persia and lands beyond it, and to the west, along the North African coastline. Throughout their subsequent history the forced exile of Jews from one country usually re-

sulted in the voluntary settlement of Jewish groups in other countries, where they came to constitute new Diaspora communities.

Roman rule. Long before the Second Jewish Commonwealth was destroyed by the Romans (70 C.E.), Jews had settled in most parts of the ROMAN EMPIRE and also to the east of it, in the Parthian Empire. The Greek geographer Strabo, writing in the first century B.C.E., stated that it was difficult to find a place in the entire world to which the Jewish nation had not penetrated. The Jewish presence in the Roman Empire prepared the ground for the spread of Christianity. By the second century C.E. Jewish communities were established in the Roman colonies of Spain, Gaul (today France), Germany, Pannonia (today Hungary), Dacia (today Romania), the Balkans, Asia Minor, the Levant coast, and in all lands of North Africa; in Arabia; and in the domains of the Parthian Empire.

From this period dates the polyglotism that was to remain a characteristic of the Jews into the twentieth century. The Jews of Palestine spoke Hebrew, Aramaic, Greek, and Latin, and those of the Diaspora also spoke a similar assortment of languages. During this period Jews translated the Bible into Aramaic and Greek, and they produced important literary works in these two languages (Aramaic: the Babylonian and Palestinian Talmuds, Midrashim; Greek: the writings of the Alexandrian philosopher Philo Judaeus, the histories of Flavius Josephus, etc.). Hebrew became restricted to synagogal use and to international communications.

Although hard-and-fast data are scanty, there can be little doubt that the constituent parts of the Diaspora maintained communication with one another. We know of several leading Talmudic rabbis who traveled between Palestine and Mesopotamia and through Palestine, Greece, and Rome. The Jews engaged in lively seafaring all along the Mediterranean. These chains of communication were the basis of strong emotional ties among the Diaspora communities as well as between them and Palestinian Jewry, so that if an attack were made on Jews or their religion in any part of the Roman Empire it provoked almost instantaneous reaction in the form of revolts in other Jewish communities.

As long as the Jerusalem Temple stood (i.e., until 70 C.E.), the relationship between the Diaspora communities and the Palestinian center found its expression primarily in the payment of the Temple tax of half a shekel. This tax was defrayed equally by Jews who lived in the Roman Empire and those who lived outside its boundaries. The Babylonian Jews sent their half-shekels to Jerusalem in a huge caravan, accompanied by a large contingent of Jews to defend it in case of brigand attack. Perhaps even more important was the fulfillment of the biblical commandment of pilgrimage to Jerusalem, which annually brought large numbers of Jews from all over the Diaspora to the Holy City. Financial support of Palestinian Jewish institutions by wealthy Diaspora Jews continued after the destruction of the Temple. The Diaspora also gave strong political support to the Palestinian Jewish community. Another link between the Diaspora and Palestine was the attendance of Diaspora Jews at the renowned Palestinian Jewish academies of religious learning, which continued, and even intensified, after the destruction of the Temple and secured Palestinian Jews the religious hegemony over the entire Diaspora until the end of the second century C.E. A direct result of this scholarly communication was the spread of religious learning and observance from Palestine to the countries of the Diaspora.

Under Islam and Christendom. Following the Arab conquest of the Near East, North Africa, and Spain, medieval civilization was divided into a northwestern Christian and a southeastern Muslim realm, between which the maintenance of communication was an almost exclusive privilege of Jews (*see* ISLAM, CLASSICAL AND MEDIEVAL ERAS; MIDDLE AGES). Christians could not trade in Muslim countries, nor could Muslims trade in the Christian lands. Yet the source of most of the luxuries demanded in Europe was in the "House of Islam." In this situation the Jews, who were tolerated in both realms as commercial intermediaries, filled a crucial need. In the eighth and ninth centuries, the Rādhānites (or Rāhdānites), as the intercontinental Jewish merchants were called, established three major trade routes between southwestern Europe and East Asia. The Rādhānites spoke French, Spanish, Slavic, and Greek as well as Arabic and Persian. They exported from Europe to the East eunuchs, slave girls and boys, brocade, beaver and marten furs, and swords. On the way back they brought musk, aloeswood, camphor, cinnamon, and other products of the East.

Jewish merchant adventurers. When Charlemagne sent an embassy to Hārūn al-Rashīd (in 797), a Jew, Isaac, accompanied it as an interpreter. The two Christian ambassadors, Sigismond and Landfred, died on the way, but four years later (in 801) Isaac returned with gifts from the caliph, including an elephant.

From the ninth to the eighteenth century dozens of Jewish travelers made their way across Europe and Asia with the prime purpose of finding the Jewish communities of distant lands and bringing back information about them. However, much greater was the number of Jews who engaged in trading between the Mediterranean and South Asia. Maimonides (1135–1204) was engaged in trading in precious stones with India and gave it up only after his brother David perished in a shipwreck in the Indian Ocean, about 1168. In the Cairo genizah numerous documents were found showing that in the Middle Ages Jews maintained commercial relations between Egypt, India, and Ceylon (today Sri Lanka), with Aden as the point of transshipment. (The genizah, meaning "hideaway," was a storeroom in the Cairo synagogue for saving any piece of paper on which the Holy Name was written, because these could not be destroyed. When discovered in the twentieth century it became a rich source of historical information, largely in the form of letters.)

Jews as cultural mediators. The contacts established by travelers and merchants had, occasionally at least, political implications. Thus it is likely that the conversion to Judaism of the Khazar kingdom (between the Black Sea and the Volga River) in the eighth century was the result of the influence of Jewish merchant adventurers. More significant for the history of global communications is the reference of Abraham ibn Ezra (1089–1164)—himself a great traveler—to a Jewish traveler who, he says, brought from India the so-called Arabic numerals.

This piece of information—if indeed based on fact—supplies but one example of the flow of ideas from the East to the West in which the Jews had a crucial role. From the eleventh century on, Sephardi (Spanish) Jews were the foremost translators from Arabic into Hebrew of the works of Jewish and Muslim philosophers, astrologers and astronomers, geometricians, and medical authors. Several of these works were themselves translations or paraphrases of, or commentaries on, classical Greek originals. Many of them were subsequently (especially from the fourteenth century on) retranslated from Hebrew into Latin, again by Jewish translators. This work of cultural transmission made, in the course of the fifteenth and sixteenth centuries, a large number of Greek, Arabic, and Hebrew works available to the Christian world. To this flow of communication was added in the seventeenth century the work of Christian translators from Hebrew into Latin, which broadened the familiarity of European scholars with the rich products of medieval Jewish thought and research as well as with the foremost works of Arab and classical Greek authors.

Also in the fourteenth to sixteenth centuries a large number of Latin works were translated into Hebrew, which made European thought accessible to Jews, and from the seventeenth century on, an increasing number of works were translated from German, French, English, Polish, Russian, and Spanish into Hebrew. In this manner the Jews were able to familiarize themselves with European culture even before the onset of the Haskalah (the Jewish Enlightenment) in the late eighteenth century induced increasing numbers of them to learn the languages of the countries in which they lived.

Mapmaking, navigation, and diplomacy. Following the Arab conquest of North Africa and Spain, the Jews played an important role in transmitting the knowledge and use of nautical aids such as the compass, the quadrant (predecessor of the sextant), the astrolabe, and astronomical tables from the Arab East to the Christian West. Majorca was the main center of Jewish craftsmen producing nautical instruments, and of Jewish mapmakers, whose charts were indispensable for seafarers (see CARTOGRAPHY). After the Spanish exile (1492) the Marranos (crypto-Jews) became dispersed along the Mediterranean, in northwestern Europe, and later in the New World, and they participated in international and transcontinental maritime trade as entrepreneurs, shipbuilders, merchants, brokers, and insurers.

From the twelfth century on, when European Christian merchants, in the wake of the Crusades (see CRUSADES, THE), began to take an interest in the Levant trade, they had it in their power to curtail the role of the Jews in international commerce, and even to exclude them from it. This, in turn, forced the Jews to turn to moneylending and led to their taking an increasingly important role in the development of the banking business.

Jews also served as diplomatic representatives of Christian states in Muslim countries and vice versa. For a Jewish trader or diplomat it was relatively easy to establish contacts in a foreign country where his coreligionists, with whom he could communicate in Hebrew, were always ready to help him. A Muslim or Christian envoy did not have this advantage.

Contacts between central and eastern Europe. A similar situation developed in the fifteenth century between central and eastern Europe. The expulsions of the Jews from German lands and their settlement in the east of Europe became the basis of commercial and intellectual communications between the two areas. The Ashkenazi ("German") Jews spoke Yiddish whether they lived in Germany, Austria, Poland, the Baltic lands, or the "Pale of Settlement" in Russia, and this, as well as family connections, gave them an advantage over the linguistically and socially more limited Christian merchants.

The phenomenal rise in numbers and in Jewish learning of East European Jews secured them the cultural hegemony of European Jewry from the seventeenth to the nineteenth century. West European Jewry remained numerically small and, after the exhaustion of the Sephardi élan in the seventeenth century, became culturally less significant. However, East European Jewish life and culture were isolated from the non-Jewish environment and became ingrown. From the sixteenth to the nineteenth century most of the Ashkenazi Diaspora was confined to ghettos, and thus whatever international commercial and scholarly communications were maintained by it had little impact on the Christian world. Talmudism and, as a reaction to it, Hasidism became the dominant modes of Jewish existence, accompanied by a rigid rejection of all manifestations of gentile culture. As for the Middle Eastern Diaspora during the same period, it shared the general cultural decline of the Muslim world; both Jews and Muslims remained largely untouched by the cultural developments of the West.

Enlightenment and emancipation. The rise of the Haskalah in the late eighteenth century and the gradual emancipation of the Jews in one European country after another in the course of the nineteenth century once more introduced Ashkenazi Jewry into the picture of global communications. Jewish participation in the cultures of countries that emancipated their Jewish populations increased at a phenomenal rate. By the end of the nineteenth century Jews could be found among the foremost scholars, scientists, artists, litterateurs, philosophers, and the like in all the countries of western and central Europe, as well as among the leading industrialists, merchants, bankers, and even statesmen. The same process could be observed also in the United States, where the Jews played a leading role especially in the development of the mass media (newspapers, MOTION PICTURES, RADIO, television) and the entertainment industries.

At the same time, the international nature of the Diaspora enabled the Jews to maintain communication with coreligionists in other countries with greater ease than was the case among their gentile counterparts. A case in point is the international character of the Rothschild banking dynasty, with its houses in Germany, Austria, France, Italy, and England. Another is the similarly international character of the political Zionist movement created by Theodor Herzl (1860–1904), owing to which it was able to conduct its struggle for the establishment of a Jewish national home in Palestine simultaneously in the major capitals of Europe.

International Jewish organizations. Intense communication among the Jewish communities all over the world was the basis for global Jewish solidarity, which led to the establishment of international Jewish organizations whose purpose was to represent Jewish interests and to defend Jews wherever and whenever they were threatened, slandered, or attacked. The foremost of these organizations were the French Alliance Israelite Universelle (founded 1860); the British Jewish Colonization Association (ICA; founded 1891), which later (1927) became the Palestine Jewish Colonization Association (PICA) and ceased to function in 1957; the German Hilfsverein der deutschen Juden (1901–1941); and the World Jewish Congress (founded 1936).

The Diaspora and Israel. After the Balfour Declaration (November 2, 1917), in which the British government undertook to facilitate the establishment of a Jewish national home in Palestine, and even more so after the independence of Israel (May 14, 1948), the Jewish community in the ancestral land of the Jews became a vital factor in Jewish life in the

Diaspora, and its most important center of communications. All over the Diaspora Jews were eager to stand by Israel, whenever the need arose to support it financially, diplomatically, culturally, and militarily, and to cooperate among themselves for these purposes. In the first few years after Israel's independence there was large-scale immigration of Jews into the new state from all over the Diaspora, including Jews who had scattered to many lands from Nazi Germany, others who had fled Nazi-occupied lands, others who had survived the Holocaust, and emigrants from various Muslim countries. In a number of these, resentment over the emergence of Israel in what had been a territory with an Arab majority was spilling over into anger against the Jewish communities that had existed in these countries for centuries. As a result of the establishment of Israel and its active encouragement of immigration, central and eastern Europe (with the exception of Soviet Russia, which did not allow large-scale Jewish emigration) as well as the Middle East have remained practically without Diaspora communities. By the 1970s this "ingathering of the exiles" had largely been accomplished, but Israel remained the most important central concern for Diaspora Jewry, attracting annually thousands of visitors, tourists, and participants in conventions.

Although Israel has thus become a focal concern for Jewish communities and their organizations in all parts of the Diaspora, the cultural achievements of Israel, which were transmitted with increasing potency to the Diaspora, became a powerful factor in maintaining Jewish consciousness and strengthening Jewish identification in the Diaspora. Because of this intensive two-way exchange, the general conviction among world Jewry is that its future depends on the continued existence of its two parts—Israel and the Diaspora—and the close interrelationship between them.

Bibliography. Étan Levine, ed., *Diaspora: Exile and the Jewish Condition*, New York, Jerusalem, and Tel Aviv, 1986; Raphael Patai, *Tents of Jacob: The Diaspora Yesterday and Today*, Englewood Cliffs, N.J., 1971; Howard M. Sachar, *Diaspora*, New York, 1985; Tom Segev, *1949: The First Israelis* (1949, ha-Yiśr' elim ha-rishonim), New York and London, 1986.

RAPHAEL PATAI

DICTIONARY. *See* LANGUAGE REFERENCE BOOK.

DIDEROT, DENIS (1713–1784)

French writer, encyclopedist, philosopher, and leader of the Enlightenment. Denis Diderot helped set a pattern for the French man of letters that has contin-

ued through such twentieth-century figures as Jean-Paul Sartre and MICHEL FOUCAULT. Diderot's most influential project by far was the monumental *Encyclopédie, ou dictionnaire raisonné des sciences, des arts et des métiers* (1751–1780), of which he was the main editor. Notable in the history of communications for its scale, the resistance it met, and its impact on French—indeed Western—life and thought, the *Encyclopédie* was in effect the scripture of European rationalism.

Born in Langres, Diderot studied there under Jesuit teachers. Later he continued his education in Paris, receiving a Master of Arts degree from the University of Paris in 1732. During the next dozen or so years he apparently lived the hand-to-mouth existence of a bohemian, sometime teacher, and writer-for-hire. At the same time he made his religious migration from Catholicism through deism to atheism. He also became a friend of that other towering figure of the French Enlightenment, philosopher Jean-Jacques Rousseau. They were friends for fifteen years, but petty differences and an underlying philosophical disagreement then led to a split.

In 1743, against the wishes of his family, Diderot married Anne-Toinette Champion, the daughter of a Paris tradesman. The marriage began as a love match but eventually became a mismatch; it endured only because the couple were devoted to their daughter, Angélique. Diderot's relationship with Sophie Volland, begun in 1755 and lasting until her death in 1784, was considerably more affectionate; his letters to Sophie are masterpieces of the GENRE.

In 1745, along with the mathematician Jean Le Rond d'Alembert, Diderot contracted to coedit what was originally conceived of as a French translation of Ephraim Chambers's *Cyclopaedia* (1728). The *Encyclopédie*, finally completed in seventeen volumes of text and eleven volumes of plates (later augmented by a six-volume supplement and a two-volume analytical index), became much more than a translation and reference work. As contributors Diderot and his coeditor enlisted a talented group of scholars, writers, and scientists imbued with a belief in the power of human reason based on knowledge of material facts. Diderot, the son of a craftsman, showed a lifelong respect for work and skills, and the *Encyclopédie* under his editorship was distinguished for being a storehouse of practical and detailed information on the sciences, crafts, and technology. But the more lasting significance of the *Encyclopédie* lay in its advocacy of facts, the scientific method, and critical thought. By helping to "transform men's values" and "make men favorable to change," the *Encyclopédie* "played an extremely important part as one of the disposing causes of the French Revolution," according to Diderot's biographer Arthur M. Wilson (*see* REVOLUTION).

Each of the *Encyclopédie*'s first seven volumes was

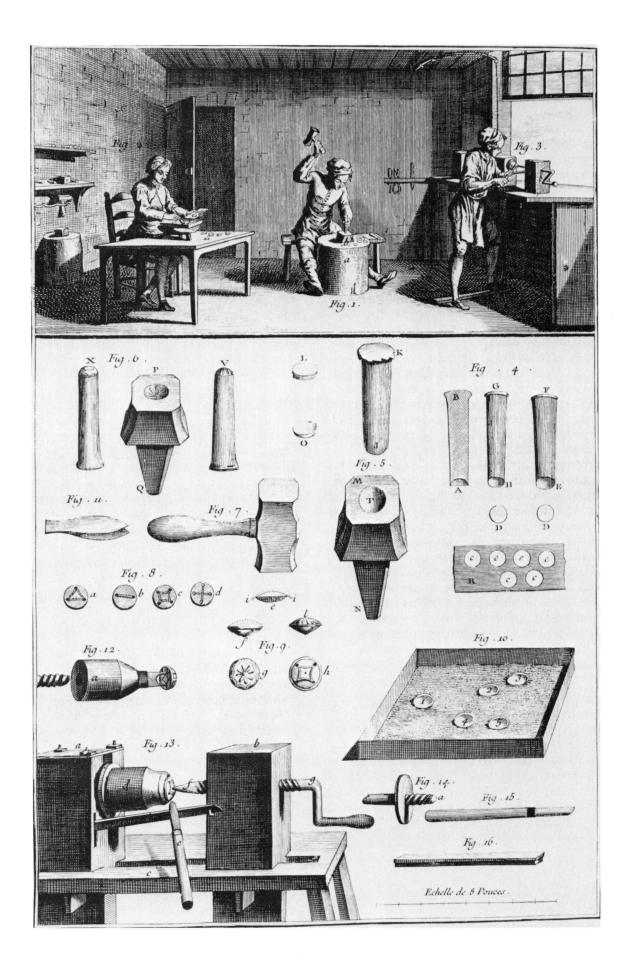

published individually when work on it was finished, and each met with a barrage of criticism from the religious and government establishments, especially the Jesuits, who felt that the work's materialism and rationalism posed serious threats to faith and the church. A personal crisis came for Diderot in 1749 after the publication of his *Lettre sur les aveugles* (Letter on the Blind), an innovative work proposing that the blind learn to read by using touch. The logical implications of the work—basing human knowledge on the senses rather than faith or authority—were not lost on the official censors, and Diderot was imprisoned for three months. A crisis for the *Encyclopédie* itself came in 1759 when a royal decree condemned it for damaging RELIGION and morality and forbade further publication. Thereafter Diderot continued as sole editor to prepare the remaining volumes of text and plates surreptitiously for delivery to subscribers who had already contracted for them. The government tacitly acquiesced in their eventual publication, but Diderot was devastated to learn that the publisher, André Le Breton, had deleted what he considered dangerous material after Diderot had approved the final galley proofs. However, the publisher's CENSORSHIP had a greater effect on Diderot than on the *Encyclopédie*.

Diderot apparently learned bitter lessons from his imprisonment and the attempted suppression of the *Encyclopédie*, and most of what he wrote after 1759 was not published until after his death in 1784. These writings included his perceptive ART criticism in the privately circulated, manuscript-format *Correspondance littéraire*; the brilliant dialogues *L'entretien entre d'Alembert et Diderot* and *Le rêve de d'Alembert*; the novels *La religieuse, Jacques le fataliste,* and *Le neveu de Rameau*; plays; and numerous essays, including especially influential ones on the theory of DRAMA, *Entretiens sur "Le fils naturel"* and *De la poésie dramatique.*

See also ENCYCLOPEDIA; LETTER; LOCKE, JOHN.

Bibliography. Lester G. Crocker, *Diderot: The Embattled Philosopher,* rev. ed., New York, 1966; Denis Diderot, *Oeuvres complètes,* ed. by Jean Varloot et al., Paris, 1975–; Douglas H. Gordon and Norman L. Torrey, *The Censoring of Diderot's Encyclopédie and the Re-established Text,* New York, 1947, reprint 1966; Jacques Proust, *Diderot et l'Encyclopédie,* Paris, 1962; Arthur M. Wilson, *Diderot: The Testing Years, 1713–1759,* New York and Oxford, 1957; idem, *Diderot: The Appeal to Posterity, 1759–1784,* New York and Oxford, 1972.

SUSAN J. STEINBERG

DIFFUSION

The dispersion or spread of a phenomenon through time and space. The phenomena of interest here are *ideas* (concepts that may or may not be related to tangible entities such as practices or products) and *innovations* (the translation of ideas into new practices, processes, or products). The diffusion of ideas and innovations is a fundamental component of social and economic change, for better (when seen as a source of advancement for society as a whole) or worse (when associated with inequalities in the distribution of resources). Because of its widespread influence the diffusion process has been extensively researched and is well documented. Communication has been found to be a key element in the spread of ideas and innovations, and it is the common link that results in similar spatial and temporal patterns of diffusion.

The Evolution of Diffusion Research

Research on the diffusion of new ideas has its origins primarily in the rural sociology tradition, with case studies focusing on the adoption of new agricultural techniques by farmers in the United States. Subsequently attention was drawn to other types of innovations such as new medical products and new industrial processes, and a more international scope emerged. The early approach also dealt largely with the "problem" of encouraging "desirable" change, particularly in developing countries, and the "solution" was often seen as instilling "progressive" ATTITUDES in a population (*see* DEVELOPMENT COMMUNICATION). In contemporary research the effects of innovations have been more thoroughly analyzed in terms of both harmful and beneficial consequences, and a more balanced approach has emerged.

Finally, the traditional approach was concerned with social processes and other demand-related factors affecting the diffusion of innovations, and not with the commercial or supply viewpoint. Reflecting this, most research on innovation diffusion concentrated on variables related to the individual or household adoption decision and emphasized the role of social networks, information flows, consumer demographics, and psychological variables such as innovativeness and resistance to adoption. Subsequent research indicates that this perspective alone does not provide sufficient explanation when—as is the case for most contemporary innovations—a diffusion process is orchestrated by those who benefit from

◁ **Figure 1.** *(Diderot, Denis)* The making of metal buttons: a page from the *Encyclopédie* of Denis Diderot and Jean Le Rond d'Alembert, Paris, 1751–1772, volume 2, plate 3. From A. Mendini, *Encyclopedie di Diderot e d'Alembert (Parigi 1751–1772),* facsimile, Milan: Domus, 1975.

stimulating the rapid and complete acceptance of an idea or innovation (e.g., through ADVERTISING). In these cases the mechanisms through which innovations are made available to potential adopters are of equal if not greater importance.

To fill this gap Lawrence Brown developed a "market and infrastructure" model of innovation diffusion that focuses on supply-oriented rather than demand-oriented factors affecting diffusion. It views the adoption of an innovation as the third of three stages. The first stage is the establishment of public or private firms, organizations, or other entities through which an innovation is distributed or made available to the population at large. The locations of these entities, the temporal sequencing of their establishment, and their operating procedures determine where and when an innovation will be available. This provides the general outline of the *spatial* pattern of diffusion. In the second stage of the diffusion process these entities conceive and implement strategies to promote adoption among the populations in their service or market areas. Frequently this entails establishing infrastructures such as service and delivery systems and water or electric supply networks. It may also involve establishment of a price for the innovation, market selection and segmentation, and the design of information dissemination programs (*see* CONSUMER RESEARCH). Taken together these stages create differing levels of access to an innovation (depending on an individual's economic, locational, and social characteristics) and hence influence the ultimate adoption or rejection decision.

Experience has shown that developing a new technology to the point at which its purchase is cost-effective to the consumer does not ensure adoption by the public. Thousands of new products are introduced each year, the vast majority of which fail. Failures to gain acceptance and use occur for both private- and public-sector innovations, but the latter are particularly frustrating because of the substantial public resources that are frequently expended on them. Public funds represent a significant portion of the total research and development (R & D) budget of most countries. The federal laboratories of the United States, as one example, employ about one-sixth of the nation's research workers. Only a small fraction of the results of this research is translated into commercial applications. As one indicator of this, only about 2.5 percent of the nearly five thousand inventions newly owned by the U.S. government each year are licensed for commercial use.

Research on a variety of public efforts to bring about life-style changes also indicates slow and limited impact. This is true, for instance, of programs to encourage seat-belt use and family planning. The limited effectiveness of technological and social change

programs has been attributed to the failure of public agencies to employ sophisticated marketing techniques and to the low frequency with which change strategies and tactics are pretested, coordinated, or evaluated (*see* EVALUATION RESEARCH).

In recognition of the importance of marketing and supply concepts to the success of public-sector efforts to induce social and technological change, a field of research has emerged that focuses on four types of strategies for planned change: (1) *facilitative* (which makes easier the implementation of changes by the target group), (2) *reeducative* (relatively unbiased presentations of facts intended to provide a rational justification for action), (3) *persuasive* (attempts to bring about change partly through biased reasoning, urging, and inducement), and (4) *power* (the use of coercion based on obligatory relationships). These strategies vary in terms of their appropriateness and effectiveness in different situations. *See* PERSUASION.

Temporal Patterns of Diffusion

A variety of temporal patterns have been associated with diffusion processes. When does an idea or innovation first begin to spread within a country, region, or organization? How quickly does it spread once introduced? What types of people, organizations, or firms tend to be early adopters, and what types of ideas and innovations spread most quickly?

The spread of ideas and innovations generally begins slowly, accelerates as the diffusion process begins to unfold more fully, slows after some turning point is reached, and levels off as saturation is approached. A graph of the cumulative level of adoption over time approximates an S-shaped (sigmoid) curve. Figure 1 shows the basic sigmoid curve and its relationship to the rate of spread of information. This graph reflects the fact that an innovation can be accepted by a person only if he or she is aware of its existence. In other words, the behavior of a population toward an innovation is closely related to the distribution of information regarding the new phenomenon, even though the availability of information does not in itself guarantee acceptance. The graph also portrays the variable adoption decision period, which is shortest among early adopters.

Another concept built into this curve is the *diffusion effect*. When only 5 percent of the individuals in a social system are aware of an innovation, there is little normative pressure to adopt. As the rate of awareness of an innovation among a population increases to 20 or 30 percent, peer pressure begins to develop, and the rate of adoption accelerates. Once this threshold is passed, a diffusion effect begins to trigger substantial influence from peer networks to accept the innovation. This diffusion or

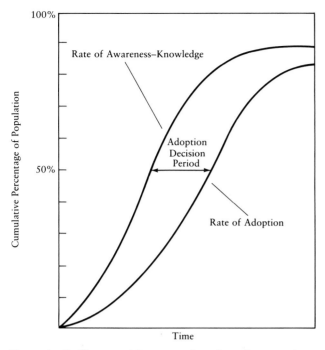

Figure 1. *(Diffusion)* The sigmoid (S-shaped) curve that describes most diffusion processes: rate of awareness-knowledge (uppermost curve), rate of adoption (lower curve), and the adoption decision period (gap between awareness-knowledge and adoption curves). Adapted from Everett M. Rogers, *Diffusion of Innovations* (1962), 3d ed., New York: Free Press, 1983.

snowball effect is particularly important in social systems that are highly connected (*see* NETWORK ANALYSIS; SOCIAL COGNITIVE THEORY).

Factors affecting diffusion. Different ideas and innovations diffuse at different speeds. Some of the following factors affect the rate of diffusion:

- *Relative advantage.* The degree to which the innovation is perceived to be superior to the product or practice it will replace, or to alternative products. It is a function of the unique benefits that the innovation provides and that other ideas, practices, or things do not. Relative advantage may be considered in terms of cost-effectiveness, a lessening of social conflict, greater comfort or security, and so forth.
- *Compatibility.* The less change a new idea or technology requires in existing sociocultural values, behavioral patterns, facilities, equipment, and procedures, the more likely is its rapid diffusion.
- *Impact on social relations.* Many ideas and innovations lead to alterations in social relationships that may inhibit or promote adoption and further diffusion. For instance, new agricultural technologies accelerated urbanization in some developing countries, and this in turn affected family and community relationships.

- *Complexity.* The degree of difficulty in using and understanding an idea or innovation. Greater complexity inhibits adoption.
- *Communicability and observability.* The more easily information about an innovation or an idea can be obtained by or communicated to the potential adopter, the more quickly it will be disseminated. If use of an innovation is observable, knowledge of its existence is facilitated. Thus the diffusion of many agricultural innovations such as new equipment and crops is facilitated by the fact that they are visible and therefore easily made known to (or difficult to ignore by) the uninformed.
- *Divisibility and reversibility.* The easier it is for an innovation to be tried on a limited and noncommittal basis, the greater the rate of adoption. If an innovation is divisible into smaller parts, then trials are possible and diffusion is promoted. Similarly, if it is possible to return to one's original condition or situation when an innovation is adopted and later rejected, then the diffusion is more rapid (e.g., there is greater resistance to surgical contraception than to birth control pills).

Classifications. The S-shaped curve of cumulative adoption is derived from a bell-shaped curve of noncumulative adoption. Using this bell or normal curve, it is possible to talk about the types of people who tend to adopt an idea or innovation during different stages of the diffusion process (Figure 2). People who adopt an idea or innovation at similar times tend to have similar characteristics. In particular, innovators and early adopters generally are better educated, have higher social status, are more risk-taking and cosmopolitan, and have greater social participation and opinion leadership than later adopters (*see* OPINION LEADER). They also tend to gain more information from impersonal sources and are less reliant on INTERPERSONAL COMMUNICATION as an influential source of information. Laggards, the last to adopt, tend to have traditional values and low social status, education, and income. Their adoption occurs only after information has "trickled down," when pressures to adopt are strong, and when prices for the new product have dropped.

Organizations. The speed with which innovations and ideas are diffused and adopted by organizations (e.g., private firms and public agencies) depends in part on characteristics of the organization's members, paralleling the trends described above. Also important, however, are characteristics of the organization. Some of these traits reflect patterns of communication, such as the degree of interconnectedness within an organization, the level of integration of the organization with external sources of information, and the extent to which the organization is open to

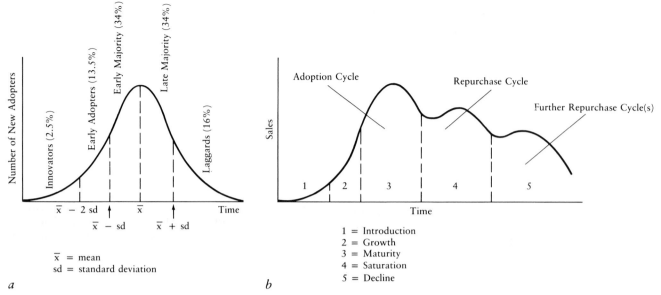

a   *b*

Figure 2. *(Diffusion)* Adoption and innovation life-cycle curves. (*a*) Adopter categories. Adapted from Everett M. Rogers, *Diffusion of Innovations*, New York: Free Press, 1962. (*b*) Innovation life-cycle stages. Adapted from David F. Midgley, *Innovation and New Product Marketing*, London: Croom Helm, 1977.

communication with its surrounding environment (*see* ORGANIZATIONAL COMMUNICATION). The extent to which an organization is functionally differentiated into many subunits and is specialized in terms of its members' expertise also correlates with innovation. Other critical organizational traits deal with the distribution of resources and power. Organizations in which power is decentralized, rules and procedures are deemphasized, and a considerable amount of uncommitted resources is available also adopt innovations more readily.

Individual adoption. The individual's decision-making process can be divided into time periods. Everett M. Rogers and Floyd F. Shoemaker developed a model describing the stages through which an individual passes from first knowledge of an innovation to a decision to adopt or reject it:

- *Awareness.* The individual learns of the existence of a new idea or innovation.
- *Interest.* The individual recognizes that he or she may have a need for this new idea or innovation and seeks more information about it.
- *Evaluation.* The individual assesses the idea or innovation in terms of its benefits and costs and decides whether or not to try it.
- *Trial.* Further evaluation of the idea or innovation occurs through small-scale or limited use. This trial reduces the uncertainties associated with the innovation.
- *Adoption.* The individual uses the new idea or innovation on a continuous, full-scale basis. Problems associated with use of the innovation or idea

may emerge at this stage, particularly when the individuals involved in the adoption decision are different from those involved in or affected by the actual implementation.

Subsequent elaborations of this A-I-E-T-A model have recognized that the adoption stage can be further analyzed in terms of different levels of use and incorporation. Postadoption steps include confirmation (through which the individual seeks reinforcement for the adoption decision) and routinization (when use of the idea or innovation has become a standard procedure).

The A-I-E-T-A model of decision making can be used to describe the role of different sources and channels of information. In general, mass media and other impersonal sources of information create awareness and interest, but later stages in the process require more personal, specific, and local sources of information. *See* MASS COMMUNICATIONS RESEARCH.

Spatial Patterns of Diffusion

Two distinct spatial patterns of diffusion have been identified: the *neighborhood effect* and the *hierarchical effect*. The neighborhood, or contagion, effect refers to the fact that the time elapsing between introduction and adoption of an idea or innovation tends to increase with distance from the nearest source of information or access. The source in question may be a nearby adopter, the distributor of an innovation, or some other propagator of information or resources. Distance to a source affects rates of diffusion for a variety of reasons. Personal communications occur more frequently across shorter than longer distances. MIGRATION is more common over shorter than longer distances, and many diffusions are the result of relocations of a population. Finally, costs of adoption generally increase with distance from the source of an innovation owing to transport costs associated with delivery, service, and repair.

Viewing the neighborhood effect over time suggests that diffusion occurs in a wavelike fashion (Figure 3). At first adoption is restricted to a compact area in which the distance decay effect is strong. As the diffusion process continues, the circle of acceptance and use expands, and distance increases between the points of origin and the ring (area) of most rapid adoption. Through time the innovation waves gradually weaken, incorporating more distant but dampened rings of adoption.

The hierarchy, or cascade, effect refers to the tendency of large urban places to adopt before smaller urban places do so. If an innovation is adopted by individuals, and any one person is as likely to adopt as another, then the most probable location for the first adopter is the largest city. Yet the per capita rate of adoption is also greater in larger cities. There are several reasons for the hierarchy effect. Inventions tend to occur in large cities, which also have the largest market areas and therefore are best able to support an innovation when demand is minimal. Large corporations tend to be located in large metropolitan areas, and they have the capital to introduce innovations. Also, as the density of the population increases, so does the amount of information (see INFORMATION THEORY).

The neighborhood and hierarchical effects frequently occur in concert, and this is portrayed by a schema developed by Torsten Hägerstrand in 1967 (Figure 4). The schema depicts diffusion as occurring through a hierarchy of social communication networks. The national, regional, and local levels of spatial aggregation each contain a network within which neighborhood effect principles of contact operate. Further, a node on one level will have contact with nodes on another level, providing mechanisms for the filtering of contacts down the urban hierarchy. Finally, if only the national scale is considered, a neighborhood effect pattern would be observed, but if the nodes on all three levels were considered together, the pattern could seem hierarchical.

Future Research Trends

Despite the recurring temporal and spatial patterns that have been found to characterize the diffusion of ideas and innovations, much remains to be learned about the processes underlying these patterns. Several

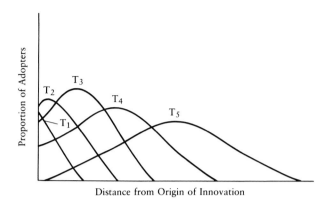

Figure 3. *(Diffusion)* The shape of diffusion in space and time: proportion of adopters at successive time periods as a function of distance from origin of the innovation. Adapted from Richard L. Morrill, "The Shape of Diffusion in Space and Time," *Economic Geography* 46 (1970): 259–268.

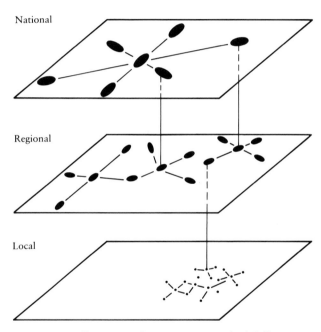

Figure 4. *(Diffusion)* Schematic portrayal of diffusion networks viewed at three different spatial scales. Adapted from Torsten Hägerstrand, *Innovation Diffusion as a Spatial Process,* Chicago: University of Chicago Press, 1967.

lines of inquiry would appear to be particularly fruitful.

First, it is becoming clear that the rapid and complete diffusion of ideas and innovations depends on performance of a set of key roles. These include

- the gatekeeper, who brings essential technical and market information into organizations and social systems;
- the idea or innovation champion, who pushes the technical idea or innovation forward in an organization or social system;

- the innovator, whose willingness to change provides an initial market for the idea or innovation; and
- the opinion leader, who is a source of advice and information about an idea or innovation.

Little is known about who the gatekeepers and champions are and how organizations and social systems can ensure that their roles are effectively played. Profiles of innovators and opinion leaders have been developed, but further research is needed to determine how they can be effectively targeted to fulfill their roles.

Transferring products from producers to consumers, the realm of market research, is fairly well understood, but moving ideas from the laboratory bench to the producer is a different matter entirely, relatively ignored as a general research question. Innovation diffusion or technology transfer from the public to the private sector has been especially neglected and should be a high priority for future research, given the sizable amount of publicly sponsored research and its potential to improve national and international standards of living.

Bibliography. Lawrence A. Brown, *Innovation Diffusion: A New Perspective*, New York and London, 1981; Torsten Hägerstrand, *Innovation Diffusion as a Spatial Process* (Innovationsforloppet ur Korologisk synpunkt), trans. with assist. of Greta Haag, Chicago, 1967; David F. Midgley, *Innovation and New Product Marketing*, New York and London, 1977; Richard L. Morrill, "The Shape of Diffusion in Space and Time," *Economic Geography* 46 (1970): 259–268; Everett M. Rogers, *Diffusion of Innovations* (1962), 3d ed., New York, 1983.

MARILYN A. BROWN

DIPLOMACY

The process and method, the means and mechanism, by which national governments conduct relations and communicate with one another, normally through their agents and representatives. The term *diplomacy* has been used in several ways, but to broaden its meaning unnecessarily, to make diplomacy synonymous with foreign policy, is unwise. As process, means, and method, diplomacy is an instrument of state policy. It involves representation, negotiation, PERSUASION, and BARGAINING as the external life of a state is conducted in pursuit of its interests, power, and order. The goals of diplomacy are understanding, compromise, and agreement. It is a generic form of state behavior, distinct from war, ESPIONAGE, and covert operations. Diplomatic activity can lead to war and play a role in war; it does not cease to operate even when war and other forms of state conduct are practiced.

Diplomacy's processes can be both formal and informal, but its agents and diplomats must be official, in residence, and accredited even if they are drawn—as they often are—from outside the ranks of the diplomatic corps and are sometimes itinerant. Diplomacy can be practiced directly by heads of government and ministers responsible for the state's external affairs rather than through special representatives. It is conducted, therefore, at several levels, from diplomatic summits down to conversations between embassy officials. Diplomacy, which can be practiced independently or in alliances, is conducted in many orthodox ways: openly and secretly, bilaterally, in blocs, multilaterally, in conferences, and at congresses (*see* INTERNATIONAL ORGANIZATIONS). Its agenda traditionally was dominated by political and strategic issues.

History

The use of diplomatic agents is as old as politics. Its modern features began to emerge clearly in the late fifteenth century in the Italian city-states, with Venice providing the lead, but the diplomatic arts had been practiced in Asia, the Middle East, Africa, and Latin America in recognizably modern forms. Diplomacy flourished most perceptibly and fully, however, as the European state system reached its mature form in the nineteenth century. Hierarchical ranks of diplomats were recognized; formal diplomatic instruments, customs, and vocabulary were fashioned; French became the official language; training of diplomats was developed; aristocrats and gentlemen created a monopoly of appointments; ARCHIVES were filled with their records; and little occurred technologically to disturb accepted practices. Ambassadors enjoyed wide latitude to conduct diplomacy and even to shape policy. The volume of transactions was manageable, the number of states active in the international system was relatively small (about twenty before 1914), and there were few international organizations and nonstate actors of significance. Ambassadors served the interest of the state exclusively.

In the twentieth century, particularly after World War I, significant changes occurred. Governments dealt increasingly not only with other governments but also with international organizations and nonstate actors such as corporations and groups operating transnationally. The agenda of diplomacy has broadened, and its balance has changed. Economic, commercial, technological, and cultural questions share the agenda. Governments have means of communicating and signaling one another beyond diplomacy, particularly the electronic mass media. The number of states active in the system increased dramatically (115 by the end of World War II), and so did the level of transactions and the flows of information. New states (many of them former European colonies) had diverse goals. The political space between the boundaries of society and the apparatus of government was reduced, partly because of the presence of organized groups and an increasingly attentive public and partly because the press and newer means of social communication such as RADIO and then television began to assert greater influence on governments (see NEWSPAPER: HISTORY; TELEVISION HISTORY). Elites lost their exclusive control but soon found ways to manipulate and co-opt these fresh sources of authority so that governments were rarely dominated by them (see GOVERNMENT-MEDIA RELATIONS). The influence of governments increased to the extent that use of the media enabled them to spread PROPAGANDA and to create and manipulate PUBLIC OPINION both within and beyond the boundaries of their states. The patterns of influence on foreign policy differed among states, but the new elements in the equation (an attentive and organized public, the new communications media) prevented a return to the relative simplicity of the nineteenth century. A form of total diplomacy has emerged, the hallmark of which is complexity.

The Influence of Technology

At the same time, advances in communications technology, changing the means and speed at which information is transmitted, decisively affected the conduct of diplomacy. The creation of a global telegraph communications system was the most significant development of the second half of the nineteenth century and the first decade of the twentieth (see TELEGRAPHY). Between 1850 and 1914, paralleling the development of a railway and shipping network, an international submarine cable system was laid down and put into operation. England was joined to France, national telegraph systems in Europe were linked together, and the European system spread eastward to the Middle East and India via the Mediterranean and westward to North America. Europe became tied to Asia and Australasia via Siberia and India, Hong Kong and Singapore, and then reached to Japan. Similarly, North America established a network across the Pacific islands to Japan and then to the Asian mainland. European and American telegraph and cable companies joined in Asia. London remained the hub in the sense that the British or British-owned share of the submarine cable system approached 80 percent before World War I, although Copenhagen, The Hague, Paris, and New York headquartered major communications companies. See NEWS AGENCIES.

Even before World War I the wireless telegraph began to challenge the monopoly of the submarine cable system. Between 1914 and 1945 wireless telegraphy and the development of the international TELEPHONE system had the greatest impact on the conduct of diplomacy and international affairs. Adolf Hitler could conduct his political coup against Austria in the spring of 1938 from his office; it was a case of *Anschluss* by phone. Winston Churchill and Franklin D. Roosevelt could direct much of their business during World War II on the transatlantic phone system. After World War II the invention of the transistor and then the microprocessor (computer "chips"), the development of computers and SATELLITE systems, and the expansion of radio and television enabled the United States to lead the world toward integrated communications systems (see TELECOMMUNICATIONS POLICY).

Every step in this technological evolution has directly affected the conduct of diplomacy. In the nineteenth century the hand-delivered LETTER or dispatch gave way—though never entirely—to the telegram and cable traffic. Face-to-face discussions, protracted meetings, and formal conferences were—with significant exceptions, as when the need for major peace settlements arose—deemed less vital, although they could be more easily and rapidly convened. Ambassadors abroad lost much of the autonomy that distance and inaccessibility had given them, though they in turn gained greater ability to influence their home governments. As the new technologies increased the volume, speed, and complexity of the message traffic, the pace of diplomacy constantly quickened, for governments were in more direct and immediate contact on a global scale. Thus both routine business and crisis management took on new features and greater urgency. Optimal decision making became a function of efficient information processing as never before. The awareness of hostile values, the probable reactions of both friends and adversaries, and the uncertainty of outcome heightened. The conduct of diplomacy and grand strategy thus challenged governments even as technological innovation lubricated the process and facilitated transactions on a global scale.

Bibliography. Jorma Ahvenainen, *The Far Eastern Telegraphs*, Helsinki, 1981; Diane B. Bendahmane and David W. McClintock, eds., *Science, Technology, and Foreign Affairs*, Vols. 4 and 5, Washington, D.C., 1984; Anne W. Branscomb, ed., *Toward a Law of Global Communications Networks*, White Plains, N.Y., 1986; Harold Nicolson, *The Evolution of Diplomatic Method*, London, 1954; Richard Rosencrance, "Diplomacy," *International Encyclopedia of the Social Sciences*, Vol. 4, New York, 1968 ed.; Ernest Satow, *Guide to Diplomatic Practice* (1917), 4th ed., ed. by Nevile Bland, London, 1957.

MICHAEL G. FRY

DIRECT RESPONSE MARKETING

Direct response marketing has been the fastest-growing form of marketing and ADVERTISING in the decades of the 1960s, 1970s, and 1980s. Its fundamental premise is the development of a direct communication and sales dialogue between a prime supplier of goods or services and the consumer.

This two-way dialogue grew as a powerful force in marketing as it became more precisely targeted, more relevant, and more service-oriented than mass distribution and general advertising. Direct marketing has been the beneficiary of all the new information processing and storage technologies. The development of the computer, the microprocessor, and personalized communication technologies such as laser printing and telemarketing has made it possible and inexpensive for advertisers to use DATA BASE marketing techniques to locate and communicate with prime new prospects and existing customers (*see* COMPUTER: HISTORY).

The Direct Marketing Association in the United States defines direct marketing as "an interactive system of marketing which uses one or more advertising media to effect a measurable response and/or transaction." This definition is sufficiently broad to encompass the many and varied forms of direct marketing that are increasingly being practiced worldwide.

Direct marketing differs from mass distribution and general advertising in its means as well as its ends. Whereas mass distribution attempts to make goods available to the broadest mass of the public by selling in bulk to wholesale and retail resellers who own the products at the point of purchase, direct marketers sell directly to the end consumer. General advertising attempts to create favorable ATTITUDES and high awareness of products owned by resellers, while direct marketing advertising tries to modify the behavior of the ultimate consumer by creating sales transactions for goods owned by the advertiser. Because responses to advertising, whether orders or inquiries, are returned to the advertiser, the results of such advertising become accurately measurable and totally accountable.

Techniques. Direct marketing has assumed many different forms and has helped to sell an increasing number of product categories and services worldwide. Perhaps the oldest form of direct marketing is the salesperson or distributor who sells door to door. Avon Products and others have used this technique worldwide to sell cosmetics and costume jewelry. Vacuum cleaners and other small appliances are sold this way as well. Encyclopedias and sets of books have been marketed door to door for the last two centuries, as have household supplies and services. The salesperson, using the technique of a personal demonstration in the home, is the medium of door-to-door, or direct-selling. Advertising is frequently used to support, target, or reinforce the salesperson's efforts.

Catalogs are another direct marketing medium that has also been used for centuries. Sears, Roebuck and Company, Montgomery Ward, and Spiegel in the United States; La Redoute and Les Trois Suisses in France; and Quelle and Neckermann in Germany, Belgium, and Holland are typical of catalogs that have acted as retail stores for people who prefer to shop at home. Specialty catalogs selling fashions, electronic appliances, horticultural products, outdoor equipment for hunting and fishing, specialty foods, and so on, have been growing at a rapid rate around the world. The growing use of catalogs for in-home shopping has been adopted by leading retailers such as Bloomingdale's and Neiman Marcus in the United States, Printemps in France, and the Seibu stores in Japan. In Great Britain mail-order sales from catalogs exceed sales made in department stores.

Another form of direct marketing is the negative-option club, which developed in the late 1920s in

Figure 1. *(Direct Response Marketing)* Sears Roebuck catalog cover, 1894. Courtesy of Sears, Roebuck and Co.

the United States and Germany. The "negative option" refers to a book-club marketing method that provides that a book club notify each member every month of the selection it proposes to send the member. If the member does nothing—the negative option—the book is sent. The member may elect to receive no book that month or select other books or products, but is expected to do so by a certain date. Today companies using the name and technique of the Book-of-the-Month Club exist in the United States, Great Britain, and Sweden.

Since 1955, with the advent of the Columbia Record Club in the United States, records have also been sold by negative-option clubs. Record clubs owned by Philips and Bertelsmann exist in Europe, and the Sony CBS Family Club sells audio products in Japan. The products offered by such clubs have expanded to include videotaped films, VIDEO games, and computer software. Specialized clubs selling books on cooking, crafts, the outdoors, history, psychology, and so on have also developed.

In many countries direct marketing has become the major medium for the sale of MAGAZINE subscriptions. In the United States almost all magazines sell mainly by subscription. *Geo* and *Capital* in Germany, *L'expansion* in France, and many magazines elsewhere have also been sold by subscription.

Direct marketing has helped to build an international industry in collectibles. Series of Olympic coins have been sold by the governments of Canada, the United States, Mexico, and the USSR. Philatelic products are marketed directly by almost every postal system in the world. Companies such as the Franklin Mint in the United States have sold gold and silver medallions, porcelain objects, books, and records in continuity programs worldwide. Continuity programs, in which a specific series of products or books is sold one at a time to subscribers, have been used by publishers such as Time-Life Books and others worldwide.

American Express, Diners Club, Visa, MasterCard, Carte Bleue, Eurocard, and Barclaycard have used direct marketing to sell credit cards worldwide. They have also used the data base of cardholders to build substantial mail-order businesses. More recently banks, insurance companies, building societies, brokers, and real estate companies have used direct marketing to sell billions of dollars of financial services.

Car rental companies such as Avis and Hertz; airlines such as American, Pan American, United, and many European carriers; and hotel chains such as Hyatt, Sheraton, Holiday Inn, Hilton, and Marriott have used direct marketing techniques to offer discounts to frequent users whose names and transaction histories are maintained in computer data bases.

Corporations such as IBM, Rank Xerox, Hewlett

Figure 2. *(Direct Response Marketing)* Advertisement for a baby buggy, from a Sears Roebuck catalog, 1899. Courtesy of Sears, Roebuck and Co.

Packard, and Honeywell have used direct marketing techniques to generate leads for salespersons and to sell supplies to current customers. In 1983 it was estimated that a business sales call by a salesperson cost more than two hundred dollars. Business-to-business direct marketing was used to generate leads that made sales calls more productive and to sell inexpensive equipment and supplies directly.

Targeting. Targeting of media and messages makes it possible to sell the right thing to the right person at the right time. It is not surprising, then, that direct marketing has also influenced POLITICAL COMMUNICATION, particularly in the United States. The national, state, and local candidates of the Republican and Democratic political parties have made intensive use of the data bases of actual or potential voters for fund-raising purposes.

The explosive growth of direct marketing has been based on its ability to use and create data bases that help direct relevant messages to the most appropriate prospects.

Bibliography. Martin Baier, *Elements of Direct Marketing*, New York, 1985; *DMA Fact Book/1984 on Direct Marketing*, New York, 1984; Edward L. Nash, *Direct Mar-*

keting: Strategy, Planning, Execution, New York, 1982; Bob Stone, *Successful Direct Marketing Methods,* 2d ed., Chicago, 1979.

LESTER WUNDERMAN

DISINFORMATION

A term that came into use in the period after World War II to designate false materials produced with an intent to deceive foreign military and intelligence agents (*see* DECEPTION). Its meaning was gradually extended to include false information intended to influence broader target populations. Disinformation also has come to be widely used as a catchall designation for views with which one disagrees. *Misinformation* is a word with broader connotations, encompassing information that is unintentionally as well as knowingly false.

Main features. Disinformation is a form of PRO- PAGANDA. When disinformation was confined to attempts to mislead foreign intelligence and military services, it was a special form of "black propaganda" (unacknowledged, purposeful, and false). But in the broader sense of the term, disinformation may be passed along quite openly, although known by its sponsors to be false. Disinformation may be disseminated in the form of forged documents, false quotations, misleading rumors (*see* RUMOR), fabricated statistics, or other false claims of events, policies, or relationships. The false information is often embedded in a body of accurate fact as a means of adding credibility to the falsified evidence (*see* PERSUASION). Disinformation designed for an enemy audience may mislead people at home (a phenomenon called blow- back) and is for this reason occasionally criticized as incompatible with a democratic order. But the bulk of disinformation is designed for the domestic mar- ket, not a foreign audience, although in every country the specialists focus on the disinformation activities of foreign enemies.

Sometimes disinformation corresponds to a reality that the creator of the fabricated evidence cannot document from valid sources. For example, in 1961 Richard Helms, then head of the U.S. Central Intel- ligence Agency (CIA), briefed a U.S. Senate commit- tee on two forgeries allegedly showing that the United States, despite claims to the contrary, was secretly supplying rebels trying to overthrow the Sukarno government of Indonesia. Former CIA officials Victor Marchetti and John D. Marks note that "they were indeed rather crude forgeries, but their message was accurate. Not only did the CIA in 1958 support efforts to overthrow the Sukarno government, but Helms himself, as second-ranking official in Clan- destine Services, knew it well." Thus, paradoxically, the forgeries were disinformation that conveyed a

valid message; the exposures and disclaimers were themselves a form of disinformation.

Origins of the term. Some Western specialists trace the word *disinformation* to the Russian *dezinfor- matsia.* They cite the claim that a Soviet Department D (for *dezinformatsia*) was organized within the So- viet KGB (Komitet Gosudarstvennoi Bezopasnosti, or State Security Committee) in the 1950s, thus sug- gesting a special Soviet role in disinformation both in etymology and fact. James Watson and Anne Hill in *A Dictionary of Communications and Media Stud- ies* (1984) assert that disinformation "derives from the Russian *dezinformatsia,* a term especially asso- ciated with the Soviet Union's secret service, the KGB." However, *dezinformatsia* is not a word with Russian roots, and it appears in Soviet dictionaries and encyclopedias only after World War II. All give the term French roots (*dés* and *information*), and into the 1970s Soviet writings translated the word as "misinformation." Thus the original Russian word has Western roots, and the translation from *dezin- formatsia* to *disinformation* appears to have been a Western initiative.

The practice. Disinformation as fact has an ancient lineage. The Indian classic *Arthaśāstra,* dating from 321 to 296 B.C.E., advises a prince desirous of win- ning battles to circulate secret agents among the enemy spreading rumors of their certain defeat. While the use of disinformation has been a long-standing feature of war and politics, it is possible that its importance has increased in modern times as a func- tion of greater wealth and technical improvements. These factors have led to a proliferation of weapons and may also have allowed a larger scope to the manipulation of both enemy intelligence and foreign and domestic populations. There is some empirical evidence for the increased use of disinformation in military strategies, but claims of its increased appli- cation in political warfare and domestic politics are only a plausible guess.

A classic case of disinformation in military use is the series of operations organized by the British in World War II to deceive the Germans about Allied intentions. According to one official, the disinfor- mation program Operation Fortitude

was responsible for containing a minimum of 20 enemy divisions during the first crucial months of the [Normandy] invasion. The enemy was led to believe—and reacted to— a long inventory of opportune untruths, the largest, most effective, and decisive of which was that Neptune [the code name for the invasion plan] itself was only the prelude to a major invasion in the Pas de Calais area. . . .

Anthony Cave Brown notes that

the British had been extremely careful to reveal to the Russians only as much of their deception machinery as was necessary to ensure their cooperation in Bodyguard [the name for the overall disinformation program]. But the Russians were quick to adopt and apply this unique method of modern warfare.

The use of disinformation in domestic politics and to engineer public consent is massive and has assumed many forms (see PUBLIC OPINION). In one famous case U.S. Senator Millard Tydings of Maryland was shown in a picture (forged) standing together with Earl Browder, head of the U.S. Communist party, a tactic that helped defeat Tydings in 1952. The U.S. Federal Bureau of Investigation's use of forged letters, cartoons, photos, and other documents to discredit, harass, and disrupt radical and other oppositional civil rights and peace groups—under the FBI program code-named "Cointelpro"—was a large-scale and well-documented disinformation effort carried out for a decade or more but officially terminated in 1971.

It has been a long-standing tradition to mobilize populations by fabricated enemy threats. During the last months of 1981, for example, U.S. officials claimed that a Libyan hit squad had been dispatched to assassinate the U.S. president. None of the varying accounts of this hit squad was ever confirmed, and the head of the FBI eventually acknowledged the absence of any such evidence. The original claim was nevertheless effective as propaganda.

See also ESPIONAGE; RADIO, INTERNATIONAL.

Bibliography. Philip Agee, *Inside the Company: CIA Diary*, New York, 1976; Nelson Blackstock, *Cointelpro: The FBI's Secret War on Political Freedom*, New York, 1975; Anthony Cave Brown, *Bodyguard of Lies*, New York, 1975; *The Etymological Dictionary of the Russian Language* (Etimologicheskii slovar' russkogo iazyka), Vol. 1, Book 5, Moscow, 1910–1916, reprint Moscow, 1958, and New York, 1978; *The Great Soviet Encyclopedia* (Bol'shaia sovetskaia éntsiklopediia), 3d ed., Moscow, 1970–1975, New York and London, 1973– ; Victor Marchetti and John D. Marks, *The CIA and the Cult of Intelligence*, New York, 1974; Harry Rositzke, *The CIA's Secret Operations: Espionage, Counterespionage, and Covert Action*, New York, 1977; Richard H. Shultz and Roy Godson, *Dezinformatsia: Active Measures in Soviet Strategy*, Washington, D.C., 1984.

EDWARD S. HERMAN

DISNEY, WALT (1901–1966)

U.S. film animator, producer, and businessman. The name Walt Disney has become almost synonymous with family entertainment. For more than forty years Disney created cartoons, films, television shows, and even giant theme parks designed to appeal to "the child in everyone." Born in Chicago, Walter Elias Disney worked as an artist and animator in Kansas City, where he met Ub Iwerks, a fellow artist who was to be his lifelong collaborator. They began an ANIMATION studio, which went bankrupt, but their second attempt, in Los Angeles, became the industry powerhouse known as the Disney Studios. In 1928 they produced the first sound cartoon, *Steamboat Willie*, featuring a character called Mickey Mouse drawn by Iwerks with voice by Disney. It was an instant success and became one of the cultural phenomena of the era. The next year Disney introduced the "Silly Symphonies" cartoons, in which the animation was precisely coordinated with a soundtrack dominated by musical effects. Best known of these are the initial *The Skeleton Dance* (1929) and *The Three Little Pigs* (1933).

During the 1930s the small studio grew into a huge enterprise under Disney's leadership. Other cartoon characters joined Mickey Mouse, including Minnie Mouse, Donald Duck, Goofy, and Pluto, all turned out by a vast assembly line of artists and technicians called designers, in-betweeners, inkers, and opaquers. The Disney organization pioneered many technical advances, such as multiplane animation, which allowed for greater complexity and sense of perspective. Disney became a leader in the use of color, obtaining exclusive rights in 1935 to employ Technicolor's three-color process in cartoons. Through merchandising agreements Disney characters turned into armies of dolls, toys, books, and premiums.

Disney had long wanted to produce full-length animated features. In 1937 he stretched his company's resources to the limit to make *Snow White and the Seven Dwarfs*, which proved a major success and was followed by *Pinocchio* (1940), *Dumbo* (1941), *Bambi* (1942), *Cinderella* (1950), and *Sleeping Beauty* (1959). Unusual among these projects was the early *Fantasia* (1940), in which cartoon ART was used to animate various classical music pieces. Though not immediately popular and scorned by some critics as a lowbrow exploitation of fine music, the film eventually found a large audience during rerelease in later years.

For many years Disney totally dominated animation in the United States, and his studio became a training school for a generation of animators. Some, on going elsewhere, carried on Disney's assembly-line methods and hyperactive style; others reacted against it, veering toward simpler, more personal, and often more sophisticated films.

During World War II the Disney organization produced innumerable training and PROPAGANDA films for government agencies, such as *Saludos amigos*, aimed at Latin America. During and after the war Disney also made a number of films combining live action and cartoon, such as *Song of the South* (1946),

Figure 1. *(Disney, Walt)* Walt Disney with Mickey Mouse. © 1954 The Walt Disney Company.

and in 1950 he made his first completely live-action film, *Treasure Island*. Other notable live-action pictures include *20,000 Leagues under the Sea* (1954) and *Mary Poppins* (1964). Disney also issued a series of documentaries on nature entitled "True-Life Adventures," starting with the short *Seal Island* (1948) and including the feature-length *The Living Desert* (1953), drawing on the work of specialists in nature photography. Though sometimes criticized for their "mickey-mousing" musical accompaniments, the films are nonetheless a fascinating look at natural phenomena. *See also* DOCUMENTARY.

Disney saw the potential of television early on. Using it as a new market for his entire backlog, he also began to produce special series for Sunday-night family viewing, including the enormously popular "Zorro" and "Davy Crockett."

In 1955 Disney realized a long-held dream by opening Disneyland, a 160-acre amusement park in Anaheim, California. A second, even larger park called Disney World was under construction in Florida at the time of Disney's death, with still others in the planning stage. In Disney's theme parks all his familiar characters were featured anew and recycled in countless forms, but the parks also gave his taste for the amazing, the whimsical, and the fantastical a

monumental form that had a major impact on TOURISM in the postwar decades.

See also CARICATURE; CHILDREN—MEDIA EFFECTS; COMICS; HUMOR; MOTION PICTURES; VIOLENCE.

Bibliography. Leonard Maltin, *The Disney Films,* New York, 1973; Richard Schickel, *The Disney Version: The Life, Times, Art, and Commerce of Walt Disney,* rev. and updated, New York, 1985.

RICHARD PILCHER

DOCUMENTARY

The term *documentary,* used as a noun, is generally equated with nonfiction work in film, RADIO, television, or VIDEO. But the boundaries of nonfiction are never clear. Some works claiming documentary authenticity use actors in dialogue invented by writers and staged by directors—elements more properly belonging to FICTION, since the aura of characters and events becomes almost wholly the creation of the artists. For such works the term *docudrama* has come into use, and it should be regarded as a branch of historical fiction rather than documentary. *See* FACT AND FICTION.

Documentarists are dedicated to *not* inventing. They prefer images and sounds found in the world around them to anything they can invent. They express themselves largely by the way they combine and juxtapose these images and sounds and, in many documentaries, by adding commentary and music.

Early History

The documentary had its beginnings in the prehistory of MOTION PICTURES. Some of the experimenters who contributed to the evolution of MOTION PHOTOGRAPHY were devising equipment to "document" some phenomenon or event—in the case of Eadweard Muybridge (1830–1904) in the United States, the motion of racehorses and, later, of other animals and of humans; in the case of the Frenchman Étienne-Jules Marey (1830–1904), the flight of birds. The recording of such actions for study and analysis has remained an important role for documentarists.

The ingenious device of the brothers LOUIS AND AUGUSTE LUMIÈRE, the cinematograph, which debuted with resounding success in Paris in 1895 (the event that launched commercial cinema), tended to propel the new medium in a documentary direction. The cinematograph was a compact, hand-cranked instrument that could, with adjustments, serve as camera, projector, or printing machine. Its small size and light weight encouraged "cinematographers" to go forth and record the world in action. In contrast THOMAS ALVA EDISON's first camera, devised to make films for his Kinetoscope (the peepshow device that had its commercial debut the year before the cinematograph), was a ponderous instrument firmly rooted in the Edison studio, where performers were brought before it to juggle, dance, box, or do rope tricks. The contrast between the cinematograph and the Kinetoscope had other historic ramifications. A Lumière-trained emissary with a cinematograph could be sent anywhere in the world to demonstrate the invention with films made by the Lumières, and could then, using the same equipment, astonish audiences anew with items shot and developed locally: in Spain, the climax of a bullfight; in Russia, the coronation of the new czar; in Australia, a glimpse of the Melbourne races. Within two years they had introduced the cinematograph in major cities in every part of the world, made more than 750 short films, and planted the word *cinema* in many of the world's languages. Diverse other entrepreneurs were by then racing the Lumière envoys far and wide and inspiring the beginnings of local filming, generally on a documentary note.

The Lumières established another media word. They called their short travel films *documentaires*. Films of this sort dominated film programs for some years, but their emphasis changed. The earliest films, shot mainly by Louis Lumière—who was also the chief cinematograph inventor—favored genre glimpses of middle-class life: men sawing and selling firewood in a city street, the arrival of a train, workers leaving a factory, a bicycle lesson—aspects of daily life seen in an astonishing new way (see Figure 1). But the touring cinematographers, for promotional reasons and to win needed access permissions, enlisted the sponsorship of king, kaiser, czar, maharajah, and their retinues. All proved eager to help introduce the new wonder—and came to expect its attentions. Royal and military panoply became standard film ritual.

The first Lumière films were less than a minute long, but the length of films increased rapidly; by 1905 ten-minute films were common. By this time fiction films were thrusting the documentary aside. Beauteous men and women, seen in unprecedented close-ups, were becoming new-age idols. And it was in the fiction film that filmmakers were expanding film techniques, particularly the wonders of FILM EDITING. The documentarists, holding too long to a successful formula, became victims of it. The world glimpses continued, but in 1909 entrepreneurs began combining them into the composite NEWSREEL. The innovation was welcomed, but it marked the decline of the early documentary.

Thenceforth fiction films, growing into multireel wonders, would dominate film history. Yet occasionally the documentary would have moments of surprising rebirth and would even—especially in times of crisis—seize the center of attention.

Between the Two World Wars

The first such resurgence came in the 1920s and revolved around two remarkable figures, ROBERT FLAHERTY of the United States and DZIGA VERTOV of the Soviet Union. In spite of differences, they showed striking parallels. Both were lone operators, embattled independents often at odds with the film industries in which they worked. Both avoided large film operations; each generally worked with his wife and was assisted by a brother. Each had a fleeting time of glory.

Robert Flaherty. Robert Flaherty (1884–1951) began his working life as a prospector. Employed by Sir William Mackenzie, Canadian industrialist and railroad builder, he explored northern wilderness areas in search of mineral deposits, serving as advance man for an industrial tomorrow. But as he pushed northward, Flaherty's interests shifted from the buried ore to the Eskimos inhabiting the land. In 1913 he began making a film about them. The process involved endless difficulties, but the result was a milestone in the history of documentary film. Flaherty had absorbed the syntax of film communication as it had evolved in the fiction film, and he applied this to real-life material. The result was *Nanook of the North* (1922; see Figure 2). It seemed so unorthodox to distributors that most of them rejected it, yet it won worldwide success, set the pattern for later Flaherty projects, and remained a film landmark.

In *Nanook of the North*—as in the later *Moana*, shot in Samoa—Flaherty was not showing indigenous peoples as he found them. He said, "I am not going to make a film about what the white man has made of primitive peoples." He involved Nanook and his people, the Inuit of Canada's Hudson Bay area, in an adventure of remembering. They would show for the camera, and for posterity, how they *used* to do things before the white man came—how they hunted, fished, built igloos, dressed, ate, slept. In a sense, Flaherty was repudiating his own industrial role. The clock was turned back. An anthropologist might call his work salvage ethnography. Flaherty was creating a sort of living museum, startling in its aliveness and intimacy.

Dziga Vertov. The work of Dziga Vertov (1896–1954) occupied a similar time span in very different circumstances. He was born Denis Arkadyvich Kaufman in the Polish city of Białystok, then within the czarist realm. His father was a librarian. As World War I began, the family moved to what seemed the comparative safety of Petrograd. When the 1917

Revolution began, Kaufman became involved. Volunteering for the cinema committee, he became a film editor. As the Bolsheviks fought back internal opposition and foreign intervention from U.S., British, French, and Japanese expeditionary forces, he edited footage of the fighting into reels that were dispatched to agitprop units. When the fighting ended late in 1920, he began proclaiming in spirited manifestos the role he felt film should play in the new socialist society. He was now Dziga Vertov, a pseudonym suggesting a spinning top, or perpetual motion.

He looked on fiction films as a dangerous new religion, an opiate. Seeing its "ikons" commanding the "prayerful emotions of millions," he urged filmmakers to "come to life." They should become "organizers of visible life," documenting the birth of a new reality. His attacks won him enemies, but also support in high places. V. I. Lenin was reported to feel that all cinema programs should include, along with fiction, items of "Soviet actuality." In 1922 Vertov received a go-ahead to create *Kinopravda* (Film Truth), a monthly collection of actuality items that continued until 1925 (see Figure 3). Vertov's wife, Elizaveta Svilova, served as its film editor; his brother Mikhail Kaufman was chief cameraman. Each day he and other cameramen sallied forth to record such moments as seemed to them historic: a Moscow trolley line, long out of operation in torn-up streets, finally back in repair and resuming its runs; an army tank leveling an area for an airport; a hospital assisting war-starved children. In the editing process, meaningful juxtapositions and superimposures were especially favored. Valued footage was reused in feature-length compilation films such as the prideful *Shestaya chast mira* (One-Sixth of the World, 1926). The work inspired similar films from others, including the admired *Turksib* (1929), by Victor Turin, on the construction of the Turkestan-Siberian railway (see Figure 4); and the historical compilation films of Esfir Shub, in which pre-Revolution newsreel shots of bread lines, munitions assembly lines, and arrests of troublemakers were juxtaposed with newly discovered home movies of life at the czar's court. Shub's films, especially *Padeniye dinasti Romanovikh* (The Fall of the Romanov Dynasty, 1927), had a great impact on Soviet audiences.

The documentary occupied a prominent role in the early years of the Soviet Union but soon lost momentum. Under Joseph Stalin the emphasis was on articulation of officially proclaimed themes rather than on the reporting of actualities. Film projects could be undertaken only on the basis of detailed proposals specifying content and message. Vertov, who looked on his work as film journalism, resisted this process and came to be regarded as "antiplanning." He worked in increasing isolation and was able to complete few major films. The work for which he would eventually become best known at home and abroad, *Chelovek s kinoapparatom* (The

Figure 3. *(Documentary)* *Kinopravda* cameraman. National Film Archive, London.

Figure 4. *(Documentary)* Victor Turin, *Turksib*, 1929. National Film Archive, London/Sovexport.

Man with the Movie Camera, 1929), met with Soviet disfavor when released. Presenting a dazzling inventory of the techniques of film reportage, it was unclear in its implications. Was Vertov proclaiming the power and significance of the medium or warning against its capacities for deception?

Spread of the movement. The films of Flaherty and Vertov were among factors attracting artists in many lands—painters, sculptors, architects, musicians—to film. Viewing and discussing films in the cineclubs and film societies formed in many cities, some artists felt the urge to experiment, and many of them leaned to documentary. Even artists associated with abstractionism found delight in maneuvering "fragments of actuality" into visual patterns in motion. The French artist Fernand Léger fused footage of gears, pendulums, eggbeaters, and other familiar objects into his *Ballet mécanique* (1925). Similarly the German Hans Richter, member of a Zurich AVANT-GARDE group, parlayed racetrack footage into a *Rennsymphonie* (Racing Symphony, 1928). Walther Ruttman, a German POSTER designer who had studied music and architecture, orchestrated images of Berlin into *Berlin: Die Sinfonie der Grossstadt* (Berlin: The Symphony of the City, 1927). All these films, documentary in their basic material, reflected a fascination with the expressive potentialities of film editing.

This trend, coming as silent film was giving way to sound film, was short-lived. Sound pushed the documentary in other directions. Documentarists, acquiring a voice, found their medium could argue, protest, plead, sell, evangelize. Spurred by the advent of a world depression and rising political tensions, the documentary of the 1930s became above all a medium of exhortation.

John Grierson. The documentary movement organized in Britain by JOHN GRIERSON, son of a Scottish schoolmaster, was dedicated to social enlightenment. Launched in 1930, it had government underwriting and occasional industry sponsorship. Grierson, influenced by WALTER LIPPMANN in the United States, felt that the problems of society had become too complex for the public to grasp, but he felt the documentary film could lead the way through the wilderness. He was not afraid of the word PROPAGANDA. He could say, "I look on cinema as a pulpit."

Praising Flaherty's *Moana* for "documentary value," Grierson brought the term *documentary* back into use. But Grierson's views on documentary diverged from those of Flaherty. He scorned Flaherty's focus on the remote and primitive and demanded attention to "the drama of the doorstep." Films made under Grierson seldom revolved around individuals. A Grierson documentary tended to be an essaylike survey of a current activity or problem, with the audience being guided through the footage by a narrator or commentator. This became a standard documentary feature in many countries. Government film units tended to favor it because it exerted a leadership role. It was also economical. Narration could be combined with footage shot silently, at a time when sound shooting was cumbersome and expensive. In many countries the word *documentary* came to connote a film in the Grierson pattern, although many artists resisted what they considered its paternalistic character.

British and U.S. documentarists. Whereas the sponsorship of the British movement was conservative, looking to foster empire unity and industrial productivity and harmony, many of the young cineasts recruited by Grierson had liberal and even dissident social views, which found their way into the films, especially in the strong focus on workers and their problems. This mixture of viewpoints had its virtues: the films were seldom simplistic. Production, begun slowly in 1930, hit full stride in 1935 with the release of diverse impressive films: *Song of Ceylon,* directed by Basil Wright; *Shipyard,* by Paul Rotha; *BBC: The Voice of Britain,* by Stuart Legg; *Housing Problems,* by Edgar Anstey and Arthur Elton (see Figure 5). They were followed closely by the most admired of the unit's productions, *Nightmail* (1938), by Harry Watt and Basil Wright, showing action on a train rushing the mails from London to the towns of northern England and Scotland. The narration included passages of rapidly tripping verse by W. H. Auden accompanied by a Benjamin Britten musical score. Major composers were constantly drawn into social documentary projects of this period.

Social concerns and internal tensions likewise marked documentary activity in the United States. Its leading figure was Pare Lorentz, who began his film career by making, under the auspices of government agencies, *The Plow That Broke the Plains* (1936)

(see Figure 6) and *The River* (1937). Both had musical scores by Virgil Thomson and narration that, in its rolling cadences, reminded people of Walt Whitman. Both had a powerful public impact—which eventually became a political danger to Lorentz's work. The films provided such persuasive rationales for the policies of President Franklin D. Roosevelt's New Deal—soil conservation, flood control, public power—that conservatives in Congress grew alarmed. Roosevelt had established a central U.S. Film Service for further projects of this sort, and Lorentz was in the field preparing them—rural electrification and unemployment were on the agenda—when Congress scrapped the budget. The U.S. Film Service came to a sudden halt.

But the U.S. documentary movement had achieved momentum, and private groups carried on with similar works. The American Institute of City Planners underwrote *The City* (1939), by Ralph Steiner and Willard Van Dyke, with an Aaron Copland score and a narration written by Lewis Mumford. It offered a vivid panorama of urban decay, along with a program for action. Parallel activities of a more militant sort were emerging from other groups, such as the Workers Film and Photo League and Frontier Films. Frontier Films, focusing some of its projects on foreign issues, released *China Strikes Back* (1937), giving U.S. audiences their first glimpse of Mao Zedong in his Yenan stronghold, resisting the U.S. ally Chiang Kai-shek.

Leni Riefenstahl. Social concerns and conflicts characterized film activities in many countries, in-

Figure 5. *(Documentary)* Edgar Anstey and Arthur Elton, *Housing Problems,* 1935. National Film Archive, London.

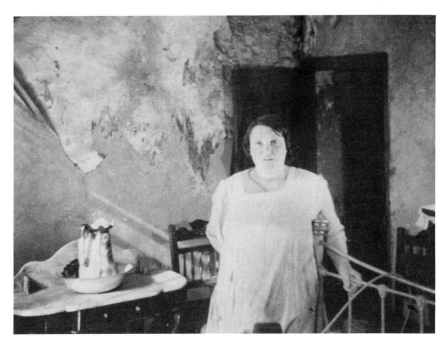

Figure 6. *(Documentary)* Pare Lorentz, *The Plow That Broke the Plains,* 1936. The Museum of Modern Art/Film Stills Archive.

cluding France, the Netherlands, Poland, and Japan. In Germany, however, social and political conflicts had been forced underground. Such activities as liberal cineclubs had been eliminated, and total coordination was the order of the day. Adolf Hitler, while planning the 1934 Nazi party rally, summoned Leni Riefenstahl. He had long admired her as the heroine of a series of mythic "mountain films," one of which she had also directed. He told her she was to produce a film record of a history-making rally to be held in Nuremberg that would signal to the whole world the rebirth of Germany. All necessary means would be at her disposal.

Riefenstahl, given sweeping authority, went to work. In Nuremberg she ordered a flagpole to be equipped with an elevator, able to carry a cameraman to the top in seconds while shooting. From fire department and utilities she commandeered trucks with extension ladders, so that cameramen would be able to soar over the historic buildings of Nuremberg while surveying massed crowds below. She ordered a ramp built along a major parade route to enable traveling cameras to move with the marchers while shooting from bird's-eye vantage. Ritual and film were planned together.

Riefenstahl did the editing. She left articulation of the message to speeches by Hitler and others. But she backed these with an overwhelming choreography of images and sounds: marching men, throngs, adoring women, children, banners, swastikas, eagles, oratory, German monuments, folksongs, clouds, uniforms, grandiose music—and amid it all, dramatic appearances by the führer. The result, *Triumph des Willens* (Triumph of the Will, 1935), seemed to many the most brilliant and certainly the most frightening of the era's films of exhortation (see Figure 7). It seemed an announcement of inevitable war.

Some years later, with the war a global reality, film director Frank Capra was summoned to the Pentagon and asked to make clear to U.S. troops, through a series of documentary films, why they were fighting. He decided to include in the *Why We Fight* films extensive passages from *Triumph des Willens.* As in many compilation films, footage lived on to play a role not intended for it.

World War II

The exhortation films gave way to war films, which were dominated by battle reports. For almost a decade they came in a relentless barrage, chronicling the crisis events. Reenactments were often used, but spectacular combat photography was the central element. Many cameramen died in action. During this period the documentary took center stage. In every warring nation people flocked to theaters to get some sense of the distant events.

Among documentarists who won honors for their war films were the Dutch filmmaker JORIS IVENS, whose *The Spanish Earth* (1937) and *The Four Hundred Million* (1939) helped propel him into an international career of filmmaking; the Russian Roman Karmen, producer of the spectacular *Leningrad v borbe* (Leningrad at War, 1942) and many other

Figure 7. *(Documentary)* Leni Riefenstahl, *Triumph des Willens* (Triumph of the Will), 1935. The Museum of Modern Art/Film Stills Archive.

crisis reports; the English filmmaker Humphrey Jennings, whose *Listen to Britain* (1942) and *Fires Were Started* (1943) were probably the least chauvinistic of war films; and the U.S. filmmaker John Huston, whose *The Battle of San Pietro* (1944) depicted the experience of battle so vividly that it was felt best not to release it until the war was almost over.

Some parts of the film record long remained hidden. Eventually, through such films as *Nuit et bruillard* (Night and Fog, 1955), by Alain Resnais, and *Requiem dla 500,000* (Requiem for 500,000, 1963), a compilation of Nazi archive footage exhumed by Polish documentarists Jerzy Bossak and Wacław Kazimierczak, audiences gradually gained some conception of the holocaust. First footage of the havoc at Hiroshima and Nagasaki, shot by Japanese cameramen under Akira Iwasaki but classified by occupation authorities, did not reach audiences until a quarter of a century later in *Hiroshima-Nagasaki, August 1945* (1970), compiled in the United States after the footage was declassified.

Postwar Rise of Television

During the war documentarists had dwelt near the center of power. The end of war seemed to leave them without a major mission. In many countries documentaries were vanishing from theaters. But a new arena opened up. Television, which had had a brief start before the war, was halted by it. But war-related developments in electronics enabled television to reappear and grow with startling suddenness after the war. By the 1950s it seemed on its way to winning the big audiences away from radio and cinema. Experimenting with diverse programming, it became the main habitat of the documentary. *See* TELEVISION HISTORY.

Several genres of television documentary emerged. One was the film-illustrated newscast. As the theater newsreel vanished, its technicians and commentators migrated into television newscasting. Grierson-style surveys of current topics, guided by commentary, likewise became a television form. Commentators became frequent on-camera instead of "voice-over" presences, which turned some into national celebrities. *See also* TELEVISION NEWS.

Another genre looked to the past. Film ARCHIVES were being formed in many countries to store the vast amounts of film that had accumulated over the decades (*see* ARCHIVES, FILM). A country's film archive generally focused on its national heritage. Reassessment of twentieth-century experience through programs based on the archival material became a widespread television genre. The idea was also applied to historic still photos, paintings, and other art works, often shown with camera motion via ANIMATION photography. The Canadian film *City of Gold* (1957), based on nineteenth-century photographs and made by Colin Low and Wolf Koenig, had brilliantly pioneered this technique.

Still another genre, reflecting new environmental concerns stimulated by war, focused on nature. Prominent in this category were the television films of Jacques-Yves Cousteau, about life on and under the ocean, and the encyclopedic BBC series by David Attenborough, *Life on Earth* (1979), which scrutinized ancient and modern species with exceptional camera wizardry. Technical advances were setting the stage for explorations undreamed of in earlier decades, including photography in outer space and within the human body, as in the National Geographic special *The Incredible Machine* (1977).

Technical developments played a part in another genre, which acquired the name CINÉMA VÉRITÉ, after Vertov's *Kinopravda*. Its adherents wanted to immerse audiences in ongoing events, as *Kinopravda* had sought to do. The sound elements had not been available to the Vertov group but were now a relatively easy matter, thanks to wireless microphones and other devices that facilitated synchronized coverage of characters on the move. *Cinéma vérité*—or *direct cinema,* as some preferred to call it—won an early vogue in the United States with *Primary* (1960), by Robert Drew and Richard Leacock; in Canada with *Lonely Boy* (1961), by Wolf Koenig and Ralph Kroitor; and in France with *Chronique d'un été* (Chronicle of a Summer, 1961), by Jean Rouch and Edgar Morin. *Cinéma vérité* won intermittent access to television, but television executives were generally wary of commissioning unpredictable projects.

Television documentary moved in still other directions. Every major special-event telecast was, in effect, an instant documentary, edited while in progress. Preserved on film or tape, it became a part of the documentary heritage, bequeathing historic footage to film archives. This was true of all kinds of events, including SPORTS events. The term *documentary* was not often linked with sports, yet sports were a concern of documentarists from the start. They

were the motive behind the first experiments of Muybridge. In later years two major documentaries, Riefenstahl's *Olympia* (1938) and Kon Ichikawa's *Tokyo Olympiad* (1965), brought documentary technology and production virtuosity to extraordinary heights (see Figures 8 and 9). Yet the television sportscast, when it acquired isolation cameras, instant replays, slow-motion analyses, and the freeze-frame, became an even more dazzling achievement. It held audiences spellbound throughout the world.

Whether viewed as a documentary triumph or a social-psychological phenomenon, all this was remote from the expectations of a Flaherty or a Vertov. Its meaning was variously assessed. Some saw the phenomenon as abetting violent drives; others as a new social opiate, beguiling and pacifying whole population strata. Still others saw it as the essence of the civilizing process—human combat reduced to order, to accepted rules, to ritual.

Further ramifications. A factor that had facilitated the postwar rise of *cinéma vérité* had been the advent of magnetic SOUND RECORDING and its diverse blessings: freedom from laboratory processing, instant review of items recorded, easy editing, and portability. These advantages fostered many other media developments. In radio they led immediately after the war to a new documentary movement. Previous radio documentaries were primarily radio equivalents of docudrama, relying heavily on studio reenactments, as in the *March of Time* radio series launched in 1931. After the war, radio documentaries based on the wire recorder and then on the tape recorder became an established genre. Once freed from studio confinement, the documentary has remained a worldwide feature of radio journalism.

Figure 8. *(Documentary)* Kon Ichikawa, *Tokyo Orinpikku* (Tokyo Olympiad), released 1965. National Film Archive, London.

Figure 9. *(Documentary)* The filming of *Tokyo Orinpikku* (Tokyo Olympiad). National Film Archive, London.

Another ramification, following the rapid evolution of magnetic picture recording, was the rise in the 1970s of video as a distinct production medium. Developing in many directions, it offered diverse advantages to documentarists. Portability made it valuable for journalistic documentaries and work in ETHNOGRAPHIC FILM. The instant-review aspect gave it special values in dance training and many other kinds of training. In education, psychiatry, and mediation the medium proved valuable in fostering self-observation. Its relatively low cost made it invaluable to independent producers. In many situations it could give an individual producer capabilities that had once required a crew. Independent filmmakers and producers proliferated in the video field. Their work had an early impact on television programming, but the ferment also stimulated exhibition in libraries, universities, schools, churches, political groups, union halls, museums, film societies, clubs, community centers, and homes. Video brought a new diffusion of production and distribution to the documentary field.

Bibliography. Erik Barnouw, *Documentary: A History of the Non-Fiction Film*, rev. ed., New York, 1983; Forsyth Hardy, ed., *Grierson on Documentary*, rev. ed., London, 1966; Lewis Jacobs, ed., *The Documentary Tradition*, 2d ed., New York, 1979; Erwin Leiser, *Om Dokumentarfilm*, Stockholm, 1967; Georges Sadoul, *Louis Lumière*, Paris, 1964.

ERIK BARNOUW

DRAMA

This entry is composed of two articles:
1. History
2. Performance

1. HISTORY

The word *drama*, like drama itself, originated with the Greeks: *dran*, meaning "to do," "to act." In fact, while drama is considered as literature, it is essentially a popular ART, written to be seen and heard. Published drama (scripts) is not unlike published music (scores): both are meaningful only when read with the ability to imagine the PERFORMANCE. Thus read, however, they furnish the instruction as well as the pleasure that have from the start been the functions of drama. See section 2, below.

Greek and Roman Drama

The earliest extant drama, which developed from religious rites, assumed a highly stylized form. Most of the speeches are choral lyrics, chanted and sung as well as choreographed. Dramatic scenes are few and brief, consisting of short emotional speeches called *stichomythia*. The tragedies (*see* TRAGEDY) feature gods and goddesses, but the protagonists are usually the mortal heroes of Greek legend and history. Their dramas communicate classic moral, spiritual, and intellectual values, which are interpreted by the chorus.

Greek drama employed formal patterns. Tragedies started with a *prologos*, followed by a choral entrance lyric (*parados*), a dramatic scene (*episode*), a choral ode (*stasimon*), and a finale (*exodos*). Each tragedy had five dramatic scenes separated by choral odes. Accompanied by instrumental music, the chorus danced, sang, chanted, and spoke its lines. The last scene ended the conflict, with either a messenger's account of the catastrophe or a god's arbitrary resolution (deus ex machina).

Only a few plays of the classical era have survived. Aeschylus (525–456 B.C.E.), who invented the second actor and thus "fathered" Western drama, wrote the *Oresteia* (the only extant trilogy), *The Suppliant Women*, *Prometheus Bound*, and *The Persians*. Characterized by the beauty of the choral lyrics and by spectacular theatrical effects, these and his other plays express Aeschylus's belief in human responsi-

Figure 1. *(Drama—History)* Comic mask from Minturnae. Roman Imperial period. The University Museum, Philadelphia. Neg. no. 23276.

Figure 2. *(Drama—History)* Tragic mask from Pompeii. Roman, first century C.E. Naples Museum. Art Resource, New York.

bility despite the operation of divine fate and in wisdom emerging from human suffering.

Sophocles (496–406 B.C.E.), who invented the third actor, increased the subtlety of characterization and complexity of plots. His plays, especially *Oedipus Rex,* are the basis of many of the critical dicta in ARISTOTLE's *Poetics.* Sophocles depicts human suffering, evil and weakness, and the parlousness of life—but also the human potential for nobility. Euripides (484–406 B.C.E.) is notable for his religious skepticism and subtle depiction of psychology, most strikingly in his portrayal of mass hysteria in *The Bacchae.* Many of his works feature women, often in desperate situations: *Medea* (infanticide), *Hippolytus* (incest), *Electra* (matricide), and *The Trojan Women* (bereavement).

Greek COMEDY, which had its origin in Dionysian fertility rites, is erotic, ribald, and sometimes scatological; in addition, it often ridicules contemporary notables who were present during the performance. Comedies opened with a dramatic scene in which a character came up with a novel course of action, followed by the entrance of a fantastically garbed chorus that remained onstage throughout the play and took part in the action, the high point of which

was a contest (*agon*) between two opposing characters. In a harangue (*parabasis*) the chorus then presented the playwright's views. This was followed by a number of short scenes, and the comedy concluded with the resolution of the *agon*. The only surviving comedies are those of Aristophanes (448?–385? B.C.E.), best known for his *Lysistrata,* which portrays women conducting a sex strike to force their men to end the war between Athens and Sparta. Aside from the broad farce, a progenitor of vaudeville and burlesque, this "old comedy" excelled in the wit associated with the later comedy of manners.

Menander, Plautus, and Terence are the principal "new comedy" writers of the Greek and Roman theaters. Menander (343?–292 B.C.E.), an Athenian, wrote polished and highly praised comedies of which only a few fragments have survived. Plautus (254?–184 B.C.E.) adapted Greek plots to a Roman milieu, adding topical events and characterizations to broad and immensely popular comedy involving disguises and mistaken identities. Many of his plots were adapted by later playwrights, from William Shakespeare and Molière to Jean Giraudoux. Terence (190?–159 B.C.E.) wrote less broadly farcical adaptations from the Greek.

Roman tragedy is best represented by Seneca (4? B.C.E.–65 C.E.). His drama is presumed to have been written to be read rather than performed, is highly rhetorical (*see* RHETORIC), and stresses the brutal. Based on Greek legends, his *Medea, Agamemnon,* and other tragedies were widely studied in the RENAISSANCE.

Classic Asian Drama

The earliest Asian drama activity was in India, reaching its golden age in the fourth century C.E. It too had its origin in religious RITUAL and featured much stylized DANCE and music (*see* MUSIC THEATER—ASIAN TRADITIONS). Indian drama is based on sacred epics such as the Mahabharata and Ramayana. Kālidāsa, the greatest Sanskrit dramatist, is believed to have lived in the fifth century. He wrote highly poetic romantic comedies, his masterpiece being *Śakuntalā,* in which the royal marriage of the title character undergoes great trials before the happy resolution. The other well-known Indian drama is *Mṛcchakaṭikā* (The Little Clay Cart), reputed to have been written by King Śūdraka around the fourth century, a romantic comedy about a ruined merchant in love with a courtesan; it became popular in late-eighteenth-century Europe and influenced Johann Wolfgang von Goethe and other writers.

Chinese drama, although also highly stylized, is less dependent on dance and less inspired by sacred texts. The thirteenth- and fourteenth-century *k'un ch'u* is a type of music drama derived from the Peking OPERA; other plays were dramatizations of popular romances (*see* ROMANCE, THE), such as *Ki-pa-ki* (The Story of the Lute) and *Hoei-lan-kin* (The Chalk Circle),

Figure 3. *(Drama—History)* Toshusai Sharaku, *Kabuki Actors,* 1794. The Metropolitan Museum of Art, New York, The Elisha Whittelsey Collection, The Elisha Whittelsey Fund. (JP 3118)

Figure 4. *(Drama—History)* Chinese theatrical scene, ca. 1860. Reproduced by courtesy of the Trustees of The British Museum.

Figure 5. *(Drama—History)* Henry Peachum, drawing on a page of manuscript, in *Titus Andronicus,* 1595: believed to be the only known contemporary representation of Elizabethan actors in costume. Reproduced by permission of the Marquess of Bath, Longleat House, Warminster, Wiltshire; and the Conway Library, Courtauld Institute of Art, London.

best known in the West because of its later adaptation by Bertolt Brecht.

Japanese drama, stemming from a period roughly paralleling the MIDDLE AGES, includes No and Kabuki. The former is Buddhist-inspired and highly stylized, performed for elite audiences, chanted and danced by masked actors, and about seven hours long. Although No dramas are informed by the Buddhist spirit, they often deal with feudal battles. One of the finest No plays is *Sobota komachi,* by Kwanami Kiyotsugo (1333–1384), the dramatization of an arrogant noblewoman's expiation of her youthful sins. Kabuki, an offshoot of No, is popular episodic drama often adapting No plots. Its most prominent practitioner was Chikamatsu Monzaemon (1653–1724), and its best-known drama is Takeda Izumo's *Chusingura* (1748), dealing with forty-seven legendary outlaws.

Medieval Drama

Medieval Europe was a religious rather than a national community, its drama consisting of church-inspired, anonymous spectacles (*see* SPECTACLE) that were extensions of religious services and sermons. Tropes, brief Latin dramatic sketches, developed into the mystery, cycle, and morality plays characterizing this period. The mystery (or miracle) plays dealt with biblical subjects and included farcical interludes. Eventually these became cycles performed by guilds (labor unions) in town marketplaces. One of the finest of these is the Wakefield cycle, whose *Second Shepherds' Play* (early fifteenth century) follows three shepherds in their devout journey to the manger amid farcical episodes of the theft of a sheep. Morality plays were allegories personifying vices and virtues struggling for the possession of the human soul, as in the anonymous fifteenth-century *Castle of Perseverance* and *Everyman.*

Renaissance Drama

Drama flourished in the sixteenth and seventeenth centuries, culminating in what are still the masterworks of Western civilization: the plays of Shakespeare and his contemporaries, including the Spanish dramatists Lope de Vega and Pedro Calderón de la Barca. The perspective changed from theological preaching to humanistic explorations as the subject changed from the biblical and legendary to the psychology of complex individuals. Subtlety increasingly marked not only tragedy but also comedy.

The preeminent genius of the Renaissance theater was Shakespeare, whose tragedies, histories, and comedies have been performed throughout the world and translated into almost all languages. His *Hamlet, King Lear, Macbeth, Othello,* and other plays are so well known that poems, novels, and plays have been written about them: Tom Stoppard's *Rosencrantz and Guildenstern Are Dead* (1966), for example, is predicated on the audience's familiarity with *Hamlet.* Christopher Marlowe and Ben Jonson are the most notable of Shakespeare's English contemporaries; Marlowe first used the blank verse that became standard in Elizabethan drama, while Jonson wrote distinguished "comedies of humour," plays like *Volpone* (1607) and *The Alchemist* (1612) that caricatured personal vices.

The chief Spanish dramatists were the immensely prolific Lope de Vega, most of whose two thousand plays are cloak-and-dagger tragicomedies—although his best-known work, *Fuente ovejuna* (The Sheep Well, 1612), is a tragedy with a peasant hero; and Calderón de la Barca, who often wrote on religious themes, although his most popular play is *La vida es sueño* (Life Is a Dream, 1635), which portrayed a romantic search for the ideal and was adapted by a number of modern poets.

Neoclassical Drama

The seventeenth and eighteenth centuries, sometimes called the neoclassic age, are characterized by increasing dramatic variety. The order and unity associated with CLASSICISM and its reemergence are exemplified by the work of Jean Racine and Molière in France, but the equally distinguished Pierre Corneille and the English playwrights of the period typify a very different kind of drama.

Racine's work represents the high point of the revival of the Greek tragic spirit and the rigorous, simple structure of classic drama. His verse tragedy—*Britannicus* (1669), *Mithridate* (1673), and *Phèdre* (1677), among others—portrays destructive passions such as jealousy. Molière accomplished something similar with his "character comedies": in the guise of simple, farcical plots without resolution of serious underlying issues, his protagonists in plays like *Tartuffe* (1664), *Le malade imaginaire* (The Imaginary Invalid, 1673), *L'avare* (The Miser, 1668), and *Le misanthrope* (1666) are destroyed by passions whose comic portrayals closely skirt tragedy. Corneille subordinated classical doctrine to original and often romantic portrayals of heroes who seek glory and achieve their ideals—as in *Le Cid* (1637), his best-known drama.

In England, Restoration comedy—especially the plays of George Etherege (*The Man of Mode*, 1676), John Vanbrugh (*The Relapse*, 1696), William Wycherley (*The Country Wife*, 1675), and William Congreve (*The Way of the World*, 1700)—is characterized by sophisticated drawing-room wit in an artificial ambience of the pursuit of riches and sensual pleasure. Despite its aberrant morality, this is possibly the finest high comedy ever written. The reaction

Figure 6. *(Drama—History)* John Barrymore as Richard III, New York, 1925. The New York Public Library at Lincoln Center, Astor, Lenox and Tilden Foundations. Billy Rose Theatre/Vandamm Collection.

Figure 7. *(Drama—History)* Molière as Sganarelle. After an engraving by Simonin. From Émile Dacier, *Le Musée de la Comédie-Française 1680–1905*, Paris: Librarie de l'Art Ancien et Moderne, 1905, p. 27.

following the outrage of succeeding generations produced only pale imitations in the sentimental comedies of Oliver Goldsmith (*She Stoops to Conquer*, 1773) and Richard Brinsley Sheridan (*The School for Scandal*, 1777) in the next century. In France the same period saw the biting satiric comedy of Pierre-Augustin Caron de Beaumarchais, whose *Le mariage de Figaro* (The Marriage of Figaro, 1784; more popular as the libretto of Wolfgang Amadeus Mozart's opera) anticipated coming political upheavals; his *Le barbier de Seville* (The Barber of Seville, 1775; also the libretto for an opera, this one by Rossini) similarly ridiculed the aristocracy.

Early Nineteenth-Century Drama

The end of the eighteenth and the start of the nineteenth century ushered in literary and artistic RO-MANTICISM. In England, William Wordsworth and Samuel Taylor Coleridge's *Lyrical Ballads* (1798) marked the start of the movement that was to flourish with poets who also wrote closet and stillborn drama such as Percy Bysshe Shelley's *The Cenci* (1819) and Lord Byron's *Manfred* (1817), meant to be read rather than produced. It was in Germany that romantic drama was most successful, however. Goethe in *Götz von Berlichingen* (1773) and in the two-part *Faust* (1808–1832; the second part being a poetic drama that almost defies stage production) and Friedrich von Schiller in *The Robbers* (1782), *Wilhelm Tell* (1804), and other plays exemplified the Sturm und Drang (Storm and Stress) movement unleashed by Friedrich Maximilian von Klinger's 1776

Figure 8. *(Drama—History)* A scene from the commedia dell'arte. Reproduced from the *Recueil Fossard*, 1577. From Cesare Molinari, *La commedia dell'arte*, Milan: Mondadorí, 1985, p. 102.

Figure 9. *(Drama—History)* John Gielgud, Cyril Ritchard, and George Hays in William Congreve's *Love for Love,* New York, 1947. The New York Public Library at Lincoln Center, Astor, Lenox and Tilden Foundations. Billy Rose Theatre/ Vandamm Collection.

play of that name. This movement's drama, often based on medieval characters and events and reflecting the gothic atmosphere of popular fiction, gloried in wild and untamed natural expression (*see* LITERATURE, POPULAR). In France the romantic call to arms was Victor Hugo's preface to his *Cromwell* (1827) and *Hernani,* which repeated the call in the poetic outbursts of the outlaw hero three years later, culminating in a hundred nights of riots championing the new freedom against the classicists.

Modern Drama: Ibsen to World War II

Modern drama started in the mid-nineteenth century with naturalism, REALISM, "well-made plays," problem plays, and various AVANT-GARDE movements that in time entered the mainstream. Well-made plays were the farces and intrigue plays of boulevard playwrights using standard formula plots predicated on a withheld secret, focused on a trivial object, and

climaxing with an "obligatory scene" in which the secret is revealed and resolved happily for the main character. Another popular type of drama was Grand Guignol, short sensational plays that titillated and terrified audiences with blood-curdling scenes of ghostly horror or frightening VIOLENCE.

Realism refers to staging as well as subject, character, and dialogue that seeks to convey the illusion of ordinary life. Naturalism is realism carried to extremes: graphic portrayals of seamy environments, poverty, misery, and sordidness. Problem plays subordinate timeless, universal issues to contemporary social ones. Such realistic types of drama should be distinguished from Soviet "socialist realism," which is optimistic, reflects political concepts, anticipates a socialist future, and depicts Soviet heroes. Avant-garde drama includes a number of types. EXPRESSIONISM characterizes drama that distorts external reality in order to express subjective inner reality. Surrealism depicts yet transcends reality by present-

Figure 10. *(Drama—History)* Karl F. Schinkel, *Decoration for Mozart's Magic Flute, Act 1, Scene 1,* Berlin, 1816. The Metropolitan Museum of Art, New York, Whittelsey Fund, 1954. (54.602.1 [13])

ing the irrational and the unconscious. And dadaism, an extreme nihilist antiwar movement originating in 1916, attempted to match the horrors of war with the meaninglessness of modern values—just as futurism had done a few years earlier with the opposite aim of repudiating human values and glorifying ruthless power and the machine age.

The Norwegian Henrik Ibsen is the acknowledged founder of modern drama. *En dukkehjem* (A Doll's House, 1879), *En folkefiende* (An Enemy of the People, 1882), *Gengangere* (Ghosts, 1881), and *Hedda Gabler* (1890) are foremost among the plays introducing realism and publicizing contemporary social problems caused by archaic laws and beliefs. Ibsen's rival, the Swedish playwright August Strindberg, an even more prolific and innovative Scandinavian, has almost equal claim to be called the founder of modern drama; naturalistic plays like *Fröken Julie* (Miss Julie, 1888) and *Fraden* (The Father, 1887) also ushered in the realism of twentieth-century drama, while *Till Damascus* (To Damascus, 1898–1904), *Spöksonaten* (Ghost Sonata, 1907), and *Drömspelet* (A Dream Play, 1902) were innovative not only for

their own time but also for later decades. A third giant is [George] Bernard Shaw, who championed and helped establish Ibsen's work and in his many plays—*Pygmalion* (1913), *Saint Joan* (1923), *Heartbreak House* (1919), *Man and Superman* (1903), and more than fifty others—wittily dealt with all areas of human endeavor, attempting always to instill fresh insights into contemporary as well as timeless problems. Still other architects of modern drama are the Russian Anton Chekhov, whose *Vishnyovy sad* (The Cherry Orchard, 1904) and other plays successfully dramatized the humdrum and nonsequential speech characteristic of everyday life, and the Italian Luigi Pirandello, whose preoccupation with the relativity of reality is powerfully dramatized in *Sei personaggi in cerca d'autore* (Six Characters in Search of an Author, 1921) and other plays notable for their mixture of cerebration and melodrama. Chekhov's and Pirandello's plays, even more than those of the other early moderns, are fusions of comedy and tragedy—the modern drama that can no longer be classified in either category.

The countless other dramas of this period include

some excellent poetic plays, such as the tragedies of Federico García Lorca (*Bodas de sangre* [Blood Wedding, 1933]; *Yerma,* 1934; and *La casa de Bernarda Alba* [The House of Bernarda Alba, 1945]) and the tragicomedies of the Irish playwrights J. M. Synge (*Playboy of the Western World,* 1907) and Sean O'Casey (*Juno and the Paycock,* 1924); the "epic" plays of Brecht (*Mutter Courage und ihre Kinder* [Mother Courage and Her Children, 1941]; *Leben des Galilei* [Galileo, 1943]; *Der kaukasische Kreidekreis* [The Caucasian Chalk Circle, 1948]; and others), whose attempts at didacticism are constantly overshadowed by his artistry; and the plays of U.S. dramatist Eugene O'Neill, whose mordant masterpieces are *The Iceman Cometh* (1946) and *Long Day's Journey into Night* (1956).

Drama since World War II

Contemporary drama takes many directions. In the United States the first important playwrights were Arthur Miller and Tennessee Williams. In *Death of a Salesman* (1949) Miller fused realism with cinematic cross-cutting that jumbles time as it portrays the thought processes of a failing businessman in a society that extols immoral values. Williams, in plays like *The Glass Menagerie* (1945) and *A Streetcar Named Desire* (1947), combined lyricism and symbolism in depicting the decline of gentility and the growth of urban savagery. In England, John Osborne's *Look Back in Anger* (1956) articulated postwar frustrations and launched a middle- and lower-class naturalistic drama.

Figure 11. *(Drama—History)* The opening night of *Hernani,* by Victor Hugo, 1830. Etching by J. J. Granville. The caption reads: "Disheveled Romans at the first performance of *Hernani.* A sixth act would have suffocated us all." Musées de la Ville de Paris © by Spadem 1987.

LES ROMAINS ÉCHEVELÉS A LA 1ʳᵉ REPRÉSENTATION D'HERNANI.

Si le drame avait eu six actes, nous tombions tous asphyxiés.

Figure 12. *(Drama—History)* Lotte Lenya in Bertolt Brecht's *Mutter Courage und ihre Kinder* (Mother Courage and Her Children). Courtesy of the German Information Center.

But it was absurdism that produced the most notable postwar drama, matching an atmosphere of existential despair with an apparent lack of form and absence of MEANING in plot and dialogue that reflect the portrayed meaninglessness of existence. The first and most purely absurdist plays were *La cantatrice chauve* (The Bald Soprano, 1950) and *La leçon* (The Lesson, 1951), by Eugène Ionesco. But elements of this dramaturgy are important aspects in the work of the playwrights Samuel Beckett and Harold Pinter. Beckett's *Waiting for Godot* (1953) became the most influential play of the century, expressing the entropy that is even more devastating in his *Endgame* (1957). Pinter's "comedy of menace," beginning with *The Birthday Party* (1958) and *The Caretaker* (1960), combined farce with terror.

Avant-garde drama has found modern expression in multimedia productions such as Robert Wilson's *Einstein on the Beach* (1976), while the social upheavals of the 1960s and 1970s are reflected in the Artaud-inspired "drama of cruelty," such as Jean Genet's *Le balcon* (The Balcony, 1956). Throughout, the commercial THEATER has continued to produce musicals and romantic comedies, yet even these have absorbed innovations that have entered the mainstream of popular drama. *See* MUSIC THEATER—WESTERN TRADITIONS.

These innovations have also entered the mainstream of other drama. Alongside the classic oriental drama, for example, the influence of modern Western drama has been felt in Asia and in Africa. It was introduced in India by the British in the nineteenth century, with the Hindu poet and philosopher Rabindranath Tagore becoming the first world-renowned modern playwright in Asia. He fused indigenous Indian folk drama and literary Western drama in some forty plays, most of them short, lyrical works like *Visarjan* (1890) and *Chandalika* (1933). Some decades later the left-wing writer Khwaja Ahmed Abbas depicted Muslim peasant life in popular drama that resembles the tendentious "Living Newspaper" theater of the 1930s and advocates harmony with Pakistan.

In Japan the first departure from classic drama occurred at the start of the twentieth century with Shimpa, a type of sentimental melodrama. The most distinguished modern Japanese drama is that of Yukio Mishima, the charismatic, militant patriot whose novels and plays received worldwide prominence; he rewrote No plays into lyrical and erotically charged dramas such as *Sotoba komachi* (1952) and *Hanjo* (1955), providing them with modern settings and a merging of oriental and occidental themes.

Modern Chinese drama began in 1907 with *hua chu* (talking drama), consisting of adaptations of popular Western plays such as *Uncle Tom's Cabin* and *La dame aux camélias*. Subsequent drama consisted principally of state-subsidized left-wing revolutionary drama. The doyen of Communist Chinese playwrights is T'ien Han, a prolific translator as well as author of many didactic plays such as *Hsieh yaohuan* (1961). Hsiung Fo-hsi was a leading popular dramatist whose plays were written to educate the peasantry. Much modern Chinese drama tends to confine itself to polemics.

African drama is relatively new and reflects centuries of COLONIZATION by various European countries. It is European in form but distinctly native in setting, atmosphere, and theme, and it often reflects the violence of national liberations as well as internecine struggles. The leading African playwrights, mainly Nigerian, have written in English. The plays of John Pepper Clark, such as *Song of a Goat* (1961) and *Ozidi* (1965), are heavily symbolic, with classical choruses and declamatory verse. Wole Soyinka is equally prominent as a poet and novelist; his works—notably *The Lion and the Jewel* (1963) and *The Trials of Brother Jero* (1964)—have reinvigorated

Figure 13. *(Drama—History)* Robert Wilson, *Einstein on the Beach,* Act IV, Scene 3C (Spaceship), 1976. Photograph copyright Babette Mangolte.

English-language drama in which tribal customs and people appear in a dramaturgical mixture of the indigenous and the European.

See also FICTION; FICTION, PORTRAYAL OF CHARACTER IN. For drama forms in new media, *see* RADIO; TELEVISION HISTORY; VIDEO.

Bibliography. Margarete Bieber, *The History of the Greek and Roman Theater,* 2d ed., Princeton, N.J., 1961; Faubion Bowers, *Theatre in the East: A Survey of Asian Dance and Drama,* New York, 1956, reprint 1969; M. C. Bradbrook, *History of Elizabethan Drama,* 6 vols., Cambridge, 1979; E. K. Chambers, *The Medieval Stage,* 2 vols., Oxford, 1903; Barrett H. Clark and George Freedley, eds., *A History of Modern Drama,* New York, 1947; *Enciclopedia dello spettacolo,* 9 vols., Rome, 1954–1964, *Aggiornamento, 1955–1965* (1966), and *Indice–Repertorio* (1968); Martin Esslin, *The Theatre of the Absurd,* 3d ed., Harmondsworth, Eng., and New York, 1980; John Gassner, *Masters of the Drama,* 3d ed., New York, 1954.

MYRON MATLAW

2. PERFORMANCE

When asked to define THEATER, John Cage answered, "I would simply say that theater is something which engages both the eye and the ear. . . . The reason I want to make my definition of theater that simple is so one could view everyday life itself as theater." Cage says the one who looks is the one who "sees theater." But the theatrical frame could also be defined by the maker of the event: anything I do that I call theater is theater. This is the attitude of many performance artists.

Both these definitional stances are extremely inclusive. By contrast the most conservative definitions apply rigorous aesthetic/structural criteria to events, as ARISTOTLE does when defining TRAGEDY: "A tragedy is the imitation of an action with enough magnitude to be complete in itself; in language pleasurably embellished . . . ; performed, not merely recited; with incidents arousing pity and fear in order to effect a catharsis of such emotions." Elegant as these kinds of definitions are, they cause trouble when frozen into rules that artists must comply with. From the late MIDDLE AGES until the nineteenth century, Western dramaturgy was hobbled by restrictive interpretations of Aristotle's description of Attic theater.

Issues in the Study of Theater

Theater is a subcategory of PERFORMANCE, a wide-spectrum term covering diverse arts, activities, and behaviors. These performative activities could be arranged on any of several continua:

- according to the relative "artificiality" of the activity or GENRE—from photo-realism and naturalism to the most fantastic representations of kathakali or Papua New Guinea masked theater (*see* MASK);
- according to the amount of formal training needed in order to perform;
- according to the presence or absence of a well-defined audience separate from the performers and the concomitant liking for or aversion to audience participation: a black church service in the United States fails if the audience does not participate, whereas a ballet fails if the audience does;
- according to the relationship between theater space and theatrical event—ranging from differences between the behavior of table servers in a diner and those in a fancy restaurant to differences between the impromptu shows of street performers in the marketplace and performers in giant performing arts centers, formal OPERA houses, and domed stadiums;
- according to the social and ontological status of who is performing and who is being performed—from sacred beings ritually summoned into the here and now by priests or other masters of sacred ceremonies to the most banal characters of a SOAP OPERA played by professional actors.

The taxonomical problem is further complicated because frequently a single performance mixes several categories.

Theater is transformative and transgressive. Its fundamental impulse is to create living beings or to summon into the here and now beings who otherwise exist only in nonordinary spheres usually inaccessible to humans. This fetching from beyond is a dangerous business, godlike in its audacity, and mischievous. That is why in so many genres around the world (and as early as the fifth century B.C.E. in Greece) tragedy was closely linked to farce. A set of three Greek tragedies was followed by a satyr play, one of which—Euripides' *Cyclops*—survives. In the Indian Sanskrit theater of the fourth to eighth centuries the stage manager (surrogate for the author/director) was also the clown who made the plot go, arranging or misarranging things. U.S. playwright Thornton Wilder used such a stage manager in *Our Town*. Of course, Shakespeare well understood "fools," whose stupidity is cleverness and whose innocence guile. In Japan, in a full day's program, five serious No alternate with four farcical Kyogen. African DANCE-theater likewise mixes the serious with the satiric and farcical. In the Arctic and elsewhere the jokes and tricks of shamans are integral parts of their healing performances.

Theater demands trained, costumed, and often masked performers enacting narratives. Some theaters—especially modern Western drama—emphasize spoken dialogue. But dialogue is not essential to theater. What counts is the systematic interplay among a complex set of behaved performance texts. The kathakali of Kerala in southwestern India combines sung poetic narration, robust dancing, and facial displays of emotion with a fully developed language of hand gestures called mudras. As the musicians drum, clang cymbals, and sing, the ornately made-up and costumed actors dance out the stories, signing dialogue and emotions with their hands, eye gestures, and expertly controlled footwork. The kathakali performer is rigorously trained in dancing, eye and facial gesturing, and mudras. Through constant practice beginning at about age eight and continuing for six to eight years, the actor's body is literally reformed to suit this demanding art. The intentions of kathakali are entirely different from those of naturalistic drama, which attempts to simulate ordinary reality. Speaking at the start of the twentieth century, Russian actor and director Konstantin Stanislavsky said he wanted spectators to feel not that they were at the theater but that they were visitors to households, looking through invisible fourth walls. Kathakali, on the other hand, creates its own worlds fabulously separate from ordinary reality. *See also* EYES; FACE; FACIAL EXPRESSION; GESTURE; SIGN LANGUAGE—ALTERNATE SIGN LANGUAGES.

In theatrical naturalism it is presumed that the roles played are being skillfully pretended by the actors. In other genres, such as Balinese Sanghyang or Yoruba Egungun, the performers are not playing roles: they are possessed. Beings—gods, demons, ancestors—take over the performers. Theater by means of spirit possession is probably very ancient, connected as it is with ancestor worship, death cults, and various other religious and shamanic rituals.

In the Ramlila—a great cycle play of Hindi-speaking northern India depicting the life of Rama—barely adolescent boys enact the deeds of Rama; his wife, Sita; and his brothers, Lakshman, Bharat, and Shatrughna. They are joined by adult actors playing such roles as Hanuman, the monkey-general, and Ravana, the ten-headed demon king of Lanka. The adults, some of whom have performed their roles for decades, are presumed to be performing in the ordinary sense. But the boys playing the gods are different.

Figure 1. *(Drama—Performance)* A kathakali performer. From Clifford R. Jones and Betty True Jones, *Kathakali: An Introduction to the Dance-Drama of Kerala,* San Francisco: The American Society for Eastern Arts, 1970, p. 100.

They are called *swarups*—literally "temple images"—and they are thought to be as sacred as any temple icon. Once the *swarups* are costumed and the headpieces signifying their divinity are in place, spectators press in to glimpse the boys-icons-gods. The *swarups'* adventures and the texts they recite form a key part of the ethical, religious, literary, and artistic education of most North Indian Hindus.

From its development in Japan in the thirteenth century No masked theater has stood between the extremes of pretending and actualization. As No actor Takabyashi Koji said, "If I know six months ahead of time that I am going to perform a given mask I can look at it everyday—I can see what the mask is, what it gives me. Or, on the other hand, if I receive a mask but don't know what to use it in, I will study the mask every day till it suggests a play

for me to use it in. The mask influences my state of mind, my body." Immediately before entering the stage the No actor looks in the mirror at himself fully costumed and masked. What he sees is not himself and not his character, but a being in between, an incompletely transformed being and therefore one still restlessly "in life."

Theater employs a variety of texts, only one of which is verbal. In addition to what is spoken or sung there is the mise-en-scène—exactly how the actions of a performance are staged. In many parts of the world mise-en-scènes are more or less fixed. The meaning of the performance is expressed more in the staging of events than in what the performers say. This is certainly true of many RITUAL performances. In aesthetic theater the mise-en-scène is frequently treated with extreme respect. It is unthinkable for a young No or Kabuki actor to revise the actions of a play. Only the most respected senior members of a company are entitled to make revisions in staging. The German playwright-director Bertolt Brecht—influenced greatly by Chinese theater—assembled *Modellbücher*, photographically detailed accounts of his mise-en-scènes. The mainstream modern Western way—wherever it is practiced, in New York, New Delhi, São Paulo, Nairobi, or Tokyo—is to invent new mise-en-scènes suiting either new or old verbal texts.

Modern Western theater emphasizes verbal texts because these persist in time and can be used as the basis for making new mise-en-scènes, which can be studied separately long after a given performance is over. But in nonmodern, premodern, and postmodern genres—street performance, popular ENTERTAINMENT, circus, performance art, and many of the performing arts of Africa, Asia, and Native America—the main weight of meaning and affect is borne by mise-en-scène, scenography, NARRATIVE, costume, mask, music, dance, and audience-performer interaction—the interplay of multiplex performance texts. Scholars are paying increased attention to this INTERTEXTUALITY.

Theater and Other Performative Genres

The performative genres—from theater to ritual, SPORTS, PLAY, and performance in everyday life—are always mixing and feeding one another. Artists even

in the most traditional cultures are frequently heedless of boundaries. Furthermore there is a continuous interplay among genres and between the so-called high arts (codified, classical, elitist) and the popular arts (improvised, widespread). Theater, like music, constantly absorbs into its classical repertory items transcribed from folk and popular culture (*see also* FOLKLORE). And, conversely, what is happening in the centers of classicism (however defined) is later reflected in the outlands. In India there is the age-old relationship between the Sanskritic and the *adavasi* (aboriginal) cultures; in late-twentieth-century theater in the United States painting, dance, music, and theater have various points of contact, as do these high arts and television (*see* TELEVISION HISTORY), movies (*see* MOTION PICTURES), sports, and questionable entertainments like PORNOGRAPHY.

Ritual and theater mix well. The Yaqui of Mexico and Arizona celebrate a Lenten cycle they call Waehma. Beginning the first Friday after Ash Wednesday and culminating with the redemption of the whole Yaqui community on the Saturday before Easter, Waehma combines Native American ritual clowns and deer dancers with early RENAISSANCE Spanish staging conventions and narratives introduced to the Yaqui by Jesuit missionaries in the seventeenth and eighteenth centuries. Waehma employs both outdoor processions around the way of the cross and more private ceremonies inside individual homes. Strictly Catholic ritual imported from Europe is balanced against the drama of pre-

Figure 2. *(Drama—Performance) Oedipus Rex,* directed by Tyrone Guthrie, at the Stratford (Ontario) Shakespearean Festival Theatre, 1954. The New York Public Library at Lincoln Center, Astor, Lenox and Tilden Foundations. Billy Rose Theatre Collection. Copyright by Mc-Kague, Toronto.

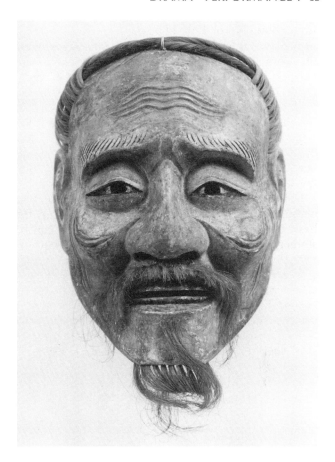

Figure 3. *(Drama—Performance)* Japanese Gigaku masks, Muromachi period. Tokyo National Museum. Photographs courtesy of the International Society for Educational Information, Tokyo, Inc.

Columbian Native American masked characters called *Chapayekas* who are enlisted in the pursuit and crucifixion of Jesus.

On Good Friday night the *Chapayekas,* led by Judas, their saint, celebrate the crucifixion by dancing drunkenly around a crèche/bier containing a small figure of Jesus on the cross. But sometime during this mock fiesta Jesus is taken away (he is resurrected) and a teddy bear is substituted. By the time the *Chapayekas* discover the trick, their anger is rendered helpless by drunkenness. But both anger and inebriation are acted: during the holy weeks of Lent no Yaqui, especially ones dedicated to the sacred role of *Chapayeka,* tastes alcohol. Defeated, the *Chapayekas* slink away. But on Saturday morning, joining with their allies, the soldiers of Rome, they storm the church three times in an attempt to recapture Christ, never suspecting that he is already resurrected. This time the forces of evil are transformed by the blood of Jesus—represented by leaves and flowers—showered on the *Chapayekas* and soldiers by pascolas (dancers), deer dancers, matachini, and a great crowd of spectators. The *Chapayekas* finally

enter the church, not as enemies of Christ but as Yaqui men desirous of redemption. Kneeling, they receive blessings. Then begins the year's biggest fiesta, featuring deer dancers, pascolas, and the life-giving matachini dancers. The deer dancers and pascolas are pre-Columbian; the matachini derive from Europe.

Categories slip. Underneath all performative genres—or, better, permeating all performative behavior—is play. Play is the essence of what anthropologist Victor Turner called the "subjunctive mood," the provisional, the open, the antistructural. What human rigidity proposes as law, settled opinion, and fixed tradition, play undermines, transforms, and recreates. Play is a manifold and subversive set of strategies, including trickery, parody, satire, and irony, that confers ontological status to lying. In the state of fecund DECEPTION humans invent unreal (as yet uncreated) worlds. Performance is the way these worlds take concrete shape in time and space, expressed as gestures, dances, words, masks, music, and narratives. Even in the Western theatrical tradition some characters and stories—Oedipus, Hamlet,

Willy Loman, Blanche Dubois, Godot—achieve a kind of archetypal/mythic status. These narratives/ characters persist over time; they are re-created by generations of actors, each of whom stamps them with a particular meaning. In addition to these characters, certain roles—the Mother, the Soldier, the Artist, the Judge, the Priest, the Wife, the Farmer, plus many others—achieve concrete shapes and rhythms.

Of course, different cultures handle their own stories/characters/archetypes differently. Specifying those differences is a way of comprehending divergent cultural processes. For example, artists, critics, and spectators of modern Western theater demand "new" and individuated versions of characters/narratives, whereas Japanese Kabuki actors happily give up their born names for the names of great actors of past generations. Kabuki performers submerge much of their individual creativity in the collective. Among the Kwakiutl of the U.S.-Canadian Pacific, masks, dances, and stories are valuable inheritable properties. The owner of a mask/dance can perform it himself or invite someone else to perform it for him, in which case the main honor of the performance goes not to the dancer but to the owner.

Developmental Phases

Although there are no universals of theater or theatricality, there is a seven-phase developmental sequence of activities that can be used interculturally to place various genres and styles. The seven phases are training, workshop, rehearsal, warm-up, performance, cool-down, and aftermath. The first four phases are preparatory; the last two follow a performance. Not every genre in all cultures uses all of these in making, displaying, and evaluating performances. What is emphasized or omitted can reveal a great deal. In No there are years of training and careful preparations before a performance but little or no rehearsal. Experimental theater emphasizes workshops during which details of the performance texts are painstakingly deconstructed and reconstructed. Stanislavsky and Brecht took up to two years to rehearse particular performances. Balinese Sanghyang is neither rehearsed nor trained for, but many preparations are made beginning several weeks before a trance dance. Western and Indian scholarship from their very inceptions have emphasized aftermath: detailed postperformance discussions, analysis, and theorizing. Whole books—like the Sanskrit *Natyasastra* (second century B.C.E.–second century C.E.) and Aristotle's *Poetics* (fourth century B.C.E.)—are devoted to specifying the exact nature of theater.

What all theatrical performances share—their underlying unity despite the tremendous diversity of styles, intentions, audiences, and occasions—is a quality of "twice-behaved behavior": "restored behavior." Such behavior—whether in a theater or in a life role, as part of a popular entertainment or a ritual, as a way to tell the truth or as a con game— is practiced, rule-governed behavior, trained for, rehearsed, previously known, or learned by osmosis (as Balinese or Pentecostals learn how to go into trance). Because performance behavior is not free and easy it never wholly belongs to the performer; it is always "other." As such it is well suited to represent or call into being nonordinary and nonhuman figures and worlds of experience; and it can be effectively codified, manipulated, reified, rearranged, and transmitted across time and space.

See also MUSIC HISTORY; MUSIC PERFORMANCE; MUSIC THEATER.

Bibliography. Keir Elam, *Semiotics of Theater and Drama*, London and New York, 1980; *High Performance* (magazine), Los Angeles, 1978– ; Kunio Komparu, *The Noh Theater* (No e no izanai), New York, Tokyo, and Kyoto, 1983; Patrice Pavis, *The Languages of the Stage*, New York, 1982; Richard Schechner, *Between Theater and Anthropology*, Philadelphia, 1985; Edward H. Spicer, *The Yaquis*, Tucson, Ariz., 1980; Victor Turner, *From Ritual to Theater: The Human Seriousness of Play*, New York, 1982; idem, *The Ritual Process*, Chicago, 1969, reprint Ithaca, N.Y., 1977; Phillip Zarrilli, *The Kathakali Complex*, New Delhi, 1984.

RICHARD SCHECHNER

DURKHEIM, ÉMILE (1858–1917)

French sociologist. Émile Durkheim, whose concept of social reality assigns a central role to communication processes, had a wide influence on methods and theories of modern social science. Born in the Lorraine area of France near Strasbourg, Durkheim studied philosophy at the University of Paris, where he obtained his Ph.D. in 1893. His interest in political and social thought led him into the newly emerging field of sociology. In 1887 Durkheim had begun teaching sociology and education at the University of Bordeaux, and in 1902 he moved on to the Sorbonne. He became a follower of Auguste Comte and pressed for a recognition of sociology as a science, stating that sociology's main goal was to show that social forces are "real." Social reality is not the same as psychological or biological reality. A social system generates a reality sui generis.

Durkheim's contributions to communication lie in his argument that people imbue a wide variety of objects, places, events, signs, and symbols with special qualities and meanings (*see* ARTIFACT; SIGN; SYMBOLISM). These qualities transform otherwise ordinary objects or events into something extraordinary. More specifically, the object is transformed from something without social implications (a profane object) into something that has social implications. Durkheim argued that such objects, which he referred to as "collective representations," acquire their significance through collective social processes and, in turn, are significant insofar as they are relevant to collective interests. One particularly interesting form of collective representation is the sacred event or sacred literature (*see* RITUAL; SCRIPTURE). The very sacredness of such literature removes it from individual criticism and grants it special collective powers that ordinary people or conditions cannot transcend. Collective representations are communicated and facilitate communication. They have the ability to generate massive collective actions. *See also* MEANING.

How this process works can be illustrated by society's definition of crime, which results from what Durkheim postulated as the "collective conscience." He observed that punishments often far exceed any kind of balanced response to possible physical or personal injuries suffered from the crime. In fact, some crimes do not appear to create any physical damage and yet may be punished with astonishing ferocity. Durkheim claimed that the intensity of the punishment was a consequence of the extent to which the criminal action violated the collective conscience. Crime does not violate the collective conscience because it is inherently bad; instead it is seen as bad because it violates the collective conscience.

Durkheim also argued that crime is normal to any society. Just as a psychologist might struggle with the idea of what constitutes a normal personality or normal behavior, Durkheim struggled with the problem of what constitutes a normal society. One of the qualities of any normal society is that crime will be a part of the system. In effect, there have to be some "wicked" people in order for there to be a group that can identify itself as "good." This was a novel argument for the late nineteenth century and remains so for the present time. It suggests that crime is a structural element of all societies and is a sociological condition as much as a psychological one.

However much social reality is merely a fabrication or construct, its effects on the individual and society are profound. For example, Durkheim's *Le suicide* (1897) was a brilliant attempt to demonstrate that individualistic actions are associated with complex social forces. One form of suicide, which Durkheim referred to as "anomic suicide," is a result, he argued, of the individual's disengagement from social constraints. Communities in which individualism is an important part of life will more likely have higher suicide rates than those in which individualistic philosophies are muted. Drawing on statistics available at the time, Durkheim noted higher suicide rates

Figure 1. *(Durkheim, Émile)* Émile Durkheim. The Bettmann Archive, Inc.

among Protestants (an individualistic religion) than among Catholics. A methodological tour de force for its time, Durkheim's study of suicide was among the earliest endeavors to bring a systematic, sophisticated use of statistical data to bear on a social issue.

In *Les formes élémentaires de la vie religieuse* (The Elementary Forms of the Religious Life, 1912) Durkheim examined the effects of social constructs on society. Here he argued that religious beliefs are associated with the forms of social organization adopted by any given people. For example, in societies organized in terms of simple clans the idea of a dominant God figure struggling to maintain equilibrium between the forces of good and evil is not likely to occur. In societies organized in terms of competing major units (e.g., the city-state) religious IDEOLOGY creates an anthropomorphized form of God in which the deity struggles with competing spiritual or otherworldly units. In other words, Durkheim claimed that religious belief is a kind of primitive sociology. It is a mythical representation of the abstract and powerful forces of social integration and disintegration. *See also* RELIGION.

The effects of social constructs, Durkheim observed, can become quite complex, with some social events the product of other social events. For example, war is a social occurrence best understood by examining other social conditions that bring it into being rather than by relying on simplistic psychological or biological factors to account for it. (The elemental argument here is that psychological and biological factors are essentially constant in large populations over time; therefore they cannot be relied on as explanations of the fluctuations between peace and war in social systems.) Durkheimian sociology was intended as an antidote to the trend in the late nineteenth century to seek biological and psychological explanations for complex social occurrences—a trend that has continued into the present time.

Thus a Durkheimian perspective makes us aware of the extent to which social reality is a "communicated" form of reality. Any kind of social observation is completely dependent on what we are told the social situation is. We cannot, for example, even observe a "professor" until we are informed in some manner that we are in the presence of a person of this status. Because social character—as opposed to purely physical qualities—is derived from complex forms of symbolic communication and resides within these communication systems, the validity of social reality can be no greater than the validity of the communication on which it rests. It is important that social reality be presented as authentically as possible if appropriate social interactions are to take place.

Bibliography. Émile Durkheim, *The Division of Labor in Society* (De la division du travail social), trans. by George Simpson, New York, 1933, reprint (new trans. by W. D. Halls) New York, 1984; idem, *The Elementary Forms of Religious Life* (Les formes élémentaires de la vie religieuse), trans. by J. W. Swain, London and New York, 1926, reprint London, 1976; idem, *The Rules of the Sociological Method*, 8th ed. (in French), ed. by George E. A. Catlin, trans. by S. Solovay and J. Mueller, Chicago, 1938, reprint New York, 1964; William D. Perdue, *Sociological Theory: Explanation, Paradigm, and Ideology*, Palo Alto, Calif., 1986.

EDITH W. KING AND R. P. CUZZORT

E *(ī)*, the fifth letter of the Roman alphabet, represents historically the Semitic ∃, which originally expressed a sound resembling that of *h*, but was adopted by the Greeks (and from them by the Romans) as a vowel, the pronunciation of which probably varied from the 'mid-front' (*e*) to the 'low front' (*ę*) vowels of Bell's system. In the Roman as in the earliest Greek alphabet, the letter represented the long as well as the short quantity of the vowel.

EAST ASIA, ANCIENT

We know a great deal about how information, ideas, and attitudes were communicated in ancient East Asia—more than we know about Europe in various comparable periods. There are several reasons for the richness of the record. The relative social stability of China, which was the dominant power in the region, made possible an uninterrupted record, throwing light on administrative, educational, and other matters. Chinese, Japanese, and Korean elites all valued LITERACY and WRITING. In addition, they aspired to serve in the central government bureaucracies, which kept exhaustive records and sponsored publication. Another factor was the written LANGUAGE—literary Chinese—which was employed throughout East Asia. Finally, for nearly a thousand years widespread PRINTING ensured the survival of books and a common stock of knowledge among those who could read.

Education. EDUCATION throughout East Asia for the last two thousand years has stressed formation of character on classical models. The overt purpose of TEACHING was not to disseminate knowledge, to socialize, or to develop individuality, but to pass on a "way" (*dao*) of living, of seeing, of doing something as it should be done. A "way" united knowledge, understanding, skill, and norm.

Children who had the opportunity to be educated spent years chanting the written classics. Only when the words of the teachings were firmly in memory did the teacher expound them. The result was profound internalization of values. This process created an elite that shared a broad and deep CULTURE and could transmit subtle meanings through allusion. Their knowledge filtered down to the illiterate, binding together a community of values that even rebels rarely challenged.

Education began in the family (although fathers did not normally teach their children) and in 500 B.C.E. still covered a variety of practical arts. By 200 B.C.E. it had become largely bookish. The state had appointed "professors" to ensure that texts of the several competing philosophic schools were kept intact and taught. By 100 B.C.E. an imperial "university" had been formed, its teachers entirely Confucian. It is said to have had three thousand students by the late first century B.C.E. *See also* UNIVERSITY.

Each new direction in ART or learning derived in principle not from the one before it, but from the canons that were required to be the source of every innovation. Chinese traditions were cumulative in the sense that writers were aware of their precursors and were expected to master earlier contributions before going beyond them. But novelty did not replace the old—least of all the oldest classics, to which the mind of the reader usually went first of all. The surest proof that one's work was valuable was to

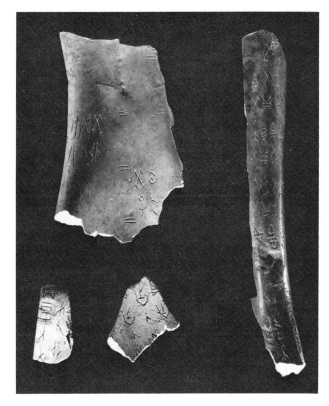

Figure 1. *(East Asia, Ancient)*   Inscribed oracle bones, Shang dynasty, China. Peabody Museum, Harvard University, Cambridge, Mass. Photograph by Hillel Burger. Photograph no. N28172.

connect it with the "way" of the ancients. Thus officials sponsoring translations of European scientific books early in the seventeenth century claimed they incorporated Chinese traditions that had died out early but had been preserved abroad. Their aim was not to disparage Western ideas but to convince readers that foreign writings could be taken seriously.

Language. Ancient East Asia was racially more diverse than today, and linguistically at least as diverse as Europe. Fifteen hundred years ago many inhabitants of what is now Xinjiang (Chinese Turkestan) were blond and spoke languages related to Persian and Latin. The predominant languages of East Asia in historical times have belonged to two families: the Sino-Tibetan (including Chinese) and, farther to the north, the Altaic. Both Japanese and Korean, which had little in common with Chinese until they borrowed lavishly from it, somewhat resemble Altaic languages such as Turkish and Manchu. Chinese differs from other widespread languages in its lack of inflection and its use of tones and in the limited role of phonetic elements in its written symbols. These characteristics complicated the highly inflected Japanese and Korean languages as they incorporated Chinese influence. *See* LINGUISTICS.

Like Latin in Europe, classical Chinese was used

a

 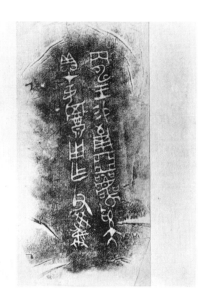

b

Figure 2. *(East Asia, Ancient)* *(a)* Ritual bronze vessel, Shang dynasty. Eleventh century B.C.E. *(b)* Rubbings of the inscription of sixteen characters on the vessel. Courtesy of the Freer Gallery of Art, Smithsonian Institution, Washington, D.C. (Acc. no. 53.83).

by all educated people over a large, linguistically and culturally diverse area, from Japan to Vietnam and on into Southeast Asia for many centuries. Even within China many so-called dialects are mutually unintelligible languages, and many non-Chinese languages survive, especially among groups descended from the indigenous peoples of the south. The classical written language that unified these variant cultures was in principle a dead language, perpetuated by memorization of classics. In practice it was continually invigorated and stylistically reshaped by its interaction with living speech, while preserving basic differences from the vernacular in structure and choice of words.

Mastery of the written language was probably restricted to 1 or 2 percent of the Chinese population in 100 B.C.E. and may not have exceeded 10 percent in 1800. But mastery in this context required staggering feats of memorization. As Evelyn Rawski and others have shown, a large proportion of the Chinese merchant and artisan classes could for centuries read and write well enough for everyday purposes, although in the eyes of their betters they remained "word-blind."

The limits of expression in classical Chinese were primarily cultural, not linguistic. Any language preserves established boundaries of thought and, when necessary, stretches to encompass new ones. It has long been recognized that classical Chinese was an adequate medium for expressive POETRY and powerful critical scholarship. As in any other language, literature balances precision about some things against vagueness about others. Over the last generation studies of early East Asian scientific, technological, and medical works have revealed traditions as diverse as those of premodern Europe, with theory and practice fully recorded. Ancient Chinese was as adaptable to the design of bureaucratic forms as modern English—because such forms were needed. Argumentation relied more often on analogy and historical allusion than on systematic proof, but the latter is often found in scientific writings. The Chinese translators of Euclid's *Elements* in 1607 had no difficulty creating classical Chinese equivalents. The alacrity with which geometry was then studied in China suggests that the language posed no inherent barriers to this least Chinese of thought patterns.

Two factors are sometimes said to give communication in classical Chinese a unique character: (1) the pictographic and ideographic origins of Chinese graphs and (2) the fact that the graphs cannot be inflected by changing the arrangement of the strokes that compose them. Both points involve misconceptions. Regarding the first point, by 200 B.C.E. only a small fraction of graphs were pictures (or combinations of pictures to signal abstract ideas), and a government reform had standardized the writing system to the point that even these were largely unrecognizable as pictures. Chinese were no more apt to see pictures while reading than English speakers are likely while reading the word *beer* to visualize an insect in its first three letters.

As for the second point, although classical Chinese does not modify graphs to express tense, gender, number, and so on, authors routinely expressed these aspects by specific words. This may add to the number of words, but it is unnecessary to inflect every verb in a text, as must be done in Indo-European languages even when all express the same tense. In Japanese and Korean, based on different linguistic strategies, phonetic elements were used between Chinese graphs to add grammatical endings.

Throughout East Asia, what could not be expressed reflected the norms and the habits of institutions. Historical change has again and again made it expressible.

Records. The earliest surviving written documents, from an archive of about 1450 B.C.E., record on tortoise shells and animal bones divinations carried out on behalf of the king. Precursors of this "oracle-bone" writing, graphs or groups of graphs incised on pottery, have been dated as early as the mid-fifth millennium. The archive has been a central function of government since its beginning. The legitimacy of a dynasty was demonstrated in part by maintaining systematic, dated records, which included diaries setting out the words and acts of the ruler, documents supporting administrative decisions, biographies of officials and other eminent persons, information on taxation, commodities, rituals, celestial events, natural disasters, and many other matters. For the last two thousand years new dynasties compiled official histories of their predecessors as evidence of legitimate succession. Activities of the central government provided a model for many kinds of private writing. Early forms of NARRATIVE fiction, poetry, and mathematical astronomy can be found in official compilations. *See also* ARCHIVES.

Divinatory documents on shell and bone were not the only ones that used specialized media. Inscriptions cast into RITUAL bronzes of the same period recorded their making, giving, and use in an ancestral cult. Carved jade tablets served for contracts and treaties.

Archival documents and books in general were written on silk rolls and bamboo or wooden slips held together with cord and rolled to make books. The earliest known specimen of paper, a lighter and more durable material than its predecessors, is dated 49 B.C.E. It too was stored in rolls until about twelve hundred years ago, when folded leaves began an evolution that yielded sewn bindings. Brush and carbon ink (india ink) were used at least as early as 1300 B.C.E. The flexibility of the former and the ease

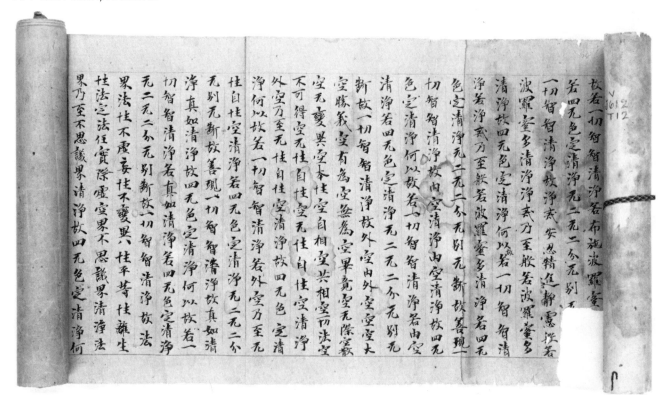

Figure 3. *(East Asia, Ancient)* Buddhist sutra, Tang dynasty. A paper scroll found in the Caves of the Thousand Buddhas, Dunhuang, Kanzu province, China. Courtesy of the Library of Congress.

with which the flow of the latter can be controlled gave Chinese calligraphy since the fourth century C.E. an expressiveness equal to that of pictorial art. *See* WRITING MATERIALS.

Over centuries of memorization and hand copying, the Confucian classics were transmitted with astonishing fidelity, but writings of lesser status were often corrupted, and the attrition was great. Woodblock printing, used at least since the eighth century in China, became standard for reproduction of books not long after 1000. Viscous water-base ink was applied to the block and transferred to the paper with no need for a press. Illustrations could be incorporated when the blocks were cut. Multicolor printing, an obvious outgrowth, appeared as early as 1340.

Because labor, wood, and storage were cheap, and any book needed thousands of different characters, there was no economic incentive to perfect movable-type printing, invented by 1050. Even if only a few impressions were taken at a time, the margin of profit was high. Protracted royal support in Korea, where wood was scarce, led to the perfection of metal movable type early in the fifteenth century. But movable type became economically important in China only with the beginnings in the nineteenth century of a mass book market, with its incentives for smaller print than could be quickly carved in blocks. Intense competition among publishers long antedated that time. Pirating was common enough that a claim to COPYRIGHT under government protection appeared as early as the 1190s.

Literature. The transition from classical to vernacular literature did not take place in China until the twentieth century, but the roots of the latter go back a thousand years. Among the few archaic books that survived to become classics of the Confucian school are precursors of history, fiction, and poetry. The *Zhou yi* or *Yi jing*, the Book of Changes of the late ninth century B.C.E., contains snatches of songs and stories alongside prognostications and divinatory proverbs. The *Shi jing*, the Book of Poetry, most of which probably originated in the next century or so, combines popular songs collected throughout the Chou domains and adapted to the language of the royal court, songs performed on ceremonial occasions in the palace, and ritual hymns used in its ancestral shrine. Nature, love, grief, spiritual awe, the resentment of the oppressed, sensual exuberance—many key themes of later poetry appear in this collection. It also prefigures a central characteristic of Chinese poetic symbolism: the poet's inner state is expressed by describing a correlate in the outside world, as when devastated chestnut and plum trees on a mountainside stand for a gentleman far from home, fallen upon bad times.

In ancient China, as in the early Occident, the boundary between historic narrative and story remained fuzzy. The earliest chronicles contain anecdotes of high adventure and divine intervention. The Standard Histories (*zhengshi*), beginning with that by Sima Qian (between 100 and 90 B.C.E.), systematically recorded every aspect of political and social life from the legendary beginnings of culture. They seldom contained an assertion not drawn from a written document. The result is a remarkably accurate account of the emperors' words and acts, of the lives of statesmen, of economic affairs and institutions. But documents also contained reports of marvels, speeches, and thoughts to which their authors were not privy, and accounts of superhuman virtue and bravery. Sima Qian's biographies of jokesters and assassins, and later accounts of magicians and immortals, provided exemplars for genres devoted to wit, knight-errantry, and prodigies. Buddhist and Taoist stories of encounters of gods and mortals and testimonies to miracles inspired secular counterparts. The boundaries of literature continued to expand beyond the orthodox preoccupation with encouraging proper attitudes and behavior.

The seventh-century *chuanqi* tales, written to entertain, can reasonably be considered prose romances. The association of their classical language with bookishness was so strong that their scholarly authors often designed them as showcases for a specimen of fine writing—a love letter or a didactic essay. The most vital development of fiction came in the freer forms invented further down the social scale, in the urban culture of merchants and artisans.

Although some Sinologists see traces of speech forms and rhythms in the classics of the first millennium B.C.E., actual writing in the vernacular began with the efforts of early Buddhist proselytizers fifteen hundred years ago to reach common people and was quickly adapted for a variety of narrative aims. Such documents depended on the immediate appeal of everyday language heightened by art. Normally alternating prose and song, they were accessible only in one dialect region at one time.

City culture put money into the purses of people who did not belong to the educated elite but who wanted entertainment. Public storytellers were an organized presence early in the eleventh century. By 1550 a great diversity of written stories drew on the classical tradition, on professional oral fiction, and on DRAMA. They include tales of detection, of suspense, of love in marriage and amorous intoxication outside it, comparable in sophistication and invention with the best of seventeenth-century European writings.

Although the literary traditions of Korea and Ja-

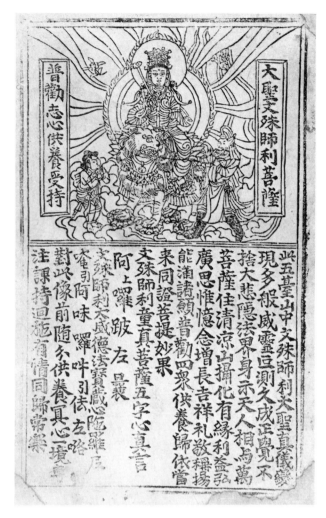

Figure 4. *(East Asia, Ancient)* Buddhist woodblock print from Dunhuang, tenth century. Reproduced by courtesy of the Trustees of The British Museum.

pan were heavily influenced by China—the Korean more than the Japanese—basic differences in culture and language are reflected in the literature, notably in poetry. For instance, the first great collection of Japanese verse, the aristocratic *Manyoshu*, written in the century before 760, includes mostly verse restricted to thirty-one syllables. This is more daunting than the contemporary twenty-eight-character Chinese form, for Japanese is polysyllabic. The GENRE succeeds by fully exploiting multiple meaning and indirection. The haiku form, cultivated by sixteenth- and seventeenth-century townsmen, was only seventeen syllables long. Equally given to controlled ambiguity, it demanded a wit and verbal dexterity probably unequaled elsewhere.

Visual arts. Pictures and diagrams were incorporated in books practically since their inception. Domestic scenes, visualizations of the afterlife, and cosmic diagrams (especially star charts) have been painted

白雲如帶束山腰石
磴飛空細路遙獨倚
杖藜舒眺望欲因鳴
澗落吹簫沈周

Figure 5. *(East Asia, Ancient)* Shen Chou (1427–1509), *Chang-li yuan-t'iao* (Poet on a Mountain Top). From a Chinese landscape album with six leaves. Ink on paper. The Nelson-Atkins Museum of Art, Kansas City, Mo. (Nelson Fund).

and carved to decorate tombs for more than two thousand years. Certain aspects of Chinese art— PORTRAITURE, SCULPTURE, and ARCHITECTURE—remained the province of artisans. For much of the last millennium, however, calligraphy, painting, and related arts such as carving of seals have been considered the province of the scholarly, cultivated amateur, though often pursued for money. The arts for which Japan is best known were created in the milieu of urban merchants and artisans. The multicolor Japanese woodblock prints, especially pictures of entertainers, that reached their peak in the eighteenth century are the most famous. Japanese considered these prints vulgar decorations until the nineteenth century, when they were avidly collected by foreigners and exerted an important influence on European modernist painters.

Travel. Because of China's size and geographic diversity, the problems posed by internal and international travel were comparable. People and goods have passed back and forth between China and other parts of the world with few interruptions since the Neolithic period. Japan and Korea were by comparison isolated. Korean isolation was furthered by dread

of being culturally overwhelmed by China. Insular Japan has tended for fifteen centuries to alternate periods of intense Chinese influence with periods in which it turned inward and assimilated them (*see* TOKUGAWA ERA: SECLUSION POLICY).

The Chinese imperial highway system by the third century B.C.E. totaled more than four thousand miles. The custom of conscripting labor for road building and other public projects during the agricultural off-season made this the best-constructed part of a road network for vehicles drawn by oxen or horses. Major highways in the third century C.E. have been estimated at twenty-two thousand miles. A government system of post stations, which by the eighth century provided accommodations, food, and fresh horses for official travelers, made possible sustained travel at a rate of about one hundred fifty miles per day. Within five hundred years, couriers could carry messages from outlying parts of the empire considerably faster than that. Camels, which can survive by foraging at considerable intervals, not only extended communications across deserts but greatly reduced the cost of long-distance shipping. *See* POSTAL SERVICE.

Large canal systems date from the Zhengguo Canal (mid-third century B.C.E.), which irrigated two-thirds of a million acres. Canals with spillways and locks connecting watercourses across mountain ranges date from the same period. This experience was applied in South China to connect an extensive system of waterways, making possible cheap long-distance transport in high volume.

The large administrative centers in the capital subsisted on tax grain. As the capital moved farther from the rich Lower Yangtze Valley, artificial waterways were needed where rivers were lacking. The Grand Canal was built for this purpose around 600 C.E. and extended northward to reach later capitals. China's long seacoast made ocean shipping practicable for domestic trade and, at certain periods such as around 1400, for forwarding of tax grain to the capital.

International trade. International trade between China and other countries predates historic times. Jade, which was needed for ritual implements, was not produced in China; expeditions in the late second century B.C.E. quickly bore fruit in trade with India and across Central Asia with Iran. The massive trade in silk that soon followed probably helped drain the finances of the ROMAN EMPIRE. Overland transport, often interrupted by political change in the many small states en route, took on major importance again in the thirteenth and fourteenth centuries, when the Mongols imposed peace in the regions between the Pacific and eastern Europe.

Chinese long-distance navigation became prominent after the third century C.E. Endless movement of cargos in native ships and those of Islamic and Southeast Asian merchants made southern coastal cities such as Guangzhou (Canton) cosmopolitan trade centers by 800. Accounts of East African coastal kingdoms appear in Chinese shortly after this time. From about 1300 on, the advanced technology of Chinese ships—the true rudder, a sail that enabled tacking to windward, bulkhead compartments, navigation with the magnetic compass—made them briefly paramount in highly competitive ocean transport.

Trade was not the only motive for navigation. Although Chinese regimes were seldom expansionist outside traditional borders, the Mongol Yuan mounted aggressive seaborne forces in the thirteenth century. In more pacific times the imperial charisma could be augmented by the tribute of foreign states. Most official EXPLORATION was carried out to establish such relationships, made attractive to the tributaries by gifts and the prospect of unofficial trade. The peoples loosely bound in this extensive system were either culturally or technologically inferior neighbors, or so distant that they could not challenge Chinese convictions about the centrality of China's civilization and the necessity for hierarchy in foreign affairs. As late as the eighteenth century China had

Figure 6. *(East Asia, Ancient)* Japanese calligraphy: Edo period, Rimpa school. Hon'ami Koetsu (1558–1637), *Poems of Thirty-six Master Poets.* Ink on gold paper. Courtesy of the Freer Gallery of Art, Smithsonian Institution, Washington, D.C. (Acc. nos. 75.20–29 and 75.20–30).

had no experience with peoples who, while posing no military threat, had to be treated as equals. Attempts by modern European powers to establish diplomatic relations were greatly confused because Chinese expected them to conform to the tributary system. It was only after China lost a series of wars and was forced to accept unequal treaties that this clash of views about the character of international communications was resolved.

See also ASIA, TWENTIETH CENTURY; SILK ROAD; SOUTH ASIA, ANCIENT.

Bibliography. G. F. Hudson, *Europe and China*, London, 1931, reprint Boston, 1961; David Johnson, Andrew J. Nathan, and Evelyn S. Rawski, eds., *Popular Culture in Late Imperial China*, Berkeley, Calif., 1985; Joseph Needham, *Science and Civilization in China*, 6 vols., Cambridge, 1954–, esp. Vol. 1, *Introductory Orientations* (travel between civilizations), Vol. 4, part 3, *Civil Engineering and Nautics* (roads and waterways), Vol. 5, part 1, *Chemistry and Chemical Technology* (T. H. Tsien on paper and printing); Evelyn S. Rawski, *Education and Popular Literacy in Ch'ing China*, Ann Arbor, Mich., 1979; Edward H. Schafer, *The Golden Peaches of Samarkand*, Berkeley, Calif., 1963; Masayoshi Sugimoto and David L. Swain, *Science and Culture in Traditional Japan, A.D. 600–1854*, Cambridge, Mass., 1978.

NATHAN SIVIN

EASTMAN, GEORGE (1854–1932)

U.S. photographic pioneer and inventor of the Kodak system. George Eastman was in large part responsible for bringing PHOTOGRAPHY to the millions. His linked development of the paper-backed film roll, the box camera, and the centralized developing service made it possible for all, whatever their age or economic status, to take photographs recording, commemorating, and adorning the world around them. *See also* PHOTOGRAPHY, AMATEUR.

When Eastman was born, the world of photography had just been revolutionized by the introduction of the wet-collodion process; in 1877, when Eastman decided to take up photography, this was still the predominant photographic process. During this period few hobbyists remained interested in photography for long, because its complexity made picture taking a chore rather than a pleasure. Eastman was mechanically inclined, however, and began experimenting with the dry-collodion process, which had recently been described in the *British Journal of Photography*. Within a year he had devised automatic equipment to make dry plates, obtaining patents both in England and the United States. In 1881 he formed the Eastman Dry Plate Company, which, after becoming the Eastman Dry Plate and Film

Figure 1. *(Eastman, George)* Frederick Church, *George Eastman with a Kodak on the S.S. Gallia*, 1890. International Museum of Photography at George Eastman House.

Company in 1884, was reorganized as the Eastman Kodak Company in 1892. It was this business that would make Eastman one of U.S. technology's greatest success stories and the city of Rochester, New York, a center of the photographic industry.

Though an improvement on wet plates, dry plates were still cumbersome. In 1884 Eastman developed flexible film, which consisted of a dry emulsion attached to a paper backing instead of the fragile and bulky glass plate; he also designed a holder for these paper-backed film rolls that would fit on any existing camera. Soon he created a completely transparent film, backed by celluloid instead of paper; it was this celluloid film, arranged in fifty-four-foot-long strips, that made possible the moving pictures shown in Edison's Kinetoscopes (see EDISON, THOMAS ALVA; MOTION PICTURES—PREHISTORY).

The second component of Eastman's success was a camera especially designed to use his new film, the Kodak, invented by Eastman in 1888. It was a camera reduced to its essentials: a lens at one end, a film holder at the other, and a shutter mechanism in between. Over the next fifteen years Kodaks became cheaper and easier to use, until in 1900 Eastman introduced the Brownie, a camera even a child could use, at a cost of one dollar.

Arguably the most important of Eastman's innovations was his factory service for processing film. The complexity of developing and printing film had been perhaps the greatest obstacle to amateur photography, and the processing service completely removed this obstacle.

The Kodak system thus incorporated three basic elements: the flexible film roll; an inexpensive, compact, easy-to-use camera; and a convenient central developing service. The aspiring photographer needed only to buy a camera, shoot some pictures, and send the camera back to the Eastman Kodak Company, which would develop the film, reload the camera with fresh film, and mail the camera and finished pictures back within the week. The system has remained much the same, although now the photographer sends only the exposed film, not the entire camera, to the developer.

Eastman, who never married, gave away nearly his entire fortune to educational institutions in Rochester and across the country. The University of Rochester's Eastman School of Music, and George Eastman House, a major film and photography archive (see ARCHIVES, FILM), are two of his best-known legacies. In 1932, weakened by illness, he left a message saying, "My work is done," and shot himself.

Bibliography. Brian Coe, *George Eastman and the Early Photographers,* London, 1973.

HARTLEY S. SPATT

EDISON, THOMAS ALVA (1847–1931)

U.S. inventor known for his work with the electric light, the telegraph, the TELEPHONE, the phonograph, and MOTION PICTURES. Thomas Alva Edison was more than an inventor. Through his imagination and capacity for endless experimentation he contributed to nearly every electrical advance of his lifetime. In addition, he devised a system of large-scale industrial experimentation that became the model for the modern corporate laboratory.

Edison's inventions all followed a pattern: identify a need, then invent the solution. Telegraph companies lacked enough operators to relay messages over long distances, so Edison invented an automatic repeater. Brokers could not obtain news of stock and commodity transactions quickly enough to respond to changing market conditions, so Edison invented the Universal Stock Printer. TELEGRAPHY consumed inordinate amounts of expensive copper wire, so Edison invented a quadruplex system that cut costs by three-quarters. The telephone suffered from inadequate transmitting instruments, so Edison invented a microphone diaphragm with a carbon button, still employed in modern telephones.

Edison's researches often led to peripheral inventions that proved of greater value than his intended accomplishments. While working on an "autograph telegraph" for transmitting handwritten messages, Edison invented an "electric pen" that left a chemical track on special paper—the mimeograph stencil. Another spin-off from the autograph telegraph proved even more important than the electric pen and the mimeograph stencil. Edison was working on a way to transform his mechanical marks into electrical impulses and was simultaneously working on the problem of the telephone transmitter, which transformed mechanical movement into sound. He combined the two lines of research, and on July 18, 1877, shouted into a microphone that was attached to the stylus of his autograph telegraph, then ran the embossed paper back through a speaker. The shout was played back to him; it was faint but distinct. Edison had invented the phonograph (see SOUND RECORDING—HISTORY). After this burst of invention he became known to the public as the Wizard of Menlo Park.

For Edison invention was a never-ending process of discovery, and rather than develop all his inventions to commercial perfection, he often moved to new fields of endeavor. He invented the carbon-filament lamp—which later became known as the electric light bulb—then invented an entire system of electrical generation and power distribution to make it available to potential users. Between 1881 and 1883 Edison obtained an astonishing two hundred

Figure 1. *(Edison, Thomas Alva)* Thomas Alva Edison in his laboratory. The Bettmann Archive, Inc.

patents, nearly all for electrical generation and lighting.

A minor problem with Edison's light bulb led to another important invention. Edison noted that his bulbs became unusable long before they blew out, because a black coating appeared on the inside of the glass. This came to be called "the Edison effect." Edison lost interest in it, but the phenomenon was investigated by two British scientists, J. Ambrose Fleming and Joseph J. Thomson, who correctly attributed the blackening to a flow of electrons (previously unknown) within the bulb. As a result the bulb was transformed from an illuminator to a rectifier in 1904 and, in the three-wire arrangement of LEE DE FOREST, to an amplifier in 1907. Thus the RADIO tube was born.

Edison's work on moving pictures was stimulated by the serial photographs of Eadweard Muybridge (*see* MOTION PHOTOGRAPHY). Edison at first conceived of such sequences of photographs being mounted on a cylinder similar to the revolving cylinder used in his phonograph, creating a device that might be used as a supplement to the phonograph. He assigned the moving-image problem to his laboratory assistant William Kennedy Laurie Dickson. Dickson, prompted by GEORGE EASTMAN's invention of photographic film on long celluloid strips, took the experiments in a different direction. Adding

sprocket holes along one edge of the film to control its movement, he developed the historic Kinetoscope (the peepshow viewing machine) and the Kinetograph, the huge camera that would provide its entertainment items. The peepshow machine and accompanying films were placed on the market in 1894; by the end of that year Kinetoscope parlors were operating profitably from Chicago to Copenhagen.

Despite the advice of Dickson, Edison resisted the idea of projecting the films onto a screen, reasoning that if many paying customers were allowed to view simultaneously what they viewed individually on a Kinetoscope, the market would soon be exhausted. But the resounding success of the 1895 Paris debut of the cinematograph of LOUIS AND AUGUSTE LUMIÈRE clearly doomed the Kinetoscope. Edison hastily arranged to take over a projector developed by U.S. inventors C. Francis Jenkins and Thomas Armat; it had its debut in 1896 as the Edison Vitascope.

The Edison company remained in film production for many years, and Edison became a leader of the Motion Picture Patents Company—"the Trust"—a group of companies that sought to control the infant industry through restrictions on the use of their patents. The effort proved unsuccessful (*see* HOLLYWOOD).

Edison was an inventor whose innovations generally reached their principal success in forms determined by others. Edison's phonograph cylinder gave way to the disc, his DC electric power to AC, his peepshow films to projection in cinemas. When he died in 1931 he did not leave behind a thriving business corporation but a legacy of visions that have changed the entire character of modern life.

Bibliography. Robert E. Conot, *A Streak of Luck: The Life and Legend of Thomas Alva Edison,* New York, 1979; Lawrence A. Frost, *The Edison Album: A Pictorial Biography,* Seattle, Wash., 1969; Gordon Hendricks, *The Edison Motion Picture Myth,* Berkeley, Calif., 1961, reprint New York, 1972.

HARTLEY S. SPATT

EDUCATION

Education may be understood as an activity, a possession, or an institution. As an activity it can be undertaken purposefully or may simply occur as a person experiences and processes the external world. As a possession education may be acquired purposefully by attending SCHOOL. As an institution education may consist of specific places with specially trained personnel, or it may consist in purposeful instruction in settings other than those designated as schools or colleges.

In its broadest sense education is nearly synonymous with socialization, the process of acquiring the norms, values, and patterns of behavior of the CULTURE and the particular social groups to which we belong. Socialization is one of the central reasons for education. That is, we educate to socialize, to equip individuals with those identities and characteristics that enable them to take membership in the culture and the social group. ÉMILE DURKHEIM referred to education as "methodical socialization" and described it as "the influence exercised by adult generations on those that are not yet ready for social life." Durkheim contended that the object of education is "to arouse and to develop in the child a certain number of physical, intellectual, and moral states that are demanded of him by both the political society as a whole and the special milieu for which he is specifically destined."

A distinction is often made between education that is purposeful and education that is not. If we set out specifically to teach someone something about the world he or she inhabits, it is clear that we are educating. It is not so clear that we are educating when that same individual "picks up" information about the world from persons who did not plan to teach this information and had no intention that someone would learn it. It is often said that travel is educational, although no one may specifically try to educate us as we move from place to place. The same notion is applicable to the mass media. Exposure to the media may be instructive even though it is not education in a purposeful sense.

The notion that education can take place when no one plans or intends it is implicit in such locutions as "Experience is the best teacher" and "The only place he ever got an education was in the school of life." On the other hand, an education can be intended and offered but not received, as when a child's teachers are said to have tried every possible way to teach him or her, but to no avail (see also TEACHING).

Informal, Nonformal, and Formal Education

Education can also be categorized as *informal, nonformal,* or *formal.* Informal education is what is picked up as we go through life—at work, in travel, at play, and from the mass media. It is largely unplanned and generally does not result from any intention to acquire or impart specific knowledge or skills. It is, in short, the everyday process of learning one's culture. Nonformal education is somewhat more systematic. It is planned educational activity but without the structures and organizations associated with such institutions as schools and colleges. Examples of nonformal education include the Boy Scouts and Girl Scouts, adult LITERACY and community

center programs, agricultural extension, and some forms of religious education. Formal education, in contrast to informal and nonformal, is the system of schooling put in place precisely to gain greater and more systematic control over the socialization processes, as well as to instruct in the content fields.

These three categories of education may overlap. Informal and nonformal education may occur within the formal context of schools. Nonformal education can occur in the normally informal setting of the home, as when parents set out specifically to educate their children (*see* FAMILY). Television generally offers ENTERTAINMENT but may educate even while serving this purpose. In addition it may present programs designed specifically to teach children to count and to read and programs aimed at teaching adults about philosophy, gardening, astronomy, and home repair that are properly understood as instances of nonformal education. *See* AUDIOVISUAL EDUCATION; EDUCATIONAL TELEVISION.

In most industrialized nations formal, informal, and nonformal education occur as parallel processes and may interact quite harmoniously. Or they may be in conflict with one another, as when one set of values and behavioral codes is learned at school; another in home, church, and club; and still another from the mass media. In most nations and cultures formal education is conducted by one or another level of government, often to secure the participation of youth in the economic and political structures supported by it. Nonformal education may be planned to supplement formal systems of education or may be offered as an alternative to formal education. For example, some religious groups may believe that government schools, as formal systems, do not teach desired values. These groups may then attempt to provide their own formal schools or may counter the influence of government-run schools by offering separate religious classes for young people. These same religious groups may also seek to form clubs and to offer radio and television programs (*see* RELIGIOUS BROADCASTING) either to supplement what is learned at school or to provide alternative conceptions to what is taught at school.

However, dividing education into the three categories here alludes only to their structural characteristics. These are critical to an understanding of education, but a more important dimension concerns the aims of education. What ends are served? With what purpose do we undertake methodical socialization?

The Outcomes of Education

When education is thought about as an intentional endeavor, a variety of philosophical issues arise: Why educate? What is an educated person? What knowledge is of most worth? Do we have the right or the obligation to educate in particular ways or to particular ends? One useful strategy in trying to answer these and similar questions is to distinguish among education for membership, education for enlightenment, and education for emancipation.

Education for membership refers to nonformal and formal education undertaken to secure the allegiance of students to the agency or institution sponsoring the educational activity. Education for enlightenment instructs students in how they may transcend everyday experience and self-interest through rigorous study of classical and modern ideas. Finally, education for emancipation attempts to achieve a measure of liberation from potentially oppressive and exploitative political economies. Each of these perspectives requires further consideration.

Education for membership. There are several forms of membership that education is generally thought to prepare persons for, among them religious, social, political, and economic. When education is undertaken intentionally (nonformally or formally), it is frequently for the purpose of preparing persons for membership in the group or entity that sponsors that education. Education may be formalized precisely because a political, social, or religious entity wants to unite a specific population in support of certain ideals and aspirations. A church, for example, may establish a formal system of education in order to ensure and strengthen the bonds of membership within it, even though the schools it establishes may also attend to matters of social, political, and economic membership. States or nations may establish formal systems of education in order to ensure the preparation of citizens for life in the state.

The desire to establish and solidify membership is often a primary objective in the formalization of education. In his *Politics,* ARISTOTLE argued that "the citizen should be molded to suit the form of government under which he lives." Modern systems of public education are frequently espoused on the basis of John Stuart Mill's rationale (in *Considerations on Representative Government,* 1861) that "the first element of good government, therefore, being the virtue and intelligence of the human beings composing the community, the most important point of excellence which any form of government can possess is to promote the virtue and intelligence of the people themselves."

This reasoning is frequently presumed to justify government-sponsored schools for the young. Yet Mill, along with many other political theorists of his time, had considerable difficulty with the idea of formal education in the hands of the state. In his essay "On Liberty" (1859) Mill argues that "a general state of education is a mere contrivance for moulding people to be exactly like one another: and as the mould in which it casts them is that which pleases the predominant power in the government, . . . it establishes a despotism over the mind, leading by natural tendency to one over the body."

Herein lies one of the major difficulties of education for membership: Is there an obligation in formal education for something more than forging bonds among its members on behalf of whatever agency or institution sponsors the schooling? In nations in which formal education is pervasive, social membership is an important aim of the early elementary grades. The emphasis in these grades is on learning how to become a member of groups, how to associate with peers, and how to respond to adults. As the learner matures, the basic skills of literacy and computation receive the major emphasis. Usually beginning when the learner is age eleven or twelve, the stress on generic skills diminishes, and the learner is introduced to the subject matter fields or disciplines. This content or disciplinary emphasis continues through all subsequent grades and into higher education.

Although these emphases may appear unobjectionable, indeed even laudable, it may be argued that they are pursued primarily to induct the learner into some political or social niche. Those who sponsor the schools are doing it for some purpose, and that purpose may not be so noble as to include the unfettered independence, freedom, and autonomy of the student. Does the formal system help the student to understand how membership may be declined, how the conditions of membership may be altered, or how the character of the sponsor may be changed to make membership appealing? Options and choices of this kind may not be present in formal systems of schooling.

It is perhaps not unusual that many cultures and societies enforce various forms of membership on the very young, for they are not able to reason for themselves and may need to adopt rules and norms of membership for simple reasons of safety. The problem arises near the time of emerging adolescence when a tribe, subculture, or political unit decides whether to forgo indoctrinary forms of education for membership and begins to introduce methods and content that permit the learner to reexamine his or her membership for the purpose of choosing it.

Education for enlightenment. The possibility of choice and the manner of making that choice involve consideration of education as a means to enlightenment. There are two primary reasons for conceiving of education as enlightenment. The first, already mentioned, is that the self-interests of the sponsors of schooling may preclude the possibility of the learner's deciding not to join the sponsor or prevent the learner from seeking membership with another sponsor. Thus education as enlightenment has as one of its purposes informing the learner of the possibilities and potentials of his or her existence, beyond the usual interests of the sponsor of the schools. Enlightenment theorists believe that personal freedom and choice are virtually defining conditions of human existence; if neither is exercised, then one defaults—from their perspective—on what may be the most precious possession one may ever have.

The second major argument for enlightenment is that no one should simply accept experience as it is presented, even if that experience is explicitly educational. Education is much too important to be left to the vicissitudes or the planned interventions of daily life. Persons must learn to think for themselves; to make independent observations, analyses, and judgments; to act from their own sets of reasonable beliefs and grounded principles. If left only to life's experiences, the person risks being trapped in the rigid and stultifying confines of convention and stereotype. This fear of being trapped within one's own limited experience was apparent in early Greek notions of human existence, leading the Greeks to place a heavy emphasis on education. As H. I. Marrou states in *A History of Education in Antiquity* (1956), "For Hellenistic man the sole aim of human existence was the achievement of the fullest and most perfect development of the personality." This notion is frequently expressed as *paideia,* the perfection of the person as an individual entity.

In *The Paideia Proposal* (1982) U.S. philosopher Mortimer Adler sets forth a program of studies not unlike—in form at least—the Hellenic curriculum rooted in the concept of *paideia.* This curriculum demands the same course of study for every student and is designed to terminate in the attainment of three primary objectives: (1) the acquisition of organized knowledge (e.g., literature, language, mathematics, natural science, and history); (2) the development of intellectual skills (e.g., calculating, problem solving, measuring, and exercising critical judgment); and (3) an enlarged understanding of ideas and values (e.g., permitting the thoughtful discussion of great ideas, enjoyment of works of art, and involvement in music and drama). The intent of this line of thought is to emphasize not only the acquisition of common basic skills and knowledge but also an understanding of central concepts and theories in the major disciplines of knowledge and the taking on of such critical traits of character as autonomy, a sense of fairness, intellectual curiosity, and a proper regard for evidence and truth. These noble educational ideals have captured the imagination of many powerful figures in human history, among them Immanuel Kant, JOHN MILTON, Leo Tolstoy, JOHN LOCKE, and JOHN DEWEY. Recently, however, the work of the enlightenment theorists has been attacked by scholars whose work has a more emancipationist foundation.

Education as emancipation. Despite the uplifting rhetoric of the enlightenment position, contemporary theorists have found ample reason to critique it. The critics begin by objecting that the enlightenment theorists, once they have made the case that the point of enlightenment is to handle the indoctrination difficulties associated with membership, go on to ignore the social, political, and economic foundations of education. These ties between systems of schooling and economic and political institutions are, the emancipationist critics contend, all too often destructive of educational ends.

Michael W. Apple addresses the point directly when he argues that "institutions of cultural preservation and distribution like schools create and recreate forms of consciousness that enable social control to be maintained without the necessity of dominant groups having to resort to overt mechanisms of domination." Everett Reimer, one of the most trenchant critics of formal systems of schooling (and a major influence on the ideas of Ivan Illich), echoes Apple's sentiments when he states that schools have been successful because "to the masses and their leaders, they have held out unprecedented hope of social justice. To the elite they have been an unparalleled instrument, appearing to give what they do not, while convincing all that they get what they deserve."

Ivan Illich, perhaps the best known of the emancipationists, laments the state of formal education in advanced societies and has suggested that developing nations should not try to imitate the educational systems of the industrialized nations. Illich argues that compulsory schools divide a society into two parts, that which is educational or academic and that which is not. This bifurcation leads to a divided social reality, in which whatever is defined as educational has little to do with whatever else is in the world, and the world outside the school possesses little that is explicitly educational. In Illich's words, "education becomes unworldly and the world becomes uneducational."

These concerns (i.e., that formal schooling simply reproduces the culture in which it occurs) have led a number of educational theorists to call for more explicit forms of nonformal education, for specifically educative events and activities without the enormous investment in formal, obligatory systems of education. The self-help (*harambe*) schools in Kenya and Nigeria and the consciousness-raising and popular-education movements in Latin America are examples of efforts to educate the masses without large-scale commitments of national resources to formal systems of schooling (*see* DEVELOPMENT COMMUNICATION).

In the mid-1980s Thomas J. La Belle examined many of the nonformal programs in Latin America and the Caribbean, reaching the conclusion that a considerable distance remains between the rhetoric and the reality. Though he supports the aims and objectives of many of the nonformal programs, he argues that they have not been successful in establishing a participatory base in local communities and in breaking away from the powerful influences of governing elites. To the emancipationist, political and economic elites control formal systems of schooling and will try to use these schools to ensure a smooth transition into appropriate levels of membership on the part of all social classes. The enlightenment theorist understands the necessity for membership but also recognizes how education for membership can be misused by those in power. The advocate of enlightenment responds to this threat by stressing attention to knowledge, understanding, and the critical traits of character needed to rise above the elemental attempts of educational systems to socialize and stratify their students. However, enlightenment theory is usually grounded in views that subordinate power to reason and wealth to morality. Thus the enlightenment theorist typically views change as rational, orderly, and subject to compromise based on evidence and etiquette. Emancipationists tend to focus more on the realities than on the hopes for human attainment. They are attentive to a history of the human species that is rooted in conflict, upheaval, and the ascendancy of power over reason and wealth over morality. *See also* IDEOLOGY.

From this survey of perspectives it becomes clear that our conceptions of what education is and should be are driven by our experiences, our values, and our theories of knowledge, culture, and history. It is taken for granted that education, at least in its formal and nonformal modes, is charged with giving each of us command of the basic skills of language, literacy, computation, and citizenship. The controversial questions are what more beyond the basics is to be attained and to what end are these skills and understandings to be acquired. These questions will not soon recede in the importance they possess or the controversy they generate.

Bibliography. Mortimer J. Adler, *The Paideia Proposal*, New York, 1982; Michael W. Apple, *Ideology and Curriculum*, London and Boston, 1979; R. F. Dearden, P. H. Hirst, and R. S. Peters, eds., *Education and the Development of Reason*, Vol. 3, *Education and Reason*, London, 1975; Émile Durkheim, *Education and Sociology* (in French), trans. by Sherwood D. Fox, Glencoe, Ill., 1956; Ivan Illich, *Deschooling Society*, New York, 1970, reprint 1983; Thomas J. La Belle, *Nonformal Education in Latin America and the Caribbean: Stability, Reform, or Revolution?* New York, 1986; Henri I. Marrou, *A History of Education in Antiquity* (Histoire de l'éducation dans l'antiquité), trans. by George Lamb, New York, 1956, reprint 1982; R. S. Peters, ed., *The Philosophy of Education*, London, 1973; Everett Reimer, *School Is Dead*, Garden City, N.Y., 1971.

GARY D. FENSTERMACHER AND
ALEXANDER CUTHBERT

EDUCATIONAL TELEVISION

Educational television (ETV) is broadly defined as all efforts to impart planned educational benefits through television. It employs either broadcast or nonbroadcast methods of distribution and is designed for use in settings as different as SCHOOL, home, hospital, and workplace. Its methods are derived from a variety of sources, including CLASSROOM teaching techniques, the behavioral sciences, drama, and the informational and entertainment patterns of noneducational television (*see* TELEVISION HISTORY).

This article is concerned mainly with the cognitive effects of educational television. For additional material on the history, organization, and broader effects of ETV, *see also* AUDIOVISUAL EDUCATION; CHILDREN; EDUCATION; MASS MEDIA EFFECTS; TEACHING; and, for its implications for national development, DEVELOPMENT COMMUNICATION.

Research Trends

A review of social science research on the uses and effects of television reveals several important trends. One is a movement away from a nearly exclusive focus on aggression and the effect of television's negative role models to an emphasis on how the medium may be used to model positively valued ATTITUDES and behaviors. Research in this changing tradition has concerned itself with the effectiveness of positive role models in helping to counteract stereotypes associated with races, cultures, occupations, sex roles, age groups, and disabilities. It has also given a great deal of attention to motivating a desire to learn.

A second trend has been an increasing emphasis on understanding the use of television's formal features (i.e., the elements of its presentational structure and design) in accomplishing its learning goals. This line of research attempts, for example, to determine the role ETV formats and special visual effects can play in directing and encouraging viewers' attention, comprehension, imitation, and active mental participation through such processes as rehearsing, comparing, guessing and checking, evaluating, and inferring.

Developments in use of CABLE TELEVISION, videodisc, teletext, VIDEOTEX, videocassettes, and related devices are altering in fundamental ways the nature of the transaction between the television screen and the learner. This is because these devices allow the learner's choices or responses to help shape the direction of the presentation. Consequently an important line of research explores the educational use and value of active learner participation in learning from television (for example, the usefulness of rehearsing what is to be learned, making choices among options opened by branching study, and making guesses and checking their accuracy through feedback).

Another important trend is the incorporation of empirical research into the process of creating ETV presentations. A result has been the emergence of a professional specialty in *formative research* that tests prototypic program materials on an audience to validate their educational effectiveness or to suggest needed revisions in their design. The more general implications of formative research are often derived from case studies of educational series. *See* EVALUATION RESEARCH.

Perhaps the most fundamental research trend, however, is one that spans both behavioral science research and applied ETV research by exploring the meanings associated with television's formal features. To practitioners the concern is to understand how television's forms and technical effects function as codes for MEANING and how this special "language" of television may be used to enhance the design of the ETV presentation.

The language of television. The interest in television's visual codes, or language, has inspired several distinct lines of research. One of these begins with the concept that the act of extracting meaning from a medium is a defining characteristic of intelligence. This view is explicated by Jerome Bruner and David Olson, who have defined intelligence in part as "skill in a medium," implying that different media engage different aspects of intellectual functioning. Research by Robert L. Thorndike in renorming the Stanford-Binet Intelligence Tests in the United States bears further on the hypothesis that extraction of meaning from television is a defining function of intelligence. He found that in 1972 U.S. children six to twelve years of age scored up to ten IQ points higher than comparable children who made up the 1930 norming sample. Thorndike points to television as the most likely source of this gain, inasmuch as it is the only substantial and widely available source of intellectual stimulation that appeared in U.S. culture during the approximately forty years in question. His student, Robin Garfinkel, reasoned that if television is in fact responsible for producing this gain, then the visually dependent items on the IQ test ought to account for more of the increase than do the items not dependent on visual stimuli. Her research bore out this hypothesis.

Another line of research, initiated by Israeli researcher Gavriel Salomon, supports the view that television's technical effects and devices are interiorized by individuals and become part of the perceptual and intellectual processes that they often use to acquire, transform, and represent real-world (as well as media) stimuli. Salomon calls this process of interiorizing the language of the media "supplantation." *See* PERCEPTION—STILL AND MOVING PICTURES.

A third line of research is concerned with developing a taxonomy of television's visual codes and with empirical studies on the role of these codes in children's development and learning. One study of this type found that children as young as three years of age could tell which of several visual effects of television are more likely to be found in advertisements directed to girls than in those directed to boys. The children in this study tended to observe correctly that boy-oriented (versus girl-oriented) advertisements are more likely to use hard and clear (rather than soft) focus, sharp and angular (rather than curved) forms, loud and fast (rather than soft and slow) music, quick (rather than slow) camera zooms, and many (rather than few) edited intercuts from scene to scene.

Another line of research is concerned with teaching children about television's visually coded meanings. The aim is to understand the extent to which training in what is often called "media literacy" enables children to understand more of what the presentation is attempting to convey and to perceive more accurately the motivation behind the producer's choice of special forms and features (*see* LITERACY).

Still another area of research consists of experimental attempts to improve on the educational effectiveness of ETV presentations by communicating with learners through the use of television's unique visual conventions. "The Electric Company," a beginning READING series produced in the United States, illustrates this line of research. This program makes extensive use of ANIMATION to portray several of the dynamic visual processes required for reading in English: scanning of letters and words from left to right; blending of successive letters to form intelligible sound sequences; fixing of attention on an ambiguous word while trying to determine its meaning from context; processing of meaningful letter groups as information "chunks," as in the case of morphemes and digraphs; and sight-reading of vocabulary. Another example is the frequent use of unusual camera angles to provide the viewer with new physical perspectives on situations and events. In general these approaches relate to the supplantation process described by Salomon.

Significance of the research. Research into the educational significance of television's unique visual codes represents a fundamental departure from the direction of most studies carried out in earlier years of ETV. Literally scores of studies were done in schools and colleges comparing television teaching with live instruction. Only rarely was the television presentation in these studies embellished in such a way as to take advantage of the medium's special visual effects. ETV was looked upon simply as a potentially more cost-effective means of presenting classroom demonstrations or lectures. Most of the earlier studies involved learners of high school age or older, and most showed no difference in learning resulting from the televised and the live teaching. ETV's advocates looked on this result as decisive evidence of television's valid role in instruction. However, apparently only a few of the broadcasters and scholars who took this viewpoint had reckoned with the extent to which classroom teachers would see television as a usurper of their function and therefore a threat, and how many would find the central scheduling of classroom ETV a hindrance to its best use in the classroom. These early studies and projects proceeded largely on the implicit premise that television's useful educational role was in replicating classroom instruction as practiced in the days before television. ETV practitioners touted the capacity of the medium to put a master teacher in every classroom.

But the result was often less than had been hoped. American Samoa, for example, after installing a very elaborate ETV system, with imported teachers broadcasting over six stations every subject offered in grades one through twelve, had to remove television from all high school and some upper elementary school grades. This happened when classroom teachers acquired more skill and began to view ETV's master teacher approach and the rigidity of central scheduling as a hindrance rather than a help. Three of the six channels were turned off, and one of the remaining three came to be used entirely for evening entertainment. Similarly one of the most carefully designed ETV operations in the United States—the Washington County, Maryland, school system centered in Hagerstown—abruptly changed its plans after ten years. It had been using cable interconnection to deliver 148 classroom programs a week. Then the school system decided to abandon the cable, record the programs on cassettes, store them in schools for use at teachers' convenience, and cut back new production to a few series per year. It was reported that the amount of use of the recorded programs increased noticeably after the classroom teachers took over responsibility for deciding when to schedule them.

As the field matured, therefore, emphasis turned away from trying to broadcast the equivalent of classroom instruction toward finding television's unique, complementary role in classroom instruction. The increasing interest in research on television's visual language is part of this trend.

The Japanese Experience

A national model of full television use in schools is to be found in Japan, where by 1983 22,500 primary schools, representing 90 percent of all Japanese primary schools, made use of programs supplied by NHK (Japan Broadcasting Corporation). NHK provided 122 television programs each week (including fifty-seven rebroadcasts) totaling thirty-three hours and thirty minutes. Programs covered all basic subjects at all grade levels. Color television sets were found in 99.7 percent of Japanese primary schools, and 88 percent of them had a color television receiver in every classroom. The outstanding popularity of natural science, social studies, and moral education programs has not changed since school broadcasting started.

Research on Japanese school television takes two forms. One seeks to document patterns of use, and the other elicits the reactions of teachers and pupils to the content and approach of individual programs, to guide revisions. In striking contrast to the situation in many other countries, the Japanese give almost no attention to summative evaluation to establish television's tested teaching effectiveness under controlled experimental conditions. Instead instructional television is looked on as a matured field with a secure role, whose value is seen in the high levels of voluntary use by teachers.

Japan's extensive school television offerings, now a tradition of more than thirty-five years, owe much to that country's extraordinary national investment in public service applications of television, perhaps greater than in any other country in the world. Total NHK revenues for 1985 reached the equivalent of $2.2 billion to support a wide range of telecommunications services, television accounting for the largest share. But substantial and stable funding accounts for only a small part of television's near universal acceptance and use in Japanese schools. Another key factor is the homogeneity of Japanese society, which allows for high uniformity nationwide in the content, sequence, and pace of school instruction. These conditions are highly favorable to central ETV programming and scheduling.

Worldwide Applications

Educational television has been called on to serve as a tool of national development in a number of countries. In many Third World nations in particular the supply of teachers is inadequate, and ETV can speed up educational reform without the country first having to build up a full quota of well-trained teachers. The incorporation of SATELLITE systems into existing TELECOMMUNICATIONS NETWORKS has enabled countries like Indonesia, Mexico, and India to increase greatly the availability of television and radio signals throughout their territories, particularly to distant or rural populations that were difficult or impossible to reach before. Some of these efforts, like the program of educational reform in El Salvador and the use of satellite television in Indonesia, have been both massive in scale and well documented by research. Some of the most impressive numbers are reported by China, which introduced a Television College and received in the first year of operation ten million applications for entrance. They could accept only half a million students, but that made a sensational difference in the number of Chinese to whom higher education was available.

And not only in the Third World has ETV been pressed into service as an extension of the school and the UNIVERSITY. For people who have to study at home because classroom attendance is for one reason or other difficult or impossible for them, ETV has come very widely into use in industrialized countries like Britain, France, the Federal Republic of Germany, the German Democratic Republic, Sweden, Italy, the Netherlands, Poland, Canada, and others. The Open University of Great Britain, which is built around television, reading, written assignments, and other study activities, is not only one of the largest universities in the country but also one that is widely admired and imitated. Japan has a national high school—the NHK Gakuen—that uses ETV, radio, and correspondence study.

The Children's Television Workshop (CTW), a privately supported institution in the United States, makes a series of ETV programs largely for children at preschool and early elementary grade levels. These are broadcast for home viewing but are also used in many school systems. ("The Electric Company," mentioned earlier, comes from this source, as does the series "Sesame Street.") CTW programs reach viewers throughout the United States and in many foreign countries, sometimes in foreign-language productions or translations.

Governments and broadcasters have become increasingly aware that the complex problems of education, interrelated as they are with political, economic, and other social factors, cannot be solved merely by solving the technological problems of delivering ETV programs. They have therefore turned increasingly to the problems of the effective use of television. Thus the problems of research on out-of-school and nonformal television move ever closer to those discussed earlier in this article.

Bibliography. Takashiro Akiyama and Sachiko I. Kodaira, *The Role of Educational Broadcasts in Japanese Schools,* Tokyo, 1984; Jennings Bryant and Daniel R. Anderson, eds., *Children's Understanding of Television,* New York, 1983; Godwin C. Chu and Wilbur L. Schramm, *Learning from Television: What the Research Says,* Washington, D.C., 1967; George C. Comstock and Marilyn Fisher, *Television and Human Behavior: A Guide to the Pertinent Scientific Literature,* Santa Monica, Calif., 1975; David Hargreaves, *Adult Literacy and Broadcasting: The BBC's Experience,* London and New York, 1980; David Hawkridge and John Robinson, *Organizing Educational Broadcasting,* London and Paris, 1982; Jerome Johnston and James S. Ettema, *Positive Images: Breaking Stereotypes with Children's Television,* Beverly Hills, Calif., 1982; Norman MacKenzie, Richmond Postgate, and John Scupham, *Open Learning: Systems and Problems in Post-Secondary Education,* Paris, 1975; John Maddison, *Radio and Television in Literacy: A Survey of the Use of Broadcasting Media in Combatting Illiteracy among Adults,* Paris, 1971; John K. Mayo, Robert C. Hornik, and Emile McAnany, *Educational Reform with Television: The El Salvador Experience,* Stanford, Calif., 1976; Manfred Meyer, ed., *Children and the Formal Features of Television: Approaches and Findings of Experimental and Formative Research,* Munich, 1983; David R. Olson, ed., *Media and Symbols: The Forms of Expression, Communications, and Education* (Yearbook of the National Society for the Study of Education, Vol. 73), Chicago, 1974; Gavriel Salomon, *Interaction of Media, Cognition, and Learning,* San Francisco, 1979.

EDWARD L. PALMER

EGYPTIAN HIEROGLYPHS

Pictorial system of WRITING that appeared in Egypt about 3000 B.C.E., just before the Dynastic period and roughly at the same time as writing developed in Mesopotamia. Very little is known about the origins of this writing system, although comparison with the CUNEIFORM system that appeared in Mesopotamia does not support the hypothesis that one system influenced the other. In its earliest form the small pictorial hieroglyphic signs were used to designate objects of everyday life, animals, people, and gods (see Figure 1). Eventually, however, the writing system became differentiated into separate scripts with fairly distinct functions. Cursive versions (called hieratic and demotic scripts) were developed for specific tasks of recordkeeping or mundane communication (see Figures 2 and 3). While hieroglyphic script is the forerunner of the other two, its function became limited increasingly to inscriptions of a sacred, religious character.

The earliest evidence of writing in Egypt shows that the basic principles known from later hieroglyphic texts were already present. Hieroglyphic script represented from the start an elaborate, pictorial, iconographic system (*see* ICONOGRAPHY). The main changes in the script from its origins to its latest use in the fourth century C.E. were an increase in the number of signs, from about seven hundred in the classical Egyptian period to more than three thousand in the Greco-Roman period; an increase in the number of meanings that could be expressed by each SIGN; and, accordingly, an increase in the number of

Figure 1. *(Egyptian Hieroglyphs)* Hieroglyphic script. From the papyrus "Ritual of the Transformations of the Soul." Bibliothèque Nationale, Paris. Giraudon/Art Resource, New York.

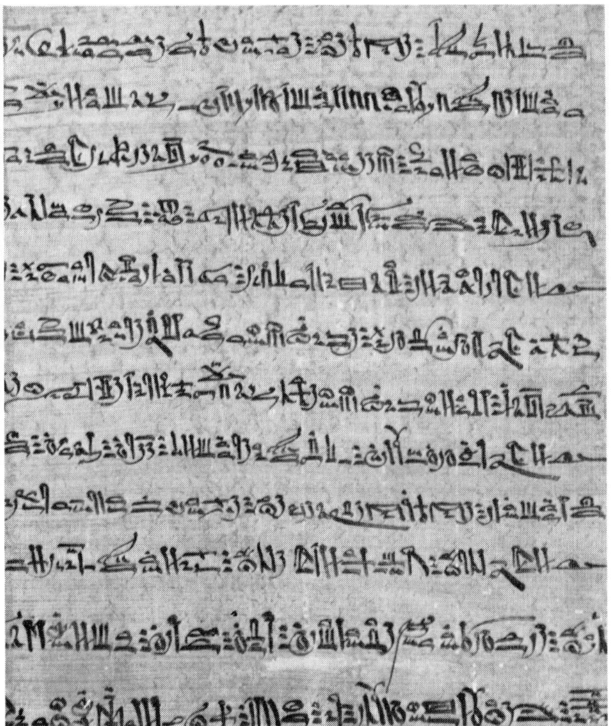

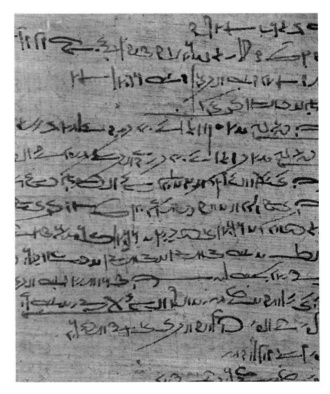

Figure 2. *(Egyptian Hieroglyphs)* Hieratic script. From "The Great Harris Papyrus." Reproduced by courtesy of the Trustees of The British Museum.

Figure 3. *(Egyptian Hieroglyphs)* Demotic script. From the papyrus "The Teaching of Onkhsheshonqy." Reproduced by courtesy of the Trustees of The British Museum.

homophones (words that sound alike but have different meanings).

Decipherment. During the RENAISSANCE, hieroglyphs were rediscovered through the classical authors who had written about them. As a result they were considered purely as pictorial symbols, with no linguistic meaning. On this ground, for instance, while the German Athanasius Kircher (1602–1680) correctly asserted that Coptic was the last stage of the ancient Egyptian LANGUAGE, he denied that this language might be conveyed by the hieroglyphs. Another theory that failed to recognize the linguistic function of hieroglyphs was propounded by such scholars as German mathematician and philosopher Gottfried Wilhelm Leibniz (1646–1716). This theory asserted that because hieroglyphic script was pictorial, it probably represented an early stage of what was termed "universal writing," a later stage of which was exemplified by Chinese script and which was thought to depict ideas in a universal form that was accessible to everyone.

Substantial progress in decipherment occurred only in the eighteenth century, when scholars guessed that demotic and hieratic were not separate scripts, but cursives of hieroglyphic writing, and began to conclude that hieroglyphs did in fact write a language. The Frenchman Jean-Jacques Barthélemy (1716–1795) surmised that the cartouches (small, usually oblong sections of an inscription, each of which encloses a name) contained the names of kings and queens, an important discovery that made it possible to locate meaningful sequences within a script that did not have clearly marked divisions between words. Next, the French orientalist Antoine-Isaac Silvestre de Sacy (1758–1838) established the method for the forthcoming decipherment with his studies of the recently discovered trilingual decree (in hieroglyphic, demotic, and Greek), the famous Rosetta stone (see Figure 4). Important progress was made by Swedish diplomat Johann David Akerblad (1760–1819) and English scientist Thomas Young (1773–1829), who pointed out the phonetic value of signs enclosed in some of the cartouches. However, their valuable efforts did not extend beyond reading alphabetically written late (Ptolemaic Greek) names.

The discovery that the script was both phonetic and ideographic and the subsequent decipherment were accomplished by French Egyptologist Jean-François Champollion (1790–1832). His basic insight arose from the exact interpretation of two cartouches enclosing the names of kings Thutmosis and Ramses. The success of the decipherment rested on some of his predecessors' contributions, his wide knowledge of the classical history of ancient Egypt, and his mastery of Coptic, which suggested to him the correct reading of sign sequences that occurred in more than one word or name.

Types of signs. Hieroglyphic script involves three classes of signs, each of which performs a distinct function: ideograms (picture signs), phonograms (pictorial signs that represent consonants), and determinatives. Ideograms, or logograms, are pictorial signs that mean what the picture represents, whether an object or an action. For example, as shown in Figures 5a and 5b, a sign depicting a bull means "bull," and a sign depicting a man building a wall means "build." The relationship between representation and meaning may be metonymic (i.e., a pictorial sign may represent something that is associated with the depicted object). For example, a sign depicting a scribe's palette means "scribe" (see Figure 5c).

Phonograms are signs that employ the rebus principle: they convey the sound of what they depict, but not its meaning. This phonetic value is always consonantal, since hieroglyphic writing does not indicate vowels. Phonograms may be uniliteral (the so-called alphabetical signs), representing one consonant; biliteral, representing two consonants; or triliteral, representing three consonants.

Determinatives are signs that express no phonetic value. Used as suffixes, they clarify the meaning of signs that would be ambiguous otherwise by indicating the family of meanings to which the word belongs. For example, the determinative depicting a sealed roll of papyrus indicates that the word to which it is added refers in some way to writing or abstract notions (see Figure 5d).

In practice signs could fulfill two or three of these functions in different contexts. The way in which spellings combined ideograms, phonograms, and determinatives was not fixed, but rather fluctuated according to the date and type of the inscription. Many words were written only with phonograms, even when they could have been expressed pictorially and/or they contained more than one linguistic unit (morpheme). There are examples of writing that employed ideograms exclusively, but what they could express was necessarily very limited. Signs that functioned solely as ideograms were indicated by the addition of a small stroke. See Figure 5e for an ideogram representing the word *FeNeDj* (nose).

More often, ideograms were combined with other signs, particularly redundant phonograms (also referred to as phonetic complements), which partially or fully conveyed the phonetic reading of the sign. See Figure 5f for a mixed phonetic and ideographic spelling of *FeNeDj*. Biliteral and triliteral phonograms could also be accompanied by redundant phonograms that provided further clarification of the word. See Figure 5g for an example of *FeNeDj* with redundant phonograms that convey both the reading of the ideogram and the phonetic value of the more complex phonograms. Regardless of the spelling, a

Figure 4. *(Egyptian Hieroglyphs)* The Rosetta stone. Reproduced by courtesy of the Trustees of The British Museum.

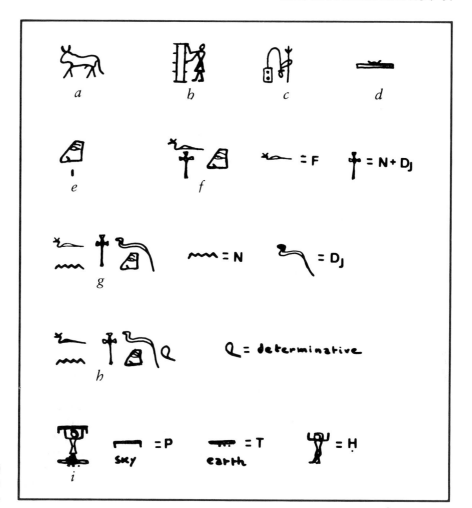

Figure 5. *(Egyptian Hieroglyphs)* Working drawing by the author: types of hieroglyphic signs.

determinative could be placed after the word to clarify the meaning even further. See Figure 5*h*, in which the determinative for words representing parts of the body follows the mixed spelling of *FeNeDj*.

It is clear, therefore, that writers had a great deal of discretion when spelling words. They exploited this flexibility to develop the specific semiotic capabilities of hieroglyphic writing, based largely on its unique combination of writing and art.

Relation to iconography. The most striking feature of hieroglyphic script is its pictoriality. The signs were drawn from the realities of Egyptian life; most of them may be identified at first glance, even by an uninitiated person. They were liable to the same conventions that otherwise governed pictorial records. For instance, like pictorial representations (but even more strictly), hieroglyphs were subject to rules of orientation. Asymmetric signs, such as human beings and animals, had to face the same direction, usually toward the starting point of the reading. Reading of horizontal lines or vertical columns moved in either direction, but usually signs faced right and were read from right to left.

However, two characteristics identify hieroglyphs as signs and not merely as pictures: (1) calibration and (2) complete use of space. Calibration refers to the size and placement of the signs relative to each other. The proportions of the signs depend on their arrangement in imaginary square frames within inscriptions, not on the actual size of what they depict, as is the case in Egyptian art. Complete use of space refers to the distribution of signs within the available space. Those imaginary square frames, which may be divided in half or into quarters, are arranged inside narrow strips of lines or columns so as to avoid large blank spaces. No such *horror vacui* prevails in artistic presentations.

In general, however, hieroglyphic writing shared many of the characteristics of iconography, and the border between script and representation was often blurred. The interplay between texts and representations was consciously manipulated to achieve a twofold semiotic function. Writing could function as a code transposing a linguistic message unit by unit, while at the same time it could convey meanings on a specific nonlinguistic level. For example, a picture of a man could function as a determinative for the caption that spelled his name. Conversely, a sign within an inscription could be significantly enlarged and stand outside the calibration to function as an autonomous picture—serving as both the picture and part of its own caption.

The nonlinguistic meanings may be independent of the message (for instance, purely playful or aesthetic), they may restate the message, or they may even function as its ideological exegesis. For instance, one can write *Ptah* (a god) in such a way that the three consonants are graphically transposed to depict the mythological duty of Ptah, namely, to lift up the sky upon the earth (see Figure *5i*).

These semiotic resources of hieroglyphic writing were exploited more or less sporadically from ancient times. During the Greco-Roman period, however, they were systematically employed in religious texts, especially temple inscriptions. Not merely an exercise in virtuosity for its own sake, these manipulations of the linguistic/pictorial ambiguity of hieroglyphs were a direct consequence of Egyptian religious beliefs. Egyptians believed that the signs were closely interrelated with their meanings, and Egyptian priests pursued scribal studies as part of their philosophical studies. The Greeks were so struck by this that they overestimated the pictorial functions of hieroglyphs and disassociated them from their linguistic function. For the Egyptians, however, investigating the expressive possibilities of hieroglyphic writing was no less than a study of the complex network of relationships that connected the elements of the world.

See also WRITING MATERIALS.

Bibliography. *Actes du colloque international de l'Université de Paris VII: Écritures, systèmes idéographiques et pratiques expressives,* compl. by Anne-Marie Christin, Paris, 1982; Madeleine V. David, *Le débat sur les écritures et l'hiéroglyphe aux XVIIe et XVIIIe siècles et l'application de la notion de déchiffrement aux écritures mortes,* Paris, 1965; *Écritures II,* compl. by Anne-Marie Christin, Paris, 1985; Henry George Fischer, *Reversals,* Part 1, *The Orientation of Hieroglyphs (Egyptian Studies II),* New York, 1977; Sir Alan Gardiner, *Egyptian Grammar, Being an Introduction to the Study of Hieroglyphs,* 3d ed., Oxford and London, 1957; *Naissance de l'écriture: Cunéiformes et hiéroglyphes,* Paris, 1982.

PASCAL VERNUS

EISENSTEIN, SERGEI (1898–1948)

Soviet pioneer film director and influential film theorist and teacher. Sergei Mikhailovich Eisenstein based his work and thought on the principle that the film medium is a synthesis of ART and science. His own early training in engineering, architecture, and THEATER gave a broad base to his filmmaking career; he saw in each new subject a need to use different parts of the worlds of science and art. Each film required its own style, composition, and invention, and in all his films he had the constant collaboration of cinematographer Eduard Tisse (*see* CINEMATOGRAPHY).

There is no single monolithic Eisenstein FILM THEORY. The pragmatist-inventor found precedents and stimulation in unfamiliar corners of art history and scientific experiment. His constantly changing film theories cannot be taught separately from his films, and vice versa. He enjoyed teaching and often declared that his time would be better spent in writing rather than in making films. Even during the wartime evacuation of the Soviet filmmaking community to Alma-Ata, his classes were as disciplined as was the filming of *Ivan Grozny* (Ivan the Terrible, Part I, 1944). Eisenstein's lectures to his students were planned along an outline intended for a series of books titled "On Direction." Although he was ill, his last two years were spent largely in trying to complete this work.

He read widely and was similarly catholic in his filmgoing. His eagerness to work with sound and color brought new ramifications to his ceaseless research. Study of the seven complete films—*Stachka* (Strike, 1925), *Bronenosets Potyomkin* (Battleship Potemkin, 1925), *Oktiabr* (October, 1928; released in the United States as *Ten Days That Shook the World*), *Staroie i novoie* (Old and New, 1929), *Alexandr Nevskii* (Alexander Nevsky, 1938), and *Ivan Grozny,* Parts I and II (the two completed portions of *Ivan the Terrible,* 1944, 1946)—should be supplemented with an examination of his detailed notes and published treatments of *Benia Krik, Capital, The Glass House, Sutter's Gold, An American Tragedy, Que Viva Mexico!, Black Majesty, Moscow, Perekop, Bezhin Lug* (Bezhin Meadow), *Great Ferghana Canal, Love of a Poet* (Pushkin), and *Ivan Grozny III,* and of the staging of Émile Zola's *Thérèse Raquin* and Richard Wagner's *Die Walküre.*

The influence of Eisenstein's films, especially after *Potemkin*'s phenomenal success in Berlin, can be traced through subsequent German and European production methods from the wider use of nonprofessional actors and real settings to the integration of montage into the whole creative process (*see* FILM EDITING). One of the many puzzles he has left with us is, where are the great works of the students of this acknowledged great teacher? His proudest moment may have been the positive reception of *Chapayev,* written and directed by the "brothers" Sergei and Georgi Vasiliev (actually unrelated), who were in Eisenstein's first formal film course in 1928. Part of the answer is surely the assignment of some of his most promising later students to the Ukrainian studios; they died in the defense of Kiev in World War II. Another factor may be that Eisenstein's goals and

Figure 1. *(Eisenstein, Sergei)* Eisenstein directing *Oktiabr* (October, 1928). The Museum of Modern Art/Film Stills Archive.

Figure 2. *(Eisenstein, Sergei)* A drawing by Eisenstein for Nikolai Cherkasov's role in *Ivan Grozny, Part 3.* From Jay Leyda and Zina Voynow, *Eisenstein at Work,* New York: Pantheon Books, 1982, p. 138.

ideals for his own works seemed unattainable by students without his cultural background. Was he too great a teacher? His effect on film spectators was apparently more lasting than the effect on his own students. Yet other students through the years have continued to read his *Film Form* and *Film Sense* while studying his films.

See also MOTION PICTURES—SILENT ERA; MOTION PICTURES—SOUND FILM.

Bibliography. Sergei Eisenstein, *Film Form: Essays in Film Theory* and *The Film Sense,* ed. and trans. by Jay Leyda, New York, 1957; idem, *Immoral Memories: An Autobiography,* trans. by Herbert Marshall, Boston, 1983; idem, *Notes of a Film Director* (Zametki kinorezhissera), trans. by X. Danko, New York, 1970; Vladimir B. Nizhnii, *Lessons with Eisenstein,* trans. and ed. by Ivor Montagu and Jay Leyda, New York, 1962.

JAY LEYDA

ELECTION

The idea of elections is closely tied to the Western ideal of "informed choice" by an "enlightened electorate"—and is thus linked to communication in several ways. In democratic societies, communication institutions may be evaluated for their contributions to wise collective decisions. But elections do not necessarily involve choice; their more universal feature is that of legitimation. In many political systems elections are used to demonstrate who holds power ("demonstration elections"). In either case an election contributes to maintenance of the polity and to the capacity to govern it.

Choice implies that leaders or policies other than those in force might be possible. This intertwines elections with communication institutions that are free from control by the government in power, a norm to which elected governments subscribe in principle but which in practice may be contrary to their interest in maintaining power. There is, then, an inherent tension between the communication sector and the governing sector of a political system. The press's responsibility for presenting political alternatives, implicit in exchange for its special freedoms, is put to the test most clearly in the context of an election campaign (*see* GOVERNMENT-MEDIA RELATIONS).

Campaigning, an organized set of communication activities directed toward a specific social goal, is not necessary to democratic choice, but pragmatically it is common in all but the most trivial elections. Occasionally a small polity might choose its leaders randomly (by lot) or by rotation, for a fixed period. But the usual election involves voting by the members, preceded by a campaign on behalf of alternative candidates. Not only the vote itself but the quality of the campaign that precedes and informs it will affect the eventual legitimacy accorded the chosen leaders and policies. Campaigns are communication institutions themselves; their interactions with media organizations and voters have important consequences for democratic governance.

To cast a vote can be considered an act of communication. But voting for a candidate is at best an uncertain means of expressing policy preferences; voting in elections that do not involve candidates delivers a clearer message (*see* PLEBISCITE). A ballot initiative (which establishes a law by popular vote) or referendum (by which an electorate can repeal a law) makes special demands on communication media because voters cannot rely on personalities or political parties to guide their choices. Voters' need for understanding of policy alternatives on the ballot typically exceeds the realization many times over.

Information Needs

Most research on elections focuses on votes for partisan candidates for major administrative offices, such as a nation's president, or choices between leading political parties that might form a governing coalition in a parliamentary system. Voters tend to be much better informed on these choices, owing to the intensive campaigning by competing sides via mass media, than they are regarding elections for lesser offices. But often voters are invited to make many choices regardless of their ignorance. In the United States, an extreme example, a voter might in a single year cast ballots for candidates for three national offices, half a dozen or more state offices, another dozen county and municipal offices, plus "yes" or "no" votes on various initiative and referendum propositions. Surveys repeatedly show that such votes are mostly cast in the absence of the strong infor-

mation base that the ideal of the "enlightened electorate" would assume.

Uninformed voters represent a chronic problem for democratic systems that prize both a free press and the goal of electoral decisions "in the public interest." One approach to this dilemma is to place greater normative burdens on the press to provide information and on voters to use it to inform themselves. In some systems voting is strongly encouraged; evidence of having voted may, for example, be required before issuing the citizen a travel permit. But in other systems voting is discouraged, as by onerous registration requirements or LITERACY tests that favor the majority linguistic group. In a more positive vein a degree of voter literacy may be fostered by printing multilingual ballots.

Norms may operate either for or against informed voting. For example, people may be encouraged to vote out of their duty as citizens; this encourages ritual voting, in contrast to the positive norm that one ought to be "informed about issues" before voting. Surveys that compare nonvoters to voters indicate that it is the less informed sector of the population that tends not to vote. This could be viewed as functional from an informed-electorate standpoint. It is, however, often dysfunctional for the nonvoters—who as a rule also tend to be less educated, less affluent, and less likely to share in the benefits and resources being allocated through the electoral process.

Election campaigns provide a wide array of possible sources from which voters can collect information of various kinds in making their decisions. Chief among these sources are the news media, notably the newspaper (*see* NEWSPAPER: HISTORY). People who get most of their news from RADIO or television—the majority in most surveys—are typically more casual voters, neither as partisan nor as informed as are regular readers of print media. But panel surveys that follow the same people over long periods of time indicate that many voters learn nearly as much about political issues and candidates from radio or TELEVISION NEWS as others learn from newspapers.

Issue, party, and image voting. Elected officials often assert that the votes they have received provide a mandate for their policies. The validity of this claim depends on the basis of voting. Relatively few voters give as a major reason for their choices specific policy differences between candidates. Many elections take place in the virtual absence of issue disputes or policy challenges; voters remain unaware of these considerations unless they are prominent in the campaign. Issue-oriented elections are the exception rather than the rule, representing a special achievement on the part of the media. More often votes are based on such factors as simple name recognition in the case of an incumbent candidate, mere acquiescence to existing policies without serious consideration of alternatives, casual judgments of candidates' personalities from one or two indicators, recommendations from other voters, heavy and clever ADVERTISING, or endorsement by a prominent source such as a newspaper.

The lightly determined character of many votes should not be taken as undermining the validity of two commonly criticized but rather complex forms of political choice. One is the traditional political act of basing vote choices primarily on *party* affiliation; the other, prominent in the era of television, is commonly called *image* voting. Issue-based voting is often viewed as a tradeoff against these other general categories of voter decision making. But both party and image voting, although they may seem quite simple on the surface, can represent communication and information collation at least as extensive as that involved in issue voting.

Political parties arise, at least informally, in almost any electoral system. Even in one-party systems there are "wings" or factions that represent interest aggregations and coalitions. An enduring party is both the product and the producer of a wide range of political communication. Revolutionary parties create their own press systems, and once in power they often convert the major media to their own perpetuation in power. This has been most obvious in Communist systems, in which the revolutionary movement incorporates a rationale for operation of the means of political mass communication by the state.

New communication media in Western democracies have partially replaced the party as a channel for distributing messages and for gaining political contributions (*see* POLITICAL COMMUNICATION—IMPACT OF NEW MEDIA). But parties, sometimes informal ones, continue to represent constellations of issues and interests in most political systems. To the extent that these interests are interrelated or at least mutually compatible, voting for a party's candidate is a surer method of issue voting than is attempting to pore over the many claims and promises of competing candidates for all offices.

The popular literature critical of television lays heavy emphasis on the charge that votes are mainly determined by candidates' personalities or "images." But research suggests that much more than presentation of candidates' superficial attributes is involved. The character of a candidate in terms of honesty, intellect, and leadership qualities is often evaluated by voters as part of a highly complex judgment. These attributes are difficult to assess even at first hand, and the more so via the media. There remains no clear-cut evidence of a systematic tendency among

citizens or media to be seduced by a photogenic fraud.

Media Coverage

The press is sometimes criticized for organizing its political reporting in terms of predictable themes. In a long campaign voting decisions are interpreted in terms of which candidate is "leading the race" and who is "the underdog," as if politics were analogous to professional sports. This means that voters, who by their choices determine who is ahead, are in turn the target of information that might influence future voter choices.

Despite considerable research no clear pattern of BANDWAGON EFFECTS (i.e., people wanting to vote for the anticipated winner) has been documented. For some voters, learning that their candidate is "trailing" may be discouraging; to others it can be a stimulus to redoubling campaign efforts. Nonetheless, restrictions on media reports of preelection polls are often proposed (*see* POLL). There has been a special concern in the United States regarding media "computer projections" of presidential election outcomes based on partial returns that are broadcast while voting is still in progress. In many countries the scope of media coverage is limited by law to avoid these journalistic influences on those who have not yet decided how to vote.

The high cost of campaigning, particularly in countries where broadcast time is sold, operates to keep the number of candidacies low. But there is a loss in the variety of political perspectives presented to the electorate when only well-established parties and leaders can afford an effective campaign. The media, because of their limited resources, may also have a stake in thinning down the list of candidates, although they also constantly need the "news" those candidates make. In multiparty systems such as those commonly found in western Europe, news media are sometimes required by law to provide coverage or equal access to *all* official entrants in an election race, not just to those they judge to have a "serious" chance of winning.

Although the press and politicians represent quite separate interests and often assume adversarial roles in an election campaign, they also share a common stake in communication. The press needs news to report, and a candidate needs publicity; successful candidates manage to generate publicity for themselves that is also news for the reporters. Much of the money raised for a campaign goes into paid advertising, which is in turn the basic economic support for a "free"—that is, commercial—press. The media and the politicians, then, combine symbiotically to inundate the public with both advertisements and publicity-news during a campaign. Much of the "campaign news" focuses on candidates' names, faces, and personalities.

Paid political advertisements, although they are often criticized as misleading, sometimes provide voters with knowledge regarding policy differences between candidates. Dependence on advertisements extends even to volunteer campaign workers, who may find out more about their own candidate from television commercials than from the local campaign office. In European democracies party broadcasts and party-aligned newspapers, which are the rule, often serve this issue-information function. In many countries elections have increasingly featured televised debates between candidates (see POLITICAL COMMUNICATION—BROADCAST DEBATES). Multicandidate presentations greatly reduce opportunity for selective exposure of an individual voter to a single party. The partisan European media probably leave greater opportunity for selective exposure in a campaign, but they also maintain wider latitude for exposition of noncentrist political positions (see SELECTIVE RECEPTION).

Incumbency. Biases in coverage based on incumbency in office are less well controlled than are partisan biases, both because officeholders have no interest in reducing the preponderant advantage they gain from heavy press coverage and because an incumbent provides the press with a convenient peg on which to hang a news article. U.S. studies show much more coverage in the media, and much more information in voters' minds, about incumbents than about the candidates challenging them for their seats. Not surprisingly, incumbents regardless of party tend strongly to be reelected.

Interpersonal channels. Interpersonal influence during an election campaign has been thought to be quite strong but has not been directly assessed. It was emphasized in the earliest studies as an alternative explanation to media influence—by researchers who could not find strong evidence of the latter. They suggested that influence proceeds in a "two-step flow" from the media to opinion leaders and then on to other voters (see OPINION LEADER). Subsequent studies, however, indicate that people as a rule get news directly from the media and attribute more influence on their opinions to the press than to personal acquaintances.

Systemic functions. Functions of an election for the political system extend beyond the manifest purposes of electing leaders and choosing among policy alternatives. By emphasizing the political community as a whole, an election—even when it offers no real choice—serves an integrative function, which can be particularly important in nations composed of diverse or dispersed populations. This is perhaps most no-

ticeable in India, a huge multilingual and multiethnic nation where elections have become a celebration of nationhood even when they are divisive on particular issues (see POLITICAL SYMBOLS). Elections have re-emerged in many Latin American countries following years of military rule.

The raising of campaign issues also serves an AGENDA-SETTING function, in that the election focuses public and governmental attention on high-priority problems. Election campaigns intensify the process of socialization of new members to the political system, both young people coming of age and immigrants from other societies (see POLITICAL SOCIALIZATION).

At the most macroscopic level of analysis elections serve to legitimize all institutions associated with them. This legitimation function is not simply a matter of acquiescence by members of the system to the choice they make. In international politics a "duly elected government" has a particularly strong claim to diplomatic recognition by other nations. (In some local situations citizens refuse to vote rather than confer this legitimacy via the election.) The democratic electoral system and the political community as a whole are also reaffirmed and strengthened by an election. So too is the communication system that serves this process.

See also MASS COMMUNICATIONS RESEARCH; MASS MEDIA EFFECTS; POLITICAL COMMUNICATION—HISTORY; PUBLIC OPINION.

Bibliography. Bernard Berelson, Paul F. Lazarsfeld, and William N. McPhee, *Voting: A Study of Opinion Formation in a Presidential Campaign,* Chicago, 1954; Jay G. Blumler and Denis McQuail, *Television in Politics,* Chicago, 1969; Steven H. Chaffee, ed., *Political Communication: Issues and Strategies for Research,* Beverly Hills, Calif., 1975; Peter Clarke and Susan H. Evans, *Covering Campaigns,* Stanford, Calif., 1983; Kathleen Hall Jamieson, *Packaging the Presidency: A History and Criticism of Presidential Campaign Advertising,* New York, 1984; Sidney Kraus and Dennis Davis, *The Effects of Mass Communication on Political Behavior,* University Park, Pa., 1976; Paul F. Lazarsfeld, Bernard Berelson, and Hazel Gaudet, *The People's Choice* (1948), 3d ed., New York, 1968; Michael B. MacKuen and Steven L. Coombs, *More Than News: Media Power in Public Affairs,* Beverly Hills, Calif., 1981; Dan D. Nimmo and Keith R. Sanders, eds., *Handbook of Political Communication,* Beverly Hills, Calif., 1981; Thomas E. Patterson, *The Mass Media Election,* New York, 1980; Percy H. Tannenbaum and Leslie J. Kostrich, *Turned-on TV/Turned-off Voters,* Beverly Hills, Calif., 1983; David Weaver, Doris Graber, Maxwell McCombs, and Chaim Eyal, *Media Agenda-setting in a Presidential Election,* New York, 1981.

STEVEN H. CHAFFEE

ELECTRONIC MUSIC

The development of electronic music stemmed largely from a desire on the part of composers to extend the sounds available to them, to go beyond the reaches of the traditional orchestra to a point at which they could even work with sounds never heard before. The development belongs by definition to the age of electronics, which began with the invention of the electron tube in the first decade of the twentieth century, but electronic music had its precursors in the previous century.

Early history. In 1837 Dr. C. G. Page of Salem, Massachusetts, reported that one could produce a ringing SOUND by toying with horseshoe magnets, a coil of copper wire, and a zinc-lead battery. Although he was at a loss to explain the phenomenon, he called the result "galvanic music" and shared his findings with others. In 1874 Elisha Gray, an early telephone experimenter, invented a one-octave keyboard instrument that was battery powered and produced sound through the use of single-tone telegraph transmitters. In 1899 English physicist William Duddell produced circuitry that could control and modulate the whining sound of carbon-arc streetlights. He attached a keyboard to this primitive voltage-controlling device and demonstrated it in numerous public performances.

The early experiments, little more than toys, were succeeded by performance instruments—that is, instruments designed to be played live before an audience, sometimes with other, more traditional instruments. The most ambitious instrument of this sort before the availability of the vacuum tube was the telharmonium of Thaddeus Cahill. He patented it in 1896, although his first operating model was not completed until 1900. His grand plan was to synthesize the sound of the orchestra—*synthesize* was the word he used. In 1906 he installed a two-hundred-ton instrument in Manhattan, with which he intended to send live music by wire to nightclubs in the city. The business was a failure, but elements of his design were applied by Laurens Hammond years later in the development of the popular Hammond organ.

The subsequent evolution of such instruments was closely related to the development of electronics. Early vacuum-tube radios sometimes squealed when a hand was brought near them. In 1920 Russian scientist Leon Theremin built a simple performance instrument that made use of this phenomenon (beat-frequency modulation). Called the theremin, the instrument was performed by waving one's hand in the air between two antennae, which caused interference between two radio-frequency signals and generated a third "beat" frequency that could be heard by the human ear. The manner in which it was played enhanced the mysterious nature of the device. The instrument produced continuous tones and was monophonic (producing one note at a time). It was used for the production of movie soundtracks through the 1960s. A transistorized version of the theremin was invented in the early 1960s by U.S. engineer Robert Moog. The principle of the theremin was also used in the sphärophon, invented in 1924 by Jörg Mager of Germany. It had a keyboard so that notes could be played more accurately. It could play quarter tones, was monophonic, and was not restricted to producing sweeping glissandi sounds like the theremin.

Another monophonic instrument similar to the theremin was the ondes martenot, invented by Maurice Martenot of France in 1928. It was designed more like a traditional keyboard instrument and therefore enjoyed popularity as a special instrument in the classical mold. The right hand changed the tone by moving a sliding metal ring up and down over a pattern of a normal keyboard. The left hand controlled volume with a pressure-sensitive key; when fully released, it would produce the silence needed to make a transition from one note to the next. A small bank of buttons controlled the filtering of the sound. Composers such as Darius Milhaud, Arthur Honegger, and Olivier Messiaen wrote music for the ondes martenot.

Among other instruments developed for the performance of electronic musical sounds were the trautonium of Dr. Frederick Trautwein (1930), the mixtur-trautonium of Oskar Sala (1950), the Hellertion of Bruno Helberger and Peter Lertes, and numerous other devices such as the emicon, the melodium, the oscillion, the croix sonore, the magnetton, the mellertion, the dynaphone, and the photophone. The electronic organ, the electric piano, and the electric guitar were other developments during this period.

Electronic music studios. The invention of the tape recorder freed electronic music from the restrictions of live performances. In the electronic music studio one could meticulously record and rerecord individual electronically generated tones to construct music from its component parts. Although the early performance instruments found a place in the early electronic music studios of the 1950s, a new breed of instrument was clearly needed that could take advantage of the studio. The early studios themselves set the pace for the field by providing examples of the kind of serious electronic music that could be produced. Three major studios dominated the field in the 1950s: the French National Radio in Paris, the Northwest German Radio (NWDR) in Cologne, and the Columbia-Princeton Electronic Music Center in New York.

Digital Synthesis	Analog Synthesis	Electronic Organs
Current Manufacturers: Casio, New England Digital, Fairlight, Ensoniq, E–MU, Roland, Kurzweil, Korg, Buchla, and others.	Current Manufacturers: Korg, Roland, Yamaha, Casio, Moog, and others.	Current Manufacturers: Hammond, Baldwin, and others.
1985: Yamaha Computer Assisted Music System		
1984: Kurzweil 250, Ensoniq Mirage		
1983: EMU Emulator	1983: Korg Poly 60	
1982: Buchla Digital		
1980: alphaSyntauri	1980: Yamaha DX–7	
1979: Fairlight CMI, Casiotone	1978: Prophet–5	
1975: Synclavier	1975: Moog Polymoog	
	1973: Oberheim	
	1971: Arp 2600	
	1970: Arp 2500	
	1969: EMS Putney, Moog Minimoog	
	1966: Synket, Buchla	
	1965: Electronium	
	1964: Moog	
	1960: Clavinet	
1957: Bell Labs experiments begin	1959: RCA Mark II	
	1956: Electronic Sackbut	
	1955: RCA Mark I	
	1952: Monochord	
	1950: Mixtur–Trautonium	
	1947: Melochord	
	1945: Ondioline, Hanert Electrical Orchestra	
	1944: Grainger–Cross Free Music Machine	1940 to present: Continued development of analog and digital electronic organs.
		1939: Hammond Solovox
	1934: La Croix Sonore	1935: Coupleaux–Givelet organ, Hammond Novachord, Warbo Format Organ
	1930: Trautonium, Vierling–Koch organ, Partiturophone	
	1929: Hellertion, Coupleaux–Givelet Automatic Musical Instrument	1929: Hammond Organ
	1928: Ondes Martenot	
	1924: Sphärophon	
	1920: Theremin	
	1900: Telharmonium	
	1899: Singing Arc	
	1874: Musical Telegraph	

Figure 1. *(Electronic Music)* Electronic music instruments time line. © 1986, Thomas B. Holmes.

In 1948 Pierre Schaeffer of French National Radio began to tinker with the composition of music using "found" sounds in the station's library of music discs. He was joined by Pierre Henry in 1949. Equipped by 1951 with tape recorders, filters, and other equipment, they established a genre of electronic music called musique concrète. Musique concrète employed only sounds that could be recorded from the real world: voices, trains, traffic, noise, and so forth. The composers then rearranged and edited the material for effect, creating massive collages of pulsating, melodramatic sounds that were on the leading edge of experimental music. The style persists today in the use of sounds from the real world in all forms of music. Musique concrète was broadened in scope by the mid-1950s to incorporate electronically generated sounds with found sounds. Further impetus for the development and dissemination of electroacoustic and computer music in France came about as a result of the establishment of IRCAM (Institut de Recherche et Coordination Acoustique Musique) at the Pompidou Center in the late 1970s.

While the French were experimenting with musique concrète, the Germans developed a style based on the use of purely electronic tone generation. Under the tutelage of musicologist Herbert Eimert, young German composers like Karlheinz Stockhausen (later director of the Cologne studio) were given the opportunity to explore the uncharted territory of electronic music. The early works of the studio used only pure electronic sounds, but later work branched out into combinations of natural sounds with electronic sounds. The result was an extension of serial (twelve-tone) music in which the composer manipulated every dynamic aspect of the sound to produce the desired effects. The German studio had some of the most elaborate equipment of the day, including a monochord (an updated version of the trautonium), sine and sawtooth wave oscillators, a variable-speed tape recorder, a four-track tape recorder, audio filters, a mixing panel, and a melochord that featured two monophonic tone generators that could be played simultaneously using two keyboards.

Although formal studio activity in the United States followed a little later than in France and Germany, its participants succeeded in constructing the most sophisticated synthesizer of the day. The Columbia-Princeton Electronic Music Center was established in 1957 and was designed to house the Olson-Belar synthesizer produced by RCA and later known as the Mark I. Employing vacuum-tube electronics and amplified tuning-fork oscillators, the instrument was very large and occupied most of one studio room. It was not actually a computer, although a paper-tape system (more like that of a player piano) was devised to feed the machine instructions. It could be programmed to control the pitch, volume, duration, and timbre of sounds, and because of this it became one of the most versatile instruments of its day. Composers from around the world came to the studio to use the machine. Some of the more familiar composers to have worked there were Edgard Varèse, Otto Luening (cofounder of the studio), Vladimir Ussachevsky (cofounder of the studio), Milton Babbit, Charles Wuorinen, Luciano Berio, Wendy Carlos, and Pauline Oliveros.

Later synthesizers. The next significant leap forward in the development of electronic music instruments came with the invention of the Moog synthesizer in 1964. Based on the principle of voltage control, this monophonic instrument provided the composer with unusual versatility in the combination and manipulation of electronic sounds. This was followed by a wide variety of voltage-controlled synthesizers made by other companies, including the Buchla Modular Electronic Music System (1966), the Arp 2500 (1970), and scores of additional units by companies like Roland, Korg, Oberheim, and EMS. Through those developmental years many new approaches to the design and control of instruments were employed, resulting in the production of polyphonic synthesizers capable of playing more than one note at a time, portable keyboards that could be held like a guitar, and models ranging in size from large studio machines to small performance keyboards for use onstage.

Until 1975 all the commercially available electronic music synthesizers were analog in design. Although the computer or digital generation of sound had been the subject of experiments for many years, it was not until 1975 that the first commercially available digital synthesizer was produced. Called the Synclavier, it featured multitracking of sounds and a wide variety of preset and programmable sound choices for the composer or performer. This was followed by the introduction of low-priced, consumer-oriented digital keyboards by the Casio Corporation in 1979 and a continuing interest in the use of digital synthesis techniques. By the late 1980s more than one hundred companies were engaged in the manufacture of electronic music instruments, software, and peripherals for making music with synthesizers and personal computers.

See also MUSIC MACHINES; MUSICAL INSTRUMENTS; SOUND EFFECTS; SOUND RECORDING.

Bibliography. Michel Chion and Guy Riebel, *Les musiques electroacoustiques,* Bry-Sur-Marne, France, 1976; Herbert Deutsch, *Synthesis: An Introduction to the History, Theory and Practice of Electronic Music,* Port Washington, N.Y., 1976; Thomas B. Holmes, *Electronic and Experimental Music,* New York, 1985.

THOMAS B. HOLMES

ELECTRONIC PUBLISHING

The term *electronic publishing,* though popular, is nevertheless ambiguous, alluding to different kinds of activities and products. It may be used to describe the production of books, magazines, newspapers, and other printed products that do not differ in general appearance from those of the past but are produced through the application of a variety of new technologies. These innovations include computers and computer programs used in conjunction with high-speed photocomposition machines or such devices as laser scanners and imaging engines (*see* FIBER OPTICS). They also include the capture of original input from writers by means of optical character recognition, on-line input and editing terminals, off-line diskettes (floppy disks) from personal computers, or remote transmission of text and GRAPHICS by TELEPHONE line, microwave, or SATELLITE.

The same term may also be used to imply production from a given DATA BASE of digital information. The use of a data base makes it possible to update, reorganize, and rearrange textual (or even graphic) information and to publish selected parts of such data for different uses or markets or at different times.

Yet another common use of the term refers to alternative PUBLISHING ventures in which the material published does not resemble the conventional BOOK or MAGAZINE. In this sense publishing consists of providing a data base of information that can be accessed by telecommunications or supplying digital data for research or referral purposes in the form of a transportable magnetic medium such as a digital computer disk. A variety of services of this character have developed, some of which not only provide information retrieval capability but may also afford a mechanism for the handling of transactions, the monitoring of equipment, access to computational facilities, and electronic messaging services. Companies have emerged with names such as Videotex, Pentel, Oracle, Ceefax, Télétel, Telidon, Compu-Serve, and The Source, as well as QL (law research and newspaper retrieval services), Vu/Text, Nexis, and Unidas. In specialized fields, various on-line services are available; for instance, Bibliographic Retrieval Services (BRS) offers BRS-MD for medical information retrieval, and the American Chemical Society provides on-line access to the data bases of many of its publications. *See* VIDEOTEX.

It may be seen that some uses of the term *electronic publishing* arise from consideration of the *technology* of publishing, while other references address the *product* itself. There is obviously a relationship between these two concepts—production technology and the nature of the product—since production technology makes possible the digital storage of textual data and even graphics. Access to this store of data can be made available in nonprint format, and its contents can also be manipulated in electronic format.

The application of computers and electronics to the publication process has caused significant changes in the way people work, the structure of the graphic arts industry, and especially the responsiveness of the publication process. For example, national newsmagazines work with input typed into the system directly by writers and reporters; editing takes place on-line, and page layout and makeup are performed on WYSIWYG ("what you see is what you get") work stations; photographs are cropped, rotated, enhanced, or sharpened; and complete pages (including text and graphics) are then transmitted via satellite to a remote printing plant. These activities can be accomplished more effectively, within a much shorter time span, and often with an editorial quality surpassing that which had previously been possible.

With the advent of microcomputers and inexpensive laser imaging devices, a form of electronic publishing known as desktop publishing can be carried on by persons who have had no formal experience or training in the graphic arts industry. They can apply computer programs that justify text with even right and left margins and hyphenate words, can check definitions and spellings with an on-line dictionary, and can even use a program capable of checking grammar. Artwork can be created in both raster (dot-for-dot) and vector (line) format, and other art can be scanned and recorded, thus affording creative opportunities for combining text and graphics. Page makeup decisions may be effected interactively by the user or by a computer-run procedure (*see* INTERACTIVE MEDIA).

With the ability to store text and graphics in digital form, *demand publishing* becomes possible. Researchers and readers may be able to command the PRINTING of selected materials for their own use, derived from an electronically stored source, rather than having to photocopy existing printed matter.

Electronic publishing is thus a ferment of processes, relationships, and opportunities for the interchange of information and the dissemination of knowledge. Publishing—only one of the forms of communication—grows and becomes ever more closely intertwined with other communications media such as radio, telephone, and television, all of which are being enhanced and extended by the achievements of modern electronics (*see* MICROELECTRONICS).

See also COMPUTER: HISTORY; COMPUTER: IMPACT; STANDARDS; TELECOMMUNICATIONS NETWORKS; TYPOGRAPHY.

Bibliography. Caroline Chauncey, "The Art of Typography in the Information Age," *Technology Review* 89 (Mar. 1986): 26–31, 79; Jean Crichton, "Turnkey Systems for Book People," *Publishers Weekly* 228 (Aug. 16, 1985): 37–41; Jerome P. Frank, "First Major Publisher to Install Computer-Assisted System (J. B. Lippincott)," *Publishers Weekly* 228 (Oct. 4, 1985): 52, 53; Steve Roth, "Turnkey Systems Revisited," *Publishers Weekly* 228 (Dec. 13, 1985): 43; *The Seybold Report on Publishing Systems*, Media, Pa., 1971–; John W. Seybold, *The World of Digital Typesetting*, Media, Pa., 1984; Allene Symons, "Technology in the Bookstore," *Publishers Weekly* 228 (Sept. 6, 1985): 36, 42; Michael Wallace, "Technological Changes in Printing: Union Response in Three Countries," *Monthly Labor Review* 108 (July 1985): 41–43.

JOHN W. SEYBOLD

ENCYCLOPEDIA

One of the world's foremost instruments for collecting and disseminating knowledge. This has been true especially since about 1500, because gradual changes in the encyclopedia's form after that time encouraged even more its use as a communicator of information. The invention of PRINTING, the growth of wealth, increasing LITERACY, and many other factors have reshaped the encyclopedia while enlarging its readership.

Etymology. The word was first used in Renaissance Latin and spelled *encyclopaedia*. Derived from a misreading of Greek manuscripts, *enkyklopaideia* was thought to be *enkyklios paideia*, meaning the "circle of knowledge," that is, the learning that the Greeks believed was essential for a general education. Then *encyclopaedia* took on a second meaning, that of a work containing information on many diverse topics. In the sixteenth century the word started to appear in various forms in BOOK titles, such as *Margarita Philosophica Encyclopaediam Exhibens* (Strasbourg edition, 1508), J. S. van Ringelbergh's *Lucubrationes, vel potius Absolutissima Kyklopaideia* (1541), and Paul Scalich's *Encyclopaediae, seu Orbis Disciplinarum, tam Sacrarum quam Prophanarum, Epistemon* (1559). The word continued to appear in titles of Latin and other works during the seventeenth century. Finally, *encyclopaedia* and its varied spellings in different vernacular languages came to be adopted more frequently than the words *dictionary* or *lexicon* for the description of a book containing extensive learning. This happened after Ephraim Chambers employed the term, in modified form, for his English *Cyclopaedia: Or, an Universal Dictionary of Arts and Sciences* (1728), and the French men of letters DENIS DIDEROT and Jean Le Rond d'Alembert used it for their *Encyclopédie, ou dictionnaire raisonné des sciences, des arts et des métiers* (1751–1772).

Three civilizations—Chinese, Arab, and European—produced most of the world's encyclopedias until well into the nineteenth century. The Chinese and Arab traditions differed markedly from the European; Chinese encyclopedias were mostly compendiums of documents, and the Arab encyclopedias were strongly influenced by Muhammadanism.

Early history. Ancient and medieval European encyclopedias cover many of the same topics as later ones, although certainly not in so much depth. Knowledge has expanded enormously and has been subdivided into numerous disciplines. Science, medicine, RELIGION, and the humanities are discussed in such influential early encyclopedias as Pliny the Elder's *Historia naturalis* (77 C.E.), Isidore of Seville's *Originum seu etymologiarum libri XX* (ca. 636), Hugh of Saint Victor's *Didascalicon: De Studio Legendi* (late 1120s), and Vincent of Beauvais's *Speculum Maius* (1244). In addition, Theophilus's *De Diversis Artibus* (probably between 1110 and 1140) describes the mechanical arts, and Gulielmus Pastregicus's *De Originibus Rerum Libellus* (ca. 1350) does the same for biographical topics. One important innovation in the contents of encyclopedias since 1350 has been the inclusion of individual biographical articles on living people. These first appear in Johann Heinrich Zedler's sixty-four-volume *Universal Lexicon* (1732–1750).

Later developments. Since 1500 encyclopedias have become even more strikingly different from their predecessors. To make the encyclopedia more ordered, intelligible, and usable, alphabetical arrangement, cross-references, indexes, and other devices gradually appeared. The first encyclopedias had been organized topically and were usually designed to be read from cover to cover, but occasional works in ancient and medieval times adopted either in part or completely an alphabetical arrangement. Then, in the sixteenth century, various Latin-language dictionaries employed an alphabetical arrangement, and in the seventeenth century the practice spread to such vernacular encyclopedias as Louis Moréri's *Grand dictionnaire historique* (1674). Since that time the alphabetical arrangement has been more common than the topical.

Domenico Bandini, in his *Fons Memorabilium Universi* (ca. 1410), used cross-references. They started to become much more effective no later than Chambers's eighteenth-century *Cyclopaedia*, in which he carefully cross-referenced over half of his articles.

Rudimentary contemporary indexes are found for various medieval, sixteenth-century, and seventeenth-century works. Pierre Mouchon added a separate two-volume index to Diderot and d'Alembert's *Encyclopédie* in 1780. However, only in the nineteenth century did systematic indexing start to become standard in encyclopedias.

Compilers of encyclopedias have also introduced various techniques in order to keep abreast of new learning. Revised editions had been a characteristic of encyclopedias before 1500, but yearbooks did not appear until the nineteenth century. From 1857 to 1864 Brockhaus published one in monthly installments, and from 1861 to 1902 *Appleton's Annual Cyclopaedia and Register of Important Events* supplemented *The American Cyclopaedia*. In addition, around 1920 several encyclopedias began the practice of continuous revisions with the hiring of permanent staffs.

The composition of the staff of an encyclopedia has also been transformed. Before the eighteenth century most, if not all, encyclopedias were compilations written by one or a few jacks-of-all-trades. The *Encyclopédie* of Diderot and d'Alembert changed all that. The work enlisted more than a hundred contributors, many of them experts on the subjects they wrote about. Then, during the nineteenth century, the *Encyclopaedia Britannica, Brockhaus,* and other large-scale encyclopedias introduced a further refinement: an editor in chief, assistant editors, and hundreds of contributors.

During the nineteenth and twentieth centuries the number of encyclopedias has grown phenomenally. Not only have the *Britannica* and *Brockhaus* continued to be published since their founding in 1768 and 1796, respectively, but many others have appeared. In fact, the creation of an encyclopedia has even become a matter of national prestige, and one European country after another has produced one. Just a few are *Encyklopedia powszechna* (Poland, 1858–1868), *Egyetemes magyar encyclopaedia* (Hungary, 1861–1876), *Enciclopedia universal ilustrada europeo-americana* (Spain, 1905–1933), *Bol'shaya sovetskaya entsiklopediya* (USSR, first edition, 1927–1947), *Enciclopedia italiana* (Italy, 1929–1939), and *Encyclopédie française* (France, 1935–1966).

The making of encyclopedias has become one of the biggest enterprises of the book trade. In the MIDDLE AGES Isidore of Seville's and Hugh of Saint Victor's encyclopedias circulated in not more than two thousand copies combined. Two of the most controversial encyclopedias ever written, Pierre Bayle's *Dictionnaire historique et critique* (1697) and Diderot and d'Alembert's *Encyclopédie,* had printing runs of little more than two thousand and forty-two hundred sets, respectively, for their first editions. On the other hand, the fifth edition of Brockhaus's *Allgemeine deutsche Real-Enzyklopädie für die gebildeten Stände* (1819–1820) printed over thirty thousand sets in the years 1819–1823 alone; the *Britannica* during the early 1960s was selling more than one hundred fifty thousand sets worldwide annually and sending its yearbook to eight hundred thousand subscribers.

Encyclopedias not only remain one of the best sources for comprehending a civilization but also are an important influence in shaping it.

See also CLASSIFICATION; LANGUAGE REFERENCE BOOK.

Bibliography. Robert Lewis Collison, *Encyclopaedias: Their History throughout the Ages,* 2d ed., New York, 1966; "Encyclopaedias and Dictionaries," *The New Encyclopaedia Britannica,* Vol. 18, Chicago, 1985 ed.; "Encyclopédie," *Trésor de la langue française: Dictionnaire de la langue du XIXe et du XXe siècle (1789–1960),* Paris, 1971 ed.; "Encyclopédies et civilisations," *Cahiers d'histoire mondiale* 9 (1966): 449–851; Frank A. Kafker, ed., *Notable Encyclopedias of the Seventeenth and Eighteenth Centuries: Nine Predecessors of the Encyclopédie* (Studies on Voltaire and the Eighteenth Century, T. 194), Oxford, 1981; Alain Rey, *Encyclopédies et dictionnaires,* Paris, 1982; Gert A. Zischka, *Index Lexicorum: Bibliographie der lexikalischen Nachschlagewerke,* Vienna, 1959.

FRANK A. KAFKER

ENTERTAINMENT

Entertainment, entertaining guests, and entertaining an idea have in common the root word *entertain* (from the Latin *tenēre*), meaning to hold or to keep steady, busy, or amused. The modern definition of entertainment is any NARRATIVE, PERFORMANCE, or other experience that can be sold to and enjoyed by large and heterogeneous groups of people. It is usually sought for its own sake rather than for informational, educational, therapeutic, or other instrumental purposes. Thus the term is useful for commercial purposes in selling cultural commodities of broad general appeal. However, the term obscures the fact that entertainment also has informational content that usually cultivates conventional themes, outlooks, and perspectives (*see* CULTIVATION ANALYSIS). This is why some analysts have called entertainment "information for those who seek no information" and consider it a powerful ideological force in any society (*see* IDEOLOGY).

The modern concept of entertainment began to evolve with the transition in societies from ORAL CULTURE TO WRITING. For the first time storytelling could transcend barriers of time and distance, reaching audiences not known to or even conceived of by the teller. With the emergence of PRINTING and, later, of other mass media—PHOTOGRAPHY, SOUND RECORDING, MOTION PICTURES, RADIO, and television (*see* TELEVISION HISTORY)—increasingly larger and more diverse audiences were able to share the same entertainment experience. These developments led by the mid-twentieth century to the creation of international audiences for media artifacts (*see* ARTIFACT) considered to be marketable commodities in world trade. Entertainment has become the business of a vast and highly differentiated industry encompassing PUBLISHING, film and television production, and performance genres (*see* GENRE) of various kinds, including popular music (*see* MUSIC, POPULAR) and SPORTS (*see also* SPECTACLE). Under such circumstances entertainment has acquired new shades of meaning. It is a trade term designating a particular category of marketed product and as such has administrative and legal ramifications.

When a film or television program is classified as entertainment, the label implies that it is intended primarily to absorb the attention and to leave agreeable feelings. Any weightier roles of communication, such as EDUCATION or PERSUASION, are assumed to take a back seat, in contrast to other types of content such as news (*see* TELEVISION NEWS), POLITICAL COMMUNICATION, or ADVERTISING. Entertainment may indeed inform or persuade, but it is generally presumed that these effects are secondary or incidental and will not interfere with the real function of pleasant diversion. This assumption is embedded in such phrases as "mere entertainment" and "pure entertainment" and in the idea of entertainment as an escape from reality.

Entertainment has thus become a crucial industry term that in the process of demarcating subject matter and approach also functions as a disclaimer of intent or effect. In HOLLYWOOD's big-studio era, for example, it was used to describe the studio product and went with the traditional dictum to writers, "If we want a message, we'll send for Western Union." The word and its implications served as a strategic defense in the 1930s and 1940s in industry struggles against CENSORSHIP boards and proposals for such boards on local and national levels in the United States and elsewhere. In the 1950s television inherited the problem as well as the strategy.

At the same time that this concept of entertainment was achieving international currency, the mass media were themselves the increasing focus of important systematic research (*see* COMMUNICATIONS RESEARCH: ORIGINS AND DEVELOPMENT). Early research helped to define the terms of the debate inasmuch as the use of entertainment as a disclaimer of intent or effect is based largely on its accepted distinction from PROPAGANDA. Propaganda is usually associated with formats that, like the DOCUMENTARY or COMMERCIALS, announce and confront their topics, and for that reason such formats may confound their purpose by alerting the audience's critical faculties and generally enmeshing it in "on the other hand" considerations. Yet the study of media messages and their effects has made clear that despite—and perhaps because of—the innocuous associations of the label, entertainment plays a significant role in the cultivation of values and beliefs and the socialization of CHILDREN. Entertainment's impact is embedded in premises that are not debated and may not even be clearly articulated but are accepted by audiences in order for the experience to have meaning. Its influence is pervasive and cumulative. In effect, entertainment in all its forms constitutes a storytelling environment that operates by principles at once implicit and widely shared to help form expectations and interpretations of the social world.

The power and appeal of this storytelling environment can be seen by examining the most widely distributed entertainment commodities. Genres that stress action and good-bad conflicts have been particularly successful in transcending time periods and national boundaries (*see* MYSTERY AND DETECTIVE FICTION; SPY FICTION; WESTERN, THE). These genres rely on essentially the same formula, inherited and adapted from numerous early forms: a community, nation, or the world can be saved if a certain evil person or group is tracked down, caught, or killed. The dramatic resolution often involves VIOLENCE, as the hero or a group of heroes prevails through superior strength, strategy, technology, or supernatural powers.

Some critics see ideological implications in almost every aspect of such a formula. Does its continuous use cultivate the view that the world's problems stem from evil people rather than from intractable social issues? Or that the law cannot effectively protect society from criminals, making necessary—even laudatory—violent action by individuals? Entertainment producers tend to dismiss such questions and to supply practical and economic reasons for all aspects of the formula. Good-evil conflicts win large audiences and lend themselves to clear-cut resolutions within limited time periods. The emphasis on resolute individual action helps to enlist STARS, who in turn attract SPONSOR support. The focus on contemporary concerns and issues allows fictional violence to be explained as simply reflecting a violent world. Finally, the producers of entertainment reject as unproved many assumptions and beliefs about entertainment's effects on ATTITUDES and behavior, and they are able to cite research results supporting a range of conclusions (*see* MASS MEDIA EFFECTS).

Members of the entertainment industry also are held responsible for the more easily visible aspects of the entertainment product. The identification of a stereotyped character or unsavory deed with a particular national, ethnic, religious, or other group often results in protests from civic groups, government officials, legal representatives, and others (*see* PRESSURE GROUP), attesting to the influence popularly attributed to fictional representation. Producers have therefore found it expedient to give much care to the selection of characters' backgrounds and occupations (*see* MINORITIES IN THE MEDIA). Choices are likely to involve a defensive web of editorial policies, which often prompts a reliance on the safety of tried and true elements of plot, theme, and treatment. Writers often have little autonomy, and series formulas may be spelled out in written guidelines. Story lines and concepts often emerge as the result of mediation and consultation among a number of different functionaries essential to the production of the entertainment commodity (*see* ARTIST AND SOCIETY).

Thus the structure of the entertainment industry itself determines to a large extent the nature of the product. In this way the "deniability" of intent or effect associated with the use of the term *entertainment* can be seen to be a structural feature of the industry. Those who see entertainment as a for-profit commodity—the result of decisions made on many levels about content, packaging, marketing, and distribution—find it easy enough to deny that the ensuing product advocates a particular position or perspective and, accordingly, to disavow responsibility for its potential reception by an audience. At the same time, however, the industry's concern with maintaining an audience mandates attention and responsiveness to what is and is not acceptable in the larger society. Formulas change as society is perceived to change, as themes and portrayals once condoned are subject to criticism and plot elements once taboo become permissible. Examining the evolution of entertainment formulas over time enables one to chart the development of a society's attitudes toward particular groups and issues as well as the relative importance attributed to them (*see* CULTURAL INDICATORS).

Entertainment, the telling and passing on of stories, is thus one of the primary ways in which cultures speak to their members and thereby maintain a sense of coherence, indeed of history. Entertainment is attentive to the norms, myths, and fears of its audiences but also serves to shape and reshape them; it reflects social trends but also nudges them into being and reinforces and furthers them. It provides a social repertoire of characters, relationships, and outcomes that is used in the ongoing attempt to make sense of the world.

See also FACT AND FICTION; FICTION; LITERATURE, POPULAR; TASTE CULTURES.

Bibliography. Heinz-Dietrich Fischer and Stefan Reinhard Melnik, eds., *Entertainment: A Cross-Cultural Examination,* New York, 1979.

ERIK BARNOUW AND CATHERINE E. KIRKLAND

ESPIONAGE

The clandestine acquisition usually of enemy or rival intentions and capabilities, often at the international level. Virtually all nations seek foreknowledge of threatening actions by attempting to break into the communication links of others. Preserving secure channels, or counterintelligence, is an inevitable concomitant.

Collected data are useless until received by authorities who can evaluate them, and intelligence operations demand rapid transmission. Through the ages spies possessed important information that could not be communicated or that arrived too late. Until the development of TELEGRAPHY and RADIO most intelligence information was carried by hand. In ancient times this often meant exposing the bearers of bad news to the murderous whims of distraught rulers. Messengers on horses represented the swiftest and most common means of communication for centuries. Other means were also employed in the dispatch of sensitive material, including trained swallows and pigeons. Carrier birds were used by the Chinese for the transmission of intelligence three thousand years ago and still served the same purpose for many military units during World War II.

Early history. Surreptitious intelligence gathering has ancient antecedents. According to the biblical account, Moses, at the command of Jehovah, ordered a dozen followers to spy on the promised land of Canaan before it was occupied by the Israelites. One of the spies was Joshua, who himself later instructed two agents, "Go view the land, even Jericho." Ancient writings abound with examples of espionage and deceptive communication devices. According to Herodotus, the Persian king Xerxes was thwarted in a planned surprise attack on the Spartans when a spy's message of alarm was sent secretly on a wax-covered wooden tablet. The Chinese military philosopher Sun-tzu wrote in *The Art of War,* "If I am able to determine the enemy's dispositions while at the same time I conceal my own, then I can concentrate and he must divide." Ancient China's political leaders made extensive use of message concealment, called *steganography.* In its crudest form, wax-covered dispatches written on silk were carried in the body orifices of couriers. To capture a courier and uncover his secreted message was the simplest form of counterintelligence, and remains so today.

The earliest CODE breaking for political purposes can be traced to early India. A book written before 300 B.C.E. urged court ambassadors in other jurisdictions to observe "signs made in places of pilgrimage and temples, or by deciphering paintings or secret writings." Codes, elementary but sometimes complex, apparently existed in all early civilizations, giving CRYPTOLOGY a universality that was further extended to cryptanalysis, or code breaking. All were developed independently and responded to the perceived requirements of security at the time.

David Kahn, in his comprehensive history of secret communications, *The Codebreakers,* states, "Cryptology was born among the Arabs. They were the first to discover and write down methods of cryptanalysis." As Islam spread across three continents, codes and ciphers were considered essential for communicating. Even the use of invisible inks was widespread. Muslim plenipotentiaries were provided with personal codes. A fourteenth-century Arab teacher, Ali ibn ad-Duraihim, provided a step-by-step method for breaking codes based on alphabetic frequency that could serve as an instruction manual in cryptanalysis today.

While Islam flourished in all disciplines, in the Western world during the MIDDLE AGES the crafts of espionage fell moribund, either for lack of need or as a reflection of the relative decline in intellectual creativity and innovation during those years. Soon, however, the West's interest in matters of espionage was reawakened. Leon Battista Alberti (1404–1472), called the "father of Western cryptology," invented a movable cipher disk in the late fifteenth century. Inspired by the inventions of JOHANNES GUTENBERG, Alberti used two copper wheels, which became the first polyalphabetic coding device and the forerunner of most modern cryptographic methods with their innumerable substitution combinations.

The publication in 1518 of *Polygraphia,* written by the German Benedictine abbot Johannes Trithemius (1462–1516), further broadened cryptographic activity. Hundreds of codes were invented for secret communications, including the famous Ave Maria cipher. This system of word substitution permitted seemingly religious material to mask hidden messages.

Code breaking. More is known about the means of communicating secretly than about code breaking successes. One of the earliest cryptanalysts of note was Thomas Phelippes, an agent in the employ of Sir Francis Walsingham. When Walsingham established the forerunner of the British Secret Service in the reign of Elizabeth I, Phelippes provided invaluable service by breaking codes in Latin, French, Italian, and Spanish as well as in English. Combined intelligence intercepts and decoding by Walsingham's group led to precise knowledge of when the Spanish Armada would sail and the discovery of incriminating plans by Mary, Queen of Scots, to overthrow Elizabeth.

It is essential that coded transmissions not be overly complicated. A misunderstood or misread ciphered message from Napoléon contributed to the defeat of the French at Leipzig in 1813. It was all the more remarkable because Napoléon relied less on cryptology than most great military commanders. His *petit chiffre* ("little cipher") was regarded as too simple, as was illustrated by the ease with which the Russians decoded French messages during the Moscow campaign.

When the telegraph was introduced in the nineteenth century, interceptions were inevitable. The earliest instance of tapping telegraphic traffic is attributed to J. O. Kerbey, a Union railroad telegrapher caught behind Confederate lines during the United States Civil War. Although a prisoner in Richmond, Virginia, he was able to break into lines of his captors and relay military data by coded mail to the Union.

Cryptanalysis achieved full growth in World War I. With radio and telegraphy in full play, coding and code breaking were to play vital roles during the conflict and even helped to determine its outcome.

Great Britain's first act of war in 1914 was to cut the German transatlantic cable off Emden, forcing Berlin to rely for diplomatic communication on interceptible wireless messages or cables controlled by neutrals. British intelligence painstakingly broke the German codes, leading to one of the most dramatic intercepts of all time, the Zimmermann telegram. The German foreign minister, for whom it is named, sent a message urging Mexico to enter the war in return for annexation of parts of the United States. Knowledge of these negotiations helped to bring the United States into the war against Germany and to crystallize anti-German sentiment.

Russia suffered a crushing blow in the Battle of Tannenberg in 1914 when field commanders dispensed with encoded messages and sent orders in plain language. The Germans monitored them and used the intelligence to inflict one of the greatest military defeats in history.

Technological innovations. Commercial use of codes progressed with twentieth-century advances in technology. International companies purchased complex electromechanical devices for secret communications during the 1930s. An adjunct of business operations, these machines were adopted by Japan and Germany as their basic diplomatic and military coded transmission vehicles during World War II. The Allied forces broke these codes, winning an incalculable advantage throughout the war. Polish intelligence duplicated the German Enigma machine, and the British completed the code breaking. Intercepted messages (distributed under the supersecret classification of ULTRA) included Adolf Hitler's communications and daily reports on German military movements. At the same time, U.S. cryptanalysts, notably William Friedman, duplicated the Japanese machine, designated PURPLE. The deciphered intercepts, known as MAGIC, gave the Allied forces an indisputable edge in the Pacific war. Germany, to a less publicized extent, was also proficient in code breaking, cracking the codes of thirty-four enemy and neutral nations.

Most agents of World War II relied on what were standard though improved covert communication methods such as concealed radio transceivers and microphotography. The cold war that followed ushered in a new dimension in communications intelligence that emphasized interceptions. The computer and other electronic advances provided new ways to unlock codes and made possible more secure channels.

The vast reaches of space became the next arenas of counterintelligence and espionage. The United States and the USSR maintain space vehicles to intercept radio communications and visually track naval and military movements.

Beyond question, the largest electronic intelligence organization in the world is the National Security

Agency of the United States. NSA was at one time believed to have operated more than half the computers that existed worldwide.

Advanced technology involves ever-increasing numbers of people in the planning, production, and use of highly secret material related to national security. Access to classified data is more widespread than ever, and easily compromised. All nations forbid unauthorized possession of restricted information, but it is during transmission of classified information that counterintelligence efforts are most likely to succeed. Most modern covert operations were uncovered by a breakdown or penetration of the spy ring's communications apparatus. Monitoring of suspects entails sophisticated eavesdropping or visual observation. For democracies, such clandestine intrusion can lead to abuses of civil liberties and invasions of PRIVACY for the innocent.

Despite scientific and technological advances, transmitting intelligence and espionage itself have remained relatively constant in technique. Codes, ciphers, and cryptanalysis originated centuries ago. Steganography has progressed little from retrievable messages swallowed by couriers to modern-day microdots. Though satellites go vastly higher than the observation balloon first used by the French in 1794 during the wars of the French Revolution, they serve essentially the same purpose. What did change was the international climate of SECRECY, which led to an escalating battle between those who wished to perfect impenetrable communications and those who sought wide access to information.

See also DECEPTION; DISINFORMATION; SPY FICTION.

Bibliography. James Bamford, *The Puzzle Palace*, Boston, 1982; Richard Deacon, *A History of the British Secret Service*, New York and London, 1969; Allen W. Dulles, *The Craft of Intelligence*, New York, 1963, reprint Greenwood, Conn., 1977; Ladislas Farago, *The Broken Seal*, New York, 1967; Jock [Chetnynd John Drake] Haswell, *Spies and Spymasters*, London, 1977; Allison Ind, *A Short History of Espionage*, New York, 1963; David Kahn, *The Codebreakers*, New York, 1967; Richard W. Rowan and Robert G. Deindorfer, *Secret Service: Thirty-three Centuries of Espionage*, new and rev. ed., New York, 1967; Barbara W. Tuchman, *The Zimmermann Telegram*, New York, 1958; F. W. Winterbotham, *The Ultra Secret*, New York and London, 1974.

ROBERT GORALSKI

ETHICS, MEDIA

Media ethics is a new but important branch of professional ethics. Recognizing the power of mass com-

munications in modern life, the Hastings Center and the Carnegie Foundation of New York included media ethics in their 1980 study of ethics teaching in higher education in the United States. Consequently occupations in the mass media were grouped with such professions as medicine, law, business, and engineering; these come under the purview of applied ethics, a burgeoning component of moral philosophy. Meanwhile, debate over the NEW INTERNATIONAL INFORMATION ORDER made SATELLITE ownership, journalistic fairness, broadcast sensationalism, and other ethical issues matters of global concern.

Media ethics as a subset of applied or professional ethics combines description and theory. The most sophisticated media ethics retains an interest in concrete moral judgments, in the way ethical decision making functions in media practice. But the concern for principle, for general ethical theory, is retained as well. Ideally the two sides are dialectically unified. Work in the larger world of applied ethics demonstrates that if description of actual morality among practitioners becomes the exclusive aim, the result is minimalist ethics. If metaethics dominates, it becomes a self-contained circle out of touch with reality.

Although concerned observers and practitioners have for three centuries leveled criticism against the media and raised moral awareness about them, the exponential growth in media ethics began in the 1980s. The ongoing challenge has been to integrate the results of case studies with moral reasoning. For the foreseeable future the question is whether media ethics can be developed with such competence that it contributes to applied ethics generally.

For the sake of convenience, media ethics can be divided into three main branches according to the typical functions of most information systems: reporting news, promoting products or services, and entertaining. In capitalist societies, however, practitioners of journalism, ADVERTISING, and entertainment often belong to the same corporation and encounter all three media areas directly or indirectly in their work. Some problems cut across all three areas. Stereotyping, for instance, is deep-seated and pervasive in every form of mass communication; sensationalism also is common to reporting, PERSUASION, and entertainment.

From that mix of interests across media functions, five substantive issues dominate the agenda: invasion of PRIVACY, truth telling, exploitation, VIOLENCE, and democratic participation. Each of these moral problems occurs to some degree in other occupations as well. Exploitation, for example, is central to business ethics and debated throughout the professional world. Media violence attracts social scientists and theorists from several disciplines. However, the media ethics component is irreducible and cannot be traded away without trivializing the problem.

Invasion of Privacy

Professors in journalism schools and PUBLIC OPINION polls agree that invasion of privacy is the premier issue in media ethics, at least in Western cultures. Intruding on privacy creates enormous resentment and damages press credibility. Privacy matters are among the most painful that humane reporters ever encounter. For all of privacy's technical gains in case law and tort law, ethicists consider legal definitions an inadequate foundation. How can the legally crucial difference between newsworthy material and GOSSIP or voyeurism be reasonably determined?

Therefore, while acknowledging legal distinctions and boundaries, the ethics of privacy is constructed from such moral principles as the dignity of persons and the redeeming social value of the information disclosed. Louis Hodges, an ethicist at Washington and Lee University, contends that privacy is a moral good because controlling intimate information about ourselves is essential to a healthy sense of personhood. However, privacy cannot be made absolute because we are cultural beings with responsibility in the social and political arena. We are individual beings, therefore we need privacy; we are social beings, therefore we need public information about one another. Since we are individuals, eliminating privacy would eliminate human existence as we know it; since we are social, elevating privacy to absolute status would likewise render human existence impossible. These considerations lead to the formal criterion that the intimate life space of individuals cannot be invaded without permission unless the revelation averts a public crisis or is of overriding public significance and all other means have been exhausted.

From an ethical perspective, legal definitions of privacy beg several questions about the relationship between self and society. A legal right to privacy presumes a sharp line dividing an individual's zone from the collective. An ethics of privacy prefers the richer connections between public and private advocated by social theorists since Alexis de Tocqueville who have centered their analysis on a viable public life. While participating in the theoretical debates over the nature of community, media ethicists have been applying moral principles to three areas: reporting personal data on various social classes from innocent victims of tragedy to criminals, confidential information stored in computer data banks, and ubiquitous advertising that intrudes on our everyday activities.

Truthfulness

The journalist's obligation to truth is a standard part of the rhetoric. In fact, communicators recognize that the credibility of words is somehow central to the communication enterprise. Many who dispense information would agree with the existentialist philosopher Karl Jaspers, who claimed that the moment of communication is simultaneously the preservation of and search for truth. See MEANING; SEMANTICS.

However, except for a focus on the obligation to accuracy in reporting, mass media education and practice do little to clarify such concepts as truthfulness and its antonym, DECEPTION. Just as advertising scholars have provided little enlightenment on the nature of persuasion, so newspeople have not developed the role of truthfulness in a way that its centrality would seem to require. With facticity discredited by the philosophy of science, media ethics is searching for a holistic version of truth-in-context similar to that advocated by the German theologian Dietrich Bonhoeffer in his *Ethics*.

Meanwhile, various dimensions of the issue are crowding in from every direction. The issue tends to be posed most frequently by specific events, such as the presentation of a "docudrama," the selective quotation of a newsmaker, or the omission of relevant information from an advertisement. But far more significant are the larger patterns of misrepresentation involved in such problems as SEXISM, racism, and hype.

Ethicist Sissela Bok correctly argues that when regard for truth is weakened, a society's well-being is threatened. But she refuses to reject all lies unconditionally. If some lies are not morally reprehensible, what are the criteria for justifiable exceptions? To media ethicists it is apparent at this stage that the current IDEOLOGY stresses the rights and privileges of the press and downplays the press's responsibilities to its audience. Someone once defined journalism as history in a hurry, and providing an accurate, representative account rarely occurs under those conditions. Bok has outlined the framework that still must be spelled out for all phases of media practice— tilting it toward the principle of veracity, toward ARISTOTLE's assumption that lies are mean and culpable.

Exploitation

Advertising, by its nature, is self-interested communication. Advertisers finance media programs in the expectation of substantial returns on their investment. They associate the good life with the acquisition of products and services in order to reap financial benefits.

Similarly self-interested, but more extreme in its methods and aims, is the PROPAGANDA emanating from media controlled by dictators and authoritarian governments. Viewers, listeners, and readers—whole populations—are exploited and truth obscured in the bureaucrats' interests. Because of its drastic effects, political propaganda has preoccupied media scholars since World War I. With totalitarianism a dominant issue after World War II, media researchers critiqued not only the work of JOSEPH GOEBBELS's war ministry for Adolf Hitler but political propaganda of all forms.

This preoccupation eventually led to a broader definition of the problem of propaganda, including theories of indirect, pervasive propaganda. French scholar Jacques Ellul advanced the notion of sociological propaganda—the mass media's propensity to socialize industrial cultures into uniform wholes. Ellul centered his analysis on technology as the determining factor, as did Jürgen Habermas in Germany. The Frankfurt school—Max Horkheimer, THEODOR ADORNO, Herbert Marcuse—also made the role of the media a central variable in its social theories. Meanwhile, Latin American scholars Ivan Illich and Paulo Freire contributed their analyses of symbol formation under conditions of oppression (*see* SCHOOL), and in the United States George Gerbner developed the theory of "cultivation"—television's long-term effect on people's view of reality (*see* CULTIVATION ANALYSIS). Finally, Stuart Hall of Britain's Center of Cultural Studies saw ideology as the heart of modern cultural life. *See also* MARXIST THEORIES OF COMMUNICATION.

The problem in ethics is establishing the boundaries between legitimate persuasive intent and exploitation, between rational appeals and demagoguery. What kinds of communication, institutional and personal, are coercive, harmful manipulation whose intent and practice are oppressive rather than liberating? Several topics are attracting the greatest interest as windows through which to clarify the ethics of exploitation:

- political advertising, particularly the thirty- or sixty-second commercials designed for emotional influence;
- market illiterates, whose meager education and submarginal incomes make them naive consumers, easily manipulated;
- sins of omission, in which audiences are uninformed because vital economic or political information is withheld in the story or advertisement; and
- the power of media monopolies to control the market and capital while decimating alternative or independent producers and writers (*see* MONOPOLY).

Ethicists, in other words, are attempting to fix legitimate responsibility in concrete cases and thereby advance the problem of exploitation from mere rhetoric to possible solution.

Violence

Few issues command as much attention from media reformers as violence in books, magazines, comics, television, and film. In the United States, for example, studies have shown that by high school graduation the average seventeen-year-old will have seen eighteen thousand murders on television. Critics vociferously protest programs that glorify brawling for its own sake, war stories that purvey frivolous militarism, and police shows that offer hyped-up violence without even a hint of normative reflection.

Media ethicists find it almost impossible to get beyond such hot-tempered moralism to systematic reflection. An ethics of violence rather than moral preachments is especially important because the specter of CENSORSHIP always shadows the debate. Against the moralists are combative libertarians who fear that any curtailment of speech heralds a retreat from democracy.

Violence is a serious ethical issue because it violates the persons-as-ends principle. In Immanuel Kant's standard formulation, we must treat all rational beings as ends in themselves and never as means only. In Kant's ethics this categorical imperative is a universal law no less binding than such laws of nature as gravity. Gratuitous cheapening of human life to expand ratings, from this perspective, is a reprehensible misuse of human beings as means to base ends. Media ethics has shown a special interest in the sexual violence so common in music VIDEO, horror movies (especially slasher films), pornographic literature, videocassettes, and the commercials promoting them. Sadistic, bloodthirsty torture in a sexual context is a particularly offensive form of dehumanization. *See also* PORNOGRAPHY.

While avoiding doctrinaire moralism, an ethics of media violence has rarely gotten beyond the arguments from AESTHETICS. In fact, media ethics typically repeats the crucial distinction between artistic realism and mindless violence, between the violence in a film like *Gandhi* and that in the "Dukes of Hazzard" television series, for example. In addition, it supports psychiatrists who broaden our definitions of violence to include not just physical damage but also psychological injury.

But a unique contribution from ethics to understanding media violence still must be made. The most likely arena lies in delineating responsibility. Applied ethics always takes seriously the matter of who should be held accountable. The important question then becomes whether producers of violent entertainment can dismiss their responsibility for quality programming by claiming to give the public what it wants. Are only parents to be held accountable for the television programs their children watch, or do advertisers and networks carry obligations also? If so, in what proportions? Does the person with greatest technical expertise have the greatest moral liability? How can paternalism that downgrades laypeople and informal social networks in the decison-making process be avoided? When is the state or the courts the final adjudicator? In professional ethics in general and media ethics specifically, clarifying accountability is an important safeguard against the human penchant for evading culpability. The ongoing challenge for media ethics, then, is establishing the appropriate levels of responsibility among the principal players in media violence: producers and writers, actors, network executives, the public, and politicians.

Democratic Participation

The spectacular progress of satellite technology has attracted media ethicists into a provocative debate over cultural imperialism and democratic participation. As the number of prime geostationary positions filled up in the late 1970s, the implications for the principle of distributive justice became inescapable. The 1979 meeting of the World Administrative Radio Conference in Geneva reaffirmed the sovereign right of member nations to their prime frequencies and satellite requirements. Instead of the first-come, first-served principle, the MacBride Commission formed by UNESCO also recommended the country-by-country concept of equal access in its 1980 report *Many Voices, One World*. Media ethics has generally supported the thesis that information is a vital resource of the future for all nations and, therefore, orbital positions ought to be reserved on the basis of land mass and population rather than the current demand of industrialized societies. The Dutch scholar Cees Hamelink, for example, has argued convincingly that new technologies such as satellites are not merely efficient machines that send international messages at one-thousandth the previous cost. Media ethics views satellites, for all their benefits, as weapons of possible control over space in the interests of technologically powerful nations. The issues, in fact, are typically construed in historical terms. That is, since World War II the smaller nations have demanded political independence from colonial powers and economic independence from transnational corporations. In the 1980s they legitimately demanded cultural independence—freedom from the films, data, television, and news of dominant nations that prevented them from achieving their own identities. *See* INTERNATIONAL ORGANIZATIONS.

While combating cultural imperialism on the *inter*national level, media ethics argues for democratic participation *intra*nationally. The same equal access principle is applied in both cases. Media structures within a nation-state are considered ethically legiti-

mate to the extent that they achieve maximum distribution and ownership based on the principle of essential needs. Freire and Illich in Latin America and Saul Alinsky in the United States all defend a model of participatory democracy grounded in a dialogic theory of communication. With the old liberal and socialist paradigms of national development both discredited, the Iranian internationalist Majid Tehranian argues for the dialogic paradigm as a revolutionary alternative to these two monologic, *I-It*, mechanized versions. *See also* CITIZEN ACCESS; CITIZENS BAND RADIO.

Overview

These five issues and their cognates dominate the agenda in media ethics, but they do not encompass it. Random samples of textbooks and journals yield a list of numerous other topics involving media ethics, such as PHOTOJOURNALISM, minority hiring, promoting nutritionless products, conflict of interest, stealing corporate money, pornography, PUBLIC RELATIONS, confidentiality, fair trial, credibility, ethics codes, professionalism, municipal ownership of cable, fabrication, checkbook journalism, TERRORISM coverage, bias, plagiarism, the adversary relationship, and lawyer advertising.

Those in the process of systematically constructing a theory of media ethics must deal with such conceptual problems in applied ethics as accountability, normativeness, individual autonomy, collective responsibility, and the logic of corporate morality. But even defining these sophisticated notions is a complicated task. Within a profession that prizes independence, for instance, accountability is a hostile idea; in order to apply it properly, one must distinguish among the public, professional colleagues, and the government without mixing categories. Norms carefully developed at the outset prevent decision makers from rationalization, but media ethics often slides from cultural pluralism into a metaphysical relativity suspicious of norms. And individual autonomy, bequeathed to the West by the eighteenth-century Enlightenment, seems unquestioned to mass media CULTURE. Or collective responsibility: on what grounds can the public as a whole legitimately be held responsible for anything not consciously chosen? Yet the communication enterprise is inherently audience- and reader-oriented, depending for its lifeblood on the supposed reality of a duty-bound public. Finally, granted that a focus on individual decision making must be replaced in media ethics by an emphasis on institutional structures, what intellectual defense, if any, can be made for an intelligible notion of corporate morality?

The earliest efforts in media ethics centered the analysis on the media system itself—codes, ombudspersons, customs of the trade, management policies, GOVERNMENT REGULATION, journals of criticism. The more advanced form of media ethics that emerged in the 1980s revolves around professional ethics generally. The inability of scholarship in media ethics to solve all the analytical difficulties involved is not just a problem with abstractions but a testimony to the fertility and complexity of the field.

See also COPYRIGHT; DISINFORMATION; FACT AND FICTION; LIBEL; MINORITIES IN THE MEDIA; PROFESSION; TELEVISION NEWS.

Bibliography. Hermann Boventer, *Ethik des Journalismus,* Konstanz, FRG, 1984; Clifford G. Christians and Catherine L. Covert, *Teaching Ethics in Journalism Education,* Hastings-on-Hudson, N.Y., 1980; Clifford G. Christians, Kim B. Rotzoll, and Mark Fackler, *Media Ethics: Cases and Moral Reasoning,* 2d ed., New York, 1987; Deni T. Eliot, ed., *Responsible Journalism,* Beverly Hills, Calif., 1986; Jacques Ellul, *Propaganda: The Formation of Men's Attitudes,* trans. by Konrad Kellen and Jean Lerner, New York, 1965; Paulo Freire, *The Politics of Education: Culture, Power, and Liberation,* trans. by Donaldo Macedo, South Hadley, Mass., 1985; H. Eugene Goodwin, *Groping for Ethics in Journalism,* Ames, Iowa, 1983; Edmund Lambeth, *Committed Journalism: An Ethic for the Profession,* Bloomington, Ind., 1986; John C. Merrill and S. Jack O'Dell, *Philosophy and Journalism,* New York, 1983; Anne Vander Meiden, ed., *Ethics and Mass Communication,* Utrecht, The Netherlands, 1980.

CLIFFORD G. CHRISTIANS

ETHNOGRAPHIC FILM

Anthropology is related to film in three ways: (1) movies can be studied as cultural artifacts; (2) motion picture footage of human behavior can be produced for research; and (3) films can be made to communicate ethnographic descriptions of a culture.

No standard definitions of ethnographic film exist. The popular assumption is that an ethnographic film is a DOCUMENTARY about "exotic" peoples. Some scholars suggest all film is ethnographic, while others wish to restrict the term to films produced by anthropologists. Scholarly literature in the field is concerned with assumed tensions between science and art; questions of accuracy, fairness, and objectivity; the appropriateness of documentary conventions to ethnography; the relationship between a written and a visual anthropology; and problems involved in collaborations between filmmakers and anthropologists.

The earliest ethnographic films were indistinguishable from theatrical "actualities"—one-reel, single-take episodes of human behavior (*see* NEWSREEL). Anthropologists, like everyone else, were fascinated with the technology of film and its promise to provide

us with an unimpeachable witness. Among the first anthropologists to produce researchable footage was the Frenchman Félix-Louis Regnault, who proposed, in 1900, that all museums should collect "moving artifacts" of human behavior for study and exhibit. Scholars, explorers, and even colonial administrators made footage for research and public display. However, the crude technology, the lack of familiarity with the equipment, and the vagueness of the filmmakers' intentions greatly limited the use of these films. In the course of time filmmaking conventions evolved that tended to conflict with scholarly needs for acceptable research data. For example, filmmakers tend to fragment and reconstitute action into synthetic sequences that suggest time relationships sometimes at variance with the photographed action. Such strategies, appropriate to fiction, created barriers between anthropologists and film professionals. *See* FACT AND FICTION.

In the 1930s MARGARET MEAD and GREGORY BATESON extended Regnault's ideas. The results of their fieldwork were "published" films like *Bathing Babies in Three Cultures* (1941), designed to make their data available for other scholars. The tradition of group research of filmed behavior championed in this way continues with Alan Lomax's CHOREOMETRICS study of DANCE as cultural behavior. In the 1950s the Institut für den Wissenschaftlichen Film in Göttingen launched its Encyclopedia Cinematographica project, which included an archive and center for the study of filmed behavior. A similar organization was established at the Smithsonian Institution in Washington, D.C.

Ethnographic film designed for the public began as part of a general educational film movement in the 1920s. Films of "exotic" peoples were produced commercially, sometimes with the assistance of anthropologists, and screened in theaters as Selected Short Subjects. For example, CHARLES PATHÉ sought the assistance of the Department of Anthropology at Harvard when producing "People and Customs of the World" in 1928.

There were a number of attempts to represent native life in feature-length theatrical films. Edward Curtis's 1914 production, *In the Land of the Head Hunters,* a romantic epic of the Kwakiutl of British Columbia, had been a box-office failure but established a precedent for ROBERT FLAHERTY's *Nanook of the North* (1922), a portrait of the struggles of an Inuit (Eskimo) family against the harsh environment of the Hudson Bay region of Canada. *Nanook's* international success prompted Paramount to finance Flaherty's second film, *Moana* (1926), and to distribute Merian C. Cooper and Ernest B. Schoedsack's *Grass* (1925), a study of the annual migration of the Bakhtari of Iran (see Figure 1).

These films caused HOLLYWOOD to become interested in productions with "exotic" locations. However, the procedures instituted at the major studios were essentially incompatible with ethnography. When Cooper and Schoedsack again departed to make *Chang* (1927) in Siam, they carried a fully approved dialogue script, ensuring fidelity to executive preconceptions. Hollywood was beginning to develop its own traditions of Asian, African, and South Sea Island adventure drama, largely ignored by the academic world as irrelevant to anthropological concerns.

A few ethnographic films were undertaken by anthropologists in the 1920s and 1930s. The rapid disappearance of native peoples as well as of the folk customs of Western cultures caused salvage ethnographic film projects to be undertaken. For example, between 1912 and 1927 the Heye Foundation supported a series of films on Native Americans produced by Owen Cattell with the assistance of Frederick Hodge. However, it was not until after World War II that substantial activity took place.

By 1952 there was sufficient interest in the field to form an International Committee on Ethnographic Film associated with UNESCO. The Festival dei Popoli in Florence, the Conference on Visual Anthropology in Philadelphia, Cinéma du Réal in Paris, and the Margaret Mead Film Festival in New York were some of the festivals organized to encourage the growth of anthropological cinema.

In Europe the pioneering work of Jean Rouch of the Musée de l'Homme brought new impetus to the field. In the early 1960s technical advances made it possible for small crews to produce synchronous sound location films. The equipment encouraged some filmmakers to record actions and events as detached observers, hoping that they were not significantly influencing the actions being followed. Rouch adopted an opposite approach: he felt that the presence of the camera could be used to instigate moments of revelation. *Chronique d'un été* (Chronicle of a Summer, 1961; see Figure 2) was produced with sociologist Edgar Morin as a CINÉMA VÉRITÉ film, drawing on ideas from both DZIGA VERTOV and Flaherty. Rouch took cameras into Paris streets for impromptu encounters in which the filmmaking process was often a part of the film. Filmmakers and equipment were in evidence in the frame, and those filmed became collaborators, even to the extent of participating in discussions of the footage that were in turn incorporated into the final version of the film.

Rouch continued his collaborative approach in a number of films made with West Africans. Some early efforts, such as *Les maîtres fous* (The Mad Masters, 1955), were criticized because of their emphasis on the bizarre. Rouch was more successful in his efforts to produce a "shared anthropology" with his so-called ethnographic fiction films, such as *Jaguar* (1965) and *Petit à petit* (Little by Little, 1968).

Figure 1. *(Ethnographic Film)* Merian C. Cooper and Ernest B. Schoedsack, *Grass*, 1925. National Film Archive, London.

A desire to let us see the world through the eyes of the natives was also the guiding principle of the Navajo Film Project (1966) of Sol Worth and John Adair in which members of the Navajo community were taught the technology of filmmaking, after which *they* determined what images of their lives should be captured on film (see Figure 3). The idea of a reflexive ethnography that actively seeks the participation of the native while acknowledging the role of the ethnographer reflects a growing concern voiced by both anthropologists and filmmakers about the ethics of documentary processes.

During the 1950s and 1960s a number of impressive ethnographic films emerged from diverse institutions and locales. *The Hunters* (1958) is the first North American ethnographic film to gain worldwide attention. It was part of John Marshall's thirty-year film study of the San (Bushmen) of southern Africa. Marshall subsequently produced dozens of African and North American films, including *Nai* (1980), a life history of a San woman, which was broadcast on U.S. public television.

Robert Gardner, a former associate of Marshall's at the Film Study Center at Harvard University, released *Dead Birds* (1964), a study of symbolic warfare among the Dani of New Guinea (see Figure 4). The film grew out of a project in which ethnographers, a novelist, and a filmmaker all described the same culture, permitting audiences to compare the presentations. Gardner later produced several films in East Africa and India and was instrumental in establishing the Program in Ethnographic Film, subsequently renamed the Society for the Anthropology of Visual Communication.

Timothy Asch, director of the University of Southern California's Center for Visual Anthropology, worked collaboratively with anthropologist Napo-

Figure 2. *(Ethnographic Film)* The meeting of Angélo and Landry. From Jean Rouch and Edgar Morin, *Chronique d'un été,* 1961. The Museum of Modern Art/Film Stills Archive.

Figure 3. *(Ethnographic Film)* Al Clah finding his own shadow. From *Intrepid Shadows,* a film by Al Clah. Navajo Film Project of Sol Worth and John Adair, 1966. The Museum of Modern Art/Film Stills Archive.

leon Chagnon on a series of films about the Yanomamo of Venezuela, among them *The Feast* (1968), *Ax Fight* (1971), and *A Man Called Bee* (1972). The films along with written ethnographies and study guides were designed to teach college undergraduates cultural anthropology.

The varied educational values of ethnographic film were exemplified in the curriculum developed by the Educational Development Corporation of Newton, Massachusetts, in "Man: A Course of Study," by Canadian anthropologist Asen Balikci and others. Films on Netsilik Eskimo life originally designed for use in a grammar-school course were repackaged for college-level courses, a commercial television special, *The Eskimo Fight for Life,* and a Canadian preschool children's series.

While most European and North American ethnographic filmmakers travel to distant places to film exotic peoples, Australians have been filming the native people of their country since the turn of the century (*see* AUSTRALASIA, TWENTIETH CENTURY). The Torres Straits Expedition of 1898 is reputed to be the first time an ethnographer took a motion picture camera into the field. The Australian government has provided one of the most consistent sources of funding for ethnographic filming found anywhere. The Australian Commonwealth Film Unit and later Film Australia have made it possible for Ian Dunlap to undertake long-term filming projects such as his "Peoples of the Western Australian Desert" series. The Australian Institute of Aboriginal Studies employs a staff ethnographic filmmaker. In that capacity Roger Sandall produced a number of films on the ceremonial life of various Australian Aboriginal peoples including *The Mulga Seed Ceremony* (1969). Recently these films have become restricted in their public showing owing to the secret quality of some of the ceremonial acts portrayed. David and Judith MacDougall are the Australian Institute's current resident filmmakers. They are noted for a series of "Turkana Conversations," including *Lorang's Way* (1979), *The Wedding Camels* (1981), and *A Wife among Wives* (1982), shot in a distinctive observational style that has caught the attention of cineastes as well as anthropologists (see Figure 5).

Figure 4. *(Ethnographic Film)* Warriors assembling for battle. From *Dead Birds,* a film by Robert Gardner, 1964. The Film Study Center, Harvard University.

The Institute for Papuan New Guinea Studies has carried on the tradition begun by its Australian colleagues and has sponsored a number of films on native life. Of special interest is *First Contact* (1983), by Bob Connolly and Robin Anderson. It employs 1930 footage of the forays of three Australian miners into remote sections of the New Guinea highlands and contemporary interviews with the two surviving miners and Papuan natives as they recall their first encounters. The film provides astonishing insights into the clash of cultures that epitomized modern world history.

With the rise of television (*see* TELEVISION HISTORY), the networks and other producing organizations gradually became a significant source of support for ethnographic film activity. In Britain, Granada's long-running series "Disappearing World" established a fruitful tradition of collaboration between field ethnographers and filmmakers, resulting in films like Brian Moser's *Last of the Cuiva* (1971), shot in eastern Colombia. BBC-TV anthropological projects have included the series "Face Values"—produced in cooperation with the Royal Anthropological Institute—and "Worlds Apart," in which pro-

Figure 5. *(Ethnographic Film)* Lorang. From *Lorang's Way,* by David and Judith MacDougall, 1979, distributed by the University of California Extension Media Center, Berkeley, Calif.

ducers Chris Curling and Melissa Llewelyn-Davies explored the impact of Leni Riefenstahl's photography in *The Southeast Nuba* (1983). In the United States the Public Broadcasting Service aired "Odyssey," a series that covered all aspects of anthropology. A similar series was maintained by Japan's Nippon TV under the title "Man," produced by Junichi Ushiyama. Television systems in many parts of the world have scheduled series for school and college use, drawing on the growing anthropological film resources.

Television has become a leading source of funds for nonfiction films of all kinds and seems likely to remain a dominant force in the future of ethnographic film. Some anthropologists will no doubt continue to make researchable footage for analytic purposes, but the preponderance of activity will be in the production of television programs that will also be used in museums and classrooms for the teaching of anthropology.

See also FILM EDITING; MOTION PICTURES; PHOTOGRAPHY; VIDEO.

Bibliography. Steve Feld and Carroll Williams, "Towards a Researchable Film Language," *Studies in the Anthropology of Visual Communication* 2 (1975): 25–32; Karl Heider, *Ethnographic Film*, Austin, Tex., 1976; Luc de Heusch, *The Cinema and Social Science: A Survey of Ethnographic and Sociological Films* (UNESCO Reports and Papers in the Social Sciences, no. 16), Paris, 1962; Paul Hockings, ed., *Principles of Visual Anthropology*, The Hague, 1975; David MacDougall, "Ethnographic Film: Failure and Promise," *Annual Review of Anthropology* 7 (1978): 405–425; Anthony R. Michaelis, *Research Films in Biology, Anthropology, Psychology, and Medicine*, Orlando, Fla., 1955; Jay Ruby, "Is an Ethnographic Film a Filmic Ethnography?" *Studies in the Anthropology of Visual Communication* 2 (1975): 104–111; Sol Worth and John Adair, *Through Navajo Eyes*, Bloomington, Ind., 1972.

JAY RUBY

ETHNOMUSICOLOGY

A discipline that combines scientific and humanistic methods of research to study human musical communication. The claims of ethnomusicology to be scientific are supported by its use of the phonograph and electrical instruments, enabling people to measure accurately the varieties of musical scales and to listen repeatedly to the subtleties and complexities of aurally transmitted PERFORMANCE. Its aims and methods are humanistic in that it does not postulate a universal definition of music but rather takes into account the socially shared perceptions and definitions of music makers. Since this includes the perceptions of ethnomusicologists, an observer may treat

Qur'anic chant as music for comparative purposes or for the study of tune-text associations, even though orthodox Muslims might not regard it as music.

Ethnomusicology arose as part of the response of people in Europe and North America to the impact of other musical systems on their listening habits and their thinking about music. A rationale for a discipline of ethnomusicology was implicitly suggested by British philologist and physicist A. J. Ellis in a paper published in 1885, shortly before Claude Debussy and other musicians were struck by the sounds of Indonesian and African music in Paris. However, the word *ethnomusicology* was not coined until the late 1940s, and the full implications of Ellis's insights were not seriously considered until the 1960s. Even in the 1980s there were still some ethnomusicologists who saw their work as "comparative musicology," a branch of the science of music concerned primarily with "ethnic" and non-Western or non-European musical systems. One of the aims of such an enterprise was considered to be that of filling gaps in the history of music (*see* MUSIC HISTORY).

Ellis's arguments and evidence challenged the idea of a unilinear evolution of music from simple to complex, reflecting people's increasingly sophisticated use of organized sound as a means of communication. He claimed in 1885 that music was a social fact and a cultural variable, and after measuring the musical scales of various nations he concluded:

The musical scale is not one, not "natural," nor even founded necessarily on the laws of the constitution of musical sound so beautifully worked out by Helmholtz, but very diverse, very artificial, and very capricious.

Ellis stressed the importance of human invention in music and suggested that musical systems are cultural systems whose organizing principles are linked to other modes of social activity. Their impact on social life depends on how people relate them to different kinds of experience.

MAX WEBER came to similar conclusions about relationships between systems of ideas and social and musical organization in *The Rational and Social Foundations of Music* (1921), in which he claimed that European music was rationalized from within the tone system. He argued that the concern with harmonic distances, as distinct from real distances on instruments (such as equidistance between frets or flute holes), was a logical application to music of the scientific attitude that emerged at the time of the RENAISSANCE (*see* MUSIC THEORIES).

Erich von Hornbostel and colleagues in the Berlin Phonogram Archive (1906–1933) produced comparative studies suggesting that musical systems had not evolved independently of general patterns of cultural history and that European music could no longer be regarded as the pinnacle of human musical invention. Not only were there other musical systems of comparable value and complexity, but also so-called European innovations, such as polyphony and the use of discords for special effects, had been invented independently at other times and in other places.

The development of ethnomusicology is inconceivable without the invention of the phonograph, which helped to transform speculations about the simplicity and complexity of musical structures into statements of fact (*see* SOUND RECORDING). Repeated listening enabled scholars' ears to become sensitized to the subtleties of unfamiliar patterns of sound. Music that was too complicated to note down by ear could be transcribed and analyzed with some degree of objectivity. Myths about the uniformity, spontaneity, or backwardness of aurally transmitted musics were dispelled. Research was further enhanced by the development of the portable tape recorder in the 1950s and 1960s and by the use of sonagrams and the invention of the melograph, which produced accurate visual displays of melodic line that could be compared with aural transcriptions and with the observations of performers and listeners.

The composers Percy Grainger and Béla Bartók were among the first to carry out systematic fieldwork with a phonograph. In 1908 Grainger produced transcriptions that revealed the creativity of individual British folksingers, and Bartók showed in the 1930s that the individuality of Hungarian folk musicians must also be set in a framework of systematic regional styles and genres that corresponded with social and cultural variations (*see* GENRE).

Studies of recorded performances, and of different musical genres in their social and cultural contexts, have shown that the quality and complexity of musical communication cannot be usefully explained by dividing the world's musics into oral and written or into categories such as folk, popular, and art. There is as much variation, or improvisation, in performances of the same written score by different orchestras and conductors as there is stability in repeated performances of a piece in an oral tradition. *See* MUSIC COMPOSITION AND IMPROVISATION; ORAL CULTURE.

Similarly, musical skills are not required any less for folk and popular music than for art music; and even if popular music were music that did not seek "to appeal to refined or classical taste" (as defined in the *Oxford English Dictionary*), this would not determine the degree of refinement of those who listen to it (*see* MUSIC, FOLK AND TRADITIONAL; MUSIC, POPULAR).

It has been claimed that certain patterns of rhythm, tone, melody, or timbre can induce physiological responses in culturally attuned performers and listeners or even in those with no such preparation. Indeed, music can be profoundly moving by means of the resonances that people can establish between tone stress and motion on the one hand and the nervous tension and motor impulse of their bodies on the other. But no music has power in itself. Music has no effect on the body or consequences for social action unless its sounds and circumstances can be related to a coherent set of ideas about self and other and to bodily feelings.

Research into the differential effects of the music of possession cults on people's attainment of trance states has shown that there are no direct causal links between musical performance and trance, because there are many other necessary symbols that relate altered somatic states to experiences of daily life. For example, performance of the right music and at the right tempo might be essential for bodily transformation, but only members of cult groups could be possessed, and even then only when they were dancing in the right place (e.g., near the home of their ancestors' lineage).

The chief task of ethnomusicology, then, is to discover how people make musical sense of what they define as music by performing, listening, and talking. Composing need not be treated as a separate activity, because musical composition is an aspect of musical performance (*see* MUSIC PERFORMANCE). It is of comparatively recent origin as a distinct category of music making, a product of the division of labor in society rather than a consequence of fundamentally different musical abilities.

Ethnomusicological discovery is best attained by context-sensitive fieldwork designed to reveal the processes by which music is made and given MEANING by different individuals in different social contexts. What ultimately account for stability and change in patterns of music making are the aesthetic force of musical symbols and people's decisions to invoke them and place them in a social context—the tensions between inner, affective states and the ways in which cultural systems enable people to make sense of them and follow them through. It is for these reasons that some ethnomusicologists have become increasingly interested both in cognitive and affective aspects of musical communication that transcend cultural conventions and in the possibility of innate musical capabilities or of a specifically musical intelligence that could be a primary modeling system of thought, as with speech.

The work of Ellis and subsequent research into the workings of "unnatural" scales, intervals, and musical systems have shown that analyses of music must not be based on tonal relations determined by the laws of acoustics, unless those laws are explicitly invoked as part of the system. However, it is possible that some of those features of human musicality that have been identified by psychologists in the context of Western music making are in fact part of the innate musical intelligence of human beings. For instance, it has been suggested that people might seek out tonal centers in melodies and clusters of tones whether or not they were explicitly employed in a given musical system. If there are such universal capabilities, they could help to explain the musical attraction of certain types of contemporary pop music in many parts of the world. Future research in ethnomusicology will need to explore how individuals mediate between innate musical capabilities in their bodies and the musical conventions of different societies.

See also CANTOMETRICS; SONG.

Bibliography. John Blacking, *How Musical Is Man?* Seattle, Wash., 1973; A. J. Ellis, "On the Musical Scales of Various Nations," *Journal of the Society of Arts* 33 (1885): 485–527; Steven Feld, *Sound and Sentiment: Birds, Weeping, Poetics, and Song in Kaluli Expression*, Philadelphia, 1982; Alan P. Merriam, *The Anthropology of Music*, Evanston, Ill., 1964; Gilbert Rouget, *Music and Trance* (La musique et la transe), trans. by Derek Coltman, Chicago, 1985; Max Weber, *The Rational and Social Foundations of Music* (Die rationalen und soziologischen Grundlagen der Musik), trans. and ed. by Don Martindale, Johannes Riedel, and Gertrude Neuwirth, Carbondale, Ill., 1958.

JOHN BLACKING

ETHNOPOETICS

Study of the verbal arts in a worldwide range of languages and cultures. Primary attention is given to the vocal-auditory channel of communication in which speaking, chanting, or singing voices give shape to proverbs, riddles, curses, laments, praises, prayers, prophecies, public announcements, and narratives. The aim is not only to analyze and interpret oral performances but also to make them directly accessible through transcriptions and translations that display their qualities as works of ART.

History

Ethnopoetics originated in the United States among poets such as David Antin, Jerome Rothenberg, and Gary Snyder, all of whom had training in anthropology or LINGUISTICS; Nathaniel Tarn, whose poetic career was preceded by an anthropological career under the name E. Michael Mendelson; and anthropologists and linguists with experience in writing POETRY, including Stanley Diamond, Dell Hymes, and Dennis Tedlock. The term *ethnopoetics* was first used in print in 1968 by Rothenberg to name his editorial department in the poetry magazine *Stony*

Brook. In 1970 he joined Tedlock in founding *Alcheringa/Ethnopoetics*, a magazine featuring transcripts, translations, and tear-out disc recordings of performances by indigenous verbal artists from Africa, Asia, Oceania, and the Americas.

Philosophy and Methodology

Practitioners of ethnopoetics treat the relationship between PERFORMANCE and text as a field for experimentation. Texts that were taken down in the era of handwritten dictation and published as prose are reformatted and retranslated in order to reveal their poetic features as defined by such formal devices as initial particles, native pattern numbers, syntactic structures, and parallelism (*see* ORAL HISTORY). In the case of a SOUND RECORDING, transcripts and translations serve not only as listening guides but also as scores for new performances. The richest single GENRE is storytelling, in which speakers depart from third-person NARRATIVE in order to take the parts of the characters. In the process they provide dramatized examples of everything from an ordinary CONVERSATION to a shamanic power SONG, while at the same time simulating voices that differentiate characters according to social position, personality, and emotional state.

An ethnopoetic score follows the original timing of a recorded performance, dividing the words into lines according to the alternation of sounds and silences. This makes it possible to distinguish rapid passages (with little pausing) from slow ones (with much), and it becomes apparent that pauses often create suspense by cutting across verse or sentence structures rather than coinciding with them. In the following passage translated from Zuni (an indigenous language of New Mexico), three sentences are broken into eight tension-filled lines. The pauses between lines average three-quarters of a second, with two dots indicating a two-second pause. The story concerns a dancer who became possessed by his MASK and tried to run away:

They brought him back, and when they
tried to unmask him
the mask
was stuck
to his face.
He was changing over.
. .
When they tried to unmask the young man, some of his
flesh peeled off.

In contrast with surprising events like this one, actions carried out according to a plan may be described with a series of one-sentence lines. In the following example, translated from Haya (a language of Tanzania), a woman is preparing for a journey into the wilderness:

She grinds a little millet for herself.
She makes it into porridge.
She finishes it.
She wraps it.
She finishes wrapping—
she goes and forges for herself nine arrowheads.
She ties them up.

Just as the Zuni passage had one line (the sixth) whose completeness momentarily relieved tension, so this passage has one line (the fifth) that introduces a tense moment into an otherwise orderly account. Instead of ending this line with a falling intonation, indicating a complete sentence, the narrator leaves it hanging with a rise (indicated by a dash) just before telling us that the woman knows not only how to prepare food but also how to make weapons.

Scoring also requires attention to changes of amplitude. In this next excerpt a Zuni narrator emphasizes the climactic third line not by loudness but by a decrease in amplitude, thus preserving the delicacy of the moment of birth:

She sat down
by a juniper tree and strained her muscles:
(softly) the little baby came out.

Other ways of giving emphasis are illustrated by a dialogue from a Yucatec Maya story in which a bereaved man consults with his guardian spirit. In the first and third lines a loud voice (shown in capitals) dramatizes the man's predicament and the forthrightness of the guardian's response; in the last two lines a slow, precise enunciation (in italics) and a focusing of loudness on isolated words give the guardian's further remarks a didactic force:

"What shall I do, small friend? My wife was CARRIED
    AWAY.
My eyes are sad since it happened."
"WOULD YOU LIKE TO GO SEE HER?"
"I'd like to go see so I could find where she is."
"Good, fine. *You'll have to go see*
BUT there is a WAY to see. You are going to SEE, friend."

Conventional transcripts make oral performances seem more repetitive than literary compositions, but ethnopoetic scores reveal that repeated words may be differentiated by changes in voicing. In the Zuni excerpt below, three identically worded phrases contrast not only because one of them is loud, but also because they are divided into three descending pitch levels by a chantlike rendition:

And ALL THE PEOPLE WHO HAD COME
        KILLED THE DEER
                    killed the deer
                            killed the deer.

Some dimensions of performance, including tones of voice, SOUND EFFECTS, and gestures, require parenthetical descriptive notes like the ones in dramatic

scripts (*see* GESTURE). Whatever a score may encompass, the notion of a definitive text has no place in ethnopoetics. Just as any translation from one language to another suggests alternative translations, so any passage from sound to visible marks suggests others. Linguistics avoids this problem by narrowing its attention to the normative side of performance, recognizing only such features as can be accounted for by general rules. Ethnopoetics remains open to the creative side of performance, valuing features that may be rare or even unique to a particular artist or occasion.

See also INSULT; ORAL POETRY; POETICS; PROVERB; RIDDLE; TRANSLATION, THEORIES OF.

Bibliography. *Alcheringa/Ethnopoetics* (New York) nos. 1–5 (old series), 1970–1973, and (Boston) Vols. 1–4 (new series), 1975–1980; David Antin, *Talking at the Boundaries*, New York, 1976; Allan F. Burns, *An Epoch of Miracles: Oral Literature of the Yucatec Maya*, Austin, Tex., 1983; Dell Hymes, *"In Vain I Tried to Tell You": Essays in Native American Ethnopoetics*, Philadelphia, 1981; Jerome Rothenberg, ed., *Shaking the Pumpkin: Traditional Poetry of the Indian North Americas*, New York, 1972; idem, *Technicians of the Sacred: A Range of Poetries from Africa, America, Asia, Europe, and Oceania*, 2d ed., rev. and expanded, Berkeley, Calif., 1985; Peter Seitel, *See So That We May See: Performances and Interpretations of Traditional Tales from Tanzania*, Bloomington, Ind., 1980; Dennis Tedlock, *Finding the Center: Narrative Poetry of the Zuni Indians*, New York, 1972, reprint Lincoln, Neb., 1978; idem, *The Spoken Word and the Work of Interpretation*, Philadelphia, 1983.

DENNIS TEDLOCK

ETHOLOGY

The biological study of animal behavior, encompassing questions of causation, development, function, and evolution. This very broad conception masks the extent to which modern ethology grew from a more narrowly proportioned field in which naturalistic observation of free-living animals (in the wild or in relatively unrestrained captivity) was informed by and gave form to notions of instinct. From the outset, concern with communication—the analysis of animal social behavior in terms of the sending and receiving of signals—has been in the forefront of ethological interest.

Classical Ethology

The founding of ethology as a school dates from the 1930s and was the achievement of Konrad Lorenz in Austria. Lorenz acknowledged a number of influences, beginning with CHARLES DARWIN. Darwin's theory of evolution by natural selection gave ethology a basic framework. More particularly relevant to behavior study was his discussion of emotional expression in animals and humans, which showed how movement and posture patterns can be interpreted in motivational, functional, and evolutionary terms as means of communication; and his theory of sexual selection, which provided an explanation for the extravagant amounts of effort expended in reproductive competition and display in numerous species. British ornithology made important contributions in the early years of this century, especially Eliot Howard's observations on bird territoriality and the uses of song and other displays in relation to it, and Julian Huxley's conception of how movements can be modified in evolution to serve a signal function, a process he called *ritualization* (the term ethologists still use for it). At about the same time, Charles Whitman in the United States and Oskar Heinroth in Germany independently recognized that behavior patterns can be as useful as anatomical features for characterizing taxonomic groups. Jacob von Uexküll, another German, presented a view of the animal as confined phenomenally to a world bounded by its sensory receptivity and motor capacity, which vary widely among different kinds of animals. Wallace Craig, an associate of Whitman, drew attention to behavior sequences consisting of actions that vary with circumstance in such ways as to bring the animal into a situation sufficient to elicit a specific stereotyped motor pattern: *appetitive behavior* leading to and apparently aimed at performance of a *consummatory act.*

From these and other sources, and observations and conjectures of his own, Lorenz drew a picture of animal behavior as, to a large extent, innately structured and instinctively controlled. Central to his reasoning was the contention that the principles applying in comparative anatomy apply in comparative behavior study as well; for example, the kind of correspondence that makes us call the proximal bone of the forelimbs of all tetrapods—be they frogs, flamingos, foxes, or Finns—by the same name (humerus) has its counterpart in patterns of behavior possessed by related species. Such correspondence, known as homology, has its best behavioral manifestations in postures and movements that serve as social signals. In his observations of ducks, Lorenz found that each species has a repertoire of such displays. The forms of these displays are species-specific in detail yet similar enough across species for lines of correspondence to be drawn and the composition of a core repertoire shared by the whole group to be deduced.

Complementing this evidence for a historical evolutionary interpretation of species-characteristic behavior was evidence of adaptive correlation: variation between related species in homologous patterns concordant with differences in the habitat conditions or life histories of the species concerned; and resemblances between unrelated species in behavior patterns not homologous but answering to similar functional requirements ("analogous" forms resulting from "convergent" adaptation). Whether in terms of phyletic origin or adaptation resulting from natural selection, the evolutionary interpretations of behavioral comparisons suggested a genetic basis. This was part of what Lorenz meant when he described the behavior with which he was concerned as innate.

But innate also has an ontogenetic connotation, which is that development of an individual's features proceeds on the basis of hereditary specification, independent of any formative contribution from experience or interaction with the environment. The patterns of behavior upon which Lorenz concentrated were so constant in form throughout a species that he assumed both the genetic and the ontogenetic senses of innate applied to them—indeed, that the two senses entailed each other. This constancy of form also seemed to be due solely to neural connection patterns, like reflexes. Unlike reflexes, however, the behavior considered by Lorenz to be instinctive was unresponsive to repeated stimulation for a time after performance and then became progressively more easy to elicit again as further time passed. At a certain point the animal appeared compelled to go in search of the eliciting stimulation, to embark on appetitive behavior aimed at release of the consummatory act. This buildup and collapse in readiness to perform instinctive behavior suggested accumulation and discharge of some internal motivating agency. Lorenz postulated generation and expenditure of "action-specific energy" and likened the mechanism of its operation to a hydraulic system.

Another important feature of these instinctive "fixed-action patterns" was their stimulus specificity. Lorenz, and later the Dutch zoologist Niko Tinbergen, demonstrated that such behavior is tuned to simple but specific features of the normally adequate stimulus object, such as a mark it carries or part of its shape. From the point of view of communication, the most interesting of these *sign stimuli* or *releasers* (as such effective fragments of stimulus objects were variously called) were those presented by "social companions." Here it was apparent that specific social responsiveness can be tuned selectively to signals emanating from individuals of the same species. These signals can be either passively presented (e.g., a color patch or a distinctive odor) or actively presented (e.g., a display posture or vocalization) or some combination of the two. Experiments showed that much social interaction consists of sequences in which the individuals alternate as signalers and responders. This led Lorenz to believe that social behavior in animals is often a mosaic of releaser/response couplings rather than an integration based on a unified internal representation of the social companion.

This view was reinforced by the study of social orientation governed by *imprinting*. Some social responsiveness, especially among birds, was found to lack a specific stimulus prior to the first performance. The particular stimulus seemed to be fixed by whatever object happened to elicit this initial performance, and that object became an individual's releaser or objective for that kind of behavior from then on. Normally imprinting is to an appropriate social companion. However, Lorenz reported cases for which the imprinting for different social responses occurred at different times (*critical periods*). By experimental manipulation, an animal could be made to be socially attentive to several different kinds of inappropriate objects. Lorenz claimed that this way of acquiring social discrimination differed from familiar forms of learning from experience in being confined to a narrowly limited critical period of development, in being irreversible, and in requiring no association with reward (*reinforcement*).

Like Lorenz, Tinbergen began making ethological observations in the 1930s, and their ideas converged. However, Tinbergen was dissatisfied with the single-level, mosaic structure of Lorenz's causal scheme. His own student, Gerard Baerends, showed how the nest-provisioning behavior of a digger wasp can be viewed as hierarchically organized: the work proceeds in steps, and at each transition point the animal has alternative courses of action open to it, the one taken being decided by the situation encountered. Tinbergen saw that this pattern applied to the organization of the major functional categories of behavior in general. For example, the reproductive behavior of a fish, such as the male three-spined stickleback, divides into territorial fighting, nest building, mating, and care of eggs; each of these activities in turn consists of several components, such as attacking, fleeing, and threatening in the case of fighting; and each of these actions can be broken down further into the particular movements of the moment—turns, fin positions, and the like. According to Tinbergen's observations, behavioral sequences typically follow this kind of order, beginning with appetitive behavior common to a class of functionally related activities, and proceeding, according to the sign stimuli encountered, to increasingly specific selections of appetitive action, and terminating in the fixed-action pattern of one of the constituent consummatory acts. He pictured the underlying mechanism as an arrangement of hierarchically ordered control centers, with, for example, a single center for reproductive behavior at the top; generating "motivational impulses," which it feeds to centers for fighting, nest building, and so on at the level below it; and each of these feeding

Figure 1. *(Ethology)* Konrad Lorenz, 1973. UPI/Bettmann Newsphotos.

into centers for its alternative action patterns at a lower level again. Outlet from each center at each level was governed by a gate tuned to open in response to the sign stimuli specific to the behavior in question.

Tinbergen followed Lorenz in thinking of the working of this mechanism in hydraulic terms, but instead of many action-specific energies he postulated a single kind of motivational excitation, which descended the hierarchy according to which gate was opened at each level, and was discharged in performance of a terminal consummatory act at the bottom. Also, in contrast to Lorenz's view that only consummatory acts should be referred to as instinctive, and since they and they only were supposed to combine all the attributes of instinct, Tinbergen preferred to regard the whole hierarchical system of a major functional category of behavior as an instinct. He had this sense in mind when he used the term in the title of the book in which he presented his motivational theory as the centerpiece, along with behavioral and physiological evidence that he felt supported it.

The Study of Instinct (1951) can be regarded as the culmination of ethology's classical phase of theory building. In addition to the concern with causal mechanism, Tinbergen discussed the functions and evolution of behavior, which was to some extent independent of the causes. Indeed, a great deal of the ethological research at this time was less directly concerned with theoretical issues than with observation and experiment aimed at comprehensive descriptions of species' behavior repertoires (*ethograms*) and understanding of what ends the behavior served and how it might have evolved. This was especially true for communication behavior. Comparisons of the forms of display postures and movements, of the situations in which they occurred, and of their sequential associations with other behavior—within species and between related species—gave evidence for their interpretations as "derived activities." Thus many such displays appear to be ritualized versions of the initial parts (so-called intention movements) of locomotory, attacking, or fleeing movements.

Another possible evolutionary antecedent of signal display is *displacement activity:* the apparently irrelevant movements many animals make when they are subject to conflicting tendencies such as attacking and fleeing. For example, many displays signifying that an animal is hesitating between alternative courses of action appear to be derived from grooming or preening movements, which are common as displacement activities in such situations. In yet other cases the display behavior appears to have become causally "emancipated" from the conditions governing its supposed unritualized occurrence; an example here is the courtship preening and drinking movements of some species of ducks, which occur in the absence of conflict conditions.

Perhaps the most intriguing example of this early ethological work on signal analysis was Austrian biologist Karl von Frisch's study of communication in honey bees, the highlight of which was discovery of a kind of symbolic representation. Worker bees returning to their hive after finding food (or a suitable place to set up a new hive if division of the colony is imminent) more than two hundred meters away perform movements on the vertical surface of the comb that convey the location of the find to other bees. This "waggle dance" consists of a figure eight, during the central straight run of which the bee wags its abdomen from side to side. Von Frisch found that the angle of this wagging run with respect to gravity corresponds with the angle of the direction to the location with respect to the position of the sun (azimuth), and that the distance to the location is given by the number of waggles or the time taken to complete a circuit of the figure eight. Adding to this extraordinary story, von Frisch discovered that bees allow for change of position of the sun with time, so that if their return to the hive is interrupted, their eventual dancing takes account of how much the sun

will have shifted in the interval. Moreover, the bees do not even have to have a view of the sun to know its position, for they can tell where it is from an ability to perceive the pattern of polarization of light from a portion of the sky. *See also* INSECTS, SOCIAL.

Reaction to Classical Ethology

The spokesmen for classical ethology took a critical stance toward other schools of animal behavior study, such as behaviorism in the United States with its emphasis on learning and European animal psychology with its insistence on the ultimate inaccessibility of animal minds to scientific analysis. Lorenz in particular was so emphatically outspoken that reaction was inevitable. For example, many comparative and physiological psychologists in the United States criticized ethology for drawing ontogenetic conclusions from evolutionary or functional premises without doing the necessary developmental study; for constructing hypothetical physiological machinery from features of the behavior it was designed to explain rather than from physiological fact, some of which was already known to be inconsistent with ethological motivational theory; and for giving insufficient consideration to the qualitative differences in the behavioral capacities of different kinds of organisms.

Dissatisfaction with classical theory also arose within ethology, partly because of the outside criticism and partly because some of its own discoveries called aspects of the theory into question. For instance, Erich von Holst, the most physiologically sophisticated of the classical ethologists, undermined the idea that consumption of behavioral energy is what consummates behavioral sequences by demonstrating the importance of *reafference*—the stimulus changes experienced by an animal as a consequence of its own movement. In particular, he showed how the reafference compares to that "forecast" at the beginning of the movement in determining whether the animal continues in what it was doing or switches to something else. No such role for sensory feedback was included in the motivational schemes of Lorenz and Tinbergen. As evidence accumulated, however, the stimulation resulting from movement rather than performance of the movement per se took on an increasing significance.

Pressure to pin terminology down to observable magnitudes led ethologists in the 1950s to abandon speculative concepts like action-specific energy and motivational impulses and replace them with measures such as behavioral tendency, which were anchored in estimates of probabilities of occurrence. Statistical procedures such as factor analysis were applied to the sequential and covariant patterning of behavior. The once clean lines of ethological theory

ETHOLOGY / 121

became buried under new data, which showed, among other hard lessons, that causal accounts of behavior in terms of unitary instinctive motivation were too crude to come to grips usefully with the variety of ways in which behavior varied.

Developmental study such as that of the British ethologist Peter Marler and his associates of vocal ontogeny in songbirds showed how the interplay between heredity and experience can be far more intricate, much more a matter of complementary contribution than an exclusive dichotomy between innate and learned. Further work on imprinting showed that the limits to the time when experience can take effect are more flexible than the concept of critical period assumed, and so led to adoption of the looser concept of *sensitive period;* that the claim of irreversibility has to be qualified according to the manner in which it is assessed; that reinforcement can be involved; and generally that imprinting has more continuity with other kinds of learning, especially perceptual learning, than was initially supposed. Other work on communication behavior was mainly either descriptive of order in social interaction or aimed at finding principles that would generate that order. The 1950s and 1960s saw ethology dividing its energies among a disparate number of areas of research, in which it increasingly joined forces with neighboring disciplines, such as physiology, experimental psychology, and ecology. The distinguishing characteristics of ethology became blurred; no longer was there a theoretical integration of the sort presented by the theses of *The Study of Instinct.*

Sociobiology

A new theoretical synthesis of animal behavior study was claimed in the 1970s, but its foremost spokesman, U.S. biologist Edward O. Wilson, represented it as an alternative to ethology rather than a part of it. Sociobiology proposed a combination of population genetics and behavioral ecology as the basis for explanation of all aspects of social behavior and social organization in evolutionary terms. In fact, the sociobiological orientation arose within ethology, where it had always been latent. It caused a surge of renewed interest in issues concerning the adaptive significance of behavioral phenomena that had seemed inconsistent with natural selection ever since Darwin had brought his theory to bear on them.

Foremost among these problems was altruism. Any genetically based tendency for an animal to act in another's interest and thus increase the other's chances for survival and reproduction (its "fitness") at the expense of its own should, according to natural selection as originally conceived, be eliminated from the population, because helped individuals will tend to leave more progeny than the helpers. In spite of

this, altruistic behavior is not uncommon. One of the answers seems to be kin selection, which applies to altruism among genetically related individuals. By promoting the reproduction of a relative, an animal can add to the copies of the kinds of genes it replicates by its own reproduction (to the extent that the two animals have genes in common) and so increase its own "inclusive fitness." Kin selection theory has led to much new insight into social patterns, such as the finding that in some species individuals can distinguish close kin from others and thus preferentially distribute their aid.

This effort to relate behavioral characteristics to genetic advantage has also encompassed communication. For example, assessments of the costs and benefits of alternative strategies in aggressive encounters have been found to favor threat display over unconditional attack or surrender. The time and effort devoted to courtship signaling by males in numerous species as well as the elaborateness and risk-exposing conspicuousness of the behavior in many cases have apparently evolved as advertisements of reproductive potential as a consequence of assessment by females prior to choosing a mate (a form of Darwinian sexual selection).

This view of signal function has led to the controversial idea that animals use signals to try to manipulate one another, rather than to inform one another. Since informing can be one way of manipulating, this may be a false dichotomy. And where the possibility of DECEPTION exists, one can ask whether it applies only to a recipient's being misled by a signal or if it extends to the proposition that a signaler acted deliberately to deceive. The latter implies intentionality, which most ethologists shy away from as too mentalistic a notion to merit scientific consideration. However, U.S. biologist Donald Griffin has reopened "the question of animal awareness" and thus has brought to the fore something he calls *cognitive ethology.* Several lines of evidence, ranging from chimpanzees to honeybees, have revealed that animals can be cognizant of much more about their social and physical worlds than used to be thought possible (*see* COGNITION, ANIMAL). This research has led to claims of syntactic structure, semantic content, and intentionality in animal signaling. Comparison between animal signaling systems and human LANGUAGE has also received a boost, but the more substantial contribution of the ethological perspective to the human case has been the attention it has drawn to NONVERBAL COMMUNICATION as part of the emergence of human ethology.

Concern with the syntactics, semantics, and pragmatics of animal communication is rife with controversial issues, yet it makes the point that more than the evolutionary questions of sociobiology must be taken into consideration in a fully developed biology of animal behavior. As Tinbergen added, after he had defined ethology in terms of the four questions of causation, ontogeny, function, and evolution, the mission of the science is to give equal attention to each of them, and to their integration.

See also ANIMAL COMMUNICATION; ANIMAL SIGNALS; ANIMAL SONG.

Bibliography. Donald R. Griffin, *Animal Thinking*, Cambridge, Mass., 1984; Robert A. Hinde, *Ethology*, New York, 1982; David McFarland, ed., *The Oxford Companion to Animal Behavior*, Oxford and New York, 1982; W. John Smith, *The Behavior of Communicating: An Ethological Approach*, Cambridge, Mass., 1977; Niko Tinbergen, *The Study of Instinct*, Oxford, 1951.

COLIN G. BEER

EVALUATION RESEARCH

In the context of communication projects or programs, the term *evaluation* refers to all those systematic information-gathering activities that close the communication loop and potentially improve the effectiveness of message delivery (*see* MODELS OF COMMUNICATION). These activities may include identifying levels of prior knowledge and the characteristics of usual practice among intended recipients, assessing the readability or clarity of messages, measuring changes in behavior (intended or not) that are associated with message delivery, or assessing the impact of an intervention in alleviating the problem it was designed to address.

This latter type of problem has been the focus of a good deal of project evaluation work (*see* DEVELOPMENT COMMUNICATION). Traditionally, evaluation has been an after-the-fact, or summative, exercise designed to determine whether a project or program attained its objectives and whether the outcome could be attributed unequivocally to project or program activities. The goal was to obtain reliable information that would allow decisions to be made about future support for the present activity or about new, related activities. Consistent with this viewpoint, choice of methodology became crucial as more threats to the validity of conclusions about causes were uncovered. Thus during the 1960s and 1970s much work was conducted on developing experimental and quasi-experimental designs that could increase the capacity of evaluators to draw conclusions about causality.

There are other consequences to the view that evaluation should address summative questions. Such evaluations are usually carried out by outside consultants, people other than those whose work is being evaluated. The outsiders are expected to contribute not only their particular skills in data gathering and analysis, but also the requisite objectivity, much in the manner of basic scientific research. In this context the relationship between project staff and evaluators is often adversarial, and the dominant mode is fault-finding.

Evaluations designed to uncover causal relationships also require a stable, well-functioning project and quite large sample sizes, particularly when the expected effects are likely to be small. Thus they are expensive and tend to be conducted quite late in the life history of a project.

Formative Evaluation

While always a feature of the evaluation landscape, formative evaluation has been gaining increasing recognition as a valuable tool for project personnel and, in many cases, a more productive use of scarce evaluation resources. Procedures to gather information about a process or product to improve quality or effectiveness are used routinely in the communications field for materials that are meant to influence or teach (although sometimes they are called *field testing*, rather than formative evaluation). However, their systematic use in all stages of project planning, design, and implementation is relatively new.

Case studies. Two cases in which formative evaluation has made an important and significant contribution to project design and implementation will illustrate the point. Both were funded by the U.S. Agency for International Development. The Mass Media and Health Practices Project was implemented in Honduras and Gambia; the Radio Mathematics Project was implemented in Nicaragua and replicated in Thailand. These two cases exemplify the variety of approaches that can be taken to gathering evaluative information. While by no means unique, they represent two substantial and well-funded efforts that produced, on the one hand, successful communication campaigns and, on the other, a successful instructional program, with the help of intensive information-gathering activities.

The Mass Media and Health Practices Project (MMHP), conducted by the Academy for Educational Development, designed and implemented a program to conduct public health education aimed at the treatment of infant diarrhea. The core of the program involved teaching mothers to prepare and administer oral-rehydration fluid. The academy used formative evaluation in three ways during project planning and implementation: (1) It conducted pre-program research, to assist planners to understand thoroughly the problem that the educational campaign would address and the cultural context in which the campaign would take place. (2) It pretested materials, including posters, radio programs, and training materials, with members of the appropriate target audience for accuracy, comprehension, and acceptability. And (3), the processes of production, distribution, use, and consumption of educational materials were systematically monitored and analyzed to create a permanent feedback loop. The information gathered measured incremental learning among target audiences and identified weaknesses in project implementation sufficiently early so that action could be taken to correct them.

A variety of qualitative and quantitative research methods were used to gather information.

1. *Focus group interview.* This practical and efficient technique for eliciting reactions was adapted from the field of marketing (*see* CONSUMER RESEARCH). The goal is to encourage the expression of as many ideas as possible and to stimulate participant interaction. Questions are open-ended, and the interviewer must be able to ask follow-up questions that probe, without leading the group toward predetermined answers. MMHP used focus groups of rural mothers to discuss traditional beliefs and practices about diarrhea and to generate the vocabulary used by rural people for objects and concepts to be incorporated in the project's educational materials.

2. *In-depth interview.* This is a one-on-one interview, usually structured around a carefully designed set of open-ended questions. The in-depth interview serves a purpose similar to that of the focus group—to probe ATTITUDES and feelings among a small number of respondents and to develop hypotheses—but it avoids the peer influence and pressure of a group setting. MMHP used the technique in one setting to probe health workers' understanding of diarrheal disease and in another to explore the concept of dehydration with rural mothers.

3. *Pretest interview.* A one-on-one or group interview is structured around specific materials. Questions are directed at determining what people see or hear in the material, how well they understand its message, and how well they like it. This technique was used extensively in developing radio spots and printed materials.

4. *Survey.* The survey is the standard method for systematically gathering quantifiable information by aggregating responses from a sample of individuals. MMHP used surveys to assess audience performance on such variables as knowledge and practice of oral-rehydration therapy, radio listenership, and awareness of the project's educational messages. *See* OPINION MEASUREMENT.

5. *Central-location intercept interview.* This special type of survey is usually conducted at some popular place within the community—for example, a street corner, market, or clinic. The questions are very short, usually requiring only yes or no or other simple answers. Intercept interviews allow the researcher to question large numbers of people quickly and require little interpretation or subjective analysis. MMHP found this technique particularly useful for pretesting simple graphic materials.

6. *Observation.* This research technique was used by MMHP during the preprogram stage, when trained observers spent several days in rural households observing child-care practices, particularly the care of sick children. As a corroborative technique complementary to other data sources *during* the campaign, observers again observed children with diarrhea and the care they received.

7. *Behavioral trials.* Such trials provide detailed information on unexpected problems and are essential for validating the potential practicality of new manual skills being promoted. MMHP conducted trials of mixing oral-rehydration fluid during the preprogram research to expose any difficulties rural mothers might have in mixing the fluid in their actual home conditions.

8. *Product preference trials.* Product preference trials seek to identify consumer preferences among a range of products and product packaging available for a particular need. MMHP asked rural mothers to identify the types of medicines they preferred (among tablets, injections, liquids, etc.) to help determine how best to package and promote oral-rehydration fluid.

9. *Broadcast monitoring.* Two types of broadcast monitoring were used. During preprogram research, project researchers monitored the number and strength of all radio station signals reaching the target area, to validate reports of radio listening by survey respondents and to guide the choice of stations for best broadcast coverage. Broadcasts of project radio spots were monitored to ensure that radio stations were adhering to the schedules agreed on with project personnel.

Each of the above techniques required slightly different skills, provided significantly different kinds of information, and was more appropriate at certain stages of the formative evaluation process than at others. The special value of combining several of these methods is in the variety of perspectives they bring to bear and the cross-validation they provide.

The Radio Mathematics Project (RMP) developed a substantially different formative evaluation model in response to the requirement to produce a daily radio lesson. The project developed full-year courses in primary-school mathematics using what has become known as *interactive radio instruction,* in which students listening to radio lessons are expected to participate actively, responding aloud, writing in their notebooks, or working with specific materials. The course of lessons, about 150 for a school year, carries the major burden of instruction and thus differs conceptually from educational broadcasts that are meant to provide enrichment or supplemental information to students (see AUDIOVISUAL EDUCATION).

In educational broadcasting for formal education (see EDUCATIONAL TELEVISION) the goals and problems are quite different from those for the kind of nonformal education undertaken by MMHP. The main goal of interactive radio instruction is the development of specific skills. The in-school audience is captive, relatively homogeneous, and can be expected to have heard most of the prior lessons in the series. Thus, in several ways, the problems of the producer of formal educational programs are less severe than those of the producer of nonformal broadcasts, who must appeal to a casual listening audience with a wide variety of backgrounds.

On the other hand, the producer of programs for formal education has problems not often found in nonformal education. He or she must impart skills that can be taught only by a structured sequence of carefully designed, integrated instructional units that build slowly but continuously toward a set of well-defined objectives. Skills such as arithmetic, GRAMMAR, READING, or LANGUAGE cannot be taught in small independent units that can be broadcast in random order; the component skills must be taught in a specific sequence, and instruction cannot proceed effectively unless the audience has mastered preceding lessons. Furthermore, adequate mastery of skills can only be expected after both effective instruction and ample practice over time.

To accommodate itself to these characteristics of educational programming, the RMP developed a system of lesson production whereby programs could be continuously adapted to the changing characteristics of the audience, even though the producers could not predict in advance the exact rates at which changes in the listeners would occur. In this system, which is modeled after industrial feedback processes, programs are produced just before broadcast, and the reactions of the listening audience are continuously monitored to determine the direction and amount of change taking place. The information collected is used in the planning and production of upcoming programs in the series. If the students are learning to respond more quickly to a particular type of oral drill, the time allowed for such responses is decreased in future lessons. If students show that they can now understand shortened instructions, the number of words used in similar messages is reduced in the future. In this way the production of a year-long series can be accomplished within a single calendar year, and the final product is well fitted to the audience for which it is intended.

The greatest difference between this feedback system of production and the more traditional field testing is that in the feedback system there is no actual revision of materials. The information collected in the field is used in the production of new programs, not in the revision of those that were already broadcast. That is, it is not a method for correcting faults but rather one for adapting design parameters for an audience in a state of flux.

The feedback method can be used only when most of the instructional and broadcast features of the lessons are approximately correct and when the production team is capable of producing good, if not perfect, programs with high face value. Work must be done in advance to make appropriate decisions about the pacing, vocabulary level, and other features of the lessons. Thus the two methods—feedback and revision—are complementary, and both can be used to good effect under different circumstances, even within the same project.

The methods used by RMP to collect data were similar to those used by MMHP, with the addition of paper-and-pencil tests of student achievement administered weekly. Systematic classroom observation was the most important of the qualitative methods used, but the project also interviewed children and teachers and administered questionnaires to teachers and other school personnel.

Evaluation as a tool. The growing appreciation of formative evaluation within communication campaigns reflects a shift toward evaluation as a tool for getting things done. Earlier evaluation work reflected a view of evaluation contributing to a body of basic research findings upon which later campaigns could build, but providing mainly after-the-fact information of little benefit to the campaign that was evaluated. Formative evaluation, integrated as it is within the campaign and during the campaign, allies the evaluation enterprise with the efforts of the campaign directors, taking away the adversarial edge and providing useful guidelines for improvement. The evaluator and the campaign director work together, and later campaigns benefit even more. Evaluation ceases to be a threat and becomes a constructive tool suited most appropriately to communication campaigns.

While summative evaluation has dominated the field of evaluation, particularly regarding methodological developments, formative evaluation techniques have long been usefully employed in the communication field. The cases described here exemplify intensive and systematic use of techniques that will continue to enhance the power of mass communication media as tools for instruction and PERSUASION.

See also MASS COMMUNICATIONS RESEARCH; MASS MEDIA EFFECTS.

Bibliography. Marvin C. Alkin, Richard H. Daillak, and Peter White, *Using Evaluations: Does Evaluation Make a Difference?* Beverly Hills, Calif., 1979; Tony Bates and John Robinson, eds., *Evaluating Educational Television and Radio,* Milton Keynes, Eng., 1977; D. J. Casley and D. A. Lury, *Data Collection in Developing Countries,* Oxford and New York, 1981; Thomas D. Cook and Donald T. Campbell, *Quasi-experimentation Design and Analysis for Field Settings,* Chicago and Boston, 1979; Lee J. Cronbach et al., *Toward Reform of Program Evaluation: Aims, Methods, and Institutional Arrangements,* San Francisco, 1980; Michael Q. Patton, *Utilization-focused Evaluation,* Beverly Hills, Calif., 1978; Wilbur L. Schramm, ed., *Quality in Instructional Television,* Honolulu, Hawaii, 1972; Elmer L. Struening and Marcia Guttentag, *Handbook of Evaluation Research,* Beverly Hills, Calif., 1975.

BARBARA W. SEARLE AND PETER L. SPAIN

EXPLORATION

The period historians label the Age of Discovery extends from 1415, when the Portuguese started to explore the coast of West Africa, to the mid-sixteenth century. At the beginning of the fifteenth century, Europe was a largely self-contained region, having only sporadic contacts with other continents and civilizations. By 1550 most of the world's coastlines had been mapped, the Portuguese had built a trading empire in the Far East, and Spain ruled vast tracts of America (Figure 1). A linking up of civilizations had occurred, and the world was no longer divided into discrete units surrounded by wastes of unexplored ocean or desert. All this had been achieved by a Europe that in the late fourteenth century contained only about 15 percent of the world's population. These discoveries led to important changes in the outlook of Europeans, as the classical Christian worldview of the early RENAISSANCE was infused by an increasing awareness of the rest of humanity. This process prompted French historian Jules Michelet (1798–1874) to define the Renaissance as "the discovery of the world and of man."

Early history. In the ancient classical world exploration had taken place. Greeks and Romans reached the Red Sea, the Persian Gulf, and even northern India. However, between 500 and 1000 much of this geographical knowledge was lost to the Latin West, although preserved in Greco-Arabic libraries in Spain and the Middle East (*see* LIBRARY). Thus, Greek astronomer Claudius Ptolemy (Ptolomaeus; 90–168), who lived in Alexandria, had a far more sophisticated grasp of cosmography than anyone in medieval Europe. A key date in Renaissance scholarship is 1406, when Ptolemy's *Geography* became available to Western readers through translation. Although Ptolemy made significant errors, his achievement was to describe a system of geographical coordinates whereby any point on the earth's surface could be fixed (*see* CARTOGRAPHY; MAP PROJECTION). The effect of the *Geography*'s availability on the European imagination was to create speculation about the world and the possibility of its exploration.

This advance did not dispel contemporary ignorance. Europe's isolation had been accentuated in the late fourteenth century by the rise of the Ottoman Turks, whose empire interposed a barrier cutting off the land route from Europe to the East. Late-medieval scholars had no way of distinguishing between, for instance, the basically accurate account of MARCO POLO (ca. 1254–1324; see Figure 2) and the entirely spurious travelers' tales of the pseudonymous and immensely popular fourteenth-century writer "Sir John Mandeville," who told of headless beings and ants the size of goats. The learned knew from classical sources that the world was round, but they had no idea what lay on its other side (Figures 3 and 4). There was also the view of the Roman author Pliny (ca. 23–79) that the equator was an impassable barrier and that crews attempting to cross it would be scorched to death.

Such beliefs were among the first casualties of the voyages. The Age of Discovery was also the age of print and of increasing LITERACY among the upper classes. Numerous editions of explorers' accounts were published, such as the *First Letter* of Christopher Columbus (ca. 1451–1506), which went into twenty editions by 1500. The first collection of documents relating to the voyages, Montalboddo's *Paesi Novamente Retrovati,* dating from 1507, rapidly went through fifteen editions in four languages (*see* PRINTING—CULTURAL IMPACT OF PRINTING). The epoch-making voyages of Columbus during 1492 and 1493, of Vasco da Gama (ca. 1460–1524) to India from 1497 to 1499, of Ferdinand Magellan (ca. 1480–1521) from 1519 to 1521, and of others not only undermined the credibility of Mandeville but also demonstrated the fallibility of Pliny, ARISTOTLE, and even Ptolemy, thus perhaps contributing to a growing awareness of the superiority of direct personal observation over reliance on traditional authority.

The clash of cultures. English historian J. R. Hale has said that the attempt of one society to comprehend another inevitably forces it to reappraise itself; this was no easy task for a Europe newly emerging from its medieval straitjacket. Intellectually, the voyages posed two separate challenges to accepted opinion. One was the discovery of the New World. (It was in 1503 that Florentine explorer Amerigo Vespucci [1454–1512] first postulated that the newly mapped coast of Venezuela might be a part of a "new world" and not, as hitherto believed, some remote part of Asia.) The other challenge involved

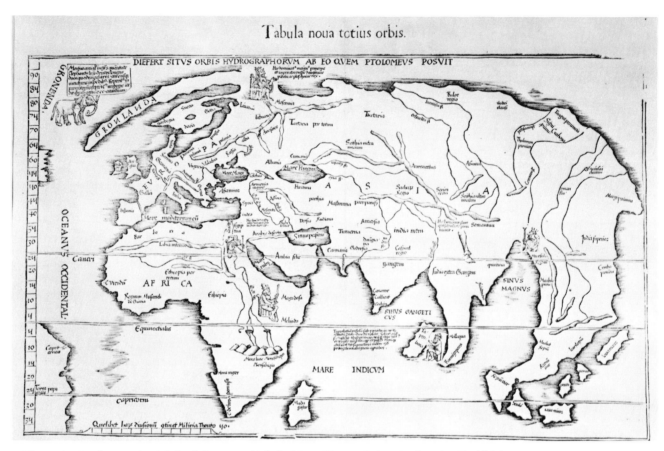

Figure 1. *(Exploration)* Michael Servetus, *Tabula Nova Totius Orbis* (Ptolemaic World Map), Vienna, 1541. Courtesy of the Royal Ontario Museum, Toronto, Canada.

a

b

Figure 2. *(Exploration)* Details from a late-fourteenth-century copy of *The Book of Marvels*, by Marco Polo. *(a)* Kubla Khan hunting. *(b)* Commerce in the Gulf of Cambay. Bibliothèque Nationale, Paris. Giraudon/Art Resource, New York.

the Portuguese encounter with advanced Eastern civilizations such as the Hindu culture of the rich city-state of Calicut on the Malabar coast of India.

Da Gama's first encounter with the Hindus in 1498 led to ludicrous misunderstanding. After insulting the elegant *samorin* ("ruler") of Calicut with presents more suited for a West African village headman, he proceeded to mistake Hindu temples for churches and to equate the goddess Kali with the Virgin Mary. Such failures of interpretation became more lethal once the Portuguese, through superior naval and warfare technology, had established local domina-

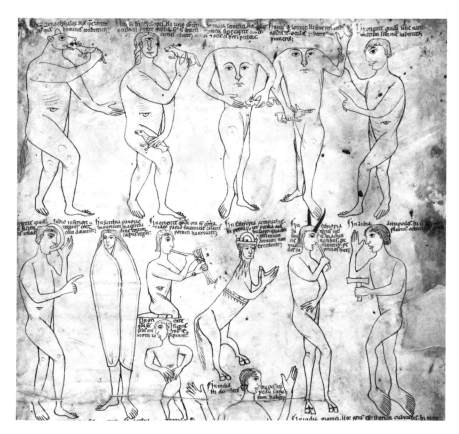

Figure 3. *(Exploration)* Detail from "The Arnstein Bible," from the Premonstratensian Abbey, Arnstein, ca. 1175. These products of a twelfth-century monk's imagination illustrate some medieval ideas about the appearance of natives of foreign lands. By permission of the British Library.

tion. The Portuguese Empire came to be thoroughly imbued with the intolerant and crusading spirit of the sixteenth-century Counter-Reformation. In Goa (India), for instance, only Christians could hold public office, and temples were systematically destroyed. This was the start of what Indian historian K. M. Panikkar has labeled the Age of Vasco da Gama, a period of imperialist domination and cultural apartheid that lasted from 1497 until 1947, the year of India's independence, and to some extent beyond.

The New World produced a different kind of challenge. Where had the American natives come from? sixteenth-century theologians asked. How was their geographical situation to be squared with biblical accounts of the creation of humanity and its dispersal after the Flood? Also, why had these peoples been excluded for so long from the benefits of Christianity? And—the more immediate question—how were they to be treated? The answer to the last question clearly depended on the answers to the other questions. Were the natives innocent survivors of a golden age, an earthly paradise, as their nakedness and tractability seemed to indicate? Or were they rather, as some among the first settlers held, degenerate and fit only to labor in the fields and mines for their European masters?

The "answers" ultimately assigned to all such

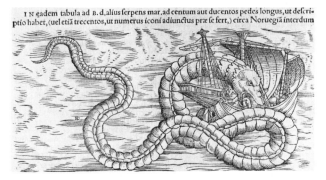

Figure 4. *(Exploration)* A large sea monster destroying a sailing ship, ca. sixteenth century. From Conrad Gesner, *Historia Animalium*, Liber III, p. 1040. Courtesy of the Library of Congress.

questions have greatly influenced the intellectual outlook of the modern world. It was Europeans, and not Amerindians, Arabs, or Chinese, who "discovered" and in most cases conquered the known world of the sixteenth century. The truculent self-confidence of the conquistadores was reinforced by their successes and deeply penetrated European consciousness. The whole world came to be locked into the conceptual embrace of the West, so that today peoples of every culture and countries at different points in economic development (*see* DEVELOPMENT COMMUNICATION) still see the world and themselves largely through Western cultural spectacles.

See also AMERICAS, PRE-COLUMBIAN; COLONIZATION; EAST ASIA, ANCIENT; HELLENIC WORLD; ISLAM, CLASSICAL AND MEDIEVAL ERAS; MIDDLE AGES; ROMAN EMPIRE.

Bibliography. Bailey W. Diffie and George D. Winius, *Foundations of the Portuguese Empire 1415–1580,* Minneapolis, Minn., 1977; John Huxtable Elliot, *The Old World and the New 1492–1650,* Cambridge, 1970; Donald F. Lach, *The Century of Discovery,* Vol. 1, *Asia in the Making of Europe,* Chicago, 1965; Kavalam M. Panikkar, *Asia and Western Dominance,* London, 1953; Geoffrey V. Scammell, *The World Encompassed: The First European Maritime Empires, c. 800–1650,* Berkeley, Calif., 1981.

DAN O'SULLIVAN

EXPRESSIONISM

A range of work in ART, literature, THEATER, and film is commonly dubbed expressionist, but the precise limits of this art movement are matters for debate. There is widespread agreement on the major geographical locus—Germany—and on a time period that, on the most generous interpretation, extends from the beginning of the twentieth century up to the rise of the Third Reich. There is also agreement that expressionism has had a continuing impact on the development of many forms of modern communication, most particularly on the cinema. So-called German expressionism remains one of the more durable movements routinely invoked by film historians.

The principal influences on cinematic expressionism in Germany lie in the visual arts and, to a lesser degree, in DRAMA. Two groups of artists are always identified in art histories of expressionism: *Die Brücke* (The Bridge), organized in Dresden in 1905 and dominated by Ernst Kirchner (Figure 1), and, six years later in Munich, *Der blaue Reiter* (The Blue Rider), including Wassily Kandinsky (Figure 2), Paul Klee, and August Macke. Often quite diverse in style, these expressionist artists were united as much as anything in their general beliefs, their weltanschauung. They shared a rebellion against traditional forms and a drive to achieve what in 1910 Kandinsky called the "great abstraction."

They argued that the established AESTHETICS of naturalism and impressionism were profoundly limited in seeking to represent only the surface of things. The task for expressionism was to delve beneath this surface in search of essences. Accordingly, expressionism was formally antinaturalistic, insistent upon

Figure 1. *(Expressionism)* Ernst Ludwig Kirchner, *Einladung zur Ausstellung der Künstlergruppe Brücke* (Invitation to the Brücke Artists' Group Exhibition), 1906. Woodcut. From Annemarie and Wolf-Dieter Dube, *E. L. Kirchner: Das graphische Werk,* Munich: Prestel-Verlag, 1967, p. 98, fig. 693. Copyright by Dr. Wolfgang and Ingeborg Henze, Campione d'Italia.

Figure 2. *(Expressionism)* Wassily Kandinsky, *Aquarelle abstraite* (Abstraction in Watercolor), 1910. National Art Museum, Paris. Lauros-Giraudon/Art Resource, New York.

Figure 3. *(Expressionism)* Otto Reigbert, set design for *Trommeln in der Nacht* (Drums in the Night), by Bertolt Brecht. Kammerspiele, Munich, 1922. Deutsches Theatermuseum, Munich.

freeing the object from its natural environment. Allied to this aesthetic rebellion—which, while genuine enough, did not necessarily lead to any single artistic style—was a wider rejection of European bourgeois culture. That is perhaps clearer in drama, where the painter's visual abstractions could be united with more easily articulated social commitments. Thus in expressionist theater—Georg Kaiser's *Gas* is one of the best-known examples—characters and events are construed in terms of their emblematic qualities rather than within the conventions of psychological REALISM. With its NARRATIVE experimentation, elaborate set design, and stylized ACTING, this theater was to prove an influential mediator of expressionist techniques for the German cinema of the early twenties (Figure 3).

Das Cabinet des Dr. Caligari (The Cabinet of Dr. Caligari, 1919) marks the beginning of German expressionist cinema (Figure 4). Its distorted sets and fierce contrasts of black and white, light and shadow, give the film the look of an expressionist painting brought to life. However, it would be misleading to take *Caligari* as typifying the German cinema of its period. Few films aspired to its aesthetic extremes, and closer examination of German cinema between 1919 and 1927 suggests a more varied output. Expressionist film encompasses far more than *Caligari*. Fritz Lang's *Metropolis* (1927), considered the end of German expressionist film, has the usual fantastic sets, sharp contrasts, geometric patterns, and stylized movements of mass workers rising in anger (Figure 5). But Lang suggests that a rational spirit may prevail in his futurist city.

There are many sources for this hybrid movement, some deriving from older German traditions. As film scholar Lotte Eisner has argued, Max Reinhardt's theatrical innovations were important, particularly his impressionistic lighting techniques and his concern with group composition onstage. This "chiaroscuro" tradition, as she terms it, combined with some of the more obviously expressionist influences, gave rise to what might more appropriately be called the German style, a body of techniques employing perspective distortions, shadows, halftones, and studied compositions to convey a peculiar sense of insecurity and threat. Borrowing themes and narratives from the romantic and gothic traditions, German silent cinema created a grotesque and displaced universe in which powerful forces combined to assail often despairing individuals (*see* ROMANTICISM).

This sense of disharmony, of a world at odds with itself, is common to expressionist work in several media. In film, however, the style was grafted onto themes that differed somewhat from those commonly found in the other arts. Where expressionists in painting and theater often held radical political views, German expressionist cinema proved predominantly conservative. Trapped in an unforgiving and constraining world, characters in these films were obliged to subject themselves to proper authority so that acceptable social order might survive. The darkly disturbing shadows of the German style, in film at least, thus served to express a fatalistic and conservative response to the stresses of Weimar society: a metaphorical defense against social chaos and a call for authoritative leadership. It is this element that allowed Siegfried Kracauer to forge the central connection of his famous thesis, seeking to establish a

Figure 4. *(Expressionism)* Robert Wiene, *Das Cabinet des Dr. Caligari* (The Cabinet of Dr. Caligari), 1919. The Museum of Modern Art/Film Stills Archive.

clear line of progression all the way from *Caligari* to the rise of Adolf Hitler.

Whatever the truth of Kracauer's analysis, German expressionist cinema itself was effectively finished by 1926. In the wake of the 1924 Dawes Plan, U.S. investment in the German film industry was exchanged for a drastic cut in the German export market. The HOLLYWOOD majors (most notably MGM and Paramount) took the opportunity to undermine their only serious competitor in Europe. Already guaranteed 50 percent exhibition in Germany, they set about luring away the industry's major talents. Many of the technicians, performers, directors, and producers central to German cinema headed for new jobs in Hollywood. *See* MOTION PICTURES—SOUND FILM.

As well as precipitating the decline of the German industry, this had the effect of accelerating the rate at which the German style came to influence U.S. film. Hollywood filmmakers were already aware of the remarkable innovations wrought in Germany, particularly in relation to camerawork. The influx of German technicians added to that influence, and the German style became a primary resource whenever filmmakers needed to suggest mystery, instability, or malevolence. Thus, the two emergent popular genres of the early thirties—the gangster movie and the HORROR FILM—both employed "German" lighting and compositional techniques to invoke their respective underworlds.

Such applications were, of course, specific and pragmatic. Yet the German style was also more diffusely influential. Those U.S. filmmakers already inclined toward a broadly pictorial aesthetic found their preferences further legitimated by the German idiom. John Ford, for example, was to use expressionist-influenced imagery in several of his critically successful films of the thirties and forties, including most notably *The Informer* (1935). In a period when it seemed important to establish the credentials of film as art, the very obviousness of the German style commended it to critical attention, though as concern with such obvious artiness has declined so too has the acceptability of expressionism's visual extravagances. Some genres, notably the horror film, remain deeply marked by the expressionist influence, and there is no doubt that our conceptions of composition and light in cinema were significantly changed by the German silent film. But the cinema's dominant ethos was to prove naturalistic in both narrative and style, precisely the restrictive aesthetic against which the original expressionists arrayed themselves. It is

Figure 5. *(Expressionism)* Fritz Lang, *Metropolis*, 1927. National Film Archive, London/Deutsches Institut für Filmkunde.

both ironic and revealing that in cinema, at least, their battle was lost almost before it began.

See also AVANT-GARDE FILM; CINEMATOGRAPHY; FILM EDITING; FILM THEORY; MOTION PICTURES—SILENT ERA.

Bibliography. Lotte H. Eisner, *The Haunted Screen*, London, 1969; Siegfried Kracauer, *From Caligari to Hitler*, Princeton, N.J., 1947; Victor H. Miesel, ed., *Voices of German Expressionism*, Englewood Cliffs, N.J., 1970; Peter Selz, *German Expressionist Painting*, Berkeley, Calif., 1957; Wilhelm Worringer, *Abstraction and Empathy* (Abstraktion und Einfuhlung), trans. by Michael Bullock, London and New York, 1953.

ANDREW F. TUDOR

EYES

Eyes are fundamentally important for communication because the direction of the gaze reveals the direction of an organism's attention. Throughout the animal kingdom, being attended to by another animal of the same or a different species is a matter of the highest possible significance. Survival depends on sensitivity to the attentions of predators, members of the opposite sex, and sometimes competitors. Because a direct gaze signifies attention, it commands attention in response. Eyes looking at us are a salient stimulus: in a roomful of people or on the street, the person who is looking at us stands out. Most people have had the experience of glancing up from some absorbing matter only to find themselves looking directly into someone's eyes, creating the sensation that the eyes have some magnetic power to penetrate into consciousness through the skull itself. A more likely explanation is that the gaze is registered in peripheral vision but not immediately recognized; the innate importance of being looked at keeps the impression from fading and brings it to awareness, so that the person looks up in the right direction. Evolution has provided us with a remarkable sensitivity to the gaze.

In the wild, visual attention from another (particularly another of a different species) typically means danger. Perhaps for this reason, various prey species of fish and insects have developed eye spots—parts of circles or rings that look like the eyes of a much larger animal and presumably serve to discourage predators. Often these "eye" displays are combined with sudden startling movement. Many other species have developed eye rings or other markings around the eyes themselves, although their evolutionary significance is still a matter of speculation.

Gaze and attention. In most species, a direct gaze is a signal of danger. In the social primates, although the gaze is still most commonly a threatening stimulus, the situation has become more complicated: the gaze serves as an important signal of an animal's intentions (or, more scientifically, of its likely future behavior) and thus serves to facilitate smooth social interactions. Eyes are particularly important in the communication of the dominance and subordination relationships that are fundamental to the group's social organization. Visual attention is directed from less dominant animals toward more dominant ones: infants look toward mothers, females look toward males (or higher-status females), subordinate males look toward dominant males. In a face-to-face interaction between a dominant and a subordinate animal, however, the subordinate animal averts its gaze in a GESTURE of submission. A steady face-to-face stare is a component of nearly all primate dominance or threat displays. If the subordinate animal does not look away but returns the gaze, that constitutes a challenge, and the dominant animal will escalate its threat display with various other signals such as an open mouth or a vocalization. The subordinate animal may then submit, or (rarely) the encounter may erupt into overt aggression. The stare is central to genuine displays of aggression. When young animals merely play at fighting, they open their jaws as in a threat, but keep their eyelids partly closed, as though indicating that the threat is just pretend. *See also* ANIMAL COMMUNICATION; ANIMAL SIGNALS; INTERACTION, FACE-TO-FACE.

It would be wrong to assume, however, that the gaze has a fixed form or a fixed meaning in primates. The form and meaning even of the threat display differ according to the situation and the animal's position in the social hierarchy. In addition, not all eye contact is associated with threat. Among the higher primates, we see the first signs of eye contact as a sign of affiliation. Mother and infant may look into each other's eyes for protracted amounts of time, perhaps because of the position of the infant in nursing. The significance of the gaze, like the significance of attention itself, is more variable than it is in species with less stereoscopic vision, less developed muscles of FACIAL EXPRESSION, and less complicated social relationships. Nonetheless, it is worth noting that most affiliative interactions, such as mating and grooming, are much more likely to involve averted gaze and presentation of the back.

In human beings, a direct gaze is a salient and arousing stimulus. By the time they are six weeks old, human infants smile, and their pupils dilate when they see faces or masks of faces; the critical stimulus seems to be the eyes. Babies do not respond as reliably to faces with the eyes covered up or with the features scrambled or to profiles as they do to a simple MASK with two dots appropriately oriented. Eyes are the first feature to be included in children's drawings of people, and both children and adults show a tendency to interpret ambiguous figures as faces when there are two spots roughly where eyes would be (*see* CHILD ART). In looking at each others' faces or at pictures of faces, human beings focus most on the eyes and remember the eyes better than other parts of the FACE; in looking at pictures of groups of people, we remember the ones who were looking directly at the camera. In our daily lives as well, a direct gaze is a salient element in the environment. It has a much higher probability of being noticed than many other aspects of behavior, such as foot movement, changes in pupil size, and subtle facial or postural changes.

A direct gaze is not only a salient stimulus, it is an arousing one. Numerous studies have shown that eye contact (or, more likely, the perception that one is being looked at) produces increases in measures of physiological arousal such as heart rate, galvanic skin response, and electroencephalogram. And in some contexts this arousal still shares some of the threatening properties characteristic of the displays of lower primates. In many (preliterate) cultures masks with prominent eye spots were used to frighten off evil spirits or to keep the uninitiated away from secret ceremonies. Although cultures differ in the overall amount of time people spend looking at each other in social interactions, all cultures have rules defining the amount of direct gaze that is appropriate for various kinds of social interactions and relationships. More often than not, these rules serve to restrict rather than to encourage looking at another's face. People feel uncomfortable when they are stared at, unless they have a clear, nonthreatening explanation of the stare, and they may try to escape the situation. The threatening properties of the stare are also reflected in the ancient and widespread belief in the evil eye. According to this superstition, some people (often people who are disfigured, diseased, or socially disfavored) have the power to harm others merely by looking at them. The gaze signals attention, and too much attention, especially from strangers, suggests danger.

Human beings, however, far outstrip their primate cousins in the range and subtlety of their personal relationships. In some circumstances people fear attention, but in others they yearn for it and feel abandoned when it is withdrawn. Thus the meanings communicated to a person by the movements of another's eyes are as diverse and complex as all the meanings of attention and inattention in human interaction. One of the most important differences between human and animal eye communication is that in humans the eyes are enormously significant in communicating affiliation: intimacy, affection, desire, and love. Eye movements are an important element of flirtation, and cosmetic decoration of the area around the eyes is as old and as general as the evil eye itself.

Eye contact. The importance of eye contact in establishing affiliative relationships begins at birth. Newborn babies soon begin to focus on their mothers' eyes (this may strengthen the mother's attachment to her child). By six weeks the infant responds to eye contact with a smile. The mother's gaze and the baby's gaze are interdependent; her looking at the baby increases the probability that the baby will start looking at her or keep looking at her. Likewise, a mother responds by smiling or talking when her baby looks at her. By the second half of the first year, the excitement of losing and regaining eye contact is the essence of one of the baby's first games—peekaboo.

In adults the attention signaled by a look may be interpreted positively or negatively. In some social contexts it is even irrelevant to emotion. For example, one of the most carefully studied communicative functions of human eye movements is the moment-to-moment regulation of the sequence of turns in CONVERSATION. Making eye contact is important in initiating a social interaction in the first place, and eye movements are also an important part of a cluster of subtle signals communicating a person's wish to begin speaking, to keep speaking, or to stop speaking and give the other person a chance. In general, people look at their companions more while listening than while speaking. While speaking, people look away at the beginning of their turns and when they are saying things that are difficult to communicate, either cognitively or personally. Looking away seems to limit incoming information for the speaker so that more attention can be given to the formulation of the difficult thought. It may also serve as a signal to the listener not to interrupt. These regulating signals are so automatic in face-to-face conversation that they are rarely noticed consciously until the normal pattern is disrupted. For example, if someone gazes straight at us while recounting an apparently painful and intimate experience, we may suspect that we are hearing a story that has been well rehearsed.

Numerous attempts have been made to pinpoint the emotional meaning of visual behavior in human interaction, some arguing that a direct gaze signals attraction, others that it is a threat, and so on. It should be clear by now that the direct gaze is a salient and arousing stimulus that signals attention, but within these limits particular directions or durations of the gaze do not have intrinsic meaning. Instead, the gaze is interpreted in terms of the surrounding behaviors, the interpersonal relationship, the social context, and the perceiver's motivations and goals in the interaction.

For example, people sometimes feel uncomfortable when they are stared at and try to escape if they can. In one study, an experimenter stared at drivers or pedestrians who were stopped at a red light and found that when the light changed, allowing them to escape, those who had been stared at crossed the intersection faster than those who had not. However, if the person gazing at us is in trouble and the remedy is clear (for example, a lost child), a stare can elicit approach and comfort. In the first case, the attention implied by the stare is ambiguous; some response seems to be called for, but it is not clear what it should be. In the second case, the meaning of the attention is clear and nonthreatening, and so is the appropriate response.

Similarly, an unusually high level of gaze is appreciated in a friendly context and increases our liking for the person, but in a critical context we prefer a person who does not look at us so much. A person who seeks contact with others welcomes eye contact and likes the gazer; a person who is feeling withdrawn or embarrassed reacts to the same gaze with tension and hostility. To some extent, a gaze serves to focus and intensify the general emotional tone of a social interaction.

A wide range of contextual factors affects the meaning of visual behavior. The face itself is an enormously important context. People can easily recognize facial expressions of fear, anger, surprise, and interest, all of which include a direct gaze as a component. All of these emotions involve heightened attention; in expressions of shame, sorrow, and disgust, involving a desire to withdraw attention, the eyes are partially closed or turned away. Age, GENDER, and status also determine the meaning of gaze, with children, females, and lower-status people expected (or permitted) to pay more visual attention.

Eyes and communication. The eyes "communicate" at many different levels. The gaze may have a direct effect on the receiver, an effect that precedes or occurs independently of an interpretation. Researchers have often found that people are not consciously aware of a companion's visual behavior, even when their own behavior is affected by it. At the next level, the receiver notices the gaze and interprets it. The ultimate interpretation may vary greatly in type and complexity, but the initial realization is the same: "That person is attending to me." In most situations this fundamental interpretation is insufficient, and the person goes on to make further interpretations and attributions, all springing from the first one.

A fully communicative situation involves a shared code and shared assumptions about the code usage, as when two people prearrange a set of eye signals with explicit meanings. But this is rare. Many nonverbal cues, and the gaze in particular, gain much of their power in social interactions from the shared assumption—not necessarily a valid one—that they are unintentional. The gaze is a central component of an undercurrent code that differs from most other human codes in that others are not likely to make explicit comments on it, and if they do the signal can be denied. The existence of a not quite conscious, not exactly systematic code that is assumed to be less conscious and less systematic than it really is allows people to express their feelings and to negotiate developing relationships without having to be held accountable until they are ready to acknowledge the developments.

Bibliography. Michael Argyle and Mark Cook, *Gaze and Mutual Gaze,* Cambridge and New York, 1976; Robert G. Harper, Arthur N. Wiens, and Joseph D. Matarazzo, *Nonverbal Communication: The State of the Art,* New York, 1978.

PHOEBE C. ELLSWORTH

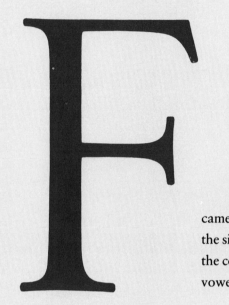(ef), the sixth letter of the Roman alphabet, represents historically the sixth letter (*waw*) of the Semitic alphabet, which expressed the sounds of *w* (approximately) and the related vowel *u*. In early Greek writing the letter had at first the same twofold power; but subsequently its accidental varieties of form came to be differentiated in function, the form F (retaining the sixth place in the alphabet) being appropriated to the consonantal use, while V or Y served for the vowel, and is the source of the Roman U, V, Y. . . .

FACE

The human face is the most conspicuous and the most varied of a person's physical attributes. Great differences in its form and structure can be observed not only between different communities but also within them. Its huge repertoire of movements, both voluntary and involuntary, gives it the power to display the most subtle feelings and sentiments, moods, intentions, and desires. It is the great silent communicator that provides the physical basis for much that is important in social decision making and judgment.

It serves also as the reference point, the locus of the personality, the embodiment of the inner self. It seems entirely appropriate that important communications should be addressed to it and that messages should in turn be received from it, since that is where the personality appears to reside. To its possessor, the face feels to be the center of waking life. If the "me" resides anywhere, it is in the face.

Emotions, personality, and the face. Whether we, as observers, always interpret correctly the messages received from a face, and whether the judgments we make about the person "behind it" are soundly based, is, however, open to question.

There is no doubt that we can be highly successful in correctly identifying emotions in FACIAL EXPRESSION. The patterns of facial movement corresponding to feelings such as joy, sorrow, and fear are similar in many parts of the world, and we can recognize them in societies quite different from our own. Although the basic "language" of expression is universal, the nature and extent of facial movements may vary in different communities; local "dialects" need to be allowed for. Individuals, too, show much variability in facial expressiveness. Some people externalize their feelings readily; others reveal them hardly at all. Furthermore, facial mobility is influenced by the expressive norms and conventions of the particular subculture in which an individual lives.

When we attempt, however, to go beyond feelings and judge from the anatomy of the face more enduring qualities of character and personality, we are likely to be unsuccessful. A review of the unhappy history of the pseudoscience of physiognomy reveals many remarkable assertions about the implications for character of particular anatomical characteristics. ARISTOTLE, for example, declared that "large ears indicated a tendency to irrelevant talk or chattering," and in the eighteenth century Johann Kaspar Lavater, the Swiss writer whose classic work on physiognomy was printed in no fewer than 140 editions, asserted that "a small nostril is an infallible sign of a timid mind." Physiognomists have not agreed about which facial parts are related to which qualities of personality, and none of the alleged relationships has ever been proved to exist. Nevertheless, anatomical characteristics such as a tall brow, closely spaced EYES, a small chin, or a hooked nose are commonly, but quite mistakenly, associated in many people's minds with particular qualities of personality. Closely spaced eyes, for example, often lead to attributions of meanness.

Race, sex, and age. The facial features on which such erroneous judgments are so often based are related not to temperament but to race, sex, and age. The overall shape of the face is determined by the skull, which in blacks, for example, tends to be longer than it is in those of Mongoloid stock (whose faces, in consequence, tend to be broader). Individual features also show considerable racial variation; the lips of blacks, for example, tend to be fuller than those of Nordic peoples. The noses of Mongolians and Eskimo do not protrude from the face nearly so much as those of Caucasians. Also, the shape of the nose, as well as other facial features, differs according to sex. Among Caucasian females, the inward-curving, turned-up nose is much more common than in males; the jaw is also less pronounced. Female eyes are larger and darker, and their skin is smoother with more underlying fat. In all faces, advancing years bring changes not only in the wrinkling, color, opacity, and texture of the skin but also in the underlying bones; shrinkage of the jaw, for example, is often quite marked. As children grow older, there is a large increase in the distance from nostrils to eyes.

Elaboration and modification of the face. The human face offers countless opportunities for elaboration and modification. Its features can be exaggerated; its surface painted, marked, scored, or cut; and its immediate context readily manipulated to produce powerful illusory effects. Such alterations have long been exploited for a variety of social purposes.

The rulers of ancient Egypt emphasized their superior status by painting their faces with malachite green, carmine, and antimony. Babylonians—both young men and women—lined their eyes with stibium and painted their faces with white lead. The Greeks in Homer's time used little makeup, but by the fourth century B.C.E. the use of cosmetics was well established. They were especially fond of ceruse, a paste of white lead and egg white, which gave the face an ethereal paleness. This highly poisonous cosmetic remained popular as a beautifier until the nineteenth century and was especially favored by women eager to proclaim their aristocratic way of life. It provided the most striking contrast imaginable to the suntanned appearance of peasant workers in the fields, and it concealed at least some of the ravages of age. In ancient Rome, Ovid recommended and wrote lyrically of the powers of cosmetics. One hundred years earlier, the Indian writer Vatsyayana, in the Kama Sutra, told women how to use cosmetics

as "extra arts" in seduction. In France, in the eighteenth-century courtly society of Pompadour, Dubarry, and Marie-Antoinette, they reached the highest peak of artificiality.

How to interpret the cosmetic codes needed to be learned. At one period during the eighteenth century in France, a red-rouged face indicated a lady of quality and a painted white face a prostitute. Across the English Channel at the same time, the ladies painted themselves white and the prostitutes used red. And there have been times, for example, in England during the reign of Queen Victoria, when the use of any cosmetic substances proclaimed immodesty and impropriety.

Such has been the belief in the power of the face to influence people and events—a supernatural power, as many equatorial peoples have believed—that facial modifications far more radical than face painting have seemed worth much effort and pain. Highly painful facial scars and weals, made by cauterizing and cutting the flesh, have often been eagerly sought. Such scarification and cicatrization follow strict rules dictated by local custom. Among the Abipone of South America techniques of this kind were used to communicate tribal membership and to confirm passage through important initiation rites, such as those attending the attainment of full adulthood. Marking or scarring the flesh of the face has also been used to declare that an appropriate relationship has been established with the gods and spirits. In the Bible there are references to "cutting for the dead," a form of facial scarification that proclaimed solemn respect for ancestors. In Germany, facial dueling scars were once much prized by young men as public marks of valor.

Facial tattooing, a far less radical but nonetheless painful procedure, still occurs in many parts of the world. The exalted rank of tribal chieftains was often indicated by their more beautiful and elaborate designs. Tattoos have been used for a variety of purposes: to declare one's totem, rank, or family connections; to record achievements, such as the number of whales killed; or simply to signify that a young woman was available for marriage. Tattoos have even recorded disgrace, as in the case of an island chief who deserted in battle. In Australia a particular style of facial tattoo could announce that a woman's child had died or might simply record the number of children she had borne.

Another method of facial elaboration, popular in equatorial countries, is the attachment of objects by forcing them through the flesh. Nose, ear, and mouth

piercing, the stretching of ear lobes by suspended objects, and the extension of lips by labrets, or circular plugs, all have particular local significance. Among the Toposa of the Sudan, for example, a brass wire piercing the lower lip signifies that a woman is married. In Malaysia teeth might be mutilated by drilling or filing to announce that the rituals of puberty, wedding, or mourning have been properly undertaken.

In Western countries, too, attached objects have sometimes been used to adorn faces. A fashion for applying patches to the face developed during the seventeenth century in Europe. Very soon a "language of patches" evolved, which became almost as elaborate as the "language of the fan," a patch at the corner of the eye indicating passion or one at the corner of the mouth signifying the expectation of a kiss. In England patches at one time served as party symbols, the Whigs patching to the right of the face and the Tories to the left.

Some highly effective methods of facial elaboration, however, are concerned not so much with the

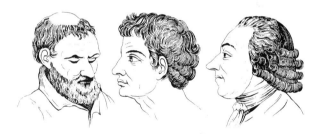

Figure 2. *(Face)* Physiognomical exercises. From Johann Kaspar Lavater, *Essays on Physiognomy,* London and New York: Ward, Lock, and Bowden, 1880s, plate xxi.

Figure 3. *(Face)* System of race determination in Nazi Germany. The Bettmann Archive/BBC Hulton.

◁ Figure 1. *(Face)* The Chatsworth head, Greek severe style, from Cyprus, ca. 460 B.C.E. Bronze. Reproduced by courtesy of the Trustees of The British Museum.

Figure 4. *(Face)* Young man of Mali. United Nations photo 153449/Ian Steele.

Figure 6. *(Face)* A Laotian refugee of the Hmong tribe. United Nations photo/John Isaac.

Figure 5. *(Face)* A girl on horseback in Inner Mongolia. United Nations photo 152120/John Isaac.

face itself as with the space around the face. The impression created by the face is much influenced by its immediate context, by the things that immediately surround it, such as jewelry, headdress, helmet, or beard. Of all these possibilities, the hair has been exploited most consistently in this way.

During the seventeenth and eighteenth centuries, coiffures of great height and bulk were much esteemed as badges of rank and wealth. Women of quality would adorn their towers of hair with flowers in bottles, candles, and even models of battleships in patriotic celebration of recent naval victories. Wigs of considerable complexity and refinement were much favored by those who could afford their very great cost (which made them a lucrative prospect for snatch thieves in the streets).

Distinctive styles of wigs evolved. Lawyers, judges, parsons, and physicians proclaimed their professions by the cut of their wigs. Officers of the Buffs and Blues indicated their regiment by the color of the dusting powder they used. British prime minister William Pitt (the Younger) almost suppressed the wig with his "guinea tax" in 1795. In France, following the Revolution of 1789, the wig became the hated

Figure 7. *(Face)* Sugutani Shichi Nin Kesho, Woman looking in mirror. Woodcut. Orion Press/Scala/Art Resource, New York.

Figure 8. *(Face)* Yanomamo man decorated for a ceremony. Napoléon A. Chagnon/Anthro-Photo.

Figure 9. *(Face)* Eighteenth-century Frenchwoman with large hat and wig. Engraving. The Bettmann Archive, Inc.

Figure 10. *(Face)* Ulysses S. Grant (1822–1885). Photograph by Matthew Brady or an assistant. The Bettmann Archive, Inc.

Figure 11. *(Face)* John Ruskin (1819–1900). Photograph by Frank Hollyes. Courtesy of the Board of Trustees of the Victoria and Albert, London.

Figure 12. *(Face)* Giuseppe Arcimboldo, *Autumn,* 1573. Oil. Louvre, Paris. Giraudon/Art Resource, New York.

symbol of the aristocracy. Then a curious reversal of meaning occurred: the wig was now reserved, apart from one or two professional groups, for footmen and servants.

The beard also has enjoyed changing meanings. In ancient Egypt it was the sole prerogative of rulers; even Queen Matshrtpdont wore an artificial beard. Yet, as a special dispensation, commoners were also allowed to wear the beard as a sign of mourning. In Greece the beard was the mark of wisdom and enlightenment, and the great god Zeus was always respectfully portrayed as bearded. During later centuries the beard exchanged places many times with the shaven face as the mark of the aristocrat. In the time of Queen Elizabeth I of England, the precise cut of the beard denoted one's profession: the soldier had his "spade," the courtier his "court," and the clergyman his spirelike "cathedral." Soon thereafter, however, beards disappeared until well into the nineteenth century.

In the United States it was a different story. During the Civil War, luxuriant beards proclaimed a proper soldierly patriotism; General Ulysses S. Grant typi-

fied a long line of U.S. presidents who wore beards. The tradition was broken only after many years by William McKinley.

In Europe it was poets, musicians, intellectuals, and reformers who boldly reintroduced the beard in the nineteenth century. Such are the curious ways of fashion and fancy, however, that by the 1890s those same freethinkers and reformers were signaling their independence of spirit by making themselves the very first to appear aggressively cleanshaven.

See also BODY DECORATION.

Bibliography. John Brophy, *The Human Face*, New York, 1946, reprint London, 1954; Johann Kaspar Lavater, *Physiognomische Fragmente zur Beförderung der Menschenkenntnis und Menschenliebe*, 4 vols., 1775, trans. by Henry Hunter (Essays on Physiognomy), London, 1789; John Liggett, *The Human Face*, New York and London, 1974.

JOHN LIGGETT

FACIAL EXPRESSION

The human FACE is an exquisitely complex structure, and its "information value" is dependent not only on specific muscular movements but also on its structural features. The human face, particularly, is notable for the degree to which it is specialized for displaying information. There are several separate sources of information used in making judgments of facial expressions. Rapid signaling is provided by muscular movements, as well as by blanching or blushing, sweat production, pupillary responses, and alterations in head position or gaze. Informative structural features include those that are relatively constant over the life span, such as bone structure, size and shape of facial features, or skin pigmentation; and others that reliably change with age, such as bags, pouches, and fatty deposits. Additional information is provided by features such as facial anomalies or, more commonly, by eyeglasses, cosmetics, hair removal or hairpieces, scars, or appliances.

The relatively constant signs are frequently, and often erroneously, judged as reflections of emotion or personality characteristics. Only a minority of facial muscular behaviors (probably about one-third) is related to emotion per se. Some are related to nonemotional functions that are not primarily communicative in nature, such as eating, drinking, breathing, and visual and auditory localization. Other facial behaviors can serve a communicative function but are not usually expressive of emotion. These include (1) gestures, such as winking; (2) self-manipulative actions, such as lip biting; (3) actions that are patterned accompaniments to SPEECH, such as eyebrow and upper-eyelid elevation in emphasis; and (4) such actions as head nods, smiles, eyebrow actions, and the like that listeners do and that play a role in regulating conversational exchanges. Psychological disorders can affect both the frequency and the intensity of facial expressions.

Origin and meaning of facial expressions. CHARLES DARWIN believed that expressions of emotion originated in our evolutionary past, a belief that has inspired attempts to determine the universality of these expressions. Several studies have demonstrated that people in diverse literate and preliterate cultures agree in identifying the emotions represented by certain distinctive facial expressions, such as those for happiness, sadness, anger, fear, disgust, and fear/surprise. Universal facial expressions have also been proposed for "interest," shame, and contempt, but the evidence is less compelling in these cases. The startle reaction shows reliable patterns of facial behavior and probably has a universal expression. However, because the startle reaction is such a stereotyped and automatic response, many researchers do not consider it an emotion. (Emotional responses to *being* startled often occur, but these responses are variable.)

While there is substantial evidence that full-blown facial expressions of fundamental emotions are the same in all cultures, the facial behavior observed in different cultures may be influenced by two factors: (1) an evaluation of the situation, which means that the "same" situation may invoke different emotions in different cultures; and (2) display rules, or social conventions for managing expressions of emotion. Display rules can stipulate that emotional expressions be minimized, masked, neutralized, exaggerated, or faked in specific situations. These rules are less evident if individuals who are responding emotionally are not aware that they are being observed.

Development of facial expressions. Discriminable facial expressions can be observed early in development. Nearly all the discrete facial muscle actions visible in the adult can be identified in the newborn. Several investigators have reported neonatal imitation of specific facial actions such as tongue protrusion and mouth opening. Complex patterned facial expressions are present from the first days of life: the "cry" face of distress; the "disgust" face to unpleasant tastes; startle responses to sudden, intense stimulation; brow knitting (interest or puzzlement) while fixating on visual objects, including faces; and "smiles" seen largely during the rapid-eye-movement phase of sleep.

Social smiling toward a caregiver begins around three to four weeks of age, and by two or three months broad smiles are seen during social interaction and in contexts suggesting successful cognitive mastery. Laughter first appears at about four months.

a

b

Figure 1. *(Facial Expression)* *(a)* Man recoiling, *(b)* woman sneering, *(c)* child sulking. Photographs by O. G. Rejlander. From Charles Darwin, *The Expression of the Emotions in Man and Animals.* Gernsheim Collection, Harry Ransom Humanities Research Center, The University of Texas at Austin.

c

Throughout the first year of life, crying is the dominant response when any strong emotion is aroused. How the discrete, differentiated expressions of fear, anger, and sadness emerge during development is less fully understood. Few studies have been conducted on how these expressions are used by two- to five-year-olds in natural interaction.

Since we do not have access to an infant's self-awareness, it is not known at what point infants' expressions reflect experienced emotion. Estimates have ranged from three to eighteen months, depending on the investigator's criterion for the ability to experience emotion. However, it is known that infants soon learn to use their expressions as signaling mechanisms to caregivers. Instrumental (purposive) use of crying and smiling is acquired by two or three months of life, and by the end of the first year infants use smiles as social greetings, display deliberate tantrum behaviors, and make visible efforts to hold back or suppress tears. By age six, children are already able to verbalize some cultural display rules for emotional expressions (e.g., "big boys don't cry").

144

Children show parallel development in abilities to recognize emotional expressions. By two months the human face becomes a meaningful stimulus, and by four to six months children can recognize smiling versus nonsmiling faces. Three- to five-year-old children can match facial expressions to emotion terms and can voluntarily produce recognizable versions of prototypic facial expressions. Children learn to take advantage of their enhanced abilities to recognize expressions of others and to produce expressions as signals. They use information conveyed by caregivers' facial expressions in evaluating ambiguous situations (strangers, novel objects, etc.); and they use facial and gestural actions during fighting, rough-and-tumble play, seeking of caretaking, and defense of desired objects.

The abilities to produce and understand facial expressions are important in adult communication. Such abilities do not seem to vary with personality characteristics. Nor are skills in producing facial expressions correlated with skills in recognizing them. The one consistent finding that has emerged from studies of production and recognition ability is a slight superiority for women in both abilities.

People base their judgments of emotion primarily on facial cues. Judgments of facial expressions alone generally correlate better with judgments made when both facial expression and speech are available than when the judge has only speech and no visual cues. However, contrary to the assumption that people can detect from facial expressions when they are being deceived, research shows that individuals do little better than chance in discerning when a facial expression reflects authentic versus simulated emotion.

Studying facial expressions. Research on facial expressions was greatly impeded until the 1970s by unsatisfactory methods for measuring facial behavior. Most studies have used either observers' judgments or direct measures of facial behavior. In the judgment approach, naive or trained observers are shown a set of facial expressions and asked to identify the emotions represented, to guess the eliciting situation, or to place the expressions along an emotion scale (e.g., "pleasantness-unpleasantness"). Observer judgment approaches are less informative because it is difficult to determine which features of facial expressions are responsible for the judgments rendered.

In the more precise direct measurement approach, photographs, films, or videotapes of facial expressions are examined by coders trained to identify specific facial actions thought or shown to represent emotion. The most comprehensive coding system is the anatomically based Facial Action Coding System (FACS), developed by psychologists Paul Ekman and Wallace Friesen, which defines nearly fifty indepen-

Figure 2. *(Facial Expression)* Nineteenth-century physiologist Dr. G. B. Duchenne produced hundreds of artificial "expressions" by applying electric current to the face of an almshouse patient who had no sensation of pain in that area. The experiments and photographs were published in *Mécanisme de la physionomie humaine.* Gernsheim Collection, Harry Ransom Humanities Research Center, The University of Texas at Austin.

a

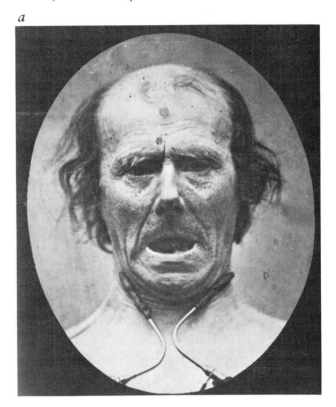

b

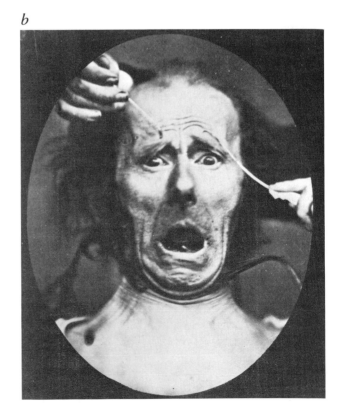

a

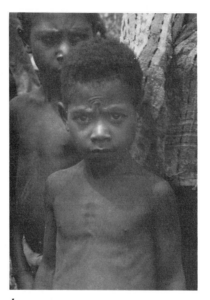 

b

c

 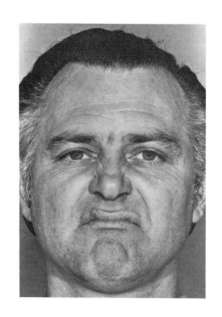

dent visible facial actions (in combination, these actions can produce more than five thousand facial expression configurations). The actions may also be detected electronically, using a procedure known as electromyography to amplify the tiny electrical discharges created by contracting muscle tissue. Electromyography can detect facial actions too small to be visible, such as the actions that occur while imagining emotional situations.

Why are particular facial expressions associated with particular emotions? Contemporary investigators agree with Darwin that many expressive movements derive from actions that once served some direct biological function (e.g., sensory or protective functions) or that represent the initial phases ("intention movements") of an act such as attacking or fleeing. Evolutionary biologists and ethologists have sought the precursors of human expressions in nonhuman primates. Explanations have been proposed for some key facial expressions.

The evolution of the smile has been traced from the protective "grimace" seen in lower nonhuman primates during aggressive encounters. In higher nonhuman primates this grimace is seen as an appeasing or reassuring signal in positive social encounters. The story remains incomplete, however, since the primate grimace (like the human fear grimace) involves a different facial muscle from that used for the smile. (The great apes do have a smilelike display involving the same muscle as the human smile, but its use has not been studied carefully.) The smile is one of the easiest facial expressions to recognize at a distance, and this may explain in part its specialization for expression of positive emotion.

The tensed or pursed lips that humans show in anger closely resemble the "tense-mouth" display seen in other primates. Anger expressions in humans, as in nonhuman primate threat displays, are accompanied by fixed, staring EYES and lowered brows. Darwin believed that the lowered brow seen in anger served to shade the eyes from light and enhance visual acuity, a strategy that is perhaps useful in assessing a threat or keeping an eye on an opponent. Gaze aversion is found in many species as an appeasement signal. More generally, looking away serves to reduce arousal in moments of uncertainty or ambivalence (e.g., flirting or shy approaches to strangers). *See also* ANIMAL COMMUNICATION; ANIMAL SIGNALS; ETHOLOGY.

Physiology and facial expression. The specific mechanisms in the central nervous system for gen-

erating the muscular actions in facial expressions are poorly understood. It is clear from neuroanatomical studies and clinical investigations of brain-injured patients that there is dual control of facial expressions. Spontaneous, "emotional" expressions seem to be controlled primarily by the pathways of the subcortical extrapyramidal nervous system, whereas voluntary expressions (e.g., those performed in response to a request) are controlled largely by the pyramidal motor tracts that emanate from the motor strip of the neocortex. Brain damage in these different systems can selectively impair spontaneous or posed expressions.

Attempts to understand further the neural bases of the generation and the perception of facial expressions have explored possible cerebral hemispheric differences. In the production of facial expressions there is greater asymmetry (lopsidedness) in posed expressions than in spontaneous expressions. However, consistent left/right differences across individuals, muscles, or even types of expressions have not been found in all studies.

There do seem to be hemispheric differences in the perception of faces. A slight right-hemisphere advantage (the right hemisphere "sees" the left half of the field of vision) is generally found in tasks that require recognition of faces flashed briefly to the left or right visual fields. This advantage may be due to the right hemisphere's bias for processing information globally rather than by attention to small local features. The right-hemisphere perceptual advantage is weak, however, and is not always seen in experiments.

Facial expression and emotion. When do facial expressions reflect real emotion rather than just social rituals, display rules, or even DECEPTION? This is a vexing issue, because there is no infallible sign of real emotion, and people's self-reports of emotion are unreliable. But there are several clues. As mentioned previously, spontaneous facial expressions are more symmetrical. They are also likely to occur more quickly, whereas posed or managed expressions tend to be slower and to last longer. Smiles that reflect felt happiness are accompanied by a crinkly-eyed appearance caused by contractions of the muscles surrounding the eyes; posed or unfelt smiles as a rule do not involve contractions of these muscles. Expressions that mask another emotion may be betrayed by "leakage cues," that is, by giveaway movements in the body or elsewhere in the face.

Facial expressions are sometimes accompanied by signs of changed activity in the autonomic nervous

◁ **Figure 3.** *(Facial Expression)* *(a)* Happy, *(b)* sad, *(c)* disgusted. Left-hand photos in *(a)*, *(b)*, and *(c)* from Paul Ekman, *The Face of Man: Expressions of Universal Emotions in a New Guinea Village*, Garland, N.Y., 1980; right-hand photos from Paul Ekman and Wallace V. Friesen, *Unmasking the Face: A Guide to Recognizing Emotions from Facial Clues*, Englewood Cliffs, N.J., 1975. Courtesy of Human Interaction Laboratory, University of California, San Francisco.

system (ANS), which is responsible for many of the most salient characteristics of experienced emotion, such as a racing heart, altered respiration rate, sweating, blanching or blushing, goose bumps, or pupil dilation or constriction. Some signs of autonomic activity are visible to the naked eye, and others can be detected using sensitive electronic procedures. The presence of these signs is often used as an additional (but not conclusive) clue that an individual is experiencing emotion.

Infants who show wariness or distress faces when approached by strangers show different patterns of heart rate from those of infants who show neutral or positive faces. In adults, viewing slides of emotional faces may be sufficient to produce some ANS changes. There does not seem to be any consistent relationship between the intensity of facial expressions shown by individuals and the degree of their ANS changes. Contrary to long-held belief, different emotions are associated with distinctive patterns of ANS change. Moreover, voluntarily producing facial expressions characteristic of emotion can elicit the corresponding ANS patterns.

See also GESTURE.

Bibliography. Paul Ekman, *Darwin and Facial Expression: A Century of Research in Review*, New York, 1973; idem, ed., *Emotion in the Human Face*, 2d ed., Cambridge and New York, 1982; Carroll E. Izard, ed., *Emotions in Personality and Psychopathology*, New York, 1979; Michael Lewis and Leonard A. Rosenblum, eds., *The Development of Affect*, New York, 1978.

ALAN J. FRIDLUND, PAUL EKMAN,
AND HARRIET OSTER

FACT AND FICTION

The distinction between "fact" and "fiction" appears, at first sight, to be simple. It would seem to be a condition of sanity that we can distinguish between something that has actually been done (the literal meaning of "fact") and something that has been thought of or imagined (the literal meaning of "fiction"). Yet there can be an unthinking transfer of this necessary everyday distinction into the theory and practice of communications, where it soon becomes clear that matters are not so simple. *See also* FICTION.

The decisive new factor in the distinction, within a context of any kind of communication, is that "fact" can no longer be taken as simply "something done." Once some fact in the simple sense is spoken or written about, reported, reconstructed, it can no longer be referred, unexamined, to the unquestionable side of the distinction. At the same time, "fiction," within any communicative practice, is no longer

a matter of simple contrast with "fact." It is true that some "facts" can be shown, by the offer of further evidence, to be fictitious. But it is also true that "fictions" of a certain kind are regularly judged by their degree of fidelity to what is taken as actuality or reality. Moreover, and crucially, there are overlaps of actual procedure, in composition and presentation, between what is offered as fact and what is offered as fiction. At least some of these overlaps are inherent in any communicative procedure.

Fact, Fiction, and the "Factional"

If we are to understand, in its necessary complexity, the real range of relationships between fact and fiction, we must begin, not from their abstract relation as polar opposites, but from the modes in which either can be communicated. This is not to surrender the most basic everyday distinction between "things done" and "things thought of or imagined." But this distinction can be retained only if we are sufficiently attentive to the diverse modes of communication within which it becomes operative.

We can begin by contrasting the two most extreme modes: the scientific report and the specified fantasy. These appear to be the archetypes of fact and fiction, but this is only because of their relatively special conditions. The scientific report, in its ideal form, is a description of things done and observed in such a way that others can do and observe them again. Yet it is clear that this MODE of the scientific report depends on a certain limited number of conditions, as in laboratory experiments. When the facts are not capable of replication in this way, the special warranty of this mode is not available, however faithfully the conventions of this kind of reporting are followed. Unless the facts can be replicated, questions about the position and interest of the reporter, about the conditions within which the observation occurred, and about the relations of the reported facts to other areas of knowledge arise as certainly, if not as controversially, as in cases of political and social reporting in which they are or ought to be crucial.

Thus there can be, and often is, a false extension from the mode of the scientific report dependent on replicable facts to modes that lack this warranty but retain its conventions of presentation: the "objective" reporter; the style of "letting the facts speak for themselves." This has important consequences in political and social reporting, but it is also an important consideration in certain kinds of scientific reporting, especially in sociology and anthropology, in which the position and interests of the observer/reporter are crucial to the nature of the observation but are often masked by conventions of objectivity and impersonality as matters of style.

The specified fantasy is less complicated. In its simplest forms the conventions of removal from any observable time or place—"Once upon a time"; "On the fourth planet of Sirius"—are explicit. Yet there are almost imperceptible gradations, within the broad category of fantasy, from what is offered as familiar (and therefore checkable) reality to the extraordinary and uncheckable event. In genuine fantasy this causes few practical problems, but there are cases—"true stories of the supernatural"; "factual reports of the paranormal"—in which the conventions no longer hold, although their styles may still be relied on.

Nevertheless, at its extremes the fact/fiction dichotomy is not especially difficult to sustain. The most difficult and most relevant problems occur in a wide area between these extremes, in which very careful distinctions are necessary in practice but in which the simple categories are often automatically applied.

A good example is what has been called *faction*—that is, a novel, play, or film explicitly based on some real-life event. What is supposed to be original about this stems from the assumption that fiction, in the broad sense, is normally not so based. Yet this is far from being as simple as it looks. What is to be said about Shakespeare's history plays, or about all historical novels? These are "imaginary" works in the obvious sense that nobody supposes them to be documents or transcripts of the events they present; but in many of them the claim is clearly implied that they have a general basis in fact, and in modern examples this is often underlined by reference to research undertaken. What then distinguishes these works from others in which all the characters and events are said to be invented? There are some conventional signals, including the use of actual names and places, in the historical as in the "factional" play, novel, or film, although precisely what this is a signal of is not always clear. Although the difference between works drawing on actual and invented elements is important, there is still an uncertain area between them. There are many cases in which characters, places, and events are seen as based on actual people, places, and events, even though these are not directly named. But what really matters in this attempted distinction is the implied claim of closeness to reality that depends on the simplest version of the fact/fiction dichotomy: those other works are fictional; these are life itself.

In practice we have only to read different versions of the same "faction" to realize that some of the basic procedures of fiction—selection of point of view, identity of narrator, INTERPRETATION of words and actions, temporal and spatial boundaries of the NARRATIVE—are necessarily involved in any such writing. We may then, as with any other kind of work, make our own judgments about whether or not a particular presentation is convincing. Here again there is a large overlap, since many judgments of this kind are based on internal evidence, of how well—how coherently, penetratingly, sympathetically, wisely—the presentation is carried out. Judgments are often also based on technical evidence—that is, whether the work is well executed. But there remains a real distinction: in the faction or in the specified historical work one can appeal to available evidence not included that would alter the treatment, whereas in pure fiction one cannot. Yet it is remarkable how often, in the reading of mainstream fiction or the viewing of film and television, the same kind of reference, though necessarily more general, is made. People do try to re-place the most absolute fictions, of a broadly realist kind, within a world of which they have other kinds of experience. Thus we have the familiar paradox of a work of fiction being judged by its truth to life.

It must be recognized that truth, in this kind of judgment, is different from simple factual accuracy or reproduction, though often there is also intense interest in these, down to the most marginal details. The truth referred to is of that broad kind underlying the RENAISSANCE claim that POETRY was more true than history because it addressed the most general and universal experiences rather than the necessarily local particularities of historical persons and events. Is there anything in this kind of thinking about "truth" and "the facts" that can be taken on into the most difficult and most controversial area of communications practice, the reporting and interpretation of current events?

Television and the Mediation of Facts

Television has raised certain old problems in some very new forms. Unlike other communications media, it appears to offer us the opportunity of seeing events for ourselves. All written accounts and all oral reports (whether by word of mouth or by RADIO) have a more observable and conventional mediation. Either the text is there, to be assessed as writing for its degree of reliability, or the intermediary is there, with at least some potential of assessment for reliability. Much is done in these older forms to establish authority or objectivity or fair-mindedness—often by fair means, often by foul. But the apparent innovation of television—in which an intermediary can also usually be identified and indeed made subject to the same kind of assessment—is that over and above this it is made to appear that we are seeing what is happening without mediation, that we are seeing the facts for ourselves.

We should not underestimate the qualitative change

in news reporting made possible by the television camera (*see* TELEVISION NEWS). In very many cases there is indeed a directness that surpasses all earlier communicated forms. Yet we are bound to hesitate at the claim that we are then seeing the facts for ourselves. Two considerations—one relatively minor, one quite major—qualify this common assumption.

First, the stance of the television reporter is typically that of the narrator. In factual reporting, as in fiction, the key decision is that of stance: where and on what terms, and with what, if any, declaration of interest does the reporter/narrator position himself or herself? The most evident cases are in reporting of battles, street fighting, and demonstrations (*see* DEMONSTRATION). It is often crucial to observe, as one of the facts, where the reporter is positioned. Usually for logistical reasons, but at times also for other, often ideological reasons, the reporter and then the field of vision of the camera are placed clearly on one side of the conflict. This is not only a limitation on the area of observable facts; it is also commonly a framework within which a theoretically common area of facts is perceived. Thus in a case in which, for example, there is charge and counter-charge between police and demonstrators, it becomes a specific fact of this chosen mode that the forward, aggressive movement is seen from one side only, and moreover that it is directed not only toward the reporter but apparently, through the camera, toward the viewer. When the alternative charge is made, it is from chosen and typically identifying ground toward relatively distant others. Many of the facts may then indeed be directly recorded, but there is a strong tendency to see them within the enclosing but less evident fact of the choice of position. This tendency is of course strongly confirmed if the reporter's commentary or narrative also comes from the same selected point of view.

More broadly, there is always a selected communicative relationship between the commentary/narrative and the images being shown. There is interpretation of incidents not always easy to make out. There are labeling and description, frequently tendentious, very often at least parti pris, of the conflicting forces. Indeed, in a significant number of cases there is actual asymmetry, or even contradiction, between the commentary/narrative and the images. Yet when only the images are seen as the facts, one can fail to notice the elements of a fiction.

Yet if only because, for all the difficulties of such cases, both commentary/narrative and images are explicit and observable, this is the lower level of the most general problem. The higher level is where the procedures of composition—in factual reporting as in the most explicit fiction—are necessarily involved. It is only on certain rare occasions that factual reporting is a camera crew working in real time. Pre-sentation typically involves the crucial, and practical, intermediary processes of selection and editing.

Selection as such, inevitable as it usually must be, is a long step from the bare simplicity of facts toward the procedures of a fiction. However scrupulously done, selection is always the exercise of comparative evaluation of importance, significance, and representativeness. Thus the "facts" are almost always subject to this ordinarily undisclosed exercise of discriminating composition. Excluded facts can through this process be deprived of their factual quality and interpreted as mere rumor or assertion.

This is the crux of a common and inevitable problem in factual reporting. But we should not assume, from its practical inevitability, that it can be safely described as a technical, professional, and thus neutral process. Some examples of undoubtedly manipulative editing throw light on the more general procedure.

It has been alleged that in the editing of a television report on the 1984 British coal strike the temporal order of two key events was reversed. In one edited version the police were shown as charging and the miners countercharging; in another the miners were charging and the police countercharging. The observable facts were much the same in each case, but the alternative order of the events had a major effect on the most central (and most disputed) fact: the identification of the aggressor and of the group responding to aggression. This came out differently, but equally "factually," in the alternative edited sequences.

Again, there have been cases in which a soundtrack from one event—the shouting of angry abuse—was edited into apparent association with a physical action that had occurred at another time and even on a different day. This is a familiar device of television and FILM EDITING; a general effect is achieved by the imaginative interweaving and composition of diverse material. Most responsible news organizations would reject such overtly misleading practices, though it must be noted that only those few with access to the primary "factual" material can really know—still less prove—whether anything of the kind, in major or minor ways, has been done.

Yet cases of malpractice, which deserve to be isolated and investigated, point to the more general problem of all editing. Is it then possible to retain the simple fact/fiction dichotomy and to refer cases of malpractice, minor or major, to an area of error or malignity in what is still, for the most part, factual reporting?

Communication as Continuum

It is important that some position of this kind should be retained. If we draw the wrong conclusions from observation of the compositional elements inherent in all factual reporting, we can deprive ourselves of any grounds for distinction between the best and the worst cases and, even more seriously, can arrive at a damaging cynicism, in which the common desire to try to establish the facts of any situation can be made to appear naive. Indeed, this has been the effect of some recent theoretical tendencies that, correctly observing some common illusions of objectivity and of positive knowledge, would reduce all communication to a series of subjective relativities and would finally deny communication itself as a possibility—all human discourse being an exchange or encounter of private fictions.

It is clear, given the weight of the evidence in the matter of composition of even the most factual reports, that this hopeless conclusion cannot be refuted by any simple reassertion of the fact/fiction dichotomy. But instead of collapsing the dichotomy, we can more usefully review it with attention to its historical formation and its specific conventions and modes. The distinction between truth and lies, and the more difficult distinction between factual truth and imaginative truth, has been attempted and on the whole successfully made in all recorded human societies. In the latter case the arguments have always been more difficult, as we should expect. Yet historically the arguments were altered by the development of methods of substantiating facts, and especially by the movement from personal or official authority as evidence to modes of proof and re-proof, notably in the physical sciences. The great gains of this development were, however, partly nullified by a related rejection of fictions, in which kinds of discourse without these methods of substantiation were indiscriminately downgraded. The popular belief not based on evidence, or even against the evidence, was compounded with forms of discourse that were not claiming provable status. The widespread prejudice against "fiction" was very damaging, but almost equally damaging was the inherent naïveté about "fact." As the role of the observer and of methods of observation as constituents of fact become more clearly understood, an equally prejudiced reaction against "fact" seems likely.

What was missing from these crude and prejudicial contrasts was any adequate understanding of modes and conventions of discourse. It is this understanding that the science of communications seeks to promote. We are learning to identify the signals by which a particular mode, in the broad spectrum from the most factual to the most fictional, is or can be announced. We are learning the conventions that make different modes possible and, within these conventions, the responses that are relevant to any particular mode. To know the signals and the conventions is not enough in itself. There can be abuses and con-

fusions of procedure within any of them: the fictional claiming an inappropriate factuality, the factual using its procedures to include inappropriate fictions. Yet none of these judgments can be made until we realize that we are dealing, not with two large and separate categories, "fact" and "fiction," but with a range of communicative modes that has become a range just because the range of human experience— of events quite beyond us, of events involving us, of speech, of thoughts, of images, of dreams—is in practice so wide and so diverse. It would be an extraordinary loss if our sense of "fact," in all the innumerable cases in which the concept is wholly appropriate, were in any way weakened. But it seems now that we can only intelligently retain it, in a world in which widespread communication and new media and institutions are central in most of our lives, if we understand it as part of the communicative process: the complex social establishment of what we are able to observe. And if this is the case, there can be no crude contrast with "fiction," which in its most serious sense is a related part of the communicative process: the complex social embodiment of what we can observe, feel, and imagine.

RAYMOND H. WILLIAMS

FAMILY

The family is generally regarded as a basic social institution that has considerable impact on children's socialization and development. The family influences several facets of children's acquisition of communication skills (*see* CHILDREN—DEVELOPMENT OF COMMUNICATION). Children are active, self-directed learners of the rules of communication, but they do benefit from parental guidance. Some aspects of communication development respond mainly to maturational factors and children's own efforts, whereas others are susceptible to external influences.

The most important source of influence in the family is the parents, along with the *home environment* they provide. Home environment is a complex concept that includes simultaneously the family's socioeconomic status, the actual living conditions, interaction patterns and activity structures in the family, and other factors such as parental ATTITUDES, goals, and orientations.

Socialization

Parents socialize their children by providing the example of their own actions, attitudes, and beliefs in ways that allow the children opportunities to learn. Willingly and unwillingly, parents model behaviors that children imitate. In the same way, parents reward and punish children, provide direct instruction,

Figure 1. *(Family)* A middle-class family at home, South Dakota, 1939. The Bettmann Archive, Inc.

and structure their environments (*see* SOCIAL COGNITIVE THEORY).

The psychological impetus for socialization seems to come initially from children's dependence on parents and from the affective relationship between parents and children. By establishing a positive affective relationship with their children, parents instill in them a willingness to acquire the behaviors of other family members. The effectiveness of socialization, indicated by the extent to which children acquire the behavior and values of their families, is further promoted by (1) the ability of parents to control the sources of information and rewards available to children and (2) parents' readiness to monitor their children's behavior and respond with appropriate rewards and sanctions. The family's influence may decrease as children grow older and gain access to other reference groups, to other reward contingencies, and to other sources of information outside the family.

These principles of socialization apply across a wide variety of cultures and social settings. They are not peculiar to the family but operate whenever a new member joins an established group (*see* POLITICAL SOCIALIZATION). The types and content of behavior that are socialized vary dramatically among cultural groups and to some degree from one family

(or any other basic unit) to another within a given CULTURE. Despite these differences the skills of special significance to human beings—such as LANGUAGE—are universal targets of socialization processes.

Basic Skills

Much research has been devoted to elucidating the family's role in the development of communication skills considered fundamental: LANGUAGE ACQUISITION (the formal elements of language), SPEECH (oral communication), and LITERACY (READING and WRITING).

Language acquisition. Language acquisition is one of the truly momentous achievements of early childhood. Within their first five years children master the basic rules of PHONOLOGY, syntax, SEMANTICS, and pragmatics. Researchers disagree about the extent to which acquisition is governed by innate factors or environmental sources such as the family. The strongest environmental position has been voiced by behaviorists like B. F. Skinner, who claimed that children's language is structured by the environment through principles of reinforcement. According to this view, parents selectively reinforce those features of infants' babbling that most closely resemble adult speech and continue to shape the utterances until they approximate adult style. Other learning theorists emphasize imitation: the child imitates adult words and phrases and is rewarded for doing so. In contrast, U.S. linguist Noam Chomsky and others have argued that language acquisition is innately preprogrammed and that we are genetically endowed with knowledge about language. For Chomsky the language to which parents and others expose children is error-ridden and incomplete, making the task of deciphering its underlying structures extremely difficult without ready-made hypotheses.

Both of these accounts have been challenged. Few linguists or psychologists take the environmental position without also referring to children's innate capacity for language and their efforts at mastery. Researchers now recognize that the language to which children are exposed is not as deficient as was once assumed; parents tailor their speech in several ways to their perceptions of children's abilities and interests. Phonological features of adult speech to children include high pitch and exaggerated intonation, clear enunciation, and slow tempo with distinct pauses between utterances. Syntactic features include sentences that are well formed and intelligible; few disfluencies or broken sentences; heavy reliance on content words; many repetitions and expansions of the child's own utterances; and avoidance of pronouns, modifiers, and functors. Semantically adults use a limited vocabulary, restrict topics to the "here and now" and to matters of interest to children, and use particular levels of generality when naming objects. Pragmatically they use more directives, imperatives, and questions.

Presumably this specialized input makes the rules of language more apparent for children and lures them into meaningful dialogue. Examples of parents'

modifications that appear to affect children's syntactic growth rate include expansions on children's prior utterances, specific uses of gestures (*see* GESTURE), and repetitions. Engaging children in routine games or rituals (*see* RITUAL) may also promote language learning because these activities make language predictable, associate it with concrete actions, and encourage children to produce utterances. In short, by accommodating children's attentional states and cognitive capacities, parents may enhance the children's ability to comprehend and express verbal meaning.

A tendency to modify the speech of young children may be universal. It has been observed in all family members and across different ethnic groups, social classes, and language communities (*see* LANGUAGE VARIETIES). However, cultural groups do vary in the degree and type of adjustments they use with young children and in the specific caretakers (e.g., parents, siblings) that employ them.

Oral communication development. In addition to learning the formal systems of language, children learn social rules governing its usage, such as cooperative rules of CONVERSATION, conventional devices to attain specific communicative goals, and methods to check on the accuracy of one's own understanding and that of one's interactional partner. As with language acquisition, developments in communication depend on both children's own efforts and environmental feedback.

Parents adopt several conversational techniques to help children participate in interaction and become aware of the communicator's responsibilities. Use of distinct gestures to gain attention and convey information is one such technique. Another is ritualized question-and-answer sequences, from which the children learn about taking turns and the functions of

Figure 2. *(Family)* Father plays with baby. Bajoeng Gede, April 30, 1937. From Gregory Bateson and Margaret Mead, *Balinese Character: A Photographic Analysis*, New York, 1942, plate 74, 2. The Institute for Intercultural Studies/Library of Congress.

questions. These games or rituals become more complex as children acquire a larger repertoire of skills.

Specific instructional sequences may be offered in some cultural groups but not in others. Cultural groups may also differ in the types of communicative lessons they provide and the specific rules they abide by. Nonetheless, all groups have some provisions for making known and reinforcing their conventions of communication.

Cultural groups and individual families within cultures vary in their reliance on patterns of communication that are used in the CLASSROOM. Parents differ in the degree to which they encourage children to specify referents clearly (as occurs in written text), familiarize them with the structure of NARRATIVE through storytelling, and draw attention to components of language such as words and sentences. In addition, parents influence children's scholastic performance in the extent to which they foster a dialect or style of communication that conforms to the expectations of educational institutions. Children encouraged to use dissimilar patterns may be hindered in their performance at SCHOOL not because they lack communication skills but because the language of the classroom does not build on the skills they do possess.

Literacy skills. A considerable body of research shows an association between resources of the home and children's literacy skills. The effects of family environment appear before children begin school and continue throughout the school years. Analyses identify several types of home resources and family interactions that may affect acquisition of reading and writing skills. Most of the available studies examine family effects on reading, but several researchers suggest that similar influences may affect writing skills.

Literacy skills are associated with access to reading and writing materials and relevant experiences provided by the home. The tendency of parents to read to their children is associated with children's reading skills. Parents of early readers are likely to acquire picture dictionaries, alphabet books, and basal readers and to provide paper, pencils, and blackboards for their children. They are also likely to take children to the LIBRARY and to expose them to a variety of other out-of-home experiences such as family trips and cultural activities. Parents also influence their children's reading through modeling. The reading habits of parents (e.g., amount and type of material read) are generally correlated with children's performance on tests of reading readiness.

In addition to these specific features of the home, other general factors are associated with children's performance. Parents' expectations for achievement in school-relevant skills are associated with performance during preschool and grade school years. The affective relationship between mothers and children is also correlated with reading activity, possibly because it indicates how supportive the learning environment is.

Summary. Parents may employ many strategies that promote children's communication skills. These include encouraging participation; tailoring communications to a comprehensible style; responding to the child's attempts; and modeling patterns of speech, reading, and writing. The variety of cultural contexts and the specific interaction patterns of each family allow for a multiplicity of individual differences in children's communicative skills and styles.

See also EDUCATION.

Bibliography. Noam Chomsky, *Aspects of the Theory of Syntax*, Cambridge, Mass., 1965; Jill G. de Villiers and Peter A. de Villiers, *Language Acquisition*, Cambridge, Mass., 1978; Shirley Brice Heath, "Questioning at Home and at School: A Comparative Study," in *Doing the Ethnography of Schooling: Educational Anthropology in Action*, ed. by George Spindler, New York, 1982; Robert D. Hess, S. D. Holloway, G. G. Price, and W. P. Dickson, "Family Environments and the Acquisition of Reading Skills: Toward a More Precise Analysis," in *Families as Learning Environments for Children*, ed. by Luis M. Laosa and Irving E. Sigel, New York, 1982; B. F. Skinner, *Verbal Behavior*, New York, 1957.

ROBERT D. HESS AND TERESA M. MCDEVITT

FAR EAST, ANCIENT. *See* EAST ASIA, ANCIENT.

FARADAY, MICHAEL (1791–1867)

British physicist and chemist (or, as he put it, "natural philosopher") whose findings played a seminal role in modern scientific developments, including many aspects of communications technology. Michael Faraday's work is often linked with that of JAMES MAXWELL (1831–1879). Their careers overlapped, and both were intent on unifying the fields of electricity and magnetism—Faraday by experiment and Maxwell by mathematics. Their work, at a time when electricity and magnetism were little understood, established principles that paved the way for the invention of TELEGRAPHY, the TELEPHONE, dynamos, RADIO, and television, as well as such basic aspects of modern life as the large-scale production of electricity.

Born of poor parents on the outskirts of London, Faraday had only rudimentary schooling. At age fourteen he was apprenticed to a bookseller and bookbinder. Faraday furthered his education by reading the books he was to bind or sell, including an encyclopedia article on electricity that drew him strongly to science. In 1813 he heard four lectures by Sir Humphry Davy, head of the Royal Institution.

Faraday sent him his lecture notes, bound and carefully illustrated, and asked for a job. Soon retained by Davy as a lecture assistant, Faraday began his lifelong association with the Royal Institution. He continued to learn from the experiments he set up for lecturers, and later in 1813 he embarked on a one-and-a-half-year trip with Sir Humphry and Lady Davy that enabled him to visit laboratories and outstanding scientists all over Europe. Thus he had an extraordinary introduction to the scientific developments of the time.

Back at the Royal Institution laboratories Faraday began the experimentation that eventually made him famous. He not only carried out his own experiments but also repeated new experiments reported by others in order to better his own understanding. He became director of the laboratories in 1825 and by 1830 had published more than sixty papers. On an annual wage of one hundred pounds plus rooms, coal, and candles he and his wife lived simply.

Faraday's greatest triumphs were the induction of an electric current by a moving magnet (the principle of the dynamo) and, almost equally important, the rotation of the plane of polarization of a polarized light wave by a magnetic field. The latter showed that a magnetic field affected a light wave. (Faraday and others had already shown that light had wavelike properties.) Faraday thus anticipated, but did not achieve, the electromagnetic theory of light and all other electromagnetic waves (radio, X ray, and many others). He used the evocative term "lines of force" to describe an electric or magnetic field and was conceptually close to modern field theory.

In acknowledgment of Faraday's achievements the electromagnetic unit of capacitance is now universally known as the *farad*. Faraday also had a law of chemistry named for him, but his work in chemistry is not so well known as that in physics. He did, however, introduce such terms as *electrode, electrolysis, anode, cathode,* and, at the suggestion of a friend, *ion*.

Faraday's leadership in establishing the core of electromagnetic theory, although entirely experimental, was the basis on which Maxwell, as the latter acknowledged, started his famous study aimed at uniting the field mathematically, which in turn resulted in the all-embracing Maxwell Equations. Faraday, ever eager to uncover new experimental knowledge, appealed to Maxwell for suggestions on how the mathematical conclusions might be developed experimentally.

Faraday received honors from many parts of the world but declined a knighthood. He and his wife continued to live simply. Lectures and a government stipend from the Civil List brought him about one thousand pounds a year during the latter part of his life. He once accepted a one-thousand-pound fee for consultation on industry matters but generally avoided such involvements to devote himself fully to his "great objective."

Bibliography. Joseph Agassi, *Faraday as a Natural Philosopher*, Chicago, 1971; J. G. Crowther, *British Scientists of the Nineteenth Century*, London, 1935; R. A. R. Tricker, *The Contributions of Faraday and Maxwell to Electrical Science*, New York, 1966; L. Pearce Williams, *Michael Faraday: A Biography*, New York, 1965.

JOHN G. BRAINERD

FARNSWORTH, PHILO (1906–1971)

U.S. inventor best known for his role in the creation of electronic television—the great turning point in TELEVISION HISTORY. Two men are regarded as chief contributors to that breakthrough: VLADIMIR K. ZWORYKIN, head of the television development staff assembled by the Radio Corporation of America (RCA) at Camden, New Jersey; and Philo Taylor Farnsworth, a largely self-taught experimenter working with slim backing in a San Francisco laboratory. The relative significance of their contributions was long contested, first in U.S. Patent Office confrontations and throughout later years in journal literature.

Farnsworth, born on an isolated Utah farm, did not encounter electricity until his early teens, when his family moved to Rigby, Idaho, and acquired a Delco machine. The youth seemed able at once to understand its workings and became an obsessed

Figure 1. *(Farnsworth, Philo)* Philo T. Farnsworth. The caption reads: "Invention of California scientist designed to permit reception of talking movies in the home." The Bettmann Archive, Inc.

reader of electrical journals. In 1922, talking to his high school history teacher, Justin Tolman, he said he had read about television experiments in the East that used a whirling disc to scan images. That was not practical, Farnsworth said, and he proceeded to astonish the teacher (who later testified about this) by covering a blackboard with diagrams showing how it might be done with electrons in vacuum tubes. Tolman encouraged Farnsworth to pursue his ideas. In Salt Lake City two years later those ideas caught the interest of George Everson, a California promoter who had come to organize the community-chest drive and had hired Farnsworth and his friend Elma Gardner. Everson offered to set up Farnsworth in a California laboratory to develop his electronic television scheme and to search for additional funds himself. Farnsworth, aged nineteen, asked Gardner, aged seventeen, to become his wife and laboratory assistant; she agreed, and they set out for California.

Farnsworth proved to be a near genius in conceiving and developing new technical ideas. After receiving instruction in glassblowing he designed and made all the needed vacuum tubes. In 1927, one year after the start of laboratory work, Farnsworth applied for his first patent; he received it in 1930. The first public demonstration (i.e., the first open to newspaper reporters) of a completely electronic television system was staged in his laboratory in 1928. It was far removed from the television of later years but was sufficient to bring wide newspaper reports.

The 1930 patent award (and supplementary patents) challenged RCA, whose president, DAVID SARNOFF, had given Zworykin's staff the task of developing and perfecting television for early introduction. Virtually all pertinent existing electronic patents were controlled by RCA; additional patents, if covering essential items, were purchased outright. Like Farnsworth, Zworykin had long seen an all-electronic system as essential and was progressing toward that end. Farnsworth and Zworykin had worked along parallel lines. In pickup tubes Zworykin had developed his iconoscope; Farnsworth had his image dissector tube. They were tubes designed for the same function but based on radically different principles. RCA first announced it would not need Farnsworth's tube but, based on picture quality, finally realized it could not do without it. Challenging Farnsworth's patents, RCA lawyers questioned him relentlessly in interference proceedings but failed to shake his position. RCA then offered to buy his patents outright, but Farnsworth would agree only to a royalty basis. Against all RCA precedent, the company yielded. Farnsworth's image dissector became a key ingredient in the television system introduced by RCA at the 1939 New York World's Fair.

Meanwhile Farnsworth had moved his laboratory to Philadelphia, where his development work was supported by Philco in exchange for patent rights.

FIRST DAY OF ISSUE

Figure 2. *(Farnsworth, Philo)* A commemorative postage stamp depicting Philo T. Farnsworth and the first television camera. Issued September 21, 1983, Washington, D.C.

After World War II the laboratory was taken over by International Telephone and Telegraph (ITT), which ultimately put Farnsworth to work on rocketry and nuclear fusion. But his health was failing, and he returned to Salt Lake City for his final years.

Farnsworth seemed indifferent to public acclaim. *Century of Honors* (1984), published by the Institute of Electrical and Electronic Engineers, notes that he was the only one among almost a thousand honored in the one hundred years of the institute's existence who did not supply the editors, or place on record, any information about himself. However, after his death a U.S. postage stamp (1983) carried his picture, in a series featuring scientists who had laid the foundations of electronic communications.

JOHN G. BRAINERD

FEEDBACK. *See* MODELS OF COMMUNICATION.

FEMINIST THEORIES OF COMMUNICATION

Feminist communication theory is nurtured and critiqued by feminist theory as it has developed in the large intercultural and international feminist movements. The histories, questions, analytical tools, and boundaries of feminist communication theory are reviewed, revised, reinterpreted, and written in ways that are themselves challenges to traditional communication theory. Although there is no general agreement about the categories of feminist communication study and theory (or even about the need for agreement), some topics are common to many of the analyses.

Feminist theory. Feminists consider most theories of communication inadequate, misleading, and dangerous because they distort women's experiences, ideas, and concerns. One problem is with what has traditionally been labeled theory. Australian feminist theorist Dale Spender argues that in a society in which men have named only themselves as theorists their theories have often been used to mystify, intimidate, and oppress others while justifying the status quo. Male theorizing has too often been used to

construct divisions between those "who know" and those who don't. Spender points out that much theorizing is based on the honoring of great men: entire systems of books, courses, and dialectics have been erected around individual men whose names are used to label theoretical frameworks. In communication research there is, for example, Marxist theory (*see* MARX, KARL), Foucauldian theory (*see* FOUCAULT, MICHEL), McLuhanism (*see* MCLUHAN, MARSHALL), and Lacanian theory. It is no accident that there is no (Mary) Dalyist theory, no (Julia) Penelopeian theory, no (Suzette) Elginist theory, no (Adrienne) Richist theory, no (Monique) Wittigian theory—even though these theorists have written extensively about communications issues, bringing together and expanding our knowledge of LANGUAGE and interaction and suggesting new problems, methodologies, and interpretations. To validate this work by labeling the theories with women's names would acknowledge that these women are experts and have created serious, impressive, contending theories. For feminists, even though recognizing the need to discover and rediscover the women whose names and intellectual work have been distorted, appropriated, or elided by men's histories, the problems with associating theories with individual names are complex. U.S. scholar Nancy Hartsock and others argue that theory is not the activity of a few but the articulation, open to all, of our practical, knowing activities; theory can be considered as making conscious the philosophy embedded in our lives—"theory in the flesh." Feminism itself is not a theory, a set of hypotheses, an institution, or a collection of principles; it is a movement, a renouncement of obedience to the systems erected by men, a search for answers to new questions, a collective process.

Thus feminists recognize that there is not a single human way of understanding interactions. U.S. philosopher Sandra Harding is joined by others in suggesting that innovative theorists welcome a plurality of perspectives to encourage the instability of analytical categories and to encourage the use of these instabilities as resources for thinking and action. Harding points out that this approach to theorizing incorporates what some believe to be a distinctive emphasis that many women put on contextual thinking and decision making, a focus on the importance and usefulness of talk, connectedness, and relationships. Such a perspective is exemplified by U.S. psychologist Carol Gilligan's *In a Different Voice* (1982), an influential and controversial study positing the existence of a distinctively female process of moral development based on intimacy and caring rather than on the more abstract principles of fairness or justice often characterizing male moral decisions.

Silencing of women. Many studies have uncovered the ways in which women's discourse is subject to male control and CENSORSHIP. For example, research conducted in the United States and elsewhere shows that in male-female gatherings men talk more and interrupt more than women. It is telling that men's talkativeness and interruptive tendencies are not among men's stereotypes about male interaction.

Formal educational structures and possibilities differ for women and men, leading to the stifling of women's creative reading, writing, and speaking. U.S. writer Alice Walker asks, "What did it mean for a Black woman to be an artist in our grandmothers' time?"—that is, an artist given no training in reading or writing, no books or other resources. UNESCO figures report that the gap between male and female LITERACY is growing in many societies. In some countries when women are permitted to go to universities they are segregated from male students and often are not allowed to participate in discussion. Women often are not permitted to study abroad. In many countries—for example, even in Japan, where the literacy rate is close to 100 percent—women have been excluded from many literary jobs and honors and are encouraged to express their subordination through "feminine" words, voice, and syntax. In all formal education what is taught is men's knowledge; the silencing of active, theorizing women takes place in almost all educational formats. U.S. theorist Berenice Carroll notes that men apply gender-specific terms to evaluate men's and women's intellectual achievements. Terms such as *original, innovative, first rank,* and *excellent* are used to exclude women, whose intellectual contributions are called derivative, unoriginal, popular.

Women are also silenced or threatened by the application of deviancy labels. Spender documents that women, particularly knowledgeable, witty women, who question or rebel against patriarchy are called aberrations, unnatural, unattractive, unsexed, unnaturally sexed, and man-haters. Women writing in the Indian journal *Manushi,* for example, frequently analyze the ways in which the labeling of women makes it very costly, in terms of reputation and economic sanctions, for women to speak out on social issues. Such analysis often concerns how assessments of a woman's behavior are based on the relations she is believed to have with men and on the deviation of her behavior from the ideal of the loyal, obedient wife.

The ultimate exercise of personal and political power is through VIOLENCE. Although this has long been an issue for feminists concerned with the victimization of women through rape and domestic abuse, some theorists have begun to acknowledge that the threat of male violence, implicit or explicit, restricts women's activities in every sphere and thus underlies all aspects of human communication.

Heteropatriarchal semantics. U.S. theorist Julia Penelope and others have explored the ways in which language itself is a conceptual frame governing how and what we think (*see* LANGUAGE IDEOLOGY). In a heteropatriarchal society such as the United States, for example, heterosexuality and male dominance are assumed to be natural and "male" and "female" to be natural, eternal categories rather than the expression of concepts essential to the maintenance of the heteropatriarchy. Similarly, French novelist Monique Wittig asserts that the fact of oppression created the categories rather than vice versa. Masculine/feminine and male/female are language categories concealing the social and political differences between men and women. A materialist feminist approach argues that although race and sex are seen as the cause or origin of oppression, they are actually the sign or mark imposed by the oppressor. Sex, race, and class are not individual characteristics but in many countries constitute the conceptual terminology supporting a white, middle-class, male elite. The categories are thus closely related in function. A major feminist contribution to social scientific theory has been the replacement of *sex* by the terms GENDER or *sex/gender system,* reflecting the fact that such categories are culturally and not biologically determined. Most feminist theorists focus on gender differences in order to draw attention to how that divisive system is socially constructed and maintained.

Feminist communication theorists consider language problematic in a way that much mainstream communication theory does not. Traditional Marxism, for example, assumes the relation "women/men" to be a natural one, outside the social order; in much Marxist theorizing women are assigned to classes of men, bourgeoisie or proletariat, an assumption that hides the class conflict between men and women (*see* MARXIST THEORIES OF COMMUNICATION). Instead of viewing language primarily as a tool for the transmission of information, the feminist approach treats language as a basically man-made construction that constricts the ways we can make MEANING. In feminist linguistic work, for example, dictionaries are studied as representative of male symbol systems and prejudices. Many feminists are engaged in recovering and inventing ways of defining, speaking, and writing female experiences and perceptions.

Writing the body. This expression is most frequently associated with some French feminists who argue in part that women need to learn to write from their bodies, their pleasures, and their experiences. A major focus is again on silences, on the absence of women's voices caused by the overpowering voices of masculinity in the structure and use of language. Rather than focusing on, for example, the documentation of a past in which women have been vocal or arguing that speech differences are grounded in sex, race, or class differences (which some French feminists find to be inadequate and traditionally North American problem-solving approaches), writers such as Hélène Cixous suggest that we write a feminine language with "mother's milk" or "the blood's language." That is, women can begin with the immediate specificity of their bodies and their psychosexuality to create a new reality.

Other feminists have criticized this particular psychoanalytical perspective for being ahistorical, ignoring or paying little attention to differences established by race and class, and overlooking the social/political institutions that support the oppression of women. Other, multilingual feminists question the existence of a single language of the body because women think and speak in different ways about their bodies depending on the categories and relationships available in various languages.

Some believe a more useful approach than neo-Freudian psychoanalytic theories is emerging in the writings of feminists who describe their multiple, shifting, often seemingly self-contradictory identities. Objecting to the ready labels often applied to them (e.g., "white," "middle class," "black," or "Hispanic"), these women claim for themselves others as well, such as "intellectual," "feminist," and "anti-imperialist." They also question the assumption that there exist, for our theorizing of language and communication, separate homes within feminism based on the imposed divisions among racial, ethnic, religious, sexual, or national identities. Used separately these labels too often leave unchallenged such polar concepts as East/West or white/nonwhite, which themselves leave unchallenged the idea that communication theory based on analyses of the situation of women in the West can be adequate for the West when they do not deal with the hierarchical East/West divide. Similarly, others point to how such concepts as "capitalism" and "Christianity" construct many of the analytical terms in communication theory.

Technologies. Feminist scholars have been very interested in the differing consequences of technologies for the construction and employment of males and females. One research area concerns the methods that are used to speak and write to others: who may or must interact with whom and how. Some feminist theorists have given explanations and implications of women's exclusions from the social histories of the technological processes involved in communication—PRINTING, RADIO, television (*see* TELEVISION HISTORY), and so on. A related area of research presents the evidence that technological processes, developed and analyzed primarily by men, have had profound and largely unexplored consequences for women's communication. The resources available to women structure the time, place, and content of their interactions.

The media as industry. Feminist criticism of the media has a long history. In the United States in 1870 Susan B. Anthony and Elizabeth Cady Stanton were conscious of how very different the structure and policies of their weekly newspaper, *The Revolution,* were from those of most newspapers (*see* NEWSPAPER: HISTORY). Anthony and Stanton wanted to publish primarily women's words because "masculine ideas have ruled the race for 6,000 years," and they insisted that women's words appear under their own names. In the late twentieth century the establishment and expansion, primarily in Europe and North America, of women's periodicals, publishing collectives, press networks, and professional organizations have been part of an unprecedented effort to provide women with access to information sources and networks. Despite such attempts, however, media industries remain largely under male control, and women remain vastly underrepresented in media management and production worldwide.

In countries with high illiteracy rates for women and with prominent gender differences in work experience, mobility, and media access, much feminist criticism involves the documentation and analysis of the values carried by media messages, including the representation of physical ideals of beauty and femininity against which all women are evaluated and the portrayal of housework and childcare as female duties. Many of these particular messages come from Europe and the United States, a fact that raises important questions about media practices and IDEOLOGY. Who is allowed to make cultural productions, and how are they used? How are media practices in the dominant cultures involved in social and political dominance throughout the world?

Feminist theorists have begun to address such issues by expanding on the perspectives and approaches characteristic of traditional MASS COMMUNICATIONS RESEARCH (*see also* MASS MEDIA EFFECTS). The impact has been felt in various fields as studies examine the ways in which women's participation in the production of ART and literature (*see* LITERARY CANON) has been ignored or restricted and how biased and distorted media images—or the absence of images—have contributed to the silencing of women and the perpetuation of dangerous stereotypes (*see* FILM THEORY; LITERARY CRITICISM; PORNOGRAPHY).

Public and private. The opposition of the concepts "public" and "private" is central to many communication histories and theories. In many cultures these concepts support a capitalist status quo and an extensive sex/gender system. Within this system the minds and words of women are considered complementary, and inferior, to those of men; masculine intellect is seen in contrast to and as transcending the feminine character, which is biologically driven and firmly bound to the body and the home. Men make the move away from the body and the home to reason and public activities.

This public/private division is present throughout mainstream communication theorizing, which is itself often divided into the study of INTERPERSONAL COMMUNICATION—focusing on such topics as male/female, intimacy, sex roles, role playing, friendships, body image, empathy and healthy interaction, styles of listening, perception processes, self-concept, and identity—and mass communication—concerned with such issues as competition, producers and consumers, technology, political power, audience, content, history, institutions, PERSUASION, and policymakers. Interpersonal communication study is the "small world" approach dealing with relationships among individuals. Much interpersonal communication research begins with an assumption of equality in the private world. Mass media study, however, is the "big world" of communication structures and policies and deals with significant political issues.

There are other areas of study that do not fit neatly into this dichotomy. Yet most cultural studies, with interest in forms of communication as everyday activities and with concern for the misuse of media, have not provided critiques of the controlling dichotomy or incorporated women's communication experiences as represented in feminist scholarship and theory. Notable exceptions include U.S. scholar Janice Radway's analysis of readers' uses of romance novels (see ROMANCE, THE) and British scholar Angela McRobbie's critique of the exclusion of girls from men's cultural studies of the working class.

Feminists have written about the dichotomy between public and private not as a natural or convenient division of labor but as a paradigm convenient for posing separate sexual spheres of activity and for exaggerating gender differences in political life. Men cannot possess a public, political life unless there is also posited a separate private, apolitical life. For centuries women have criticized masculinist assumptions in many cultures about a "women's sphere." For example, Westerners often are critical of purdah, the man-made rules and sanctions that seclude women, govern their behavior toward men, and control their speech and movement in the home and community. Yet related rules and sanctions can be seen to operate in many forms in all patriarchal societies, even in men's harassment of women in "public" streets throughout the world. The history of women's attempts to "make sense"—to speak and write for themselves, to control their own knowledge, and to transmit this knowledge to others—has been virtually ignored in men's histories. Feminist communication theory exposes that divisive, distorting category system of private and public and offers a more diversified, holistic understanding of communication.

See INTERPRETATION; SEXISM.

Bibliography. Donna Allen, ed., *Media Report to Women*, Washington, D.C., 1972–; Katherine Fishburn, *Women in Popular Culture*, Westport, Conn., 1982; Carol Gilligan, *In a Different Voice: Psychological Theory and Women's Development*, Cambridge, Mass., 1982; Fran P. Hosken, ed., *Women's International Network*, Lexington, Mass., 1975–; Cheris Kramarae and Paula Treichler, with Ann Russo, *A Feminist Dictionary*, New York, 1985; Cheris Kramarae, ed., *Technology and Women's Voices: Keeping in Touch*, London, 1987; Teresa de Lauretis, ed., *Feminist Studies/Critical Studies*, Bloomington, Ind., 1986; Toril Moi, *Sexual/Textual Politics: Feminist Literary Theory*, London and New York, 1985; Cherríe Moraga and Gloria Anzaldúa, eds., *This Bridge Called My Back: Writings by Radical Women of Color*, Watertown, Mass., 1981; Dale Spender, *Women of Ideas and What Men Have Done to Them: From Aphra Behn to Adrienne Rich*, London, 1982; Barrie Thorne, Cheris Kramarae, and Nancy Henley, eds., *Language, Gender, and Society*, Rowley, Mass., 1983.

CHERIS KRAMARAE

FESSENDEN, REGINALD (1866–1932)

Canadian-born electrical engineer who made important contributions to the evolution of RADIO in the United States. The course of his career was set by GUGLIELMO MARCONI's 1895 invention of wireless TELEGRAPHY, but Reginald Aubrey Fessenden was intent on the next step, the transmission of voice—a step analogous to the progression from SAMUEL F. B. MORSE's telegraphy to the TELEPHONE of ALEXANDER GRAHAM BELL. Leaving an academic career to pursue his interests, Fessenden first took a position with the U.S. Weather Bureau, which was serving farmers with wireless weather bulletins in Morse code and was willing to let him experiment with voice transmission—or radio, as some called it. He later secured backing for his own company, the National Electric Signaling Company. Marconi's wireless system used a separate radiomagnetic burst for every dot and dash. Fessenden envisioned a radical departure: a continuous carrier wave on which he hoped modulations capable of carrying recognizable voices and tones could be introduced. To produce his carrier wave he ordered a high-frequency alternator from General Electric, whose engineers were skeptical of the idea but were willing to fill the order. Fessenden soon had success with experimental voice transmissions, and on December 24, 1906, he staged a historic demonstration. Wireless operators on ships on the Atlantic, alerted in advance, heard through their earphones a woman singing, a violin playing, a man talking. It was Fessenden wishing them a merry Christmas and asking them to let him know at his laboratory in Brant Rock, Massachusetts, if they had heard his transmission.

Throughout that winter Fessenden maintained radio transmissions between two stations eleven miles apart. The American Telephone and Telegraph Company (AT&T) showed interest in this demonstration of radiotelephony, but nothing came of the negotiations. Meanwhile LEE DE FOREST's invention of the Audion vacuum tube, used as a detector and an amplifier, brought a big leap forward in the quality of voice transmission. Radio became a hobby for countless amateurs, but neither De Forest nor Fessenden found it easy to translate this enthusiasm into steady income. Fessenden's backers grew restive. A 1909 navy contract failed to check their disillusion, and two years later Fessenden was dismissed from his own company. He subsequently focused on naval electronics—depth finders, underwater communications devices, and the like. His reputation revived in 1926, when his antitrust suit against Radio Corporation of America (RCA) won him $500,000.

Fessenden's career was one of beginnings. Among his notable early achievements was his 1901 invention of the heterodyne circuit, which greatly increased the strength of an incoming signal. Later combined with De Forest's Audion, it led to EDWIN H. ARMSTRONG's superheterodyne, which became the basis for radio amplification throughout the industry.

HARTLEY S. SPATT

FESTIVAL

An ancient and resilient cultural form, richly varied in organization and function across the world's societies. For all their diversity, however, festivals display certain characteristic features. They occur at calendrically regulated intervals and are public in nature, participatory in ethos, complex in structure, and multiple in voice, scene, and purpose.

Festivals are collective phenomena and serve purposes rooted in group life. Systems of reciprocity and of shared responsibility ensure the continuity of and participation in the festival through the distribution of prestige and production. Most festivals provide the opportunity for individual religious devotion or individual PERFORMANCE, and this opportunity is a primary motive for the occasion. Other unstated but important purposes of festivals are the expression of group identity through ancestor worship or memorialization, the performance of highly valued skills and talents, or the articulation of the group's heritage. Rarely do such events use the term *festival,* employing instead a name related to the stated purposes or core symbols of the event: Mardi Gras (Catholic), Sukkot (Jewish), Holi (Hindu), Shalako (Zuni), Adae (Ghanaian), Calus (Romanian), Namahage (Japanese), Cowboy Reunion (American), and Feast of Fools (French). Those events that do have *festival* in their titles are generally contemporary modern constructions, employing festival characteristics but serving the commercial, ideological, or political purposes of self-interested authorities or entrepreneurs. *See also* SPECTACLE.

Consideration of terminology also raises the question of festival's relationship to RITUAL. The separation of the two types of symbolic enactment evolved as a consequence of modern religious systems' attempts to obliterate native religions. Quite commonly, however, indigenous practices survived under a new name, disguising their origins. These became known as festival or fiesta, in contrast to ritual, which became the serious occasions focusing on male authority legitimated by modern official RELIGION. In an effort to denigrate indigenous religious practices, modern religion thus assigned festival to a position peripheral to the core of ritual life. The most recent modern religions, such as Protestantism, completely dissociate festival from religion, and it then becomes a secular event. As a result ritual is associated with official religion, whereas festival designates occasions considered to be pagan, recreational, or for children. Like PLAY and creativity, festival explores and experiments with MEANING, in contrast

Figure 1. *(Festival)* Boy's Day (May 5), Japan. Carp streamers on the roofs of houses. Courtesy of Japan National Tourist Organization.

to ritual, which attempts to control meaning. Both forms utilize multiple codes and channels (*see* CODE). Examples of contemporary festivals and holidays with ancient roots include celebrations of saints' days, the Virgin Mary, Christmas, the new year, Easter, May Day, and Halloween, all of which represent a fusion of early Indo-European and/or Native American religious rituals with modern official religion and CULTURE.

Ritual and festival occur in modern cultures as separate events, but older religions integrate the calendrical rites we are labeling festival into the larger ritual cycle. For this reason much of the literature on religion, ritual, festival, fiesta, or carnival does not distinguish between the two related forms.

Festival Communication

Festival communication actively engages the participants. It is this feature that distinguishes festival from those large-scale forms that may be observed from a distance or by television or those events in which the participants passively receive messages but have no choice in their roles. Therefore, we can describe festival action as a combination of participation and performance in a public context. Very little festival action is private; those acts that are, such as courtship or religious devotion, are nevertheless made possible and defined by the special purposes of a particular festival. Moreover, what is spoken, acted, or displayed in festival—public or private—anticipates a response, social or supernatural. This active mode, then, makes demands on participants, requiring their attention. And this concentration of attention heightens consciousness, creating an intersection of individual performance and social reflexivity.

Festival communication involves a major shift from the frames of everyday life that focus attention on subsistence, routine, and production to frames that foster the transformative, reciprocal, and reflexive dimensions of social life. Such a frame shift does not rule out the mundane or the dangerous; commercial transactions flourish in many festivals, and MASK and costume have on occasion disguised bloody violence. The shift in frames guarantees nothing but rather transposes reality so that intuition, inversion, risk, and symbolic expression reign.

The messages of festival concern the shared experience of the group and multiple interpretations of that experience. Shared experience may be enacted as myth, music, or DRAMA; it may also be the marked representation of a segment of everyday life such as harvesting; it dominates the rhetoric as well as the action of an event clearly defined as "ours." In all socially based festivals, however, the messages will be directly related to the present social circumstances as well as to the past. Because festival brings the group together and communicates about the society itself and the role of the individual within it, every effort either to change or to constrain social life will be expressed in some specific relationship to festival.

Festival Structures

The structures that operate to create festival reality may be characterized as (1) event structures and (2) social structures of participation.

Event structures. The multiple activities of festival do not occur randomly but rather in an order, officially or unofficially agreed upon. The following events generally are included in a genuine festival.

(a) *Opening ceremony:* A ceremony such as a parade or procession, simple or elaborate, provides the official opening. The display of individuals and institutions and sometimes characters in costume in this ceremony can reveal the social structure of the community and confirm dominant community values as well.

(b) *Ritual:* In festivals linked to religion the ritual will enact a religious purpose: promises made to a saint or to the Virgin, the acknowledgment of the ancestors, a sacred DANCE for rain or a feast in honor of the harvest. In secular festivals the ritual event

Figure 2. *(Festival)* Musicians at a festival in Languedoc, France. From Daniel Fabre and Charles Camberoque, *La fête en Languedoc*, Toulouse: Privat, 1978, p. 187.

Figure 3. *(Festival)* Dragon dance. New Year celebration, Taipei. Courtesy of the Information and Communication Division in New York, Coordination Council for North American Affairs.

may provide the means for addressing death and the affirmation of life, or it may be the ceremonial coronation of the festival queen.

(c) *Drama and contest:* Through the genres of folk drama, contest, or other dramatistic forms the community expresses social conflicts and concerns rooted in social relationships and/or survival issues. In ritual drama such as Mexican *pastorelas,* British mummers' plays, and Jewish *Purimspiel,* or in ritual contests such as the Indianapolis 500 or cowboy rodeo, experience can be symbolically addressed from any point in history or from any domain of social experience. Thus pagan and modern religious themes are often combined with ease, the actions and characters of one period of history can be shuffled with those of another, animals can represent human behavior and relationships, and the sacred and secular can be reversed.

While dramatistic forms are not required to resolve conflicts or to provide solutions, these forms interpret conflict and identify sources of tension through continued enactment and the display of alignments and oppositions. They can confirm the social order, introduce change, foster REVOLUTION, or express alternative viewpoints or resistance to oppression, depending on what forces are in control of social reality and in charge of performance.

(d) *The feast:* FOOD plays a very important role in festival. Some festivals contextualize food in a feast event, such as a barbecue or a pig roast, scheduled and set aside in a special place where large groups can eat together. Especially relevant is the nature of festival food. It will embody the identity of the group and represent the occasion, so festival foods are always specific: *posole,* haggis, shrimp jambalaya,

homentashn, mutton stew. Thus what food is served, who serves it, how it is prepared, the spices or condiments associated with it, the bread, and the drink all communicate about "our tradition." No one confuses tortillas with croissants or croissants with cornbread. Festival also emphasizes the *social* act of eating, for in this setting many people ingest their tradition simultaneously, confirming their identity as a group by eating certain foods during a certain period of time.

(e) *Dance and music:* Like food, dance involves the individual in action that is performed within a group, most of whose members are engaged in the same action. Specialists will provide music or drums to accompany the dance, though musicians will also perform in settings other than those involving dance. Dance may be performed for religious purposes, as part of folk tradition, or as a social act. Music and dance permeate festival, so much so that they set the pace for most activities and key the emotions of the participants.

(f) *Concluding event:* Festival follows a pattern from formal opening to informal conclusion, characterized by increasing spontaneity and intensity. The concluding event, in contrast to the opening ceremony, exhibits less structure and more creativity or personal expression. Noise and participation increase as drumming, dancing, drinking, and displays of fireworks accompany courtship, singing, and socializing.

Social structures of participation. Although festivals share many features, they may differ radically in appearance, sound, and purpose. The route to comprehension of a specific festival is through the concept of *participation.* In a community-based fes-

163

tival individuals have many alternatives for participation, and not everyone attends the same activities. But if those in attendance are primarily observers or consumers rather than participants, the event is not based in the social life of the community.

Festival offers opportunities for wide participation because its general purpose is relevant to all group members. It therefore attracts separate social interests, recognizing difference within the confines of the social group. Both women and men will have roles, the young and the old attend, outsiders and insiders alike have spaces accorded to them, and the rich and the poor walk on the same ground (though not necessarily together). Because socially based festival recognizes difference and strives for participation and integration, it defies external ideological control.

As we have seen, the particular activities available in a given festival reflect the concerns of the community. Thus if the community consists of several ethnic groups, ethnicity will be reflected in the activities, and participants will make choices on that basis. When age and sex divisions are important in a social group, festival activities especially designed for the old or the young or for females or males will be found.

Common to festival is one category of activity that is definitively not of the community: the traveling people and their entertainments and wares. At some festivals an entire carnival may be set up on the festival grounds, while others may concentrate on individual specialists such as fortune-tellers and magicians, and still others on craftworkers. These marginal, traveling people offer the exotic, strange, and different to the community for consumption. In contrast to the local performers, the itinerant specialists offer the strange in a commercial interaction, and often the souvenir object, the memory of the freak, or the hopes of the fortune raised by the fortune-teller remain with the participants long after other memories have dimmed.

Motivation for participation in festival includes the demonstration of religious commitment, the display or gain of social prestige, the public statement of political sentiments, participation in competitive events or the display of special skills, and social interaction that allows for the exploration and negotiation of many kinds of relationships.

Symbolic Processes

Two symbolic processes contribute heavily to the festival mystique: the manipulation of temporal reality and transformation.

The manipulation of temporal reality. The temporal reality of festival incorporates time in at least two dimensions. In the first the principles of periodicity and rhythm define the experience. Not sur-

prisingly, this cyclic pattern is associated with the cycles of the moon in cultures in which the lunar CALENDAR is or has been used in recent history. With the passage of time festival occurs again and again, marking the cycles of the moon, the annual repetition of the seasons, and the movements of the planets governing the solar calendar. Festival occurs calendrically, either on a certain date each month or on a specific date or periodic time each year. The cycles of time are the justification for festival, independent of any human agent. Unlike rites of passage, which move individuals through time, and unlike private parties, which structure a way out of time, festival yokes the social group to this cyclic force, establishing contact with the cosmos and the eternal processes of time.

In the second of these dimensions of temporality, expressions of tradition and change confront each other. Meaning in festival derives from experience; thus festival emphasizes the past. Yet festival happens in the present and for the present, directed toward the future. Thus the new and different are legitimate dimensions of festival, contributing to its vitality.

Transformation. In the festival environment principles of reversal, repetition, juxtaposition, condensation, and excess flourish, leading to communication and behavior that contrasts with everyday life. These principles can be applied to every code in use for communication. Repetition, for example, operates so that the sound of drums, fireworks, or singing voices may be continuous throughout an event, or the major visual symbol such as an image of a bear or the symbol of corn or the cowboy/gaucho may be shown in many circumstances.

Festival use of symbolic form has captured the interest of a number of scholars in different disciplines, from Jane Ellen Harrison to Victor Turner and MIKHAIL BAKHTIN, all of whom noted the transformative potential in rites and festivals. Transformation in festival takes the form of symbolic manipulation using the principles listed above. Among the most common is *inversion*, the reversal of the established social order, including social hierarchy and GENDER roles. In hierarchical societies symbolic inversion creates an upside-down world with the "inferior" at the top and the "superior" at the bottom, or it declares egalitarianism to be in order for the duration of the festival. Special characters such as clowns may assume the role of agent in bringing about the symbolic action. In societies in which egalitarianism is the stated norm, symbolic inversion may create a royalty of queens and princesses (especially common in festivals in the United States), demonstrating the reversal from egalitarianism to aristocracy and from a male-dominated to a female-dominated social structure. Competitions in festival serve the same purpose, creating competitive performers and dividing them into the victorious and the defeated, creating differentiation out of sameness.

The principle of juxtaposition permits the enactment of cultural themes that may be deeply rooted in concepts of difference and contrast or may derive from oppositions or conflicts in social experience. For example, until the modern era, most societies were preoccupied with survival and thus concentrated attention on fertility rites and reproductive acts, emphasizing gender differences. Today festivals continue to represent an opportunity for the enactment of gender roles and for courtship and romance.

Almost any theme selected by festival will be repeated in many codes, and most behaviors and actions can be found in excess. Symbolic forms permit the communication of a large quantity of cultural knowledge because symbols condense messages and carry multiple meanings, offering some ambiguity in meaning. Among the most dramatic symbols associated with festival are masks and costumes (*see* CLOTHING). They draw upon both the familiar and the strange but distinctly transform the human inside into a message bearer—carrying information that may be supernatural, exotic, condensed, bizarre, or mysterious in nature. LANGUAGE, music, objects, actions, and humans are all available for symbolic communication. Marching band music will carry different messages from those of dance music, clown action will communicate something other than what a queen's behavior conveys, a procession of pilgrims speaks about a different subject from that of a parade of automobiles, and riding a bull sends a message other than that of killing a bull.

Scholarly interpretations of festival stress the licensed relaxation of norms and rules, a negation of the social order that opens doors of risk and con-

fronts destruction and re-creation. Closely associated are themes of revitalization, suggesting that the principles of excess, reversal, repetition, juxtaposition, and condensation lead participants to experience transformation and regeneration. This may take many forms: personal affirmation, political action, courtship and marriage, social revitalization, and so on.

Conclusion

Taken as a whole, festival facilitates regeneration through the rearrangement of structures, thus creating new frames and processes; consequently, it can strengthen the identity of the group and thus its power to act in its own interest, or it can contribute to the articulation of social issues and possibly conflict if more than one interpretation prevails on the same subject. Because of the social power of these regenerative forms, however, festival thrives in both ancient and modern societies, always enacting social life and shaping the expressive enterprise of human society.

Bibliography. Barbara Babcock, ed., *The Reversible World: Symbolic Inversion in Art and Society,* Ithaca, N.Y., 1978; Mikhail Bakhtin, *Rabelais and His World* (Tvorchestvo Fransua Rable i narodnaiâ kul'tura srednevekov̂ia i Renessansa), trans. by Hélène Iswolsky, Cambridge, Mass., 1968, reprint Bloomington, Ind., 1984; Victoria R. Bricker, *Ritual Humor in Highland Chiapas,* Austin, Tex., 1973; Harvey Cox, *The Feast of Fools,* Cambridge, Mass., 1969; Alessandro Falassi, *Time Out of Time,* Albuquerque, N. Mex., 1987; Jane Ellen Harrison, *Themis: A Study of the Social Origins of Greek Religion* (1911), reprint (2d ed., 1927) London, 1963; Gail Kligman, *Calus: Symbolic Transformation in Romanian Ritual,* Chicago, 1977; Em-

Figure 4. *(Festival)* Carnival, Rio de Janeiro, Brazil. From Bina Fonyat, *Carnaval,* Rio de Janeiro: Editora Nova Fronteira S.A., 1978, p. 53. © 1978 Bina Fonyat.

manuel Le Roy Ladurie, *Carnival in Romans* (Le carnaval de Romans), trans. by Mary Feeney, New York, 1979; Robert J. Smith, *The Art of the Festival: As Exemplified by the Fiesta to the Patroness of Otuzco*, Lawrence, Kans., 1975; Victor Turner, *Dramas, Fields, and Metaphors: Symbolic Action in Human Society*, Ithaca, N.Y., 1974; Yoshiko Yamamoto, *The Namahage: A Festival in the Northeast of Japan*, Philadelphia, 1978.

BEVERLY J. STOELTJE

FIBER OPTICS

Communication system using hair-thin glass fibers or plastic strands through which light from a laser transmitter serves as a carrier for voice, VIDEO, or data signals. Fiber optics differs from more conventional communications technologies in that photons are the particles of energy used rather than electrons.

Background

Smoke signals were an early example of optical communications. ALEXANDER GRAHAM BELL, after his major work on the TELEPHONE, introduced in 1880 a device he called the photophone. He claimed that the sun's rays could be harnessed to transmit messages, suggesting that light could be transformed into a source of electrical energy and into an electrical signal as well. However, no practical applications were developed until laser technology came about in the late 1950s. The semiconductor laser, the tiny transmitters that literally pulse millions of times every second and are the workhorses of a fiber-optic system, resulted largely from research at AT&T Bell Laboratories. By 1970 these lasers, coupled with the availability of sophisticated light-sensitive devices (photodetectors) that receive and decode the signals they emit and with advances in low-loss glass conductors, gave scientists the components necessary for a workable system.

Prior to that, scientists had considered and then rejected sending light signals through the atmosphere; fog, clouds, and physical obstructions presented problems that were difficult to overcome. It was the search for a "controlled atmosphere" through which laser light could be sent that ushered in the research and development of optical fibers. In their article "Dielectric-fiber Surface Waveguides for Optical Frequencies" (1966), K. C. Kao and G. A. Hockham suggested that thin pieces of pure glass could carry laser signals at a loss level of twenty decibels per kilometer or less, even though to that point only losses in the thousands of decibels had been recorded. Researchers at Corning Glass Works achieved this goal in 1970, meaning that fiber-optic signals could be sent in a manner competitive with existing communications technologies.

By the mid-1970s AT&T and GTE began installing the first fiber-optic links in the United States. Although these early networks provided only a fraction of the capacity of later systems, they demonstrated that fiber-optics technology was technically feasible, generating widespread interest. Proponents emphasized that fibers, despite their smaller size, could carry much larger amounts of data than other technologies such as microwave systems and coaxial cables, with the added advantage that fibers were immune from cross talk, lightning, and other types of atmospheric interference.

The new technology rapidly gained international prominence. GTE installed systems in Belgium and Canada. "Hi-Ovis" (Highly Interactive Optical Visual Information System) was a prototype project carried out in Japan in the late 1970s using fiber-optics technology. A computer and transmission center provided video services to 158 homes in a small community near Osaka. Customers received a multitude of television channels and had access to airline and train timetables, stock-market quotations, and weather reports. They could also prepay theater, travel, or restaurant reservations; access newspapers via telecopier; and have two-way video access to city hall, hospitals, and libraries. *See also* VIDEOTEX.

Applications in Telecommunications

In 1981 Saskatchewan Telephone, a Canadian company, announced its plans to build a three-thousand-kilometer fiber-optic network devoted primarily to CABLE TELEVISION services to rural areas. In the United States the first long-distance application of fiber was proposed and implemented by AT&T in 1983 in the area known as the Northeast Corridor. Originally proposed as a 611-mile network between Cambridge, Massachusetts, and Moseley, Virginia, that network has become part of AT&T's nationwide fiber-optic system. Advantages in cost, capacity, and quality of signals played a key part in this decision, which was soon emulated by other telephone companies providing long-distance services.

The advent of long-distance fiber-optic networks in the 1980s led proponents of fiber to believe that this new technology could be competitive with the SATELLITE. Arguments in its favor included immunity from interference and interception, lower initial cost, greater cost-effectiveness, and rapid standardization.

Even though long-distance applications brought fiber optics to the market in a substantive way, shorter routes could become even more lucrative because of greater demand for installed capacity at the local-exchange level. The local exchange is considered the next frontier, and telephone companies have already begun installing fiber optics.

Whereas fiber-optic technology has been incorporated into networks in Europe, Asia, Australia, Latin

America, and South Africa, it has always been clear that fibers could also be used in other than land-based applications. The first transoceanic fiber-optic system was under construction by the late 1980s. And it seemed likely that a worldwide Integrated Services Digital Network (ISDN)—a widely discussed idea—would utilize mainly fiber-optic technology. *See* TELECOMMUNICATIONS POLICY.

Bibliography. Allen Boraiko, "Harnessing Light by a Thread," *National Geographic* 156 (Oct. 1979): 516–535; C. David Chaffee, *The Rewiring of America: The Fiber Optics Revolution*, Cambridge, Mass., 1987; Alan G. Chynoweth, "The Fiber Lightguide," *Physics Today* 29 (May 1976): 28–30, 32, 34, 36–37; *Fiber Optics News* (formerly *Fiber/Laser News*), Potomac, Md., 1982–; K. C. Kao and G. A. Hockham, "Dielectric-fiber Surface Waveguides for Optical Frequencies," *IEE Proceedings* 113 (July 1966): 1151–1158; W. T. Tsang, ed., *Semiconductors and Semimetals*, Vol. 22, *Lightwave Communications Technology, Part A, Material Growth Technologies*, Orlando, Fla., 1985.

C. DAVID CHAFFEE

FICTION

In its largest sense, a category including all that is imagined or invented. In a more restricted sense, fiction comprises that body of PROSE works including novels and short stories.

In the broader sense fiction originates in prehistory. Humans are storytelling animals, and so we can assume that fiction came into being with the dawning of consciousness. The earliest cave people sitting around the fire likely told one another stories that were not bound strictly to fact. The element of NARRATIVE in some cave paintings suggests the importance to them of—doubtless embellished—tales of the hunt and of the natural world.

However, the term *fiction* tends to be used specifically to describe written and disseminated prose work. The standard definition includes any form of literature or narrative that does not attempt to relate a true, historic, and documented set of circumstances. The categories so defined include fable, romance (*see* ROMANCE, THE), fairy tale, conte, prose pastoral, novel, and short story. The word *fiction* is usually not used of DRAMA, POETRY, or MOTION PICTURES—even when these forms are based on fictional material.

The term itself is derived from the Latin verb *fingere*, meaning "to form, mold, or feign." Initially it was used in English to indicate the action of fashioning or forming an object. But its second meaning of feigning or counterfeiting was also invoked, and in this sense to make a fiction meant to create a lie or deception. Only later, in the eighteenth and nineteenth centuries, did *fiction* take on the more positive meaning of a prose literary work based on the creation of events out of the imagination.

This evolution in meaning has parallels in the cultural history of fiction. English culture in particular was slow to accept fictional works as having value or as being anything other than lies. In the seventeenth century strict Protestant groups such as the Puritans and the Dissenters felt that reading fiction, particularly novels, was undesirable because it amounted to no more than reading falsehoods. In the eighteenth century another trend arose, asserting that reading novels was a morally beneficial activity. Novels such as Samuel Richardson's *Pamela* (1740) and *Clarissa Harlowe* (1747–1748), Oliver Goldsmith's *The Vicar of Wakefield* (1766), and, in France, Jean-Jacques Rousseau's *Émile, ou traité de l'éducation* (1762) and *Julie, ou la nouvelle Héloïse* (1761) served to convince people that this "feigning" form could present morally consistent lessons. Despite the apparent popularity of novels during the eighteenth century, however, the form was not very widely accepted and accounted for only a small fraction of book sales. It was during the nineteenth century that novels were published in large numbers and became the dominant form of fiction.

The acceptance of fiction was largely a function of the social and historical contexts in which it was presented. The earliest fictions were oral (*see* ORAL CULTURE) and functioned in preliterate cultures (*see* LITERACY). Those oral works were of two genres (*see* GENRE): the epic and the FOLKTALE. The earliest epics that have survived include the ancient Greek Iliad and Odyssey, the Babylonian Gilgamesh, and the Indian Ramayana and Mahabharata. The epic is a form that tends to arise during periods in which a feudal type of aristocracy dominates, and it serves to unite the members of the hierarchy by emphasizing the feats of their collective ancestors. Sung or chanted to groups by bards who memorized these lengthy stories, epics required the presence of listeners and ratified the experience of the group.

The tale could be told and retold more informally, either by a local storyteller or, for example, by parent to child. Early tales tend, like the epic, to be about aristocratic heroes in supernatural settings and have been hypothesized by critics such as the psychoanalyst Bruno Bettelheim to channel collective and unconscious wishes into narrative form. Both epic and folktale were based on collective myths and legends, not on original material as would be required of later fiction.

These earlier forms of fiction, usually authorless in today's sense of that term (*see* AUTHORSHIP), existed in cultures in which little attention was paid to the distinction between FACT AND FICTION—at least in its narrative forms. Before the seventeenth and eighteenth centuries most epics, tales, contes, and the like did not make a point about being either factual or fictional, any more than history or journalism was bound to strict standards of facticity (*see* HISTORIOGRAPHY). In this sense the epic and the tale are not truly fictional because there did not then exist a correspondingly strong sense of the factual.

During the seventeenth and eighteenth centuries there were increasing attempts to distinguish the factual from the fictional in all realms—in the writing of history, the presentation of news, and the determination of LIBEL in courts of law (*see* LAW AND COMMUNICATION). The category of fiction became more clear-cut. Fiction was not legally actionable, but fact was; fiction was not "news," and neither was it history. During this period the novel became its dominant form.

Unlike the epic, the early novel was an essentially middle-class form addressing the particular problems and ideological concerns of that class (*see* IDEOLOGY). Its central character was not a hero in the old sense of a superior being but an ordinary person who was usually the victim of some social injustice or abuse—whether falsely accused of a crime, forced to marry some undesirable person, deprived of financial or social support, or isolated either physically or emotionally from others. Plots often revolved around marriage and inheritance. As its name implies, the novel also required new or original stories and not the retelling of traditional tales and legends.

Since this period the dominant MODE of the novel and of much of popular fiction, including film and television narrative, has been REALISM, which seeks to conceal the artistic conventions on which it depends behind the events of the story itself, thus making what is in fact art appear as a direct transcription of life. In this way the signs and structures of storytelling are made to appear natural rather than artificial. Thus most fictions have appeared to readers to be units of experience rather than structures of fantasy, and realism has served to justify the seemingly frivolous nature of fiction by giving fantasy a utilitarian cast. When we read a novelist like Charles Dickens, for example, we may have the impression that we are seeing the world of nineteenth-century London rather than the highly artificial view of one middle-class Englishman.

By confining themselves to the fictional and at the same time creating the illusion of factual subject matter, novelists created a new mode of writing that could comment on the social world while remaining immune from legal attack. By keeping to the safety of fiction, early novelists like Daniel Defoe, Henry Fielding, Laurence Sterne, and Jane Austen could satirize society, with the result that such criticism had a special status as social commentary. Because the form was confined to the fictional, readers knew that they were protected, in effect, from engaging with the factual, and novel reading became a self-contained and socially quietist activity.

Throughout the nineteenth century writers aimed to expand the scope of the novel. Walter Scott extended its historical range; Honoré de Balzac transcended the limitations of a single volume by having his *La comédie humaine* (1842) encompass more than fifty volumes, all dealing with the same society and reintroducing the same characters; Dickens, Victor Hugo, George Eliot, William Makepeace Thackeray, Leo Tolstoy, and Émile Zola, among others, included within single works all classes of society and used the novel as a kind of ENCYCLOPEDIA of humanistic knowledge. It was thought that novels could and should represent as much as possible in life. Implicit in most such works were criticisms of social practices from child labor to penal reform to the role of women. One might describe this period as characterized by the domination of fictional representation.

At the end of the nineteenth and the beginning of the twentieth century, however, the novel, though at its height, began to suffer a crisis in self-confidence. Writers such as Joseph Conrad, Ford Madox Ford, James Joyce, and Virginia Woolf began to question the conventions of realism and the limits of LANGUAGE and wrote works in which fundamental truths were shown to be ultimately incapable of being captured in words. Such novels demonstrate the struggle between the desire that fiction represent life through verisimilitude and a recognition that the most crucial aspects of life—love, beauty, horror—cannot ultimately be represented in a realistic work of prose or perhaps in any language at all.

During this crisis of the novel other forms of fiction came into their own. The short story, for example, as practiced by writers such as Edgar Allan Poe, Guy de Maupassant, and O. Henry, reflected the recognition that the encyclopedic nature of the great nineteenth-century novels was a falsification. Short stories could best represent the fragmentary nature of reality and true perception. Fragmentation, whether in the short story or in the narratives of Joyce and Woolf and later those of John Barthes, Thomas Pynchon, the Italian writer Italo Calvino, and the French practitioners of the *nouveau roman* such as Alain Robbe-Grillet and Marguerite Duras, set the pattern for experimental fiction. In such works questions of representation, of the limits of language, of the fragmentary nature of experience, and of the inadequacy of rational explanation become central issues. The traditional hero often becomes an antihero or a patently unheroic figure. The conclusive ending that raised the eighteenth- and nineteenth-century hero to some kind of satisfactory and fulfilling role in society gave way in the twentieth century to unresolved endings often indicating the increased alienation from society of the central character. *See* AVANT-GARDE; FICTION, PORTRAYAL OF CHARACTER IN.

An increased attention to psychology was linked to the decline of realism. The theories of WILLIAM JAMES, SIGMUND FREUD, and CARL JUNG helped to bring to authors an awareness of the role of unconscious motivation in human behavior, thus transforming the depiction of reality. Increasingly novels began to represent less of the objective world and more of the state of mind, of the consciousness (or unconscious motivations) of characters. Writers such as Henry James, Edith Wharton, Woolf, Joyce, and William Faulkner allowed the state of mind or point of view of a particular character to determine the content of the novel. The traditional form of narrative exposition might give way to one modeled on the flow of thought or "stream of consciousness."

Popular literature continued to depend on realism as a mass market for fiction developed (see LITERATURE, POPULAR). Mass-market fiction of all forms is characterized by traditional heroes and heroines, strongly realistic scenarios and settings, decisive endings, and action-oriented plots.

Another feature of the development of fiction in the twentieth century was the recognition that fact and fiction are themselves arbitrary categories that are not necessarily mutually exclusive. Writers such as Norman Mailer and Hunter Thompson have produced works that are ostensibly about historical events but are nonetheless novels, and the boundary between DOCUMENTARY and fictional film has been blurred by directors such as Frederick Wiseman, Jean-Luc Godard, and Michelangelo Antonioni (see AVANT-GARDE FILM). The influence of STRUCTURALISM and poststructuralism has meant that even genres such as history and journalism can no longer be seen as value-free and objective but rather as bound by the conventions and biases of fictional narrative. Even the legal system recognizes the factual status of fiction by awarding libel damages to people who have been negatively represented in fictional works even if their names have been changed.

The recognition that all fictional forms depend on conventions and ideological structures has led to an expansion of the subject matter of fiction. Increasingly issues and groups not usually represented by the dominant discourse—women, nonwhites, non-Westerners—are demanding and to some extent are achieving fictional representation (see LITERARY CANON). This in turn may have the effect of creating new fictional forms, just as the rejection of realism has spurred attempts to return to earlier, traditional sources of fiction such as folktales.

See also ART.

Bibliography. Wayne C. Booth, *The Rhetoric of Fiction*, 2d ed., Chicago, 1983; Peter Brooks, *Reading for the Plot*, New York, 1984; Lennard J. Davis, *Factual Fictions: The Origins of the English Novel*, New York, 1983; Georg Lukács, *The Theory of the Novel* (Die Theorie des Romans), trans. by Anna Bostock, Cambridge, Mass., 1971; Robert Scholes and Robert Kellogg, *The Nature of Narrative*, New York, 1966; Ian P. Watt, *The Rise of the Novel*, Berkeley, Calif., 1957, reprint 1974.

LENNARD J. DAVIS

FICTION, PORTRAYAL OF CHARACTER IN

Before the days of nonrepresentational ART it used to be said that every picture tells a story, because the viewer identified the historical personages or the social class and type being illustrated, and by an almost automatic process of psychological metonymy extrapolated the relevant aspects of the characters that the artist was using to suggest a NARRATIVE situation. The writer of FICTION has traditionally worked in the same way. The differences among fictional characters are the most important ways of indicating to us what is going on and what the author is trying to do.

The notion of character in literature begins in ancient BIOGRAPHY. Greek philosopher Theophrastus (ca. 372–ca. 287 B.C.E.) and Roman historian Suetonius (ca. 69–after 122 C.E.) were alike interested in the oddities and quirks of human nature and in the difference between inadvertent private habits and deliberate public image. In *The Lives of the Caesars* Suetonius did not flatter his subjects but showed their strengths with their weaknesses, thus revealing incongruity and inconsistency as the mainspring of literary character.

Theophrastus was more interested in the dominant trait in an individual's nature, or, as Elizabethan dramatist Ben Jonson was to say, one's "humor." In his *Characters,* Theophrastus presents portraits of the coward, the flatterer, the chatterbox, the miser, and so on. This kind of CLASSIFICATION was soon in alliance with the medical doctrine of the "four humors," the preponderance of one or more of which was said to determine character; and it anticipated modern typologies such as the introvert and extrovert nature or U.S. psychologist W. H. Sheldon's correspondence of three physical types—the ectomorph, the mesomorph, and the endomorph—with certain mental attributes.

Early interest in character was thus, on the one hand, quasi-scientific and, on the other, concerned with biography and anecdote. Class and sex were important. Great and influential people were psychologically interesting; the masses were not. Nor, on the whole, were women; their character was determined by their sex. Homer portrayed human beings as individuals, but individuals determined by their roles in society as warrior, wife, or child. We are moved by the scene in the Iliad when Hector bids farewell to his wife Andromache, and his little son shrinks back in fear of the waving plume on his helmet. Everyone in the scene behaves, as it were, "in character." We should be startled if Homer told us that Hector was inordinately fond of cheese, that Andromache had affairs and breakdowns, that their child was psychopathic. Yet examples such as these are the concealed, incongruous matters that concerned Suetonius, just as they do the modern novelist.

In *The Canterbury Tales* (ca. 1387), one of the great literary works of the MIDDLE AGES, Geoffrey Chaucer follows the principle of decorum, derived ultimately from Homer by way of his critics and imitators, which prescribes the correct image and behavior for characters in all walks of life—the knightly, the ladylike, the worldly, the pious, the coarse, the comic. With this he mixes the personality based on humors, so that his Miller, for example, is not only coarse and churlish as befits his station ("A churl has told a churl's tale"), but has all the physical and psychological attributes of the angry man, whose temperament is based on an excess of choler. In his other long poem, *Troilus and Criseyde* (ca. 1386), Chaucer demonstrates a quite different way of looking at character, based on humane gossip and speculation. What was Criseyde really like? What was her motivation? Is she to be blamed or pitied? For his absorbing interest in these and other questions, in which he seems to enlist the cooperation of a circle of civilized listeners, Chaucer has been called the first psychological novelist.

The twentieth-century English novelist E. M. Forster distinguishes the "round" from the "flat" character in fiction. The former, like Shakespeare's Hamlet or Jane Austen's Emma, is constantly surprising us by unexpected behavior or by revealing a wide and contradictory spectrum of being and awareness. The latter, like Charles Dickens's Mr. Pickwick in *The Pickwick Papers* (1837), pleases and reassures us by remaining predictable and consistent through all the events of the story. Forster's distinction is convenient and sums up the frequently cited literary practice of basing character either on convention and type or on a creative process of speculation and inquiry. At the same time it does not answer the real question: on what grounds do we feel that a character has come alive or has failed to do so? There is no doubting the vitality and convincingness of Mr. Pickwick, which we may confirm, for example, by calling a friend's behavior Pickwickian. But many "round" characters, closely and ingeniously examined by their authors, may nonetheless strike the reader as intelligently constructed rather than alive and kicking. Other characters seem imagined as "flat" and yet during the course of a long novel may become so intimate and so familiar to the reader as to appear "round."

Arguably, we only recognize and respond to characters in fiction as alive if we have met people like them in life. Some writers give the impression that they see and enjoy their characters in the same way as they enjoy people they meet in life. Others appear to invent purely literary characters whom neither they nor their readers would or could ever meet. In the first case the unconscious element is important. The writer cannot say how the character arrived or why it seems so real. The Russian poet Aleksandr Pushkin, who greatly admired Shakespeare, was one of the first to perceive that Shakespeare's characters appear independent of the plot and action in which the play requires them to take part. Shylock in *The Merchant of Venice* is a more interesting and complex person than the play needs. In the same way descriptions of some of the most successful fictional characters such as Falstaff (fat, cowardly), Hamlet (melancholy, indecisive), or Austen's Emma (handsome, clever, and rich) seem not to coincide with the impression we actually receive of them. Their success as characters depends on their not resembling an objective view of themselves.

Here the author seems to create a parallel to the psychological fact that we appear different to ourselves than to others. "Consciousness" in this sense is different from "character," and a master novelist like the Russian Leo Tolstoy could invent a consciousness, as if from the inside, before also shaping it as a character. Some decades later English writer Virginia Woolf made the operation of consciousness paramount for all her characters, representing their "stream of consciousness" (a phrase coined by U.S. philosopher WILLIAM JAMES) rather than their appearance, distinctive manners, or habits of speech. Consciousness in Woolf's novels tends to become uniform—her own—and the idea that all consciousnesses are much the same both enables the reader to identify with the generic consciousness in her fiction (and in that of other writers) and diminishes the older notion of character as an observation of human types. Instead of observing others, judging them, perhaps laughing at them, the reader is invited to partake in a more universal awareness of being. Similarly, English author D. H. Lawrence rejected "the old stable ego" of the character and replaced it with a generic physical "blood awareness" of characters as men and women, spiritually alive or dead, saved or damned.

Other twentieth-century novelists like the French writer André Gide have explored the artistic possibilities in the notion that, far from our actions being determined by the way our characters have formed, anyone might do anything at any time. Such so-called gratuitous acts express a basic anarchy of being that the Russian author Fyodor Dostoyevsky earlier conveyed in his novels, and they relate also to the British novelist Joseph Conrad's vision of the inexplicable moment, arranged by chance, that may determine what the individual is and will become.

Such a concept of character may itself become a convention associated with a particular kind of novel or writer, and such conventions are often very persistent, perpetuating at their crudest a stock type of character—the English gentleman, the omniscient detective, the femme fatale. Successive writers try to evade such archetypes (which essentially resemble the "characters" of Theophrastus) by merging consciousnesses and removing distinguishing marks of class, type, or sex. But structuralist critics have objected that any attempt by the novelist to represent the reality and the people "out there" in life shows a misunderstanding of the nature of fiction. Fiction and fictional characters are inevitably based not on an imitation of life but on a CODE of signifiers, conventional signs like those of LANGUAGE itself, representing nothing but "literariness" (see STRUCTURALISM).

The abandonment of the assumption that fiction and its characters are based on a representation of external reality has had important consequences. It confines characters to books and to the relation of books to one another. Yet however important type or GENRE is in the construction of MEANING, all character is ultimately created by the relation between the self and some person out there, in life or in literature, who is not the self.

Bibliography. John Bayley, *The Characters of Love: A Study in the Literature of Personality*, London, 1960; W. J. Harvey, *Character and the Novel*, London, 1965; Jean de La Bruyère, *Les caractères*, Paris, 1688, reprint 1965; J. W. Smeed, *The Theophrastan 'Character': The History of a Literary Genre*, New York and Oxford, 1985; P. F. Strawson, *Individuals*, London, 1958.

JOHN BAYLEY

FILM. *See* MOTION PICTURES.

FILM EDITING

The process of selecting and arranging discrete film shots (and, in the sound era, recorded sound elements) in a manner designed to serve the overall purposes of a film project. A shot is a continuous moving image of a person, object, or event—that is, a moving image in which there are no temporal jumps in the action. A shot is the integral space-time image unit that is produced between the moment the motion picture camera is turned on and the moment it is turned off. In the broadest sense, film editing is the arrangement of these integral image units into larger wholes.

Each shot corresponds to a discrete strip of film. At its most basic level, film editing is the manual process of connecting strips of film. However, most films have some communicative function: to tell a story, to convey information, to promote aesthetic experience. Thus the process of connecting film strips is informed by these purposes, and the history of film editing traces the refining of the techniques that serve such purposes and of defining new purposes and related techniques.

Usually more than one shot, or "take," is executed of the subject before the camera. Alternate takes are made both to increase the probability that at least one version of the subject will be usable and to try out different ways of portraying the subject. Film editing involves selecting preferred takes. Also, a shot may be longer and may contain more information than a scene or sequence requires. In such circumstances the editor will shorten the scene by removing extraneous material from the film strip. Furthermore, in the production of most films, more images and even scenes are photographed than are used in the finished film. One task of the editor, often in consultation with the director and/or producer, is to make decisions about which takes and which shots to use, and how much of a shot to use, given the purpose of a film or film sequence as a whole.

There was little call for editing in the earliest days of cinema, because films were composed of single shots. This was true of the first films of the brothers LOUIS AND AUGUSTE LUMIÈRE. However, their later films—largely travel films—were often composed of a number of shots, each lasting about a minute. These might be images of parades, newsworthy personages, and exotic locales (see DOCUMENTARY). Editing here amounted to little more than trimming the length of the shots and manually splicing film strips together, with perhaps a minimal concern that there be sufficient variety among the views selected. This was not film editing as we presently know it, for that requires a conception of a film as a unified whole rather than as a collection of shots. Around the turn of the century, however, with such films as Georges Méliès's *Cinderella* (1899), cinema became committed to the function of telling stories. NARRATIVE came to provide standards of wholeness, and editing began to evolve.

Early film narratives were subject to certain constraints. First, their temporal organization was strictly chronological; for example, the birth of Christ could only be shown before his encounter with the wise men in the synagogue. Second, the visual organization of these early narratives tended to be invariant. The camera took a position vis-à-vis filmed events that was roughly like that of a THEATER spectator in relation to onstage action. Each scene, often enacted as a tableau, was seen from a medium-range view.

Film editing grew more sophisticated with an increase in the number and variety of temporal and visual patterns available to the filmmaker. The period dating from Edwin S. Porter's *The Great Train Robbery* (1903) and culminating with D. W. GRIFFITH's *The Birth of a Nation* (1915) was marked by a number of significant developments. Strict chronology ceased to be the sole connective between events. Events might be arranged in strict temporal order, but they could also be portrayed as happening simultaneously (through parallel editing) or represented out of chronological order through the use of flashbacks or flash-forwards. In a related development one could also cut between modalities—from actuality, for example, to dreams. Thus, the kinds of relations between depicted events became more flexible.

Similarly, the visual organization of the narrative image became more complex. In contrast to the "theatrical distance" of early film narratives, the space inside scenes became the subject of intensive articulation. In addition to middle-range views, the camera could move in for a close view of a detail (a close shot), or it could fill the screen with a face (a close-up). Certain aspects of a scene could be singled out for emphasis. The camera could also pull back from a detail to a medium view or a long view, thus contextualizing that item in a larger constellation of objects and actions where its significance becomes apparent. Here the issue of simultaneity assumes special importance. If one cuts from a close shot of a gun to a medium shot of someone pointing the gun at a character, intelligibility requires that the audience presume that these are roughly simultaneous views of the same event rather than, say, views separated by a significant temporal distance.

In addition to the introduction of variable camera positions—close shots, medium shots, long shots—and their alternations, the frontal, approximately eye-level tableaux of early films were also augmented by the use of overhead shots (high-angle shots), shots from below (low-angle shots), and shots in which the camera is not held parallel to the action (oblique-angle shots). These devices, along with point-of-view editing (in which a shot of a character looking at something offscreen is followed by a shot of that offscreen something), supply the basic elements from which the film editor composes scenes. The editor then combines scenes or sequences by means of temporal ordering patterns such as chronology, simultaneity, flashbacks, or flash-forwards. This was the core system of narrative editing that had evolved by 1915 and is still in wide usage.

Soviet film theoreticians and filmmakers of the 1920s, including Lev Kuleshov, V. I. Pudovkin, SERGEI EISENSTEIN, and DZIGA VERTOV, were so impressed by Griffith-style editing that they declared editing, referred to as "montage," to be the sine qua non of film. In their writings and films they refined and expanded upon already existing editing patterns. They employed a type of editing, sometimes called the montage of attractions, to make metaphorical comments about narrative events—for example, cutting from a shot of a disreputable official to one of a peacock in order to underscore the official's pride. And in films such as Vertov's *Chelovek s kinoapparatom* (The Man with the Movie Camera, 1929), a veritable cine-poem in which editing is devoted to cataloging comparisons and contrasts between myriad aspects of everyday life, the Soviets experimented with patterns of editing not primarily subordinated to narrative purposes.

With the coming of sound to film, there was a danger that film would regress to the sort of canned theater that had predominated before the editing breakthroughs associated with the name of Griffith. However, Russian theoreticians and filmmakers as well as the literary critic ROMAN JAKOBSON extended the principles of montage editing to the organization of the soundtrack. In montage, shots were juxtaposed for expressive purposes. These theoreticians and filmmakers advocated that asynchronous aural elements (such as offscreen sounds) should also be juxtaposed against the image, affording a contrapuntal means of expression. Thus, in *M*, by Fritz Lang, we hear the ominous whistle of the child-killer offscreen, while on-screen we see his innocent victim, a juxtaposition that makes the scene all the more foreboding. This type of contrapuntal use of sound was pioneered in such films as Carl Dreyer's *Vampyr*, Lang's *M* and *Testament of Dr. Mabuse*, Vertov's *Enthusiasm* and *Three Songs of Lenin*, Pudovkin's *The Deserter*, LUIS BUÑUEL's *L'âge d'or*, and René Clair's *À nous la liberté*. Modeled on montage, this use of sound makes the aural track an element in the editing.

Although most editing is narrative in form, the AVANT-GARDE FILM movement has explored other options. In the 1920s the cubist Fernand Léger choreographed moving images of industrially produced goods to alert viewers to their aesthetic properties, while surrealists such as Buñuel and Salvador Dalí used editing to portray and celebrate unconscious thought by imitating the disjunctive logic of dreams. More recently collagist Bruce Conner juxtaposed images culled from other films to create what are called "found footage films." Here the function of editing is to call attention to the bizarreness of contemporary ICONOGRAPHY by dislodging the images of advertising and popular films from their normal contexts. The development of editing through avant-garde experimentation is a matter of determining new aesthetic purposes and of discovering shot arrangements and rhythms that communicate those purposes.

See also CINEMATOGRAPHY; FILM THEORY; MOTION PICTURES.

Bibliography. Sergei Eisenstein, *Film Form: Essays in Film Theory,* and *The Film Sense,* ed. and trans. by Jay Leyda, New York, 1957; Lev Kuleshov, *Kuleshov on Film,* ed. and trans. by Ronald Levaco, Berkeley, Calif., 1974; V. I. Pudovkin, *Film Technique: Five Essays and Two Addresses,* trans. and annot. by Ivor Montague, London, 1933; Karel Reisz and Gavin Millar, *The Technique of Film Editing,* 2d enl. ed., New York, 1968.

NOEL CARROLL

FILM MUSICAL. *See* MUSICAL, FILM.

FILM THEORY

The discipline that aims at an exploration or understanding of issues related to the film medium as a whole—as distinct from film criticism, which has as its goal the description, INTERPRETATION, or evaluation of a given film. Film theorists for a long time considered themselves aestheticians, but have come to treat film AESTHETICS as but one of the many subdisciplines of film theory.

In the early decades of the twentieth century there were many speculations about the social and psychological consequences of this new system of representation; but the writings that come down to us, those that established a tradition that continues to grow, sought to define the status and possibilities of film as ART. Those who felt an immediate sympathy for film and wanted to see it blossom on its own realized that they had first to free it from sheer mechanical reproduction on the one hand and the slavish imitation of theater on the other. In short, cinema had first to be deemed not only an art but an independent art with its own principles.

Predictably, those first decades saw countless interarts comparisons. Cinema was said to function like the other arts because it imposed on the chaos and meaninglessness of the world a self-sustaining structure and rhythm. Poet Vachel Lindsay, the first person in the United States to publish a theory of film, showed that cinema enjoyed the properties of all the other arts, including ARCHITECTURE. In France a whole coterie of film enthusiasts compared film to music, concentrating on its ability to shape the flow and look of reality. Following the initial steps of Ricciotto Canudo, and under the banner raised by Louis Delluc, leader of the French AVANT-GARDE FILM movement until his death in 1924, this group insisted that cinema was an independent art. Numerous essays of the early 1920s suggested that, because cinema in its infancy was economically obliged to record theatrical performances, it had seldom looked beyond the theater for its own essence. In contrast, the AVANT-GARDE perspective of the twenties stressed the qualities of rhythm, image, and, above all, dream inherent in the film experience. Delluc tried to sum up his conception of the new art in one word, *photogénie*—a special quality available to cinema alone that can transform both the world and the viewer in a single gesture. Cinema is PHOTOGRAPHY, to be sure, but photography that has been raised to a rhythmic unity and that in turn has the power to give solidity to our dreams. The writings of Germaine Dulac, Jean Epstein, and Abel Gance similarly abound with lyric statements about the uniqueness of cinema.

Around 1925 a new center of film theory grew to rival that in Paris. The Soviet Union had established its famous State Film School (VGIK) in 1919, and around it there developed heated and productive discussion. Lev Kuleshov, DZIGA VERTOV, V. I. Pudovkin, and especially SERGEI EISENSTEIN are the names most often associated with this period. Nearly all questions pertaining to cinema were framed by this group as questions of FILM EDITING. Eisenstein's ideas went furthest here, but his writings were composed in the context of a vast and vibrant atmosphere of debate, in which the famous literary formalists, the constructivists, and the FEX (Factory of the Eccentric Actor, a futurist theatrical group) participated.

Formalist film theory. Two strains of early formalist theory can be distinguished, which for convenience might be termed Western and Eastern. The Western strain is a direct descendant of Kantian aesthetics. It accords an essential value to art, one we participate in through contemplation. Hugo Münsterberg and Rudolf Arnheim, both German expatriates who settled in the United States, updated Kant with Gestalt psychology. Münsterberg felt that cinema, imitating the motions and emotions of mind and spirit, was the modern art par excellence. Arnheim hoped to protect the new art from popular and technological corruption. For both thinkers the medium would become valuable only when its specific temporal and spatial characteristics were shaped in such a way as to turn cinema's bare recording capability into an object of imagination. They proposed various techniques of style in their quest for an expressive cinema. Their work has spawned most of the introductory textbooks in film analysis, each addressing the possibilities of camera angles, editing, sound, color, and so on. *See* CINEMATOGRAPHY.

The Eastern tradition, flourishing under the sign of an emergent Marxism, certainly could never have accepted the "essentialist aesthetics" of neo-Kantianism. For Pudovkin, Eisenstein, Vertov, and other Russian formalists, the cinema was a medium ripe for the radical representation of social life. They too wanted cinema to do something other than reproduce life. All insisted that only through the conscious shaping of images and through their violent or subtle juxtaposition could cinema perform its only valuable mission, the representation of a revolutionary consciousness. When the Western theorist called for a cinema of contemplation and spiritual values, these Soviet theorists and their Eastern European followers argued for a cinema of action, the action of the film on the spectator or the action of the spectator on the film.

The end of the silent film triggered many important essays on film. By 1929 the number of journals devoted to film theory indicated that a significant world community regarded cinema as an art form. Aestheticians rose up everywhere to debate the new direction that cinema should take after sound had disturbed its equilibrium. Today we can see that the coming of sound marked the decline of the great age of formalist film theory. Nevertheless, by 1935 it was taken for granted in most educated circles that cinema was an art, independent of all other arts, yet having in common with them the process of transformation whereby dull matter is shaped into scintillating and eloquent statement. If film devotees still see cinema in much this way, if most articles on cinema still hold to this general perspective, it is in large part because of the powerful viewpoint propounded between 1915 and 1935.

Realist theories. The combination of a worldwide economic depression and the transition to sound film effectively quashed silent-film aesthetics. The Russian formalists were stilled, the German film community emigrated, and the great French film clubs and journals ceased to exist (*see* MOTION PICTURES—SOUND FILM). Social rather than aesthetic issues came to the fore in the cinema and in discourse about the cinema. The British documentarists, particularly Paul Rotha and JOHN GRIERSON, insisted on the primacy of film for the education and social cohesion of the masses (*see* DOCUMENTARY). Their views were later systematized by Siegfried Kracauer, a German émigré whose influential *Theory of Film* was published in the United States in 1960.

But while this Western European realist theory vied with Soviet social-realist thought, the French anthropological tradition that began at this time became more influential than both. André Malraux, Gilbert Cohen-Séat, André Bazin, and Edgar Morin may all be taken as anthropologists of the medium, since their primary endeavor was to understand the place of a new technology, the cinema, in social and psychological life. Bazin's position, for example, was based on the intuition that before being an art—that is, a construction of the imagination—cinema is a fact of nature impinging directly on our psychological relation to reality, however defined. This form of REALISM, in contrast to that of Kracauer or Grierson, permitted Bazin to deal with many types of films as he sought the human impact of home movies, medical films, documentaries of exploration and of art works, fantasy films for children, and of course the

mainstream fictional genres. For him and his followers at the journal *Cahiers du cinéma*, the language of the cinema depends on the phenomenological stance toward the image that the spectator is asked to take. For example, in filming a magic trick a director is permitted every ploy of mise-en-scène but may not construct the trick on the editing table without betraying the viewer's belief that the event has actually occurred. Entire periods (such as NEOREALISM or NEW WAVE FILM) and auteurs (JEAN RENOIR, ORSON WELLES) are constituted first by the relation they ask the spectator to adopt vis-à-vis reality and the image.

Evidence of this phenomenological turn in film theory, apparent in the interest in the medium shown by philosophers Jean-Paul Sartre and Maurice Merleau-Ponty, can also be seen in the work of the Institut de Filmologie, headed by Cohen-Séat from 1946 into the 1960s. In the pages of the *Review* published by the Institut, studies of the perception of space, time, and causation sit side by side with audience studies examining depth perception and the development of cinematic comprehension in children. For these theorists, the facticity of the image, even as it strives to engage the imagination, makes it a peculiarity in the world of culture and separates it absolutely from the standard canons of art. Even the conservative GENRE of literary adaptation underwent a change in this era, at least as chronicled by Bazin, who applauded Robert Bresson, Jean Cocteau, Welles, and others for refusing to remake some literary structure into a cinematic structure; instead, the original was taken as a kind of objective fact to be documented. This was the age of Alexandre Astruc's "camera-stylo" and of new auteurs like Jean Rouch, Nicholas Ray, and Roberto Rossellini, who rejected traditional notions of art in the quest for a vibrant notion of cinema.

Semiotics. During the 1960s film theory began to draw away from broad and casual reflection as it embedded itself deeper into the life of the university. Now a certain type of film, the art cinema of Cocteau, Federico Fellini, INGMAR BERGMAN, and others, found easy acceptance on European and U.S. campuses; such films became part of legitimate culture. Some humanities scholars used this base to formalize auteur theory and genre theory. These approaches, designed to legitimate a larger number of films that might otherwise have been consigned to the cluttered drawers of popular culture, are not properly theoretical at all, but critical methods. Jean Mitry was a pivotal figure in lifting theory beyond mere critical application. He both summarized the traditions that went before him and demanded a new philosophic rigor in film theory, although his work still resides within the humanistic paradigm of theory.

Once inside the walls of the university, film theory was open to changes and influences from many other, "nonhumanist" disciplines. As one outgrowth of the expanding fields of structural anthropology and LINGUISTICS, the first developments of a SEMIOTICS of the cinema found their way into seminars and dissertations in France and Italy in the mid-1960s. Christian Metz, whose career parallels that of modern theory, sought to distill from Mitry's works the rules by which films are constructed and comprehended. Metz invited a thorough scientific analysis of signification in the cinema.

Semiotics prospered in Italy as well with the work of Gianfranco Bettettini, Emilio Garroni, and Pier Paolo Pasolini, all of whom influenced Metz's French school. In the Soviet Union, Jurij Lotman began to synthesize his views, updated from the Russian formalism of the 1920s and 1930s. His essays arrived in the West in the early 1970s and lent a needed social dimension to what might otherwise have become a largely grammatical undertaking.

Poststructuralism. Whereas Metz's first writings depended on CLAUDE LÉVI-STRAUSS, FERDINAND DE SAUSSURE, and Louis Hjelmslev, a second wave of work derived from intellectuals clamoring for a serious Marxist interpretation of cultural artifacts such as films. Louis Althusser's influence was an important factor in the complete redirection of the formerly auteurist *Cahiers du cinéma* in the late 1960s. *Cahiers*, along with *Cinéthique* in France and *Screen* in England, promoted a kind of theory best termed "ideological analysis," which gave to Metz's semiotics a potent political thrust. Their analyses of films and filmmaking practices showed just how conventional our sense of cinematic realism is. And they went on to suggest that the semiotic rules of naturalness help keep in place the reigning IDEOLOGY of bourgeois society, thwarting other ways of making sense of reality, other styles of representation and of life. Simultaneously, these journals and their key contributors—among them Jean Narboni, Jean-Louis Comolli, Stephen Heath, Laura Mulvey, Colin McCabe, and Peter Wollen—promoted alternative modes of filmmaking that escaped the codes of standard NARRATIVE and forced the spectator into more constructive relations with the images. Bertolt Brecht became a significant figure whose greatest disciples in film included Jean-Luc Godard, Jean-Marie Straub, and Danièle Huillet, and the political avant-garde in England.

This trajectory made film theory important not only to a growing number of scholars but also to cultural critics not formerly drawn to the cinema. The development of ROLAND BARTHES's influential literary theory from phenomenology to a rigid STRUCTURALISM, then to ideological analysis, and on to PSYCHOANALYSIS, helped to pull film studies into maturity in the 1970s. At the same time, an avant-garde wing of feminist scholars found in the cinema

a perfect site for a kind of unified field theory seeking to organize diverse disciplines (*see* FEMINIST THEORIES OF COMMUNICATION). From this perspective the semiotic codes of cinema produced by a cultural institution like HOLLYWOOD may be seen as reaffirming the existing patriarchal societal order. Cinema is thought to create rather than merely reflect reality by "constructing" viewers in certain ways. Such a functionalist approach is also exemplified by Heath's detailed psychoanalytic examinations of films.

Perhaps in response to the frequently speculative nature of this type of criticism, some scholars reduced their focus to more negotiable objects of analysis— to the minute ways any given film is seen to function and to the larger ways the whole system of cinema (genres, traditions of style and production) operates. Many theorists found the interplay between film history and film theory indispensable. Others reacted to the poststructuralist period of the 1970s by applying philosophical concepts and methods to the study of cinema. In France, for example, philosophers like Gilles Deleuze and Jean-Louis Schefer advanced their own theories of film.

Yet another approach, what might be termed "neoformalism," is concerned with the objective, systematic analysis of films as texts that exhibit rational cinematic laws. In the United States, David Bordwell, a representative of this approach, has attempted to map the findings of cognitive psychology onto those of film theory. Here observable mental laws are taken as essential for the understanding of intertextual factors that guide the comprehension of films. At the opposite extreme from the neoformalists are followers of the French philosopher Jacques Derrida, such as Marie-Claire Ropars, whose analyses aim not at reconstructing the laws of cinema but rather at generating fresh meanings. Theory here is concerned with the fluid interaction of viewer and film.

The blossoming of film theory in universities throughout the world during the late 1960s and 1970s may have slowed, but the breadth and energy it afforded the field will be felt for a long time. As it always has, the cinema continues to mix aesthetic, logical, and anthropological speculation. Film theory remains an extraordinary spectacle on the margins of the cinema itself.

Bibliography. Dudley Andrew, *Concepts in Film Theory*, New York, 1984; idem, *The Major Film Theories*, New York, 1976; Stephen Heath, *Questions of Cinema*, Bloomington, Ind., 1981; Brian Henderson, *A Critique of Film Theory*, New York, 1980; Gerald Mast and Marshall Cohen, eds., *Film Theory and Criticism: Introductory Readings*, 3d ed., New York, 1985; Bill Nichols, ed., *Movies and Methods*, Vols. 1 and 2, Berkeley, Calif., 1976, 1985; Phil Rosen, ed., *Narrative, Apparatus, Ideology: A*

Film Theory Reader, New York, 1986; Elizabeth Weis and John Belton, eds., *Film Sound: Theory and Practice,* New York, 1985.

DUDLEY ANDREW

FLAHERTY, ROBERT (1884–1951)

Pioneer U.S. documentarist known especially for his startlingly intimate portrait of Inuit life, *Nanook of the North* (1922)—which earned Robert Joseph Flaherty the title "father of the DOCUMENTARY"—and for three other features of similar style: *Moana* (1926), shot in Samoa; *Man of Aran* (1934), shot in Ireland's rugged Aran Islands; and *Louisiana Story* (1948), shot in Louisiana's Cajun bayou country. In each of these Flaherty sought to capture on film a vanishing (or vanished) way of life that he saw threatened or doomed by the advance of modern society. He worked on many additional film projects, long and short, in most cases controlled by others. Some were never completed. From some he withdrew because he found himself at odds with studio views and practices. Flaherty's career gave full meaning to the term *independent filmmaker.* He wanted always to work alone or in small units, which included in almost all cases his wife, Frances Flaherty. Studio hierarchies

and large production crews were anathema to him. His work was achieved mainly outside the film industry world as he struggled for funds and for distribution of his films. His career presaged that of generations of independent documentarists.

Born in Michigan, son of a mining engineer who often worked in Canada, the young Flaherty spent years as an explorer and prospector before turning to film. During the period from 1910 to 1915 he made four subarctic expeditions for Sir William Mackenzie, builder of Canadian railroads, with the task of determining the mineral deposits along proposed northern railway routes. Flaherty fulfilled his mission, but his interests shifted to the Inuit of the area, from whom he learned much about frontier survival. During his last two expeditions he made a film about them, but the film was lost in a fire. Five years of fund-raising efforts to make another film about the Inuit finally led to the support of Revillon Frères, French furriers, and to *Nanook of the North.* The film was so different from cinema successes of the day that all U.S. distributors rejected it, but Pathé took a chance and won worldwide success, which brought Flaherty a contract from Paramount (one of the companies that had rejected *Nanook*) to go to Samoa for "another *Nanook.*" The result, the idyllic

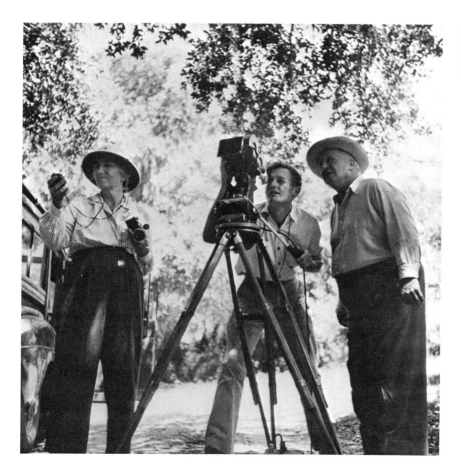

Figure 1. *(Flaherty, Robert)* Robert Flaherty *(right)* with Frances Flaherty and Richard Leacock. National Film Archive, London.

Moana, was a box-office failure, and it virtually ended Flaherty's relations with big-studio HOLLYWOOD. His next feature, *Man of Aran* (his first sound film, and a substantial success) was financed by British film interests. His last film, *Louisiana Story,* was backed by Standard Oil of New Jersey, which hoped to assure the public that oil exploration of wilderness land was in safe hands. A film of rare beauty, it was for Flaherty another chance to celebrate the wonders of the wilderness and those who lived there.

Years of frontier isolation had given Flaherty minute powers of observation. For him the first task of a filmmaker was to see what was before the lens, not to get the lens to record what one expected and wanted to see. He developed his footage on location, often under the most inhospitable circumstances, and screened the rushes over and over, always sharing the ongoing filmmaking experience with those in the film, while searching for patterns of meaning to emerge. On the screen, in projection, the film took shape. Filmmaking was a new kind of exploring. If one went on location with a firm plan of action, as executive producers tended to expect, one went—it seemed to Flaherty—with blinders. Alert to the unanticipated moment, he was always ready to amend his plans. The people in his films, his cocreators, suggested many of the film episodes and seemed endlessly ready for the reenactment of events that characterized their lives. Moments of exceptional intimacy, almost unknown in the actualities of earlier days, often resulted.

Flaherty did much to rescue film from the studio. At a time when studio ingenuity could produce astonishing things, Flaherty showed that a close-up look at an actual segment of humanity could provide its own kind of astonishment. Thus *Nanook* marked a watershed. Flaherty's on-location achievements influenced fiction as well as nonfiction films. Of special significance has been his influence on such genres as Italian NEOREALISM, ETHNOGRAPHIC FILM, and CINÉMA VÉRITÉ.

See also MOTION PICTURES.

Bibliography. Arthur Calder-Marshall, *The Innocent Eye: The Life of Robert J. Flaherty,* London, 1963, reprint Baltimore, Md., 1970; Frances Hubbard Flaherty, *The Odyssey of a Film Maker,* Urbana, Ill., 1960; William T. Murphy, comp., *Robert Flaherty: A Guide to References and Resources,* Boston, 1978; Paul Rotha, *Robert J. Flaherty: A Biography,* ed. by Jay Ruby, Philadelphia, 1983.

WILLIAM T. MURPHY

FOLKLORE

Term coined in 1846 by the British antiquarian William John Thoms, apparently a translation of the German term *Volkskunde,* introduced in 1787.

Thoms's "good Saxon compound, Folklore" has achieved wide currency in the world's languages (including prominently Romance and Slavic languages), though sometimes in conjunction or competition with more local coinages. Thoms defined folklore essentially by enumerating some of its forms: "The manners, customs, observances, superstitions, ballads, proverbs, etc., of the olden time." Folklore names both the traditional cultural forms and the discipline devoted to their study, though in recent years the term *folkloristics* has gained increasing currency for the latter.

The concept of folklore emerged in the late eighteenth century as part of a unified vision of LANGUAGE, CULTURE, literature, and IDEOLOGY in the service of romantic nationalism. For Johann Gottfried von Herder (1744–1803), the German philosopher whose romantic conception of *das Volk* and folk tradition informs all subsequent understandings of folklore, the possession of a common language was the touchstone of a people's distinctiveness, the source that gave rise to and sustained their sense of themselves as a separate, unique, social entity; language embodied the character, the inner being, of a *Volk.* Moreover, language represented the means of transmitting the distinctive traditions of a *Volk* across the generations, thus representing the instrument for that progressive cultivation of faculties that Herder identified as culture. In Herder's conception, culture and tradition found their highest and truest expression in the poetry of the folk, its folk song and folklore. With the modern fragmentation of humanistic thought and the concomitant quest for disciplinary autonomy, however, that formerly unified vision has largely come undone. Anthropologists, linguists, literary scholars, and folklorists have all continued to maintain an interest in folklore but have defined it from their own disciplinary vantage points, emphasizing certain features or aspects at the expense of or in opposition to others. Instead of proposing a single definition of folklore, it seems most useful to identify those definitional foci that have remained salient (though in various guises and formulations) as guides to the concerns that continue to attract interest and attention to folklore. *See also* ROMANTICISM.

Traditionality

There is no single idea more central to conceptions of folklore than tradition. Tradition has figured prominently in definitions of culture in general, but folklorists tend to place especially great emphasis on traditionality as a criterial attribute of folklore. This emphasis, in its various guises, was a response to the powerful challenge to traditional authority, in MAX WEBER's classic sense, by the modern ideologies of the Protestant Reformation, the Enlightenment, and industrial capitalism, in which reason, individualism, innovation, and progress were paramount values. The deepening consciousness of the great transition to modernity that stimulated the discovery of folklore rested in part on a perceived contrast between those societies in which traditional authority was dominant and those emergent forms of social organization governed by the rule of practical reason. The interest in folklore that burgeoned in the nineteenth century was part of the intellectual effort of that watershed era to comprehend the fundamental changes represented by the advent of modernity. The legacy of this effort still colors the popular but distorted conception of folklore as folly, superstition, and falsehood, anachronistic leftovers from an earlier stage in human social development since transcended by the scientific rationalism of modern civilization.

There is, however, a counterimage of folklore that is no less a product of the intellectual currents just mentioned, namely, the view of folklore as attractive, colorful, emotional, natural, and authentic. This may be termed the romantic view of folklore, in contrast to the rational one. Part of the Herderian legacy, this romanticization of folklore stemmed in part from a reaction against the cold rationalism of the Enlightenment, insisting instead that in folklore lay the foundation for an authentic national culture, true to the spiritual and historical integrity of a people. This view provides the source of romantic nationalist glorifications of folklore, the nostalgic quest for cultural roots, folk arts, crafts, and music revivals, the "folklorico" phenomenon, folklife preservation programs, and so on. From either the rationalistic or the romantic perspective, however, folklore is viewed overwhelmingly as declining in the face of modernity, and this consciousness of epochal change provides much of the stimulus for our interest in folk traditions.

The term tradition is conventionally used in a dual sense, to name both the process of transmission of an isolable cultural element through time and also the elements themselves that are transmitted in this process. To view an item of folklore as traditional is to see it as having temporal continuity, rooted in the past but persisting into the present in the manner of a natural object. There is, however, an emergent reorientation taking place among students of tradition, away from this naturalistic view of tradition as a cultural inheritance rooted in the past and toward an understanding of tradition as symbolically constituted in the present. Tradition, so reconceptualized, is seen as a selective, interpretive construction, the social and symbolic creation of a connection between aspects of the present and an INTERPRETATION of the past. This view of tradition as an interpretively assigned meaning not only provides an illuminating

basis for the critical understanding of the idea of folklore itself as a symbolic construct, but also opens the way for investigations of folklore-based cultural revival movements, the use of tradition as a mechanism of social control, the modern construction of invented traditions (such as Royal Jubilees or May Day rallies) as ways of giving symbolic resonance and authority to modern social formations, and the very need for traditionalization itself—the social need to give meaning to our present lives by linking ourselves to a meaningful past. Such lines of investigation may seem to challenge the insistence of more conservative folklorists on distinguishing between folklore and folklorism, the genuine and the spurious, the authentic and the concocted, but they need not diminish our interest in demonstrably old forms. Rather, they provide an integrative critical perspective that comprehends both the materials and processes of folklore and the discipline devoted to their study in terms of the continuous social process of traditionalization.

A further implication of the centrality of tradition to conceptions of folklore has been the tendency to emphasize the collective, ready-made, stereotyped nature of folklore forms. Traditionality implies supraindividuality, insofar as it involves intergenerational transmission, continuity, and customary authority within a social group. In addition, prevailing models of the nature of folk society tend to view it as essentially homogeneous; in the words of U.S. anthropologist Robert Redfield, "in the ideal folk society, what one man knows and believes is the same as what all men know and believe." Linguistic theory has also been influential in this regard, as scholars have extended FERDINAND DE SAUSSURE's linguistic distinction between *langue* and *parole* to the contrast between folklore and written literature, seeing folklore as *langue,* collectivized, socialized, persistent traditional form, the creation and possession of the community at large. While folkloric variation has long been of real interest to folklorists and much scholarly effort has been devoted to the comparative analysis of versions and variants of particular items of folklore, the standard of reference has been the idealized, generalized folk tradition, seen as a communal product. Hence, too, the imputed anonymity of folklore; individuality of expression is seen as totally subsumed by the homogeneity of the collective.

In recent years, however, largely under the influence of performance-centered approaches, greater emphasis has been placed on individuality and creativity in folklore. Examination of the PERFORMANCE of folklore in concrete situations of use has provided a productive framework within which to study the interplay of tradition and innovation in the actual conduct of social life. Folklore texts have come to be seen not simply as realizations of a normative standard, but as emergent, the product of the complex interplay of communicative resources, social goals, individual competence, community ground rules for performance, and culturally defined event structures. Tradition, the collective, the communal, the conventional, are not forsaken here; rather, the individual and the creative are brought up to parity with tradition in a dialectic that is played out within the context of situated action, viewed as a kind of practice.

Social Base

The prefix "folk" in folklore suggests that part of the essence of folklore resides in its social base. The question "Who are the folk?" looms large in any consideration of the nature of folklore and the history of the discipline devoted to its study. Conceptions of the social base of folklore may be summarized in terms of three broad perspectives, with the understanding that each perspective involves nuances and further distinctions.

The term folk was first introduced into social theory in late eighteenth-century Germany and became one of the formative concepts in the development of nineteenth-century sociology as part of the great evolutionary and typological tradition represented by the work of Wilhelm Wundt (1832–1920), William Graham Sumner (1840–1910), Ferdinand Tönnies (1855–1936), ÉMILE DURKHEIM (1855–1917), and others. The features attributed to the ideal folk society are most concisely summarized in the abstract of Redfield's synthetic essay, "The Folk Society," published in 1947: "Understanding of society may be gained through construction of an ideal type of primitive or folk society as contrasted with modern urbanized society. Such a society is small, isolated, nonliterate, and homogeneous, with a strong sense of group solidarity. . . . Behavior is traditional, spontaneous, uncritical, and personal. . . .''

Redfield, like the great majority of his predecessors, constructed his model of the folk society as an ideal type, acknowledging that "No known society precisely corresponds with it." In Redfield's schema, folk stands in opposition to urban society, which he leaves for his readers to define by assembling the logically opposite characteristics of folk society. The polar types in these constructions represent the opposite ends of a continuum, along which all empirically occurring societies may be expected to fall. In historical terms, though, the continuum is seen as a directional one: it represents the great evolutionary progression from premodern to modern society. The effect of such theoretical constructs is to reinforce the point that folk society is steadily giving way to progress and that folklore is increasingly incompat-

ible with modern life. Thus, many folklorists orient their work toward rural peoples; members of ethnic groups less far removed from their agrarian past than those who are full participants in modern, urban, technological, mass society; and occupational groups like cowboys, loggers, seamen, or miners, whose work keeps them in close contact with the natural environment.

Another significant aspect of Redfield's formulation is his inclusion under the rubric *folk* of both "tribal and peasant groups." This inclusive scope, however, has been the subject of extensive debate. Many *folk* theorists, including most folklorists, have reserved the designation folk for peasant peoples, village artisans, and other occupational groups that constitute the lower, less advanced stratum of a complex society. Tribal societies have been seen as qualitatively different social forms, whole—not part—societies in which the primitive modes of existence have retained their full functional integrity. Others, like Redfield, have emphasized the continuities between tribal and peasant societies and have brought these societies within a more unified frame of reference. The issues continue to be debated, often as the basis for the disciplinary differentiation of folklore from anthropology.

Notwithstanding the continuing influence of the traditional conception of folk society, recent thinking about the social base of folklore has begun to depart from the classic view in significant ways. One influential formulation has been advanced by U.S. folklorist Alan Dundes: "The term 'folk' can refer to *any group of people whatsoever* who share at least one common factor. It does not matter what the linking factor is . . . but what is important is that a group formed for whatever reason will have some traditions which it calls its own." Here the notion of the folk has been detached from the evolutionist and typological assumptions of much classic folk theory, but certain key features are retained. Shared tradition remains the essential criterial attribute of the folk group, grounded in shared identity. Crucially, however, this is a limited homogeneity; in place of the essentially complete homogeneity of ideal folk society, Dundes falls back on any single feature of shared identity that can constitute the basis for the formation of a social group. Any such group, as it persists through time and accumulates a body of experience in common, will have its own core of traditions, hence its own folklore. Thus we can find jokes shared by astronauts, proverbs current among computer programmers ("Garbage in, garbage out"), and so on. In these terms "Every group has its own folklore" and will continue to do so as long as people continue to come together in groups. The nature and extent of the folkloric repertoire in these various groups remains to be discovered.

Still another substantial departure from classic folk theory is represented by recent social-interactional and performance-centered approaches to folklore that focus on the structures of social relations that organize the actual use of folklore forms in the conduct of social life. To be sure, certain of the older formulations accord a central place to the kinds of social relations that constitute the essence of folk society, but the new approaches go further yet in their investigations of the social base of folkloric expression by treating it as an empirical problem, examining the structure and dynamics of identity and role relationships in situations of use. Such investigations reveal that folklore may be an expression of differential as well as shared identity, relationships of conflict as well as group unity, social diversity as well as homogeneity. Most important, it appears, the empirical investigation of the social base of folklore in use highlights the ways in which folkloric expression may be constitutive of social relationships, not merely reflections, projections, or correlates of them.

Finally, in Redfield's enumeration of the attributes of the ideal folk society is the criterion of nonliteracy. As elaborated later in his essay, "The folk communicate only by word of mouth; therefore the communication upon which understanding is built is only that which takes place among neighbors, within the little society itself." The prominence of the verbal channel and oral, face-to-face communication has been a feature of folklore since its inception. Folklorists ever since the late eighteenth century have continued to give pride of place to oral folklore; indeed, some would define folklore itself as "oral literature" or "verbal art" or "literature orally transmitted," though others would insist on the inclusion of customary behaviors and beliefs, material folk culture, and the like. As a rule, modern anthropological folklorists tend to concentrate their efforts on oral genres of folklore, in large part because they have other theoretical frameworks for the comprehension of other aspects of culture. *See also* ORAL HISTORY.

Another correlate of the emphasis on orality is a widespread emphasis on oral transmission as a criterial attribute of folklore. This has dual implications, highlighting both the medium of transmission and the social configuration of the learning situation. As for the medium of communication, the focus on the oral channel has traditionally been invoked to distinguish folklore from written—especially print—communication. Perhaps the major difference between oral and written language, in the eyes of folklorists, has been the relatively greater capacity of WRITING to fix a verbal text, inhibiting the kind of flexibility and variability that reliance on oral transmission alone will allow. Such variability, of course, will be conditioned by a range of social and generic factors; forms of oral folklore run the gamut in performance from word-for-word fidelity to a fixed textual standard, as in a curing chant or a PROVERB, to great textual flexibility, as in the telling of a legend. Nevertheless, print and LITERACY do make a difference, and folklorists tend largely to draw the boundaries of the field to exclude forms that depend on the written word, with the exception of a few genres, such as graffiti and autograph verse, which share with the spoken genres the qualities of traditionality, anonymity, and variability.

Also conventionally excluded from the domain of folklore are the modern mass media, such as commercial recordings, radio, film, or television, that use oral language but in ways that contrast significantly with face-to-face spoken interaction. The mass media are disqualified on three counts: (1) they are not rooted in community life but commodified and imposed from without, (2) they are not participatory but are meant to be consumed by a mass audience, and (3) as with print, they are not variable but fixed by the media in which they are communicated.

Modes and styles of learning are implicated by the insistence on orality. Literacy is acquired by formal, institutionalized teaching and learning, largely foreign to classic folk culture, where informal learning—personalistic, context-linked, and traditional—predominates. To be sure, not all informal learning relies on spoken interaction; folklorists or folklife scholars whose interests extend beyond the verbal forms to include customary behaviors and material folk culture add to the criterion of orality the mechanism of transmission by imitation or customary example. The American Folklife Preservation Act of 1976, for example, stipulates that the forms of expression that constitute folklife "are mainly learned orally, by imitation, or in performance, and are generally maintained without benefit of formal instruction or institutional direction," taking account of both the media of transmission and the social configuration of the learning situation.

Aesthetics

Clearly, orality is only one element in each of such labels as "verbal art," "oral literature," and "literature orally transmitted" that designates what is for some folklorists the essential core of folklore; the other is artfulness. Indeed, it was the aesthetic appeal of certain folklore forms that first excited attention in the eighteenth century, well before the coining of the terms *Volkskunde* or folklore or the emergence of a sociology of folk society. The source of one major impulse that led to the discovery and study of folklore was the romantic movement, especially in its more nationalistic guises. In the ideology of romantic nationalism, a distinctive language and literature are the principal vehicles for the expression of national identity, pride, and spirit. Thus a quest for the roots of an authentic, indigenous national literature in folklore began in the eighteenth century with such powerfully influential compilations as Thomas Percy's *Reliques of Ancient English Poetry* (1756) and Herder's *Volkslieder* (1778–1779) and reached an apogee, perhaps, in Elias Lönnrot's *Kalevala* (1835), the rallying symbol for Finnish national culture. The romantic aesthetic glorified folk songs, ballads, fairy tales, legends—the folk genres of poetry and prose—for their vigor, spontaneity, naturalness, emotional impact, and lack of contrivance, and the celebration of folk art has continued to be sustained by such aesthetic standards ever since. *See also* FOLKTALE.

Interest in verbal art and folk AESTHETICS has become one of the most vigorous sectors of contemporary development in folklore theory. An especially influential definition of folklore that highlights interest in the aesthetic dimension has been put forward by Dan Ben-Amos: "folklore is artistic communication in small groups," that is, groups "in which people confront each other face to face and relate to each other directly." *See* INTERACTION, FACE-TO-FACE.

One line of analysis, now becoming increasingly influential, centers on the nature and conduct of performance, influenced by the insights of literary theory and symbolic anthropology. Here, the principal interest lies in what constitutes artfulness in SPEECH and action, not only in the formalized genres of verbal art and the symbolic enactments of RITUAL and FESTIVAL but also in the less marked ways of speaking and acting. Those who explore folklore as performance also study the functional role of artfulness in the conduct of social life: to enhance rhetorical efficacy, to elicit the participative energies of an audience, as a medium of reflexivity or self-aggrandizement, as entertainment, and so on. Related to such performance-centered perspectives is ETHNOPOETICS, centrally concerned with the aesthetic patterning of oral literary forms and the problems of translating and rendering them in print in such a way that the artfulness of their oral performance is not lost. A still broader enterprise is ethnoaesthetics, the ethnographic investigation of native systems of aesthetics in their own terms, as these condition the making, consumption, and interpretation of aesthetic productions.

All of these efforts are integrative, in the great intellectual tradition of folklore, resistant to intellectual or disciplinary compartmentalization as folklore has always been since the first emergence of the concept more than two centuries ago. While the forms of folk expression and the discipline devoted to their study are continuously transformed, the symbolic construction of folklore remains a significant social force, energized by the dynamic processes of traditionalization, ideology, social thought, and the artfulness of everyday life.

See also ARTIFACT; ETHNOMUSICOLOGY; HUMOR; MUSIC, FOLK AND TRADITIONAL; ORAL CULTURE; ORAL POETRY; RIDDLE; SPEECH PLAY.

Bibliography. William R. Bascom, ed., *Frontiers of Folklore*, Boulder, Colo., 1977; Dan Ben-Amos, ed., *Folklore Genres*, Austin, Tex., 1976; Jan Brunvand, *The Study of American Folklore*, 2d ed., New York, 1978; Giuseppe Cocchiara, *The History of Folklore in Europe*, Philadelphia, 1981; Richard M. Dorson, *The British Folklorists*, Chicago and London, 1968; idem, ed., *Handbook of American Folklore*, Bloomington, Ind., 1983; Alan Dundes, ed., *The Study of Folklore*, Englewood Cliffs, N.J., 1965; Åke Hultkrantz, *General Ethnological Concepts*, Copenhagen, 1960; Américo Paredes and Richard Bauman, eds., *Toward New Perspectives in Folklore*, Austin, Tex., 1972; J. Barre Toelken, *The Dynamics of Folklore*, Boston, 1979; William A. Wilson, *Folklore and Nationalism in Modern Finland*, Bloomington, Ind., 1976.

RICHARD BAUMAN

FOLKTALE

Refers to oral NARRATIVE in general or to a particular GENRE of oral tales. As a general term *folktale* succeeds but does not replace the term *fairy tale*, which continues to be in literary and popular use. Fairy tale, in English at least since 1749, is a translation of the French *conte de fée*, a term that Comtesse d'Aulnoy (Marie-Cathérine le Jumel de Barneville de la Motte) used in the title of her book published in 1697. Folktale is a translation of the German *Volksmärchen*, which appeared first in *Volksmärchen der Deutschen* (1782–1786), by Johann Karl August Musäus. The term, like other German compounds such as *Volkslied* (1778) and *Volkskunde* (1785), derives from Johann Gottfried von Herder's thought, use, and coinage, particularly his formulation of the concept of *das Volk*. Folktale, hence, is an oral narrative told by peasants, lower classes, or traditional people whose LITERACY, if existing, is minimal. In their verbal art these groups were thought to embody the spirit of a nation. Today the term extends to tales of groups with strong traditional, ethnic, or regional bases or their literary imitations.

As a particular genre, folktale, together with *myth* and *legend*, constitutes the primary European generic CLASSIFICATION of oral narratives that has been adopted in scholarly discourse. These three genres are taken to differ from one another in their relation to cultural conceptions of truth and reality. Myth (from Greek *mythos*) is believed to be true, legend (from Latin *legenda*) purports to be true, and folktale is inherently untrue—only FICTION and fantasy. As a function of their distinctive relations to belief, these three genres also differ from one another in terms of their narrative figures, times, and locations. Myths are about supernatural beings that exist beyond the boundaries of human time and space; legends involve identifiable personalities, dates, or places, yet their events have an extraordinary quality, often involving interaction between humans and supernatural beings or forces. In contrast, in the folktale the human characters, as well as the times and places, are unidentifiable in social, historic, or geographic terms, thus suspending reality and letting fantasy rule.

This division of oral narratives into myth, legend, and folktale is not universal. Societies differ in their categorizations of narratives, the choice of distinctive features that differentiate among them, and the number of categories they perceive and name. Cultural ideas, conventions, purposes, means, and meanings of narratives can potentially function as distinctive features of genres. These factors not only can vary from one culture to another but also can change over time within a single society.

Before the rise of the German term *Märchen* in the late eighteenth century and the acceptance of the term folktale in the English of the nineteenth century, speakers and writers in these languages used other terms to designate fictive oral tales. In German *Fabel* and later *Mährlein* served that purpose before *Märchen* and *Volksmärchen* replaced them; in English *tale*, *fairy tale*, or even *old wives' tale* were in use. The equivalent of the last term served a similar purpose in classical Greece (as is suggested by PLATO in *Lysis* and *Gorgias*).

History of the Folktale

Essentially oral, folktales could not have left historical records until the introduction of literacy. The paradoxical dependence of oral tales on WRITING has resulted in four types of historical documentation of the folktale in which the variables are the tellers, the writers, and the literary contexts.

Intracultural recordings of folktales. With the emergence of literacy, scribes and sages, chroniclers and teachers committed to writing religious, philosophical, historical, and judicial texts. Within them they incorporated the oral literature of their societies, including folktales. However, these folktales are not characterized as fiction in the contexts in which they appear. On the contrary, their inclusion in documentation of other subjects depends on their cultural acceptance as historical reality rather than fiction. They offer sanction to social values, institutions, or dynasties. Their fictive nature becomes apparent only anachronistically and comparatively. For example, the biblical story of David, who killed Goliath and married King Saul's daughter to become a king himself, has the pattern of the dragon-slayer folktale

variety (Types 300–359 in Antti Aarne and Stith Thompson's *The Types of the Folktale,* "The Ogre [Giant, Dragon, Devil, Cobold, etc.] Is Defeated") detailing the hero's rise from humble to royal status. In the Bible the narrative recounts the historical foundation of the Davidic dynasty, but comparative research could point to its folktale features.

Folktales in intercultural contacts. In the past as well as the present, contact between literate travelers and nonliterate natives has resulted in the recording of the latter's folktale traditions. In their accounts the nonnative writers describe the tales, together with the histories, institutions, customs, or landscapes of the natives' countries. For example, in the fifth century B.C.E. Herodotus included in his description of Egypt a rendition of the "Pharaoh Rhampsinitus' Thief" tale (Type 950, "Rhampsinitus"). In modern times traders, missionaries, and anthropologists have recorded the folktales of the peoples they visited and studied and have made them available in print.

Literary writing of folktales. After the emergence of literacy, authors from different oral traditions documented in their own writings the occurrence of folktale themes and plots in specific languages and historical periods. If their own writing launched a tale into oral circulation, the written evidence could mark the earliest-known version of a tale. None of these literary texts resembles an oral narrative, nor do they purport to; nevertheless, even if they are relatively remote from their oral renditions and are currently available only as short stories, romances (*see* ROMANCE, THE), framed stories, or even dramas, they are milestones marking the history of particular folk stories. The tale of "The Two Brothers" (Type 318, "The Faithless Wife"), for example, was written down by a scribe called Ennana in Egypt around 1210 B.C.E. (New Kingdom); the apocryphal Book of Tobit (Types 505–508, "The Grateful Dead") probably dated from the fourth century B.C.E., and the story of "Susanna" that is included in the apocryphal Daniel draws upon folk themes and later became part of the medieval folk-religious and religious literatures. Petronius, a first-century Roman writer, presents the realistic anecdote of the "Matron of Ephesus" (Type 1510) in a storytelling context in his *Satyricon;* and Apuleius, a second-century North African philosopher and rhetorician, inserts in his *Metamorphoses* the tale of "Amor and Psyche" (Type 425A, "The Monster [Animal] as Bridegroom") as an old wives' tale.

Writers used the storytelling situation as an artistic device for the presentation of narratives, some their own, some traditional. So framed are, for example, the Indian collection *Pañcatantra* ("The Five Chapters," second century B.C.E. or 300 C.E.) and the Arabic *1001 Nights* (ninth century). Later in Europe this literary device was used by Giovanni Boccaccio

(1313–1375) in the *Decameron* (ca. 1358) and by Geoffrey Chaucer (ca. 1342–1400) in *The Canterbury Tales*. The literary tradition of framed narratives as a method of folktale presentation continued up to the height of the RENAISSANCE and the threshold of the Enlightenment. The *Piacevoli notti* (1550–1553), by Gianfrancesco Straparola (ca. 1480–ca. 1557), was molded after Boccaccio's *Decameron*, and the narratives in *Il pentamerone* (1634, 2d ed. 1674), by Giambattista Basile (ca. 1575–1632), are presented as if told to a woman during the last five days of her pregnancy before the onset of labor. These last two collections include several tales that later were identified as part of the core of the European folktale tradition. Whereas the early Asian narrative frames have a didactic, ethical purpose, the later European frames are concerned primarily with social entertainment.

Anthologies of tales that lacked a narrative frame had functional purposes: their writers intended them to be either rhetorical aids or written substitutes for storytelling entertainment. These editors did not necessarily draw on their oral traditions directly but culled the texts from former sources. These collections thus have a mnemonic function—as do current professional Japanese storytellers' notebooks—to help memory that has declined with the increase of literacy. In the transition from oral to written texts, writers could make an additional transformation and versify the tales, which was done more than once to the Aesopian fables.

European medieval collections such as *Gesta Romanorum* (end of the thirteenth century, printed in 1473) contained tales from different written and oral sources. These collections had both entertainment and moralistic functions, similar to the Italian collection of tales from the same period—*Cento novelle antiche*—and the literary genre *faraj*, which flourished earlier in Arabic literature.

Modern authors who present folktale collections often are ideologically and/or nationalistically motivated; they resort to these tales as a symbol and resource of traditionality. However, during the nineteenth and twentieth centuries some writers without scholarly responsibility changed, rewrote, and "improved" the oral texts to bring them up to the aesthetic standards of a READING audience and to meet readers' expectations of their national rustic literature. Since the romantic period authors who have been influenced by oral tales have developed a distinct genre and literary tradition of artistic tales, *Kunstmärchen*, that is separate from and cannot become part of the history of the folktale. *See also* ROMANTICISM.

The deliberate recording of folktales. In Germany the work of the brothers Grimm, Jacob (1785–1863) and Wilhelm (1786–1859), established yet another reason for the recording of folktales: they were attributed a cultural literary import of their own. The tales were recorded by scholars who shared a native language with the tellers—the peasants and lower classes of their own society. Although historically the work of the brothers Grimm marks the inception of purposeful folktale recording by natives from natives and for natives, some of the literary writers in Italy and France were their precursors. For example, Basile's *Il pentamerone* is written in a local Neapolitan dialect that attests to the author's regard for local speech. However, these early collectors lacked the ideological motivation of the brothers Grimm and their followers concerning the recording of folktales.

The Grimms also affirmed the scholarly-literary goal of an accurate documentation of storytelling, reflecting the vocabulary, style, and narrative exposition of the oral narrators themselves. For many years this had been an ideal that could only be approximated rather than achieved—even the Grimms themselves deviated from their rule—but it became the guiding principle of folkloristic documentation of folktales. Modern recording techniques and awareness of ideational constraints now make this goal obtainable.

Research Methods

Theoretical speculations in the nineteenth century derived principally from comparative philology and comparative anthropology. On the one hand, because of the discovery of the connection between Indic and European languages, a single country—India—was thought to be the cradle of European folktales. On the other hand, the application of the theory of cultural evolution to folktale research led to the belief that the folktale emerged in a single cultural stage, one common to all peoples all over the world. The two theories are known as *monogenesis* and *polygenesis*. The research that evolved early in the twentieth century purported, in part, to resolve the conflict between these incompatible theories.

The historic-geographic method. The historic-geographic method purports to reconstruct, locate, and date the primary form of a tale through a systematic comparison of all its available written and oral versions. In the course of analysis the tale dissemination routes are delineated, and its subforms are established. The two fundamental concepts of the historic-geographic method are *type* and *archetype* (or *Urform*). Folklorist Stith Thompson defined the type as a "traditional tale that has an independent existence," but in practice a tale type is not an existing story but a construct formulated in the course of classification of themes and episodes. Its correspondence to actual tales told around the world is variable, depending on the tradition in which the tale is told and the tradition on which the typology is based. For example, European tales have a better fit with standard types than do African tales. When the correspondence between tales and types becomes too weak, a new typology is needed in order to carry out research effectively. A narrative text could be a fragment of a type, or it could combine episodes that belong to several types. On occasion folklorists reify narrative types and consequently refer to such specific texts as fragments or conglomerates of types. A tale type is constructed inductively on the basis of all known versions and their variations, thus representing the possible thematic combinations and plot boundaries of tales that manifest similarities in spite of historical and cross-cultural differences.

Folklorists have long been aware of the fact that in oral tradition tales exist but types do not, yet they have maintained simultaneously that types have independent existence in tradition, and therefore their primary forms are describable and retrievable from among currently available versions. These primary forms are the tale archetypes. Consequently the fundamental theoretical difficulty that the historic-geographic method has had to confront is the weak link between its two basic concepts, type and archetype, often requiring reification of the former in order to recover the latter. The historic-geographic method incorporates principles of comparative philology. To a certain extent the concept of type corresponds to the notion of *root*—the ultimate constituent element common to all cognate words. In that respect type is the thematic core of a tale that is found in all its versions in different cultures and historical periods.

The relationship among the numerous versions that share a thematic core is based on three assumptions that are sometimes considered the "laws" of the dynamics of tales in society. First, tales are disseminated centrifugally, "like ripples in a pond," independent of human MIGRATION, trade contacts, and linguistic affinities. Second, tales maintain their thematic similarities through a self-correcting principle that guides narrators toward median versions: each storyteller learns the tale from multiple sources, and the eventual synthesis then serves as one of the many sources for subsequent narrators. Third, innovations (mostly through errors and faulty memory) that trigger a positive response can be established in a community and generate a subtype of a tale.

The morphological method. The morphological method moves the historical quest from the particular tale to the genre in general, seeking to uncover the historical roots of the folktale. Russian folklorist Vladimir Propp (1895–1970), the chief proponent of this method, shifted folktale studies from a focus on change in a folktale over a period of time (diachronic analysis) to a focus on the elements in a folktale at a particular time (synchronic analysis). He proposed a morphological description of the folk-

tale, examining the integration of narrative elements into the whole. This is in contrast to the historic-geographic method, which compares narrative elements across many versions of a single type.

The basic concepts in Propp's morphological analysis are *function* and *role*. The functions are the fundamental components of a tale. Each function is an act of a character, described in terms of its significance for the tale's course of action. Whereas the historic-geographic method considers acts and characters independently, the morphological method sees them in relation to each other and to the tale as a whole. The definition of each function is an abstract descriptive term: absence, violation, departure, and so forth, expressing the importance of a particular function to the general development of the plot. The folktale functions do not exceed thirty-one, following each other in a distinct sequence that characterizes the folktale as a genre. Often the functions occur as sets of logical pairs of cause and effect, action and consequence, such as pursuit and rescue, struggle and victory. The development from a conflict to its resolution is a *move*. A move can constitute a sequence of functions that encompasses a single episode or an entire tale.

The folktale characters fulfill seven roles: villain, donor, helper, princess, dispatcher, hero (seeker or victimized), and false hero. Each has a sphere of actions consisting of appropriate functions. When a single character is involved in several spheres of actions, the roles played change during the course of the story. The import of the morphological method exceeds its initial goal of historical inquiry or even conclusions that remain inevitably speculative. This method allows formal narrative regularities to be discovered and a story GRAMMAR to be formulated in many tales that lack an established literary text and theoretically can be transformed with each telling.

On this foundation other tale morphologists, such as Alan Dundes in the United States and Claude Brémond in France, have formulated methodological strategies and theoretical concepts that are only implicit in Propp's own study, exploring in particular the ideas of pairing of functions, the notion of the move, and the structural SEMANTICS of the folktale. Both Dundes and Brémond maintain a syntagmatic principle of analysis, describing the tale in terms of the sequence of its elementary parts. A group of Russian morphologists, headed by Eleazar Meletinsky, has proposed a transformation of the morphological into a structural analysis of the folktale. Such a method builds on the semantic significance of the folktale functions and roles and analyzes them in terms of oppositional and paradigmatic sets that constitute the deeper structures of the tale. Actions and characters do not simply follow each other narratively but relate to each other in terms of their values, meanings, and positions in the social structure, and the significance of their actions. *See also* STRUCTURALISM.

Quite apart from the trend in morphological studies of the folktale that Propp initiated is the formal description proposed by U.S. linguist William Labov. He defined the elementary part of a narrative not in terms of its significance but in terms of its sequential position and rhetorical function in the narrative. His analysis uses personal experience narratives, but it can be related to folktale morphology as well. Labov's descriptive terms are abstraction, orientation, complicating action, evaluation, result or resolution, and coda.

The morphological method began with a historical quest but has developed into a method in its own right, the ultimate goal of which is the description of narrative grammar or grammars of the folktale told in different cultures by different peoples of different genders and ages.

The ethnographic method. The ethnographic method extends the goal of systematic description of the tale to its telling, exploring narration in society and culture. In ethnographic research the holistic conception that is the basis for morphological analysis encompasses the entire system of storytelling in society. The major concepts of the ethnographic method are *storyteller, performance,* and *context,* thus grounding the narrative tradition of a culture in the verbal activity of its individual members and its social institutions. The storyteller is the vehicle for the articulation of a narrative tradition, for its rise and demise, for the creativity and placidity in its delivery, and for its continuity and transformation. Storytellers differ from one another in age, GENDER, and verbal proficiency, and their tales and tellings are dependent on these variables. In addition, personal temperament and experience potentially affect their tales. In the past most studies have concentrated on the most proficient narrators in a community. However, in principle the ethnographic method requires the exploration of storytelling by community members who have not received, and perhaps rightly so, any public recognition for their narrative ART.

Women's tales often differ from men's tales. The generic designation of old wives' tales need not be derogatory but may be indicative of a thematic sphere that older women articulate best. Narrators of either gender vary their repertoire of tales as they move from childhood to adolescence and then to adulthood and old age, narrating culturally and developmentally age-appropriate tales. The focus on the storyteller implies that in spite of commonly shared aesthetic standards and cultural values, narrators differ in style, themes, vocabulary, and rhythm, as do writers in literate societies. *See also* LANGUAGE VARIETIES.

PERFORMANCE, as Richard Bauman defines it, is a communicative MODE of artistic responsibility that the storyteller assumes publicly as a teller of tales. It involves a shift from ordinary speaking into performance that involves dramatic use of gestures (*see* GESTURE), a higher frequency of formulaic and rhythmical language, as well as the possible use of instrumental accompaniment, interspersing PROSE with songs.

The nature of oral narrative performance is context dependent. Context consists of such variables as the listening community and the occasion for narration. The listening community could be children or peers of the narrator's age and gender; itinerant listeners such as pilgrims or traveling companions; or a stable audience such as FAMILY, friends, and the native village population. The occasion could be formal entertainment associated with rites, such as a wake, or an informal aside in a daily CONVERSATION; it could take place in the market or at the bedside of a child. The tale text and its performance would vary accordingly.

The goal of the ethnographic method is to describe the total narrative potentialities and their actualizations in a single society. In practice, so far, most studies have concentrated on individual storytellers, their art, styles, and repertoires, or their performance in culturally appropriate occasions. The ethnographic approach particularizes the narrative tradition of a society, describing the general notion of tales of a nation (such as "Japanese tales" or "Zuni tales") as a system of narratives that are dependent not only on shared AESTHETICS, common cultural values, social-historical experiences, and a common stock of themes and figures but even more so on individual narrators, their verbal proficiency, their performances, and the social institutions in which society enables them to tell stories.

Interpretation of Folktales

What do folktales mean? There have been countless interpretations of these narratives, as if fantasy without reason is senseless, and folktales cannot just be but must have MEANING. These explicative analyses interpret folktales in terms of a specific frame of reference, and in most cases the validity of such interpretations depends on the correspondence between the tales and the theoretical construct that serves as a key for their explanation.

Psychoanalytical interpretations. Probably the most controversial of these interpretive frameworks has been formulated by either Freudian (*see* FREUD, SIGMUND) or Jungian (*see* JUNG, CARL) psychoanalytic theory. Most likely, the objections to this kind of INTERPRETATION are based at least as much on its content as on its logic. Since PSYCHOANALYSIS, perhaps more than any other theory, emphasizes the sexual dimension of symbols, and since adults often have a conception of childhood as the age of sexual innocence, it is difficult to accept an interpretation of tales told by and for children that dwells on sexuality. However, from psychoanalytic perspectives consciousness controls neither dreams nor folktale fantasy, and therefore the two are an ideal match for mutual interpretation. The meanings of symbols in dreams can be explained in light of their significance in folktales, and folktale fantasy makes sense in terms of its meaning in dreams. Thus conceived, the folktale is a cultural or even universal dream fantasy, reflecting emotions that individuals as well as society suppress because they are unable to confront directly the ambivalent feelings of children growing up within a family.

Although all psychoanalytic interpretations share these premises, they involve three distinct though not mutually exclusive modes: symbolic, dynamic, and equivalentic. Symbolic analysis treats figures, objects, and actions in the folktales in terms of their significance in either Freudian or Jungian analytic theory. The tales become a symbolic CODE that represents concepts in either theory. Dynamic interpretations deal with the psychological effect the tales have or—in the words of Bruno Bettelheim's apt title—with the uses of enchantment. Accordingly, the traditionality of the folktales and their preoccupation with family figures enable children to experience their family-related fears in their fantasies and overcome them in reality. The equivalentic interpretation draws on the variability of folktales themselves. The substitution of actions and figures that the narrators themselves make in different renditions of the same story offers a key, according to Dundes, to their symbolic significance. When a narrator substitutes "beheading" for "castrating" when talking to a more refined audience, an implicit interpretation is given to the verb used earlier.

Anthropological interpretation. Along with the recording of folktales of nonliterate cultures, anthropology has developed several paradigms for the interpretation and explanation of the significance of tales in society and their relation to culture. Folktales, along with other narrative genres, have complemented direct observation of and participation in the life of traditional peoples. These stories are the tales people tell to themselves about themselves, their fantasies, and their past. The tales evoke a responsive chord among the listeners only if they correspond to their worldview, their aesthetic standards, and the ethical values that were partially shaped by these tales to begin with. Hence folktales are valuable primary testimony about a society's view of itself. The validity of the interpretation of folktales depends on its agreement with observations of social conduct, analysis of language and religious symbols, and information about sociopolitical structure and history.

On the basis of these premises anthropological interpretations have taken three directions. First is the consideration of tales as a reflection of culture and history. The world of the imagination must draw on knowledge of reality, history, and a specific belief system. Hence it should be possible to read in, and not into, these tales the past and present life of the people who tell them and to consider the tales as a mirror of culture, a worldview, and modes of thought.

Often, however, direct observations of social life contrast with the folktales' popular themes. Peaceful people tell about wars, and tribes that enjoy family cohesion tell about the abandonment of children. In these cases folktales offer a reversed picture of actual conduct, and interpreting them often calls for the integration of psychoanalytic theory with anthropological observation and the suggestion that folktales reflect family tensions, unconscious wishes, and interpersonal dynamics that often stand in direct contrast to observed behavior. Hence in this second trend of anthropological interpretation, folktales, together with social acts, art forms, and RITUAL, might provide glimpses into the inner workings of the mind in traditional societies.

Third is the functional interpretation of folktales that purports to explain their significance in terms of a contribution to social and cultural cohesion. Functional interpretations depend on observation and inference. The consideration of the entertainment function of the folktale depends on ethnographic observation or examination of historical records concerning the occasions in which storytelling occurs in society. Similarly the idea that folktales have an educational function has its basis in observation and thematic analysis of the narrative. But the notion that folktales function as an outlet for psychological frustrations, ambivalences, and tensions incorporates psychoanalytic assumptions into anthropological interpretations, drawing on the assumed rather than the observed.

Literary interpretation. Often the applicability of psychological and anthropological interpretations has obscured the validity and import of the literary interpretations of tales. Furthermore, vestiges of nineteenth-century thought, according to which folktales represent the childhood of fiction and hence its primitive literary stage, impeded modern interpretive abilities that would have revealed the literariness of the folktale. The morphological method has made a partial contribution to literary analysis of the folktale, but since the method is concerned with narrative actions and characters in the abstract, divorced from their representation in language, its concepts and terms have but a limited application to literary interpretation of folktales. However, the necessary concepts for literary interpretation have been formulated in two contrasting trends: ETHNOPOETICS and folktale criticism.

Ethnopoetics has emerged in recent years as a research trend and an interpretive mode that seeks the poetic principles according to which nonliterary societies create and perform their verbal art. Though not aimed at folktales in particular, ethnopoetic interpretation has been applied to folktales and has demonstrated its effectiveness in their analysis. Ethnopoetic interpretation builds on the locally defined genres as a system to frame and communicate meanings; it explores the use of poetic imagery and cultural verbal symbols as a way to interpret emotions and ideas the narrators wish to convey artistically to their listening community, and it analyzes the linguistic means by which storytellers shift from speaking and (to use U.S. anthropologist Dell Hymes's apt phrase) "break into performance." *See also* ORAL POETRY.

Contrasted with ethnopoetic interpretation is folktale criticism. Although the two trends seek to explore the folktale's own artistic merit, ethnopoetics is based on the group's own terms, concepts, and linguistic phrases in the texts, whereas folktale criticism, particularly as formulated by the Swiss folklorist Max Lüthi, proposes a set of critical concepts that would allow folktale interpretation on its own appropriate terms. Accordingly, Lüthi suggests that the folktale is one-dimensional, depthless, and abstract. The terms are taken from the critical vocabulary of modern art. Drawing on the historical connections between the emergence of modern abstract art and the European discovery of primitive art, Lüthi suggests that the very qualities that have been discerned in the visual expression of nonliterate societies are also intrinsic to their verbal art; they are the source of the folktale, its aesthetic value, and the foundation of its literary value.

Conclusions

Folktales are oral narratives. However, after centuries of interdependence on script and print their themes and figures have become an integral part of literate and now electronic society. The process began quite early. Sophocles drew on the oral traditions of his time in the writing of *Oedipus the King,* as did Shakespeare when he wrote *The Taming of the Shrew, King Lear,* and other plays. In modern literate societies, folktale themes have become the subjects of operas and ballets (*see* DANCE; OPERA), children's stories, and animated movies. They are the references for cartoons and POETRY alike. Some are concerned that folktales have all but disappeared from oral tradition. They have tried to renew the art of their telling in children's library story hours and even special festivals, doing so in an exaggerated fashion, wishing to resuscitate a dying art. But neither print nor film has so far silenced the narrators in pubs and

in the marketplace, in the moonlit village square or the pilgrimage van, or even on the airplane. Storytelling and folktales may change, but they do not go away. They thrive in the nonliterate societies of the world and survive even in the multimedia environment of the modern world. *See also* ORAL CULTURE.

Bibliography. Antti Aarne, *The Types of the Folktale* (Verzeichnis der Märchentypen), 2d ed., trans. and enl. by Stith Thompson, Helsinki, 1961; Dan Ben-Amos, ed., *Folklore Genres,* Austin, Tex., 1976; Dan Ben-Amos and Kenneth S. Goldstein, eds., *Folklore: Performance and Communication,* The Hague, 1975; Bruno Bettelheim, *The Uses of Enchantment: The Meaning and Importance of Fairy Tales,* New York, 1976; Claude Brémond, *Logique du récit,* Paris, 1973; Linda Dégh, *Folktales and Society: Story-Telling in a Hungarian Peasant Community,* Bloomington, Ind., 1969; Richard M. Dorson, gen. ed., *Folktales of the World,* 14 vols., Chicago, 1963–1987; Alan Dundes, *The Morphology of North American Indian Folktales,* Helsinki, 1964; Gonthier-Louis Fink, *Naissance et apogée du conte merveilleux en Allemagne, 1740–1800,* Paris, 1966; Bengt Holbek, *Interpretation of Fairy Tales,* Helsinki, 1987; Melville Jacobs, *The Content and Style of an Oral Literature,* Chicago, 1959; Kaarle Krohn, *Folklore Methodology* (Die folkloristische Arbeitsmethode, 1926), trans. by Roger L. Welsch, Austin, Tex., 1971; William Labov, *Language in the Inner City,* Philadelphia, 1972; Wilhelm Laiblin, ed., *Märchenforschung und Tiefenpsychologie,* Darmstadt, 1969; Max Lüthi, *The Fairytale as Art Form and Portrait of Man* (Volksmärchen als Dichtung), trans. by Jon Erickson, Bloomington, Ind., 1984; Vladimir Propp, *Morphology of the Folktale,* 2d ed., rev., trans. by Laurence Scott, Austin, Tex., 1968; Kurt Ranke, ed., *Enzyklopädie des Märchen,* Berlin and New York, 1975–; Lutz Röhrich, *Märchen und Wirklichkeit,* 2d ed., Wiesbaden, FRG, 1964; Stith Thompson, *The Folktale,* New York, 1946; Jack Zipes, *Fairy Tales and the Act of Subversion,* New York, 1983.

DAN BEN-AMOS

FOOD

Essential for human biological survival, food is also a cultural domain that is often elaborated into complex systems of MEANING. CLAUDE LÉVI-STRAUSS remarked that food is not only good to eat but "good to think." Food is both physically manipulated to feed us and intellectually manipulated to refer metaphorically to important aspects of existence. The unique, incorporative nature of eating (assimilating) makes food an important sacred and social symbol (*see* SYMBOLISM). Relationships between a group and its gods, as well as between members of the community, are manifested in events of food sharing and exchange. Relationships between competing and conflicting class and ethnic groups are often symbolized in food preferences and avoidances.

Food items themselves can be used to mark an individual's status as well as the boundaries of an ethnic or class group. However, other more complex levels of food manipulation (dishes, meal structures, and cycles) are also used to transmit social and cultural messages. Finally, eating events themselves can be major communicative events reserved for transmitting basic messages about social roles and relationships.

In the process of moving from nature to CULTURE, food items are produced and/or acquired, transformed through cuisine rules, and then combined with other dishes in expected arrangements and sequences to comprise meals or eating events. Such meals or eating events are scheduled to interrupt or punctuate social time. Ordinary meal cycles punctuate regular activity/LEISURE cycles. Special events occur to mark major breaks in productivity (weekends, harvests, successful hunts), in the life cycle (births, weddings, deaths), and in the maintenance of the group (political and religious commemorations). At each stage in the movement from food production to consumption, food is used to communicate. However, the degree to which the domain of food is elaborated symbolically differs among societies.

Lévi-Strauss has argued that humans universally distinguish between "the raw and the cooked" as a METAPHOR for nature versus culture. Cooking represents human ability to transform nature. In his ambitious scheme labeled the "culinary triangle," one point in the triangle—the raw—is contrasted with two other points—the cooked and the rotted. Cooking signifies a transformation through culture, but rotting (used to process many foods such as cheese) is a transformation by nature. Within the domain of the cooked, two common processes—roasting and boiling—are discussed. Roasting involves direct contact between food and fire, but boiling is mediated by both a pot and a cooking medium. According to Lévi-Strauss, boiling is thus more culturally mediated, and roasting is closer to rawness and to nature. Through several more steps of logic, boiling is ascribed to "endo-cuisine"—that which is for domestic use in a small, closed group; roasting belongs to "exo-cuisine"—what one offers to more distant guests.

This general scheme is not borne out by systematic cross-cultural research. However, many societies do use such aspects of their culinary systems to distinguish between insiders and outsiders and between the good or pure versus the defiling, polluting, and dangerous. Thus relationships between social actors and groups as well as those between groups and the forces that govern existence are controlled by rules for food use that define inclusion and encourage discipline, solidarity, and the maintenance of social boundaries.

Ritual purity: Inclusion and exclusion. In the Hindu food system food plays a major role in underscoring the caste system. Caste relations are explicitly manifested in food transactions. The food-giving and food-receiving relationships among castes mark their relative position in the hierarchy of RITUAL purity. Higher castes may receive only raw (natural and unpolluted) food from lower castes. The lowest caste groups are defined by their willingness to take any kind of cooked food from any group.

The Hindu food system distinguishes between two types of cooked foods: *pakka* and *kacha*. Pakka food is domestic-group food. It is boiled (grain and legumes) and is thought to be highly susceptible to pollution. In high-caste Hindu homes such food cannot be touched by servants. High-caste women prepare the food with elaborate ritual precautions, as described by R. S. Khare in *Hindu Hearth and Home*. Kacha food is FESTIVAL food, fried in a highly valued cooking medium (ghee or clarified butter), which is viewed as a purifying substance. Different foodstuffs are usually used for kacha food, and kacha food is exchanged more freely between groups. At a higher level, foods for Hindu gods are set even more apart. Food offerings are elaborately cooked and sanctified in rituals exclusive to the highest-caste priests.

Kashruth provides another example of the use of food to signify ritual purity and separateness. British anthropologist Mary Douglas, in "The Abominations of Leviticus," points out that the rules concerning which animals are kosher and which are not involve the appropriateness of an animal's form and locomotion for its epistemological class (land, air, or water animals). By eating only animals that are not anomalous to their class in appearance or movement, the individual and the group maintain purity and avoid danger. Others have pointed out that such rules qua rules also serve to discipline members of a group and create and maintain a strong sense of exclusiveness. Taboos on totemic animals (animals associated with the origin of a descent group or clan) reflect the mystical association of a food source with the forces that control the continuity of the world. Such food avoidances simultaneously affect spiritual and social solidarity. In the Christian religion communion is an inversion of such an association. Here the consumption (incorporation) of the essence of a supernatural force (rather than its avoidance) communicates similar spiritual and social messages.

Food taboos are often not part of such coherent epistemological systems as we find elaborated in the Old Testament or in Hindu sacred writings. Many food taboos are not as basic to the worldview of a society. They refer not to the controlling forces of

Figure 1. *(Food)* Feast given by Louis XIII for the Cavaliers of the Holy Spirit at Fontainebleau, May 14, 1633. Engraving after Abraham Bosse. The Bettmann Archive, Inc.

the universe but to systems of health beliefs (what is good or bad for the body) or to systems of social status. The latter are of central concern to food and communication.

Social, cultural, and political factors. Food items are frequently associated with particular social statuses and are selected accordingly. GENDER is often marked by food. A recent study of restaurant eating in Chicago indicated that in such public settings where food choices were open (not controlled by the household cook) and observed by others, men's and women's choices differed in distinctly patterned ways. Moreover, in restaurants whose clientele was predominately couples, gender differences in food choice were more marked than in other settings. In family restaurants food choices tended to mark age more than gender differences.

In U.S. popular culture men eat red meat and potatoes and avoid white meats and quiches. There is some indication that these ideas go back to nineteenth-century associations between red meat, blood, and strength on the one hand and eggs, light meats, and procreation on the other. Gender-marked food items are found in most cultures. Similarly food is used to mark age. In the classic ethnographic film *The Hunters,* about the !Kung of the Kalahari Desert in southern Africa, it is noted that the scavenged contents of a bird's nest (newly hatched birds and eggs) would never be eaten by adults but would be made into soup for CHILDREN. Cross-culturally children's food tends to be easy to chew and digest. Mass ADVERTISING has targeted age groups for certain foods and beverages in contemporary society. Such close associations between particular statuses

and particular foods severely constrain one's food choices if one wants them to communicate social-status competence.

In societies with structured social inequality foods are strongly associated with class position and prestige. Studies of food consumption in societies moving from agricultural subsistence economies to those dependent on markets and industrially processed food frequently find an association between prestige and the consumption of newly available, highly processed foods. This phenomenon was noted in several studies conducted during the 1940s in the rural United States and is now common worldwide in the transformation of Third World societies. At the same time new metropolitan elites in major world cities have restored the highest prestige rank to homemade items—those "made from scratch"—and to the authentic one-pot dishes of exotic ethnic cuisines that were once thought of as poor people's food.

In his recent book *Cooking, Cuisine and Class,* British anthropologist Jack Goody attempted to relate the nature of internally differentiated cuisine styles, particularly distinctions between high (haute) and ordinary cuisine, to types of societies. He finds differences in cuisine variation between preindustrial Africa and preindustrial Europe, Asia, and the Middle East. He relates these patterns of variability to differences in the systems of production.

Food has also frequently become a political symbol in social movements against the state. Food riots are a familiar event in the history of state-organized societies. The focus on food shortages as a potent symbol of political discontent is a major means of mobilizing large groups to action. Studies of food as an important symbol in political movements cover such historically and culturally diverse systems as early China and Rome, twentieth-century India, and the recent Solidarity movement in Poland.

Ethnic identity. It is almost a cliché to say that food items are used to mark ethnic groups. Foods are both eaten and avoided in the name of ethnic identity. Sharing certain special foods communicates a positive identity and solidarity, as in, for example, the use of the crawfish in Cajun cookery and the tamale for Tejanos (Mexican-Americans), as described in *Ethnic and Regional Foodways in the United States.* Similarly the food items closely identified with other groups can be consciously avoided. High-caste Hindus refer to nonvegetarian Hindus in derogatory terms, distinguishing levels of pollution that rank beef eaters lower than other meat eaters. Italians often make fun of "American" bread. The Oglala Sioux view negatively the American foods they eat daily; in contrast, as William and Marla Powers's work illustrates, they imbue the puppy meat reserved for ceremonial activities with the essence of Siouxness.

However, ethnicity is less often marked by particular items than by the complex rules for how to prepare the items and when to eat them. Many people in the United States eat as many bagels as Jewish-Americans or as much pasta as Italian-Americans, but they do not follow the rules for how to prepare these foods, when and with whom to eat them, and how they should be served.

For many groups, particular dishes (transformed food items) are imbued with meaning and signify group membership. For example, distinctions in the way a food is cleaned or cut, the way heat is applied (roasting, broiling, steaming, boiling), the cooking medium used (water, oil, broth), and the proportions of spices used to flavor it can all be used to distinguish the cuisines of different groups that use similar ingredients. All Asian cuisines use similar spices and soy sauce, but proportions and combinations generate major variations in taste traditions and regional styles.

Chinese cuisine is very eclectic in the food items it incorporates in its cuisine structure, but cooking rules are specific, and the repertoire of dish structures is limited. Thus new items are incorporated into a basic cuisine pattern that K. C. Chang has found persisting over thousands of years. It is the structure of dishes, the way they are combined in meals, and certain flavors that communicate "Chineseness."

For Italian-Americans in the northeastern United States two types of food-preparation styles exist: Italian and American. The basic Italian dish is a one-pot mixture called "gravy," which is a slowly cooked, meat-based, highly spiced tomato sauce that is served mixed with pasta. The other dish is the "platter," which is the typical Anglo meal of meat, starch, and vegetables, cooked quickly and separately, and presented simultaneously but in a segregated fashion on the plate. Similar items could be used in both dishes (a platter could contain meat loaf, noodles, and stewed tomatoes). However, the two types of cooking and presentation signify opposing identities for the two dishes. This food system uses both types of culinary rules alternatively and recursively in the

Figure 2. *(Food)* A ceremonial post-mortuary feast, Bajoeng Gede, July 10, 1937. From Gregory Bateson and Margaret Mead, *Balinese Character: A Photographic Analysis,* New York, 1942, plate 29, 1. The guests sit sideways, hunched over the food, in two rows facing opposite directions, so that each person's right hand is toward the food. (In Bali the eating of meals is accompanied by a sense of shame.) The Institute for Intercultural Studies/Library of Congress.

patterning of meals. Gravy meals are alternated with platters throughout the week. Gravy items and platter items are served together at most holiday and life-cycle feasts. Thus culinary rules play a major role in communicating the hyphenated identity of the group.

Within any single cuisine tradition, food is used to create solidarity in individual families and lineages. Particular recipes and kitchen utensils are passed down to perpetuate the family's special taste preferences and style. Thus family continuity is deliberately conveyed through the transmission of unique practices in those aspects of the system in which variety and creativity are permitted. Family distinctiveness is also displayed at extended-family and community gatherings, during which differences in practice are publicly recognized.

Organization of eating events. The activities related to organizing meals for special occasions and the actual PERFORMANCE of these occasions are even more explicitly related to communication. Rules exist for the appropriate composition of a meal. Dishes must be organized in time sequences or spatial arrangements to comprise a meal appropriate for the occasion. Meals and feasts involve presentation rules. In what order are dishes presented? What combination can be served simultaneously? Course sequences are a specific way of encoding group differences, and they are often hard to change. Americans eating Chinese meals have forced restaurants to adapt to American sequence rules in which soup is served first and sweets last. How are foods arranged on the table or on the plate or banana leaf? In the elaborated Hindu food system in one region the spatial arrangement of feast foods on the banana leaf is very formal. The feast foods are also placed in formal temporal sequence as well. The left or "sinister" side of the leaf holds raw or fried (kacha) foods, which are least susceptible to pollution. The right or ritually purer side holds and protects boiled (pakka) foods. In the middle, two foods that mark the meal are placed: rice—the staple—which is present at every meal, and a sweet—unique to special occasions—which marks its festive nature. It is the ritualized nature of the procedures at a feast as well as the special food markers (sweets, special meats, or baked goods) that is used to underscore the significance of the occasion.

The planning of feasts or special food events is particularly significant for communicating the identity, status, and power of a group, family, or individual. Important aspects of family, extended family, friendship, and community relationships can be revealed by watching the menu negotiations for an event. In many major community feasts the planning may be a major diplomatic event in which the fight for control over the invitation list, the menu, and food-preparation assignments may be used to demonstrate, exacerbate, or resolve long-term conflicts. Interfamily cooperation or status competition can be generated. Members of the community can be flattered or insulted by the negotiations. Being asked to bring food may be an honor or a sign of subservience, but it is always socially significant.

Menu decisions for events in which the social context is larger than the family depend very much on who the social audience will be and what message is intended to be conveyed. In a study of a community of Italian-Americans decisions about what to serve at three daughters' weddings were strongly influenced by the nature of the match and what the family wanted to communicate through food choice. In a match involving a non-Italian groom from outside the community the menu was unusual in that it consisted entirely of homemade traditional Italian dishes. In a match involving an Italian-American groom from outside the community an expensive American catered dinner was served that included only one specific traditional item made collaboratively by the close female relatives and friends of the bride's family. However, a match with a local member of the close-knit enclave led to a dinner with no Italian items.

In the first wedding a need to demonstrate a strong ethnic tradition to the outsider was satisfied. The second wedding format communicated both family status through the quality of the menu and a solid and appropriate support group through the collaborative baking. For the last wedding there was less need to convey either ethnicity or status.

Often feasts are used to display status through conspicuous consumption. It has often been noted that the potlatches of the Indians of northwestern North America as well as pig feasts in Melanesia were used to demonstrate and validate social status through the lavish provision of both quantity and quality by the host. Analogies can easily be drawn to contemporary wedding feasts for upwardly mobile families or families with social power that display their status by using the most prestigious foods in the catering repertoire for that year. Competitive entertaining events are also increasingly important among metropolitan elites, who compete through the media of French, nouvelle, and exotic cuisines. For them quantity—the former hallmark of Euro-American hospitality—has been replaced by the search for light, fresh, scarce, and esoteric ingredients.

Eating events themselves are fraught with rules of precedence and deference as well as etiquette. By controlling when one begins to eat, how fast one eats, how much one eats, and the like, individual groups communicate their civility and separate themselves from disdained ethnic or class groups.

Prestige and power statuses are often clearly marked by the order in which a person is served as well as

Figure 3. *(Food)* Thanksgiving dinner at a rural home in Pennsylvania, 1940s. The Bettmann Archive, Inc.

by the amount he or she is served. Sometimes the types of food permitted are status specific. The most desirable parts of animal or plant food may be mandated for the most powerful or respected person present; the converse is also frequently true.

Communication occurs at eating events indirectly as privilege and power are revealed by deference, precedence, and control. Personal traits are also inferred from eating behavior associated with gluttony or waste.

Eating occasions are also settings in which messages are transmitted directly through CONVERSATION. The act of eating together in private family settings provides an opportunity to communicate about appropriate role behavior. Ethnographic observations of conversations at mealtimes in societies as different as those of the United States and Bangladesh indicate that a great deal of socialization occurs during this time. Women in Bangladesh are told directly and indirectly that they are subservient

to men, that their food needs are secondary, and that the constraints on their eating are much more severe. Similarly at dinner tables in the United States children learn gender and age roles, and the talk of adult males and females gives evidence of unequal power distribution, both specifically through non-food-related discussion and indirectly through commentary about the food itself. Conversation about how food was selected, prepared, and served offers commentary about the appropriateness of the role behavior of the cook and how these behaviors conform to the community standard.

The roles of women as food givers and men and children as food receivers are characteristic of most cultures. This often leads to eating patterns in which women spend a great deal of time and effort serving their families and catering to individual needs rather than participating in the social interaction of the meal. Women's eating is often temporally separated from the rest of the family. In Islamic countries, where women are viewed as potentially polluting, they are often strictly segregated spatially from men during eating. In the Sudan, for example, men eat in one part of the home and women in another. Such temporal and spatial segregation powerfully conveys gender differences.

Summary. As one of the basic human drives, the need to eat provides many opportunities for communication. Human groups select raw foods from nature, transform them through cuisine, compose meals, create cycles of meals to punctuate seasons and stages of life, and create rules of etiquette for meal performance. With each of these steps they use food to mark social status, power relationships, and group identity. Food transactions and sharing underscore major social relationships. Domestic events reveal relationships of dominance and subservience between gender and age groups. Community food events have the potential to display relations of cooperation, exchange, solidarity, and sometimes conflict within friendship and extended-kinship networks. In many societies large public feasts and transactions as well as patterns of preference and avoidance communicate relationships of inequality and exclusion between major class and ethnic groups. Finally, many cultures use food systems as elaborated domains of meaning to express important messages about relationships to sacred forces.

Bibliography. Linda Keller Brown and Kay Mussell, eds., *Ethnic and Regional Foodways in the United States,* Knoxville, Tenn., 1984; Kwang-chih Chang, ed., *Food in Chinese Culture: Anthropological and Historical Perspectives,* New Haven, Conn., 1977; Mary Douglas, "Abominations of Leviticus," in *Purity and Danger: An Analysis of Concepts of Pollution and Taboo,* New York and London, 1966, reprint 1978; idem, ed., *Food and the Social Order,* New York, 1984; Peter Farb and George Armelagos, *Consuming Passions: The Anthropology of Eating,* Boston, 1980; Jack Goody, *Cooking, Cuisine and Class,* Cambridge and New York, 1982; R. S. Khare, *The Hindu Hearth and Home,* Durham, N.C., 1976; Claude Lévi-Strauss, "The Culinary Triangle" (in French), trans. by Peter Brooks, *Partisan Review* 33 (1966): 586–595.

JUDITH GOODE

FORENSICS

In current usage, those communicative activities in which argumentation plays a major role—primarily PUBLIC SPEAKING, discussion, and debate. It also refers to an argumentative perspective for investigating any communication, whether or not it is overtly argumentative in nature. Forensics has served both as a means of public decision making on controversial questions and as a pedagogical instrument providing training in the skills of analysis and advocacy.

Origins and Philosophical Assumptions

ARISTOTLE defined forensics as a branch of ORATORY concerned specifically with argumentation in a court of law, focusing on past events, and involving issues of justice and injustice. Elements of debate can be found in passages of Homer, but the father of debate is considered to be the Sophist Protagoras of Abdera (ca. 481–ca. 411 B.C.E.), best remembered for his statement that "man is the measure of all things." Protagoras taught his students to argue both sides of a question. In classical Greece citizens were expected to defend their own claims in assemblies and courts of law, so forensic skills were valuable for pragmatic reasons (*see* HELLENIC WORLD).

These skills remained useful during the Roman and early medieval periods, although the emphasis was increasingly pedagogical. Students recited the *suasoriae* and *controversiae,* speeches arguing opposite sides of fictitious legal cases (*see* ROMAN EMPIRE). Public debates over abstract theological questions characterized the MIDDLE AGES and the RENAISSANCE; these debates took the form of disputation—defending a thesis by means of formal logic.

Forensics is rooted in several philosophical presuppositions. First, it is assumed that much in human affairs is uncertain and contingent, not susceptible to absolute knowledge or empirical measurement. Forensics emphasizes resolution of such matters through argument. Second, knowledge is socially constructed through the forensic encounter. What the arguers take to be true is influenced by the ability of a resolution to withstand close scrutiny and argument. Forensics may be considered a means of testing the probable truth of hypotheses put forward in the form of resolutions. Third, forensics emphasizes the rigorous scrutiny of ideas through such formalistic conventions as the presence of committed advocates, the opportunity for full and free discussion, and the adjudication of the dispute by disinterested parties. Fourth, forensics is intimately related to the theory of freedom of expression as the system best calculated to promote truth and justice. What gives confidence that truth will emerge from such an exchange is the careful scrutiny of proffered claims and the Aristotelian assumption that truth is by nature stronger than its opposite. Forensics, therefore, is an important element of democratic governance.

Varieties of Forensic Activities

During the twentieth century there have been four major forms of forensic activities: parliamentary debate, political campaign debate, advocacy systems in special fields, and academic contest forensics.

Parliamentary debate. Debate has long been a major feature of legislative bodies. Tradition, law, or other influences may determine procedures. In the United States, for example, congressional debate rules derive from centuries-old British precedents, from the U.S. Constitution, from the *Manual* written by Thomas Jefferson as U.S. vice-president, and from rules adopted by each of the legislative branches for its own proceedings. Interpretations of these rules by the presiding officer may also have an impact on procedures.

Debates in parliamentary style, though less elaborate, have also been a common feature of state and local governments, annual meetings of corporations, and a variety of private voluntary organizations. These groups may evolve their own procedural rules or adopt some established codification such as the widely used *Robert's Rules of Order,* compiled by Henry M. Robert in 1876 and later amended by him.

Political campaign debate. The joint appearance of opposing candidates on the same platform, dividing time in a debate format, is a relatively recent democratic innovation. It gained considerable impetus on the U.S. frontier, where candidates for local office often met in debate. Among the most celebrated political debates of the nineteenth century were the seven debates between Stephen A. Douglas and Abraham Lincoln in the 1858 campaign for the U.S. Senate seat from Illinois. A modern adaptation of the idea came a century later when John F. Kennedy and Richard M. Nixon, respectively the Democratic and Republican candidates in the 1960 U.S. presidential election, engaged in four television debates, also heard on radio. Each debate featured brief opening and closing remarks from each candidate, with the bulk of time given to responses to questions posed by a panel of journalists. Such campaign debates, at various governmental levels, have been staged frequently but irregularly since that time in the United States and elsewhere. The idea has been welcomed enthusiastically but also criticized as leading to superficial responses. It seems likely to remain one of the options of democratic government. *See also* POLITICAL COMMUNICATION.

Advocacy systems in special fields. While courts of law remain an especially notable arena for the resolution of issues through forensic procedures, the forensic approach to the resolution of disputes has proved valuable in many other fields, such as RELIGION, science, medicine, and the arts. The publication in 1958 of British philosopher Stephen Toulmin's *The Uses of Argument* did much to stimulate interest in organized argumentation as a social technique. He urged that individual fields avoid formal logic as a model and evolve their own standards for the conduct and resolution of disputes.

Academic contest forensics. Since the late nineteenth century debating contests have become a prominent activity at universities, colleges, and high schools in a number of countries. Academic study of argumentation has burgeoned during this same period, usually in speech departments. This study has led to interscholastic, intercollegiate, and international debates, in which debating teams from Australia, Great Britain, Japan, New Zealand, the Soviet Union, the United States, and many other countries have participated. Various tournament formats have been used. In the most common, opposing two-person teams are assigned to debate alternately for and against a resolution. Each speaker delivers one constructive and one rebuttal speech and cross-examines one member of the opposing team.

Forensics as a Perspective for Inquiry

In addition to designating a variety of speaking activities, the term *forensics* also has been used to refer to an argumentative perspective on communication studies, one that focuses on people's giving of reasons to justify beliefs and values and to influence the actions of others. This perspective is applied not only to formal speaking situations but also to informal interaction. Research topics include children's acquisition of argument skills, argument in informal CONVERSATION, and the argumentative dimension of works of literature and ART.

See also PERSUASION; RHETORIC.

Bibliography. J. Robert Cox and Charles Arthur Willard, eds., *Advances in Argumentation Theory and Research,* Carbondale, Ill., 1982; Douglas Ehninger and Wayne Brockriede, *Decision by Debate,* 2d ed., New York, 1978; Austin J. Freeley, *Argumentation and Debate: Reasoned Decision Making,* 5th ed., Belmont, Calif., 1981; Ray E. Keesey, *Modern Parliamentary Procedure,* Boston, 1974; Sidney Kraus, ed., *The Great Debates: Kennedy vs. Nixon, 1960,* Bloomington, Ind., 1962, reprint 1977; James H. McBath, ed., *Forensics as Communication: The Argumentative Perspective,* Skokie, Ill., 1975; J. W. Patterson and David Zarefsky, *Contemporary Debate,* Boston, 1982; Richard D. Rieke and Malcolm O. Sillars, *Argumentation and the Decision Making Process,* 2d ed., Glenview, Ill., 1983; Stephen Toulmin, *The Uses of Argument,* Cambridge, 1958, reprint 1964.

DAVID ZAREFSKY

FORGERY, ART

It is not entirely clear what makes ART forgery a crime. Some aesthetes claim that the sole legitimate reason for collecting art resides in the aesthetic qualities of the work; thus forgery should not be an issue, much less a crime. Such a perspective is, however, naive. Art markets treat works as investments and as historical artifacts (*see* ARTIFACT). Art touched by the hand of a particular artist gains value from that fact alone. So forgery is a crime, even when buyers deceive themselves.

Art forgeries have been divided into four categories: the copy, the PALIMPSEST, the pastiche, and what might be called the original forgery. The *copy* is designed to be an exact replica of an original work of art, including its signature if the work is signed. It is sold either as the work itself or as a second version of the work by the original artist. A *palimpsest* is a basically authentic artwork, but one that has been partially restored or painted over by a second person, often to increase its value and with the side effect that the artist's intention has been lost. The primary example of a palimpsest is the addition of a false signature. A *pastiche* is probably the most common type of forgery. This is a work in the style of an artist and includes images and themes the artist used in other works; it is a work the artist might have created. The *original forgery* is an original composition, not composed of elements previously painted by the artist, but designed to be seen as the artist's own work. The most famous example of an original forgery is Han van Meegeren's *Christ at Emmaus,* a picture Jan Vermeer might have painted had he been influenced by Michelangelo da Caravaggio and had he decided to paint religious pictures.

As long as particular works of art have had a value attached to them because they are originals, forgers have been willing to reap the rewards. Forgeries occurred in ancient Egypt, and forgers apparently were common in ancient Rome. The growth of collecting art works for the sake of owning them as objects also contributed to the growth of forgery. Extensive forgeries of works of art began in the late MIDDLE AGES with the rise of princely collectors. By the RENAISSANCE forgeries were common, and artists we now describe as great, such as Michelangelo, Peter Paul Rubens, and Andrea del Sarto, forged the work of others to satisfy patrons or to demonstrate their own virtuosity.

Statistics on the scope of the problem of forgery are difficult to establish. One art expert, Leonard DuBoff, speculates that between 1 and 10 percent of all art transactions involve forgeries and fakes. A classic anecdote illustrates the problem: George de Cornell, director of the Fine Arts Guild of America, reportedly claimed in 1935 that "out of three thousand Corots, eight thousand are in the United States." Incredibly, New York customs statistics indicate that more than 103,000 "Corots" were imported from Europe over a twenty-year period.

This history refers to Western art worlds. In other societies attitudes toward originality, hence forgery, have been quite different. Tribal and folk societies typically do not place the same premium on novel creativity and the role of the individual artist as do modern Western art worlds. In many societies, such as classical India or Mesoamerica, the individual artist was unimportant, although the art might be highly esteemed. In such contexts exact copying was

Figure 1. *(Forgery, Art)* Han van Meegeren, *Christ at Emmaus,* 1937. Oil on canvas. Museum Boymans-van Beuningen, Rotterdam.

Figure 2. *(Forgery, Art)* Forged Corot *(ouvrage en dé-trempe), Landscape with Stream*. Drawing. Reproduced by courtesy of the Trustees of The British Museum.

valued, and change was not desired. Likewise, in an advanced non-Western civilization such as Ming China (seventeenth century), creativity as Westerners define it was not essential. As critic Laurence Sickman wrote, "When a Chinese artist reproduces a composition of an old master or paints in his style, it is no more plagiarism than when Horowitz plays a composition by Brahms." The art is seen as fundamentally separate from the artist. To capture the style of another is a mark of success, not dishonesty, and so "forgery" has quite a different meaning in such a society.

Basically, two techniques can be used to determine whether an artwork is genuine: scientific analysis and critical (or aesthetic) analysis. Numerous advances have been made over the past few decades in the scientific dating of art works. For example, certain paints are known to have been used in particular historical periods. Even the crackle in the paint can indicate the age of a picture. X rays are helpful for seeing what is beneath the outside covering of paint. These techniques do not aid in the identification of modern works. Further, they prove only that a painting is *not* genuine, not that it is. For this, the art expert's discerning eye is necessary.

How can the critic determine who painted what?

Leaving aside historical traces, such as certificates of authenticity (which can be forged more easily than the work itself) and provenance (which can be created like any good story), the expert must look at the work and its style. This is inherently problematic, and in legal trials involving forgeries experts have testified for both parties. Such a judgment may seem almost mystical, as in the comment of Klaus Perls, a prominent forgery hunter:

It is difficult to explain how you recognize a fake. The first look at a work of art has to give you the emotional response of truth or fake. You can write whole books on what this first look implies. It is the summing up of all the knowledge you've acquired, all the things you've seen of the artist, all you've read.

The skill in creating forgeries is to ensure that they do not raise suspicion, that they do not look like forgeries. In the words of Ernst Bloch, "A forgery can be distinguished from an original because it looks more genuine."

Style, of course, is not an objective feature of an artwork but an abstraction of the essence of the work as viewed by an individual or group. Style is known only through social, historical, and personal contexts. What a Rembrandt "looks like" changes from generation to generation. Successful forgeries capture the spirit of the age's perception, underlining and exaggerating those features that contemporary critics deem most significant.

The Aesthetic Valuation of Artistic Forgeries

Forgery poses particularly thorny questions for both philosophers of art and those associated with the crime. Does authenticity by itself bestow some value? This question was raised most directly by critic Aline Saarinen:

If a fake is so expert that even after the most thorough and trustworthy examination its authenticity is still open to doubt, is it or is it not as satisfactory a work of art as if it were unequivocally genuine?

Some, such as Arthur Koestler and Alfred Lessing, adopt a position that has been termed "appearance theory." They suggest that our only concern should be the work itself, abstracted from the whole of its surroundings. According to this view, condemning forgery is simply a means by which an artistic establishment maintains its own power, legitimacy, and credibility. Forgery may be a problem historically, biographically, legally, and economically, but not aesthetically. Philosopher Jack Meiland argues that we must distinguish between the primary value and the derivative value of a work. Forgery is relevant to the derivative value.

An important approach to understanding forgeries focuses not on the work but on the individual creator. Every work of art has a history of production.

A forgery misrepresents this history. Its meaning is fundamentally dishonest. Part of the aesthetic meaning of a work is that it was completed in a particular period by a particular hand. Such a view grounds AESTHETICS in historical circumstance. In the West creative artists are defined as those who can transcend the unstated limits of what constitutes artistic traditions; they break free of the conventions of the age. The forger has by comparison an easier job; the conventions have already been laid out by others. Creativity has become mimicry. Critics are concerned with the original use of a technique, not the second. Leonard Meyer suggests that knowingly to admire a forgery or to claim that it does not differ from the original is reverse snobbery. He argues that an object can only be understood in context, not through intrinsic qualities alone. This approach finds no difficulty with the changed evaluation and value of a

forgery after its unmasking because of the change in its social context.

In certain AVANT-GARDE art movements the question of a forgery becomes more complex. Can one forge Marcel Duchamp's *Fountain* (1917), a real ceramic urinal? The display of "found objects" presents the same problem to those who wish to draw an uncrossable line between creator and deceiver. Where are the boundaries of art? Likewise, if we choose to label as forgery the work of one person passed off as the work of another, can we protect the legitimate art restorer? Of course, as participants in the art world we can make these distinctions because of our tacit knowledge, but this does not provide a formal method of distinguishing "real" from "forged."

A final issue, and one that differentiates forgery from many other crimes, is that the forger wishes to

Figure 3. *(Forgery, Art)* G. F. Ioni, *Madonna and Child with Angels*, nineteenth century. Forgery in the style of San di Pietro (Siena, 1406–1481). Tempera on panel. The Cleveland Museum of Art, Bequest of James Parmelee.

have a say in our moral evaluations. Many of the more prominent forgers of our century have been willing to tell their own stories, either revealing themselves or after being revealed. They have an argument to make, in line with what was earlier referred to as appearance theory. Many forgers do not consider themselves criminals; rather, they conceive of their actions as a protest against a corrupt art world. For example, Tom Keating, an English forger of the 1960s and 1970s, claimed that his motive was simply "a protest against merchants who make capital out of those I am proud to call my brother artists, both living and dead." The comment is self-serving but is supported by those in the art world who suggest that the greed of the buyer is partially responsible for the crime. According to some, museums turn a blind eye when fakes are donated to them by wealthy collectors, on the assumption that if they were to turn down collectors who would not be able to get their tax write-offs, the museums might not receive future gifts.

By blaming their victims, forgers contend that they are great artists. If their works are accepted as the creations of famous painters, they must have equal talent. Given that the structure of the art world is based on patronage, today in the form of critics, MUSEUM officials, and wealthy collectors, unsuccessful artists may feel that their work is not accepted because *they* have not been accepted. The art world from this perspective has become a social and political arena.

In sum, forgery poses complex problems that touch on reputation, originality, value, and expertise. As fraud, forgery surely poses a major problem for all members of the art world. However, as an aesthetic enterprise, opinions are mixed. As long as we value particular artists rather than beauty, forgery will be with us and will continue to be discussed heatedly.

See also ARTIST AND SOCIETY; AUTHORSHIP.

Bibliography. Daniel P. Biebuyck, ed., *Tradition and Creativity in Tribal Art*, Berkeley, Calif., 1969; Leo M. Drachsler and Harry Torczyner, eds., *Forgery in Art and the Law*, New York, 1956; Denis Dutton, ed., *The Forger's Art: Forgery and the Philosophy of Art*, Berkeley, Calif., 1983; Gary Alan Fine, "Cheating History: The Rhetorics of Art Forgery," *Empirical Studies of the Arts* 1 (1983): 75–93; John FitzMaurice Mills and John M. Mansfield, *The Genuine Article*, New York, 1979.

GARY ALAN FINE

FOTONOVELA

The fotonovela, or photonovel, tells a story through the combination of still photographs and the written word. The union of PHOTOGRAPHY and the captioned story was used as early as 1855 in France in the presentation of a romantic story (*see* ROMANCE, THE).

It was not until after World War II, however, and the advances made in offset printing, that the fotonovela received extended distribution. It is popular in several European countries, particularly Italy, Spain, and France, and in many parts of the Third World, notably North Africa and Latin America.

The fotonovela is a product of advancing technology in the production and mass reproduction of images (*see* GRAPHIC REPRODUCTION). Beginning in Italy and then in France with the use of captioned stills from films, it was seen first as simply a means of retelling motion picture stories in MAGAZINE form, thus allowing a wider distribution of the film medium. In Italy these early film-based fotonovelas were known as *fumetti*, or "clouds of smoke," for the balloons placed above characters' heads indicating speech or thought. Content often included film gossip and publicity and astrological predictions along with the main story. As the fotonovela became more popular, stories were written specifically for the medium, most of them simple romances depicted in a sequence of staged and photographed scenes.

During the 1950s European colonies or dependencies proved fertile ground for the export and sale of fotonovelas. New marketing techniques and content variations were developed for these areas. Established publishing empires in Spain and Italy produced fotonovelas that were then translated and printed in Latin American countries such as Brazil, Chile, and Argentina.

By the 1960s the fotonovela's potential for profit in Europe and Latin America, combined with an increasing availability of press capacity and a policy in many countries of subsidizing paper and ink manufacture, led to a vast expansion in fotonovela creation and production. Spain and Italy were no longer the major producers for developing nations. Production centers arose in countries with strong film industries, particularly Argentina and Mexico. Local variations were created to appeal to regional audiences. In Brazil and other southern Latin American countries domestic production began to compete with fotonovelas whose copy was imported from Italy and translated.

Mexico became the heart of fotonovela production for North America and northern Latin America in the 1970s. The photographic stills were shot in Mexico, but a majority of the Mexican fotonovelas were printed in the United States, usually in Miami or Los Angeles, cities with large Spanish-speaking populations. As with the exported Italian products, the mounted photographs and captions produced in Mexico were sent to publishing houses in such countries as Colombia and Venezuela, where they were printed. Some of the language, particularly the highly local Mexican slang, was altered for regional taste.

Fotonovelas are usually aimed at a female audience, although they are also read by men. In some

Figure 1. *(Fotonovela)* Page from an Italian fotonovela. From *Charme*, Rome, September 11, 1975, p. 40. Copyright Lancio Film 1975–Edizioni Lancio SpA.

areas, as in France, they were originally included as inserts in popular women's magazines, indicating a largely middle-class readership. With the development of a separate format, however, the fotonovela could be directed to a working-class audience whose members were not likely to purchase or read women's magazines. The separate format thus tends to attract less ADVERTISING, and profits depend on direct sales. The GENRE has also spawned numerous offshoots appealing to specific audiences, such as the *fotoaventura* or the *fotonovela picaresca,* whose content is male-oriented and more often overtly sexual.

Fotonovela readers are usually young and primarily urban. Because fotonovelas are generally regarded with some disdain as a type of subliterature, readership tends to be underestimated by surveys. This may be compounded by the fact that reading often takes place in a group setting. Anthropological studies in Latin America have suggested that particularly in small regional centers fotonovelas are often read aloud by the literate member of a group. Fotonovela readership in Latin America is also greater than the estimated weekly circulation of 20 million. Many issues are recirculated through trading arrangements with family or community members. Most working-class neighborhoods and market towns have women entrepreneurs who set up fotonovela rental libraries where for a small fee one can rent and read on the spot a fotonovela that may be several years old.

Fotonovela subgenres stress different themes or types of content. The *fotonovela rosa,* which dominated early production, presented variations on a Cinderella story in which a poor but virtuous heroine attracts and marries a handsome millionaire. This type of story soon lost its appeal in Europe and Latin America. As the production arena expanded, the social class of the hero in particular became more representative of that of most fotonovela readers. The problems resolved in the course of the story changed from class differences over which love could prevail into more mundane confrontations with parents, friends, or career goals that seemed to block the fulfillment of true love.

In Latin America a notable shift of content first occurred with the *fotonovela suave,* in which middle-class young people faced middle-class romantic problems. An even bigger innovation came from Mexico in the form of the *fotonovela roja,* which focused on working-class protagonists. Romance was no longer the solution to problems; instead, stories generally ended with the violent death of one or more characters. The juxtaposition of sexuality and death was a recurrent and striking theme. Stories tended to strongly reinforce traditional moral codes; punishment or retribution for wrongdoing is always exacted and yet is not usually the result of any deliberate action on the part of the main characters.

There is a strong emphasis on trusting to fate and the ability of faith and true love to overcome obstacles.

It has been theorized that each fotonovela type fulfills a different function for its audience and stresses specific components of cultural IDEOLOGY. The *fotonovela rosa,* for example, provides a mechanism of escape from real problems; its emphasis on female virtue and passivity and the obligatory happy ending (usually the prospect of a marriage) foster traditional notions of femininity. The *fotonovela suave,* which attracts more advertising than the others and is largely distributed in the more affluent southern Latin American countries, encourages readers to aspire to middle-class life-styles and promotes the consumption of middle-class goods. The *fotonovela roja,* concerned with the portrayal of urban values such as individualism and law and order, may serve to integrate rural and working-class readers into an urban way of life.

Fotonovelas have been attacked by critics on several grounds. Feminists see them as contributing to the cultural oppression of women by portraying stereotyped roles and romance as the solution to problems (*see* FEMINIST THEORIES OF COMMUNICATION). Fotonovelas have also been denounced as escapist fare whose themes downplay issues of class and social conflict and thus reduce class consciousness and the possibility for change. Fotonovela readers point out that at least the *fotonovela roja* deals with problems largely ignored by polite society, such as rape, incest, and illegitimacy. While plots do not end in the resolution of such problems, at least it is made clear that these things are not the fault of the victim.

While it is true that fotonovelas ignore political, economic, and social issues in favor of the more easily resolved love story of two individuals, the medium has also been seen in terms of its potential for eliciting reaction and change and has been the subject of experimentation in Europe and Latin America. In France a number of alternative fotonovelas have been produced by state agencies trying to adapt the form for different, progressive messages. In Latin America both private and government groups have attempted to use the fotonovela form for straightforward self-improvement messages ranging from encouraging nonformal education or better hygiene to feminist consciousness-raising or the propagation of radical political views. In this way the fotonovela's role in the formation and influence of group values and its significance as an interpersonally mediated form of mass communication can become an important basis for community organization.

See also DEVELOPMENT COMMUNICATION; LITERATURE, POPULAR; SERIAL; SOAP OPERA.

Bibliography. Fernando Curiel, *Fotonovela rosa, fotonovela roja,* Mexico, D.F., 1980; Cornelia Butler Flora, "Fotonovelas: Message Creation and Reception," *Journal of Popular Culture* 14 (1980): 524–534; Cornelia Butler Flora and Jan L. Flora, "The Fotonovela as a Tool for Class and Cultural Domination," *Latin American Perspectives* 5 (1978): 134–150; Angeluccia Bernardes Habert, *Fotonovela e indústria cultural: Estudo de uma forma de literatura sentimental fabricada para milhões*, Petropoles, Brazil, 1974; Serge Saint-Michael, *Le roman photo*, Paris, 1979.

CORNELIA BUTLER FLORA

FOUCAULT, MICHEL (1926–1984)

French philosopher, historian, and political theorist. Michel Foucault's ideas on social power and its concealed roots in LANGUAGE and socially constructed meanings had wide implications for the study of communication. Born in Poitiers, Foucault studied philosophy at the Sorbonne. After a brief spell as a member of the French Communist party, he turned from philosophy to psychopathology and published an early book on mental illness. In the 1950s he left France to teach in Sweden, Poland, and Germany, returning to an academic post in France in 1960. After the widespread acclaim that greeted his *Les mots et les choses* (*Words and Things*, 1966) he received an academic appointment in Paris, where he taught philosophy at the avant-garde University of Vincennes and was deeply influenced in his political thought by the student uprisings of 1968. Foucault edited the leftist weekly journal *Libération*, became active in campaigns for prison and homosexual reform, and was hailed as a master of the fashionable new intellectual current of STRUCTURALISM (an allegiance he consistently denied). In his later years his work turned increasingly to themes of social power, and his final study was of the history of sexuality. He died of a cerebral tumor in 1984.

Although he was praised by many as the single most important European philosopher of his time, Foucault's lifelong work actually constituted a set of intellectual guerrilla raids against what he took to be the insidiously repressive, violent character of Western philosophical thought and social practice. His early, vastly influential study *Madness and Civilization* (1964) is on the surface a documentary history of Western society's treatment of the supposedly insane, charting the epochal shifts from medieval ATTITUDES toward the mentally ill to the gradual growth of techniques for incarcerating and institutionalizing those labeled psychologically deviant. The secret subtext of the work, however, is a powerful polemical challenge to what Foucault regards as the repressive project of stringently dividing a dominative "reason" from its monstrous "other"—a project inherent both in Western philosophy since René Descartes and in the nature of Western social and polit-

ical institutions. From the outset, then, Foucault championed in both his theoretical work and his political practice groups marginalized by the prevailing social order. The political passion that fueled this enterprise is curiously dissembled by the meticulously clinical techniques of documentation and analysis evident in his major published works.

Foucault's abiding concern is less to pass moral or political judgment on the repressive phenomena he recounts than to expose the profound relativity of all modes of thought and political regimes, which absolutize and idealize forms of knowledge that are in fact intimately bound up with the institutional disciplining, control, and "normalization" of human subjects in society. His chief philosophical work, *Les mots et les choses,* seizes upon changing notions of language from the MIDDLE AGES to the modern period, but it does so as a way of uncovering the hidden logics by which societies organize their "discursive formations," legitimating certain areas as proper objects of inquiry and excluding others. In this work, as in *The Archaeology of Knowledge* (1969), Foucault's concern is with the concealed epistemes or structural sets of rules that govern the definition of evidence, license certain forms of social authority, and permit certain objects to be interrelated in particular ways. Thus Foucault's apparently neutral methodological inquiries in fact secretly serve the radical political impulses that emerge more explicitly in his later publications.

In *Discipline and Punish* (1975), with its detailed examination of techniques of penal correction, Foucault discovered that his real theme is less epistemology than power—more particularly the varied microtechniques by which power is "imprinted" on the human body to render it a docile, well-drilled agent of dominant social forces. Yet power, Foucault insists, is not to be viewed purely negatively as an oppressive force stifling the free expression of the human subject. On the contrary, power is positive and productive; it is less what crushes the human subject than what constitutes it, in a complex range of internalized disciplines and "technologies." It is humanism, to which Foucault is implacably opposed, that would view the human subject in sentimental fashion as some rich interior space of potential freedom rather than as the product and effect of social technologies. Because this consistent antihumanism looks forward eagerly to the passing of the ephemeral historical construct known as "Man," Foucault has been ranked with the structuralists from whom he sought to distinguish himself.

Turning in his final work to the history of sexuality, Foucault warns against the romantic view that would regard sexuality as bound up with our free, "natural" identities, awaiting its appropriate expression. On the contrary, he describes sexuality as being of rather recent historical birth, a construct of many varied forces (including the PSYCHOANALYSIS that purports to "treat" it) rather than a biological given. The steady proliferation of post-Freudian discourses on sexuality and of techniques for its management and normalization is for Foucault simply a dramatic instance of the manipulation of human subjects at the hands of social power. The subject who "freely" confesses in the psychoanalytic scene colludes with such powers rather than emancipating himself or herself from them.

Briefly a Marxist in his youth and a pupil of French Marxist philosopher Louis Althusser, Foucault turned under the influence of the May events of the 1968 French student revolt to a more local, pluralistic, strategic politics, rejecting all "global" political programs as inherently oppressive, yet with increasing skepticism about the possibility of any total break with a social power that he now saw less as centralized than as all-pervasive. His thinking about power and its capacity to produce forms of knowledge was deeply shaped by the work of Friedrich Nietzsche; indeed Foucault could be best described as a neo-Nietzschean thinker, passing to that point from orthodox Marxism by the precarious bridge of late-1960s Western Maoism. His work is relentless in its ingrained suspicion of all humanist or idealist illusion, scornful of all notions of "truth," and produced out of a sense of solidarity with the mad, victimized, imprisoned, categorized, and sexually "deviant." Foucault's final position could perhaps best be summarized by claiming that he is an anarchist without being a libertarian—doggedly committed to a fundamental refusal of the given social order but profoundly skeptical of any positive, "totalizing," or liberatory alternative to it.

See also BARTHES, ROLAND; COMMUNICATION, PHILOSOPHIES OF; DURKHEIM, ÉMILE; MARX, KARL; MARXIST THEORIES OF COMMUNICATION.

Bibliography. Michel Foucault, *Madness and Civilization* (Histoire de la folie), trans. by Richard Howard, New York, 1965; idem, *Discipline and Punish: The Birth of the Prison* (Surveiller et punir), trans. by Alan Sheridan, New York, 1977; idem, *The History of Sexuality*, Vol. 1, *An Introduction* (Histoire de la sexualité), trans. by Robert Hurley, New York, 1978.

TERRY EAGLETON

FREUD, SIGMUND (1856–1939)

Austrian physician and founder of PSYCHOANALYSIS, whose theories have had reverberating effects on ideas about human communication and have been a major influence on communications study and research. The name of Sigmund Freud is inextricably linked to fin de siècle Vienna, where he based his initial work in laboratory research and then private medical practice on the assumptions of the natural sciences. But after early studies in neurology and hysteria that emphasized physiological presuppositions, Freud moved increasingly toward a psychological understanding of nervous diseases. His contribution to the study of communication begins with his first major work in psychoanalytic theory, *The Interpretation of Dreams* (1899), in which he argued that the dream has a symbolic or an expressive function.

In this autobiographical confession Freud established that dreams are expressions of unconscious wishes that are unrecognized as such by the untrained individual. He eventually identified a veritable language of the unconscious in seemingly meaningless behavior such as jokes, facial tics, SLIPS OF THE TONGUE, compulsions, and daydreaming. In simple terms, Freud developed a technique of reading the unconscious, which was, according to his theory, unavailable to direct observation because of the psychic mechanism of repression. Freud's insistence on the

Figure 1. *(Freud, Sigmund)* Sigmund Freud. The Bettmann Archive, Inc.

fundamentally instinctual nature of the unconscious and the ineliminable opposition of repression to the instincts separates him from many of his best-known disciples, such as CARL JUNG, Alfred Adler, and Wilhelm Reich.

Freud's theoretical and case studies identify two levels of communication: the intrapsychic and the interpersonal. Intrapsychic communication becomes problematic when repressions fail to prevent otherwise forbidden impulses from disturbing consciousness. The purpose of psychoanalytic therapy is to work toward the conscious control of unconscious conflicts by drawing them out in INTERPERSONAL COMMUNICATION between analyst and patient, which circumvents failing repressions. The analyst encourages uninhibited talk by the patient—a technique that Freud's famous early patient Anna O. dubbed "the talking cure." Within the privacy of the analytic session each individual becomes something of an artist revealing the most private details of inner life. Indeed, Freud discovered a bit of the artist in every person in fantasies and dreams. But the artist in every person remains merely potential, lacking the power to communicate until released by the psychoanalyst. With the analyst's guidance the patient grows into a successful but limited artist by constructing a system of interpersonal MEANING.

Freud argued that the patient inevitably develops resistances to revealing the most significant intimate details. Among the most desperate but predictable strategies is the phenomenon of transference, in which the patient projects onto the analyst both hostile and affectionate feelings in order to avoid communicating what the patient most wants to keep unconscious. The analyst's task, as in the case of most resistances, is to press for a conscious honesty about tabooed wishes. Successful therapy results in more honest interpersonal and intrapsychic communication.

Freud also encouraged honesty about the private motives behind public communicators and communications. He understood public figures (e.g., Woodrow Wilson, Leonardo da Vinci) and cultural products (e.g., novels, paintings) as private symptoms rather than public symbols. In reading public meanings backward to private motives Freud helped to inaugurate an era in which communication has come to be understood as a psychological art, the art of symbolically shaping and expressing our most private lives.

Freud's writings have had a considerable influence on theories about communication in other disciplines and have had practical applications as well. His ideas on sexuality, repression, and the unconscious have helped form modern notions of personality and GENDER and have found application in such fields as ART, EDUCATION, and ADVERTISING. Freud's views on SYMBOLISM and the unconscious have contributed to various artistic theories and techniques—inspiring, for example, a school of LITERARY CRITICISM and the stream-of-consciousness technique in novels. Along with such figures as CHARLES DARWIN and KARL MARX, Freud is one of the seminal thinkers of the modern era, helping to furnish the vocabulary of the modern mind and contributing to the mass of assumptions that underlie most thinking about communication.

See also IDEOLOGY; STRUCTURALISM.

Bibliography. Sigmund Freud, *General Psychological Theory*, ed. with an intro. by Philip Rieff, New York, 1963, reprint 1966; idem, *Therapy and Technique*, ed. with an intro. by Philip Rieff, New York, 1963, reprint 1967; Philip Rieff, *Freud: The Mind of the Moralist*, 3d ed., Chicago, 1979.

ALAN N. WOOLFOLK

FUNCTIONAL ANALYSIS

A theoretical framework for the analysis of social phenomena and structures. Also known as structural-functional analysis, it emphasizes social rather than individual-level explanations of phenomena, pointing—in general—to the functions (consequences) of the phenomena under study for the social system.

Sociology in the United States is often credited with advancing the structural-functional approach to the study of mass communication. Early traces of a functional orientation can be found, for example, in the treatment of society's communication system by Albion W. Small and George E. Vincent in their introductory sociology textbook published in 1894. These authors likened a society's communicating apparatus to a "social nervous system," with ramifications throughout the social organism. Such early allusions to the social functions of mass communication, sometimes suggested by biological analogies, usually were not articulated explicitly and systematically in terms of sociological functional theory. *See also* COOLEY, CHARLES HORTON.

A major step in the explicit codification and paradigmatic presentation of functional theory for U.S. sociology was the publication in 1949 of ROBERT K. MERTON's critical essay on *manifest* and *latent* functions as part of his work on social theory and social structure. In clarifying the nature of functional analysis Merton identifies three postulates common to early functional theory, which he suggests have proved debatable (thus leading to ideological criticisms of the functional approach) and which he regards as unnecessary to the functional orientation: (1) functional unity (the idea that any practice must be functional or dysfunctional for the total society), (2) universal functionalism (the idea that all persisting forms of social or cultural practices must be functional), and (3) indispensability (the idea that society has certain functional requirements that can be met only by certain specific social or cultural forms). These three dispensable early postulates of functionalism have led, according to Merton, to charges that functional analysis "inevitably involves certain ideological commitments," usually that it is conservative and insensitive to problems of social change.

Merton reformulates the functional approach to avoid these troublesome postulates and their associated ideological criticisms. First, he proposes that, rather than assume unity throughout society, functional analysts should specify the unit or system that is of concern for a particular functional analysis (e.g., society, subgroups, individuals). One can then examine the functions that a social practice has for this and other specified units, allowing for the empirical possibility that a practice may have positive functions for certain units and not for others—that is, being functional for one subgroup but not others. Second, rather than assume universal functionalism, one should accept the possibility that a social practice can have either functional or dysfunctional consequences (or both) for the unit under analysis. Finally, rather than assume indispensability of any particular social item or practice, the analyst should attempt to specify the functional prerequisites for a society and then study how any particular function may result (more or less effectively) from alternative social and cultural forms and practices.

In 1959 Charles R. Wright explicitly applied Merton's paradigm of functional analysis to the study of mass communication. From this perspective it is useful to regard mass communication as a social activity and to examine its role in the maintenance and change of social structure. Functions, as conceived by Wright, refer to the contributions that an organized system of communication, some element in it, or other regular communication activities make toward the ability of a system (personal, social, cultural) to survive and to maintain itself in working order, thereby making appropriate adjustments to changing conditions outside or within the system. Dysfunctions refer to those consequences that impede necessary adjustments and responses to changing external or internal demands on a system.

The aim and focus of functional analysis differ from those of other theoretical and research approaches to MASS MEDIA EFFECTS, which usually center on the effects of a specific instance of mass communication. For example, while media-effects research might focus on the immediate impact of a televised scene of VIOLENCE on the ATTITUDES or behavior of individual viewers, functional analysis would direct attention to the consequences that the

practice of regularly presenting such content in mass entertainment might have for society and its members, especially consequences for stability, adaptation, and change.

The first step in applying functional analysis to the study of mass communication, then, is to identify or stipulate the items to be the subject of analysis. These should be regular, patterned, or repetitive features of communication. Mass communication is conceived of as a special kind of social communication involving relatively large, socially heterogeneous audiences, mostly anonymous to the mass communicator. Media content is produced and distributed by social organizations or by persons working in complex organizations, involving extensive division of labor and costly resources. And its messages are communicated publicly, rapidly, and in a transient form.

At the broadest level one may examine the functions of mass communication itself, taking this regular form of social communication as an item for analysis. For example, James Beniger argues from a historical-sociological view that the current modes of mass-communicated information serve to cope with society's ever-increasing social needs for control over the production and movement of manufactured goods. In this sense mass communication is functional for contemporary, so-called information society.

A second level is to consider the functions of a particular way of organizing mass communication and the mass media, taking the specific form of the mass media system found in a particular society as the item for analysis. To do so requires the specification and identification of types of communication systems. Often this CLASSIFICATION is made in terms of the major institutional ownership and control of the mass media (e.g., state or private ownership) and the governing philosophy of the system (e.g., totalitarian or democratic). Thus one might be concerned with the functions of centrally organized and controlled systems of mass media for a totalitarian or for a democratic society. See GOVERNMENT-MEDIA RELATIONS.

A third level (or type of item) for analysis is some regular practice within the mass communication process, such as the practice of presenting national news on network television at a specific time every day or the practice of assigning news reporters to news beats (see TELEVISION NEWS).

Once the communication item to be studied has been specified, the next consideration is how such an item contributes functionally or dysfunctionally to the system under study (i.e., society, its members, subgroups, CULTURE, or some other unit). As an example, the regular broadcasting of weather forecasts enables a society to take the steps necessary to survive the potentially disruptive and even devastating social, economic, and human costs that could follow from unforeseen storms. To that extent one may interpret such commonplace weather broadcasts as functional. On the other hand, the routine broadcasting of weather predictions might lead to public apathy, indifference, boredom, satiation, or similar responses so that warnings of imminent danger go unheeded and steps necessary to avoid social disruption, even disaster, are not taken. Then one might interpret routine mass-communicated weather predictions as dysfunctional. A third possibility is that routine predictions have no significant effect on the ability of a society and its members to adjust, survive, or operate normally.

An item may be perceived as functional for one system but not for another. As an example, a tightly controlled mass media system, involving regular practices of CENSORSHIP and GOVERNMENT REGULATION, might be regarded as functional for the stability of a totalitarian society but dysfunctional for a participatory democracy. See POLITICAL COMMUNICATION.

It is this aspect of functional analysis—the interpretation of consequences—that leads to concern that ideological judgments may bias the analysis. Clearly the analyst must make an assessment of what is to be regarded as functional or dysfunctional from some point of view. Sociological functional theory has stressed the adaptive maintenance of the social system, its perceived tendency toward an equilibrium. This does not imply a total lack of change by society but rather an overall ability to survive without being destroyed or paralyzed, seriously disrupted, or essentially transformed through sudden internal social conflict, REVOLUTION, external threats, or other dangers to the existing system. Thus through its attention to questions of adaptation or failure to adapt, dysfunctional and functional consequences, and forces pressing for change as well as for stability, functional analysis allows for consideration of social change as well as for the maintenance of the social order. It thereby avoids a conservative bias. Functional analysis focuses attention on the potentials of mass communication for both beneficial and harmful effects, thereby protecting investigators from biased viewpoints that consider only the positive or only the negative consequences of, for example, mass-communicated news and entertainment.

A framework for a functional inventory that has proved useful in organizing claims and findings about mass media effects has been suggested by Wright. Adapting distinctions suggested in the writings of political scientist and communications scholar HAROLD D. LASSWELL, this framework specifies four basic communication activities engaged in by members of a society: (1) *surveillance* of the environment ("news

activity"), (2) *correlation and interpretation* of these events and prescriptions for reactions to them ("editing and persuasion"), (3) *socialization,* or the transmission of culture and values to new members of the society, and (4) *entertainment.* Clearly these communication activities can be performed through INTERPERSONAL COMMUNICATION, mass communication, or both. A functional approach raises questions about what happens when these basic communication activities are carried out regularly by means of mass communication.

More specifically, the functional framework poses the comprehensive task of specifying the manifest (intended) and latent (unintended) functions and dysfunctions of mass-communicated news, editing, PERSUASION, socialization, and entertainment for the society, its individual members, specific subgroups, and cultural systems. This framework guides a functional approach to examining the social consequences of mass communication.

Efforts to determine the functions or dysfunctions of carrying out surveillance, correlation, socialization, or entertainment by means of mass communication are complicated by the fact that in most societies these communication activities are usually conducted through both interpersonal and mass communication, as noted above. Sociologically oriented communication studies in the 1970s and 1980s also have drawn attention to the interdependent roles of mass communication and interpersonal communication in people's lives and in social processes. These studies often bear on the functions of mass-communicated news and entertainment even when the research is not explicitly framed in terms of functional theory.

One function of mass-communicated news, suggested in the early writings of PAUL F. LAZARSFELD and Merton, is to confer status and public legitimacy on those people, organizations, or public issues that get mass media attention. This conferred status, in turn, may play a role in organized social action by affecting a candidate's chances for leadership, an organization's public role, public discussions and PUBLIC OPINION concerning the issue, or some other social process or mechanism. Sociological studies have examined the complex ways through which mass communication and interpersonal communications affect the public's awareness of and response to social crises, including the status conferred on social issues and the subsequent conditions and patterns of organized social action. Such studies examine the contributions of mass communication and interpersonal communications to society's ability to cope with social crises and social problems, including such diverse phenomena as national political scandals or the threat of natural disasters. The findings of these and similar studies are consistent with a functional orientation even if it is not explicit.

Functional analysis presents a distinctive sociological orientation toward the formulation and interpretation of MASS COMMUNICATIONS RESEARCH. Its use provides researchers with a theoretical framework for examining the social consequences of mass communication phenomena, especially their contributions to social order and social change.

Bibliography. Jeffrey C. Alexander, ed., *Neofunctionalism,* Beverly Hills, Calif., 1985; James R. Beniger, "The Information Society: Technological and Economic Origins," in *Media, Audience, and Social Structure,* ed. by Sandra J. Ball-Rokeach and Muriel G. Cantor, Beverly Hills, Calif., 1986; Lyman Bryson, ed., *The Communication of Ideas,* New York, 1948; Harold A. Mendelsohn, *Mass Entertainment,* New Haven, Conn., 1966; Robert K. Merton, *Social Theory and Social Structure,* Glencoe, Ill., 1949, reprint (rev. and enl. ed.) 1962; A. R. Radcliffe-Brown, *Structure and Function in Primitive Society,* New York, 1952, reprint 1965; Albion W. Small and George E. Vincent, *An Introduction to the Study of Society,* New York, 1894; Charles R. Wright, *Mass Communication: A Sociological Perspective,* 3d ed., New York, 1986.

CHARLES R. WRIGHT

(dʒī), the seventh letter of the Roman alphabet, was originally a differentiated form of C; for its early history see that letter. In Latin G represented the voiced guttural stop; but in the later period of the language it must have been pronounced before front vowels as a palatal, its representation in the Romance languages being precisely the same as that of Latin *i* consonant, (j). . . .

GALLAUDET, THOMAS (1787–1851)

U.S. educator of the deaf and general educational reformer. In 1817 Thomas Hopkins Gallaudet founded the first free U.S. SCHOOL for the deaf in Hartford, Connecticut, following in the tradition of eighteenth- and early nineteenth-century European pioneers in EDUCATION for the deaf, such as the Abbé de l'Épée in France, Samuel Heinicke in Germany, and Thomas Braidwood in Scotland and England. With his Hartford school Gallaudet effectively launched the movement for free, formal, and general education for the deaf in the United States. By the late 1800s this movement had culminated in the development of one of the largest and most respected systems of free education for the deaf in the world.

Born in Philadelphia and raised in Hartford, Gallaudet graduated from Yale in 1805. After work in law, teaching, and commerce, he studied for the ministry and was ordained but declined a church post because of poor health. During this same period, through his acquaintance with a deaf neighbor child whom he had tried to teach privately, Gallaudet became interested in the education of the deaf, which at that time in the United States took place only individually, irregularly, and unsystematically. Backed financially by the child's father and several friends, Gallaudet went to Europe in 1815 to study the methods of education in schools for the deaf there. After a disappointing reception in England, Gallaudet was warmly welcomed at the Institut Royal des Sourds-Muets in Paris, where he studied for several months. In 1816 Gallaudet returned to the United States with the Paris school's Laurent Clerc, who became the first deaf teacher of the deaf in the United States. The following year Gallaudet founded his school in Hartford, and the school soon won government funding. Similar schools in other states quickly followed—in New York in 1818, Pennsylvania in 1820, and Kentucky in 1823—and by 1863 there were twenty-two schools for the deaf throughout the United States. Gallaudet was principal of the Hartford school until 1830, when poor health forced him to retire.

Gallaudet continued his educational efforts for the deaf after his retirement. He also devoted himself to other educational reform causes, including the education of blacks and higher education for women.

Deafness and its concerns were also central in Gallaudet's family. Gallaudet married a deaf woman, Sophia Fowler, who had been one of his first pupils at the Hartford school. His eldest son, Thomas, became a well-known minister to the deaf in New York. His youngest son, Edward, helped found the first U.S. college for the deaf, in Washington, D.C., in 1864. This institution was renamed Gallaudet College in 1894 in honor of the senior Gallaudet. In 1891 the school established the first U.S. college

training center for teachers of the deaf. In 1986, in recognition of the institution's role in research on the deaf and in training teachers, the school was renamed Gallaudet University.

See also NONVERBAL COMMUNICATION; SIGN LANGUAGE.

JOSEPH CADY

GALLUP, GEORGE (1901–1984)

U.S. pollster who pioneered the development of scientific methods for measuring PUBLIC OPINION. A measure of George Gallup's influence is that, before he reached the age of forty, all sample surveys of public opinion had come to be called "Gallup polls."

Born in Jefferson, Iowa, Gallup earned a Ph.D. in psychology at the State University of Iowa in 1928. One year later he was made head of the Department of Journalism at Drake University; he also taught journalism at Northwestern University during 1931–1932. Then he was hired by Young and Rubicam, the New York ADVERTISING agency, to conduct sample surveys for the agency's clients. In 1935 he founded the American Institute of Public Opinion to conduct his own opinion studies.

In 1936 came one of the important turning points in Gallup's career and in the history of public opinion studies. As usual in a presidential election year, *The Literary Digest*, then an influential U.S. weekly magazine, conducted a preelection POLL to forecast the winner. The magazine's theory was that the more people surveyed, the greater the poll's accuracy: it

Figure 1. *(Gallup, George)* George Gallup. The Bettmann Archive, Inc.

mailed out sample ballots to ten million people—its subscribers plus automobile owners. Meanwhile, working independently, three young survey researchers—Gallup, ELMO ROPER, and Archibald Crossley—also conducted preelection polls. Each interviewed only a few thousand voters, but, having learned something in college about the theory of sampling, they selected their interviewees to represent as well as possible the voting population of the United States. On the basis of two million returned ballots, "one in every five voters," *The Literary Digest* confidently predicted that Alfred M. Landon would win. The three researchers predicted that Franklin D. Roosevelt would win by a margin very near what the election returns soon showed.

As a result of his success, Gallup began to conduct and publish polls approximately every three weeks from his American institute. In late 1936 he founded the British Institute of Public Opinion; thereafter he cooperated in establishing institutes or other programs for opinion studies in some thirty countries. He was instrumental in developing methods for determining relative interest in different news items and different advertisements. He also pioneered in establishing time series of opinion data; for example, the polls on presidential popularity that he initiated in 1936 have become one of the devices by which U.S. presidents are compared and held accountable. In addition to starting such trend lines, he was also able to make some of the first international comparisons of opinion data.

The professional performance of pollsters continued to concern Gallup. He urged his colleagues to make more effort to separate informed from uninformed opinion, to study the intensity with which opinions are held, and to learn to predict when an opinion is likely to be translated into action. Above all, he urged pollsters to inform readers in detail how a given poll was made so that they would have some idea of how much it could be trusted.

See also OPINION MEASUREMENT.

Bibliography. George Gallup, *The Sophisticated Poll Watcher's Guide*, Princeton, N.J., 1972.

WILBUR SCHRAMM

GANDHI, MOHANDAS (1869–1948)

Indian leader, apostle of nonviolence. A master of moral communication able to stir masses of people to action, to sway the world press, and to disarm opponents, Mohandas Karamchand Gandhi was known to his people as mahatma ("great soul") and led them in struggles that in 1947 achieved Indian independence. He saw in nonviolence a technique of political resistance for the oppressed and eventually

a new way of REVOLUTION. His ideas were influenced by the Quakers, U.S. author Henry David Thoreau, and Russian writer Leo Tolstoy, but of primary importance were Indian religious doctrines that emphasized respect for all life. From the Bhagavad Gita, the principal Hindu SCRIPTURE, Gandhi derived important concepts, including *satyagraha* ("holding to the truth," resisting wrong without feeling enmity or using violence). As a leader in this new kind of revolution Gandhi adopted an unusual and striking uniform—the loincloth, or dhoti—by which he became known to the world.

It was a different Gandhi who at the start of his career had gone to London to train as a lawyer. There he wore Bond Street clothes, took dancing lessons, and sported a silver-topped stick. He returned home to take up practice in Bombay, but his first case found him tongue-tied and ended in disaster. In 1893 his brother arranged for him to work for an Indian firm in South Africa. There the shock of his encounter with the brutal racism of colonial rulers awakened his conscience and began to shape his ideas for combating oppression with what he then called passive resistance. Meeting violence with nonviolent suffering inspired his followers and disconcerted the oppressors. Here, urged Gandhi, was the true way to fight evil and cleanse the soul of hatred for the evildoer. He furthered his ideas with eloquent speech, prolific writing, and the force of his example, as well as by a shrewd choice of occasions on which to put his views into action for the greatest impact.

Back in India in 1915, already widely known for his African work, he continued his prolific writings. In 1919 he helped establish the periodical *Young India*, which later became *Harijan*, published in nine languages. His doctrine of *ahiṃsā* ("nonviolence") developed into a more comprehensive program of civil disobedience that began to challenge British imperial dominance and included boycotts of British manufactured goods. Gandhi showed a rare gift for symbolic action to dramatize issues and conflicts. His decision to wear the dhoti, identifying himself visibly with the millions, including the lowliest, was an example of this. Another was his emphasis on the spinning wheel, symbol of a program of Indian self-sufficiency that challenged the might of Britain's textile industry. The symbol acquired deep emotional meaning. A glimpse of a spinning wheel in a motion picture sometimes prompted an Indian audience to burst into applause. Censors began to excise such shots from MOTION PICTURES.

In 1929 the Congress party of India adopted total independence as its goal and asked Gandhi to lead the country to it. This set the stage for one of the most extraordinary of Gandhi's symbolic actions, his famous march to the sea to break the law protecting

Figure 1. *(Gandhi, Mohandas)* Mohandas Gandhi. The Bettmann Archive, Inc.

the British monopoly in salt manufacture. It was an event both bizarre and awesome. With his thin legs setting a brisk pace, followed by struggling thousands including reporters and NEWSREEL cameramen, he walked two hundred miles. Reaching his destination, he entered the surf, dipped up saltwater, and, while crowds roared, placed it on a fire. It spurred resistance to the salt monopoly and to payment of the hated salt tax. Film of the event was banned for years from Indian theaters but was shown abroad. In India the message went by word of mouth, electrifying the country.

In 1933 Gandhi started a "fast unto death" to make his countrymen renounce the practice of untouchability. The thirteen days he went without food shook the age-old institution to its foundations and robbed it of its moral sanction. In later years he sought in the same way to allay religious strife. In 1948, his assassination by a fanatical Hindu made him a martyr to the cause of Hindu-Muslim unity.

Gandhi's doctrine of nonviolence proved relevant again in the U.S. civil rights movement (1950s–1960s) led by Martin Luther King, Jr., and had echoes elsewhere in marches, boycotts, demonstrations, vigils, fasts, and other symbolic actions. The vigilance of the mass media and the growth of international communications in the global village suggest the continuing relevance of such actions.

See also ASIA, TWENTIETH CENTURY; COLONIZATION; DEMONSTRATION; POLITICAL SYMBOLS.

Bibliography. Louis Fischer, *The Life of Mahatma Gandhi*, New York, 1950; Mohandas Karamchand Gandhi, *The Story of My Experiments with Truth*, 2 vols., trans. by Mahadev Desai, Ahmedabad, 1927–1929; Vithalbhai K. Jhaveri and D. G. Tendulkar, *Mahatma: Life of Mohandas Karamchand Gandhi*, 8 vols., Bombay, 1951–1954.

CHIDANANDA DAS GUPTA

GENDER

In the scholarly literature on sex differences and on the difference between sex and gender, *sex* refers to biological differences, whereas *gender* characteristics are learned cultural constructions. Differences in the biological functions of males and females may be genetically determined and immutable, but the significance of those differences for social roles is determined by cultural belief systems. The values and meanings attributed to gender identity are encoded, preserved, and transmitted in public symbols that are shared by members of a particular society. At the most basic level these symbols are the vocabulary and conventions of LANGUAGE itself. Of even greater significance for thought and behavior, however, are the complex images and representations of gender that are communicated through religious doctrine and RITUAL in traditional societies, through the mass media of industrial societies, and in the conversational habits of daily interaction everywhere. *See also* CULTURE.

Research and theories. MARGARET MEAD was one of the first to draw attention to cross-cultural variation in the behaviors expected of men and women. Her pioneering study in 1935 suggested that all cultures may have institutionalized male and female roles, but little consensus exists about what these roles should be. Furthermore, many role-specific behavioral characteristics are irrelevant to actual differences in male and female biological functioning. Nevertheless, in *Male and Female* Mead concluded that "men may cook, or weave, or dress dolls or hunt hummingbirds, but if such activities are appropriate occupations of men, then the whole society, men and women alike, votes them as important. When the same occupations are performed by women, they are regarded as less important."

Debate continues over whether female occupations, and by implication women themselves, are thought to be inferior to those of the male in all cultures and in all historical periods. Those who support the universalist position regarding gender inequality fall into several categories, of which two are the most widely known. According to a traditional school of thought, women are universally devalued because they are naturally less aggressive and physically weaker than men. A related position proposes that women and men were apportioned different life tasks by God, and therefore women should confine themselves to the concerns of the home.

One controversial theory states that women have lower prestige than men in all human societies for structural rather than biological reasons. Best represented by anthropologists Sherry B. Ortner and Edwin Ardener, this analysis follows from CLAUDE LÉVI-STRAUSS's proposition that all humankind values "culture" above "nature." Nature, in this view, represents the fact that each individual is a biological organism subject to the vicissitudes of illness, death, and other sorts of experiences that are beyond human control. Culture, by contrast, represents those human activities that are creative, that are more lasting than the physical body, and that allow individuals to "transcend" their biological destinies. The structuralist position argues that women, because they alone experience biological processes such as menstruation, pregnancy, and lactation, are universally identified more closely with nature than are men. Men are thus seen as being more transcendent, and this has far-reaching implications for the social valuation of the sexes.

A number of theorists, however, oppose the idea that women are universally devalued. One group of feminist anthropologists, perhaps best represented by Eleanor Leacock, has suggested that the universalist notion is based on ethnocentric reporting. Furthermore, most anthropologist field researchers have been male and have talked primarily to male informants. Feminist anthropologists have begun to make a point of discussing this question with female informants. In their view ethnography from a female point of view will yield a contrasting picture of the social valuation of women.

Some scholars have taken an intermediate position, insofar as they acknowledge that gender asymmetry is common to most or all documented societies, but they argue that this asymmetry had its origin at a specific point in human history. The significance of history for a feminist agenda for action is implicit in historian Gerda Lerner's assertion that "patriarchy as a system is historical: it has a beginning in history. If that is so, it can be ended by historical process."

One of the first historical theorists to address this problem was German philosopher Friedrich Engels. He argued that the ultimate source of women's subjugation was the development of private property, which led in turn to the institution of monogamous marriage and the control of female sexuality by men. Subsequent research, however, has supported the notion that male dominance exists in societies without inheritable private property and may have pre-dated this institution in the history of Western civilization.

Origins of male dominance. The search for the origins of male dominance has led a number of scholars to scrutinize existing data on the earliest prehominid ancestors. The traditional view of human evolution emphasizes the role of large-animal hunting, which is primarily a male occupation, in the emergence of humanity. In this model the transition to upright stance improved survival by allowing hunters to carry and use weapons against their animal prey. In addition, the development of language was related to the need for planning among hunters and cooperation during the hunt. An alternative viewpoint is outlined by Nancy Tanner and Adrienne Zihlman. They suggest that it was not hunting per se that was the driving force in evolution but rather the movement of the ancestral apes from a primarily forest to a primarily savannah niche. The gathering of FOOD (generally a female occupation) was critical to the exploitation of the new environment and may have given rise to tool use through the production and use of containers to hold the gathered food and convey it to offspring. In this model, kinship systems evolved from small, mother-centered groups to more complex units through sibling cooperation and sharing. Females would have been socially central in this model, and by implication they would have wielded considerable influence as the source of socialization and as the pivotal figures in food-sharing groups.

This model does not account for the fact that in most known societies women are not socially central, at least not in public life. Other theorists have advanced the argument that the development of the sexual division of labor may account for women's loss of public influence. The sexual division of labor is common to most, if not all, human societies. The rigidity and exclusiveness of sex-specific occupations vary widely, but in the simplest societies such large-game hunting as exists is identified as a male occupation. This is probably because women, burdened during most of their adult lives by pregnancy or the care of small CHILDREN, have a diminished capacity for participation in long-distance chases in pursuit of prey. Because both hunting and the gathering and identification of numerous plant species may require years of training and preparation, it behooves these societies to teach children of each sex the skills they will best be able to utilize. Thus in most cases women reach adulthood without the skills of the hunter. Although the woman's contribution to the caloric intake of the group may be no less than that of the male (and in many cases is far greater), her prestige may suffer because the vegetable foods she gathers are usually shared only within her FAMILY group. Large animals, on the other hand, are normally distributed more widely throughout the group and among social groups, because meat must be disposed of immediately. A sort of common historical precedent is established, whereby women's concerns are viewed as private and familial, but men's activities and influence are seen as more social in nature. In anthropologist Michelle Rosaldo's view this parallels the tendency of more complex societies to relegate women's activities to the domestic sphere but to allow men to be active in the extradomestic public sphere.

Nevertheless, most researchers agree that women in hunting/gathering societies experience greater autonomy and power than they do in more complex societies. Lerner has proposed that the real beginning of women's oppression may be traced to the development of agriculture. In foraging societies an increase in population is thought to be undesirable because it strains the carrying capacity of the land. Women's reproductive capacity has only a neutral value under these circumstances because it is not seen as a valuable resource. In agricultural systems, however, children are desirable because of the labor they can provide. Under these conditions women's power to reproduce (and perforce women themselves) becomes a desired "object" to be controlled, traded, or raided. Thus women lose their identity as autonomous subjects and become a form of objectified property. The concept of women as objects underlies Lévi-Strauss's analysis of tribal kinship and marital exchanges in which the exchange of women between groups forges intergroup linkages that are essential for human survival and the development of culture. To feminist theorists such as Gayle Rubin this signifies that men have assumed rights over their female kin that women do not have over their male kin or over themselves.

Determining the status of women. All of these analyses fail to address the fact that women's status is not uniform in all societies at a given level of complexity. For example, women's status is high in some tribal societies, such as that of the Hopi, but much lower in some tribal areas of Papua New Guinea. A number of ethnographic studies have attempted to establish the sorts of conditions under which women may be accorded high or low status. These field studies have focused almost invariably on the sex-gender system in a single culture. However, some efforts to uncover generalities about the determinants of women's status cross-culturally have been undertaken.

The results of these cross-cultural comparisons are inconclusive. Nevertheless, some promising avenues of research have been revealed. For example, anthropologists have compared the social condition of women under different systems of social organization. Results suggest that in matrilineal systems, in which property and social affiliations pass through the female line, women seem to experience somewhat greater autonomy than in patrilineal systems. Nevertheless, even under conditions of matriliny, a woman seldom controls the major share of the family's or group's property because it is commonly passed from her brother to her son.

Another area of intensive research concerns the extent to which women produce food or material wealth for the family or kin group. One theory holds that women have greater power when they make significant contributions to the production (rather than only to the processing) of food or wealth.

Systematic comparisons of the ethnographic record, however, suggest that there is no simple answer to the question of what factors determine women's status in society. Martin King Whyte reviewed a sample of ninety-three preindustrial cultures and found that none of the popular hypotheses concerning these determinants was strongly supported. Although women's contribution to subsistence was not found to have general status implications, Whyte found that matriliny and matrilocality (residence of the husband with his wife's natal group) do exhibit minor benefits for women and that the existence of private property is associated with a low social estimate of the value of women's labor.

The strongest pattern Whyte uncovered was an association between social complexity and loss of formal female authority. In more complex societies women experience greater sexual restriction, have fewer property rights, and have less independent solidarity with other women than in simple societies. One of his most significant findings, however, was that there is no simple measure of women's status. Components of high status—such as women's personal autonomy, control over property, and participation in group decision making—are not necessarily found together in the same society. These variables seem to occur independently, and Whyte concludes that there is no such thing as *the* status of women cross-culturally.

One problem with cross-cultural comparisons is that they fail to account for the fact that societies themselves vary in terms of the factors that confer status on individuals. For example, it may be that the power and prestige of women suffer to the extent that their society excludes them from the kinds of achievement that are culturally valued. Among the Thakali-speaking peoples of Nepal women have relatively high status (as evidenced by considerable personal autonomy, substantial control over family finances, and a relative absence of negative female imagery in the culture) even though they are excluded from participation in the complex political system of decision-making meetings and public offices. These offices, however, are assigned by rotation, and thus occupation of them does not confer status in itself. Instead status is achieved by the accumulation of wealth among this mercantile trading population. Women, because they participate actively in commerce, not only are valued as economic contributors but also are highly esteemed as individuals if they demonstrate a shrewd talent for bargaining. The economic values of the Thakali contrast sharply with the religious values of the high-caste Hindus to the south. There ritual purity is a supreme social value. Hindu women, who are seen as more subject to impurity than men by virtue of their ritual pollution through childbirth and menstruation, have far less autonomy and access to public influence than Thakali women.

Sherry B. Ortner and Harriet Whitehead have proposed that cross-cultural variations in ideas about sex and gender are related to the ways in which women and domestic relations fit into various male-dominated prestige systems. For example, because a kinswoman's sexual chastity is so critical to a man's prestige in certain Mediterranean societies, women are often represented as dangerous and disruptive beings in need of strict control. In those societies in which men's prestige is not dependent on the behavior of women there may be less representation of cross-sex relations as threatening and less inclination to restrict women's autonomy.

Representations of women in public communications. The relationship between female oppression and negative representations of women in the symbols of communication has been another highly controversial but profoundly important topic of theory and research. It is unclear what impact exposure to sexual and gender imagery through the media, in literature, and particularly in PORNOGRAPHY has had on the actual behavior of individuals. One position holds that human behavior, both individual and institutional, is shaped primarily by the realities of economic distribution. If so, negative female imagery is merely a reflection of women's economic powerlessness and is not a direct cause of their oppression. According to an alternative view, public representations manipulate and direct social ATTITUDES. Therefore, negative representations of women in public communications may encourage the public to stereotype all women as passive, incompetent, overly emotional, and so on. Stereotypes of this kind may in turn become economically damaging if they prevent women from achieving promotions or appointments to positions of responsibility that would give them economic power and independence.

The commonly understood symbols of human communication are also the basic units of human thought in every society, whether technologically simple or complex. Commonsense perceptions of appropriate social behavior are shaped by the symbolic terms in which social actors conduct their interactions. According to Melvin DeFleur and Sandra Ball-Rokeach, "As people communicate intensively over the years, selected assertions become regarded as true or correct metasymbolic representations of specific aspects of reality. Because of this process, our interpretations of reality, as well as folkways and other social norms, are *constructed* as by-products of the biosocial process of communication." Cultural conceptions of gender are embedded in this socially shared interpretation of reality. The culturally constructed reality is learned by all members of a communicating group, and so it generally remains unquestioned. Thus gender roles, as part of this unquestioned worldview, appear to be supported by common sense and seem as natural and inevitable as the anatomical differences between the sexes.

The gender content of these symbolic representations has come under increasing scrutiny now that children are partially socialized by their exposure to television, films, and popular songs (*see* MUSIC, POPULAR). Mass media research has frequently focused on the problem of whether the media shape social attitudes or merely reflect them. In his review of this research social psychologist Kevin Durkin explored the link between television viewing and the preference for traditional sex roles among children. Content analyses of television programming revealed that men appear far more often than women, that they are represented as being more dominant and in control, and that women are represented as being subservient more often than men. This is more true of programs aimed at adults than of children's television and is especially pronounced in ADVERTISING. *See also* CONTENT ANALYSIS; MASS MEDIA EFFECTS.

Studies of the association between traditional sex stereotyping and amount of viewing time have been inconclusive, however; some results have supported such a link and others have not. Durkin concludes that attempts to detect direct, linear causation between mass media and children's social learning are unproductive. In his view the child's reaction to television may not be confined to passive absorption; and, what is more, television messages are always interpreted in the light of experiences and information received in familial and other social contexts. This observation serves as a reminder that sex and gender symbols do not exist in a social vacuum. They can be best understood as part of a larger system of cultural assumptions regarding prestige, power relations, and the achievement of social status.

See also FEMINIST THEORIES OF COMMUNICATION; SEXISM.

Bibliography. Frances Dahlberg, ed., *Woman the Gatherer,* New Haven, Conn., 1981; Kevin Durkin, *Television, Sex*

Roles, and Children: A Developmental Psychology Account, Milton Keynes, Eng., 1985; Gerda Lerner, *The Creation of Patriarchy*, New York and Oxford, 1986; Margaret Mead, *Sex and Temperament in Three Primitive Societies*, New York, 1935; Sherry B. Ortner and Harriet Whitehead, eds., *Sexual Meanings: The Cultural Construction of Gender and Sexuality*, Cambridge and New York, 1981; Rayna Reiter, ed., *Toward an Anthropology of Women*, New York, 1975; Michelle Rosaldo and Louise Lamphere, eds., *Woman, Culture, and Society*, Stanford, Calif., 1974; Martin King Whyte, *The Status of Women in Pre-Industrial Societies*, Princeton, N.J., 1978.

BARBARA PARKER

GENRE

Literature has traditionally been organized on the basis of genres, or types of works. Genre makes possible the communication of content: its coded signals prompt readers to take up a work in an appropriate way. Genres used to be regarded as fixed, hard-edged classes, but in actuality they change and overlap so much and so untidily that it is best to regard them as loose groupings or families. Each has its own family resemblances, its characteristic features, but none need contain all the characteristics of its family.

These characteristics are of both form and content. Thus an epic is a long, continuous NARRATIVE focused on a great action; an epigram is a brief, pointed, witty, or touching poem with freedom of subject. Readers learn genres gradually, usually through unconscious familiarization, as when children learn broad types like story or SONG. In such ways expectations of genre are built up that writers can capitalize on so as to surprise or innovate. The system of generic expectations amounts to a CODE, by the use of which (or by departure from which) composition becomes more economical. In fact, genre serves the purposes of communication as much as those of taxonomy or CLASSIFICATION.

History

How many genres are there? In one sense there are as many thousands of groupings as writers and readers have ever recognized, although the nonspecialist probably makes do with as few as a dozen or so: song, TRAGEDY, COMEDY, farce, joke, novel, thriller, romance (*see* ROMANCE, THE), and a few others.

In the fifth century B.C.E. Homer was already regarded as the inventor of RHETORIC and hence of genre. Ancient rhetoricians identified many genres, and there is no doubt that Virgil, Horace, and other Roman authors practiced such kinds as epic and satire conscious not only of predecessors but also of the forms they shared with them. From late antiquity

on, Christian writers took up the pagan classical kinds with a greater sense of difference, adapting such forms as the epithalamium (wedding poem) to radically different purposes, in the process arriving at new genres like the allegorical epithalamium of the fifth-century writer Martianus Capella. Medieval Christian genres—romance, sermon (*see* HOMILETICS), carol—constitute a completely transformed set of genres, which superficially appear to have little connection with those of pagan antiquity. Two classical phases followed: the RENAISSANCE, when ancient genres were revived in vernacular guises; and the Augustan period, when a return was made to "purer" or more "correct" versions (*see* CLASSICISM). From the second of these movements emerged the fatal notion of genre as minutely prescriptive, which was to lead even so sensible a critic as SAMUEL JOHNSON to condemn William Shakespeare for using the word *knife* in a tragedy and JOHN MILTON for introducing Christian pastors into a pastoral.

The so-called fixed historical genres have changed almost beyond recognition. Greek tragedy began with Aeschylus, as a musical form more akin to OPERA than to modern DRAMA. It had only two characters, and its text was divided between episodes of dialogue and lyric choruses. But in the MIDDLE AGES tragedies were narratives, like those of Giovanni Boccaccio's *De casibus*. And when tragedy returned to the stage in the Renaissance, it had large numbers of characters, onstage VIOLENCE, and a range of diction quite foreign to ancient tragedy. Again, the modern PROSE tragedy of Henrik Ibsen or Anton Chekhov abandoned the classical tragedy's reversal of fortune (peripeteia) and even, in the cases of Eugene O'Neill and Arthur Miller, its elevated nobility. Forms change, with or without change of labels.

Nonetheless, writers and critics have abstracted from the various forms of the main kinds certain irreducible elements or modes (*see* MODE). These can be used to form mixtures between one genre and another. From the late sixteenth century in Britain, and earlier on the Continent, writers have made deliberate attempts to produce mixed genres or to explore intermediate possibilities between two genres, as in Fletcherian tragicomedy, which seeks an elusive mood between the comic and the tragic. When Shakespeare makes Polonius in *Hamlet* speak of "pastoral-comical, historical-pastoral, tragical-historical, tragical-comical-historical-pastoral," he is not ridiculing the idea of generic combination but only Polonius's tedious account of it.

In the nineteenth century generic mixture was entered into with new energy. Greek, neogothic, and exotic forms (romance, Eastern tale, and countless others) were brought into play so polymorphously that formal diversity outstripped critical generalization. Eventually the Italian aesthetician Benedetto

Croce could plausibly argue that genre was a chimera—that every work was unique, of its own kind (*see* AESTHETICS).

It is a common modern assumption that genres are things of the past, if indeed they were ever more than illusions. But in fact communication is impossible without the agreed codes of genre. And distinctively modern genres exist, many created or transformed by the electronic media, although most new genres have not yet been named. In literature, for example, the novel is partly being replaced by the characterless "fabulation" (Italo Calvino, Franz Kafka); by "self-begetting fiction," or writing about writing (Vladimir Nabokov's *Pale Fire*, Doris Lessing's *The Golden Notebook*); and generally by "metafiction," which creates fictional illusion only to demolish it (*see* FICTION). And there are other new forms, such as "faction" (*see* FACT AND FICTION) or the semifictional "documentary" novel (E. L. Doctorow, Truman Capote).

In the same way, individual BIOGRAPHY is partly being replaced by biography of a FAMILY or social group or by a set of short biographies illustrating a thesis. In POETRY the American long poem and, even more, the sequence of short interconnected lyrics have gone far to replace epic. Much LITERARY CRITICISM is now concerned with identifying these new groupings. A revived interest in genre was given a strong impulse by Northrop Frye's *Anatomy of Criticism* (1957), and many works of a theoretical nature have followed, most of them based on the analysis of modes.

The Study of Genre

In the nineteenth and early twentieth centuries theorists mostly speculated about the essential character of very broad divisions of literature. They divided it into dramatic, lyric, and narrative categories, which they regarded as necessarily constitutive of all literature, and they engaged in philosophical meditations designed to arrive at an understanding of the "vision" each category embodied. This sort of theorizing works at such a high level of generalization that it is often in danger of failing to correspond very closely to actual instances. For example, it does not always take account of the complexities of mixture found in real literary works or of a host of awkward instances that tend to falsify the approach via broad categories.

Later theorists have preferred to come to grips with more restricted or at least more specific groupings, with individual modes if not with historical kinds. Francis Cairns has much to say about the *propemptikon* ("valediction") in ancient Greek literature, Renato Poggioli and T. G. Rosenmeyer concern themselves with variant forms of pastoral, Tzvetan Todorov describes the operation of fantasy as a mode, and Fredric Jameson traces changing structures of the romance. Much of the late-twentieth-century theory is still analytical rather than historical in approach, but at its best it tends to take account of historical change, even while treating genre as a system and disengaging inner structures common to the generic tradition in question. This is bound to be so, because literary interest—certainly all literary innovation—consists in modulations or changes of generic signals. It is in departures from rules of genre that writers show their originality. It might almost be said that genre criticism is more useful the more specific it gets. For example, notions of tragedy in general may not take critics very far in interpreting *Hamlet*, but a knowledge of Elizabethan and Jacobean revenge tragedy will allow them to appreciate the weight of many features of the play more accurately.

At the other end of the scale theorists have been concerned with the relations among genres in the whole canon of literature (*see* LITERARY CANON)—with their arrangement in systems of various sorts. In earlier times the arrangement was hierarchic, the kinds being ranked higher or lower. Even ARISTOTLE discussed whether tragedy or epic is the best of the various genres. To some extent, however, the relations within systems were dynamic. Thus in the seventeenth century, epigram, georgic, and satire all changed position from the lower end of the hierarchy of kinds to places much closer to the top. Nor is this sort of ordering altogether outmoded: critics may still talk of major and minor forms. But modern systems tend to be constructed on a more descriptive basis. There are exceptions, as with the construction of systems in which large numbers of genres are arranged in spectra, according to the degree to which they exemplify certain arbitrarily chosen factors. These (sometimes very elaborate) maps purport to locate the genres in mental space: they may be of local illustrative use but can have no general validity and for the most part are purely fanciful.

If the genre of a work is mistaken, spectacular misreadings may occur. Unless one sees that John Dryden's *Mac Flecknoe* (1682) is satire, that it is not to be taken as serious panegyric, one cannot appreciate it for what it is. But this is an extreme case; more often readers and critics misinterpret because their ideas of the genres involved are merely crude or vague. Such misinterpretations may, however, be interesting or even significant and may put the work into creative new propinquities that give rise to previously unknown groupings. Thus in the course of history works gradually change their generic affiliations in such a way as to preserve their interest for each new generation. Yet the genre's tradition embodies a compensating continuity that may keep readers in touch with older meanings and values. *See also* READING THEORY.

For additional discussions of genre, *see* ART. For

additional entries on popular genres, *see also* COM-ICS; LITERATURE, POPULAR; MYSTERY AND DETECTIVE FICTION; SCIENCE FICTION; WESTERN, THE. For genres in film and broadcasting, *see* MOTION PICTURES; RA-DIO; TELEVISION HISTORY; and also entries on specific genres: AVANT-GARDE FILM; CINÉMA VÉRITÉ; DOCUMENTARY; HORROR FILM; MARTIAL ARTS FILM; MUSICAL, FILM; MYTHOLOGICAL FILM, ASIAN; QUIZ SHOW; SOAP OPERA; TELEVISION NEWS.

Bibliography. Rosalie L. Colie, *The Resources of Kind: Genre-Theory in the Renaissance*, Berkeley, Calif., 1973; Heather Dubrow, *Genre*, London and New York, 1982; Alastair Fowler, *Kinds of Literature: An Introduction to the Theory of Genres and Modes*, Cambridge, Mass., and Oxford, 1982; Northrop Frye, *Anatomy of Criticism*, Princeton, N.J., 1957; Claudio Guillén, *Literature as System*, Princeton, N.J., 1971; Paul Hernadi, *Beyond Genre: New Directions in Literary Classification*, Ithaca, N.Y., 1972.

ALASTAIR FOWLER

GESTURE

Bodily action other than SPEECH that is recognized as being done in order to express something. It is considered separate from emotional expression and separate from other bodily actions such as tics, mannerisms, and nervous movements. These expressions and actions may be very revealing of a person's current level of physiological arousal, emotional state, unconscious motives, social class, or cultural background, but to the extent that they are thought not to be under voluntary control, they are not regarded as gesture.

The topic of gesture includes bodily movements that occur in close association with speech (gesticulation); expressive movements that can be used independently of speech and can serve as complete utterances on their own, such as the thumb-up gesture (Figure 1), the shoulder-shrug, or shaking of the fist (autonomous gesture); gestural codes used in certain occupational circumstances in which speech is difficult or impossible, primary sign languages used in communities of the deaf, alternate sign languages used in some tribal and religious communities during periods when speech is forbidden, and the special elaboration of gesture found in religious RITUAL, as in the complex systems of mudras developed as part of the ritual of prayer in Tantric Buddhism; and the complex gestural systems found in some DANCE traditions, especially in India. *See* MIME.

Gesture has attracted the attention of scholars for many centuries. In the eighteenth century, especially in France, such writers as DENIS DIDEROT and Étienne Bonnot de Condillac thought the study of gesture provided a key to understanding the nature of thought

Figure 1. *(Gesture)* The OK version of the thumb-up gesture. From Desmond Morris, Peter Collett, Peter Marsh, Marie O'Shaughnessy, *Gestures: Their Origins and Distribution*, New York: Stein and Day, 1979, p. 190.

and the origin of LANGUAGE. This view continued to be expressed in the nineteenth century. Important contributions include those by the British anthropologist E. B. Tylor (1868) and the German psychologist Wilhelm Wundt (1900). In the twentieth century gesture was little investigated until the beginning of the 1970s. Since then it has attracted increasing attention with the development of the linguistic study of sign languages, the study of the role of gesture in the development of language in infants, and the study of the relationship between gesture and speech (gesticulation), which is considered to have implications for theories of utterance production. There has also been renewed discussion of the place of gesture in theories of language origins. The discussion of gesture that follows will not include SIGN LANGUAGE and other highly specialized elaborations of gesture.

Types of Expression in Gesture

There are at least four ways in which gestures achieve expression: pointing, characterizing, act ritualization, and arbitrary convention.

Pointing. A body part is moved in a certain direction, thereby serving to direct the recipient's attention to what is being referred to. Although pointing is often done with an extended index finger, it need not be, and in many cultures the lips, nose, chin, or head may be used more commonly. In fact, any body part that can be moved directionally may be used for pointing. Pointing may be done to referents present in the immediate environment, to indicate directions and locations, or to direct attention to abstract referents, as when a speaker points in different directions when referring to different points of view or different components of the discourse. A pointing gesture may be a simple directional movement or it may describe a path in space. Pointing gestures that do more than merely direct attention to the referent and, by virtue of the movement employed, provide some representation of the features of the referent merge with the next mode of gestural expression.

Characterizing gestures. Here movements are made that characterize aspects of the referent, either by pantomimic action or by sketching or modeling. Characterizing gestures are often used to refer to concrete activities or objects, to characterize the manner or reaction of another person, or to characterize the speaker's own reactions in a situation being talked about. Characterizing gestures may also be employed to provide concrete visual images that are metaphors for abstract referents.

Act ritualization. Gesture plays an important role in the regulation of interaction. Thus there are gestures of greeting, assent, and negation; gestures that signal the relinquishment or the resumption of turns at talk; and gestures such as those of the waiter or police officer that regulate the movements of others, as in beckoning or in signaling "wait" or "halt." Many of these gestures can be understood as abbreviated and conventionalized forms of an actual interpersonal action. Thus the headshake of negation may be seen as a reduced and conventionalized version of turning away, the outstretched arms with exposed palms often seen in greeting may be understood as derived from grasping and embracing actions, raising the hand with palm forward to command another to halt may be seen as derived from the act of holding back another's forward movement. In this respect, many human gestures may show analogies with the displays of animals, which are interpreted by ethologists as ritualizations of acts of withdrawal, approach, aggression, and the like. *See also* ANIMAL COMMUNICATION; ANIMAL SIGNALS; ETHOLOGY.

Arbitrary convention. Novel forms of gesture may be created when needed. Gesturing, however, is much influenced by social convention, and many forms within a given community have become highly stable in both their performance and their meaning. In some cases of such highly stable forms, it is not possible to account for any relationship between form and meaning in terms of any of the three preceding principles, and the gesture remains significant purely because of a shared convention. In such a case, the gesture is said to be arbitrary. Very few gestures appear to be completely arbitrary in this sense, although many are so highly conventionalized that they function as if they were. Examples include such western European gestures as thumbing the nose as an INSULT (Figure 2), crossing the fingers when wishing for a desired outcome, or tapping the side of the nose as a gesture of warning (used in parts of Italy).

Gesticulation

When a person speaks, muscular systems besides those directly involved in vocal articulation often become active. There are movements of the FACE and EYES; of the head, arms, and hands; sometimes of the torso and legs that, even to a casual observer, are seen to be patterned in relation to the flow of speech. Most commonly noted are those more or less complex movements of the hands and arms that appear as accompaniments to speech and are usually thought to emphasize what is being said or to illustrate it in some way.

Bodily movements that accompany speech have for a long time been considered an important part of the presentation of public speeches. In the first systematic treatment of RHETORIC (by the Spanish Roman Quintilian in the first century C.E.), extensive attention was given to how the speaker should manage bodily expression. Detailed descriptions were given of a number of gestural forms with instructions on when and how they should be used. With the revival of classical learning in the seventeenth century several treatises devoted to this topic appeared, such as those by Louis de Cressolles (1620) and Valentin Conrart (1689) in France and by John Bulwer (1644) in England. Textbooks such as *Chironomia* (1806) by the Irish divine Gilbert Austin and the many that followed in the nineteenth century gave extensive and detailed instructions on the use of gesture in PUBLIC SPEAKING.

The scientific study of gesticulation has been concerned mainly with how such bodily movements are patterned in relation to speech as observed in situations such as interviews or informal conversations. Close analysis has shown that gesticulation in the forelimbs and head is organized into phrases that are patterned in close association with the phrases of speech production. Speech is normally produced in phrases that may be defined in terms of patterns of stress and intonation (depending on the school of linguistic analysis, these are known as phonemic clauses, tone units, breath groups, or syntagmata). Such phrases are widely regarded as minimal units of speech production, each usually serving to express

Figure 2. *(Gesture)* The tandem version of the nose-thumb gesture. Red devil figurine. The Pitt Rivers Museum, University of Oxford.

a single idea unit (a minimal unit of meaning at the discourse level). The discovery that phrases of gesticulation are matched closely to these phrases of speech production suggests that speech and gesticulation are the products of a single underlying process of utterance production. It appears that, in this process, units of content may be given expression partly in speech and partly in gesture. Phrases of speech and phrases of gesture are matched because they are components in the expression of a single unit of content.

Content may be expressed in gesticulation in many different ways, so that the relationship between what is expressed in speech and what is expressed in gesticulation can vary. For example, "beat" or "baton" gesticulations are simple in form and appear to function as markers of units of discourse organization. Complex characterizing forms may present sketches or pantomimes, displaying aspects of the objects or actions the speaker is talking about; or they may have a metaphorical significance, as when a speaker uses containerlike gesticulations to suggest boundaries to the discussion or provides gestures suggestive of actions that can serve as concrete images for abstract processes. Speakers may also use gesticulation to clarify the meaning of a potentially ambiguous word, to complete an incompletely spoken sentence, or to convey aspects of meaning that are not conveyed directly in words.

Since in gesticulation a speaker may simultaneously present part of an utterance in verbal form and part in gesture, the mental representation of the content of the utterance cannot be exclusively linguistic in format, as has sometimes been maintained. It is thought that the study of how gesticulation is related to speech will help to advance understanding of the nature of mental representation and of the processes by which such representation gets translated into utterance form.

Cultural Variation in Gesticulation

Although all speakers gesticulate, the forms of movement employed and the extent to which it is done are matters of considerable variation, not only among individuals, but also among cultures. A study by David Efron (1941) of European immigrants in New York City established that there were marked differences in gesticulatory style among different cultural groups. He showed that southern Italians made much use of pictorial or pantomimic gesticulations. East European Jewish immigrants, on the other hand, employed gesticulation to portray visually the logical structure of what they were saying but almost never used pictorial illustrative forms (Figure 3). Efron also showed that whereas the Italians had a rich repertoire of standardized, autonomous gestures, the East European Jews did not. By comparing the gestural practices of the descendants of these two groups of immigrants, Efron further showed that the more the descendants were integrated into the mainstream of English-speaking life in the United States, the less these gestural differences became. Thus gestural style is learned as part of the culture.

Since Efron's work, few other investigations have explored cultural differences in gesticulation. However, we may suppose that cultural differences in gesticulation and other gestural usages reflect cultural differences in how members of the culture make use of the information gesticulation can provide.

Figure 3. *(Gesture)* Ghetto Jews: symbolic gestures. From David Efron, *Gesture and Environment*, New York: King's Crown Press, 1941, figs. 32–36.

Autonomous Gesture

Most communities share a repertoire of gestural forms that are more or less standardized in the manner of performance and relatively stable in meaning. Communities differ considerably in the extent to which they make use of such gestures and in the extent and nature of the repertoire at their disposal. A survey of a selected number of distinct gestural forms of this sort undertaken by Desmond Morris and colleagues in forty locations widely distributed from north to south in western Europe showed many differences, both in the number of forms recognized and in the meanings they were said to have. (The gestural forms examined are given in Figure 4.) A few gestures in the sample studied (for example, the "nose thumb" in Figure 4c) were found to be known throughout the region and were everywhere regarded as having the same meaning. Other gestures—for example, the "cheek screw" (Figure 4e)—were found to be quite limited in distribution and restricted in meaning. On the other hand, a gesture such as the "ring" (Figure 4i) was recognized widely but varied sharply in meaning from one part of Europe to another. Thus in southern France and Italy it was said to mean "good" or "OK." In northern France it was said to mean "zero" or "nothing." In Greece and Turkey it was taken as a gesture of homosexual insult.

Although lists of autonomous gestures have been published from several different countries, little is understood about how the gestures are employed in everyday interaction and the conditions that favor their emergence. A comparison of the range of meanings attributed to them suggests, however, that the majority have developed as gestural devices for the regulation of interpersonal conduct and the management of turning points in interaction, such as greetings and farewells. Gestures that serve as a way of making a comment on another's actions or on one's own situation are also very common. Autonomous gestures that are given a meaning like a word, such as a noun or a verb, are quite rare, however. Autonomous gestures of the conventionalized sort are almost always used singly, and they serve as a complete utterance. They are not used in combinations as components of utterances.

Development of Gesture

Studies of infants have suggested that the close relationship between hand movements and speech characteristic of adults is present at birth. Gestures such as lifting the arms as a request to be picked up or pointing as a way of referring to objects develop before speech, but gestures become more complex as speech develops. While older children gesticulate more than younger ones do, there are important changes in the kinds of gesticulations that occur and how they relate to speech. There is a shift away from elaborate enactments that serve instead of speech toward a more precise speech-concurrent usage in which gesticulation occurs more selectively. There is also an increasing use of abstract, discourse-marking gesticulation. Characterizing gesticulation becomes more symbolic and more restricted in the aspects of meaning it is called upon to display.

Neurological Bases of Gesture

Clinical neurologists have long recognized that patients suffering from brain damage that impairs speech (left-hemisphere damage in most cases) also show impairment in their ability to use gestures. Some maintain that this impairment is a result of interference with motor control, but other neurologists believe it results from interference with symbolic capacities. Detailed studies of gesticulation in aphasics have suggested that the disorganization in gesticulation observed in these patients parallels closely the kind of disorganization observed in their speech. Studies of hand preferences in gesticulation in healthy people show that, at least as far as characterizing gesticulations are concerned, these are almost always produced by the dominant hand. Since the dominant hand is regarded as being under the control of the same side of the brain as the side controlling speech (left side in right-handed people), this finding has been taken as further evidence that gesticulation and speech are under the guidance of the same fundamental process.

Universal Aspects of Gesture

The employment of gesture, either as gesticulation, in autonomous forms, or (in appropriate circumstances) in gesture systems or sign languages, appears to be a universal feature of human communicative behavior. The principles governing the creation of gestural forms also appear to be universal.

Almost all gestures, no matter how arbitrary, originate as pointings, characterizations, or partially completed interpersonal actions. They do not derive historically from other gestures in the way that words in a language usually derive historically from other words. Probably for this reason similar gestural forms can be found in widely separated cultures. For example, in one study autonomous gestures collected among four tribal groups in East Africa were compared with those that had been recorded among Spanish-speaking urban dwellers in Colombia. Of the sixty-eight East African forms examined, twenty-two were found to be highly similar to the Colom-

a The Fingertips Kiss	*f* The Eyelid Pull	*k* The Horizontal Horn–sign	*p* The Thumb Up
b The Fingers Cross	*g* The Forearm Jerk	*l* The Fig	*q* The Teeth Flick
c The Nose Thumb	*h* The Flat–hand Flick	*m* The Head Toss	*r* The Ear Touch
d The Hand Purse	*i* The Ring	*n* The Chin Flick	*s* The Nose Tap
e The Cheek Screw	*j* The Vertical Horn–sign	*o* The Cheek Stroke	*t* The Palm–back V–Sign

Figure 4. *(Gesture)* Examples of gestures. From Desmond Morris, Peter Collett, Peter Marsh, Marie O'Shaughnessy, *Gestures: Their Origins and Distribution*, New York: Stein and Day, 1979, p. xxvi.

bian gestures. These similar gestures turned out to be ones that are found in many other parts of the world. They included the use of the headshake for "no," the shoulder-shrug for "don't know," and a hand placed with the palm against the cheek for "sleep."

These worldwide similarities may be accounted for in most cases not so much in terms of diffusion of particular forms but as parallel formations arising from the fact that the means for representing such common activities as sleeping and eating are quite limited. A few widely distributed gestures may share a basis in forms of expression that are biologically inherited. Some writers have included the eyebrow-raise often observed in greeting and the shoulder-shrug for "don't know" in this category.

The widespread occurrence of similar gestural forms in different cultures and communities is one of the main reasons for the persistence of the idea that gestural expression can be more readily understood than spoken expression and that it thus constitutes a sort of universal language. Writers on gesture throughout the eighteenth and nineteenth centuries often took this view, and it was widely supposed that there was but one "sign language" common for all of humanity. However, recent work on sign languages has shown beyond doubt that these differ from one another much as spoken languages do. It is quite clear also from comparative studies of autonomous gestures and gesticulation that there are many differences from one culture or community to another.

Such differences arise for at least three reasons. First, in the creation of a characterizing gesture, the features of the object or activity to be characterized can vary. Second, the object or action depicted can vary in how it relates to the meaning of the gesture. For example, the "horns" hand (Figure 4j) in both Italy and Texas makes reference to the horns of cattle. In Italy horns are associated with a cuckold, and the gesture is highly insulting. In Texas, on the other hand, the gesture is used to show that one supports the Texas Longhorns, a football team associated with the University of Texas at Austin. Third, as a gesture becomes established as a stable, economical form of expression it becomes simplified, often losing its representational character. The way in which this simplification comes about can vary markedly from one community to another. In short, though the principles that govern the formation of gestures appear to be universal, the consequences of the operation of the principles are not predictable, with the result that very different forms become established in different parts of the world.

See also BODY MOVEMENT; CHOREOMETRICS; CONVERSATION; INTERACTION, FACE-TO-FACE; KINESICS; NONVERBAL COMMUNICATION.

Bibliography. David Efron, *Gesture, Race and Culture*, The Hague, 1972; Adam Kendon, ed., *Nonverbal Communication, Interaction, and Gesture*, The Hague, 1981; A. Lock, ed., *Action, Gesture, and Symbol: The Emergence of Language*, London, 1978; Desmond Morris, Peter Collett, Peter Marsh, and Marie O'Shaughnessy, *Gestures: Their Origins and Distribution*, New York, 1979; J. L. Nespoulous, P. Perron, and A. R. Lecours, eds., *The Biological Foundations of Gestures: Motor and Semiotic Aspects*, Hillsdale, N.J., 1986.

ADAM KENDON

GOEBBELS, JOSEPH (1897–1945)

German high-ranking National Socialist politician, Adolf Hitler's close collaborator, and controller of communications in the Third Reich. Paul Joseph Goebbels was born in the industrial town of Rheydt in the lower Rhineland. His father was a factory clerk, his mother the daughter of a blacksmith. As a child he contracted polio, which left him with a crippled foot and a permanent limp. Rejected for military service in 1914, he suffered throughout life from what he regarded as the stigma of failing to serve his country in wartime. The crippled little man with slight frame and black hair had to preach publicly the virtues of a tall, blond, blue-eyed Aryan "race." Nazi colleagues, envious of his intelligence and demagogic brilliance, later ridiculed him (behind his back) as "that bourgeois little mouse-doctor."

After 1918 Goebbels turned to a bohemian lifestyle and wrote poetry and drama. His literary efforts were unsuccessful. In 1922 he became a disciple of Hitler, whose manner and speech he imitated. For the next decade he had two goals: to promote Hitler as Germany's savior from Jews and Communists and to popularize Nazi IDEOLOGY as Germany's salvation. He presented Hitler as "either Christ or St. John," "the greatest German of all time." In 1929 Goebbels emerged as PROPAGANDA leader of the Nazi party. He now functioned as Nazi political campaign organizer, effectively using his powerful, resonant voice, which almost matched that of Hitler, to spread Nazi ideology. He used U.S. ADVERTISING and promotional methods in his own newspaper, *Der Angriff* (The Assault), and in many pamphlets (*see* PAMPHLET). He followed the editorial capitalization technique of shrieking TYPOGRAPHY favored by U.S. publishing tycoon WILLIAM RANDOLPH HEARST (e.g., "War against profiteers! Peace with the workers! THE GERMAN ALWAYS BEFORE THE FOREIGNER AND THE JEW!"). As master propagandist, Goebbels had a significant role in Hitler's rise to political power.

On March 12, 1933, shortly after Hitler became chancellor, Goebbels was appointed minister for public enlightenment and propaganda. He was empowered

Figure 1. *(Goebbels, Joseph)* Joseph Goebbels giving a speech at a Nazi rally. The Bettmann Archive, Inc.

to use the full resources of the state for National Socialist *Gleichschaltung,* "coordination" of every national institution—the press, MOTION PICTURES, publications, visual arts, the THEATER, RADIO, and SPORTS—for the advancement of Nazi doctrine. In this capacity he controlled the media and entire communications system, including all information, ideas, and attitudes allowed in the closed society of the Third Reich (*see* CENSORSHIP); from 1933 to 1945 he was the supreme arbiter of German cultural life.

In accordance with the Nazi leadership principle (*Führerprinzip*), Goebbels successfully maintained rigid control over German media through indoctrination and socialization mechanisms. His conduct may have been attributable in large part to overcompensation for his lack of physical virtues. Hurling sarcastic barbs at real or supposed enemies, he had an overwhelming need to transfer his own feelings of hatred and rage to the masses. Examples of his modus operandi include a rabble-rousing speech at the symbolic burning of the books on May 10, 1933 ("Spirits are awakening, O century! It is a joy to live!"), and his organization of the flamboyant Party rallies at Nuremberg ("I'm half-crazy with pride that such a genius as Hitler should see eye-to-eye with me toward the future!"). The delirium these produced was tellingly recorded in Leni Riefenstahl's DOCUMENTARY *Triumph des Willens* (Triumph of the Will), the official Nazi film of the 1934 rally.

During World War II Goebbels made able use of his propaganda machine to maintain public morale by accentuating magnificent German victories, discontent in the Soviet Union, U.S. inefficiency, and the certainty of final victory. This task became more

difficult as the tide of war changed in favor of the Allies. In 1944 Hitler named him general plenipotentiary for the mobilization of the war effort.

Goebbels remained loyal to Hitler to the end and even stage-managed his own death. On May 1, 1945, he and his wife, Magda, after poisoning their six children ("They must not grow up in a non-National Socialist Germany"), committed suicide in Hitler's Berlin bunker.

Bibliography. Paul Joseph Goebbels, *The Goebbels Diaries, 1942–1943* (in German), ed. and trans. by Louis P. Lochner, Garden City, N.Y., and London, 1948; idem, *The Goebbels Diaries* (Joseph Goebbels, Tagebücher, 1945), trans. by Richard Barry, ed. by Hugh Trevor-Roper, London, 1978; Roger Manvell and Heinrich Fraenkel, *Doctor Goebbels: His Life and Death,* New York, 1960; Curt Reiss, *Joseph Goebbels: A Biography,* Garden City, N.Y., 1948.

LOUIS L. SNYDER

GOFFMAN, ERVING (1922–1982)

Canadian-born sociologist whose work was devoted to the study of face-to-face interaction (*see* INTERACTION, FACE-TO-FACE) in various public and institutional settings. The impact of his work on various disciplines, from communication to political science, has grown steadily.

Erving Goffman was born in a small town in the province of Alberta. After three years of general undergraduate education at the University of Manitoba and some time in the artistic milieu of Ottawa, where he worked for the National Film Board, he completed an A.B. in sociology at the University of Toronto in 1945 and moved to the University of Chicago. There anthropologist Lloyd Warner and sociologist Everett Hughes became his mentors. In 1949 Goffman went to the University of Edinburgh and did fieldwork in "Dixon," on a small Shetland island. The doctoral dissertation that developed from his research, "Communication Conduct in an Island Community" (1953), laid out the major themes of his life's work: the various ways the social order is broken, repaired, and ultimately maintained through face-to-face interaction (a domain of investigation he later labeled the "interaction order").

Goffman found evidence for the organization of social interaction in the many small behaviors of everyday life. For example, in Dixon people were enabled to interact socially with a minimum of uncertainty by a pool of what Goffman called "safe supplies." Such supplies were, among other things, small talk about animals, children, or the weather as well as tasks like eating, smoking, or knitting, which allowed people to keep silent for a while without being considered offensive.

This example shows the kind of empirical evidence Goffman used—everyday life situations that were so common that no social scientist had looked at them systematically until Goffman detrivialized them through his exceptional capacity for observation and analysis. The example also shows that from a theoretical point of view Goffman can be seen as a Durkheimian microfunctionalist (see DURKHEIM, ÉMILE): interactions are "little social systems," as he once phrased it, and the social function of talk and related activities is to keep these systems running efficiently. Goffman kept a delicate balance between a strictly sociological perspective and a more psychologically oriented mode of interpretation. In this respect, the feeling of embarrassment played a key role in his thinking; people were seen as constantly trying to manage their interactions in order to avoid the sanction of embarrassment.

But the scope of Goffman's ideas must be seen in a much wider context: the complex articulation between individual action and the social order set forth in his work. In his early books, such as The Presentation of Self in Everyday Life (1959), Goffman used a dramaturgical model to consider all face-to-face behavior as the presentation of the situationally fitted social identity. In later years he moved toward a sophisticated cognitive conceptualization, based on GREGORY BATESON's notion of "frame," defined as a social matrix of PERCEPTION and interpretation of the reality at hand (Frame Analysis, 1974, and to a lesser extent Forms of Talk, 1981). In this view life appears as loose "strips of activities" that are composed of multiple layers of MEANING.

One only needs to follow the threads of Goffman's career, most of which was spent in the United States,

to realize that he left legacies to several fields. After his dissertation research, his next major project was an ethnographic study of St. Elizabeths Hospital in Washington, D.C. There he tried to observe and understand the lives of mental patients in the wards from their own point of view. The book that followed from this research, Asylums (1961), has had a wide-ranging influence on psychiatric practice and policy, contributing to the reduction in size of large mental hospitals and the establishment of community mental health programs during the 1960s in the United States and in Europe.

Goffman joined the Department of Sociology at the University of California, Berkeley, in 1958 and contributed to research then in progress in both criminology and anthropological LINGUISTICS. In 1968 he moved to the University of Pennsylvania as Benjamin Franklin Professor of Anthropology and Sociology. Although he usually worked independently and had few regular graduate students, he ultimately had international influence on a variety of disciplines beyond anthropology and sociology, including linguistics, FOLKLORE, communication, political science, and ETHOLOGY.

Scholars in the field of communication have quoted Goffman extensively, but they have rarely applied his ideas to their work in any systematic fashion. Goffman's approach to communication processes is potentially fruitful not only for interpersonal and health communication specialists but also for mass media researchers, as evidenced by his original analyses of photographic ADVERTISING (Gender Advertisements, 1979) and radio announcements (Forms of Talk, 1981). He used mostly naturalistic methods and demonstrated how a qualitative approach could lead not only to a descriptive account of behavior but also to theoretical insights about the underlying structure.

It should be said, however, that using Goffman's work is not necessarily easy. It is deceptively simple merely to attach his labels to diverse items. The temptation to do this comes partly from the fact that there is no obvious cohesiveness to Goffman's theoretical frame. Indeed, Goffman can be considered a sort of sociological bricoleur, creating numerous terms, reshuffling others, and not always remaining consistent from one book to the next. Because of this, the application of his legacy appears easy at a surface level but is actually quite difficult at a deeper level. Perhaps Goffman's ultimate contribution to the study of communication is the vision of the social world he presents in his superb prose: one of intimate strangeness with one's fellows, achieved through a combination of sympathy and detachment. Only a gradual immersion in Goffman's works, coupled with a similarly estranged yet accepting eye for observation, may bear the fruit of his legacy. Seen this way, Goffman's contribution is neither the creation of a single school of thought nor a single theoretical insight but a complex attitude toward the world.

Bibliography. Jason Ditton, ed., *The View from Goffman*, London, 1980; Paul Drew and Anthony Wooton, eds., *Erving Goffman: Exploring the Interaction Order*, Cambridge, forthcoming; Dell Hymes, "On Erving Goffman" (621–632), Michael Schudson, "Embarrassment and Erving Goffman's Idea of Human Nature" (633–648), Gary T. Marx, "Role Models and Role Distance: A Remembrance of Erving Goffman" (649–662), Paul Creelan, "Vicissitudes of the Sacred: Erving Goffman and the Book of Job" (663–695), *Theory and Society* 13 (1984).

YVES WINKIN

GOSSIP

Talk about absent others, often talk about those very characteristics and activities they would least like having discussed. Even when its contents are not scandalous, gossip has a somewhat illicit air, as gossipers are telling someone else's story, one to which they have no right. On the other hand, gossip also provides opportunities for the expression of moral values, for making sense out of aberrant or outrageous behavior, and for the creation of a clear definition of who one is by the delineation of who one is glad not to be. It is a complex communicative phenomenon, serving a range of functions, both intended and not. Gossip—or ways of speaking very much like it—is found in many communities worldwide, especially in face-to-face social groups. In this apparently near universal distribution lie one of the reasons for scholarly interest in gossip and also the danger of overgeneralization from any one instance.

Approaches to the study of gossip. Any definition of gossip depends on both its content—what it is about—and its character as a social activity. The four major approaches to gossip are concerned with these two dimensions in different degrees. Many scholars and researchers with a communications perspective have considered it primarily as a means of transmitting and manipulating information. Some researchers concerned with the informational content of gossip have gone further in arguing its role in creating knowledge.

A second approach likewise focuses on content but is concerned with the moral element of gossip and with locating this moral element in general patterns of social process in the community. Some anthropologists argue that gossip, while making moral appeals, is primarily a device used strategically by individuals or groups to advance their own interests. From both these perspectives, the critical element of gossip is its topic; they disagree on how these topics and their implications are to be evaluated. Both approaches find some degree of cross-cultural similarity in the functions that gossip serves.

A third group of scholars—primarily folklorists

Figure 1. *(Gossip)* Two women gossiping. Hellenistic statuette from Myrina, ca. second century B.C.E. Reproduced by courtesy of the Trustees of The British Museum.

and anthropological linguists—have been concerned with gossip as an aesthetic and expressive act, concentrating on its formal and stylistic features and its role in the expressive repertoires of particular communities. In contrast to the preceding approach, this perspective stresses highly variable aspects of gossip. While all are concerned with gossip in terms of cultural notions of verbal art, license, and decorum, the results from Gary Gossen's study of a Mayan Indian community and Roger Abrahams's study of Afro-Caribbean ones depict formally very different phenomena. This approach is inherently very particularistic; gossip takes different forms and is related to other forms of talk in quite different ways in various societies.

A final approach is to study gossip as social interaction, specifically through the application of conversational-analytic techniques to gossip texts. Such work combines a concern for small-scale social process with a detailed methodology for describing the organization of talk. There have been few cross-cultural applications of this approach.

Research findings. Research from these perspectives suggests four general findings about gossip that should be taken into account in such studies. First, gossip is about something and is something in itself; any study of gossip should consider it as both text and social activity. Second, two kinds of social relationships are involved in any gossip event: those between the gossipers and their subject and those between the gossipers themselves. Gossip is both talk about and talk with others. Third, gossip should be considered not as an isolated phenomenon but as part of the expressive and communicative repertoire of a community. Its character and implications are related to those of other ways of speaking. Finally, how gossip is conducted in any community—its style and interactional organization—is as critical for the parties involved as are its topics; indeed, its aesthetic and expressive qualities may make gossip possible as well as satisfying.

It is clear that a unifunctional interpretation of gossip would be misleading. The specifics of how it works and how it influences social life vary considerably from one culture to another. Gossip can serve at the same time to further partisan ends and reinforce group values. Similarly, while it can threaten to disrupt relations with some—those talked about—it also can be an essential way of building and sustaining sociability, of weaving together a social web by weaving words together.

See also CONVERSATION; INTERACTION, FACE-TO-FACE; INTERPERSONAL COMMUNICATION; NARRATIVE; SPEAKING, ETHNOGRAPHY OF.

Bibliography. Roger D. Abrahams, *The Man-of-Words in the West Indies: The Emergence of Creole Culture*, Baltimore, Md., 1983; Elizabeth Colson, *The Makah Indians*, Manchester, Eng., 1953, reprint Westport, Conn., 1974; Ronald Frankenberg, *Village on the Border*, London, 1957; Gary Gossen, *Chamulas in the World of the Sun: Time and Space in a Mayan Oral Tradition*, Cambridge, Mass., 1974, reprint Prospect Heights, Ill., 1984; John B. Haviland, *Gossip, Reputation and Knowledge in Zinacantan*, Chicago, 1977; Ralph L. Rosnow and Gary Alan Fine, *Rumor and Gossip: The Social Psychology of Hearsay*, New York, 1976.

DONALD BRENNEIS

GOVERNMENT-MEDIA RELATIONS

Long before social science began debating questions of media impact, governments had already assumed an effect great enough to merit tight legal controls. At no time in history has any political system ever extended complete freedom of action to any mass medium. Even in the United States, generally regarded as having a very libertarian press system, print and broadcast news organizations are subject to LIBEL suits by government officials (as well as private citizens), PORNOGRAPHY statutes, antitrust legislation (*see* MONOPOLY), national security regulations, and, in the case of broadcast news sources, regulations requiring "fairness" in news content. All modern nations develop laws, regulations, and procedures for defining the limits of press freedom. *See* GOVERNMENT REGULATION.

In Great Britain the common law still provides punishment (public reprimand or even jail) for journalists who report defamations about a sitting Parliament or its members, and libel recoveries are allowed even if a defamation is true. In Italy the government plays a formal role in licensing journalists, and the Ministry of Justice is involved in sanctioning reporters who violate the professional code of journalism. Mexico and other countries have established systems in which newsprint is controlled by a public-private corporation. Newspapers are dependent, at least in part, on the government for something as essential as the paper on which their copy is published. In the last analysis all governments establish formal and legal means for ensuring that press-government relations are never totally beyond their control.

Patterns

So obvious is the importance of law and regulation in the ties between government and press that most studies concerning the two have focused on the legal aspects of the relationship. The single most famous typology offered about the press-government relationship focuses almost completely on the role of the governmental system. *Four Theories of the Press* (1956), written by Fred S. Siebert, Theodore Peterson, and WILBUR SCHRAMM, presents "authoritarian," "libertarian," "communist," and "social responsibility" models of press-government interaction. Past analyses have seldom examined ways in which media organizations tend to look at government and to define their own task of reporting and assessing activities of government. If we survey the range of media perspectives, focusing on societies in which the press and other news sources are not wholly under government control—setting aside regimes in which government has taken over the press functions—six basic patterns seem to emerge. The sources may be (1) antithetical, (2) adversarial, (3) symbiotic, (4) bureaucratic, (5) partisan, or (6) obeisant.

The antithetical press. The antithetical press rejects several of the basic values of the political system and refuses to relate to governmental elites in any ongoing way. In essence, the antithetical press does not "cover" political leaders; it rejects them and their system. Intensely ideological, the antithetical press also disdains partisan ties, something that differentiates it from the obeisant press, a press type that embraces both IDEOLOGY and party.

In antilibertarian societies the antithetical press is outlawed. In liberal societies the antithetical press is often called the underground press, not because it is necessarily illegal but because it is politically radical and clearly outside the power structure. Journalists who work in the antithetical press, like the *Nation* in the United States, prefer not to rely on government officials as sources, but instead to interpret conditions and reflect on events.

In a commercial press system the antithetical press is often small in number and in size, and economically vulnerable. Most antithetical press sources either move toward adversarialism in their relationship to government or, more often, fail to sustain themselves. In fact, owing to their lack of financing through ADVERTISING, party, or government, most antithetical press sources publish infrequently, usually on a monthly basis.

The adversarial press. The adversarial press accepts the basic political values of the system but defines its relationship to political leadership in an aggressive and "negative" way. Adversarial news sources cover politicians but in their reporting focus on the failures and problems of leadership. The adversarial news source also practices investigative journalism, news gathering that emphasizes discovery of facts and deemphasizes the pronouncements and public actions of government elites.

Although the Western press is often described as adversarial in nature, most social scientists believe that the Western media are not particularly adversarial. Most day-to-day commercial news sources in the West do little investigative journalism and give considerable deference to political leaders, relying heavily on the government for news and quotations.

Le monde in France is one of the more famous examples of an adversarial daily. Begun as an experiment after World War II, *Le monde* has generally had a liberal viewpoint, but compared with most major Western dailies the paper has related adversarially to leaders of all political colorations and has chosen not to practice the sort of "objective reporting" one usually associates with most of the daily press.

In most pluralist democracies, the periodical press is more likely to be adversarial than the day-to-day press. According to some observers, the United States has recently experienced some increase in adversarial treatment of the news. However, press historians regard the late-nineteenth-century newspapers of WILLIAM RANDOLPH HEARST and JOSEPH PULITZER as substantially more adversarial in nature than the contemporary media. *Muckraking*, a higher order of adversarial news reporting, was widely practiced by both newspapers and magazines toward the end of the nineteenth century.

There is a school of thought that argues that adversarialism is, in the daily press, something of an illusion. One contemporary author speaks of a "bounded adversarialism," a modern media system that becomes adversarial only when it believes that the government or its officials have broken the basic rules of the game.

Symbiotic news organizations. Symbiotic sources are those that are more likely to rely on government than to defy government. Symbiotic news organizations practice a form of objective reporting that lends itself to covering what government leaders routinely say and do on a daily basis. Instead of defining their role as oppositional to that of the sitting government, these symbiotic news organs recognize that they need the government at least as much as the government needs them. Relationships are, therefore, transactional and mutually beneficial.

Commercial wire services practice a form of journalism that implies a symbiotic relationship. Typically, wire services remain symbiotic in practice until government action elicits an adversarial response. Media historian David Halberstam argues that the wire services covered the early stages of U.S. involvement in Vietnam by relying heavily on official releases and news provided by the Department of Defense, a practice that Halberstam believes inhibited other news sources from moving to a more adversarial posture during the early part of the war (*see* NEWS AGENCIES).

Certain types of media seem more likely then others to accept a symbiotic relationship with government. Commercial radio appears more symbiotic in its behavior than commercial print media, at least in the United States. Political scientist David Paletz has demonstrated a tendency for the local press to be more symbiotic in its relationships with government than are the larger national newspapers. It is generally accepted that all forms of Western media are most likely to behave symbiotically at the outset of a newly elected government, a time during which the press desperately needs access to the new leadership, and little hard news about policy-making is available; hence the "honeymoon" period.

One school of media theory argues that all commercial media are symbiotic in their news practices. These theorists regard press and government elites as so close in background and/or values that the relationship may be even less than symbiotic—in a word, "hegemonic," or given to a single dominant value system in which the press plays the role of safety valve for the ruling elite.

The hegemonist theory is among the most controversial concerning media-government relationships. In fact, the conflict among those who consider the commercial press in democratic societies to be basically adversarial, basically symbiotic, or basically hegemonic has dominated much of the academic debate concerning interactions between press and government.

Bureaucratic. Much of the Western media structure is not commercial. Much of it is actually governmental, which is to say formally tied to the state. Governmental newspeople are themselves of two types: those who are directly employed as part of the nation's press secretariat and those who work as government-funded or subsidized journalists.

To distinguish between the two types—press secretaries and government-linked reporters—one might call the first type government news officials and the second type news bureaucrats. Of the two, news bureaucrats are far greater in number and more related to our concerns.

As a rule, news bureaucrats work in broadcast journalism. Virtually every Western nation has a broadcast news organization that is maintained by government funding, many based on the British Broadcasting Corporation (BBC) model originally formulated during the 1920s.

Even the most commercial news systems inevitably establish some form of bureaucratic press. The United States has no functional equivalent to the BBC, but the U.S. government does operate the United States Information Agency (USIA), a bureaucratic news organization that, by law, disseminates news only outside the United States. USIA is bigger and more heavily funded than the news divisions of the three principal U.S. television networks combined (*see* RADIO, INTERNATIONAL).

There are print sources, too, that could easily be classified as bureaucratic both in nature and in their relationship with the government. *Al ahram* in Egypt is a bureaucratic print source, semi-independent of government at the reportorial level but tied to government at the editorial level: the nation's president appoints the editor in chief. In Yugoslavia, a socialist country, the government employs and funds *Borba,* the official daily newspaper. The socialist countries have print sources that meet our definition of bureaucratic; in the West, however, bureaucratic news media are mostly electronic: Canadian Broadcasting Corporation (CBC) in Canada, Radiotelevisione Italiana (RAI) in Italy, Télédiffusion de France (TDF) in France.

Because bureaucratic news sources are funded or subsidized by the state, most media theorists reasonably assume that the relationships between bureaucratic sources and government officials will be comparatively friendly and only rarely adversarial. In the Federal Republic of Germany bureaucratic news sources have been quite unwilling to adopt an adversarial position in covering the major parties or the government. Research indicates that the CBC in Canada (a government-backed system) is considerably less aggressive in its news practices than CBS (a commercial system) in the United States. In France government pressure has kept French television news bureaucrats from behaving as adversarially as commercially sponsored reporters, causing a pattern of resignations and press crises in French television news. The history of recent years does suggest that the commercial media—adversarial or symbiotic—are more likely to cover scandals or to present bad news about government leaders than are bureaucratic news media.

Partisan. The essence of a partisan medium is that it has direct, often formal ties to an active political party. In the nineteenth century, particularly in the United States, those ties were frequently announced in the very name of a newspaper.

For the most part the history of free press often begins with the free but partisan press (*see* NEWSPAPER: HISTORY). By the late eighteenth century, the partisan press was essentially the only form of press that covered politics and government. In the United States the two original capital newspapers were controlled quite directly by Thomas Jefferson (a Republican) and Alexander Hamilton (a Federalist), each at the time a sitting member of President George Washington's cabinet.

Because partisan sources are tied to or directed by the party, the relationship to the government by a partisan paper is, at once, variable and predictable. Partisan press sources treat government leaders favorably if their party controls the government, negatively if their party does not. Indeed, parties pioneered the newspaper business in the eighteenth and nineteenth centuries in the Western democracies for two reasons: first, in order to win elections, and second, to ensure themselves favorable coverage once they had succeeded. During the 1800s, a newspaper's reporters were essentially employees of the party that published it, paid either directly by the party or indirectly through patronage-based subsidies. Even as late as the early twentieth century the major Canadian newspapers were so tied to their patron party that the reporters themselves sat in the Parliament galleries in accordance with their party label.

The partisan press has, however, accounted for less and less in all the media systems of the late twentieth century. Even in the most partisan of political systems the majority of daily newspapers have broken their formal ties to political parties. And the newest systems have tended not to adopt partisan news sources or have tended to drop them quickly along the way to political development. Israel, a comparatively young and intensely partisan nation, has not been able to support a partisan press. Between 1948 and 1976 the number of party-affiliated newspapers in Israel dropped by almost two-thirds. The one major daily, which began in the 1940s as a party paper, has since announced its independence from the Labor Party. In Scandinavia and in western Europe, with Italy the major exception, the same pattern holds: the partisan press maintains its significance only rarely, and most of its worth is as press history.

The obeisant press. Extremist parties, however, have not been as willing as centrist parties to accept the decline in party-based journalism. *Humanité* in France and *L'unità* in Italy are the most famous examples of Communist party papers in Western society. But extremist right-wing parties also work hard at preserving their obeisant press organs; the Movimento Socialista Italiano (MSI) in Italy, for example, publishes *Il secolo d'Italia,* a newspaper that is almost as much an official organ as *L'unità.*

Like the partisan press, the obeisant press treats government in a predetermined manner—hostile when the government is the opposition, sympathetic when the government is the sponsoring party. The main differences between partisan and obeisant sources are two. First, the partisan press has a directorate that is *linked* to party; the obeisant press has a directorate *chosen* in large measure by party. Second, obeisant press sources usually represent extremist parties, so by definition their party is less likely to control government. Therefore, obeisant press sources often reflect the same sort of relationship to sitting governments that antithetical press sources exhibit.

Change and Evolution

Scholars disagree about the reasons for a news source practicing one type of journalism or another. Constitution and law play a large part in defining limits and establishing practices, most especially for bureaucratic news sources, which are tied formally to the government. Perhaps more interesting are those interpretations of why a source (or group of sources) shifts among the three most common commercial types (symbiotic, adversarial, and partisan) or why, for that matter, an entire press system moves from one general approach to another.

Beyond the formality of law, four general interpretations of change exist. First is a historical interpretation, which focuses on cataclysmic events. For example, the BBC adopted a more adversarial relationship with the government of Margaret Thatcher after it was disclosed that during the war with Argentina over the Falkland (Malvinas) Islands in 1982, the government had permitted the sinking of an Argentine naval vessel, the *General Belgrano,* despite the fact that the ship was not in the designated war zone and was moving away from the combat zone. The war did serve to make the bureaucratic British press less bureaucratic. In the United States as well conduct of the war in Vietnam and the Watergate affair (1972–1974) have been considered the two events that helped to shift U.S. news sources away from symbiosis toward "bounded adversarialism" and, in some cases, adversarialism.

Demographics have also been used to explain shifts from one type of system to another. An increasingly educated public may prefer a less symbiotic relationship between its news source and its government; so, too, may an increasingly educated press corps. Indeed, one plausible explanation for the recent shift away from symbiosis in many systems is that reporters have been drawn increasingly from more prestigious educational backgrounds and higher social strata.

Some press theorists invoke political culture to explain systemwide or localized changes in press behavior and media-government relations. In the twentieth century the single greatest change has been the decline in partisan press practices and styles. Some believe that partisanship has become less important in political culture because the parties themselves gave up on the partisan press; the more widely accepted notion is that as partisanship as a cultural force declined, the partisan press approach was incongruent with political culture and therefore doomed to a far less important role in journalism.

Political culture leads directly to the last interpretation of change in media-government relations—the commercial interpretation. One can obviously employ audience tastes to explain the decline of partisan press in the United States: the general public wanted more objective reporting and got it. But one can also use audience tastes to explain the weak and ephemeral nature of the antithetical press: there are too few antisystem readers to buy, and sustain, those sources. Indeed, one can even use commercial pressure to explain one of the most surprising changes in press-government relations, the nearly universal shift during the first half of this century toward a more symbiotic relationship. As technology made possible a closer look at political leaders, and as publics were given greater opportunity for personalized news about those leaders, commercial press organs were themselves forced to draw closer to leadership; personalized information demanded the closer tie. In order to please readers (viewers, too), reporters had to sacrifice adversarial practices to gain moment-by-moment access to politicians.

No matter which interpretation of change is best, one truth seems to hold historically: whoever *pays* for the news organization—be it party, government, or public—plays more than a modest role in determining the way in which that news organization interacts with political elites.

See also CENSORSHIP; ELECTION; NEWSMAGAZINE; NEWSPAPER: TRENDS; POLITICAL COMMUNICATION.

Bibliography. Richard Fagen, *Politics and Communication*, Boston, 1966; Itzhak Galnoor, ed., *Government Secrecy in Democracies*, New York, 1977; Dan Nimmo and Michael W. Mansfield, eds., *Government and the News Media: Comparative Dimensions*, Waco, Tex., 1982; Richard L. Rubin, *Press, Party, and Presidency*, New York, 1981; Colin Seymour-Ure, *The Political Impact of Mass Media*, Beverly Hills, Calif., 1974; Fred S. Siebert, Theodore Peterson, and Wilbur L. Schramm, *Four Theories of the Press*, Urbana, Ill., 1956, reprint Freeport, N.Y., 1973.

MICHAEL J. ROBINSON

GOVERNMENT REGULATION

Governments have regulated the flow and content of information and communication in all societies throughout history, although some societies have valued freedom from such regulation. Governments have imposed systems and bureaucratic structures of CENSORSHIP and control as a way of compelling adherence to religious, social, political, or ideological ends and values. Government regulation has acted as both an enforcer of accepted standards and an eradicator of views deemed to threaten the existing order. Government regulation also exists (1) as a convenience to modern communications industries to ensure that the operations of individuals and companies are confined within rules to their mutual benefit and (2) as a protection of the public against excessive bias in the presentation of a single point of view and excessive emphasis on VIOLENCE, obscenity, or sexual explicitness. Regulation also exists as a protection for government in helping to maintain SECRECY or to shield the powerful from criticism or exposure. No society, even those most firmly committed to freedom of expression, can altogether avoid government regulation of communications.

History

In ancient Rome the censor enumerated and classified the population and assessed its morals. To protect Rome against both immorality and political treason, the institution of public informers was developed. Banishment was imposed by the censor on offending philosophers and teachers, and actors in offending dramas lost their citizenship. The censors regulated the admission of Greek arts and writings into Rome through control of the movement of individuals. In turn, Judaism, Christianity, and Islam confronted the laws of the decaying ROMAN EMPIRE with their different versions of theological exclusivism, all refusing to participate in the pluralistic, idolatrous practice of Rome. Each of these religions created a canon of texts deemed to be authentic and regulated their practice through the listing of schismatic and heretical works.

However, the systems of religious and secular censorship based on centrally authorized prohibition that are still familiar today have more recognizable origins in the conflicts between the new sciences and RELIGION during the twelfth and thirteenth centuries. At that time the universities were the battlegrounds for struggles between new and inherited beliefs. Thus in 1215 the University of Paris banned ARISTOTLE's works on physics and natural sciences (although his logic remained in the curriculum), and the works of Arabic and Persian philosophers were similarly squelched. These regulations occurred while the universities were themselves becoming involved in the new debates about academic freedom. *See* UNIVERSITY.

Even before the arrival of PRINTING, university and educational authorities, operating within broader civil authority, were building systems of control through manipulation of the commerce in and production of texts. Booksellers and stationers were licensed to deal in prescribed categories of material. With the coming of printing in the fifteenth century, systems for licensing presses were backed up by the establishment of both clerical and government censorship of books prior to publication and the prohibition, after publication, of works that had not been censored. These methods of control, under varying degrees of vigilance, lingered on in parts of Europe and Asia until the national revolutions of the nineteenth century. The central texts for these elaborate machineries of intellectual and confessional control were the 1559 Index of Forbidden Books of Pope Paul IV and the Index of the Council of Trent five years later, which set out the methods for the prepublication examination of books and arranged for the inspection of printing presses and stationers' premises. *See* BOOK.

Evolving scientific theories as well as the changing industry of printing exerted great pressure on these systems of control. The coming of the ENCYCLOPEDIA and the drastically altered nature of state institutions in the seventeenth century also influenced the methods of censorship and regulation. A rash of indexes broke out in various parts of Europe, mutually denunciatory and impossible to enforce. While in earlier times the universities had carried out the task of prejudging manuscripts, with church and state enforcing their judgments, the institution of printing complicated the situation and made the distinction between the manuscript and the printed edition paramount. Gradually the universities lost their power of jurisdiction.

Each system constructed in European societies for limiting and inspecting printing establishments broke down under the sheer pressure of the demand for printing services. Through the Stationers' Company successive English administrations after 1556 attempted to control the entry of apprentices into the printing trade and to ensure their compliance. Censorship by the Privy Council and by means of royal patents had broken down during the reign of Henry VIII. Parliament's increasing difficulty in controlling the stationers during and after the civil war of the 1640s was followed by a period of extreme repression after the return of Charles II in 1660 and then, in 1695, by the abrogation of press licensing altogether.

Censorship in the eighteenth and nineteenth centuries. English governments turned to another form of regulation—industrial—in their pursuit of social order through the control of controversial material. In 1712 the first of a series of Stamp Acts forced newspaper prices dramatically upward by obliging all periodicals publishing news to use only stamped sheets of paper. Newspapers were confined thus to the wealthier classes. The system survived through various transitions until 1865—after decades of struggle between illegal unstamped radical newspapers and the legal stamped middle-class press. A wide variety of other controls was also imposed on the press; these were gradually reduced or removed from the late eighteenth century onward (*see* NEWSPAPER: HISTORY). (The charge of *scandalum magnatum,* or defamation of those in power, was finally removed from common law—although it continues to echo even into the late twentieth century—and evolved into the still stringent civil laws against LIBEL. Controls over obscenity and official secrecy remain in place for all forms of media.)

Different traditions of censorship took root in France and Germany and elsewhere in Europe. In the eighteenth century France acquired a prepublication code, operated by the chancellor with the help of nearly eighty censors, each specializing in a different category of material. A vigorous debate ensued on the disadvantages of a censorship that varied in nature and intensity from one year to the next. Jean-Jacques Rousseau, Voltaire, and others were published outside France (Holland, Switzerland, England) and secretly imported. In France, perhaps more clearly than elsewhere, censorship was conducted in the name of learning, the censors being acknowledged authorities in the subjects concerned and desirous of protecting the public against the unfamiliar, the damaging, and the inaccurate. Absolutist censorship (as practiced, for example, in the Holy Roman Empire) was not dissimilar in scope and intention from that of twentieth-century totalitarian administrations, in which associations of writers, scientists, and philosophers provide sanction and intellectual cover for a censorship designed to prevent or retard political discussion outside a very small elite.

The French Revolution of 1789 suddenly and briefly opened the floodgates of a totally free press; five hundred publications sprang into existence but were rapidly extinguished as censorship—far more oppressive than that of prerevolutionary decades—was enforced. By the time of Napoléon's empire only a single news publication, edited by the emperor, survived. In England fear of REVOLUTION led to the passage of the Six Acts, by which Parliament attempted to stamp out radical publications and free assembly—a repression that ultimately made establishment of the free press into a basic liberal cause. John Stuart Mill's tract *On Liberty* (1859) was the most widely influential text of the nineteenth-century movement toward intellectual liberty in stable societies, and Henry Jephson's *The Platform* (1894) followed the evolution of the argument for freedom of SPEECH and assembly as the counterpart of a free press.

Some of the ideas and practices of European states spread to the Americas. Both North and South America saw experiments in new forms of absolutism and liberalism. In many societies new state machinery was devised to cope with the paradoxes of postcolonialism: media institutions born of liberal struggle found themselves subjected to the demands of dominant groups and classes identified with new regimes.

The colonies that became the United States carried on a concentrated discussion and practice of censorship that enabled them to pass through and beyond the various stages undergone by European societies. Freedom of speech and publication were not established in the early communities of colonists, fleeing though they were from intolerance and repression. Quakers were persecuted and their publications repressed in Massachusetts, but they themselves refused toleration to other sects and religions elsewhere in the colonies. In contrast to the narrow theocracies of other settlements, Rhode Island was established as a center for freedom of worship and speech.

In the eighteenth century there were several celebrated prosecutions of newspaper publishers, but the 1734 trial of JOHN PETER ZENGER for articles of an allegedly seditious nature published in his *New-York Weekly Journal* failed, and the case helped to mark the rapid development of free-press thinking in America. Common law continued to prohibit treason, blasphemy, sedition, and obscenity (the four universal targets of censorship) as forms of libel, but gradually defenses against the charge of libel became firmly established. Under the 1791 First Amendment to the U.S. Constitution, Congress was prohibited from passing laws prohibiting freedom of speech or publication, and upon this declaration a vast superstructure of libertarianism was gradually created, the amendment having been taken to imply that censorship prior to publication is illegal. In the United States, government controls took the form of preventing distribution (e.g., by forbidding certain kinds of material to pass through the U.S. mail system). However, special laws of a censoring nature—such as the Alien and Sedition Act of 1798 and the Comstock Act of 1873, prohibiting the dissemination of obscene material through the postal services or U.S. Customs—have also attempted to protect the U.S. government or society from malicious publications (*see* POSTAL SERVICE). Efforts to expand First Amendment rights were undertaken continuously by radical and labor organizations and also by the media industry, which attempted to push back government licensing of the radio SPECTRUM.

Censorship in the twentieth century. The major struggles in the United States in the 1970s and 1980s (paralleled in many other societies) revolved around access to governmental information. The controversy over the publication of the Pentagon Papers during the administration of Richard Nixon helped to establish the importance of freedom of information legislation, based on the (much-disputed) notion that the First Amendment guarantees the right to know as well as the right to speak and publish. Freedom of information acts have been introduced in many countries, including several in Scandinavia, but in Britain the view has remained entrenched in official circles that secrecy of government documents of all kinds must be protected, even to the extent of imprisoning civil servants who reveal politically sensitive material to journalists. U.S. practice inspired a movement throughout the journalism of democratic societies toward more openness of government, but in the mood of the 1980s it experienced more setbacks than progress.

The position of the press in the Soviet Union and its closely allied societies is instructive in comparison with the prevailing doctrines of Western countries. Russia in the nineteenth century modeled its press laws closely on those of France despite Russia's more active secret repressive apparatus. With the 1905 revolution censorship prior to publication was abolished, and after the Bolshevik Revolution a new

Soviet Constitution was drawn up offering a free press of an extreme kind. However, special exceptions (which included the protection of socialism and of the Communist party of the Soviet Union) were quickly applied, amounting to an abrogation of guaranteed rights. Soviet practice, echoed in a large number of developing societies, is based on the idea that the state as representative of the rights of the people, and of the party as the people's instrument, should suppress all forms of dissident literature and news publication. According to the theories of V. I. Lenin news media of all kinds are such crucial tools for the building of a new society that those who flout edicts of the party are guilty of frustrating socialism itself.

After World War II Asia and Africa went through a generation of highly concentrated change. Previously the basic communication systems of those continents, as well as the doctrines of governance, had largely been constructed to suit the needs of imperial powers (*see* COLONIZATION). Newspapers, RADIO, and other telecommunications tended to be the possessions of private companies located in the imperial countries. The independence movements all were founded on newspapers molded by the traditions of the nineteenth-century European nationalist movements. As colonialism ebbed, particularly after World War II, a host of new nations faced their own regulatory decisions—and often began by sweeping away hated controls, then enacting quite similar systems themselves. The struggle to legitimize and consolidate authority and the quest for national identity played a part in these processes, precipitating struggles still far from resolved. *See* AFRICA, TWENTIETH CENTURY; ASIA, TWENTIETH CENTURY.

The Debate over Deregulation

The censorship debate has nearly always been part of the larger debate about industrial regulation by government. Since the 1960s government regulation of the communications industry has been explicitly linked in the United States to the issue of how best to preserve and fulfill the principles of the First Amendment.

The historical context is crucial to an understanding of the deregulation debate. Commerce has been regulated by various governmental authorities for many centuries. There are numerous examples. Authorities controlled the prices and quality of medieval markets. The Holy Roman Empire instituted and regulated a messenger service that covered the entire central region of Europe from Turkey and Poland to the English Channel. The early postmasters of the American colonies were obliged to copy and pass on the newspapers to the more distant groups of settlers. Japanese authorities ensured the existence of the tile newspapers of the seventeenth century. The English

Tudor and Stuart administrations established wage levels and price levels for a range of basic goods to protect the public against unwarranted inflation and to ensure the well-being of workmen. In the United States the legislation of the New Deal, under which the 1934 Communications Act was passed and public administration models for the airplane and aviation industries were established, was simply a continuation of practices that had existed throughout the era of industrial capitalism and had long preceded it. The building of canals and railways, the organization of banking, the issuing of currency—all of these commercial undertakings were deemed to require quite sophisticated forms of regulation.

In the United States during the 1970s and 1980s a fundamental debate sprang up about the conflict between regulated industry and the doctrine of the open market. Government-run and government-regulated industries alike were increasingly felt to infringe on the rights of consumers because they were, by virtue of their status, exempted from the rigors of competition. A parallel discussion sprang up throughout western Europe and Australia in the wake of new antisocialist dissent. To many, regulation had been proved inadequate where, as in Britain and France, for example, poor TELEPHONE services could be blamed on the existence of public, protected monopolies. In the United States there was steady pressure to revise the powers and duties of the Federal Communications Commission (FCC). In both national and industrial forums, such as the successive World Administrative Radio Conferences of the International Telecommunication Union (ITU), U.S. spokespersons argued with increasing decisiveness against further governmental and intergovernmental control over the rapidly expanding telecommunications services. U.S. dissent stopped short of outright resignation from the ITU, but within the United States and later in the United Kingdom the administrations of Ronald Reagan and Margaret Thatcher forced the radio, television, cable, SATELLITE, and telecommunications services increasingly into the private sector, reducing the regulatory functions of government to those of essential protection of the public and maximal encouragement of free-market forces. *See also* TELEVISION HISTORY.

The existence of public franchising through the FCC of radio and television stations (justified by the limits of the spectrum as a resource and the consequent need to protect "public interest, convenience, necessity," in the words of the 1934 Communications Act) led almost inevitably to the FCC's intervention into the control of content. In the name of public interest the Fairness Doctrine and the equal-time rule were imposed, obliging all controversial issues to be handled with enforced pluralization of coverage. Later the Prime Time Access Rule obliged networks to allow local stations an additional half hour early in the evening for local programming within peak time. (It quickly proved to be an ineffective regulation, since the time was taken up by programs of pure entertainment rather than local information.) Concern that such regulations were rarely effective helped to defeat the attempts of public-interest groups in the 1970s to force the three networks to offer more and better children's programming and to reduce or eliminate ADVERTISING aimed at children. Gradually the climate of opinion turned against such interventions and toward free use of the air by those who had acquired de facto command of it.

The roots of the U.S. dilemma over television regulation lay in the Sixth Report and Order of the FCC of April 1952, which created allotments of spectrum space to 617 VHF stations and 1,463 UHF stations (both later expanded). Unwittingly the FCC had created the basis for three parallel groups of stations, controlled by three network companies able to dominate, control, and greatly profit from the medium of television. By imposing quite arbitrary and technically unnecessary limits on television coverage of the nation, the FCC had played the role of confining the total number of voices and images actually available to the public. The superstructure of further control and inspection, imposed amid an extraordinary quantity of litigation and cross-litigation, then became inevitable.

In the 1980s context of a wholly new set of technical possibilities—VIDEO, CABLE TELEVISION, satellites, and other systems for distribution of signals—the accepted forms of regulation were questioned. The position of the three networks, allegedly more in control of the FCC than disciplined by it, was challenged. Under President Nixon there had been many threats of interference in the news coverage of the networks, whose supporters tended to argue that the courage of professional news providers rather than the fear of the open market had succeeded in protecting the content of news against political pollution.

By the mid-1980s radio was enjoying drastic reductions in day-to-day supervision by the FCC. Cable television services were permitted greater leeway, since they were not subjected to the same controls as television stations, which were dependent on the FCC-regulated radio frequency spectrum. The growing use of videocassette machines in the home meant that viewers could free themselves from the planned schedule of programs. Successive FCC chairmen agreed that only through greater diversity and more open competition could the consumer be properly served. The process of creating, justifying, and implementing new regulation is so slow, they agreed, that a new rule is often superseded by the time it is enforced.

The FCC's rule making had spread throughout a variety of tangential industries such as that of HOL-LYWOOD, whose film companies were barred from direct ownership of television outlets. Gradually, as the deregulation movement spread from industry to industry (airlines, telecommunications), the rules governing television administration and content started to become more flexible. By the end of the century broadcast services, under the impact of technological proliferation and ideological change in Washington, could perhaps become as easy of access and as diverse in ownership as the newspapers of the nineteenth century.

In Europe the ideological backwash of the U.S. debate swept over the discussions about implementing the new technologies. The scarcity of spectrum space had long been among the leading arguments adduced for the retention of monopolies or "duopolies" in the national radio and television services of European societies. This position was challenged repeatedly in the 1970s and 1980s. In Britain the vast national telephone and telecommunications administration, British Telecom, was sold off on the Stock Exchange, its telephone MONOPOLY broken. The existence of nationally regulated or chartered broadcast institutions, such as the BBC in England, RAI in Italy, and ARD and ZDF in Germany, was also challenged. In Italy during the early 1970s the constitutional court broke the monopoly of the RAI, and a totally unregulated swarm of television stations sprang up, to the amazement of other European television administrations. Within a decade, however, France, the whole of Scandinavia, Germany, Belgium, the Netherlands, and Great Britain were all in the midst of political controversy over the allocation of cable stations, radio stations, and satellite channels—and even over whether and how to continue the collection of viewers' television set license fees, the monopoly reception of which had long helped to maintain the power and creative resources of the national television organizations. In every one of these societies new interests, sometimes emerging from the world of the press, sometimes from cinema, were ready to enter the domestic moving-image market.

While the meaning of regulation was fairly clear, the term *deregulation* was seen to have a diversity of meanings. Measures announced to be deregulatory in the context of one country looked very much like the regulatory systems of others. What was happening was the application of the same free-market doctrine to a variety of different circumstances. Under the welter of argument and reform a great restructuring of capital took place from public to private sectors, with government nonetheless retaining a great deal of control over the rate and state of diversification and the methods and levels of financing. It will not be possible before the end of the century to see clearly whether government regulation actually increased or diminished as a result of this great international ideological deregulatory project.

Bibliography. Erik Barnouw, *A History of Broadcasting in the United States*, 3 vols., New York, 1966–1970; Michael Botein, David M. Rice, and Edward B. Samuels, *Development and Regulation of New Communications Technologies*, New York, 1980; Asa Briggs, *The History of Broadcasting in the United Kingdom*, 4 vols., London and New York, 1961–1979; idem, ed., *Essays in the History of Publishing*, London, 1974; Benjamin M. Compaine, Christopher H. Sterling, Thomas Guback, and J. Kendrick Noble, Jr., *Who Owns the Media?* 2d ed., White Plains, N.Y., 1982; Margaret Dickinson and Sarah Street, *Cinema and State: The Film Industry and the British Government, 1927–1984*, London and Champaign, Ill., 1985; Elizabeth L. Eisenstein, *The Printing Press as an Agent of Change: Communications and Cultural Transformations in Early Modern Europe*, 2 vols., Cambridge and New York, 1979; Thomas I. Emerson, *Toward a General Theory of the First Amendment*, New York, 1966; Walter B. Emery, *National and International Systems of Broadcasting: Their History, Operation, and Control*, East Lansing, Mich., 1969; Fred W. Friendly, *The Good Guys, the Bad Guys, and the First Amendment*, New York, 1975; Harold A. Innis, *The Bias of Communication*, Toronto, 1951; Hiroshi Inose and John R. Pierce, *Information Technology and Civilization*, San Francisco, 1984; Jeffrey Kieve, *The Electric Telegraph in the U.K.: A Social and Economic History*, Newton Abbot, Eng., and New York, 1973; Ithiel de Sola Pool, *Technologies of Freedom: On Free Speech in an Electronic Age*, Cambridge, Mass., 1983; Anthony Smith, *The Newspaper: An International History*, London, 1979; John Wicklein, *Electronic Nightmare: The New Communications and Freedom*, New York, 1981.

ANTHONY SMITH

GRAMMAR

The study of the structure of words, phrases, and sentences is as old as recorded history. One of the first and most enduring goals of grammarians has been the codification of norms of LANGUAGE usage, especially of WRITING. In modern times linguists have sought to develop scientific theories of language structure and change, concentrating on spoken language. The latter enterprise has had three principal objectives: first, to trace the development of modern languages from ancient languages; second, to describe the differences and similarities among the languages of the world; and third, to gain insight into human psychology through the study of language.

The term *grammar* (from the Greek *grammata*, meaning "letters") refers to the study of linguistic structure. This may be construed either broadly, to include the investigation of MEANING (SEMANTICS) and sound patterns (PHONOLOGY), or narrowly, covering only the forms of words (morphology) and the ways they are put together into sentences (syntax). Except where explicitly noted, the narrow interpretation will be assumed here.

Among the most central concerns of grammarians are:

- the CLASSIFICATION of words into categories (parts of speech), based on their distributional patterns and semantic functions
- the order of elements in a sentence (e.g., the relative order of an adjective and the noun it modifies may differ across languages, as in the case of English and French)
- variations in the form of a word, depending on the context in which it appears, as in agreement *(He sings* versus *They sing)* and case marking *(Pat saw them* versus *They saw Pat)*

History

Like so much else in Western culture, the tradition of grammatical scholarship began in ancient Greece. PLATO is credited with first making the distinction between nouns and verbs. Dionysius Thrax, author of the oldest surviving systematic grammatical description of Greek (ca. 100 B.C.E.), identified eight parts of speech. Thrax's grammar served as a model for subsequent works on Greek and also for the Latin grammars of the Romans. Because Latin was the language of scholarship in the MIDDLE AGES, grammar in this period was concerned almost exclusively with Latin, the most influential work being Priscian's grammar (ca. 500 C.E.).

Throughout the classical and medieval periods, one major focus of grammatical studies was the identification of "faults" and "barbarisms" in common usage. This prescriptive aspect became increasingly important in later works, which were concerned not with the language of their own time but with the Latin of CICERO and Virgil. The notion that the grammarian's role is to define correct and incorrect uses of language persists into the present, though it has been rejected emphatically by modern academic linguists. *See also* LINGUISTICS.

The RENAISSANCE saw the rise of studies of the vernacular languages of Europe. This work was modeled on the classical Greco-Roman grammars, employing the same grammatical categories and focusing on literary language. Clear evidence of the importance of the normative view of grammar in this period was the establishment in the seventeenth century of the French Academy, whose task it was (and still is) to define "the art of speaking and writing correctly." The same century, however, also saw the emergence of "rational" grammars, which sought to demonstrate a common logical basis for the structure of human languages. The most famous of these was the *Grammaire générale et raisonnée,* published in 1660 by the teachers of Port Royal. *See also* LANGUAGE REFERENCE BOOK.

A major turning point in the history of linguistics came in the eighteenth century with the discovery by European scholars of the Indian grammatical tradition and the concurrent recognition of the historical kinship among Sanskrit, Greek, and Latin. Grammatical scholarship in India can be traced back to the second millennium B.C.E., the most famous of the ancient Indian grammarians being Pāṇini (probably fourth or fifth century B.C.E.). This tradition developed out of the desire to preserve certain orally transmitted religious texts from the inevitable changes in the language. Despite this normative motivation, the Sanskrit grammarians developed theoretical apparatuses for the description of languages far more sophisticated than anything available in Europe before the nineteenth century. In particular, their superiority in the transcription of pronunciation stimulated interest in the sound systems of languages among European linguists. The discovery that Sanskrit was related to Greek and Latin gave an enormous boost to the study of the history of what we now call the Indo-European languages.

The combination of these two trends resulted in the dominant focus of nineteenth-century linguistic scholarship, namely, determining what sound changes had taken place in the Indo-European language family and reconstructing the evolution of the members of that family. Probably the most famous results to emerge from this line of research are known as Grimm's law and Verner's law. Both were concerned with explaining certain systematic correspondences among the consonants of different languages, such as the fact that Germanic languages often have *f* where other Indo-European languages have *p* (as in English *father* versus Latin *pater).* Jacob Grimm postulated a prehistoric sound change in Germanic to account for these, and Karl Verner showed that a number of apparent exceptions to Grimm's law could be accounted for systematically. Late in the century a group of scholars known as the *Junggrammatiker* ("neogrammarians") argued that all sound changes operated without exceptions and that all apparent exceptions would fall under the scope of further laws.

In describing the history of languages, the grammarians of the nineteenth century turned away from the prescriptivism that had dominated earlier linguistic scholarship. In seeking exceptionless laws, the *Junggrammatiker* attempted to bring to the study of language the explanatory rigor associated with such fields as physics and chemistry. The twentieth century has been characterized by the extension of this more scientific approach to the synchronic description of languages—that is, to describing the state of a language at a given point in time.

The Swiss linguist FERDINAND DE SAUSSURE is usually credited with establishing the importance of (nonnormative) synchronic studies, but it was in the New World that this goal was most influential. Faced with a myriad of exotic Native American languages lacking any written records, linguists in North America found little in the prescriptivist or historical traditions of European grammatical scholarship that was applicable.

Some influential American linguists in the first half of the twentieth century concentrated on the development and employment of rigorous techniques of data collection and classification. This was in part a reaction to earlier work that had imposed the traditional Greco-Roman grammatical categories on non-Indo-European languages and in part a result of the importance of behaviorism in social science in the United States during that period. Many emphasized the diversity of languages and the importance of analyzing each language in its own terms. While some (notably EDWARD SAPIR and BENJAMIN LEE WHORF) speculated about the underlying thought processes of the speakers of exotic languages (reviving themes raised in earlier centuries by the German scholars Johann Gottfried von Herder and Wilhelm von Humboldt), others followed Leonard Bloomfield in eschewing "mentalistic" notions in their work.

In the 1950s and 1960s the study of grammar changed radically with the development of transformational grammar, first by Zellig Harris and his student Noam Chomsky and then later in a different direction by Chomsky and his followers. A number of factors made the time ripe for the emergence of a rigorous and explicit theory of language structure. These factors included advances in mathematical logic, the advent of computers (sparking interest in machine translation and other natural language applications), and the weakening of the behaviorist hold on the social sciences in the United States. The impact of Chomsky's 1957 monograph, *Syntactic Structures,* has been called revolutionary, and since the mid-1960s generative ideas have dominated grammatical scholarship.

Generative Grammar

The fundamental observation that was the starting point for generative grammar had been made at least as far back as the early nineteenth century by von Humboldt. It was simply that human languages are infinite, in the sense that there is no limit to the number of sentences in them. Hence, Chomsky argued, the Bloomfieldian emphasis on methods for compiling and organizing finite corpora was misguided, as were the informal heuristics of which traditional grammars are composed. Chomsky advocated the formulation of precise systems of rules that would distinguish sentences of a language from arbitrary strings of words. Much as the axioms and rules of inference in a mathematical theory will generate infinitely many theorems, the rules of a generative grammar should generate all and only the sentences of a language.

Beginning in the 1950s a branch of MATHEMATICS known as formal language theory was developed, based on this conception of grammar. Chomsky defined a hierarchy of types of grammars, differing in the sorts of formal operations permitted in their rules. Some types of grammars proved incapable of generating certain types of languages (where language, in this context, means simply a set of finite strings of symbols). Generative grammarians used these results, together with data from English and other languages, to argue for the inadequacy of some types of formal grammars as theories of natural language structure. Formal language theory has turned out to be important for computer science, in particular for the development of new computer languages and for the theory of compiling.

Having argued against various models of grammar for the description of natural languages, Chomsky put forward his theory, known as transformational grammar. A transformational grammar consists of two parts: a base grammar, which generates a set of abstract structures (called underlying or deep structures in some versions of transformational grammar), and a set of transformations, which are rules that turn the underlying structures into the actual sentences of the language. Among the most widely discussed transformations proposed for the grammar of English are a rule to derive passive sentences (e.g., *Wine was being drunk by children*) from active underlying structures (in this case, the deep structure of *Children were drinking wine*) and a rule to prepose question words (deriving *What did you eat?* from an underlying structure in which *what* follows *eat*). Various formulations (employing several notations) have been proposed for these rules and for the many other transformations that have been posited.

It is important to note that the inputs to transformations are not themselves sentences. Rather they are representations of the phrase structure of the sentences, often containing elements distinct from anything that appears on the surface. In the examples above, for instance, the underlying structures would not specify the inflectional forms of the verbs (e.g., *was* versus *were*), since these are affected by the operation of the transformations.

Chomsky explicitly rejected behaviorism, arguing that the reason for studying linguistic structure is the insight it can provide into the nature and organization of the human mind. Indeed, he uses the term *grammar* ambiguously to mean either the mental representation of a speaker's knowledge of a language or the linguist's codification of the structure of a language.

Chomsky goes on to advocate a rather strong version of nativism, claiming that the only way to account for the speed and ease with which children acquire language is to assume that much of what they appear to learn is genetically determined (*see* LANGUAGE ACQUISITION). Since any normal child will acquire whatever language he or she is exposed to, Chomsky's position entails a commitment to the claim that all human languages share a common core of structure. The goal of generative grammar is to determine what this core—or "universal grammar," as it is often called—consists of. The search for a common structure shared by all natural languages is reminiscent of the work of the seventeenth-century rational grammarians; indeed, as Chomsky himself has emphasized, modern transformational grammar resembles the earlier rational grammars not only in its general philosophical outlook but also in some of its specific analyses.

Given the enormous variation among the languages of the world in such features as word order, agreement, cases, genders, and word structure, generative grammarians have argued that linguistic universals must be rather abstract. Specific proposals regarding universal grammar have taken the form of general conditions on the form and functioning of grammatical rules. One specific example often cited by Chomsky is the fact that rules are always structure-dependent, in the sense that they are sensitive to the groupings of words in a sentence into phrases. For example, the English rule for forming yes-no questions involves preposing a tensed auxiliary verb, as in *Are you sleeping?* (corresponding to the declarative *You are sleeping*). If there is more than one tensed auxiliary verb in a sentence, it is the one in the main clause that gets preposed. Thus the yes-no question corresponding to *Someone who is working was talking about someone who is sleeping* is *Was someone who is working talking about someone who is sleeping?*, not *Is someone who working was talking about someone who is sleeping* or *Is someone who is working was talking about someone who sleeping*. (An asterisk before an example is used to indicate that it is not a well-formed sentence.) Which element gets preposed can be identified only with reference to the "main clause," which is a structural notion. No natural language, it is claimed, could have a rule that picked the first tensed auxiliary, regardless of its place in the phrase structure of

the sentence; nor could a language form questions by taking the words of the corresponding declarative in reverse order. Many other, more specific, constraints on the operation of grammatical rules have been proposed in the literature. Such constraints are claimed to provide insight into the nature and organization of the language faculty and hence of the human mind.

Over the years, generative grammarians have divided into a number of schools, each with its own formalism, terminology, and theoretical assumptions. Among the most influential have been generative semantics, relational grammar, lexical-functional grammar, generalized phrase-structure grammar, and government-binding theory. Though they all fall within the generative paradigm, they differ on such issues as the relationship between grammatical structure and meaning, the role of relational notions like *subject* and *object* in grammatical theory, and the need for transformations. Despite this factionalism Chomsky has remained a dominant figure, with his ideas largely defining the mainstream of generative research.

Alternatives to Generative Grammar

Although generative grammar has held center stage in grammatical scholarship since the early 1960s, other approaches to the study of linguistic structure have been pursued as well. Although there are far too many schools of thought to permit a comprehensive list, a few especially influential developments deserve some mention.

One line of research not really entirely separate from generative grammar is Montague grammar, named after the logician and philosopher Richard Montague. He attacked early generative work for its failure to deal with meaning in a serious way. Generativist semantic analyses at that time consisted of providing translations of natural language sentences into representations built up out of elements called semantic markers; no systematic interpretations for these elements were provided. Montague argued that semantic theory must specify a relationship between expressions of a language and things or states of affairs in the world, not just a translation into another language. Drawing on the formal tools of mathematical logic, he developed a rigorous system of rules for simultaneously constructing sentences of English and specifying the conditions under which they would be true. Although linguists were critical of the syntactic naïveté of this work, many were greatly impressed with the precision and sophistication of the semantics. Many of Montague's ideas have been incorporated into subsequent research, both within and outside the generative paradigm, and they have had a lasting effect on the way in which grammarians think about problems of meaning.

In the area of linguistic universals an approach different from the generative paradigm has been developed by Joseph Greenberg and his followers. Rather than investigating a small number of languages in depth looking for absolute laws of grammar, Greenberg surveyed hundreds of languages looking for strong statistical tendencies in observable distributional patterns. This effort has been extremely fruitful, yielding many previously unknown generalizations and leading to new proposals about the classification and historical relationships of languages. These generalizations have also been used by generativists as a source of evidence for grammatical universals.

Finally, one widespread criticism of Chomskyan linguistics is that it treats language strictly as a matter of individual psychology, failing to consider it as a social institution. Hence it has little or nothing to say about variations in language usage due to class, race, social context, or other external factors. The tradition of dialectology, whose concern with rigorous procedures of data collection and classification culminated in the great dialect atlases of Europe and the United States, was given a deeper theoretical foundation by U.S. linguist Uriel Weinreich. Weinreich's work has been continued in a more explicitly quantitative style by his pupil William Labov. The philosophers John Austin and Paul Grice independently pioneered the investigation of the uses to which language can be put and the mechanisms people employ to achieve various ends with language. These lines of research (as well as other work) have led to an increased appreciation of the ways in which linguistic communication can go beyond the conveyance of the literal meanings of words and sentences, and to the recognition that the structure of language is heavily influenced by its communicative functions. Indeed, even generativists now are aware that grammatical research cannot be confined wholly to intrasentential relations but must look at the wider context—linguistic and nonlinguistic—to correlate forms of language with facts about who is using them and to what end. *See also* LANGUAGE VARIETIES; SPEAKING, ETHNOGRAPHY OF.

Bibliography. Noam Chomsky, *Language and Mind,* enl. ed., New York, 1972; John Lyons, *Introduction to Theoretical Linguistics,* London, 1968; Frederick J. Newmeyer, *Linguistic Theory in America,* New York, 1980; R. H. Robins, *A Short History of Linguistics,* London, 1967, reprint (Indiana University Studies in the History and Theory of Linguistics) Bloomington, Ind., 1968; Neil Smith and Deirdre Wilson, *Modern Linguistics: The Results of Chomsky's Revolution,* Bloomington, Ind., 1979.

THOMAS WASOW

GRAMOPHONE. *See* SOUND RECORDING.

GRAMSCI, ANTONIO (1891–1937)

Italian theoretician and politician. Born in Ales, Sardinia, the son of lower-middle-class parents, Antonio Gramsci began his studies at the University of Turin in 1911 with the aid of a scholarship. There he was much influenced by the philosophy of Benedetto Croce and at the same time came into contact with the Turin working-class movement. He joined the Italian Socialist party (PSI) in 1913 and wrote for socialist newspapers. In 1919 he helped to establish a new weekly journal, *L'ordine nuovo,* to express the ideas of the factory council movement and to relate them to the Russian Revolution; in 1921 he became one of the founders of the Italian Communist party (PCI). He was arrested by the Fascist government in 1926, sentenced to more than twenty years' imprisonment, but was moved in 1935, critically ill, to a clinic in Rome, where he died in 1937.

Gramsci was one of the most original Marxist thinkers of this century. Many of his most important studies were written in prison and subsequently published as *Quaderni del carcere* (Prison Notebooks). His distinctive ideas concern the role of intellectuals in society and the complex of ideas, interpretations of the world, and social relations that they construct, which he terms *hegemony.* According to Gramsci all human beings are intellectuals in a broad sense, in that they possess rational capacities, but at present only some of them actually have an intellectual function. Those who have such a function he divides into two categories: traditional intellectuals, who expound and develop the body of ideas (e.g., religious ideas) inherited from earlier periods and in general help to sustain historical continuity and the status quo; and organic intellectuals, who are the thinkers and advocates of particular interests—especially class interests—and are particularly needed by a rising class that is trying to enhance its power and to establish a new social order.

Hegemony, for Gramsci, is the element of PERSUASION and consent that helps to sustain the rule of a dominant class. Thus on one side Gramsci defines the state as a system of force plus consent, in which the influence of a "dominant ideology," transmitted through all the institutions of civil society, is a crucial factor in maintaining class rule (*see* IDEOLOGY). On the other side he contests the "economistic" versions of Marxism, which involve "the iron conviction that there exist objective laws of historical development similar in kind to natural laws, together with a belief in a predetermined teleology like that of religion," and asserts the importance for a social group that is striving either to preserve or to establish its supremacy of "intellectual and moral leadership" by means of which it can dominate antagonistic groups and attract allies.

Gramsci's writings provide a major starting point

for studies of the role of intellectuals in modern societies; of the communication of ideas and beliefs that sustain, modify, or undermine an existing form of social life; and of the nature and significance of consent as against coercion in the overall regulation of behavior. Some later critics, however, have suggested that Gramsci overemphasized the element of consent and the influence of a dominant ideology in the modern state.

See also MARX, KARL; MARXIST THEORIES OF COMMUNICATION.

Bibliography. Alastair Davidson, *Antonio Gramsci: Towards an Intellectual Biography,* London, 1977; Quintin Hoare and Geoffrey Nowell Smith, eds., "Introduction," *Selections from the Prison Notebooks of Antonio Gramsci,* London, 1971; Anne Showstack Sassoon, "Gramsci, Antonio," in *A Dictionary of Marxist Thought,* ed. by Tom Bottomore, Oxford, 1983.

TOM BOTTOMORE

GRAPHIC REPRODUCTION

The term *graphic reproduction* refers to any technological process that can copy, duplicate, replicate, multiply, and serve in the distribution of pictures. Graphic reproductions may include copies of paintings intended as framed wall decorations, BOOK and MAGAZINE illustrations based on drawings or paintings, photographs transformed into PRINTING processes for all manner of publication, and even paper prints mounted on stereograph cards. They also include posters (*see* POSTER), postcards, and other formats for multiplying and distributing copies of original pictures.

Most frequently graphic reproduction refers to some aspect or product of the graphic arts. These involve paper and printers' inks and include the traditional printmaking techniques such as wood engraving, etching, aquatint, mezzotint, and lithography as well as the multitude of photographic technologies developed in the nineteenth century and brought to a high degree of color sophistication in the twentieth (*see* PHOTOGRAPHY). Among the most common types of photographic technologies, aside from the simple multiplication of prints from an original negative, were heliotype, collotype, photogravure, halftone process engraving, and photolithography, which developed into offset printing. During the transition period between the use of the traditional graphic arts to multiply images and the success of the photographic technologies, experimental graphic reproduction processes bore fanciful names like Artotype and Heliogravure. The transition, lasting from approximately 1870 to 1893, ended with the domination of graphic reproduction processes by photography, even to the extent that the chromolithograph, widely enjoyed as a relatively cheap method of reproducing paintings, gave way to the four-color halftone process and a variety of gravure color techniques.

As major vehicles for the mass distribution of visual information in pictures, the graphic arts and printing processes have influenced the sciences as well as the visual arts. More broadly, analysis of the social impact of the visual media indicates that the graphic processes of reproduction, especially the photographic technologies, revolutionized the ways in which people perceive reality. Permanently altering the relationship between the fine arts and the popular arts, the graphic reproduction processes expanded educational strategies for young people and helped to establish entire new industries of communication. The implications of graphic reproduction processes therefore extend to far more than the study of their technologies and encompass aspects of communications theory beginning with theories of visual perception (*see* PERCEPTION—STILL AND MOVING PICTURES)

HERODOTI HISTORICI INCIPIT.
Laurentii Vallen. conuersio de Græco in Latinum.

h ERODOTI Halicarnasci historiæ explicatio hæc est: ut neq; ea quæ gesta sunt: ex rebus humanis obliterentur ex æuo: neq; ingentia & admiranda opera: uel a Græcis edita: uel a Barbaris gloria fraudêtur: cum alia: tum uero: qua de re isti inter se belligerauerût. Persarû eximii memorât dissensionû auctores extitisse Phœnices qui a mari quod Rubrum uocatur: in hoc nostrum proficiscentes: & hanc incolentes regionem: quam nunc quoq; incolunt: longinquis continuo nauigationibus incubuerunt: faciendisq; Aegyptiarum & Assyriarum merciû uecturis in alias plagas: præcipueq; Argos traiecerunt. Argos & enim ea tempestate omni

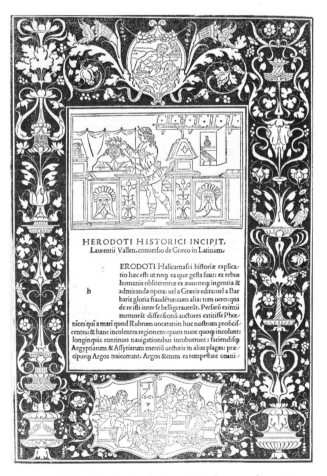

Figure 1. *(Graphic Reproduction)* Title page from Herodotus, *Historiae* (Venice: Gregoriis, 1494). Woodcut. The Metropolitan Museum of Art, New York, The Elisha Whittelsey Collection, The Elisha Whittelsey Fund, 1959. (59.508.93)

I have seen full many a sight
Born of day or drawn by night:
Sunlight on a silver stream,
Golden lilies all a-dream,
Lofty mountains, bold and proud,
Veiled beneath the lacelike cloud;
But no lovely sight I know
Equals Dinah kneading dough.

15

Figure 2. *(Graphic Reproduction)*   Paul Laurence Dunbar, *Candle-Lightin' Time*, New York, 1901. Two pages with photograph and poem. Butler Library, Columbia University in the City of New York.

and continuing into mass PERSUASION and symbolic structures.

Considerable human effort has been dedicated to inventing techniques for multiplying pictures. These techniques often paralleled but are considered to have preceded the invention of movable metal type (*see* TYPOGRAPHY) used for distributing ideas expressed in words, a process ordinarily called printing, although this term applies equally to pictorial processes. Many of the relief processes like woodcut were invented in East Asia as early as the first century B.C.E., along with the paper needed to support ink images (*see* EAST ASIA, ANCIENT; WRITING MATERIALS). The dispersion of both the idea of a repeatable image and the manufacture of paper can be traced through Central Asia to the Arab centers of culture, finally reaching Europe sometime around the eleventh century. European metalsmiths in the Gothic period probably can be credited with discovering the action of acids on copper and zinc, leading to the

development of the intaglio process of etching. These same smiths had already engraved designs on chivalric armor of the medieval knights and on sword pommels, goblets, jewelry, and seals cut into rings (*see* HERALDRY). In engraving, as in etching, the DESIGN to be printed was cut into a metal or wood surface so that the ink was below the surface of the printing plate. In the relief process the designs were on the surface of the printing block, with the areas not printed cut below the surface.

The relief processes were predominant in many early RENAISSANCE books, in both illustration and text, simply because woodcut was compatible with the relief metal types invented by JOHANNES GUTENBERG and his colleagues during the mid-fifteenth century. Because they could not be printed simultaneously with type, etchings and engravings had to be printed separately on special intaglio presses and then inserted into the text; sometimes pages had to run through two different types of presses to accommo-

Figure 3. *(Graphic Reproduction)* Pierre Bonnard, page 27 from *Parallèlement,* by Paul Verlaine (Paris: Ambroise Vollard, 1900). Lithograph, printed in color, page size: 11⅝ by 9½ in. Collection, The Museum of Modern Art, New York. Louis E. Stern Collection.

Figure 4. *(Graphic Reproduction)* Vladimir Lebedev, illustration for *Circus* (1925), a children's book. From Szymon Bojko, *New Graphic Design in Revolutionary Russia,* New York: Praeger Publishers, 1972.

Figure 5. *(Graphic Reproduction)* David Lucas, after John Constable, *Noon*, 1830. Mezzotint. The Metropolitan Museum of Art, New York, Harris Brisbane Dick Fund, 1925. (25.51.14)

date the mode of graphic reproduction. Obviously such double press runs were expensive and not conducive to speed of publication. *See* PUBLISHING—HISTORY OF PUBLISHING.

The major modern technique for multiplying pictures was invented at the end of the eighteenth century by an enterprising music publisher seeking a way to print and distribute music scores. The process was lithography, based on the discovery that printing ink and water mutually repel. While this planographic method was at first an artist's medium, enjoyed by such masters as Eugène Delacroix and Théodore Géricault, by about 1830 lithography began to be used in the manufacture of books, posters, and illustrations in both Europe and North America. As an illustration medium, lithography had several advantages: artists could draw directly on the prepared lithographic stone, and freshly inked type pages could be transferred to the same stone. There had been developed a reasonably inexpensive method of combining text with picture, an essential characteristic of modern communication.

The number of pictures distributed through the relief, intaglio, and planographic processes, along with their photographic equivalents, must be counted in the millions. The lucrative practice of copying paintings dominated the market, but graphic reproductions included political satires, memento mori of the deaths of royalty, celebrations of important events, religious symbols and stories, architectural drawings, botanical representations, pictures of far-off places both real and fanciful, fashion plates, and other subjects used in educational tracts and commercial catalogs. To keep up with demand a new practice involving a strict division of labor was firmly established by the nineteenth century. An artist or drafts-

man created the original image, a specialist in the selected printing medium transformed that image into lines suited to reproduction in that specific medium, and another specialist printed the final plate. This division of labor eventuated in the cutting up of large boxwood blocks used for illustration in the pictorial press—for example, *Harper's Weekly* in the 1870s—giving sections of the blocks to specialists in cutting various textures for sky, skin, trees, horses, or city scenes. The block was then reassembled for printing.

In studying the complex history of graphic reproduction processes, William Ivins, Jr., formerly curator of prints at New York's Metropolitan Museum of Art, came to the conclusion that the development of specialized textures over the centuries raised issues about what he called "the syntax of visual communication." Ivins's *Prints and Visual Communication* (1953) was the first attempt to document visually the progress of the graphic arts toward what he believed to be the only graphic medium without interfering syntax: photography. If the traditional graphic arts did away with the copying errors of the medieval manuscript illuminators, it was not until the invention of photography in the early nineteenth century that nature could be recorded directly. For Ivins photography's greatest benefit was the elimination of both the artist-draftsman and the transfer specialist, since both represented further removes from reality. With the invention of technologies that enabled photography to become a graphic reproduction medium compatible with metal relief type, Ivins was persuaded that the major technical problems of visual communication had been solved, at least in terms of ink and paper. He was satisfied that photographic reproductions were faithful to originals, despite the fact that they, like the older graphic arts, suffered considerable losses of scale, color, and the three-dimensionality of painting textures. Further research by other historians suggests that photography too has a visual syntax, as must all media that translate reality into two-dimensional images. *See* VISUAL IMAGE.

Most important to Ivins was that the advent of photography had altered judgments about reality. As he observed, "Up to that time very few people had been aware of the differences between pictorial expression and pictorial communication of statements of fact." Gradually but inexorably photographic technologies assumed the task of pictorial communication of statements of fact, and photography became the standard for truth in visual communication.

Long before Canadian philosopher of media MAR-SHALL MCLUHAN offered similar theories, German critic WALTER BENJAMIN observed that human sense perceptions altered as the MODE of existence of entire cultures changed. For Benjamin the manner in which perception is organized through specific media is determined by historical circumstances. These include the technologies available for the transmission of visual images at any time in the history of a society. In his influential essay "The Work of Art in the Age of Mechanical Reproduction" (1936) Benjamin stated that the mechanization of graphic reproduction destroys the "authenticity" of an object. Authenticity refers to the essence of an object, ranging from its duration in time to the history it experiences as an enduring physical presence. Reproducing

Figure 6. *(Graphic Reproduction) Sioux Chiefs' Delegation in the East Room of the White House, 1877.* Engraving from a photograph by Matthew Brady. From *Frank Leslie's Illustrated Newspaper*, October 13, 1877, p. 81. Courtesy of the Library of Congress.

Figure 7. *(Graphic Reproduction)*   Charles R. Parsons and Lyman W. Atwater, *An American Railway Scene, at Hornesville, Erie Railway.* Chromolithograph. Printed by Currier and Ives, New York, 1874. Amon Carter Museum, Fort Worth, Tex.

an object for mass distribution removes the original ARTIFACT from the crucial social nexus of tradition and RITUAL for whose purposes it was originally created. Benjamin prophesied that many ART objects, including paintings, would be created for the sole purpose of sales as graphic reproductions, thereby substituting commodity mechanization for original authenticity.

Following Benjamin's lead, English art critic John Berger, in *Ways of Seeing* (1972), claimed that modern reproductions do more than diminish the authority of an original object: "For the first time ever, images of art have become ephemeral, ubiquitous, insubstantial, available, valueless, free." While the general illusion is that reproductions make it possible for the masses to appreciate art, the reality is that originals remain high-priced commodities for the elite. Both Benjamin and Berger saw discussions of graphic reproduction as belonging to the realms of politics and class struggle.

French art historian André Malraux was less pessimistic about the influence of graphic reproduction on society, observing in his influential *Musée imaginaire* (Museum without Walls, 1965) that photographic technologies had opened the riches of all cultures to artists and the public alike. Malraux noted that through graphic reproduction the arts of Oceania, Africa, the Eskimo, and the Australian Aborigine as well as pre-Columbian SCULPTURE and Gothic ARCHITECTURE have become not only available but incorporated into the visual experiences of the twentieth century, just as Chinese and Japanese arts were incorporated into European arts in the nineteenth century, especially through the introduction of the Japanese woodcut. Owing to ever more sophisticated methods of graphic reproduction, art books are becoming the universal substitute for the MUSEUM; they are "the museum without walls." For Malraux the effect of exposure to the multiplicity of cultures would be beneficial to the development of an international consciousness.

Because the photographic print itself is implicated by some critics as a multiplied object having no definable authenticity, photography has come under attack as being nothing more than a graphic reproduction medium, unable to join painting, for example, as having the authority of the unique. As the electronic media and holography enter into the technologies of graphic reproduction, issues such as this will continue to arise. The act of multiplying images as a means of mass visual communication has serious implications for the sociologist, the political scientist, the aesthete, the art historian, and the economist.

See also AESTHETICS.

Figure 8. *(Graphic Reproduction)* José Guadalupe Posada, *Ballad Sheet for All Souls' Day: The Bicycles,* 1890s. Metal cut. The Metropolitan Museum of Art, New York, Gift of Jean Charlot, 1930. (30.82.112)

Bibliography. Walter Benjamin, "The Work of Art in the Age of Mechanical Reproduction," in *Illuminations* (Illuminationen, Frankfurt, 1955), ed. with an intro. by Hannah Arendt, New York, 1969; John Berger, *Ways of Seeing,* London, 1972; William M. Ivins, *Prints and Visual Communication,* London, 1953, reprint Cambridge, Mass., 1969; Estelle Jussim, *Visual Communication and the Graphic Arts: Photographic Technologies in the Nineteenth Century,* New York, 1974; André Malraux, *Museum without Walls* (Musée imaginaire), trans. by Stuart Gilbert and Francis Price, Garden City, N.Y., 1967.

ESTELLE JUSSIM

GRAPHICS

Means for the visual display and communication of information, including diagrams, networks, matrices, and maps. Through graphics we can exploit the properties of visual PERCEPTION to display and communicate information. Because graphics involves the organization and display of previously given data, it constitutes the rational part of the world of images. The main issues of modern graphics discussed here are matrix theory, the semiology of graphics, and the choice of a graphic construction.

Matrix theory utilizes the notion of information level to define the purpose of graphics. We construct a graphic in order to understand a problem—that is, to simplify it by reducing a vast amount of elementary data to a small number of categories of information that we are capable of taking into account at a given moment.

The semiology of graphics describes the properties and functions of the graphic SIGN SYSTEM. The different visual variables lead to a variety of possible constructions, which with the aid of matrix theory we may analyze and define in terms of their utility. The reorderable matrix offers a solution to most graphic problems. First the data set is represented in the form of a double-entry table, in which x and y are the orthogonal dimensions of the table and z is depicted by a variation in light energy at each meaningful point in the table. The data on x and y are then permuted to reveal the groups that constitute the pertinent information. However, with certain problems the nature of the data requires other types of constructions.

The choice of a graphic construction thus depends on the number of characteristics involved, the nature of the series of objects to be represented (ordered or reorderable), and the types of relationships existing among the objects. A synoptic table of graphic constructions will be used to show the most appropriate construction for each case.

The Matrix Theory of Graphics

We represent data graphically to better understand a problem, to more readily read the numbers, to more easily attain the highest level of information (i.e., the overall level). This notion of level enables us to determine the most useful construction for a given problem.

Information levels. Information implies the answer to a question. The following simplified example illustrates the nature and level of questions we can ask in approaching a data table.

In 1966 the five ministers of the European Economic Community (EEC) met to discuss meat production. They had numerous statistics at their disposal. Figure 1 shows the production of five types of meat (the columns) in the five countries (the rows); as with any table, we can consider three types of questions:

- questions involving x: A given meat is produced in which country? (a)
- questions involving y: A given country produces which meat? (b)

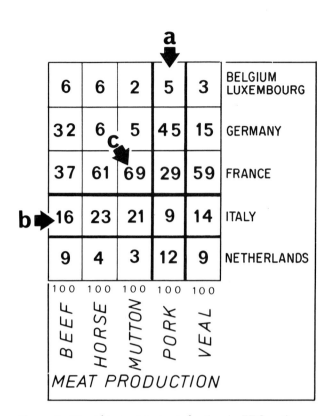

Figure 1. *(Graphics)* Meat production in EEC nations.

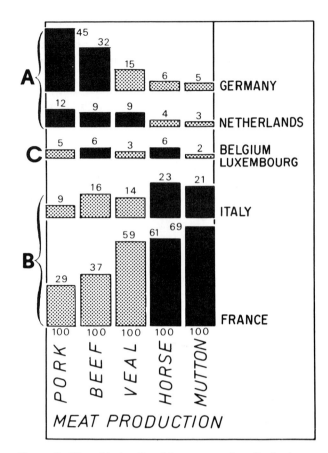

Figure 2. *(Graphics)* Graphic construction displaying essential information from Figure 1.

• questions involving *z:* Where do the highest percentages occur? (c)

For each type of question there are also three levels: elementary, intermediate, and overall. Elementary questions (e.g., What percentage of the total pork production does Italy account for?) can be answered by looking at the number in the box. This is elementary data, the raw material that information processing must work to transform. Our memory cannot retain the multiplicity of elementary data; understanding means reducing, simplifying, discovering similar elements, grouping them, and classing them—that is, processing them. This is the first goal of modern graphics. Intermediate questions (e.g., What kinds of meat production does Italy have?) correspond to all the subsets generated by the data table. Overall questions (e.g., How are the countries grouped?) cannot be answered visually by referring to the data table; we need to look at a construction like that in Figure 2, which displays the essential information. The Federal Republic of Germany and the Netherlands are similar in structure, based on the predominance of pork and beef. They form one group (A), in contrast to another group (B), formed by France and Italy, that has the opposite structure. Consequently, within the framework of these data,

the policies of groups A and B can only be opposed or complementary.

Reducing these four countries to two groups makes the most useful information appear. Whether the dimensions of the table are 5, 50, or 500, in every case the goal is to reduce these dimensions to the smallest possible number of groups.

The overall level is the high ground of understanding and responsible decision making. Moreover, when we can answer a question on this level, questions on the other levels also elicit a meaningful answer, one that either confirms the general structure of the data or constitutes a meaningful exception to it. As illustrated in Figure 2, for example, the deciding vote in case of a tie would obviously belong to the Belgo-Luxembourg Union (C), which marks an exception to the main structure defined by A and B. Understanding also means interpreting the exceptions.

Three basic questions. Utilizing a graphic thus involves three successive steps: identifying the data, defining the overall structure, and discovering the exceptions. This amounts to asking three questions:

1. What is the problem? More specifically, what are the *x, y,* and *z* components of the data table?
2. What is the information? More specifically, what are the groups formed by the data in *x, y,* and *z*?

3. What are the exceptions to these groups?

This approach means that we do not "read" a graphic; we "question" it. The answer to the first question is relatively easy if the graphic arrangement is simple, the writing legible, and the wording precise and concise. The answer to the second question excludes constructions that are not permuted and those that answer only elementary questions. The answer to the third question depends on the definition of the overall structure (i.e., on the answer to the second question). These three basic questions provide the means of determining the most appropriate construction among a variety of possibilities derived from combinations of different visual variables (see Figure 3).

The Semiology of Graphics

Graphics exploits the means and properties of visual perception in order to represent data. Essentially data can be seen as a relation between two elements that takes one of the following forms:

- a simple difference: A is different from B ($\neq$)
- an order: B is between A and C (O)
- a proportion: A is two times greater than B (Q)

The visual variables. To represent these relations, graphics utilizes the eight types of perceptual variation distinguishing two marks. Not all of these variables can express order or proportion. Figure 4 classes the variables according to their properties.

On the plane formed by the graphic there are three types of marks: the point, the line, and the area. The combination of points and lines produces two types of data representation: the network and the matrix. The network results from representing the elements by points and the relations by lines, as in Figure 5. This construction is appropriate for representing relations among the elements of a single set (Figure 6). However, it will be legible only for a small number of relations. The area can be used to represent relations of inclusion, as in Figure 6.

The matrix results from representing the elements by lines and the relations by points, as in Figure 7. This construction, almost always legible, is appropriate for representing the relations between two different sets. The double-entry table is the most widely used example of the matrix construction, which favors the analysis and transformation of what we shall call the image, the meaningful visual form perceptible in the minimum instant of vision.

Properties and limits of the image. The image has three dimensions. The meaningful form constituting

Figure 3. *(Graphics)* Constructions derived by combining different visual variables. None of these constructions answers the three basic questions. ▷

BEEF VEAL MUTTON HORSE PORK

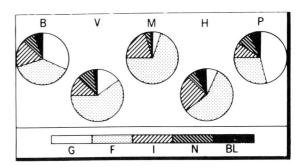

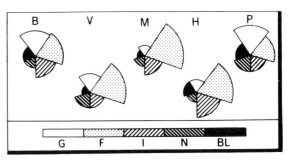

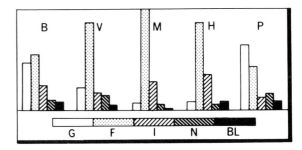

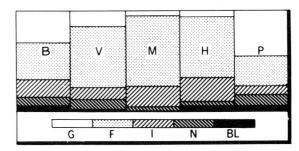

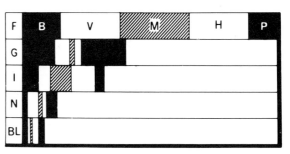

G. GERMANY   F. FRANCE   I. ITALY

N. NETHERLANDS   BL. BELGIUM LUXEMBOURG

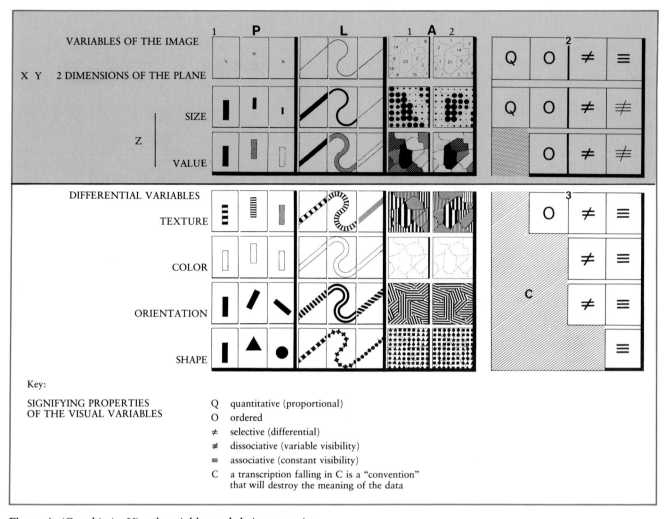

Key:

SIGNIFYING PROPERTIES
OF THE VISUAL VARIABLES

Q quantitative (proportional)
O ordered
≠ selective (differential)
≢ dissociative (variable visibility)
≡ associative (constant visibility)
C a transcription falling in C is a "convention"
   that will destroy the meaning of the data

Figure 4. *(Graphics)*   Visual variables and their properties.

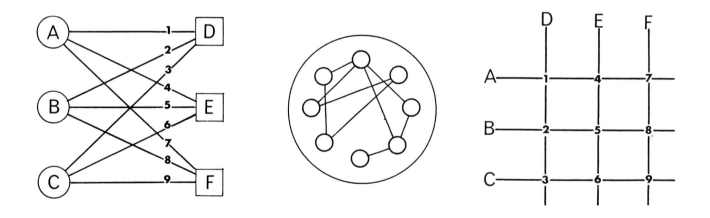

Figure 5. *(Graphics; left)*   Network construction.

Figure 6. *(Graphics; center)*   Network construction
showing relations among elements of a single set.

Figure 7. *(Graphics; right)*   Matrix construction.

an image is produced by the x and y (orthogonal) dimensions of the plane and a z variation in light energy obtained by differences in the size and value of the marks (see Figure 4). An image can represent the relationships among three independent sets (Figure 8).

The image has only three dimensions. Individual images (Figure 9) will be destroyed by a superimposition (Figure 10); we see only their sum. If that sum is not meaningful, the overall form is useless. To represent the relationships among n sets, graphics offers three solutions:

- A juxtaposition of images, each with two or three dimensions (Figure 9). We can, for example, establish collections of tables or maps, whose permutation (Figure 11) produces a partial answer, involving x or y, to the second basic question (i.e., concerning the groups formed by the data).
- A superimposition of images (see Figure 10). This will only produce an answer on the elementary level, but that level can be useful, as in the reading of a map. Distinguishing among superimposed images involves the use of differential variables (see Figure 4).
- The reorderable matrix. This construction combines the perceptual properties of the eye with the technical possibilities of permuting rows and columns. The eye can perceive leaves, a branch, or the entire tree; that is, it operates on all three levels of information. The perception of similarities and differences enables us to control the regrouping of elements in such a way as to construct an image that answers all three types of basic questions.

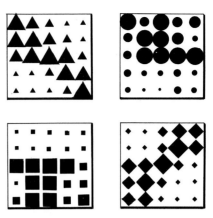

Figure 9. *(Graphics)* Juxtaposition of individual images.

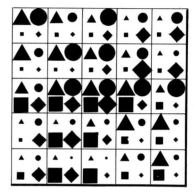

Figure 10. *(Graphics)* Superimposition of images from Figure 9.

The xyz structure of the data table. Before constructing a graphic, we represent the data in the form of a double-entry table whose structure approximates that of the image. The series of objects (individuals, dates, places, products, objects) is on x, the series of characteristics attributed to these objects is on y, and the answer, or relationship of each object to each characteristic, appears in z (i.e., in the boxes, or cells, of the table). This answer can be a quantity, an order (good, average, bad), a yes/no (binary) alternative, an unknown (?), or not applicable. When the data come from different tables, we must rework the tables in order to utilize a single *xyz* structure. This is termed the *matrix analysis of the data.*

Construction of the reorderable matrix involves reproducing the *xyz* structure of the data table, representing the z dimension by a variation in size or value, and permuting rows and/or columns to discover groups, thus displaying the overall information. This permutation of rows and columns can be done by simply cutting out the various forms on pieces of paper so that they can be rearranged. Although larger matrices obviously require special equipment, the personal computer has made permutation a routine matter. Whatever the equipment, we

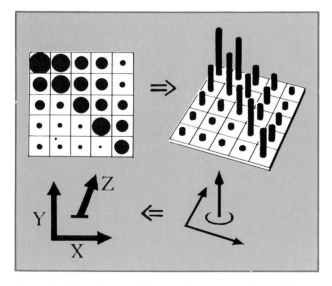

Figure 8. *(Graphics)* Relationships among three different sets.

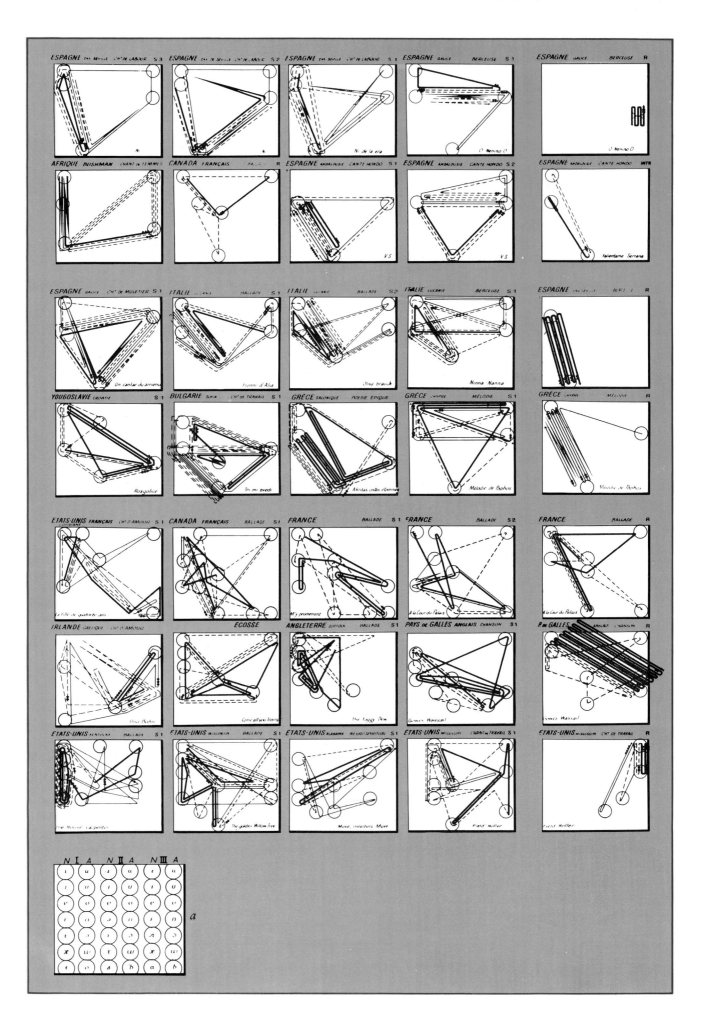

◁ **Figure 11.** *(Graphics)* Permutation of collections. In order to compare various folk songs, the vowels are used as the basis for a "vocalic map" *(a)*. The succession of vowels in each stanza of a given song traces a characteristic image of the song on the map. This classification reveals three levels of complexity among the songs and displays the refrains on the right. From Alan Lomax and E. Trager, *Phonotactique du chant populaire*, Paris, 1954.

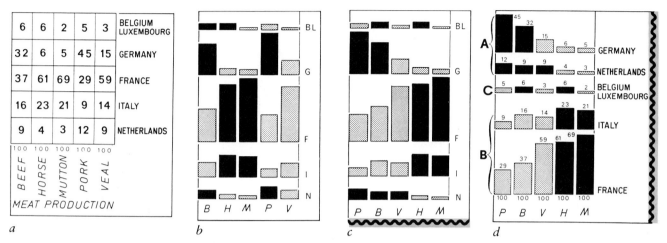

a   *b*   *c*   *d*

Figure 12. *(Graphics)* *(a)* Data table; *(b)* construction of image based on order of table; *(c)* regrouping of similar columns; *(d)* regrouping of similar rows.

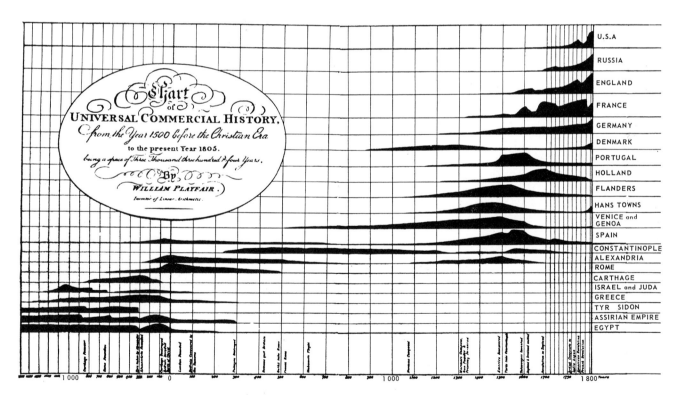

Figure 13. *(Graphics)* Playfair's reclassification of civilizations according to era and longevity. From William Playfair, *An Inquiry into the Permanent Causes of the Decline and Fall of Powerful and Wealthy Nations*, London, 1805.

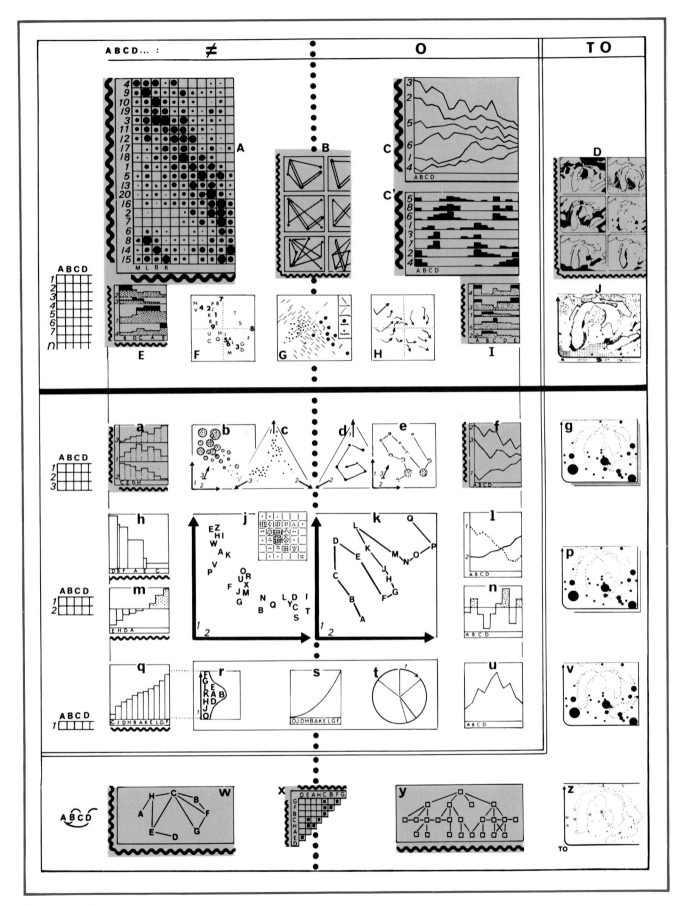

Figure 14. *(Graphics)* Main types of graphic constructions.

first construct, based on the order of the table (Figure 12 [a]), the image (b). Next, exercising strict visual control, we regroup the similar columns (c), then the similar rows (d). This process of reclassing is the visual form of information processing; it adds to the classic concept of the immutably constructed graphic image the notion of the transformable, mobile image that characterizes modern graphics. This notion is by no means of recent invention: as early as 1805 William Playfair reclassified various civilizations according to their era and longevity (Figure 13). If the data table is extensive, we have to use some automated means of permuting, but there are hundreds of methods with different results, thus posing the

problem of interpretation. The reorderable matrix then becomes the basis for this interpretation.

The Choice of a Graphic Construction

The synoptic table in Figure 14 shows the main types of graphic constructions. The choice of a construction depends primarily on the structure of the data table, that is, on the number of characteristics and the properties—ordered (O), reorderable ($\neq$), or topographic (TO)—of the series of objects.

If the table has more than three characteristics, the solution stems from the transformable nature of the modern graphic image. The standard construction is

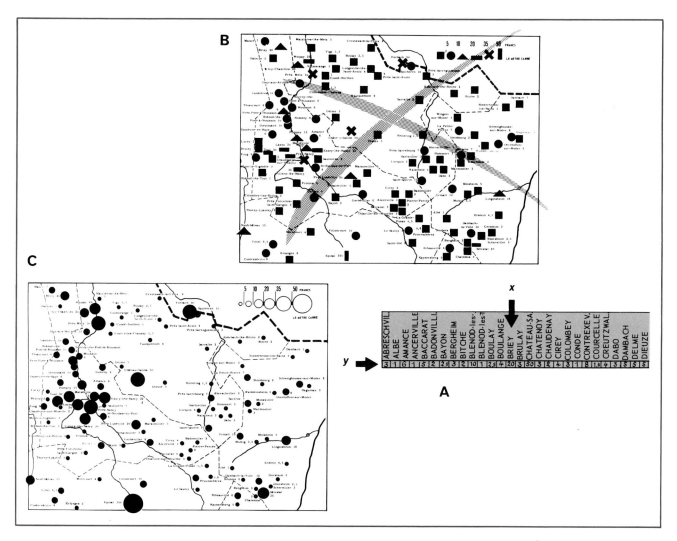

Figure 15. *(Graphics)* Maps with one characteristic. Maps B and C display the information in table A, where *x* lists cities and the single row in *y* shows land prices. Map B, which represents the prices by a variation in shape, answers only questions involving *x* ("What is the case for a given place?"). This map must be "read" point by point. Map C, which represents the prices by the size of the marks—that is, by a variation in light energy—also answers questions involving *y* ("Where do we find a given case?" and "Where are the expensive areas?"). Because this map can be "seen," it answers questions of all types and levels.

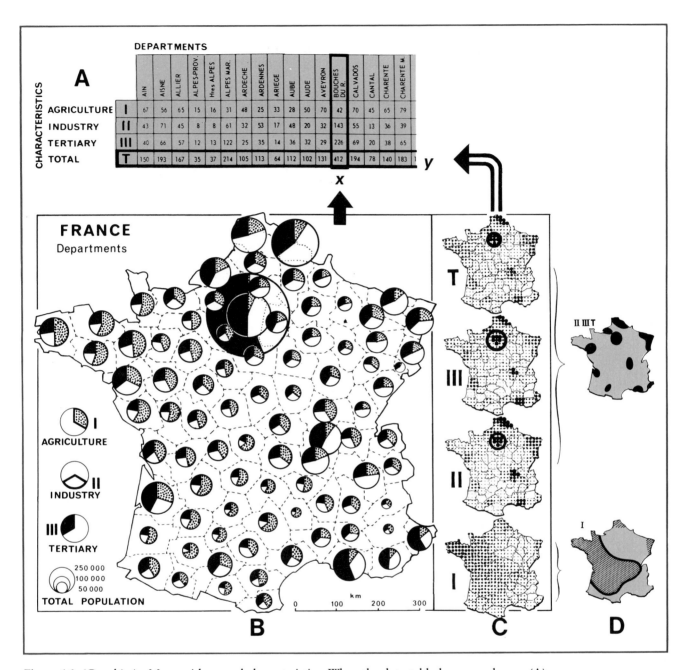

		AIN	AISNE	ALLIER	ALPES-PROV.	Htes ALPES	ALPES MAR.	ARDECHE	ARDENNES	ARIEGE	AUBE	AUDE	AVEYRON	BOUCHES DU R.	CALVADOS	CANTAL	CHARENTE	CHARENTE M.	
AGRICULTURE	I	67	56	65	15	16	31	48	25	33	28	50	70	42	70	45	65	79	
INDUSTRY	II	43	71	45	8	8	61	32	53	17	48	20	32	143	55	13	36	39	
TERTIARY	III	40	66	57	12	13	122	25	35	14	36	32	29	226	69	20	38	65	
TOTAL	T	150	193	167	35	37	214	105	113	64	112	102	131	412	194	78	140	183	1

Figure 16. *(Graphics)*   Maps with several characteristics. When the data table has several rows (A), a superimposition map answers questions involving *x* ("What is the case for a given place?"). A superimposition is useful whenever the map is to function as a precise reference instrument (e.g., tourist maps, architectural drawings, industrial plans). In these instances we use the differential variables— texture, color, orientation, or shape—to distinguish each characteristic. But such a map will not answer questions involving *y* ("Where do we find a given case?"). Only maps with a single characteristic can answer all such questions, and they alone can make groups appear (D). When both types of questions are pertinent, we use a collection (C) along with a superimposition (B).

the reorderable matrix (A), which can take the following forms:

- the array of curves (C) and the image-file (C'), when the objects are ordered
- the weighted matrix (E) and the weighted file (I), when the overall total of the data table is meaningful
- the collection of tables (B) and the collection of maps (D), when the best discrimination is produced by either two ordered characteristics or topographic order

Factorial clusters (F, H) can represent the results of various mathematical classings. The superimposition of tables (G) or maps (J) is appropriate with a small number of characteristics but involves a problem of visual differentiation.

If the table has fewer than four characteristics, each is represented by one of the dimensions of the image, and the relations will appear directly, without reclassing. The standard construction is the scatterplot with two characteristics (j), which takes the form of (k) when the objects are ordered. Depending on the problem, we can use (b) and (e), scatterplots with three characteristics, or (c) and (d), triangular constructions (generally appropriate when the sum of the three characteristics is meaningful). A small number of objects will lead to matrix constructions—(a), (f), or (l)—or to a histogram (h). A meaningful difference between two characteristics will lead to (m) or (n).

If the table has only one row, the standard constructions are the distribution diagram (r) and the time series, or "chronogram" (u). The repartition, or "cumulative curve" (q), and the concentration (s) respond to specific questions. With a very small number of objects, we can use a pie chart (t).

If the relations involve the elements of a single set, we use a reorderable network (w) or an ordered network whose order is based on a single dimension of the plane (y). A network can also take the form of a matrix (x).

A map is an ordered network whose order is based on both dimensions of the plane (z). The nature of the order is determined by that of the object being represented (e.g., geographical space, the heavens, a human being, a piece of furniture). A map represents relations of proximity among the elements of an object (see CARTOGRAPHY). This is accomplished by using the xy dimensions of the plane, which means that if the z dimension of the image is used to represent quantities, there are no further dimensions available for representing n characteristics. In topography it is advisable to distinguish maps with one characteristic (Figure 14 [v] and Figure 15) from those with n characteristics (Figure 14 [j] and Figure 16). The properties of color enable us to superimpose two maps (p) or three maps (g), each with one characteristic. Beyond that, we need to use a collection (D) coupled with a superimposition (J) to answer all the pertinent questions.

Graphics and the Computer

Graphics owes a great deal to the computer. By minimizing the constraints of traditional drafting and facilitating the permutation of rows and columns, the computer enables us to cross the three-dimensional barrier imposed by the image and tackle problems with n dimensions (see COMPUTER: IMPACT). But the computer also owes a great deal to graphics, which constitutes its most powerful language for processing and communicating information, provided of course that the universal laws governing visual perception are understood, respected, and exploited.

Bibliography. Jacques Bertin, *Graphics and Graphic Information-Processing* (La graphique et le traitement graphique de l'information), trans. by William J. Berg and Paul Scott, Berlin and New York, 1981; idem, *Semiology of Graphics: Diagrams, Networks, Maps* (Sémiologie graphique), trans. by William J. Berg, Madison, Wis., 1983; Serge Bonin, *Initiation à la graphique*, Paris, 1975; Willard C. Brinton, *Graphic Methods for Presenting Facts*, New York, 1914; Otto Neurath, *Basic by Isotype*, London, 1937; William Playfair, *The Statistical Breviary*, London, 1801; Edward R. Tufte, *The Visual Display of Quantitative Information*, Cheshire, Conn., 1983; Howard Wainer and David Thissen, "Graphical Data Analysis," *Annual Review of Psychology* 32 (1981): 191–241.

JACQUES BERTIN
(Translated by William J. Berg)

GREELEY, HORACE (1811–1872)

U.S. editor and publisher. Horace Greeley began his career as a youth setting type for small New England newspapers and PRINTING houses. After his father failed at farming and went west, Greeley moved to New York. He ran a printing house for several years before becoming associated with Thurlow Weed and William Seward as publisher of various political newspapers such as the *Constitution,* the *Jeffersonian,* and the *Log Cabin,* all of which were intended to advance Whig candidates. He also published the *New-Yorker,* a weekly miscellany that borrowed its contents liberally from other publications. His first attempt at a "cheap-for-cash" newspaper was as printer in 1833 for the *New York Morning Post,* which failed to attract a mass readership and folded.

Greeley issued the first copies of the *New York Tribune* in 1841 and with it began his rise to fame as a newspaper publisher at a time when the new

Figure 1. *(Greeley, Horace)* Thomas Nast, caricature of Horace Greeley, 1866. Historical Pictures Service, Chicago.

sensational penny press was beginning to capture the interest of New York readers. Journalism historian Frank Luther Mott notes that the *Tribune* was nicknamed the "Great Moral Organ" because of Greeley's high moral and ethical standards and his expressed aversion to "the immoral and degrading police reports, advertisements and other matter which have been allowed to disgrace the columns of our leading Penny Papers." Yet he soon found that to compete for circulation he must use crime stories, advertisements, and even theatrical reports.

Greeley's greatest impact came through the pages of the *Weekly Tribune,* which he founded about six months after the daily version by combining the *New-Yorker* and the *Log Cabin.* This weekly publication, which eventually reached over two hundred thousand in circulation, led U.S. historian Samuel Eliot Morison to observe that "under Greeley's editorship, the *Tribune* became a liberal power of the first magnitude" and caused English visitors invari-

ably to remark, and often to deplore, the fact that "shop clerks, mechanics and even common laborers subscribed to newspapers."

Greeley became the best-known U.S. newspaper editor during the first half of the nineteenth century because his paper reflected, and at times advocated, most of the social reforms of the time. Greeley concerned himself with such reform efforts as the labor movement, limited socialism as advocated by French philosopher Charles Fourier, women's rights, prohibition, a protective tariff, abolition of hanging, and the use of fertilizers as a form of scientific farming. Greeley's two greatest causes were westward expansion and the abolition of slavery (*see also* SLAVE TRADE, AFRICAN). He may have been one of the first to express the concept of U.S. manifest destiny after he visited Europe and noted what he thought was corruption and decay in those countries. His constant espousal of the U.S. system and the democratic process, his belief in the people of the United States, and his overwhelming concern for the poor, the unemployed, and degraded and underpaid workers led the average citizen to support him. According to one quip, the typical Midwesterner would not decide on any issue before reading what "Uncle Horace" had to say.

Ironically, Greeley himself was a frustrated politician who supported the Whig party originally and eventually the new Republican party. He was unsuccessful in eight attempts for public office, including an 1872 race for the presidency (as a liberal Republican endorsed by the Democrats) against the Republican incumbent, Ulysses S. Grant. But in a day of personal journalism, when newspapers supported the causes and reflected the beliefs of the editor, Greeley was the model. The *Tribune* was what it was because of Greeley.

See also ETHICS, MEDIA; NEWSPAPER: HISTORY; POLITICAL COMMUNICATION.

Bibliography. James Parton, *The Life of Horace Greeley,* New York, 1855, reprint Boston, 1896; Don C. Seitz, *Horace Greeley: Founder of the New York Tribune,* Indianapolis, Ind., 1926, reprint 1970; Glyndon G. Van Deusen, *Horace Greeley: Nineteenth-Century Crusader,* Philadelphia, 1953.

PERRY J. ASHLEY

GRIERSON, JOHN (1898–1972)

British filmmaker. Scottish-born John Grierson exerted a pervasive influence on the development of DOCUMENTARY film and gave the GENRE its most enduring short definition: "the creative treatment of actuality." Trained as a moral philosopher, Grierson saw film and other popular media exerting a public

Figure 1. *(Grierson, John)* John Grierson in the early days of the National Film Board of Canada. National Film Board of Canada.

influence that had formerly been the unchallenged domain of church and school. He viewed the cinema as a pulpit; through film he believed he could dramatize social issues and lead citizens to a more active, participatory role in democracy. Recognizing that there were many audiences outside those in cinemas, he initiated the exhibition of films in union halls, church basements, and school meeting rooms, reaching targeted audiences for his film messages. His vision of the documentary film was influenced by the cinema-poetics of ROBERT FLAHERTY, the editing technique of SERGEI EISENSTEIN, and the storytelling skills of HOLLYWOOD narrative films. *See* MOTION PICTURES.

Grierson directed his first film, *Drifters*, in 1929. Produced for the Empire Marketing Board, whose role was to knit together the far-flung British Empire by promoting trade and unity, *Drifters* saluted the teamwork of people and machines in the herring fisheries. It typified the Grierson documentary—the short film with a commentary articulating a socially relevant point of view. This tendentiousness differentiated Grierson documentaries from those of Flaherty. Both men believed that documentary film had to be based on the actual, on real people playing out their life roles, not on the use of actors and scripts, and they shared each other's distrust of Hollywood and commercial cinema. But Grierson was indifferent to the art of film except insofar as it made his message more persuasive and provided insight into the social consequences of the industrial world.

Grierson's strategy for securing an economic base for documentary was to organize talented filmmakers into production teams motivated for public service and sustained by enlightened government or corporate sponsorship. He designed and developed the

Figure 2. *(Grierson, John)* John Grierson. Photograph by Virginia Haggard Leirens.

prototype Empire Marketing Board Film Unit in 1929, the General Post Office Film Unit in 1933, and the National Film Board of Canada in 1939, and drafted proposals leading to the establishment of the Australian Commonwealth Film Unit and the New Zealand Film Unit.

The POLITICIZATION of documentary was a world phenomenon during the 1930s, but no one in the West better understood how to make films of social concern a government enterprise than Grierson. A talented politician in his own right, he served as a buffer between his filmmakers and their corporate and government sponsors, successfully lobbying for support of liberal (some would say socialist) films from a Tory administration. *Housing Problems* (1935), by Edgar Anstey and Arthur Elton, focused on London slums, with on-location testimony by slum occupants talking directly to the camera, pointing to the horrors around them—anticipating a technique that would later be used extensively in television. Grierson persuaded the Gas Light and Coke Company to sponsor this film by assuring them that the construction of new housing would be a boon to the gas industry. Basil Wright's *Song of Ceylon* (1935), which was sponsored by the Ceylon Tea Propaganda Board, reflected the filmmaker's admiration of the Ceylonese and their culture while simultaneously making clear the role of the colony's tea in the imperial economy. Such ambiguity was also present in films that gave dignity to British workers while serving to render that labor force more amenable to industrialization. Grierson's commitment to securing

institutional support for documentary production often conflicted with his urge to promulgate a radical notion of documentary. In such instances he tended to subordinate his theoretical interests to practical concerns, tempering public pronouncements in order not to arouse the documentary movement's enemies or disturb its sponsors.

Although he urged his staff to avoid the "aestheticky"—reminding them that they were propagandists first and filmmakers second—Grierson nevertheless selected people steeped in montage and eager to experiment with film form. He attracted a diverse assortment of talented artists: the classic film *Night Mail* (1936), directed by Harry Watt and Wright, was a collaborative enterprise enlisting the services of poet W. H. Auden, composer Benjamin Britten, and Brazilian-born filmmaker Alberto Cavalcanti, whose experiments with sound were a major contribution of the British documentary. An unconventional, daring, and charismatic administrator, Grierson inspired the careers of Wright, Paul Rotha, Humphrey Jennings, Norman McLaren, Colin Low, Tom Daly, and many others. His most enduring organizational achievement was the National Film Board of Canada, which he headed until 1945 and which remained a world leader in documentary and ANIMATION during the following decades.

See also CINÉMA VÉRITÉ; NEWSREEL.

Bibliography. Gary Evans, *John Grierson and the National Film Board: The Politics of Wartime Propaganda,* Toronto, 1984; John Grierson, *Grierson on Documentary,* ed. by Forsyth Hardy, London, 1946, reprint 1979; Forsyth Hardy, *John Grierson: A Documentary Bibliography*, London, 1979.

D. B. JONES

GRIFFITH, D. W. (1875–1948)

The first great U.S. film director, David Wark Griffith remains controversial. His innovations in film technique are unchallengeable: between 1908, when he directed his first one-reeler, *The Adventures of Dolly*, and 1914, when he directed his three-hour epic of the Civil War and Reconstruction, *The Birth of a Nation* (released 1915), he established virtually all the conventions of film grammar still in use today. Although no longer credited with the first close-up or crosscut, Griffith was the first to reveal the full dramatic potential of film form. There is, however, little denying that Griffith's ideology remained that of an anti-Reconstruction Southerner and that his sense of dramatic conflict remained at the level of low melodrama (rising, at its best, to Dickensian verve).

Griffith grew up in Louisville, Kentucky, and aspired to theatrical fame through ACTING or writing but had only limited success in either. After acting briefly in MOTION PICTURES from 1907, he became the principal director for the American Biograph Company the following year, turning out more than 450 one- and two-reelers by late 1913. (Even more astonishing, all but 8 of those Biograph films survive, in contrast to his lost Paramount features of the late 1910s.) Arguably this rapid output contains his greatest work—concise, technically innovative, socially conscious dramas, as early as *A Corner in Wheat*, *The Lonely Villa*, and *The Country Doctor* (all 1909). Near the end of the Biograph period are films with previously unseen sophistication in filmic (as opposed to theatrical) acting—among them *The New York Hat* (1912), with Mary Pickford and Lionel Barrymore, and *The Battle at Elderbush Gulch* (1913), with Lillian Gish. For his heroines Griffith regularly preferred resourceful child-women—Pickford, the Gish sisters, Blanche Sweet, and Mae Marsh.

Only in a literal sense was Griffith the founding father of HOLLYWOOD. From 1910 on, he did take summer trips from New York to the sunshine of Los Angeles with his cameraman and collaborator, G. W. "Billy" Bitzer, and the Biograph players. However, Griffith was never able to accommodate himself to the regimented production patterns of Hollywood (in the sense of the community of film studios that flourished there from the late 1910s). In 1919 he joined with Pickford, Douglas Fairbanks, and CHARLES

CHAPLIN to found United Artists, but that was essentially a distributing organization. For production space Griffith built his studio that year in Mamaroneck, New York. But his debts prevented true independence.

Griffith's ongoing financial woes had begun with the commercial failure of the $2.5 million *Intolerance* (1916). The single greatest film in the view of some filmmakers (Vsevolod Pudovkin, King Vidor) and critics (Pauline Kael), its complex intercutting among four historical epochs baffled most audiences at release. Perhaps holding up better today are such less ambitious features as *True Heart Susie* and *Broken Blossoms* (both released in 1919 and starring Lillian Gish). And at least three of his films from the early 1920s must be counted among the great works of silent filmmaking: *Orphans of the Storm*, set amid the French Revolution; *Isn't Life Wonderful*, shot on location in the ruins of postwar Germany; and *Way Down East*, a bravura melodrama with an astonishing chase across an ice floe, and Griffith's only film since the foundation of United Artists that did not lose money. Forced into the Hollywood studio system, he thereafter produced undistinguished silents and two sound films that were ridiculed and quickly forgotten. But notwithstanding his troubling provincialism and sad decline, there is no more significant figure in the history of U.S. filmmaking.

Figure 1. *(Griffith, D. W.)* D. W. Griffith on the set. The Bettmann Archive, Inc.

Figure 2. *(Griffith, D. W.)* The destruction of Babylon, from *Intolerance*, 1916. The Museum of Modern Art/Film Stills Archive.

Bibliography. Karl Brown, *Adventures with D. W. Griffith,* New York, 1973; Robert M. Henderson, *D. W. Griffith: His Life and Work,* New York and London, 1972; Richard Schickel, *D. W. Griffith: An American Life,* New York, 1984.

SCOTT SIMMON

GROUP COMMUNICATION

The study of the process of group communication traces its origins to the fourth and fifth centuries B.C.E. in Greece and the study of dialectics, a process of arriving at agreement through the exchange of opinions and dialogue. During the twentieth century the "group" came into its own as the most pervasive unit of sociological analysis. Probably the greatest single influence in directing scholarly thinking about groups was KURT LEWIN's application of field theory to the social psychology of groups. This approach reached its greatest popularity during the 1950s and spawned the term *group dynamics.* Inquiry into group phenomena during this heyday of small-group research focused on environmental influences on groups, the internal structure of groups, and compositional characteristics of groups based on differences among members. Scholarly inquiry in subsequent decades has focused on the central role of communication in the formation, maintenance, and performance of small groups.

The centrality of communication is explicit in the standard definition of group that has come into general use. U.S. social psychologist Marvin Shaw defines a group as "persons who are interacting with one another in such a manner that each person influences and is influenced by each other person." The unit of analysis, sometimes called "small group," occasionally has been defined in terms of its size. Group usually refers to a social system comprising a minimum of three members. Dyad typically refers to a sociological unit of two persons. With the addition of a third person to the dyad, the complexity of sociological and communicational variables increases markedly. The upper limit on the size of a group, however, is indefinite. Although scholars typically limit the group to a maximum of fifteen to twenty persons, the crucial definitional limitation on a group's size is the extent to which each member interacts with every other member so that mutual influence is possible among all members.

The nature of communication in groups has also been redefined during scholarly inquiry of the past several decades. The traditional approach has been to visualize communication in terms of its *transmissional* properties: direction of information flow and number of messages sent and received among group members, who are seen as nodes in a communication "network." The more recent conceptualization of group communication emphasizes its *pragmatic* properties: multiple functions performed by communicative actions, sequences of interactive functions within the conversational flow, and social relationships among group members created by the sequencing of interactive functions. The key difference between these two conceptualizations of communication is the emphasis on the linear quality of transmission of messages contrasted with the emphasis on the functional quality of pragmatic properties of communicative actions or events. Both conceptualizations of communication are necessary for an understanding of the sociological properties of a group.

Leadership

Perhaps the most widely researched phenomenon in group communication is leadership. Traditionally leadership has been identified with certain transmissional properties of communication. The leader most often emerges in a central position in the network, a node that requires the fewest number of transmissional relays to disseminate information to all other members. Leaders also were typically found to be those members who sent and received the most messages, a natural consequence of the centralized network position. Leaders also serve a gatekeeping function in information dissemination and are thus subject to the problems associated with information overload (receiving a number of messages exceeding the capacity to process them).

More recent communications research has examined the functions of leaders and the communicative properties of acts most typically performed by them. Such research has shown that leaders often initiate more themes or topics than other members, engage in more frequent orientation behavior, and are perceived to demonstrate more goal-directedness, to give more directions and summaries, to be more assured,

and to exhibit more argumentativeness in their communicative behaviors. Despite such findings, functional dissimilarities idiosyncratic to specific leaders and specific groups abound. Consequently, a definitive list of leadership functions has eluded scholars in the field.

Recent exploratory research into the pragmatic properties of leaders' communications suggests that leadership is more likely to be a social relationship between leaders and followers created through group interaction than a leader's independent performance of specific functions directly attributed to leadership. This social relation between leaders and followers is probably a function of the greater complexity of communicative behaviors displayed by leaders. That is, leaders, interacting with followers, tend to exhibit the greater variety of communicative functions compared with nonleaders, and they continue to exhibit the greater complexity of communicative functions throughout a group's interactional history. Leaders also tend to employ different communicative strategies with different group members, thereby creating different social relationships. By contrast, nonleaders tend to interact very similarly with every other member throughout the group's history. Only with leaders do followers tend to vary their communicative styles. The pragmatic properties of communication associated with leadership, then, emphasize the social relationship between leaders and followers created by communication and are probably more important than the transmissional properties of a leader's central position in an information-flow network.

Leadership itself is a phenomenon that appears in a variety of social systems other than the group. Within the group, however, a distinction is often made between leader and leadership. *Leader* typically refers to the high-status role or position occupied by a member who achieves that role in a variety of ways, principally through appointment or designation by some external authority. The emphasis on communication often distinguishes the designated or legitimate leader from an emergent leader—a member who, as a result of interaction, earns the recognition of other group members as having achieved the role of leader. The process of leadership emergence occurs during and is a direct outgrowth of communication among group members.

Leader emergence is often viewed as a multistage process of contention for the leadership role. The emergent leader, unlike the legitimized leader, occupies the position only as a result of recognition and acceptance by followers. Maintaining an emergent leader's role requires maintaining that acceptance. Emergent leadership thus implies a relationship between leader and followers that is not necessarily present in (and is less stable than) the status of the legitimate leader. The emergent process of group leadership is similar to the creation of an informal role structure in larger social organizations. *See also* ORGANIZATIONAL COMMUNICATION.

Decision Making

Groups serve a number of functions within a society, but the one that has attracted the most scholarly interest has been the process of social decision making. This process traditionally has been viewed as a step-by-step progression to social agreement. This linear progression toward consensus emphasizes the influence of human rationality. The epitome of the rational linearity of group decision making is embodied in social philosopher JOHN DEWEY's stages of reflective thinking: (1) a difficulty is felt or expressed; (2) the nature of the problem is defined; (3) the problem is analyzed; (4) possible solutions are suggested; (5) the best solution is selected by testing each solution against selected criteria; and (6) the best solution is implemented. This linear approach views group decision making as identical to problem solving and is typically prescriptive in that it outlines an agenda to guide groups along an orderly path toward achieving consensus.

Some lines of inquiry are based on the assumption that groups evolve or develop cumulatively toward achieving consensus but do not necessarily do so in a certain standard fashion. U.S. social psychologist Robert Bales probably initiated this kind of inquiry when he studied the pragmatic properties of communicative acts performed by group members during discussions. He concluded that groups accomplish decision-making tasks through a cumulative but non-linear process.

Subsequent inquiry employing a similar descriptive approach to communication has emphasized the sequential properties of interactional functions and the temporal connectedness among communicative acts, and has expanded upon Bales's three-phase model. Although idiosyncratic variations occur among different groups, the descriptive approach to group development has emphasized that group decision making appears less rational than individual decision making, at least in the sense of linear path-goal progress toward solutions. The group decision-making processes appear to reflect the influence of the social relationships among group members on their interaction.

Other Functions of Groups

Groups perform many functions in society in addition to decision making. For example, groups are established for brainstorming (generating a variety of new ideas), personal improvement (such as interpersonal awareness groups), therapy (treatment of mental illness), and social support (such as helping ex-alcoholics adjust). Other groups exist as units within larger organizations. The groups vary not only in purpose but also in susceptibility to influences from the larger environment.

The pragmatic functions of communication are related to the group's reason for existence. The most significant pragmatic functions of communication in therapy groups, for example, are quite different from the primary functions performed by members of decision-making groups. Although the transmissional properties of communication are quite similar in groups with different goals, the pragmatic properties of communicative functions performed by group members are closely aligned with and directly relevant to the group's goal.

Approaches to the Study of Groups

The group has, of course, been an object of interest in many social science disciplines. Sociologists and psychologists have long exhibited interest in a variety of group processes without considering their relevance to communications. A typical mode of social scientific inquiry asks group members to provide paper-and-pencil responses after a period of interaction, and these perceptions, associated with compositional or structural properties of the group, become the information on which most claims about group actions are based. Among others in the social sciences, U.S. social psychologists Joseph McGrath and Irwin Altman have lamented that group research was becoming a "science of the independent variable." Knowledge claims based on this input-output model of inquiry emphasize the impact of a group's structural or compositional variables on outcomes of group interaction (defined as perceptual responses of members after interaction) and virtually ignore characteristics of interaction itself. The current emphasis in group communication study on the pragmatic properties of communicative functions has added new dimensions to many of the traditional sociological approaches to groups. Furthermore, the emphasis on communicational pragmatics has also alleviated much of the criticism of past group research, namely, that it tended to trivialize understanding and confirm the obvious.

Sociologists typically have defined deviance within a "labeling" perspective. That is, the deviant is the group member who is labeled or perceived by other group members as being a deviant, the one who has violated the group's norms. In terms of the transmissional properties of communication, deviant members usually appear in one of two places in the communication network: on the periphery (an outcast who exchanges fewer messages with other group members) or in a central position (the object of social pressure from other group members). Viewing communication in terms of its pragmatic functions has shed new light on the concept of deviance. Deviance from this perspective is a communicative act performed by one or more group members. During the normal process of group interaction, nearly all group members exhibit deviant behaviors and thereby violate the social norms of the group. Furthermore, many of the functions associated with leadership have also proved to be deviant behaviors. Deviant behavior may be detrimental to the group's overall functioning when it impedes progress toward a goal, but it may also enhance group functioning when it allows an innovation that furthers progress toward a goal. In addition, innovation is frequently associated with leadership functions.

Group members form coalitions or temporary alliances, it has been argued, in order to increase their relative power within the larger social system. Viewed in terms of communication, coalition formation involves far more than the unequal distribution of power. Transmissionally, members of a coalition send and receive more messages among themselves, while the number of messages between members of differing coalitions is significantly fewer. Pragmatically, functions of intracoalition communication include positive reinforcement—coalition members agree with and support one another. Interaction between members of different coalitions is more likely to be argumentative and to reflect social conflict. In the normal course of group development, however, coalitions typically dissipate as the group nears its goal.

Conflict, when viewed as a purely sociological or psychological variable, can be defined in personal or social terms, but when viewed communicationally, conflict is exclusively social, that is, between group members. The functions served by conflict messages are not entirely negative. In its pragmatic sense, social conflict is what occurs in the interaction of incompatible activities, such as an argumentative sequence between group members who favor and oppose a specific idea.

Many scholars view conflict as important and even necessary for achieving consensus on a decision-making task. Those who have studied conflict in groups from a communicational perspective have also found that conflict is likely to be a normal and inevitable part of the evolutionary development of a group. The communicational view thus has shifted the focus from the need to resolve conflict (because it impedes the group's progress toward goals) to the importance of managing conflict (determining whether the conflict is beneficial to the group's functioning and to be encouraged, or detrimental and to be resolved).

Social-psychological research during the decades of the 1950s and 1960s contained the implicit assumption that the group was a unique sociological entity, worthy of study in its own right. The emphasis in group communication in subsequent years has been increasingly to treat the group as only a setting in which human communication occurs. Group is a level of sociological complexity existing between the social systems of dyad and organization. The group is the smallest social system in which a communication network can appear. In a two-person system only one link (A-B) exists. Three links are possible in a three-person group (A-B, B-C, and A-C). A transmissional network is possible only when members of the social system have a choice when sending and receiving messages, and this requires that there be a minimum of three nodes (A, B, C).

Understanding of group communication has been based on inquiry devoted almost exclusively to face-to-face communicative situations. However, modern technological advances in electronically mediated linkages among individuals signal a potentially new mode of group communication, a form of electronic decision making. The use of computer terminals and modems among geographically separated individuals and its effect on our understanding of communication processes are likely to become important topics for communication scholars.

See also FAMILY; INTERACTION, FACE-TO-FACE; INTERPERSONAL COMMUNICATION; NETWORK ANALYSIS.

Bibliography. Robert F. Bales, *Interaction Process Analysis: A Method for the Study of Small Groups,* Reading, Mass., 1950; Dennis S. Gouran and B. Aubrey Fisher, "The Function of Human Communication in the Formation, Maintenance, and Performance of Small Groups," in *Handbook of Rhetorical and Communication Theory,* ed. by Carroll C. Arnold and John Waite Bowers, Boston, 1984; Paul A. Hare, *Handbook of Small Group Research,* 2d ed., New York, 1976; Randy V. Hirokawa and M. Scott Poole, *Communication and Group Decision Making,* Beverly Hills, Calif., 1985; Marvin E. Shaw, *Group Dynamics: The Psychology of Small Group Behavior,* 2d ed., New York, 1976.

B. AUBREY FISHER

GUTENBERG, JOHANNES (1390/1400–1468)

German inventor, credited with developing the process of PRINTING from movable, precisely cast, and fitted metal types—a process that revolutionized BOOK production and has had an immense cultural impact. Johannes Gensfleisch zur Laden zum Gutenberg's invention was a confluence of the elements necessary to produce multiple, identical copies of text emulating the quality of careful scribal writing. The key element was a hand-held, adjustable mold for casting, from inserted matrices, individual types, one at a time, of uniform height and perfect alignment for use on the bed of a press. Other elements were the adaptation of a screw-operated winepress or binder's press; use of an alloy of lead, tin, and antimony for the types; and preparation of an oil-based ink of the kind used by some artists. The casting process, with the press, set Gutenberg's system distinctly apart from the woodblock printing and metal stamping already known in Europe, China, and Korea.

Details of Gutenberg's life and activity are traced largely through scattered legal documents and the scholarly study of types, inks, paper, presswork, and hand illumination of the period. Statements made shortly after he died by persons who knew him assert that it was indeed he who originated the process of printing from movable type. Trained in the skills and exacting standards of a goldsmith and craftsman in metals, Gutenberg was a member of the goldsmith's guild and belonged to a patrician family. About 1430 civil strife in Mainz forced him into exile in Strasbourg; he returned to Mainz permanently no later than 1448.

Meanwhile he was teaching gem polishing and other "arts" to a craftsman, Andreas Dritzehn, and in 1438 formed a partnership with him and two others to teach them further "secrets." Litigation after Dritzehn's death in 1438 cites purchases of lead and other metals; use of a word, *Formen*, denoting "types"; description of what must have been the casting mold; and payment for "that which pertains to printing." After returning to Mainz, Gutenberg obtained several loans, beginning in 1448, to continue his work. One of these was for eight hundred guilders from a lawyer, Johann Fust. Gutenberg later mortgaged all his tools and equipment to Fust and accepted him as a partner for another eight hundred guilders.

What emerged, not later than 1456, was the superb forty-two-line Latin Bible, which had two columns per page and 643 leaves and was set in type copied from the best black-letter script. Some sets were printed on vellum, some on paper; at least forty-seven survive in substantial form.

Late in 1455 Fust sued for repayment of the entire debt and interest; the inventor could not pay. Fust took over the business and continued it, with Gutenberg's foreman, Peter Schöffer. Gutenberg is believed, however, to have had a part in the beautiful Latin Psalter, which was the first printed book to bear a date (August 14, 1457) and the names of the printers (Fust and Schöffer).

A Mainz official lent Gutenberg printing equipment, but what, if anything, he produced with it is uncertain. Gutenberg may have printed the thirty-six-line Bamberg Bible and perhaps the undated *Missale Speciale Constantiense* and the 1460 *Catholicon*. Several grammars, indulgences, and a PAMPHLET are attributed to him. In 1465 he was granted a court sinecure with allowances and tax exemption. By 1471 his system of printing was sweeping Europe, and by 1500 presses had been established in 242 cities.

See also PUBLISHING; TYPOGRAPHY.

Bibliography. Warren Chappell, *A Short History of the Printed Word*, New York, 1970, reprint Boston, 1980; Elizabeth L. Eisenstein, *The Printing Revolution in Early Modern Europe*, Cambridge and New York, 1983; Hellmut Lehmann-Haupt, *Gutenberg and the Master of the Playing-Cards*, New Haven, Conn., 1966; Victor Scholderer, *Johann Gutenberg: The Inventor of Printing*, 2d ed., London, 1970; S. H. Steinberg, *Five Hundred Years of Printing*, 3d ed., Harmondsworth, Eng., and Baltimore, Md., 1974; Margaret Bingham Stillwell, *The Beginning of the World of Books 1450 to 1470: A Chronological Survey of the Texts Chosen for Printing . . . with a Synopsis of the Gutenberg Documents*, New York, 1972.

CHANDLER B. GRANNIS

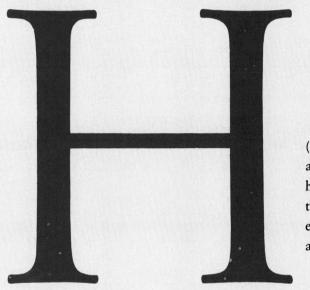

($\bar{e}^{\mathrm{i}}$tʃ), the eighth letter of the Roman alphabet, ancient and modern, representing historically the Semitic 日, *hheth* or *kheth*, through the Greek H, *heta, eta*, originally the eighth [letter], but, in the later Greek alphabet, after the omission of F . . . , the seventh letter.

HEARST, WILLIAM RANDOLPH (1863–1951)

U.S. publisher who built a successful chain of newspapers through "yellow journalism"—an emphasis on the sensational, lurid, entertaining, and scandalous in news coverage. William Randolph Hearst's father, Senator George Hearst of California, had made a fortune from the Comstock silver lode in Nevada and other mining interests. Senator Hearst launched his son's career in 1887 by making him a present of the San Francisco *Examiner,* a struggling paper he had bought some seven years earlier. Until then the younger Hearst had shown little talent for anything, having dropped out of Harvard in his sophomore year. On frequent trips to New York he had been fascinated by JOSEPH PULITZER's New York *World,* and he decided not only to imitate this paper but also to surpass it. Pulitzer had carried JAMES GORDON BENNETT's earlier formula of sensationalism in the news columns and strong convictions on the editorial page to new heights, but Hearst thought he could do it better.

He was right. His *Examiner* was even more flamboyant because it lacked the *World*'s idealism. Arthur McEwen, the chief editorial writer on Hearst's brilliant staff, summed up the owner's method when he said that readers should look at the front page and say, "Gee whiz!"; look at the second page and say, "Holy Moses!"; and look at the third page and exclaim, "God Almighty!" The emphasis was always on mass appeal, the human-interest story, and, most important, the sensational.

This was the formula Hearst brought to New York in 1895 when he took over the New York *Morning Journal* and pitted it against the *World.* It was a battle of the giants, with Hearst and Pulitzer trying to outdo each other. Hearst adopted his rival's ideas wholesale, carrying them a step further in extravagance and boldness, meanwhile hiring away some of Pulitzer's best staff members. In an effort to boost circulation Hearst decided to create a Sunday supplement that would surpass Pulitzer's. He lured Richard Outcault, creator of the immensely popular comic cartoon "Yellow Kid," away from Pulitzer and made extensive use of color. Soon both the comic strip (*see* COMICS) and color had become indispensable. Hearst's editorial page, like Pulitzer's, carried on crusades, but in time Hearst traversed the entire political spectrum from radical left to radical right.

The climax of the Hearst-Pulitzer conflict was the Spanish-American War, which Hearst was popularly credited with starting; it was even said that he had conspired to sink the *Maine.* However, Hearst's was only the most strident voice in a general clamor for war by the press. Hearst covered the war in Cuba himself, with a staff he brought along in a tramp steamer he had chartered. Among U.S. newspapers the *Journal*'s coverage of the war was arguably the most flamboyant. Other newspaper editors and publishers were incensed at what they considered Hearst's exploitation of the conflict, but by the end of the war Hearst's *Journal* claimed a circulation equal to that of Pulitzer's *World.*

Another controversy—this one adversely affecting Hearst's standing with the public—was the assassination of President William McKinley. Because of the frequent and vitriolic anti-McKinley editorials that had run in Hearst's papers, some accused him of being behind the president's assassination, and the *Journal* was burned in public and removed from libraries. Hearst survived the furor and went on to

Figure 1. (*Hearst, William Randolph*) William Randolph Hearst, drawn by cartoonist Oliver Herford as a spider with political ambitions: one hand is on the governorship of New York state, and another is reaching for the Capitol in Washington, D.C. The Bettmann Archive/BBC Hulton.

play an equally controversial role in World War I, staunchly opposing U.S. entry into the conflict and maintaining a marked anti-British bias.

Hearst frequently used his PUBLISHING concerns to propagate his own constantly shifting political views. Candidates for public office whose opinions diverged from his could expect to be vilified in Hearst's publications, while those with whom he agreed were glowingly praised. Hearst also entertained political ambitions of his own. From 1903 to 1907 he served in the U.S. House of Representatives, from which he was mostly absent. He also made two unsuccessful runs for mayor of New York City (in 1905 and 1909) and one for governor of New York (in 1906).

At their peak Hearst's properties constituted one of the most remarkable publishing empires the country had seen, comprising a string of newspapers extending from coast to coast; magazines (*see* MAGAZINE), including *Harper's Bazaar, Cosmopolitan,* and *Good Housekeeping;* and allied news services such as King Features Service, International News Service, and International News Photos (*see also* NEWS AGENCIES). On Sunday Hearst's papers reached more than three million readers; on weekdays, twice that. It was an empire that began to decline in the early years of the depression, however, and some holdings had to be sold or consolidated.

Together, Hearst and Pulitzer ended the era of personal journalism that had dominated the nineteenth century. In its place they created a pattern of sensationalism that has persisted, chiefly in less reputable publications and in segments of the London press.

See also NEWSPAPER: HISTORY.

JOHN TEBBEL

HELLENIC WORLD

Although Greek was spoken in the region that is now Greece (Hellas in the Greek language) before 2000 B.C.E. and was written by perhaps 1600 B.C.E., there is little that can be said about communication before the destruction soon after 1200 B.C.E. of civilizations now conventionally called Minoan (in Crete) and Mycenaean (on the mainland). The only attested use of WRITING in the earlier period was restricted to very short documents on clay tablets recording various aspects of the domestic economy in the palaces. The scripts employed were clumsy and suitable only for their special purpose, evidently a kind of code learned within a closed circle of professional scribes, and the practice disappeared with the palaces, as did the scribes themselves.

When the art of writing returned to this area about 800 B.C.E., it was in the highly advanced form of an ALPHABET, borrowed from the Phoenicians but fundamentally improved by the introduction of vowel signs. The rapid diffusion of this alphabet was one of the greatest cultural revolutions in history. Its importance is virtually self-evident in its detailed manifestations. Yet it is essential to define carefully the limits of the Greek revolution.

The role of written communication. In all premodern societies there were two severely limiting conditions to written communication. The first was the lack of cheap WRITING MATERIALS and of PRINTING (movable type). Hence the number of copies of any written work available for circulation was rigidly restricted. Distribution was limited to copies prepared by hand and passed by hand from person to person. This method of production and distribution also reduced the ability of the authorities to prevent the dissemination of "objectionable" matter, but that is insignificant against the limits within which any copies were available.

The other limiting condition was widespread illiteracy. No valid statistical picture is available except for the last two centuries or so of the modern era, and historians have commonly clouded the picture by defining LITERACY as the ability to sign one's name. In reply it is essential to note how little occasion most ancient Greeks had to read (or write) seriously at any time in their lives. This is symbolized by a story told by Plutarch in the *Life of Nicias,* that of the many thousands of Athenian soldiers captured in the unsuccessful invasion of Syracuse in 413 B.C.E., a few were released because they could recite some of the choruses of Euripides. For the Sicilians, Plutarch comments, "had a passion for his poetry greater than that of any other Hellenes outside Greece proper. They committed to memory the little samples and morsels brought to them by visitors, and then shared them delightedly with each other." The tale may not be true, but it is at least ben trovato: the Sicilian Greeks depended on snatches quoted by visitors, not on the copies of the text of Euripides, which were simply too scarce.

The situation in classical antiquity with respect to literacy, and therefore within the whole field of communications, was filled with paradoxes. There was widespread use of writing once the alphabet had been invented, though there is a tendency in the modern historical literature seriously to exaggerate its indispensability in all disciplines. One contrast is illuminating: although it is the case that science and philosophy could not have advanced as they did without the use of writing, the law had become relatively sophisticated during centuries when it was deliberately kept unwritten. Only popular demand eventually forced the Roman pontiffs and similar functionaries to relinquish their monopoly of legal knowledge by the production of written codes, with undoubted consequences in further refinement of legal analysis; yet in classical Athens, to give a particularly revealing example, the bulk of private legal transactions continued to be conducted orally, without a scrap of paper from beginning to end of the affair, whereas in Ptolemaic and Roman Egypt, everything, even a receipt for a paltry sum, was recorded. That distinction reflects the difference in the bureaucratic structure of the regime, not a distinction in the substantive needs of the legal system as such.

It is, perhaps surprisingly, not easy to give a proper account of genuine literacy in the Hellenic world. Those who read and wrote occupationally—scribes and notaries—were a feature of Egypt and other eastern areas conquered and brought within the Greek sphere by Alexander, but they were neither numerous nor important in the old Greek world. All intellectuals of course read and wrote fluently. But how regularly? Personal correspondence, letter writing, offers one test, but we simply do not know enough about the practice outside Egypt, where all sorts of letters have been preserved on papyrus: appeals to officials, letters home from soldiers, instructions to business agents, and so on. However, the total number of known letters is infinitesimal, and it is a serious question whether the letters were written because there were professional scribes available, not the other way around. Collections of literary letters, a small number of which are known though not always with certain authenticity, prove nothing. It is perhaps more revealing that the messenger, whether in a political role or in private affairs, is regularly a transmitter of oral communications. The Roman *tabellarius*, the courier in the literal sense, seems to have been virtually unknown. Who, outside the Egyptian sphere, would have penned a letter for an illiterate soldier, and who would have read it to his mother in her native village?

The difficulties go deeper still. It is undeniable that all Greek intellectuals were literate (at least from the sixth century B.C.E.), that they possessed and read books—poetry, scientific treatises, history. But what did that mean in practice, in real life? What are we to make of PLATO's notorious attack on books in the *Phaedrus*, that they destroy the memory and replace self-knowledge and the further advance of knowledge by the illusion of permanent and unchanging data? Is that just one more, especially extreme instance of Platonic "archaism," or does it reflect a fundamental conviction that the true learning process depends on the dialectic, which can only be conducted orally in a face-to-face situation? Does it reflect what the distinguished classicist Georg Rohde asked in a 1951 lecture, "On Reading in Antiquity," in the rhetorical question, "Can we imagine Socrates reading?"

A time of change. Although the evidence is very sparse and lends itself to contradictory interpretations, there seems little substantial reason for denying the view that a radical change came in the later fourth century, symbolized by ARISTOTLE, the man who invented research, so to speak, of a kind that

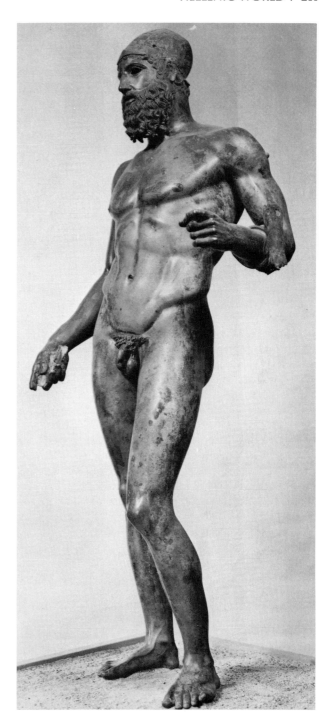

Figure 1. *(Hellenic World)* Life-size bronze warrior B from Riace. Mid-fifth century B.C.E. National Museum at Reggio Calabria, Italy. Alinari/Art Resource, New York.

depended heavily on the written word. It was only thereafter that we have evidence for silent reading, of enough copies of (some) books to warrant speaking of a knowledge among intellectuals of books much more widespread than one can imagine at the time Herodotus and Thucydides were writing. Books in their day have been tellingly described as prompt

Figure 2. *(Hellenic World)* White-ground lekythos in the style of the Achilles Painter, 440 B.C.E. Courtesy, Museum of Fine Arts, Boston. Francis Bartlett Fund.

Figure 3. *(Hellenic World)* The portico of the Temple of Minerva Polias, Athens. A drawing from *The Antiquities of Athens. Measured and Delineated by James Stuart F.R.S. and F.S.A. and Nicholas Revett, Painters and Architects.* London, 1787, vol. 2, chap. 2, pl. 8, reprinted New York: Benjamin Blom, 1968. ▷

copies, aide-mémoire. And even in the Hellenistic, and then the Roman, world, books remained the preserve of a small minority with a scientific or philosophical interest or with enough skill, money, and interest to read (and first to possess) poetry, books of travel, and novels for entertainment or edification.

The story of technical literature—of manuals of rhetoric, grammar, medicine, agronomy, architecture, horsemanship, military science—is particularly revealing. The beginnings go back to the later fifth century, notably with the earliest Hippocratic writings in medicine, and to Aristotle's *Politics,* in which he could refer interested readers to agronomic writers, of whom he named two (whose works, like all the rest in this genre, have failed to survive). However, this kind of writing was in the overwhelming bulk post-Aristotelian, the product of the Hellenistic and Roman ages. What is less clear is the extent to which such works circulated, in particular among practical men as distinct from "professional" scientists and philosophers like Aristotle himself. That the small cultivators, whether free or slave, landowners or tenants, never saw, let alone read, a manual on farming cannot be doubted, and there appears to be no evidence that the wealthier ones—Xenophon, for example—did so either. Or that master builders, architects, or even doctors normally learned their trade otherwise than by experience, by apprenticeship (whether within the family or through outsiders). In the history of communications, oral transmission of knowledge was the rule until very recent time, virtually without exception, and that applied among the Hellenes to social and political activity as much as to the practical skills by which people gained their livelihood. That is the significant measure of literacy in any society, not the conventional one of whether individuals could write their own names, a test that had no visible bearing on behavior within the society. Fluent literacy, Eric Havelock has acutely observed, going one step further, depended "on the mastery not of the art of writing by a few, but of fluent reading by the many."

An important indicator of the failure of fluent reading by the many to develop was the absence of the simplest devices for the assistance of readers. This was not a matter of genuine technological advance, such as the invention of either cheap paper or movable type, but of rudimentary steps that we take

Fig. 3.

Fig. 4.

Fig. 2.

Fig. 1.

Publish'd Oct.r 27th 1787 According to Act of Parliament.

Figure 4. *(Hellenic World)* Epitaph for the Athenians who fell in the battle of Potidaia, 432 B.C.E. Reproduced by courtesy of the Trustees of The British Museum, London.

Figure 5. *(Hellenic World)* Vase stand in black-figured style, with signatures of Ergotimos (the potter) and Kleitias (the painter). The Metropolitan Museum of Art, New York, Fletcher Fund, 1931. (31.11.4)

for granted. Punctuation hardly existed, nor even separation of words. The evidence for a genuine cursive script, necessary for rapid writing, is also negligible. These "inventions," it need hardly be said, required even less imagination or creative originality than the invention of the vowel sign, which had been the decisive step in the creation of a "true" alphabet by the Greeks. Nor was it only the many, the marginally literate, who suffered. It was, for example, impossible to cite a passage in a longer work, and it was even cumbersome to look up an earlier passage for one's private study before the papyrus roll was replaced by the BOOK (the codex). For complicated reasons that shift was achieved only among the Christians, so that it did not occur on any scale before the Byzantine period. Pagan Greeks, not sur-

prisingly, tended to quote the printed word from memory rather than rewind a papyrus roll in search of a passage or data.

Recordkeeping. Related were the paucity of records and the low level of recordkeeping, though it is hard to establish a clear cause-and-effect relationship. In the private sphere accounting practices were rudimentary before the invention of double-entry bookkeeping at the end of the MIDDLE AGES, and recordkeeping was unknown for analytical purposes, as distinct from the mere "police" function of checking on crude inputs and outputs. More significant were the poor state of public records and the fairly close link between the political regime and the publicity given to public acts. The situation is illustrated by the relatively detailed account in Thucydides of the difficulties faced by the Athenians in acquiring elementary knowledge about the various Sicilian cities with which they were negotiating (or which they thought of attacking), not only because of "diplomatic" obstacles but equally because information was not readily available in documentary form. In another passage Thucydides reports that, during negotiations in 413 B.C.E. with emissaries from Chios who were preparing a revolt from the Athenian Empire, the Spartans sent someone to inquire whether Chios actually had sixty warships in readiness and generally whether the island-state deserved its reputation. Nor does the change that set in with the Hellenistic age, already noted, seem to have produced any qualitative change in the public sphere, as is evident from a reading of the knowledgeable second-century-B.C.E. historian Polybius. The mountainous *paperasserie* of Greco-Roman Egypt is illusory in this respect: the vast quantity of documentation did not bring about any qualitative change in the archives.

One must ask, then, what control the Spartans had over the reliability of the report brought back in 413 B.C.E. by their emissary to Chios. Reliability is of course a crucial question in all communication, foreign or domestic, but it is always more acute when the transmission is oral, as was regularly the case in antiquity. Oral communication was normal at all times; even when the final step in the chain was in writing, the basis was a verbal one. That was of course true for most of history, even in the centuries after governments began the practice of more or less permanent, identifiable embassies abroad. The historian of communication must distinguish, in looking at the millennia since the early Greek period, between on the one hand developments that rested on technological change—the introduction of cheap paper and movable type, then of steam navigation, the telegraph, and the telephone—and on the other hand changes attributable to the social structure and the nature of politics.

Social and political context. There was nothing in antiquity comparable, in the public sphere, for instance, to the detailed day-by-day instructions and records of the Consiglio of Venice in the late Middle Ages pertaining to Venetian possessions in Greece and the Aegean; or to the diplomatic reports sent to Italian governments by their "ambassadors" in various European capitals; or, in the private sphere, to the accounts and the correspondence with agents abroad of the Fuggers in Germany or the Medici in Florence. Without any technological advance a revolution in communication had occurred in Europe in the later Middle Ages; the employment of writing, of documents, of recordkeeping, had taken a qualitative leap forward. The proceedings of the Roman Senate were not recorded until the dictatorship of Julius Caesar, by which time Rome ruled a large part of the known world. But the affairs of the republic of Venice or of the duchy of Milan at the end of the Middle Ages were recorded in minute detail, as was the information on which governmental decisions were based. That is a measure of the new complexity of public affairs, including a new notion of public accountability.

Even when communication was purely oral at all stages, some machinery, or at least particular circumstances, was indispensable if information and ideas were to be communicated. The basic distinction was obviously between communication within the community and external communication. Internally the smallness of the population that mattered and the narrowness of the space involved were permanently decisive factors. During the city-state period, Athens and Syracuse, the most populous communities, never numbered more than thirty-five or forty thousand adult males, and there were not a dozen city-states with more than ten thousand. In the vast majority of the communities, in other words, the whole citizenry could literally be assembled in one place at any one time. Even in the Hellenistic period, when some of the cities grew to unprecedented size, the numbers involved in the public affairs of the no longer independent cities remained small enough to permit retention of the illuminating phrase, a "face-to-face society." And behind the formal, institutional channels of communication there lay a whole network of smaller, informal channels—daily intercourse in the markets and public squares; at temples, shrines, and altars; in the gymnasia, public baths, and fountains.

Externally, across political boundaries, more complicated distinctions have to be drawn. In the field of public affairs formal machinery was largely restricted to ad hoc ambassadors (including military negotiators) and spies, backed up by the men called *proxenoi* who in a private capacity performed what today would be called consular services. In the cultural fields—literature, philosophy and science, architecture, and the crafts—there was a large amount of more or less formal communication through direct personal contacts. Travel was common in these circles, and there were schools, public lectures, and debates. This was clearly the area in which communication was most rapid and most extensive. A third group of activities consisted of business affairs, the communication of information about harvests, prices, markets, industrial techniques (to speak loosely) through agents, associates, friends, or accidental sources. And finally there was the vast range of informal, unofficial, unclassifiable means of communication not immediately directed to any of the three categories already mentioned, through casual voyagers, merchants, and soldiers. The volume of such communication was considerable, but its reliability is doubtful and not measurable. No one could depend on it for public or private decision making. The contrast between the documentation available in the Hellenic world and the records of either the Roman Senate from the time of Caesar or the Venetian Council of the later Middle Ages reflects the "backwardness" of the ancient Greeks in the field of communication, and it shows that major advances did not necessarily require technological change.

See also COINS; HISTORIOGRAPHY.

Bibliography. Moses I. Finley, "Censorship in Classical Antiquity," in *Democracy, Ancient and Modern*, 2d ed., ed. by Moses I. Finley, New Brunswick, N.J., and London, 1985; Stewart Flory, "Who Read Herodotus' *Histories?*" *American Journal of Philology* 101 (1980): 12–28; E. A. Havelock, *Origins of Western Literacy*, Toronto, 1976; idem, *Preface to Plato*, Oxford, 1963; F. G. Kenyon, *Books and Readers in Ancient Greece and Rome*, 2d ed., Oxford, 1951; Friedmar Kuhnert, *Allgemeinbildung und Fachbildung in der Antike*, Berlin, 1961; Diego Lanza, *Lingua e discorso nell'Atene delle professioni*, Naples, 1979; Oddone Longo, *Tecniche della comunicazione nella Grecia antica*, Naples, 1981; Gianfranco Nieddu, "Alfabetismo e diffusione sociale della scrittura nella Grecia arcaica e classica," *Scrittura e civiltà* 6 (1982): 233–261; Georg

Rohde, "Über das Lesen im Altertum," in *Studien und Interpretationen zur antiken Literatur, Religion und Geschichte*, Berlin, 1963.

MOSES I. FINLEY

HERALDRY

Derived from the word *herald,* dating from the MIDDLE AGES and designating a professional who served as an ambassador, a messenger of war and peace, or a proclaimer or announcer at court gatherings and tournaments of arms. The herald thus had to be able to recognize the personal markings or coats of arms of individuals and nations.

Origin of Heraldry as a System

During the Crusades (*see* CRUSADES, THE) the need to distinguish friend from enemy on the battlefield led to the development of a system of markings making it possible to identify individuals whose features were obscured by helmets and armor. The social structure of feudalism was thus mirrored in the equipment of combatants, expressed through the size and form of buntings carrying markings, colorful designs on shields and helmets, and types of helmet crests. *See also* BODY DECORATION; CLOTHING.

Between the First and Second Crusades national capacities for waging warfare were exercised and tested by means of tournaments, displays of military skill that proceeded according to certain rules and regulations. As the court personnel who made a specialty of identifying tournament participants, heralds attained great status, and the range of their activities continued to expand. Heralds served as court recordkeepers, provided eyewitness accounts of battles, and kept official lists of casualties. At a time when most of the population was illiterate (*see* LITERACY) heraldry and its practitioners were of central importance.

Both on the European continent and in England a rivalry arose between heralds and other court members such as minstrels. The great significance of military arms and indicators of rank in feudal society eventually resulted in the greater influence of heralds as bearers of ORAL CULTURE and ORAL HISTORY. They performed a valuable service by centralizing the information they gathered, resulting in registers or rolls of armorial marks that are vital to the modern science of heraldry. Regional or local rolls were incorporated into general rolls that included the coats of arms of real sovereigns as well as those of legendary historical figures such as Adam and Eve, the seven Roman kings, or Alexander the Great. Some general rolls even provide fictional coats of arms for God the Father, the Holy Trinity, or Christ. Such examples are generally quite unheraldic, indicating

that early collectors were aware of their historical invalidity. "Occasional rolls" were often compiled for specific events such as tournaments or military actions. Heralds frequently produced rolls of arms as part of their apprenticeships or as gifts for royal patrons.

Early heroic ART and literature indicate that by the second quarter of the twelfth century the use of heraldic emblems for identification was firmly established. One of the first surviving examples is the monument of Geoffrey Plantagenet, later count of Anjou (Figure 1). During the ceremony in which he was knighted by his stepfather, Henry I of England, he received a shield decorated with heraldic lions that can still be seen on his enamel tomb-plate (*see* ART, FUNERARY).

In the feudal system the inheritance of power and wealth by successive generations consolidated the status of heraldry. Coats of arms indicated one's FAMILY, rank, and holdings and could reflect adjustments in these over time, as through marriage, inheritance, and knighthood. The practice of securing ownership with written documents led to an increase

Figure 1. *(Heraldry)* Geoffrey of Anjou. From *Boutell's Heraldry,* rev. ed., London: Frederick Warne, 1978, p. 5. Revised by J. P. Brooke-Little (Frederick Warne & Co., 1950, 1983), copyright © Frederick Warne & Co., 1983. Reproduced by permission of Penguin Books Ltd.

in the use of seals, which up to that time had been a privilege accorded only to royalty. Seals were used in ancient Egypt, Babylonia, Assyria, and China to mark private property. Seal engraving was established as an art in these cultures because there was a need for devices that could not be easily forged. Seals affixed to official parchments often featured monarchs in a characteristic pose, perhaps seated on a throne. The medieval knight was usually pictured on horseback and in full armor, bearing the heraldic markings identifying him even in the thick of battle (Figure 2). When not engaged in military activities the knight was entitled to use his heraldic emblems for other, civic purposes. As they became more common, seals were used almost exclusively as legal signatures. Much knowledge about heraldry in the Middle Ages has come from the study of armorial seals.

Development of the Heraldic Style

The effective use of *cognizances,* a term usually replaced today by *coats of arms* or *achievements,* was derived from the conditions and technology of early warfare. In order to protect the body from injury during sword fights and long-distance combat using projectiles, especially arrows, soldiers wore armor covering most of the body and carried shields attached to the left arm by straps. The shield's relatively large, firm surface provided a particularly suitable place for mounting easily visible markings.

The choice of such markings was arbitrary, although it was important to select patterns that were clearly identifiable and unique within a surveyable geographic area. Two types of graphic designs predominated: abstract geometrical divisions of the shield into two or more colored areas (giving rise to the development of what are known in modern heraldry as the "ordinaries"; Figure 3); and decorative figures ("charges") from the environment or the cosmos (Figure 4). These charges include living beings (people, animals, birds, fish, reptiles, and chimeric beasts), plants (trees, branches, leaves, and flowers), heavenly bodies, and implements of all kinds. One characteristic of the heraldic style is to fill all available space with detailed ornamentation: the hairy part of a lion's mane; animal tails, claws, beaks, and tongues; a fish's fin; rose petals; the stamen of a fleur-de-lis. Some charges were particularly preferred, such as the lion and eagle among animal figures and the rose and ornamental lily among plants.

The choice of colors and charges was also governed by particular considerations. Canting arms, for example, play upon the bearer's name in the form of a pun or rebus (e.g., sheaves of oats for *Candavène* [in modern French, *Champ d'Avoine*] in the French province of Artois; in Spain, a winged hand for

Figure 2. *(Heraldry)* Seal of Thomas de Beauchamp, third earl of Warwick, 1344. From *Boutell's Heraldry,* rev. ed., London: Frederick Warne, 1978, p. 7. Revised by J. P. Brooke-Little (Frederick Warne & Co., 1950, 1983), copyright © Frederick Warne & Co., 1983. Reproduced by permission of Penguin Books Ltd.

Manuel, from the Latin *manus-ala*). Some coats of arms were designed as variations on the coat of arms of one's feudal lord (resulting, for example, in the lion group of the Netherlands and the lower Rhine region). Others were variations on the coat of arms of a highborn ancestor. Avoiding the duplication of heraldic arms was possible only within a circumscribed geographic area, which explains how identical coats of arms could develop independently in different regions (e.g., those of Flanders, the margravate of Meissen, and the county of Mahlberg in southern Baden all featured a black lion on a golden background).

Tinctures. The easy recognition of emblems from a distance was made possible by the use of a few contrasting tinctures, either metals, colors, or furs. English blazons, or technical descriptions of heraldic devices, are based on old French models: yellow (or gold) is known as *or;* white (or silver), *argent;* red, *gules;* blue, *azure;* black, *sable;* and green, *vert.* The metals gold and silver are usually represented by the colors yellow and white, respectively. Colors appear in a particular order of frequency: red, blue, black, and green.

The two most common furs used in heraldry are ermine (represented by black on white) and vair (silver or white and blue, representing gray squirrel; Figure 5). Furs were introduced into heraldry during the Middle Ages as the result of far-reaching cultural and trade connections. Heraldic terminology reflects

Figure 3. *(Heraldry)* Examples of ordinaries: *(a)* bars, bars gemelles, fess cotised, fess double cotised; *(b)* pale, pallets, pale endorsed, pale counterchanged. From *Boutell's Heraldry,* rev. ed., London: Frederick Warne, 1978, pp. 40 and 41. Revised by J. P. Brooke-Little (Frederick Warne & Co., 1950, 1983), copyright © Frederick Warne & Co., 1983. Reproduced by permission of Penguin Books Ltd.

the influence of Middle Eastern languages dating from the time of the Crusades. This military origin can also be seen in the way blazons assume that the achievement is described from the bearer's own point of view. Thus what one sees on the left is described as being on the right or, in heraldic terms, *dexter;* what is seen on the right is actually on the bearer's left and is known as *sinister.*

Graphic characteristics. In early heraldry coats of arms were used in ways such that colors could not be shown, as on tombstones or in seals. During the fifteenth century PRINTING made possible one solution to the problem by allowing letters indicating color to be placed in or next to fields or figures. Early in the seventeenth century this method was replaced by the more efficient technique of hatching, a means of indicating color by patterns of dots and lines. This meant that particular heraldic devices could be appropriately interpreted in different countries, transcending the language barrier. *See also* GRAPHIC REPRODUCTION.

Role of the Coat of Arms

An important element of medieval armor was the helmet covering the wearer's skull and eyes. The combination of shield and helmet shown by the bearer when on horseback and the way they hung on a hook after being removed built the basics for the design of a complete achievement. Patterns originally painted onto the surface of the helmet were eventu-

ally replaced by more easily visible three-dimensional structures called heraldic crests. Elements other than the shield in the complete coat of arms were influenced most by developments in the arts. The helmet as featured in heraldic emblems of the Middle Ages corresponded to actual armorial models. Mantlings or lambrequins, pieces of cloth extending from the top of the helmet to shield the metal from the hot eastern sun, at first functioned merely as protection against climate and temperature changes. In the coat of arms they developed into a decorative framework allowing the heraldic artist to display his skills when drawing or painting the ornamental panels of fabric. To the shield, the helmet, the crest, and the mantling may be added in the modern coat of arms such features as a wreath, an insignia of an order of knighthood, supporters (often human or animal figures bearing up the shield of arms), and a motto (Figure 6).

In the sixteenth century crowns or coronets became an important component of the coat of arms. Before that they had been used solely by monarchs as an insignia of rank in paintings as well as on shields (*see* PORTRAITURE). Crowns eventually replaced the helmet and even the mantling in some achievements, particularly in Latin nations, and coats of arms began to follow the architectural and DESIGN features of RENAISSANCE art (*see* ARCHITECTURE).

The heraldic style developed differently in different regions, so that typical features of an achievement often reveal its specific area of origin. Coats of arms

Figure 4. *(Heraldry)* Examples of charges: *(a)* cockatrice, erect; *(b)* deer, at gaze; *(c)* English dragon, rampant. From Hubert Allcock, *Heraldic Design: Its Origins, Ancient Forms, and Modern Usage,* New York: Tudor Publishing Company, 1962, p. 18.

designed (or redesigned) in Britain, Scandinavia, Middle Europe, Italy, Spain, Portugal, Poland, or Hungary may differ in terms of the preponderance of two- or three-dimensional drawings, the shape of the shield, the division of the shield's area, a preference for certain motifs, the skill of the mantling design, or the type of crown or coronet depicted.

Quartering. The practice of dividing the surface of the shield into several parts can be traced to early Spain. The union of the two Iberian kingdoms, Castile and León, around 1230 was expressed in the "marshaling" of their coats of arms—Castile's a golden castle in a red field, León's a purple lion in a silver field—into a single quartered shield. A quartered shield is divided into at least four sections by vertical and horizontal partition lines, each section displaying a complete coat of arms. Eleanor of Castile brought this method with her when she married King Edward I of England in 1254. In the same manner the later English monarchs combined the coats of arms of England and France, calling themselves rulers of both countries from 1337 to 1801.

During the fourteenth century the number of quartered coats of arms increased considerably throughout Europe. The practice made possible the display of inheritances and inherited titles; even tokens for specific persons or items could be designed and placed in the second or third quarter of a shield. When appropriate a second helmet with crest might be added to the coat of arms. Quartering flourished in Germany and especially in England (Figure 7), where several dozens of quarterings could accumulate for each shield based on ancestral coats of arms. This system reflected the class-based structure of European society, a structure that remained basically stable until the mid-eighteenth century and the turmoil giving rise to the French and American revolutions. Classic heraldic rules and graphics thus functioned as a SIGN SYSTEM for the communication of institutionalized power and privilege.

National coats of arms. The equation of ruler and state in many early political hierarchies was reflected in the identical coats of arms of nation and sovereign. When a ruler was head of more than one state or even a number of smaller territories such as dukedoms, a separate coat of arms could be used for each. These achievements were usually shown as a group, but after the invention of quartering they were incorporated into a single shield. The escutcheon (shield) of pretense gained importance in cases in which

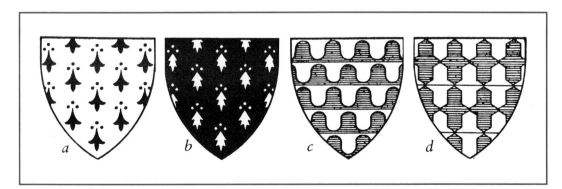

Figure 5. *(Heraldry)* Examples of tinctures: *(a)* ermine; *(b)* ermines; *(c)* vair; *(d)* countervair. From *Boutell's Heraldry,* rev. ed., London: Frederick Warne, 1978, p. 28. Revised by J. P. Brooke-Little (Frederick Warne & Co., 1950, 1983), copyright © Frederick Warne & Co., 1983. Reproduced by permission of Penguin Books Ltd.

Figure 6. *(Heraldry)* Spanish coat of arms. From El Marqués de Avilés, *Ciencia heroyca reducida a las leyes heráldicas del blasón,* Madrid, 1780. Facsimile, Barcelona: Círculo del Bibliófilo, vol. 2, 1979, frontispiece.

arms. Most socialist republics avoid the use of a shield as a background for figurative emblems. Instead the frame usually consists of plants (often ears of grain), twigs, and an inscribed ribbon or band. The function of national representation is now often taken over by the national flag, which in many cases is geometrically divided into rectangular planes just as in traditional heraldry. As the number of independent nations increases, so does the range of patterns and designs. This has resulted in the explosive growth of one aspect of the study of heraldry—vexillology, or the study of flags. *See also* POLITICAL SYMBOLS.

Civic heraldry. The practice of ascribing heraldic achievements to individual communities is increasing in popularity. Up to the early twentieth century only cities or towns were customarily entitled to coats of arms, but now in some areas (as diverse as Switzerland, Finland, or the state of Rhode Island in the United States) every community, however small, is equipped with its own coat of arms. Almost every European city or town has long had its own achievement. Elsewhere the granting of coats of arms may be a more confusing matter dependent largely on colonial developments; in much of Latin America, for example, they are the result of grants by Spanish kings (*see* COLONIZATION).

Civic heraldry generally follows the rules of conventional heraldry. However, while a family may freely choose its coat of arms, a civic or municipal achievement must be granted or at least approved by some authority. In the late twentieth century it is usual for civic heraldic emblems to consist only of a shield, although there are exceptions that make use of historical themes. In socialist countries civic heraldry has developed quite differently. Hungarian examples employ progressive applied graphics similar

foreign monarchs or commoners attained positions of national leadership. In this way it became possible for the coat of arms of a reigning family to differ from that of the country, especially in new nations that arose from the division or defeat of old states. Paralleling this development is the still-observed medieval custom in which each member of a ruling dynasty (e.g., those of twentieth-century Britain, Sweden, and the Netherlands) has additional devices, or marks of cadency, incorporated into his or her coat of arms.

Many republics established after the late eighteenth century have attempted to create coats of arms based on historical events or designated national symbols (e.g., animals, trees) rather than monarchical emblems such as crowns (Figure 8). A seal consisting of pictures or images not at all related to heraldry often performs the same function as a state coat of

Figure 7. *(Heraldry)* Examples of quartering: *(a)* the royal arms of the house of Plantagenet, ca. 1400–1603; *(b)* the arms of Richard II. From *Boutell's Heraldry,* rev. ed., London: Frederick Warne, 1978, p. 209. Revised by J. P. Brooke-Little (Frederick Warne & Co., 1950, 1983), copyright © Frederick Warne & Co., 1983. Reproduced by permission of Penguin Books Ltd.

Figure 8. *(Heraldry)* Coats of arms of republics, ca. 1960: *(a)* Bolivia; *(b)* Cuba; *(c)* Guatemala. From Hubert Allcock, *Heraldic Design: Its Origins, Ancient Forms, and Modern Usage,* New York: Tudor Publishing Company, 1962, pp. 76 and 77.

to those commonly used in the design of contemporary badges or buttons. There is even an increasing interest in national heraldry, in a conservative way, in Poland and the Soviet Union.

Political and social circumstances directly influence the observance of heraldic rules and regulations as well as the form of heraldic insignia. In societies in which nobility constitutes a social class, institutions are established just to enforce these rules. When civic coats of arms are created, such institutions are relied on for their knowledge of heraldry, a task that exceeds their original duties. In Britain this function is performed by the College of Arms, also known as The Heralds' College; in the Netherlands, by the Hoge Raad van Adel. In some countries civic heraldry is the province of a special department in the state's records office.

The legacy of classical heraldry can be seen not only in personal and national coats of arms and in the revival of interest in heraldry but also in the long-standing use of heraldic emblems and devices on COINS and currency, on STAMPS, and in the symbols adopted by SPORTS clubs, schools and universities (Figure 9), Masonic lodges, military bodies, and groups of all kinds to proclaim identity by means of a unique VISUAL IMAGE. Even traffic signs and signals reflect the influence of graphic techniques first devised for heraldic purposes. Perhaps most apparent is heraldry's contribution to the widespread use of ADVERTISING logos and corporate trademarks that prompt immediate recognition (Figure 9).

See also ICONOGRAPHY; REPRESENTATION, PICTORIAL AND PHOTOGRAPHIC; SIGNAGE.

Bibliography. Alan Beddoe, *Beddoe's Canadian Heraldry,* rev. by Strom Galloway, Belleville, Ont., 1981; Charles

Figure 9. *(Heraldry)* Examples of the use of heraldry in advertising. From Hubert Allcock, *Heraldic Design: Its Origins, Ancient Forms, and Modern Usage,* New York: Tudor Publishing Company, 1962, pp. 40–42.

Boutell, *Boutell's Heraldry*, rev. ed., rev. by J. P. Brooke-Little, London and New York, 1983; Richard Marks and Ann Payne, eds., *British Heraldry from Its Origins to c. 1800*, London, 1978; Ottfried Neubecker, *A Guide to Heraldry*, New York, 1979; Ottfried Neubecker with John Philip Brooke-Little, *Heraldry: Sources, Symbols and Meaning* (Heraldik), New York, 1976; Michel Pastoureau, *Traité d'héraldique*, Paris, 1979; Gustav A. Seyler, *Geschichte der Heraldik*, Nuremberg, 1890, reprint Neustadt an der Aisch, FRG, 1970; Karl-Alexander von Volborth, *Heraldry: Customs, Rules and Styles*, Dorset, Eng., 1981; Anthony Richard Wagner, *Heralds and Heraldry in the Middle Ages* (1939), 2d ed., London, 1956.

OTTFRIED NEUBECKER
(Translated by Barbara G. Potzka)

HERMENEUTICS. *See* INTERPRETATION.

HISTORIOGRAPHY

The writing of history. The term derives from two Greek words, *historia* ("inquiry") and *graphein* ("to write"), marking it as a communicative activity that renders an account of the past to present and future generations. Initially a general inquiry into the phenomena of the world, *historia* later became a systematic inquiry into the past. The course of human affairs had always threatened to limit each generation's perception of the world to the here and now unless a link with the past could be established. Historians made possible communication between past and present when they compiled historical accounts—oral or written—and, in doing so, tempered change with the other basic aspect of human life: continuity. The identification of stable or recurrent features in different historical periods made possible a connection between the account of the past, the experience of the present, and the resultant expectations for the future. In this sense history is communication on the grandest scale, spanning centuries of human life, informing and transmitting.

There have been numerous varieties of historiography, although, particularly from the viewpoint of communication between past, present, and future, two broad types can be discerned: traditional and modern. They differ sharply in what they have tried to convey from generation to generation as well as in their methods and goals.

Traditional Historiographies

The traditional model of historiography was characteristic of societies that stressed continuity over change; looked to the past for guidance, ideals, and legitimacy; and did not envision a radically different future. They emphasized tradition (from the Latin *tradere*, "to hand on"), which could only function through uninterrupted communication of an accepted view of the past. Traditional historiography spoke most strongly of the human origin and the early past, linking authority in knowledge and government to that period. With continuity prevailing over change the critical and innovative ingredients were commensurately small, limited to guarding the purity of tradition.

Ancient Asia. The traditional histories of ancient India, China, and Japan evoked a deep sense of continuity as they communicated to successive generations a shared sense of the past and its lessons for human conduct (*see* EAST ASIA, ANCIENT; SOUTH ASIA, ANCIENT). The Indian story of the remote period of human origin was told by the historical material in the Vedic literature, the *Itihāsa*. It spoke of a steady decline in four stages from a perfect to a corrupt stage and communicated unvarying lessons for proper human conduct. Chinese historiography lacked the ample mythological base and the story of decadence of its Indian counterpart, but the crucial fifth-century *Spring-and-Autumn Annals,* in the version of CONFUCIUS, also told its story of states and power struggles with clear lessons for human conduct. The influence of these annals can be discerned in both Chinese and Japanese examples.

These traditional historiographies tended to encourage respect for the existing order, especially the legitimacy of the rulers. Many Indian histories, often composed by court historians, gave genealogies of ruling dynasties that reached well back into mythological times, carrying a clear message of legitimacy. In Chinese historiography the concept of a mandate from heaven provided a cosmic-mythological sanction for the ruling dynasty but also justification for the revolt against it when the dynasty did not preserve the proper social order. Japanese historiography traced the lineage and authority of the imperial line back to the Sun-Goddess. Not surprisingly, the sources for these stories of the past were frequently official or quasi-official records. In China the History Office (*shi kuan*) produced accounts of the life of the empire. A similar historiography, stimulated by the Chinese example, began in the eighth century C.E. in Japan (the *Kojiki* and the *Nihon Shoki*); here, however, the anchor of stability and continuity was the divine origin of the emperors. When in feudal Japan (eleventh to seventeenth centuries) imperial rule was at a low ebb, histories reflected the shifting power centers in the *Historical Tales* and the *Military Tales*. The sense of uneasiness of that turbulent period was best conveyed in the *Gukansho* (1219) with its mix of the Shinto concern with the imperial order, the Buddhist concept of cycles of growth and decay, and the Confucian insistence on order and harmony. The renewal of a quasi-official national history under the Tokugawa shoguns (1600–1868) signaled the return of centralized order although not of a true imperial rule (*see* TOKUGAWA ERA: SECLUSION POLICY).

The emphasis on the preservation of the traditional order, on the communication from generation to generation of a shared image of the past, prevailed over any aspiration to assess and revise historical accounts critically. The three Asian historiographies were eventually challenged by an alternative account, the Buddhist account of the past (for the period after the Buddha), but none of them found it a serious rival.

Ancient Greece and Rome. Western civilization's traditional historiographies differed in many ways from those of Asia. As early as the sixth and fifth centuries B.C.E., in a decisive development, Greek historiography broke the hold of mythological interpretations on the past. Into the place of tales about gods and heroes Greeks put the stories of ordinary human beings. By the time of Herodotus and Thucydides (both fifth century B.C.E.), the link to the mythological past had become insignificant. Accounts of the polis (city-state) provided a sense of historical continuity until Alexander the Great and the subsequent Hellenistic monarchies introduced another sharp break in the Greek tradition. While local and regional histories continued in Greece proper, these accounts of the pre-Alexandrian past communicated little of value to the large non-Greek populations. In the non-Greek regions, scholars cultivated the Homeric past in critical text studies or searched for a unity of history beyond the monarchies. Studies in text criticism yielded many insights into the Homeric texts, but their rationalistic approach undermined much of the force of the Homeric tradition; attempts to write history with a wider focus never really succeeded until Diodorus Siculus (first century B.C.E.). *See* HELLENIC WORLD.

Roman historiography evolved from several historical traditions. In part it was linked to the venerable Homeric tradition through the story of Aeneas, fleeing westward from the burning Troy and becoming the ancestor of Rome. Coexisting with the Aeneas narrative was the native tradition of Romulus and Remus. And a nonmythological account of the early past, the *Annales Maximi,* prompted by the needs of the Roman state, consisted of records of officeholders, events, and religious functions kept by the high priest. Attempts to synchronize these varied accounts of the earliest past into a coherent tradition continued until the age of Augustus.

Roman historiography proper began late in the third century B.C.E. Reflecting Greek cultural dominance, its early works were written in Greek, thus barring communication with most Romans. This Greco-Roman historiography—its peak achievement being Polybius's *Histories* (second century B.C.E.)—met eventually with resistance from Romans who wished their history to be communicated in Latin and from a Roman perspective. Marcus Porcius Cato the Elder (234–149 B.C.E.) began that work, although Greek models never lost their impact. Subsequently the aims, character, events, concerns, and decline of the Roman Republic were all recounted by Roman historians in annals (a favorite Roman genre since the *Annales Maximi*); compilations of traditional lore (*antiquitates*), especially those by Marcus Terentius Varro (116–27 B.C.E.); and monographs, such as the strongly moralistic or sociocritical works of Sallust. There were also exhortations to a proper civic life in biographies and memoirs; the analysis of historical works as a special genre by rhetoricians such as CICERO (106–43 B.C.E.); and accounts by outsiders, mostly Greek scholars. The subsequent transition from the republic to the empire was recorded in the works of both Livy (59 B.C.E.–17 C.E.) and Tacitus (56–120 C.E.), which were characterized by sympathy for the "Old Rome." Other histories attempted to diminish the distance between the Roman and Greek histories (Dionysius of Halicarnassus, first century B.C.E.); to show the corruption of the emperors (Suetonius, second century C.E.); and to celebrate great individuals (Plutarch, 46?–?120). By the fourth century little genuine appreciation of the Roman past remained, as illustrated in the account by Ammianus Marcellinus and the increasingly popular "brief history" genre, which communicated the bare essentials of the continuous Roman past to a people, including emperors, who no longer had either a true reverence for or a sufficient knowledge of the republican past—a past that was shared by only a minority of the empire's population. *See* ROMAN EMPIRE.

Christian historiography. After the fourth century C.E. Christian historiography radically changed the substance of what was communicated about the past. The ancient history of the Homeric tradition or of the Roman tales was replaced by the story of the Jewish people. Earlier stories about the rise and fall of states yielded to accounts of the path from the Creation to redemption, the world acquired a definite end in the Last Judgment, and time acquired a particular structure based on the historical and religious role of Jesus. Yet the style of written histories changed much less radically than the substance. Even though Christian writers insisted on using the *sermo humilis* (the artless speech of daily life), many of the Greek and Latin models with their sophisticated array of literary forms and rules endured.

Jews and Christians began the counting of years

with Creation, but this scheme was replaced, beginning with the sixth century, by that of Incarnation years (*anno Domini,* "in the year of the Lord"). Since the seventeenth century this system was also used for years prior to the Incarnation (B.C.). Thus time had been anchored in the Christian historical framework. However, historical accounts continued to incorporate other, more secular themes and institutions. For example, the continuity between past, present, and future was thought to be guaranteed by the anticipated survival of the Roman Empire. Of course, those who saw in the Catholic Church the only visible, divinely willed institution of continuity opposed such views. In the *City of God,* St. Augustine (354–430) denied the claim by any institution of this world (the Earthly City) to represent the purity of the City of God. Even so, medieval chroniclers regularly claimed divine sanction for partisan secular matters when they employed spiritual arguments to endow rulers with legitimacy, to integrate ethnic groups into Latin Christendom, and to support political causes.

Despite its universal and spiritual tenor, much of medieval history remained local or regional in scope because historians, faced with an ill-developed network of communications, wrote about those events that fell within their range of experience and interest. This tension between the universal message of Christianity and local or regional interests pervaded all of medieval historiography, which included annals, chronicles, *gesta,* and biographies of rulers and saints. Annals and chronicles were typically year-by-year accounts, whereas *gesta* referred to the story of deeds by one or a series of officeholders (e.g., abbots, bishops, or the rulers of a dynasty). As the centuries went on, ever fewer histories began with an account or a digest of the biblical story, often choosing to begin with the birth of Jesus. Nevertheless, the biblical authority was used to affirm the continuity of history through divine providence and prophecy, which interpreted events described in the Bible as prophecies and explanations of future events. The structural element most often used as an argument for universal continuity, prevailing even in local and regional accounts, was the endlessly repeated cycle of human sin and divine retribution. Such a history was congenial to monks, the authors of most chronicles well into the thirteenth century, who wrote for the greater glory of God and the edification of their fellow monks. Because they assumed that the chaos of this world was part of a divine order invisible to human beings, they did not feel the need to strive for an overall interpretation of events for accounts that supplied explanations of causes.

From 1200, the ever-accelerating increase in knowledge created problems for medieval historiography. Higher levels of mastery and organization were required, and historians found the earlier, noninterpretive styles of historical writing to be of little help. As late-medieval universal chronicles overflowed with material, various solutions were attempted: new encyclopedic works (Vincent of Beauvais's *Mirror of the World,* ca. 1250); rudimentary methodological categories for structuring accounts (Ranulf Higden's *Polychronicon,* fourteenth century); grand, most often tripartite order schemes (Joachim of Fiore's three ages of Father, Son, and Holy Spirit, twelfth century); the revival of St. Augustine's dualistic structure; and the pre-Christian concept that all of world history was encompassed by four consecutive empires with Rome being the last (Otto of Freising, twelfth century); and, finally, chronicles in digest versions, the *florilegia.* See MIDDLE AGES.

Modern Historiographies

In the fifteenth century there began a radical change that over the next three hundred years ended traditional Western historiography. Its main elements were the development of text criticism, which subjected texts, formerly revered for their age or sacred origin, to critical analysis; the interpretation of history as the story of the development of secular ideals; the emphasis on a continuous, well-organized, and well-written narrative that attempted to interpret and explain causes; the discovery of archaeological materials as sources; the view that the past was a source of knowledge about life; and the replacement of the spiritual meaning and universal scope of history by a secular framework that expressed the interests of the state. While these innovations first appeared during the RENAISSANCE, the Reformation furthered their development by ending the ecclesiastical and spiritual unity of the West.

Although elements of traditional history remained—particularly the history fashioned after rhetorical patterns that provided lessons for life and a narrative in good style (such as Lord Bolingbroke's view of history as the teacher of philosophy by examples)—they were not the building blocks of future historiography. Instead, under the impact of the above innovations, there began in Western civilization a search for a new way of interpreting history, one that no longer could assume a well-established and generally shared view of the past.

New methods and sources. Text criticism, viewed as guarantor of historical truth, supported the methodological views characteristic of the seventeenth- and eighteenth-century erudite historians (Jean Mabillon, the Bollandists, and the Maurists), who collected and critically assessed primary sources. The range of historical methods and subject matter was widened by the Göttingen scholars of the eighteenth century, typified by Leopold von Ranke (1795–1886), who helped bring about scientific history (*Geschichtswissenschaft*) as an ordered, methodologically structured, and critical inquiry with close ties to philology. The most influential legacies of that school are a sophisticated body of historical methods and the great nineteenth-century text editions (*Monumenta Germaniae Historica* and the Rolls Series).

The universal manner of history writing, so dominant in Christian historiography, provided, in a secularized mode, a path to a new synthesis for historians. The need for a new synthesis was made more urgent by the great geographical discoveries, but the integration of ever new peoples and areas into historical schemes tailored to traditional Latin Christendom proved difficult. Traditional attempts included accounts written by Sir Walter Raleigh (ca. 1552–1618) and Jacques-Bénigne Bossuet (1627–1704); a more modern, geographically oriented approach was written by George Hornius (1620–1670).

The role of progress. In eighteenth-century Europe some French philosophes proclaimed the general progress of humanity (*see* UTOPIAS). History acquired a new driving force—the growth of rationality—and a new future—the triumph of reason. It meant, however, that interpretations of the past and the present were based on a constant devaluation of the past and a perceived ideal state of human existence in the future. Generations no longer communicated to their successors the wisdom or lessons of the past but measured the authority of the past and all actions in the present by an ideal future to be achieved. Change toward such a future dominated some grand nineteenth-century interpretations of history. Georg Wilhelm Friedrich Hegel (1770–1831) constructed a grand philosophy of history in which change and continuity were merged into a process, the self-realization of the Absolute Idea in time, whereas KARL MARX (1818–1883) viewed history as a process driven by economic changes that transformed all of life and led to the ultimate redemption of human beings from history itself. In a less speculative way American history, too, accepted this view: from the Puritan image of America as the shining "City upon a Hill," a model for humanity, to John Adams's insistence on the universal import of the American Revolution and the American mission in human history, to George Bancroft's (1800–1891) fusion of God's Providence and America's democratic mission.

Connected with the scheme of progress were the attempts to see past, present, and future linked by the gradual emancipation of the masses. In a speculative mode, Thomas Carlyle, Jules Michelet, and John R. Green emphasized that message, and so did

the twentieth-century American Progressive historians with their vision of the future universal victory of liberal democracy. In contrast, twentieth-century historians of "the people" preferred the soberly empirical approach that characterized the rise of social history in contemporary historiography, one of its most noted schools being the *Annales* group—Lucien Febvre (1878–1956), Marc Bloch (1886–1944), Fernand Braudel (1902–1985), and Emmanuel Le Roy Ladurie (1929–).

Scientific history's rejection of the speculative and grand style of historical writing in favor of empirical and more narrowly focused studies, along with the surging tide of nationalism, diminished the possibility of a universal history. Yet the aspiration to explain the whole sweep of history has remained alive and has resulted in two approaches: the continued belief in history as the story of progress, especially linked to the growth of science and technology; and cyclical views in which history was presented as a sequence of separately developing cultures or civilizations. This latter model had its best-known advocates in Oswald Spengler (1880–1936) and Arnold Toynbee (1889–1975).

By 1900 the existence of many conflicting views on history as well as the trend toward a "scientific" history with a strictly empirical verification helped to erode the philosophical and religious certainties about the world that had been shared and expressed in historical writings for centuries. In the absence of an accepted synthesis change in historical writing as well as in world events prevailed over continuity, posing the question of what of lasting value could be communicated from generation to generation. On the answer depended the feasibility of a "scientific" history and, for some, the relevance of history to the modern world. One group of historians followed the precepts of Comtean positivism and tried to establish long series of objective facts tied together by cause-and-effect chains in order to arrive eventually at a verifiable historical synthesis. Although the early "scientific" historians in the United States affirmed the older Rankean precepts, they were also inspired by the English positivist historians H. T. Buckle (1821–1862) and William E. Lecky (1838–1903). Their opponents objected that the positivist approach was too mechanical and distinguished insufficiently between the human and natural realms. They included the U.S. New Historians, most notably James H. Robinson (1863–1936) and Charles A. Beard (1874–1948), who were inspired by pragmatism and progressivism and advocated an activist historiography based on the continuing affirmation of progress. German historians such as Wilhelm Dilthey (1833–1911) searched for a theory of history without metaphysical elements while still affirming a human cosmos safely separated from that of nature. Finding such a theory elusive, they generally adhered to an approach in which each historical period is appreciated and studied on its own terms (historicism).

Since the 1940s other attempts at a positivist historiography included Carl Hempel's attempt to introduce the scientific requirements of general laws into history (the Covering Law Theory), while a broad group of scholars, the so-called narrativists, have tried to preserve the difference between natural and historical sciences. They considered the narrative form as central and indicative of the autonomy of history. The debate on the proper reconciliation of past, present, and future continues, with the theoretical discussions accompanied by ideological controversies (particularly the various Marxist views), and, outside Western culture, with attempts to master the historiographical aspects of nation building among developing countries.

See also IDEOLOGY; ISLAM, CLASSICAL AND MEDIEVAL ERAS; ORAL HISTORY; RELIGION.

Bibliography. Ernst Breisach, *Historiography: Ancient, Medieval, and Modern,* Chicago, 1983; Peter Gay, *Style in History,* New York, 1974; Michael Grant, *The Ancient Historians,* New York, 1970; John Higham, *History: Professional Scholarship in America,* Baltimore, Md., 1983; Michael Kraus and Davis D. Joyce, *The Writing of American History,* rev. ed., Norman, Okla., 1985; Savoie Lottinville, *The Rhetoric of History,* Norman, Okla., 1976; Beryl Smalley, *Historians in the Middle Ages,* London, 1974; Haydn V. White, *Metahistory: The Historical Imagination in Nineteenth-Century Europe,* Baltimore, Md., 1973.

ERNST BREISACH

HITCHCOCK, ALFRED (1899–1980)

British-born film director. Known for technically innovative and morally and psychologically complex thrillers, Alfred Hitchcock earned critical respect and wide recognition as the "master of suspense." His aim, he said, was to arouse audiences through "pure film," and his contributions to the language of cinema include an entire movie—*Rope* (1948)—shot without dissolves, in ten-minute takes. Also seminal are such arresting depictions of terror as Janet Leigh's shower murder in *Psycho* (1960) and Cary Grant being chased by a crop duster in *North by Northwest* (1959). But more than his genre's consummate craftsman, Hitchcock was the artist who stretched its limits (*see* GENRE). Beyond style (for Hitchcock, indistinguishable from subject), his more than fifty MOTION PICTURES—from *The Pleasure Garden* (1925) to *Family Plot* (1976)—share macabre humor and a disturbing personal vision: good and evil are proximate, guilt is nebulous, and chaos lurks beneath a veneer of social order.

Hitchcock's career was divided between the studios of England and HOLLYWOOD. During both periods he achieved a remarkable independence, usually choosing his own writers and STARS and, from the early 1950s on, producing his own work. His success within the system as well as his transcendence of genre served as a model for personal filmmakers everywhere.

Born a Catholic grocer's son in Edwardian London, Hitchcock studied engineering and then art before devoting himself to film. His first movie job (1921–1922) was as a designer of silent-film titles for the London office of Famous Players-Lasky. By 1922 he had begun writing scripts, and soon—at Michael Balcon's Gainsborough Studios—he was directing as well. With his 1926 *The Lodger,* the formula for a Hitchcock plot was set: there must be the threat (or fact) of murder, at least one morally suspect character, and a vulnerable woman (preferably a blonde). The major British films followed: *The Man Who Knew Too Much* (1934), *The Thirty-nine Steps* (1935), *The Lady Vanishes* (1938). Though influenced by EXPRESSIONISM, these films were also earthily realistic in style.

In 1938 producer David Selznick invited Hitchcock to Hollywood, where together they made *Rebecca* (1940). Though their partnership dissolved, Hitchcock remained in the United States, producing over the next four decades what many consider his greatest works. Ranging from the stylized clarity of *North by Northwest* to the surrealism of *Vertigo* (1958), their styles varied, as did their subjects: seething small-town America in *Shadow of a Doubt* (1943), voyeurism in *Rear Window* (1954), obsessive passion in *Vertigo.* Always, though, there was the issue of physical danger and the fascination with evil.

Almost always, too, there was popular success, and along with it both critical acclaim and inquiry. Genre experts questioned the plausibility of Hitchcock's plots, whereas for scholars the issue was his seriousness. Some, such as new wave critics Claude Chabrol and Eric Rohmer, found Hitchcock a profound—and also profoundly Catholic—moralist who used the metaphor of criminal transgression to pursue the themes of metaphysical guilt (the transfer of guilt was, for them, Hitchcock's most consistent theme) and redemption. Others rejected the influence of the Catholic impulse but concurred about Hitchcock's metaphysical subtext. Detractors—often pointing to his cool humor, "happy endings," and "McGuffins" (his characteristic plot-triggering devices)—insisted that Hitchcock was a technician and entertainer first, if not exclusively.

Figure 1. *(Hitchcock, Alfred)* Alfred Hitchcock directing *The Thirty-nine Steps*, 1935. National Film Archive, London. By courtesy of The Rank Organisation PLC.

Undisputed, though, is Hitchcock's tremendous iconographic and stylistic impact, particularly on the French NEW WAVE FILM and on the U.S. cinema of the 1970s and 1980s. His transformation of the thriller into a vehicle for personal expression influences both how genre films are made and how they are perceived.

Bibliography. Eric Rohmer and Claude Chabrol, *Hitchcock: The First Forty-four Films* (in French), trans. by Stanley Hochman, New York, 1979; Donald Spoto, *The Dark Side of Genius,* Boston, 1983; Robin Wood, *Hitchcock's Films,* London and New York, 1965.

DIANE JACOBS

HOLLYWOOD

Place name referring to the main production center of the U.S. film industry in southern California, but also conveying various other meanings. To some the term more readily signifies the oligopoly of major studios that have long dominated theater and television screens in many parts of the world and have controlled related enterprises. It also connotes for many a dreamworld revolving around STARS and a legendary way of life projected through fan magazines and other media and exercising a hegemony over fashions, hairdos, and life-styles worldwide. To some it suggests a modern Babylon, a world of titillation and moral danger to be combated by CENSORSHIP and the PRESSURE GROUP. The word also functions as a shorthand for standardized culture and may be used by some critics as a synonym for kitsch. Behind all these meanings, all connoting influence, lies the fact of economic power, often monopolistic in nature, that has evolved throughout film and TELEVISION HISTORY and has been strengthened by numerous developments.

Beginnings

The industry did not begin in Hollywood. It began across the continent in greater New York, where projected motion pictures were introduced to U.S. audiences in 1896, first appearing in vaudeville houses, amusement parks, club halls, and improvised screening rooms and later in storefront theaters known as nickelodeons. As exhibition spread, film production likewise erupted in a host of small units in and around New York, Philadelphia, Chicago, and elsewhere. Competition was chaotic and sometimes violent, with much improvisation of equipment and charges of patent piracy. But quick profits were possible. *See* MOTION PICTURES—SILENT ERA.

MONOPOLY trends made an early appearance. In 1908 ten of the pioneer units led by two of the largest, Edison and Biograph, tried to win industry control through their patents by forming the Motion Picture Patents Company, soon known as the Trust. Producers and exhibitors licensed by the Trust, using equipment covered by patents it controlled, were to do business only with each other, freezing out independents using unauthorized equipment, who were

Figure 1. *(Hollywood)* David Butler, *Thank Your Lucky Stars*, 1943. The Museum of Modern Art/Film Stills Archive.

constantly accused of patent infringement. The Trust was eventually ruled illegal and in any case never won complete control. But meanwhile some independent producers trickled to southern California. As movie tastes veered toward action films, especially westerns *(see* WESTERN, THE)—and after 1914 to feature-length spectacles of the sort favored by D. W. GRIFFITH and others—the westward trickle became an increasing migration of people and companies. A grand choice of terrain, year-round good production weather, and room for expansion welcomed them. The migration became "Hollywood."

Rise to Power

World War I furthered the rapid growth of the industry. Before the war a number of countries had been film exporters. France, which in 1895 had been the first to show films commercially, had generally been the export leader, followed by the United States, Italy, England, and Germany. But the war brought French, Italian, and British production almost to a standstill and isolated the German industry, while audiences far and wide remained ravenous for film. Hollywood proceeded to fill the vacuum, as one of the most spectacular booms in history began under the California sun. Such emerging stars as Mary Pickford, Douglas Fairbanks, and CHARLES CHAPLIN became international legends, of incalculable value to their studios, and able to command such unheard-of salaries as $10,000 a week. Their fame soon affected trade practices. By 1915 a European theater wanting to obtain a Chaplin film from its distributor, Essanay, found it had to contract for the entire Essanay output. Block-booking thus entered the film world and became a factor in Hollywood's international status. After the war European film industries, reactivating production, found it difficult to win reentry into their own domestic markets, as leading theaters were block-booked in extended contracts. Audiences seemed untroubled—by now, films meant Hollywood. Some countries adopted import barriers and exhibition quotas for cultural as well as financial reasons, but the efforts did not greatly impede the U.S. industry; economics favored its continued hegemony. Because the U.S. domestic market included a third of the world's theaters, Hollywood features regularly earned back their investments at home and could undersell local products almost anywhere. Meanwhile the U.S. market seemed impenetrable to foreign producers. Many of the leading theaters had become producer owned, while others were under block-booking contracts. Hollywood, scarcely a decade old, was already an entrenched power.

Industry consolidation. By the 1920s the leading elements of the long-defunct Trust—Biograph, Edison, Essanay, Kalem, Kleine, Lubin, Gaston Méliès, Pathé, Selig, Vitagraph—had vanished from the top hierarchy, replaced by such names as Fox, Loew, Paramount, Universal, and others. With growth came huge new corporate mergers and realignments aided by Wall Street interests. Producers sought market security by acquiring chains of theaters; large chains of theaters sought to assure themselves of films by acquiring production companies. Out of the maneuvers emerged an industry dominated by giants. As they came under attack—from religious groups that increasingly saw films as an immoral influence, and independent producers and distributors contesting the amalgamation process—the giants grew close together.

Sound film. The advent of sound, which might have loosened the industry structure, in the end hastened its consolidation. Experiments to link sound and image had long been in progress, with leading studios only cautiously interested because fortunes were being made with silents. But when a lesser studio, Warner Brothers, ventured into sound to improve its precarious industry position and in 1927 won a reverberating success with *The Jazz Singer,* starring Al Jolson, the events precipitated an industry upheaval. The large companies with Wall Street connections had little difficulty financing the changeover to sound, and did so with remarkable speed, but many smaller producers and exhibitors simply closed down or sold out to the giants. By 1930 the transformation of the industry into a virtual oligopoly had been completed. Warner, having in the process become one of the giants, was part of it. The oligopoly now consisted of eight companies, which for the next two decades would constitute the aristocracy of Hollywood. This was the era of the big studio, which would give Hollywood its global image, one that would prevail even after the reality had changed. *See* MOTION PICTURES—SOUND FILM.

Studio World

Most powerful of the eight were the "Big Five": Loew's (including MGM), Paramount (formerly Famous Players-Lasky), Twentieth Century-Fox, Warner, and RKO (an amalgamation of various production and exhibition interests). These five companies were fully integrated; that is, they produced motion pictures, distributed worldwide, and owned theater chains where their pictures were guaranteed showings. In alliance with them were the "Little Three": Columbia, Universal, and United Artists. Columbia and Universal were producer-distributors that supplied the Big Five mostly with low-cost pictures for double features; United Artists, which had been created in 1919 by Pickford, Fairbanks, Chaplin, and Griffith, was solely a distributor for a small number of independents. These eight constituted the majors.

"Poverty Row" existed on the periphery. Small studios such as Monogram, Republic, Grand National, and Producers' Releasing Corporation serviced theaters in small towns and rural areas. As a group they had a marginal impact on the industry.

Corporate headquarters for the industry remained in New York, close to sources of finance; production was centered in Hollywood, which by now had fine-honed an efficient means of mass production: the studio system. Double features had become an exhibition standard, and Hollywood produced two classes of pictures to fill the need: class A, with name stars, big budgets, and high production values; and class B, economy films needed to meet distribution commitments. Each studio aimed to release an average of a feature film per week, plus short subjects. In terms of variety, studios produced a range of genres including crime films, musicals (*see* MUSICAL, FILM—HOLLYWOOD GENRE), westerns, melodramas, and screwball comedies (*see* COMEDY). Production was hierarchically organized and highly departmentalized, with a complex web of controls.

Censorship

The industry had long been troubled by multiplying censorship systems. Several U.S. states, a number of cities, and many foreign countries had set up official censors or censor boards, who sometimes banned films outright or required specific excisions before films could be shown. Their criteria varied widely. Some boards charged a fee for their review "services." To combat these distribution obstacles, the majors in 1930 adopted a Motion Picture Production Code, proclaiming moral principles they pledged to observe. The hope was that this "self-censorship" would arrest and even reverse the censorship trend. But two years later the Roman Catholic church, declaring compliance with the code to be too lax, created the Legion of Decency, which established its own rating system. Catholics were pressed to boycott films condemned by the Legion. To counter this economic threat the majors put teeth into their own

Figure 2. *(Hollywood)* Busby Berkeley, *Gold Diggers of 1935*, 1935. The Museum of Modern Art/ Film Stills Archive.

code by setting up a Production Code Administration under Joseph I. Breen, with power to penalize any of the studios overstepping the code or violating Breen office rulings on permissible topics, plotting, dress, lovemaking, language, and other matters— including ADVERTISING. Strict as the system was, it did not replace other censorship systems; in fact, new layers of supervision were added by World War II. With war films in demand, the studios looked to the federal government for cues on subject matter and treatment and received crucial support in facilities, consultants, and uniformed extras, resulting in a close collaboration. Soon after the war the cold war began, bringing a "red scare" to the major U.S. media. Film industry leaders, prompted by accusations in congressional hearings—especially those of the House Committee on Un-American Activities (HUAC)—instituted secret personnel blacklists that for years influenced production planning. Safe topics were the order of the day. Throughout this era films from Hollywood appeared to be the most censored of media. Yet working within the web of controls, the men and women of big-studio Hollywood—an extraordinary international assemblage of artists and technicians—were able to mass-produce work that defined for much of the world what a motion picture could be. Many observers have looked on the big-studio period as Hollywood's golden age.

Crises

But suddenly it all seemed to unravel. Around mid-century Hollywood encountered three devastating, virtually concurrent crises. Coming on the heels of years of prosperity, the reversals seemed almost unbelievable and for a time seemed likely to overwhelm Hollywood. The Hollywood that eventually emerged from the crises was, in fact, very different.

Antitrust. The first blow came from the U.S. Supreme Court. In 1948, climaxing a historic antitrust suit against the eight majors—*United States* v. *Paramount et al.*—the Court ruled that the companies had formed an illegal combination to control film exhibition. The Court ordered the integrated companies to divest themselves of their theater chains, which had been an important element in their control of the industry. It also outlawed block-booking and other trade practices that had kept independent exhibitors in a subordinate position and had virtually barred independent producers, including foreign producers, from leading U.S. theaters.

In the upheaval that followed the ruling, a new mode of production gradually replaced the studio system: independent production. As the majors retrenched, scrapping production plans and paring studio payrolls, many of the actors, directors, and others set adrift by the process turned to independent production. They saw the possibility of market access and welcomed the fact that the majors, having lost control of the market, had lost their power of censorship. (An advisory rating system eventually replaced the Hollywood code and its enforcement machinery.) The majors too shifted into a different role. Following procedures in effect at United Artists, they began functioning mainly as financiers and distributors of films rather than as producers. The independents became the source of much of Hollywood's creative initiative; but, crucially dependent

Figure 3. *(Hollywood)* Cecil B. DeMille directing a scene in *Triumph,* 1924. The Museum of Modern Art/Film Stills Archive.

on finance and effective distribution, they tended to become satellites of the old majors. Most of these leading companies, as financiers and distributors, ultimately proved able to retain their central power, but in a more loosely structured industry.

Television. About the same time as the Supreme Court decision, another devastating crisis struck Hollywood. Box-office attendance had begun a decline, and it continued for a decade; in the United States attendance dropped by 50 percent during this period. The reason was clear: television was rapidly replacing movies as the dominant LEISURE activity. Theaters closed; profits plummeted. Hollywood was close to panic and had reason to make further retrenchments.

It tried various competitive strategies. Television appearances by contract stars were vetoed. The majors barred their films, old and new, from television. (The films of Poverty Row were, however, earning a bonanza on the tube.) To lure the audience back, Hollywood tried 3-D and such wide-screen processes as Cinerama, Cinemascope, and Vistavision (*see* CINEMATOGRAPHY). The innovations succeeded, but audiences did not resume their former ways. They flocked to the occasional blockbuster, then back to television. The mid-1950s brought a reversal of strategy. One after another, leading studios contracted with the networks to produce filmed series—mainly westerns at first—for commercial network sponsorship. On the heels of this move they began releasing their backlog of features for television use, earning lifesaving cash infusions. While transforming Hollywood, they also transformed television. By 1960 U.S. television schedules, which had been three-quarters

live, were at least three-quarters film. The television industry had made Hollywood its main production center. The move and its timing had even wider significance: television was beginning or about to begin in scores of other countries. The filmed series might have worldwide markets. In midcrisis Hollywood began to glimpse a new and different future, one that would actually extend its power. But it would also involve new hurdles.

Trade barriers. In the devastation left by World War II, many nations sought to protect their economies by new means. The freezing of funds was one of these measures. Many European and Asian nations, while giving Hollywood free access to their screens, limited the earnings that the industry could remit. As a result, the majors acquired large foreign bank accounts in foreign currencies, which they could not convert into dollars or transfer to the United States. But the funds could buy local goods and services, so Hollywood had reasons to produce abroad, creating the phenomenon of runaway production. Blocked funds were thus turned into international assets—for theatrical and television distribution. Authentic locales, low labor costs, and tax advantages were additional incentives. Many countries were also using subsidies to boost local production; the U.S. companies, through their foreign subsidiaries, became eligible for such subsidies. The films could also be included in the quotas widely imposed on theaters, which mandated a minimum proportion of domestic productions. The various protective devices thus stimulated a greatly increased U.S. involvement abroad. Hollywood became truly international in scope, producing films on every continent and tailoring its products to world markets. Its distribution activities were meanwhile expanding in other ways, challenged by new technologies. The potentialities of CABLE TELEVISION, SATELLITE transmission, VIDEO in its various uses, the laser videodisc—all offered new vistas and possible crucial gambles. Hollywood saw the need to move into all. As costs mounted, it explored marketing strategies involving the entire leisure field. Amusement park exhibits, soundtrack tapes, book tie-ins, and the merchandising of toys, games, and clothing all created profit centers to amortize rising development and production costs. But uncertainties likewise mounted.

Conglomerate Era

During these postwar decades the expanding involvements and risks stimulated a trend toward the formation of conglomerates. Film companies diversified into other fields or merged with or were absorbed by corporations in other businesses. In the 1960s Paramount was acquired by Gulf and Western, which had holdings in steel, hydraulics, mining, plastics, and other industries. United Artists was absorbed by Transamerica Corporation, Warner Brothers by Kinney Services. In the 1970s MGM was taken over by Kirk Kerkorian Enterprises, and Columbia Pictures became part of Coca-Cola. A reason for such moves was the quest for security. A downturn in any one line of business could be offset by involvement in others. Conglomeration appeared to have a stabilizing effect, giving Hollywood room to maneuver in a difficult time. But it also heightened concerns about the widening hegemony of the U.S. media abroad. Consumption of Hollywood's products had grown worldwide, and cries of "cultural imperialism" were increasingly heard as relationships between media and society came everywhere under closer scrutiny.

Bibliography. Tino Balio, ed., *The American Film Industry*, 2d ed., rev., Madison, Wis., 1985; Michael Conant, *Antitrust in the Motion Picture Industry*, Berkeley, Calif., 1960, reprint (ed. by Garth S. Jowett) New York, 1978; Thomas H. Guback, *The International Film Industry: Western Europe and America Since 1945*, Bloomington, Ind., 1969; Benjamin B. Hampton, *A History of the Movies*, New York, 1931; I. C. Jarvie, *Movies and Society*, New York, 1970; Garth S. Jowett, *Film: The Democratic Art*, Boston, 1976; James Monaco, *American Film Now*, New York, 1979; Robert Sklar, *Movie-made America: A Social History of American Movies*, New York, 1975.

TINO BALIO

HOMILETICS

The science of liturgical ORATORY. The word *homiletics* is derived from the Greek *homilētikos* ("of conversation") and *homilia* ("converse or dealings

with another"). In ancient Christian usage *homilia* denoted a religious discourse adapted to concerns of the people assembled for worship. Homiletical discourse and the science of homiletics are to be distinguished from several related speech acts: exegesis (philological analysis), catechesis (instruction), kerygma (evangelistic proclamation), *paranesis* (ethical admonition), prophecy, theology, apologetics, hermeneutics (science of INTERPRETATION), and catechetics (science of instruction).

Homiletics prescribes methods for effective preaching. Paradoxically, the effectiveness of the preaching is attributed not to the method but to the initiative of God, who speaks through the SPEECH of the homilist. This paradox is fundamental for an understanding of the Abrahamic religious traditions, particularly Judaism and Christianity, which conceive of God as a transcendent personal being who communicates with humanity in a way that invites and allows free response. The divine-human relationship resulting from this communication is understood to be a historical dialectic generating scriptures as well as communities for whom those scriptures are sacred and reality defining. Other religious communities, most notably the Buddhist, have also developed a tradition of preaching, especially after contact with the West. Neither Buddhist nor Hindu preaching, however, is mandated scripturally or confined within a RITUAL. Because homiletical exposition is an act of worship meant to enable ancient texts to continue to function as contemporaneous words of God, homilists need authorization. Some denominations restrict the power and privilege of homiletical discourse by law to the ordained and by custom to those whose personal morality lends credibility to their speech. *See* RELIGION.

Historical overview. Christian homiletical history begins with Jesus and his companions, who themselves stood within a well-established Hellenistic Jewish tradition of discussing the SCRIPTURE in the synagogues. The Jewish and Christian canons provide models for their own homiletical interpretation. The Book of Deuteronomy (or "second law") is a series of discourses, attributed to Moses, explaining the Law. In the Gospel of Luke, Jesus begins his career in the Nazareth synagogue by delivering a homily on the Book of Isaiah, while the Acts of the Apostles describes the preaching of the first generation of Christians. By contrast the Qur'an (or Koran, meaning "recital") takes the form of a direct personal address by God, through the Prophet Muhammad's mouth, confirming and giving an authoritative interpretation of previous scriptures. Being itself an extended homily, the Qur'an has seemed to its adherents to be less in need of contemporizing interpretation than the Hebrew and Christian scriptures have seemed to theirs. *See also* ISLAM, CLASSICAL AND MEDIEVAL ERAS.

Since the homily is an interpretation of text, the homilist must be able to read. The high LITERACY rate in the Hellenistic world supported a rich homiletic tradition in Christian antiquity. Influential in the third- and fourth-century Mediterranean world were Origen, John Chrysostom, and Cyril of Jerusalem; the Cappadocian church fathers Gregory of Nyssa, Basil the Great, and Gregory of Nazianzus (all speaking Greek); and the Latins Ambrose of Milan and Augustine of Hippo, whose death in 430 closed an era (see HELLENIC WORLD; ROMAN EMPIRE). The subsequent decline in EDUCATION brought a decline in the quality and in some places the frequency of preaching in the early MIDDLE AGES. Many homilists had difficulty reading the scripture, particularly as Western Christians forgot Greek and Hebrew and found their native tongues diverging from the Latin into which the scriptures had been translated.

To overcome the language difficulties and to help integrate the in-migrating tribal peoples into the settled Christian populations in and around the territories of the old empire, monasteries fostered bilingualism by taking in Christian and tribal children and raising them together. This did facilitate vernacular preaching. However, homiletic themes were more likely to be drawn from marvelous tales of divine miracles and punishment than from the canonical texts. Collections of model homilies and edifying anecdotes were circulated in a move to improve preaching; those anthologies are considered precursors of European FICTION. Numerous collections of them survive, although works of homiletical theory are less common.

Better homilies were not forthcoming until the general educational level of western Europe improved, around the twelfth and thirteenth centuries. Medieval homilists of note included Bernard of Clairvaux, Francis of Assisi, and Dominic. Their era saw the organization of preaching orders, whose friars were more literate and articulate, centrally administered, and commissioned to travel widely to garner support for consolidation of church power. Among the causes these preachers regarded as contemporary implications of the scriptural word of God were the identification and persecution of heretics, the solicitation of funds for local and Vatican projects, and the launching of military campaigns in which civilians as well as soldiers would be sacrificed to the cause.

Ironically, then, both the tactical success of such preaching and its failure to effect a feeling of relationship between God and hearers led to the Reformation of the sixteenth century, a watershed in the history of Christian homiletics. Protestant Christianity, aided by the PRINTING press, restored the primacy of scripture in the ritual celebration, reemphasizing the word as medium of contact with the divine. MARTIN LUTHER, Philipp Melanchthon, and many other reformers wrote theoretical or practical works of homiletics, which attained the critical methodological self-consciousness of a science for the first time since Augustine. Catholicism and Orthodoxy (the Eastern church) saw God's address through scripture within a larger context in which church traditions, the nonverbal aspects of the cult, and other created things became means of contact with the divine through homiletic interpretation.

Secular influences. Historically Islamic expansion and Christian missionizing have at times allowed the homily to escape its traditional place within the liturgy and also inside religious buildings. This may be observed in the "electronic church," a term that identifies the sense of intimacy and gathering experienced by millions who hear televised or radio sermons while alone (see RELIGIOUS BROADCASTING). The homily has also gone beyond its scriptural frame of reference and has become a political address; but even as political address it celebrates the nation's transcendent values and promotes fidelity to national traditions. In this sense, the nineteenth- and twentieth-century RHETORIC of U.S. national destiny may be seen as neither purely secular nor purely religious.

This interplay of secularizing and religious factors has been a controlling feature of the development of the science of homiletics and its articulation of objectives. Principles of effective preaching have been debated extensively, but generally they have paralleled secular rhetorical principles. Persuasive speech was a political and diplomatic tool prized in the ancient world. Egyptian and other Near Eastern principles of statecraft, including oratory, found their way into the Hebrew Wisdom literature. Hellenistic TEACHING and rhetorical forms were already present in the Christian scriptures and increasingly gave structure and content to Christian address in the first few centuries of the common era. For example, Origen and Augustine adapted allegory as a key to the meaning of Jewish and Christian texts. Platonism shaped the preachers' quest to find God's communication as a transcendent meaning hidden by the literal meanings of texts.

By medieval times Christian liturgical address itself was informing secular oratory. The Jewish and Christian notion that free human decision affects history and that speech precipitates decision shaped the Western view that people—first monarchs, then the masses—could make history by communicating. This conception may be deemed the survival of the Greek idea of democracy but with a difference: human decision here is prompted by God's invitation, so historical events may be seen to bring about a transcendent or divine purpose.

In medieval and modern times the divine purpose often has been linked with or displaced by a military or political interest. Preaching mobilized Europe for expeditions (crusades) against the Muslim administrations in Eastern territories (*see* CRUSADES, THE). The COLONIZATION of the Americas, the continental expansion of the United States, several nonviolent liberation movements, and the foundation of the modern state of Israel all illustrate the secularization of the homiletic dynamic: a transcendent purpose receives oratorical expression so that people are moved to try to achieve what has become through communication their mission. This view may be distinguished from both capitalist and dialectical-materialist paradigms, which emphasize inevitable laws of economic and historical process operating independently of communication (*see* MARXIST THEORIES OF COMMUNICATION—ORIGINS AND DEVELOPMENT). However, works of homiletical theory and practice written from a denominational perspective generally do not credit the interdependence of the homily and secular political rhetoric but instead hold that a pure presentation of God's scriptural word without admixture of pagan or secular techniques is both possible and desirable.

See also PUBLIC SPEAKING.

Bibliography. Henry Ward Beecher, *Yale Lectures on Preaching* (Lyman Beecher Lectureship, 1st–3d series), New York, 1872–1874; Sacvan Bercovitch, *The American Jeremiad,* Madison, Wis., 1978; Yngve Brilioth, *A Brief History of Preaching* (Predikans historia), trans. by Karl E. Mattson, Philadelphia, 1965; Abraham Cohen, *Jewish Homiletics* (Sieff Lectures on Preaching, 1936), London, 1937.

MARIANNE SAWICKI

HORROR FILM

Cinematic GENRE that seeks to bring delight through a therapeutic use of fear. Its characteristic themes and motifs lend themselves to sensationalism and exploitation, but it has deep roots in human psychology, social life, FOLKLORE, and literature. The horror film draws strength from humanity's universal fear of its dead; from dread of the unknown, the deformed, the deviant; from sadistic and masochistic impulses; and from the need to face these and other fears in the safety of ART.

The horror film may articulate our apprehensions of those above or below us in social position, tensions within the FAMILY situation, the consciousness that things have gone wrong in the way we have ordered our lives, and the suspicion that we are at the mercy of powers over which we have no control—together with the desire to achieve such control. It draws on familiar elements from folktales and ballads—devils,

demons, ghosts, vampires, and lycanthropes. The genre reworks themes familiar from a vast literature and subliterature of terror, including the English Gothic novel, German and French romantic tales from Ludwig Tieck and E. T. A. Hoffmann to Charles Nodier and Théophile Gautier, and the American uncanny tale from Nathaniel Hawthorne and Edgar Allan Poe to Henry James (*see* FOLKTALE; LITERATURE, POPULAR). Although some of the masterpieces of cinematic art—from the works of SERGEI EISENSTEIN to those of INGMAR BERGMAN—contain elements derived from the horror film, the most characteristic representatives of that genre lean more toward folktales and pulp fiction. It is an art form of the grotesque in which the terrible is in constant danger of being submerged by laughter, a danger that masters of black humor from James Whale to Roman Polanski have turned to their advantage.

The first classics of the horror film appeared in Germany just before and after World War I: *Der Golem* (1915) and *Der Student von Prag* (1913), both remade several times, and especially Robert Wiene's *Das Cabinet des Dr. Caligari* (1920). Wiene's film brings together structures, themes, and motifs that would henceforth be the staples of the genre— the confusion of waking and dream states, the tension of pursuit ending in a terrible revelation, hypnotists imposing their will, men and women forced into actions and situations the conscious mind denies but the unconscious may desire, strangers invading our personal space, sexual tensions leading up to the climactic moment in which a dark "monster" bends over or carries off a woman in white, and sinister shadows suggesting dark deeds. Other German films of the silent period add the doppelgänger, or double, a feature particularly suited to the trickery of the fantastic film; the golem, or monster of human creation; and the vampire, whose most famous silent avatar is portrayed by Max Schreck in F. W. Murnau's *Nosferatu* (1922; Figure 1). *See* MOTION PICTURES—SILENT ERA.

In the United States the developing genre was shaped and enriched by Lon Chaney, whose ability to combine grotesque physical deformity with pathos in such films as *The Hunchback of Notre Dame* (1923) and *The Phantom of the Opera* (1925) paved the way for the art of Boris Karloff. Some of the German masters of the uncanny (Paul Leni, Paul Wegener, Murnau) also found their way to HOLLYWOOD and helped to forge links between the silent horror film and its early successors in the sound era (*see* MOTION PICTURES—SOUND FILM). The era began in the early 1930s with the release of Carl Dreyer's *Vampyr* (1932) in Europe and Tod Browning's *Dracula* (1931) and James Whale's *Frankenstein* (1931) in the United States. U.S. films soon came to dominate the field. Although their themes—vampiric pos-

Figure 1. *(Horror Film)* Max Schreck as the vampire in *Nosferatu*, 1922. The Museum of Modern Art/Film Stills Archive.

session, witchcraft or voodoo, the dangers of science, humans usurping the place of God—recalled those of their German, Danish, and French predecessors, the trend was now toward more realistic presentations. However stylized the horror films of Universal Studios may have become, they were far from the distortions of decor and gesture that films like *Das Cabinet des Dr. Caligari* and *Waxworks* (Leni, 1924) shared with German expressionist theater (*see* EXPRESSIONISM). *Frankenstein* and *Dracula*, soon joined by werewolves (*The Werewolf of London*, 1934; *The Wolf Man*, 1941), zombies (*White Zombie*, 1932), and new versions of *Dr. Jekyll and Mr. Hyde* (1932, 1941), spawned a host of sequels and imitations. Saturation caused their terrors to evaporate until they were played for laughs as horror figures encountered comedic characters like Abbott and Costello, the Dead End Kids, and Old Mother Riley. This left the field free for a team led by Val Lewton at RKO to experiment with films whose sometimes sensational titles belied their tendency to suggest rather than to show (*Cat People*, 1942; *I Walked with a Zombie*, 1943).

Until the end of World War II most horror films used black-and-white photography, although some early examples had been released on tinted stock and some works had experimented with color sequences. In the 1950s and 1960s, however, two new ventures broke away from the reticence the Val Lewton team had shown in the actual depiction of horror and made graphic use of the red of blood and the green of putrescence (*see* CINEMATOGRAPHY; SPECIAL EF-

FECTS). One of these was Hammer Films, a British company that began its color series with remakes of old Universal classics featuring Dracula, Frankenstein, and the Mummy. The other was U.S. director Roger Corman, who took his cue from such black-and-white classics as Edgar Ulmer's *The Black Cat* (1934) and Lew Landers's *The Raven* (1935), giving his films titles culled from the writings of Poe (e.g., *The Fall of the House of Usher*, 1960; *The Pit and the Pendulum*, 1962) while deviating further and further from Poe's texts. These films brought to the forefront a number of actors—Peter Cushing, Christopher Lee, and Vincent Price—who became as closely linked in the public imagination with horror films as Karloff and Bela Lugosi had been in the 1930s.

Sexual taboos were increasingly ignored in the 1960s and 1970s, especially in a series of vampire films derived from the works of Irish novelist Sheridan Le Fanu rather than Bram Stoker, and in such elegant exercises in European devilry as Mario Bava's *The Mask of the Demon* (1960), distantly based on the work of Russian writer Nikolay Gogol. Once again, familiarity bred laughter rather than fear. Corman turned to black humor, as in *The Raven* (1963), which brought together Karloff, Price, and Peter Lorre, while the cinema-going public was given stronger meat in a series of sadistic horror films beginning with *The Texas Chainsaw Massacre* (1974) and *Rabid* (1976). Significant innovations in the genre included George Romero's *Night of the Living Dead* (1968), a remarkable symbolization of middle-American anomie (Figure 2); Peter Bogdanovich's

Targets (1967), in which such anomie confronted the conventions and STARS of traditional horror movies; and exercises in modern Grand Guignol from Robert Aldrich's *Whatever Happened to Baby Jane?* (1961) to John Carpenter's *Halloween* (1978). Filmmakers in Japan, Mexico, and Spain made contributions to the genre; socialist filmmakers generally avoided it.

Trends in the history of the horror film have often been linked with social issues and concerns. For example, what some saw as a deep disturbance in family relationships was felt by some critics to be reflected in such films as *Rosemary's Baby* (1968), *The Exorcist* (1973), and *The Omen* (1976), which centered horror on demonically possessed children who turn against the adult world. Another trend may be seen in the confluence of SCIENCE FICTION and horror, epitomized in such films as *Godzilla* (1956), *The Invasion of the Body Snatchers* (1956), and *Alien* (1979). There has been much speculation linking the monsters portrayed in these films with the social and political fears of the time, but the connection of science fiction and the horror film itself has a long history dating from the earliest attempts to bring to the screen nineteenth-century novels like Mary Shelley's *Frankenstein* and Robert Louis Stevenson's *Dr. Jekyll and Mr. Hyde*. The horror film is an abiding genre whose further development seems assured by the human needs to which it answers.

See also MYSTERY AND DETECTIVE FICTION.

Bibliography. Lotte Eisner, *The Haunted Screen*, London, 1969; William K. Everson, *Classics of the Horror Film*, New York, 1974; idem, *More Classics of the Horror Film*, Secaucus, N.J., 1986; Siegfried Kracauer, *From Caligari to Hitler*, Princeton, N.J., 1947; David Pirie, *The Vampire Cinema*, London, 1977; S. S. Prawer, *Caligari's Children: The Film as Tale of Terror*, New York, 1980.

SIEGBERT S. PRAWER

HOVLAND, CARL (1912–1961)

U.S. pioneer in communications research. During World War II Carl Iver Hovland, an experimental psychologist at Yale University whose work dealt with problems of conditioning and learning, was appointed chief psychologist and director of experimental studies for a research branch of the War Department. His assignment was to study the nature of morale in the army—specifically, to evaluate the effectiveness of a series of army orientation films entitled *Why We Fight*. The effect of communication on ATTITUDES was a relatively new field, and the army needed reliable guidance in dealing with its use.

After the war Hovland returned to Yale, where he became chair of psychology, Sterling Professor, and director of the new Yale program on communication and attitudes. It was a remarkable research program both because of its rigor and because of the extraordinary group of young psychologists and psychology students Hovland assembled. The new program used the detailed, practical findings of Hovland's army research to derive broad, theoretical conclusions. He insisted on tightly controlled experiments, testing a few variables at a time, varying one and holding the others constant. In this way he was able to illuminate, one by one, many of the questions that had puzzled students of communication.

The program addressed many long-standing ques-

Figure 2. *(Horror Film)* George Romero, *Night of the Living Dead*, 1968. The Museum of Modern Art/ Film Stills Archive.

tions concerning the processes of PERSUASION. Is giving one side of an argument more effective than giving two? Is a direct approach more or less effective than an indirect one? Is a communicator who is perceived as trustworthy more effective than one who is not? What makes a communicator credible? Is it possible to "inoculate" audiences against undesired attitudes? How effective are fear appeals and emotional appeals? How does belonging to a group affect the kind of attitude change a person will accept?

Hovland and his group also studied the nature of persuasibility, addressing such topics as the advantage of a certain order of presentation and the effect of changing one component of a person's attitude on the whole pattern of his or her attitude. The matter of "cognitive consistency" was thus brought into focus (see COGNITIVE CONSISTENCY THEORIES). Hovland also worked out some remarkable computer simulations of thinking and made an impressive "communication analysis" of concept learning.

When the American Psychological Association gave Hovland its medal for distinguished scientific contributions, the award said, "His work has been of central importance in advancing attitude research from the early stage of merely demonstrating that changes can be produced to the point of being able to predict when and where they will occur. His work has provided a convincing demonstration of the values of a sustained and integrated program of research."

See also COMMUNICATIONS RESEARCH: ORIGINS AND DEVELOPMENT.

Bibliography. Carl I. Hovland, Irving L. Janis, and Harold H. Kelley, *Communication and Persuasion,* New Haven, Conn., 1953; Carl I. Hovland, Arthur A. Lumsdaine, and Fred D. Sheffield, *Experiments on Mass Communication,* Princeton, N.J., 1949; Wilbur L. Schramm, *The Science of Human Communication,* New York, 1963.

WILBUR SCHRAMM

HUMAN-ANIMAL COMMUNICATION

The belief that animals have LANGUAGE and that people and animals can talk to each other is widely held among the world's cultures. The popular interest in the purported ability of primates to learn and conduct SIGN LANGUAGE with a grammatical context reflects a belief that communication with animals is both possible and somehow desirable.

In experimental work with animals words are used as conditional stimuli to produce an emotional state or response (whether the animal is responding to the word or to some other vocal quality such as intonation patterns is another question). Following the response will be a reward or punishment, which can also be a word or words. These uses of words are studied through conditioning techniques that exam-

ine the ability of the animal to discriminate among different signs and to learn and remember contingencies (rewards or punishments) associated with different verbal signs.

Outside the experimental setting people talk to their pets, and to work and farm animals as well. This talk is associated with behavior that is reinforced by the talk; for example, a person speaks to a dog, the dog wags its tail (as if in response to what the person has said), and the person then "replies" to the dog's behavioral response by speaking to it again. However, this informal discourse and accompanying behavior cannot be resolved into a defined series of signs and rewards or punishments. Instead it has to be examined as communication in which both person and animal are using species-specific behavior to maintain a rewarding interaction. How people talk to animals and sustain affectionate or playful interaction with them has been poorly described. The only reliable information consists of ethnographic accounts of human-animal interaction in nonindustrialized societies and recent research that focuses on interactions between urban residents and their pets. There is no reliable published information on how rural residents talk to farm animals.

Interaction with pets. In industrialized countries pet ownership varies greatly. For example, dog ownership ranges from 3.9 per 100 people in Japan to more than 15 per 100 in the United States, France, and Australia. Of subjects surveyed in these countries, almost all urban owners talk to their pets. Frequency of discourse has not been reliably studied, although subjects report spending as many as four hours a day in close interaction with their animals. The talk occurs during periods in which the owner is engaging in affectionate interchange, playing with, walking with, or working with the animal—shepherds, police dogs, and seeing-eye dogs, for example. It also occurs at other times when the owner seeks to establish a "human" dialogue. As it has been observed in public places using ethological techniques and in controlled laboratory conditions using experimental techniques, the dialogue has a form that sets it apart from discursive SPEECH between adults.

In affectionate interactions with pets, people talk to and touch their animals. The physical interaction takes the form of stroking, patting, holding, grooming, and directing attention by controlling the animal's head. The forms of these tactile interactions are not influenced by the presence or absence of human speech. When speech occurs it is distinctive. Voice volume is lowered, and pitch is raised. Phrases are short and are terminated with rising intonation. Pauses are inserted between phrases, or questions are framed, permitting the talk to assume the form of a dialogue. The person either waits for the animal's behavior to serve as a reply or answers for the

Figure 1. *(Human-Animal Communication)* A 114-year-old man on Shima Island in Japan. United Nations photo 148561/Bruno J. Zehnder.

animal. The style of the discourse changes when the affectionate behavior lapses into PLAY, and voice volume and rate of utterance increase and pitch changes become less pronounced. Similarly, when the animal exhibits unwanted behavior, the person will lapse into harsher, louder, and lower-registered voice sounds associated with verbal command or punishment.

The distinctive affectionate speech is also associated with typical facial expressions. Subjects exhibit more subtle smiling, less wrinkling of the eyebrows, and more relaxation of the eyelids when talking to their pets than when talking to relative strangers (the experimenters). The head is frequently tilted to one side. When subjects are seeking face-to-face interaction during a period of dialogue, the jaw is moved forward and the eyes are more completely closed. *See also* FACIAL EXPRESSION; INTERACTION, FACE-TO-FACE.

When other people are present, subjects will shift rapidly between talking to the person and talking to the animal, changing pitch and voice volume as well as style of discourse appropriately. *See also* CONVERSATION.

The verbal style used with animals resembles the dialogue style caregivers use with young infants. This verbal style probably enhances the value of the animal as an intimate companion because the human can use more of his or her repertoire of intimate and affectionate behavior with it.

Some have suggested that pets can evoke affectionate behavior from people who cannot interact affectionately with other humans. Pets have been used in therapy with prisoners, inpatients and outpatients with mental disorders, and the institutionalized aged. However, there is only anecdotal evidence suggesting that contact with pets facilitates changes in behavior toward other humans.

Future research. There is now a renewed interest in RHETORIC and form of dialogue. The relationships between humans and animals permit the investigation of affectionate verbal behavior that has a stylized form. Moreover, the phenomenon is easy to study, as most subjects in the United States are relatively unselfconscious about interacting with animals under observation. Unfortunately, we have almost no well-recorded or well-documented studies of such interactions from other societies. *See also* COGNITION, ANIMAL.

Bibliography. Alan M. Beck and Aaron H. Katcher, *Between Pets and People: The Importance of Animal Companionship*, New York, 1983; Aaron H. Katcher and Alan M. Beck, eds., *New Perspectives on Our Lives with Companion Animals*, Philadelphia, 1983; Thomas A. Sebeok and Robert Rosenthal, *The Clever Hans Phenomenon: Communication with Horses, Whales, Apes, and People*, New York, 1981.

AARON H. KATCHER AND ALAN M. BECK

HUMOR

A significant amount of human communication is devoted to humor. Humor influences listeners' views and persuades them to accept or reject ideas; it gives pleasure, creates playful moods and an atmosphere of conviviality, induces feelings of social solidarity, permits venting of aggression, and relieves tension. It is also used for criticism and ridicule. In short, it is one of the most powerful tools available to humans in their communicative endeavors. Yet its nature has been a mystery and a subject of fascination since antiquity, and efforts to analyze it have often foundered.

Historically there has always been a great interest in understanding the nature of humor. Scholars have investigated its antecedents, form, content, use, and consequences since ancient times. Literary critics have explored the nature of COMEDY, a dramatic form of humor with a long tradition.

During the twentieth century, humor has been subjected to rigorous empirical scrutiny by social scientists, especially by psychologists, who have conducted various kinds of experiments to determine its nature and role in human social interaction. Attention has also been focused on the evolutionary and developmental aspects of humor, with particular emphasis on the relationship between humor and PLAY and the emergence of the concept of a sense of humor.

Conceptualizations of Humor and Theoretical Perspectives

Since humor is basically a mental experience, it is difficult to pin down its exact nature. No single definition in the history of humor research has included all its essential attributes or has been acceptable to all scholars. Some researchers even refuse to define it.

Originally the term *humor* meant body fluid or moisture, and it was used in this sense in premodern physiology. It was believed that the four fluids in the human body—phlegm, blood, yellow bile, and black bile—determined a person's overall disposition. This linkage to disposition gradually led to the associated meaning of mood or state of mind in general, which finally led to the current primary usage of the term, namely, a mirthful state of mind caused by some events, ideas, or objects perceived as being comical, absurd, incongruent, ludicrous, and so forth.

The concept of humor overlaps many others such as fun, amusement, joking, wit, laughter, and play. These share some attributes of meaning with humor, but the denotational and connotational range of each is difficult to determine.

While no single definition of humor can cover its complex nature, there is a consensus in the scholarly literature that humor generally includes three phases: (1) some event in the external world acts as a trigger for a specific mental response; (2) a cognitive and intellectual process receives and evaluates the event, resulting in a mirthful state of mind; and (3) there is an immediate overt behavioral reflection of the mirthful state—smiling or laughter. The nature of the triggering antecedents generates the most debate and controversy, but there is also disagreement over what psychological and physiological conditions cause smiling and laughter, what exactly these expressions reflect, and whether or not either is required to express a humorous state of mind.

Given the elusive nature of humor, it is not surprising that many theories have been proposed to explain it and the reasons for its occurrence. No single theory, however, has thoroughly explained the complex nature of humor. Existing humor theories reflect biological, physiological, sociocultural, linguistic, cognitive, literary, aesthetic, and philosophical perspectives, among others. Broadly speaking, three major approaches can be discerned, but many theories appear to be a combination of two or more.

Intellect-based theories. The premise common to these theories is that the human mind recognizes accidental or deliberately evoked incongruity, ambiguity, and/or oppositional dualism in external events and tries to resolve them by finding new relationships or by mediating among them. The success of such mental activity provides satisfaction and mirth. Implicit in the intellect-based theories is the premise that the logic in potentially humorous experiences is peculiar to them and contrasts with the logic underlying normal situations and messages, requiring creative and unusual ways of comprehending it.

Emotion-based theories. Theories in this category link humor to such preexisting feelings and emotions as hostility, aggression, disparagement, superiority, or malice toward others. These emotions then create a humorous state of mind when others suffer from various kinds of misfortunes, such as mental defects, physical deformity, suffering, and punishment. Many of these theories appear to be extensions of the theory of English philosopher Thomas Hobbes, who argued that laughter was nothing but "sudden glory" as the mind compares one's eminence with the follies and infirmities of others.

Theories of cathartic release and relief. According to these theories humor permits the release of pent-up energy or suppressed impulses, producing a mirthful state of mind. It is relief from the strain of excess energy or repressed impulses that leads to mirth. Humor and the resulting laughter lead to a psychological or physiological state of equilibrium. The most prominent exponent of the release-relief theory of humor was SIGMUND FREUD.

Humor in Communication

The relationship of humor to ongoing social interaction has fascinated scholars in many disciplines. Just as communication is a two-way process, so is humor. The act of communication requires a sender, a receiver, a medium, and a message. So does humor, which can be on occasion both the medium and the message. Humor is overt when it is directed solely at creating mirth but is covert when it occurs as part of general social interaction, and it may include such motives and emotions as aggression, resentment, ridicule, solidarity, and criticism. Much depends on the social context, the predisposition or the mental state of the listener, and the ways in which a message is interpreted. Humor is generally a cooperative venture, not only in face-to-face communication but also across time and space. Since individuals differ in their perceptions of humor in both verbal and nonverbal events, humor may be intentional or unintentional either from the speaker's or from the listener's point of view.

Sociocultural Determinants of Humor

Sociocultural factors that influence the occurrence, form, content, and function of humor as a communicative act are the time, place, and nature of the social event; the participants and their respective backgrounds and roles; the topics involved in the interaction and the resulting verbal exchanges; and the participants' cultural values and expectations concerning appropriate behavior in a particular social situation. Some general observations can be made, however, regarding the influence of the above-mentioned factors on the occurrence of humor.

Social situations range from small-group interactions to events in which most members of a community get involved. Social events can be public or private and can center around work, leisure activities, religious functions, political activities, feasts, SPORTS, and games, among others. The atmosphere at social events can be formal or informal.

Institutionalized humor generally is found in public social situations, although its occurrence depends on cultural norms about humor initiation and its appropriateness in different contexts. In general, types of institutionalized humor have relatively fixed topics, genres, and contexts, and audiences for them have definite expectations about what will take place. An example of institutionalized humor in the United States is the "roast," at which a famous person (often a politician) is subjected to ridicule and mockery by his or her friends and cohorts in front of a crowd of spectators. Institutionalized humor in mainstream U.S. culture is generally considered inappropriate in the context of religious ceremonies such as church services, weddings, and funerals; however, initiation ceremonies, funerals, and calendrical rituals celebrating seasonal changes have been used as public occasions for ritual clowning and humor development in many African, Asian, and American Indian societies. In many societies institutionalized humor involves group activities or PERFORMANCE by well-established humorists; examples are pantomime, burlesque, impersonation, CARICATURE, parody, clowning, joke telling, and comedy.

Small-scale, private social gatherings are appropriate settings for individualistic, impromptu, or extemporaneous kinds of humor (teasing, joke telling, banter, repartee, punning, etc.). There is much leeway for creativity in this setting, as individuals are relaxed and the social occasion includes other activities such as CONVERSATION, eating (see FOOD), and drinking.

In certain social situations participants use humor to reduce boredom, tension, and other similar feelings. When a job is tedious, mechanical, or dangerous, for instance, individuals often establish joking relationships, play practical jokes, or engage in obscene banter, horseplay, and name calling (see also INSULT).

Factors such as the age and sex of participants affect the nature of humor in social situations. The form and content of humor in CHILDREN's social interaction, for example, is different from that in adult interaction. When children get together they often combine play and humor; many games become the source of humor initiation, such as riddling, verbal duels, tongue twisters, and practical jokes. At a certain age children are also very interested in scatological humor. They often engage in outrageously exaggerated imitations of adult activities and roles. Many of the types of humor mentioned here suggest children's concern with the acquisition and mastery of their language and of appropriate behaviors commensurate with different social roles (see also LANGUAGE ACQUISITION).

Cultural notions of politeness and decorum apply to many situations in which both men and women participate. Activities that involve members of only one sex, however, are often free from such constraints. For example, scatological and obscene humor is generally considered inappropriate in mixed-sex social situations. In men's interaction, however, such humor is quite common. In some preliterate societies men generally gather in the men's hut when they are not hunting, eating, or otherwise engaged. The relaxed atmosphere in these huts is conducive to GOSSIP, teasing, obscene joking, banter, and horseplay, much as one hears in clubs and bars in the West. In rural India a village well is commonly the site where women gather to fetch water or to wash clothes and in the process engage in teasing, gossiping, joking, banter, repartee, and so on.

In many societies women seem to be under greater constraints than men in their use or enjoyment of humor as part of social communication. In such societies notions of modesty and passivity associated with what is considered appropriate behavior for women may lead to their exclusion from public social events at which only men may engage in humor. As women get beyond the reproductive age, however, these restrictions are often relaxed.

In situations involving competition, antagonism, alienation, and schism, humor is frequently used to convey group solidarity and to reinforce group identity. Humor developed for such purposes is disparaging because it ridicules members of groups other than one's own and portrays them as possessing negative attributes. Much ethnic humor is of this nature because it is based on pejorative stereotypes of members of other cultures. Another type of humor is in-group humor, based primarily on knowledge shared by members of a group, who could be persons in the same profession, the same work place, the same religious or political group, and so on.

Norms of appropriateness for humorous communications are not always explicit and may vary not only cross-culturally but also from individual to individual within a society. Institutionalized humor, however, thrives because a majority of the people in a society accept the norms surrounding its form, content, occurrence, and usage in certain social situations.

Genres of Humor

Works on LITERARY CRITICISM, POETICS, and LINGUISTICS generally include descriptions of humor genres. The existing typologies of humor use different classificatory criteria, such as form, technique, content, subject matter, intentionality, and performance, which often overlap. For instance, the category *ridicule* is based on the intentionality of the speaker, whereas the category *pun* is based on the technique of deliberate ambiguity. The genres of *joke* and RIDDLE are identified on the basis of both form and content, but a category such as *obscene humor* is based entirely on content. Some genres of humor seem restricted only to certain modalities—for instance, burlesque or vaudeville, which are based on the criterion of performance onstage or in a movie.

A major dichotomy among genres of humor is verbal versus nonverbal, although such genres as comedy combine both. Pantomime and practical jokes are examples of nonverbal humor, whereas language structure is the primary underpinning of such genres of verbal humor as pun, malapropism, and spoonerism. Tall tales are examples of humor based on breach of cultural norms or exaggerated actions.

A pun sets up an ambiguity in meaning because of a play on words. What is said can be understood literally or as having a more subtle INTERPRETATION. The speaker may intend the pun or may form it accidentally. In either case the onus of interpretation is on the listener, who may or may not choose to recognize the subtle meaning.

A malapropism involves the misuse of a word because of its confusion with a similar-sounding word.

Such a misuse results in an utterance that does not make sense and is comprehended only by the invocation of the appropriate word; for example, "Capital punishment is a detergent to crime." Malapropisms can occur in the initial stage of learning a foreign language because of inadequate knowledge of the vocabulary.

A spoonerism occurs when sounds in words or words in a sentence are transposed, resulting in an utterance different from that intended by the speaker. The result may make sense but be incongruent in the social situation in which it is produced (*see* SLIPS OF THE TONGUE).

Humor can be a pleasant as well as very effective form of communication in a variety of settings. In many situations direct communication is not possible, but communicating through humor is acceptable. Humor reflects the human mind's creative abilities and helps to ease the burdens of human sociocultural existence.

Bibliography. Mahadev L. Apte, *Humor and Laughter: An Anthropological Approach,* Ithaca, N.Y., 1985; Antony J. Chapman and Hugh C. Foot, eds., *It's a Funny Thing, Humour* (International Conference on Humour and Laughter, Cardiff, Wales, 1976), Oxford and New York, 1977; Evan Esar, *The Humor of Humor,* New York, 1952; Sigmund Freud, *Jokes and Their Relation to the Unconscious* (Der Witz und seine Beziehung zum Unbewussten, Vienna, 1905), trans. and ed. by James Strachey, New York, 1960; Paul McGhee, *Humor: Its Origin and Development,* San Francisco, 1979; Paul McGhee and Jeffrey H. Goldstein, eds., *Handbook of Humor Research,* New York, 1983; D. H. Monro, *Arguments of Laughter,* Melbourne, 1951; Elliott Oring, ed., *Humor and the Individual,* Los Angeles, 1984; Victor Raskin, *Semantic Mechanisms of Humor,* Boston, 1985; Christopher Wilson, *Jokes: Form, Content, Use and Function,* New York, 1979.

MAHADEV L. APTE

HYMAN, HERBERT H. (1918–1985)

U.S. sociologist and social psychologist who introduced theoretical and methodological innovations that have become part of the academic heritage of PUBLIC OPINION and communications research. Herbert H. Hyman is best known for his contributions to the study of reference groups, POLITICAL SOCIALIZATION, PUBLIC OPINION, survey research methods, and secondary analysis of sample surveys.

Born in New York City, Hyman graduated from Columbia College in 1939 and earned an M.A. (1940) and a Ph.D. (1942) in psychology from Columbia University. His doctoral dissertation, *The Psychology of Status* (1942), provides early examples of his conceptual innovation, namely, *reference groups* and *reference individuals,* terms Hyman coined to signify the groups or individuals that people use for self-comparisons in assessing their own status. Subsequently the concept of reference groups (and to some extent, reference individuals) was further developed and refined and became widely accepted in social psychology and sociology. In the field of communications it has been applied to studies of mass communication producers and mass media audiences, for example.

After earning his Ph.D., Hyman held research positions with several government agencies engaged in applied survey research related to World War II. These early experiences provided a practical background for his later methodological contributions to both academic and applied survey research. After the war he became affiliated with the University of Chicago's National Opinion Research Center (NORC), working there with Paul B. Sheatsley and others on a full- or part-time basis from 1945 to 1957. His best-known publication in communications from this period is "Some Reasons Why Information Campaigns Fail," written with Sheatsley in 1947. This widely cited work was one of the first empirical studies of psychological barriers to mass communication information campaigns.

At NORC Hyman also directed a large-scale collaborative inquiry into the process of interviewing as a method of data collection. The report on this six-year series of studies on interviewer effects, *Interviewing in Social Research* (1954), became a methodological landmark in survey research.

In 1951 Hyman accepted an appointment to Columbia University's graduate department of sociology, joining such well-known sociologists as Edmund de S. Brunner, PAUL F. LAZARSFELD, Robert S. Lynd, and ROBERT K. MERTON. He also participated in Columbia's Bureau of Applied Social Research, becoming an associate director in 1957. At Columbia he wrote his influential treatise on the principles of survey research, *Survey Design and Analysis: Principles, Cases and Procedures* (1955), which soon became the standard work for graduate training in survey research methods and later served as an important reference work on the logic of survey analysis.

Hyman's monograph *Political Socialization: A Study of the Psychology of Political Behavior* (1959) introduced political socialization as a potentially fruitful area for social research. The term *political socialization*, another Hyman coinage, referred to those processes of political learning that are shared by most members of a group or society and that contribute to regularities, uniformities, and stability in political systems. Hyman explicitly addressed the role of the mass media in political socialization in a 1963 paper on POLITICAL COMMUNICATION in developing societies. Consistent with his earlier view of socialization

as a social process, the focus was on the socializing influence of *patterns* of communication shared by members of a society, rather than on individualistic political learning. The concept of political socialization has since been broadened, and its study has developed into an academic specialty, particularly in political science and communications research.

In 1969 Hyman left Columbia to join the sociology department at Wesleyan University, where he continued to explore the subjects of communications and socialization, moving beyond politics to consider, for example, the role of mass communications in affecting social sentiments. His best-known work during this period, however, is his methodological development and scholarly use of secondary analysis—the strategy of reanalyzing social sample survey data originally collected for one purpose in order to study another problem, such as the long-term impact of EDUCATION or the relations between communications behavior and social structure. Hyman's *Secondary Analysis of Sample Surveys* (1972) was the first book to codify the methodological principles of secondary analysis, a research method now widely used in social science.

Hyman completed three major secondary analyses of national sample survey data while at Wesleyan. *The Enduring Effects of Education* (1975) reexamined data from more than fifty U.S. national sample surveys to investigate the lifelong impact of schooling on people's knowledge and receptivity to new information from the mass media and other sources. *Education's Lasting Influence on Values* (1979) investigated the impact of schooling on a range of values held by nationwide samples of U.S. adults, including views on freedom of information and communication. The third study, *Of Time and Widowhood: Nationwide Studies of Enduring Effects* (1983), examined the long-term social and psychological consequences of widowhood.

Hyman staunchly advocated the application of survey research to studies of social problems and social change at home and abroad, especially in developing societies. He taught survey research methods and conducted applied social surveys in a variety of countries. Hyman died in the People's Republic of China on December 18, 1985, while participating in a conference on the uses of sociology.

Bibliography. Herbert H. Hyman, *Political Socialization*, New York, 1959, reprint 1969; idem, *Secondary Analysis of Sample Surveys: Principles, Procedures, and Potentialities*, New York, 1972, reprint 1986; idem, *Survey Design and Analysis*, New York, 1955, reprint 1960; Hubert J. O'Gorman, ed., "Herbert H. Hyman: His Life and Work," in *Surveying Social Life: Papers in Honor of Herbert H. Hyman*, Middletown, Conn., 1986.

CHARLES R. WRIGHT

(əi), the ninth letter and third vowel of the Roman alphabet, going back through the Greek *iota* to the Semitic *yod*. The simple form I of the character in Greek from about 500 B.C., and in the Roman alphabet, was reduced from a more complex Early Greek form ⟨, which originated in the Phœnician Ƨ. . . . In the Latin alphabet, . . . it was used with . . . values . . . of *i* vowel (long and short) and *y* consonant, as in *ibīdem, ībis; iacui, Iupiter, Iouis.*

ICONOGRAPHY

Branch of the history and study of the VISUAL IMAGE that, according to its classic formulation by U.S. art historian Erwin Panofsky in 1939, "concerns itself with the subject-matter or meaning of works of art, as opposed to their form." So understood, iconography implies an approach to ART objects, and especially those of the western European tradition, in which specific, intended meanings can be identified to some extent independently of the form or style of their expression. Simply to describe the subject of a work of art by naming what is shown in it—the martyrdom of a saint, a particular episode in history or myth, the representation of the ancestors of Christ in the form of the Tree of Jesse—is iconography in a limiting sense only. To go further is to enter into the play of symbolic meanings and how they have been understood, which is commonly termed *iconology* for distinction's sake. Typical topics of investigation would then be the role of light as a symbol of divine grace in the paintings of Jan van Eyck (Figure 1) or the different emblematic images and subjects used throughout history to underscore the theme of death (*see* ART, FUNERARY).

The distinction here corresponds to the semiological distinction between icon and symbol (*see* SEMIOTICS). While icons are related to what they represent by virtue of some denotational quality of resemblance, symbols are related to what they signify in an arbitrary sense only, by virtue of the connotations with which they are invested. And if the topic of study embracing both of these processes is taken to be the systems of visual signification prevailing in a particular CULTURE and period (rather than the contributions of individual artists), then its pursuit can be extended to non-Western traditions, such as the representation of Buddha in East Asian art (Figure 2).

As an account of the workings of SYMBOLISM, however, this definition needs to be extended. Critical objections are that it leaves out the relationships of analogy and substitution that enable artists to deal in symbolic objects of a made-up kind (as in Hieronymus Bosch's *Garden of Earthly Delights*), to suggest resemblances between things (fire screen and halo, nose or mouth and sex organ), or simply to introduce patterns of GESTURE or behavior that are understood as saying something in themselves (the swearing of an oath, the manner in which Judas betrays Christ with a kiss). It also schematizes artificially the processes of apprehension. Today semiology and cognitive psychology deal in their separate ways with the bases on which one arrives at a grasp of MEANING that entails the recall of earlier images, built-in references of a special or condensed kind, and a layering of implications. Recognition and identification of a direct kind, as in a child's response to the appearance

of a horse, may well serve as a preliminary step toward that apprehension, but it cannot be that they are the precondition of it in any universal sense applying to all media. The delimitation of the iconographic branch of study must therefore arbitrarily seek to separate content from formal organization and presentation for the purposes of analysis in a way that would hardly be possible if the cultural ARTIFACT being considered were a textile, an illuminated manuscript page, or a carved stone.

When *iconography* was first introduced into critical terminology in the nineteenth century, it connoted

Figure 1. *(Iconography)* Jan van Eyck, *Madonna in a Church*, ca. 1426. Light coming through the church windows and infusing the interior is used to convey the Virgin Mary's role as instrument of the divine purpose and vessel of grace. Gemäldegalerie, Staatliche Museen Berlin-Dahlem. © Bildarchiv Preussischer Kulturbesitz, Berlin (West). Photograph by Jörg P. Anders.

dard elements or features are shown in these cases in a changing fashion means that particular instances can be compared and contrasted, according to type, with earlier representations. An extension of the same principle allows for the study of how everyday themes and genres are represented, as in Dutch art of the seventeenth century (Figure 3), and how they are transformed over time. The idea of a series entailed here applies also to artists' self-portraits and to group portraits such as those of company or family members. These examples lead in an obvious way toward psychological or content forms of explanation to account for change and development in a particular artist. New stimuli from outside or new internal sources of inspiration provide the bases for such explanation.

Iconology has been distinguished from iconography in the twentieth century on the ground that it consists of iconography turned interpretative so that it goes deeper into intrinsic meanings or content. German art historian Aby Warburg, in reviving the term in 1912, explained it as the study and INTERPRETATION of historical processes through visual images, and it has been increasingly recognized that such a reading of visual evidence from the past makes

Figure 2. *(Iconography)* Śākyamuni Buddha, Wei dynasty, China, 477 C.E. The Metropolitan Museum of Art, New York, Kennedy Fund, 1926. (26.123)

a classificatory process of study that was typologically oriented in scope (*see* CLASSIFICATION). Such a usage survives today in one area, the study of face masks in PORTRAITURE, which represent distinctive versions of a basic physiognomic structure from which further or secondary images are then seen to derive. Examples of motifs in art that are simply classifiable, like church-screen decorations, include subjects, such as the Annunciation, that are depicted in a schematized form; the emblems of saints or emperors; and heraldic devices (*see* HERALDRY). The fact that stan

Figure 3. *(Iconography)* Jan Vermeer, *A Girl Asleep,* 1650s. The painting on the wall, the objects in the still life, the mirror, and even the pose of the girl are all details open to interpretation in emblematic terms, although their primary role is to set the scene. The Metropolitan Museum of Art, New York, bequest of Benjamin Altman, 1913. (14.40.611)

Figure 4. *(Iconography)* Sandro Botticelli, *The Calumny of Apelles,* ca. 1498. Uffizi, Florence.
The allegorical content reflects the intellectual influence of the Medici court and its humanist scholars.
Alinari/Art Resource, New York.

for a relationship to IDEOLOGY as embodied in the conventions, beliefs, or assumptions of a society. The standard art-historical practice of iconography has tended to trace these connections through texts, a method suited to works of art that were addressed in the first instance to learned humanists, men and women of the church, or members of a court or privileged circle. The work then counts as evidence of a program, its presumed aim being to communicate in equivalent visual form values read into those texts, or spiritual and intellectual significances found in them (Figure 4), which may be so general that they are independent of period.

But a relationship to ideology can equally be found in gestures, costume (*see* CLOTHING), ornament, or building types (*see* ARCHITECTURE). The visual stimuli or cues that the eye receives here are not simply the expressive accompaniment to a preconstituted message or embellishments in its rendition (as with an actor going through a familiar speech); they are its communicative vehicles. Structuralists recognizing this (CLAUDE LÉVI-STRAUSS, ROLAND BARTHES) have widened the terms of discussion accordingly to in-

clude such purely physical features as the contributions of texture and color, relationships of shape, and formal contiguities, as well as overall qualities such as atmosphere and mood (*see* STRUCTURALISM). The parallel that this implies to forms of THEATER or SPECTACLE leads to the idea of a broad-based form of cultural study focusing on particular performances (*see* PERFORMANCE). Topics such as court masques or the decorations for triumphal entries, Jacques-Louis David's enactment of a shared spirit of purpose in his Oath subjects, and Francisco de Goya's responses to the loss of liberty in Spain show how this way of thinking about art in its socially mediated aspects proves true to what Warburg later in life conceived of as the study of "expressive human communication and the transformation of its language."

We move here, in fact, to what is sometimes called *imagery*—namely, subject matter and its presentation in visual form. Traditionally this term referred to or included in its scope popular art forms, in which the relation of image to text is different from that previously described: more complementary, as in the case of printed images of MARTIN LUTHER from the time of the Reformation (Figure 5), or more integrally interactive, as in CARICATURE or the comic strip (*see* COMICS), in a way that resembles naive art. The subject of study is then not just the occurrence of motifs but their ordering to make up a form of communicative discourse, so that iconography becomes, as Panofsky thought of it, a way station on the path to iconology.

Over time the scheme of thought underlying images often has become obscure and puzzling, and therefore its rationale must be revealed through study and put into relation to the circumstances of creation. Insofar as the study of symbolism implies a deciphering of cryptic features, identifying its presence is a learned and sometimes arcane discipline. But there is also a symbolic cast present in the choice of images themselves and the way in which these choices and the modes of presentation condense or bring into

focus beliefs and values. The Russian soldier caricatured as a monster and the NARRATIVE devices of the comic strip may seem quite akin here to Panofsky's favored subjects of study. But there is also a crucial distinction that allies those kinds of image with RITUAL and with ADVERTISING, as forms of cultural expression and PERSUASION. This entails a move away from the tenets of iconography toward what may be called a visually oriented semiotics. Accordingly, in studying the cult of Napoléon one may work from the premise that its impact can be measured from the sheer number and range of images, and one's sense of it can be enriched by reference to illustrated biographies and novels and the veneration of mementos. Similarly, the feelings attending the westward movement of the U.S. frontier can be reconstructed from media images of the railroad and of the tree felled by an ax (Figure 6).

Figure 5. *(Iconography)* Hans Sebald Beham, *The Complaint of the Godless against Luther,* ca. 1520. At the head of a group of peasant folk, Luther points to the Scripture in response to his accusers, whose wealth and privilege are endangered by his proclamation of true doctrine. Above, Christ mediates the dispute and indicates approval of Luther and his followers. Germanisches Nationalmuseum, Nuremberg.

Figure 6. *(Iconography)* Currier and Ives, *Across the Continent.* "Westward the Course of Empire Takes Its Way," 1860. The Harry T. Peters Collection, Museum of the City of New York.

Alternatively there is a narrower, contextual version of iconography that focuses on such factors as the circumstances of patronage, the physical context of a work's display, or the functional adaptations that the work undergoes. The religious, social, and political dimensions seen in this way as entering into the creation and apprehension of visual imagery are conducive to what may be thought of as a "reconstruction of intentions." But reconstruction need not be taken here as implying a finite set of ideas and purposes, as in the classic definition of iconography. Rather, different meanings to different audiences or in different periods form part of the identity that is studied. The work of art represents a special kind of cultural object, physically unchanging for the most part and persisting as a constant through differing approaches to its character. The attempt to recover the work's identity must necessarily remain speculative, however systematic methods of re-creative description and hermeneutic linkage to external data (such as BIOGRAPHY) may have become. Since the early modern period the fact that the visual image has become generally more private in character opens up the possibility of personal and psychoanalytic

readings of the artist's mental and physical processes (*see* PSYCHOANALYSIS). These are often distinct from readings that the *artist* would formulate or endorse. But it is still possible within the scope of iconography to chart on more than one front the artistic response to such a development as the cold war or to consider to what extent at a given time different modes of expression such as POETRY and painting parallel one another (*see* MODE).

Bibliography. Ernst H. Gombrich, *Symbolic Images*, 2d ed., Oxford, 1978; Robert Klein, *Form and Meaning: Essays on Renaissance and Modern Art* (La forme et l'intelligible), trans. by Madeline Jay and Leon Wieseltier, New York, 1979; Erwin Panofsky, *Meaning in the Visual Arts*, Garden City, N.Y., 1955, reprint Chicago, 1982; Mark Roskill, *What Is Art History?* London and New York, 1976.

MARK W. ROSKILL

IDEOLOGY

Patterns of ideas, belief systems, or interpretive schemes found in a society or among specific social groups.

Traditionally those who study ideologies want to know, among other things, how ideologies arise and how they are disseminated and transformed. They want to know how to identify and analyze ideological structures and whether they necessarily distort, falsify, or bias our thinking. They are interested in the nature of ideas: Are ideas determined by their material or social basis, or are they autonomous? Do ideologies correspond to class, GENDER, or ethnic identities? Some have studied the functions of ideology and have speculated about its role in shaping consciousness, legitimating a particular set of power relations, or producing consent to a specific type of social order.

Since its inception MASS COMMUNICATIONS RESEARCH has been concerned with how the meanings and messages of the media influence social thought (or, more accurately, how media content influences individual behavior, perhaps by influencing opinions, ATTITUDES, or values). In this general sense mainstream media research can be said to have always implicitly addressed ideological questions. However, the explicit analysis of ideology as such has been absent for much of its history, especially in the more behavioristic, empirically oriented types of research that have dominated the field. This absence has been paralleled in sociological theory in the United States more generally. The concept of ideology has had more consistent treatment in European social theory, and in recent years ideological questions have once again come to play a more central role in both U.S. and European media studies, especially among practitioners employing a "critical" approach. Any account of the role of ideology in media research must therefore try to explain this uneven visibility of the concept itself as well as the significant contrasts between U.S. and European emphases.

The critique of RELIGION and of superstitious or prescientific ideas was integral to the rise of rational and scientific thought in the West. Niccolò Machiavelli (1469–1527) argued that the way people understand things depends on their "appetites . . . interests . . . standpoints"; he connected their ideas with the use of force and fraud to secure and maintain power. In his *Novum Organum* (1620) Francis Bacon defined positive science as a critique of the "ideas of the tribe." These emphases on the unmasking of false or distorted thinking and on the links among ideas, interests, and power are sustained in varying ways by such thinkers as Thomas Hobbes (1588–1679), Claude-Adrien Helvétius (1715–1771), Paul-Henri-Dietrich d'Holbach (1723–1789), and others into the Age of Enlightenment. During the French Revolution Antoine-Louis-Claude Destutt de Tracy (1754–1836) first coined the term *ideology* to mean the "science of ideas."

Certain critical formulations concerning the social determination, class origins, and illusory character of ideology first appeared as part of the elaboration of historical materialism by KARL MARX (1818–1883). Marx used the term *ideology* negatively, to characterize the influence of idealism in German philosophy (e.g., G. W. F. Hegel, 1770–1831) and as an aspect of the critique of religion (e.g., Ludwig Feuerbach, 1804–1872). Marx and Friedrich Engels set out deliberately to invert idealism. Material processes and socioeconomic relations, they argued, form the "bases" and ideas only the "superstructure" of society: "It is not the consciousness of men that determines their being, but . . . social being that determines consciousness." In his subsequent critique of bourgeois society Marx linked ideas to class position and class interests. Political economy is the commonsense ideology of the capitalist. Ideology therefore legitimates capitalist exploitation. Ruling classes maintain their position through their MONOPOLY over the cultural institutions that produce "ruling ideology." Subordinate classes, whose ideas do not reflect their "true" class interests, have been deceived into "false consciousness."

Later developments of the Marxist conception of ideology can be found, for example, in works by V. I. Lenin; in the work of György Lukács (1885–1971), who analyzed how the "world visions" of different classes are expressed in literature; and in the much-expanded and antireductionist conception of ideology and CULTURE that underpins ANTONIO GRAMSCI's (1891–1937) theory of "hegemony" (i.e., how a dominant social bloc wins social, moral, and intellectual "leadership" and authority over a whole society). Elsewhere, in the (non-Marxist) German "sociology of knowledge" tradition, theorists like Wilhelm Dilthey (1833–1911) and Karl Mannheim (1893–1947) analyzed different "world outlooks" (*Weltanschauungen*) as expressed in philosophy, ART, and social thought. MAX WEBER's *The Protestant Ethic and the Spirit of Capitalism,* which examined the role of Puritan ideas in the rise of capitalism, was a founding text of modern sociology. In France the positivist social theorist Auguste Comte (1798–1857) divided the progress of rational enlightenment into an ascending sequence of "thought stages." Another founding father of sociology, ÉMILE DURKHEIM (1858–1917), studied the social basis of the ideas and religions ("collective representations") of different groups and the normative function of these ideas in organizing social behavior, as well as the classificatory systems found in primitive societies.

In the 1920s and 1930s THEODOR ADORNO, Max Horkheimer, Herbert Marcuse, and others belonging to what became known as the Frankfurt school (which was much influenced by Hegel, Marx, and SIGMUND FREUD) began to theorize about the manipulative role of ideology and the mass media (the "cultural industries") as key factors in the tendency of modern mass societies to collapse into authoritarianism. Members of the school emigrated from Nazi Germany to the United States, where their theses provided the first critical theories of ideology that the emerging science of mass communications felt obliged to test, confirm, or reject.

The first major phase of mass communications research in the 1940s was shaped by the attempt to test these hypotheses empirically in a U.S. setting. Some of the studies done during this period dealt with the influence of the media on electoral choice (e.g., *The People's Choice*, by PAUL F. LAZARSFELD, Bernard Berelson, and Hazel Gaudet, 1948), the creation of "fantasy worlds" (e.g., studies of HOLLYWOOD and of the daytime radio SERIAL, reported in *Communications Research 1948–1949*, edited by Lazarsfeld and Frank Stanton), and the shaping of PUBLIC OPINION. The communications researchers concluded that the media's impact on values, attitudes, and beliefs tended to be consensual. Media influence was a more mediated process—less powerful and direct in shaping attitudes, when examined empirically—than had been hypothesized. Thus the Frankfurt school's critique of the manipulative role of the mass media was rejected as being too elitist, too pessimistic, too speculative, and overly ideological.

This early work on the mass media gave U.S. communications research its distinctive stamp for three decades. During this period ideology was diffused into the looser concept of "values," redefined in terms of individual attitudes, or reduced to immediate behavioral effects. It lost its theoretical advantage and historical specificity and for some time effectively disappeared as an issue in its own right. For example, in an influential paper on "The Structure and Function of Communication in Society" (1948) HAROLD D. LASSWELL, analyzing media content in terms of its effects on values, listed power, wealth, respect, well-being, and enlightenment as the key values, adding that "with this list . . . we can describe . . . the social structure of most of the world."

ROBERT K. MERTON has accurately traced the transition that occurred in this period from a European-style sociology of knowledge, with its emphasis on "systematic ideological analysis," to U.S.-style empirical mass communications research. In *Social Theory and Social Structure* (1949) he said: "The American variant . . . studies the isolated fragments of information . . . the European variant . . . thinks about a total structure of knowledge (systems of doctrine)." Parallel with this shift, critical modes of inquiry were replaced by a more rigorously empirical methodology based on survey, questionnaire, and audience research data and quantitative CONTENT ANALYSIS. Par-

adoxically the pioneer of the new empirical methodologies—Lazarsfeld—had himself been loosely associated with the Frankfurt school. In influential works summarizing these trends (e.g., *Personal Influence*, by Elihu Katz and Lazarsfeld, 1955; *The Effects of Mass Communication*, by Joseph T. Klapper, 1960) the concept of ideology played no significant role.

The most notable—but partial—exception to this trend was the mass communication and public-opinion-conducted research within political science. Here a concept of ideology (meaning rigid, well-formulated but "biased" systems of political belief) remained, alongside an interest in PROPAGANDA and PERSUASION and what earlier (1927) had been described as "the management of collective attitudes by the manipulation of significant symbols." However, by the 1960s political scientists like Seymour Martin Lipset and sociologists like Daniel Bell had declared "the end of ideology" in the Western liberal democracies, and the term ideology was reserved largely for the analysis and decoding of political propaganda in the context of the cold war. Quantitative content analysis procedures became considerably sophisticated in this period. In general Lasswell observed (in 1964) that "political scientists are increasingly aware of the strategic significance for arenas of power of the control of communication."

The virtual silence on the topic of ideology in mainstream communications research was broken by two developments, one internal and one external. Interactionist sociological models (in U.S. social science research in the 1960s), with their focus on microsocial interactions and the power of the media to "define situations" and to label groups and individuals as deviant (as well as by their commitment to more qualitative methodologies), began to challenge the dominant positivistic or behavioral perspectives in media research. More generally the social and political unrest in the United States in the late 1960s and early 1970s, which increased ideological polarization, brought the consensus model of American pluralism into question. The turmoil drew attention once more to the role played by the media in interpreting situations of conflict and in the exercise of symbolic or interpretive "power" as a form of social and ideological control. With the reintroduction of these questions of power, legitimation, and social control, the paradigm of ideology once more appeared in U.S. communications theory and research, alongside more mainstream approaches.

Simultaneously in Europe in the 1970s new theoretical developments in LINGUISTICS (especially in France) and in cultural studies (especially in Britain) revived the study of ideology in the humanities and social sciences and at the same time transformed many of its earlier emphases. Ideologies now were conceptualized less as discrete messages with a determined content and more on the model of LAN-GUAGE itself. Ideologies were the underlying interpretive frameworks that generated meanings through the operation of different codes or sign systems (see CODE; MEANING; SIGN SYSTEM). Thus, for example, CLAUDE LÉVI-STRAUSS and ROLAND BARTHES, influenced by the structural linguistics of FERDINAND DE SAUSSURE (1857–1913) and the Prague school, developed a semiotic approach to the analysis of myths and other ideological phenomena (see SEMI-OTICS; STRUCTURALISM). Ideologies were understood to be organized within distinct discursive chains or forms of narration. They did not reflect one prees-tablished meaning, already fixed in the activity or event in the real world, that the media merely re-ported to the audience (the notion of "content" embodied in traditional content analysis). Instead, depending on which ideological framework was being used, different, often conflicting or contradic-tory, meanings (interpretations) could be produced, using the practices of signification (sign-ifi-cation). Cultural studies analyzed media *content* in terms of the ideological codes used by producers to encode a specific meaning and *effects* in terms of the codes that audiences used to decode. It redefined culture in terms of the inventory of interpretive frameworks or systems of representation distributed within any one society (see INTERPRETATION). Both approaches redefined media influence as operating symbolically rather than in a directly behavioral fash-ion (i.e., mediated by language, signs, symbols, ideas) and treated texts not as the transparent bearers of meaning and influence but as arenas in which mean-ing was socially and symbolically constituted and contested.

These theoretical approaches restored the theoret-ical centrality of ideology to the analysis of cultural and communicative forms and gave greater auton-omy to ideology than it had been accorded in tradi-tional (e.g., Marxist) formulations. The new approaches mounted an extensive critique of the tendency toward class and economic reductionism in classical Marxist theories of ideology. Using semiotic and structuralist approaches, Barthes analyzed mass media and popular cultural forms as modern myths or "fragments of ideology" (mythologies). Louis Al-thusser retained a classic Marxist interest in how ideology reproduces the social relations of domina-tion and in the media as "ideological apparatuses" but described ideology, according to the semiotic or discursive model, as consisting of "concepts, sym-bols, images . . . systems of representation." MICHEL FOUCAULT, who took discursive analysis furthest (dropping the term ideology altogether), nevertheless restored the classical stress on the indissoluble link between power and knowledge—the way ideological discourse both constructs what we know about the world and validates its own truth claims ("regimes

of truth"). Influenced by the same linguistic trends and by feminism, psychoanalytically informed criti-cal theories began to study how individuals are con-structed as subjects of—and for—ideology and how they are set into positions of knowledge or recogni-tion in relation to dominant ideological discourses (e.g., the influence of Jacques Lacan's rereading of Freud on film, television, and GENRE theory and criticism). *See also* PSYCHOANALYSIS.

The political upheavals of the 1960s and the the-oretical developments of the 1970s thus provoked a rupture in the models of society, influence, and effects around which mainstream empirical mass commu-nications theory and research had consolidated (both in the United States and elsewhere). This prompted a renewed interest in (1) the influence on audience behavior, attitudes, and belief in the "pictures of the world" that the media circulate; (2) the question of which representations, whose interpretations or def-initions of the situation prevailed, and thus the links among the media, power, and social conflict; and (3) the role of media-circulated images and ideas in legitimation, securing consent to social order, and the exercise of social and symbolic control by pow-erful or dominant groups over subordinate, marginal, or so-called deviant social groups. This opened the door to a renewed concern with ideology within media research.

In the 1970s the impact of these new, more ideo-logically oriented paradigms of theory and research can be seen in, for example, (1) large-scale, "main-stream" studies like *Violence and the Media: A Staff Report to the National Commission on the Causes and Prevention of Violence* (U.S., 1969) and the Surgeon General's Scientific Advisory Committee on Television and Social Behavior, *Television and Growing Up: The Impact of Televised Violence* (U.S., 1972); (2) a broader, more symbolically oriented or culturally informed approach among senior com-munications research specialists (e.g., U.S. scholar George Gerbner's work on CULTURAL INDICATORS, 1970); or (3) the numerous studies of news (see TELEVISION NEWS), entertainment shows, soap operas (see SOAP OPERA), and domestic serials and the rep-resentations of different groups (class, ethnic, gender) or issues (Palestine, the Third World, TERRORISM) that began to appear in the expanded media studies field. These were all characterized in their different ways by more systematic attention to the underlying ideological structures of media discourse.

In the 1980s the continuing development of semi-otic, structuralist, psychoanalytic, and poststructur-alist theories has provided more sophisticated critical models for the analysis of mass media texts and institutions, which are seen as having their primary societal effect symbolically—that is, in the realm of ideas through the production and transformation of meaning—thereby strengthening the emphasis on their ideological character. Other critical approaches, influenced by a return to a "political economy of the media," deal with questions of ideology through economic and institutional analysis of media ownership and control and through the use of such concepts as *international flow* and *cultural imperialism*. Together these have constituted the basis for more critical approaches in mass communications theory and research, both in the United States and elsewhere, and in a grounding of the field in the wider framework of cultural studies, as an alternative to the more empirical and behavioral emphases of mainstream theory and research.

See also COMMUNICATIONS, STUDY OF; COMMUNICATIONS RESEARCH: ORIGINS AND DEVELOPMENT; MARXIST THEORIES OF COMMUNICATION; MASS MEDIA EFFECTS.

STUART HALL

INDUS SCRIPT

Script used in the Indus Valley around 2600–1800 B.C.E. It is little understood, but it is important for the history of communication as one of the oldest systems of WRITING, created by a great urban civilization that had well-established contacts with the ancient Near East.

Historical background. A stone seal with the image of a unicorn bull and a text in an unknown script was published in 1875 in an archaeological report about the ruin mounds at Harappa in the northern Indus valley. In the 1920s large-scale excavations were undertaken at the site and at Mohenjo-Daro, six hundred kilometers to the south on the Indus River. The urban civilization discovered there had been completely unknown. It is not even mentioned in the earliest historical records of India—the hymns of the *Rig Veda*—which are believed to date from the last quarter of the second millennium B.C.E.

Later archaeological research has located about one thousand Harappan settlements over a large area that extends from Shortugai in Afghanistan to Daimabad near Bombay, and from Sutkagen-dor near the Iranian border of Pakistan to Alamgirpur near Delhi (see Figure 1). The Indus civilization, which developed from Early Harappan Neolithic cultures that are several millennia older, flourished around 2600–1800 B.C.E.

The Indus script apparently came into being around the beginning of this period, or even earlier. It is thus older than the oldest known purely syllabic script (linear Elamite), which dates from around 2350 B.C.E., and the oldest alphabetic script, which dates from about 1600 B.C.E. Its appearance at such an early date suggests that the Indus script represents the earliest type of real writing, the logosyllabic (or morphemographic) script, in which each sign stands

for a word or a morpheme of one or more syllables.

Many artifacts—including seals bearing Indus script—found in contemporary strata in Mesopotamia and the Persian Gulf attest to the existence of well-established trade and communication links between the Indus civilization and the Near East (*see* ARTIFACT). From the Old Akkadian period (2350–2150 B.C.E.) onward these contacts were probably carried mainly over the sea route. Many scholars contend that the realm of the Indus civilization was in fact the country of Melukha mentioned in the CUNEIFORM texts of the twenty-fourth to nineteenth centuries B.C.E.

Evolution and texts. The Indus script is a distinctive writing system. It cannot readily be related to any other known script. The "potter's/owner's marks" on the ceramics of Early Harappan Neolithic cultures (at Damb Sadaat, Amri, and Rahman Dheri) may represent a forerunner which, in combination with influences from the West, developed into actual writing. It is also possible, because the art of the nearby and contemporaneous Proto-Elamite culture (ca. 3100–2900 B.C.E.) had a strong influence on Harappan carvings, that the vaguely similar Proto-Elamite script was a model for the Indus script.

Fully developed Indus script first appears in the miniature tablets that are characteristic of the early levels of Harappa, tentatively dated about 2600 B.C.E. Some of the signs differ slightly from the later forms. Also, the direction of writing varies, unlike later examples in which the writing runs almost invariably from right to left.

The great majority of the preserved Indus texts are on stamp seals made of steatite. Some seals are rectangular and contain text only, but most are square with a pictorial motif—usually a naturalistic animal figure—on the lower part. Occasionally, there are scenes with humanlike deities which give some insights into the Harappan religion. Ancient seal impressions on clay were used for sealing merchandise; packing materials have left their traces on the reverse of these clay labels (see Figure 2).

Other principal sources of text include molded tablets of terra-cotta or faience that may have been used as amulets, graffiti on pottery fragments, ivory sticks of unknown use, and inscriptions on axes and other items. Financial records—perhaps written on palm leaves as they were later in India—probably existed, but they have perished.

In late Harappan times seals with nothing but geometric patterns—like the swastika—became common. After the collapse of the urban civilization in the Indus valley, the Indus script gradually fell into disuse. The latest example is from Daimabad, dating from about 1600 B.C.E. The oldest known script of India, the Brahmi (attested ca. 250 B.C.E.), is not descended from the Indus script but from the Semitic consonantal ALPHABET.

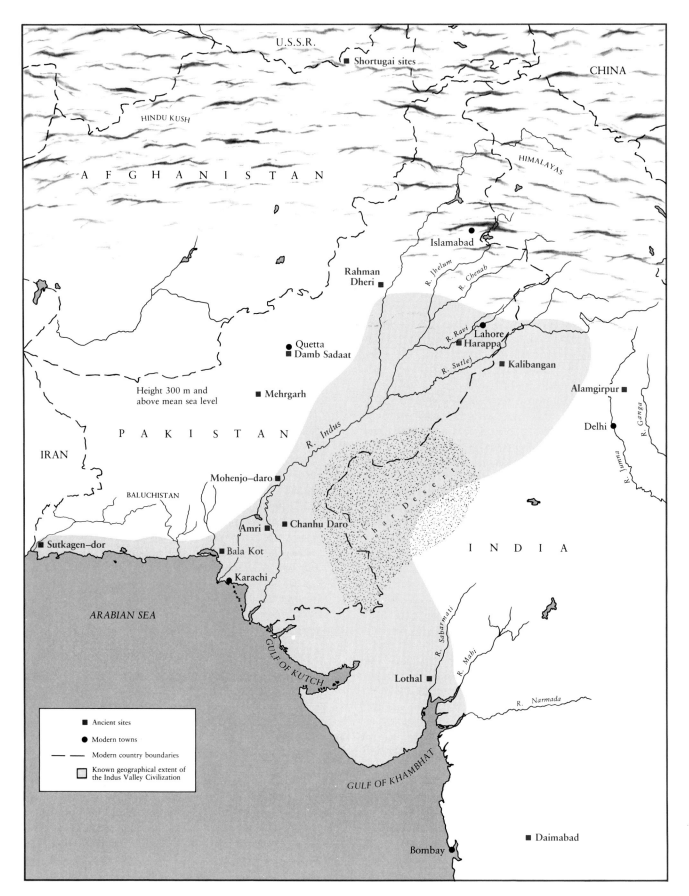

Figure 1. *(Indus Script)* Ancient sites in the Indus Valley.

Figure 2. *(Indus Script)*   Seal impressions, Mohenjo-Daro, ca. 2600 B.C.E. National Museum, New Delhi.

Obstacles to decipherment. Ancient scripts of unknown languages usually have been deciphered by comparing them with existing translations and/or by identifying the proper names of gods or kings that are known from other sources. However, there are no bilingual texts, that is, texts that provide two versions—one in Indus script and one written in a known script. And since nothing is known from external sources about the political history of the Indus civilization, no names of gods or kings, let alone of ordinary people, are available to help in the task of decipherment. Moreover, the texts are limited in scope. There are altogether about thirty-five hundred texts, but all are extremely short, comprising five signs on the average. The longest text has twenty-six signs on three sides; the longest single side has seventeen signs divided among three lines. In addition, the nature of the underlying language is completely unknown. For all these reasons the Indus script is very hard to decipher; some scholars consider it an impossible task unless bilingual texts are found.

Tools for decipherment. Techniques that can assist the task of decipherment—once the type of writing has been established—include the rebus principle and the contextual use of the signs. If Indus script was in fact logosyllabic, it must also have employed the rebus principle, as did the other logosyllabic scripts such as Sumerian and Egyptian. According to the rebus principle, each sign symbolized not only the object it represented pictorially but also linguistic units that were phonetically similar to the word naming the depicted object. Because this principle is dependent on phonetic values—which are, of course, language-specific—the use of the rebus principle may make it possible to identify the language underlying the script and, therefore, to decipher individual signs. Four conditions are necessary for this method to succeed: (1) the object depicted by a given pictogram (pictorial sign) must be recognizable, (2) this pictogram must also have been used phonetically, that is, in a meaning different from the pictorial meaning,

(3) the intended (phonetic) reading must make sense in context, and (4) linguistically satisfactory homonyms (phonetically similar words with different meanings) are found in a likely language.

Unfortunately, very few signs are pictorially clear. The great majority are so simplified and stylized that their pictorial meaning is likely to remain a permanent enigma. However, the fact that most of the Indus texts are seals and that some of them have been found in the Near East gives a valuable clue to their contents. The inscriptions engraved on Indus seals can be assumed to be largely parallel to Mesopotamian seal inscriptions, which have been deciphered. The latter consist mainly of proper names and official titles, with or without attributes and dedicatory formulas. Consistent with the Mesopotamian seals, and also based on later Indian studies of proper and place names, it is probable that names of gods and priestly titles occurred on the Indus seals in large numbers.

Underlying language. The language underlying the Indus script is uniform throughout the area and the duration of the Indus civilization. This is shown by the sign sequences, which remain uniform throughout this period. By contrast, several Indus seals found in the Near East, especially those with a form resembling the local seal form (cylindrical or round), have totally different sign sequences; they may record Sumerian or Semitic names of acculturated Indus merchants.

It is not certain what language group is the most direct successor to the language of the Indus civilization. One possibility is Indo-European, particularly Indo-Aryan. However, this is not supported by some of the cultural evidence, such as the absence of horses among the animals depicted on the Indus seals and attested by bone remains. Studies in historical LINGUISTICS suggest that Dravidian (still spoken in Baluchistan and Afghanistan) is the most likely successor to the underlying language of the Indus script.

See also CLAY TOKENS; WRITING MATERIALS.

Bibliography. Kimmo Koskenniemi and Asko Parpola, *Corpus of Texts in the Indus Script, Documentation and Duplicates of the Texts in the Indus Script, A Concordance to the Texts in the Indus Script,* Department of Asian and African Studies Research Reports, nos. 1–3, Helsinki, 1979–1982; Iravatham Mahadevan, *The Indus Script: Texts Concordance and Tables,* New Delhi, 1977; Asko Parpola, "The Indus Script—A Challenging Puzzle," *World Archaeology* 17 (1986): 399–419; idem, "Tasks, Methods, and Results in the Study of the Indus Script," *Journal of the Royal Asiatic Society* (1975): 178–209.

ASKO PARPOLA

INFORMATION SCIENCE. *See* LIBRARY.

INFORMATION THEORY

A calculus capable of accounting for variation and information flow within systems regardless of whether they are biological, social, or technical. Information theory is characterized by a few axioms from which many measuring functions, accounting equations, theorems, limits, and, above all, its notion of information and communication can be derived. The information theorist treats quantities of information much like a physicist traces energy uses and losses within a mechanical system or an accountant measures cash flows and capital distributions within a company. Although quantities of information do not behave like energy and matter and have little to do with truth or value, once information flows are assessed they can be related to and shed light on other organizational features of the system in which such flows are observed.

Origins

The idea of information theory emerged in the late 1940s and came to several researchers virtually independently. NORBERT WIENER, the founder of CYBERNETICS (the theory of communication and control in humans and machines), came to it while working on statistical aspects of communication engineering. Soviet mathematician A. N. Kolmogoroff came to it from probability theory, and CLAUDE SHANNON of the Bell Telephone Laboratories in the United States developed it while working on problems of coding and deciphering messages. Earlier, British statistician R. A. Fisher, known for his analysis of variance, suggested a quantitative expression for the amount of information an experiment provides. Nearly a century before all four of them, Austrian physicist Ludwig Boltzmann had measured thermodynamic entropy by a function that resembles the one now used in information theory. However, it was Shannon who published the most elaborate account of

the theory in 1948, offering proof of the uniqueness of its form and twenty-one theorems of considerable generality. WARREN WEAVER anticipated that any theory clarifying the understanding of information and communication was certain to affect all fields of knowledge. He gave a popular account of Shannon's work and coauthored with him *The Mathematical Theory of Communication* (1949). Subsequently, U.S. statistician Solomon Kullback linked information theory to statistics, and British cybernetician W. Ross Ashby generalized it to many variables.

Historically, information theory was a major stimulus to the development of communication research. It made the heretofore vague notions of information mathematically tractable, liberated it from the conflicting claims by diverse disciplines concerned with knowledge and communication technology, and legitimized research on communication and information processes whether they occurred in society, in electronic information systems, or within the human brain.

Three versions of the theory are discussed here: the possibilistic and semantic theory of information, the probabilistic or statistical theory of communication, and its extension to a method for testing complex models of qualitative data.

Semantic Information

The semantic theory quantifies information in ways similar to ordinary uses of the term: we might judge one report to be *more* informative than another, we might experience *how little* we can say in a telegram, and we might admit to having *not enough* information to decide how to resolve an issue. To obtain information we may ask questions. Questions admit uncertainty and are designed to elicit answers that help the questioner decide among several uncertain possibilities. The knower selects an answer from a repertoire of possible responses. The questioner decides what that answer means and which uncertain alternatives it thereby excludes. Information is always selective among a set of preconceived alternatives, and the theory quantifies this selectivity in terms of the number of questions we need to have answered.

The semantic theory presupposes a distinction between two sets of elements, languages, or symbol repertoires, connected by a code. One contains the set of messages, answers to questions, statements, or meaningful actions exchanged; the other contains the set of meanings, referents, things, people, ideas, concepts, or consequences the former refer to, indicate, or are about. The semantic theory suggests that information is manifest in what the elements in one set imply about those in the other set. From the point of view of the questioner or receiver the theory expresses the amount of information, I, a message conveys as the *difference between two states of uncertainty*, U, before and after that message became known:

$$I\left(\text{message}\bigg|\begin{array}{c}\text{state of}\\\text{knowledge}\end{array}\right) =$$
$$= U\left(\begin{array}{c}\text{before receipt}\\\text{of message}\end{array}\right) - U\left(\begin{array}{c}\text{after receipt}\\\text{of message}\end{array}\right)$$

The message is an element in one set; the uncertainties concern elements in the other set, for example, the interpretations such messages could have; and the amount of information indicates the selectivity that a message induces within the domain of possible interpretations.

Accordingly, information is *positive* when a message, answer, or report reduces the receiver's uncertainty about what he or she wishes to know. A sequence of informative messages, such as would be received during an interview or a conversation, reduces the receiver's uncertainty or enhances his or her state of knowledge stepwise and results in *additive* quantities of information associated with each message. A message whose content is already known does not alter the receiver's uncertainty and is *redundant,* simple repetition being one example. A message that says something unrelated to what the receiver needs to know is *irrelevant*. A message that denies what previously appeared certain and thus increases the receiver's uncertainty conveys *negative* amounts of information. Except for some syntactic limitations, the formal complexity or material composition of the message does not enter the definition of information and does not affect what or how much it conveys. Semantic information measures not what a message is but what it does in someone's cognitive system of distinctions.

The unit of measurement in information theory equals the amount the answer to a yes-or-no question conveys and is called one *bit* (for *bi*nary dig*it*). Since N alternatives can be exhaustively distinguished by $\log_2 N$ yes-or-no questions, the state of uncertainty becomes simply $U = \log_2 N$ bits. Thus, if U is an integer, U equals the number of times N alternatives can be divided in half until only one alternative remains. The remainder is elementary algebra:

$$I\left(\text{message}\bigg|\begin{array}{c}\text{state of}\\\text{knowledge}\end{array}\right) =$$
$$= \log_2 N_{\text{before message}} - \log_2 N_{\text{after message}}$$
$$= -\log_2 \frac{N_{\text{after message}}}{N_{\text{before message}}}$$
$$= -\log_2 P_{\text{after|before}}$$

Thus information—the difference between two states of uncertainty—is seen to be a *measure of the con-*straint a message imposes by singling out a subset of the initial number of uncertain possibilities N. With P as the logical probability of this subset, it may also be interpreted as a *measure of the difficulty of selecting* among a set of alternatives *by chance* and thus becomes equated with that message's surprise value. For example, because ignorant students can answer 50 percent of all yes-or-no questions correctly merely by choosing at random, teachers expect that knowledgeable students will perform significantly above that logical probability. Therefore, the semantic theory can also be seen to equate information with choices that deviate from what would be expected under conditions of ignorance.

When the alternatives are enumerable, information theory offers a precise instrument for quantification. The answer to the question "Did she have a boy or a girl?" conveys one bit of information. To make appropriate choices among eight different subway trains requires three bits of information. To locate one criminal among, say, a million Bostonians requires nearly twenty bits of information, which is the minimum amount that Boston's police department has to process per individual crime. A Hollerith card with eighty columns by twelve rows, whose positions may be either punched or not, can store up to 960 bits of information. Two such cards can store twice as much. According to Bremmermann's Limit, which states that no computer can do better than 10^{47} bits per second and per gram of its mass, the limit on computability on earth is about 10^{72} bits and is not achievable in practice.

When the alternatives are less clear or known only in relation to each other, the theory offers possibilities of quantitative comparisons. The statement "She plays a stringed instrument" conveys three to four bits less information than one asserting that "She plays the viola," because the former leaves uncertain which stringed instrument she plays. For the same reason, "about noon" conveys less than "at 12:03 P.M.," although the additional quantity conveyed by minutes may be irrelevant in a particular situation. Information quantities can also be associated with the logical structure of complex messages. For example, two statements connected by an inclusive *or* convey less information than either statement does by itself; when the logical conjunction *and* is used to connect them, they are more informative together than either is alone.

Note several properties of the semantic theory. First, quantities of information are not tied to physical entities. The length of the silence between the signals of the Morse code is as critical as the absence of a letter from a friend is informative to the usual receiver.

Second, quantities of information are always expressed *relative to someone's cognitive system of distinctions,* including the distinctions an "objective" measuring instrument makes for a scientific observer. An X-ray photograph may be more informative to the physician than it is to the patient precisely because the former tends to have a more elaborated conceptual system and language for interpreting such images. It follows that one can observe that person A said X to person B, where X is a vehicle of communication or the material form of a message, but it is only when the codes relating the cognitive systems of A and B to X are known that one can assert how much semantic information A communicated to B.

Third, quantities of information are always *contextual* measures. They are not attributable to a single message but express what this message does in the context of all possible messages or conditions. The larger this repertoire, the greater the amount of information a particular message may convey and its receiver needs to process in order to make an appropriate selection. Where there are no options there is no information. When the context of communication is not clearly understood, quantities of information may become at best approximate.

Fourth, a valuable oddity of the theory is that paradoxical or contradictory messages turn out to convey quantities of information that are infinite, indicating the logical inadequacy or powerlessness of a cognitive system to cope with such messages. This is particularly true when messages are *self-referential.* For example, "Ignore this command" asserts how it is to be taken, its illocutionary force or its truth value, and is impossible in a system that insists on the distinction or asymmetry between language and action or between statements and what these statements refer to. *See also* SEMANTICS.

Statistical Theory of Communication

In the mathematical theory of communication the statistical analog of uncertainty is called *entropy* and is defined by the famous Shannon-Wiener formula:

$$H(A) = -\sum_{a \epsilon A} p_a \log_2 p_a$$

where the variable A consists of mutually exclusive categories, values, or symbols a, and p_a is the probability with which a is observed in A. The entropy is a measure of variability or diversity not unlike the statistical concept of variance, except that it does not require variables to express magnitudes and is hence entirely general. When all observations fall into one category the entropy is zero; otherwise it is a positive quantity whose maximum depends on the number of distinctions drawn within a sample.

In social research, entropy measures have served

to assess occupational diversity in cities, the variability of television programming, the consensus on preferences for political candidates, the specificity of financial reports, the diversity of opinions, and the richness of vocabularies. Entropy measures may be used comparatively, for example, to differentiate between different genres of literature (newspaper English is low in entropy compared with avant-garde poetry); or they may be correlated with other variables, for example, to ascertain how diversity of opinion is related to number of newspapers serving a community or to predict the reading ease of a text. However, taking full advantage of the additivity of entropy and information quantities, the theory's most important contribution is the calculus it defines on top of such entropies. Already the relationship between entropy and the aforementioned uncertainty is instructive in this regard.

When there are N_A alternatives a and each is observed the same number of times, that is, $p_a = 1/N_A$, then in this special case, the entropy equals the uncertainty, $H(A) = U(A) = \log_2 N_A$. When n individual observations are differentiated into mutually exclusive classes $a = 1, 2, \ldots$, so that $n = n_1 + n_2 + \ldots$ and $p_a = n_a/n$, then

$$H(A) = \sum_{a \epsilon A} \frac{n_a}{n} (\log_2 n - \log_2 n_a)$$

in which $\log_2 n$ is the quantity of uncertainty in the sample of size n with each observation considered unique, $\log_2 n_a$ is the quantity to which the uncertainty reduces after knowing an observation to be of type a, and $\sum n_a/n$ renders the expression as an average reduction of uncertainty. Thus the entropy $H(A)$ is the average uncertainty or diversity in a sample when its n observations are considered in categories. The entropy formula is the same whether one considers the entropy in one variable, A, in a matrix of two variables, say, A and B, or in a cross-tabulation of many variables A, B, C, $\ldots$, Z:

$$H(ABC \ldots Z) = -\sum_a \sum_b \sum_c \ldots \sum_z p_{abc \ldots z} \log_2 p_{abc \ldots z}$$

The mathematical theory of communication relates a sender, who emits symbols a from a set A with a certain entropy $H(A)$, to a receiver, who receives symbols b from a set B with a certain entropy $H(B)$, by means of a channel that converts input symbols a into output symbols b and associates a probability with each transition. In the ideal channel, symbols sent and symbols received are related one-to-one (Figure 1*a*). Variation at the receiver for which the sender does not account is called *noise* and is manifest in one-to-many relations (Figure 1*b*). Variation at the sender omitted by the receiver is called *equivocation* and is manifest in many-to-one relations

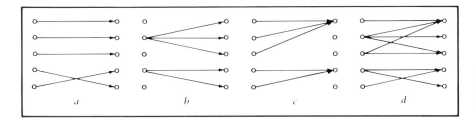

Figure 1. *(Information Theory)* Four examples of symbol-transition diagrams: *(a)* error free; *(b)* noise only; *(c)* equivocation only; *(d)* mixed.

(Figure 1*c*) with the most typical example being a mixture of these (Figure 1*d*). Noise and equivocation distract from perfect communication but in different ways. The term *noise* is borrowed from acoustical distortions and is generalized here to cover all kinds of random alterations, blurred images, and uncertainties about how a sent symbol is received. Equivocation shows up in a receiver's simplification of what has been sent or the ambiguity about the sender's intentions. The theory has three ways of expressing the *amount of information transmitted*, $T(A:B)$, through a channel:

(1) $T(A:B) = H(B) - H_A(B)$
(2) $T(A:B) = H(A) - H_B(A)$
(3) $T(A:B) = H(A) + H(B) - H(AB)$

The first expresses communication as the difference between the entropy at the receiver and that part of its entropy that is noise, $H_A(B)$. The second expresses communication as the difference between the entropy at the receiver and that part of its entropy lost as equivocation, $H_B(A)$. Both formally resemble the expression for the semantic information by being the difference between the entropy without and the entropy with reference to a second variable. The third expresses communication as the difference between the entropy that the sender and the receiver would exhibit if they were entirely unrelated and the joint entropy, $H(AB)$, that is in fact observed. It follows that noise and equivocation can be obtained algebraically by $H_A(B) = H(AB) - H(A)$ and $H_B(A) = H(AB) - H(B)$, respectively. Communication is symmetrical, $T(A:B) = T(B:A)$, can be interpreted as *shared variation*, and the quantities involved may be depicted as in Figure 2.

Although communication always involves some kind of covariation, it speaks for the generality of the theory that senders and receivers need not share the same symbol repertoire. Indeed much of communication proceeds by conversions of mental images into verbal assertions, of sound into electrical impulses, of temporal representations into spatial ones, of expressions in one language into those of another, and so forth, during which some patterns are retained.

Regardless of the nature of the media involved, *the amount of communication possible is limited by the number of options available.* More specifically,

no channel can transmit more information than its weakest component. For the simple channel between a sender and a receiver $T(A:B)_{max} = min[H(A),H(B)]$.

Considering that messages can take many material forms and information can be carried by rather different symbols, much of early information theory was concerned with the construction and evaluation of appropriate codes for efficient and/or error-free communication. The coding function may be part of the communicator (e.g., a natural language) or part of the medium (e.g., a microphone or loudspeaker) (Figure 3).

In his fourth theorem Shannon shows that, given enough time, it is always possible to encode a message for transmission even through a very limited channel. However, with C as the channel capacity (in bits per second) and H as the entropy in the source (in bits per symbol) no code can achieve an average rate greater than C/H (symbols per second). In other words, different languages, different signaling alphabets, and different media may make communication more or less efficient, but none can exceed C/H.

Redundancy is another important concept provided by the theory. Redundancy is measured as the difference between the amount that could be and the amount that is in fact transmitted:

$$R = T_{max} - T$$

Redundancy may be caused by duplication of channels of communication, repetition of messages sent, or a priori restrictions on the full range of symbols or symbol combinations used for forming messages (by a GRAMMAR, for example). Although redundancy appears to measure the inefficiency of transmission, in human communication it is a valuable quantity because it can compensate for transmission errors and the effects of selective inattention. For example, the detection of misspellings in a written text, the simplifications used in forming a telegram, and speed reading are all possible only because of redundancy. Shannon estimated that the English language is about 50 percent redundant; subsequent researchers revised his calculation to nearly 70 percent. Shannon's tenth theorem states that the effect of noise in a channel of communication can be compensated for by an amount of redundancy equal to or exceeding the amount of noise in that channel. This redundancy

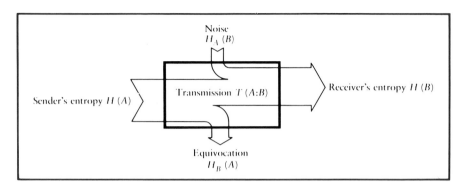

Figure 2. *(Information Theory)* Informational account for simple communication channels.

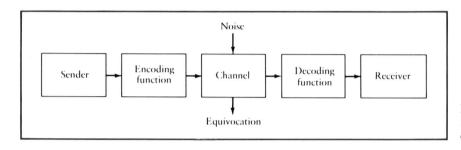

Figure 3. *(Information Theory)* Multicomponent communication process. (After Claude Shannon.)

may stem either from an additional correction channel or from a suitable coding of the messages transmitted.

In complex systems of many variables the total amount of information transmitted within it is

$$T(A:B:...:Z) = H(A) + H(B) + ... + H(Z)$$
$$- H(AB...Z)$$

To analyze this quantity, various equations are available. For example,

$$T(A:B:...:K:L:...:Z) = T(A:B:...:K) + T(L:M:...:Z)$$
$$+ T(AB...K:LM...Z)$$

decomposes this total into two quantities within and one quantity between the subsystems *AB...K* and *LM...Z*. Or

$$T(A:B:...:Z) = T(A:B) + T(AB:C) + T(ABC:D)$$
$$+ ... + T(AB...Y:Z)$$

expresses the total as the sum of the amounts transmitted between two variables plus the amount between the two and a third, the amount between the three and a fourth, and so on.

$$H(Z) = T(A:Z) + T_A(B:Z) + T_{AB}(C:Z)$$
$$+ ... + T_{AB...X}(Y:Z) + H_{AB...Y}(Z)$$

explains the entropy in *Z* in terms of the amount of information transmitted from *A* plus the amount of information transmitted from *B* controlled for by *A*, and so on, plus the unexplainable noise in *Z*. In this manner complex information flows within a system may be analyzed.

Structural Models

Structural modeling searches for models of qualitative data that represent an optimum balance between structural simplicity and the insignificance of their errors of information omission. Thus models may be found that fit the data best and model the flow of information throughout a system with the least amount of error. Shannon's originally chainlike conception is just one such model.

In the previous examples the total amount of information found in the multivariate data about a system is seen as defined by two kinds of quantities. The sum $H(A) + H(B) + ... + H(Z) = H(m_{ind})$ can be interpreted as the maximum entropy that a model m_{ind} exhibits whose variables $A,B,...,Z$ are statistically independent. The quantity $H(AB...Z) = H(m_o)$ is the entropy actually observed within a model m_o capable of representing all complexities contained in the data. If the two quantities were equal, the data could be said to fit the model of independent variables and show no structure. The total amount, $T(m_{ind}) = H(m_{ind}) - H(m_o)$, can be seen to express the amount of information by which the model m_{ind} is in error. Between the two models, m_o and m_{ind}, on which classical information theory is based, a host of other models could be constructed and tested. Consider four structurally different models within six variables each (Figure 4).

Just as for m_{ind}, each model m_j can be used to generate its own maximum entropy distribution, yielding $T(m_j)$ (for models with loops, as in m_1, this quantity must be obtained by iterative computation,

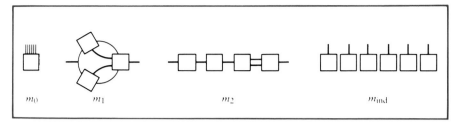

Figure 4. *(Information Theory)* Four examples of structural communication models in block diagrams: *(from left to right)* undifferentiated whole; with circularities; linear chain; with independent components.

whereas for other models algebraic techniques are readily available). In these terms the total amount of information in the data can be decomposed by

$$T(m_{ind}) = T(m_j) + [T(m_{ind}) - T(m_j)]$$

where $T(m_j)$ is the amount of information the model m_j fails to capture, whereas $[T(m_{ind}) - T(m_j)]$ is the amount of information represented by m_j.

Limitations of Information Theory

Some writers have argued that information theory is biased by its early applications in engineering, that it is unable to account for semantic aspects of communication, and that it is limited to linear models (allowing no feedback). None of these arguments is correct.

According to Shannon's second theorem, whose proof is corroborated by many others, the form of the entropy and the information functions is unique, given the axioms of the theory. This puts the theory on a rather unquestionable basis. The critics' burden is to reveal possible inadequacies of the theory by showing the unreasonableness of its axioms, which may be stated here as follows:

(1) $H_2(p, 1-p)$
   is continuous for $0 \le p \le 1$ and $H_2(\frac{1}{2}, \frac{1}{2}) = 1$
(2) $H_r(p_1, p_2, \dots, p_r)$
   is a symmetrical function of its arguments,
   $\sum_{a=1}^{a=r} p_a = 1$, and
(3) for any $0 \le \lambda \le 1$:
   $H_3(\lambda p, (1-\lambda)p, 1-p) = H_2(p, 1-p) + pH_2(\lambda, 1-\lambda)$.

Inapplicabilities of the theory could be encountered, for example, when probabilities do not add to one—a condition that would already fail the first axiom. This condition may arise when the universe of events is undefined, observations in a sample are nonenumerable, or distinctions are fuzzy (do not yield mutually exclusive categories). Information theory presupposes the applicability of the theory of probability (logical possibility, relative frequency, proportion or percent), which is a rather basic demand. The second axiom would become inappropriate, for example, when the ordering of the events

1,2,...,r would make a difference in the amounts the whole set carries. This condition may arise when data are nonqualitative (magnitudinal, for example), in which case the information contained in these proximities is ignored. The third axiom would fail when information quantities are nonadditive and/or probabilities are not multiplicative—for example, when two messages jointly convey more information than the sum of what they convey separately. This situation may arise in irony or when metacommunications and communications are mixed up. The fact that information theory cannot reflect its own context and is, hence, *morpheostatic* in character is common to most social theories and not unique to this one.

Extensions of Information Theory

The basic idea of information theory—equating information with selectivity—may be extended. Effective decisions, one could argue, organize the world, create unusual material arrangements. Messages ranging from blueprints, computer programs, and DNA to political speeches and votes convey information to the extent that they bring about thermodynamically nonentropic pattern, like the assembly of a piece of equipment, a network of computations, the biological structure of an organism, or new forms of social organization. Thus information could be conceived as a measure of the organizational work a message can do, selection being a simple case of this. Information in this sense can be processed (combined, transformed, or encoded in different media) or duplicated at comparatively little cost. Information creates its own context of application. When it organizes an information-processing system it may become amplified, elaborated, and expanded beyond its original scope. Information also becomes part of any living organization, social or biological, that maintains its structure against natural processes of decay or organizational infringements from its environment. Because the thermodynamic laws and the economic costs of production and dissemination apply only to its material carriers, which are largely arbitrary, information is not a commodity. It provides relatively independent accounts for the escalating organizational changes in contemporary society. Information controls a society's rate of thermodynamic decay and directs its economic developments while escaping many of the traditional socioeconomic constraints.

See also MODELS OF COMMUNICATION.

Bibliography. Klaus Krippendorff, *Information Theory: Structural Models for Qualitative Data*, Beverly Hills, Calif., 1986; Claude E. Shannon and Warren Weaver, *The Mathematical Theory of Communication*, Urbana, Ill., 1949, reprint 1964.

KLAUS KRIPPENDORFF

INNIS, HAROLD (1894–1952)

Canadian political economist and geographer, author of several influential works on communications. Harold Adams Innis devoted most of his scholarly life to producing detailed studies of aspects of Canadian commerce and industry (e.g., fisheries, the fur trade, and railways). As an outgrowth of these studies, he undertook during the last decade of his life an extensive analysis of forms of communication and produced two major works, *Empire and Communications* (1950) and *The Bias of Communication* (1951). His focus was on power and how it is exercised through control of areas of space and periods of time. He saw communications technology as the key to this economic and political process, for such technology determines the social coordinates of space and time—the forms of social organization that are possible, the distribution of power among social groups, and the forms of knowledge possessed by a people.

After studying at the University of Chicago, where he became interested in the work of U.S. economist and sociologist Thorstein Veblen, Innis attacked the "frontier hypothesis"—the belief that the source of inspiration and action in Western CULTURE was not at its center but at its margins. Every frontier, Innis pointed out, was controlled by a "back tier." The back tier drained away the products of the frontier, and the interests of the back-tier economy constituted the dominant force in geographic expansion. The first back tier of North America was Europe, and to that extent North American economic and communications development was part of the trajectory of European history. With the gradual decline of European influence the back tier shifted to North American metropolitan centers, particularly Washington and New York. Innis's studies of the confrontation between American Indian ORAL CULTURE and the European literate tradition, of the exploitation of Canadian timber resources to fuel the growth of North American newspapers, and of the ease with which these same newspapers penetrated Canadian life led him to examine the progression from oral to print/literate and then to electronic civilizations.

Innis argued that the ways in which communication systems structure (or "bias") relations of time and space are at the base of social institutions. He divided communication and social control into two major types: those achieved through space-binding media and those achieved through time-binding media. Because they are easy to transport, space-binding media, such as print and electronic communication, are connected with expansion and control over territory and favor the establishment of commercialism and empire. Because they are more difficult to transport, time-binding media, such as the manuscript and human speech, favor the cultivation of memory, a historical sense, relatively small communities, and traditional forms of authority. For Innis the tragedy of modern culture is the intrinsic tendency of the PRINTING press and electronic media to reduce both space and time to commercialism and expansionism. The bias of modern technology is its reduction of signaling time (the gap between when a message is sent and when it is received). Print solved the problem of producing standardized communications rapidly and in sufficient quantities to administer large areas. Although it allows for efficient production, print does not possess an efficient distribution system and depends on ship, rail, and air transportation to gain rapid and widespread circulation. The development of electronic communication—beginning with TELEGRAPHY and culminating in RADIO and television (*see* TELEVISION HISTORY)—solved simultaneously the problems of rapid production and distribution. These technologies not only eclipsed space but transformed time, eventually obliterating memory and reducing message duration to the hour, minute, second, and microsecond.

There is always a price, Innis believed, for technological advance. Modern media widen the area of distribution but narrow the range of response. Large audiences receive but are unable to respond directly or to otherwise participate in vigorous discussion. Innis's remedy was always the same: reduce the control of modern technology, reestablish the oral tradition, create avenues of fuller democratic discussion and participation, reawaken memory, cultivate an interest in time and history, restore the roots of a genuinely republican tradition.

Though his work was somewhat overdrawn, Innis provided a theory of communications that is historical and materialistic; that accounts for the effects of economics, geography, and politics; and that is profoundly liberal and humanistic in outlook. His ideas influenced, and ultimately were transformed by, his University of Toronto colleague MARSHALL MCLUHAN.

Bibliography. Donald Creighton, *Harold Adams Innis: Portrait of a Scholar*, Toronto, 1957; Harold A. Innis, *The Bias of Communication*, Toronto, 1951; idem, *Empire and*

Communications (1950), rev. by Mary Q. Innis, foreword by Marshall McLuhan, Toronto, 1972; William H. Melody, Liora Salter, and Paul Heyer, eds., *Culture, Communication and Dependency: The Tradition of H. A. Innis,* Norwood, N.J., 1981.

JAMES W. CAREY

INSECTS, SOCIAL

The social insects include all the termites, all the ants, and certain species of wasps and bees. Most of the communication is by means of odors—usually species-specific chemicals known as pheromones—and most of the rest is tactile, including vibrations that humans perceive as SOUND. The best understood of the social insects is the temperate-zone honey bee, *Apis mellifera.* Because its signaling behavior is the second most complex known in the animal kingdom (only human speech can carry more information), and because the other elements of its communication illustrate the general patterns in the social insects, the discussion here will concentrate on honey bees.

A typical temperate-zone honey bee colony consists of twenty thousand to fifty thousand worker bees, a single queen, and (in the spring and summer) some hundreds of drones. The colony lives in a hollow cavity, usually in a tree, and constructs a series of parallel combs that hang as vertical sheets. The cells in the comb are used to rear new bees and to store food; the food consists of pollen (the bees' protein source) and honey (the carbohydrate store), which is made from nectar. The interior of the hive is dark. Unlike all other social bees and wasps in the temperate zone, the colonies overwinter (as opposed to being started anew each spring by overwintering females, as is the case with bumble bees, yellow jackets, and so on). The overwintering is possible because the cavity provides insulation and the bees store massive quantities of honey, which they "burn" throughout the winter to keep warm.

The queen produces a variety of pheromones, of which two are especially important. One, which is secreted onto her body and ingested by her attendants as they constantly groom her, is spread to all members of the hive through bee-to-bee food exchange (trophallaxis). This pheromone represses the vestigial ovaries of the workers (all of whom are females) and prevents the rearing of new queens. When the queen dies or the colony grows so large or so crowded that the pheromone cannot be distributed effectively, workers begin rearing new queens and initiating preparations for swarming.

Swarming, during which the old queen and about half the population of the hive depart in search of a new cavity, will occur when the new queens are ready to hatch and the weather is favorable. The readiness of the new queens is monitored by acoustic communication. From time to time the old queen presses her body against the honeycomb and vibrates the muscles normally used for flight. This sets up a vibration in the comb with a frequency of about two thousand hertz, which is pulsed according to a particular pattern. Any developing queen mature enough to respond replies with another pattern of pulses. These sounds are detected with vibration detectors located in the hollow legs of the workers and queens. As soon as the weather is acceptable, swarming is triggered by another acoustic signal, this time produced by a worker running over the crowded combs.

The other pheromone serves to attract drones for mating. Once a new queen has hatched she locates the other developing queens by odor and by sound (they respond to the pulsing of the new queen) and kills them; then she leaves the hive to mate. Mating takes place in special drone congregation areas, where drones from many different hives circle, waiting for virgin queens. How drones and queens agree on where these mating areas should be located is not known; the areas are the same year after year, yet no drones survive the winter, and queens only mate just after birth. In any case, the queen flies through the drone cloud, emitting her species-specific pheromone, and the drones give chase. A queen will make several passes through the drone area, mating five to ten times, before returning to the hive to begin several years of egg laying.

Young workers tend the queen and developing larvae, recognizing each class by odor. Later they guard the hive entrance, admitting only those bees that carry the hive odor; this odor is a combination of genetically determined scents and odors permeating the hive as a result of the various sorts of food being stored. The odors cling to waxy hairs on the bee's body. Intruders are attacked and stung, a process that is facilitated by other pheromones. One pheromone, released from the sting apparatus itself when stinging takes place, draws other bees to the site of attack and encourages further stinging. Another, less well understood, is released from the mouth and seems primarily to alarm other bees.

Most of the communication in the hive concerns foraging for food. Scout bees search the area around the hive for several hundred meters (though up to fourteen kilometers at times) looking for undiscovered patches of flowers. Especially high-quality patches are advertised on the scout's return by means of a dance (Figure 1). The dance is generally in the form of a figure eight, with the straight runs crossing in the center emphasized by a "waggling" of the body from side to side at thirteen hertz and a series of sound pulses at about two hundred eighty hertz bursted thirty times a second. In the darkness of the hive both the waggling and the bursting are detected

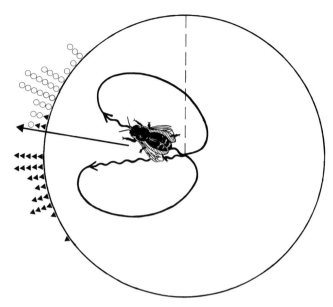

Figure 1. *(Insects, Social)* The dance of forager honey bees consists of a straight, waggling run, followed by a turn and a semicircular return, another waggling run, a turn in the other direction, a return, and so on. At distances less than about one thousand meters, the runs tend to alternate left and right of the true direction, this angular divergence declining with distance. In the example shown here, the orientation of the runs after right-hand turns is indicated by filled triangles, runs after left-hand turns by open circles. The direction of the food is given by the angle between vertical and the dance: "up" is taken as the direction of the sun, so that a dance oriented (as is this one) eighty degrees to the left of vertical corresponds to food eighty degrees left of the sun's direction. Distance is given by the duration of the waggle run or one of the dance features that correlate with run duration. Courtesy of James L. Gould.

one waggle run to the next in the same way. Different races of *Apis mellifera* have different distance "dialects" (Figure 2), reflecting differences in foraging ranges that correlate with the severity of the local winter. The three species of honey bees in the tropics have their own dialects as well. The dialects are entirely genetic: rearing a short-dialect Egyptian bee (*A. m. fasciata*) in a long-dialect German hive (*A. m. carnica*) has no effect on either dialect, and misunderstandings inevitably result. The up-is-the-direction-of-the-sun convention essential to direction communication is also innate. Food very close to the hive is indicated by dances with no waggles at all; these maneuvers are known as round dances.

The information content of the dance can be calculated by considering the accuracy of the dance and therefore the number of different locations (messages) that can be specified. The divergence in dance direction and the variability in distance indication from cycle to cycle make the dance "noisy"; the tendency of recruits to attend several cycles and average them partially compensates for this problem. Careful experiments indicate that the dance noise has evolved to spread out recruits in a controlled manner, a strategy well adapted to exploiting food found in patches. (In the tropics, where the flowers are usually in trees rather than in fields, the dance noise is much smaller.) The decreasing angular divergence of the dance exactly compensates for increasing distance, and the distance scatter precisely matches the amount of direction scatter (Figure 3).

In addition to the radial coordinates of the food

with the antennae by potential recruits attending the dance.

The radial coordinates of the food are specified by the waggling runs. The direction is indicated by the orientation of the dance on the vertical comb: a dance with waggling runs pointing directly up indicates food in the direction of the sun; waggling runs aimed eighty degrees to the left of vertical indicate that the food is eighty degrees to the left of the sun's direction. When the food is nearby, the waggle runs alternate left and right of the true direction; at greater distances this divergence declines, reaching essentially zero at about one thousand meters.

The distance to a food source correlates with the duration of the waggling run, though whether recruits measure duration or count either waggles or sound pulses is not known; any of these measurements would suffice, and each varies slightly from

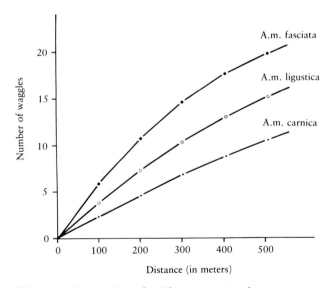

Figure 2. *(Insects, Social)* The conversion from run duration (or number of waggles or sound bursts) depends on the species and race. The dialects for three of the fifteen or so races of the temperate-zone honey bee are shown here. Redrawn after James L. Gould.

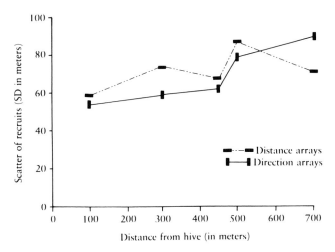

Figure 3. *(Insects, Social)* The decreasing angular divergence of the dance at greater distances results in a constant degree of recruit spread and just matches the spread caused by the constant amount of scatter in distance indication. As a result, recruits are dispatched to a general area of fixed size around the discovery; this area reflects the tendency of temperate-zone flowers to grow in patches. Redrawn after James L. Gould.

patch the dancer returns with several other important pieces of information. Waxy hairs on the dancer's body carry the odor of the food, which will be very important in the recruit's subsequent search once she reaches the general area of the food. The odor is detected by receptors on the attenders' antennae. The quality of the food is also signaled by the intensity of the dance and (if it is nectar) by actual samples of the food, which the dancer provides when signaled by means of a short sound pulse at about three hundred thirty hertz for about one-quarter second. During these food transfers, as during all trophallaxis, the antennae of the two bees move rapidly, tapping each other repeatedly; this behavior is thought to serve some communicatory function. The dance may also advertise pollen (available for inspection in the "pollen baskets" on the dancer's rear legs), water (used to cool the hive on hot days), propolis (tree sap used to strengthen comb in hot climates, entomb foreign matter too large to eject from the hive, polish the inside walls, narrow the entrance, and so on), and, during swarming, suitable new nest sites. At especially rich sources of food and at potential nest sites foragers often release yet another pheromone from a gland in the abdomen, which helps attract other bees. Altogether a dance can transmit one of perhaps three hundred million messages.

The dance behavior of the three species of tropical honey bee casts some light on the evolution of this remarkable communication. The Indian honey bee, *Apis cerana,* is very similar to the temperate-zone honey bee though noticeably smaller; it nests in dark cavities and dances on vertical sheets of comb in the dark. The giant honey bee, *A. dorsata,* builds a large single sheet of exposed comb under large, high, overhanging structures like thick tree limbs and projecting rocks on cliffs. The dance is performed on the vertical surface of the comb, using the same dance conventions but with two interesting differences: the dances are silent, and the attenders do not crowd behind the dancer but rather stand back in a circle; because these dances occur on exposed comb, the attenders can actually see the dancer.

The dances of the dwarf honey bee, *A. florea,* also occur in the open. This species, however, builds its single sheet of exposed comb up and over a narrow branch, and the bees dance on the horizontal top surface of this structure. The dances, exposed as they are to the sky overhead, point directly at the food source. Like the dances of *A. dorsata,* they are silent, and the dancer holds her abdomen high in the air as though to make the dance easier to see. The dance probably evolved in this horizontal form as part of a takeoff maneuver, became ritualized into a figure eight with the distance correlation, and then was modified for use on a vertical surface by adding the sun-to-gravity conversion; indeed, many insects spontaneously convert sun angles to gravity angles while walking. Sound probably evolved as an adaptation to dancing in the dark and must now communicate at least distance.

Some species of social bees have a system for locating food involving a generalized rousing by an excited forager, who carries on her body the odor of the food but provides no information about that food's location. Successful ant foragers frequently lay a pheromone trail. Wasps, however, generally lack any mechanism of food recruitment.

Bibliography. Karl von Frisch, *The Dance Language and Orientation of Bees* (Tanzsprache und Orientierung der Bienen), Cambridge, Mass., 1967; James L. Gould, *Ethology: The Mechanisms and Evolution of Behavior,* New York, 1982; James L. Gould, F. C. Dyer, and W. F. Towne, "Recent Progress in the Study of the Dance Language," in *Experimental Behavioral Ecology and Sociobiology* (Fortschritte der Zoologie, Vol. 31), ed. by Bert Hölldobler and Martin Lindauer, Stuttgart and New York, 1985; Thomas D. Seeley, *Honey Bee Ecology: A Study of Adaptation in Social Life,* Princeton, N.J., 1986; Edward O. Wilson, *The Insect Societies,* Cambridge, Mass., 1971.

JAMES L. GOULD

INSULT

Originally a figurative jump over someone else; hence, later, a triumph over someone, an attack intended as an affront. Today insult is used somewhat more broadly to refer to a range of rude or insolent expressive acts which, intentionally or not, create animosity.

The study of insults. Those who study language in social contexts approach insults as units of ongoing speech that are contrived acts of rudeness or personal challenge intended to intensify a conflict relationship between the insulter and those to whom the insult is directed. In Western speaking systems, which value the appearance of spontaneity, the study of such turns of phrase shows them to be conventional and learned, part of a practiced conversational repertoire, like proverbs and other traditional examples of verbal art (*see also* PROVERB; SPEAKING, ETHNOGRAPHY OF).

In speaking systems that value formality and eloquence more highly, insults serve—along with curses, charms, personal praises (encomia), and boasts—as powerful expressive acts used by performers as weapons under conditions of high intensity in conflict. Insults actively manipulate symbolic objects and actions regarded as good and bad, pure and impure, clean and contaminated, within a specific culture's system of order and values. An insult identifies its target with an unclean or impure object or activity, or, even more powerfully, with an anomaly in the system, something that challenges the order of the culture because of its unclassifiability. The most powerful and most common insults categorize a person as a cannibal, carrion eater, coprophage or coprophile, or an incestuous person or the child of such a union—that is, one who does not live by the rules of membership within the human community. Also very common are accusations of not fitting into the system at all, as in insults equating humans with amphibians—snakes, toads, lizards—because such creatures live neither wholly on land nor in water, and while they are animals, they are cold-blooded and have scales rather than skin.

Insults are primarily improvised, fixed-phrased formulas and are most powerful when they are employed at points of greatest stress in community life. Insulting is usually a responsive activity, arising in verbal competition. Indeed, with many groups the competition of insults is an obligatory prelude to other agonistic activities: games of strength and skill or physical combat. This is, of course, precisely how insults enter into cheering at an athletic contest, where the strengths of one's own players are paralleled in verbal formulas with the insufficiencies of the others. Traditional rivals have often developed an extensive repertoire of insults that are called forth under licensed conditions when members of the two groups meet, a practice called *blasons populaires* in the folklore literature.

In some cultures, there is such a strong relation between skill in battle and skill in invective contests that official "shouters" are appointed to sing the praises of past victories and to curse as well as insult the enemy. Such singers of praise, whom we know best through the figure of the bard, scop, skold, and nidpoet of northern European tradition, were regarded not only as purveyors of powerful agonistic language but also as court entertainers; many remnants of their combative shows revealing their invective skill can be found in the manuscript literature. Thus, some of the most important studies of invective have been written about the singers of insults rather than the insult system itself. Because these extemporizers are also the singers of praise and thus the composers of epics, the literature on ritualized abuse is often found in studies of epic composition.

Insults and other performance traditions. Two other important areas of scholarship in which insults are central are discussions of joking relationships and reports of PERFORMANCE traditions featuring the trading of verbal abuse. Both of these areas focus on the playful rather than the bellicose character of invective contests.

A joking relationship is a term used by anthropologists to describe an obligatory relation of familiarity, expressed usually in ribald, licentious, playfully abusive forms of reference or address. Insults arise as a matter of convention between individuals characterized by their group identification. These groups may operate wholly within one culture, such as a sister's son and a mother's brother. (Teasing might be the better term, were the badinage not so abusive.) In other cases, the formal joking has become a means of accommodation between peoples who in the past have gone to war against each other.

The earliest description of such abuse within conventional relationships was made by the British social anthropologist A. R. Radcliffe-Brown, pursuing a functionalist line of argument: such joking occurred in relationships that contained both divergent interests that could lead to hostility and conflict and convergent interests that required the maintenance of friendly relations. An example of such a relationship would be one between a husband and his mother-in-law. Recent studies of such relationships have viewed joking as an activity within an expressive economy, operating in the same range of interactive relationships as greetings and other matters of a formal, ceremonial sort, though joking calls for a special license to use obscenity and insult playfully. Those standing in such categorical social relations have greater expressive flexibility; abusive joking is not obligatory but is only one option among many that can be chosen in interaction. Similar licensed abuse has been widely found among those in less formally structured relationships: age-mates who have formalized palships or members of a special-purpose group (such as a funeral society) in which the insulting may go on during the specially marked and framed ceremony with which the group is associated.

Folklorists and sociolinguists have devoted special study to occasions that produce performances calling for the invention of artful abuse. These range from the spur-of-the-moment encounters between Afro-American youths called most commonly *playing the dozens* to the hours-long singing improvisations of "the warrior" abuse singers found in many parts of Latin America. Equally artful are the festival and funeral verses improvised throughout the Mediterranean. Because there are stray literary remnants of such *flytings* and *scoldings* between bards in many places, and because of the association of this kind of activity with specific social types (e.g., shepherds, horse traders, barbers), the future study of insults is likely to call on complementary research by comparative linguists and literary historians, sociologists and ethnographers, folklorists, sociolinguists, and other students of heightened and stylized communication.

See also HUMOR; SPEECH PLAY.

Bibliography. Donald L. Brenneis, "Fighting Words," in *Not Work Alone*, ed. by Jeremy Cherfas and Roger Lewin, Beverly Hills, Calif., 1980; Robert C. Elliot, *The Power of Satire: Magic, Ritual, Art*, Princeton, N.J., 1960; Thomas Kochman, ed., *Rappin' and Stylin' Out: Communication in Urban Black America*, Champaign-Urbana, Ill., 1972; A. R. Radcliffe-Brown, *Structure and Function in Primitive Society*, New York, 1952, reprint 1965.

ROGER D. ABRAHAMS

INTERACTION, FACE-TO-FACE

The primary form of communication for humans, the one from which all other forms have developed. Both intuition and the work of investigators indicate that face-to-face interaction is essential in the development of individuals and in the maintenance and transmission of CULTURE. Interaction is generally accepted as the vehicle for such crucially important and interrelated functions as establishing the parent-infant bond, nurturing and guiding the social and cognitive development of the child, defining and sustaining cultures and subcultures, and providing a medium for transactions between individuals—the CONVERSATION, PLAY and games, religious and secular RITUAL, commercial exchanges, greetings, and the like that make up everyday life.

The term face-to-face interaction most immediately suggests occasions when people join together in talk or otherwise jointly sustain a single focus of attention. However, also pervasive in everyday life is less focused interaction in which participants make adjustments in their actions in response to the presence of others, such as changing one's course on the sidewalk to avoid an oncoming pedestrian, changing one's position in a theater seat to let another move across the aisle, or standing in a certain position and with a certain body tonus in the presence of others in an elevator.

Phenomenologically, face-to-face interaction may be said to come into being when each of at least two participants is aware of the presence of the other, and each has reason to believe the other is similarly aware. In these conditions interaction may be said to have occurred even if there is no perceptible communicative action by either participant. This is because, given a state of reciprocal awareness, interaction might have occurred, and thus even its absence becomes meaningful.

However, investigators cannot rely on a phenomenological definition. Participants' states of awareness are not readily accessible for direct observation. For research purposes we must focus on participants' overt actions. From this viewpoint, interaction occurs as soon as the actions of two or more individuals are observed to be mutually interdependent. Through detailed studies of films or videotapes of interactional events such as greetings, it has been possible to show how people engage in an elaborate process of mutual adjustment of their actions, including their bodily orientations, movements in space, and direction of gaze. In typical, everyday interactions, participants' actions appear to embody strong regularities that lend themselves well to systematic research.

A full analysis of interaction would include many different kinds of action. Use of LANGUAGE is a frequent component: the way words are pronounced, elements of intonation or prosody, syntax, and semantics. In addition to intonation there is quality or manner of speaking, such as variations in loudness and pitch beyond that involved in intonation, tempo, resonance, pauses, and nonfluencies, as well as nonlanguage sounds such as laughing and sighing. Nonspeech actions include FACIAL EXPRESSION and bodily movements such as posture and GESTURE; the way in which interactants space themselves and orient their bodies to one another and how they arrange themselves in relation to the physical layout of the environment; and the part played by TOUCH and SMELL and the use of cosmetics, CLOTHING, and artifacts such as pencils, pipes, and canes. *See also* BODY DECORATION; BODY MOVEMENT; INTERPERSONAL DISTANCE; PROXEMICS; SPEECH.

Traditions of Research

One of the earliest attempts to analyze the process of interaction was undertaken by U.S. psychologist Eliot Chapple in 1939. He proposed that any instance of interaction could be treated as a sequence of actions and inactions by the participants. In a conversation, for example, periods of talk by a participant could be treated as stretches of action and periods of silence as stretches of inaction. The patterning of these periods could be subjected to quantitative analysis. To facilitate data gathering, Chapple developed the interaction chronograph, a device on which investigators could record the length of speech and silence or other actions and inactions by pressing keys. Chapple used such information to investigate the process of interaction and the characteristic interaction styles of the participants. Chapple also proposed that social structure could be analyzed in process terms as a complex system of interaction. His emphasis on objective analysis of interaction events was highly influential in the great expansion of work on face-to-face interaction that took place shortly after World War II, especially in the United States.

Beginning in the early 1950s considerable interest developed in what has come to be known as NONVERBAL COMMUNICATION. This term draws attention to the complex and subtle ways in which people provide information for one another in interaction through what they do and how they do it, in addition to what they say and how they say it. Much research on nonverbal communication has been carried out by experimental social psychologists intrigued with the possibility that certain nonverbal actions might be used as indicators of other phenomena, such as type of interaction, attitudes or feelings of the participants, their hidden motives, and the like; or of other personal characteristics, such as individual differences. Most of this work has been concerned with measurement of just one or two nonverbal actions at a time. Gaze direction in interaction has proved a particularly popular object of investigation (*see also* EYES).

More relevant to the issue of the process of face-to-face interaction has been another line of research that has examined how participants are able to accomplish a given interaction. Normal everyday interaction is governed in part by a system of rules known by all participants that renders action intelligible, gives rise to a set of mutual expectations regarding appropriate conduct, permits routinely coordinated action by the participants, and—of particular interest to investigators—introduces strong regularities in participants' actions. The research focus here is on the organization (or structure) of interaction, including as far as possible all the actions relevant to that organization. Emphasis is also placed on analyzing sequences of actions involving all participants in the interaction, thus centering on interactive regularities rather than regularities in messages produced by individual participants.

Certain investigators, including GREGORY BATESON, Ray Birdwhistell, ERVING GOFFMAN, Norman McQuown, and Albert Scheflen, were particularly instrumental in the development of this approach

during its formative period in the early 1950s. Bateson and Birdwhistell were trained as anthropologists, Goffman as a sociologist, McQuown as a linguist, and Scheflen as a psychiatrist. Given this diversity, the intellectual influences on these founders cannot be briefly summarized. However, two authors are prominently cited by almost all of them. Sociologist GEORG SIMMEL emphasized interaction as a basic constituent of society and thus an activity of central importance to sociology. Linguist EDWARD SAPIR similarly stressed the centrality of interaction to society, as well as the importance of nonlinguistic elements of interaction. Sapir's work was influential in giving current structural work on interaction its strong linguistic cast.

Bateson, Birdwhistell, and McQuown were among the participants in a year-long study group in 1955 that focused on the systematic and comprehensive investigation of interaction. "Natural History of an Interview," a two-volume manuscript resulting from that collaboration, was essentially completed in 1959 but never published. Nevertheless, this work and the contributors to it have exerted considerable influence on the shape of research on face-to-face interaction. In addition, Birdwhistell brought the study of body motion to the attention of investigators; his term for the area—KINESICS—is widely used.

Several lines of structural research have been pursued, distinguishable mainly by differences in methodology rather than in underlying conceptual frameworks. Greatly influenced by the contributors to "Natural History of an Interview," Scheflen developed context analysis. This was an attempt to adapt for interaction research the methods developed by structural linguists in the United States. Scheflen's substantive work began with detailed analyses of rather unorthodox approaches to psychotherapy but expanded to include general treatments of interaction and territoriality.

Goffman was perhaps the most prominent writer on interaction. An innovative and influential sociologist, Goffman firmly established the study of small-scale interactional processes as a legitimate area of research. Drawing on his own participant observation and on examples derived from many sources, including news reports and books of etiquette, Goffman was unexcelled at articulating the subtlety, complexity, and diversity of interaction and at illuminating the order underlying it.

Conversation analysis, though deriving from the school of sociology known as ethnomethodology, is very similar to the previously mentioned approaches in its conceptual framework. As implied by its name, primary emphasis is on the study of conversation. Under the early leadership of U.S. sociologists Harvey Sacks and Emanuel Schegloff, conversation analysts have focused on the linguistic elements of conversations, although there are notable exceptions. Among the many contributions of conversation analysts are discussions of the design features of interaction systems and demonstrations of the complex ways in which syntax is used in the service of interaction, as well as of the ways in which interaction process can affect the production of linguistic utterances.

Components of Interaction

There is more to interaction than structure, however. A complete description of an interaction would have to range beyond signals, rules, and other structural elements. At least two other major components would also have to be included: strategy and situation. Each of the three components—structure, strategy, and situation—is closely linked to the other two.

Situation or context involves an apparently large set of cultural categories that applies to the participants, their relationship, the social setting of the interaction, and other factors. A participant's definition of the situation—that is, the assignment of values to relevant categories—for a given interaction permits choice of appropriate conventions. This matching of convention to situation is possible because each convention carries a set of situational requirements specifying the categories and their respective values that must apply in order for the convention to be appropriately used.

Work on forms of address provides an interesting example of research on situation. In one study U.S. linguist Susan Ervin-Tripp, observing her own rules of address, sought to identify the categories and values underlying the use of such forms as title-plus-last-name, Mr.-plus-last-name, and first name. Using a dichotomous category system, she found, for example, that she used first name in several situations, one of which was when the setting was not status marked and the partner was a friend or colleague who was neither of higher rank nor fifteen years older.

Because of the situational requirements of conventions, the use of a given convention by participants provides information on the categories and values respectively assigned by them. When one participant first uses a convention in an interaction, thus disclosing an attendant set of situational information, it becomes an interactional issue whether or not the partner chooses to ratify or join in the enactment of the convention, thereby tacitly agreeing to the participant's definition.

Strategy, the third major component of a description of interaction, derives from the choices participants make regarding both structure and situation. In either case, strategy involves choice among legitimate alternatives and failure to act appropriately (violation of applicable rules). In its relation to struc-

ture, strategy is roughly analogous to the notion of strategy in games. If structure is similar to the rules of a game, then strategy is the way the participants operate within or break the rules. A move in a chess game would be a single element of strategy: the exercise of an option when more than one move is available within the rules. One cannot operate within a structure without simultaneously engaging in a strategy. At the same time, it is structure that makes the choice of actions meaningful.

Strategy becomes involved in situation through a participant's choices in assigning values to social categories, selecting and ratifying conventions congruent with those assigned values, and selecting and ratifying conventions at variance with those values (a violation). Situation and its attendant strategy may be the sources of much of the richness and complexity we experience in interaction. The general notion of strategy includes but extends beyond the study of individual differences in interaction.

A theme that has emerged in virtually all structural research is that interaction is constructed through the common participation of all those involved. Significantly extending the earlier notions of message or information exchange and of sequential influence of actions, the notion of common participation has been fundamental to the structural analysis of interaction process from its beginning. From this perspective, interactional events such as the exchange of speaking turns are achieved only through the joint, coordinated action of relevant participants. One effect of common participation is that the frequency, duration, and other characteristics of actions such as gazes or smiles, once regarded by many investigators as belonging exclusively to one participant, can be deeply affected in various ways by the actions of the partner.

The notion of common participation emphasizes the deep interconnectedness of things in interaction. The full implications of this basic phenomenon continue to be explored by investigators. On the one hand, common participation appears to complicate some more traditional approaches to interaction research. On the other hand, common participation provides a powerful resource for investigators. By capitalizing on the complex network of relationships among the many different actions by all participants, investigators not only can facilitate research on the process of interaction itself, but also can make more effective use of interaction processes in examining other phenomena of interest, such as individual differences and cognitive processes.

Bibliography. Ray L. Birdwhistell, *Kinesics and Context: Essays on Body Motion Communication,* Philadelphia, 1970; Eliot D. Chapple, *Culture and Biological Man,* New York, 1970; Starkey Duncan, Jr., Donald W. Fiske, Rita

Denny, Barbara G. Kanki, and Hartmut B. Mokros, *Interaction Structure and Strategy*, New York, 1985; Erving Goffman, *Frame Analysis*, Cambridge, Mass., 1974; Robert G. Harper, Arthur N. Wiens, and Joseph D. Matarazzo, *Nonverbal Communication: The State of the Art*, New York, 1978; Adam Kendon, *Studies in the Behavior of Social Interaction*, Lisse, The Netherlands, 1977; Albert E. Scheflen, *Communicational Structure: Analysis of a Psychotherapy Transaction*, Bloomington, Ind., 1973; Jim Schenkein, ed., *Studies in the Organization of Conversational Interaction*, New York, 1978.

STARKEY DUNCAN, JR.

INTERACTIVE MEDIA

Technologies that provide person-to-person communications mediated by a telecommunications channel (e.g., a TELEPHONE call) and person-to-machine interactions that simulate an interpersonal exchange (e.g., an electronic banking transaction). Most scholars would not classify as interactive media those technologies that permit only the selection of content such as a broadcast teletext service with one hundred frames of information, each of which can be selected on demand by a viewer. However, the boundary between selection of content and simulation of an interpersonal communication exchange is not always definable in a specific application or service.

The importance of interactive media is associated, first, with their capability to extend person-to-person communication beyond face-to-face settings. Through audio, audiovisual, and electronic text channels individuals can communicate with others who are geographically dispersed. Second, interactive media offer the potential to overcome a few important limitations of one-way mass media. Whereas the public is a receiver of one-way mass communications, the public can send and receive communications through interactive media. And although mass media are controlled by a relatively small number of individuals working in large institutional settings, some forms of interactive media are controlled by individuals or small groups working in a wide range of settings.

The most common form of interactive media communications is a telephone call. The telephone network may also be used to provide audio communications among groups at two or more locations. This form of communication is generally classified as audio teleconferencing. When a video channel is added to an audio link between groups by means of SATELLITE transmission, microwave transmission, or a two-way CABLE TELEVISION system, the communication exchange is generally classified as a video teleconference. The communication of electronic text messages over the telephone network or other means of transmission is classified as electronic

mail, computer conferencing, or personal computer bulletin boards, depending on the size of the group exchanging messages, control of the system by an individual or organization, and the type of content exchanged. In each of these media content is created largely or entirely by the individuals who use the technology.

However, there is another class of interactive media in which most of the content is created by a centralized production group or organization. Here individual users interact with content created by an organization. For example, in some interactive cable television systems, viewers can respond to questions posed in programming. Typically their response is limited to pressing one of a few alternative buttons on their cable converter box, thereby indicating agreement with one of the opinion statements set out by the program producers. Similarly, much of the content in computer-based interactive media such as VIDEOTEX is created by production groups or the host organization for the system. With the exception of message sending, the interaction consists largely of selecting and manipulating content provided by the service.

Applications. The modern era in interactive media may be traced to the New York World's Fair in 1964, when AT&T demonstrated a picture telephone and predicted that the device would enter millions of homes and businesses within a decade. The picture telephone of the 1960s was a failure owing to its high cost and low demand for such a service. Concurrently the picture telephone received much publicity and focused attention on other potential applications for interactive media. Contributing to the interest in interactive media were the energy crisis in the early 1970s, which focused attention on ways to reduce travel costs through telecommunications; the dispersal of the work force in some industries and government agencies, which underlined the need to link separated work groups; general inflation, which encouraged efforts to reduce operating costs and improve worker efficiency; and advances in cable, satellite, and computer technology, which made it possible for a variety of groups to explore new services.

During this period a range of demonstration projects in Europe and North America examined how government, education, and business services might be delivered through interactive media. British government agencies developed audio and video teleconferencing systems to link geographically dispersed civil servants. In the United States the National Science Foundation supported a series of trials in interactive cable television for providing social service information to senior citizens as well as for training fire fighters, teachers, and day-care workers. Other interactive media projects in North America and

Europe linked doctors at a major hospital via two-way microwave transmission to patients in a small island clinic, allowed public defenders to speak over picture telephones to their clients in a city jail, and linked remote classrooms throughout a state to a professor on a UNIVERSITY campus who provided instruction to the learners at each site. At the same time many commercial applications emerged. In Britain a major videotex service, Prestel, began to offer electronic text information services to homes and businesses in the late 1970s. Similar services followed in other European countries and in Australia, Japan, and North America.

Policy issues. These trials, demonstrations, and services were investigated by scholars from a range of disciplines. They examined the use of interactive media as a substitute for travel and studied the role of interactive media in linking a geographically dispersed work force, including some individuals who work at home, and the impact of such media use on the composition of the work force. On a larger scale, they debated the value of an information-based economy in which interactive media would perform a major role.

Communication scholars also examined the adoption or rejection of interactive media in organizations, along with the problems that might accompany implementing new interactive media services. In addition, they explored the economic, social, and psychological factors that lead individuals and groups in organizations to accept or reject telecommunications innovations. Moreover, researchers documented many of the ways in which interactive media can change patterns of work. Along with expected concerns about the cost and perceived benefit of the technology to an organization, research findings indicate that potential users are often concerned about the threat a new technology may pose to their jobs, how it may change their status within the organization, and whether it may cause them social embarrassment. Although the new technology may be adopted as a replacement for a former way of doing business, it often leads to new work patterns and therefore alters rather than substitutes for the old way.

Focusing more narrowly on the behavior of those using interactive media, communication scholars studied the development of communication codes, the shared rules or pacts that allow individuals to communicate with and be understood by others in a specific social and technological context. The new generation of interactive media increased the number of channels by which individuals could exchange messages, but the development of widely shared communication codes to govern the exchange of those messages will require more time. By studying how new communication codes evolve, researchers hope to gain some understanding about this fundamental component of human communication.

Interactive media also pose many challenges to the development of communication policies. Policy analysts have addressed issues of PRIVACY, access, and ownership of interactive media, among others. Privacy issues are associated, first, with interactive media content such as electronic mail that is created by users of the technology. Because this content is processed by computers, there is a potential for abuse by government or private agencies that might intercept mail and process the contents. In addition, the use of interactive media often creates information about individuals for billing purposes. Even if one assumes a benign environment in which government and private agencies do not seek to obtain or use this information, its mere existence raises privacy issues.

Several applications of interactive media raise important questions of compliance with a legislative statute or constitutional right. Issues of legal compliance will receive increased attention from scholars if interactive media are applied to courtroom settings, voting in elections, and securities trading.

Access to interactive media is another issue for concern. Unlike mass media, which are relatively available to all (as readers, viewers, or listeners), access to interactive media is restricted—in some instances by high cost and in others by the technical skills required to use the technology. Some analysts have voiced a concern that this may lead to a new society of information haves and have-nots. Indeed, the new-technology environment might return Western society to a pre-twentieth-century model of information flow, when access to and ownership of information was restricted and thereby became an important instrument of economic, political, and social power.

On the other hand, interactive media offer the possibility of extending the number and types of information sources available to the public. Unlike mass media programs, which are expensive to produce and can be distributed only through a limited number of available channels, some forms of interactive media can be inexpensive to produce. Furthermore, the potential number of distribution channels for interactive media is greater. This expectation was expressed frequently during the 1970s. However, as trials and demonstrations ended and commercial services emerged, the economic environment that led to centralized control of the mass media by a few organizations began to have its effect on the interactive media industries. It remains unclear whether interactive media at the turn of the century will indeed provide a greater diversity of information sources to the public.

In response to these policy issues, a few European

countries, notably Sweden, developed policies to manage the interactive media environment. In other countries a long-term trend of deregulation for mass media and telecommunication services was extended to interactive media policies. In these countries interactive media services grew unhampered by policies about privacy, access, and ownership, or they were loosely regulated by policies and laws created for earlier mass media and telecommunication services.

See also AUDIOVISUAL EDUCATION; CITIZEN ACCESS; VIDEO.

Bibliography. Martin C. J. Elton, William A. Lucas, and David W. Conrath, eds., *Evaluating New Telecommunication Services,* New York, 1978; Sven Gustafson et al., *New Views: Computers and New Media—Anxiety and Hopes* (Commission on New Information Technology), Stockholm, 1979; Ithiel de Sola Pool, ed., *The Social Impact of the Telephone,* Cambridge, Mass., 1977; Ronald Rice et al., *The New Media: Communication, Research, and Technology,* Beverly Hills, Calif., 1984; John Short, Ederyn Williams, and Bruce Christie, *The Social Psychology of Telecommunications,* New York, 1976; "Symposium on Experiments in Interactive Cable TV," *Journal of Communication* 28 (1978): 142–208; Ederyn Williams, *Research at the Communications Studies Group, 1970–1977,* Cambridge and London, n.d.

JOHN CAREY

INTERCULTURAL COMMUNICATION

The process of communication across cultural boundaries; also, the academic discipline studying it. As a process it involves the concept of CULTURE, which from this perspective is assumed to represent a unitary whole best understood from the point of view of the actors (e.g., individuals, institutions) involved.

As an academic discipline intercultural communication involves an examination of LANGUAGE and other constituents of interactions in different cultural settings, determinations of their relative importance for the actors involved, and an analysis of other factors that may have an influence on the process. So far three major theoretical perspectives have emerged to account for the phenomena of interest in the field: (1) empiricist, (2) phenomenological, and (3) systems.

The empiricist approach. Greatly influenced by work in both experimental psychology and communications research, this view assumes that the characteristics of sender(s) and receiver(s) are somehow different because of their different cultural backgrounds. All types of exchanges, including NONVERBAL COMMUNICATION, are assumed to be affected by these differences. Three main areas of research have evolved: (1) characteristics of senders and receivers,

with an emphasis on the identification of similarities (*see* SEMANTIC DIFFERENTIAL); (2) message characteristics, that is, how "standard" forms of intracultural communication vary across cultures (*see* FOLKTALE; ORAL HISTORY); and (3) characteristics of "good" receivers, with emphasis on the identification of personality and other types of traits that may allow a person to function without much difficulty in a culture different from his or her own (also known as "intercultural competence").

The phenomenological approach. Emphasis here is on the point of view of the participant. U.S. researcher Fred L. Casmir suggests that after elimination of "unexamined preconceptions or presuppositions," phenomenology proceeds to analyze the specific communication event

through the consciousness of interactive communicators by way of their intuition, imagination, and experience. By doing so, phenomenologists feel they are able to gain substantial insight into the essential *structure* and *relationships* of these events, based on concrete examples supplied by experience or imagination, or a combination thereof. Further investigation is often conducted in an intentional sense with the senders, in order to determine what were the motives behind communication events which they initiated.

Thus this approach relies on interpretation: by the participants, of the events they initiate or participate in; and by the researcher seeking to make sense of the phenomena under study.

The systems approach. This represents an effort to synthesize, but also broaden, the scope of the discipline. The systems view considers the previous two approaches as component parts. P. E. Rohrlich has suggested that intercultural communication is best regarded "as a set of interacting elements, actors, interacting in a physically and culturally compounded environment. While the environment exists apart from the system, its cultural relevance derives from cultural perception of it by the system's actors. . . . The elements of the system maintain socio/psycho/cultural depth of cognitive perception which they bring to both intentionally and unintentionally communicated messages." Rohrlich argues that three distinct but interrelated levels—intrapersonal, interpersonal, and synthetic—can be identified, each having specific attributes, research interests, and areas of application. For example, at the intrapersonal level problems of "culture shock" can be addressed through cross-cultural counseling. At the interpersonal level semantic and/or linguistic issues such as translation and interpretation problems can be dealt with through orientation or through training in cross-cultural "management." And at the synthetic level, according to Rohrlich, broader questions derived from general and specific cultural differences can be handled through both positive and negative feedback mechanisms, for example, in the context of GROUP COMMUNICATION.

Issues

The major deficiency in intercultural communication theory is an inability to specify how culture is learned or transmitted. This limitation is related to the vagueness characteristic of most definitions of culture. Nevertheless, knowing how people "learn" their culture seems crucial for any analysis (empirical or otherwise) of intercultural communication. Because the observation of children learning cultural facts and behavior raises theoretical and methodological problems, an alternative is to study how adults go through the process of accommodating to a new culture ("acculturation").

Much work has focused on techniques for improving interactions between people from different cultural backgrounds. All three theoretical approaches described above have contributed to this line of research.

From a training perspective, the empirical approach has paid considerable attention to the "culture assimilator," a technique of programmed instruction derived from work by Harry Triandis and others. Early work on assimilators—perhaps *facilitators* is a more precise term—was based on extensive interviewing, trying to identify situations in which cultural conflict (or communication difficulties) could arise. Triandis, for example, outlined a procedure that specified a priori a set of conflict dimensions around which episodes were then constructed. The fact that this is an expensive research procedure has limited its development and use, and less expensive protocols still have to prove their effectiveness.

The phenomenological approach, by contrast, has paid very little attention to training techniques. However, experiential learning techniques (e.g., "simulations" and "immersions") may have a relation to phenomenological analysis because of their emphasis on viewing the world from a different perspective.

Systems theory, like phenomenological analysis, has yet to develop unique training approaches. The more germane are those using the concept of "synergy," found in industrial and organizational applications where there is a need to place personnel in foreign cultures. Although the term is less than clear, N. Adler suggests that cultural synergy "attempts to recognize both similarities and differences between nationalities that compose the organization or team. This approach suggests that cultural diversity be neither ignored nor minimized. Rather, cultural diversity can be viewed as a resource in the design and development of the training process and content."

Developments in telecommunications and trans-portation have had an impact on ideas about contacts between members of different cultures. The task of dealing effectively with foreign situations can be addressed not only through "cultural training" but also by learning rules governing specific interactions. The notion of "microcultures" suggests that such rules of exchange have developed as the world has become more internationalized, so that many interactions no longer represent or critically involve any of the traditional, geographically based cultures. Once the rules are understood, the locale becomes less relevant, and communication is facilitated because participants share knowledge of the rules governing the type of interaction they find themselves in.

At a different level two other related issues have been investigated. One has to do with the effects of TOURISM on local cultures, the other with the potentially negative and/or positive consequences of media materials imported from one culture to another. Although it is difficult to deny the positive outcomes associated with tourism, such as improved economic conditions and increased knowledge of different cultures, questions remain about the unintended changes in the "host" culture derived from the presence of large numbers of visitors. For example, it has been observed that traditional arts and crafts sometimes change in the direction of perceived preferences of the tourists, not always resulting in products of quality or truly reflective of the culture that generated them.

The introduction of new communication technologies and accompanying materials diffused through them has also been a matter of study and concern. Perhaps the major questions have centered on the possible negative consequences on a culture receiving substantial amounts of ENTERTAINMENT, news, films, and other materials produced in foreign countries. The hypothesized effects include both individual-level and societywide outcomes such as changes in consumption patterns, preferences in media use (foreign over locally produced material), and even political and ideological issues (*see* MARXIST THEORIES OF COMMUNICATION—THIRD WORLD APPROACHES). These are, however, unresolved issues that continue to be studied by academics and several INTERNATIONAL ORGANIZATIONS such as the United Nations Educational, Scientific and Cultural Organization (UNESCO).

Bibliography. Molefi K. Asante, E. Newmark, and C. A. Blake, eds., *Handbook of Intercultural Communication,* Beverly Hills, Calif., 1979; R. W. Brislin, K. Cushner, C. Cherrie, and M. Yong, *Intercultural Interactions: A Practical Guide,* Beverly Hills, Calif., 1986; Fred L. Casmir, ed., *Intercultural and International Communication,* Washington, D.C., 1978; Pierre Casse, *Training for the Cross-Cultural Mind,* 2d ed., Washington, D.C., 1981;

Edward T. Hall, *Beyond Culture*, Garden City, N.Y., 1976; Dan Landis and R. W. Brislin, *Handbook of Intercultural Training*, 3 vols., Elmsford, N.Y., 1983; Charles E. Osgood, William H. May, and Murray S. Miron, *Cross-Cultural Universals of Affective Meaning*, Urbana, Ill., 1975; Harry C. Triandis, Varso Varsilian, et al., *The Analysis of Subjective Culture*, New York, 1972.

DAN LANDIS

INTERNATIONAL COMMUNICATION.

For a discussion of the formal contacts between nations, see DIPLOMACY; INTERNATIONAL ORGANIZATIONS. The entry INTERCULTURAL COMMUNICATION discusses a somewhat related topic.

A historical background is offered in the entries COLONIZATION; EXPLORATION; MIGRATION; SILK ROAD. An increasingly significant form of international communication is discussed in TOURISM.

Several entries deal with communication developments in different regions: AFRICA, TWENTIETH CENTURY; ASIA, TWENTIETH CENTURY; AUSTRALASIA, TWENTIETH CENTURY; ISLAMIC WORLD, TWENTIETH CENTURY; LATIN AMERICA, TWENTIETH CENTURY. Disparities between developed and developing societies in their influence over the flow of communication are discussed in COMPUTER: IMPACT—IMPACT ON THE WORLD ECONOMY; NEWS AGENCIES; SATELLITE; TELEVISION HISTORY—WORLD MARKET STRUGGLES. Efforts to combat such disparities are reviewed in DEVELOPMENT COMMUNICATION and NEW INTERNATIONAL INFORMATION ORDER and are further analyzed in MARXIST THEORIES OF COMMUNICATION—THIRD WORLD APPROACHES. Various problems arising from the use of communications for international political purposes are addressed in DISINFORMATION; PROPAGANDA; RADIO, INTERNATIONAL.

INTERNATIONAL ORGANIZATIONS

As settings for interactions among nations and for collective problem solving in particular, international organizations have especially important functions in the field of communications. Communication issues inevitably transcend national boundaries. There are two kinds of international organizations: governmental and nongovernmental. The governmental organizations—often called intergovernmental—are the setting for interactions in which official representatives are the main legal actors. Nongovernmental organizations, on the other hand, consist primarily of private citizens, groups, or both, who cooperate on the international level.

Many international organizations are global in nature, with members in every region of the world. In some, membership is open to all concerned, as is the case with the Universal Postal Union. Others have a limited membership relating to their more restricted purposes and scope of activities. Many of these, such as the European Broadcasting Union and the Organization for Economic Cooperation and Development, are regional or specialized in structure but also engage in international activities. These are usually referred to as regional or specialized organizations.

History

International organizations active in communications are among the oldest in existence. The first modern international governmental organization, the Central Commission for the Navigation of the Rhine, was established in 1851 by the Congress of Vienna. During the nineteenth century the number of international organizations in the fields of transportation and communication grew rapidly, primarily in response to the growth in transportational commerce and communication that accompanied industrialization as well as the development of TELEGRAPHY and the TELEPHONE.

The oldest international governmental organization still in existence, the International Telecommunication Union (ITU), traces its history back to 1865, when the conference of the International Telegraphic Union, composed of twenty European states, met in Paris to establish rules for the transmission of telegraph messages across national boundaries (*see* TELECOMMUNICATIONS POLICY). Earlier such messages had to be transmitted to the border, walked across the frontier, and retransmitted. This arrangement resulted in distortion, loss, or interception of the information, and a great deal of frustration. The treaty established international regulations in telegraphic communications and granted the participant nations the right to correspond by telegraph, providing protection for PRIVACY and SECRECY in the transmission of such messages.

The advent of the telephone in 1876 prompted the International Telegraphic Union to add *telephone* to its name, thus becoming the International Telegraph and Telephone Union. From 1903 to 1906 attempts were made to achieve interference-free RADIO communication. Another union was founded in Berlin in 1906 by twenty-seven maritime states to regulate radio communication to ships at sea and to set STANDARDS for radio frequencies and technology. It was through the realization of the advantages of this type of international communication cooperation that in 1932, at the Madrid International Telecommunications Conference, these two international intergovernmental organizations (the International Telegraph and Telephone Union and the Radio-Telegraphic Union) merged to form the International Telecommunication Union. At the 1947 Atlantic City Plenipotentiary Conference ITU became a specialized agency of the United Nations, linking ITU in many ways to that newly established international organization.

The earliest international response to the international flow of information through POSTAL SERVICE systems was the establishment in 1878 of the Universal Postal Union. This organization negotiated and developed international protocols and regulations.

The development and spread of LITERACY and modern EDUCATION, accompanied by the development of mass communication—especially the growth of the book PUBLISHING industry and the support for freedom of expression in Europe during the late nineteenth century—prompted the development of international COPYRIGHT agreements. The Bern Convention in 1886 laid down the principles of the Universal Copyright Convention, in which many nations participated.

The number of international organizations, both intergovernmental and nongovernmental, grew even more sharply after each world war. Membership in these organizations increased as the result of decolonization and struggle for political, economic, and cultural independence. During World War I there were more than 80 intergovernmental and close to 500 nongovernmental organizations, of which approximately 20 and 200, respectively, were in the fields of communication and transportation. By the beginning of the 1980s these numbers had increased to roughly 350 intergovernmental and 2,600 nongovernmental organizations, of which about half in each category dealt with some aspects of communications, transportation, education, and cultural activities (see Figure 1).

The increase in the number of international organizations of all kinds since the mid-nineteenth century has been due mainly to the following factors:

- the development of modern telecommunications technologies, especially satellites and computers (*see* COMPUTER: IMPACT; SATELLITE)
- the increase in the number of nation-states, transnational organizations, groups, and individuals involved in communication activities
- the call for regulation and standardization, aimed at promoting efficiency and the "free flow" of information
- protection of national sovereignty, individuals' rights, and privacy
- international and regional development and co-operation
- allocation of communication resources (e.g., of the radio SPECTRUM) and prevention of unwanted interferences
- increased promotion of international cooperation, understanding, and peace
- negotiation of demands, disputes, and arbitration
- the design of international legal regimes and policies in regard to information flow across national boundaries
- research and development
- exchange of scientific, technical, and cultural information

Speed in communication is a prerequisite for stable world development, as it helps bridge sociopolitical and resource distribution disparities (*see* DEVELOPMENT COMMUNICATION). Since international communication can assist development in such fields as trade, health, and scientific knowledge, the coordination and smoothing of the flow of information through international organizations become essential to world peace and security. *See also* DIPLOMACY.

The United Nations

The most important intergovernmental organization established since World War II is the United Nations (UN). It is essentially different from the former League of Nations, established in 1920, in that it operates

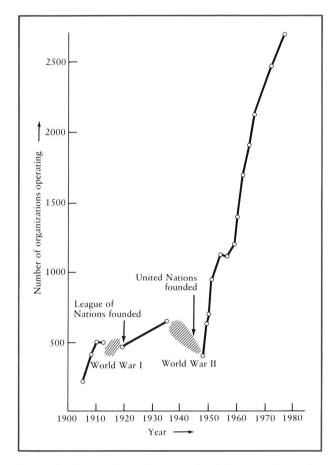

Figure 1. *(International Organizations)* Pattern of growth in the number of international organizations, governmental and nongovernmental, during the twentieth century. Redrawn after Colin Cherry, *World Communication: Threat or Promise?* Chichester, Eng., and New York: John Wiley and Sons, 1978, p. 124.

in economic and social fields rather than being limited to political debate. The UN is able to make provisions for actual cooperation through specialized, autonomous bodies like the United Nations Educational, Scientific and Cultural Organization (UNESCO). A unique feature of the UN is the separation maintained between the political and operational spheres, to guard against infringement on national sovereignty. The UN also allows nonmember states to be "associates" (e.g., Switzerland, a nonmember, participates in most specialized areas).

Twenty-four UN agencies (with related organizations) deal with education, science, CULTURE, sociology, economics, health, mass communication, agriculture, aviation, postal service, maritime issues, and other essential and practical areas of international development. Of these, five major organizations besides UNESCO are concerned directly with world communications: the Universal Postal Union (UPU), the World Intellectual Property Organization (WIPO), the ITU, the International Civil Aviation Organization (ICAO), and the International Maritime Consultative Organization (IMCO).

In a sense, all UN agencies are concerned with communication in that their tasks are to improve international organization, which inherently requires communication and the collection and dissemination of information. UNESCO in particular deals directly with international communication through examination of the uses of modern communication technologies, literacy, textbooks, mass communication, sociological and demographic data, exchanges of cultural and scientific information among countries, translation, and the wide variety of issues related to human communication and culture.

UNESCO's principal activities in the information field include technical assistance to the developing areas, its contribution to the copyright laws, and its concern with problems of imbalance in the world flow of information. The organization has been in the forefront of the debate over the need for a NEW INTERNATIONAL INFORMATION ORDER and has been the major forum for the promotion of national and international communication policies, especially through the work of the International Commission for the Study of Communication Problems (the MacBride Commission, named for its president, Sean MacBride). The so-called MacBride Report led to the establishment of the International Program for the Development of Communications (IPDC), which operates within the UNESCO framework and is supervised by an intergovernmental council elected from UNESCO members. Its main task is to assist the developing countries in improving their capabilities in the field of communications, mainly by supplying trained personnel and technical infrastructure.

The WIPO protects proprietary rights in published work. Its Patent Information Network, with nearly seven million citations, is a major activity in international recordkeeping and dissemination. Its primary task is to administer the 1952 Universal Copyright Convention.

The UN's four other main specialized organizations responsible for world communications planning (the ITU, UPU, ICAO, and IMCO) work together closely because their spheres of interest overlap to a large degree: international postal service depends on air transport; air transport relies on radio communications, telex, and, increasingly, use of satellites; and telecommunications is essential for safe and efficient navigation and for international shipping. The common factor is telecommunications, without which none could operate on a global scale (see TELECOMMUNICATIONS NETWORKS). The ITU and UPU are concerned with message traffic; the ICAO and IMCO, with transport communications. Each has its own constitution, methods of operation, budget, and forms of representation. The highest administrative bodies of these organizations work with their permanent secretariats to deal with general policy, while consultative committees may be set up to deal with technical questions. The strength of this arrangement is that agencies can draw on the expertise of a wide range of actors in particular fields, and commercial independence is not violated. One weakness is the lack of enforcement ability, as such committees are strictly advisory organs.

The most complex organizational structure belongs to the ITU, which has three permanent organizations other than its secretariat: (1) the International Telegraph and Telephone Consultative Committee, (2) the International Radio Consultative Committee, and (3) the International Frequency Registration Board. This collective provides technical assistance, including training, to members. The ITU had the most challenging task of dealing with technological developments in communication—from telegraph to communication satellite—all achieved in less than a century. Its work is crucial to NEWS AGENCIES, data communication services, and navigation, as well as broadcasting. This expansion of the tasks assigned to the ITU is reflected in its World Administrative Radio Conference (WARC), which deals with a complex set of technical—and often controversial—questions, including the allocation of international radio frequencies.

The UN has also been involved in other communication-related issues and problems through its specialized committees and related organizations in the fields of social and economic development. Its Committee on the Peaceful Uses of Outer Space (COPUOS) was assigned numerous tasks, among them the study of the legal problems arising from outer space activities (e.g., direct broadcast satellite and remote

INTERNATIONAL ORGANIZATIONS / 335

sensing), and has produced documents that are generally considered basic to space law. Other UN organizations and agencies such as the International Bank for Reconstruction and Development (commonly referred to as the World Bank), the General Agreement on Tariffs and Trade (GATT), the United Nations Development Program (UNDP), and United Nations University (in Tokyo) have been active in the areas related to telecommunications and socioeconomic development.

Other Organizations

The development of satellite technology has greatly enhanced the importance of international organizations beyond the UN system. The International Telecommunications Satellite Consortium (known as INTELSAT) provides common-carrier satellite service to most countries of the world, and as a major component in the international infrastructure for transborder data flow, it plays an important role in economic communication across national boundaries. As an intergovernmental organization INTELSAT has been viewed as one of the most successful efforts in global cooperation and international development. Similar in function but smaller in size is the intergovernmental system INTERSPUTNIK, with membership composed of the Soviet Union, the socialist countries of eastern Europe, and a number of other socialist and nonsocialist nations in Asia, the Middle East, and Latin America. INTERSPUTNIK coordinates its activities with the ITU and has established agreements with other organizations and nations on areas and methods of cooperation.

One of the earliest uses of satellite communications was for navigation. This led to the establishment of a new international intergovernmental organization called the International Maritime Satellite Organization (INMARSAT), whose satellites provide links to ships at sea with a combined system of computer networks and DATA BASE access.

An essential function of international organizations has been their ability to identify specific communications technologies of interest to different groups and nations. It is in this context that another major organization, the Intergovernmental Bureau of Informatics (IBI), was established. Its aim is to coordinate and set standards for the field of informatics—the design, construction, evaluation, use, and maintenance of computer- and satellite-based information systems, as well as their policy implications.

An increasing number of international organizations, while limited in their domain, are united by some geographical, cultural, technological, or historical associations. Many of these "regional" organizations are active in some aspects of communications technologies and their policy implications. Intergov-

ernmental organizations of this type include the European Economic Community (EEC), the Council of Europe, the Organization of American States (OAS), the Organization for Economic Cooperation and Development (OECD), the Organization of African Unity (OAU), and the Arab League Educational, Cultural, and Scientific Organization (ALECSO). Operational agencies and professional organizations (both intergovernmental and nongovernmental) include the European Conference of Postal and Telecommunications Administration (ECPTA), Arab Telecommunications Union (ATU), Pan African Telecommunications Union (PATU), European Broadcasting Union (EBU), Asia Pacific Broadcasting Union (ABU), Islamic Broadcasting Union (IBU), and World Association for Christian Communication (WACC).

There are also large numbers of nongovernmental professional media organizations in the communications field, such as the International Organization of Journalists, the International Press Institute, the International Federation of Journalists, the International Federation of Information Processing, the International Documentation and Communication Center, and the International Press Publishers. Active in the scholarly and professional fields are such organizations as the International Association for Mass Communication Research (IAMCR), the International Communication Association (ICA), and the International Institute of Communications (IIC). Because these organizations have no direct governmental authority, they exert only indirect influence on major international communications policies, but they have great impact on the "climate" of the international decision-making process.

Many aspects of the activities of international organizations involve political, economic, and cultural —as well as bureaucratic and organizational— BARGAINING, which can best be described as international political discourse (see POLITICAL COMMUNICATION). In addition, states often use international organizations as part of their own policies to advance their economic and political preferences. In general, cooperation and problem solving among states have been more extensive in the technical, regulatory, and cultural areas of international communication than in the political and economic aspects of the field.

Bibliography. Anne W. Branscomb, ed., *Toward a Law of Global Communications Networks,* White Plains, N.Y., 1986; Colin Cherry, *World Communication: Threat or Promise?* rev. ed., Chichester, Eng., and New York, 1978; George A. Codding, Jr., and Anthony M. Rutkowski, *The International Telecommunication Union in a Changing World,* Dedham, Mass., 1982; George Gerbner and Marsha Siefert, eds., *World Communications: A Handbook,* New York, 1984; Harold K. Jacobson, *Networks of Interdependence,* New York, 1979; David M. Leive, *Inter-*

national Telecommunications and International Law: The Regulation of the Radio Spectrum, Dobbs Ferry, N.Y., and Leiden, Holland, 1970; Hamid Mowlana, *Global Information and World Communication: New Frontiers in International Relations*, White Plains, N.Y., 1986; Kaarle Nordenstreng, *The Mass Media Declaration of UNESCO*, Norwood, N.J., 1984; Edward W. Ploman, *International Law Governing Communications and Information*, London, 1982; Union of International Associations, *Yearbook of International Organizations* (Annuaire des organisations internationales), biennial, Brussels, 1948–.

HAMID MOWLANA

INTERPERSONAL COMMUNICATION

The most general meaning of the term *interpersonal communication* is simply "communicating between persons," but scholars insist on a narrower and more rigorous conceptualization. The anchor points for such a conceptualization are (1) at least two communicators intentionally orienting toward each other, (2) as both subject and object, (3) whose actions embody each other's perspectives both toward self and toward other. In an interpersonal episode, then, each communicator is both a knower and an object of knowledge, a tactician and a target of another's tactics, an attributor and an object of attribution, a codifier and a CODE to be deciphered.

Beyond this basic conceptualization the question "What makes communication interpersonal?" has been answered in several quite different ways. *Interpersonal* has been defined in terms of

1. The *channels of communication* available to the interactants. Applying this criterion, interpersonal communication is equivalent to face-to-face interaction because only in this context do interactants have access to visual, tactile, *and* vocal messages (*see* INTERACTION, FACE-TO-FACE).
2. The *degree of structure* in the interactional situation. In contrast to the predictable patterns of communication found in highly ritualized, formal, or typified situations, interpersonal communication is associated with informal, spontaneous, and unstructured situations.
3. The *number of interactants*. Accordingly, as one moves from dyadic to increasingly larger units, communication among interactants becomes less interpersonal (*see* GROUP COMMUNICATION).
4. The *closeness of the relationship between interactants*. Communication in intimate relationships, therefore, is viewed as more interpersonal than communication in role relationships.
5. The *kind of knowledge used by communicators*

when making predictions about the consequences of their messages. By this standard, predictions based on cultural or sociological knowledge produce impersonal communication. Conversely, predictions based on psychological knowledge produce interpersonal communication.

Not only has interpersonal communication been defined in different ways, but as a specific field of inquiry it encompasses all the disciplines concerned with social behavior or human interaction. The cross-disciplinary nature of the field is reflected in its historical development. Early in the twentieth century a number of influential sociologists drew attention to interpersonal communication by observing that the self evolves out of interaction with significant others. The implications of this insight were examined thoroughly by GEORGE HERBERT MEAD, whose work became the foundation of socialization theory and an explanation for how cultural norms are internalized by individuals. Strongly influenced by Mead's "interactionist" sociology, the psychiatrist HARRY STACK SULLIVAN gave a series of lectures in the 1940s in which he introduced an interpersonal orientation to the field of psychiatry. Sullivan's approach shifted the focus of psychiatric study from inside the individual to relationships between individuals. This relational emphasis was reinforced and extended by GREGORY BATESON, who attempted to formulate a general theory of communication applicable to individuals, groups, and cultures. At about the same time Fritz Heider, a social psychologist, wrote *The Psychology of Interpersonal Relations*, a book that set an agenda for empirical research on attraction, attribution, and communication. During the 1960s U.S. involvement in the Vietnam War inspired outspoken criticism of U.S. social ideals. Searching for alternatives to conventional ideals, a group of self-styled "third-force" psychologists offered a humanizing approach to interpersonal relations based largely on Martin Buber's interhuman philosophy of "dialogue" and the virtuous ideals of confirmation and authenticity.

Perspectives

There is no general theory of interpersonal communication, but there are several distinctive perspectives on the subject. Underlying each perspective are certain premises about the nature of interpersonal life. Although these premises are not always stated explicitly, they become quite evident when one examines the lines of investigation associated with a particular perspective. Each perspective can be seen as a set of premises about the relation between self and other on the basis of which specific research problems are formulated (see Table 1).

Table 1. Perspectives on Interpersonal Communication

Model	Relations	Focus
Monadic	Control	Individual
Dyadic	Coordination	Collective
N-adic	Self-regulation	Contextual

Interpersonal relations as control. Interpersonal communication has been viewed as a problem of control in which self seeks to control the outcomes of other. Interpersonal situations are seen as uncertain, but it is assumed that the problem of how to act can be decided rationally on the basis of social knowledge. Thus interpersonal communication is described as a goal-oriented activity in which the probability of success is determined largely by whether self has enough social knowledge and/or social skill to predict and control other's responses. Since primacy is granted to self—the individual "knower"—the control perspective is highly individualistic. The focus is on what is happening inside the individual. Interpersonal communication is reduced to an outcome of psychological processes.

The control perspective has given rise to several lines of research emphasizing strategic communication. One approach has been to define the goal of interpersonal communication as compliance and to examine the factors associated with self's ability to elicit compliance from other. Compliance gaining has been conceptualized as an ability to select an appropriate message strategy. As a result, research on compliance gaining has focused on developing taxonomies of message strategies and also on determining the conditions under which communicators select different strategies. Unfortunately this research has not progressed beyond the point of asking individuals which strategies they would select, or have selected in the past, to "get their way." The responses of other to self's selections have not been observed. Also, compliance typically has been studied as an event that occurs at one point in time rather than as a sequence of interaction involving maneuvers and countermaneuvers between self and other.

A second approach has focused on the processing and application of social knowledge. Referred to as the social cognition approach, this line of research emphasizes the structures of knowledge that self brings to an encounter with other and examines how self gathers, retrieves, processes, and applies social information during the course of an interaction. One program of research representative of this approach is the constructivist perspective, which hypothesizes

a causal relationship between an individual's system of constructs and the messages the individual will produce in an interpersonal encounter. The system of constructs is the organized cognitive structure by which self anticipates, interprets, and evaluates other's responses. The more differentiated and abstract self's system of constructs, the more likely it is that self will form multiple goals and identify multiple obstacles to achieving these goals. An individual with a complex construct system is thought to possess a more highly developed repertoire of strategies. This type of individual has learned to approach interpersonal communication as a situation involving complex communication tasks and has developed a wide variety of interpersonal tactics to cope with this complexity. The constructivist perspective extends the scope of research on interpersonal strategies beyond compliance by acknowledging the multiple intentions that self may have when encountering other. However, message selection and production still are examined only from the individualistic perspective of the message producer. *See also* SOCIAL COGNITIVE THEORY; STRUCTURALISM.

Interpersonal relations as coordination. Interpersonal communication has been construed as a problem of coordination in which self and other must coordinate their lines of action in order to achieve their personal goals. In contrast to the monadic model of communication represented by HAROLD D. LASSWELL's famous equation—"Who says what in which channel to whom with what effect?"—the coordination perspective is tied to a dyadic model of communication that views the relation of self to other as a coorientation process involving something more than an aggregate of individual processes (*see* MODELS OF COMMUNICATION). The dyadic model can be traced back to JOHN DEWEY and Mead in interactionist psychology, to Theodore M. Newcomb in social psychology, and to ALFRED SCHUTZ in phenomenological sociology. Terms such as *role-taking, intersubjectivity,* and *joint-consciousness* have been coined to reflect how each person projects part of the other's consciousness onto his or her own, thus joining together, at least temporarily, into a single interaction system.

Much of the empirical work associated with the coordination perspective was inspired by British psychiatrist R. D. Laing's observations on interaction and interpersonal perception in dyads. Laing observed that each person's behavior toward the other is mediated by the experience by each of the other, and the experience of each is mediated by the behavior of each. This deceptively simple statement provided the foundation for a series of collective representations of experience in a dyad, referred to as levels of coorientation. These levels include

1. level of agreement (what self thinks; what other thinks);
2. level of understanding (what self thinks other thinks; what other thinks self thinks); and
3. level of realization (what self thinks other thinks self thinks; what other thinks self thinks other thinks).

By taking into account the levels of experience of self and other as a dyad, investigators are able to study the relations between the two persons systematically. A coordination model of measurement has been applied in investigations of consensus, superior-subordinate relations, family socialization, and disturbed communication in marriage.

The coordination perspective is rooted in the premise that reality is socially constructed and must be socially sustained. The premise of a socially constructed reality embodies three important assumptions: (1) meanings are learned through SPEECH, (2) speech is a social process governed by rules, and (3) without rules there can be no meanings (see MEANING). These assumptions draw attention to the inextricable connections among speech behavior (verbal and NONVERBAL COMMUNICATION), rules, and meanings. This corpus of concepts is central to an approach to the study of interpersonal communication referred to as *rules perspectives*.

One of the most widely discussed rules perspectives is the coordinated management of meaning, a theory of interpersonal communication that attempts to explain the procedures by which individuals coordinate their actions. The theory defines rules as cognitions existing in the heads of individual actors. Rules organize the meanings of actors and subsequently regulate their actions. Since individuals will frequently be guided by different rules, the theory draws attention to cases in which coordination requires self and other to assign different meanings to the same messages. Thus the theory emphasizes managing meanings rather than sharing them.

The theory of coordinated management of meaning calls into question the assumption that interpersonal communication accomplishes a sharing of the same meanings between individuals. Meanings are not fixed by messages. In fact, only the most trivial messages are transparent. Although it is commonly assumed that "whatever can be meant can also be said and understood," this "principle of expressibility" may have no meaningful application outside the realm of unequivocal literal expressions. In the world of ordinary discourse between human beings the main qualities of expression are nonliteralness, ambiguity, vagueness, and incompleteness. Speakers are rarely able to say exactly what they mean. Typically self and other have different knowledge and beliefs about the world, and encounters between such different private worlds cannot be expected to produce "shared meaning" in the ordinary sense of that term. Rather than the ideal of a pure intersubjectivity based on the possibility of a free and complete interchangeability of dialogue roles, the "real" world of interpersonal relations is only a partially shared one in which a sense of sharing is the product of mechanisms of control over meanings as well as mutual faith in a shared social world. *See also* AUTHORSHIP.

Interpersonal relations as self-regulation. Interpersonal communication has been viewed as a problem of self-regulation in which self and other form a system that controls itself by following largely implicit rules established through a process of trial and error over a period of time. In contrast to the monadic and dyadic models of communication, the principles of self-regulation may be thought of as "N-adic" in that they assume "it is always the most complex that explains the most simple." This contextual orientation implies that an analysis of any communication system must extend the boundaries of the system to include other interactants implicated in or by the system.

Self-regulation has been used to describe the functioning of naturally evolving groups such as families and work teams (see FAMILY). These bonds evolve over a period of time through a sequence of transactions and feedbacks until the members become a unit governed by stable rules unique to them alone. The systemic orientation holds that members of such groups should be seen as elements in a circuit of interaction. While it is acceptable to assume that every member has influence, it is unacceptable to conclude that any one member's behavior causes the behavior of others. As elements in a circuit, none of the members has unidirectional power over the whole. Causality is circular insofar as every member influences the others and is influenced simultaneously by them. The part cannot control the whole, or, as systems theorists have expressed it, "the power is only in the rules of the game," which cannot be changed by the people involved in it.

The principles of self-regulation are sometimes classified as part of a school of thought about human communication referred to as the *interactional view*. Most closely associated with the cybernetically informed writings of Bateson, the proponents of the interactional view have successfully applied transactional and systemic concepts to the analysis of communication systems. This corpus of work has emphasized

1. the coexistence of analogical and digital messages;
2. metacommunication and its power to frame "a context of contexts";
3. how interactional circularity is reflected in the report and command levels of communication

and embodied in the arbitrary punctuation of interaction sequences;

4. the necessity of defining relationships and the symmetrical and complementary forms that relational definitions typically assume;
5. the tendency of interactional sequences to perpetuate themselves; and
6. interactional paradoxes.

Many of these seminal ideas about communication systems were incorporated in the famous double-bind theory of schizophrenic transaction. The double bind is a description of a repeated sequence of interaction that, because of the conflicting, unresolvable messages being sent, produces the kind of confusion associated with feeling "damned if you do and damned if you don't." An injunction is made and simultaneously disqualified by the same person. This double message is accompanied by another message that rules out any possibility of commenting on the bind or leaving the field. "Victims" of repeated occurrences of this sequence will inevitably learn to distrust their perceptions, thus accounting for the once-puzzling tendency of schizophrenics to use communication to deny that their communication is a communication.

Research Domains

As the different perspectives show, there is no widely accepted framework for organizing the large volume of research on interpersonal communication. Yet it is possible to discuss some particular research objectives in terms of the conventional categories of structure, function, and process.

Structure. One of the most productive lines of inquiry has been the effort to determine universal parameters of interpersonal behavior. The accumulated evidence strongly suggests that influence and affection are fundamental processes of communication found in some form everywhere. Most of the variation in individual behavior can be accounted for by these two behavioral dimensions and by some measure of interactional frequency. There is also conclusive evidence of an "interpersonal reflex," a tendency for certain behaviors to elicit certain responses. Although reciprocity is limited by fluctuations in the situation and relationship between partners, regular patterns of mutual influence have been observed in a wide variety of linguistic, vocal, and kinesic behaviors (*see* KINESICS). Structural studies of long-term relationships have focused on relationship boundaries, such as rules of participation, and structural hierarchies, such as rules of power and authority. This work has pointed the way to methods of intervention conducive to therapeutic and organizational change.

Function. There are numerous ways of classifying the desired or potential consequences of interpersonal communication. Research has strongly suggested that interpersonal communication is multifunctional. Almost every message has the potential to produce more than one outcome. Traditionally researchers have insisted on classifying behavior in terms of mutually exclusive categories, but that arbitrary rule is no longer viewed as useful. The following are usually included among the most central functions of interpersonal communication: (1) to organize, (2) to manage impressions, (3) to validate, (4) to disclose, and (5) to protect. Researchers have identified a number of highly generalized contradictions that have substantial force in determining communication outcomes. They include stability/change, autonomy/interdependence, and expression/protection. These contradictions often take the form of mixed motives, making it difficult to decide precisely how to act or what to say in a particular interpersonal situation.

Process. Research on process focuses generally on how interpersonal relationships develop over time and, specifically, on how properties of time constrain interpersonal transactions. Much of this research has been confined to one time period only, largely owing to the methodological and sampling problems associated with longitudinal research. Initial interactions have been shown to be highly predictable transactions that seem to be governed by a principle of uncertainty reduction. Beyond initial interaction, there is very little conclusive research on the development of interpersonal relationships. The development of an interpersonal relationship is not a systematic and orderly process but seems instead to be characterized by retreats and advances that are episodically conditioned by the particular interaction experiences of the participants.

See also CONVERSATION; DECEPTION; SOCIAL SKILLS.

Bibliography. Carroll C. Arnold and John Waite Bowers, eds., *Handbook of Rhetorical and Communication Theory,* Boston, 1984; Dean C. Barnlund, ed., *Interpersonal Communication: Survey and Studies,* Boston, 1968; Gregory Bateson, *Steps to an Ecology of Mind,* New York, 1972; Michael Brenner, ed., *The Structure of Action,* New York, 1980; Frank E. X. Dance, ed., *Human Communication Theory: Comparative Essays,* New York, 1982; Fritz Heider, *The Psychology of Interpersonal Relations,* New York, 1958; Mark L. Knapp and Gerald R. Miller, eds., *Handbook of Interpersonal Communication,* Beverly Hills, Calif., 1985; R. D. Laing, Herbert Phillipson, and A. Russell Lee, *Interpersonal Perception: A Theory and a Method of Research,* London and New York, 1966; George Herbert Mead, *Mind, Self, and Society,* ed. with an intro. by Charles W. Morris, Chicago, 1934, reprint 1962; Mara Selvini Palazzoli, Luigi Boscolo, Gianfranco Cecchin, and

Guiliana Prata, *Paradox and Counterparadox* (Paradosso e contraparadosso), trans. by Elisabeth V. Burt, New York, 1978; W. Barnett Pearce and Vernon E. Cronen, *Communication, Action, and Meaning*, New York, 1980; Harry Stack Sullivan, *The Interpersonal Theory of Psychiatry*, New York, 1953; Paul Watzalawick, Janet Helmick Beavin, and Don D. Jackson, *Pragmatics of Human Communication*, New York, 1967; C. Wilder-Mott and John H. Weakland, eds., *Rigor and Imagination*, New York, 1981.

ARTHUR P. BOCHNER

INTERPERSONAL DISTANCE

The spacing of individuals whenever they are in each other's presence. The distances adopted are affected in the first place by the situation and the nature of the interactional activity, but individual preferences, goals, and expectations also may play an important part. Thus the distances adopted may be quite variable from one circumstance to another. The term *personal space*, coined by U.S. psychologist Robert Sommer, has also been widely used. This term has sometimes been taken to refer to a "bubble" or sphere of space that surrounds the individual, providing protection from intrusion by others. Because the spacings between people are always a function of their interaction, interpersonal distances may be quite variable for an individual over time. Consequently, the term personal space can be misleading if it implies that individuals carry a protective spatial zone around them that is constant in size.

Situational Influences

The role of the situation in structuring spatial patterns is a pervasive one, yet one that enters awareness infrequently once the situational norms are learned. The kinds of activities characteristic of different settings are critical in determining appropriate interpersonal distances. For example, the demands of games or SPORTS may lead players to congregate closely as in football or spread themselves widely as in baseball. In general, the hitting, throwing, or kicking of a ball requires substantial spacing among at least some of the players, whereas the direct physical competition of wrestling or boxing requires intense bodily contact. In other activities, such as military marching band drills, spacing is controlled to within fine limits of tolerance. In such settings it is very likely that neither one's personality nor interpersonal affect is much of an influence on spacing. The requirements of different work settings can also impose fairly specific constraints on spacing. In many work settings the activity norms and the physical design of the setting determine the spacing among employees (e.g., workers on an assembly line or clerks in an open office area). In other settings the activity norms determine the spacing between the professional and the client (e.g., between a physician and a patient or between a barber and a customer). In general, these prescribed spacing norms may be seen as serving specific task or service functions. That is, the completion of the task or service requires, or is at least facilitated by, a particular spatial arrangement. Furthermore, individuals are substitutable in the sense that replacements will occupy spatial arrangements comparable to those they replaced.

Although the situational determinants of spacing are very important, most empirical research tends to overlook the role of the situation. In fact, most studies focus on relatively artificial interactions between strangers meeting in a laboratory room, hardly a circumstance representative of everyday exchanges. Many other studies simply examine people's conscious schemas for spacing behavior by having them arrange miniature cutout figures representing themselves and others. This latter technique can provide useful information on people's cognitions about relative spacing preferences, but such conscious preferences may not be representative of spontaneous spacing patterns.

Regulating Interaction

In addition to serving specific task and service functions in various settings, spatial behavior also facilitates the regulation of interaction. U.S. anthropologist Edward T. Hall has written extensively on the manner in which distance determines the form of specific interactions. In general, closer distances that permit TOUCH and olfactory input are appropriate for intimate exchanges (*see also* SMELL). As interactions become more formal, less personal, and less intense, interpersonal distances increase. Thus distance and arrangement set limits on the nature of the interaction and the intensity of the exchange between individuals.

The selection of specific distance arrangements can also help to restrict unwanted interaction. When individuals enter relatively large social gatherings (e.g., parties or receptions), small groupings of several individuals typically orient themselves into roughly circular arrangements. These arrangements help to define distinct groups and, at the same time, reduce potential interference from nearby conversations and activities. Occasionally people enter settings in which they expect and prefer no interaction at all with others (e.g., a library, a doctor's waiting room, or a train station). The choice of more remote seats will usually discourage others from initiating an interaction.

Intimacy and Social Control

Interpersonal distance may also serve functions linked to interpersonal motives. Preferred distances between

Figure 1. *(Interpersonal Distance)* Noncontact behavior: starlings on telephone wires. Animals Animals © E. R. Degginger.

individuals are partially a product of their relationships. In that sense distance reflects the intimacy function. That is, one's affective reaction toward another person, in terms of liking, love, or commitment to that person, may be indicated by interaction distance. Closer distances are preferred between good friends, lovers, and family members. Those preferences are, of course, limited by cultural and situational norms, personality, and GENDER differences. The intimacy function may be manifested more commonly in interactions that are relatively less structured and less evaluative in nature, such as casual interactions among friends, exchanges between family members, or conversations between coworkers on a coffee break.

When the setting of an interaction is more structured and highly evaluative, then behavior may be more a product of the social control function. Social control describes what happens when one's behavior is purposely managed to influence the behavior or judgments of others. This more deliberate behavior can be independent of one's feelings toward another person. For example, an applicant may be very sensitive to managing his or her own behavior in an employment interview. An intense dislike of the personnel manager probably would not prevent the applicant from approaching at a moderately close (but not too close) distance, maintaining a high level of gaze, and reacting favorably to the personnel manager's comments. Interpersonal distance may be managed not only to create a positive impression, but also to control or intimidate another person. Very close approaches or "spatial invasions" can put the recipient on the defensive and lead to flight from the intruder. Even when spatial invasions do not cause the victim to leave the setting, other compensatory responses may occur, such as turning or leaning away from the intruder to lessen the impact of the close physical presence. In general, as the consequences of one's social behavior become more salient and important, the strategic management of one's behavior will most likely increase.

Group and Individual Differences

Situational and activity norms, like personal relationships, lead to general expectations about appropriate distancing in interactions. With the exception of those settings in which spacing is very finely restricted (e.g., military drill formations), these expectations probably define a range of appropriate spacing. These ranges themselves may vary as a function of CULTURE. Hall's observations in different societies led to his proposing a contact-noncontact continuum to classify the comparative intensity of social exchanges within cultures (*see also* PROXEMICS). In general, Hall proposed that Arabs and both Mediterranean and Latin American peoples were on the contact end of the continuum because they preferred close, intense interactions. In contrast, the British and northern Europeans were on the noncontact end of the continuum because they preferred less proximate and less intense interactions. The effects of cultural background, race, and ethnicity on spatial behavior, however, do seem to be diluted when examining those differences within a single society, such as in the United States.

Within a culture, at least within most Western cultures, *gender* and *personality differences* may be important determinants of spacing preferences. In same-sex interactions, females typically interact at closer distances and, more generally, prefer higher

Figure 2. *(Interpersonal Distance)* George Cruikshank, *Inconveniences of a Crowded Drawing Room,* 1818. Reproduced by courtesy of the Trustees of The British Museum.

levels of nonverbal involvement (in behaviors such as gaze, touch, and smiling) than males do. In cross-sex interactions, interpersonal distance is highly related to the degree of commitment or liking between individuals. That is, for unacquainted male-female pairs, relatively distant patterns are common, but for lovers or good friends much closer patterns are common. It is important to appreciate that these gender differences are affected not only by the type of relationship between the interactants, but also by the cultural differences previously described. In some Mediterranean countries, for example, close contact, including touching and hugging, is socially acceptable in public between males but not for mixed-sex pairs. Gender differences seem primarily to be a product of both different social learning experiences for males and females in childhood and later sex-role expectations, although some genetic component may also enter.

Personality is another potentially important determinant of spatial behavior. The influence of personality is most apparent in the broad contrast between "normal" and "abnormal" groups. In general, individuals classified as abnormal are more likely to select and maintain greater distance from others than are normal individuals. A strong preference for maintaining large interpersonal distances is especially characteristic of one subgroup: violent prisoners. The contrast between violent and nonviolent prisoners has been reported in a number of studies that included samples of subjects from different cultures, races, and age groups. Within the normal range of personality differences, three traits representative of a general social approach-avoidance dimension—extraversion, affiliation, and social anxiety—have received considerable attention. Across studies, a general pattern is discernible: decreased interpersonal distance was correlated positively with extraversion and affiliation and negatively with social anxiety. Numerous other personality dimensions, including self-esteem and dominance, may also be related to spatial preferences, but those relationships are not as well supported as those with the social approach-avoidance variables.

It is important to recognize that the influence of factors such as gender and personality can be quite variable depending on the situation. In many casual exchanges among friends, acquaintances, or coworkers, there is considerable latitude in what might be considered appropriate spacing. In such instances gender and personality differences may be expressed in spacing behavior without attracting undue attention. In contrast, in formal, highly constrained settings, spacing patterns may be determined almost completely by the task and setting norms, and minor variations from the norm would be judged as inappropriate.

A Multivariate Perspective

An understanding of interpersonal distance or any other social behavior is facilitated by an appreciation of the broader behavioral context in which it occurs. Selection and maintenance of comfortable distances in interaction are very much related to involvement behaviors such as gaze, orientation, facial affect, posture, and various paralinguistic cues. In addition, the content of CONVERSATION can promote or discourage a close and involved interaction. It may be convenient for the sake of analysis to examine behaviors in isolation, but such an approach tends to overemphasize the significance of the focal component and ignore related cues.

Although interpersonal distance is an important component in the overall level of involvement between individuals, it is still just one component. Much of the research on distance in social interaction has examined the behavioral adjustments that follow movement toward or away from a partner. In some situations changes in distance seem to precipitate compensatory adjustments in other behaviors such as gaze, orientation, or smiling. That is, if one person moved considerably closer to another, the latter might decrease gaze toward and turn away from the person who moved. The apparent purpose of these compensatory reactions is the maintenance of a comfortable level of intimacy. In other situations, particularly between good friends, lovers, or family members, increasing intimacy in the form of a close approach, touch, or gaze will often result in a reciprocation of intimacy. Again, that adjustment can occur in any one or more of the component behaviors, such as distance, touch, gaze, or smiling. Understanding and explaining these various patterns of exchange in interaction has been a major focus of theoretical work in psychology and communication.

See also CROWD BEHAVIOR; NONVERBAL COMMUNICATION.

Bibliography. J. R. Aiello, "Human Spatial Behavior," in *Handbook of Environmental Psychology*, ed. by Daniel Stokols and Irwin Altman, New York, 1987; Edward T. Hall, *The Hidden Dimension*, New York, 1966; Nancy M. Henley, *Body Politics: Power, Sex, and Nonverbal Communications*, Englewood Cliffs, N.J., 1977; Albert Mehrabian, *Silent Messages: Implicit Communication of Emotions and Attitudes*, 2d ed., Belmont, Calif., 1980; Miles L. Patterson, *Nonverbal Behavior: A Functional Perspective*, New York, 1983; Albert E. Scheflen and Norman Ashcraft, *Human Territories: How We Behave in Space-Time*, Englewood Cliffs, N.J., 1976; Robert Sommer, *Personal Space: The Behavioral Basis of Design*, Englewood Cliffs, N.J., 1969; idem, *Tight Spaces: Hard Architecture and How to Humanize It*, Englewood Cliffs, N.J., 1974.

MILES L. PATTERSON

INTERPRETATION (HERMENEUTICS)

Hermeneutics is the science of interpretation. Although there were treatises on interpretation among the ancients (e.g., ARISTOTLE, St. Augustine), hermeneutics as a particular philosophy based on particular theories of interpretation emerged in the modern period with the work of German philosophers Friedrich Schleiermacher (1768–1834) and Wilhelm Dilthey (1833–1911). The former, a theologian and interpreter of both PLATO and the Bible, founded what came to be known as romantic hermeneutics, grounded in an alleged romantic faculty of empathy for what is "other" and strange, and grounded also in grammatical-linguistic study (*see* GRAMMAR; LINGUISTICS). Dilthey, who understood his aim as uniting the critical philosophy of Immanuel Kant with the romantic hermeneutics of Schleiermacher and the emerging historico-critical method, attempted to develop a hermeneutical theory that would prove to be "a critique of historical reason." Despite their many individual contributions to modern hermeneutics, the writings of both Schleiermacher and Dilthey are ordinarily considered versions of romantic hermeneutics and thus of relatively little value to modern hermeneutical theory related to the field of communications. The latter developments may be found in the distinct but related contemporary hermeneutical theories of Hans-Georg Gadamer, Jürgen Habermas, and Paul Ricoeur. It is their influential positions and controversies that ordinarily constitute what is called hermeneutics in modern linguistic and communication circles.

Interpretation as a problem or even as an explicit issue has tended to become a central concern in periods of cultural crisis. So it was for the Stoics and their reinterpretation of the Greek and Roman myths. So it was for those Jews and Christians who developed allegorical methods for interpreting their scriptures (*see* SCRIPTURE). So it has been across the disciplines since the emergence of historical consciousness in the eighteenth and nineteenth centuries. The sense of historical distance that scholars find in their relationships to the classics of their CULTURE (or of a broader cultural tradition, both religious and secular) has impelled an explicit interest in the process of interpretation itself. If scholars focus only on their sense of historical distance from the classics they will formulate the problem of interpretation as primarily a problem of avoiding misunderstanding, which even Schleiermacher often tended to do. The two aspects of Schleiermacher's hermeneutics reflect conflicts that are still unresolved: his emphasis on the interpreter's need for "empathy" and "divination" of the original author's feelings and intentions, which encouraged the development of romantic hermeneutics; and his emphasis on developing methodological controls that would help interpreters avoid misunderstanding, which encouraged the development of, first, historico-critical methods, then several formalist methods, and, later, structuralist and semiotic methods (*see* SEMIOTICS; STRUCTURALISM).

There is little doubt among most contemporary interpreters that historico-critical methods are needed to avoid ethnocentric and anachronistic interpretations of other cultures or texts of earlier periods of one's own culture. Most contemporary hermeneutical theorists not only accept but also demand the controls and the clear gains that historical methods have allowed. Several hermeneutical theorists also accept the gains provided by semiotic and structuralist methods—gains that permit attempts at serious cross-cultural interpretations. *See also* HISTORIOGRAPHY.

Gadamer's Contributions

It is impossible to summarize briefly the complex debates on hermeneutics in the modern period and to contrast hermeneutics with all the other theories of interpretation. It is clear, however, that Gadamer, a German hermeneutical theorist, has made a fundamental contribution to the development of contemporary interpretation theory. His interpretation theory is historically conscious without being strictly historicist. Moreover, he maintains this position without retreating into earlier romantic understandings of empathy with "the mind and/or spirit" of the author, as do Schleiermacher and Dilthey. Of major interest here is not the Heideggerian ontology (on "historicity") of Gadamer's position. It is important to note, however, that Gadamer's principal philosophical mentor, Martin Heidegger, is the first philosopher in the phenomenological tradition to shift philosophical study from a search for "eidetic," "genetic," or "transcendental" "essences" into an explicitly hermeneutical stance. Hermeneutics emerges in Heidegger's work *Being and Time* (1927) as an ontology for all understanding. In Gadamer the philosophical concern with all understanding as hermeneutical continues but is expanded into a study of hermeneutics itself in ART, history, philosophy, and theology in his magnum opus, *Wahrheit und Methode* (Truth and Method). Gadamer's influential interpretation of hermeneutics on the model of the CONVERSATION can be described in the following terms.

In the first place, every interpreter enters the task of interpretation with some preunderstanding of the subject matter addressed by the text. Contemporary historical consciousness helps to clarify the complex reality of the interpreter's preunderstanding. Historical consciousness is, after all, a post-Enlightenment and, in some ways, even an anti-Enlightenment phenomenon. More exactly, for Gadamer, the Enlightenment belief that the interpreter can in principle and should in fact eliminate all prejudgments was at best a half-truth. The truth operative in the Enlightenment's "prejudice against pre-judgments" was classically expressed by Kant as "aude sapere": dare to think for yourself and free yourself from the mystifications and obscurantisms present in all the traditions. Indeed, that critical force released by the Enlightenment was a liberating moment that inevitably forms part of the horizon (the preunderstanding) of most modern scholars.

Yet the reason why this Enlightenment truth is only a half-truth must also be clarified. If the expression *historicity* is not merely a philosophical abstraction, if the phrases *socialization* and *enculturation* are other than disciplinary jargon, they all bespeak, Gadamer argues, the other truth missed by Enlightenment and modern methodological polemics against prejudgments and traditions. The fact is that no interpreter in any discipline approaches any text or any historical event without prejudgments formed by the history of the effects of the interpreter's culture. There does not exist any anthropologist, social scientist, humanist, or historian as purely autonomous as the Enlightenment model promised. This recognition of the inevitable presence of tradition in all preunderstanding, moreover, does not mean that the interpreter has to share the tradition to which the text to be interpreted belongs. For example, interpreters of the Bible do not have to believe in the particular tradition they are interpreting in order to interpret it properly. However, every interpreter does enter into the act of interpretation bearing the history of the effects, both conscious and preconscious, of the traditions to which all interpreters in every age ineluctably belong. In Gadamer's controversial formulation, each of us belongs to history far more than history belongs to us. Any claim that the interpreter can ignore the history of those effects, including the history of former receptions or readings of the text, is said to be illusory. At this point, in Gadamer's work and in hermeneutics more generally, the problem of LANGUAGE becomes the principal hermeneutical concern.

Hermeneutics has become focused primarily on the question of language and communication, as has much contemporary philosophy since the linguistic turn of LUDWIG WITTGENSTEIN, FERDINAND DE SAUSSURE, and Heidegger. The explicitly hermeneutical concern takes the following form. Every language carries with it the history of the effects, the traditions, of that language. The word RELIGION, for example, as used in the English language, carries with it the history of the effects of both the Roman notions of civil religion and Jewish and Christian notions of faith, as well as Enlightenment notions of natural and positive religion. No interpreter enters the process of interpretation without bearing some prejudgments or pre-judices; included in those prejudgments through the very language we speak and write is the history of the effects of the traditions forming that language.

Yet to say that the interpreter "enters" the process of interpretation also allows us to recognize a second step in that process. The clearest way, for Gadamer, to observe this second step is to consider our actual experience of any classic text, image, symbol, event, RITUAL, or person. Indeed, any classic text (such as the texts of Homer, the Bible, or Shakespeare) can be considered paradigmatic for the interpretation of all texts. First, every culture has some loose or strict canon of classics for that culture (*see* LITERARY CANON). Those classics, both consciously and preconsciously, deeply influence the history of the effects of the preunderstanding of all participants in that culture and thereby all prospective interpreters of the culture. Every Westerner, for example, is initially startled when attempting to interpret the seeming dissolution of the self in classic Buddhist texts on "no-self." The belief in individuality among Westerners is not limited to substance notions of the self. Even radical critiques of the notion of the self-as-substance in the West live by means of the history of the effects of Greek, Jewish, Roman, and Christian senses of the self, which have become, since the RENAISSANCE, the modern Western notion of the individual.

Moreover, any classic text in the Western tradition bears a certain permanence and excess of MEANING that resists a definitive interpretation. Thus we recognize the first productive paradox of the classic. The actual experience of any classic text (e.g., the Bible) vexes, provokes, and elicits a claim to serious attention that is difficult to evade. And just this claim to attention from the classic text provokes the reader's preunderstanding into a dual recognition: first, of how formed our preunderstanding is and, second, of the vexation or provocation elicited by the claim to attention of this text. In sum, the interpreter is now forced into the activity of interpreting in order to understand at all. One's first recognition is the claim to attention provoked by the text. That experience, as Gadamer's successors in reception theory in modern hermeneutics have insisted, may range from a tentative sense of resonance with the possibilities suggested by the text through senses of import or even "a shock of recognition."

At this point the interpreter may search for some heuristic model to understand the complex process of interaction now set in motion by the claim to attention of the text and its disclosure of one's preunderstanding. This search for a heuristic model for the de facto process of interpretation provides the third step of interpretation. Gadamer's now famous and controversial suggestion of the model of the "game of conversation" for this process of interpretation becomes clear here. Gadamer's insight is that the model of conversation is not imposed on our actual experience of interpretation as some new de jure method, norm, or rule in the manner of Dilthey's neo-Kantian search for a "critique of historical reason." Rather the phenomenon of the conversation aptly describes anyone's de facto experience of interpreting any classic text, ritual, or cultural symbol. To understand how this comes about, Gadamer first considers the more general phenomenon of the game before describing the game of conversation itself.

The key to any game is not the self-consciousness of the players in the game but rather the release of self-consciousness into a consciousness of the phenomenon of the to-and-fro, the particular back-and-forth movement that constitutes any particular game. The attitude of the authentic players of any game is dependent above all on the nature of the game itself, not on their own consciousness. If the game is allowed, then the back-and-forth movement takes over the players. When we really play any game, it is not so much we who are playing as it is the game that plays us. If we cannot release ourselves to the back-and-forth movement, then we cannot play. But if we can play, then we experience ourselves as caught up in the movement of the game. We realize that our usual self-consciousness cannot be the key here. Rather we may even find, however temporarily, a sense of a new self given in, by, and through our actual playing, our release to the to-and-fro movements of the game.

This common human experience of the game is, for Gadamer, the key to the basic model of conversation for the game of interpretation. For what is authentic conversation (as distinct from debate, GOSSIP, or confrontation) other than the ability to become caught up in the to-and-fro movement of the logic of question and response? Just as the subject in any game releases herself or himself from self-consciousness in order to play, so too in every authentic conversation the subject is released into a particular subject matter by the to-and-fro movement of the questioning. It is true, of course, that conversation ordinarily occurs between two living subjects or even one subject reflecting on a question (as in Plato).

Yet the model of conversation, Gadamer insists, is also in fact applicable to our actual experience of the interpretation of texts. If interpreters allow the text's claim to serious attention to provoke their questioning, then they enter into the logic of question and response. And that logic is nothing other than the particular form that the to-and-fro movement of this singular game—the conversation as inquiry or questioning—takes. To repeat, the kind of interaction that occurs when we converse is the central model for interpretation, an interaction of the logic of questioning whereby a particular question and not our own subjectivity is allowed to take over. If we cannot converse, if we cannot allow for the demands of any subject matter or any questions provoked by the claim to attention of the text, then we cannot interpret. But if we are willing to enter into any genuine conversation, then we are willing to admit that conversation can be a model for the process of interpretation itself. In contemporary hermeneutics the model of conversation (and thereby reflections on Plato's models of dialogue) has become the principal model for hermeneutical theorists, despite their otherwise significant differences (see below).

Along with the earlier demands of the historico-critical method in romantic hermeneutics, therefore, modern language-oriented hermeneutical theorists insist on the model of conversation with the formed subject matter, consisting of questions and responses provoked by any text or any other cultural ARTIFACT. On this Gadamerian hermeneutical model, therefore, the primary meaning of the text does not lie behind it (in the mind of the author, the original social setting, the original audience) or even in the text itself (as in the New Criticism). Rather the meaning of the text lies *in front* of the text—in the now common question, the now common subject matter of both text and interpreter. Historically conscious interpreters do not seek simply to repeat, to reproduce, the original meaning of the text in order to understand its questions. Rather they employ all the tools of historical criticism and then seek to mediate, translate, and interpret the meaning into their present "horizon of understanding." Interpreters seek, in Gadamer's often misunderstood phrase, to "fuse the horizon" of the text (the horizon of meaning in front of the text, not behind it) with their own horizon of understanding on a particular question.

Moreover, by recognizing the experience of the interaction of interpreter and text as an experience modeled for its communication possibilities on conversation, Gadamer maintains that interpreters also recognize the inevitable finitude and historicity of even their best acts of interpretation. For they recognize the fate of all interpretation of all classics as a fate that can become an explicitly hermeneutical communication destiny. That destiny—present in all the classic conversations, especially the Platonic dialogues, and in all the great interpreters—is the insight that "insofar as we understand at all we understand differently."

Hermeneutics, therefore, is insistent that gains of the historico-critical method are essential for any historically conscious interpretation. Hermeneutics on the Gadamerian model is equally insistent that interpreters do not finish their task after using that method.

Interpretation after Gadamer: Hermeneutics of Suspicion and Explanatory Methods for Interpretation as Communication

Within the hermeneutical tradition two crucial questions have been posed to Gadamer's theory. Both have direct relevance for the use of hermeneutics for communication theorists. The first question is whether Gadamer's theory involves too sanguine a notion of tradition. One need not retreat to Enlightenment polemics against the inevitable presence of tradition in all understanding in order to share the insistence of several of Gadamer's critics (especially Habermas, a philosopher of the Frankfurt school) that Gadamer's notion of tradition bears its own dangers.

One way of clarifying that danger is to recall the central insight of the Enlightenment itself, namely, its belief in the emancipatory power of critical reason. Yet this clarification, however acceptable to most modern theorists, will not suffice as a charge against Gadamer's own general program of interpretation but only against his particular interpretation of the Enlightenment. For, at best, the truth of Gadamer's interpretation of the Enlightenment can be said to be the partial truth of the corrective of Enlightenment polemics against all traditions. This same critique of the Enlightenment is now widely shared by most historians and cultural anthropologists. In sum, there is nothing intrinsically hermeneutical in Gadamer's interpretation of the antitraditional stance of most Enlightenment thinkers. His hermeneutics does not stand or fall on the truth of his highly particular (and romantic) interpretation of the Enlightenment. Gadamer, as much as such critics as Habermas, allows for—indeed demands—moments of critical reflection by the interpreter as intrinsic to the process of interpretation. The fact that his position is grounded in the conversation between text and interpreter (and not simply the text, as in most forms of purely formalist criticism) indicates this. The kind of "critical reflection" that Gadamer characteristically endorses is the kind of classic reflection expressed in the notion of dialectic in the dialogues of Plato and the critical phenomenology of Aristotle rather than in modern critical theories.

However, even those differences need not mean that Gadamer's hermeneutics is simply traditionalist and thereby unconcerned with critical analysis of the tradition. The real difficulty seems to lie elsewhere. Gadamer's retrieval of the classical tradition's enrichment of the interpreter's preunderstanding does include forms of critical reflection that can undo error and falsity in any interpretation. His explicitly hermeneutical interpretations of the critical principles of Plato, Aristotle, and G. W. F. Hegel (often against his own hermeneutical mentor, Heidegger) should be sufficient warrant for this fact. Yet it remains an open question whether Gadamer's understanding of the kind of critical reflection available to the modern interpreter can account for those modern critical theories developed to expose not error but illusion, not normal cognitive and moral ambiguity but systematic distortions. Here, other hermeneutical theorists charge, is where Gadamer's anti-Enlightenment polemic severely damages his case. His apprehension is that any move to critical theory will inevitably become yet another futile attempt to provide a mythical "presuppositionless" interpreter. Because of that apprehension Gadamer seems to discount the occasional necessity of some critical theory in some conversations—including conversations with all the classics of the Western humanist tradition. The basic developments in modern hermeneutics (as, for example, in liberal and modernist theological interpretations of the Bible) have been geared to various modern critical theories. Those theories were forged to expose the latent meanings of texts, especially those latent meanings that enforce not mere error but illusion, not occasional difficulties but systematic distortions.

But Gadamer's own position does not really allow these so-called hermeneutics of suspicion to join his "hermeneutics of retrieval or recovery." Yet even his model of interpretation-as-conversation should alert hermeneutical theorists to the occasional need for a hermeneutics of suspicion and its attendant critical theory. This intrahermeneutical debate can be clarified by returning to the model of conversation itself, on the interpersonal level. For example, if in the course of any conversation someone begins to suspect (the verb here is crucial) that a conversation partner is psychotic (in the strict psychoanalytical sense), that person would consider himself or herself justified in suspending the conversation. In a post-Freudian culture the need for a hermeneutics of suspicion—and the need for critical theories (such as psychoanalytic theory and Marxist IDEOLOGY critique) to spot and possibly heal systematic distortions in our personal and, beyond that, our cultural and social lives—has become an indispensable aspect of many modern interpreters' preunderstandings, including several hermeneutical theorists (such as Habermas). It is true, of course, that this kind of interpretation of latent, hidden, repressed meanings unconsciously operative as systematic unconscious distortions is easier

to develop through the various interpretative techniques of psychoanalytical theory on the personal and interpersonal levels than it is on the social, cultural, and historical levels. However, even on those levels various forms of revisionary Marxist ideology critique, of feminist hermeneutical theories, and, more recently (with thinkers such as MICHEL FOUCAULT), of Nietzschean "genealogical methods" exist to try to locate the systemic but largely unconscious distortions in both the preunderstanding of the interpreter and the classic texts and traditions of the culture. Every one of these hermeneutics of suspicion, moreover, cannot rest simply on the model of conversation. Each needs a critical theory to aid its hermeneutical operation. *See also* FEMINIST THEORIES OF COMMUNICATION; MARXIST THEORIES OF COMMUNICATION; PSYCHOANALYSIS.

For any interpreter who suspects that there may be systematic distortions in a particular tradition, a hermeneutics of suspicion can be a helpful correlate to a hermeneutics of recovery. At any such points of recognition of systematic distortion (e.g., by a cultural anthropologist) the hermeneutic model of conversation becomes inadequate to describe the full process of interpretation. Recall the idea of psychoanalytic models of interpretation on the interpersonal level of interpretation, for example. The analyst and the analysand are not, in fact, engaged in an ordinary conversation. Rather they are engaged in a process of interpretation whereby one "conversation-partner" (the analyst as interpreter) employs a critical theory (psychoanalytic theory) to interpret the analysand's unconscious experience. Thereby the interpretation may emancipate the analysand from the systematic distortions repressed but still distortingly operative in experience. Only after that kind of psychoanalytical emancipation is the kind of hermeneutics based on Gadamer's model of conversation possible again. Yet not to face the demand for a hermeneutics of suspicion in interpreting both ourselves and all the cultural, social, and political traditions seems to leave interpretation theory unwittingly without the hermeneutic resources that contemporary hermeneutics in its full range makes available. Just as Gadamer's hermeneutics of recovery on the model of conversation can complement exegesis of a strict historico-critical sort, so too any legitimate hermeneutics of suspicion can complement the hermeneutics of recovery.

Conversation can remain the key heuristic model for hermeneutics. And yet, as such hermeneutical theorists as Habermas have argued and as such hermeneutics of suspicion as psychoanalytical theory, feminist theory, ideology critique, and Nietzschean genealogical methods imply, the model of conversation alone is a necessary but not a sufficient model for the needs and aims of contemporary hermeneutical theory in its full complexity. It is also important to insist that this correction of Gadamer's position need not demand a retreat to an Enlightenment polemic against all tradition. It does demand, nonetheless, the development of modern critical theories whose emancipatory thrust continues the kind of critical reflection present in the logic of questioning in the Platonic dialogues, in the legitimate demands of historico-critical methods, and in the hermeneutical model of interpretation-as-conversation set forth by Gadamer himself.

This first difficulty with Gadamer's position has occasioned within hermeneutical theory itself a basic acceptance of his model for interpretation-as-conversation but also an insistence on a correction of his critique of the role of critical theory in the interpretive process as a whole. The second question posed by post-Gadamer hermeneutics is related not to the model of conversation but to the notion of the text and its subject matter. The crucial issue here is that the subject matter that becomes the common subject matter of both interpreter and text in the process of interpretation-as-conversation is one whose claim to attention is expressed in the form of a text. This point is worth emphasizing in order to understand the fuller contemporary debates on hermeneutics.

Once again, it is not that Gadamer is unaware of the importance of form and structure for *expressing* any particular subject matter in a text and thereby, in his terms, for causing the claim to serious attention of the meaning "in front of the text." But insofar as the interpreter recognizes that the text produces its claim to attention by structuring and forming the subject matter into a work, an ordered whole, *a text*, some hermeneutical theorists argue for the legitimacy of using some explanatory methods in hermeneutics itself. It is true, as Ricoeur insists along with Gadamer, that for the hermeneutical tradition understanding envelops the entire process of interpretation. The hermeneutical question becomes whether explanatory methods grounded in explanation (*Erklären*) as distinct from understanding (*Verstehen*) can develop a hermeneutical understanding of how the meaning of a text is produced through the very form and structure of the text.

The fuller model of hermeneutics-as-conversation thereby suggests itself in the influential work of Ricoeur, the French hermeneutical theorist, whose position is that the entire process of interpretation encompasses the arch of some initial understanding yielding to an explanation of how the referent (the world of meaning in front of the text) is produced through the meanings-in-form-and-structures (the sense) in the texts. After those explanatory moments provided by such explanatory methods as semiotics, structuralism, and communication theories, the interpreter has, in fact, a better understanding of the subject matter (as an *in-formed* subject matter) than any interpreter does without them. Indeed, without the use of such explanatory methods as the formalist methods of LITERARY CRITICISM or semiotic and structuralist methods on the codes (*see* CODE) of a text, it is difficult to see how the hermeneutical theorist is not in danger of simply extracting "messages" (under the rubric "subject matter") from the complex, structured, formed, encoded subject matter that is the text.

Every text, after all, is a structured whole. Every subject matter comes to us with its claim to serious attention in and through its form and structure. For hermeneutical theorists to resist explanatory methods seems pointless. Such methods can show how expression occurs from the semiotic level of the word, through the SEMANTICS of the sentence, through the structured whole of the text (achieved principally through composition and GENRE) to the individuating power of style (*see* STYLE, LITERARY). So apprehensive can some hermeneutical thinkers become of how explanation (or *Erklären*) can turn into a means to undo the hermeneutical model of a conversation between text and interpreter (and therefore undo authentic hermeneutical understanding, or *Verstehen*) that they are sometimes tempted to discount explanatory methods altogether.

Several hermeneutical theorists now insist that any explanatory method that shows how meaning is produced in the text should be used (e.g., through genre and style analysis in literary studies). Structuralist methods, for example, are not identical with the antihistoricity of some structuralist thinkers any more than Gadamer's own hermeneutics is identical with his commitments to the Greek and German humanist traditions in his polemics against the Enlightenment and modern critical theories. Rather, structuralist and semiotic methods—such as the formalist methods of the New Critics, the explication-de-texte methods of earlier Continental critics, the semiotic methods or the more familiar use of literary criticism by historical critics, or even some variants of deconstructionist methods and modern Anglo-American communication theories—have demonstrated their hermeneutical value even to those interpreters who do not share the larger explanatory claims of some of their proponents. In that sense modern hermeneutics, first formulated in Gadamer's theory of the model of conversation, has itself become one major conversation partner in the conflict of interpretations on interpretation itself across the disciplines in our period.

See also AESTHETICS; AUTHORSHIP; INTERTEXTUALITY; READING THEORY.

Bibliography. Wilhelm Dilthey, *Descriptive Psychology and Historical Understanding* (in German), trans. by Richard M. Zaner and Kenneth L. Heiges, The Hague, 1977; Hans-

Georg Gadamer, *Philosophical Hermeneutics* (selections from *Kleine Schriften*), trans. and ed. by David E. Linge, Berkeley, Calif., 1976; idem, *Truth and Method* (Wahrheit und Methode), trans. from 2d ed. by Garrett Barden and John Cumming, New York, 1975, reprint 1986; Jürgen Habermas, *Knowledge and Human Interests* (Erkenntnis und Interesse), trans. by Jeremy J. Shapiro, Boston, 1971; idem, *Theory of Communicative Action*, Vol. 1 (Theorie des kommunikativen Handelns), trans. by Thomas McCarthy, Boston, 1984; Martin Heidegger, *Being and Time* (Sein und Zeit), trans. by John Macquarrie and Edward Robinson, New York, 1962; Paul Ricoeur, *The Conflict of Interpretations* (Le conflit des interprétations: Essais d'herméneutique), ed. by Don Ihde, Evanston, Ill., 1974; idem, *Freud and Philosophy: An Essay on Interpretation* (De l'interprétation: Essai sur Freud), trans. by Denis Savage, New Haven, Conn., 1970; idem, *Interpretation Theory: Discourse and the Surplus of Meaning*, Fort Worth, Tex., 1976; F. D. E. Schleiermacher, *Hermeneutics: The Handwritten Manuscripts* (Hermeneutik), ed. by Heinz Kimmerle, trans. by James Duke and Jack Forstman, Missoula, Mont., 1977; Joachim Wach, *Das Verstehen: Grundzüge einer Geschichte der hermeneutischen Theorie im 19. Jahrhundert*, Tübingen, 1926–1933, reprint Hildesheim, FRG, 1966.

DAVID TRACY

INTERTEXTUALITY

As a theoretical concept, intertextuality came into currency in the late 1960s. Its most generally accepted definition is the relation of one literary text to other texts. In this broad sense intertextuality therefore encompasses allusion, parody, burlesque, travesty, pastiche, imitation, quotation, and other forms of textual echoing, with the important exceptions of influences, sources, or plagiarism. Historically intertextuality developed in the wake of various North American and European textual theories that attacked the then-prevalent views both of the nature of MEANING in literature and of how texts related to other texts. These theories included Russian formalism, French STRUCTURALISM, and modern reworkings of certain ideas of SIGMUND FREUD and KARL MARX. Although the definition of intertextuality has varied slightly with each particular orientation and has continued to vary depending on the discipline using it, the concept proved particularly attractive in the field of LITERARY CRITICISM because it appeared to offer a new way to understand literary INTERPRETATION. The text was no longer to be read only historically or in relation to either the author (as tended to be the case in the romantic period [*see* AUTHORSHIP; ROMANTICISM]) or the world (as in theories of REALISM). Instead intertextuality would offer a way for criticism to restrict itself to describing the relationships between one text and other related texts. Sometimes this notion of related texts was extended to include the broader systems of signification that exist and operate within a given culture or society. *See also* IDEOLOGY; SIGN SYSTEM.

In either case, however, intertextuality differs deliberately and significantly from those studies of literary influence, sources, or plagiarism that are all oriented toward the author's writing of the text. The process of writing was now considered to precede the text's existence and to be both inaccessible to the reader and also not particularly necessary for the interpretation of the text. This questioning of the value and availability of the author's intention (and therefore of any influences, sources, and possible plagiarism) was also a central issue of American New Criticism from the 1930s on. Later theories of intertextuality in the 1970s and 1980s shared the New Critical assumption that literary texts in particular exist as separate and autonomous entities in the sense that once published they are independent of their authors or the world outside and are meaningfully connected only to other texts.

The term *intertextuality* was first coined and defined by Julia Kristeva in her 1966–1967 lectures in Paris. The idea grew out of her work on Russian theorist MIKHAIL BAKHTIN, especially his view of the multiple "voices" that exist in literary texts. For Kristeva intertextuality *was* the text's meaning; that is, its meaning depended solely on those voices (or other texts) that a given text transforms and absorbs. From this initial, if somewhat vague, definition, the concept of intertextuality both broadened and narrowed as it migrated across various communications disciplines. At its most specific it came to be a tool of specifically literary interpretation, a means of studying the textual and hermeneutic history of a text in a new and different way from traditional literary history. These two new kinds of history (textual and hermeneutic) are related but distinct. To read the novels of Thomas Hardy, for example, as the "intertexts" of John Fowles's contemporary novel *The French Lieutenant's Woman* (1969) would be to read for *textual* history, for Fowles's novel textually recalls the earlier ones. But to read Fowles's story as the intertext of Hardy's *Tess of the D'Urbervilles* (1891) would be to read for *hermeneutic* history, for here it would be the reader whose reading history is called into play. Intertextuality can and does violate historical time in this second—hermeneutic—MODE. Readers connect up the texts they have previously read, and their reading is rarely, if ever, totally chronological in terms of the dates of publication of what they read.

At its most general the term *intertextuality* has been used to refer to that which defines all textuality and, especially but not exclusively, all literature. By this view "literature" actually comes into being and has meaning by virtue of its relations to other texts as perceived by the reader. This is a move away from the most common and dominant thematic and expressive (author-oriented) definitions of literature, such as the familiar one that asserts that literature consists of those significant texts that express the authors' awareness of the universal, timeless themes of humankind. The radical nature of this change was sensed immediately by literary critics and has had important theoretical repercussions. Among the most significant of these was the new possibility that the text's meaning could now be conceived not as a "product" fixed in the text—that is, put there by the author in order for the passive reader to find it with ease—but as a "process" or result of the active participation of the reader as cocreator of the text.

Although the early definitions of intertextuality in literary theory (by the French critics Gérard Genette and Laurent Jenny, for example) concentrated on the textual nature of the process at the expense of the notion of the reader's role, this radical change had implicitly been made. Theorists at first referred to the change in terms of the "death of the author" (MICHEL FOUCAULT, ROLAND BARTHES) and the rise of self-reflexivity—the view that texts refer only to themselves or to other texts. It was not long, however, before it became clear that the death of the author had directly brought about the birth of the reader. If early definitions of the concept had downplayed the reader's role in favor of the text's relations to other texts, this was both natural and understandable as a reaction against the basically nineteenth-century theories of literature still prevalent in the years prior to 1960. Both realism and romanticism had made the text itself secondary to what it was said to reflect or represent (the world or the author). Nevertheless, according to the extensive theoretical work of Michael Riffaterre, the real intertextual dialogue was to be seen as a complex process, provoked in the act of reading, between readers and their memory of other texts.

The experience of literature, by this definition, has no longer anything at all to do with the world outside or with the author; it consists of a reader, a text, and the reader's reactions. These reactions take the form of systems of words grouped associatively in the reader's mind. Two texts could share these systems without one having influenced, been a source of, or plagiarized the other because it is the reader, not the author, who is central to making meaning, to interpreting, for instance, *The French Lieutenant's Woman* in light of the Hardy intertext (or vice versa). This does not reduce intertextuality to a clever, supplementary noticing of textual analogies by a particularly cultivated reader. Instead it is argued to be the necessary process by which any text takes on its full meaning for any reader. The question that arises from the obligatory nature of this process is, which is the controlling agency in interpretation—the reader or the text? For some theorists the reader is free to associate texts more or less at random, limited only by individual idiosyncrasies and personal culture. For them *The French Lieutenant's Woman* may be read intertextually through either a television SOAP OPERA like "Dynasty" or William Makepeace Thackeray's *Vanity Fair* (1847–1848). For others the text as a structured entity demands a more conditioned and therefore much more limited and controlled reading. From this perspective only the Thackeray text, with its structural parallels to the Fowles novel, would qualify as a true intertext.

Many such radical consequences followed from the rise of intertextuality as an important theory of textual and hermeneutic meaning. One was its overt challenge to any simple notion of what literary texts, in particular, refer to. If a text's first and foremost relationship is to other texts, then there can be no simple realist concept of the relation of literature to the world. The world of literature will always be filtered through the prism of other texts' versions of it. There are also ideological implications in this same process: if textual meaning is not inherent in the world outside the text but exists in the relations within and between texts, then there can be no transparent relation of imitation between literature and reality; there are inevitably going to be social and political assumptions both in the text's language and in the reader's interpretation of it. Another seemingly opposite consequence of the theory of intertextuality was its implied questioning of any view of texts as closed, totally self-sufficient entities with fixed meaning. Instead texts reverberate with echoes of other texts and are opened up to a continual process of meaning making. It all depends on the reader. *See also* READING THEORY.

Intertextuality has frequently been used as a generic term to encompass any form of textual interrelation: parody, pastiche, allusion, quotation, and so on. However, there are important distinctions to be made among types of intertextuality. These depend on two considerations. The first is the intended effect on the reader of the textual confrontation: is the reader to mock, to laugh, to respond to a call to authority? The second is the particular nature of the textual linkage: is it one that stresses difference or similarity between texts? The basic concept of intertextuality does not deal specifically with either of these considerations, but no discussion of the particular kinds of textual interrelation listed above is possible without them. The humor usually associated with the intertextual modes of parody, pastiche, travesty, and burlesque, but not necessarily with allusion, imitation, or quotation, is one example of differences in intended response. Parody, however, is particularly rich in its possible responses. *The French Lieutenant's Woman* does not so much ridicule as revere the Victorian novels it parodies. The range of response in twentieth-century parody in all the arts is wide, extending from the playful to the scornful to the respectful. There is much playful toying with Leonardo da Vinci's *Last Supper* in Arakawa's painting called *Next to the Last*. Diego Velázquez's *Las Meninas* (1656) is as respectfully treated in Pablo Picasso's cubist variants of it as is Ludwig van Beethoven's music in George Rochberg's modern parodies or classical architectural forms in postmodernist constructions like Charles Moore's *Piazza d'Italia* in New Orleans. The more traditional notion of parody as being scornful or derisive in intent was dominant in the nineteenth century and can still be found in modern works like Robert Nye's *Faust*.

The one constant in all of these responses to parodic intertextuality is irony, and it is irony that defines the particular nature of parody, which is a form of ironic difference between texts. Pastiche, imitation, and allusion, on the other hand, try primarily to achieve correspondence or similarity, not difference, in their relations with other texts. Quotation, of course, while involving more or less structurally identical repetition, can always involve a recognition of difference as well. Even the most literal quotation can have a different meaning when inserted into a new context.

Despite these distinctions based on intention and form, in all of these types of intertextuality it is the productive and dynamic interaction of text and reader that is held to determine meaning. For the reader it will not be to Fowles himself that one looks for the meaning of *The French Lieutenant's Woman* but to those other texts by Hardy, Thackeray, Henry James, Charles Dickens, and others that form the intertexts of the novel. The concept of intertextuality has offered a methodology of reading and an important tool for textual analysis, one that has radically refocused literary study in particular, although its influence soon spread to other cultural realms: music, the visual arts, architecture, television, film—in other words, to any domain in which interpretation is the fundamental task of criticism.

See also POETICS.

Bibliography. Gérard Genette, *Palimpsestes*, Paris, 1982; Linda Hutcheon, *A Theory of Parody*, London and New York, 1985; Julia Kristeva, *Séméiotiké: Recherches pour une sémanalyse*, Paris, 1969; Andrew Oliver and Brian T. Fitch, eds., *L'intertextualité: Intertexte, autotexte, intratexte* (special issue), *Texte* 2 (1983); Jean Parisier Plottel and Hanna Charney, eds., *Intertextuality: New Perspectives in Criticism*, New York Literary Forum 2 (1978); Michael Riffaterre, *Semiotics of Poetry*, Bloomington, Ind., 1978; idem, *Text Production* (La production de texte), trans. by Terese Lyons, New York, 1983; Wolf Schmid and Wolf-Dieter Stempel, eds., *Dialog der Texte: Hamburger Kolloquium zur Intertextualität*, Vienna, 1983.

LINDA HUTCHEON

ISLAM, CLASSICAL AND MEDIEVAL ERAS

The subject of classical Islam involves an immense area of the greatest possible cultural diversity and a span of many centuries. The elements that shaped the processes of communication in the world of Islam and between Islam and the non-Muslim world from the seventh century C.E. to about 1500 were basically three: the introduction of paper, the creation of a unified empire, and the establishment of one LANGUAGE, Arabic, as the medium of learned communication.

By far the most important factor was the introduction of paper. Originating in China, paper became known in Muslim central Asia in the second half of the eighth century, reportedly through Chinese prisoners of war brought to Samarqand. It relentlessly spread westward, replacing papyrus and parchment for all practical purposes within about two centuries. While it remained rather expensive, this was less true for paper than for the other generally used WRITING MATERIALS. Paper was less fragile than papyrus, and above all it could be manufactured anywhere in any desired quantity. The explosion of scholarly and literary activity in Islam and the production of ever more voluminous writings, combined with an increasing trend toward specialization, must be credited mainly to the new WRITING material. As a consequence, all kinds of ideas became more accessible throughout the Muslim world, even in remote fringe areas.

Communication was greatly facilitated by the fact that Islam created a unified empire larger than its two great predecessors in the region, the Achaemenid Empire and the ROMAN EMPIRE. It soon broke up into de facto independent territories under rulers who were often bitter rivals. However, the unity was not based on ethnic or geographical factors or on political configurations but on a religious IDEOLOGY. While the world of Islam was exposed to massive sectarian splits and hostilities, the RELIGION of Islam remained a unifying factor making for geographically unimpeded communication. The unified world of Islam, moreover, occupied a central location with respect to the then-known world and thus constituted a potential bridge for transmitting material and intellectual achievements in all directions.

Because it is the prime tool for communication, the widespread use of the same language makes for the most efficient transmission of ideas. Though the variety of languages spoken by Muslims was great, Islam succeeded in establishing one language, Arabic, as the medium of science and scholarship, including the fundamental religious and legal disciplines. Native languages continued to play a role in such areas as POETRY—the literary art form universally practiced and enjoyed by Muslims of all classes—and entertaining literature, as well as other subjects such

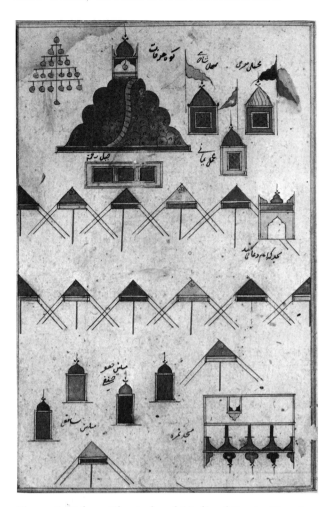

Figure 1. *(Islam, Classical and Medieval Eras)* Drawing from a poem on the rites of pilgrimage, showing pilgrims' tents ranged before Mount ʿArafāt. Persian, sixteenth century. By permission of the British Library.

as HISTORIOGRAPHY and mysticism that touched large sections of the population, but even in these genres Arabic was the admired model. However limited and even nonexistent the knowledge of Arabic may have been among people of low educational level, it was indispensable for educated people, including the intellectual leaders and those concerned with the transmission of the cultural heritage.

Communication within the Muslim World

The domination of one religion and language in Islam simplified communication to a degree not known before on such a large scale, but it also created a rather marked distinction between communication within the Muslim world and as it applied to contacts with the non-Muslim world. In some ways, then, intra-Muslim relations and, to use an anachronistic term, "international" exchanges followed different courses.

Travel and oral transmission. Probably the most important vehicle for the accelerated spread of ideas in medieval Islam was the intensive and far-flung caravan travel on land and the flourishing travel by sea. Travel being a strenuous and often dangerous activity, it was rarely undertaken by individuals on their own, although there were mystics and ascetics who on occasion traveled by themselves over long distances, propagating their views and causes along the way. Land and sea travel were essentially economic activities organized by merchants, but it was also customary and necessary for scholars and other intellectuals to travel all over the Muslim world and seek (religious) knowledge or further their careers in distant countries. Such travel usually required joining caravans organized by groups of merchants. Thus the two most influential and closely interrelated classes of Muslim society were brought into intimate contact over extended periods of time. Long-distance caravans and ocean-going ships accomplished the transportation of books, including newly released publications, and provided an opportunity for the exchange of ideas and the discussion of research in progress.

A different kind of travel peculiar to Islam was the hajj, the pilgrimage to Mecca, to be performed at least once during a Muslim's lifetime. This travel, too, was done mainly by caravan. Scholars performed the pilgrimage repeatedly if possible and then joined colleagues and teachers resident in Mecca and Medina for extended stays in the holy cities. As a regular annual event encompassing the entire vast realm of Islam, the pilgrimage was, and is, a unique institution in human history. As a by-product of its essential purpose of religious rededication, it served as a forum for personal meetings of members of all professions and occupations and thus as a center for the continuous exchange of information.

The courts of rulers and the salons of the wealthy and powerful also served to establish personal contacts among members of the intellectual elite and thus created conditions suitable for propagating new insights and accomplishments. Their effectiveness, of course, fluctuated greatly with changing political and economic fortunes.

Oral transmission and transmission in written form were recognized in Islam as basically different means for the dissemination of knowledge, and their comparative usefulness and reliability were much debated. In higher EDUCATION there developed a continuous and heated discussion about whether oral instruction by a teacher or self-study by means of books was preferable. Oral transmission was presumably common in pre-Islamic Arabia. It was natural in a bedouin society such as then existed in much of the Arabian peninsula. With the spread of the Arabic language and the growing LITERACY in it, followed by the introduction of paper, the situation changed. Muslim civilization became primarily a civilization of the written word. Oral transmission, however, retained a significant place in it. For example, the careful indication of sources was considered indispensable for the validation of information, and while they were often clearly stated to be written sources, religious scholarship early introduced a special method of citing oral sources that became the norm for scholarly activity. It focused on the *isnād* (chain of transmitters), the indication of the various authorities participating in the process of transmission viva voce from one authority to another back to the original source. A vast literature was produced that elaborated on the criteria determining the qualifications of the transmitters and thereby the reliability of the information itself. Entertaining literature, such as romances or tales narrated by storytellers in public, was often orally transmitted and only secondarily put into writing. Poetry was seen as orally transmitted by individuals who became the official transmitters of a given poet (*see* ORAL POETRY). However, in contrast to folk poetry, art poetry usually depended on writing for its spread and preservation. More significantly, this also applied to the vast corpus of religious and juridical writings.

Books and writing. With books and writing established as the dominant means of communication, three basic institutions helped to determine the extent and character of communications: the educational system, the institutions for PUBLISHING and preserving books, and the problem of CENSORSHIP. Education was seen as a lifelong task. Students were expected to continue the acquisition of knowledge, and many did. An appropriate curriculum, beginning at an early age with learning the Qur'ān (Koran) by rote, was more or less uniform, although there were sporadic attempts to develop a pedagogically more

Figure 2. *(Islam, Classical and Medieval Eras)* Disputation in a school in Aleppo. Illustration from the second Maqāma of al-Harīrī's *Maqāmāt.* Phot. Bibl. Nat., Paris.

suitable course of study. Many works were written setting out in detail the technical, practical, and moral aspects of the educational process. Higher education was connected principally with the mosque, but since the eleventh century the *madrasah* (college) provided a highly structured institution for the cen-

Figure 3. *(Islam, Classical and Medieval Eras)* Brass writing box with copper and silver inlay. Mogul, thirteenth century. Reproduced by courtesy of the Trustees of The British Museum.

Figure 4. *(Islam, Classical and Medieval Eras)* Frontispiece to the ninth section of a thirty-volume Qur'ān, Egypt, end of fourteenth century. By permission of the British Library.

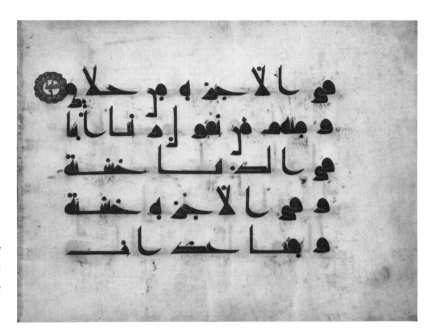

Figure 5. *(Islam, Classical and Medieval Eras)* Page from a Qur'ān in kufic script on parchment. Ninth to tenth centuries. Courtesy of the Freer Gallery of Art, Smithsonian Institution, Washington, D.C. (Acc. no. 37.6).

tralization and administration of advanced study. A *madrasah* was exclusively concerned with the legal/religious sphere of knowledge (which was peripherally interested in other subjects such as aspects of historiography). As is only natural for educational institutions, the *madrasah* tended to reinforce accepted values rather than to develop and disseminate new ideas. In general, however, Islam's stress on education ensured the transmission and elaboration of the cultural heritage through successive generations.

The way in which books were "published" and put in circulation before the invention of PRINTING—near the end of the period considered here—was not much different from procedures in classical antiquity. All or part of a work was entrusted to copyists connected or identical with booksellers, or was commissioned by a wealthy patron. Several copies would be produced for distribution or sale. The system was necessarily slow and clumsy; at times it probably prevented the circulation of books that should have been more widely known. BOOK production was greatly assisted by the copying labors of students taking down the dictation of their teachers and by the fact that there never was a shortage of those who wanted to earn a modest livelihood by copying manuscripts. Substantial private and, in a way, public libraries existed in large numbers, many of them famous for their size and quality. Much effort was expended on their efficient administration, as their indispensability for the dissemination of ideas was recognized and appreciated. Libraries and bookshops were, in addition to mosques and salons, meeting places where intellectual life was concentrated and ideas were exchanged. *See* LIBRARY.

Figure 6. *(Islam, Classical and Medieval Eras)* Page from a Qur'ān in thuluth script on paper. Egypt, Mamluk period, fourteenth century. Courtesy of the Freer Gallery of Art, Smithsonian Institution, Washington, D.C. (Acc. no. 30.59).

The impediment to the free circulation of ideas called censorship did not visibly exist as a formal institution in medieval Muslim society, as far as is known. The office of *muḥtasib* (market supervisor) had charge of the control of public morality. The *muḥtasib* would, for instance, warn against the teaching of lewd poetry to children. It was his duty to suppress views that were not in agreement with accepted religious teachings. The danger inherent in any activity of this sort was clearly recognized. Only if the *muḥtasib* could distinguish right from wrong on the basis of his own knowledge and judgment or by following the opinions of established contemporary scholars was he to exercise such censorship, for, it was said, "the danger is great, and if an ignorant *muḥtasib* delves into something he does not know, he may do more harm than good."

However, a kind of censorship was built into Muslim society by virtue of its attunement to what was religiously and socially acceptable at a given time in a given environment. Censorship was thus basically self-imposed. The banning and burning of books by concerned authorities were not infrequent occurrences. Writings considered heretical stood little chance of attaining wide circulation and an even smaller chance of surviving, unless those heretics formed well-knit social entities that endured over the centuries. The famous "unorthodox" thoughts of Muslim mystics managed to spread and survive attempts to suppress them because they gained majority support and were somehow adapted to what was broadly conceived as orthodoxy. The ecstatic utterances of a clearly objectionable sort ascribed to eighth- and ninth-century mystics seem often to have been propagated orally rather than in published writings vulnerable to suppression. Thus censorship, all but nonexistent on one level, was omnipresent and quite powerful on another. It did not stop the flow of ideas but could, and did, inhibit their gaining ground.

Communication with the Non-Muslim World

Powerful societies are apt to think of themselves as self-sufficient and to cultivate a sense of superiority over and hostility toward outside groups. Interaction in either direction is thereby hampered. The situation in the Muslim civilization was exacerbated by its religious basis. Proclaiming the attainment of bliss in the other world as humanity's real and only goal in life, it was accustomed to denying true value to anything foreign that was not expressly sanctioned by Islam. This led to skepticism toward ideas that were recognized as coming from outside and also sustained opposition to them, often lasting long after they had found wide acceptance. But intellectual curiosity, the main motivation for communication, was alive and active.

Translation of texts from non-Muslim civilizations. Translation provided the most effective means of establishing lasting contact with foreign ideas. Extensive translation activity from Greek into Arabic was responsible for bringing about the formation of what is meant by Muslim civilization. The process of assimilating Hellenism had been a continuous one before the advent of Islam. It can be documented in the Persian Sassanian Empire and was dominant in Syriac-speaking Christianity, which provided crucial intermediaries. With the early Muslim conquests of the first half of the seventh century, Islam took over

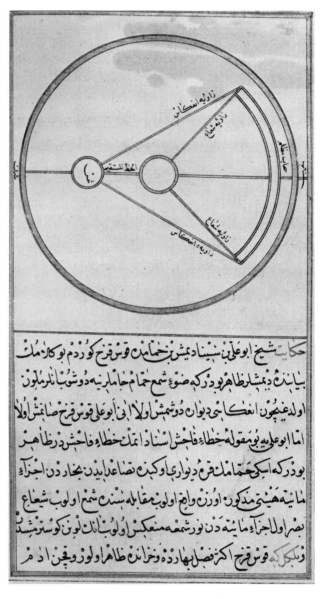

Figure 7. *(Islam, Classical and Medieval Eras)* Diagram from al-Qazwīnī's *Wonders of Creation* illustrating Avicenna's theory of the rainbow. By permission of the British Library.

Figure 8. *(Islam, Classical and Medieval Eras)* Aristotle. From a manuscript of the *Description of the Animals,* by Ibn Bakhtīshū', early thirteenth century. By permission of the British Library.

the homeland of Persian civilization and entered vast Hellenized territories. Indian, Persian, Syriac, and Greek books were found to be sources of useful knowledge needed by the new state if it was to flourish. Very soon, some literary and scholarly works were translated or at least somehow made available. The most important and readily accessible storehouse of practical and theoretical knowledge was classical Greek literature. An organized effort to translate it into Arabic started around 800 and continued in full force throughout the ninth century, only to diminish rapidly thereafter. The caliph al-Ma'mūn (r. 813–833) is credited, traditionally and for good reasons, with being the principal promoter of the movement. The Christian scholar from al-Ḥīrah on the Euphrates, Ḥunayn ibn Isḥāq (808–873), stands out as the single most influential translator and the founder of a school of translators. *See* TRANSLATION, LITERARY.

Science (including medicine) and philosophy possessed the greatest attraction for Muslims because these disciplines provided practical information and theoretical foundations to build on. Greek medicine, already established in Sassanian Mesopotamia, was represented principally by the large corpus of works by Hippocrates and Galen, and they were translated

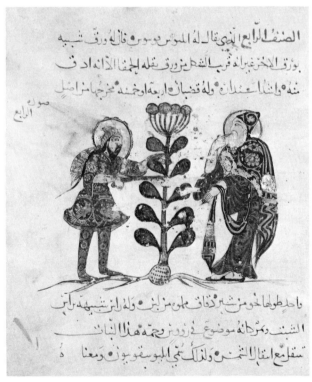

a

b

Figure 9. *(Islam, Classical and Medieval Eras)* Two illustrations from an Arabic translation of the *Materia Medica of Dioscorides,* written by Abdallah ibn al-Fadl. Iraqi painting on paper, Baghdad school, 1224 C.E. *(a)* Physician and attendant cutting a plant; *(b)* Autumn crocus. Courtesy of the Freer Gallery of Art, Smithsonian Institution, Washington, D.C. (Acc. nos. 38.1 and 43.2).

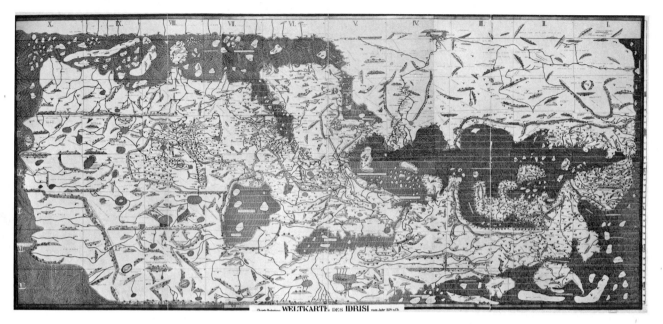

Figure 10. *(Islam, Classical and Medieval Eras)* Al-Idrīsī, map of the world, 1154 C.E. Courtesy of the Library of Congress.

in their entirety. Astronomical and mathematical classics, such as the works of Euclid and Ptolemy, soon found their way into Arabic. Astrology and oneirocritics (the interpretation of dreams), to name some of the pseudosciences, were thought by many to be of great practical value. Works on alchemy, representing a very late stratum of Hellenistic civilization, soon entered Islam. Aristotelian logic headed the list of works expounding Greek abstract thought; it was adopted, if often attacked, by Muslims and furnished the conceptual framework for later scholarship. Most of ARISTOTLE's other works were also translated. His ethics, together with the ethical thought of other Greek writers and large compilations of easily quoted wisdom sayings, exercised a far-reaching influence. Aristotelian metaphysics became a strong force in Muslim theological speculation, as did the more congenial Platonic and especially Neoplatonic thought from works made available in translation. Some popular literature was known, but drama and poetry and the great historical works of antiquity were not translated, as they had lost ground already in Near Eastern schools before Islam and were in many respects not communicable to a society with a totally different outlook.

Ḥunayn made use of all the tools known to philology. Greek manuscripts were collected, requiring extensive searches in Byzantine territory. They were collated, and a reliable text was established, whenever possible, before translation began. The inherent problems of translation were understood and discussed. The creation of a viable translation vocabu-

lary was seen by Ḥunayn as a prime task. In this way he and his school were able to discard the popular mechanical translation method and to make translations that were exact without being incomprehensible and that rendered the meaning of the originals faithfully. With the Muslims' growing estrangement from contact with speakers of Greek, direct knowledge of Greek texts was already becoming more and more difficult for them to acquire during the tenth century. The existing translations constituted the sole means of access to Greek knowledge for the great Muslim philosophers, physicians, and scientists of the following centuries. They thoroughly reworked, adapted, and incorporated that body of knowledge, influencing not only Muslim secular thought but also Islam as a religion and even to some degree as a legal system.

The seepage of other information from the outside into the world of Islam was considerably slower and more haphazard. International merchants made a large contribution, reporting on foreign countries with an eye for the marvelous and unusual, or for geographical and economic information and, on a much smaller scale, for political and historical data. Another interest, explainable by the role of religion in Islam with its numerous sects and religious mi-

Figure 11. *(Islam, Classical and Medieval Eras)* Interior, ▷ Great Mosque at Córdoba, Spain. Arcades of 'Abd ar-Rahman I, ca. 786 C.E. Lauros-Giraudon/Art Resource, New York.

norities, was foreign religious beliefs and how others thought about Islam. The resulting new discipline of comparative religion provided an acquaintance with foreign religious ideas and widened the Muslims' religious horizon.

Muslim influence on other civilizations. For spreading the accomplishments of Islamic civilization into Christian Europe, a translation movement proved again the most important medium. Its principal locus was, naturally enough, the Iberian peninsula. The motivation was the European desire for scientific knowledge and interest in philosophical speculation. A lesser factor, not involved in the earlier translation enterprise, was the necessity to learn about adversaries by translating their works. Philosophical, scientific, and medical translation served the purpose of improving the Western acquaintance with Greek writings then imperfectly known in Europe in the originals. In translation Arabic works based on the Hellenistic heritage, such as some of the works of al-Fārābī (870–950) and, most important, the works of Ibn Rushd, also known as Averroës (1126–1198), became strong catalysts in the formation of European thought. Here too, a minority group often intervened in the translation process, in this case the Jews. Some Latin translations from the Arabic went through the medium of Hebrew. The common translation procedure, repeated in numerous variations, involved collaboration between someone, frequently a Jewish scholar, who knew Arabic and some Spanish vernacular and thus was able to give a rough oral translation, and a European Latinist. The overall result was again an increase in knowledge and the inauguration of a fertile process of integration and development.

A variety of influences coming from the Muslim world matched the translation movement in overall importance, but the channels of transmission are by no means as obvious. Their existence can be suspected without decisive proof being obtainable. The most celebrated cases are the possible connection of troubadour poetry with Spanish Arabic poetry and the influence of Muslim religious mythology (concerning visits to the other world and related matters) on Dante Alighieri (1265–1321). In the case of Dante it has been established that some of the relevant Arabic literature may have been known to him in translation. Possible relations in the realm of poetry remain likely but mainly on the shaky ground that similar trends making themselves felt in close geographical proximity are unlikely to be totally unrelated, and poets and connoisseurs might well have been in occasional touch across the political boundaries. Institutions such as colleges show remarkable parallels in certain places, but concrete influence remains to be proved.

ART and ARCHITECTURE, FOLKLORE, fables, and games exhibit many features of undeniable Muslim origin. Literary and artistic motifs can be traced on their migrations with comparative assurance. Among games, chess is the outstanding example, but other games too, such as playing cards, are documented as having reached Europe from the Muslim world. The transmission may have been the result of contacts with expert artisans, merchants, and travelers, or simply of contacts with ordinary people close by, especially under political conditions such as existed in Spain and southern Italy.

The exact circumstances of the communication of a large array of technological inventions, many of them singularly potent forces in shaping history, are similarly clouded. Rarely do we have substantial literary documentation such as exists in connection with automata such as clocks or fountains, where at least the transmission from antiquity to Islam is well attested. As in the case of paper, much technological invention would seem to have had its origin in eastern Asia. This would make the Muslim world the logical area of transit, but a direct northern route through central Asia and Russia cannot be ruled out. A case has also been made for the frequent movement of technology from Europe into Islam; for instance, the lateen sail and the stirrup, which, while apparently originating in the East, was developed and its function expanded in Europe.

The carriers of the new inventions remain anonymous. Skilled artisans, prisoners of war (as we have seen in connection with the introduction of paper), soldiers, merchants, and other travelers, as well as Christian monks and perhaps even slaves—a list as plausible as it is unspecific—may have played a role in the transmission. In the history of the transfer of technology, the decisive constant is less the point of entry than the improvements made after it has reached its destination. It is the innate stubborn resistance to innovation that determines the history of technology's diffusion, as is illustrated, for instance, both in the Muslim world and in Europe, by the long time it took for the Indian/Arabic numerals to be accepted, despite their obvious advantages. Many crucial details of the process of transmission, which probably cannot easily be reduced to one common denominator, remain to be learned, if they are not lost to us forever.

See also CRUSADES, THE; EAST ASIA, ANCIENT; HELLENIC WORLD.

Bibliography. Enrico Cerulli, Il *"Libro della Scala"* e la questione delle fonti arabo-spagnole della Divina commedia, Vatican City, 1949; Ibn Khaldūn, *The Muqaddimah,* trans. by Franz Rosenthal, New York, 1958, reprint 1967; George Makdisi, *The Rise of Colleges: Institutions of Learning in Islam and the West,* Edinburgh, 1981; Joseph Needham, *Science and Civilization in China,* New York and Cambridge, 1954; Johannes Pedersen, *Den Arabiske* *bog* (The Arabic Book), trans. by Geoffrey French, Princeton, N.J., 1984; Franz Rosenthal, *The Classical Heritage in Islam*, London, 1975; Joseph Schacht and C. E. Bosworth, eds., *The Legacy of Islam*, 2d ed., Oxford, 1974; Ibn al-Ukhūwah, *The Maʿālim al-qurba fī aḥkām al-ḥisba*, ed. and trans. by Ruben Levy, London, 1938; Gustave E. von Grunebaum, *Medieval Islam: A Study in Cultural Orientation*, 2d ed., Chicago, 1954; Lynn T. White, Jr., *Medieval Religion and Technology: Collected Essays*, Berkeley, Calif., and London, 1978; idem, *Medieval Technology and Social Change*, New York, 1962.

FRANZ ROSENTHAL

ISLAMIC WORLD, TWENTIETH CENTURY

Communication patterns in the Islamic world have undergone considerable change since the advent of twentieth-century life-styles and the introduction of new technologies. However, the mainstream concept of reaching out with the Word of Allah and keeping the Islamic *Umma* (Muslims of the entire world) well informed through all available channels has never changed. New trends and models emerged from increased contact with other cultures and their communication systems and from the far-reaching economic and social developments of the latter part of the twentieth century. World trends have included an increasing flow of information, new international communication systems, a focus on DEVELOPMENT COMMUNICATION, a growing role of RELIGION in the mass media, and—within Islam—an emphasis on communication from an Islamic outlook.

Modern Islam

Geographically and demographically, the core of the Islamic world extends along a broad band through the continents of Africa and Asia, but Islamic communities exist throughout the world. Muslims number roughly one billion worldwide. MARSHALL MCLUHAN's idea of a "global village" also applies to the Islamic world, where new communication technologies have created what may be called a "global mosque." Far from being isolated cultural pockets in alien environments, remote Islamic communities employ both traditional and modern channels of communication to maintain an active relationship with one another and with their cultural roots.

Conceptually the Islamic faith transcends national boundaries and ethnic differences as well as LANGUAGE barriers. It has a built-in function of both vertical and horizontal communication, for which twentieth-century communication technologies have offered channels with unlimited capacity. Traditional channels have sometimes had to be phased out or modified to cope with new needs and priorities, but in many cases they have been amply supported by the new technologies.

Along with breakthroughs in technologies, the impact of two world wars, countless regional and domestic conflicts, and new sources of material wealth in a few Islamic countries have affected the life and thought of the Islamic world. Some Islamic countries were more directly involved than others in regional conflicts, but such conflicts had far-reaching communication implications with respect to the use and abuse of communication capabilities, particularly in RADIO broadcasts and psychological warfare.

It is often argued that contact with the West throughout the twentieth century has only superficially westernized the lives of Muslims without reaching into their inner souls. Especially significant in this context is the spectrum of value systems applied in CENSORSHIP of film and other media in Islamic countries. The countries may be politically, socially, or economically worlds apart, but they share an Islamic background that dictates ideological and moral criteria for film censorship and the admissibility of certain topics or ATTITUDES for treatment by the print or electronic media. Atheism, paganism, adultery, usury, gambling, and drinking, for example, cannot be tolerated in domestic or imported productions. Faith in God, honesty, justice, equality, charity, the family, and the work ethic are, on the other hand, Islamic ideals that have to be upheld within a framework of AGENDA-SETTING that varies according to the degree of twentieth-century secularization permitted by the religious authority in a given state. All this is part of the deep-rooted Islamic identity that the modern media have challenged but have also, in many ways, reinforced.

Although the media are not directly run by religious institutions (except broadcasts and publications devoted entirely to religion or located in countries controlled by a religious hierarchy), complete secularization of the media has never been an objective of communication policy. Religious content may vary in volume and intensity but has always been a conspicuous element even in broadcasts beamed to the Islamic world from non-Islamic countries (e.g., BBC broadcasts). A measure of state control, however, is almost universal in Islamic countries as a safeguard.

Modern Islamic Media

The Pan-Islamic movement of the turn of the century and the Pan-Arab movement of the 1950s were supported by a powerful press, but the innovative revival of Pan-Islamism in the 1960s, 1970s, and 1980s used more diversified media. Communication technology enabled two daily newspapers in the Islamic world to publish simultaneous editions at different locations. Offset PRINTING processes became highly developed. Millions of copies of the Qurʾan, the Islamic SCRIPTURE, were turned out by ultramodern printing

Figure 1. *(Islamic World, Twentieth Century)* Muslims being called to prayer. Mopti, Mali, 1967. United Nations photo 106,724.

equipment in several Islamic countries. Film production in the Islamic world, particularly in Egypt and elsewhere in North Africa, also made remarkable progress. Films that dealt with Islamic topics and Islamic history became very popular, and some won regional and international awards.

However, the electronic media can be singled out for achieving the most conspicuous progress. In the Arab countries of West Asia and North Africa, where Arabic, the sacred language of Islam, is the common language of the region, radio lent its overwhelming power to governments as well as to operators of pirate or dissident broadcasts (*see* RADIO, INTERNATIONAL). The religious content of most scheduled and unscheduled radio transmissions became more intensive when nationalistic or Pan-Arab grievances were more or less identical with Islamic issues.

Other languages spoken in the Islamic world include Persian, Pashto, Turkish, Urdu, Malay, Indonesian, Swahili, and several additional Turkic and

African languages, besides English, French, and Russian. Some languages use Arabic characters (e.g., Persian and Urdu), and others use Latin or other characters. New word-processing and photocomposing techniques have solved many of the problems related to this mosaic of symbols, but the basic communication problem is offset by the unifying factor of the Islamic faith and the Qur'an.

The Qur'an has always been the core of Islamic communication in countless formats. The first technological innovation after printing was the amplification of the human voice in Qur'an recitals by microphones and loudspeakers. Then came radio, which opened worldwide vistas for Qur'anic recitals. A significant development was the early 1960s launching in Egypt of a radio network completely dedicated to the Qur'an. This was followed by another originating from Saudi Arabia. An unfailing by-product was the introduction of complete sets of Qur'anic recitals on cassettes, which are often used in combination with printed editions of the Islamic scripture.

Television brought to the Islamic world a new dimension of communication plus all the problems associated with television in developing countries (see TELEVISION HISTORY). Among these was the precarious balance between domestic and imported productions. Some Islamic countries resented the image-assisted "cultural invasion" that introduced alien or un-Islamic concepts and values (see NEW INTERNATIONAL INFORMATION ORDER). However, television survived the unrest in those countries by maintaining a tradition of religious censorship and religious content.

There were also technical problems. When television appeared in the Islamic world during the late 1950s and early 1960s, each individual country had its own plans irrespective of future regional and international development. These differences were further accentuated when the time came for choosing PAL or SECAM as a system for color television. Divergent choices made it very difficult and expensive to exchange programs, even between neighboring countries, or to form a Pan-Islamic or Pan-Arab network. The problem was eventually solved by technological advances and multisystem equipment.

SATELLITE capabilities also caught up with the emerging needs of the global mosque. One striking example is the annual radio and television coverage of hajj, the once-in-a-lifetime pilgrimage to Mecca. Around three million Muslims from all over the world gather in Mecca for the most spectacular of all Islamic RITUAL events and the annual "convention" of the Islamic faith. Until the late 1940s any intrusion of the major media into events of the hajj was taboo, but one by one radio broadcasters, still photographers, and then motion picture and VIDEO photographers were permitted to cover the pilgrimage. By the 1980s the hajj had become, via satellite, an event shared by all Islamic countries simultaneously.

Another area of Islamic ritual enhanced by communication technology is the call to prayer. Aside from public-address systems that have functionally replaced the traditional minaret towering high above the structure of the mosque, the call to prayer is carried by radio and television five times a day in many Islamic countries.

One serious consequence of television has been its effect on the lives of working people in rural areas. The traditional working day used to start at dawn and conclude with the evening prayers about two hours after sunset. Usually people would retire at that time and get up early in the morning. With the attraction of prime-time television ENTERTAINMENT and home video, many people stay up late and consequently get up late. Apart from considerations related to program content, this situation has significantly changed social and work patterns and has interfered with agricultural productivity.

Economic developments during the 1960s and 1970s encouraged waves of temporary MIGRATION. Migrant workers flocked to oil-rich countries, where relatively lucrative job opportunities were abundant. It was observed that shortwave radio-cassette recorders and later videocassette recorders were among the migrants' first acquisitions. Radio-cassette recorders kept them abreast of news at home and provided other information and entertainment. The demand for such recorders created a sizable market in affluent Islamic countries, and the migrant workers remained devotees of this combined medium even after they returned to their old homes. The availability of the medium then created a demand for prerecorded cassettes. Some were domestically produced, but others could readily be transported— perhaps smuggled—across national borders, with far-reaching social and political implications. The role of cassettes in the REVOLUTION organized from exile by the Ayatollah Ruholla Khomeini, which in 1979 overthrew Moḥammad Reza Shah Pahlavi and took control of Iran, is a telling example. Cassettes recorded in Paris were smuggled into Iran and duplicated for distribution to revolutionary units for indoctrination and coordination of action.

The satellite is a medium of somewhat similar implications. The geographic location of many countries in the Islamic world made them prime targets for satellite communication. Through a network of ground stations, INTELSAT is accessible almost everywhere in the Islamic world via Atlantic and Indian Ocean satellites. To serve the specific purposes of certain areas of the Islamic world, two major satellite systems were developed: PALAPA for the

Indonesian archipelago in Southeast Asia and AR-ABSAT for the Arab countries of West Asia and North Africa.

Education and research in the specialized field of Islamic communication as distinct from communication in general have been carried out by Al-Azhar University in Egypt, Omdurman Islamic University in Sudan, and Imam Muhamed Ibn Abdel Wahhab University in Saudi Arabia. There are also training facilities in Mecca, Medina, Islamabad, and Kuala Lumpur and courses offered by several other institutes in the Islamic world. Scholars in Egypt and Saudi Arabia have theorized about the relationship of traditional Islamic models to modern MODELS OF COMMUNICATION.

The need to coordinate within the framework of a worldwide Islamic community was behind the creation of the Organization of Broadcasting Services in Islamic Countries, with headquarters in Jedda, Saudi Arabia. Membership in the organization did not exclude membership in various preexisting organizations, such as regional organizations. The most active among these is Gulfvision, which serves Arab countries of the Persian Gulf area.

In spite of all the conflicts and contradictions that have beset the Islamic world during the twentieth century, the development of communication has been guided not only by national priorities but also by Islamic motives. Constructive plans developed by INTERNATIONAL ORGANIZATIONS have had Islamic support. Most Islamic countries participate in the International Program for the Development of Communication (IPDC), which started in 1982.

The twentieth-century upheavals in communications technology have had dual meanings for the Islamic world. Often posing threats to Islamic values and unity, they have at the same time provided means to deflect the threats and strengthen the unity. All new media have been enlisted in the service of the global mosque.

Bibliography. Yehia Aboubakr, Saad Labib, and Hamdy Kandil, *Development of Communication in the Arab States,* Paris, 1982; John Esposito, ed., *Voices of Resurgent Islam,* New York, 1983; Munir Hijab, *Nazariatul I'lam Al-Islami* (Theories of Islamic Communication), Cairo, 1981; Marjorie Kelly, ed., *Islam: The Religious and Political Life of a World Community,* New York, 1984; Bernard Lewis, ed., *Islam and the Arab World,* New York, 1979; Malise Ruthven, *Islam in the World,* New York, 1984; Edward W. Said, *Covering Islam,* New York, 1981; W. Montgomery Watt, *What Is Islam?* 2d ed., London, 1979.

YEHIA ABOUBAKR

IVENS, JORIS (1898–)

Dutch filmmaker. Ivens was a pioneer documentarist whose filmmaking, spanning more than half a cen-

tury, ranged over five continents and influenced generations of filmmakers, particularly those engaging the medium in the cause of revolutionary social change. In at least four genres of activist DOCUMENTARY he set a tradition in motion (*see* GENRE).

In *Misère au Borinage* (1933), made with Henri Storck of Belgium and focusing on impoverished striking miners, he inaugurated the contextual social action documentary aimed at community mobilization. In *The Spanish Earth* (1937), on struggles of the beleaguered Spanish republic against Fascist forces led by Francisco Franco, he inaugurated the international solidarity documentary, a summons for world aid. In *Komsomol* (1932), a tribute to the first Soviet Five Year Plan, made by Ivens during a visit to the USSR sponsored by director Vsevolod Pudovkin, he inaugurated the utopian genre of the exemplary portrait of an exotic revolutionary society (*see* UTOPIAS). And in *Nieuwe Gronden* (New Earth, 1934), a bitter juxtaposition of Dutch workers heroically winning land from the sea with stock shots of harvests being destroyed elsewhere in a depression-stricken globe, Ivens provided the first Western variant of the radical compilation genre pioneered by Soviet documentarists. Much of our inherited lexicon of the documentary was first tested and consolidated during the 1930s by Ivens and his editor, Helen van Dongen, from contrapuntal sound to individual characterization and narrative mise-en-scène and editing, but such innovation was always in the service not of modernist dislocation but of improved social access and POLITICAL COMMUNICATION.

Ivens as filmmaker came of age as Amsterdam's delegate to the cosmopolitan AVANT-GARDE of the 1920s with the urban cinepoem *Regen* (Rain, 1929), his most enduring work from this period. As the depression spread, Ivens's long-standing Communist commitment became increasingly the determining principle of his work, and his ensuing "proletarian" period was marked by heroic epics of work ranging from the Zuider Zee to the Urals. The late 1930s gave rise to Ivens's best-known "Popular Front" period. His home base during these years was the United States, and he filmed on behalf of not only the Spanish Loyalists but also Chinese soldiers repelling the Japanese invaders (*The Four Hundred Million,* 1938) and Ohio farmers organizing to electrify their lands under the benevolent aegis of the New Deal (*Power and the Land,* 1941).

World War II saw Ivens busy first with the U.S. "Second Front" movement and then, under the auspices of the Netherlands government, with preparations for a Grierson-style educational film apparatus for a postwar Netherlands East Indies. The result was instead a vibrant appeal for Indonesian independence (*Indonesia Calling,* 1946), the prophetic prototype for later Third World variants of the solidarity genre. Ivens was thereupon stripped of his Dutch

Figure 1. *(Ivens, Joris)* Joris Ivens, *The Spanish Earth*, 1937. National Film Archive, London. Copyright Joris Ivens.

Figure 2. *(Ivens, Joris)* Joris Ivens. Photograph by Virginia Haggard Leirens.

citizenship and settled in for a cold-war exile in Poland and the German Democratic Republic, another prolific period whose best work is the epic manifesto of union internationalism, *Das Lied der Ströme* (Song of the Rivers, 1954).

In 1957 Ivens settled in Paris, the city that was to become his permanent home and to which he dedicated his poetic essay *La Seine a rencontré Paris,* made the same year. Some critics welcomed the return of the lyrical landscapist to what they saw as his true calling, but they were to be disappointed. The following decade saw many more lyrical travel essays, but always infused with Ivens's socialist celebration of human labor and class struggle. Ivens earned his new nickname, "the Flying Dutchman," working with the new post-Stalin generation of young leftist filmmakers in China, Cuba, Chile, Italy, and France. The Vietnam War provoked yet a new phase in the sexagenarian's career. The author of four films on Indochina, Ivens became the figurehead of European artistic efforts on behalf of the Vietnamese cause. At the same time, after Prague, Ivens quietly joined other European Communists in breaking ties to Moscow, looking instead to the East for an alternative model of the revolutionary dream. Returning to China for a third time, Ivens, together with his partner, Marceline Loridan, produced his final masterpiece, the eleven-hour, twelve-part series on the cultural revolution, *How Yukong Moved the Mountains* (1976), a direct-cinema epic on the process of collective political change (*see* CINÉMA VÉRITÉ).

Ivens had much in common with the other three founding parents of the documentary cinema, ROBERT FLAHERTY, DZIGA VERTOV, and JOHN GRIERSON. Flaherty's lyrical and heroic romanticism often surfaced in Ivens's images of revolutionary heroism and of collective work amid the natural elements in every corner of the globe. Sharing both Vertov's commitment to Marxism and his roots in the futurist-constructivist currents of the 1920s avant-garde, Ivens's idealism and efficacy far outlasted Vertov's, being grounded in the oppositional undercurrent of the Western democracies rather than the congealing cultural bureaucracy of the Soviet state. As for his friend Grierson, who hired him to make the Canadian *Action Stations!* in 1942, Ivens shared both his pragmatism and his populism, his commitment to documentary film as a means of stirring popular audiences in the age of mass media. Yet, despite Ivens's many Grierson-style state commissions over the years, his most important work remained the articulation of opposition, the elaboration of models of survival, resistance, and alternative values under the global hegemony of capitalism.

Although Ivens was born in the same year as Grierson and SERGEI EISENSTEIN, his career extended into a much later period. His pioneering legacy has been the beneficiary of at least a dozen book-length studies around the world and of many more major retrospectives in almost every world cinematheque from New York to Beijing. Yet the critical consensus suggested by this acclaim is not unanimous in a country whose documentary legacy he helped found—the United States—where many of his major works are unavailable and where his reputation is still clouded by a cold-war mystique of the separation of politics and art. Ivens's accomplishment has been to refute that separation and to provide each decade since the 1920s with its most lingering images of radical hope.

See also AVANT-GARDE FILM; MOTION PICTURES; NEWSREEL.

Bibliography. Rosalind Delmar, *Joris Ivens: Fifty Years of Filmmaking,* London, 1979; Joris Ivens, *The Camera and I,* New York and Berlin, 1969; Joris Ivens and Robert Distangue, *Joris Ivens ou la mémoire d'un regard,* Paris, 1982; Thomas Waugh, ed., *"Show Us Life": Toward a History and Aesthetics of the Committed Documentary,* Metuchen, N.J., 1984.

THOMAS WAUGH

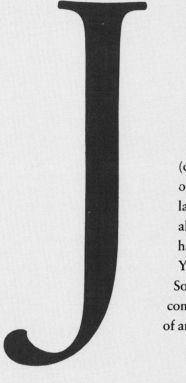

(d$_\textrm{Ʒ}$ $\bar{e}^{\textrm{ı}}$), the tenth letter of the alphabet in English and other modern languages, is, in its origin, a comparatively late modification of the letter I. In the ancient Roman alphabet, I, besides its vowel value in *ibīdem, mīlitis*, had the kindred consonantal value of modern English Y, as in *iactus, iam, Iouem, iūstus, adiūro, maior, peior*. Some time before the sixth century, this *y*-sound had, by compression in articulation, and consequent development of an initial 'stop', become a consonantal diphthong. . . .

JAKOBSON, ROMAN (1896–1982)

Russian-born linguist. A founder of the Prague school of structural LINGUISTICS, Roman Osipovich Jakobson also did work in literary theory, LITERARY CRITICISM, and FOLKLORE and was a major figure in the study of Russian and Slavic languages and literature, POETICS, SEMIOTICS, child LANGUAGE, and aphasia (see SPEECH AND LANGUAGE DISORDERS). Human communication in general and language in particular as its primary vehicle were concerns that permeated every period of his life and unified every facet of his work.

Born and educated in prerevolutionary Moscow, Jakobson in 1915 became a founding member and the first president of the Moscow Linguistic Circle, which examined questions of poetics and the poetic use of language and many of whose members were associated with a school of thought known as Russian formalism. Jakobson himself acknowledged that his fascination with linguistics grew out of his love of literature and was particularly ignited by the innovations of the Russian AVANT-GARDE poets Velemir Vladimirovich Khlebnikov and Vladimir Vladimirovich Mayakovski.

In 1920 he moved to Prague and in 1926 cofounded the Prague Linguistic Circle, whose members pursued the structure and function of PHONOLOGY, morphology, and poetics. FERDINAND DE SAUSSURE's ideas of the bipartite nature of the linguistic SIGN as signifier and signified in *langue* and *parole,* the linguistic sign's relations on the paradigmatic and syntagmatic axes, and its opposition to other signs formed the basis of much of the group's investigations. However, the Prague linguists rejected Saussure's dichotomy of a synchronic view of language as a static system opposed to a diachronic view of it as dynamic. They believed that the system is always interacting with itself. They also questioned the Saussurian doctrine of the arbitrariness of the linguistic sign, which was that there was no connection between the elements of a sign that would make any particular signifier (the "sound-image") the natural vehicle for a particular signified (the concept associated with the sound-image). *See also* STRUCTURALISM.

During the 1920s and 1930s Jakobson, together with N. S. Trubetzkoy, developed the central notions of the distinctive features in phonology and their operation in binary oppositions. One term of the opposition was "marked" for the feature; the other term, "unmarked." Jakobson took this work a step further by analyzing the semantic structure of morphological as well as phonological units in terms of markedness and the binary organization of conceptual features. At the root of these advances is the idea of *relational invariance*—that is, of the integrity of linguistic units, which vary contextually but maintain systematic relations to the other units in the system.

When the Germans occupied Czechoslovakia, Jakobson fled to Scandinavia, where he found more confirmation of the distinctive features of his groundbreaking work on LANGUAGE ACQUISITION in children and language loss through aphasia. In 1941 he arrived in New York, where he flourished as a teacher, first at the École des Hautes Études and then at Columbia University. In 1943 he cofounded the New York Linguistic Circle.

In 1949 Jakobson moved to Harvard University, where he exercised a profound influence on the next several generations of U.S. Slavicists. This period is also characterized by collaborative research with scientists in the fields of acoustics, communication theory, and MATHEMATICS. From 1960 until his death in 1982 he taught at both Harvard and the Massachusetts Institute of Technology.

The repercussions of Jakobson's ideas are evident in much subsequent work in linguistics in the United States. His student and collaborator Morris Halle modified the phonological distinctive features into generative phonology in the early 1960s. U.S. linguist Noam Chomsky, in his transformational GRAMMAR, reversed the principle of relational invariance by resolving syntactic variations into hypothetical deep structures. The surface variations could be derived by rules, but at the cost of what Jakobson considered the semantic focus of those variants. The opposition of conceptual features, however, remained the hallmark of the morphological and lexical work of Jakobson's student C. H. van Schooneveld.

See also SEMANTICS.

Bibliography. Elmar Holenstein, *Roman Jakobson's Approach to Language: Phenomenological Structuralism,* Bloomington, Ind., 1976; Roman Jakobson, *Selected Writings,* 2d ed., 7 vols., The Hague, 1971–1982; Roman Jakobson and Krystyna Pomorska, *Dialogues,* Cambridge, Mass., 1983.

ROBERT A. FRADKIN

JAMES, WILLIAM (1842–1910)

U.S. thinker and educator. Originally a physical scientist (with an M.D. from Harvard Medical School), William James then became a psychologist and scholar of RELIGION and ethics, but he is best known as the leader of the influential movement in U.S. philosophy called pragmatism. Eldest child of the eccentric philosophical theologian Henry James, Sr., and brother of the novelist Henry James, William James contributed crucially to the transition from Victorian to modern conceptions of reality and of human COGNITION. His persistent opposition to abstraction and absolutism and his emphasis instead on the experiential and conditional had a telling influence on twentieth-century

Figure 1. *(James, William)* William James. The Bettmann Archive, Inc.

developments in communications theory. James's work demonstrated a marked continuity across his several fields, each of which he taught, in succession, as a Harvard faculty member from 1872 to 1907. In each instance he took an established subject and worked a similar kind of modern transformation on it—away from abstract, a priori reasoning and static, transcendental, and absolute understandings toward concrete, functional emphases and dynamic, experiential, and conditional outlooks.

James's work in psychology, epitomized by his classic two-volume *Principles of Psychology* (1890), rejected the atomism and mechanical associationism of older schools. Instead James proposed a "functional psychology" that defined mental life not as passive before phenomena but as purposive and continually changing and that focused not on the mind's supposedly fixed, abstract structure but on the experiential consequences of the mind's actions. James's view of cognition emphasized the importance of symbolic knowledge of the world, in addition to that known through direct, unmediated observation. He thus participated in the emergence of modern conceptions of the role of symbols in the formation and communication of human thought processes (*see* SEMIOTICS; SIGN; SYMBOLISM). In his 1894 presidential address to the American Psychological Association, he introduced this point with a famous example:

There are two ways of knowing things, knowing them immediately or intuitively, and knowing them conceptually or representatively. Although such things as the white paper before our eyes can be known intuitively, most of the things we know, the tigers now in India, for example, or the scholastic system of philosophy, are known only representatively or symbolically.

James's next major works, *The Will to Believe and Other Essays in Popular Philosophy* (1897) and *The Varieties of Religious Experience* (1902), subjected religion to the same kind of empirical scrutiny he believed all phenomena must undergo. He characteristically went for evidence not to religious institutions or theological systems but to spontaneous religious experience itself. Radically reconstructing certain fundamental religious ideas, James held here that experience did not support the traditional notions of an infinite, omnipotent, and personal God and of life after death but did suggest the existence of a diffused "higher part of the universe" that works for the good and helps humankind to achieve it.

Pragmatism was first used as a term in the 1870s by U.S. philosopher CHARLES S. PEIRCE but was more fully developed and altered by James in popular works such as his 1907 *Pragmatism: A New Name for Some Old Ways of Thinking.* (The philosophy should not be confused with notions of expediency or commercial efficiency.) James rejected the metaphysical idealism that prevailed in the philosophy of his day, holding instead that the MEANING or validity of any idea or value can ultimately be found only in the succession of experiential consequences it leads to. James's view here of truth—not as an a priori, static imperative transcending experience but as arising concretely out of what he called "agreement with reality"—generated a vigorous new movement in Western philosophy and intellectual culture at the dawn of the twentieth century, inspiring younger philosophers such as JOHN DEWEY, who became one of its best-known later exponents. *See also* WITTGENSTEIN, LUDWIG.

Not a complete materialist or relativist, James confessed to a "piecemeal supernaturalism" (i.e., based on the evidence he saw for a "higher part of the universe"), and his pragmatism does imply the existence of an objective reality outside individual consciousness. James's modernism lay instead in his emphasis on the fluidity of that external reality and on the conditionality of any knowledge we can ever have about it—beliefs that led him to exhort a constant skepticism about any absolute, fixed understandings of reality and a constant reevaluation of our own conceptions against the ever-changing particulars of what he called "the total context of experience." These beliefs form almost a manifesto for modern communications.

Bibliography. Gay Wilson Allen, *William James: A Biography,* New York and London, 1967; Jacques Barzun, *A*

Stroll with William James, New York, 1983; Gerald E. Myers, *William James: His Life and Thought,* New Haven, Conn., 1986; Ralph Barton Perry, *The Thought and Character of William James,* 2 vols., Boston, 1935; Andrew J. Reck, *Introduction to William James: An Essay and Selected Texts,* Bloomington, Ind., 1967.

JOSEPH CADY

JOHNSON, SAMUEL (1709–1784)

English man of letters, lexicographer, biographer, and journalist. Samuel Johnson was the leading literary figure in the Britain of his time, which scholars often call "the Age of Johnson." He not only achieved great fame in his lifetime, but, as the subject of one of the most famous biographies in any LANGUAGE, James Boswell's *Life of Samuel Johnson* (1791), his life, conversation, and correspondence have become intimately known to more than two centuries of readers. Johnson is the most frequently quoted writer of English PROSE in the world today. His contributions to the history of communications are manifold, from his youthful attack on CENSORSHIP (*A Complete Vindication of the Licensers of the Stage,* 1739) to his popularization of literary BIOGRAPHY (*Lives of the English Poets,* 1779–1781), but most important are his role in the establishment of the writer as an independent person free from the influences of patronage, and his *Dictionary of the English Language* (1755).

The son of a struggling provincial bookseller, Johnson was born in Lichfield and was educated locally; he started college at Oxford in 1728. His poverty compelled him to leave college after just thirteen months, ending his formal education. He later received honorary degrees from Trinity College, Dublin, in 1765 and from Oxford University in 1775. After five years of desultory reading, writing, translation, and teaching, Johnson married a widow some years older than himself, Elizabeth Porter, in 1735. His effort to found a school, using much of his wife's small inheritance, failed, and in 1737 Johnson moved to London to commence a career of writing for his living. The next twelve years show the emergence of all the major projects that distinguished his career. Between 1737 and 1749 he undertook a variety of journalistic tasks, writing book reviews and composing parliamentary debates (Parliament's proceedings in the mid-eighteenth century were still secret, but Johnson, writing for the *Gentleman's Magazine,* actually composed debates on the legislative issues of the day so plausible that they were taken for originals well into the next century). He produced his first biographies, began the editing of Shakespeare's works that would lead to his influential edition of all the plays (1765), wrote his two imitative satirical poems (*London,* 1738, and *The Vanity of Human Wishes,* 1749), and started work on his *Dictionary.* In the

1750s he turned to periodical essays, writing or contributing to three different series, one of which, *The Rambler* (1750–1752), is without parallel among collections of English essays, comparing equally with the *Essays* of Francis Bacon. He produced a philosophical novel, *Rasselas,* in 1759, the same year as the appearance of Voltaire's *Candide,* with which it is often compared. In addition to his edition of Shakespeare and some able political pamphlets (*see also* PAMPHLET), Johnson published *A Journey to the Western Islands of Scotland* (1775) and a series of biographies of English poets for a multivolume edition of their writings. In his later years Johnson's persistent poverty was somewhat alleviated by a small annual pension from the crown and considerably reduced by his intimacy with the wealthy Thrale family, especially Mrs. Hester Thrale. His last years are notable for the intimacy in which he lived with a number of friends who would become his biographers in the years after his death. More biographies of Johnson appeared in the decade after his death than of any other figure in literary history in a comparable period, and, through the version of Boswell, Johnson's has become the best known of all literary careers.

In 1746 Johnson signed a contract with a group of publishers for his *Dictionary;* soon thereafter he addressed an ambitious *Plan* for this work to the fourth earl of Chesterfield, one of the nation's richest

Figure 1. (*Johnson, Samuel*) Joshua Reynolds, *Samuel Johnson,* 1756. National Portrait Gallery, London.

men and most active literary patrons. From Chesterfield's initial encouragement of this project and his later neglect of Johnson while the work was under way derives Johnson's great contribution to authorial independence. Early in 1755, when the work was nearly ready for publication, Chesterfield renewed his interest in it, but Johnson, unwilling to acknowledge support from someone who had not materially aided him, spurned the earl's interest in a splendid LETTER that has become both an evocation of the age of the independent writer and the most famous single literary epistle in the English language. Although this letter was not published in Johnson's lifetime, his position on authorial independence and patronage became widely known.

The contribution of the *Dictionary* to modern lexicography is enormous. Johnson did not set forth deliberately to fix the MEANING of words, although his work has sometimes been thought to have that effect. Instead, he tried to "register" the meanings of words as representative English authors of the previous two centuries had used them. What he did that was new for his time was to extend to the English dictionary the techniques of the RENAISSANCE lexicons of the classical and biblical languages, which had illustrated the various uses of individual words with quotations from the best authors. The *Dictionary* was the first English lexicon to employ illustrative quotations, often in a copious manner suggesting that Johnson sought to record the intellectual history of his times through his dictionary. Just as the idea of Johnson's *Dictionary* derives from JOHN LOCKE's call for STANDARDS of usage, so subsequent English dictionaries derive directly from Johnson's seminal work, down to the nineteenth-century *New English Dictionary* (completed in the twentieth century and now called the *Oxford English Dictionary*). Publication of Johnson's *Dictionary* brought him fame, if not fortune, and through its many abridgments and editions would carry Johnson's name, ideas about language, and clear definitions on into our own century.

Johnson's career is notable for the number of genres in which he specialized; one of his early biographers listed twelve areas in which he had achieved excellence (*see* GENRE). Yet through his miscellaneous output runs an important thread for communications history: Johnson's reliance on the publishers of his century for his livelihood. Before Johnson, authors had to rely on some form of patronage, but in his time it became possible for a writer successfully to negotiate with the new lords of the press, the publishers. Johnson's role in the evolution of the concept of literary property is pivotal for his century. During his life as well as through his influence, the encyclopedic quality of Johnson's knowledge and achievement best characterizes his contribution to the history of communications.

See also ARTIST AND SOCIETY; AUTHORSHIP; LANGUAGE REFERENCE BOOK; LITERARY CRITICISM; PUBLISHING; WEBSTER, NOAH.

Bibliography. W. Jackson Bate, *Samuel Johnson,* New York and London, 1977; James L. Clifford, *Dictionary Johnson: Samuel Johnson's Middle Years,* New York, 1979; Robert De Maria, Jr., *Johnson's Dictionary and the Language of Learning,* Chapel Hill, N.C., 1986; Alvin Kernan, *Printing Technology, Letters and Samuel Johnson,* Princeton, N.J., 1987; James H. Sledd and Gwin J. Kolb, *Dr. Johnson's Dictionary: Essays in the Biography of a Book,* Chicago, 1955.

PAUL J. KORSHIN

JOURNAL. See AUTOBIOGRAPHY; DIARY.

JOURNALISM. See COMMUNICATIONS, STUDY OF; NEWSPAPER: HISTORY; NEWSPAPER: TRENDS; PHOTOJOURNALISM.

JUDAISM

The Jews are a people scattered throughout the countries of the world yet connected ultimately by a sense of shared origins, historic destiny, and common identity. The development and continuity of Judaism, despite centuries of dispersion and MIGRATION (*see* DIASPORA), can be traced to elements in the heritage of the Jewish people that contribute to processes of communication linking diverse communities of the Jewish world.

From the early beginnings the Jews interacted with other nations and civilizations, but they preserved a distinctive consciousness. As a small minority among the peoples of the ancient Near East, Persia, Greece, and Rome, and within Islamic and Christian societies, the Jewish people were subject to the impact of these environments. At the same time, mutual influence through the ages led the surrounding cultures to adopt certain features of Judaism.

Judaism has many similarities to such other members of the monotheistic family of religions as Christianity and Islam, but a variety of practices and assumptions are not shared (*see* RELIGION). Adherence to monotheism, the main tenet of Judaism, set the Jews apart from other nations beginning in the ancient Near East. This self-image as a people with a sense of religious mission found expression in the belief in a covenant contracted between God and the ancestors of the Jews, introducing the notions of the divine election and future redemption of the nation.

Jewish law and writings. The traditions and ethical teachings that have become associated with Judaism are contained in the law and prophetic writings collected in the Hebrew Bible, which is the foundation of Jewish life and thought. The Torah, considered the holiest and most authoritative text, is read in synagogues from manuscript scrolls that continue to be copied by hand by highly skilled scribes. This care for the transmission of the written law from generation to generation is one symbol of the divine authority accorded the canonized books of the Bible. Supplementary to the written law there developed a body of oral law claimed to have been communicated from teacher to student since the time of Moses, which is accepted as binding by mainstream or Rabbinic Judaism. *See* SCRIPTURE; WRITING.

The principles of Rabbinic Judaism characterize the most widespread and influential belief system of Jewry to the present day. According to Rabbinic Judaism, Jewish law is continually adapted and interpreted by commentators, or rabbis, whose discussions contribute new layers of meaning to the prescriptions regarding RITUAL and practical matters. These opinions and decisions, the dissenting ones alongside those of the majority, were eventually codified in the Talmud, which consists of the basic texts of Rabbinic Judaism—the Mishnah and the Gemara. In addition, a body of popular interpretive literature known as the Midrash elaborates on the literal text of the Bible by employing legends, parables, and aphorisms.

Succeeding generations of scholars reinterpreted the opinions of their predecessors, creating a body of doctrine that was meant to preserve the essential features of Judaism in light of new social realities. Deliberations and interpretations of the Talmud continued in the various academies that emerged in all parts of the Jewish world community. They are also discussed in rabbinic Responsa, discursive written replies to inquiries on all aspects of Jewish law. This legalistic and poetic literature on the governance of ritual observance and social behavior, in general, embodies the basis of Judaism as a cultural system and facilitates communication among Jews throughout the world.

Institutions and community. Judaism advocates the merits of studying the Torah and other traditional texts for knowledge of the regulations that guide Jewish life. This emphasis on learning and EDUCATION for the whole people resulted in the obligatory establishment of religious schools by every Jewish community. Another institution in which Jews assembled for study of sacred writings, public discussion of communal issues, and prayer is the synagogue. Although the ARCHITECTURE and interior of synagogues reflect contemporary styles of the local society, these structures exhibit common classic features prescribed by tradition, as well as distinctive Jewish motifs and symbols. The synagogue has become a center of Jewish life, functioning as a house of assembly that supports a variety of activities within the community.

The communal structures developed by Jews to mediate internal affairs and to communicate with the surrounding non-Jewish populace have varied in range and scope depending on place and time. However, in attending to the needs of its members, the organized Jewish community (the kehillah) proceeded in accordance with Jewish principles. In addition to establishing synagogues, cemeteries, religious courts, and ritual baths, aid to the needy was carried out at the community level by voluntary associations whose services were funded through charity contributions and a special tax. Conformity to the norms of the community was virtually guaranteed by a kind of excommunication (herem) administered by the elders, which banned the outcast from any contact. Community leaders also served as liaisons in the collection of levies that were transferred to the local authorities.

The administrative systems that Jewish communities established to manage their everyday affairs allowed them a wide measure of autonomy. Although it was not the purpose of the rulers of the countries who enforced segregation of the Jews from the rest of society, the modes of self-governing community life to which Jews adhered throughout the Diaspora enabled them to develop their group life independently. Communication among the various individual administrative bodies was made possible by centralized decision making and legislation on the part of regional councils that convened representatives to resolve issues common to the area's communities. These gatherings occurred, for example, when major Jewish settlements flourished in Babylon, the Ottoman Empire, and eastern Europe.

The era of reforms. The structure provided by the Jewish community for organizational life and cultural continuity was challenged by the processes of modernization and secularization. The leadership of the kehillah, perpetuated in the hands of the rabbinate whose judicial power as communal and religious authorities allowed them to guide Jewish life until the late eighteenth and early nineteenth centuries, was threatened by the Enlightenment and its promotion of Jewish emancipation and secular education.

One impact of reforms in western and eastern Europe was to shake the religious unity that had lasted from the first to the seventeenth century. Forces that were altering the social and political climate of Europe questioned the Jewish traditional mode of life and offered new views on the state of Jewry. Rather than separateness, an IDEOLOGY of integration and equal citizenship led to varied responses on the part of Jews. Many enlightened intellectuals converted to Christianity in an attempt to resolve the problematic dilemma of gaining entry into European

Figure 1. *(Judaism)* Cornell Capa, *Talmudic Scholars, Israel, 1955.* © Magnum Photos, Inc., New York.

society as members of a group whose rituals, CUL-TURE, LANGUAGE, and CLOTHING marked them as different.

Another path was taken by many others who chose to balance acceptance of emancipation with preservation of Jewish identity. Out of this new trend to adapt traditional Judaism to contemporary conditions there eventually evolved the main denominations of modern Judaism—Reform, Conservative, Orthodox, and Reconstructionist—and the expression of secular interpretations of Jewish identity.

The encounter with modernity is characterized by increased communication between Judaism and the non-Jewish world, which provoked a multiplicity of responses and redefinitions of Jewish identity. New attitudes in Europe regarding the possibility of na-tional independence influenced the reawakening of Jewish nationalism. Although Jewish prayer recurrently expresses a yearning for return to the homeland, the idea of Jewish national rebirth in Israel—Zionism—was crystallized as a modern political movement only in the nineteenth century.

Anti-Semitism and the Diaspora. A significant impetus to the growth of Zionism was the spread of anti-Jewish sentiments throughout western Europe, central Europe, and particularly in Russia, as the spirit of emancipation that granted equal rights to Jews reversed itself in manifestations of anti-Semitism. The hostility and violence that Jews suffered in their attempt to integrate into the local society heightened their support of the idea of settlement in the land of Israel as a solution to their problem. Discriminatory policies, economic hardships, and government-sponsored anti-Semitic pogroms in this period also spurred Jewish migration to other refuges, including the United States.

Although wandering and immigration characterize the Jewish nation from its early origins, the map of the Jewish world was visibly changed by migrations and persecutions of the late nineteenth and twentieth centuries. Between 1880 and 1920 more than two and a half million Jews left eastern Europe. The end of World War II marked another period of mass migration, mainly to Israel on the part of survivors of the Nazi holocaust in Europe and Jews in Muslim countries who had been uprooted from their homes. The modern state of Israel, established in 1948, maintains close ties with Jewish communities in the Diaspora for whom activity of various kinds on behalf of Israel has become one of the most visible signs of Jewish affiliation.

Jewish life has long been characterized by the existence of autonomous Jewish settlements under foreign power linked to the focal point of Israel. This dispersion resulted in differences among Jewish ethnic communities as time went on. Similarities were reinforced by emissaries who traveled to the various communities in the first and second centuries C.E., for example. They relayed the regulations and recommendations established by the Sanhedrin, a court of Jewish sages that formulated rulings to enable Jewish life to continue uniformly. In other periods contact was also maintained among Talmudic scholars and as a result of the commerce and trade activities of Jewish merchants. The rhythm of the Jewish CALENDAR and FESTIVAL timetable, the Jewish week (which culminates in a Sabbath day of rest), and the Jewish life cycle guides the shared cultural framework of diverse Jewish communities.

Language. Nonetheless, it is important to mark the varieties of languages, customs, ART forms, and creativity that distinguish Jewish ethnic groups. Influenced by the culture of their adopted region of settlement, Jews have generally spoken the language of their neighbors, often developing their own dialect versions of these or evolving a distinctive language of their own. Hebrew was retained as the dominant language of worship and was taught to children at an early age. LITERACY, as a result, has been generally high among Jews. In recent times Hebrew has been revived as a spoken language and has become the official language of Israel.

The linguistic map of Jewry reflects the process by which local tongues were combined with Hebrew and Aramaic components to form written and spoken Jewish languages. The Hebrew ALPHABET, as the basic medium of education, is used for writing these other languages, the most widespread of which are Judeo-Spanish (Ladino and Judezmo) and Yiddish.

The first emerged from the experience of descendants of the Jewish exiles from Spain and Portugal, expelled in 1492 during the Inquisition, who settled in North Africa, the Balkans, and other areas in the Ottoman Empire and later in parts of Europe. This category of Jews has come to be known as Sephardim, a term often used to include Jews from Muslim countries of Asia and Africa. Yiddish, on the other hand, is the language closely associated with Ashkenazim, the other principal designation that encompasses Jews of European and Slavic extraction. These two major groupings and the many Jewish subcommunities they represent exhibit distinctive dress, music, art, foodways, and observances in addition to their particular patterns of linguistic and literary productivity.

Along these lines there were also two characteristic forms of Hebrew script, Ashkenazi and Sephardi, which remained intact even after the invention of PRINTING with movable type in the fifteenth century. The art of producing and illustrating Hebrew manuscripts had always been valued in Jewish society, but Jewish and Christian printers facilitated the dissemination of many copies of Hebrew editions of biblical texts and other books, which had a major impact on the spread of Jewish culture and scholarship. Changes in the standardized printed Hebrew letter forms did not occur until the nineteenth and twentieth centuries. These trends in Hebrew printing parallel the rise of Jewish national social movements in Europe, which introduced new developments in modern Hebrew and Yiddish culture.

Under the influence of the European Enlightenment, modern Jewish literature in Hebrew and Yiddish blossomed in a new, secular domain. In pre–World War II eastern Europe this literary activity flourished alongside a vital Jewish press, a thriving network of Jewish schools, research institutes, and Jewish theatrical innovation. Estimates are that in Poland, for example, two hundred Jewish journals in Polish, Hebrew, and Yiddish were published before the destruction of this vibrant community by the Nazis.

In 1939 there were approximately ten million Yiddish speakers in the world, mainly concentrated in the eastern European centers of Jewish culture. As a result of the holocaust as well as the natural process of linguistic assimilation, dwindling numbers of Jews maintain active use of a specifically Jewish language, except for the case of Hebrew in Israel. Jews have always contributed in the language of the prevailing society to the national literature and other cultural spheres, including the mass media. The award of the Nobel Prize for literature to Isaac Bashevis Singer in 1978 drew attention to Yiddish literature and helped to spur renewed interest in that language.

As ethnic identification is reexamined and reevaluated in the United States and other nations, especially on the part of the grandchildren of immigrants, Jews join other minorities in the search for ways to communicate their identity, albeit in new forms. Modern Jewish identity is a fusion of ethnic, national, religious, and historical components. The transmission of Judaism occurs in a variety of ways as the cultural system unfolds and changes. In the post–World War II era the Nazi holocaust and the rise of the state of Israel have had an important effect on Jewish group solidarity and self-preservation. Despite the wide variety of possible affiliational paths that Jews can adopt, the unity of the Jewish people in many lands is maintained through the observance and preservation of shared traditions.

Bibliography. *Algemeyne Entsiklopedye: Serye Yidn*, Vols. 1–7, Paris and New York, 1934–1966; Salo W. Baron, *A Social and Religious History of the Jews*, 2d ed., Vols. 1–18, New York, 1952–; Lucjan Dobroszycki and Barbara Kirshenblatt-Gimblett, *Image before My Eyes: A Photographic History of Jewish Life in Poland, 1864–1939*, New York, 1977; Louis Finkelstein, *The Jews: Their History, Culture, and Religion* (1949), 4th ed., 2 vols., New York, 1970–1971; Jewish Encyclopedic Handbooks, *The Jewish People, Past and Present*, 3 vols., New York, 1946–1952; Elihu Katz and Michael Gurevitch, *The Secularization of Leisure: Culture and Communication in Israel*, Cambridge, Mass., 1976; Cecil Roth, *The Jewish Contribution to Civilisation*, Oxford, 1945, reprint London, 1956.

HANNAH KLIGER

JUNG, CARL (1875–1961)

Swiss psychological theorist who ranks as one of the most important psychologists of the twentieth century. Carl Gustav Jung is best known as SIGMUND FREUD's chosen successor to lead the psychoanalytic movement, also as the first president of the International Psychoanalytic Society and the founder of his own school of analytical psychology after his break with Freud in 1914. His formative teachers in psychiatry were Eugen Bleuler (Zurich) and Pierre Janet (Paris). After early studies in word association and dementia praecox that initiated his contact with Freud, Jung went on to develop an influential classification of personality types and eventually a theory of the collective unconscious that has important implications for the study of communication as well as of CULTURE, mythology, and RELIGION.

The contribution of Jung to the study of communication developed primarily in response to Freudian psychoanalytic theory. Although he accepted Freud's general concept of the unconscious, Jung denied its instinctual—especially its sexual—nature, asserting instead the religious ground of our "undiscovered self." He also rejected the necessity and dynamic quality of what Freud called the psychic mechanism of repression. In place of the instincts Jung proposed a series of universal cultural archetypes that underlie the personal unconscious, originating in the impersonal "collective unconscious." These archetypal motifs, such as the "persona" and "shadow," the "anima" and "animus," define the basic forms of the psyche. They are suprahistorical, transcultural, and not reducible to their particular individual and collective representations. According to Jung, archetypes specify a transcendent order.

Jung implicitly identified two levels of communication: the intrapsychic and the interpersonal. Intrapsychic communication is problematic insofar as the individual psyche develops a neurotic imbalance that prevents conscious expression of archetypal representations. The task of Jungian psychotherapy is to work toward the recognition of hidden parts of the personality and to correct the imbalance with compensatory expressions. This task is accomplished through INTERPERSONAL COMMUNICATION in which the analyst helps the patient to bring repressed contents to light—for example, by interpreting fantasies and dreams. As in the case of Freudian therapy, each individual becomes something of an artist of private life because there is a touch of the artist in every person. However, this artist in every person remains merely potential, lacking the power to articulate and to communicate until released by the analyst. With the analyst's help the patient grows into a successful but limited artist by creating a set of interpersonal meanings. But in contrast to Freudian theory this set of meanings constitutes a personal myth that integrates the individual into a universal and saving symbol system that can fairly be described as religious in function.

In Jung's vision the modern individual suffers from the failure to experience and therefore to communicate eternal archetypal forms in a cold and rationalist world. Ironically, the more successful one is at creating a personal, saving myth, the more one is authorized to withdraw from the public world into the therapeutic security of a private religion.

See also ARTIST AND SOCIETY; FOLKLORE; PSYCHOANALYSIS.

Bibliography. Frieda Fordham, *An Introduction to Jung's Psychology*, 3d ed., London, 1966; C. G. Jung, *Modern Man in Search of a Soul*, New York and London, 1933, reprint 1961; idem, *The Portable Jung*, ed. by Joseph Campbell, trans. by R. F. C. Hull, New York, 1971; idem, *Psychology and Religion* (1938), 2d ed., Princeton, N.J., 1969; Philip Rieff, *The Triumph of the Therapeutic: Uses of Faith after Freud*, New York, 1966.

ALAN N. WOOLFOLK

K

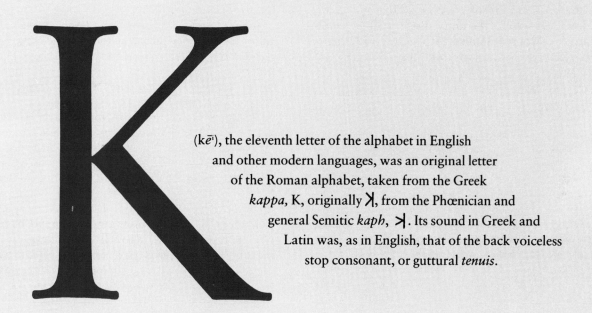

(kē¹), the eleventh letter of the alphabet in English and other modern languages, was an original letter of the Roman alphabet, taken from the Greek *kappa*, K, originally ⪫, from the Phœnician and general Semitic *kaph*, ⪫. Its sound in Greek and Latin was, as in English, that of the back voiceless stop consonant, or guttural *tenuis*.

KELLER, HELEN (1880–1968)

U.S. author, lecturer, and champion of the communication needs of the handicapped—a subject illuminated by her own life. At the age of nineteen months Helen Adams Keller was stricken with a disease that was diagnosed as acute congestion of the stomach and brain. She was left deaf, blind, and mute and became a wild and destructive child, existing in a private world of darkness and silence. Her father, publisher of a weekly newspaper and a local government official, contacted the Perkins Institute in Boston, which specialized in the rehabilitation of the blind. The director at Perkins recommended a recent graduate, Anne Sullivan, herself partially blind, who traveled to the Keller home in Tuscumbia, Alabama, and began her celebrated and determined efforts to penetrate Helen's isolation and to make possible communication between her and the world around her.

To gain ascendancy over Keller, Sullivan used a mixture of stern discipline and loving tenderness. Into Keller's hand she spelled out the names of objects, using a manual ALPHABET. Keller readily learned and could repeat the alphabetic signs but could not at first comprehend how they were related to objects until, two weeks after they had begun, Sullivan held Keller's hand under a pump and spelled the word *water*. Within a few months of this event she had learned three hundred words and had written a letter to her mother.

Keller and Sullivan traveled together to Boston, where they became associated with the Perkins Institute and where Keller began to develop an interest in helping others who were impaired in similar ways. In 1894 they moved to New York so that Keller could attend the Wright-Humason School, which specialized in TEACHING the deaf to speak. Two years later Keller enrolled in the Cambridge School for Young Ladies to prepare for entry into college. Within nine months she had passed the first admission tests to Radcliffe; in 1900 she was admitted. Sullivan attended every class with Keller, tirelessly spelling the lectures into her hand. In 1904 Keller graduated cum laude with distinction in English. In the meantime, with the help of Sullivan and Harvard instructor John Macy, she had written her AUTOBIOGRAPHY, *The Story of My Life*, which was published in 1903.

For the career of advocacy she now undertook, Keller depended largely on patrons, but she also proved adept at raising money on her own, writing steadily and even delivering lectures on the vaudeville circuit. In 1917 she produced a feature motion picture, *Deliverance*, dramatizing her emergence into human society; for this she and Sullivan jointly coached the actors. A more telling enactment of her story came late in her long life with the television play *The Miracle Worker* (1957), by William Gibson, later

Figure 1. *(Keller, Helen)* Helen Keller, Anne Sullivan Macy, and Alexander Graham Bell. Courtesy of the Alexander Graham Bell Association for the Deaf, Volta Bureau Library, Washington, D.C.

developed into a successful stage play (1958) and still later into two motion pictures (1962, 1979) under the same title. Keller and her story became an invaluable aid to the American Foundation for the Blind in carrying its message to the public. She was especially proud of helping to bring the subject of ophthalmia neonatorum (blindness of the newborn) into the open; caused by venereal disease, it had been an unmentionable subject.

Keller lived until 1968, the recipient of honorary degrees from Temple and Harvard Universities and of a presidential Medal of Freedom.

See also NONVERBAL COMMUNICATION; SIGN LANGUAGE; SPEECH AND LANGUAGE DISORDERS; TOUCH.

Bibliography. Helen Keller, *The Story of My Life*, New York, 1903, reprint 1954; Joseph P. Lash, *Helen and Teacher*, New York, 1980.

ROBERT BALAY

KENYATTA, JOMO (1893?–1978)

Kenyan journalist who became a leader in the African nationalist movement and, in 1964, the first president

Figure 1. *(Kenyatta, Jomo)* Jomo Kenyatta.
UPI/Bettmann Newsphotos.

of independent Kenya—a position he held until his death. A member of the Kikuyu tribe, the largest ethnic component of Kenya, Jomo Kenyatta spent his early years as a shepherd guarding his father's flock. He started schooling late but soon showed literary and linguistic gifts. While in school he assisted in the translation of passages of the New Testament into Kikuyu. In his mid-twenties he served as interpreter for the Supreme Court in Nairobi. About this time he dropped his original name, Johnstone Kamau, and took the name Kenyatta. To make Kenyans aware and proud of their heritage became his overriding concern. Appointed general secretary of the Kikuyu Central Association, he became the first editor of its journal, *Muiguithania* (The Reconciler), the first periodical published by indigenous Kenyans. It voiced the grievances of tribe members whose lands had been taken by settlers. Kenyatta often represented such cases at hearings, both in the colony and before commissions in London.

During a sixteen-year stay in Europe (1930–1946), based in England, he served constantly as spokesman for African nationalist viewpoints and demands. In articles and books such as *Facing Mount Kenya* (1938), *My People of Kikuyu* (1942), and *Kenya: The Land of Conflict* (1945) he wrote eloquently about his land and its people, describing their way of life as superior to that of Europeans and criticizing the colonial system (*see* COLONIZATION).

In 1946 he returned home to take up a teaching appointment and soon afterward was elected president of the Kenya African Union (KAU). He skillfully developed this into a political organization, the Kenya African National Union, focusing on the nationalist struggle. In 1952 the colonial government charged him with secretly instigating the Mau Mau uprisings. His arrest, trial, and nine-year detention tended to enhance his status as the father of the nationalist movement. He was released in 1961. When Kenya won independence two years later, Kenyatta became prime minister. A year later, when the country was proclaimed a republic, he became its president.

Mzee ("Old Man") Kenyatta used all his oratorical and writing skills to exhort his people to the tasks of national development, unity, and reconciliation. The political stability and steady socioeconomic progress that Kenya witnessed under President Kenyatta favored the development of communications. Private and foreign ownership of newspapers and magazines was permitted, and Kenyan newspapers were among the best in Africa (*see* NEWSPAPER: TRENDS—TRENDS IN AFRICA). RADIO and television broadcasting systems and telecommunications facilities were expanded, though largely concentrated in the few urban areas. The Kenyan capital, Nairobi, developed into a communications center and focal point for INTERNATIONAL ORGANIZATIONS and conferences.

See also AFRICA, TWENTIETH CENTURY.

Bibliography. Guy Arnold, *Kenyatta and the Politics of Kenya*, London, 1974; Jeremy Murray-Brown, *Kenyatta*, London, 1974.

S. T. KWAME BOAFO

KINESICS

Defined by the U.S. anthropologist Ray L. Birdwhistell in 1952 as the study of the communicative functions of body motion in face-to-face interaction. The term now has wider application, but its original use referred to an approach in which patterns of body motion such as FACIAL EXPRESSION, GESTURE, bodily carriage, and posture are viewed as culturally patterned and learned by individuals in the course of becoming competent users of the face-to-face communication systems of their culture. The socially coded nature of bodily communication was discussed earlier by the linguist EDWARD SAPIR, but Birdwhistell was the first to suggest that it could be analyzed using techniques developed in LINGUISTICS.

Complementing the work of the U.S. linguist George L. Trager on paralanguage, Birdwhistell proposed a terminology and conceptual framework for kinesics parallel to that employed in American structural linguistics. The least discriminable contrastive unit of body motion was termed the *kineme*, on analogy with the phoneme. Kinemes were postulated to occur in regular combinations, or *kinemorphs,* and these in turn were thought to be organized into *kinemorphic constructions.* For example, for a given cultural group only one kineme of eyebrow raise would be established if the members of the group distinguished only two facial configurations as communicatively significant, according to whether the brows were raised or not, regardless of the different degrees of eyebrow raise that could be found by measurement in different individuals or on different occasions. The combination of different eyebrow-raise kinemes with kinemes of mouth and eyelid movement produces different facial kinemorphs. Such facial kinemorphs themselves may combine in various ways with different combinations of kinemes of arm and hand movement, head movement, and the like. In greeting, for instance, the head may be thrown back at the same time as the eyebrows are raised and lowered rapidly, the mouth opened in a smile, the arm raised in a wave. The smile combined with eyebrow movement, the wave, and the head movement are all examples of kinemorphs. Their combination in this pattern is a kinemorphic construction. The communicative significance or "meaning" of this construction would then be determined through a study of the interactional contexts of its occurrence, following procedures of context analysis developed by Birdwhistell's colleague Albert Scheflen, a psychiatrist.

For kinesics to be possible, film or VIDEO recording and appropriate stop-frame and slow-motion replay apparatus are essential. The use of film for kinesic analysis was pioneered by GREGORY BATESON and MARGARET MEAD, who also contributed much to the development of the general theoretical outlook of which kinesics is a part. This outlook regards the kinesic code as a subsystem of communication along with others such as SPEECH, TOUCH, SMELL, spacing, and orientation (*see also* NONVERBAL COMMUNICATION). Communication in face-to-face interaction, thus, is seen as a complex, continuous, culturally patterned, multichannel process. The aim of kinesics is to provide a systematic analysis of the body motion system and to show how it is related to these other systems.

See also BODY MOVEMENT; BODY MOVEMENT NOTATION; FACE; INTERACTION, FACE-TO-FACE.

Bibliography. Ray L. Birdwhistell, *Kinesics and Context: Essays on Body Motion Communication,* Philadelphia, 1970; Albert E. Scheflen, *Communicational Structure: Analysis of a Psychotherapy Transaction,* Bloomington, Ind., 1973; Thomas A. Sebeok, Alfred S. Hayes, and Mary Catherine Bateson, eds., *Approaches to Semiotics,* The Hague, 1964.

ADAM KENDON

KUROSAWA, AKIRA (1910–)

Japanese film director. After his debut in 1943 with *Sanshiro sugata,* Akira Kurosawa went on to make a body of twenty-eight films that has placed him among the most celebrated film directors. He is world renowned for such pictures as *Rashomon* (1950), *Ikiru* (1952), and *Shichinin no samurai* (The Seven Samurai, 1954).

Trained as a painter, Kurosawa—unlike more traditional Japanese film directors—sees film mainly as a NARRATIVE of visuals, and this is as true for his earlier films as for the spectacular *Ran* (1985). His extraordinarily visual language perhaps also accounts for his popularity outside Japan.

Figure 1. *(Kurosawa, Akira)* Akira Kurosawa. The Museum of Modern Art/Film Stills Archive.

At the same time, however, the moral concerns of his films—and Kurosawa is as driven by moral concerns as Robert Bresson or INGMAR BERGMAN, directors he in no way resembles otherwise—deepen their effect and underlie the philosophical statements that give his films universal appeal. These statements often involve education—in films such as *Sanshiro sugata*, *Sanjuro* (1962), and *Akahige* (Red Beard, 1965), the hero is taught how to be himself, how to achieve a reality that is his, or, as in *Ikiru*, how to redeem what must be. In many films Kurosawa defines the nature of reality (the "true" in philosophy) by showing its counterfeit, the "false." The theme of illusion versus reality occurs in many of his films. Often he shows a rehearsal for an event and then, in contrast, the event, as in *Ikiru, Seven Samurai, Yojimbo* (1961), *Warui yatsu hodo yoko nemuru* (The Bad Sleep Well, 1960), and—a film devoted entirely to this question—*Rashomon*. Or we are shown a "false" man who learns to be "true" (*Kagemusha;* Shadow Warrior, 1980). However, the films are not didactic and are only rarely sententious. Image and editing (*see* FILM EDITING) unite in an endless and exhilarating flow that makes the Kurosawa film a pleasure to watch. As a film technician he is without peer.

This results in a language that is easy to understand. It also makes for a moral simplicity that can be seen as either idealistic or unrealistic. In Japan Kurosawa has often faced a highly critical press, partly for this reason and partly because his later films were made with foreign funding—the result of his difficulty in obtaining domestic funding. Indeed, unfriendly Japanese critics have described Kurosawa as making films for the West. This is untrue. Western appreciation has been a by-product of Kurosawa's deep moral concern and stunning cinematic technique, both aimed entirely at an explication of Japan and the Japanese.

See also MOTION PICTURES—SOUND FILM.

Bibliography. Donald Richie, *The Films of Akira Kurosawa*, rev. ed., Berkeley, Calif., 1984.

DONALD RICHIE

L

(el), the twelfth letter of the modern and the eleventh of the ancient Roman alphabet, represents historically the Greek *lambda* and ultimately the Semitic *lamed*. The earliest known Semitic forms of the character are 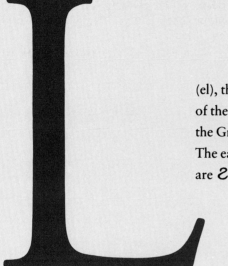 and ; both these occur in early Greek inscriptions; the latter was adopted from the Greek into the Latin alphabet, and is the ancestor of the modern Roman forms, but in Greece itself was superseded by the inverted form Γ, which eventually became Λ.

LAND, EDWIN (1909–)

U.S. physicist and inventor of the Polaroid one-step photographic process. Having been interested in PHOTOGRAPHY since childhood, Edwin Herbert Land began, as a student at Harvard in 1926, to experiment with polarized light. He left Harvard before graduation to continue work on a synthetic sheet polarizer, which he was able to produce by embedding crystals of iodoquinine sulfate in a sheet of plastic. To exploit his discoveries Land joined George Wheelwright III of Harvard's physics department to form the Land-Wheelwright Laboratories and in 1937 the Polaroid Corporation. This firm began to discover uses for sheet polarizers, including polarizing filters for cameras and sunglasses and, during World War II, optical elements for infrared night-vision instruments, periscopes, range finders, and bombsights.

But it was not until after the war that Land made his most fruitful discoveries. On a vacation in Santa Fe, New Mexico, his daughter asked after taking a photograph why she could not see the picture right away, and during an hour's walk through the streets Land conceived the system that would result in the Polaroid Land Camera. As first marketed in 1948 the camera contained a film pack consisting of silver halide negative, positive print paper, and a developing reagent. After taking a picture the operator pulled the photographic paper between two steel rollers, rupturing a pod of developer and spreading it over the paper. In about a minute the positive print was fully developed. The photographic system was an instant success, bringing sales of some $5 million in its first year.

Other inventions from Land's Polaroid Corporation included the vectograph, which permitted aerial photographs to be viewed as three-dimensional images and later resulted in the "3-D" movie craze of the 1950s, and cameras that provided instant color photographs, ejecting the print from the camera as soon as the shutter was released and developing the film in ambient light. Land's cameras and optical discoveries have been widely used by industry and the military, but his lasting contributions—his instant cameras—have brought a new kind of photographic experience to millions, enabling a picture to be viewed immediately after it is taken.

See also PHOTOGRAPHY, AMATEUR.

Bibliography. Mark Olshaker, *The Instant Image: Edwin Land and the Polaroid Experience*, New York, 1978.

ROBERT BALAY

Figure 1. *(Land, Edwin)* Edwin H. Land, 1947. Courtesy of the Polaroid Corporation.

LANGUAGE

The principal medium of human communication. In its primary form language is a spoken CODE of richly patterned combinations of signal elements (audibly distinct features of SPEECH sound) and message units (clumps of SOUND features conventionally associated with meanings or functional features). Serving as the principal means of transmission of CULTURE and belief systems, language has profound effects on the constitution of social life and in turn reflects by the variegation of usage patterns within a community the social organization of its speakers, down to the level of individual differences. *See also* MODE; SEMIOTICS; SIGN; SIGN SYSTEM.

Estimates of the number of different languages now spoken range from some two thousand to more than four thousand. The magnitude of the uncertainty is partly due to the difficulties of distinguishing between different languages and varieties of one language in particular cases and partly because of inadequate information for many areas.

Written and other representations of the spoken system are secondary to it both in historical date of development and in uniformity of acquisition within a social group. READING and WRITING must be learned, typically by instruction; speaking and understanding skills are acquired by all normal CHILDREN as part of the ordinary processes of development and socialization (*see* LANGUAGE ACQUISITION). Among the hearing impaired, strictly gestural sign systems have developed and have been transmitted in much the same way as spoken language; secondary systems of fingerspelling stand in the same relation to these as writing (*see* GESTURE; SIGN LANGUAGE).

The Nature and Origin of Language

Consideration of the nature and origin of language has accompanied a wide range of intellectual activities throughout history and doubtless longer still. Much of this long tradition consists of myth and religious doctrines holding that language, and often a particular language, was divinely inspired. Moreover, the connection between sacred texts and the language that conveys them has in many instances conferred a quasi-sacred status on the particular variety represented in the texts, sometimes "freezing" it virtually without change for many centuries and influencing the constantly changing popular usage in various ways. Sanskrit in India, Latin in much of western Europe, Greek and Church Slavonic in eastern Europe, Ge'ez in Ethiopia, and Classical Arabic in North Africa are all examples of this process. A comparable but less extreme instance of this effect is to be noted in the attitude of many English-speaking Protestants toward the language of the King James translation of the Bible. *See also* SCRIPTURE.

Broadly philosophical speculation about the origin of language has a very long and complex history of its own, impossible to summarize here. Whether language has one or a number of origins has been an important issue in this tradition. On this point, however, it is noteworthy that studies of the processes accompanying language contact underscore how very quickly and sweepingly language can change under the pressures of close contact between speech communities, as in political or economic COLONIZATION. The predictable types of change found in such circumstances include grammatical simplification and massive borrowing of vocabulary. With an undetermined number of such episodes possible in the prehistory of any language or language family, there seems to be no reasonable basis for conclusions on this issue.

Although there is a scholarly tradition of discussion of the origins of language as well, much of it shares with the speculative tradition the weaknesses necessarily found in any line of reasoning that is based only on data from attested languages but that seeks to reveal the place of origin or the original character of language. The problem of evidence appears insuperable. If language begins with Homo sapiens or earlier, hundreds of thousands of years ago or more, and if the average rate of change in this long period is comparable to that in data from attested languages, ancient or modern, then related forms (words or affixes) for comparison and reconstruction become more and more scarce as one moves back in time. In general, evidence is available only for reconstruction at relatively shallow time depths of a few thousand years earlier than the oldest attested records. The hundreds of thousands of years of linguistic evolution beyond this barrier constituted by the loss of evidence through the ordinary action of language change are apparently forever beyond the reach of linguistic science.

What can plausibly be said about the development of language as we know it must be based on a broader comparative perspective, drawing evidence from studies of ANIMAL COMMUNICATION as well as LINGUISTICS to find the parallels between ANIMAL SIGNALS and language. We must take the best-informed and broadest view of the range of variation and heterogeneity of human language itself, in place of the often parochial sample of familiar Western languages leavened with a few exotic specimens that is found in so much of the speculative and older linguistic literature.

Both human language and primate communication systems employ combinations of vocal and gestural signs; they both serve as channels for passing messages and also for constituting and maintaining social arrangements. Human speech is structured in a particular way in all known languages, however, and this structure is apparently not present in primate vocalization or in other animal communication systems, at least not on the same scale that it is found in language.

The essence of this structure is a duality of patterning of messages. In traditional terms an utterance is at the same time a sequence of syllables and a sequence of words. The speech sounds or sound features making up the vocal signals combine with each other according to patterns that are partly universal and governed by the physiology of speech and partly arbitrary and specific to the particular language variety. Message elements are combined in patterns largely independent of the sound patterns but also are manifested through the arrangements of sound elements that simultaneously make up the utterance or signal. There is thus an interaction between the combinatory patterns of the signal units or sounds and the message units or forms.

The Production and Patterning of Speech Sound

Speech sound is produced by the organs of the so-called vocal tract, all of which have other functions besides phonation. Respiration is the main function of the lungs; the larynx acts to protect the upper end of the airway to the lungs; the lips, teeth, and tongue serve to chew and swallow food; the tongue also plays a role with the nasal passage in olfaction. However, comparative physiology suggests that in humans these organs of breathing, eating, and smelling have undergone evolutionary changes specifically related to their use in speech. In turn, the constitution of these vocal organs in humans assures certain universal aspects of human language. The action of the chest cavity in speech, for instance, differs from ordinary respiration, with a shorter, sharper intake of air and a longer, slower exhalation, with relatively steady air pressure sustained in the lungs until an abrupt decline at the end of phonation, followed by another short intake phase, and so on. Utterances are thus ordinarily as long as one of these modified respiratory cycles, and they end ordinarily in a falling pitch with other characteristic effects because of the sudden drop in lung air pressure. To be sure, pitch contours do not necessarily fall, nor does a single respiration set the limits of an utterance. But these are the ordinary values, with other contours and the bridging of the inhalation pause requiring some special audible marking by the speaker.

The larynx, a boxlike structure of bone and cartilage suspended by muscles and other tissue atop the trachea, contains the vocal folds, popularly known as the vocal cords but in fact shaped more like lips. These are two symmetrical, complex organs made up of a number of muscles and ligaments and are connected to both fixed and movable anchoring structures, allowing the speaker to vary their length, stiffness, shape, and degree of approximation to each other. The rate and mode of vibration, and consequently the character of the sound they produce, changes as these factors change.

Speech seen in this way is a succession of rapid, intricately coordinated movements of the organs of the mouth, acting on the pulses of energy delivered by the buzzing of the vocal folds as air from the lungs is forced between them. These articulatory movements of speech are thus a complex kind of valving of this airstream and the acoustic signal formed by it. The hearer is able to interpret the acoustic cues, the traces in the signal of the rapidly changing shapes of the interior cavities of the speaker's vocal tract, and in effect to reconstruct the movements from their characteristic signatures. Moreover, hearers are able to compensate for individual, sex, and age differences in the vocal apparatus whose output they are interpreting and to reconstruct the same articulatory pattern as underlying quite different acoustic signals.

There is experimental and observational evidence that the syllable, consisting of a vowellike nucleus with optional flanking consonantal margins, is a neurological as well as a linguistic unit for the coding and decoding of the speech signal. In the vowel phase of a syllable the vocal tract is relatively open to the egress of air and acoustic energy. The vocal folds are (usually) vibrating, and the movements of the oral organs as an initial consonantal constriction is released and a final consonantal constriction is later imposed on the vowel position leave their audible traces in the changing distribution of energy across the frequency spectrum and through the time of articulation. Speech at this level is a succession of syllables, each composed of an initial constriction of the oral tract by a consonant articulation, followed by a relatively open, voiced, vocalic segment, followed again by a constriction phase before the next syllable with its onset, nucleus, and coda.

Syllables vary, then, in their consonantal onsets; in the color, uniformity, length, loudness, and pitch pattern of their vocalic nuclei; and again in their consonantal codas, if any. Each of the primary classes of speech sounds—consonants and vowels—has subclasses. Stop consonants are produced with complete closure of the vocal tract by one or more articulators; fricatives involve nearly complete closure, with audible turbulence produced at the point of greatest constriction. Nasal consonants are produced with the soft palate held away from the back wall of the nasal passage, thus dividing the airstream and producing a characteristic pattern of energy absorption quite different to the hearer from that of a strictly oral consonant made at the same point of articulation ([m] versus [b], for instance).

Speech communities differ in the selection and use they make of phonetic resources from the range of possibilities offered by the vocal tract. The foregoing summary has deliberately been kept at the level of nearly universal generality. Some additional, apparently universal, features can also be noted. These include the use of voicing (vocal-fold vibration) as a feature of syllabic nuclei (usually of all of them) and of some but not all consonantal articulations; the distribution of consonantal margins and vocalic nuclei in syllablelike units; the use of controlled pitch changes during voicing as part of the signaling system; and the use of more than one active articulatory zone (often the lips, as in [p f m]; the front of the tongue, as in [t s n]; and the back of the tongue, as in [k x ŋ]) as well as more than one manner of articulation (stop, spirant, nasal) in determining consonant types. The consonant inventories of some languages, such as those of the Caucasus or of the northwest coast of North America, are unusually large, distinguishing more positions and manners of articulation than the few mentioned here, whereas those of Polynesia are usually limited. Vowel systems typically (perhaps universally) include [i a u] sound types at least as variants, though not always as distinctive signaling elements. Like consonant inventories, they are subject to considerable difference from language to language.

Language Structure

Both signal units and message units in language are elements in a structured system. These elements are discrete rather than continuously varying in their qualities and can be said to be present or absent altogether from a signal rather than present to some degree. The principal relation used to demonstrate and map out the structure of a language is contrast. This is the relation between two linguistic signs—words will do as examples—that are different from each other in both sound and MEANING. For example, if we consider utterances corresponding to the written representations

"I'm looking for a pin," and
"I'm looking for a cat,"

it is evident that they are in part different in sound and in meaning and thus in contrast. Setting aside the like parts for now, we are left with the English words *pin* and *cat*. They too are contrastive by the above definition; so are *pin* and *pan*, *cat* and *kin*, and indeed many other words. Utterances that are partly alike and partly different in sound and meaning are compared in this way, with the different segments extracted and grouped according to sound, meaning, and distribution relative to other forms. *See also* SEMANTICS.

In this way, by exhaustive comparisons and sorting according to difference of sound and meaning or the lack of it, one can accumulate a stock of discrete message units. Carried to completion, the process of contrastive analysis will take many individual words apart in just the same way that words are extracted from phrases or sentences: *cat* and *cat-s, pit* and *pit-s,* and so on.

Some of the complexity of the manifold structural relations among language elements can be understood from the traditional accounts of word formation and GRAMMAR of our own or other languages as taught in the schools (*see* LANGUAGE REFERENCE BOOK). Modern linguistics seeks to go much farther in precision, coverage, and explicitness and in so doing has brought to prominence some aspects of this multidimensional complexity. For instance, it emphasizes the infinite scope and extensibility of language, such that from the decidedly finite inventory of signaling units—perhaps as few as a dozen or so distinct sound features combined into a few dozen distinct sound segments—a literally infinite number of sentences, each of indefinite length, can be generated. That is, this infinite number of possible sentences is implied by the set of rules of formation and transformation of grammatically acceptable structures. Accordingly, modern linguistics uses powerful mathematical systems to represent these formations and their relations, distinguishing in most

approaches a phonological component (a subset of rules) dealing with features of the sound system and their combinations and a syntactic component to account for sentence structure. The lexicon, the stock of message units or elementary meaningful forms spelled out as combinations of signaling units or elements of the sound pattern, is the bridge between the phonological and grammatical aspects of language descriptions (*see* PHONOLOGY). Other aspects of everyday creativity in the use of the structural resources of language have also received a share of attention from contemporary linguistics, in particular the intricately patterned choices of alternative expressions governed by social and interpersonal factors and serving, in the words of ERVING GOFFMAN, to give off information about speakers and hearers at the same time that they are giving information to each other (*see* INTERACTION, FACE-TO-FACE).

Patterning of Message Units: Morpheme, Word, and Sentence

Just as syllables are grouped by stress (prominence) differences into metrical units and these in turn into phrases by intonation contours and pauses, so too are words (many having their own internal structure of roots and affixes) grouped together by various grammatical markers into phrases and clauses. Conjunctions, prepositions, pronouns, particles, and the other "function words" serve to link together the constituents of the hierarchy of grammatical form, grouping head noun with modifier, distinguishing subject and object roles, relating the time of onset and duration of events marked by verbs and in other ways, and generally indexing the organization and guiding the interpretation of utterances for the hearer. Languages differ significantly in the details and relative complexity of this organizational apparatus. For some, English among them, the order of constituents is the principal means of identifying major sentence roles such as subject and object; for many other languages, including the older Indo-European languages of the Western classical tradition, the grammatical role of most forms is overtly marked by inflectional and derivational affixes, most of them suffixes. In still other languages, prefixes are the commonest means of indexing these functions; in some, still other formal mechanisms are found. Classical Arabic, like other Semitic languages, displays a striking pattern based on consonantal roots that are nearly always made up of three consonants and vocalic patterns interdigitated with them, as well as prefixes and suffixes. Thus, *ktb* is the triliteral root for writing; *kataba* means "he wrote," *kutiba* "it is written," *yaktubu* "he is writing," *kitaab* "book," and so on.

It testifies to the effectiveness of human speech as

a signaling system that out of a relatively few audibly distinguishable elements, combined in a highly patterned way so that the arrangements are quite redundant, a great many message units are constructed, and from these, in turn, a literally infinite number of messages may be created. The redundancy in the signal (e.g., the predictable alternation of consonant and vowel groups) protects users against damage to communication from noise in the auditory channel, allowing the listener to fill in missing elements by reference to context.

Language Use

The stock of signal and message elements, the conventions governing their patterns of combination, and of course the messages conveyed all differ in varying degrees from group to group, but language use is a universal feature of human social life. Indeed, one dimension of the patterning of language use is its subdivision into repertoires of closely related but easily distinguishable LANGUAGE VARIETIES, some associated with geographically or socially distinct groups of speakers and others used in alternation by the same speakers for specific purposes or in particular social contexts in their daily lives. The geographical distribution of differences among language varieties is the province of dialectology, one of the older branches of linguistics; the study of socially distributed language varieties, sociolinguistics, is a recent offshoot of it. All speech communities, even the smallest and least complex societies, exhibit some degree of heterogeneity and variability in the norms of speech and in the individual speakers' degree of mastery of these norms and the basic resources of the language.

One truism of linguistics is the close relationship between expert knowledge and finely subdivided terminology. This applies not only to individual experts, such as herbalists, healers, priests, warriors, and the like, but also to some degree to the culture as a whole, as in the ecologically defined preoccupation of northern peoples (or avid skiers) with snow in its many forms or of native Central American peoples with the swidden system of cultivation of maize and associated crops. Some occupational specialties, such as the priesthood or political leadership, may call for specific linguistic skills, such as ORATORY, the mastery of more than one dialect or language, or the rote learning of large bodies of text.

In some communities more than one variety or language may be in current use, with the roles of each regulated by culturally defined situations. In Greece, German-speaking Switzerland, Haiti, and much of the Arab world, for instance, a situation prevails that has been called diglossia by U.S. linguist Charles Ferguson. Diglossic societies use two for-

mally and functionally distinct varieties of the same language. One, called Low (or just L), is the language of family life and intimate acquaintanceship and consequently of informal settings generally. The other, High or H, is used in formal settings. Typically, as in the speech communities mentioned above, the two varieties differ appreciably both in grammar and in vocabulary. In other societies, for example, in Paraguay, two quite different languages are in use in a pattern of this kind, in this case Guaraní, an American Indian language, as L, and Spanish as H. Many Paraguayans use both to some extent, and it would be as odd to court one's future spouse in Spanish as to address a courtroom in Guaraní. Some societies, among them some large communities, are multilingual. In Ethiopia and many parts of sub-Saharan Africa, as well as in significant parts of Asia, the Americas, and Europe, the ordinary level of linguistic competence of an adult involves fluency in two or more languages. The social or functional distribution of use reflects, as always, the internal structure of the speech communities.

Language use has always played a significant role in political movements of many kinds. Multiethnic nation-states with one or more politically dominant groups and additional linguistic and ethnic minorities have for centuries been the source of nationalist and other ideological movements with strong linguistic components. Other groups, essentially monolingual, idealize the virtues of their own and the imagined defects of their neighbors' forms of speech. This phenomenon can be observed at all levels, from villages to nations. *See* LANGUAGE IDEOLOGY.

Language Change and Relatedness

Language change was long considered paradoxical by linguists, who were aware from the study of a wide variety of speech communities over the whole span of written and spoken records that language change is forever in progress and yet is never directly observable. Nor does its pace ever disturb communication between generations. How then could the complex structure of the communicative system be in constant flux and yet retain its negotiability within a speech community as a medium of communication?

Phonological change, in particular, was troublesome for this view of language change as ever present but imperceptible. Because of its regularity, that is, its freedom from exceptions under the stated conditions, sound change was the object of intense study in the linguistics of the nineteenth and early twentieth centuries. Some sound changes could be accepted readily as gradual, perhaps imperceptibly so, as for instance a shift of vowel quality from midfront unrounded to a lower midfront unrounded articulation. There were no articulatory barriers to the possibly smooth and gradual transition over time between one norm of pronunciation and the other. But some sound changes, including some rather well-documented episodes in the history of western European languages, could not be explained easily in this way. The type of trilled [r] produced by vibration of the tip of the tongue at or near the alveolar ridge behind the upper teeth, as in modern Spanish or Italian, was once the standard pronunciation in French and German too. Over a period of time in the seventeenth century it was replaced by the [R] produced by vibration of the uvula against the back of the tongue. There is no possible smooth transition between the two, because the middle of the tongue lying between them will not support a trill type of articulation. Thus the French and German users of the old [r] must have borrowed the new [R] from other speakers. Borrowing, then, or replacement, rather than modification, has come to be understood as the general mechanism of language change. The consequences of this unification of the mechanism of change, in turn, have led to a far-reaching integration of our understanding of the evolution of language families, the process of the formation of new varieties through contact (pidginization and creolization), and the relationship between language differences and social differences within communities. Change, then, came to be understood as the generalization of one alternative means of expression at the expense of others, so that one takes over a portion of the range of environments formerly occupied by the other or others. If this change of distribution goes to completion, the one is said to replace the other; if it has not gone to completion, the two continue to serve as alternatives under some statable pattern of distribution.

Other types of change can also be understood as changes in the distribution of alternatives, as the extension of one pattern at the expense of others. A celebrated example, chronicled by Swiss linguist FERDINAND DE SAUSSURE, is the phonological change, in early Latin, of intervocalic *s* to *r* and the irregular but highly patterned analogical consequences of this regular sound change. The paradigm of the Old Latin word for "tree," unlike the Classical form, was presumably *arbos, arbosis,* and so on. After the change of intervocalic *s* to *r,* the oblique forms, which fit the conditions for the change, have an *r* in place of the *s,* making the paradigm morphologically irregular: *arbos, arboris.* Most Latin noun stems, of course, are regular in the sense that the root-final consonant does not change. In relation to the model constituted by these numerous forms, the new products of the sound change are irregular. Three possible resolutions are available: no further change but maintenance of the irregularity, leveling of the oblique forms back to *s,* or analogic reformation of the nominative form to *r.* In the case of "tree" it is the

last of these that prevailed, giving the familiar form of the Classical paradigm: *arbor, arboris.* The otherwise comparable "flower," however, did not undergo analogic change, remaining as *flos, floris.*

Language change, then, is merely the effect over time of shifts in the pattern of choice among alternative means of expression. Alternatives are constantly present, being generated socially through the action of borrowing from inside and outside the immediate community and through the action of regular sound change and analogic or other forms of change. Thus language change is the ordinary outcome of language use, and our notion of language structure has accordingly been enriched to include this added dimension of variability.

See also COMMUNICATION, PHILOSOPHIES OF.

Bibliography. Hans Arens, ed., *Sprachwissenschaft: Der Gang ihrer Entwicklung von der Antike bis zur Gegenwart,* Freiburg and Munich, 1969; Barbara F. Grimes, ed., *Ethnologue,* 10th ed., Dallas, Tex., 1984; Archibald A. Hill, "A Note on Primitive Languages," *International Journal of American Linguistics* 18 (1952): 172–177; Henry M. Hoenigswald, *Language Change and Linguistic Reconstruction,* Chicago, 1960; Dell Hymes, ed., *Language in Culture and Society,* New York, 1964; Louis G. Kelly, *Twenty-five Centuries of Language Teaching,* Rowley, Mass., 1969; *Linguistic Bibliography/Bibliographie linguistique,* Utrecht and Antwerp, 1939–; Edward Sapir, *Language: An Introduction to the Study of Speech,* New York, 1921; Rulon Wells, "Distinctively Human Semiotic," in *Essays in Semiotics/Essais de sémiotique,* ed. by Julia Kristeva, Josette Rey-Debove, and Donna Jean Umiker, The Hague, 1971.

JOHN G. FOUGHT

LANGUAGE ACQUISITION

Critical to communication is competence in understanding and using LANGUAGE in society. To communicate effectively CHILDREN and other language acquirers must gain a tacit understanding of grammatical and appropriate language use in their speech community. In the words of U.S. linguistic anthropologist Dell Hymes, acquiring language entails not only acquisition of grammatical competence but acquisition of communicative competence as well.

The study of first-language acquisition has two major goals: (1) to explain how language is acquired, and (2) to specify and analyze children's grammatical and communicative competence over developmental time. The former concern has focused on issues of nature and nurture in the emergence of language. Currently most researchers maintain that children bring to the task of language acquisition an active and structured mind. This view has been reinforced by cross-cultural research indicating that caregivers do not universally simplify the grammatical form of their SPEECH to young children. The implication of this literature is that language acquisition is not dependent on a particular type of language environment, namely, exposure to grammatically simplified speech. This does not mean, however, that environment does not play a part in language acquisition. Cross-cultural research provides substantial evidence, for example, that acquisition of systems of MEANING and discourse structures in spoken and written language are deeply affected by the social and cultural milieu in which language acquisition takes place.

Issues in Research

An unresolved issue in acquisition research is whether the capacity to acquire a language is part of a more general cognitive capacity (see COGNITION) or an autonomous, language-specific ability. Scholars such as U.S. linguist Noam Chomsky argue that humans have an independent, specific mental faculty for constructing grammars. This faculty (referred to as Universal Grammar) sets limits or parameters on the possible grammars that the human mind will construct. U.S. psycholinguist Stephen Pinker and several other researchers have related acquisition strategies in specific languages to these parameters and have proposed a theory of language learnability in these terms. In this perspective the child is a hypothesis tester, sifting through principles of Universal Grammar to discover those that apply to the language data in the child's particular environment.

On the other hand, other researchers follow the ideas of Swiss developmental psychologist JEAN PIAGET and argue that (1) language is part of a more general semiotic or symbolic system, and (2) linguistic intelligence is rooted in general cognitive abilities developed in infancy and early childhood. These researchers point out that several critical properties of language are part of children's nonverbal competence prior to language or at the point of emergence of language. For example, children have been observed representing concepts in nonverbal imitation and PLAY prior to or along with their use of language as a symbolic system. Further, the earliest meanings encoded in language appear to match those expressed in children's nonverbal behavior prior to language. For example, relations among agent, action, and object affected by an action encoded early in children's speech are already part of children's sensorimotor intelligence before the emergence of language.

The capacity of language to express topics and comments or old and new information is also brought to bear on the issue of the autonomy of language vis-à-vis other forms of behavior and competence. Several researchers have argued that grammatical devices such as word order, subject-verb agreement, and ellipsis serve as markers of topic and comment or old and new information and that precursors to these devices can be found in children's prelinguistic communicative development. The distinction between old and new information in language has roots in children's prelinguistic attention to what is perceptually salient in their environment and children's rudimentary awareness of knowledge states of others acquired in the sensorimotor period of development. From this perspective GRAMMAR emerges out of functional considerations; grammar is to be seen as an efficient alternative to other means of carrying out these functions.

Those arguing for language and its acquisition as an autonomous phenomenon point out that linguistic structures are far more complex than these functional explanations admit. Looking only at the rules constraining phonological and morphosyntactic forms in language, we have no evidence of any other behavioral structure of this complexity. Since the latter part of the 1970s a number of psycholinguists, including Annette Karmiloff-Smith and Dan I. Slobin in the United States, have been working to resolve this dilemma. A compromise position that has been proposed is that whereas certain structures and properties of language are rooted in sensorimotor intelligence and reflect a non-language-specific, general cognitive ability, other structures and properties of language are specific to language alone. Slobin suggests that while children's early grammars draw on prelinguistic cognitive and social understandings, each language is a complex formal system for encoding notions that present learning problems not encountered in children's prelinguistic experience. Karmiloff-Smith proposes that at a certain developmental point language in itself becomes a "problem space" for children. On the other hand, in this perspective language development is not the result exclusively of preformed, innate grammatical structures. Rather, what is or may be innate is a capacity or predisposition to acquire language. In Slobin's terms children are predisposed to perceive and structure speech in certain systematic ways. Slobin presents a series of procedures or operating principles guiding children's construction of grammar. These principles delineate the language-universal and language-particular parameters of this predisposition.

One of the major interests of language acquisition research has been not only explaining but also documenting children's strategies for verbally encoding notions about the physical and social world. Several scholars have proposed that children initially use a *rigid word order* to encode elements of proposition, reserving different positions for specific elements, such as agent or patient. It is claimed that children will use a rigid word order in their language production and comprehension even when the language they are acquiring permits a variety of possible word orders. The universality of this claim has been challenged by Slobin, who reports that children acquiring a language that has a regular case-inflectional system (such as Turkish) will rely on morphology rather than a rigid word order to encode and decode meanings.

A related claim is that where children do rely on word order, the word order they prefer reflects a natural ordering of elements within a proposition. For example, it is claimed that regardless of language acquired children prefer to encode agents before patients (objects affected by actions of agents). This preference corresponds to a statistical preference among the world's languages for word orders in which subject precedes objects (e.g., subject-verb-object, subject-object-verb, and verb-subject-object word orders). While observations of children acquiring languages such as Kaluli (spoken in Papua New Guinea) and Turkish indicate that the preference for encoding agents before patients is by no means universal, the preference does hold for a wide range of language acquisition situations.

A number of child language researchers in the United States have argued that initial word-order preferences in children's speech and comprehension reflect a natural preference for encoding new and old information. Psycholinguist Patricia Greenfield stated that at the single-word stage, children tend to use their one-word utterances to encode only new information. Elizabeth Bates and Brian MacWhinney have argued that when children acquire a language with more than one word order (e.g., Italian or Hungarian), the natural tendency of children beyond the single-word stage is to encode the newest, most informative element first and then relatively old information (comment before topic). In many languages old information very often is not expressed within a clause. In these languages both children and adults prefer to introduce objects, persons, and other entities as part of a predicate and in the immediate subsequent discourse to make statements about them without explicitly referring to them. Looking at the flow of information across a sequence of clauses, we see a preference for old information to precede new information. This preference appears to be a universal organizing principle of discourse.

Acquiring competence in language involves, then, knowing how to encode and decode new and old information as well as information concerning actions and states. Language, however, is more than a vehicle for making logical propositions about the world. It is also a means of organizing social behavior and dispositions, and in acquiring language children must acquire an understanding of this social potential of language. One of the basic functions of language is the carrying out of social acts and activities. Chil-

dren are able to perform basic social acts, such as asserting and requesting, through action and vocalization in the first year of life, anticipating the use of language to achieve these ends. By the time children start producing two- and three-word utterances they are able to produce and respond to a wide range of speech acts, including begging, teasing, warning, greeting, announcing, requesting permission, test questions, answers, challenges, and indirect requests for action.

During this early period of language development, children are developing an ability to participate in conversational exchanges of two or more verbal acts, such as question-answer, question-answer-evaluation of answer, or question-clarification request-clarification response-answer to question. All studies of children's CONVERSATION indicate the expected, namely, a developmental trend toward greater similarity between children's and others' conversational acts. Cross-cultural research indicates that caregivers the world over facilitate children's acquisition of conversational competence. In the societies observed caregivers routinely prompt children, telling them what to say in a given conversational exchange. In certain societies, such as Anglo-white middle-class society, caregivers facilitate children's understanding of verbal acts (and hence their ability to respond to those acts) by supplementing the verbal message with actions and gestures that provide cues as to what verbal act is being performed.

Language in a Social Context

One of the important trends emerging in the literature on children's development of conversational competence is that as children are acquiring knowledge of language they are acquiring knowledge of society and CULTURE. Children do not produce and comprehend language in a social vacuum. Rather, they acquire language in socially and culturally constituted contexts. Particular expressions, grammatical structures, and verbal acts and activities are closely associated with particular contexts, and these contexts become part of children's understanding of language. That is, language has sociocultural meaning. Because it is such a rich encoder of social order and cultural beliefs and values, language is also a powerful vehicle for socializing children. Language socializes not simply through message content but also through patterns of use, such as social constraints on who can perform particular verbal acts and activities with whom, when, and where.

We know that children are sensitive to such social constraints early in their language development. Before the age of three children acquiring language in a hierarchical society such as that in Samoa will know to avoid performing verbal acts appropriate only to higher-ranking persons. Similarly, by the age of three English-speaking children growing up in the United States are already acquiring the linguistic features of speech associated with different social roles, such as mother, father, teacher, student, doctor, and patient. Further, in several societies children have displayed awareness and understanding of politeness norms expected in their communities early in their development. These norms may involve use of complex linguistic constructions that soften or indirectly convey a particular verbal act. *See also* FAMILY.

In addition, children in several societies have been observed to display early awareness and understanding of the grammatical expression of emotion. At the single-word stage, for example, children produce and recognize intonation contours associated with different emotions. In the latter part of the single-word stage, children are able to use morphological forms that either intensify affect or specify a particular type of affect (usually anger or sympathy for self or another person). Additionally, children become skilled quite early in a variety of verbal acts that convey some attitude or feeling, such as teasing, begging, and complaining.

In acquiring language, then, children learn ways of using language for a variety of functions: to encode activities, states, and events; to provide foreground and background for different elements of these activities, states, and events; to perform social acts and activities; to create and validate social relationships; and to convey emotions. Each one of these functions affects linguistic form. What constitutes the nature of these form-function relations is the essential problem of language acquisition.

Bibliography. Catherine Garvey, *Children's Talk*, Cambridge, Mass., 1984; Michael McTear, *Children's Conversation*, Oxford, 1985; Bambi B. Schieffelin and Elinor Ochs, eds., *Language Socialization across Cultures*, Cambridge, 1986; Dan I. Slobin, *Psycholinguistics*, 2d ed., Glenview, Ill., 1979; idem, ed., *The Crosslinguistic Study of Language Acquisition*, Hillsdale, N.J., 1986; Eric Wanner and Lila R. Gleitman, *Language Acquisition: The State of the Art*, Cambridge, 1982.

ELINOR OCHS

LANGUAGE DISORDERS. *See* SPEECH AND LANGUAGE DISORDERS.

LANGUAGE IDEOLOGY

A variety of integrated assertions, theories, and goals that attempt to guide collective sociopolitical beliefs and actions regarding LANGUAGE choices in communication systems. Such language values and decisions prescribe one language or language variety (including dialect, register, and style) over another and attempt to dictate the linguistic preferences and practices of international alliances, as well as nation-states, national and regional institutions, and local communities. Language ideologies can be elaborate or simple, highly salient or hardly noticeable. *See also* IDEOLOGY; LANGUAGE VARIETIES.

Though all societies have some standards for language evaluation, the extent to which such judgments become ideologies varies greatly from one society to another. Relationships between ideologies and behaviors are extraordinarily complex and often difficult to discern: groups may espouse ideals they ignore or subvert in actual use, distinctions may blur between evaluations of language and estimations of speakers, and language ideology may be a covert part of a body of ideals held about specific institutions of the society. All language decisions carry implicit and explicit symbolic as well as instrumental values. Many communities find their language superior to others, and some judge their language inferior, but features of distinction and criteria of judgment may differ. Some may think their language more poetic (or more direct, sacred, logical, romantic, etc.) than others and promote language choice on the basis of this feature (*see* CLASSIFICATION). However, there is no way to validate these claims, and those who hold firm to their ideologies decry or ignore research that shows the difficulty of rating languages on almost all of these scales.

Language Choice and Standardization

Language choice is an issue for international and national organizations, regional and ethnic communities, voluntary associations, and religious and sociopolitical institutions throughout the world. For some international and national groups the preferred language is one through which things get done; information, ideas, and beliefs can be transmitted efficiently across vastly different groups and great distances. For such instrumental purposes groups have contributed consciously at different times in history to the spread of languages such as Latin, English, or Esperanto (an artificial international language based largely on words common to the major European languages). For those groups whose language ideology is closely tied to RELIGION, appointed or anointed leaders perpetuate myths about the origins of their language, the extent of its supernatural powers, and the need to preserve the classical form of the sacred texts.

Modern national language ideologies vary greatly in terms of acceptance of the extent to which language can and should be regulated by the national body politic. People of the Scandinavian-Baltic nations, for example, endorse efficient, rational, and relatively frequent policy setting by political leaders, language planners, and educators who select, codify, and bring up to date standards of language use from time to time. In recent centuries France decreed French as the language of the state, established a language academy to watch over changes in the language, and charged educational institutions with TEACHING a chosen variety of French to nationals and French colonials alike. Central European nations newly independent after World War I encouraged language scholars to consider the functionalism of a national language, ways of building its resources, and distinctions between workaday technical language and poetic language.

Some newly independent nations have within their borders speakers of many unwritten languages. More than four thousand languages are spoken in the world. The vast majority are unwritten; only about three hundred are in regular use in written form, and fewer than one hundred of these have more than a scant written literature. New national leaders have had to settle on a language of oral exchange among individuals and groups and to standardize this choice for the written records of government. The selection of a national language has been central in the modernization of new nations. Political leaders depend on formal schooling to promote a single language CODE that will mark the educated person. Often underlying the promotion of a single linguistic medium in such nations is a language ideology that regards language as a medium of exchange for verbal transactions in a linguistic marketplace of buyers and sellers who obtain certain goods and services and have an underlying profit motive. Linguistic capital, like any other form of capital, enables those who have it to get ahead of those who do not. *See also* DEVELOPMENT COMMUNICATION.

However, any SPEECH community, regardless of size or relative power in the national or world marketplace, can harbor intense language ideologies. Members may believe their language to be a core sociocultural marker of ethnic or regional identification whose importance transcends the acquisition of wealth or membership within the national socioeconomic system. On the other hand, the fundamental definition of the community's language may be as an oral communication system, inappropriate either in written form or on the tongues of outsiders. Thus language loyalties may penetrate deeply into human values and habits.

Linguistic and Literary Aesthetics

In nations with long-established choices of a national language for affairs of state (or religion), leaders may favor certain varieties and styles of language over others. Special written texts (such as dictionaries, grammars, and key writings from earlier eras) may codify the linguistic norm (*see* LANGUAGE REFERENCE BOOK). Recommendations to preserve older forms,

eschew borrowings, and create words for new cultural items from older resources in the language are attempts to conserve what may be regarded as a pure form of the language. Formal schooling may prescribe GRAMMAR rules in an attempt to prevent changes in the language, which could be interpreted as signs of the deterioration of the society.

Regional or social dialects are typically the candidates for what will become the most prestigious variety of the language. Generally the chosen standard variety is the dialect of a particular region and/or social class. But the ideology may not recognize this at all and may give a totally different justification.

Within each language certain uses or styles achieve a higher valuation than others. A register of a particular language is a variation according to use: physicians, lawyers, sportscasters, and teachers use a special register of their language as part of daily communication within their occupational roles. To the extent that such registers become associated with formal EDUCATION and high social status, certain features of these registers, especially vocabulary, will be borrowed by those who esteem both the norms and the goals of these professional groups. The valuation of registers shifts in accordance with society's estimation of the speakers who use them.

Far more stable as a highly valued norm across speech communities is the language of the literature most highly valued in the society. In both oral and written literary language, performers, writers, and audiences recognize nonordinary uses and forms of language set apart from ordinary styles. Literary language reflects ordinary life and language and yet portrays and inspires interpretations and responses that transcend the mundane. Both the essence and the form of expression live beyond any single PERFORMANCE or reading. Those who create, perform, and interpret literature receive differing degrees of recognition and sponsorship in their societies. In some systems, governments or national academies support literary artists and print codifications of the literary norm, as well as works of literature, which they hold up as language models for the nation. Other societies separate political and artistic sectors to preserve artists as independent critics of all aspects of daily existence. In virtually every society in which written language plays a significant role, literary language represents an ideal form of the language that some members strive to create and others to understand and appreciate.

Linguistic Deprivation and Incompetence

All assertions, theories, and goals that attempt to value some language varieties while denouncing or ignoring others reflect distorted ideas about language varieties. In addition such ideologies often exaggerate the extent to which certain language values and habits can be institutionalized and perpetuated by the government, schools, or literary academies.

Sectors of society that equate certain language varieties with power or socioeconomic or moral worth tend to prescribe rules of language use and to judge individuals who do not meet these prescriptive norms as deficient or incompetent. Informal indirect practices of exclusion and stratification close off from employment and social opportunities those who do not or cannot meet these language norms. For example, in complex modern states those speakers of a high socioeconomic class regard their language variety as a marker of relative prestige, intelligence, morality, and good citizenship. For them and for those who aspire to upward social mobility, speakers who do not share their linguistic norms are rightly denied opportunities and given derogatory character evaluations and low estimations of their motivation and morality. Selective vision, distorted conclusions, and exaggerated claims operate together to ensure maintenance of certain language ideologies despite empirical research demonstrating that although languages differ from one another, one is not inherently better structurally than any other.

Modern Linguistic Research

Linguists and other social scientists who study language provide systematic statements about uniformities of process in language systems and their uses and users. Since the beginnings of modern LINGUISTICS in the nineteenth century scholars of language have regarded it primarily as a means of referring and predicating. Most linguistic research focuses on the representational value of language, its rules and ways of standing for objects, situations, and feelings. This objectification and representational function of language depends, however, on epistemological presuppositions that regard language as object of inventory and description through patterns of rule generation.

Yet the functional powers of language go beyond its capability for labeling to its constitutive values in a system of shifting social relations. Social groups construct both cognitive understandings and linguistic forms and performances in accord with urges to present themselves, control the behavior of others, and transcend the immediate frame of any manifest utterance or verbal exchange. Such intentions lie behind the actual language used or the immediate reality represented to interrelations of social role, notions of time, and recognitions of multiple levels of MEANING. Speakers negotiate these meanings at the moment as well as in remembered reconstructions, and audiences interpret language according to their emotional needs, levels of analytical expertise, and membership in interpretive communities.

A science of language that merely objectifies linguistic material cannot capture the value-constituting relations of language. Thus language scientists have to recognize that the epistemology of their own language research reflects a language ideology just as much as a mythic ideology of some nonliterate society. Science in the relatively advanced societies has been said to permit a constant rational process of orderly revision and reform of sociopolitical institutions. However, explanations of language and its complex interdependence with sociocultural phenomena, which can themselves be ideologically based, must penetrate further language ideologies in order to move beyond theoretical statements to programs for policy or practice. Language ideology by its very nature yields only rarely to scientific criticism.

See also COMMUNICATION, PHILOSOPHIES OF; FEMINIST THEORIES OF COMMUNICATION; SEXISM.

Bibliography. Basil B. Bernstein, *Class, Codes and Control,* 2d rev. ed., 3 vols., London, 1971–1977; Noëlle Bisseret, *Education, Class Language, and Ideology,* London, 1979; Edward Finegan, *Attitudes toward English Usage,* New York, 1980; Jürgen Habermas, *Theory of Communicative Action, Vol. 1* (Theorie des kommunikativen Handelns), trans. by Thomas McCarthy, Boston, 1984; Frederic Jameson, *The Prison-House of Language,* Princeton, N.J., 1972; Gunther Kress and Robert Hodge, *Language as Ideology,* London, 1979; William Labov, *Sociolinguistic Patterns,* Philadelphia, 1972; Ferruccio Rossi-Landi, *Linguistics and Economics,* The Hague, 1975; Aldo D. Scaglione, ed., *The Emergence of National Languages,* Ravenna, 1984; Raymond Williams, *Marxism and Literature,* Oxford, 1977.

SHIRLEY BRICE HEATH

LANGUAGE REFERENCE BOOK

Traditionally language reference books have been both scientific and popular and have served both descriptive and prescriptive functions. They codify LANGUAGE, examine its past, argue or gently push for reform, offer information to the puzzled or the curious. Even the most descriptive works cannot avoid making judgments, which in turn serve as recommendations to readers. And even the most prescriptive works take as their point of departure a description of some aspect of language. Created in response to linguistic needs, real or perceived but always socially or politically motivated, language reference books both affect and reflect cultural attitudes toward language (*see* LANGUAGE IDEOLOGY).

We take our language seriously because we perceive it as an essential feature of our humanity and our individuality. Consequently we tend to resist attempts to tamper with our traditions of language use. This resistance may be mild, as when a student ignores a teacher's efforts to dictate a preferred pronunciation, or it may be violent. Although the classically based standard written language of Greece had long since lost its ties to spoken Greek, great resistance accompanied attempts earlier in this century to modernize Greek WRITING, and riots resulting in several deaths followed the translation of the New Testament into demotic (modern) Greek in 1901.

Functions

The functions of language reference books are many and varied, as are their users. They may be directed toward foreigners to help them learn a new language or toward native speakers to assist them with difficult words or to resolve usage questions. In either case their purpose, as British lexicographer SAMUEL JOHNSON put it in the preface to his influential *Dictionary of the English Language* (1755), is to *ascertain* ("to fix, or make certain") particular linguistic forms in explicit or implicit preference to variants. In some cases the result of this fixing of forms is to favor a particular dialect as the standard for a nation. In other cases it is to create a standard form of written communication for a society with one or more competing spoken dialects or languages. *See also* LANGUAGE VARIETIES.

The creation of reference books is frequently tied to the emergence of a new nation, the industrialization or modernization of an already existing nation, or a shift in the international importance of a nation with a consequent shift in the load its written language must bear. In some cases the movement toward standardization occurs after a period of energetic linguistic growth. In the sixteenth and seventeenth centuries, for example, English underwent a period of sudden expansion, flourishing as a literary as well as an administrative language, enlarging its vocabulary through borrowings from French and Italian, coinages based on the learned languages, and revivals of archaic words. During this period the power of the English monarchy greatly increased, England emerged as an international colonial power, and the Reformation threw increased emphasis on the English vernacular as the language of religion at the expense of Latin. During this time there was heightened interest in the study of the English language and its history and in the creation of artificial "philosophical" languages that would serve the burgeoning field of international scientific communication. In addition frequent recommendations were made for the regulation of the English language, particularly in the areas of word coinage and spelling. However, it was not until the eighteenth century, with the growth and solidification of power of the English middle class and the spread of LITERACY accompanying industrial expansion, that the first generalized movement toward linguistic standardization and the first large-scale publication of language reference books

occurred. In that century dictionaries, grammars, usage guides, and language commentaries first established themselves as authorities for the regulation of the English language.

The Idea of a Standard Language

In order to bring about reform some language standardizers sought to identify a historical period, whether past or present, to set up as a golden age whose language should be both preserved and imitated. For the Greeks of the Hellenistic period it was the golden age of Athens (*see* HELLENIC WORLD). For the Latin grammarians Aelius Donatus (fourth century C.E.), Priscian (sixth century C.E.), and their colleagues the golden age was exemplified by CICERO's writing (first century B.C.E.) (*see* ROMAN EMPIRE). In contrast the editors of the dictionary of the French Academy (1694) looked to their own century for linguistic precedents. They perceived modern French to be flourishing and supposed the language may even have reached perfection. However, perfect French was spoken by only a small percentage of the population. According to Claude Favre de Vaugelas, the French academician and author of the first usage commentary of the language, *Remarques sur la langue françoise* (1647), good usage belonged to the elite, defined as the best elements of the royal court and the best writers of the day, while bad usage characterized the majority of speakers and writers. The fifth edition of the dictionary of the French Academy, issued in the seventh year of the First Republic, similarly defended the need for an elite body of linguistic judges; like its predecessors it also described the language not of the masses but of the select few who spoke and wrote correctly. This dictionary showed the effects of Enlightenment thinking; the preface recommended the work as something necessary for the good sense and rationality of the people, not simply as a record of correct or fashionable language. It also stressed the notion that a word must be allowed one and only one meaning if language is to be logical and efficient.

For the English language the golden age was not the Elizabethan period, frequently perceived as a time of unchecked growth, which in itself provided reason enough for language reform. Instead authorities like Johnson looked to the era before the Restoration for the best English writers. According to Johnson (1755), English, which "was employed in the cultivation of every species of literature, has been hitherto neglected, suffered to spread, under the direction of chance, into wild exuberance, resigned to the tyranny of time and fashion, and exposed to the corruption of ignorance, and caprices of innovation." Influenced by the spirit of the Enlightenment, Johnson and his European contemporaries regarded language as one of many natural phenomena that could be improved

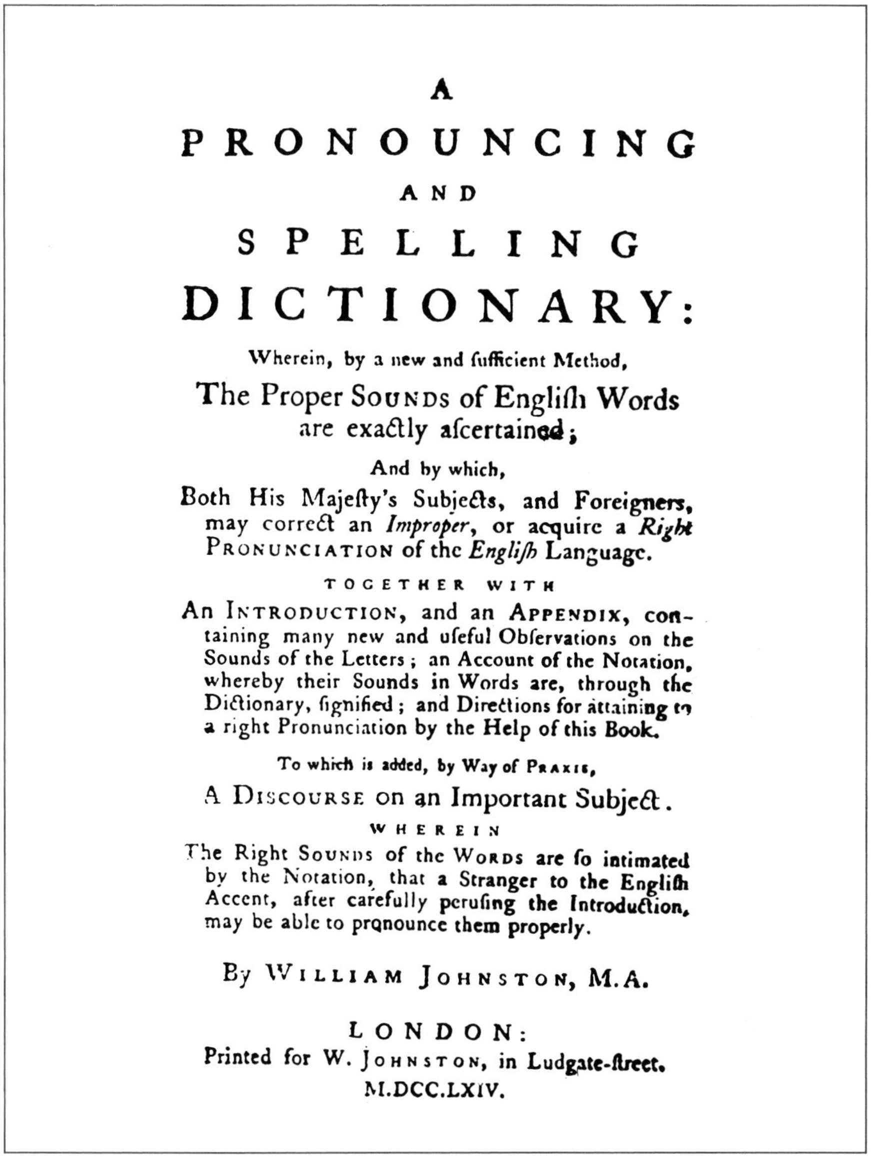

A

PRONOUNCING

AND

SPELLING

DICTIONARY:

Wherein, by a new and fufficient Method,

The Proper SOUNDS of Englifh Words
are exactly afcertained;

And by which,

Both His Majefty's Subjects, and Foreigners, may correct an *Improper*, or acquire a *Right* PRONUNCIATION of the *Englifh* Language.

TOGETHER WITH

An INTRODUCTION, and an APPENDIX, containing many new and ufeful Obfervations on the Sounds of the Letters; an Account of the Notation, whereby their Sounds in Words are, through the Dictionary, fignified; and Directions for attaining to a right Pronunciation by the Help of this Book.

To which is added, by Way of PRAXIS,

A DISCOURSE on an Important Subject.

WHEREIN

The Right SOUNDS of the WORDS are fo intimated by the Notation, that a Stranger to the Englifh Accent, after carefully perufing the Introduction, may be able to prqnounce them properly.

By WILLIAM JOHNSTON, M.A.

LONDON:

Printed for W. JOHNSTON, in Ludgate-ftreet.

M.DCC.LXIV.

Figure 1. *(Language Reference Book)* William Johnston, *A Pronouncing and Spelling Dictionary,* 1764. Title page. From R. C. Alston, ed., *English Linguistics 1500–1800 (A Collection of Facsimile Reprints),* Menston, Eng.: The Scolar Press, 1968. By permission of Scolar Press.

if subjected to rational reform and brought under the constraints of reason and logic. A somewhat different spirit of reform motivated the compilers of the Oxford English Dictionary, who began work in the mid-nineteenth century to correct what they felt were deficiencies in the English dictionaries of their time. Their objective was to account for all the words in the English vocabulary from the earliest records to the present and to record for each word its pronunciation, etymology, and examples of its use in context—a historical treatment of all words and idioms. The intent of the dictionary of the French Academy (fifth edition) was similarly to fix the language without hemming it in but in tracks that would always lead to rational advancement, not poor usage. Today's reformers of English exhibit this same spirit of linguistic idealism. They do not posit a golden age but instead look to a perfectible, rational form of English that can exist only if we follow their advice.

Language Reform

The social role of language is seldom ignored by the writers of reference works, and authors seem both pessimistic and optimistic in their goals. Citing examples of linguistic forms to which they object, they may warn against the dangers of linguistic decay, exhorting their readers to return to or to create anew a form of language that will both reflect and guarantee the survival of their civilization. On a more practical level they may cite the educational needs of the young, of immigrants or foreign merchants, and of the less fortunate classes. For example, Scottish rhetorician Hugh Blair intended his *Lectures on*

Rhetoric and Belles Lettres (1829) "for the initiation of youth" into a subject that had been cultivated with the greatest of care among civilized nations because a well-regulated language was also thought to be a rational one. Language commentators in the United States further stressed the value of good, standard speech and writing to a democratic society. While such practical aims are frequently subordinated to idealistic or philosophical treatments of language as reflecting both beauty and truth, it is a commonplace of eighteenth- and nineteenth-century English grammars that "grammar is the art (or science) of speaking and writing correctly" (*see* GRAMMAR).

Johnson's explicit goals all tended toward the correction of English. In the preface to his dictionary he stated that his aim was to regulate confusion, bring choice out of variety, detect adulteration, establish authority, and adjust orthography. Although Johnson's dictionary carried great weight as a standard for its time, Johnson himself was not a true language reformer in the sense that NOAH WEBSTER was. To Johnson's aims Webster, in *An American Dictionary of the English Language* (1828), added correcting the pronunciation of the common people, explaining new words not found in earlier dictionaries, classifying common roots among languages, noting those aspects of English that are particularly American, and ultimately ascertaining "the true principles of the language." Elsewhere Webster explained that his purpose was to eliminate pronunciation differences in the speech of Americans and to rationalize the spelling of English words to better reflect their proper pronunciation and in some cases their etymology. At the beginning of his career he was strongly influenced by a sense of American nationalism, and he once urged that British usage be rejected even if correct for the simple reason that it was British.

While Webster was able to accomplish some of his ends—he did, for example, lend authority to the "American" spellings of such words as *ax, humor, plow, jail,* and *center* (compare the "British" *axe, humour, plough, gaol,* and *centre*)—many of his idiosyncratic ideas about pronunciation and spelling met with opposition. Thus Webster's insistence that *deaf* be pronounced /dif/ and that *bridegroom* be respelled *bridegoom* were instantly rejected and had to be retracted.

Impact of Reference Books

The intention of most reference works may be to establish authority and certify correctness, but their effectiveness is extremely difficult to judge. Their role is frequently little more than symbolic, and it has been suggested that the true standardizing forces for many languages have not been the basic reference works or the works of classical writers but the editorial practices of large PUBLISHING houses, which determine principles of spelling, punctuation, diction, and usage. The standardization of pronunciation is even less certain. Printed reference works like Webster's dictionary, H. W. Fowler's *Dictionary of Modern English Usage* (1926), or the frequently reprinted pronunciation guides of Daniel Jones may serve to authorize geographical or social variants, but they are little more than starting points in the determination of national standards. Even in spelling, which is thought to be fairly conventional in English, some significant variation does occur from dictionary to dictionary, as well as in general use. Sometimes spelling variation becomes a usage crux as well, as in the case of the disputed form *alright* for *all right,* which has been discussed in usage books and dictionaries for the past thirty years or more.

While the publication of a language reference book does not usually draw much partisan response, the appearance in 1961 of *Webster's Third New International Dictionary* provoked some sharp reactions that reveal an ambivalence about the purpose of a language reference work. Critics objected to the new editorial practice that eliminated some of the usage labels traditionally found in English dictionaries, and they asserted the need for more lexicographical prescription. They claimed that readers of dictionaries want to know not just how a word is spelled and what it means, but when and when not to use it. The dictionary editors, on the other hand, maintained that the function of an unabridged dictionary is to describe rather than prescribe, to record with scientific objectivity the English language as it is, not as it should be. Ironically, a century earlier Webster himself was called to task by a reviewer in the *Atlantic* (1860) for thinking that "the business of a lexicographer was to *regulate,* not to *record.*"

Reference works are but one element in the complex system that forms our attitudes toward and knowledge of any given language. Their influence within that system is based on a number of variables. On the one hand, they are highly visible cultural artifacts whose authority is both sought by the perplexed and alluded to by speakers and writers in defense of particular language issues (*see* ARTIFACT). (It is often not a problem that the authority of one reference work may be disputed by another, for few except scholars consult more than one dictionary, grammar, or usage guide to find what they need.) On the other hand, it is not clear that people follow the advice or even the descriptions provided by language reference works. The power of reference works to promote language change is limited, and they may in fact be as productive of change as they are of standardizing a language. Imperfectly understanding the prescriptions in question, speakers and writers

Figure 2. *(Language Reference Book)* James A. H. Murray, editor of the *Oxford English Dictionary,* published between 1884 and 1928. From K. M. Elisabeth Murray, *Caught in the Web of Words: James A. H. Murray and the Oxford English Dictionary*, New Haven, Conn.: Yale University Press, 1977, frontispiece.

may produce new variants in their efforts to be correct; words take on new meanings, hypercorrect idioms evolve, and spelling pronunciations become the norm rather than the exception.

Language regulation for English is an informal process of self-regulation, one not generally dependent on language experts. It is true that the use of English is affected by writers on language, authors, journalists, teachers, and even occasionally linguists and to a very small extent by government intervention. As a consequence the definition of standard English is a loose one, embracing a certain degree of variation even in formal registers, and even the most prescriptive English reference works not only allow but encourage some degree of individual choice. The regulation of French, in contrast, is highly centralized and has been for some centuries directed by the specific authority of the French Academy and its dictionary, and the national system of education with its official language texts. Despite such formal efforts at control, variation in spoken and written French remains great, and in recent years movements to revive local dialects and languages have grown stronger.

It is quite likely that the effect of standard reference works is strongest in situations involving the modernization of a language or the creation of a written form for a previously unwritten language. It is also likely that once modernization has occurred (as, for example, in the case of modern Hebrew) and the standard language has been launched, it will take on a life of its own, and the various forces of linguistic control—academies, government edicts, educators, critics, and language scholars—will have less direct influence over its development.

See also EAST ASIA, ANCIENT; ENCYCLOPEDIA; ISLAM, CLASSICAL AND MEDIEVAL ERAS; MEANING.

Bibliography. Dennis E. Baron, *Grammar and Gender,* New Haven, Conn., 1986; idem, *Grammar and Good Taste: Reforming the American Language,* New Haven, Conn., 1982; Claude Hagège and Istvan Fodor, *Language Reform, History and Future* (in German, French, and English), 3 vols., Hamburg, 1983.

DENNIS BARON

LANGUAGE VARIETIES

The term LANGUAGE is, from a linguistic point of view, relatively nontechnical. Most linguists prefer to use the concept of *variety* as a neutral term to refer to any particular kind of language spoken by an individual, group, or community that they wish for some purpose to consider as a single entity. As a very general notion a variety includes what could also be called a *language,* a *dialect,* a *register,* or a *style.* To understand the reasons why certain varieties are thought to belong to the same language and others to different languages we must understand the kinds of social and linguistic distinctions to which these labels relate.

The study of language varieties has taken a central place in modern LINGUISTICS. The variability of language within a community is intimately related to the process of language change, as both its product and its prerequisite. Language changes as speakers borrow features from their fellow speakers, so that the new features replace the old in more and more instances of an ever-wider range of their possible uses. For this borrowing to take place easily and frequently, the lenders and borrowers must be able to communicate easily and frequently. Looking at the community as a whole, then, one sees that changes spread inside communication networks within the larger community more readily than they spread between them. The expected patterns of greater similarity within social groups and within spaces bounded by geographical barriers are indeed what one finds.

Dialect, Register, and Style

The term *dialect* has generally been used to refer to a subordinate variety of a language. For example,

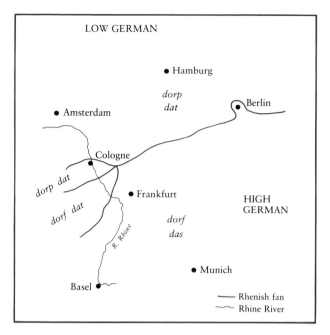

Figure 1. *(Language Varieties)* The Rhenish fan. Redrawn after Werner König, ed., *dtv-Atlas zur deutschen Sprache*, Munich, 1978, p. 64.

the English language has many dialects. A *regional dialect* is a language variety associated with a place, such as the Yorkshire dialect. Dialects of a language tend to differ more from one another the more remote they are from one another geographically. The term *dialect* also has historical connotations. Historical linguists, for instance, speak of the Germanic dialects, by which they mean the ancestors of language varieties we now recognize as modern Germanic languages, such as English, Dutch, and German. The entities we label as the English language or Flemish dialect are not discrete entities. Any variety is part of a continuum in social and geographical space and time. The discontinuities that do occur, however, often reflect geographical and social boundaries and weaknesses in communication networks.

Some classic cases of related dialects are the West Romance and Germanic dialect continua. The West Romance dialect continuum stretches through rural communities from the Atlantic coast of France through Italy, Spain, and Portugal. Mutual intelligibility exists between adjacent villages, although speakers of the standard varieties of French, Italian, Spanish, and Portuguese find one another mutually unintelligible to varying degrees. Similarly the Germanic dialect continuum connects a series of historically related varieties that differ from one another with respect to one or more features. The linguistic boundaries between varieties are called *isoglosses*. Major dialect boundaries are often characterized by a bundle of isoglosses.

One example is the *Rhenish fan,* which separates Low German from High German. As can be seen in Figure 1, the set of isoglosses runs from east to west across Germany (slightly north of Berlin) and Holland. The features comprising the isoglosses include the pronunciation of final consonants such as *p* and *f* and *t* and *s* in words such as *dorp/dorf* ("village") and *dat/das* ("that," "the"). The first member of each of these pairs is the Low German variant, as found in modern standard Dutch, and the second is the High German variant, as found in modern standard German. The point at which the isoglosses meet the Rhine is marked by a fanning out of the isoglosses. In villages along this area speakers may have some Low German features and some High German features—for example, both *dat* and *dorf*.

The dividing line between the languages we call Dutch and German is linguistically arbitrary but politically and culturally relevant. Certain varieties of the West Germanic dialect continuum are considered to be dialects of Dutch and others dialects of German because of the relationship these varieties have to their respective *standard languages*. The process of standardization is connected with a number of sociohistorical factors such as LITERACY, nationalism, and cultural and ethnic identity. It results in the selection and fixing of a uniform norm of usage, which is promoted in dictionaries, grammars, and TEACHING (*see* LANGUAGE REFERENCE BOOK). A standard language is a variety that has been deliberately codified so that it varies minimally in linguistic form but is maximally elaborated in function.

Thus the Dutch dialects are dependent on, or *heteronomous* with respect to, standard Dutch; German dialects are dependent on standard German. This means that speakers of German consider that they speak German; they read and write in German and are taught German in school. They look to standard German as a reference point. The relationship of heteronomy is shown in Figure 2. The term *language* is employed for a variety that is autonomous, together with all those varieties that are heteronomous with respect to it.

Because heteronomy and autonomy reflect political and cultural rather than purely linguistic factors, they

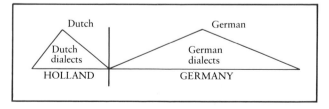

Figure 2. *(Language Varieties)* West German dialect continuum. Redrawn after J. K. Chambers and Peter Trudgill, *Dialectology,* Cambridge: Cambridge University Press, 1980, p. 11.

can change. Formerly heteronomous varieties can achieve autonomy, often because of political developments. Speakers of English in the United States, for example, used to look to British English norms of usage; now, however, an autonomous American variety of standard English must be recognized.

Some linguists make a further distinction between *accent* and *dialect*. An accent consists of a way of pronouncing a variety. A dialect, however, varies from other dialects of the same language simultaneously on at least three levels of organization: pronunciation, GRAMMAR or syntax, and vocabulary. Thus educated speakers of American English and British English can be regarded as using dialects of the same language because differences of these three kinds exist between them. In practice, however, speakers of the two varieties share a common grammar and differ from each other more in terms of vocabulary and pronunciation. Some examples of these differences are illustrated in Table 1.

Geographical distance is but one factor in dialect differentiation. We can draw an analogy between geographical and social space. A dialect continuum can be social rather than geographical. A good example is found in Jamaica, where at one time those at the top of the social scale—the British—spoke English, while those at the bottom spoke Jamaican Creole. Over time the gap between the two has been filled by a range of varieties that are either more like the creole or more like English. Most speakers use several varieties that span a range on this so-called post-creole continuum and shift among them according to context or addressee. Any division of the Jamaican social dialect continuum into English versus Jamaican Creole would be linguistically as arbitrary as dividing the Germanic dialect continuum into Dutch and German. There is no social, political, or geographical reason for saying that English begins at one particular point and Jamaican Creole at another.

A variety is thus a clustering of features. In addition to dialect two other varieties are register and style. A *register* is a variety associated with particular professions, contexts, or topics. Two lawyers discussing a legal matter use the register of law; the language of police detectives reviewing a case reflects a register particular to their profession and the topic under discussion. Vocabulary differences—either a special vocabulary or special meanings for ordinary words—are most important in distinguishing different registers. Language *style* can range from formal to informal depending on social context, relationship of the participants, social class, sex, age, physical environment, and topic. Stylistic differences can be reflected in vocabulary, as in "The teacher distributed the new books" versus "The teacher gave out the new books"; syntax, as in an increased use of the passive

Table 1. Differences between American and British English

	American	British
Pronunciation ate	/eit/ (rhymes with *mate*)	/ɛt/ (rhymes with *met*)
Grammar/Syntax Past participle of *get*	Jane had *gotten* used to it.	Jane had *got* used to it.
Vocabulary	Sam took the *elevator* rather than the stairs.	Sam took the *lift* rather than the stairs.

voice (in English) in formal speech ("The meeting was canceled by the president" versus "The president called off the meeting"); and pronunciation (see Tables 2 and 3).

Social Aspects

The social dimensions of language varieties have been investigated since the nineteenth century. Since the development of quantitative techniques for analyzing variable features of language in the late 1960s, much work has focused on urban dialectology. Sociolinguists have focused on patterns of language use that require reference to social factors such as class stratification, sex, age, and context for their explanation.

One of the first features to be studied in this way was the pronunciation of postvocalic /r/, as in *cart*, *bar*, and *farm*. Varieties of English can be divided into two groups with respect to their treatment of this variable: those that are *r*-pronouncing and those that are not *r*-pronouncing. Today in Britain accents that have lost postvocalic /r/ as a result of linguistic change generally have more prestige than those, like Irish English, that preserve it. In many parts of the United States the reverse is true, although this has not always been the case. Table 2 compares the pronunciation of postvocalic /r/ in New York City (based on research by linguist William Labov) and Reading, England (based on linguist Peter Trudgill's research). The results show that in New York City the lower one's social status, as measured in terms of factors such as occupation, EDUCATION, and income, the fewer postvocalic /r/s one uses, while in Reading the reverse is true.

Like many features investigated by sociolinguists the pronunciation of postvocalic /r/ shows a geographically as well as socially significant distribution. Just as the DIFFUSION of linguistic features may be halted by natural geographical barriers, it may also be impeded by social class stratification. Similarly the boundaries between social dialects tend for the most part not to be absolute. The pattern of variation

Table 2. Percent of Postvocalic /r/s Pronounced (based on Labov 1966 and Trudgill 1974)

New York City	Reading	Social class
32	0	upper-middle class
20	28	lower-middle class
12	44	upper-working class
0	49	lower-working class

for postvocalic /r/ shows *fine stratification* or continuous variation along a linguistic dimension (in this case a phonetic one) as well as an extralinguistic one (in this case social class). The indexes go up or down in relation to social class, and there are no sharp breaks between groups.

The use of other features can be more sharply socially stratifying. That is, a social barrier between the middle class and the working class may be reflected in the usage of some linguistic feature. In English such features are more likely to be grammatical or syntactic, such as the use of multiple negation (e.g., "I *don't* want *no* trouble"), than pronunciation variables. A major finding of urban sociolinguistic work is that the differences among varieties of English are largely quantitative rather than qualitative. Language use is conditioned by both internal linguistic constraints and external social ones.

Not only do some of the same linguistic features figure in patterns of both regional and social dialect differentiation, but they also display correlations with other social factors. Table 3 shows that whether or not one pronounces the final ending of words like *reading* or *fishing* (or omits it, as in *readin'* and *fishin'*) is an indicator of social class as well as style. The behavior of each social class group varies according to whether its style is casual or formal. Although each class had different average scores in each style, all groups *style shift* in the same direction in their more formal speech style, that is, in the direction of the standard language.

It has also been found in a number of sociolinguistic studies that women tend to use higher-status

Table 3. Percent of Forms without Final *g* (results from Trudgill's study of Norwich, England, 1974)

Social class	Style	
	casual	formal
middle-middle class	28	3
lower-middle class	42	15
upper-working class	87	74
middle-working class	95	88
lower-working class	100	98

variants more frequently than men. This pattern was found, for example, with both postvocalic /r/ and final *g*. Women of each social class group use the more prestigious variants more often than men of equal social status. Similar results have been found in other places, such as Sweden. Some researchers have argued that, in the case of spoken English at least, men's and women's speech are two distinct varieties of language. They point to studies that have shown differences in phonological features (pronouncing the final *g*, as noted above), intonation patterns, choice of vocabulary (certain adjectives and intensifiers appear more frequently in women's speech), use of tag questions (addition of a question—such as "isn't it?"—to a statement in order to get agreement or affirmation, something women seem to do more than men), and other features of verbal repertoires. Many of these studies are preliminary, and the features mentioned need to be investigated more thoroughly and systematically. *See also* GENDER; SEXISM.

Multilingualism

Of course, not all language communities are organized in the same way. Widespread bilingualism and multilingualism are actually more common than monolingualism. It has been estimated that there are some four to five thousand languages in the world but only about 140 nation-states.

In many multilingual communities speakers switch among languages or varieties as monolinguals switch among styles. Often each language or variety serves a specialized function and is used for particular purposes. This situation is known as *diglossia*. An example can be taken from Arabic-speaking countries in which the language used at home may be a local version of Arabic. The language that is recognized publicly, however, is modern standard Arabic, which takes many of its normative rules from the classical Arabic of the Qur'an. The standard language is used for "high" functions such as giving a lecture, READING, WRITING, or broadcasting, while the home variety is reserved for "low" functions such as interacting with friends at home.

The analogy has been extended to other communities in which the varieties in diglossic distribution have the status of separate languages, such as Spanish and Guaraní (an Indian language totally unrelated to Spanish) in Paraguay. Spanish serves here as the high variety and is used for high functions.

In some multilingual communities speakers who do not share a native language use a lingua franca to communicate in certain contexts, such as in commercial transactions. The chosen lingua franca can be indigenous to an area, as Swahili is to Africa, or nonindigenous, as English is to India. It may be, but does not have to be, the native language of any of the speakers. A pidgin language is one that is created from one or more languages and is used as a lingua franca but has no native speakers. The language from which the pidgin is derived has been simplified, and vocabulary and grammatical complexities have been reduced. Often vocabulary and pronunciation conventions from other languages (other than the one on which the pidgin is based) are introduced into the pidgin by those who use it. As with other lingua francas, the uses and occasions for using a pidgin will depend partly on how widely it is known.

Linguistic diversity thus occurs in both monolingual and multilingual communities. Differences among language varieties are likely to emerge in response to geographical, social, and functional factors. Political considerations are becoming increasingly relevant as well. With the end of colonialism and the formation of new nation-states, the question of which language (or which version of which one) will become the official national language arises and has often led to bitter controversy. Even countries with more than one official language, such as Canada, have not escaped attempts by various factions to gain political advantage by exploiting issues of language loyalty. Language varies according to its users and uses, and research on language varieties will have to take into account all the relevant factors that affect these choices.

See also LANGUAGE IDEOLOGY; MEANING; SPEAKING, ETHNOGRAPHY OF.

Bibliography. J. K. Chambers and Peter Trudgill, *Dialectology,* Cambridge, 1980; R. A. Hudson, *Sociolinguistics,* Cambridge, 1980; William Labov, *The Social Stratification of English in New York City,* Washington, D.C., 1966, reprint 1982; Peter Trudgill, *The Social Differentiation of English in Norwich,* Cambridge, 1974; idem, *Sociolinguistics,* Harmondsworth, Eng., 1983.

SUZANNE ROMAINE

LASER. *See* FIBER OPTICS; SOUND RECORDING.

LASKER, ALBERT (1880–1952)

U.S. advertising executive. Long considered the doyen of U.S. ADVERTISING and its most articulate apostle, Albert Davis Lasker had a career that spanned the industry's most spectacular decades of growth and in many ways epitomized them. His promotional and propagandistic wizardry became legendary and earned him great wealth and political influence, but in his final years he changed his opinions on many subjects, including advertising and politics.

In 1898, at the age of eighteen, Lasker entered the Lord and Thomas advertising agency in Chicago at a salary of ten dollars a week, but he proved so adept at winning new clients that he soon dominated the

Figure 1. *(Lasker, Albert)* Mary and Albert Lasker. From John Gunther, *Taken at the Flood,* New York: Harper and Brothers, 1960.

agency, earned huge bonuses, and by 1903 was able to buy out one of the partners, D. M. Lord. A few years later he and a colleague, Charles R. Erwin, bought out Ambrose Thomas's share. When Lasker bought out Erwin in 1912, he became sole owner of Lord and Thomas; he would soon take home more than a million dollars a year from the agency's earnings.

His fame spread. In 1917 former U.S. president Theodore Roosevelt invited him for a visit to Oyster Bay, New York, and welcomed him with, "They tell me you are America's greatest advertising man." Lasker replied, "Colonel, no man can claim that distinction as long as you are alive." The jovial encounter led to a prominent Lasker role in Republican party politics. He became assistant to Will Hays, chairman of the Republican National Committee, for which his first task was to organize a campaign against U.S. entry into the League of Nations. Lasker's PAMPHLET, *After the Peace, What?* was distributed in millions of copies. The success of the drive led to another role, as coordinator of all publicity for Warren G. Harding's 1920 "front porch campaign" for the presidency, and to brief service under President Harding. Lasker was invited to become czar of HOLLYWOOD, which was awash with scandal, but instead recommended his friend Hays and returned to his agency.

Expounding to staff members at length about the glories of advertising, he now led them in vigorous drives for Lucky Strike, Pepsodent, Kotex, Kleenex, Palmolive, Frigidaire, Goodyear, and a host of other clients. His leadership was marked by verve, decisiveness, and a flair for terse expression. Asked how Kleenex (an unprecedented new product) was faring, he answered, "Fine. Women are beginning to waste it." For Pepsodent he decreed a secret ingredient, ordering his staff to devise a name for it consisting of two consonants and three vowels. They came up with *irium*, which would dominate Pepsodent commercials during its sponsorship, beginning in mid-1929, of the "Amos 'n' Andy" series on NBC, one of the first great successes of network RADIO. Lasker plunged heavily into radio; for a time almost half of NBC's revenue came from Lord and Thomas. In Lasker's Lucky Strike campaigns the focus was on women. At the start of the 1920s few women smoked. If they could be persuaded to do so, the market would double. Lasker built his strategy around opera singers ("Luckies are kind to my throat") and movie stars—figures of glamour, status, and daring. The depression scarcely slowed Lasker; in 1932 he personally netted almost three million dollars. Near Lake Forest, Illinois, he built a fifty-room mansion on a 480-acre tract with 97 acres of formal gardens, an eighteen-hole golf course, a theater, and a swimming pool; he employed fifty servants. The rich and famous came and went.

In the 1940s, after his first wife had died, he married a Hollywood actress, Doris Kenyon, but they were divorced within months. He entered psychoanalysis, then married again. With his new wife, Mary, he seemed to become a different person. The man who had helped scotch U.S. membership in the League of Nations became an ardent internationalist and backer of the United Nations. He gave up the Lake Forest estate, calling it "the kind of place that's going to be surrounded by an angry mob some day. . . . I intend to be part of the mob." He turned his agency over to his chief staff members (it became Foote, Cone, and Belding) and embarked on new interests. He wrote to his friend Robert Hutchins, president of the University of Chicago: "I am the most superficial man on earth, and yet I am the dean of my profession . . . there must be something wrong with the profession." The man who had set out to persuade millions of women to smoke began to give huge sums to cancer research. After his own death from cancer much of his fortune went into medical research and international causes.

Bibliography. John Gunther, *Taken at the Flood*, New York, 1960.

ERIK BARNOUW

LASSWELL, HAROLD D. (1902–1978)

U.S. political scientist. Harold Dwight Lasswell was one of the most productive and influential political scientists of the twentieth century. Both his scholarly interests and his preparation were wide-ranging. A doctorate from the University of Chicago, when some of the pioneers of modern social science were teaching there, was supplemented by a period in Europe during which he attended seminars with such scholars as economist John Maynard Keynes, campaigned for philosopher Bertrand Russell when Russell was running for Parliament, studied the work of SIGMUND FREUD and KARL MARX, and for six months underwent analysis with Theodor Reik (author of *Listening with the Third Ear*, 1948) to experience personally the workings of PSYCHOANALYSIS. Later Lasswell became noted for applying psychoanalysis to the study of political power, seeing (like Freud) public actions in terms of private motives and personalities. Like many of his fellow pioneers in politics and sociology, he also saw communication as one of the fields of thought and action a modern social scientist ought to understand, and it became a central focus of his studies.

From 1922 to 1938 Lasswell taught political science at Chicago, where among his students were many of the leading political scientists of the next academic generation. When he came up for promotion, however, he was refused a permanent appointment. He resigned from the university, packed his books and research notes into a truck, and started east. The truck caught fire, and all the contents burned, leaving the young teacher without either a job or work materials. Ten years later he got his professorship, but it was at the Yale Law School.

More than anyone else Lasswell pioneered the use of CONTENT ANALYSIS as a major methodology in the study of communications. His published doctoral dissertation (1927) was titled *Propaganda Techniques in the World War* (World War I). During and after World War II he supervised two large content studies—one at the U.S. Library of Congress, the other at Stanford University—examining PROPAGANDA symbols, opinions of the world elite, and the world "prestige press." He was especially interested in using the massive amounts of data collected during such studies to establish world trend lines—"world weather maps of public opinion"—on the basis of which political scientists could practice "social psychiatry" and "preventive politics" (*see* PUBLIC OPINION).

Lasswell also posed three "developmental constructs" or paradigms of possible future states: (1) the Marxist state, (2) the "skill commonwealth" run by a managerial elite, and (3) the "garrison state" run by the police or military. These and other concepts in his writings influenced U.S. communications policies in the cold war. His article "The Strategy of Revolutionary and War Propaganda" (1933) analyzes the Marxist use of POLITICAL SYMBOLS and utopianism (*see also* MARXIST THEORIES OF COMMUNICATION; UTOPIAS). His *National Security and Individual Freedom* (1950) is a handbook for policymakers on how to maintain maximum freedom—including freedom of the press—under cold war conditions.

Thus Lasswell's concerns with communication were by no means limited to content analysis. Among his numerous publications are works that every communication graduate student reads. One of these is "The Structure and Function of Communication in Society" (in *The Communication of Ideas,* edited by Lyman Bryson, 1948), containing Lasswell's theory of the functions of communication: *surveillance* of the environment, *correlation* of society's response to it, and *transmission* of the social heritage. Perhaps no definition of communication has been more widely quoted than the Lasswell formulation: "Who says what, in what channel, to whom, with what effect?" Lasswell also helped found *Public Opinion Quarterly* and was a member of various important committees and commissions, including the 1947 Hutchins Commission on Freedom of the Press. He became president of the American Political Science Association in 1955.

Lasswell was a leader in what he termed the "policy sciences" and an advocate of communications research as the scientific study of policy-making. In an influential article titled "Communications Research and Public Policy" (1972), published in *Public Opinion Quarterly,* he called for the monitoring of flows of information that enter the public opinion and policy-making process. His initiative and encouragement contributed to the development of the concept of CULTURAL INDICATORS.

See also COMMUNICATIONS RESEARCH: ORIGINS AND DEVELOPMENT.

Bibliography. Lyman Bryson, ed., *The Communication of Ideas,* New York, 1948; Harold D. Lasswell, *Politics: Who Gets What, When, How,* New York, 1936, reprint 1950; idem, *World Politics and Personal Insecurity,* New York, 1935, reprint 1965; Dwaine Marvick, ed., *Harold D. Lasswell on Political Sociology,* Chicago and London, 1977; Arnold A. Rogow, ed., *Politics, Personality, and Social Science in the Twentieth Century: Essays in Honor of Harold D. Lasswell,* Chicago, 1969.

WILBUR SCHRAMM

LATIN AMERICA, TWENTIETH CENTURY

Latin America has a long tradition of strong cultural manifestations. The important civilizations existing before the Spanish conquest in the sixteenth century (e.g., Aztec, Inca, Maya) are notable for their cultural and scientific achievements (*see* AMERICAS, PRE-COLUMBIAN; CALENDAR; NUMBER). Nearly four centuries of colonial life left imprints in the populations, LANGUAGE, traditions, and systems of social organization that are still visible in the patterns of expression and communication of the countries in this vast region of the world.

The Latin American media industries that developed during the twentieth century have been primarily commercial in nature and privately owned. They include giant enterprises such as Televisa in Mexico and TV Globo in Brazil that produce in various media and have access to international distribution networks. But the prevailing pattern has been marked by limited production capacity with heavy dependence on U.S. sources for equipment, programming, investment capital, and ADVERTISING revenues. Direct ownership by U.S. corporations has become less prevalent. Thus the overall picture continues to be one of relatively small-scale local activity supplemented by large-scale imports—of news services, television programming, films, and other media materials. Cuba and Nicaragua are exceptions because their respective revolutions introduced important changes in terms of ownership, programming, and even equipment.

Evolution

The general trend may be said to have started in the early years of the century, when the international NEWS AGENCIES began extending their cable services to major Latin American capitals (*see also* NEWSPAPER: TRENDS—TRENDS IN LATIN AMERICA). By the 1930s the U.S. film industry had achieved worldwide dominance, and local film industries with far more limited budgets found it almost impossible to compete against HOLLYWOOD products. U.S. predominance is expected to continue unless policies are formulated to address the social and cultural impact of the mass media and their relation to the international communications industry (*see* NEW INTERNATIONAL INFORMATION ORDER).

The financial stakes are substantial because Latin America has become a significant market for communications technology and content. Importation of broadcasting technologies for RADIO and television has been followed by the adoption of computer, SATELLITE, CABLE TELEVISION, and VIDEO technologies, especially since the late 1970s. In the early 1980s Latin America accounted for 10 percent of the international theatrical film market, which was estimated at $5 billion, and 51 percent of the international television and video sales by U.S. distributors. In contrast, a 1982 UNESCO study estimated that Latin America produced less than 1 percent of the world's cultural products, including media materials.

The spread of the private, commercial model of broadcasting coincided with the global expansion of U.S. transnational corporations (TNCs) during the 1950s and 1960s and with efforts to promote rapid modernization throughout the region (*see* DEVELOPMENT COMMUNICATION). The TNCs were searching for new markets for their consumer products and relied extensively on available media to promote them. The high economic growth rates during the 1960s and early 1970s allowed national corporations and governments to spend considerable amounts of money on promotion through the mass media. Advertising revenues thus fueled the growth of broadcast media in Latin America, along with state collaboration in the expansion of communications infrastructures and the emergence of large urban populations. The private, commercial model of broadcasting was challenged during a brief period in the late 1960s and early 1970s when some emerging political forces attempted to introduce changes in ownership, financing, and media content patterns so that these would be more in line with national development objectives. However, the reform movement was unable to cope with the opposition presented by private national and transnational interests.

Television

During the 1950s Latin American countries began adopting television technology. Transmitters, production equipment, receivers, and programs were imported from the United States. A majority of countries later also adopted the National Television Systems Committee (NTSC) color system and the 525-line video scanning format developed in the United States, both of which are thought to be of lower quality than other systems (mainly PAL and SECAM) used in Europe, the Soviet Union, and Africa. The private, commercial model of broadcasting became standard throughout the region, except in Chile between 1958 and 1973, in Cuba after 1959, and in Nicaragua after 1979.

Television quickly surpassed other media in economic and cultural impact. The largest proportion of advertising expenditures is regularly allocated to television, and people increasingly devote more of their LEISURE time to that medium. Since the 1960s imported U.S. television series have been a major element in program schedules because they cost less than local productions and attract substantial audiences as well as national and transnational advertisers. Table 1 gives a comparative breakdown of advertising expenditures by media in seven Latin American countries.

Media systems in Latin America are characterized by heavy concentration in urban areas, a tendency toward media and extramedia conglomeration (participation in various media and in other industries), a predominance of ENTERTAINMENT over other types of programming, and a ratings system that mediates relations between broadcasters and sponsors (*see* RATING SYSTEMS: RADIO AND TELEVISION). Critics ascribe to advertisers (*see* SPONSOR) considerable economic and cultural influence, including the socialization of labor within a corporate environment. On the other hand, it is held that television in Latin America, in spite of its imported aspects, has successfully adapted itself to the social, economic, and cultural circumstances of the region, as, for example, in the enormous popularity of *telenovelas* (*see* SOAP OPERA).

It is difficult to ascertain the economic viability of media industries in the region. Observers have argued that even some television stations, normally quite profitable, exist more for political than for economic reasons. By contrast, attempts to establish national film industries have largely failed despite the fact that individual filmmakers from Brazil, Argentina, Chile, Cuba, and other countries have won praise and recognition in film festivals around the world. In general, however, the cinema has been limited to small-scale local productions or variously successful efforts at regional and international coproduction and distribution arrangements. *See* MOTION PICTURES—SOUND FILM.

Media Content

The expansion of media industries has not resulted in a significant increase in the local content of programming. Considerable attention has been paid in research to the proportion of imported versus national television content (*see* CONTENT ANALYSIS). Findings suggest that the intraregional exchange of television programs—especially soap operas—increased during the late 1970s and early 1980s, with Brazil, Argentina, Venezuela, and Mexico as the largest exporters. However, material imported from outside the region, predominantly the United States, generally accounts for 50 to 80 percent of total transmission time despite legislation in many countries establishing minimum requirements in terms of national production and screen time and airtime (e.g., 60 percent in Peru, 50 percent in Venezuela and Colombia, 30 percent in Ecuador and Bolivia). Broadcasters have definite economic incentives to maintain the existing pattern because local production costs are much higher than comparable costs for imported series (e.g., a regional average of about $1,500 for a local one-hour show compared to about $250 for an episode of a U.S. series). In addition, Latin American audiences have acquired a taste for Hollywood genres, so that imported programming

Table 1. Advertising Expenditures in Selected Latin American Countries, 1983

Total Advertising Expenditures, 1983 (U.S.$)	Argentina N.A.	Brazil U.S.$ 2 Billion	Chile U.S.$ 105 Million	Colombia U.S.$ 337.8 Million	Mexico U.S.$ 220 Million	Peru U.S.$ 74 Million	Venezuela U.S.$ 186 Million
Breakdown by media	%	%	%	%	%	%	%
Television	29.6	61.0	45.1	52.0	50.6	53.9	50.5
Newspapers	23.5	14.7	35.1	18.0	12.3	25.7	25.9
Radio	8.4	8.0	10.8	25.0	16.9	12.2	17.1
Magazines	5.7	12.9	6.1	5.0	9.2	3.8	2.0
Outdoor	7.6	2.3	2.8	—	3.0	{ 4.4	2.3
Cinema	2.4	0.4	0.1	—	1.5		0.9

Source: *Advertising Age*, July 5, 1984. Amendments by authors.

often commands the largest audiences. *See also* TELE-VISION HISTORY—WORLD MARKET STRUGGLES.

The advent of new technologies during the 1980s led some analysts to expect greater diversity in media material; this, however, has not been the overall result. Cable television, videocassettes, and satellite technology have tended to reinforce (and perhaps increase) the traditional reliance on foreign programming. In a replay of the early history of radio and television in the region, issues of content have again been ignored while the technology is rapidly diffusing and practices become entrenched. Thus the audience for these—and other—new technologies has been reduced to the few who can afford to pay for them.

Cultural Implications

Throughout Latin America there are marked discrepancies between mass media content and the cultural and socioeconomic conditions of both urban and rural populations. In Peru it was estimated in 1972 that about half of the 18 million total population could not meet its basic health and nutrition needs. More than 4.5 million people were considered to live at a level of absolute poverty, meaning that they could not satisfy their most basic needs even if they devoted all their disposable income to that end. The irrelevance of the life-styles and values usually depicted in the mass media to the needs of such population groups is a frequent source of criticism. It is argued that the diversity of modern technologies should afford some means for assisting the people of the region to cope with their environment and even to influence it through active participation in the media. The difficulty (or impossibility) of gaining access to established mass media channels has led to multiple experiments in cultural expression through "alternative" communication media, channels, or formats, including small presses, music, and video exchanges. *See also* CITIZEN ACCESS; MINORITY MEDIA.

Work on the concept and practice of alternative communication has been carried out mainly by two distinct groups: popular organizations (such as labor unions, neighborhood associations, and women's groups) and technical, professional, and religious organizations. These two groups have collaborated on three types of projects, involving information, EDUCATION, and organization. The shared or similar political goals have not been enough, however, to smooth out the inevitable differences between groups of people with different backgrounds, experiences, and training. Although successful in some ways, the widespread call for new, participatory forms of communication in society has been followed by few projects implementing the principles promoted. Thus there is an evolving consensus in the region about the need to develop further the theoretical, research, and practical bases that will contribute to the movement's efficacy.

Alternative communication experiences are not restricted to printed media. Radio stations operated by trade unions, peasant organizations, and the Catholic church have a long history in Bolivia, where they play crucial political and cultural roles. A newer medium, video, is being used by more than one thousand groups working for popular organization, education, and development. Additionally, new distribution channels (e.g., the Latin American Video Network created by the Institute for Latin America, IPAL) have joined existing regional organizations such as the Latin American Association of Radio Schools (Asociación Latinoamericana de Escuelas Radiodifusoras, ALER) in promoting alternative uses of the media.

Meanwhile, national governments—sometimes in collusion with national and transnational interests—continue to expand Latin America's communications infrastructure without due consideration of the social and cultural implications. For example, cable television systems have been started in Mexico and Peru, and investments in satellite networks have grown significantly. All the countries in the region are uti-lizing INTELSAT's satellite services, and countries such as Brazil and Mexico have had since 1985 their own satellites for domestic communications, used extensively by the leading private media companies (Televisa in Mexico, TV Globo in Brazil).

This process of cooperation (or collusion) between governments and private media owners subjects many Latin American journalists and other media profes-sionals to both direct and indirect CENSORSHIP. On the one hand, governments pressure the media either through explicit censorship (as in Chile since 1973) or through the control of newsprint, taxes, and of-ficial advertising. On the other hand, media owners often establish procedural guidelines that amount to censorship in efforts to protect their individual or corporate interests.

The television industries are at the cutting edge of a trend toward the eventual integration of the mass media and the new communications technologies (e.g., video, cable, satellites, computers). Qualitative changes in the economic and organizational pro-cesses involving this sector can be expected. The trend may aggravate the traditional dependence on relatively inexpensive information and entertainment supplied by U.S. sources, but it may also allow for innovative production and distribution arrangements within the region, thus stimulating the production of local materials. For instance, films with limited the-atrical audiences could reach wider audiences when distributed in videocassette format, and television programs could overcome physical limitations if shown through cable or satellite systems that are largely immune to atmospheric conditions.

Perspectives

Despite the phenomenal expansion of media indus-tries in Latin America during the second half of the twentieth century, little interest has been shown in reforming the systems in order to promote national cultural expression. Government efforts in Peru, Chile, Venezuela, and Mexico during the late 1960s and early 1970s were unsuccessful either because their proponents lost political power or because of the sustained opposition of private interests.

At a different level, the scarcity of reliable research on media industries has made the task of assessing their cultural and economic impact—as well as that of formulating policies for them—substantially more complex. The private, commercial model is firmly entrenched within the economic systems of the coun-tries in the region, and thus it would not be very realistic to expect any of the Latin American govern-ments to be able to change their communications industries fundamentally by the end of this century. Most states simply could not afford any major inter-vention in the sector (e.g., by establishing nationwide

television or radio networks of their own). Even in such a limited domain, however, there is room for innovative policy measures that might stimulate na-tional cultural production (e.g., through fiscal incen-tives) and promote the regional integration of the media industries (e.g., through coproduction and ex-change agreements). Intergovernmental bodies in the region, such as the Latin American Economic System (Sistema Económico Latinoamericano, SELA), the Latin American Institute for Economic and Social Planning (Instituto Latinoamericano de Planificación Económica y Social, ILPES), and the Council of the Cartagena Agreement (Junta del Acuerdo de Carta-gena, JUNAC), have moved in this direction by in-corporating social communication as one of their concerns and fields of cooperation. For all of them it is clear that regional cooperation may be the most effective way to achieve the development of endog-enous cultural industries and media.

Bibliography. Elizabeth Fox de Cardona and Héctor Schmucler, *Comunicación y democracia en América La-tina*, Lima, Peru, 1982; Valerio Fuenzalida, *Estudios sobre la televisión Chilena*, Santiago, Chile, 1984; Thomas H. Guback and Tapio Varis, *Transnational Communication and Cultural Industries*, Paris, 1982; Armand Mattelart, *Multinacionales y sistemas de comunicación: Los aparatos ideológicos del imperialismo*, Mexico, D.F., 1977; Luis Peirano, ed., *Educación y comunicación popular en el Perú*, Lima, Peru, 1985; Diego Portales, *Poder económico y libertad de expresión*, Santiago, Chile, 1981; Fernando Reyes Matta, ed., *Comunicación alternativa y búsquedas democráticas*, Mexico, D.F., 1983; Jorge A. Schnitman, *Film Industries in Latin America: Dependency and Devel-opment*, Norwood, N.J., 1984; Anthony Smith, *The Geo-politics of Information: How Western Culture Dominates the World*, New York, 1980; UNESCO, *Cultural Indus-tries: A Challenge for the Future of Culture*, Paris, 1982.

HENRY GEDDES AND RAFAEL RONCAGLIOLO

LAW AND COMMUNICATION

At the least, law and legal systems operate to pro-mote order within a society by providing an institu-tionalized process to regulate disputes. At the most they exist to direct the thought and behavior of individuals along channels approved by their political superiors. In either case communication of the rules and their purpose to the affected parties seems central to the notion of law. In fact, though, communication in law is less prized than one would expect.

Sources

The Western world has made use of four sources of law, in the sense of bases of legitimacy that courts habitually regard as determinative for their decisions:

(1) custom, (2) judicial precedent, (3) juristic opinion, and (4) legislation. Each source has different implications for communication.

Custom. The traditional theory of custom is that habitual behavior comes to have legal force when people observe it, in the belief that it is already binding as law. In practice a supposed custom becomes law when court decisions based on it become accepted as a statement of customary law. In fact, there may have been no preceding custom, with people doing different things, or if there was it may not have been widely known. Customary law is found primarily in small societies with no powerful central administration, and it is a typical feature of customary legal systems that either the law is not known or there are many gaps in it. But a judge, faced with an issue, has to decide the case at hand, whether or not customary behavior can provide an answer. The judge frequently borrows, as if it were the custom, a rule from an admired system or follows the opinion of a writer who is not authoritative and who frequently has made up a rule or borrowed one from elsewhere. When an authoritative account of custom is produced, it becomes law, but as statute. Custom is not today a powerful source of law in the developed world, but it has been in continental Europe, especially during the MIDDLE AGES, and still is in parts of Africa and elsewhere.

Judicial precedent. As a form of lawmaking, judicial precedent is not a satisfactory way of communicating knowledge of law and its aims. The law is buried in a very large number of cases contained in multiple volumes, and usually several cases have to be studied to extract even the beginnings of a rule. Even when textbooks report judge-made law, they leave the impression that the cases must still be read. Law becomes very remote from laypersons, including the very people who are expected to follow it. Besides, law created in this way cannot be systematic. Judge-made law is a bad communicator not just because it is hard to find but also because it waits on events and decides what was the right thing to have done in the past according to a law that then was unknown and unknowable. Yet judicial precedent is a powerful source of law in the common-law countries, such as England and the United States, and is coming to be more highly regarded in civil-law countries, comprising most of Europe and Latin America.

Juristic opinion. Juristic opinion was a powerful source of law in ancient Rome; in the development of the learned law beginning in medieval Europe and still existing today in civil-law countries; and to a lesser though still marked extent in the United States. For communication, juristic opinion has the advantages that it can be forward looking, can set out an issue or a whole area of law systematically and clearly, and can formulate reasons for the adoption of rules. It suffers from the defect that it is not law and hence cannot be known to be the law until its authority is accepted either by a court or in legislation. Most systems that treat juristic opinion as important for finding the law fail to set up a system for deciding which jurists or which opinions are to be given precedence when jurists disagree, as is frequently the case. Often a juristic opinion may come to shape the law only a considerable time after it was expressed. Thus, insofar as it is a source of law, juristic opinion cannot be given high marks for communicating the law.

Legislation. At least in theory, legislation can be the most powerful form of lawmaking. It also has the greatest power to shape legal thought, direct human behavior, and censor knowledge (*see* CENSORSHIP). Only legislation can break sharply with preceding law and make a new beginning. A good modern example is the adoption in 1925 of the Swiss Civil Code (with only minor modifications) by Turkish leader Kemal Atatürk, and the subsequent acceptance of commercial law from similar European sources. Atatürk aimed at secularizing, modernizing, and westernizing Turkey, and law was one of his tools (*see* DEVELOPMENT COMMUNICATION). Although these aims were not achieved at one stroke, the new law was nonetheless successfully adopted.

Not only can statute law seek to change human behavior, but the legislators can set out their ends in a *preamble*—a device apparently invented by PLATO and, in the eighteenth century, favored by English political theorist Jeremy Bentham. Legislation, moreover, can be systematic on a single branch of law or, as in modern codifications, cover whole fields of law.

Thus, law as communication, as an institutionalized way to regulate and direct human behavior, is best served by legislation. Some features of legislation should be noted. First, legislation until modern times was relatively rare. Second, although legislation may break with the past, it does so only at the time when it is promulgated. It is a feature of legislation, especially marked perhaps in codification, that once it is in place it tends to remain unaltered, possibly for centuries. The courts may reinterpret it away from its original purpose, but then the resulting law is as difficult to find and know as any judge-made law. Third, very little statute law and very few codes are original in the sense that they are made fresh for the territory in which they operate, without a great dependence on law from elsewhere. Atatürk's reforms are typical. It is easier to borrow than to create, even if the law is not precisely dovetailed to the aims of the society. Whatever Atatürk may have desired and whatever he may have achieved, it is difficult to think of two societies more different in geography, economy, politics, and religion than Switzerland at the turn of the century and Turkey in the 1920s. Yet the law of the one was taken over by legislation for the law of the other. Fourth, even "original" legislation has roots, usually hidden, in the (often distant) past that are not present in the consciousness of the legislator and that affect the attempt to direct behavior. Fifth, apart from topics of consuming passion to them, legislators are generally not interested in law reform, especially in the field of private law. Change by legislation may be a long time coming.

The conclusion seems unavoidable even if surprising. In general, lawmakers are little concerned with communicating the law and their message in it, or even with having a particular message in it. The example of criminal law in nineteenth-century England is illuminating on these points. If one wanted an example of law used to communicate ideals of behavior and to restrain behavior regarded as wrongful, criminal law should have a special place. In 1833 criminal-law commissioners were appointed with the initial task of showing the need to put statutory and common-law principles in one code; then they had to prepare a restatement of the existing law in the code. Despite much previous legislation a great deal of the law was in judicial precedent and was hard to find. Five reports were produced between 1839 and 1845, and a revised commission then produced another five reports between 1845 and 1849. Judges at that stage objected to the notion of a code as being too rigid a framework for the law. Members of Parliament, who also sat as jurors or as justices of the peace, were not enthusiastic about reform. The final result was nothing more than a statute consolidating the law that was already in statute—all this against the background of a penal code for British India drafted by Lord Macaulay and successfully promulgated. Sir James Fitzjames Stephen, who had experience of the Indian codes, produced in the 1870s his own draft of a criminal code that at one time looked as if it would be successful before Parliament but was again defeated by the opposition of the judges. It did not pass in England but was a success in some colonies (*see* COLONIZATION). Since then, there has been some, but little and slow, progress. Scholars may disagree about the motivation of the reluctant lawmakers, whether as judges or legislators, but the lesson is simply that they showed no great desire to communicate knowledge of what the law was or even to produce a precise message in the law. This lack of interest in communication on the part of lawmakers is not unusual.

Qualifications. To all of the foregoing there are three particular qualifications. First, a desire for communication seems a predominant motive in the minds of many who have fought successfully for a codification of the law. This is true, for example, of Moses, Hammurabi, Justinian, Frederick the Great, Napoléon, and Atatürk. It is also true of some who unsuccessfully wished codification, such as Julius Caesar and Bentham. Dissatisfaction with the actual substance of the rules was usually a much lesser motivation. Usually the need to communicate the rules of law is made express. Those who wish law communicated by codification usually stand outside the legal tradition; they are impatient with the tolerance of other lawmakers for obfuscation. In addition they wish to communicate knowledge of law, not a particular social message in the law.

Second, in some countries communication of certain branches of law is taken so seriously that the countries may become best known in the outside world for these legal attitudes: for example, the Republic of Ireland for its refusal to give legal recognition to divorce and its criminal sanctions against abortion and contraception; and the Republic of South Africa for apartheid, laws against mixing of the races. The legal rules will often be communicated in a simplified form through media such as radio or newspapers. The law in question usually maintains or promotes social conditions and attitudes that are regarded by the state as vital to its interests and that distinguish it from other societies. The law is here used to communicate and preserve social values. One cannot lay down general rules regarding the branches of law on which attention to communication will be focused. It is not the case that a special desire to communicate rules will always be seen in criminal law (as the example of nineteenth-century England shows) or in family law. Likewise, attention is not necessarily centered in capitalist societies either on the clarity or even the formation of business law. The late development in the nineteenth century of commercial law in England—to MAX WEBER's bewilderment—is sufficient proof of this.

Third, written constitutions are typically used to communicate the highest ideals or the PROPAGANDA values embraced by the leaders of a state. This is true for countries as diverse as the United States and the Soviet Union. In contrast to the rest of law, constitutions are usually nontechnical in language, widely disseminated in inexpensive or even free editions, and often referred to rhetorically by politicians and others. They are treated as basic law, knowledge of which is a duty for citizens, but their practical use for enforcing rights in the courts may in actuality be limited. They are used to induce loyalty in the citizen to the state (*see* POLITICAL SYMBOLS).

Society's Knowledge of the Law

Though law regulates human behavior and must be communicated in order to do so, there is, in general, relatively little social interest in making knowledge of the law accessible to those affected by it or even in setting out clear aims in the law. This lack of interest in communication is best seen as indicating that the needs served in a particular society by law are, above all, the establishment of some kind of order, but not that some precise ordering of society is behind every law. To a considerable extent law is an expression of the culture of the lawmaking elite, and in making law one lawmaker signals to another: judges write opinions for other judges or top practitioners, jurists write texts for other scholars, legislators legislate to impress other parliamentarians. Only in very particular circumstances do lawmakers attempt to set out a clear message in law for the populace at large or to set out the law clearly. Outside of these particular circumstances states seem largely interested in communicating only the most basic notions: "Thou shalt not steal"—but not the nature of the act and intention that constitutes theft; "Contracts are binding"—but not what is a contract or the rights and duties of a party under a contract.

See also POLITICAL COMMUNICATION; TESTIMONY.

Bibliography. Alan Watson, *Legal Transplants: An Approach to Comparative Law*, Charlottesville, Va., 1974; idem, *Sources of Law, Legal Change, and Ambiguity*, Philadelphia, 1984.

ALAN WATSON

LAZARSFELD, PAUL F. (1901–1976)

Austrian-born U.S. sociologist. Born and raised in Vienna, Paul Felix Lazarsfeld moved to the United States in 1933 as a Rockefeller Foundation fellow and became a U.S. citizen; for three decades he was a professor of sociology at Columbia University. Along with his contemporaries HAROLD D. LASSWELL, CARL HOVLAND, and WILBUR SCHRAMM, he was a principal founder of communications research as a social science discipline.

In 1925 Lazarsfeld received his Ph.D. in applied mathematics from the University of Vienna and soon after established the Wirtschaftpsychologische Forschungsstelle, a research institute dedicated to the application of psychology to social and economic problems, which among other studies undertook a survey of RADIO listeners. The Forschungsstelle was the first of four university-related applied social research institutes founded by Lazarsfeld; the others were the Research Center at the University of Newark, the Office of Radio Research at Princeton University, and the Bureau of Applied Social Research (now the Center for the Social Sciences) at Columbia University.

In 1937 the Rockefeller Foundation granted funds to HADLEY CANTRIL for a large-scale program of research on the nature and social effects of radio, the first such study of radio ever undertaken. On the recommendation of Robert S. Lynd, a professor of sociology at Columbia, Lazarsfeld was chosen as its director. Cantril and Frank Stanton—who was then research director but would subsequently become the longtime president of the Columbia Broadcasting System—were appointed associate directors of the project, and an intensive study of radio programs and listeners was begun. The project emphasized (1) the secondary analysis of existing audience data, (2) the CONTENT ANALYSIS of radio programs, and (3) the use of the Lazarsfeld-Stanton Program Analyzer, a device for instantly recording the likes and dislikes of experimental groups of radio listeners.

The research conducted by Lazarsfeld and his associates during the project and at the Office of Radio Research virtually created the empirical sociology of mass communications (*see* MASS COMMUNICATIONS RESEARCH). In particular, this research focused on the uses and gratifications of radio in people's lives. Examples include Herta Herzog's studies of the audiences of daytime radio soap operas (*see* SOAP OPERA) and (with Cantril) of the reactions of radio listeners who heard ORSON WELLES's 1938 "The War of the Worlds" broadcast (which described an invasion from Mars), as well as THEODOR ADORNO's studies of the social roles of popular music (*see* MUSIC, POPULAR) and classical music. Other communications research projects carried out during these early years by Lazarsfeld's associates included ROBERT K. MERTON's 1944 study of a marathon eighteen-hour radio broadcast during which Kate Smith sold war bonds, Bernard Berelson's study of the functions that newspapers serve in the lives of their readers (made possible by a 1945 newspaper strike in New York), and LEO LOWENTHAL's 1944 analysis of the biographies (*see* BIOGRAPHY) of culture heroes published in popular magazines (*see* MAGAZINE). Lazarsfeld's own research (1940) on the comparative effects of radio listening and reading was an imaginative examination of this important question. His influence on the field outlived him: in the mid-1980s the directors of social research at the nation's three broadcasting networks—CBS, ABC, and NBC—were all former students of his.

In 1937, when Lazarsfeld began to examine the effects of radio, he realized that because of the private nature of radio listening new methods of study were needed. Through the detailed analysis of responses to the opinion POLL—at that time used mainly for descriptive purposes, to measure such features as the popularity or audience size of radio programs—he developed ways to measure the impact of radio on ATTITUDES. This transformation of the opinion poll into the methodological tool called survey research constitutes one of Lazarsfeld's major accomplishments.

An important finding of Lazarsfeld's research on

radio listening is that listeners tend to be self-selected; that is, they listen to programs that are compatible with their own tastes and attitudes. Accordingly, in order to sort out the causal sequences in such problems as the effect of listening on attitudes versus the effect of attitudes on patterns of listening, a method of determining the time order of variables was required. Drawing on a research project in Vienna in which repeated observations were made of the same children over time, as well as on the earlier research of Stuart A. Rice and Theodore M. Newcomb among college students, Lazarsfeld developed what he called the panel method, in which a sample of respondents is reinterviewed at periodic intervals (*see also* OPINION MEASUREMENT).

Lazarsfeld used the opportunity provided by the 1940 U.S. presidential election to test and extend the panel method as a research technique. The study was published in 1944 as *The People's Choice,* a spare and elegant book that has become a classic. The substantive findings of the study are as important as the methodology. First, a great deal was learned about the psychological and social processes that delay, inhibit, reinforce, activate, and change voting decisions. People subject to cross-pressures, for example, delay making a decision longer than do others. Second, the study uncovered an influence process that Lazarsfeld called opinion leadership. It was found that the critical flow of information from the mass media to the public is often mediated by persons who serve as opinion leaders (*see* OPINION LEADER). This process was termed the two-step flow of communication (*see also* MODELS OF COMMUNICATION).

Lazarsfeld's major contributions to communications research were his demonstration of how the media permeate people's political, social, and economic activities and his methodology for studying this permeation. He was a major trainer, and the wide-ranging work that he published influenced the generation of opinion and mass communications researchers that matured in the decades following World War II. He helped create mass communications as a field of scholarship, and through his own research and his influence on the research program of the Voice of America during World War II, he helped create the field of international communications research. *See also* COMMUNICATIONS RESEARCH: ORIGINS AND DEVELOPMENT; PROPAGANDA.

These contributions were made relatively early in his career in the United States, and by the mid-1950s he had turned largely to other interests: mathematical sociology, the history of empirical social research, and the utilization of social research. Thirty years later a debate arose about the reasons for the alleged intellectual poverty of the field of communications, and there was a subsidiary debate over the role that Lazarsfeld and others played in this intellectual decline.

During his lifetime Lazarsfeld was widely recognized as an outstanding scholar; he served as president of two major professional associations and received many honorary degrees. He was also much sought after as a consultant, speaker, and teacher. But his lifelong practice of working intensively with colleagues and students has led to another, equally important, kind of recognition: his influence persists in the research of his students and their students, and this pattern shows no signs of diminishing.

Bibliography. Elihu Katz and Paul F. Lazarsfeld, *Personal Influence,* Glencoe, Ill., 1955; Paul F. Lazarsfeld, *Radio and the Printed Page: An Introduction to the Study of Radio and Its Role in the Communication of Ideas,* New York, 1940, reprint 1971; Paul F. Lazarsfeld, Ann K. Pasanella, and Morris Rosenberg, eds., *Continuities in the Language of Social Research,* New York, 1972; Robert K. Merton, James S. Coleman, and Peter H. Rossi, eds., *Qualitative and Quantitative Social Research: Papers in Honor of Paul F. Lazarsfeld,* New York, 1975; John Durham Peters, "Institutional Sources of Intellectual Poverty in Communication Research," *Communication Research* 13 (1986): 527–559; David L. Sills, "Paul F. Lazarsfeld: 1901–1976," in *Biographical Memoirs,* Vol. 56, National Academy of Sciences, Washington, D.C., 1987.

DAVID L. SILLS

LEISURE

A distinctive feature of technologically advanced societies is the degree to which mass media are a center of daily life. One way to assess the impact of the mass media in behavioral terms is through data on the amount of time ordinary people devote daily to the media.

Empirical studies of how people use time indicate that more than half of all free time is devoted to the media in certain modern societies. A common observation is that when a television set arrives in the home (*see* TELEVISION HISTORY), less time is spent not only with other mass media (e.g., RADIO) but also on nonmedia activities such as socializing, sleeping, and gardening. As it becomes a more permanent fixture in a society, television affects other free time and obligatory activities as well (*see* CULTURAL INDICATORS).

Ratings service data. There are several methods for measuring the time people are exposed to certain mass media. Broadcast ratings services in the United States and other Western countries employ mechanical devices (usually called audimeters) installed with permission in a sampling of homes to record the time television and radio sets are on and the stations to which they are tuned (*see* RATING SYSTEMS: RADIO AND TELEVISION). Ratings services often supplement these mechanical recordings with "media diaries," in which people are asked to record their exposure to a single medium for a one-week or two-week period, or with "telephone coincidental" calls in which respondents are asked to report whether or not they were attending to the medium at the time the telephone rang and, if so, to what program. Occasionally, direct observational studies of media behavior are conducted in people's homes, although with smaller and less representative samples. Such observational studies are sometimes coupled with some sort of intervention, as when studies are made of people whose television sets are in need of repair or who are paid a substantial sum of money to give up viewing for a week or longer.

Time-diary data. A technique that seeks to provide leisure time-use data in a wider context is the time diary, which asks for a full accounting of twenty-four hours of a respondent's daily activities. Generally, time diaries have been considered to generate reliable and valid estimates of daily activity, although definitive tests have been difficult to conduct. These activity time diaries provide no cues to respondents about which activities are most important to report, require respondents to separate media exposure into primary and secondary usage, and put media exposure into the full context of other free-time and daily activities. Time diaries thus provide estimates of the total free time respondents have available, and their media exposure during non-free-time periods (e.g., at work, during meals), outside one's own home, or under other unusual circumstances. The time-diary approach thus provides a unique perspective on how the mass media relate to (or displace) other activities.

The most detailed international data on mass media exposure and free time come from a twelve-nation study conducted in 1965–1966 in which time diaries were collected from over twenty-five thousand respondents. As shown in Table 1, the predominant use of television in free time was apparent even in a period when less than 50 percent of respondents in some countries had television sets. In addition to the minutes per day spent with television as a primary activity, up to 60 percent more viewing was recorded in diaries as a secondary activity. Almost 90 percent of radio listening was also recorded as a secondary activity, accounting for its relatively small time expenditure in Table 1. Amounts of time spent READING were considerably lower than for watching television and varied widely across countries and

Table 1. Mass Media Usage across the Survey Sites in 1965 (weighted to ensure equality of days of the week and of respondents per household) *

	Kazanlik, Bulgaria	Kragujevac, Yugoslavia	Gyor, Hungary	Maribor, Yugoslavia	Pskov, USSR	Lima-Callao, Peru	Torun, Poland	Six cities, France	100 elec. districts, Fed. Rep. Germany	Olomouc, Czechoslovakia	Belgium	Osnabruck, Fed. Rep. Germany	Hoyerswerda, German Dem. Rep.	Forty-four cities, USA	Jackson, USA
N	2096	2123	1992	1995	2891	782	2754	2803	1501	2193	2077	978	1650	1243	778
Time spent as a primary activity (in minutes per day)															
Radio	20	16	11	6	11	8	10	5	7	11	8	4	4	4	3
TV	16	37	43	41	42	54	70	58	63	66	84	74	81	92	101
Read paper	14	20	12	19	17	10	16	14	12	13	16	13	13	22	22
Read magazine	1	1	1	1	6	6	3	4	12	3	5	13	2	6	4
Read books	21	7	14	8	30	2	17	7	5	20	14	6	7	5	3
Movies	10	7	5	6	16	6	4	3	3	4	4	3	1	3	2
All mass media	79	87	85	81	116	87	120	91	98	116	137	112	108	131	135
Total free time	231	311	200	222	249	309	262	245	264	239	297	300	233	301	310
Percentage with TV set	26%	35%	45%	49%	52%	54%	59%	65%	66%	72%	72%	76%	85%	97%	98%
Percentage TV/free time	7	12	22	18	17	17	27	24	24	28	28	25	35	31	33
Percentage TV/set owner	27	34	49	37	35	31	46	37	37	39	39	33	41	26	34

* Adapted from Alexander Szalai et al., *The Use of Time*, The Hague, 1972, p. 177.

according to types of print media most prevalent in a country. In general, television took up about 15 to 25 percent of the free-time activities reported in the study, and closer to 35 percent among those people who had television sets in their homes. Total (primary activity) reading time totaled about 12 percent of free time, radio listening took 3 percent, and cinema attendance took 2 percent.

Since the 1965 study people have had access to both more free time and more television sets, and television viewing has increased both in absolute hours and as a proportion of free time. In the United States, Canada, and Japan, time-diary data suggest that the gain for television was over 25 percent of free time on a per set-owner basis; in England, France, and Norway the gain was closer to 15 percent. Several factors may account for this increase beyond that due to ownership alone, including longer broadcast days, more channels, more than one set per household, color television, improved program content, and, more generally, improved adaptability to social conditions in each society. The data generally indicate little adverse effect of increased television viewing on reading time, although some increase in reading time might otherwise have been expected given the higher LITERACY levels and years of formal EDUCATION that had occurred in these time periods.

Time displacement. Time-diary data provide an ideal method to examine the effect of new media on all aspects of daily life including usage of the pre-existing media that they displace. Comparison of television set owners and nonowners in the 1965 multinational study, for example, showed a number of differences that held up across countries and across social classes. Television owners generally spent less time in functionally equivalent activities such as listening to the radio, going to the movies, or reading light FICTION. Reading newspapers and "serious" books and magazines, on the other hand, seemed unaffected.

Television "effects" were found for other free-time and non-free-time activities as well: CONVERSATION and social life decreased in television households, as did time spent sleeping, performing outdoor gardening, and caring for pets. Television owners also spent less time away from home and in the company of FAMILY members. These differences persisted after controlling for social class, GENDER, and employment status differences.

Concern has often been expressed about television's adverse effects on reading. However, time-diary studies have yet to show either that heavier television viewers read less or that people read less in societies in which television is more prevalent. Nonetheless, there is evidence of selective effects on reading. For example, reading light fiction magazines and books declined in the early days of television in

the United States. More recently, in the United States at least, some decline in newspaper reading has appeared, possibly due to local television news stations becoming more efficient in catering to audience interests in terms of community news coverage, to audiences becoming increasingly familiar with, and accommodated to, television's scheduling and style of news presentation, or to newspapers' decreased community ties as a result of increasing out-of-town chain ownership (*see* NEWSPAPER: TRENDS—TRENDS IN NORTH AMERICA). With the spread of high-quality movies through specialized movie channels and videocassette rentals, the television set might well displace some of the time spent reading more serious forms of literature (e.g., novels, short stories).

While time spent with television does tend to be higher for people with more free time, that does not hold true for all groups or in all situations. In addition, television viewing does not increase disproportionately with greater amounts of free time, and greater free time is not associated with greater viewing for all groups. For example, unemployed people do not spend proportionately more of their "extra" free time watching television, but rather in social interaction; nor do housewives spend higher proportions of their free time viewing than women in the paid labor force who have less free time. And while viewing time does increase on weekends when more free time is available, it declines significantly on vacation days and holidays. Much the same pattern holds true for the relatively low viewing habits of teenagers, who, as a group, have higher than average amounts of free time. By contrast, another group with almost limitless free time—people past retirement age—do spend far more of their free time with television.

Relation to other activities. Research has shown that activities requiring more effort and involvement than television do not depend as much on the amount of free time people have available, and that attendance at ENTERTAINMENT events or participation in outdoor recreation does not require having significantly more free time. Even people who have long workweeks or large households to manage are just as likely to attend as those without such obligations. In contrast, people with more such obligations do watch less television, although they are relatively more likely to watch cultural or artistic programs on television. These results indicate that people who are attracted to these more active forms of leisure do find some way of managing their time to fit them into their schedules.

This same sense of single-mindedness or integrated purpose is found in studies that deal with whether non-free-time activities spill over into free time (as when people pursue the same type of free-time activities, values, and goals as they do in their work), or whether the effect is more compensatory (free-time activities differ in character from work activities). Although the evidence is again not definitive, results more consistent with spillover effects than for compensation effects are found, as exemplified by the tendency of those in higher-status occupations to spend more time reading, while those in lower-status, machine-dependent occupations spend more time with television.

Allied to both of these sets of findings is the principle of "the more, the more" that characterizes the correlation among free-time activities. Thus, the more an individual participates in one leisure activity, the more likely it is that she or he will partake in another. However, the correlations between television and most other free-time activities are negative because (as the time-diary method reminds us) as more hours are spent away from home, fewer hours will necessarily be available for at-home activities.

The general picture emerging from these studies to date, then, is of a mass audience that is divided into away-from-home doers and at-home spectators. However, the strength of the divisions and correlations is modest at best, indicating that the variety of ways in which the mass media are incorporated into people's lifestyles, and their use of free time in particular, are undergoing continuous if seldom rapid change.

See also MASS MEDIA EFFECTS.

Bibliography. Rolf Meyersohn, "Television and the Rest of Leisure," *Public Opinion Quarterly* 32 (1968): 102–112; John P. Robinson, "Television's Impact on Everyday Life: Some Cross-National Evidence," in *Television and Social Behavior*, Vol. 4, ed. by Eli A. Rubinstein, George A. Comstock, and John P. Murray, Washington, D.C., 1972; Alexander Szalai, Philip E. Converse et al., *The Use of Time*, The Hague, 1973; Walter Weiss, "The Effects of the Mass Media of Communication," in *Handbook of Social Psychology*, 2d ed., Vol. 5, ed. by Gardner Lindzey and Elliot Aronson, Lexington, Mass., 1969.

JOHN P. ROBINSON

LETTER

Letters belong both to the world of social and business activity and to the domain of ART. It is not possible to keep these altogether separate, and any account of the letter in its historic evolution will shift between the two. We therefore need to consider letters as a simple means of passing on information and as purveyors of more refined messages in which the form takes on a quasi-creative or even fictive purpose.

The Western tradition in this branch of expression goes back to Rome. Indeed, it has been stated that letter writing was, next to satire, Rome's most distinctive legacy to world literature. The first great master was the humanist and philosopher CICERO, who can also claim priority in setting down a serious CLASSIFICATION of various species within the GENRE. In a letter to G. Scribonius Curio in 53 B.C.E., Cicero remarks that "letter-writing was invented just in order that we might inform those at a distance if there was anything important for them or for ourselves that they should know." This constitutes what might be called the simple NEWSLETTER function. Cicero goes on to add two further kinds: the "intimate and humorous" kind, passing between friends, and the "austere and serious" kind, exemplified by letters of consolation or bereavement. Cicero himself practiced all three kinds, but he is perhaps most renowned for sixteen books of letters addressed to T. Pomponius Atticus—a prolonged "conversation" beginning about 68 B.C.E. and providing at times an almost hour-by-hour NARRATIVE of Roman life. Cicero's surviving correspondence runs to more than eight hundred letters and contains a further sixteen books addressed "To his Friends." The title is more significant than it might instantly appear, for at the heart of Cicero's work is the cult of friendship (on which he wrote a treatise), and letters have always played an important part in strengthening feelings of group solidarity, in promoting movements, and in developing coteries and alliances.

Latin writers also pioneered the adaptation of the epistolary MODE to a more oblique literary purpose. The classical examples here are the epistles of the poet Horace, two books dating from about 20 to 15 B.C.E. The idea of a whole collection of verse epistles was altogether novel, and Horace produced a strikingly individual tone and texture. A second type of letter is that used by Ovid in his *Heroides,* in which famous women of legend, such as Dido and Phaedra, write to absent lovers; a second series is organized in pairs, with both man and woman contributing letters. They were completed before Ovid's banishment to the Black Sea in 8 B.C.E., after which he sent poems of exile known as *Tristia* back to Rome in a quasi-epistolary form.

Little survives of the highest importance from the MIDDLE AGES, though church fathers such as St. Augustine of Hippo and, many centuries later, St. Bernard of Clairvaux expounded on some major devotional topics in their letters. The moment of revival may be placed in 1345, when the Italian poet Petrarch discovered Cicero's letters in a LIBRARY at Verona. He took up the cult of friendship and modeled his own collections of letters, written in Latin, on those of Cicero and Seneca. Here, at the very birth of the humanist movement, letters occupied a prominent place, and as the RENAISSANCE spread across Europe many other distinguished writers followed where Petrarch had led. The single outstanding case in point is the Dutch scholar Erasmus; as well as being a masterful practitioner, Erasmus wrote in Latin a widely influential textbook on letter writing, which appeared about 1498. By this time humanist thinkers gave the subject an important role in EDU-CATION, a position it was not to lose until very recent times. Even when young women were discouraged from most serious literary activity, they were permitted to write letters, and this proved to be an important breach in the defenses of masculine dominance of the world of AUTHORSHIP.

After the high Renaissance, epistolary fashion followed a wider political and cultural trend, finding a new home in France. At first the greatest contemporary influence was exerted by Jean-Louis Guez de Balzac, whose Lettres began to appear in 1624 and were soon copied, translated, pillaged, and held up (especially to the young) for admiration. Balzac's sententious, rhetorically contrived style lost favor as the seventeenth century advanced, and a new model emerged in the person of Vincent Voiture, a lighter and more intimate writer. Although Voiture died in 1648, his works were not published until after his death, and in the last quarter of the century he came fully into vogue, in England as well as France. Above all he was renowned as the standard for letters of "affairs, love and courtship," that is, effusions of gallantry, compliment, and gentle badinage. Purely as literature, the works of both Balzac and Voiture seem artificial and limited today, especially when set alongside the breezy, vigorous, and almost offhand descriptions of life at the court of Louis XIV supplied by Madame de Sévigné. She left fifteen hundred letters, mostly to her daughter, which began to be published in 1725, thirty years after their author's death. A more oblique and satiric version of the form appears in French philosopher Blaise Pascal's Lettres provinciales (1656–1657), an attack on Jesuit theology.

As the fame of these works spread, England for the first time started to attempt serious emulation of Continental letter writers. This may have something to do with the improvement in roads and POSTAL SERVICE; it must also be connected with the spur given in JOHN LOCKE's highly influential work Some Thoughts concerning Education, first published in 1693. In it he singled out letters as an educational instrument, by which children should be taught

to express their own plain easy sense, without any incoherence, confusion or roughness. And when they are perfect in this, they may, to raise their thoughts, have set before them the example of Voiture, for the entertainment of their friends at a distance, with letters of compliment, mirth, raillery, or diversion; and Tully[Cicero]'s Epistles, as the best pattern, whether for business or conversation.

It is noteworthy that a copy of Locke's Thoughts was given to the heroine of Samuel Richardson's novel Pamela (1740–1741), the first important example of epistolary FICTION in English. Richardson was indeed prompted to become a novelist by accepting an invitation to compile domestic advice in the form of an exchange of correspondence.

The eighteenth-century novelists found the epistolary mode highly congenial. In England the device was extended by Tobias Smollett in The Expedition of Humphry Clinker (1771); by Fanny Burney in Evelina (1778); and, as a formal framing device at the start, by Mary Shelley in Frankenstein (1818). Jane Austen began her literary career with novels in letters, notably Lady Susan (composed ca. 1793–1794). Although she subsequently abandoned the method, a good deal of the essential narrative work in her later books is carried out through letters in the text. Many works of literature in this period are formally cast in letters, though this is often merely a loose principle of organization, with no real epistolary basis.

Richardson's influence extended outside England, particularly through his masterpiece Clarissa (1747–1749), in which an extraordinary tension is built up through a long series of letters that serve to dramatize the heroine's isolation and the manipulative schemes of the seducer Lovelace. In France similar themes were lent a greater directness of sexual import or emotional charge in novels such as Lettres d'une Péruvienne (1747), by Madame de Graffigny, La nouvelle Héloïse (1761), by Jean-Jacques Rousseau, and Les liaisons dangereuses (1782), by Pierre Choderlos de Laclos. In addition, a number of satiric or critical works were given polemical edge by being set out in the form of a series of letters, with the writer cast either as "impartial" observer, as in Voltaire's Lettres philosophiques on England (1733), or as a naive foreign visitor, as in Baron Montesquieu's Lettres persanes (1721). One of the most famous of all narratives nominally presented as letters is Die Leiden des jungen Werthers (The Sorrows of Young Werther, 1774), by the German poet and dramatist Johann Wolfgang von Goethe, a cult book that has outlasted the fashionable frissons set up by its daring exploitation of suicide as a climactic gesture of despair.

As we approach the romantic era we come to a new literary situation in which the author's personality is of prime interest, and hence there is a taste for autobiographical revelations (see AUTOBIOGRAPHY; ROMANTICISM). When the English poet Alexander Pope had arranged for the publication of his own letters in 1735, he had to go through elaborate subterfuges to conceal his responsibility for their appearance, owing to a well-established rule of decorum condemning such self-publicizing as vain and ill-bred. By the time of the romantics there was far less scrupulosity on such points, and very soon after Lord Byron's death his remarkable letters and journals began to appear before an avid public, which understandably saw these productions as more or less continuous in theme and interest with *Childe Harold* or *Don Juan*.

The nineteenth century saw a vast increase in BIOGRAPHY and bardolatry, so that the letters of famous authors were more eagerly prized than in any previous era and have thus survived in far greater numbers. We reach a point where it is likely nowadays that a new cache of letters by Emily Brontë would be more hungrily devoured than a new novel, or a new journal by Emily Dickinson more discussed than a trawl of forgotten poems. This taste can be amply satisfied, for many great authors, including Aleksandr Pushkin, Charles Dickens, Gustave Flaubert, Mark Twain, Henry James, and Anton Chekhov, left a splendid body of correspondence. So, too, did many later literary figures.

And so have many diplomats and politicians. The extraordinary surviving correspondence of the Adams family of Massachusetts—John Adams, Abigail Adams, John Quincy Adams, and others—not only lets us in on their domesticities but also, in the course of government service in Washington, D.C., and missions to Paris, London, Berlin, and St. Petersburg, gives us a backstage view of world politics. In a world of electronic telecommunications, treasure troves of this sort no longer seem likely to materialize.

But an echo of Cicero's political and philosophic letters, as well as Ovid's epistles from exile, may be found in the letters written by Jawaharlal Nehru during three years in various prisons of the British raj. When he began a term for sedition in 1930, his daughter Indira was thirteen years old. Intent on providing in absentia some supervision of her education, he began a long series of letters to her detailing his view of the history of the world. They were later published as *Glimpses of World History* in numerous editions beginning in 1938. The fact that both sender and receiver of these letters later became prime ministers of independent India (she as Indira Gandhi) gives a unique interest to these fatherly letters.

The letter has a life outside literature, but it has traditionally been one of the places where literature has capitalized most immediately and powerfully on that life outside.

See also STYLE, LITERARY.

Bibliography. Howard Anderson, Philip B. Daghlian, and Irvin Ehrenpreis, eds., *The Familiar Letter in the Eighteenth Century*, Lawrence, Kans., 1966; Robert A. Day, *Told in Letters: Epistolary Fiction before Richardson*, Ann Arbor, Mich., 1966; William H. Irving, *The Providence of Wit in the English Letter Writers*, Durham, N.C., 1955.

PAT ROGERS

LÉVI-STRAUSS, CLAUDE (1908–)

French anthropologist known as the founder of structural anthropology. Born in Brussels, Claude Lévi-Strauss studied at the University of Paris in philosophy and law. In 1935 he was appointed professor of sociology at São Paulo University in Brazil, and during his four years there he first came into contact with Amazon Indians. He moved to New York in 1942 and taught at the New School for Social Research until 1945. Returning to France after World War II he became, successively, associate director of the Musée de l'Homme, director of studies at the École Pratique des Hautes Études, and editor of *L'homme: Revue française d'anthropologie*. In 1960 he became professor of social anthropology at the Collège de France. He was the first anthropologist elected to the French Academy.

When Lévi-Strauss came to New York and joined the New School faculty, he encountered fellow émigré ROMAN JAKOBSON, who introduced him to what he later referred to as "the revelation of structural linguistics" and inspired him to invent a structural anthropology with which to make scientific sense of his observations among the Brazilian Indians. The results of his structural analyses were published in *Les structures élémentaires de la parenté* (The Elementary Structures of Kinship, 1949) and *Tristes tropiques* (1955), the work that brought him general fame in French intellectual circles. Perhaps Lévi-Strauss's most influential claim is the one first articulated in *Tristes tropiques* (and later in *La pensée sauvage* [The Savage Mind], 1962), namely, that all humans think in the same way and that all cultures—despite varying levels of technological sophistication—are fundamentally the same in intellectual complexity. The savage mind is no different from that of the civilized anthropologist.

Lévi-Strauss decided that anthropologists must follow the lead of the structural linguists and undertake a structuralist analysis of cultural phenomena. That is, they must study the unconscious infrastructure rather than the surface manifestations of phenomena. They must focus not on the terms or the units of phenomena but on the relationships among them. Only thus could their MEANING be discovered. Lévi-Strauss argued that entire domains (such as LANGUAGE or kinship) must be seen as organized systems governed by general laws. Whether confronting a kinship pattern, a social organization, a program of

CLASSIFICATION, or a myth, the anthropologist must find the units of meaning and discover how they relate to one another within a coherent and organized system. In this manner, he argued, we can understand the most important feature of any CULTURE: the ways in which the human mind takes in, classifies, and interprets information.

Lévi-Strauss views these ways as chosen from among a limited set of possibilities. In *Tristes tropiques* he wrote, "I am convinced that the number of these systems is not unlimited and that human societies, like individual human beings, . . . never create *absolutely*: all they can do is to choose certain combinations from a repertory of ideas which it should be possible to reconstitute." Thus in his massive four-volume undertaking, *Mythologiques* (1964–1971), Lévi-Strauss analyzed more than eight hundred American Indian myths from different periods and cultures dispersed over two continents. He concluded that there is a single logic of myth underlying all of these different manifestations and that, like all human patterns and behaviors, myths are codes that embody universal problems of existence.

Although Lévi-Strauss sees language as the fundamental model for all human thought, he is concerned with and sensitive to other modes of symbolic behaviors (*see also* MODE). He has said that myths share principles of COGNITION with music, and his *Mythologiques* was constructed according to an elaborate musical framework, with sections given titles such as "Overture," "Recitative," "Theme and Variations," and so forth.

In a more general sense Lévi-Strauss sees the arts as systems of shared meanings that help integrate and sustain culture in so-called primitive societies. In modern Western societies he feels that the arts have lost their collective role—in part as a result of the individualization of the arts following the RENAISSANCE and, later, ROMANTICISM—and no longer perform their traditional function. He explains this loss of shared meaning by analogy to the place of language in society: "We would never manage to understand each other if, within our society, we formed a series of coteries, each one of which had its own particular language, or if we allowed constant changes and revolutions to take place in language, like those that we have been able to observe now for a number of years in the fine arts." *See also* ART; ARTIST AND SOCIETY.

See also SAUSSURE, FERDINAND DE; STRUCTURALISM.

Bibliography. Georges Charbonnier, ed., *Conversations with Claude Lévi-Strauss* (Entretiens avec Claude Lévi-Strauss), trans. by John Weightman and Doreen Weightman, London, 1969; Edmund Leach, *Lévi-Strauss*, London, 1970; Claude Lévi-Strauss, *Mythologiques: Le cru et le cuit* (The Raw and the Cooked, New York, 1969), Paris, 1964; idem, *La pensée sauvage* (The Savage Mind, Chicago, 1966), Paris, 1962; idem, *Tristes tropiques* (World on the Wane, London, 1961), Paris, 1955.

LARRY GROSS

LEWIN, KURT (1890–1947)

German-born U.S. psychologist. Perhaps more than any other scholar Kurt Lewin put the human group into communication theory and research. A widely respected teacher at the University of Berlin, he emigrated to the United States in 1933 after the Nazis came to power in Germany. After spending two years at Cornell, Lewin was appointed to the faculty of the Iowa Child Welfare Research Station at the state university in Iowa City, where he taught social psychology and attracted a remarkably able group of graduate students.

Lewin was at his best with graduate students, better at informal group discussion than lectures. His enthusiasm and helpfulness in planning research with students were legendary. In Iowa City he reintroduced a device he had used to supplement his classes in Berlin. In Europe it was called the Quasselstrippe (*quassel* means "to ramble on"; *strippe*, a "string"); in Iowa it was named the Hot Air Club. In both places it met on Saturdays and sometimes went on all day because the chance to exchange ideas and plans with Lewin was genuinely exciting. It was not a lecture or a credit course; any student could attend and everyone could talk. Few stayed away.

Lewin's basic approach to communication was through field theory, which drew on Albert Einstein's definition of a field as "a totality of existing facts which are conceived of as mutually dependent." To understand behavior, Lewin said, one must understand the field in which it occurs—an individual's "life space," which includes all of his or her mutually dependent experiences (i.e., the total interaction of a person and his or her environment). No act of behavior could be fully understood, Lewin believed, unless the entire field was known.

Observation rather than quantification was his chief tool for psychological experiments. At Iowa he and his colleagues devised a series of remarkable experiments, all done by observation of the related fields and most of them about group relations. One of the first of these concerned the effect of frustration on children. Lewin found that frustration made children not only less happy but also less competent in learning and problem solving. Another experiment dealt with the effect of democratic versus authoritarian styles of leadership. The results indicated that under an authoritarian leader, discontent, hostility, aggression, scapegoating, loss of originality, and lack of cooperation were prevalent, while cooperation and group spirit prevailed under a democratic leader.

At the beginning of World War II Lewin became interested in the government's efforts to persuade U.S. housewives to change their food-buying habits— for example, to buy less desirable cuts of meat so that the better cuts could be saved for soldiers. To accomplish this the Department of Agriculture invited housewives to participate in discussion groups. Lewin and his students found that direct PERSUASION in such discussion groups was relatively ineffective but that "decision" groups, in which group members committed themselves to a course of action (in this case to use the less desirable cuts), were much more likely to accomplish the desired result. One important idea that emerged from Lewin's work at Iowa was the "gatekeeper" concept as a way of describing communication networks.

Lewin's project attracted a notable group of scholars. Many of the best young social psychologists in the United States from the 1950s to the 1970s were trained or at least strongly influenced by Lewin.

In 1945 Lewin left Iowa for the Massachusetts Institute of Technology, where he planned to continue his group studies in a center for group dynamics. At the same time he planned to organize the National Training Laboratories at Bethel, Maine, and a center for community relations. Before any of these was well established, however, Lewin died.

See also COMMUNICATIONS RESEARCH: ORIGINS AND DEVELOPMENT; GROUP COMMUNICATION.

Bibliography. Alfred J. Marrow, *The Practical Theorist: The Life and Work of Kurt Lewin,* New York, 1969, reprint 1980; James A. Schellenberg, "Kurt Lewin and Field Theory," in *Masters of Social Psychology,* New York, 1978.

WILBUR SCHRAMM

LIBEL

In law, libel is written communication thought to damage a person's reputation or standing in the community. Assumptions about libel and slander within the disciplines of communication and law at one time ran parallel. Just as early communication research included notions of powerful, uniform effects, the modern libel tort has operated on the assumption that communication in the form of a defamatory newspaper article or a televised news bulletin can affect PUBLIC OPINION. Communication research no longer uniformly accepts powerful effects models, but assumptions about reputational damage in libel law often appear to be based on just such cause-and-effect relationships. Legal scholar Dean William Prosser (1898–1972), summarizing accepted

judicial practices, wrote, "Normally, the publication of false and defamatory matter about the plaintiff is circumstantial evidence in and of itself that there was some impairment to reputation."

History. The basic concept of libel has changed little in the thousand years it has been documented. People have been and continue to be punished or fined for their criticism of individuals, corporate institutions, and national governments. For centuries satisfaction has been demanded for perceived INSULT. Duels and bloodshed were the common response to defamatory remarks, whether printed or spoken, in many societies. As with much law in England prior to the Norman Conquest, the strongest individual or the individual with the largest army would emerge victorious when accusations of libel were leveled. It was at least in part the state's desire to avoid such combat, rather than a right to receive compensation for damaged reputation, that led to official sanctions against defamatory expression. Only gradually did courts consider the actual harm done to reputation. English authority to punish slander can be found as early as the ninth century, and historians trace the first English codified sanctions against libel to a 1275 statute enacted by Parliament against "any slanderous news . . . or false news or tales whereby discord or occasion of discord or slander may grow between the king and his people or the great men of the Realm."

Trials for defamatory expression were at first located in secular courts, although the courts took into consideration religious doctrine. Victims of libel received no compensation beyond the satisfaction of a court-ordered public apology. The process remained essentially unchanged in England after the 1066 Norman Conquest when libel trials were moved to ecclesiastical courts. Libelers were made to confess their sins. Their possessions might be forfeited and they might be expelled from the church, but the victim still received no financial recompense.

As the law gained experience with libel, differentiations among various types of defamation were recognized. Seditious libels were words spoken or written against the state, and until 1792 English courts treated speech that threatened the stability of the state or the aggrieved governor under the theory "the greater the truth, the greater the libel." By the mid-fourteenth century English common law recognized civil libel actions as well as seditious or criminal libels. Unlike criminal libels against the state, however, some trials for civil defamation allowed defendants to plead truth as defense.

The practice of requiring defendants to pay plaintiffs for damage to their reputations grew with the merchant class, which feared the negative impact on their businesses of verbal and written assaults. Until the civil courts began to award such damages, however, merchants not content with simple public apologies by their critics to clear their names held their own courts. Eventually the practice of awarding damages to plaintiffs in the form of monetary compensation spread even to the Star Chamber.

The slander/libel dichotomy. The infamous Court of the Star Chamber was pivotal in establishing a recognized difference between libel and slander. The Star Chamber heard cases of libel that were political in nature and then only when they involved defamations against state officials or other important figures. By contrast, sixteenth-century courts of common law heard cases of slander, which by definition included all defamation cases not governed by the Star Chamber. Current folk wisdom holds that the slander/libel distinction began as the difference between spoken and written defamations. This is historically incorrect. The difference between libel and slander was based on whom the libel was about rather than how the defamation was transmitted.

The accepted practice in U.S. courts has been to incorporate an oral/written speech distinction. In a broad sense libel has come to encompass that which is transmitted through the mass media, whereas slander refers to defamations delivered in a face-to-face setting. The slander/libel dichotomy is more than semantic, however. The body of evidence required to win a slander suit is more exacting than that required in a libel trial. In essence slander trials require greater proof that the defamation has actually harmed the plaintiff. The rationale for the distinction rests on the conviction that defamations transmitted through the mass media are not only more powerful than simple spoken communication but are often in fact inherently damaging.

The nature of these rationales has raised special problems when it comes to RADIO and television broadcasting (*see* TELEVISION HISTORY). The norm is to treat defamation involving radio and television, despite its oral nature, as libel. Yet some jurisdictions have gone as far as distinguishing between broadcasters who read from a script and those who do not in determining whether a case will be tried as libel or slander. And in the final decades of the twentieth century jurists and legislators were only beginning to come to grips with the problem of deciding whether defamations transmitted through an electronic medium such as a computer DATA BASE or information stored on a laser video disk generally viewed only by single individuals or tiny audiences should be treated as libel or slander.

The modern libel tort. Libel law in the United States is based on civil rather than criminal law. It is among the most tolerant approaches toward freedom of expression, owing in great part to the First Amendment to the U.S. Constitution, which states, "Congress shall make no law . . . abridging the freedom

Individual's Reputational Interests	Societal Interest
Publication–Identification–Defamation	Fault

Figure 1. *(Libel)* Two-segment litigation model.

of speech or of the press; or the right of the people peaceably to assemble and to petition the government for a redress of grievances." The libel tort is composed of four elements that in turn make up a two-segment litigation model (see Figure 1). The model addresses both the issues of the individual's interest in harm to his or her reputation and society's interest in freedom of expression. Each of the four elements must be proved for a plaintiff to prevail.

Harm to reputation is considered under the elements of publication, identification, and defamation. The plaintiff first must prove that the alleged defamation was published, that is, seen by at least one person in addition to the plaintiff and the defendant. Next, it must be clear that people reading or viewing the information would understand that it was, in fact, intended to be about the plaintiff. Was the plaintiff identified? And third, once the judge has determined that the offending words are capable of a defamatory interpretation, the jury must decide whether in the case at hand the words in question were both false and defamatory. Information that is probably true, even if highly defamatory, is not actionable under common law or statute in most states. It is the jury's task to determine that truth from evidence presented in court.

In their consideration of whether defamation occurred, juries must also make a determination about the severity of the damage. A libel suit filed by Nobel laureate William Shockley, for example, culminated in a jury award of one dollar. The jury believed that technically and legally Shockley was libeled but questioned whether any real damage to the professor's reputation had resulted.

A defendant who cannot prove truth has not necessarily lost. Much of libel law is based on common and statutory law. Under this system each state may set its own standards of liability for defamatory falsehoods. A widespread practice has been the granting of immunity from judgments for defamatory falsehoods that are in fact accurate reports of official government actions such as trials, legislative sessions, and even some law enforcement. This doctrine is called qualified privilege and is based on the theory that full participation in the democratic process requires the unhampered ability to view and discuss government conduct. Another common-law defense to libel often available to the media is called fair comment. Under this doctrine reviewers may render negative conclusions about issues of public interest such as DRAMA, ART, MOTION PICTURES, and restaurants as long as their comments have a factual basis that is shared with the reader or viewer.

Constitutional protection. Within the context of the turbulent and sometimes volatile U.S. civil rights movement, the Supreme Court radically changed the rules of libel law as they apply to the mass media. Leaving intact the right of states to provide immunity to libel judgments through doctrines such as qualified privilege, the high court greatly expanded the protection provided the press when government officials are involved. The *New York Times* ran full-page ADVERTISING matter that accused Montgomery, Alabama, police and other officials of harassing civil rights leader Martin Luther King, Jr. Six Montgomery officials sued the *Times* for libel. L. B. Sullivan, although never referred to by name in the ad, was a Montgomery commissioner with responsibility for the police department. Based on state law, the Alabama courts awarded Sullivan five hundred thousand dollars. The Supreme Court overturned the decision in the 1964 landmark ruling *New York Times* v. *Sullivan.* Justice William Brennan argued that the First Amendment required "a federal rule that prohibits a public official from recovering damages for a defamatory falsehood relating to his official conduct unless he proves that the statement was made with 'actual malice'—that is, with knowledge that it was false or with reckless disregard of whether it was false or not."

The *Sullivan* ruling was based on constitutional interpretations developed by philosopher Alexander Meiklejohn (1872–1964). Citizens in a democracy must be exposed to the open discussion of current events if they are to carry out responsibly the duties of self-governance, such as voting. Only through an open marketplace of ideas could truth sort itself out, the Court reasoned. To uphold the constitutionally mandated freedoms of speech and the press, Justice Brennan said, "breathing space" would have to be accorded the press and the risk of honest mistakes tolerated. In effect the *Sullivan* ruling put an end to any possibility of successful seditious libel prosecutions against the media by requiring a fourth element—actual malice—in all libel suits involving public officials.

The actual malice fault requirement was quickly expanded by the Court to apply in cases involving public figures as well as public officials. Public figures are defined as those who enter the public limelight voluntarily with the intention of swaying public opinion about important issues. And in 1974 in *Gertz* v. *Welch* the Supreme Court ruled that the First Amendment requires proof of a minimum level of fault called "simple negligence" even when "private per-sons" sue the mass media for libel. Simple negligence usually is defined as a lack of reasonable care. By requiring private as well as public persons to prove fault the Court effectively ended the doctrine of strict liability in suits against the press. The Court also ruled in 1974 that all opinions, as opposed to statements of fact, have absolute constitutional immunity from libel suits.

The actual malice controversy. The fault requirement has created its own set of controversies, not the least of which has been defining who is a public person and who is to be considered private. Critics point to case law that includes examples of banks suing for libel as private persons.

Other critics say it is too difficult for juries to deal with the subtleties of doctrines such as actual malice. Studies show that in fact two-thirds of libel suits decided by juries are decided against the press but that the majority of those decisions are eventually overturned on appeal. The process is slow and costly.

A 1985 libel suit against *Time* magazine by Israeli defense minister Ariel Sharon focused renewed attention on the actual malice rule. When *Time* reported that Sharon had discussed the need for revenge with the family of murdered Lebanese prime minister Bashir Gemayel two days *before* the 1982 massacres in two West Beirut Palestinian refugee camps, the Israeli official launched a $50 million libel suit in New York. The jury decided that *Time* had defamed Sharon, that the defamation was untrue, and that *Time* had acted "negligently and carelessly." But the jury ruled *Time* was not guilty of actual malice. Advocates of the fault requirement pointed out that the jury's verdict in effect cleared Sharon's reputation and questioned *Time*'s handling of the story without seriously damaging freedom of the press. That decision also amplified one of the loudest criticisms of U.S. libel law: even if a public figure can prove libel caused by careless reporting, the press can still emerge seemingly unscathed. The almost insurmountable actual malice fault requirement erects nearly impenetrable barriers for plaintiffs such as Sharon.

Underscoring the inherent difficulty of using the courts to provide a satisfying arena for libel disputes, a $120 million suit by U.S. general William Westmoreland ended close on the heels of the Sharon case—but this time without a verdict for either side. After a costly four-month trial the general withdrew his suit against CBS television, which had produced a documentary, "The Uncounted Enemy: A Vietnam Deception," suggesting that Westmoreland had condoned reports that underrepresented the strength of the Vietcong. Westmoreland's attorneys attempted to prove that the documentary painted an inaccurate picture of his war record. Trial judge Pierre Level in dismissing the jury commented, "It may be best that the verdict is left to history."

Libel in Europe and the Third World. The 1985 Sharon case was graphic proof that libel prosecutions are not always confined by national borders. As the decade of the 1980s continued, journalists attempting to cover the antiapartheid movement in South Africa found themselves subject to what amounted to seditious libel laws. The result was a sometimes effective blockade of information both within the country and to outsiders by the government. The line between seditious libel and what governments often prefer to call national security issues tends to blur, although the effect is clear: the channel of information is blocked.

In Europe libel laws differ from nation to nation, although most utilize three types of law: civil and penal laws apply to individuals, and competition law focuses on corporate and product disparagement. The system in the Federal Republic of Germany is perhaps the most complex and is closely mirrored in Austria and Switzerland. Civil remedies for libel in Germany are available but are not popular among plaintiffs. The civil laws provide a chance to clear a reputation but do not include monetary compensation.

The operational theory of German libel law is rooted in the fact/opinion distinction. Opinions and statements of fact that are provably true are subject to claims under civil law but under stricter standards than defamations that are false. Truth is not an absolute defense. This system does not rely on the U.S. system of differentiating between public and private persons. Instead a qualified privilege is available when the information in question concerns public issues.

Civil libel law in Great Britain also lacks the public/private person distinction and relies instead on the public value of the issue discussed rather than on the prominence of the individual. Public officials, however, do receive some additional protections. Whereas the press may use a qualified privilege when reporting on much of government, newspapers, except when reporting on Parliament, may be required to print official clarifications and explanations. And it is a crime to publish defamatory falsehoods about candidates for Parliament in particular. Similar to those in the United States, British libel defenses include truth and fair comment. The British also recognize unintentional defamation—a defense that carries requirements for retraction and apology. And the British maintain a national press council. A quasi-official organ lacking enforcement powers, the council hears complaints against the press and provides written opinions that may be published in the media.

Like other European nations, France recognizes actions against insults as well as against libels. The French include statements of opinion within the category of insult and reserve defamation law for fac-

tually untrue statements. Two defenses are available to the press in libel cases: truth and good faith. Both, however, are extremely difficult to prove under French jurisprudence.

Truth is also a consideration in libel cases in Japan, but it wields limited power in some circumstances. Japanese libel law recognizes truth as a defense only in cases that explicitly involve issues of public importance. Private individuals are not fair game to the Japanese media.

The research agenda. Until the mid-1970s, libel research was almost exclusively traditional legal analysis. Communications and legal scholars studied case law and concentrated on normative legal theory. Research priorities began to change, however, toward the close of the 1970s. Studies were initiated to identify who sues for libel and why. Other research systematically examined the outcome of libel suits in order to discern long-term trends. Some journalists claim that even the threat of large libel awards has a chilling effect on in-depth reporting, but there is a dearth of research and reliable data to back up such assertions. Little effort has yet been put into interdisciplinary studies to examine libel law from a communications perspective. It is clear that phenomena such as the creation of reputation and the effects of media on reputation have implications in both communications and law.

See also CENSORSHIP; ETHICS, MEDIA; GOVERNMENT-MEDIA RELATIONS; NEWSPAPER: HISTORY; NEWSPAPER: TRENDS; PRIVACY.

Bibliography. American Law Institute, *Restatement of the Law of Torts*, 2d ed., 4 vols., Philadelphia, 1975; W. Page Keeton et al., eds., *Prosser and Keeton on the Law of Torts*, 5th ed., St. Paul, Minn., 1984; Robert M. Kundstadt, *The Protection of Personal and Commercial Reputation: A Study of the Law in Western Europe and the United States*, Munich, 1980; Don R. Pember, *Mass Media Law*, 4th ed., Dubuque, Iowa, 1987; Robert D. Sack, *Libel, Slander, and Related Problems*, New York, 1980; Bruce Sanford, *Libel and Privacy: The Prevention and Defense of Litigation*, New York, 1985.

JEREMY COHEN

LIBRARY

This entry consists of two articles:
1. History
2. Trends

1. HISTORY

A library is a collection of books (and often other materials) assembled for a specific purpose or range of purposes and housed to accommodate both the materials and those who will consult or study them. Libraries have had a long, uneven, checkered evolution. *See also* BOOK.

The earliest known libraries can be divided roughly into two classes: collections of administrative records and collections of literary and other works. The first category includes the library of baked clay tablets and cylinders of Nineveh's King Ashurbanipal (668–627 B.C.E.), which served mainly to provide the king and his civil servants with the records indispensable for the efficient administration of a great empire (*see* NINEVEH). They facilitated what has become known in the modern world as information retrieval, one of the earliest recorded examples of which was the successful search instigated by Darius I, king of Persia, in the fifth century B.C.E., to check the authenticity of the permission that was allegedly granted by his predecessor, Cyrus, to the Jews to rebuild the Temple in Jerusalem.

It would be reasonable to expect ancient Greece to have had at least examples of the second (literary) type of library, but there is little or no evidence of them prior to the conquest of Egypt by Alexander the Great and the foundation of the new city of Alexandria in 331 B.C.E. (*see* HELLENIC WORLD). The splendid new stone buildings erected after Alexander's death in 323 B.C.E. included the museum, to which was attached the legendary library with its subsidiary in the Temple of Serapis. These libraries were planned and built up during the reign of Alexander's successor in Egypt, Ptolemy Soter, and of his son Philadelphus. The latter's librarian, Demetrius of Phalerum, was, according to Josephus,

anxious to collect, if he could, all the books in the inhabited world and, if he heard of, or saw, any book worthy of study, he would buy it; and so he endeavoured to meet the wishes of the king, for he was very much devoted to the art of book collecting.

Demetrius informed his master that the Alexandrian library had already collected two hundred thousand books and that he looked forward to its reaching five hundred thousand. It is impossible, however, to estimate the number of separate works indicated by these totals since individual papyrus and parchment scrolls (the modern codex form was uncommon until the first century C.E.) may have contained more than one work or, alternatively, may have been merely single parts of larger ones. But their numbers at least suggest that some works must surely have found their way to Alexandria from otherwise unrecorded libraries at PLATO's Academy and ARISTOTLE's Lyceum.

The Alexandrian libraries were easily the greatest in the world prior to PRINTING and made Alexandria one of the most important centers of learning. Readers there were served by a succession of distinguished librarians of whom at least Zenodotus, Callimachus, Eratosthenes, and Aristophanes of Byzantium deserve to be mentioned. The modern world of learning owes them an immense debt for their work in establishing definitive texts of the Greek classics. Callimachus was also responsible for compiling the first known national bibliography, which unfortunately has not survived. The other great library of the ancient world, at Pergamum (modern Bergama), was founded a century later than those at Alexandria, and less is known about it. All were the victims of time, decay, and war. Legends ascribe their destruction to such varied causes as Julius Caesar's and Aurelian's civil wars, Antony's gift of the Pergamum library to Cleopatra, and the determined anticlassical activities of the early Christians and Arabs. It seems clear, however, that by 400 C.E. all had been destroyed or dispersed.

Little is known of libraries in the Roman Republic and the ROMAN EMPIRE prior to the breakdown of organized rule in the fifth century C.E. Many libraries, including public libraries in Rome and provincial cities, appear to have existed, but they were probably less comprehensive and worse equipped than the private ones built up by such wealthy individuals as CICERO and the younger Pliny. The Alexandrian traditions passed to the capital of the Eastern Empire, Constantinople (modern Istanbul), and were maintained there for more than a thousand years (until the capture of the city by the Turks in 1453) by great libraries, notably the Imperial and the Patriarchal. Like the Alexandrian libraries, these attracted scholars from many parts of the world. Although many of their literary productions came in the form of commentaries and edited versions of earlier authors, it is largely because of these libraries that the literary legacies of ancient Greece and Rome were preserved for later generations.

By 400 C.E. the political situation in the Roman Empire had become chaotic, and the library tradition was maintained mostly in the book collections of individuals such as Sidonius, Boethius, Bede, and Alcuin. The latter names indicate the role played by the Christian church in the next major period of library development, which was furthered by the Benedictine rule prescribing a minimum of holy READING for individual monks. During the early MIDDLE AGES some of the most important libraries were collected in the cathedrals of northern Italy, southern Germany, and, to a lesser extent, England. Books were also accumulated in individual monasteries, although hardly systematically, and were often kept in odd corners rather than in designated library rooms. Although monasteries were basically self-contained communities, they frequently held land outside their own boundaries; they were therefore liable to be involved in lawsuits and hence needed law books. Monasteries also needed texts relevant to their educational responsibilities and even more. For example, the short list of books belonging, during the late thirteenth or early fourteenth century, to the small Premonstratensian abbey of St. Radigund, near Dover in England, included works on law, medicine, and grammar as well as the more obvious theology, psalter, missal, and service books. Larger establishments such as its near neighbor, Dover Priory, and establishments at Canterbury, Durham, and elsewhere had many more. All church libraries were gradually overshadowed by that of the Vatican at Rome, whose development, inevitably impeded by the papal exile to Avignon during the fourteenth century, reasserted itself in the sixteenth. Meanwhile the diffusion of Arab culture encouraged the production of translations, which found their way into at least some of the cathedral libraries (*see* ISLAM, CLASSICAL AND MEDIEVAL ERAS).

Many of the educational responsibilities of the church passed to the new universities, of which, from the eleventh century on, that of Paris provided a greatly admired model for the West, exerting an influence particularly on developments at both Oxford and Cambridge (*see* UNIVERSITY). The early growth of the universities was based largely on individual colleges, and book collecting tended to be associated with them rather than with the central university. By the end of the fourteenth century, however, there were also small central libraries at the Sorbonne in Paris and at Oxford and Cambridge. They and their college libraries were able subsequently to retrieve and preserve at least some of the valuable manuscript material that the dissolution of religious establishments had put greatly at risk. Over the same period books and records of various kinds were accumulated in royal palaces and in the developing departments of state, although, as they tended to follow the perambulations of the monarchs throughout their dominions rather than stay in a fixed library location, the possibilities of damage and loss were considerable. The introduction of printing into western Europe in the fifteenth century obviously facilitated library growth, but the new materials made available tended to be regarded, initially and for many years following, as vastly inferior to their predecessor manuscripts. University libraries in America began in the seventeenth century soon after the first settlements.

Modern Libraries

Library services in the modern world are highly specialized and differentiated. They include national libraries; university, college, and school libraries; special libraries; and public libraries.

National libraries. Most countries have acquired a national library, but only some twenty were founded prior to 1800. Some of the earliest foundations were based on existing royal libraries, as in France and Denmark; others were based at least partly on private libraries, as with the U.S. Library of Congress and the United Kingdom's British Museum (since 1973 the Reference Division of the British Library). Some of the later ones, in common with the Library of Congress, were founded in close association with or in order to serve federal or national governments, as in Australia, Canada, and New Zealand. Many of the newest foundations, including those in the emergent African states, were created by the new governments themselves. Some countries have more than one national library, as in the United Kingdom with its National Library of Scotland and National Library of Wales, and also in Italy and Yugoslavia. Nearly all national libraries rely on the legally required deposit of books by publishers for at least part of their accessions, the privilege of COPYRIGHT being frequently linked with legal deposit.

The functions and responsibilities of national libraries vary from country to country. All normally collect and preserve their national production of books. Some also maintain large and representative collections of the literatures of other countries and, increasingly, of nonbook items including maps, music, phonograph records, tapes, film, and microforms. Some coordinate the services and facilitate the cooperation of other libraries within and outside their own countries. A few train their countries' librarians.

The services of national libraries may be available to all readers or at least to those readers unable to satisfy their library needs elsewhere. Some provide a stock that is available for consultation and reference purposes only; others make at least part of it available for home reading. National library book stocks range from the more than 10 million volumes of the Library of Congress, the British Library, the Bibliothèque Nationale in Paris, and the Lenin State Library in Moscow to the still very small collections in some of the emergent states.

In the United Kingdom, the National Library for the Blind lends books in embossed and enlarged type to visually handicapped readers, including those residing in other countries. This is an unusual pattern; most libraries for the blind and physically handicapped form departments of the larger central libraries, such as the Library of Congress.

University, college, and school libraries. Although the university and college libraries in a limited number of countries have long histories, as in Paris, Vienna, Louvain, Oxford, Cambridge, and Edinburgh, and at Harvard University in the United States, most of their systematic stock building began only

Figure 1. *(Library—History)* The public library at Hulwan. Illustration from al-Harīrī's *Maqāmāt*. Thirteenth century. Phot. Bibl. Nat., Paris.

Figure 2. *(Library—History)* Michelangelo, Biblioteca Laurenziana (Laurentian Library), Florence, begun 1524. Alinari/Art Resource, New York.

during the second half of the nineteenth century or even during the twentieth. In England this expansion was pioneered by the Cambridge University Library and the Bodleian Library in Oxford when they attempted to enforce their legal deposit entitlements (unusual for university libraries). This occurred approximately at the same time as Ainsworth Rand Spofford's comparable activity on behalf of the Library of Congress and Antonio Panizzi's for the British Museum. These book accumulation drives can be regarded as the modern equivalents of that by Demetrius of Phalerum on behalf of the Alexandrian libraries of the ancient world.

School libraries were much slower to develop than university and college libraries. Their expansion during future years would appear to offer more opportunities than for most other types of libraries.

Special libraries. The so-called special libraries, usually provided, at least initially, to serve a restricted readership, are largely a creation of the twentieth century. Some, such as medical and law libraries and libraries serving government agencies, began earlier, but the collections built up by a wide variety of businesses and professional and trade associations developed mostly after World War I. Although some grew into very large libraries, many are small and very highly specialized; their small staffs were appointed primarily to make information readily available to other employees. Because of this prime responsibility of information provision—and information that is as up-to-date as possible—the book has always tended to be less important than the

periodical in these collections. Indeed the staffs of special libraries are normally required not merely to provide the periodicals but also to draw the attention of readers to their contents. Special libraries were pioneered mostly in the industrial nations of the West and particularly in the United States, United Kingdom, France, and Germany, but later appeared in other countries.

Public libraries. Libraries provided for and accessible to the general public began predominantly in the form of eighteenth-century circulating libraries, although there were earlier examples of free public libraries. During the first half of the nineteenth century subscription and institutional libraries became much more numerous and, particularly in the United States and the United Kingdom, prepared the way for free and freely accessible libraries. The latter, supported mainly from local taxes and administered by staffs responsible to boards of local citizens, began to appear in many countries during the late nineteenth century. Grants for building such libraries became for a time a favorite form of philanthropy for wealthy individuals such as Andrew Carnegie.

Public libraries—with varying levels of coverage and efficiency—have become almost universal, and it is impossible even to estimate the total number of such systems throughout the world. Whereas the other main types of libraries mostly provide readers with material that may generally be described as educational, informational, cultural, and for research, public libraries also usually attempt to address their readers' recreational and leisure needs; it is hence much more difficult to define their specific duties and areas of responsibility. In the United States and the United Kingdom, for example, the controversy over provision of light, mostly fictional reading has persisted over more than a century and remains unresolved. Public libraries, too, have experienced more harassment than other types of libraries because of CENSORSHIP—religious, political, and sexual.

Prior to the twentieth century, readers' access to library stocks was limited primarily to those of libraries that they could visit. There is limited evidence that monastic libraries lent books to one another for reference, checking, and copying, but the vast national and international networks for interlibrary cooperation and lending are creations of the twentieth century. The encouragement of such cooperation has been one of the many useful activities of library associations throughout the world, of which the pioneers were the American Library Association, founded in 1876, and the Library Association of the United Kingdom (since 1898 the Library Association), founded one year later.

Modern methods of economical storage, including the use of mobile shelving, reducing dramatically the number of necessary access gangways, have greatly increased the number of books that can be stored on a given floor area. The growing use of microforms saves infinitely more space. Both expedients are essential if the buildings containing ever-growing library stocks are not themselves to grow beyond economic limits.

Computerization has provided many significant innovations for the way libraries function. From the immediate point of view of the individual library or library system, it can facilitate and speed up cataloging as well as the many mundane but essential routines connected with the registration of readers and the records of books consulted or circulated. Computer terminals can take the place of the card catalogs and other card records that have served library users and library staffs for so long. Much more important, however, are the vast improvements possible in the field of information retrieval. The individual library can now link itself with and obtain full advantage from the various outside networks from which it can

Figure 3. *(Library—History)* Henri Labrouste, reading room of the Cabinet des Éstampes, Bibliothèque Nationale, Paris, 1861–1869. Lauros-Giraudon/Art Resource, New York.

obtain not only bibliographical information in support of its traditional service to readers but also general and/or specialized information. There are also, of course, dangers in excessively centralized information sources. Not the least of the many values inherent in the library service of the past has been the ready access to differing opinions and alternative points of view, and the computerized library must offer no less.

See also ARCHIVES; LITERACY; PAMPHLET; WRITING MATERIALS.

Bibliography. John W. Clark, *The Care of Books: An Essay on the Development of Libraries and Their Fittings, from the Earliest Times to the End of the Eighteenth Century,* 2d ed., London, 1909, reprint (1909 ed.) Norwood, Pa., 1978; Allen Kent and Harold Lancour, eds., *Encyclopedia of Library and Information Science,* 39 vols. in progress, New York, 1968– ; E. A. Parsons, *The Alexandrian Library,* Amsterdam and New York, 1967; James W. Thompson, *The Medieval Library,* Chicago, 1939, reprint (with supp. by B. B. Boyer) New York, 1957; Robert Wedgeworth, ed., *ALA World Encyclopedia of Library and Information Services,* Chicago, 1980.

WILLIAM ARTHUR MUNFORD

2. TRENDS

The library has been the repository for written communication since the dawn of WRITING. More than five thousand years ago it housed the first clay tablets. Then as now it had three main functions: to collect, to preserve, and to make available. As WRITING MATERIALS evolved through papyrus to paper to film to magnetic tape, the library adapted, while still accomplishing its three basic functions. The library in the 1980s has incorporated new information technologies into its services just as easily as its predecessors adjusted to the printed word. The modern library houses microfiche, videotapes, and compact discs along with its books, and it uses computer terminals to provide management and user services. See section 1, above.

New information technologies, however, have created changes far beyond the simple storage and retrieval of information. The information environment itself has changed: the value of information, its use, and its dissemination are widely discussed. The library stands on the threshold of an explosion in the methods by which information is stored, viewed, interpreted, retrieved, and disseminated. Although the library has adapted to the use of technological equipment, it has not yet addressed fully the overriding changes needed to adjust to the Information Age.

Technology trends in public services. To the public, the changes occurring in the library because of automation become evident when a BOOK is checked out. Bar codes and laser scanners have replaced hand-stamped cards; due dates and patron fines are stored in a DATA BASE, not in file drawers.

There are other changes that are not so apparent to the patron. For instance, the long-standing tradition of interlibrary borrowing and lending is evolving. At one time the library's individual resources limited its patrons. Now the patron may gain access to materials from around the world through on-line data bases that provide millions of citations stored in computer memories thousands of miles away (*see* COMPUTER: IMPACT). Through a computer terminal, on-line data bases, such as DIALOG, INSPEC, and the WORLD PATENT INDEX, provide references to articles in any subject field. These services are growing quickly to provide enhanced access to the citations themselves. In 1978 only 3 percent of the citations available in on-line data bases provided full text reference. By 1985 the balance had shifted, with more than 50 percent of the citations providing the full text of the actual document. This enables the searcher to read entire articles stored in the data base rather than simply locating the author, title, and subject citations. Every year more than 6 million unique references are added to data bases; more than 70 million records are available in the late 1980s.

Advances in miniaturization and telecommunications (*see* TELECOMMUNICATIONS NETWORKS) have also simplified locating and requesting materials not owned by a particular library. Microfiche, floppy disks, RAM (random access memory) disks, and CD-ROMs (read-only memory) are examples of the storage formats available to libraries to facilitate sharing records of their holdings. Even an isolated library will be able to locate an item owned by another library by searching its record of the other library's holdings. Electronic mail and telefacsimile transmission of documents speed the actual transfer of materials from one library to another.

ARTIFICIAL INTELLIGENCE is enhancing on-line data-base searching. An "expert system" is a computer system designed to simulate human problem-solving behavior. Using artificial intelligence the computer system learns from the searches it has already done. An expert system will locate and connect to the appropriate on-line data base, translate various search languages, and recall previous searches. The U.S. National Library of Medicine is already using a prototype expert system as a cost-effective consultant in making medical diagnoses.

Groups of libraries that share resources are called library networks. These networks stretch across the nation and recently have crossed international boundaries. The Online Computer Library Center (OCLC) is a good example. OCLC provides telecommunications links among the United States, Canada,

Central America, Great Britain, Japan, and France. This maturing network, founded in 1967, celebrated its eleven millionth interlibrary loan transaction in 1986.

Library services in the home have been made possible by new technologies. With many library services already automated, patrons with a terminal and modem in their own home or place of business are able to search the on-line catalog for a book, place a book on hold or reserve, and request an interlibrary loan. Some libraries offer community information bulletin boards with notices for job-placement opportunities, car-pooling details, community activities, government services, and public documents. France's government-supported MINITEL system is a pioneering effort in this realm. It provides in-home services across the nation, allowing TELEPHONE access to regional libraries from any equipped home.

Technology trends in collection development. Many new types of media have joined the book on the library's shelves. The library of the late twentieth century collects film, videocassettes and disks, computer disks, records, maps, and other items in addition to books in order to assimilate the many forms of communication. "Media center" has become an increasingly popular label for a library that collects book and nonbook materials.

Form as well as content must be considered when developing a library collection. The library is only beginning to address the problems presented by the use of this vast variety of formats. The librarian may choose a hardback or paperback book, microform, or computer disk in order to match the information in the collection with the needs of the potential users. A well-balanced collection is no longer just a group of books that reflects the interests and needs of the library community but a collection that provides the proper format as well. These format decisions have a profound effect on the use of space and budget in the library.

Looking toward the future the library will continue to grapple with the consequences of the new variety of formats. As technology advances, and it becomes easier to reformat information from one material type to another, the library will be pressed, not to choose among types of formats, but to present information to the patron in its most desirable and usable form. A related problem will revolve around the storage and organization of cultural and historical information available on nontraditional formats. TELEVISION NEWS, for instance, has become an important form of journalism and a valuable source of cultural information. Videotapes used in assembling newscasts can be erased and reused—an economic advantage—but historic material may be lost in the process. Libraries are already playing a role in preserving this significant part of twentieth-century culture. *See* ARCHIVES, FILM; TELEVISION HISTORY.

Technology trends in cataloging. Historically, preparing a library book for use required a labor-intensive effort. Each library determined the correct bibliographic information and subject descriptions for every book obtained. Today the library accesses automated systems that provide a record of the cataloging done by other libraries. By sharing these bibliographic records the cost and time of duplicating the cataloging effort are avoided.

One result of the increase in shared cataloging information is an effort to standardize. The machine-readable cataloging (MARC) format was designed to standardize the creation of a bibliographic record. There are several different MARC formats to accommodate the variety of types of information material available. The MARC formats allow a computer to understand and manipulate the information that the library has stored on the catalog card. International standard book description (ISBD) numbers are another means of standardizing access to a particular title. These are unique numbers issued to each new book title published. Using this system a book can be identified by its number even if different cataloging methods have been used. Standardization efforts are also being made at the computer-software level to allow different computer systems to "speak" to each other. A major project at the U.S. Library of Congress is to develop interfaces among various computer systems to allow existing records to be transferred from one data base to another. *See* STANDARDS.

Library issues. The library faces growing complexities as it looks toward the next century. Individuals as well as businesses are called upon to make decisions based on knowledge far beyond their daily experiences. Information is widely discussed; how it is used and how it is distributed are important issues that are being affected by rapidly changing technologies. However, people do not turn instinctively to the library for the information they need, and the demand for libraries will not necessarily increase in the Information Age. In fact, as other information services become available the library may increasingly be ignored.

This problem may result from the library's traditionally multifaceted activities. It has tried to fulfill several roles, providing educational and LEISURE services and materials while also attempting to provide a useful collection for serious readers. These ambiguities will increase as new uses and types of information emerge and as the difference between the "information-poor" and the "information-rich" grows. Other information providers, unburdened by a tradition of attempting to fill every information need, focus on particular services. The library, faced with so many avenues of development, has incorporated new technologies into existing services without directly addressing changes in the information environment. The library will need to rethink its goals and policies in order to continue to provide useful and needed library services.

Strategic planning. Unfortunately, the library has not responded well to the Information Age challenge. Some libraries simply maintained a low profile as the entrepreneurial maelstrom continued. Others made piecemeal attempts to be more responsive to the masses. A wide variety of library activities resulted as the library wandered from one program to another, attempting to prove its utility. There is concern that library development is spurred by the availability of technology rather than by the information needs of the library community.

One approach to this problem is coordinated strategic planning. A hard look at the library, the current environment, and what will develop in the future will help in planning viable services. The library must examine the information environment and determine which services and resources will be most needed and whether the library or a profit-making service is better suited and motivated to fill the need. Current library services need to be closely examined and their costs and benefits reevaluated. New services should be planned based on the evaluation of the information environment and a careful analysis of users and potential users.

Strategic planning will involve change: the possible reassignment of staff from one department to another or reorganization to reflect services centralized by automation. Traditional services may be changed or dropped, and the onus of starting new ones may be added. But strategic planning also helps develop a frame of reference much needed in the library's changing environment. It provides opportunities to examine important issues, and it encourages the development of objective goals based on the library's mission rather than its operational needs.

Philosophy. The driving force behind a renewed and vigorous library will be a new philosophy: a change from an acquisition- and preservation-oriented institution to a service-oriented institution. This does not mean that the careful collection and cataloging of books will be abandoned but rather, as the library takes advantage of the cost- and time-saving technologies it has installed, that staff has more time to provide extended public services. There has been some doubt expressed about the library's ability to make this philosophical shift. A Carnegie Foundation report stated recently:

Library personnel, while now fully competent to handle the library automation that has taken place, have neither the education nor the emotional commitment to prepare for the shift in outlook required to change from owning, cataloging, and lending, to becoming electronic data sleuths

ready to link a student or faculty member to someone else's data bank.

The library's importance as a keeper of all information (not just profitable information) and a preserver of historical, cultural, and scientific knowledge will ensure its continued survival. However, if the library is to thrive and offer truly desirable services to its public, it must make this shift toward greater emphasis on service.

Such a philosophical shift must be accomplished by a greater effort to make the public aware of the benefits of the library and its willingness to serve. It is the library's responsibility to tell the community of its services and materials. Strategic planning, a new philosophy, and new services are only half the job. These will never be appreciated by the public at large unless the library undertakes to educate the community about the benefits and usefulness of the library.

Education. The librarian of the future needs a variety of new attitudes and skills. Library educators must address this challenge. Robert S. Taylor summarizes six major areas that provide a framework for future professional education in library and information science:

- *Organization of information.* The study of information as a malleable asset rather than a package dictated by format.
- *Information environment.* The study of the history, context, and dynamics of knowledge and information processes in society. How information is used, acquired, organized, processed, retrieved, and disseminated in the community.
- *Information media.* The study of the choices and functions of different media for different messages and for different audiences.
- *Systems and technologies.* The study of formal analysis, design, and evaluation to orchestrate effective combinations of people, machines, and information for the effective use of information.
- *Research methods.* The attainment of skills that will enable the student to become an effective participant in the research process, both to provide needed, quantitative assessments of libraries and library methods and to be a critical consumer of others' research.
- *Management.* The study of organizational behavior, marketing, strategic planning, decision making, costs and budgeting, policy and politics.

These points shift the emphasis of library education from archival studies to true information management. They prepare the librarian for the multifaceted role that a library director must play today. Integral to the library education process must be an acculturation into the new library philosophy, one that espouses service and active participation in the community.

The library has a unique role to play in the Information Age. It can add a "people perspective" to the development of information technologies and the use and availability of information. The library must focus on people in determining its services and attitudes, for ultimately it will be the users who will identify the ways in which information can help.

See also ARCHIVES.

Bibliography. Ruth Alston, "Hunger for the Poor?: Some Observations on Information Provision in India," *Journal of Information Science* 6 (1983): 115–122; Patricia Battin, "The Electronic Library: A Vision for the Future," in *New Information Technologies and Libraries,* ed. by H. Liebaers, W. J. Haas, and W. E. Biervliet, Boston, 1984; "Bibliographic Databases Provide Enormous Online Knowledge Pool," *The Futurist* 15 (1981): 49; James Ducker, "Futures Dossier: Electronic Information—Impact of the Database," *Futures* 17 (1985): 164–169; Frank Newman, *Higher Education and the American Resurgence,* Princeton, N.J., 1985; Robert S. Taylor, "Reminiscing about the Future: Professional Education and the Information Environment," *Library Journal* 104 (1979): 1871–1875.

ANNE J. MATHEWS AND DAYNA E. BUCK

LICENSING. *See* COPYRIGHT; DATA BASE; GOVERNMENT-MEDIA RELATIONS; GOVERNMENT REGULATION; NEW INTERNATIONAL INFORMATION ORDER; SATELLITE; TELECOMMUNICATIONS POLICY. *See also* MILTON, JOHN.

LINGUISTICS

The historically developed body of LANGUAGE-directed approaches and of reflexive activities concerning these approaches. The extant language-directed approaches can be organized in a systematic way when we take into account their proper object: human language and SPEECH in its various aspects. Human language and speech also include, apart from natural languages, speech (or speech fragments) guided or stimulated through human intervention, as in the various branches of computational linguistics. ANIMAL COMMUNICATION is not part of the proper object of linguistics but falls under the study of communication by means of signs (*see* SIGN; SIGN SYSTEM), which is the central concern of SEMIOTICS. Through much of its history linguistics has focused on the formal-semantic system (GRAMMAR and lexicon) of language; since the nineteenth century, however, the sound system has also been an object of systematic study, yielding many insights of great importance to the field as it now stands.

In the history of linguistics the study of the formal system has been dominant. Next to this "internal" aspect one must mention the link between language (speech) and mind (thought), which has been the object of both speculative and empirical studies on the nature of conceptualization and its possible culture-boundedness, on the interplay between rational and emotional behavior as reflected in language, and on the expression of polarities ("good"/"bad"), negative contents ("absent"), and all kinds of abstract relationships (often rendered in metaphorical terms). In pre-nineteenth-century language study such subjects were assigned to the philosophy of language or to psychology, but they now belong to distinct professional branches of linguistics, such as psycholinguistics (a term coined in the 1940s) and neurolinguistics. Important topics of research here are LANGUAGE ACQUISITION, speech production and PERCEPTION, aphasic speech (including all kinds of SPEECH AND LANGUAGE DISORDERS), and the localization of a speech area in the brain.

Another link that has been explored throughout the history of linguistics is that between language and society/culture (*see* CULTURE). Language as a means and as a process of socialization leads to a range of issues associated with its variation across social groups and within individual usage: diastratal (according to social group, education) and diaphasic (according to age) variation, styles of speech and ways of speaking, and code switching (in bilingual or diglossic situations, for example). Among the variables influencing and affecting language use are differences of GENDER and age (*see* SEXISM); social, educational, and professional background; power and solidarity relationships between language users; and the degree of formality of the communicative situation (allowing for a further typology according to text GENRE).

At a global level one can study—as is usual in the tradition inaugurated by the German philosopher Wilhelm von Humboldt—language as a cultural good. Specific themes here are the degree of determination of language patterns by cultural patterns and vice versa, linguistic acculturation, the cultural importance of language, and so on. A major difficulty of this type of research is finding noncircular parameters, free from any a priori assumptions (a problem evidenced, unfortunately, in studies of language as a mirror of the structure of society). On the practical side the link between language and society is the specific focus of language policy and attitudes. Issues here include promotion, discrimination, or repression of languages; choosing an ALPHABET; language purity; language loyalty; international and artificial languages; and norms of translation (*see* LANGUAGE IDEOLOGY; LANGUAGE VARIETIES; TRANSLATION, THEORIES OF). The relationship between language and society/culture is now the focus of two separate offshoots of the language sciences: sociolinguistics and anthropological linguistics. The sociolinguistic and anthropolinguistic perspectives can and should be integrated within the study of the formal-semantic system. In fact, a long-standing tradition exists in which linguistic MEANING is studied within its social and cultural context, a tradition now forcefully embodied within recent ethnopoetic work (*see* ETHNOPOETICS).

Apart from the formal-semantic system of language and its relationship to the human mind and to culture and society, another topic of research consists of the specific communicative uses of language. Included here are a number of logico-linguistic themes: language and truth/falsity; reference; quantification; logical relations within discourse, such as contradiction, presupposition, implication, implicature; modalities; and, on a more global level, language as an object and medium of logical analysis—all of which have been recently integrated within semiotics (and/or pragmatics). Other themes include the use of language in sciences (terminological apparatus, formulation of statements or laws, model construction and axiomatization of theories) and in literature (definition of style, text grammar, semantic analysis of literary texts). *See also* LITERARY CRITICISM; STYLE, LITERARY.

The practice of language study has also aroused a number of reflexive approaches, taking language-directed activities as their object. Among these reflexive approaches are the history (or HISTORIOGRAPHY) of linguistics and the epistemology of linguistics (the study of methods and types of argumentation found in linguistic works, focusing on the evaluation of goals and principles of linguistic theories). This reflexive work is of crucial importance for the construction of a general theory of linguistics and of language, which should be the proper object of theoretical linguistics.

The Object of Study

The core object of linguistics is the formal-semantic system of language, understood as *genus* (English *language* or *speech;* French *langage*) or as *species* (English *language;* French *langue*). This object necessarily involves a certain amount of idealization and systematization by the investigator. All approaches to language rely on the constitution of data, and in the case of linguistics this constitution can be achieved through various means. Note that linguistic data typically manifest both formal and phonological elements and that much analysis bears on the interaction of these two layers of language structure. In a growing order of determination of data by theory or theories the following means of data constitution can be sorted out: (1) recording of data (fieldwork), (2) philological interpretation of recorded data, (3) reconstruction of data (either on the basis of one language or dialect, as in strictly interpreted internal reconstruction, or on the basis of evidence from two or more languages or dialects, as in the much more common comparative reconstruction), and (4) the theoretical postulation of data or of relationships among data.

A preliminary distinction should be made between oral and written language. The problem of the status of written versus oral language is not so much one of priority but rather one of description of the competence or linguistic knowledge of the subject (within literate cultures). Are written and spoken language integrated within the subject's linguistic competence, or do they constitute autonomous blocks? The structure of written language, which does not have the complete formal-semantic organization of spoken language, is the object of graphemics (or theory of WRITING), which also deals with the history and typology of writing systems or scripts (alphabetical, consonantal, syllabic, morphophonological, morphological, ideogrammatical, pictographic). *See also* LITERACY; ORAL CULTURE.

In general, when speaking of the systematic organization of language, what is meant is spoken language. This is especially true when speaking of the formal-semantic system of language, which comprises the following components or levels:

1. Phonetics: the study of speech sounds, from the articulatory, acoustic, or perceptual point of view.
2. PHONOLOGY: the (intralinguistic) study of the functionally distinct(ive) sound classes, often codified already in the alphabet (e.g., the case of *t* in English, with its various, functionally nondistinctive word-initial, word-internal, and word-final realizations). For distinctive nonsegmental units (pitch, stress, tone), the term *tonology* is used, although it should be noted that much dealt with under tonology has a morphological function (compare the stress opposition between English *tránsport* and *transpórt*).
3. Morphology: the study of the smallest "form plus meaning" units or, in other terms, the study of the internal structure of words (e.g., *books* = *book* + *s*).
4. Syntax: the study of the combinations of words into larger units (sentences, texts) and of the rules governing these combinations.
5. SEMANTICS: the study of meaning (and reference) within a particular language. The domain of meaning can stretch from morpheme over word

and sentence to text. Semantics is essential for the definition of lexical items (the vocabulary of a language) and is intrinsically linked with lexicology and lexicography.

(In some models, levels 1–4 are subsumed under *grammar,* but this term has also been restricted to the levels of morphology and syntax; for level 5 the less theoretical terms *dictionary* and *lexicon* are also used.)

In the organization of language some issues should be kept in mind. First, not all linguistic models make the same distinctions. Some blend morphology and syntax into "morphosyntax"; others do not make a distinction between syntax and semantics. In some models even more levels are postulated, such as "morphophonology"—the study of phoneme alternations within morphemes, such as the alternation between voiceless *f* and voiced *v* in English *shelf/shelves.* Second, the interactions between the various levels are differently conceived of and accounted for (in stratificational linguistics the description is focused on these interactions). Third, the above-mentioned directionality (from the smaller to the larger units, i.e., a "bottom-up" approach) is typical for most traditional and structuralist practice but is reversed in more recent "top-down" models. Fourth, the description of the system of a language is never based on data obtained from all its speakers at a particular time. Pragmatic factors, such as number of speakers (especially true for extinct languages), make it necessary to extrapolate from more or less reduced corpora that are taken to be representative.

Finally, the formal-semantic system of language is integrated within a particular focus of approach. In a synchronic focus the description refers to data situated with respect to a particular time and place. In a diachronic focus the descriptions correlate data from one or more languages that pertain to distinct temporal periods and possibly also to distinct places. A panchronic or achronic description can combine the synchronic and diachronic perspectives, and it purports to formulate generalizations or correspondences without regard to relative position in space and time. The term *panchronic* can be reserved for descriptions aiming at typological generalizations and *achronic* for contrastive descriptions—either of two languages (say, English and French) or of two sets of languages (as in BENJAMIN LEE WHORF's contrasting Hopi and Standard Average European).

History of Interests and Methods

Linguistics, like its object (language), is a social product with a very complex history of continuities and discontinuities, including traditions of divergent interests and descriptive frameworks. The development of linguistics has been one of growing sophistication, extension of various traditions, and, naturally, accumulation of data and insights. The evolution of linguistics has been shaped by a number of variables such as types of contacts between languages, the linguistic needs of various groups, and the state of scientific methodology (descriptive techniques, terminology, or metalanguage). Another is the changing climates of opinion internal or external to linguistics: idealism, historicism, the cultural-anthropological outlook, STRUCTURALISM (and instrumentalism), the romanticist-creative conception, and the like. Still another factor is individual and collective achievements in the field: university programs, pedagogical reforms, learned societies, journals, collections, wartime enterprises, and so on.

It may be useful to articulate the history of linguistics by appealing to the notion of *program* as a cover term for a number of theoretical orientations that pursue basically the same goals and that favor specific approaches and exclude others. Major programs in the history of linguistics could be called

1. The *correspondence* program, which takes language as an instrument and which studies the (inter)relationships among language, thought, and reality.
2. The *descriptivist* program, which takes language as a set of formal data that have to be organized systematically.
3. The *social* program, which sees language as a social and intrinsically variable fact. Linguistic variation (correlating with social differences), which presupposes a multiple competence in the speaking subject, is the basis for language change.
4. The *projection* program, in which a logical-formal model is applied to a fragment of natural language (e.g., tense system, mechanisms of reference).

It is interesting to note that each of these programs subsumes various theories and that programs exist simultaneously.

The notion of program opens vistas for a comprehensive history of linguistics, including various types of folk linguistics—for example, speculations on the origin of language, creation of a (rudimentary) metalanguage, attitudes concerning languages and their use, historically and/or areally spread formulaic expressions, popular etymology, and especially the development of writing systems. Also of relevance would be various studies bordering on philosophy, psychology, theology, and other related subjects. The various traditions resulting from specific orientations must be seen in the light of particular needs, such as the case of bilingual lexicography in Mesopotamia, of Indian grammatical description of Sanskrit and philosophy of language, and of ancient Chinese lexicography.

These national orientations were soon superseded by international trends, such as the development of a grammatical model centered on the study of letters (as representing classes of sounds) and word classes. This was the merit of the school of Alexandrian grammarians, whose model was taken over by the Latin grammarians. Parallel to this grammatical trend was a philosophical trend, taking language as an object of study. In PLATO's case language became the object of an etymological (*Cratylus*) or logical (*The Sophist*) analysis. ARISTOTLE's much more detailed study of linguistic categories (in his *Organon*) led in late antiquity and during the MIDDLE AGES to a powerful tradition of linguistic reflection, either on the sign nature of language (St. Augustine, Boethius, Anselm of Canterbury, William of Ockham) or on the categories of grammar (more specifically, morphology and syntax). The latter part of the tradition is exemplified in the work of William of Conches, Petrus Helias, and the group of speculative grammarians (*modistae*). The linguistic horizon was very restricted then, and the study of Latin eclipsed to a large extent that of the vernaculars (also of Greek and Hebrew).

With the RENAISSANCE there was an increased interest in the study of the vernaculars and exotic languages from Asia, Africa, Oceania, and the New World described by missionaries. The Latin model was still much in favor as a descriptive format or as a standard for comparison. Sixteenth-, seventeenth-, and eighteenth-century studies also produced a large body of didactic works (manuals, school grammars, conversation books) with an utterly contrastive design. The creation of national academies in Europe, the diplomatic exchanges between courts and governments, and the organization of national administrations caused an explosion of linguistic tools and also of larger synthetic enterprises such as grammars and dictionaries (*see* LANGUAGE REFERENCE BOOK). The growing cosmopolitism and the vicissitudes of philosophical trends such as rationalism, idealism, empiricism, and sensualism influenced the development of a philosophical analysis of language (also of humans as speaking animals) and of grammatical categories (culminating in the vogue of "philosophical grammar" or *grammaire raisonnée*). There also developed an important body of knowledge on the relationships among languages. The theoretical and methodological advances in these fields of linguistic activity were major ones, as can be gathered from the construction of a theory of grammar in eighteenth-century France, from the reflections on the origin of language and on the relationship between nature and culture (Thomas Hobbes, JOHN LOCKE, Pierre-Louis Moreau de Maupertuis, Jean-Jacques Rousseau, Étienne Bonnot de Condillac, Adam Smith, Johann Gottfried von Herder), and from the inception of comparative studies (Indo-European and Finno-Ugric).

The nineteenth century saw the rise, development, refinement, and institutionalization of historical-comparative grammar (with Franz Bopp, Rasmus Rask, Jacob Grimm, August Pott, August Schleicher, Karl Brugmann, Berthold Delbrück, FERDINAND DE SAUSSURE, William Whitney), but it also witnessed the spread of Humboldtian linguistics, with a strong interest in (evolutionary) typology and the links among language, thought, and society/culture. Other specific disciplines developed, such as dialectology, phonetics and phonology, psychology of language, neurolinguistics, and semantics (or semasiology). Major achievements were the recognition of regular sound change, the development of the method of reconstruction and of models for genetic relationships, the discovery of the internal history of languages (most fruitfully applied within the study of lexical units), the awareness of (phonemic/morphemic) patterns in language, the idea of linguistic relativity as evidenced on the level of grammatical categories, and the formulation of criteria for typological CLASSIFICATION. If one adds to this the increased interest in the study of dialects and exotic languages one can easily see the groundwork laid in the nineteenth century for twentieth-century linguistic practice and theorizing.

The main trends of twentieth-century linguistics—excluding traditional grammar and broad speculations on the function and origin of language—should be seen in the light of a general concern with methodology and descriptive analysis. The various structuralist schools in Europe and the United States share the view of language as a hierarchical system of forms fulfilling specific functions. Divergences exist in the construction of the theoretical frameworks (integration of various layers or language styles, universalistic versus relativistic orientation, etc.), in the emphasis on the synchronic approach, in the role accorded to meaning, and in the focus on the system of forms or on their function, but it would be wrong to create an impression of the various structuralist schools as opposing monolithic blocks. The structuralist schools each claimed a number of major figures: Saussure (Geneva school); ROMAN JAKOBSON, N. S. Trubetzkoy, and Vilem Mathesius (Prague school); Louis Hjelmslev and H. J. Uldall (Copenhagen school); J. R. Firth (London school); FRANZ BOAS, Leonard Bloomfield, and EDWARD SAPIR (American structuralism, with its complex variations). Some of the exciting developments in the first half of the twentieth century were the fascinating work on exotic languages, the interest in descriptive techniques (and with grammatical forms), the creation of standard handbooks, and also the institutionalization of linguistics as an autonomous discipline. This resulted in a neater division and compartmentalization of linguistic analysis. Articulatory/acoustic phonetics was separated from phonology, and traditional grammar was replaced by a descriptive model embracing morphophonology, morphology, syntax, and, at times, semantics.

From the 1950s on, the field of syntax became open to less rigid techniques of analysis and to increasing theoretical speculation. This led to the development of transformational (generative) grammar by Zellig Harris, Noam Chomsky, and their followers, which was methodologically rooted in American structuralism but from which it diverged by adopting a mentalist and (eighteenth-century) idealist epistemology. The new period has its own social history and fashions in models and research that often reflect a total ignorance of earlier work, its specific interests (autonomous syntax; integration of syntax and semantics; the study of meaning in its pragmatic context or in the larger context of cultural behavior; the structure of the suprasegmental level: tone, pitch, prosody; morphological productivity), and above all its specific techniques and terminological apparatus. Parallel to the development of a formal theory of grammar and language has been an increasing interest in the study of language as a dynamic set of variable subsystems adapted to specific communicative and social ends. This has resulted in an impressive number of studies on (1) synchronic variation, (2) languages in contact and specific situations such as diglossia and bilingualism, (3) speech styles, and (4) language as a semiotic product and/or activity. The sometimes very narrow orientation of formal grammar/theory of grammar is also counterbalanced by the encyclopedic orientation of some traditional disciplines, such as lexicology, onomastics, dialectology, anthropological linguistics, and especially by the flourishing trend of typological linguistics (which constitutes a fertile source of data for present-day comparative linguistics). Language typology is not only directly relevant to the issue of classification but also the most appropriate way to learn and understand how language functions, how languages vary, and how they change.

Present-day Linguistics: Problems and Tasks

Almost ironically the main problems faced by present-day (general) linguistics are not caused by its primary object (language data) but by its practice and practitioners. Adopting Mario Bunge's distinction between the indirect referent (the data or some idealized version of the data base) and the direct referent of a particular scientific theory (the direct referent being the model associated with that theory), one can say that the proliferation of direct referents in modern linguistics has caused an identity crisis of the discipline. In addition to the theoretical diversity there is little overlap in the sometimes extremely narrow sets of data being investigated, and, most important, there is no agreement about argumentation in linguistics. These divergences in linguistic analysis, theory construction, and its justification fully sustain the "incommensurability view" held by some epistemologists of linguistics.

Apart from the identity crisis of linguistics as a whole, evidenced by the isolation of theories and models because of the use of separate "circuits" (journals, associations, institutions, "theory-internal" quotation) for exchanging information, there are a number of major specific problems that every theory has to face. The first concerns the linguist's attitude toward the primary object: is it language as a formal-semantic system or the use of language(s)? If the latter, the ultimate goal will be the description of language as a means and as a product of socialization. Such a view aims at an ethnography of speaking (*see* SPEAKING, ETHNOGRAPHY OF), but the extant theoretical models prove insufficient and too narrow. It is clear that the ethnography of speaking requires its practitioners to transcend the boundaries of traditional and modern linguistics, although it is at present far from clear how a full-fledged theory can be constructed for the study of "linguistic culture."

This type of research, based on linguistic data that extend well beyond the sentence, leads to a problem that is internal to linguistic description: the organization of grammar. Basically, three types of solutions can be conceived, and all are now in contention. In the first type of solution, which characterizes both traditional and (post-)structuralist descriptions, the organization of the grammar (or grammatical model) is determined by the levels of segmentation that result from the application of more or less explicit descriptive procedures. A second type of solution, characteristic of more recent work within the generative framework, is to dissolve the grammar into a number of modules (claimed to be components of universal grammar). These modules (syntactic, phonological, and logico-semantic) are interrelated, but there is no fully and consistently developed theory on the nature and effects of these interrelations. A third type of solution consists in organizing the grammar from a socio- or ethnolinguistic perspective on discourse, emphasizing CODE switching. A third problem, or set of problems, concerns the specific object of the various linguistic disciplines and its relation to a global theory of language (and linguistics). Apart from epistemological and methodological problems, which concern the susceptibility of linguistic data to mathematical, logistic, and sociological treatment, the problem of linguistic variation and language change must also be mentioned. Although the general conditions and also the specific factors are adequately diagnosed, the exact nature of variation and change, as well as their historical context, will be a major target for future linguistic research.

Bibliography. W. Abraham et al., *Terminologie zur neueren Linguistik,* Tübingen, FRG, 1974; *Bibliographie linguistique/Linguistic Bibliography,* The Hague, 1949–; Theodora Bynon, *Historical Linguistics,* Cambridge, 1977; Noam Chomsky, *Knowledge of Language: Its Nature, Origin, and Use,* New York, 1986; David Diringer, *Writing,* New York and London, 1962; *Language and Language Behavior Abstracts,* Ann Arbor, Mich., 1967–1974, La Jolla, Calif., 1974–; Edward Sapir, *Language: An Introduction to the Study of Speech,* New York, 1921; Thomas A. Sebeok, ed., *Current Trends in Linguistics,* 15 vols., The Hague, 1963–1976; Charles F. Voegelin and Frances M. Voegelin, *Classification and Index of the World's Languages,* New York, 1977.

PIERRE SWIGGERS

LIPPMANN, WALTER (1889–1974)

U.S. journalist and political philosopher. Born to a well-to-do New York family, Walter Lippmann completed requirements for a Harvard University A.B. in three years, also finding time to help found the Harvard Socialist Club. Among his professors were three who had a particularly important influence on his thought: the philosophers WILLIAM JAMES and George Santayana and the English social scientist Graham Wallas. Also influential during these years was the muckraking journalist Lincoln Steffens. Lippmann left the university during his fourth year, shortly before he was to be awarded an M.A. in philosophy, to become a reporter with a Boston newspaper.

Journalism appealed to Lippmann because it offered the possibility of combining study and writing with direct contact with decision makers. He soon left Boston to assist Steffens with a series of articles on Wall Street for *Everybody's Magazine.* Shortly thereafter he became an editor of *New Republic,* remaining with this MAGAZINE, with interruptions, for nine years.

One of these interruptions was caused by World War I. An army captain, he served as chief writer of front-line PROPAGANDA leaflets for the Inter-Allied Propaganda Commission and, briefly, as an adviser to the U.S. delegation at the peace conference.

In 1921 Lippmann was hired by the New York *World.* He soon became editorial-page director, and during nearly ten years with the newspaper he wrote some twelve hundred editorials, approximately a third on foreign policy. Simultaneously he wrote several books, a regular column for *Vanity Fair* magazine, and numerous articles. When the *World* was sold in 1931, he accepted what was then a princely salary from the New York *Herald Tribune* to write a syn-

Figure 1. *(Lippmann, Walter)* Walter Lippmann. From Larry L. Adams, *Walter Lippmann,* Boston: Twayne Publishers, 1977, frontispiece.

dicated column, "Today and Tomorrow," which soon became a prominent feature in U.S. POLITICAL COMMUNICATION. It was bought by the Washington Post Syndicate in 1963; the last regular column appeared in 1967. *See also* NEWSPAPER: HISTORY.

Lippmann's writing earned attention and respect from the politically powerful. He worked closely with former president Theodore Roosevelt; President Woodrow Wilson borrowed his "Peace without victory" slogan from Lippmann; Franklin D. Roosevelt and John Kennedy valued his advice. Lippmann's career offers a fascinating case history of interplay between mass media and politics.

Of his more than two dozen books, two are of particular interest to students of communication: *Public Opinion* (1922) and *The Phantom Public* (1925). In the former are Lippmann's insights on PERCEPTION, propaganda, opinion leadership (*see* OPINION LEADER), journalism, and related subjects. He held that information from the news media is refracted by pictures in our heads (which he labeled stereotypes) and that the content of the news is shaped by characteristics of journalists and the press. Despite its title the book's major contribution is less to PUBLIC OPINION than to media sociology, of which it remains one of the finest expositions. It concludes that government by a mystical force called public opinion is a chimera and that the machinery of knowledge is not organized in a way that provides responsible decision makers with the information they need.

The Phantom Public drives home Lippmann's conclusion that the average person cannot be expected to form intelligent opinions on major political questions. Lippmann was not opposed to the ideal of an informed citizenry, characterizing it as "bad only in the sense that it is bad for a fat man to try to be a ballet dancer," but he emphasized that most people are unable to take the time and trouble to become informed.

Several of Lippmann's briefer works also treated aspects of communication. *Liberty and the News* (1920) anticipated ideas on media sociology included in *Public Opinion*. A forty-two-page supplement to the August 1920 *New Republic* (with Charles Merz) reported on a CONTENT ANALYSIS of news about the Bolshevik Revolution carried in the *New York Times*. The authors concluded that reporters tended to see what they wanted or expected to see rather than what actually happened.

Bibliography. Marquis Childs and James Reston, eds., *Walter Lippmann and His Times*, New York, 1959, reprint Freeport, N.Y., 1968; Heinz Eulau, "From *Public Opinion* to *Public Philosophy:* Walter Lippmann's Classic Reexamined," *American Journal of Economics and Sociology* 15 (1956): 439–451; Ronald Steel, *Walter Lippmann and the American Century*, Boston, 1980.

W. PHILLIPS DAVISON

LITERACY

The set of organized, culturally specific practices that make it possible to understand, use, and create written texts. The term is sometimes loosely used as a synonym for competence in a variety of cultural skills, but a strict definition limits its meaning to practices associated with written LANGUAGE. Minimum and normative standards of literate achievement vary among *textual communities,* a term historian Brian Stock has coined to describe groups that consider texts or types of texts—and their designated interpreters—authoritative. A textual community that embraces a characteristic set of practices specifying skillful PERFORMANCE in READING, WRITING, composition, and even speaking, along with an interpretive framework that gives meaning to these performances, constitutes a *literate community.* A literate community may be a school system that subscribes to standards and practices codified in explicit testing procedures, a nation-state whose leaders promulgate literacy training in the service of patriotic goals, a cult devoted to a sacred text, an AVANT-GARDE literary circle, or a group of graffiti artists. Literates may belong to more than one literate community, and literate communities may overlap.

The proficiencies demanded for membership in particular literate communities depend on the kinds of literate tasks those communities practice. Some of these proficiencies may be formally schooled, but their usual range is much wider. Oral skills, for example, are an important but often unrecognized dimension of literate performance. Literacy-related oral skills may include reading aloud or recalling the words of a text, speaking about texts, or speaking with implicit reference to them, as when "grammatical" speech identifies the speaker with a textual community that contends that correct speech imitates certain features of written discourse. *See* GRAMMAR; ORAL CULTURE.

Contemporary popular notions of literacy often define it as reading and writing skills with general applicability, able to be specified independently of any social group or setting, and unrestricted to any particular canon of texts. That notion has its roots in the extension of literate skills through popular education to persons of modest or low social rank in industrializing nations during the nineteenth and twentieth centuries. This expansion marked a significant departure from centuries of an elite, restricted literate tradition embodied in both East and West in a narrow textual canon and a highly structured initiation procedure. What are counted as the most advanced literary skills in particular societies are traditionally the possession of privileged groups, usually males of a specific hereditary or socioeconomic status. In ancient Egypt literacy was an esoteric "mystery" presided over by an elect priesthood. Literacy in medieval Europe was a collection of craft skills reserved almost exclusively to the clergy as the guardians of all written knowledge. Literacy was apparently universal among the two highest classes of Gupta India (fourth century B.C.E.): the Brahmans (priests, lawgivers, and scholars) and the Kshatriyas (rulers and soldiers). Comparable literacy levels may also have characterized periods of high culture in traditional China. A majority of the 25,000 to 30,000 adult male citizens in classical Athens are thought to have been literate in a total Attican population of 250,000 to 350,000, including women, slaves, and the foreign-born (*see* HELLENIC WORLD).

The term *literacy* has not always had an exact synonym in other languages and cultures. A man who could read was described as *grammatikos* in classical Greece, but this connoted no positive sense of education or cultivation. During the ROMAN EMPIRE, the word *litteratus* signified a person familiar with literary culture. The same word described persons with training in Latin grammar and syntax during the MIDDLE AGES. It was used interchangeably with the term *clericus,* since churchmen had a virtual monopoly on literate skills and training. Both the fragmentation of clerical authority after the Middle Ages and efforts by printers to expand their secular markets accelerated the written codification of oral vernaculars in Europe and contributed to the gradual dissociation of literacy from clerical control.

The growth of popular literacy in the West was supported by a religious IDEOLOGY, which viewed reading as a form of receptivity to the word of God, and by a democratizing ideology, which cast literate skills as more utilitarian than intellectual and deprecated the cultivation of elite literacy and classical cultures with which literacy had long been identified. Contemporary notions of functional literacy as the minimal level of literate skill necessary to cope with the ordinary demands of daily life reflect this perception of democratized literacy as broad but shallow. Literates in the everyday, urban industrialized world of the twentieth century, for example, are more likely to use their skills for writing checks and interpreting tax forms, traffic signs, and ballots than for reading and debating works of great literature.

Medieval literacy, by contrast, was focused around the monastery and the scriptorium and oriented to the authority of the Bible (*see* BOOK). Some literate artisans were scribes, others were readers, and still others were skilled in the art of composition. Highly educated individuals might be adept at all three skills, but specialization was (and remains) a characteristic pattern of restricted literacies around the world, especially in traditional preindustrial literacies. A contemporary example may be found in computer literacy, defined as skill with computer texts, since users who are able to execute or read computer programs (texts) at a given level of proficiency may not be able, and may not be expected, to write such programs themselves (*see* COMPUTER: IMPACT—IMPACT ON EDUCATION; EDUCATION).

Despite the cultural and historical variability of literate goals and practices, most efforts to promulgate literacy standards on behalf of a particular literate community have presented those standards as natural and universal. Most are nevertheless ethnocentric, prescriptive, and associated with membership in ideal cultural groups. That fact prompts some scholars to speak of a variety of literacies or socially situated textual practices, instead of a single literacy or set of literacy standards. As definitions of literacy have moved away from attempts to specify universal cognitive achievement criteria, they have moved toward what are taken to be broadly consensual social achievement criteria. A good example is the definition of literacy put forward in 1951 by the newly formed United Nations Educational, Social and Cultural Organization (UNESCO), which declared that "a person is literate who can with under-standing both read and write a short, simple statement on his everyday life." While leaving specific cognitive criteria to be identified in local situations and circumstances, contemporary programmatic definitions of literacy frequently emphasize its social purposes and may link its practice to the exercise of personal pride and dignity, to the ability to realize goals for oneself and one's family, or to creative participation in community and nation building.

Cognitive effects. If efforts to arrive at universal standards of literacy have largely been abandoned in descriptive definitions of it, the notion that literacy has universal effects remains widespread. In individuals, literacy has been said to have an enabling effect on higher intellectual and logical processes, often defined as the capacity for abstract thought, decontextualization, propositional logic, or psychic mobility. Such claims are difficult to demonstrate, however. This is because every empirical measure of literate achievement appeals to some criterion of success in interpreting messages, where success in interpreting messages is a socially constructed rather than an objective category, subject to complex variation across literate communities. Literacy is always learned, practiced, and evaluated as interpretive strategies in which every "correct" interpretation reflects the cultural framework within which it occurs and which gives it meaning. Research on the cognitive effects of literacy, therefore, has the special challenge of identifying cultural influences that affect the cognitive performances of literates. One team of researchers working on this problem compared the cognitive behaviors of persons from different literate communities within the same Nigerian tribal culture with one another and with the cognitive behaviors of nonliterates in that culture. Although the evidence is not entirely clear, the studies by U.S. scholars Sylvia Scribner and Michael Cole in Nigeria suggest that strong literacy effects are not general and that different literacies cultivate specific skills in the exercise of tasks that vary significantly from literacy to literacy. In sum, literacy cannot be assessed independently of its socially embedded practice because it has no existence apart from a social situation.

Literacy as a mechanism of social control. Since cultural knowledge is manifest in symbolic representations for which literate modes may be especially efficient, literacy is closely associated with social control. Historically literacy has been an instrument to exert control and to challenge it alike. To achieve a wide level of cultural currency and stability, literate practices require the support of powerful institutions, such as the church or the state, which sponsor and promote literacy by providing occasions for its exercise and even by coercing participation in its practice. The development of bureaucratically complex, populous, and far-flung social and political units unsuited to traditional oral mechanisms of control propelled literate training and practice forward throughout the modern period. At the same time, a variety of nonschooled or informally schooled literacies existed in societies in which literate training was (or still is) a craft apprenticeship distinct from standardized, hierarchically stricter forms of state-sponsored literacy training.

The relationship between literacy and the distribution of power in society has been vigorously debated. A central question is whether literacy is primarily an instrument for diffusing and sharing power or a device for its exercise over the many by the few. In the modern West literacy is regarded as essential to the well-being of individuals in civil society. In the tradition of liberalism descended from the Enlightenment (including Marxism, which favors enlightened class consciousness) universal literacy is held in high esteem. Literacy is thought to be an implicit condition for open expression, which is necessary to discover truth, which in turn is necessary for a just and stable civil society. Literacy is thus a prerequisite for shared political power, a means of ensuring informed participation by democratic electorates, and an instrument of upward social mobility, particularly at the lowest levels of society. The extension of literacy through public schools to nonelites in Europe and the United States in the nineteenth century was justified by an appeal to its presumed capacity to increase its practitioners' political knowledge and maturity, to prevent civil disturbances by including literates within the circle of state power (insofar as that power was manifest in written form), to elevate political discourse above uninformed oral rumor, and thus to increase political stability.

Belief in the positive value of literacy precedes the Enlightenment, however. The labor of copying manuscripts was believed by medieval monks to be in the service of their own and the world's spiritual redemption. By the sixteenth century, Reformation clerics were enthusiastically promoting reading literacy as the key to spiritual salvation. Since the Enlightenment, competing political states have sponsored mass literacy campaigns in the hope that literates would prefer the political programs and ideals of the sponsors to those of rival states and ideologies. So deep is the commitment of modern states to mass literacy that any apparent decline in its level is a source of public concern. Great outcry was raised in the United States when levels of high school literacy measured by academic achievement tests dipped dramatically during the 1960s and 1970s. It is unclear whether this "crisis" was due to lax standards, as some critics charged, or whether it reflected a temporary adjustment to the absorption of large new student constituencies that had previously been excluded from the educational system.

A different version of the Enlightenment tradition grants the efficacy of literacy but sees it as a means for elites to restrict and control nonelites in order to maintain and extend their own power. Many scholars such as David Cressy, Harvey Graff, Lee Soltow, and François Furet have demonstrated that historical opportunities for acquiring and practicing literacy are related to a variety of social factors, including class, gender, occupation, ethnicity, birth order, and whether one's residence is urban or rural. According to this account literacy is an instrument of social power selectively granted or withheld by elites who wish to preserve the gap between themselves and outsiders in order to enjoy the rewards of their own literate status, or because they fear its extension to those lacking in or resistant to elite values. Centuries of reluctance to offer women full educational opportunities available to males and prohibitions on teaching literacy to slaves in the American South are good examples.

Still other elites have forcibly imposed literate practices on subject populations in order to transmit systems of ideology and authority implicit in those practices. During the nineteenth century the American Indian Bureau instituted compulsory education for Indian children in English-language literacy in order to demonstrate the superiority of white culture. A common conquistadorial practice during the sixteenth-century conquest of Peru was to burn the written artifacts of the Incas and establish mission schools to teach Spanish-language literacy. European settlers in North America frequently refused to recognize Indian claims to traditional tribal lands because these claims were not codified in writing. Historians of the nineteenth and twentieth centuries have argued that literacy training is also a mechanism of social control by which the labor forces of modern industrial states learn obedience and efficiency, practice taking orders, and become accustomed to routinized work. Other scholars have challenged the assumption that the acquisition of literacy automatically leads to social mobility, at least within the first generation.

Historically there appears to be no necessary relation between popular literacy and political structure. Political cultures with high participation have existed in the absence of popular literacy, and authoritarian regimes have flourished in its presence. The sense of urgency many modern states feel to achieve mass literacy among their populations may have less to do with the participatory character of their political structures than with perceived threats from rival states, or with the rationalization of economic production on a world scale and the growth of science and technology, all of which are facilitated by literate modes.

Literacy as a molder of world views. Still another body of theory assigns the effects of literacy not at the level of individual cognition or political power but to cultural perception and organization. Walter Ong, Jack Goody, and others have argued that the physical form of the dominant mode of communication in each historical period shapes the character of political and social order, the quality and texture of individual experience, and even the moral spirit of the culture it presides over. In this view differences among literate practices are trivial since the essential effects of literacy flow from certain universal features of script as an exteriorization of language in discrete signs and from the physical and technological requirements of recording, storing, and retrieving written or printed texts.

A variety of historical consequences have been derived from these assumptions. U.S. historian Elizabeth Eisenstein has argued that the accuracy of textual reproduction that printing made possible offered unprecedented opportunities for access to texts and scholarly cross-comparison (see PRINTING). This led in turn to a flowering of intellectual activity in the fifteenth century that could never again be halted or lost by the diversion of cultural energies to emergencies like war and famine. Other scholars have argued that the historical appearance of the rational, impersonal procedures of modern science required a level of symbolic abstraction that is said to be more characteristic of literate than oral communication. It has been claimed that literacy promotes cultural homogenization by giving many people access to the same ideas; individualism by making possible personal access to sources of authority, standards, and ideas foreign to one's immediate community; and psychological alienation by substituting literate solitude for face-to-face exchange. Goody has argued that religions of conversion are religions of the book because their fixed point of reference, the sacred text, is less flexible than that of more syncretistic, orally based religions. Writers such as HAROLD INNIS have claimed that literacy fosters a modern secular concern with territorial expansion, since the ease with which written materials may be transported relative to other symbols of authority facilitates political and administrative control of distant territory.

These claims confront the same obstacles to empirical demonstration as those discussed earlier, but with two added difficulties. It is not clear whether written forms of communication are more pervasive or influential than the oral ones they are assumed to displace and with which they are contrasted. It may be truer to say that written and oral practices continually collide with and transform each other. Additionally, the attempt to demonstrate that literacy causes large and often vaguely defined social effects that would be absent without it requires adopting a strong, monocausal explanation for complex differences among cultures and historical epochs.

For example, anthropologist Kathleen Gough has challenged the hypothesis that literacy promotes concepts of linear time, interest in historical precision, and the development of skeptical thought across cultures, as well as the related hypothesis that these results are fostered more by alphabetic traditions than by literacy alone. Gough argues that whether or not such hypotheses describe historical experience in the West, they do not account for important contrasts between the literate premodern high cultures of India and China. These two nonalphabetic written traditions show marked distinctions that suggest that the experience of literacy is not culturally uniform. The nature of these differences also argues against large claims of uniform difference between literate and nonliterate discourse and between alphabetic and nonalphabetic discourse, since (written) Indian traditions contain important features associated exclusively with orality, and (nonalphabetic) Chinese traditions contain features associated exclusively with alphabetic writing. Whereas the Chinese produced reliable chronologies of societal events as early as the ninth century B.C.E., for example, traditional Indian literature had nothing comparable before the Muslim period (1000 C.E.). Elaborate theories of cyclical time also characterized Indian astronomy. Similarly, Buddhist, Hindu, and Jainist thought in India cast the material world as unreal, while secular monarchs and literate bureaucracies in China fostered a fascination with correct, this-worldly social relations.

If the enthusiasm with which contradictory effects have been attributed to literacy does not resolve the question of what these effects are, it does suggest the close association between literacy and acculturation. In this view literacy is less important as a cause of particular cognitive or social effects than as a sign of its practitioners' participation in a social system of written messages. Beyond the socioeconomic factors that may control admission to training in a given array of literate skills lies a coded discourse of literate practice that continually marks and regulates social relations around written language, whether these skills are carefully restricted or widely diffused.

Measures of literacy. Contemporary emphasis on the importance of literacy may obscure the fact that even with the arrival of paper, printing, bureaucracy, and schools, reading and writing were not practiced by large numbers of persons until perhaps the eighteenth century. Although it has been argued that literates may exercise control over certain features of the lives of the less literate, many literate practices may also be irrelevant to large domains of experience for those with expertise in other communicative codes. While mass literacy may be counted as a twentieth-century achievement for many industrialized and industrializing countries, universal literacy is still an elusive attainment. Less developed countries that lack formal institutional mechanisms for teaching popular literacy have perhaps the highest rates of illiteracy in the world. Like the term *literacy,* however, the term *illiteracy* is relative. If signatures are used as a criterion for literacy (as in most studies of pre-nineteenth-century literacy, for example), literacy may be considered a widespread phenomenon in the twentieth century. If the chosen standard is a critical ease and reflective familiarity with a canonical tradition for which intensive, specialized training is required, the number of literates will be small even in societies in which rudimentary reading and writing skills are widely diffused. Nor are quantitative measures of popular literacy completely informative. The depth of a literate tradition may be indicated by the existence of literate institutions such as libraries, universities, public inscriptions, village schools, and literatures.

Daniel and Lauren Resnick have shown how dramatically literacy standards have changed throughout history. The purposes of literacy tests have been equally various. Before the late nineteenth century, most direct tests of literacy were oral tests of recitation and memorization of familiar texts. Much Qur-'anic (Koranic) literacy is still taught and examined this way today. Michael Clanchy has described how persons who could read aloud a prescribed scriptural passage (the "neck verse") in late medieval England were exempt from secular prosecution and punishment by virtue of the clerical status imputed to all literates. This practical literacy test discriminated those with benefit of clergy, or immunity from prosecution, from those without. Literacy levels have also been inferred by measuring signatures from early marriage registers, parish catechetical examination records, conscript records, nineteenth-century school attendance records, and public censuses. Precise estimates of literacy are not possible before the modern evolution of state recordkeeping and written involvement in citizens' lives, which provide data for direct or indirect measures of the literate skills of large numbers of citizens. Twentieth-century literacy tests have been devised by educators, military authorities, social scientists, and international agencies like UNESCO. These tests have had a variety of purposes, including understanding the nature and distribution of literacy skills, classifying some persons as qualified for particular tasks and opportunities, and evaluating literacy training.

Contemporary issues. Widespread popular literacy cannot be said to have existed anywhere in the world before the eighteenth century. Even after a century of public education in the United States more than 20 percent of the adult population is estimated to be less than functionally literate. While some critics argue that literacy is overvalued and that excessive emphasis on literacy may obscure the importance of nontextual modes of communication, many citizens, educators, politicians, intellectuals, and others who articulate and enforce standards of literate practice are concerned about limitations on the life opportunities of nonliterates because of their exclusion from a significant part of the communications mainstream. In a world in which science, technology, and the world economy are largely organized by literate modes, literate skills provide individuals with occupational entry, security, and mobility. They also provide tools for self-defense against literate centers of power, as well as the opportunity to take advantage of the vast range of human knowledge and experience in textual form.

See also ALPHABET; CODE; EAST ASIA, ANCIENT; ISLAM, CLASSICAL AND MEDIEVAL ERAS; LIBRARY; MUSIC THEORIES—NOTATIONS AND LITERACY; NEWSPAPER: HISTORY; PAMPHLET; PUBLISHING; READING THEORY.

Bibliography. Michael T. Clanchy, *From Memory to Written Record: England 1066–1307,* London and Cambridge, Mass., 1979; David Cressy, *Literacy and the Social Order: Reading and Writing in Tudor and Stuart England,* Cambridge, 1980; Elizabeth L. Eisenstein, *The Printing Press as an Agent of Change: Communications and Cultural Transformations in Early Modern Europe,* 2 vols., Cambridge and New York, 1979; François Furet and Jacques Ozouf, *Reading and Writing: Literacy in France from Calvin to Jules Ferry* (Lire et écrire, Vol. 1), New York and Cambridge, 1982; Jack Goody, ed., *Literacy in Traditional Societies,* Cambridge, 1968, reprint Cambridge and New York, 1975; Daniel P. Resnick and Lauren B. Resnick, "The Nature of Literacy: An Historical Exploration," *Harvard Educational Review* 47 (1977): 370–385; Sylvia Scribner and Michael Cole, *The Psychology of Literacy,* Cambridge, Mass., 1981; Lee Soltow and Edward Stevens, *The Rise of Literacy and the Common School in the United States: A Socioeconomic Analysis to 1870,* Chicago, 1981; Brian Stock, *The Implications of Literacy: Written Language and Models of Interpretation in the Eleventh and Twelfth Centuries,* Princeton, N.J., 1983.

CAROLYN MARVIN

LITERARY CANON

Those literary works that at any given moment in a CULTURE's history are regarded by educated people as the best their culture has to offer. Though one often speaks of the canon of Western literature or of the Asian classics, literary traditions are usually associated with the character and ideals of ethnic and national groups. The close relationship between these groups and their literary traditions both requires and guarantees a certain stability in the makeup of literary canons. Thus the works of William Shakespeare, inseparable as they are from England's conception of itself, will probably never disappear from the canon of British literature. At the same time that canons represent cultural continuity and duration, they also reflect cultural change. Since literary works embody the values of the society that produces them, and since such values are almost always in dispute, the question of which books ought to be accorded canonical status is frequently a subject of controversy. Arguments over whether this or that text achieves literary greatness need to be understood in the context of debates over which moral standards, social arrangements, and political goals the culture will publicly endorse.

Changes in historical circumstance bring with them corresponding changes in the literary canon. Following the French Revolution, for example, romantic (*see* ROMANTICISM) definitions of POETRY in Britain (antiauthoritarian, alienated, individualistic) brought a resurgence of interest in *Paradise Lost* (1667), with JOHN MILTON, the seventeenth-century republican, being seen as "of the devil's party." During the 1930s, anthologies of U.S. literature mirrored the economic conditions and political consciousness of the depression by including workers' songs and excerpts from political speeches; later, in the conservative 1950s, these selections were dropped.

While debate over which works ought to be considered canonical is as old as literature itself, the historical study of canon formation, of how and why certain literary works achieve classic status, is relatively new. Students of canon formation investigate the mechanisms that create and sustain or, alternatively, abort or destroy a literary work's reputation, and attempt to account for changes in the literary canon over time by delineating the emergent conceptions of literature and literary value that accompany such changes, as well as the historical processes in which they are embedded. Rather than concentrating on the features of literary texts themselves, students of canon formation examine the contexts within which literary works were originally written and read in order to understand the conditions that guaranteed that the works of some authors would remain in the foreground of literary study while the works of others would gradually be forgotten.

The main reason for the emergence of canon formation as a subject of study is the entrance into the professoriate of people from outside the culture's dominant group, combined with a heightened consciousness of the way a person's race, GENDER, and social class affect his or her social status, political power, and cultural influence. Scholars who study canon formation usually belong to or identify with groups that have been socially marginal or oppressed and whose literary production, accordingly, is not part of the cultural mainstream. Working-class people, women, homosexuals, blacks, and members of ethnic minorities look at the literary canon and find that their interests, their experiences, and their concerns are not reflected there. Unable to believe that people like themselves have never written anything that deserves to be called great, they study the mechanisms that create and sustain literary reputations in order to discover why the authors who represent their sense of themselves have not survived the process of selection. They conclude that the reasons why literary works appear in anthologies and on university reading lists have more to do with considerations of class and race, religious background, economic and social status, educational opportunity, and institutional affiliation than with considerations of aesthetic merit. Some question whether aesthetic standards can ever be separated from practical, political concerns. Believing that circumstances have favored authors who belong to certain social groups rather than others, these critics want to revise the literary canon so that it will become more representative of all the groups that constitute the social whole. *See* AESTHETICS.

The idea that the canon should represent the interests of social groups in somewhat the same way that the governing body of a democratic nation represents political constituencies does violence to traditional notions of the canon and of literature itself. From the traditional perspective, works now in the canon are assumed to reflect not the workings of a political process but the judgment of generations of readers who have responded to the work's intrinsic superiority. In this view Shakespeare and Milton, rather than the works of black or women writers, are taught in the schools not because they represent the values and interests of a particular social group or literary critical trend but because they are great in themselves, their genius having been recognized over time by people whose education, taste, and experience enabled them to identify true literary merit.

This standard conception of how canons are formed rests on a definition of literature that emphasizes its timelessness and universality. At least for the last hundred years literature has been distinguished from other forms of discourse on the grounds that its truths transcend the special interests of parties and rise above the limitations of historical time and place. Literary classics, it is said, appeal *across* time and space to people of diverse backgrounds and experience without regard to their particular conditions of existence (race, class, gender, nationality, etc.). From this perspective, insisting that works written by members of every minority group be included in a nation's literary canon robs literature of its universality, denies its transcendence, challenges its disinterestedness, and reduces it to the level of RHETORIC or PROPAGANDA, which is to say, of discourse that is committed to furthering the interests of one faction over another. To preserve literature from POLITICI-ZATION, proponents of the traditional view seek to preserve the existing canon on the grounds that it represents enduring values.

The problem with this position, from the viewpoint of people who find members of their own race, sex, or ethnic group excluded from the canon, is that it means accepting the idea that people like themselves are or have until now been incapable of producing great ART. Not wishing to accept the imputation of racial, sexual, ethnic, or class inferiority, these scholars prefer to assume that canonization is not a neutral process in which the best work rises to the top through natural selection; instead they set out to demonstrate exactly the reverse, that canonization is a means by which the class of people that exercises power in a society maintains control of the society's systems of value. For these scholars, the literary canon, far from being a protected zone that preserves the best that has been thought and said, becomes an arena of ideological struggle in which contending visions of the world vie for mastery. *See* IDEOLOGY.

In this view literary texts enter the complex interaction of social and institutional structures that mutually reinforce one another. The correlation between the behavior, manners, customs, and vested interests of the dominant social class and the standards of critical judgment ensures that only works written by people with access to certain educational and social opportunities will be able to compete. An author's social and cultural milieu, moreover, will determine his or her access to PUBLISHING outlets; publishing with a certain press will affect the nature and number of reviews an author receives. The personal, social, and institutional relationships that obtain between authors and critics, between authors and journal editors and influential publishers, between the professoriate and the reviewing media, between the judges of literary contests (who belong to all of the above-named categories) and the prizewinners—all work to determine whose books will be printed, distributed, advertised, purchased, read, reviewed, cited, reprinted, taught, written about, and declared or not declared "classic." Once the canon is in place, differing tastes in literature (canonical, noncanonical) serve to distinguish members of different social classes from one another and thus to preserve the hierarchical social distinctions on which the canon is already based.

The study of canon formation that reveals the ways in which certain social groups have been discriminated against by these processes is, in effect, a literary suffrage movement seeking to enact in academic and cultural spheres the principles that in democratic nations are supposed to regulate political life. Thus the study of the canon is not a politically neutral activity but one way for previously marginalized groups to advance their own interests. To see this political motivation as grounds for dismissing the enterprise, however, is not to adopt a neutral stance but to buy back into the conservative position that regards the literary status quo as, so to speak, interest-free.

An example of canon formation may clarify this process. In the 1970s, Harriet Beecher Stowe's *Uncle Tom's Cabin* (1852), though a standard text for historians of the antebellum era in the United States, was seldom written about, taught, or referred to by literary critics. It was considered maudlin, trite, melodramatic—a piece of sentimental propaganda, not a serious work of literature. As a result partly of the feminist movement, partly of neohistoricist criticism, and partly of a growing interest in U.S. popular culture, Stowe's novel came to be taught regularly in courses on U.S. literature and became the kind of text that younger critics can prove themselves by writing on.

The addition of a text to the literary canon is not an isolated event. The act of taking seriously a novel like *Uncle Tom's Cabin* required a shift in critical perspective that sprang from a series of interlinked circumstances—social, cultural, and institutional—whose effects have begun to alter the nature of canonical works as well by changing the shape of the attention paid to them. That Stowe's text could become an object of legitimate discourse silently validates the perspective it represents and opens the way for other works to enter the canon that previously would have been inadmissible. The presence of these texts will presumably alter the social environment in unforeseeable ways, leading to new possibilities for change. It is conceivable that as the circumstances surrounding the production and reception of literary texts evolve, canons will cease to function as symbols of national identity and will serve purposes that are as yet unthought of.

See also LITERARY CRITICISM; POETICS.

Bibliography. Pierre Bourdieu, *Distinction: A Social Critique of the Judgement of Taste* (La distinction: Critique sociale du jugement), trans. by Richard Nice, Cambridge, Mass., 1984; Joan Hartman and Ellen Messer-Davidow, eds., *Women in Print I: Opportunities for Women's Studies Research in Language and Literature*, New York, 1982; Paul Lauter, ed., *Reconstructing American Literature: Course, Syllabi, Issues*, Old Westbury, N.Y., 1983; Deborah S. Rosenfelt, "The Politics of Bibliography: Women's Studies and the Literary Canon," in *Women in Print I: Opportunities for Women's Studies Research in Language and Literature*, ed. by Joan Hartman and Ellen Messer-Davidow, New York, 1982; Barbara Herrnstein Smith, "Contingencies of Value," in *Canons*, ed. by Robert Von Hallberg, Chicago, 1984; Jane Tompkins, " 'But Is It Any Good?': The Institutionalization of Literary Value," in *Sensational Designs: The Cultural Work of American Fic-*

tion, 1790–1860, New York, 1985; Raymond Williams, "Traditions, Institutions, and Formations," in *Marxism and Literature,* Oxford, 1977; Richard Yarborough, "In the Realm of the Imagination: Afro-American Literature and the American Canon," *ADE Bulletin* 78 (1984): 35–39.

JANE TOMPKINS

LITERARY CRITICISM

The history of literary criticism, with its many different concerns—the nature of literature, the social role of the poet, the response of the reader, and questions of value and INTERPRETATION—is usually regarded as having begun with PLATO, who for nearly two thousand years stimulated defenses of POETRY and poets against his attack. Plato denigrated poets on the ground that they were secondhand imitators—imitators of external appearances, which were themselves only imitations of "ideas." Actually, in the guise of this attack on poets, he was criticizing the teachers known as Sophists for their employment of RHETORIC rather than strict dialectic. For Plato rhetoric, with its reliance on tropes, or figures of speech, was an abuse of reason and therefore of LANGUAGE. Rhetoric appealed to the baser senses, not to the rational powers; hence, in the *Republic,* Plato had Socrates advise the young to study MATHEMATICS and not poetry. At best the poet was possessed of a divine madness, and though Socrates acknowledged poetry's charm, he suggested that the poets be banished from the state—but with garlands on their heads.

ARISTOTLE's *Poetics* (ca. 330 B.C.E.), lost for centuries until its rediscovery in the RENAISSANCE, defended poetry by revising Plato's doctrine of ideas and the meaning of imitation. For Aristotle poetic imitation re-created actions and always added something of its own, which was the shape, form, or integrity of the whole. Thus was begun the opposition between the Platonic idea of imitation and an objectivizing formalism that has been with criticism in some shape ever since. The other early effort to cope with Plato was that of the Neoplatonist Plotinus, who in the third century C.E. argued that beauty is incarnate in the symbol itself, which is thus something more than a false simulacrum, or imitation of reality. Though Plotinus never discussed literature, his general remarks came to be regarded as relevant to literary matters.

Rhetoric was not successfully dispatched by Plato, who was himself an effective rhetorician. Aristotle asserted that the prime requisite of the poet was a command of METAPHOR, and in the Roman period both Horace and Longinus defended poetry, one on the ground that as a "speaking picture" it both delighted and instructed, and the other on the ground that in inspired and well-prepared hands it was capable of conveying powerfully moving experience. To both of these critics imitation of ideas had become imitation of revered precursor poets. Much later the eighteenth-century English poet Alexander Pope was to proclaim, along similar lines, Virgil's understanding that to copy Homer was to copy nature.

Generally speaking, literary criticism has followed the same lines as philosophy. Its history can be divided into three great ages: the long age of ontology that began with the Platonic critique, the age of epistemology coincident with the rise of modern science, and the age of linguistic thought, which was brought to birth in the nineteenth century. The first, ontological age was concerned with Being and Truth, either a being that poetry attempted to copy in vain (Plato) or successfully (Plotinus), or a being of the work itself, as in Aristotle's treatment of the poem as a whole that orders the parts by its own principles of unification—"not to know that a hind has no horns is a less serious matter than to paint it inartistically." The Aristotelian notion of unity solidified in Renaissance Italian and French criticism when the *Poetics* was rediscovered, and by the time of the seventeenth-century French dramatist Pierre Corneille it had become the standard employed to restrict treatment of time and place on the stage. Renaissance critics tended to invoke Plato to defend poetry in a strenuous misreading of his arguments; the work of the Italian Jacopo Mazzoni in the late 1500s is perhaps the most daring and interesting.

The earliest critical reading of texts in Western culture presumed that they were allegorical representations of spiritual truths or historical events. Such interpretive practice was early dominated by the reading of Homer and of SCRIPTURE. The Homeric epic tended to be treated as moral allegory with a Platonic flavor; scripture was given elaborate allegorical readings by Jewish writers, while Christian interpreters were often concerned about its losing historicity and developed a MODE of typological interpretation suggested by New Testament authors in which symbols, or "types," of the Old Testament were read as historical prefigurations of the events and people of the New. Thus the Bible was given the unified shape of a sequence proceeding from Creation to Apocalypse that history was itself declared to possess (*see* HISTORIOGRAPHY). Elaborate medieval schemes grew out of this tradition: the levels of interpretation developed by John Cassian and appropriated with certain variations by St. Thomas Aquinas and Dante Alighieri, who in his famous letter to Cangrande della Scala transferred the same conventions to a reading of his own secular text of *The Divine Comedy* (1321).

The history of criticism through the Renaissance is in many respects a long series of disputatious footnotes to Plato and, after rediscovery of the *Poetics,* to Aristotle. The unity of a work of literature was treated as imitative of the unity of being that literature was said to imitate; but from Neoplatonism and the *Poetics* the argument was derived that the work's unity (and fictive character) produced an improvement on nature, the "golden world" of, for example, Sir Philip Sidney's *Apology for Poetry* (1583).

In the seventeenth century, with the rise of modern science, ontology gave way to epistemological concerns, and criticism followed. In the long period of ontological dominance, readers, it was declared, were delighted, instructed, and/or transported by literature. In the age of epistemology the task soon became that of distinguishing the effects and value of ART from those of science. With truth now taken principally to be objective scientific knowledge, poetry's truth and what it taught (if anything) had to be reconsidered. A variety of theories developed that proposed to divide its "affect" (if there was a knowable object, there had to be an experiencing subject) into elements of the "beautiful" and the "sublime." These categories were to be the concern of the new science of AESTHETICS, a term invented by the eighteenth-century German theorist Alexander Baumgarten. The subject-object distinction created by Renaissance science and developed philosophically on both empiricist and rationalist lines resulted in a need to find a place for experience categorizable as neither wholly subjective nor wholly objective. The great systematizer of aesthetic theory was Immanuel Kant, whose *Critique of Judgment* (1790) treated the experience of the beautiful and the sublime as falling under what Kant, adopting another Baumgarten term, called the *judgment.* In aesthetic situations our normal purposiveness is absent from our relation to the object, and aesthetic experience is neither utilitarian nor related, except by analogy, to the idea of the good.

The new emphasis on viewers and readers was paralleled by an increased attention to authors (*see* AUTHORSHIP). Until the late eighteenth century the little interest that was taken in authors had scant effect on the treatment of their work. SAMUEL JOHNSON's *Lives of the Poets* (1781) tends to separate discussion of the life from discussion of the art. But works such as William Wordsworth's preface to the second edition of the *Lyrical Ballads* (1800) make the author the focus of criticism and poetry the utterance of personal feelings. This expressivist aesthetic, the other side of the somewhat earlier interest in affect, continued to be dominated by epistemological concerns, particularly by a sense of the gulf between subject and object or, in the Wordsworthian version, consciousness and nature. The theories of imagination developed at the time in Germany and in England reflected a desire to see the human mind as not merely the passive receptor of sense data, as in the prevailing associationist psychology, but an active creator of its own experience and even, to some extent, of the external world. Poetic theory emphasized individual imaginative power, denigrated imitation as a passive reception of fixed externality or slavish adherence to tyrannical rules of art, and developed interest instead in the inner authorial self. This in turn led to attention being given to fantasy, to dreams, and to the grotesque. *See* ROMANTICISM.

The opposition between this new sense of active creativity and the older notion of an orderly nature to be faithfully rendered is well illustrated by William Blake's spirited annotations to the *Discourses* (1797) of Sir Joshua Reynolds, first president of the British Royal Academy. But the most important single text may be the brief and truncated thirteenth chapter of Samuel Taylor Coleridge's *Biographia Literaria* (1817). Following a chapter in which he borrows wholesale from Friedrich Schelling's *System des transcendentalen Idealismus* (1800), which adopts a view of the mind as creative and holds that whether one begins from the pole of the subject or that of the object one ends in a creative idealism, Coleridge goes on to define *imagination* and *fancy.* The primary imagination is the repetition in the finite human mind of God's eternal creativity—PERCEPTION itself; the secondary imagination is artistic creativity, which "dissolves, diffuses, dissipates in order to recreate"; the fancy is the mind operating only passively, as in associationism, with "fixities and definites." Coleridge's argument, like Kant's, was an effort to avoid identifying literary art with radical subjectivity. Approaching the problem from the side of the auditor, viewer, or reader, Kant had proposed the "subjective universality" of aesthetic judgment, which is a judgment not verifiable according to scientific categories but nevertheless one that the judge, exercising no self-interest, is willing to declare everyone else should share. In his *Principles of Genial Criticism* (1814), Coleridge introduced into English thought this same distinction between a judgment of what is beautiful and a judgment of what is good or useful.

But these efforts to mediate did not hold, and criticism on the whole tended to divide in the nineteenth century between objectivist and subjectivist theories, accepting what Blake had aptly named a "cloven fiction." Objectivist theory is well characterized by the popular terms *realism* and *naturalism* as applied to literature and is perhaps best exemplified by Émile Zola's *The Experimental Novel* (1880), in which he imagines the writer as proceeding in respect of the external world like a medical researcher (*see* REALISM). Subjectivist theory is illustrated in an extreme form by the notorious conclusion Walter Pater wrote (and later suppressed) for his *Studies in the History of the Renaissance* (1873), in which solipsism is acknowledged as the primary fact of experience: "Experience, already reduced to a swarm of impressions, is ringed round for each one of us by that thick wall of personality through which no real voice has pierced on its way to us, or from us to that which we can only conjecture to be without." This view spread into criticism at the end of the nineteenth century, in, for example, Anatole France's famous statement in *La vie littéraire* (1893) that a critic should announce that he was speaking of himself when he was presumably speaking of Shakespeare or whomever.

The principle of art for art's sake, enunciated by Oscar Wilde and others, was derived from the Kantian idea of a separate aesthetic judgment as it was affected by the subjectivist current. The emphasis now fell on the idea of the artistic work as an independent entity with its own internal being apart from the vulgar world of utility. This was a sort of objectifying of the subjective. The opposite view emphasized the social function of art, its propagandistic powers, and its radical political role. Matthew Arnold, perhaps the major British critic of the nineteenth century, sought to proclaim poetry as a cultural substitute for RELIGION, which had been shaken in his time by scientific developments. His notion of art's social function is, however, perhaps closer to the idealist than to the realist view.

As the twentieth century dawned, these opposed camps produced contending theories almost everywhere in Western culture. In Russia the Marxists opposed and finally suppressed a formalist movement. In the United States a battle for control of academic literary study was waged in the 1930s and 1940s between the entrenched literary historians and the so-called New Critics, whose views were generated from a variety of sources, including the antiromantic CLASSICISM of T. E. Hulme and T. S. Eliot, the psychologistic poetic theory of I. A. RICHARDS, and the study of poetic ambiguity by Richards's student William Empson. Richards exhibited intense interest in the workings of language and MEANING, Empson's interests were linguistic, and Eliot treated the language of poetry as fundamental in his well-known utterance, "The poet has, not a 'personality' to express, but a particular medium, which is only a medium and not a personality." The New Criticism tended to formalism, appropriating from Coleridge the idea of organic unity and elevating irony, paradox, and drama to principles of structure.

All of these critics reflected a movement into the linguistic age, the first stirrings of which (apart from some prophetic precursors like Giambattista Vico in the early eighteenth century) had occurred early in the nineteenth century, when language became a

matter of study among syncretic mythographers and the disciplines of philology were being established. One of the principal intellectual developments of the twentieth century, STRUCTURALISM, spread from LINGUISTICS into anthropology, PSYCHOANALYSIS, and literary criticism. The seminal text was FERDINAND DE SAUSSURE's *Cours de linguistique générale* (1913), which makes central to the theory of language the principle of difference, that is, the notion that language is a system of signs (*langue*), each one of which is definable by its difference from every other SIGN (*see also* SIGN SYSTEM). This is the notion of a "differential structure." Literary texts now began to be treated as miniature *langues*, following Saussure. In France structuralist analyses of myths were made by CLAUDE LÉVI-STRAUSS, Jacques Lacan developed a structuralist psychoanalysis, and ROLAND BARTHES and other European critics applied structuralist principles to literary and other sorts of texts. Though in approach there was some similarity to Anglo-American criticism, from the New Critics to the influential work of Canadian critic Northrop Frye, the language of structuralist analysis, taken from linguistics, was different.

By the time this new language had invaded U.S. criticism, structuralism had already given way in France to the poststructuralist critiques of philosopher Jacques Derrida, who showed that taken to its logical conclusion structuralist theory required abandonment of any notion of the unity of a text based on the principle of a "transcendental signified," or ultimate meaning lying outside the text itself. The ancient Aristotelian concept of unity having been "deconstructed" on the principle that language is an infinite chain of signifiers down which meaning endlessly escapes, indeterminacy won the day. Texts were now regarded as "open," not "closed," and respect for the "play" of language was advocated.

Determinate meaning had been called into question by other critical theories as well, but not with such wholesale results. The principal opposition to structuralism in Europe came from phenomenological criticism, which emerged mainly out of German philosopher Edmund Husserl's attack on the subject-object problem, resulting in his famous assertion that consciousness was always the consciousness *of* something. Phenomenology created a new form of textual interpretation, or *hermeneutic,* as the German critics following in the tradition of biblical interpretation liked to call it. Phenomenology, however, soon ran up against the complications of language theory. Rather than detaching language from consciousness, as was the tendency of structuralism, phenomenological hermeneutics saw it as mediating between the author and the world and time. Interpretation was seen to be deeply implicated in temporality, and important consideration was given to the relation between so-called temporal horizons, both a reader's horizon and a text's. Hermeneutics had to read the difference between the two horizons rather than look upon the text as something independent of the temporal location of its interpretation.

Meanwhile deconstructive criticism, under the influence of its major practitioner in the United States, Paul de Man, emphasized the radically tropological and therefore rhetorical nature of all language and the unreliability—from the point of view of a desire to find in it stable meaning—of any text. Under de Man's gaze a text constantly undermined (in its tropes) the meanings apparently intended.

Three other critical movements showed the influence of these same tendencies, sometimes by opposition to or at least from anxiety about them. In Germany various attempts were made to relocate the center of a text—lost in deconstruction—in the reader (see READING THEORY). *Receptionsästhetik* sought to establish such a center in the relationship between a text's production and its reception as a historical process. Other reader-oriented theories in the United States sought to appropriate notions of competence, or intuitive understanding of literary texts, from Noam Chomsky's linguistics, or fell back on some concept of cultural consensus. There was also a revival of a socially oriented criticism, usually with Marxist roots and sometimes identified with the Frankfurt school of critical theory that had flourished in the 1930s (see COMMUNICATIONS RESEARCH: ORIGINS AND DEVELOPMENT; MARXIST THEORIES OF COMMUNICATION). Considerable uneasiness was expressed with deconstruction, which appeared to be a renewal of the formalism attacked decades before. Finally, the literary wing of the feminist movement attacked the exclusion of women writers from the "patristic" canon of great literary works and subjected the whole question of canon formation to study (see FEMINIST THEORIES OF COMMUNICATION; LITERARY CANON). Literary criticism by now had greatly enlarged the range of what interested it. History, BIOGRAPHY, AUTOBIOGRAPHY, scientific writing, and, above all, philosophy were subjected to critical readings. Indeed, *literature* threatened to become so inclusive a term as to mean anything written, and *text* had come to mean anything, verbal or not, that might be subject to treatment as a differential structure. And so what Plato had regarded as dangerous deviation came in many quarters to be the norm. It can fairly be said that these recent events have greatly disturbed the critical world and brought it to a crisis that may very well presage a new age beyond the linguistic one.

See also POETICS.

Bibliography. Hazard Adams, compl., *Critical Theory since Plato*, New York, 1971; Hazard Adams and Leroy Searle, eds., *Critical Theory since 1965*, Tallahassee, Fla., 1986; G. M. A. Grube, *The Greek and Roman Critics*, Toronto, 1965; Christopher Norris, *Deconstruction: Theory and Practice*, London and New York, 1982; John Sturrock, ed., *Structuralism and Since: From Lévi-Strauss to Derrida*, Oxford and New York, 1979; Bernard Weinberg, *A History of Literary Criticism in the Italian Renaissance*, Chicago, 1961; René Wellek, *A History of Modern Criticism, 1750–1950*, 4 vols., New Haven, Conn., 1955–1965; William K. Wimsatt, Jr., and Cleanth Brooks, *Literary Criticism: A Short History*, New York, 1957.

HAZARD ADAMS

LITERATURE. *See* FACT AND FICTION; POETICS; PROSE; STYLE, LITERARY. *See also* specific genres of literature.

LITERATURE, POPULAR

Much critical controversy surrounds popular literature, but the term itself is difficult to define. *Popular* can be taken to mean "of the people, democratic" or "best-selling, widely consumed." It is paradoxical that on occasion "elite" works of literature (such as Lord Byron's) can be popular even though "the people," politically understood, have little to do with them as either subject matter or consumers. *Literature,* for its part, is a term used both for canonized works of agreed cultural value (see LITERARY CANON) and, more neutrally, for anything circulated in printed form. Thus a "literary" writer like Charles Dickens can be regarded as popular, and a private-eye writer like Mickey Spillane, whose fiction can by no stretch of definition be termed "literary," is undeniably in the business of producing popular literature. Perhaps closest to the widely accepted meaning of popular literature is the German term *Trivialliteratur,* which denotes mass-produced READING matter of no cultural pretension.

Origins

In a sense, the history of literature is the history of its inexorably growing popularity. An advancing reproductive technology has played a leading part in this process (see PUBLISHING—HISTORY OF PUBLISHING). The successive inventions of papyrus and parchment in the ancient world, followed by the arrival of paper in Europe from China via the Arabs around the twelfth century, allowed for an ever-wider circulation for the written word. In fact, British historian James W. Thompson has asserted that the use of paper in Europe was the largest single factor responsible for the RENAISSANCE. The transformation from manuscript roll to manuscript codex (bound sheets) presaged the form of the BOOK before the innovation of the PRINTING press in the mid-fifteenth century. It is estimated that by 1500 there were some

THE

𝕸𝖊𝖗𝖗𝖞 𝕷𝖎𝖋𝖊 𝖆𝖓𝖉 𝕸𝖆𝖉 𝕰𝖝𝖕𝖑𝖔𝖎𝖙𝖘

OF

CAPT JAMES HIND

The great Robber of England.

The true Portraiture of Captain *JAMES HIND*, the Robber, who died for Treafon.

NEWCASTLE: PRINTED IN THIS PRESENT YEAR.

Figure 1. *(Literature, Popular)* Page from an English chapbook, 1652. From John Ashton, *Chap-books of the Eighteenth Century*, London: Chatto and Windus, 1882, p. 433.

twenty million books in Europe for a population of about eighty million. But cost and limited LITERACY meant that the reading of books was an elite activity for a century or so after WILLIAM CAXTON published the first English book in 1477. Nor was it only the common people who were excluded; in early modern Europe a substantial number of the nobility and churchmen were illiterate.

In general, European popular CULTURE remained an oral, instrumental, visual, and physical set of practices centered on songs, simple musical performances, games, and repartee (*see* MUSIC, FOLK AND TRADITIONAL; SONG). But in the fifteenth and six-

teenth centuries it was made literary by the circulation of almanacs, broadside ballads, jestbooks, anecdotal or folkloric narratives, and simplified romances of chivalry (*see* ROMANCE, THE). In the Elizabethan period FICTION was already stratified into high literary romance, like Sir Philip Sidney's *Arcadia* (1580), vernacular romances and tales aimed at the artisan middle class, and crude tales for street sale in inexpensive PAMPHLET form.

Before the arrival of early forms of newspaper, broadside ballads were often sharply political and topical. Jestbooks—loose collections of anecdotes, riddles (*see* RIDDLE), and comic tales—represent temporary solidification in printed form of spoken comic monologue and badinage. Some have proved remarkably durable. The escapades and witty sayings of "Howleglas" or Till Eulenspiegel, for instance, originated in Antwerp, Belgium, in the early sixteenth century and circulated throughout Europe. They survived as chapbooks in the nineteenth century and can still be found in children's literature in the twentieth. Almanacs, which were often posted on walls, served as calendars (*see* CALENDAR), horoscopes, and entertaining compendia of trivia.

All these popular literary commodities multiplied in the 150 years after Caxton and represent a broad and ragged edge between literary and ORAL CULTURE, never quite belonging to either category. They continued as ephemeral and fugitive street wares among the semiliterate at least until the mid-nineteenth century. The popular almanac and jestbook did not disappear but were absorbed into popular journalism. One can trace this legacy to modern scandal sheets like the *National Enquirer* in the United States. *See also* NEWSPAPER: HISTORY.

From Oral to Literary Culture

A significant technical advance occurred around the beginning of the eighteenth century, in the form of the chapbook (*Volksbuch* in German; *bibliothèque bleue* volumes in France). These were small paper-covered pamphlet-size booklets, measuring about three and a half by six inches, embellished with crude woodcuts. They were sold by chapmen, or peddlers, in England, *colporteurs* in France, usually for one penny or two sous (the price of a pound of bread in pre-Revolutionary France). The chapbook survived well into the nineteenth century, catering to the sizable marginally literate segment of the population (Figure 1).

Assessing the size and competence of reading publics is difficult. It has been estimated that in the seventeenth century as much as half of the British adult population was in some sense literate. In Russia, by contrast, 90 percent of the population was illiterate until as late as 1850, which may account for the extraordinary vitality of the orally transmitted FOLKTALE in that country. But the illiterate were not necessarily excluded from reading matter. Oral and literary cultures interconnected at innumerable points. It is clear, for instance, that a great deal of public reading aloud took place, in which a lettered citizen would disseminate books to a less literate audience. For the semiliterate, eighteenth-century favorites like *Robinson Crusoe* in England and poet Ludovico Ariosto's works in Italy, although originally written for upper-class readers, were adapted as short, simple chapbooks (just as the same works were later simplified for children).

Vital and attractive as it frequently is, the content of early popular literature tends to be highly repetitive. This sameness has a complex relationship to the anonymous and essentially collective nature of early popular literature. It did not originate in a single mind and was not legally protected as private property. Hence it was subject to countless reproductions and represented a stock to which individual interpreters or performers might add their own personal seasoning.

In the eighteenth century there emerged a kind of core curriculum of staple printed texts, usually for Sunday reading, such as the Bible in one of its vernacular forms or, for the English reader, John Bunyan's *Pilgrim's Progress*. Originally published in 1678, this work, an allegory of the individual's hard passage through life, had gone through at least two hundred editions by the end of the eighteenth century. Other core texts were John Foxe's *Book of Martyrs* (1563) and Daniel Defoe's *Robinson Crusoe* (1719; Figure 2). The durability of these classics of early working-class literature is remarkable. The working-class FAMILY typically might have one limited set of books, as it might have one set of bedroom furniture to last a lifetime and to be passed on to children. The notion of a diet of constantly changing reading matter for the masses is a relatively modern development.

In the mid-eighteenth century in Europe, and particularly in Germany, an awareness that popular literature could be something more than primitive subliterature emerged. The critic Johann Gottfried von Herder celebrated the German *Volkslied* (folk song) as the embodiment of the national sensibility. The Grimm brothers are said to have done the same for the German folktale early in the nineteenth century. The cult of folk literature during this period had an important influence on the growth of ROMANTICISM and European nationalism. Essentially it was valued as the pure emanation from the soul of the people. Herder's dictum was *"Das Volk dichtet"* ("The people make poetry"). More recently popular literature has usually been seen as something directed to rather than originating from the people.

CRUSOE MEETS FRIDAY

Figure 2. *(Literature, Popular)* "Crusoe meets Friday." From Daniel Defoe, *The Life and Adventures of Robinson Crusoe*, London: J. C. Nimmo and Bain, 1882 ed., vol. 1, p. 262.

The Novel as a Popular Form

Eighteenth-century England also saw the rise of the novel, the principal vehicle of the modern popular culture industry. Samuel Richardson's *Pamela* (1740), Henry Fielding's *Tom Jones* (1749), and most influentially *Robinson Crusoe* established patterns for a multitude of imitators. The novel (as opposed to mere NARRATIVE in print) required the confluence of many elements: a cultivated reading public, a large disposable income (an early novel like *Pamela* cost as much as feeding a laboring family for a week), LEISURE time (middle- and upper-class women were an important part of the novel's audience), legislative initiatives (the first COPYRIGHT act was passed into law in 1709), and advanced productive and distributive capacities, which in turn entailed metropolitan centralization. Circulating LIBRARY systems, established around the 1740s in Germany and England,

Figure 3. *(Literature, Popular)* *Kit Carson on the War-Path*, a nineteenth-century dime novel. The Bettmann Archive, Inc.

gave the middle class wide access to an item priced in bookshops as a luxury. The novel was a recognizable commodity by the end of the eighteenth century—so much so that in the 1790s there was a widespread conviction that as a form it had had its day and, like the chivalric romance, was to be relegated to literary history.

In fact, the novel gained in strength in the early nineteenth century with the worldwide popularity of Sir Walter Scott, who paved the way for Dickens. Using SERIAL issue and illustration (both pioneered in France), Dickens expanded the middle-class readership of fiction into the millions. Although the eighteenth-century novel and its Victorian successor were essentially bourgeois (both as a commodity and in terms of IDEOLOGY), they set up the apparatus by which popular literature in the nineteenth century was to be packaged, merchandised, and sold back to the working class. In the process the old fluidities of oral popular culture were lost. The German critic WALTER BENJAMIN asserted, paradoxically, that the

novel entailed the death of storytelling. The story (Benjamin was thinking principally of the Russian folktale) is a democratically owned thing passed on from person to person. The novel is a fixed, unalterable commodity, sold in the marketplace and largely protected as the author's private property. The various stories and ballads based on Robin Hood mutated with the accidents of place and period; Dickens's *The Pickwick Papers* is the same text that it was when first published in 1836.

Rise of the Mass Reading Public

For all their unprecedented sales, the kinds of fiction produced in the nineteenth century by Eugène Sue and Alexandre Dumas in France or by Dickens in Victorian England were not popular in the sense of appealing to the least literate classes. In France school inspectors sent out by the government in 1833 were appalled to find chapbooks in the hands of pupils throughout the country. In England up to the 1840s there was a vigorous underworld of penny serials and street ballads catering to the influx of newly urbanized semiliterates from the countryside. Fiction for the masses in the early nineteenth century was mostly ultraviolent "penny bloods," or "dreadfuls." Some have achieved popular folkloric status. For example, J. M. Rymer's *Varney the Vampyre* (1847), as gentrified by Bram Stoker's *Dracula* in 1897, has become a twentieth-century perennial. The universal EDUCATION acts implemented in Europe from the mid-nineteenth century on homogenized the reading public. The rich store of penny bloods did not disappear but was laundered and recycled for juvenile readers. This constituency grew explosively in later decades. The British *Boy's Own Paper* (1879–1967), for instance, claimed a readership of a quarter of a million in the 1880s. The *Boy's Own Paper* was in fact one of the more successful middle-class attempts to sanitize popular literature, the unlicensed vigor of which often makes authorities uneasy.

Homogenization of the reading public was accompanied by commercial rationalization. The turn-of-the-century book trade efficiently served as a mosaic of distinct reading publics. Juveniles made up one such market. Women were catered to by specialist magazines and romances. Men had adventure tales, crime stories, and (clandestinely) PORNOGRAPHY. Within each category there were social stratifications, between, for instance, the library-supplied romance for the middle-class woman and the sixpenny magazine sold in the sweetshop to the mill girl.

One of the most interesting developments of the late nineteenth century was the revelation that for the first time in history works might be ambitious in literary terms and also achieve mass sales. There emerged the so-called middlebrow best-seller, the first of which was probably Mrs. Humphry Ward's

United States of increasingly efficient ways of selling the product. This was most spectacularly evident in the dime-novel phenomenon. The innovation is usually attributed to New York publisher Erastus Beadle, whose dime edition of Anne S. Stephens's *Malaeska, the Indian Wife of the White Hunter* (1860) sold in the hundreds of thousands and inspired a flood of affordably priced imitations, all with lurid pictorial covers. Like *Malaeska*, many celebrated pioneer values of the frontier and popularized Western history among the Eastern urban masses (*see* WESTERN, THE; Figure 3). The idealistic Horatio Alger rags-to-riches tales were among the most successful dime novels produced by the new fiction factories.

The best-seller list and the apparatus of promotion that went with it were developed in the United States in the 1890s, and the history of popular literature in the twentieth century became the history of the best-seller. Best-sellers had been around for some time: Harriet Beecher Stowe's *Uncle Tom's Cabin* (1852) sold millions worldwide (Figures 4 and 5), and the novel *St. Elmo* (1866), by Augusta Evans [Wilson],

VOL. I.

BOSTON:
JOHN P. JEWETT & COMPANY.
CLEVELAND, OHIO:
JEWETT, PROCTOR & WORTHINGTON.
1852.

Figure 4. *(Literature, Popular)* Title page from the first edition of Harriet Beecher Stowe's *Uncle Tom's Cabin*, 1852. Courtesy, O. T. Smith Collection, Wake Forest University Library, Winston-Salem, North Carolina.

Robert Elsmere (1888). This high-minded thesis novel sold by the millions in Britain and the United States. The wide appeal of subsequent best-sellers bears witness to a significant embourgeoisment of modern popular literature.

Printed POETRY ceased to be a popular item in the twentieth century, except in the Soviet Union, where state patronage kept it alive. Working-class poetry, as originally found in the oral ballad (*see* ORAL POETRY) and later in the printed broadsheet, was absorbed into the music hall and vaudeville, from there into the sheet music industry, and then into the modern popular record industry (*see* MUSIC, POPULAR).

Marketing Popular Literature

One of the main contributions to popular literature in the nineteenth century was the development in the

A CABANA DO PAE THOMAZ

ou

OS NEGROS NA AMERICA.

CAPITULO I.

ONDE O LEITOR TOMA CONHECIMENTO
COM UM HOMEM HUMANO.

N'um dia de fevereiro, gelado e inclemente, dois *gentlemen*, a uma hora adiantada, bebiam juntos n'uma casa de jantar ricamente mobilada d'uma pequena cidade do Kentucki. Não existia presente nenhum criado, e os dois personagens, cujas cadeiras estavam proximas, pareciam occupar-se d'um assumpto d'alto interesse.

Julgâmos dever denominá-los gentlemen, ou pessoas finas, por decoro. Um delles, to-

1

Figure 5. *(Literature, Popular)* First page of a Portuguese translation of *Uncle Tom's Cabin*. From Harriet Beecher Stowe, *A Cabana do Pae Thomaz*, Lisbon, 1853, p. 1.

was so popular that at least a dozen U.S. towns were named after its hero. But the U.S. book trade of the twentieth century succeeded in attuning and directing the reading public's enthusiasms, making popular literature a secure, multimillion-dollar industry.

Twentieth-century best-sellers are characterized primarily by their immense sales, usually in paperback. It is not easy to see why certain books appeal at particular historical moments. Why, for instance, was the western writer Zane Grey sensationally popular after the 1929 stock-market crash or Erich Segal's *Love Story* (1970) the favorite novel in the United States at the height of the Vietnam war? The term *best-seller* acquired a new significance in the 1970s when a generation of blockbusters led by Mario Puzo's *The Godfather* (1969), Peter Benchley's *Jaws* (1974), and William Peter Blatty's *The Exorcist* (1971) sold ten million copies or more in two or three years. New tie-ins, by which films sold books and books sold films, combined to produce supersellers on a massive scale. Alex Haley's imaginative AUTOBIOGRAPHY of a black family, *Roots* (1976), went from a best-selling book to worldwide success as a television miniseries. In 1983 Colleen McCullough's romantic saga of Australian life, *The Thornbirds*, was made into a U.S. television miniseries that reached an estimated two hundred million people across the globe within a few months—probably the largest simultaneous consumption of a single work of fiction in history.

Critical Approaches

These blockbusting single titles are not the whole of modern popular fiction; they are partnered by a GENRE system that concentrates not on single items but on a category of works. Among the most popular are MYSTERY AND DETECTIVE FICTION, SCIENCE FICTION, gothic and horror, romance, and westerns, each with its own distinct group of readers. Genre fiction has been fruitfully examined in terms of its relatively few basic "formulas." Historically, the dominant genres can be traced back centuries. The horror fiction of a writer like Stephen King, for example, owes an evident historical debt to the late eighteenth-century gothic tales of Ann Radcliffe, and it is not too difficult to find links with the witchery pamphlets that were popular reading in sixteenth-century Europe.

Studies of popular literature have dealt not only with its content and history but with the conditions under which it is produced (*see* ARTIST AND SOCIETY; AUTHORSHIP). Contemporary theorists have also begun to investigate the social influences at work in the consumption of popular culture, such as the existence of particular TASTE CULTURES, and the role of the reader in constructing MEANING and defining the reading experience (*see* READING THEORY). These varied approaches go beyond conventional dismissals of popular literature as trivial and escapist, adding depth to LITERARY CRITICISM's exploration of the values and themes that it may be said to embody, as well as to our understanding of its functions.

Bibliography. Brian W. Aldiss, *Billion Year Spree: The True History of Science Fiction*, New York, 1973; Richard Altick, *The English Common Reader: A Social History of the Mass Reading Public*, Chicago, 1957; Peter Burke, *Popular Culture in Early Modern Europe*, New York and London, 1978; John G. Cawelti, *Adventure, Mystery, and Romance*, Chicago, 1976; James D. Hart, *The Popular Book*, New York, 1950, reprint Westport, Conn., 1976; Richard Hoggart, *The Uses of Literacy*, London, 1957; Victor E. Neuburg, ed., *The Batsford Companion to Popular Literature*, London, 1984; John Sutherland, *Bestsellers*, Boston and London, 1981; Ian P. Watt, *The Rise of the Novel*, Berkeley, Calif., 1957, reprint 1974.

JOHN SUTHERLAND

LOBBYING

A term coined in the United States in the 1830s to describe the gathering in the lobbies of Congress of agents representing special interests to further their causes. Viewed as communication, lobbying involves the identification of appropriate decision makers, techniques to establish and sustain communication channels with officials, selection and transmission of persuasive messages, and reinforcement of effective networks of influence.

Dimensions. Lobbying presents two dimensions of communication that allow comparisons of lobbying activity across political systems. First, lobbying ranges in character from formal to informal. Nations with formal systems recognize the role of the lobbyist as legally designated and defined. In the United States, for example, the rights of association and petition are protected in the Constitution; at national and lower levels, specific legislation requires lobbyists to register their backing and expenditures for public scrutiny. Considerably less formalized are the tacit exchanges and understandings by staff members of organized groups that delegate the function of representing group interests to one another and to official functionaries, despite the absence of clear-cut legal sanctions.

On a second dimension, lobbying ranges from the full-time, paid, professional activity of designated specialists (i.e., lobbying as a vocation) to the part-time, ad hoc discussions among members of influential elites with no direct responsibilities for communicating group interests (i.e., lobbying as an avocational by-product). These two dimensions yield four categories of communication activities: formal-vocational, formal-avocational, informal-vocational, and informal-avocational lobbying. Although there are cross-national differences in emphases, no political system is completely without any one of the four.

Formal channels. Foremost among the formal-vocational lobbying strategies are PRESSURE GROUP activities. These consist of direct efforts by legally designated group representatives to persuade public officials. In the United States, for example, it is commonplace for lobbyists to talk directly with legislators, promising future support in exchange for favorable consideration in legislation pending before the deliberative body. That talk might include promises of financial support in an upcoming ELECTION, vote trading on the floor of the legislature, or even bribery. More commonly, however, pressure strategies consist of lobbyists providing services to legislative, administrative, and judicial officials. Organizations devote considerable resources to researching relevant arguments, statistics, assessments, and other forms of information that they channel to governing officials via testimony before legislative committees, administrative appeals, amicus curiae briefs, and other means. More common in European political systems is legal representation on policy-making bodies of agents of organized groups. Organizations may be asked to designate representatives to governing bodies or, alternatively, have policy authority vested in them by legal means. For example, in Great Britain both labor (through the Trades Union Council) and business (through the Confederation of British Industries) have had appointed membership on a variety of public bodies, and in the Federal Republic of Germany many occupational groups exercise formal regulatory authority.

Although formal relationships between governing officials and interest-group advocates on an avocational basis take numerous forms, two occur in a sufficient variety of political systems to warrant specific mention. One strategy involves strengthening contacts between governing and nongoverning elites. Thus, in the United States, formal discussions linking administrative and legislative officials with leaders of business, agriculture, labor, science, technology, civil rights groups, citizen lobbies, environmentalists, and other special interests are commonplace. Which communication patterns take precedence is a function of the political party in power and the matters perceived as mutually antagonistic or beneficial.

In European political systems the practice is more institutionalized, with nongovernmental elites granted formal, representative contacts with administrative and legislative officials. Such ties blend into a second strategy of formal-avocational communication, consultation, which may involve explicit representation of organizational spokespersons on policy or advisory boards—as in Great Britain—or ad hoc conversations between private and public leaders. In any case the purpose of the strategy, as with interaction between private and public elites generally, is to make consultation timely in order to bring group views into the policy process *before* rather than after decisions are made. This opens the process to group representation while building widespread support for government decisions.

Informal channels. Informal contact and communication between lobbyists and official audiences are no less important strategies than formal means. A major portion of the professional lobbyist's efforts goes toward sustaining informal ties. Organizations desirous of protecting and enhancing their influence positions—the "haves"—budget large sums for entertaining public officials, providing honoraria for speaking engagements, expenses-paid tours, and both overt and covert gifts. Organizations aiming at opening communication channels—the "have-nots"—can ill afford to shortchange their paid lobbyists either. Less at issue in informal arrangements are efforts to influence official decisions on specific policies than attempts by haves and have-nots to secure access, that is, to build a relationship of mutual trust between the professional lobbyist and the public official. In that relationship of informality, even ambiguity, each political actor depends on the other. Through reciprocal trust and interdependence the very definition of the continuing policy situation, a necessary prelude to defining specific policies, is forged by lobbyist-official communication.

Finally, lobbying takes place informally through intermediaries rather than by face-to-face contacts between governing officials and professional or amateur lobbyists. In the United States strategies include efforts to influence officials by persuading their constituents to support policies the lobbyists advocate. These extend to forms of "grass roots lobbying"—arranging direct contacts between constituents and the officials in public and private forums, lobbying officials' personal friends, letter and telegraph campaigns inundating officials with constituents' pleas, PUBLIC RELATIONS campaigns, corporate ADVERTISING, contributions to election campaigns, and so on. In other nations, including Italy, lobbyists attach themselves to a favored political party; thus group and party fortunes ebb and flow together.

See also AGENDA-SETTING; POLITICAL COMMUNICATION; PUBLIC OPINION.

Bibliography. Raymond A. Bauer, Ithiel de Sola Pool, and Lewis Anthony Dexter, *American Business and Public Policy*, 2d ed., Chicago, 1972; Lewis Anthony Dexter, *How Organizations Are Represented in Washington*, Indianapolis, Ind., 1969; Henry W. Ehrmann, ed., *Interest Groups on Four Continents*, Pittsburgh, Pa., 1958; Carol

S. Greenwald, *Group Power*, New York, 1977; Lester W. Milbrath, *The Washington Lobbyists*, Chicago, 1963; David Bicknell Truman, *The Governmental Process*, New York, 1951.

DAN D. NIMMO

LOCKE, JOHN (1632–1704)

English philosopher and founder of modern epistemology. John Locke played a vital part in the development of modern scientific thought and communication. Educated on the medieval model, he was nevertheless deeply influenced by the writings of French mathematician and philosopher René Descartes. Descartes's theory that a distinct idea of oneself is the key to personal identity would become one of the foundations of Locke's philosophy. Locke could have remained an Oxford scholar during his entire life, but in 1667 he became adviser to Lord Ashley (later the earl of Shaftesbury). Through Ashley he became interested in colonial affairs, in economics, and in the controversy over the Protestant succession to the throne. This controversy forced Locke's mentor to flee to Holland in 1682; a year later Locke also had to leave England. His exile lasted until 1689. When he returned to England Locke brought with him *An Essay Concerning Human Understanding,* the work for which he is known today. The last fifteen years of his life were marked by increasing fame, wide-ranging correspondence, and material comfort; he died in 1704.

It is Locke's *Essay* that is of greatest interest to the student of communications. It laid the foundation of modern epistemology—the study of human knowledge—and remains one of the clearest descriptions of empiricism. Locke's *Essay* contains three significant points: his definition of the mind as a "white sheet of paper" written on by sense-impression, his treatment of the creation of complex ideas, and his analysis of words as signs of ideas rather than of things.

Locke asserted that the newborn's mind is a tabula rasa, or clean slate. Knowledge arises through the accumulation of sense-impressions and through reflection on their connections. A child sees a coin, for example, and notes its shape, its mass, and its markings and coloration. Over time the child sees other coins identical in some respects (what Locke calls primary qualities) but slightly different in other respects affected by external conditions (secondary qualities). If an unknown piece of metal is presented the child recalls those other examples, with their known range of appearances, and either places the new sample in the existing set of coins or creates a new category.

Thus the mind develops ideas corresponding to

Figure 1. *(Locke, John)* Michael Dahl, *John Locke,* ca. 1696. National Portrait Gallery, London.

each set of memories; these ideas can be integrated to yield new ideas not directly related to immediate sense-impressions. In this way abstractions—what Locke calls "modes, substances, and relations"—are developed (e.g., the concepts of magnetism or cause and effect). This pattern was later incorporated by Scottish philosopher David Hume into his theory of association of ideas, a theory crucial to modern psychology.

Finally, Locke devotes a long section of his *Essay* to the way we communicate with others: through words that signify ideas, not things. Traditionally it was believed that words represented things; Locke was the first to propose that words actually signify our ideas of things, mental pictures we employ in a kind of verbal shorthand. The word *gold,* he notes, stands not for a particular lump of metal but for a substance corresponding to a complex idea of "colour, weight, fusibility, fixedness, &c, which gives it a right to that name." People fail to communicate clearly because they use words that signify different things to themselves and their listeners, or because the words they choose do not truly reflect their own ideas. The only way to eliminate such flaws in communication, Locke argues, is "to use no word without a signification." Locke's call for a descriptive dictionary that would serve as the standard for word use was finally answered at the end of the nineteenth century with the publication of the *Oxford English Dictionary*, which was based on his principles. *See also* JOHNSON, SAMUEL; LANGUAGE REFERENCE BOOK.

Modern theorists have rebutted many of Locke's assertions about logic and psychology, but by highlighting the question of knowledge and by interposing the idea between stimulus and response, between things and words, Locke created a model of human experience that remains valid.

Bibliography. Richard I. Aaron, *John Locke*, 3d ed., Oxford, 1971; Maurice William Cranston, *John Locke: A Biography*, London and New York, 1957.

HARTLEY S. SPATT

LOGIC. *See* SYMBOLIC LOGIC.

LOWENTHAL, LEO (1900–)

German-born U.S. sociologist, literary historian, and media scholar. In the discordant debate over popular CULTURE few observers have argued as voluminously and persuasively as Leo Lowenthal. His dominant thesis has been that mass culture, particularly as studied in terms of its historical antecedents, is deleterious to modern living. Through numerous books, articles, and monographs, over a fifty-year period Lowenthal has decried the "decline of the individual in the mechanized working process of modern civilization." The resulting displacement of folk ART (*see also* FOLKLORE) and of "high" art, in his view, has brought about a standardized and mendacious mass culture whose main characteristics are stereotypes and manipulated consumer goods.

In a well-known study Lowenthal examined biographies in popular U.S. magazines from 1900 to 1941. By sorting out national heroes along political, business-professional, and ENTERTAINMENT lines, he found that "idols of work" (i.e., those in business, politics, and industry) were dominant in the early years of the twentieth century but were displaced by "idols of consumption" (i.e., persons from entertainment and SPORTS) as the country moved ahead to World War II. That *People* magazine would surpass its parent, *Time*, in circulation in the 1980s was not a surprise to Lowenthal.

In *Literature, Popular Culture, and Society* (1961) Lowenthal foresaw the media's constantly growing use of reports about the lives, loves, squabbles, and divorces of celebrities. He termed these so-called human-interest stories "a kind of mass gossip." However, these stories are not to be confused with simple trivia better confined to the gossip column. In a highly selective way the stories cover situations that the managing editors of such financial bonanzas as

People and *Ebony* take to be representative of the lives of their readers, who can thus identify with their favorite surrogates.

Throughout his career Lowenthal utilized CONTENT ANALYSIS to study the nexus between society and culture. By relating historical changes in society to dominant themes and images of content he was able to delineate what he called the "unbridgeable difference between art and mass culture."

Although his academic affiliation in the United States was primarily as a sociologist, Lowenthal was equally at home in history, philosophy, and particularly literature. He frequently drew on the works of writers such as Friedrich Nietzsche, Blaise Pascal, and Gustave Flaubert to expostulate against today's popular culture. In a mass-acculturated society, he contends, the media essentially gratify only lower needs and ipso facto are irrevocably doomed to serve as vehicles of inferior products. He questions whether social science methodology is able to deal adequately with the problems of contemporary social culture. As a humanist he voices concern lest too many social scientists engage themselves solely with the mere quantifiable aggregates of people.

Lowenthal was consistent in his critique of mass culture from the time he came to the United States in 1933, a refugee from Nazi Germany. Before his emigration he had served as a senior research associate at Frankfurt's famed Institute for Social Research with such noted scholars as THEODOR ADORNO and Max Horkheimer. From 1940 to 1954 he was a lecturer in sociology at Columbia University, where he worked with another distinguished refugee, PAUL F. LAZARSFELD, at the Bureau of Applied Social Research. He also served as director of research for the Voice of America from 1949 to 1954. Subsequently he became a professor at the University of California, Berkeley, for the remainder of his academic career. A four-volume collection of Lowenthal's essays and monographs was published in 1982–1984.

See also COMMUNICATIONS RESEARCH: ORIGINS AND DEVELOPMENT.

Bibliography. Leo Lowenthal, *Literature and the Image of Man*, Boston, 1957; idem, *Literature, Popular Culture, and Society*, New York, 1961, reprint 1968; idem, *Literature and Mass Culture*, Vol. 1, *Communication in Society*, New Brunswick, N.J., 1984.

DAVID MANNING WHITE

LUCE, HENRY (1898–1967)

U.S. editor and publisher, cofounder, editorial chief, and principal owner of *Time*, *Fortune*, and *Life* magazines and related enterprises that profoundly

Figure 1. *(Luce, Henry)* Miriam Troop, *Henry Luce*, 1955. National Portrait Gallery, Smithsonian Institution, Washington, D.C.

influenced U.S. journalism and PUBLISHING (*see* MAGAZINE). Born in Shantung Province, China, Henry Robinson Luce was one of four children of missionary parents. He was raised in an atmosphere of Calvinist moral principles, belief in EDUCATION, sympathy for the emerging republican REVOLUTION in China, and love for the United States.

After strict training at home and at an English school in Chefoo, Luce went to the Hotchkiss School in Connecticut and to Yale. At Yale he and a classmate, Briton Hadden, speculated about one day starting a publication that would make people better informed about public events. After they graduated in 1920 Luce studied at Oxford and then worked at the *Chicago Daily News*. The two rejoined at the *Baltimore News* in 1922.

Almost immediately they agreed to start a weekly NEWSMAGAZINE, planning at first to call it *Facts* but settling on the title *Time*. Using family and Yale connections, they raised eighty-six thousand dollars and on March 3, 1923, launched the first issue. Aimed at "the busy reader," *Time* was refreshingly different from older, soberer media. It was breezy, opinionated, terse, and witty, spurning "objectivity."

At first it had no regular correspondents; its editors interpreted, rewrote, and condensed daily newspaper reports. A fast-growing audience liked its neat summaries and unique writing style. Introduced by Hadden, this style was marked by reversals of sentence structure, the linking of colorful adjectives to names in the news, and often the juxtaposition of facts more for effect than for fairness. "Timestyle," as it became known (portmanteau words were one of its features), was at once entertaining, infuriating, and open to satire. At its best it reflected Luce's demand that his editors and writers avoid "commonplace" language. After about 1940, however, the regular correspondents' field reports were often rewritten and distorted to reflect Luce's intensely conservative, pro–Chiang Kai-shek policies, and several writers resigned in anger.

At the beginning Luce managed the business end and Hadden the editorial side. Hadden died in 1929 at age thirty-one, and Luce became editor in chief, holding that post actively until 1964. He held no corporate posts himself, but he sought out as executives talented, creative men who shared his aims and could develop his strategies. At the same time, he monitored operations closely, constantly challenging staff members.

In 1930 came the launching of the luxurious monthly *Fortune*. Its aims were to "give business a literature," "show how business works," and report on business personalities. *Fortune* did not shrink from exposing corporate sin.

Luce's early interest in broadcasting led in 1931 to a RADIO series, "The March of Time," adapted to NEWSREEL film in 1935. The episodes were often overly dramatized, even to the use of actors and simulated dialogue. But they were extremely popular for almost twenty years, and from the beginning they spurred Luce's interest in PHOTOJOURNALISM. Since 1932 he had been studying the journalistic use in Europe of miniature, wide-lens, fast-shutter cameras such as the Leica. By 1936 he was ready to launch the immensely successful *Life* magazine. He envisioned *Life* as an educational medium, reporting, through pictures and some major articles, a wide range of world and domestic news, using topflight photographers and writers and a slick, oversized format. During World War II *Life*'s vivid photographs of war and home-front scenes had strong impact. Further photographic technology was a factor in launching, in 1953, the pace-setting *Sports Illustrated*.

Books engendered by the firm's materials were published sporadically after 1930, and in 1959, under the corporate name Time, Inc., Time-Life Books was established as a major enterprise, issuing mail-subscription series of informative books, profusely illustrated, spiritedly written, and stylishly produced.

Additional developments under Luce included film and television ventures; talks leading to the acquisition of the book firm Little, Brown; and a graphic arts laboratory, highly influential for some years. Luce in his last years poured his energies into promoting a theme he called "the American Century." Meanwhile he had created an aggressive communications complex that was able to grow and change with the times.

Bibliography. Robert T. Elson, *Time, Inc.: The Intimate History of a Publishing Enterprise*, 2 vols., ed. by Duncan Norton-Taylor, New York, 1968, 1969; John Kobler, *Luce: His Time, Life, and Fortune*, New York, 1968; Curtis Prendergast and Geoffrey Colvin, *The World of Time, Inc., 1960–1980*, New York, 1986; W. A. Swanberg, *Luce and His Empire*, New York, 1972; Theodore H. White, *In Search of History*, New York, 1978.

CHANDLER B. GRANNIS

LUMIÈRE, LOUIS (1864–1948) AND AUGUSTE (1862–1954)

Leading French manufacturers of photographic equipment, chiefly renowned for their invention of the cinematograph, the device that on December 28, 1895, at the Grand Café in Paris, first showed projected MOTION PICTURES to a paying audience and launched the cinema era. The brothers Louis and Auguste Lumière had an agreement that all their innovations would be jointly credited, but Louis seems to have been the chief inventor of the cinematograph and to have shot many of the first Lumière films, which were mainly vignettes of French middle-class life: a baby being fed; a train arriving at a provincial station; workers leaving a factory; fishermen and their nets; the demolition of a wall—followed, in a trick reversal, by its sudden resurrection from the rubble.

The cinematograph had an unusual feature that decisively influenced film history. A compact portable camera, it could with adjustments become a projector or a printing machine. This meant that an *opérateur* trained by the Lumières could go to a foreign country, hold showings of Lumière films, and meanwhile shoot and exhibit local items (developed in a hotel room) that would enrich the Lumière collection. With this strategy in mind the Lumières embarked on an extraordinary exploitation plan. They held up the Paris premiere until they had trained more than a dozen *opérateurs*. Then, immediately after the triumphant debut, these were dispatched far and wide. Within two years they had introduced the cinematograph on six continents. By the end of 1897 the Lumière collection comprised some 750 short films, including such items as a Spanish bullfight, gondolas on a Venice canal, camels at the pyramids in Egypt, an elephant procession in Phnom Penh, German dragoons leaping hurdles, a New York street scene, and the coronation of Czar Nicholas II in Russia. Each *opérateur* handled a succession of premieres. The man who introduced the wonder into India went on to Australia and from there sent back film of the Melbourne races. Meanwhile, another had reached Tokyo. Throughout this two-year period the Lumières had refused to sell cinematographs, maintaining total control of the invention.

Figure 1. *(Lumière, Louis and Auguste)* Louis and Auguste Lumière. National Film Archive, London.

Figure 2. *(Lumière, Louis and Auguste)* A Polish poster for the Lumière cinematograph, Krakow, 1896. State Historical Society of Wisconsin, Erik Barnouw Collection.

At the end of 1897, as abruptly as the campaign had begun, the Lumières announced their intention of withdrawing from production and exhibition in order to concentrate on what they considered their specialties, manufacture and invention. Cinematographs would now be for sale. By that time a host of cinematographers, with rival equipment from many sources, were traversing the globe.

The Lumière whirlwind campaign had left its mark in many ways. Motion picture production was beginning almost simultaneously at various locations throughout the world. The word *cinema* (from *Cinématographe*) had been planted firmly in many of the world's languages. And the film industry had begun with a DOCUMENTARY emphasis that would continue for some years, until the ascent of the fiction film. The Lumières meanwhile went on to other

interests, including a remarkable color process for still PHOTOGRAPHY, the *autochrome,* which produced works that closely resembled pointillist paintings. It continued in use until the 1920s.

Bibliography. Georges Sadoul, *Louis Lumière,* Paris, 1964.

ERIK BARNOUW

LURIA, ALEKSANDR (1902–1977)

Soviet psychologist, neuropsychologist, aphasiologist, and semiotician whose primary interest was the relationship between LANGUAGE and mental functioning (*see* SEMIOTICS). After finishing his university education in Kazan, where he had been born and raised, Aleksandr Romanovich Luria undertook several research studies motivated by diverse psychological theories, including the psychoanalytic theories of SIGMUND FREUD and CARL JUNG (*see also* PSYCHOANALYSIS). In 1923 he joined the staff of the Institute of Psychology in Moscow, and in 1924 he met Soviet psychologist and semiotician LEV VYGOTSKY, with whom he worked closely until Vygotsky died of tuberculosis in 1934. During this decade Luria helped develop a theoretical framework that would guide the research he and many other Soviet psychologists carried out for the next several decades. This framework, which was grounded in Marxist theory as well as in the findings of psychology and other social sciences, came to be known as the cultural-historical approach to mind. The primary goal of the approach was to devise an account of human mental processes that would specify how they are related to particular sociocultural contexts. Among its fundamental tenets were the claim that human communicative and psychological processes are shaped by the tools and signs (*see* SIGN) that mediate them, and the claim that the origins of human mental processes are to be found in social life.

Luria's post-Vygotskian research revolved around three related issues. First, he carried out cross-cultural studies in cognitive functioning. To test some of the claims of the cultural-historical approach, he conducted, in Soviet Central Asia in the late 1920s and early 1930s, the first of several studies that focused on how forms of mental functioning such as abstraction, deduction, reasoning, problem solving, and self-awareness are related to the emergence of LITERACY and other characteristics of modern sociocultural settings. *See* COGNITION.

The second topic that concerned Luria in his research and clinical practice was the regulative function of SPEECH. Building on his own ideas about the relationship between internal and external processes as well as on Vygotsky's ideas about social, "egocentric," and inner speech, he performed a series of studies on the development of self-regulative speech in children. His focus was on the ways in which social speech gives rise to self-regulative speech and on the neuropsychological processes involved in the transition of self-regulative speech from an overt to an internalized form. These studies led him to make a series of claims about the social-communicative origins and semiotic structuring of self-regulation in CHILDREN and about the cerebral organization of inner speech.

The third focus of Luria's research was the neuropsychology of language and mental functions. In this area he made many of his most original and significant contributions to the understanding of human mental processes. Much of this research was motivated by the clinical work he carried out after finishing medical school in the late 1930s. On the basis of his experience in treating patients with war-related brain injuries during World War II, Luria devised a systematic account of various types of traumatic aphasia (*see* SPEECH AND LANGUAGE DISORDERS), which served as the foundation for refining his account of the "functional systems" involved in neuropsychological processes. This functional-system approach, in turn, led him to produce what is perhaps the twentieth century's most comprehensive analysis of neuropsychological disturbances of communicative, perceptual (*see* PERCEPTION), and cognitive processes. At the time of his death Luria was deeply involved in the formation of the new discipline of neurolinguistics.

Bibliography. Aleksandr R. Luria, *The Working Brain: An Introduction to Neuropsychology* (in Russian), trans. by Basil Haigh, New York, 1973; idem, *The Making of Mind*, ed. by Michael Cole and Sheila Cole, Cambridge, Mass., 1979; idem, *Language and Cognition*, trans. and ed. by James V. Wertsch, New York, 1981.

JAMES V. WERTSCH

LUTHER, MARTIN (1483–1546)

German theologian. Martin Luther set off the movement that became known as the Protestant Reformation, a religious and social upheaval that owed much of its impact to its coinciding and interreacting with another radical development: the unprecedented possibility for large-scale communication created by the invention of PRINTING. The central contribution that printed documents made to the success of the Reformation signaled the catalytic role that printing would thenceforth play in Western social, cultural, and political life. Fundamental changes in Western beliefs and social structures emerged from the meshing of these two revolutionary developments.

While still an Augustinian monk and parish preacher in Wittenberg and professor of biblical theology at that city's new UNIVERSITY, Luther arrived at the two basic views that would later become central to Protestantism and that constituted a fundamental challenge to prevailing Catholic teachings and practices. He asserted (1) the sole authority of the Bible as the source of God's word (as opposed to the Catholic emphasis on the authority of the papacy and of clerical councils) and (2) salvation by the inward act of individual faith alone (in contrast to the traditional Catholic idea of salvation by works and participation in the sacraments). Luther posted his Ninety-five Theses on the door of the Schlosskirche (castle church) in Wittenberg on October 31, 1517. That document originated in specific protest against the Catholic church's sale of indulgences (*see* CRUSADES, THE) but also reflected his new general beliefs. The action thrust Luther into the public eye as a religious re-

Figure 1. *(Luther, Martin)* Lucas Cranach, *Portrait of Martin Luther*, 1529. Uffizi, Florence. Alinari/Art Resource, New York.

former and can be thought of as the single precipitating event of the Reformation.

Between then and 1521—when in January Pope Leo X finally excommunicated him and in April the secular Diet of Worms declared him a criminal and banned his writings—Luther came into increasing conflict with ecclesiastical authorities, grew increasingly popular with students and the German people (among his chief supporters were the German nobles who resented the secular power of the papacy and its draining of finances away from their regions), and published a series of what in retrospect can be called Reformation manifestos. In such writings as "Address to the Christian Nobility of the German Nation," "A Prelude concerning the Babylonian Captivity of the Church," and "Of the Freedom of a Christian Man," Luther expanded on his religious ideas (e.g., defending the moral validity of the individual conscience, asserting the priesthood of all Christians against a separate and privileged hierarchy, and denying the validity of the Mass and of the doctrine of transubstantiation) and called for secular action when the church would not reform itself from within (see PAMPHLET). In the following year Luther was forced to live in hiding at secluded Wartburg Castle under the protection of the elector of Saxony, beginning while there his monumental and unprecedented translation of the Bible into the German vernacular (New Testament, 1522; Old Testament, 1534).

From 1522 on, Luther had to devote himself to the consolidation of the new church that, in effect though not by original intention, he had founded. Steering between the Catholics on the one hand and the more extreme German religious reformers whom he denounced on the other, and aided substantially by associates like Philipp Melanchthon and Justus Jonas, Luther created reformed rituals—including a liturgy in the vernacular—that became basic statements of the new faith (see RITUAL). However, because of disagreements with foreign reformers like Huldrych Zwingli and John Calvin over the doctrine of the Eucharist, Luther was not successful in maintaining a transnational Protestant unity, and in 1530 the newly designated Lutherans drew up their separate articles of faith in the Augsburg Confession.

By the time of Luther's death, the individualistic tendencies within his reformation movement had helped produce a markedly different European social, political, and cultural order. European society was no longer united under a single church but was marked by the existence of several; many individual nobles found in the new Protestantism a useful basis for revolt against imperial or otherwise centralized political structures (in Germany the new Lutheran churches even became territorial churches, subject to the authority of the local Protestant princes); and the "ordinary individual" gained a potentially greater status than ever before known in Western, and perhaps world, culture.

Writing, especially writing in the vernacular LANGUAGE of the common people, was one of Luther's chief tools for communicating his reform beliefs. It is unlikely that those beliefs would have had the transforming scope and impact that they did without a medium like printing that could disseminate them widely and bring them into the experience of the common person, either by the act of private READING for the literate (see LITERACY) or simply by a large-scale distribution that made them potentially available for discussion by all. The Reformation thus became one of the first arenas to demonstrate the power that printing could have as an agent of widespread cultural and social change.

See also RELIGION; RENAISSANCE; SCRIPTURE.

JOSEPH CADY

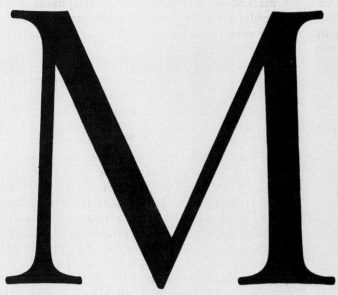

(em), the thirteenth letter of the modern and twelfth of the ancient Roman alphabet, represents historically the Greek *mū* and the Semitic *mēm*. The Phœnician form of the letter is Ⓜ, whence the early Greek and Latin Ⓜ, Ⓜ, M. Its phonetic value has varied little. . . .

MCLUHAN, MARSHALL (1911–1980)

Canadian literary and communications scholar. During the 1960s Herbert Marshall McLuhan enjoyed widespread fame for his work on the cultural implications of the mass media. Imitating the sloganizing style of ADVERTISING, a number of his oracular pronouncements became international catchphrases.

A Catholic convert who took his doctorate in English at Cambridge in 1942, McLuhan's early academic career in both the United States and Canada was unexceptional—until the publication in 1962 of *The Gutenberg Galaxy: The Making of Typographic Man.* The book built on nonliterary interests McLuhan had first displayed more than a decade earlier in *The Mechanical Bride: Folklore of Industrial Man* (1951). The body of ideas was further developed in *Understanding Media* (1964), McLuhan's most enduring and widely disseminated work. Thereafter he returned to many of the same themes, at times in increasingly idiosyncratic and picture-magazine-like texts (e.g., *The Medium Is the Massage,* 1967).

Canada and Canadian scholarship sparked McLuhan's interest in communications. The critical importance of physical communications in Canadian history and the interaction of technology and society were major themes in the work of some of his contemporaries, especially HAROLD INNIS, an economic historian. Innis argued that communication technologies confer monopolies over knowledge and "bias" the time and space dimensions of social life. Accordingly, for McLuhan technology was largely an external force that conditioned society far more than technology was conditioned or determined by society. However, McLuhan's examination of technologies did not include any consideration of their histories or the social circumstances affecting their DIFFUSION.

Catholicism informed his central vision of typographic man—that is, humankind after the PRINTING press—as somehow "fallen" from the state of grace enjoyed by tribal peoples. McLuhan argued that phonetic writing transformed the oral (i.e., spoken word) into the visual (i.e., printed word). Printing also shaped private and individualized logic and consciousness. Typographic man lives by eye rather than by ear. Declaring that aural communication demands greater imaginative work on the part of receivers than does visual communication, McLuhan suggested that it is richer. In his view print is the model of all subsequent industrialized processes, confining and limiting imagination because of its strict lineality. In McLuhan's individual terminology, print is a "hot" medium, whereas television is "cool" in that its relatively "low definition" (e.g., poor picture quality) engages the viewer more actively than does print, which, with its "high definition," encourages detachment (i.e., less involvement) as well as relative isolation. In general there is little evidence to support McLuhan's psychological arguments. Critics assert that they represented, at the very least, technological overdeterminism or very imprecise metaphors.

McLuhan was also deeply influenced by his Celtic ancestry, the poetic source of the arresting and unique style of presentation he developed. Increasingly distanced from the norms of academic discourse, he attempted to sum up his ideas as a series of aphorisms, or "probes" as he called them. These were designed to goad his audience into a greater awareness of the situation created by modern media technology. Probes such as "the medium is the message" or "the global village" gained wide currency. But the core of his theoretical contributions is that the new media, new communications technologies, are extensions of our bodies. They create new environments whose major effects, inherent in their existence, are the creation of new modes of perception, new types of sensory experiences, and new social relationships.

McLuhan particularly impressed the world of advertising and television (*see* TELEVISION HISTORY). A charismatic and provocative performer when interviewed, he appeared to be suggesting that television, and COMMERCIALS in particular, marked the road back to the lost preprint Eden. That his vision was darker than this remained hidden from those in the media promoting him.

He was a very controversial figure, feted by many but also rudely dismissed. "Impure nonsense, nonsense adulterated with sense," was the view of one contemporary critic of *Understanding Media.* By the mid-1970s the critics had prevailed. McLuhan's most enduring contribution lies in the fact that he helped to establish the mass media among the intelligentsia as a proper object of study, perhaps more by his own celebrity than by his methodology or the weight of his ideas.

See also COMMUNICATIONS, STUDY OF; MASS COMMUNICATIONS RESEARCH; MASS MEDIA EFFECTS.

BRIAN WINSTON

MAGAZINE

Periodical publication that contains in each issue an assortment of items. The term *magazine,* meaning "storehouse," originally suggested diverse content, but in recent times most magazines have become highly specialized, each attracting a sharply defined audience with items relating to a specific range of interests—which are usually, at the same time, designed to attract support from advertisers serving those interests. Most periodicals can be squeezed, sometimes uncomfortably, into four broad categories: consumer magazines, trade and technical magazines, public relations or company publications, and literary and scholarly journals.

Consumer magazines, usually ADVERTISING-

Figure 1. *(Magazine)* Newsstand in Paris. Courtesy of the French Government Tourist Office.

supported, find their constituencies among the general public, although most aim at segments of it. Trade and technical magazines, including specialized business magazines, are directed at relatively small, highly specific audiences in trades, businesses, industries, and professions to which they carry news and specialized information about their occupational fields. PUBLIC RELATIONS periodicals are issued by corporations, government agencies, colleges and universities, and other institutions to promote their interests among employees, customers, clients, and opinion leaders. Most literary and scholarly journals are published without commercial intent, though they may solicit advertising to help defray costs.

No precise statistics on the number of magazines have been compiled, but it is clearly enormous. In 1984 *Facts on File* estimated as follows: Africa, 863; North America, 12,947; South America, 3,550; Asia, 41,164; Europe, 70,602; Oceania (including Australasia), 8,415; and the USSR, 4,772.

History

The magazine was born in Europe in the seventeenth century, a few decades after the newspaper (*see* NEWSPAPER: HISTORY). One of the earliest was the *Journal des Scavans,* founded in Paris in 1665. Originally it carried abstracts of books, but later it ran original material as well. Like successful magazines ever since, it was widely imitated, both on the European continent and in England. In a wave of European magazine making in the late seventeenth and early eighteenth centuries, some periodicals forsook sober edification for sheer amusement; some answered questions supplied by their readers; others, like the *Tatler* and Addison and Steele's *Spectator,* introduced a high literary quality to magazine journalism.

Perhaps the first magazine recognizable as a prototype of what magazines were to become was the invention of Edward Cave of London (1691–1754), a cobbler's son who had worked as printer and editor. His *Gentleman's Magazine* (1731–1907) is generally credited with being the first periodical to use the designation *magazine.* Both the term and the basic format had spread to Germany by 1747. Both were also adopted by publishers in the British North American colonies.

A decade after the birth of *Gentleman's Magazine,* the first two magazines appeared in the American colonies, three days apart. They were Andrew Bradford's *American Magazine* and Benjamin Franklin's *General Magazine and Historical Chronicle,* both published in Philadelphia and dated January 1741. However, magazines were slow to take root in American soil: Bradford's magazine died after three issues, Franklin's after six. Until 1794 there were never more than three magazines at one time in the United States, and probably none had a circulation of more than fifteen hundred. A period of growth began in the nineteenth century—from a dozen magazines in 1800 to a hundred in 1825 to six hundred in 1850. They generally circulated only within a fifty-mile radius until the mid-nineteenth century, when magazines of national outlook and circulation began to emerge.

A boom in magazine making after the Civil War pushed the number of periodicals from seven hundred in 1865 to thirty-three hundred in 1885. But publishers tended to neglect the great and growing middle class. Between the genteel monthlies like *Atlantic* (founded in 1857) and *Harper's* (founded in 1850) at one extreme and trashy story papers at the other, there was a sparsity of magazines.

Rise of consumer magazines in the United States. When the modern magazine was born in the last years of the nineteenth century, it was, in retrospect, an almost inevitable consequence of the changes that had begun to alter the U.S. landscape after the Civil War. The industrial and technological revolution was changing the economy from an agricultural to an industrial one and was providing the publisher with improved tools such as speedier PRINTING presses to reach large audiences and photoengraving to replace handcrafted illustrations. Mass production and improved transport were opening up national markets beyond local or regional ones. Steady increases in population, abetted by a flood of immigrants, and higher levels of LITERACY, the result of the spread of popular EDUCATION, were creating a middle-class audience with considerable buying power and LEISURE time that made it a desirable target for advertisers. Meanwhile, Edward W. Bok (1863–1930), editor of the *Ladies' Home Journal* for three decades after 1889, had begun to demonstrate the enormous potential of a magazine that closely matched its readers' concerns.

Beginning in 1893, publishers like Frank Andrew Munsey (1854–1925), S. S. McClure (1857–1949), and Cyrus Curtis (1850–1933) capitalized on those changes and cut the basic pattern that magazine publishers traced thereafter. By filling their magazines with content reflecting popular taste and often selling them for less than production cost, they attracted an advertising volume that supported their enterprises. They opened new markets for magazines, which continued to grow with the new century and gradually spread throughout the world. The flood of consumer magazines took in all continents, especially after World War II.

The rise of new media competing for public attention—MOTION PICTURES, RADIO, television (*see* TELEVISION HISTORY), and others—was for a time seen as a mortal danger to magazines. But in fact their rise encouraged a worldwide proliferation of magazines catering to enthusiasts for the new media. By the 1980s, for example, India was reported to have seven hundred magazines aimed at film fans. Countries throughout the world had specialized magazines for television viewers, often modeled on *TV Guide* (see Table 1). And as broadcast media heightened interest in SPORTS, they seemed to bring a new spurt to sport magazines, usually with a national emphasis.

Rise of trade and technical magazines. The trade and technical press can trace its ancestry back to the Dutch and English lists of current commodity prices in the seventeenth and eighteenth centuries and to the shipping lists and public sale reports in the United States in the eighteenth and nineteenth. By the early nineteenth century forerunners of the specialized business press had begun to emerge in the United States. However, they encountered difficulties similar to those of the early general magazines: reader indifference, lack of advertising support, high production costs, a primitive distribution system.

The growth of the specialized business press in industrialized nations paralleled the growth of commerce and industry. In the United States the first trade and technical publications dealt with manufacturing, commerce, mining, and transportation. Their second broad phase saw the rise of publications directed at the professions (*see* PROFESSION). By the early 1970s the specialized business press had begun to edge into yet another direction—high technology. Thereafter periodicals covering research and advances in such fields as computers, electronics, robotics, and genetic engineering appeared in escalating numbers (*see* COMPUTER: IMPACT).

The thrust of editorial content changed over time. In new or young industries and professions, specialized business publications found their first need as teachers. As timely continuing textbooks, they concentrated on practical, didactic, readily applied information. Their editorial staffs were hired more for technical knowledge than journalistic skills. But as basic knowledge became codified and new means arose for its dissemination, the magazines increasingly stressed news of advances in their specialized fields. Their staffs became persons with communications expertise rather than exclusively technical knowledge.

The strength and importance of trade and technical periodicals seem especially related to the state of a country's commercial and industrial development. The specialized business press is both a force for and a beneficiary of such development. It is the only communications medium with a natural MONOPOLY; no other medium reaches its audiences with the kinds of specialized information that it carries.

Table 1. TV Magazines

In 1985 each of the following was among the ten highest-circulation magazines in its area.	
Australia	TV Week
Austria	Hörzu
Belgium	Télémoustique
Denmark	TV Bladet
Egypt	Al-Izaawal Television
France	Télé 7 Jours
Federal Republic of Germany	Hörzu
Ireland	RTE Guide
Italy	TV Sorrisi e Canzoni
Japan	TV Guide
Mexico	Tele-Guia
Netherlands	Avrobode
New Zealand	New Zealand Listener
Norway	Se og Hor
Portugal	TV Guia
Spain	T. P. Teleprograma
Switzerland	Tele
United Kingdom	Radio Times
United States	TV Guide

Source: *The World Media To-day* [1985] (Les temps médias), Paris, 1984–.

Company publications. Once known as "house organs," company publications are of three broad types: internal, for readers within the sponsoring organization; external, for opinion leaders, customers and potential customers, shareholders, and the like (*see* OPINION LEADER); and combination, for both internal and external audiences. They range in circulation from a few hundred copies to more than a million, in quality from the amateurish to the professionally polished and handsomely illustrated.

Their origins can be traced to ancient Chinese court circulars. An early U.S. example is Franklin's *Poor Richard's Almanack.* A scattering of the periodicals appeared in the nineteenth century. But their big growth has been in the twentieth century, especially after World War II. No doubt contributing to their rise were the sense of public relations that permeated business and industry, the growth of labor unions and the labor press, the complexity of modern industry, and management's desire to explain and defend the free enterprise system in a period of widespread GOVERNMENT REGULATION.

Literary and scholarly journals. Literary magazines have been characterized by brief lives, uncertain funding, low circulations, and high hopes. They have been a medium for experimentation in literature and the arts, sometimes a herald of new ideas, trends, and movements. Many celebrated writers such as T. S. Eliot, Robert Frost, and Eugene O'Neill published their early work in them. Scholarly journals have experienced similar uncertainties, although support from universities and scholarly societies has sometimes provided for some stability.

Medium

The importance of magazines as a communications medium—the number of magazines, the range and nature of their content, the use people make of them, and their relative prestige—varies from nation to nation. Their importance is tempered by historical, cultural, economic, and political factors. The penetration of magazines into the adult population is generally highest in the most industrialized nations, whether capitalist or socialist, but magazines are considerably less numerous in socialist countries. In the more orthodox socialist societies government supervision is a controlling factor, but magazines cater to a wide variety of interests, serving both mass and specialized audiences. In the Soviet Union they may issue from industry groups, worker organizations, educational associations, and other entities. As disseminators of information and attitudes regarded as desirable, magazines seem to be secondary in importance to newspapers but are a significant supplement. In the less orthodox socialist countries material from outside circulates with varying degrees of freedom, mainly in urban centers. Yugoslavia has been comparatively free of barriers in this respect. *See* CENSORSHIP.

Role of advertising. In most of the leading capitalist nations, advertising, by defining the role of the publisher as basically a dealer in audiences, has influenced the nature as well as the relative prominence of magazines. Whether consumer magazines can flourish depends on several conditions: the size, educational level, and affluence of markets for goods and services; the extent to which producers are able and willing to spend money to reach those markets; the availability of other media for reaching those markets; and the amount of competition from magazines beyond a nation's borders.

Ultimately the vitality of consumer magazines in any given nation depends to a large extent on the nature of the newspaper and broadcasting industries. Whether a country has mainly national dailies or mainly local ones, whether it has large-circulation newspaper supplements akin to magazines, whether its television system bans or severely restricts advertising, whether television time is costly or relatively inexpensive—all these conditions affect the volume of advertising and the prosperity of advertising-supported magazine industries.

So does the amount of competition that a native magazine industry gets from magazines published outside the nation's borders. As early as 1906 one writer complained that Canadians read more U.S. magazines than Canadian ones. Because U.S. publishers amortized their costs at home, he said, they could compete unfairly with Canadian publishers. Some seventy years later the Canadian government took measures to foster indigenous periodicals. In the decade after 1973 the number of Canadian magazines increased substantially, as did the volume of advertising placed in them. In Austria, where magazines from the Federal Republic of Germany predominate, development of a native industry has been inhibited. Other European countries in which outside magazines compete strongly with the local product include Belgium, Ireland, and Switzerland.

Role of publisher. The role of the publisher has given a certain family likeness to magazine publishing in various nations throughout most of the Western world. As dealers in audiences, publishers need invest comparatively little in capital equipment unless they choose to. Printing, subscription solicitation, subscription fulfillment, audience and market research—those and other service functions can be contracted out to others (*see* PRINT-AUDIENCE MEASUREMENT). The publisher's basic stock is editorial content that will engage readers and an audience that will attract advertisers. Hence the industry has remained relatively accessible to the entrepreneur with an idea for a new magazine and with the capital to start and nurture it.

Industry

One family likeness is in the structure of the industry. Although there are local variations, the basic pattern is similar in nation after nation: Australia, Canada, Finland, Italy, the Netherlands, Portugal, Spain, Sweden, the United Kingdom, the United States, the Federal Republic of Germany, and others. In each a handful of dominant publishers accounts for a disproportionately large share of circulation and advertising linage. But beneath those corporate peaks lies the body of the industry, a large number of ever-changing smaller magazines that serve an ever-changing spectrum of interests. The large publishing houses may have an overall competitive edge, yet the total number of magazines, their growth in numbers, and the range of interests they appeal to suggest that the industry generally is not closed to newcomers. In the United Kingdom six major companies account for about 70 percent of consumer magazine advertising. Nonetheless, the period 1966–1974 saw the birth of between 59 and 173 new consumer magazines each year. Altogether there were 1,013 new consumer magazines, 1,317 trade and technical. (However, the gain in total numbers was reduced by the deaths of 892 consumer and 1,034 trade and technical publications.) In Denmark three large companies once dominated the industry—Aller, Det Berlingske Hus, and Gutenberghus-Bladene. Palle Fogtdal, whose experience had been limited to editing a trade paper, broke into publishing in 1954. He sensed that specialized publications could compete successfully with the general-interest family magazines that dominated the scene. Thirty years later his company stood among the majors.

Circulation. Several nations have magazines with circulations that exceed a million each issue, among them Canada, Finland, France, the Federal Republic of Germany, Italy, Great Britain, the Soviet Union, and the United States. However, not even in the United States, where two magazines have each maintained sales of more than 17 million, is the magazine with multimillion circulation typical. The number of U.S. magazines with circulations of a million or more grew from about twenty-five in the mid-1920s to about seventy three decades later. Although some publishers continued to push for huge circulations, the race for enormous numbers that began with the advent of television in the mid-1950s had all but ended by the late 1960s and early 1970s with the deaths of the *Saturday Evening Post* (1969) and the picture magazines *Look* (1971) and *Life* (1972). Of the four hundred magazines belonging to Audit Bureau of Circulations in 1979, 41 percent had circulations of under 150,000 and 70 percent under 500,000. Many of the new magazines in the 1970s and 1980s started with circulations of 50,000 or under. In France the circulations of consumer magazines in the early 1980s ranged from 10,000 to 3 million; the average for the specialized press was around 37,000.

Specialization. The specialization that characterizes U.S. magazines has become a feature of periodicals in many parts of the world. Although U.S. magazines have long been specialized, their editorial focus began narrowing after World War II. Increases in leisure time and disposable income gave millions of people the time and money to engage in a host of activities that had formerly been the perquisites of the privileged; television surely sharpened public interest in some of those activities. In the 1960s and 1970s editorial focus became even finer. For instance, the traditional women's home-service magazines were joined by periodicals for liberated women, university women, weight-conscious women, sports-minded women, health-conscious women, working mothers, military wives, and so on. On a less grand scale than in the United States, specialization affected parts of the industry in much of Europe, accompanied by the growth of magazines catering to hobbies and leisure activities.

Internationalization. After World War II magazine publishing took on an international cast, although a few publishers had essayed markets abroad long before then. *Harper's* published a British edition as early as the 1880s; its British rival, *Strand*, had a U.S. edition in the 1890s. In the 1920s and 1930s Conde Nast, Hearst, and Macfadden all issued magazines abroad. *Reader's Digest* began its international operations in 1938, Time Inc. in 1941. Other U.S. publishers got a taste of publishing on a global scale during World War II when a number of them brought out special overseas editions for the armed forces. From then on one U.S. magazine after another sought readers abroad.

In the early 1980s *Reader's Digest* had some forty international editions in seventeen languages. *Business Week, Newsweek,* and *Time* issued editions—mainly for government, business, and opinion leaders—in major areas of the world. The Soviet Union, whose domestic trade and technical magazines carried advertising from western Europe and the United States, exported periodicals in many languages to promote the sale of Soviet goods and the idea of Soviet trade.

A few publishers from abroad looked to the United States not only for editorial concepts but also for markets. In 1969 Robert Guccione brought his *Penthouse,* already a success in Great Britain, to the United States. Daniel Filipacchi, a major French publisher, unsuccessfully tried to revive *Look* in 1979. The British *Economist* in 1981 launched a North American edition printed in the United States. Gruner + Jahr of Hamburg, the Federal Republic of Germany's largest magazine company, in 1978 chose New York as its second publishing capital because of limits on expansion at home. Its U.S. properties included *Parents* and a company that printed more than a hundred magazines for other publishers.

Adaptability. Throughout its history the magazine has been a remarkably adaptive medium. It has adapted to what some observers once perceived as technological threats to its vitality or even its existence: the automobile, sound movies, radio, television. It has adapted to a shifting social scene and to changes in the nature, tastes, and concerns of its audience. Since the mid-1960s some observers have seen new ways of generating, storing, and disseminating information as ultimately diminishing if not eliminating the role of the magazine in the communications system. Once again the magazine will more likely adapt than perish.

See also PUBLISHING.

Bibliography. Elliott Anderson and Mary Kinzie, eds., *The Little Magazine in America: A Modern Documentary History*, Yonkers, N.Y., 1978; Benjamin M. Compaine, *The Business of Consumer Magazines*, White Plains, N.Y., 1982; David P. Forsyth, *The Business Press in America, 1750–1865*, Philadelphia, 1964; Walter Graham, *English Literary Periodicals*, New York, 1930; George T. Kurian, ed., *World Press Encyclopedia*, 2 vols., New York, 1982; Frank Luther Mott, *A History of American Magazines*, 5 vols., Cambridge, Mass., 1938–1968; Theodore Peterson, *Magazines in the Twentieth Century*, 2d ed., Urbana, Ill., 1964; Starch INRA Hooper, *World Advertising Expenditures*, 17th ed., Mamaroneck, N.Y., 1983; *Stern* Magazine, *Consumer Magazines in Europe*, Hamburg, 1981.

THEODORE B. PETERSON

MAP. *See* CARTOGRAPHY; GRAPHICS; MAP PROJECTION.

MAP PROJECTION

The transformation of a spherical surface (earth) to a flat surface (map projection) will somehow distort angular relationships, directions, and possibly sizes (see Figure 1). In terms of communication there are four categories of map projections with the following objectives:

1. To preserve true relative sizes of surface areas. Called *equivalent* or *equal-area*, they necessarily distort angles and shapes.
2. To preserve true angular relationships around each point although not among distant points.

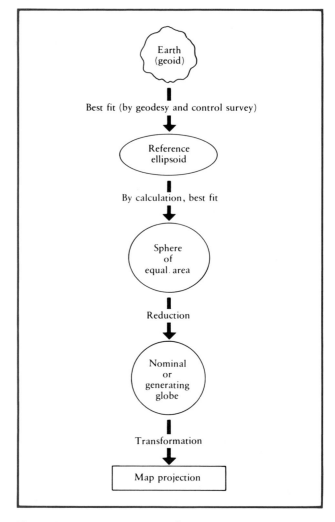

Figure 1. *(Map Projection)* The map projection process: the systematic rearrangement of the planet's meridians and parallels. Redrawn after B. D. Dent, *Principles of Thematic Map Design*, © 1985, Addison-Wesley Publishing Company, Inc., Reading, Mass., p. 45, fig. 2.10. Reprinted with permission.

Called *conformal* or *orthomorphic*, they necessarily distort relative sizes and most shapes.
3. To preserve true directions (azimuths) from one point to all others. Called *azimuthal* or *zenithal*, their property may be combined with either equivalence or conformality.
4. To present an acceptable image. Often called *compromise*, an imprecise term, they distort both sizes and shapes to some degree.

Equivalence and conformality are mutually exclusive. Except for precise measurements, the distortion in small areas in most commonly used map projections is negligible but is readily apparent in maps of large regions.

Map projections may also be described by the developable surfaces (can be flattened without stretching) to which the sphere has been projected in fact or in theory. Thus there are *cylindrical, conic,* and *azimuthal* (plane) projections, some of which are equivalent, conformal, or compromise. Equivalent or compromise projections that show the entire earth within a bounding shape, such as an oval, are named *pseudocylindrical.*

The projections used by the ancients, primarily for the celestial sphere, were azimuthal, developed by projecting the spherical surface to a tangent plane from some point. All great circles through the center of the projection are straight lines, and all azimuths from the center are correct. They began to be used for terrestrial maps in the fifteenth and sixteenth centuries, when the display of the sphericity of the earth was an important objective. Some azimuthal projections were used in the ancient world as well as today. For example, a *gnomonic* projection is from the center of the sphere, which is one's position when viewing the firmament. All great circles appear as straight lines, useful for a navigator laying out a course. An *orthographic* projection is from infinity, which provides the realistic effect of looking at a globe map. And a *stereographic* projection is from the point on the sphere opposite the tangent plane. It is conformal, and any circle or circular arc on the sphere remains truly circular on the projection. Since the sixteenth century other azimuthal projections have been devised, most notably one that adds the property of equivalence to the attributes common to the azimuthal class (see Figure 2).

In the fifteenth and sixteenth centuries the greatest achievements in geographical communication were cartographic. The writings of Claudius Ptolemy (ca. 90–160 C.E.) were introduced to Europe during the fifteenth century and made scholars and artists aware of the geographical coordinate system and of the problem of arranging the *graticule* (the system of lines indicating latitude and longitude) as a base for maps. Many projection systems were devised.

Sailing charts also began to show the graticule, but as perpendicular straight lines, usually spaced equally. These plane (or plain) charts were useful only for right-angle sailing, that is, either east-west or north-south. Any other constant bearing plotted on them as a straight line was incorrect because a *rhumb,* a bearing maintaining a constant oblique angle with the meridians, is a complex curve (*loxodrome*) on the earth. In 1569 the famous Flemish cartographer Gerardus Mercator (1512–1594) devised a projection on which all rhumbs plot as straight lines (see Figure 3). The graticule is rectilinear, but the parallels poleward are spaced increasingly farther apart to match the meridian expansion, with the poles at infinity. Mercator's projection (also conformal) has been employed for several hundred years for all nautical charts but is a poor choice for any other use

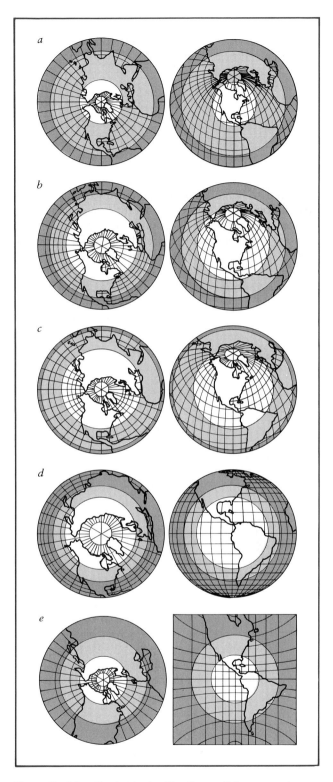

Figure 2. *(Map Projection)* The five well-known azimuthal projections, developed by projecting the spherical surface to a tangent plane from some point: *(a)* stereographic, *(b)* Lambert's equal area, *(c)* azimuthal equidistant, *(d)* orthographic, *(e)* gnomonic. Redrawn after A. H. Robinson, R. D. Sale, J. L. Morrison, and P. C. Muehrcke, *Elements of Cartography,* 5th ed., New York: John Wiley & Sons, 1984, p. 101.

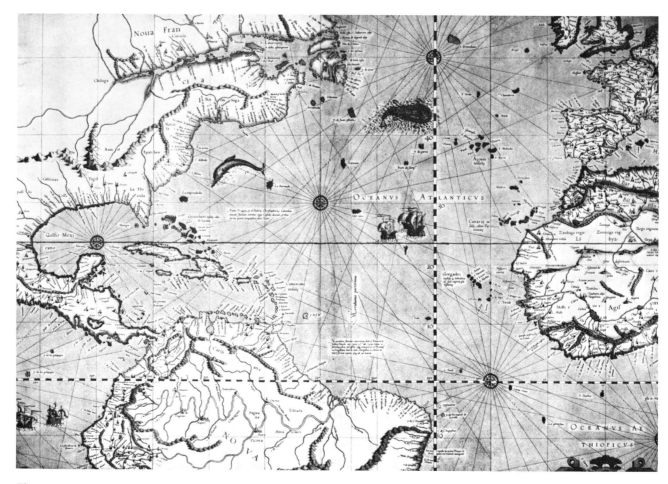

Figure 3. *(Map Projection)*   A section of Mercator's Map of the World (1569) in atlas form. Courtesy of the Library of Congress, Geography and Map Division.

because of extreme size and shape distortions in the middle and high latitudes. Nevertheless, it is commonly seen.

Since the fifteenth century interest in the subject of map projections has steadily expanded. Hundreds have been devised, and it is not uncommon for a new projection or a variant to be used for a particular map or map series (see Figure 4). Maps on which angles and directions are important, such as meteorological maps, air and sea navigation charts, topographic maps, and all maps showing rectangular grid coordinates, employ conformal projections. Maps

for general use, such as those in atlases, books, and census reports, usually employ equivalent or nearly equivalent compromise projections, of which there are scores from which to choose. SATELLITE images are on very complex projections.

See also CARTOGRAPHY; EXPLORATION; GRAPHICS.

Bibliography. D. H. Maling, *Coordinate Systems and Map Projections*, London, 1973; Arthur H. Robinson, Randall D. Sale, Joel L. Morrison, and Phillip C. Muehrcke, *Elements of Cartography*, 5th ed., New York, 1984.

ARTHUR H. ROBINSON

Figure 4. *(Map Projection)*   Three world map projections all derived from the same generating globe, ▷ that is, they are all the same nominal scale. Mollweide's pseudocylindrical projection (A) is one of many equivalent (equal-area) transformations that display all regions in their correct relative sizes. Unfortunately, equal-area projections that show the earth within a single shape, such as an oval, necessarily greatly distort some shapes. Mercator's projection (B) is conformal, and its unique merit is that all rhumbs plot as straight lines, an attribute of immense value for navigation. It grossly enlarges sizes and distorts shapes in high latitudes, and the poles are infinitely distant. Robinson's projection (C) is neither equal-area nor conformal. It is one of several compromise projections that attempts to achieve a balance between the distortions of sizes and shapes. Note, for example, the relative sizes and shapes of Alaska (586,412 sq. mi.) and Brazil (3,286,470 sq. mi.), Africa (11,677,240 sq. mi.) and the USSR (8,649,489 sq. mi.) in each projection. Graphic by the University of Wisconsin Cartographic Laboratory.

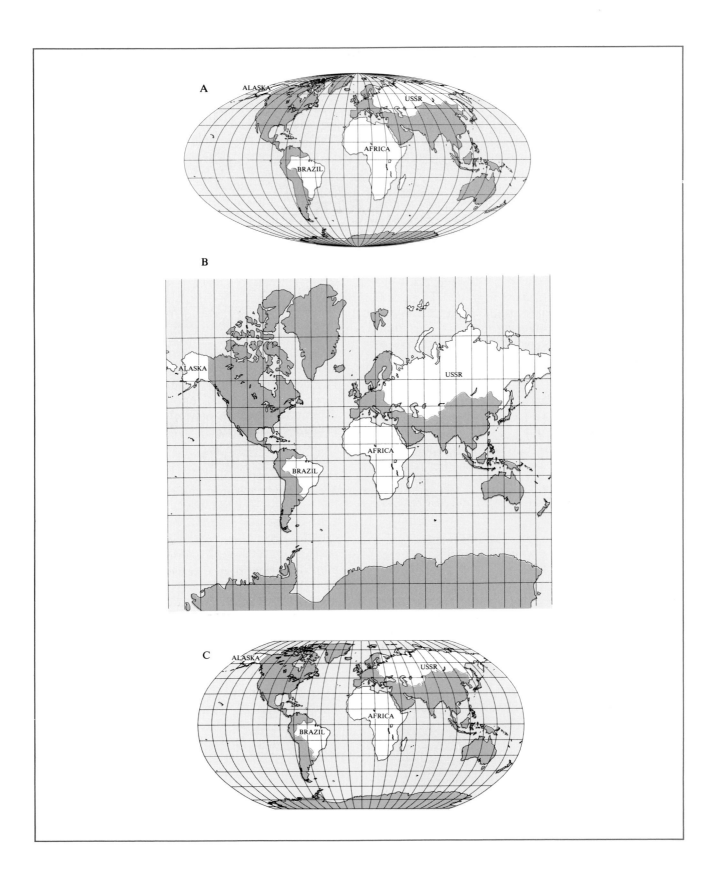

471

MARCONI, GUGLIELMO (1874–1937)

Italian inventor whose demonstration of wireless TE-LEGRAPHY set the stage for the development of RADIO and later television (*see* TELEVISION HISTORY). Guglielmo Marconi's mother, who was Irish, left home to marry the much older Italian gentleman her family had wanted her to forget. Guglielmo was raised on the Marconi estate in northern Italy and received part of his education from tutors. Rejected for admission to the University of Bologna, he busied himself at home with electrical experiments. It was a time of widespread speculation about electromagnetic waves—called Hertzian waves because German physicist Heinrich Hertz (1857–1894) had shown how to produce them via a spark leaping across a gap. It was widely theorized that the waves might be used to send messages, and numerous scientists were working on means to do so. At home, Marconi's activities worried his father, who saw Guglielmo doggedly moving pieces of metal around the estate, burying some and then digging them up. The youth was, in fact, perfecting something he called an *antenna* and testing the effects of grounding both his sending and receiving apparatus. By 1895, using Morse code dots and dashes, Marconi showed that he could send a message one and a half miles, and his father began to take his experiments seriously. Information about the invention was sent by letter to the Italian Ministry of Posts and Telegraphs. When it expressed no interest, Marconi's mother resolved to take her son and his invention to England.

Sir William Preece of the British Post Office, himself a wireless experimenter, perceived the magnitude of what Marconi had achieved and the implications for the British Empire and its far-flung shipping. Long-distance demonstrations on land and then off-shore quickly raised investment capital, and in 1897 the Wireless Telegraph and Signal Company, later renamed Marconi's Wireless Telegraph Company, was formed, with Marconi in charge of development. The equipping of ships and of shore stations to communicate with them was promptly begun. For the next twenty years England was the center of Marconi's career, but the Marconi enterprise quickly became international.

In 1897 the young inventor traveled to the United States, invited by the *New York Herald* to report the America's Cup race by wireless so that the *Herald* could have the news on the streets before the ships returned to shore. It became the sporting event of the year and also gave Marconi a chance to negotiate with the U.S. Navy and to form a subsidiary, the American Marconi Company, which would ultimately evolve into the Radio Corporation of America (RCA).

In 1901, sending the single letter *S*, Marconi achieved the first transatlantic wireless transmission. During the following decade he advanced wireless technology with many innovations: the tuning dial, directional antennas, magnetic detectors. In 1909, in recognition of his role in creating the age of wireless communication, he was awarded (jointly with the German Karl F. Braun) the Nobel Prize in physics. During the following years, and throughout World War I, military applications of his inventions were the chief focus of Marconi's work.

In the postwar period he played a part in the evolving technology of radio, interesting himself especially in the use of shortwaves and microwave relays to achieve global distances. He devised a worldwide communications system linking the British Empire. Marconi eventually settled in Italy and won numerous awards from his native land. At his death, in accordance with his wishes, he was buried at Bologna near the scene of his boyhood experiments.

Bibliography. W. J. Baker, *A History of the Marconi Company*, London, 1970; W. P. Jolly, *Marconi*, New York, 1972; Degna Marconi, *My Father, Marconi*, New York, 1962.

HARTLEY S. SPATT

Figure 1. *(Marconi, Guglielmo)* Guglielmo Marconi. Smithsonian Institution, Washington, D.C.

MARTIAL ARTS FILM

Popular film GENRE dating from around 1970 and featuring heroes and heroines skilled in the martial arts, particularly Chinese boxing, karate, and judo. Most early martial arts films were made in Hong

Figure 1. *(Martial Arts Film)* Bruce Lee, in *Enter the Dragon*, 1973. The Museum of Modern Art/Film Stills Archive.

Kong with Asian actors and settings, but they have been profitably exported throughout the world. The films are notable for their action scenes of mostly hand-to-hand combat, and the depiction of fighting is often gruesome and explicit. Chinese boxing traditions make use of hardened fists and feet, crushing grips, leaps, magic, and a philosophy of rigorous training and self-discipline, all ingredients that Westerners think of generically as kung fu.

Martial arts films have been termed the "cinema of vengeance" because revenge is frequently employed as a plot device. This allows the graphic depiction of VIOLENCE and permits the hero or heroine to exact retribution with self-righteous fervor, a sentiment the audience is encouraged to share. Sex is strikingly absent; only the most chaste romances are permitted, and female leads are almost invariably covered from neck to ankle in trouser suits. A recurring feature of the films is mutilation—blindness, amputation, severe wounds from which much time and training are needed to recuperate. Stories often require the main character to undergo a period of intensive study under a martial arts expert or master, learning the special techniques and advanced fighting skills needed to avenge a wronged family member or friend. Other plot elements sometimes introduced include rival martial arts schools, one bad and one good; the arrival of experts in other martial arts traditions such as Thai, Korean, or Japanese; and the acquisition of supernatural powers. In many of the early films principal villains were Japanese or Occidentals, indicating an appeal to a particular audience.

The genre has antecedents in Asian THEATER,

FOLKLORE, and literary tradition, but its immediate precursors were the Japanese samurai or sword-fight films (*Chambara*), which became an immense commercial success in Japan in the 1950s and, as wartime anti-Japanese sentiment receded, were profitably exported to much of the rest of Asia. Their emphasis on boldly drawn protagonists and on action rather than dialogue made them Asian versions of the popular "spaghetti westerns" and action films that they followed into the markets of the Middle East, Africa, and South America. The sword-fight film evolved rapidly from an early reliance on theatricality and obvious tricks. The American western (*see* WESTERN, THE) introduced an element of individualism in the form of the one-on-one duel, and it polarized the dramatic struggle into one between good and evil. These influences were apparent in director AKIRA KUROSAWA's classic sword-fight films *The Seven Samurai* (1954), *Yojimbo* (1961), and *Sanjuro* (1962), which owed much to the shoot-out tradition of the western film. Kurosawa's works established an entirely new style of "Eastern" western, and their worldwide success inspired many imitations in Japan itself, most notably a series about a blind swordsman called Zatoichi. The protagonists in these films were no longer the haughty samurai of historical fact but became instead the quirky individualists of movie myth, fighting for justice rather than privilege and using cunning and skill to achieve their ends. These characteristics were embodied in such STARS as Toshiro Mifune in the Kurosawa films and Shintaro Katsu as Zatoichi.

The early center of film production in China was Shanghai, but production began in Hong Kong when

Figure 2. *(Martial Arts Film)* Chuck Norris in *Forced Vengeance,* 1982. The Museum of Modern Art/Film Stills Archive.

the arrival of sound technology in the 1930s *(see* MOTION PICTURES—SOUND FILM) created a demand for films utilizing different Chinese dialects, traditions, and stars. The Japanese invasion of China and the 1949 civil war caused much moviemaking talent and capital to flee Shanghai for Hong Kong, which in the 1950s became a base for Chinese-language film production in several dialects. The market for these films was mainly among overseas Chinese in Taiwan, Malaysia, Singapore, Thailand, Vietnam, Indonesia, Borneo, the Philippines, and North and South America.

Throughout the 1960s, as business conditions in Asia boomed, Hong Kong film producers sought ways to break out of the confines of the overseas Chinese market. Dialect films were dying out, and fewer big-budget films were being made in Mandarin, the national dialect. After some attempts at coproduction with Japan and other countries it became apparent that action films were the key to success. Hong Kong filmmakers seized on the Japanese sword-fighting formula and began to vary it for Chinese audiences by introducing Chinese martial arts traditions and stars.

Just as Japanese stars Mifune and Katsu served to focus and enhance the tradition in which they worked, Chinese star Bruce Lee refined and became identified with the emerging martial arts film. Lee was only one star among many in Hong Kong—including Wang Yu, Lo Lieh, Angela Mao, Ti Lung, and David Chang—and his routines were often derived from other films. But Lee's films were the first to achieve crossover success in the North American market, leading to international publicity for himself and for the martial arts genre. The worldwide success of *The Big Boss* (1971) and *Fist of Fury* (1972) enabled Lee to write and direct *Way of the Dragon* (1972) and to coproduce his last film, *Enter the Dragon* (1973), with Warner Brothers. His sudden death in 1973 helped to make him a legend offscreen as well as on. While most martial arts films had been set in the past and derived characters and events from historical narratives, Lee's films used contemporary settings, and some of his villains were Westerners. Lee presented the forbidden to Asian and Third World audiences: the Oriental vanquishing the Occidental, nonwhite overcoming white.

Martial arts films draw on diverse traditions in theater and cinema, both Eastern and Western. Fight scenes are an integral feature of Chinese and Japanese popular DRAMA, yet although the combat techniques of the martial arts film are indigenously Eastern, much of their NARRATIVE style and character psychology derive from the American western. Just as westerns inspired Kurosawa's samurai films, which in turn spurred imitations in Japan and Hong Kong, the martial arts genre has fed back into U.S. popular cinema its characteristic elements of self-righteous revenge and exultant violence. Its influence can be discerned in the work of Chuck Norris, a world-class karate champion, who, after playing the chief villain in Lee's *Way of the Dragon,* carried the martial arts genre back to the United States and into a series of films showcasing his own talents and even into the phenomenally popular Rocky and Rambo films of Sylvester Stallone, which depict the hero's single-minded and ultimately successful quest for revenge.

Bibliography. Verina Glaessner, *Kung Fu: Cinema of Vengeance*, New York and London, 1974; I. C. Jarvie, *Window on Hong Kong*, Hong Kong, 1977; Marilyn D. Mintz, *The Martial Arts Films*, New York, 1978.

IAN JARVIE

MARX, KARL (1818–1883)

German political philosopher. Karl Heinrich Marx studied law and philosophy at the Universities of Bonn and Berlin, and at the latter he came into contact with a group of radical thinkers, the "Young Hegelians," who expressed a liberal intellectual opposition to the Prussian autocracy. But he soon became dissatisfied with the persisting influence of German idealist philosophy on their thought and with the purely cultural nature of their criticism. As Marx declared in an 1837 letter to his father describing the reorientation of his interests, he determined to seek "the Idea in the real itself," and from 1843 on he turned to the study of political economy as an indispensable foundation for a realistic theory of society and established his first contacts with the developing socialist movement.

The social theory at which Marx arrived, generally known as historical materialism, asserts that the crucial factor in the development of human society has been the growth of productive forces and the successive changes in the organization of labor and production, from which changes in the whole structure of society follow. The principal agents in this historical process, after the early stage of "primitive communism," when human beings first appeared in the evolutionary chain, are the major social classes—owners of the means of production on one side and those who contribute their labor, the "direct producers," on the other—and Marx and Friedrich Engels roundly declared in the *Communist Manifesto* (1848) that "the history of all hitherto existing society is the history of class struggles." Marx's subsequent life work was devoted to the analysis (mainly economic) of modern capitalist society and its development, the growth of the working-class movement, and the conditions for a transition to socialism.

Marx did not write systematically or at any length on LANGUAGE and communication. In his brief references to language in his early writings he emphasized above all that language, like consciousness in general, presupposes human interaction, and Engels later elaborated this view by relating the emergence of language to the development of human labor as a cooperative activity (*see* MARXIST THEORIES OF COMMUNICATION). Nevertheless, there are two aspects of Marx's thought that have an important bearing on communication. One is his conception of IDEOLOGY as a phenomenon that arises directly out of class divisions but also plays a partly independent role in sustaining the rule of a dominant class by helping to unify that class and creating a degree of consent among the ruled. Furthermore, Marx attributed great importance in the political struggles of his own time to the development of class consciousness in the working class, and this clearly involves the elabora-

Figure 1. *(Marx, Karl)* Portrait of Karl Marx carried in a parade of striking coal miners in the Borinage district of Belgium. From Henri Storck and Joris Ivens, *Borinage*, 1933. Storck collection.

tion of a counterideology, namely, socialism. All class conflicts, it may be said, are ideological conflicts in which rival worldviews, constructed through language and communication, confront each other. Some later Marxists may have overemphasized the critique of ideology or of CULTURE, at the expense of economic analysis, in what has been called the "dominant ideology thesis," but such critique has an important place in Marx's own thought, although it is not systematically developed.

A second theme that links Marx's ideas with communication is to be found in his discussion of the later development of capitalism and the transition to socialism. In the *Grundrisse* notably, Marx gives particular attention to the implications of the "knowledge revolution" in modern societies: "to the extent that large scale industry develops, the creation of real wealth becomes less dependent on labour time and on the amount of labour used than on the power of the agents which are set in motion. . . . Their 'powerful effectiveness' . . . depends upon the general state of science and the progress of technology." Later in this passage Marx notes "the extent to which general social knowledge has become a *direct force of production*, and . . . the conditions of the social life process have been brought under the control of the general intellect." In broad outline, therefore, Marx foresaw the development of automation and the advent of the "information society," but this aspect of his analysis of economic development has not yet received the attention it deserves.

Bibliography. Tom Bottomore, ed., *Karl Marx*, Oxford, 1979; David McLellan, *Karl Marx: His Life and Thought*, London, 1973; Maximilien Rubel, *Marx: Life and Works*, London, 1980.

TOM BOTTOMORE

MARXIST THEORIES OF COMMUNICATION

This topic is discussed in two articles:
1. Origins and Development
2. Third World Approaches

1. ORIGINS AND DEVELOPMENT

Neither KARL MARX nor Friedrich Engels wrote directly and explicitly on communication, but it is clear that they recognized the importance of specifically human means of communication through LANGUAGE and symbols. The distinctive feature of Marx's theory is that communication is essentially a social phenomenon in two senses: first, that language itself, like consciousness, presupposes human interaction and "only arises from the need, the necessity, of inter-

course with other men"; and second, that the communication of ideas and the transmission of CULTURE in all societies beyond the earliest tribal communities take place in a distorted "ideological" form because "the ideas of the ruling class are in every age the ruling ideas."

Language

The first of these conceptions was developed further by Engels in his unfinished essay on "the part played by labour in the transition from ape to man" (1876), in which he argued that "the development of labour necessarily helped to bring the members of society closer together by increasing mutual support and joint activity. . . . In short, men in the making arrived at the point where *they had something to say* to each other"; and he concluded that "comparison with animals proves that this explanation of the origin of language from and in the process of labour is the only correct one." Later Marxist writers generally emphasized the social and historical nature of language in opposition to theories (such as that of U.S. linguist Noam Chomsky) of an innate, biologically determined human capacity to speak a language. However, differences emerged between those who laid stress on the universality of linguistic structures, which could be related to work as a universal condition of human life, and those who conceived of language mainly as an ideological phenomenon that had, consequently, a class character.

In the USSR the conception of language as a class phenomenon that originates as a means of class rule and is determined in its development by class struggle was expounded by N. Y. Marr in the 1930s, and his views became the dominant influence in Soviet LINGUISTICS. Marr's views overshadowed those of MIKHAIL BAKHTIN, who also treated language as an ideological phenomenon but argued that since the same language is spoken by various classes, it is not determined by class struggle and is rather a locus within which class struggle takes place. Subsequently the preeminence of Marr's doctrine was ended by the publication of Joseph Stalin's article "Marxism and Linguistics" (1950), which argued that language lies outside the base/superstructure model and should be seen as a working tool that can serve different social systems.

In a different Marxist tradition the Hungarian philosopher and literary critic György Lukács suggested in his earlier writings (e.g., *History and Class Consciousness*, 1923) that the development of language might be studied from the aspect of "reification" and "alienation," and this approach has been followed by some later scholars. The Italian linguist Ferrucio Rossi-Landi, in *Linguistics and Economics*

(1977), begins by outlining a conception of the production and circulation of commodities and the production and circulation of sentences as being "the same thing," in the sense that everything that has value (and hence MEANING) is always a product of human work. In later chapters he analyzes the notions of "linguistic capital," "linguistic private property," and "linguistic alienation." He concludes with some comments on the programming of social behavior, which involves three conditioning factors: modes of production, ideologies, and programs of communication (verbal and nonverbal).

Rossi-Landi's conception has some affinities with the ideas of French sociologist Pierre Bourdieu and his colleagues at the Center for European Sociology (Paris) concerning "cultural capital" and the "pedagogic action" through which a dominant group or class is able "to impose meanings and to impose them as legitimate by concealing the power relations which are the basis of its force," thus adding a "specifically symbolic force to those power relations." More generally this work emphasizes the role of language and culture in the reproduction of an existing form of society, and the attention given to the processes of social and cultural reproduction is characteristic of much recent Marxist theory.

This focus is particularly evident in the theory of language and communication deriving from Marxism but involving a systematic reconstruction of Marx's thought that has occupied a central place in the work of German social theorist Jürgen Habermas. In *Communication and the Evolution of Society* (1979) Habermas establishes a clear distinction between "purposive-rational action" and "communicative action" and argues that both forms of action have played an essential part in the evolution of human societies: "We can speak of the reproduction of *human* life, with homo sapiens, only when the economy of the hunt is supplemented by a familial social structure. This process . . . represented an important replacement of the animal status system . . . by a system of social norms that presupposed *language*." His proposed reconstruction of historical materialism is summarized as follows: (1) the concept of social labor is fundamental, because the evolutionary achievement of socially organized labor and distribution precedes the emergence of developed linguistic communication; (2) the specifically human mode of life can be adequately described only if the concept of social labor is combined with that of the familial principles of organization; (3) rules of communicative action cannot be reduced to rules of instrumental or strategic action; and (4) production and socialization, social labor, and care for the young are equally important for the reproduction of the species. Thus the familial social structure, which controls the integration of both external and internal nature, is fundamental.

Habermas's basic ideas are developed more comprehensively in his two-volume *Theory of Communicative Action*, the main theme of which—the process of rationalization in modern societies—is related to a philosophical analysis of reason as embedded in language use and communicative action. His intention is to show the different forms of rationality of action by an analysis of the "interconnections of action orientations, types of knowledge, and forms of argumentation" and of the general contextual conditions in which discourse takes place. Habermas's argument makes possible an analysis of "systematically distorted communication" produced by the intrusion of power relations or other disturbances into the context of discourse (and there is a resemblance here to Bourdieu's notion of symbolic VIOLENCE) and also the establishment of a connection between the concept of society and the concept of underlying "life worlds" that are reproduced through the medium of communicative action.

Marxist conceptions of language have been diverse and in recent years have been strongly influenced by general developments in linguistics (including psycho- and sociolinguistics). Katalin Radics and János Kelemen have concluded that even though a Marxist theory of language (in several versions) gives primacy to the social character of language and to social communication, "this focus on the social character may be suspended in the course of devising a formal representation of grammatical structures" (*see* GRAMMAR). The question of whether a theory has a Marxist character, they observe, is not to be decided at the level of grammatical description "but on that level where our knowledge of human language is integrated with the totality of our knowledge." It is evident that in the past few decades language and communication, as elements in social reproduction, have acquired a much more prominent place in Marxist thought as a whole.

Ideology

The second major concern of Marxists with communication has produced a large and diverse literature on IDEOLOGY. Marx's theory of ideology was set out in *The German Ideology* (vol. l, pt. l), a joint work with Engels that was completed in 1846 but not published until 1932, and in a famous passage in the preface to *A Contribution to the Critique of Political Economy* (1859):

The totality of these relations of production constitutes the economic structure of society—the real foundation, on which legal and political superstructures arise and to which definite forms of social consciousness correspond. The mode of production of material life determines the general character of the social, political and spiritual processes of life. It is not the consciousness of men that determines their being, but on the contrary, their social being determines their consciousness.

Later Marxists interpreted this statement of the influence of the economic base on the cultural-ideological superstructure in various ways. Engels presented the "materialist conception of history" in a series of letters written in the 1890s to J. Bloch, C. Schmidt, Franz Mehring, and W. Borgius. After referring to different realms of ideology distinguished by their closer or more remote connection with the economic basis of society, he asserted that the production and reproduction of real life is the "ultimately determining element in history," not the *only* one, and emphasized that there is an interaction of the various elements in all historical situations.

Others in the first generation of Marxists began to study in detail particular spheres of cultural communication. In Germany Mehring published a pioneering work, *Die Lessing-Legende* (1893), which helped to establish a Marxist sociology of literature and of intellectual history; and G. V. Plekhanov, the "father of Russian Marxism," analyzed the socioeconomic influences on ART in *Art and Social Life* (1912), arguing that whereas art has a utilitarian origin in the needs of social life, aesthetic enjoyment eventually becomes a pleasure in its own right. A leading Austro-Marxist, Karl Renner, in his classic study *The Institutions of Private Law and Their Social Functions* (1904), reviewed the changing functions of legal norms in response to changes in society and more particularly to changes in its economic structure (*see* LAW AND COMMUNICATION). He claimed that law played an active part in maintaining or modifying social relations and was not a mere passive reflection of economic conditions.

However, Italian Marxist ANTONIO GRAMSCI developed most fully the idea of an independent influence of cultural communication in his conception of hegemony as the exercise by a dominant class of moral and intellectual leadership, the content of which is provided by those intellectuals who "give the class homogeneity and an awareness of its own function not only in the economic but also in the social and political fields." Gramsci argued that the relationship between intellectuals and economic production is not as direct as in the case of social classes but is mediated by the whole fabric of society, and that there is a gradation of functions and superstructural levels from the economic base upward. A major distinction is that between the sphere of civil society, in which hegemony is exercised as a means of securing the consent of the mass of the population to the general direction of social life imposed by the dominant class, and the sphere of state coercive power, which legally enforces compliance.

Two principal themes have emerged, therefore, in Marxist discussions of the communication of ideas, values, and ATTITUDES: the dependence of mental life on the "relations of production" constituted by the ownership of productive forces and the consequent class relations, and the (relatively) independent role of mental life in the reproduction or transformation of a form of social life. Much Marxist scholarship since the early studies by Mehring and Plekhanov has been devoted to analyses of the dependence of cultural products of all kinds—RELIGION, morals, law, art, and literature—on the economic structure of society. One major field of inquiry has been the "worldviews" of different classes, which Lukács analyzed in *History and Class Consciousness* in terms of the consciousness of the bourgeoisie and the proletariat. The attention given by Marxist thinkers to class ideologies stimulated the development of a general sociology of knowledge, largely through the work of German sociologist Karl Mannheim (especially in *Ideology and Utopia,* 1936). Lukács's work was also the starting point for the studies by French sociologist Lucien Goldmann. In *The Hidden God* (1956) Goldmann related the "tragic vision" expressed by Blaise Pascal and Jean Racine to the "closed situation," and consequent impossibility of effective action, of the rising bourgeoisie—the *noblesse de robe*—in seventeenth-century France. Later, in *Towards a Sociology of the Novel* (1964) and *Cultural Creation in Modern Society* (1971), he presented his views on the development of the novel and cultural creativity in capitalist societies.

In Lukács's *History and Class Consciousness* there was already a very strong emphasis on the quasi-independent role of consciousness and communication in maintaining, reproducing, or changing the existing form of society. It was expressed in the view (also formulated by V. I. Lenin) that a "correct" class consciousness of the proletariat, which is essential for a successful political struggle, can be brought to it only from the outside, by socialist intellectuals. This presents, in a stronger form, ideas similar to those of Gramsci about the important role of those intellectuals, organically related to social classes, who elaborate social doctrines that either sustain an existing culture or prefigure a new civilization. In recent Marxist thought the emphasis on intellectual and cultural processes in social life has become still more pronounced. Thus in the structuralist Marxism of French philosopher Louis Althusser a society, or social formation, is conceived as a hierarchy of structures or practices—economic, political, ideological, and scientific—in which the economic is causally primary or determining only in "the last instance" (in Engels's phrase), and the other structures have a large degree of autonomy. Ideology—the whole cultural realm excluding what can be defined as science—is conceived as the representation of "the imaginary relationships of individuals to their real conditions of existence" and as being "indispensable in any society if men are to be formed, transformed and equipped to respond to the demands of their conditions of existence." The construction and communication of ideology as a system of images, myths, ideas, and concepts is thus presented as having a vital role to play in every society, although the limits of that role are not precisely defined and the nature of economic determination "in the last instance" is not clearly explicated.

It is in the critical theory of the Frankfurt school, however, that consciousness and ideology assumed their most prominent and independent character as factors in social life, to such an extent that many commentators regard the later work of the school as a radical abandonment of Marxist thought. The fundamental themes of critical theory—the sustained attack on positivism and scientism in social thought and on the whole scientific-technological culture of the advanced industrial societies—were stated in essays published by Max Horkheimer in the 1930s and in his later work, in collaboration with THEODOR ADORNO, on the "culture industry" (*Dialectic of Enlightenment*, 1947). These themes were developed further during the period of the school's greatest influence in the 1950s and 1960s. In its last phase, and notably in Herbert Marcuse's *One-Dimensional Man* (1964), critical theory presented a conception of modern capitalist societies as being dominated not by a particular class but by an ideology ("instrumental rationality" or "scientism") and asserted a necessary connection between the domination of nature through science and technology and the domination of human beings. The strength of this ideology, according to Marcuse, has virtually eliminated the possibility of revolt and a radical transformation of society through its incorporation of the working class into the existing social system. A vestigial hope of emancipation is to be found only in the practice of cultural criticism and the appeal that a counterculture may have for diverse marginal social groups.

The idea of ideology as the most powerful force in assuring social cohesion and continuity by the pacification of subordinate and potentially rebellious groups has itself been vigorously criticized, and the successors of the Frankfurt school have in some respects qualified the doctrine. Habermas, in his essay on "technology and science as 'ideology'" (1970), argues that class antagonisms in the advanced capitalist societies have become latent but have not been abolished and that any reformulation of Marx's social theory needs to retain the model of forces of production and relations of production, though expressed in a different form as "work" and "interaction." In more recent writings, as indicated earlier, he specifies these two processes as being equally vital in the evolution of human societies.

Overview

The Marxist contribution to studies of communication has been important and influential, above all in raising questions and formulating theories about the social context of the production and diffusion of ideas and values in very diverse realms, from that of the mass media to the social relations in which science and technology are developed and applied. More recently Marxist thinkers have also contributed more directly to the analysis of language and discourse, again with an emphasis on the social context, and have entered more fully into current sociological controversies about the relationship between objectively constituted structures of society and the intentional actions of language-using human agents.

See also COMMUNICATIONS RESEARCH: ORIGINS AND DEVELOPMENT.

Bibliography. Tom Bottomore, *The Frankfurt School*, Chichester, Eng., and London, 1984; Pierre Bourdieu and Jean-Claude Passeron, *Reproduction in Education, Society and Culture* (La reproduction), trans. by Richard Nice, London, 1977; Lucien Goldmann, *Cultural Creation in Modern Society* (La création culturelle dans la société moderne), trans. by Bart Grahl, Oxford, 1977; Antonio Gramsci, *Selections from the Prison Notebooks* (Quaderni del carcere), ed. and trans. by Quintin Hoare and Geoffrey Nowell Smith, New York and London, 1971; Jürgen Habermas, *Theorie des kommunikativen Handelns*, 2 vols. (The Theory of Communicative Action, Vol. 1, trans. by Thomas McCarthy, Boston, 1984), Frankfurt am Main, 1981; Dave Laing, *The Marxist Theory of Art*, Brighton, Eng., 1978; Jorge Larrain, *Marxism and Ideology*, London, 1983; Herbert Marcuse, *One-Dimensional Man*, Boston, 1964; Katalin Radics and János Kelemen, "Linguistics," in *A Dictionary of Marxist Thought*, ed. by Tom Bottomore, Oxford and Cambridge, Mass., 1983; Ferrucio Rossi-Landi, *Linguistics and Economics*, The Hague, 1975.

TOM BOTTOMORE

2. THIRD WORLD APPROACHES

Marxist theories of communication fall under the general category of *critical theories*, which are characterized by a variety of approaches and contributors, many of them from the Third World. The periodization adopted below is somewhat arbitrary but useful for purposes of discussion. The chronological order in which theoretical questions appear does not mean that old and new theories cannot coexist and compete against each other (*see* CLASSIFICATION).

Communication and Wars of Liberation (after 1945)

The principal contribution of the Third World to theoretical reflection on communication springs from the communication practices of the many national liberation movements in Africa, Latin America, and Asia after the end of World War II (*see* AFRICA, TWENTIETH CENTURY; ASIA, TWENTIETH CENTURY; LATIN AMERICA, TWENTIETH CENTURY). The lessons to be learned from those practices are recorded in several important texts that show the strategic role information and communication have in the context of a general struggle against oppression. Some examples are the now well-known works of the Chinese leader Mao Zedong (1893–1976) and those of the Argentinian revolutionary Ernesto "Che" Guevara (1928–1967). Both leaders recognized the importance of information management and communication as decisive elements in the acquisition of power. Mao argued, for example, that "to overthrow the existing political system, it is always necessary, above all else, to create public opinion and to work in the ideological domain. It is thus that the revolutionary classes proceed as well as the counterrevolutionary classes" (*see* PUBLIC OPINION).

Perhaps because of its technical characteristics (transportability, ease of use, low cost, etc.), RADIO has played an important role in liberation movements. Frantz Fanon (1925–1961), a psychiatrist from the French Caribbean colony of Martinique, closely linked to the Algerian National Liberation Front (FLN), wrote in *This Is the Voice of Algeria*:

Before 1954, the radio was, in the psychopathological realm, an evil object, anxiogenic and accursed. After 1954, the radio assumed totally new meanings. . . . The foreign technique, which had been "digested" in connection with the national struggle, had become a fighting instrument for the people and a protective organ against anxiety.

La voix de l'Algérie libre (The Voice of Free Algeria) started broadcasting from Tunis at the end of 1956 and was followed in 1958 by *Radio Rebelde,* an initiative of Guevara, through which Cuban guerrillas provided support with broadcasts from the liberated territory of Sierra Maestra.

Every national liberation movement has produced its own analyses on the use of media (e.g., the POSTER, newspaper, radio, and film) based on the specific conditions of its struggle (*see* NEWSPAPER: TRENDS). This tradition extends from the Vietnamese war of liberation beginning in the 1940s against the French through FRELIMO (Mozambique Liberation Front)

in the 1960s to the Farabundo Martí Front in El Salvador in the 1980s. In this context the essential questions addressed by critical MODELS OF COMMUNICATION have been (1) With what classes and groups should one ally oneself to form a front of resistance? and (2) How should one establish links and define common interests with and between these classes and groups? The contributions of the various liberation movements to critical communication theory differ considerably because of the diversity of origin of these movements.

One of the most important contributions is rooted in the concepts of mass war, popular war, or the mass line, which inspired Mao in particular. Here communication becomes relevant mainly in relation to a decisive objective: educating, mobilizing, and organizing a whole people to participate in resistance. Unlike Guevara, for whom PROPAGANDA was to serve an immediate armed struggle, Mao placed communication within a more general cultural context. One of the issues Mao analyzed was the role of intellectuals (e.g., writers, artists) as mediators. In his talks on literature and art at Yenan (May 2, 1942) he discussed the links between intellectuals and other social classes within the perspective of a mass line. Like the Italian Marxist ANTONIO GRAMSCI several years earlier, Mao wanted to establish organic links between the people and the intellectuals (producers and transmitters of knowledge). This theme was to be at the center of the Chinese Cultural Revolution (1966–1969), during which sharp attacks on the social division of labor between intellectual and manual work were made.

Another major contribution of Mao was the rupture with the economistic tradition and class reductionism, which was the predominant theoretical outlook in the Communist world movement up to the 1950s. Mao tried to grasp the specificity of the anti-imperialist contradictions in terms that were different from mere class contradictions. Apart from class contradictions (capitalist–working-class antagonism), Mao analyzed another contradiction—the people on the one hand, the leaders or dominant sector on the other—and insisted on taking into account the changing composition of "the people."

The concept of mass war has had a profound effect on liberation movements throughout the Third World, particularly on those against Portuguese colonization in Guinea-Bissau, Angola, and Mozambique. From a communications perspective the contributions of Amilcar Cabral (1921–1973), head of the African Party for the Independence of Guinea-Bissau and Cape Verde (PAIGC), are important. Cabral defined the war of liberation as a cultural act ("a cultural fact and an act which is productive of culture") and analyzed the concept of *cultural identity* in all its contradictions. The need to take into account ethnicity and the diversity of groups within classes meant that the problem of cultural identity could not be reduced to class alone (as orthodox Marxism would argue).

Before the ethnic question became prominent through African revolutionary movements and the writings of their leaders (like Cabral's *National Liberation and Culture,* published in English in 1970), one of the few theoreticians to have tackled this problem was the Peruvian José Carlos Mariátegui (1895–1930) in the 1920s. A journalist and founder of a politico-cultural journal, *Amauta,* Mariátegui was considered one of the first Marxist theoreticians in Latin America. He criticized the eurocentric orientation of the Third International (1921) and what he thought was its inability to address the question of the Indian (80 percent of the population of the Andean countries) as a revolutionary figure. Through his criticism of the Western tendency to focus on the urban, industrialized proletariat, Mariátegui began to lay foundations for reflection on popular cultures.

Cultural Dependency (after 1960)

During the 1960s the second phase of critical communication theories in the Third World began to emerge. The construction of these theories followed three main lines: (1) criticism of the theory of modernization, (2) the emergence of dependency theories, and (3) the global critique of a functionalist sociology of the media (*see* DEVELOPMENT COMMUNICATION).

The first steps toward a Marxist theory of social communication in Latin America are closely tied to criticisms of the notion of development prevalent during the 1960s and to efforts to show the links between the processes of communication in society and evidence of foreign political domination and socioeconomic exploitation. Theories of economic dependency and the reproduction of inequalities between the industrialized countries (the "center") and the underdeveloped countries (the "periphery") were to supply the first models for analyses of *cultural imperialism*. This was seen not only as unequal power relations among countries in the production and distribution of cultural commodities (e.g., television programs, films, and books) but also as the imposition—explicit and implicit—of organizational models for the media. Subsequent analyses also have attended to the internal inequities existing in many Third World countries.

Among the Marxist and critical theories of communication produced in the Third World in the 1960s and the first half of the 1970s, works by Latin American researchers are the most prominent. Interest in this area can be explained as much by the level of capitalist "development" of the means of communication (Latin America accounts for more than 60 percent of Third World media, the greater part of it in private hands) as by the radicalization of many intellectuals linked to the popular classes. This helps explain why critical research circles in Latin America have had such a strong influence in the debates on a NEW INTERNATIONAL INFORMATION ORDER, which began in earnest during the 1970s. If this period can be characterized globally by an increased consciousness of the mechanisms of international subordination, one should not, however, forget the conceptual advances forged in other domains. The genesis of critical research in Latin American countries again provides a model.

The first center of critical research appeared in Venezuela in 1967 and focused on two concerns. One was linked to the world of journalism, analyzing the dependence of national media on international press agencies (Héctor Mújica and Eleazar Díaz Rangel). The other included the first studies of television, which questioned functionalist theories on the effects of the media (Antonio Pasquali, Marta Colomina, and Eduardo Santoro). Through Pasquali Venezuelan critical research developed its own epistemology, largely inspired by the Frankfurt school. In the 1970s the specific contribution of Venezuelan research was the idea of planning and developing national communication policies (Osvaldo Capriles and Alfredo Chacón). This idea would be refined through contacts between researchers and various social and economic actors capable of participating in the development of a national communication policy for Venezuela.

The second center of Latin American critical research appeared in Chile (Michèle and Armand Mattelart and Mabel Piccini) and Argentina (Eliseo Verón) around 1968. In the beginning European STRUCTURALISM (represented by ROLAND BARTHES, Louis Althusser, etc.) was an important influence, but it was not the only one. Historical studies on the nature of the local bourgeoisie and its hegemony over the media were carried out from 1969 on. In Chile the period of Popular Unity government (November 1970–September 1973) marked an increasing distance from structuralism. The principal activity during this period was no longer making ideological readings of the dominant media or demystifying the messages of power but addressing the question of what to do about the media. It was time to measure the inadequacy of orthodox Marxist theories on agitation and propaganda. The presence of a bourgeoisie that remained in control of the majority of the media forced researchers to pose new questions on the nature of mass cultural production. Studies appeared on genres, the ideology of professionalism in journalism, popular participation in the media, and the process of media reception (*see* SELECTIVE RECEPTION). In these studies, done between 1971 and September 1973, the receivers no longer were seen as passive consumers operating within a stimulus-response model but as capable producers of their own communications and decoders of messages on the basis of their own social experiences. This first phase of the formation of critical theory in Chile was inseparable from the context surrounding the creation of media under popular control during the Popular Unity government (workers' and peasants' newspapers, television programs open to popular participation, etc.). The coup d'état of General Augusto Pinochet marked the end of this phase. The second phase took off with the development of numerous analyses of popular cultures and popular resistance under the military dictatorship from 1976 onward.

The third focus of Latin American critical research is less localizable geographically, for it was to be found in many Latin American countries during the 1960s. It developed from a critique of the theories and policies inspired by *diffusionism*, particularly the policies applied within the framework of agrarian reform and the "modernization" of rural areas. The different philosophical and political theories had one common concern: to break with the vertical schema of diffusionist communication and to develop *horizontal* communication by using the experience of learners in the learning process. In the field of popular EDUCATION and LITERACY one pioneer stands out: the Brazilian Paulo Freire, who applied his ideas on consciousness-raising first in Brazil before the military coup in 1964 and then in Guinea-Bissau. His conceptions have profoundly marked pedagogical theories, not only in Latin America but also in Europe and North America. In the field of the media two pioneers of the critique of diffusionism have been the Bolivian Luis Ramiro Beltrán and the Paraguayan Juan Díaz Bordenave.

Major contributions were also made by researchers from other cultures during the same period, especially from Asia. Many were inspired by the philosophy of *self-reliance*, promoted by both MOHANDAS GANDHI in India and Mao in China. Theories of communication that acknowledge a debt to the philosophy of self-reliance have guided numerous studies critical of the expansion of advanced technologies, demanding respect for cultural identity and diversity. In India and Tanzania, for example, the notion of self-reliance has guided research on the question of appropriate technologies for developing countries and has provided the basis for a radical critique of development models in both East and West. This critique applies to both capitalism and orthodox Western Marxism.

Through the philosophy of self-reliance, popular participation has been recognized as a fundamental need on the same level as education, FOOD, and shelter. This recognition has implications not only

for the development of horizontal forms of communication but also for the very conception of research. In assessments of the research to be done, questions about the nature of the social actors under study have also arisen. With these questions in mind ideas of *research-action, participative research,* and *militant research* have appeared. This new methodological approach is counter to traditional research in which researchers see the people and/or groups making up the universe of their study only as sources of information and basic analytical data. In proposing the integration of the relevant actors into the very process of research, an old idea of Marx is revived: it is not enough to interpret reality; one must also transform it. Thus a new model of national development and national communication that is closer to local needs and resources has gained ground, as has a new perspective on international relations and relations among different cultures.

Popular Cultures (after 1980)

The studies carried out during the 1960s were characterized by the reliance on monolithic theories of power, of which the most prominent representative was the French Marxist philosopher Louis Althusser. By the 1980s Althusser's influence had faded in favor of Gramsci's theory of *hegemony*, a concept better suited to account for power as a site of negotiation, mediation, and construction of alliances between groups and classes. The determination of social uses for communication technologies has become the central question: What is the relation between the media and society? What is the link between construction of democracy and the system of communication?

These concerns fit in with the evolving strategies of resistance by specific social groups. In addition to the traditional organizations of the working class (e.g., trade unions, political parties) various social movements have emerged and have cut across class divisions to represent a new social consciousness: feminist, antinuclear, ethnic and popular movements, and others (*see* FEMINIST THEORIES OF COMMUNICATION). The appearance of specific movements broke up the centralizing tendencies characteristic of orthodox Western Marxism. In this context the demand for popular cultures arose in opposition to a single culture organized from above.

The concept of popular culture as it has been defined by critical research in the Third World should not be confused with its definition in the United States or with that of the functionalist sociological tradition that has equated popular culture with mass culture. Popular culture is here defined as a series of practices of resistance by groups and social classes that do not have the power to define what is to be the legitimate culture. These practices of resistance to a social order are also practices of construction of a collective identity and of new social relations. But while there is a large consensus on this basic definition of popular culture within critical research, approaches have been extremely varied. Because of its different shades of meaning popular culture is of interest to many disciplines: sociology, anthropology, history, linguistics, literature, and so on (*see* LITERATURE, POPULAR). However, because "the people" and "popular" are susceptible to numerous political interpretations, some have preferred to define *popular* in terms of so-called popular classes (workers, peasants). Others have gone beyond this exclusively class vision and have tried to define its multiclass aspects.

Beyond these differences the concept of popular culture has for some years guided a new type of study, especially in Latin America, on the consumption of the media. It has also oriented a series of analyses and experiments of popular participation in various technological media (VIDEO, computers, radio, press) and, particularly in Africa, has been behind the revival of so-called traditional media (THEATER, puppets, songs, folktales, etc.). Furthermore, the concept of popular culture has inspired renewed research on mass culture. The principal question has become how to set up within the capitalist media systems a dialectical exchange, albeit unequal, between popular culture and mass culture. Because of the issues raised by this question, new forms of research on popular genres in radio and television have begun.

See also COMPUTER: IMPACT; DRAMA—PERFORMANCE; FOLKTALE; MUSIC, FOLK AND TRADITIONAL; PUPPETRY.

Bibliography. Frantz Fanon, *Studies in Dying Colonialism* (L'an V de la révolution algérienne), New York, 1965; Elizabeth Fox de Cardona and Luis Ramiro Beltrán, *La comunicación dominada*, Mexico, D.F., 1981; Paulo Freire, *Pedagogy of the Oppressed* (Pedagogía del oprimido), trans. by Myra Bergman Ramos, New York, 1970; International Association for Mass Communication Research, *New Structures of International Communication: The Role of Research*, Leicester, Eng., 1982; Mao Zedong, *On Literature and Art*, Beijing, 1967; Armand Mattelart and Seth Siegelaub, eds., *Communication and Class Struggle: An Anthology*, 2 vols., New York, 1979, 1983; Tran Van Dinh, *Independence, Liberation, Revolution: An Approach to the Understanding of the Third World*, Norwood, N.J., 1986.

ARMAND MATTELART

MASK

The mask is used on all the continents of the world and has a long history. The English words *person* and *persona* derive from *persona*, the Latin word for "mask." Although masks are often admired as works of ART in themselves, their communicative character cannot be understood without considering their use, which is generally in PERFORMANCE, as part of a costume. They communicate meanings through transforming the wearer.

One can dispute whether people are masked when they put on makeup, or even dark glasses, which have also come to be used in some Melanesian and African masquerades, along with ringing the eyes in contrasting pigment. Formally comparable mask ensembles can be used for very different occasions. On the other hand, an African community's masking repertoire may include a mask that is never seen, but only heard, as an eerie cry in the night. It is possible to relate such different manifestations by comparing and contrasting the type of transformation intended and its degree of distance from ordinary humanity.

Masks very often seem to present a supernatural world by appearing and being used in ways that are taken to be nonnatural. Often the mask and its ensemble are both larger than life, and the FACE is oddly placed in relation to the body, as when a masker is covered in raffia and the mask is borne on top of the head. It may even disappear, the masker being enveloped in a cylinder of cloth. Maskers do not walk, but DANCE, or wear stilts, and may appear to levitate. They do not talk, but squeak, growl, or roar. They are believed to incarnate spirits, to be ancestors, deities, or mythical animals. When masks on their own communicate power, this seems derivable from their transformative and therefore recreative capacity. Some masks, for instance, embody ancestral powers when used by their descendants, rather like the effigies that in so many times and places have represented and therefore reproduced the dead. However, the French anthropologist CLAUDE LÉVI-STRAUSS has analyzed variants in mask DESIGN, along with other artifacts (*see* ARTIFACT), as significant of patterns in their communities, without referring to their transforming character in performance.

It seems that the face is the main point at which human identity is communicated, and communication largely passes through the face. If cognitive and affective growth depends on interaction, much of this comes from the imprinting on the infant of the speaking, smiling, or frowning adult face. Children also learn through their interactions with others that something hidden is still there (what psychologists have called the "peekaboo" phenomenon). This paradox is also a component of masking.

To change, replace, or obliterate a face by a mask signals at the least a change of identity. At the most, this real transformation of appearance is identified with a transformation of essence. The meanings communicated by donning masks differ between audience and wearers—since these at least must know who they originally are—as well as between individuals and cultures (*see* MEANING). Viewers may also re-

Figure 1. *(Mask)* Xipe Totec mask. Mesoamerican, fifteenth century. Basalt. Reproduced by courtesy of the Trustees of The British Museum.

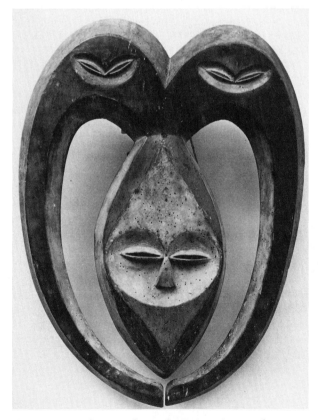

Figure 2. *(Mask)* Kwele mask, Zaire, nineteenth to twentieth century. Wood, coloring. The Metropolitan Museum of Art, New York, The Michael C. Rockefeller Memorial Collection, Bequest of Nelson A. Rockefeller, 1979. (1979.206.8)

spond to the detailed SYMBOLISM of mask ensembles, since this is a part, and sometimes a key part, of symbolism in the wider CULTURE. Face masks contradict the ordinary expressiveness of faces by their fixity, but this suits the communication of single, stereotypic aspects of personality. When animals are enacted, they are identifiable by selected characteristics in mask and in movement. Very often they too are spirits in a community's cosmology, mythical beasts or monsters. The overall shapes and movements of masked dancers may be more significant, communicatively, than the mask per se or its internal symbolism.

Maybe because masks in performance conjoin opposites, they often dramatize crossovers from one state to another, including life and death (*see* ART, FUNERARY). They may become ancestors, appearing from the world of the dead to connect with the world of the living. Masks are widely used in rites of transition, which move participants from one social state to another. They are used in initiation ceremonies marking the passage into adulthood. In Africa such masks may be represented as "living in the forest": they have a secret, nighttime side and are owned by cults restricted mainly or wholly to men; in their daytime manifestations, out of the forest into the community, they may also be taboo to women. Although it is often thought that illegal viewing may result in barrenness, women are sometimes allowed to touch masks in order to gain fertility. In the forest initiates may be "eaten" or "killed" by giant masks and required to crawl through the wearers' legs, signifying rebirth. Such rites present females as part of the natural world, males as part of human cultural achievement, while day and night are metaphors for openness and secrecy (*see* METAPHOR). Masks often deal with GENDER differences. Some New Guinean masquerades, for example, have been explained as permitting male display through the guise of animals.

Besides being used to induce growth and plenty, the arrival and departure of performing masks may effect periodic or seasonal alterations in a community's life. In West Africa, masks "come out" at stages in the agricultural cycle. Although mask use there as elsewhere is generally reserved for men, even if women are depicted, some communities in Liberia, Guinea, and Sierra Leone divide themselves into gender-distinct groups that alternately "rule the land" and initiate their members. Chinese dragons "beat the bounds" and clear the community's way to the New Year. When masks are used in rites of exorcism, as in Sri Lanka, they signal a special time for curing and act to transform patients as well. The carnivals of Europe and the Americas (which can include elements of African origin) mark a special time when everyday roles are set aside, and the world is turned topsy-turvy. Masks can be the signs of or means to larger-scale inversions in "rites of reversal," as when masters and slaves change places. Circus clowns, with their masklike painted faces and bulbous noses, offer audiences a holiday from real life, but serious rituals to transform participants' status may also include clowning as well as transvestism, obscenity, or other travesties. Is social order being reaffirmed or subverted?

Other mask events mock human efforts to classify and control. The masquerades so popular in eighteenth-century Europe freed participants from normally rigid conventions of class and gender relations. At masked balls or masquerading parties, guests put on dominos—eye masks—to signal the abeyance of social identity, just as they wore cloaks to conceal clothing that indicated precisely one's rank and gender. Plays and novels from that period suggest that the convention of masking afforded women in particular "unofficial" sexual freedom. The domino still serves as a sign of romance and discreet sexual adventure and evokes images of period glamour. Because it merely defamiliarizes the face, the domino is alluring rather than frightening.

Masks in rituals and carnivals rarely speak: they appear, and this is their message. When they are believed to be spirits or means of channeling supernatural energy and fertility to the human environment, the sounds they make may be interpreted by their attendants as authoritative messages. Some masks are considered embodiments of order and justice. In West Africa, young Okpella men *en masque* legitimately enforce rough justice. Medieval European mummers sometimes made their disguises a cover for real attack. Similarly the "portrait masks" of American Northwest Coast Indians incarnated ancestors and were used in healing rituals and by secret societies that danced enactments of cosmological myths at community feasts or potlatches. These performances apparently upheld the legitimacy of the existing social order, its ranks and limitations of privilege.

If one accepts that the superhumanness of a masked figure is an illusion, then one can see this illusion might benefit the mask's controllers. Clearly, masks have been and are used to legitimate human decisions and statuses, to instill fear in subordinates, and to keep women "in their place." These functions are aided by the rules of SECRECY that so often organize masking. Such rules exclude all but a few people from knowing how a mask assemblage is put together and can mean that others do not realize there are human wearers. The uses to which some masks are put cannot, however, explain their existence, still less all their occasions of use, for instance in FESTIVAL and carnival, where pretense is frank and social control is not a major aspect of a performance. Excluded outsiders do in fact very often know that men are dancing as masks and even who they are.

Figure 3. *(Mask)* José Rodríguez, devil mask, Acatepec, Guerrero, Mexico, ca. 1938. Carved and painted wood. Mask collected by Donald and Dorothy Cordry and presently in the Mexican Mask Collection of the Institute of Latin American Studies, The University of Texas at Austin. Photograph by Gibbs Milliken.

Figure 4. *(Mask)* Seneca cornhusk mask from the Six Nations Reserve, Ontario. Cornhusk and black fur. © Denver Art Museum 1985. Photograph by Otto Nelson.

◁ **Figure 5.** *(Mask)* Helmet mask of the Elema tribe of the Gulf of Papua, Papua New Guinea, twentieth century. Barkcloth, paint, raffia. The Metropolitan Museum of Art, New York, The Michael C. Rockefeller Memorial Collection, Gift of Nelson A. Rockefeller, 1958. (1978.412.725)

In seventeenth-century England the royal family and court acted in allegorical "masques," the most famous produced by Inigo Jones and written by such figures as Ben Jonson. Shakespeare's *The Tempest* includes both a masque and an antimasque, a frequently accompanying reversal of the masque's themes. These early musicals can be compared with other festivals and "triumphs" performed for the glorification of RENAISSANCE rulers, but here masquerading flattered the performers, not the populace, that rulers had superhuman virtues. For all their lavishness, these masques were simple in terms of plot and character, presenting typifications that are comparable to far more meagerly endowed performances of folk art, to the European commedia dell'arte, or to contemporary masking in Mexico. Such anonymous maskers claim authority through their roles, in which they often satirize contemporary conditions and mock stereotypic errors.

If masks are understood as a means of communication, we can see their suitability for what they are commonly supposed to do: support belief in ancestral spirits, effect social transitions, heal the sick, legitimate power or criticize it. We want to know what masks meant in past times, for instance in Greek and Roman rituals, but have only incomplete representations and references. The uses of masks, however, are so widespread, if varied, that they may be plausibly adduced. Masks are nevertheless not intrinsically necessary to achieve the stated tasks, which indeed are often carried out by different means, in communities otherwise comparable to those of mask users. Islam and Christianity, for example, are inimical to beliefs in the spiritual power of masks. With conversion to these religions, as with secularization, mask performances tend to become ENTERTAINMENT or are forbidden altogether. The abnormal and simplifying characteristics of face masks are more suited to the public displays of festival and carnival, or the huge arenas where classical Greek tragedies were solemnly performed, than to modern, naturalistic ACTING, though masks have been adapted to create Brechtian alienation, antinaturalistic and ritualistic effects in the THEATER.

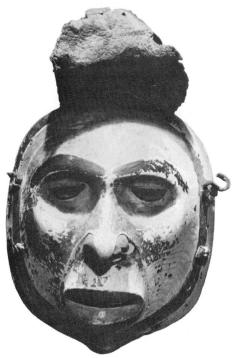

◁ **Figure 6.** *(Mask)* Tlingit Dead Man mask, Alaska, nineteenth century (?). Wood, paint, metal, leather. The Metropolitan Museum of Art, New York, The Michael C. Rockefeller Memorial Collection, Bequest of Nelson A. Rockefeller, 1979. (1979.206.440)

Figure 7. *(Mask)* Jacques Callot, *Bello Sguardo and Coviello.* Courtesy of the Library of Congress.

Figure 8. *(Mask)* Ku Klux Klan: two Klansmen during a night meeting on Long Island. The Bettmann Archive, Inc.

When masks are used to make actors collectively anonymous, they reverse contemporary individualist expectations, in which masks are assumed to hide the real personality, not to contribute a revealing transformation. Mask use always implies a philoso-

phy of personality, but not a single, specific one. In a fresh context, there will be reinterpretation, as when Westerners admire masks detached from their use to become aesthetically appealing MUSEUM objects. Yet among all the modern conditions that inhibit the power of some mask performances, maskers still create uncanny surprise, as at Halloween. The most frightening are terrorists in stocking masks. Such disguises create fear by the same means as helmets and monstrous visors in earlier times: they seem inhuman because they are faceless.

Bibliography. Donald Cordry, *Mexican Masks*, Austin, Tex., 1980; Alfred Gell, *Metamorphosis of the Cassowaries*, London, 1975; J. C. H. King, *Portrait Masks from the Northwest Coast of America*, London, 1979; Michael Leiris and Jacqueline Delange, *African Art*, New York, 1968; Emmanuel Le Roy Ladurie, *Carnival in Romans*, New York, 1979; Claude Lévi-Strauss, *The Way of the Masks*, Seattle, Wash., 1982; David Napier, *Masks, Transformation, and Paradox*, Berkeley, Calif., 1986.

ELIZABETH TONKIN

MASS COMMUNICATIONS RESEARCH

Research into mass communication belongs neither to any single academic discipline nor exclusively to the social sciences, although it has its center of gravity in sociology and psychology. The problems with which it deals are essentially those posed by the actual working of mass media institutions—the press, cinema, radio, television, and so on—rather than by any body of theory.

Certain basic and problematic features of mass

communication have shaped the field of research: the volume of messages transmitted, their public character, and their relevance to many aspects of personal and social life and to the working of modern societies. First, there is the problem of accounting for the output through a systematic description of what is produced and distributed (*see* CONTENT ANALYSIS). Second, because mass communications involves the dissemination of messages with little record of or control over reception, it is the task of research to supply the means of accounting for an audience that might otherwise be invisible and unknown (*see* RATING SYSTEMS: RADIO AND TELEVISION). Third, there are questions about the effects and the effectiveness of mass communication—what happens in consequence of the media and how well the media achieve their chosen goals (*see* MASS MEDIA EFFECTS). Although emphasis has been placed here on practical questions stimulated by an established and growing social institution, these seemingly simple and global questions have provoked controversy and theoretical activity as well as research.

If there has been any dominant or overarching theory, which is arguable, it has probably been a version of "mass society" theory, which emphasizes the power of mass media as high-status, remote, and one-way sources of standardized messages with considerable attraction for and influence on audiences. The main questions for mass communications research will be dealt with according to the threefold division established (at the risk of some distortion), because most questions eventually call for attention to all three areas. It will be readily apparent how numerous and interrelated are the subquestions that can be generated by the specified topics. To deal with each area, some attention must be given to the history of research traditions and to the variety of approaches that are in evidence (*see* COMMUNICATIONS RESEARCH: ORIGINS AND DEVELOPMENT). The variations of emphasis over time and place often reflect changing historical circumstances and climates of opinion, so closely are mass media related to their societies. British scholar Jeremy Tunstall suggested, with some justification, that mass communications research is essentially a U.S. invention, but such research activities, like the telecommunications institutions themselves, are now diverse and worldwide, and the salient questions for research quite often differ from one country or area to another.

Media Output Research

Two lines of research must be distinguished from the outset. One relates to *mass communicators*, their organizations, and the media institutions of a given society; the other relates to the *messages* made and sent. The latter has a somewhat longer history, which began mainly as an offshoot of effects research, in such matters as the power of the press to shape political events (*see* POLITICAL COMMUNICATION). This issue stimulated the wish to assess the degree and direction of editorial (or proprietary) influence in news reporting.

To some extent, content research was coextensive with research into PROPAGANDA in the early decades of the twentieth century. Subsequently, attention was directed to the analysis of MOTION PICTURES, RADIO, and popular literature (*see* LITERATURE, POPULAR) out of a concern with behavioral and moral effects in matters of crime, VIOLENCE, or sex. The motive was often that of social regulation, and in early content research there was a tendency to substitute the more available evidence of content for the largely missing evidence of effect—a confusion that later investigators tried to avoid. From the 1930s onward there has been a broader interest in the social and personal values disseminated by way of mass media, and in the implications for the quality of social and cultural life. An important early impulse in this direction was provided by the emigration to the United States of members of the Frankfurt school, including THEODOR ADORNO, Max Horkheimer, and LEO LOWENTHAL.

The arrival of content analysis as a field of research was marked by a classic statement from Bernard Berelson, in which he defined it as "a research technique for the objective, systematic and quantitative description of the manifest content of communication." Since then there have been major developments of theory and method reflecting two main and contrasting features: (1) the availability of computers to carry out the otherwise very laborious task of actual analysis, allowing elaborate multivariate studies of complex texts and large sets of data; and (2) a shift of emphasis toward qualitative analysis and a concern with latent or connotative MEANING. The latter has called for a revision of methods and a borrowing from the humanities, especially from SEMIOTICS and STRUCTURALISM (*see* LÉVI-STRAUSS, CLAUDE). The demands of qualitative analysis, particularly of nonverbal messages, have put a considerable strain on the concepts and methods of content analysis as envisaged by Berelson, because of the departure from quantitative and systematic procedures that is usually involved. In many respects, however, the scope and appeal of content research has been enhanced.

Aside from the fundamental matter of finding relevant category systems for media content, five research questions representing somewhat different concerns have been central:

1. Does content reflect or correspond to the reality of the society in which it originates, and if not, in which direction does it deviate, and whose or what reality is represented?
2. Which values are promoted or symbolically rewarded in content, and which are neglected or punished?
3. Does media information meet criteria of quality in such matters as objectivity, diversity, independence, balance, and accuracy?
4. Is there bias, whom does it favor, and what accounts for it?
5. More fundamentally, what is the essential structure of media texts and forms, and how is this related to the symbolizing modes employed in the surrounding culture?

The methods of content research are diverse and still developing, tending to distribute on a continuum. At one end content is broken up into units of meaning that can be treated statistically (as in surveys of populations), while at the other end a text or a genre has to be treated as a complex whole in which many meanings are encoded and require expert and sensitive decoding procedures. In consequence, the results of content research are almost as diverse as content itself, although a general conclusion is that media content does not and cannot reflect the society directly, but rather offers a selective view (or views) of the social world, shaped by the social and cultural context of production and by the presumed expectations and interests of the particular audience envisaged.

Research on Media Institutions

The tradition of research on media organizations appears to have begun with an interest in the special occupations that developed around mass communication, especially those of filmmaker and journalist. It was further stimulated by an awareness of the significance of the selection process that media interpose between the "social reality" and the audience (see SELECTIVE RECEPTION). This awareness was captured in the concept of the gatekeeper, a term coined by KURT LEWIN in the 1940s. A fuller consideration of media selection led to research into the whole process of production and to a concern with the many possible influences, not only on selection but also on the shaping of the message to meet the practical needs of the production process. These influences stem from several main sources: the culture and politics of the society expressed through pressure from other social institutions, the economics of the media operation, the technologies employed to col-

lect or transmit media content, the relevant professional and craft norms and requirements, and the specification of functions for the intended audience. The main questions tackled in research on media institutions are indicated by these categories and are closely connected with questions of content, since they relate primarily to the kind and degree of influence on the message sent.

Two other lines of research address questions of similar importance. First, there are issues derived from the relationship that mass communicators and their organizations have to their society (e.g., the degree of scope for creativity and independence for communicators within an organization, and the internal relations of conflict or cooperation among the various mass communicator roles). Second, there are questions concerning the relationship between the media organizations and the audience, especially how the latter is to be known and regarded. The methods of media organization research are mainly those of participant observation or surveys of chosen categories of media workers, although one should not forget the role of historical, legal, and political research on media policy and law (see LAW AND COMMUNICATION). Given that it is hard to generalize about findings, it has nevertheless become clear that media content bears strong marks of its context of production and that the latter is shaped by a network of formal and informal ties to the rest of the society.

Audience Research

The initial phase of audience research derived from the needs of the media industry to plan its activities rationally and to render account to advertiser, SPONSOR, or society. The need to quantify audiences for media with no sales or user record (initially radio) was rapidly supplemented by requirements to know much more about all media audiences. From an early point in the history of research, attention was given to the motivations of the audience and to the functions that media reception might exercise in the rest of social life. The name of one of the pioneers of mass communication research, PAUL F. LAZARSFELD, is closely associated with this and other kinds of audience research undertaken at Columbia University (New York) during the 1940s.

Aside from commercial requirements, an interest in special publics has developed out of a concern with social effects, and attention has been paid to the child audience and to other audiences based on group characteristics or particular kinds of content (see CHILDREN—MEDIA EFFECTS). While *quantitative* ratings (measures of audience size) have always taken first place in audience research because of their relative lack of ambiguity and their practical utility, there has been a persistent concern with assessing the *qualitative* response of the audience to try to discover the degree of, and basis for, attraction to many kinds of media output. Thus the purposes of audience research may be summarized as beginning with relatively "hard" matters concerning who attends to what content in what degree, and extending into "softer" areas concerning the motives for choices; the processes of selective attention, PERCEPTION, and interpretation; and the ATTITUDES and attachment of audiences to content and sources.

Early definitions of mass communication presented it as a somewhat impersonal, unidirectional flow from remote sources to many scattered individuals. Although much research into media consumption has incorporated this view and has been conducted much like other market research, an important strand of research has been concerned with the social character of audiences. Here the focus of attention is on the degree to which audiences interact internally, share a conscious social identity, have ties of attachment or loyalty to chosen media, and actively choose and use media content. A landmark in the history of audience research was the discovery that audiences do have an internal structure and may be stratified according to interest in particular content and to status relations affecting the relay of messages and influence (*see* OPINION LEADER).

Subsequent efforts in audience research reflect some of the concerns mentioned, especially the attempt to measure motivation and expectation and to grapple with the consequences of media fragmentation and abundance. The balance of power has shifted somewhat away from the sender and toward the receiver, and audience research problems are increasingly defined by the needs and interests of the receiver. The basic methods of audience research have not changed greatly over time, relying mainly on the survey of persons, the automatic recording of television reception, and the keeping of media time-budget diaries, but there has been much conceptual and methodological development in the area of audience motivation and satisfaction. Researchers have tried to establish the reasons for media use, the expected or obtained satisfactions, and the application of what is gained from media to other areas of social experience. This so-called uses-and-gratifications research tradition has connections with content as well as effects research, because it offers a way of categorizing (according to the audience's type of motive or satisfaction) and may identify intervening variables for studying media effects (given that certain audience motives may be a precondition of certain effects). The results of audience research are largely to be found in the many quantitative descriptions of audiences, but there has also been a growth in understanding of the determinants and functions of media reception.

Media Effects Research

Neither the basic problems nor the methods of media effects research have changed greatly over several decades. Problems include all manner of responses to media content, especially those that concern change or reinforcement in line with the direction of messages (*see* PERSUASION). Methods are still mainly those of the experiment or the survey of audience and content, by way of which correspondences can be sought between the message and the knowledge, beliefs, attitudes, and opinions of the receiver. What has changed, however, are ideas about the processes at work and about the ways in which media effects are likely to be manifested. In turn, this carries certain implications about methods of inquiry.

Early research sought to establish simple correspondences between media stimuli and immediate responses. It was quickly discovered that the relationship between message (as sent and apparently received) and response (as observed) is always mediated by numerous conditions that can affect the outcome. These conditions have to do with characteristics of the source, of the message itself, of the channel, of the receiver, and of the context of reception. Without knowledge of such variables, no prediction or interpretation of effect is possible, and each potential effect situation is in some respects unique. Most early research concentrated on small-scale experiments of persuasive influence in which media presentation (source) variables could be manipulated or of campaign situations thought of as field experiments in which many variables could be studied simultaneously. Experiments produced more precise information but little basis for generalization outside the laboratory. The more naturalistic settings of the campaign revealed the working of processes of relay and diffusion from message to effect, involving those variables of context and audience structure already noted.

The campaign is itself only one of numerous ways in which potential influence reaches the media public. The phenomena that have received the most attention reflect the dominant expectations and fears in relation to mass communication: various kinds of campaigns, including political (*see* ELECTION), commercial, and public information; use of media for EDUCATION and training (*see* AUDIOVISUAL EDUCATION); the promotion of development, especially in rural areas and the Third World (*see* DEVELOPMENT COMMUNICATION); the possible effects of media on behavior and attitudes in issues like aggression or criminality; and the socialization of the young (*see* CHILDREN—DEVELOPMENT OF COMMUNICATION).

Research in all these areas continues to take place, modified by a greater awareness that all kinds of content can have a wide range of effects, often unintended or unpredicted.

A landmark in the history of effects research was provided by Joseph Klapper's (1960) assessment of the field, in which he placed a good deal of emphasis on the selective role of the audience in any effect process and assessed the media as more likely to reinforce than to change or convert. Research findings indicating that INTERPERSONAL COMMUNICATION and DIFFUSION can play an important part in the flow of information and influence made a contribution to this assessment. The so-called limited-effects model of the media has been much debated and modified in the ensuing years, but subsequent theory and research have given support to something more like the original version of the media as a powerful mechanism of change and control in society, albeit often in indirect or concealed ways.

The grounds for this revision may be explained by recalling several observations supported by research. First, media of all kinds generally carry messages having other sources of social support. Second, effects often show themselves in the long run and may be missed by relatively short-term experiments or surveys. Third, the basis for effect is often cognitive rather than affective, irrational, or directly behavioral. The media provide a certain range of materials that contain information and ideas about the social environment and about values, norms, and opinions. The audience can fashion a view of the world and a set of values and opinions from these materials. The media can also offer models for social behavior (see SOCIAL COGNITIVE THEORY). They tell their publics about wider relations of power and status in society. The ubiquity, volume, and relative consistency of this flow of messages make some influence probable, especially where alternative sources are few and dependency on the media is great. Because the media have become a legitimate institution for recognizing social status and directing attention in society, they can have an influence on the standing of other institutions and of social groups. Fourth, the media have increasingly provided the channels of communication for other institutions, such as the political system, and are consequently involved with other lines of force in society. Finally, the culture made and disseminated by mass media has come to be the culture of the society, or of most of its members. It is now necessary to acknowledge long-term institutional and cultural effects as well as effects on individuals. All this imposes a strain on a research apparatus that has been developed mainly for short-term studies of individuals and aggregates, and presents a challenge that has not yet been fully met. Some attempts to grapple with it can be seen in projects concerned with CULTURAL INDICATORS and "cultivation," which seek to measure the significant features of the media "message system" and to relate changes in this to changes over time in society, culture, and opinion (see CULTIVATION ANALYSIS).

Divisions and Directions

Not surprisingly, mass communication research is not only diverse but also subject to internal debate and conflict about problem definitions, methods, and the interpretation of findings. A small number of principal dimensions structure the field and can be briefly described. One concerns the choice between more subjective, cultural, and humanistic approaches and those that are more objective, scientific, and quantitative. The difference affects choice of problem as well as of method. Adherents of the former approach pay more attention to content, culture, and meaning, while those of the latter tend to concentrate more on the measurement of audience and effects. A second dimension separates those who put more weight on the media themselves as prime movers from those who emphasize society and social structure as determinants of whatever influence mass communication may exert. To hold the former view implies an emphasis on the medium and the message, and the attachment of significance to the sensory characteristics of the vehicle by which messages arrive—to print or to electronic media as such, as did the Canadian scholars HAROLD INNIS and MARSHALL MCLUHAN.

A third, more ideological division derives from alternative philosophies of society and political theories. On the one hand, the media may be regarded as a rather unified, hegemonic instrument of power for a dominant elite or class; on the other, as a pluralistic system, responding to multiple and changing needs of society and public. The former view is represented in some early mass society theory (e.g., in the work of C. Wright Mills) and in more recent Marxist versions of media theory (see MARXIST THEORIES OF COMMUNICATION). There are implications for research in that the "dominant media" view directs attention to questions of ownership, control, and ideology in messages, while the "pluralist" view pays more attention to differential audience choice, use, and response.

In the history of mass communication research, certain other divisions have surfaced, of which the most significant may be that between what Lazarsfeld termed *critical* and *administrative* research. The former stresses the role of the researcher as independently representing the interests of society or a chosen theory; the latter refers to work directed at assisting and evaluating the work of the media, usually from within media organizations themselves. Both kinds of research continue to coexist, using similar methods often enough but separated sharply by purpose. At some point the question "Research for what?" has to be addressed. The alternative answers lead researchers in different directions and, often, to different conclusions.

The main challenges and choices facing mass communication research may be briefly summarized. The first concerns changes taking place in the media, as they multiply and take new, often less "massive" forms, posing new problems for studying a more diversified media institution, output, and audience. These problems are both conceptual and methodological. A second issue is that of the internationalization of media, requiring a shift of focus from a local or national level to media research on questions of global political and social change. Here the international flow of information and possibilities of "cultural imperialism" are the main objects of attention (*see* NEW INTERNATIONAL INFORMATION ORDER). Third, there are more vocal demands by minorities and social groups and more access and control of media channels, and research is often associated with these demands (*see* MINORITIES IN THE MEDIA). Fourth, the inextricable involvement of mass communication with other social institutions tends increasingly to invalidate the boundaries that have been drawn around this research field. *Mass* communication research is no longer easy to keep separate from other kinds of communication research or from wider questions of social life.

See also AGENDA-SETTING; CONSUMER RESEARCH; PRINT-AUDIENCE MEASUREMENT.

Bibliography. Bernard Berelson, *Content Analysis in Communication Research*, Glencoe, Ill., 1952, reprint New York, 1971; Elihu Katz and Paul F. Lazarsfeld, *Personal Influence*, Glencoe, Ill., 1955; Joseph Klapper, *The Effects of Mass Communication*, Glencoe, Ill., 1960; C. Wright Mills, *The Power Elite*, New York, 1956; Jeremy Tunstall, *The Media Are American*, New York, 1977.

DENIS MCQUAIL

MASS MEDIA. *See* CABLE TELEVISION; MAGAZINE; MINORITIES IN THE MEDIA; MINORITY MEDIA; MOTION PICTURES; NEWSPAPER: HISTORY; NEWSPAPER: TRENDS; RADIO; TELEVISION HISTORY.

MASS MEDIA EFFECTS

Although empirical research on mass communications is traditionally divided into studies of audiences, content, and effects (*see* MASS COMMUNICATIONS RESEARCH), the predominant concern is with effect. In this view, audience research and CONTENT ANALYSIS are efforts to infer the likely effects of a message

or medium from its RHETORIC and its reach. Such inferences, however, tend to attribute more power to the media than empirical studies of effect are able to substantiate. Nor do these studies support popular belief—shared by politicians and advertisers—that the media are able to change the minds of ("brainwash") vast numbers of people. Rather, empirical research is generally satisfied with evidence that the media are effective under certain conditions ("indirect" effects) and only on some fraction of the audience, not so much by "conversion" as by "reinforcement" or "activation" ("limited" effects). Such influence on even 1 percent of smokers or voters or consumers, for example, implicates large numbers of people and may be of considerable social significance (*see* CONSUMER RESEARCH).

Research Traditions

Early empirical research sought to measure the effectiveness of media campaigns. These campaigns were thought capable of directing the atomized, alienated individual in the mass society in what to think, choose, or do (e.g., to make a decision between candidates for political office or consumer products or to look with favor or disfavor on a cause such as intergroup tolerance, the United Nations, or a wartime enemy). When these hypothesized effects proved to be elusive, researchers turned their attention to specifying (1) the complexities of the influence process, that is, the conditions of greater and lesser effect, and (2) alternative conceptualizations of effect. The history of the field may be read as a persistent search for effects that better describe the social roles of the mass media. Thus successive traditions of media research have considered whether the media can tell us *what* to think, *with what* to think, *when* to think, *who* should think, what to *believe*, what to *think about*, *how* to think, what *not* to think, *where* to belong, and what to *feel* (see Table 1). The search for alternative conceptualizations of effect is motivated, at least in part, by the belief that more adequate conceptualizations will unveil more powerful effects. *See* COMMUNICATIONS RESEARCH: ORIGINS AND DEVELOPMENT.

Persuasion studies. The view of mass communications as agencies of PERSUASION found that media influence is mitigated (sometimes enhanced) by the rhetoric of message and of medium; by the "defensive" behavior of audiences in their selective exposure, perception, and retention of messages (*see* SELECTIVE RECEPTION); and by the networks of interpersonal relations (*see* NETWORK ANALYSIS) in which opinions, ATTITUDES, and actions are anchored and diffused. In the course of specifying these intervening variables early work made plain that the process of media influence was less total (exposure is selective),

Table 1. Summary Descriptions of Media Effect Traditions

Research Tradition	Image of Audience Member	Societal Context	The "Text"	Basis of Involvement	Hypothesized Effects		Theory Roots	Typical Method	Key Question	Some Basic References
					Individual	Societal				
campaign studies	atomized decision maker	mass society	persuasive appeals	ubiquity of message; consonance of appeal	change opinion, action	mobilization, participation, control	social, behavioral psychology	field experiment; panel survey	what to think, choose, do (short term)	Hovland, Janis, Kelley (1953); Klapper (1960)
gratifications; dependency	active seeker; multiple needs, roles	differentiated, pluralistic	resource material; "toolbox"	needs, interests, dependency	gratify needs, interests; unanticipated effects	societal stability	functional sociology	retrospective survey	with what to think; from what to choose	Blumler & Katz (1974); Ball-Rokeach & DeFleur (1982)
diffusion	active seeker	social networks	information, innovation	need to keep up	improve situation or status	evolutionary change, development	rural sociology, anthropology, epidemiology	ethnography; retrospective and sociometric survey; measures of time of adoption	when to think	Rogers (1983); Katz, Levin, and Hamilton (1963)
knowledge gap	information processor	stratified	instrumental information	needs, interests, problems	gain information	widen social gap	cognitive psychology	field experiment	who should think	Tichenor et al. (1970)
child socialization	tabula rasa; seeks adult status	other socializing agents	role models, values	identification	crystallize beliefs, behavior, self-concept	societal stability, reproduction	sociology, social psychology	longitudinal survey	what to believe, how to behave (long term)	Comstock et al. (1978); Wright (1986)
agenda-setting	citizen	forum of public opinion	social issues	need for orientation	revises, adopts agenda	shared social focus	political science; journalism	content analysis, survey	what to think *about*	McCombs (1981)
technological	information processor	social formations	media attributes, codes	ubiquity of medium; participation in decoding	patterns of thought, personality	social organization; integration	technological determinism; humanities	neuropsychology; historical research	how to think, where to belong	Innis (1951); McLuhan (1964); Eisenstein (1979)
ideological (critical)	passive, atomized	mass society	hegemonic	need for orientation, belonging, escape	accept hegemonic reality; false consciousness, reassurance	legitimate status quo; control	neo-Marxism	message analysis	what not to think	Horkheimer & Adorno (1972); Gouldner (1976)
psychoanalytic (cinema); textual	regressive, lonely voyeur	malaise, discontent	teasing, nonstop flow	need for identification; escape	frustration; vicarious pleasure; arousal; identity	consumerism	psychoanalysis (Lacan); symbolic interactionism; humanities	introspection, content analysis; experiment	what to feel	Tannenbaum (1980); Metz (1982); Horton & Wohl (1956); Houston (1984)
sociological	role in institution, class; demography	differentiated	social reality; conflict management	membership	belong; conform	social integration, consensus, control	Durkheim, symbolic anthropology	survey	where to belong (with whom to think)	Lazarsfeld & Merton (1948); Lang and Lang (1984)

less direct (response is contingent on others), and less immediate (influence takes time) than had been assumed. Theoretical room had to be made for the countervailing power of individual selectivity and interpersonal relations—two of the most elementary processes of social psychology—and for time (*see* INTERPERSONAL COMMUNICATION).

In addition to yielding only limited and indirect effects, early studies prematurely narrowed the concept of effect to the success of (1) persuasive messages (2) on the opinions (3) of individuals (4) in the short run. Research concentrated on the message rather than the medium; on purposive influence rather than information, IDEOLOGY, or ENTERTAINMENT; on isolated individuals rather than small groups (*see* GROUP COMMUNICATION) or social institutions; and on the short run rather than the long run.

Uses and gratifications. Alternative conceptualizations are evident in two other traditions of work known as "uses and gratifications" and DIFFUSION. Both follow from and react against the assumptions of campaign studies. Gratifications research builds directly on the notion of selectivity, adding that viewers choose messages and media not only to defend prior opinions and habits but also to satisfy needs, interests, and strivings. The use of the media for escape, for the achievement of social mobility, or for reassurance are examples of the foci of this work, which links communications research with the study of popular culture. Studies of the gratifications provided by the SOAP OPERA, for example, anticipated current humanistic interest in the genre of television as a focus for problems of identity, gender conflict, and even our anxiety about survival. The world, says the soap opera, will continue, albeit from crisis to crisis.

The media are seen here as a social utility and the "reader" (receiver) as a selective consumer. The earliest work in this tradition coincided with the earliest campaign studies but became more central as greater power came to be attributed to the audience. Whereas campaign studies see the media as a force-feeder, gratifications researchers see the media as a cafeteria or "toolbox." Methods of the former are field experiments, panels, and before-and-after surveys; the latter use retrospective interviews that credit audiences with high self-awareness. Rooted in FUNCTIONAL ANALYSIS, gratifications research has contributed to the proposition (see below) that the nature of the involvement, role, or dependency in which "readers" contact the media constrains uses, gratifications, and potential effects.

Diffusion. Gratifications research may be said to build on the notion of cognitive selectivity, but diffusion research builds on the idea that interpersonal networks filter media messages and influence their interpretation and evaluation. Studies of the diffusion of new fashions, products, technologies, and ideas show how the media stimulate awareness of an innovation over time, space, and social structure and trigger interest in other sources of influence in the adoption process. Diffusion studies shifted attention from the individual to the small group of interacting individuals and, to a certain extent, to characteristics of the larger society such as stratification or centralization that affect the flow of influence. This work also reconnected the study of mass communication with the more traditional communications concerns of disciplines such as anthropology, archaeology, history of religion, and epidemiology. If campaign studies may be said to address the proposition that the media can tell us *what to think*, diffusion studies suggest that the media tell us *when to think*—when it is our turn to be in fashion, for example—and gratifications research proposes that the media tell us from what to choose or *with what to think*.

The knowledge gap. Two further traditions of work on effect that are also anchored in the intervening variables of selectivity and interpersonal relations, respectively, are "knowledge-gap" studies and research on the role of the media in socialization. Knowledge-gap studies explore the possibility that the media may widen rather than narrow the information differential between social classes. Researchers, therefore, are particularly interested in the role of the knowledge-gap phenomenon in perpetuating inequality and in the conditions under which gaps may be overcome. Knowledge-gap studies may be said to address the proposition that the media tell us *who should think*.

Socialization. Socialization studies address the questions of *what to believe* and *how to behave*, framed in the long run and as a function of the interaction among media and other agents of socialization such as parents (*see* FAMILY), peers, and teachers (*see* POLITICAL SOCIALIZATION). Thus, for example, learning from television is enhanced if CHILDREN view with a parent or are members of certain types of families. Some researchers in this area are convinced that there is evidence to warrant the attribution of direct effects, given the primacy of children's experience with the media. It is argued, for example, that a diet of television programs that feature incidents of VIOLENCE increases the likelihood of aggressive behavior in both the short run and the long. Evidence on the effect of media depiction of real and fictional violence—especially "justified" aggression, as in prizefights or retaliation—argues for a small but significant modeling or imitative effect, tempered, however, by factors such as social approval. *See* SOCIAL COGNITIVE THEORY.

Because each of these traditions of research has had to account for factors that intervene between a message and the targeted attitude or action, they are called models of limited or indirect effects. By contrast, three other traditions of work have proposed models of direct (i.e., unmediated) effects. They are AGENDA-SETTING studies, technology studies, and ideological studies.

Agenda-setting. Agenda-setting studies address the proposition that the media tell us *what to think about.* Broadly defined, the power of the media to focus and shift public attention underlies concepts such as "status conferral," "media amplification," "moral panics," and "media events," as well as the idea that the media—not only the news—constitute a forum or bulletin board in which society's central issues are aired for consideration. Agenda-setting, in turn, affects decision making. The evaluation of a candidate for political office, for example, may be influenced by whether domestic or foreign-policy issues dominate the agenda. As in diffusion research, a measure of time is needed to establish priorities among the agendas of the media, the political parties, and the public. See POLITICIZATION.

At first it was supposed that such effects would not be affected by prior personal and interpersonal commitments, but this is not the case. Media agendas are more acceptable to those in "need of orientation," and media are more successful in mobilizing attention to issues that are not salient in the personal lives of the public. Agenda-setting studies, therefore, are better classified as a tradition of limited effects.

The technological approach. Technological theorists such as MARSHALL MCLUHAN, on the other hand, believe that for any epoch the predominant medium of communication powerfully shapes personality and social structure by enlisting a particular mental regimen to process the information encoded in the technology. Thus decoding of print is said to lead to sequential thinking, which involves notions of before and after, causality, rationality, and—because linear decoding takes time—deferred gratification. In other words, the media are said to teach us *how to think.* Because the medium rather than its content is the causal agent, the defensive processes that intervene in the flow of messages are theoretically irrelevant. Technological theories positing long-term effects on mind and society have not been the subject of much empirical research on individuals.

At the level of *institutions,* however, research on the social history of media technologies connects papyrus and highways with bureaucratic empires (*see* WRITING MATERIALS), the diffusion of print with the Protestant Reformation (*see* PRINTING), the mass-circulation newspaper with European nationalism (*see* NEWSPAPER: HISTORY), TELEGRAPHY with the integration of the U.S. economy, television with the breakdown of PRIVACY, and so on. These studies emphasize physical (rather than message) attributes of the media such as precision (Elizabeth Eisenstein's "fixity," McLuhan's "hot"), ubiquity, and simultaneity. They also account for the ways in which social definition, deployment, and control of the media are harnessed and contested by competing social forces. They argue, on the whole, that media technologies contribute to the shaping of social organization; that is, they tell us *where to belong* or with whom to think. They are also linked with mass-society theories in sociology and political science that conceive of the media as establishing direct connections between leaders and masses at the expense of secondary institutions such as political parties, parliaments, or churches (*see* GOVERNMENT-MEDIA RELATIONS; POLITICAL COMMUNICATION). Franklin D. Roosevelt's "fireside chat," early national advertising campaigns, and television evangelism are examples of attempts to establish remote loyalties over the heads of local politicians, retailers, and churches, respectively (*see* ADVERTISING—HISTORY OF ADVERTISING; RADIO).

Ideology. Ideological effects, the other tradition claiming powerful and direct effects, is also of long standing and has also been little studied empirically. So-called critical or cultural studies are often contrasted with empirical studies, but this is a confusion of theoretical orientation and methodology. Drawing on the neo-Marxism of the Frankfurt school and its successors (*see* ADORNO, THEODOR), ideological theorists consider that all other traditions of communications research have wrongly focused on change, whereas the "true" effect of the media is in the *thwarting of change.* For the critical effects traditions the strengthening of prior opinions, attitudes, and actions as a result of exposure to media "reinforcement" is not simply a residual effect—the result of selectivity and interpersonal communication—but *the* powerful effect achieved by propagating the legitimacy and taken-for-grantedness of common sense and existing social arrangements. Reinforcing these extant views of "social reality" serves the stability of the system and the well-being of its elites. Once considered manipulative, current ideological theories perceive the process of hegemony as endemic to media representation and reproduction of "reality." Empirical research in this tradition presents the media as purveyors of a coherent image of social reality to heterogeneous mass audiences for whom media consumption forms an increasingly important bond and who often favor mass media (television in particular) over interpersonal influence and alternative sources of information (*see* CULTIVATION ANALYSIS; CULTURAL INDICATORS). Methodologically, the ideological tradition raises the question of how to study an effect such as the slowing or absence of change.

Other Approaches

In addition to ongoing work within the above-mentioned traditions, research on media effects continues to explore (1) still other conceptualizations of effect that may reveal the elusive power of mass communications and (2) still more subtle processes that intervene among media, messages, and their audiences. Further conceptualizations of effect are pointed in several directions. One direction goes counter to the cognitive bias of media research and focuses on the hypothesis that the media tell us *what to feel*. Examples may be drawn from the psychological work on the role of the media in stimulating and channeling "arousal" and from the psychoanalytically inspired studies of the gratifications and frustrations of cinema audiences and television viewers in their interactions with what they see on the screen. These studies contribute importantly to the redemption of the neglected concept of entertainment.

On the whole, however, most studies of media effects tend to deepen the existing cognitive bias. Indeed, it is possible to suggest that there is a shift away from the sociopsychological study of persuasion and influence toward the study of information— its control, its diffusion, its processing, its utility, its effects (*see* INFORMATION THEORY). Traditions of research on diffusion, knowledge-gap, agenda-setting, and to a certain extent campaign studies have been concerned with information, but the new media technologies have made this concern even more salient. At the individual level these studies treat the effect of the new media on patterns of accessing and managing information and on the new media's consequences for what to think, how to think, and so on. At the institutional level, the new media have reverted attention toward social theories of media technologies, somewhat neglected because of their overdeterminism. The case studies of the institution-building roles of the printing press, the telegraph, and other media still await a sociologically informed effort to generalize about the "careers" of new media and their effects that have resulted from the interaction of technological potential, elite and professional control (*see* PROFESSION), and patterns of popular usage. *See* COMPUTER: IMPACT.

An example that combines all these emphases— cognitive, affective, and integrative—comes from a tradition of study of the live broadcasting of public ceremonies. Pioneered by Kurt Lang and Gladys Lang, current research on televised events such as the pope's pilgrimages, royal weddings, the Watergate hearings, and the Olympics focuses attention on the ability of live television to declare "time out," to evoke the sense of occasion, to highlight a value, to define what is "real," to engender what anthropologist Victor Turner has called *communitas*. This integrative effect of the media, acting also to link individuals to one another and to the "center," corresponds to one of the major concerns of French sociologist ÉMILE DURKHEIM. These studies remind us again of the hypothesized power of the media to define, but also to defy, social boundaries.

There is a revival of interest in societal-level effects of the media both as technology and as content. One finds renewed attention, originating in both functional and critical schools, to the role of journalism in exacerbating, suppressing, and smoothing processes of conflict and change. Sociologists and political scientists are equally interested in institutional effects of media that are *not* mediated by effects on the mass, such as the role of the media in the making of foreign policy, in the design of political campaigns (*see* ELECTION), and in the organization of RELIGION. Ironically some of these effects are based on the assumptions made by institutional elites about the powerful (but unproved) effects of the media on the masses.

The continuing search for better or more varied conceptualizations of effect is joined with the continuing effort to specify the conditions and processes by means of which such effects are achieved. Thus major media events provide one of the rare examples in which early assumptions about the conditions of maximal media influence are fulfilled: attendance is almost "total," and message delivery is unmediated (direct) and immediate (simultaneous). Moreover, viewers don ceremonial and institutional roles such as mourner, juror, or sports fan, and effect is thereby enhanced.

In this respect the notion of patterns of involvement, arising from psychological theories of COGNITION and affect and from sociological theories of role, serves as a basis for a multidisciplinary attack on the neglected questions about the experience of viewing (or reading) and why people devote so much time and attention to the media (*see* LEISURE). Moreover, it serves as a call to humanists and sociologists to rejoin the ranks of communications researchers. For example, the concept of reader involvement or role—expanding the notions of audience selectivity and activity—has become the focus of a notable convergence among critical, literary, and functional theorists. Certain critical theorists have recently turned from their own readings to the empirical study of audience readings. The idea that a text may be read oppositionally, not just hegemonically, by real readers makes room in critical theory for ideological change. At the same time, and related to the revival of the idea of polysemic texts, literary theorists are finding interest in the roles that real readers assume in the "reception" of texts. For their part, gratifications researchers are occupied with the idea of "negotiated" readings in which meanings, and consequent effects, emerge from the interaction between texts and readers-in-roles (*see* MEANING).

Thus election campaigns, as conceived by the group of researchers headed by Jay Blumler, encounter readers in different roles, and these role differences influence patterns of meaning, use, and effect. Related work suggests that the differential availability of "public space" for political discussion is what accounts for the differential use of TELEVISION NEWS in different societies. Reader decodings of the same texts are seen to vary by the nature of reader involvement, which in turn is a function of the role of reader or viewer in different cultures, different societal contexts, different educational levels, and so on. The concepts of involvement and role add psychological and sociological depth to the persistent concern with the conditions under which the media and their messages vary in meaning, use, and effect.

Further study of media effects, therefore, will have to choose among competing assumptions about the nature of viewer involvement and decoding. The elementary debate over the extent of audience "activity" is still unresolved. At the individual level there will be greater emphasis on shared information and affect, less on persuasive influence. Greater formalization will be given to the variety of media effects and to the conditions of their maximization. Methodologies for the study of long-run effects will be further developed. At the societal level emphasis will be placed on the role of media technology and content in defining social boundaries, in the management of conflict, and in the organization of institutional realms such as politics, markets, religion, EDUCATION, and leisure.

Bibliography. Sandra Ball-Rokeach and Melvin L. DeFleur, "A Dependency Model of Media Effects," in *Intermedia*, 2d ed., ed. by Gary Gumpert and Robert Cathcart, New York, 1982; Jay G. Blumler and Elihu Katz, eds., *The Uses of Mass Communications*, Beverly Hills, Calif., 1974; Jennings Bryant and Dolf Zillmann, eds., *Perspectives on Media Effects*, Hillsdale, N.J., 1986; George Comstock, Steven Chafee, Nathan Katzman, Maxwell McCombs, and Donald Roberts, *Television and Human Behavior*, New York, 1978; Aimee Dorr, *Television and Children: A Special Medium for a Special Audience*, Beverly Hills, Calif., 1986; Elizabeth L. Eisenstein, *The Printing Press as an Agent of Change: Communication and Cultural Transformation in Early Modern Europe*, 2 vols., Cambridge and New York, 1979; Alvin W. Gouldner, *The Dialectic of Ideology and Technology*, New York, 1976; Lawrence Grossberg, "Strategies of Marxist Cultural Interpretation," *Critical Studies in Mass Communication* 1 (1984): 392–421; Max Horkheimer and Theodor Adorno, *The Dialectic of Enlightenment* (Dialektik der Aufklärung), trans. by John Cumming, New York, 1972; Donald Horton and Richard Wohl, "Mass Communication and Para-Social Interaction," *Psychiatry* 19 (1956): 215–229; Beverle Houston, "Viewing Television: The Metapsychology of Endless Consumption," *Quarterly Review of Film Studies* 9 (1984): 183–195; Carl I. Hovland, Irving L. Janis, and Harold H. Kelley, *Communication and Persuasion*, New Haven, Conn., 1953; Harold A. Innis, *The Bias of Communication*, Toronto, 1951; Elihu Katz, Martin L. Levin, and Herbert Hamilton, "Traditions of Research on the Diffusion of Innovation," *American Sociological Review* 28 (1963): 237–252; Joseph Klapper, *The Effects of Mass Communication*, Glencoe, Ill., 1960; Gladys Engel Lang and Kurt Lang, *Politics and Television Re-viewed*, Beverly Hills, Calif., 1984; Paul F. Lazarsfeld and Robert K. Merton, "Mass Communication, Popular Taste, and Organized Social Action," in *The Communication of Ideas*, ed. by Lyman Bryson, New York, 1948; Maxwell E. McCombs, "The Agenda-setting Approach," in *Handbook of Political Communication*, ed. by Dan Nimmo and Keith Sanders, Beverly Hills, Calif., 1981; William J. McGuire, "The Myth of Massive Media Impact," in *Public Communication and Behavior*, Vol. 1, ed. by George Comstock, New York, 1986; Marshall McLuhan, *Understanding Media: The Extensions of Man*, New York, 1964; Christian Metz, *The Imaginary Signifier* (Le signiant imaginaire), trans. by Celia Britton, Annwyl Williams, Ben Brewster, and Alfred Guzzetti, Bloomington, Ind., 1928; Everett M. Rogers, *Diffusion of Innovations* (1962), 3d ed., New York, 1983; Michael Schudson, *Advertising, the Uneasy Persuasion: Its Dubious Impact on American Society*, New York, 1984; Percy H. Tannenbaum, ed., *The Entertainment Functions of Television*, Hillsdale, N.J., 1980; P. J. Tichenor, G. A. Donohue, and C. N. Olien, "Mass Media and Differential Growth in Knowledge," *Public Opinion Quarterly* 34 (1970): 158–170; Charles R. Wright, *Mass Communication: A Sociological Perspective*, 3d ed., New York, 1986.

ELIHU KATZ

MASS OBSERVATION

Mass observation (M-O) was created in Great Britain in the years immediately preceding World War II. Although it was a unique enterprise, to be understood it must be placed in the context of the DOCUMENTARY movement. That is, it was part of a number of ways of using different cultural forms to represent everyday life. The idea of using impersonal forms of recording to express faithfully the experiences of ordinary people lies at the heart of the documentary desire to use art in the service of society. More specifically, M-O pioneered methodologies of social research to discover what ordinary people felt and thought about contemporary events and to disseminate its findings to the public at large.

M-O was created, following a correspondence in a radical British weekly, by Tom Harrisson, Humphrey Jennings, and Charles Madge. (Jennings largely dropped out after the first major study was published to work in documentary film, although his first film, *Spare Time*, is thought to display the influence of M-O concerns.) The first phase of M-O was therefore governed largely by the interests and activities of Harrisson and Madge. Harrisson had worked in ornithology and anthropology, particularly in East Asia, whereas Madge was a reporter—with a reputation as a poet—who worked for a popular tabloid in 1935–1937.

The initial impetus that brought these men together was a conviction that democracy, in the sense of a mass electorate, had not yet developed adequate means of mass participation in opinion formation. They felt that although contemporary society had greater facilities for information than ever before, people were isolated and alienated, resulting in and reinforcing a climate of ignorance, fear, and hunger for symbolic integration. The founders shared a critical concern with the prevalence of RUMOR, superstition, GOSSIP, and "mass wish-situations" in popular life, particularly with regard to the responses people made to national and international events. In setting up M-O the organizers saw themselves as providing both a scientific study of popular life and a means through which ordinary people could regain a sense of social identity. The knowledge M-O was to collect was a counterweight to the illusions of politics and ADVERTISING, a necessary foundation for a more democratic social order.

M-O was therefore partly a reaction to perceived inadequacies in conventional measurements of PUBLIC OPINION but also, more positively, an expression of a conviction that social changes, particularly new forms of mass communication and entertainment, had generated new modes of social consciousness that required corresponding innovations in forms of representation. M-O was to provide an "anthropology of ourselves" that would transmit public ATTITUDES from the people to the people.

The history of M-O can be divided into three phases. The first was the years 1937–1940, when a number of initiatives were pioneered; the second phase was during the war, when M-O redefined its work in the context of needs for more effective domestic PROPAGANDA; and finally, the years since 1949, when M-O became a market research agency. Later interest has been particularly engaged by the innovations in social documentary that M-O pioneered in its first phase. (Attempts to revive the spirit and practice of the original project occurred even in the early 1980s.)

The uniqueness of the M-O enterprise in this initial phase lay in the recruitment of amateur observers who either responded to questionnaires or sent in day reports and diaries. The rationale for this policy was that a corpus of observations by ordinary people would provide unique insights into popular feelings and behavior. The accumulation of a mass of observations would transform subjective impressions into objective knowledge. It would provide a chart or map of collective habits and social behavior. An attitude that contemporary society was a strange cultural landscape that needed novel methods of exploration was consistent with other types of documentary initiative but was also a challenging elaboration of innovations in community studies in the United States. M-O was, however, fiercely independent of conventional academic concerns. Its founders wished to document a collective social reality, but only in ways that would be immediately accessible to those who lived that reality so that it would in turn help to reshape that reality.

It was probably inevitable that the innovations in ideas and methods that inspired M-O in the early years should have generated several different types of observational study. From the beginning M-O had two headquarters—one based in Madge's home in London and the other based around Harrisson in Bolton (called Worktown in M-O publications). The London group collected reports from observers nationwide on a very wide range of topics, most characteristically focusing on the observers' experiences on specific days. It was hoped that the heterogeneity of the responses would enable the editors in London to compile an authentic picture of public opinion and behavior. The most famous of the day studies concerned the Coronation Day of George VI in 1937 (published as *May 12th*). It was a particularly interesting example, since it was the first time a royal ritual had been made instantly available nationally through mass broadcasting.

The work in Bolton was more akin to participant observation than the collection of unstructured diaries and observations. A number of people traveled north to paint, photograph, observe, and work in Bolton and associated towns such as the holiday resort of Blackpool. Once again a very rich archive of contemporary life was accumulated, but the profusion of material was generally too great to be handled (the only publication exclusively based on this material is *The Pub and the People*). Fascinating pictures of British tastes and attitudes were rescued from the many projects, and these had a strong political as well as cultural impact. However, the outbreak of the war precluded further developments in opinion formation through popular research.

In fact the initial objectives of M-O were changing quite quickly under the pressures of experience, greater realism, and changing circumstances. The onset of the war against fascism, however, catalyzed arguments within the organization. Madge and Harrisson had increasingly been at odds personally, and Harrisson's decision to make the services of M-O available to the Ministry of Information led to Madge's resignation. He felt that the dangers of research as a form of social control, which had been sensed from the beginning, were intensified when a method of popular observation became a servant of government rather than of the people. The politics of social knowledge had always been fundamental to the M-O enterprise, and the relationship with government raised issues that altered the character of the research enterprise. Subsequent work became more dominated by full-time research workers; it became a specialist rather than a popular form of inquiry.

This is not to imply a simple equation of politicized research with the earlier work and more "professional" research with the latter. The studies of popular responses to the "phony war" (*War Begins at Home*) and the mobilization of women workers in industry (*War Factory*), for example, were useful and important studies, but the research was increasingly administrative rather than expository. As part of this process statistical information became more important, although the element of qualitative observation remained a defining feature and gave the research a distinctive character that remained controversial.

Financing a novel enterprise such as M-O had always been tricky. In the early days the support of people such as the publisher Gollancz had been crucial, in combination with an ingenious mixture of lecture fees, royalties, gifts and subsidies, and small pieces of sponsored research. In the second phase the opportunities for market research were more thoroughly explored. During the war years several M-O books and pamphlets were published under the auspices of the Advertising Service Guild, which in itself marks a distinctive step away from the polemical engagements of the early years toward more manipulative studies of public opinion. The personnel also changed during these years. Harrisson, who was in the army from 1942 to 1946, could not adapt to England after the war and went back to East Asia. Although a number of committed individuals had remained with the organization, in the postwar years there was a lack of clear objectives. Eventually in 1949 M-O became Mass Observation Limited, an unusual but nevertheless strictly commercial market research organization. Partly in order to attract clients and partly to meet the criticisms of the rapidly growing world of academic social science, M-O's research practices became more standardized with more emphasis on quantitative research profiles. A unique research initiative had been absorbed into the domains of conventional knowledge.

In the history of social research M-O has usually been dismissed as an eccentric, if fascinating, digression from the mainstream. M-O was always populist rather than academic in orientation, theory was deliberately eschewed, and the somewhat indiscriminate enthusiasm for information meant that the researchers were often swamped by their material. The lack of rigor in designing the collection of observations also meant that while the ARCHIVES of the organization proved fascinating for students of recent social history, they were difficult to use. Despite these drawbacks, however, M-O's importance lies in the challenge it posed to the status of science and exper-

tise in interpreting public opinion. While its methods remained vulnerable to the criticisms of academic social science, in retrospect we can see that the group was attempting to pioneer an entirely different relationship between researcher and community, a prospect that remains to be explored.

See also CINÉMA VÉRITÉ; MASS COMMUNICATIONS RESEARCH; MASS MEDIA EFFECTS; PERSUASION; POLITICAL SOCIALIZATION.

Bibliography. Angus Calder, "Mass Observation, 1937–1949," in *Essays on the History of British Sociological Research*, ed. by Martin Bulmer, Cambridge, 1985; Angus Calder and Dorothy Sheridan, eds., *Speak for Yourself: A Mass Observation Anthology, 1937–1949*, Oxford, 1984; Thomas H. Harrisson, *Living Through the Blitz*, London, 1976; Tom Jeffery, *Mass Observation: A Short History* (Centre for Contemporary Cultural Studies, occasional paper, SP no. 55), Birmingham, Eng., 1978; Humphrey Jennings and Charles Madge, eds., *May 12th Mass-Observation Day Surveys: An Account of Coronation Day*, London, 1937; Charles Madge and Thomas H. Harrisson, eds., *Britain*, London, 1939; idem, *Mass Observation*, London, 1937; idem, *War Begins at Home*, London, 1940; idem, *War Factory*, London, 1943; J. Sommerfield and Bruce Watkin, *The Pub and the People*, London, 1943, reprint (with a new introduction by Tom Harrisson) 1971.

DAVID CHANEY

MATHEMATICS

There are two principal factions in modern mathematics: "pure" mathematicians develop the subject for its own intrinsic value; "applied" mathematicians develop the subject in order to solve practical, real-life problems. Purists compare themselves to architects and their applied colleagues to skilled laborers. As they see it purists are the truly creative persons, coming up with the ideas that applied mathematicians then merely use as tools. Applied mathematics, well-known purist Peter Halmos once said, is "just plain bad mathematics. [I]t solves problems about waterways, sloping beaches, airplane flights, atomic bombs, and refrigerators; but just the same, much too often it is . . . badly arranged, sloppy, untrue, . . . unorganized, and unarchitectured mathematics."

In rebuttal, applied mathematicians see themselves as having all the qualifications of purists plus the additional credential of wanting and knowing *how* to apply the fruits of their creativity to serve humanity. As applied mathematician Morris Kline once put it, "the greatest contribution mathematicians [have] made, and should continue to make, [is] to help Man understand the world about him."

This disagreement among mathematicians has had great impact on how and what children are taught

Figure 1. *(Mathematics)* Facing the impossible. According to Gödel's theorem, trying to prove that pure mathematics is logical is as futile as trying to make sense of this visually ambiguous figure. From R. L. Gregory, *Eye and Brain: The Psychology of Seeing,* London: Weidenfeld and Nicolson, 1966, detail from cover.

about mathematics. The highly publicized and ill-fated "new math" of the 1960s, for example, was largely the brainchild of pure mathematicians. The unprecedented emphasis on rigor and fundamentals overtaxed both teachers and parents, many of whom found themselves unable to help with their children's homework. "The movement to teach rigorous mathematics was and is a mistake," says Kline. "The mathematics that is most important . . . and attractive to students is the kind that applies to their world."

Origins and Development

Historically, applied mathematics preceded pure mathematics. The Egyptians first used mathematics four thousand years ago for agricultural and commercial reasons. They used formulas to compute acreage, storage space, profits, taxes, and other such practical matters. These formulas were surmised from real experience, not abstract reasoning. They were mathematical rules of thumb akin to today's Dolbeer's law, which describes the relationship between air temperature and the chirping of crickets (air temperature in degrees Fahrenheit is equal to one-quarter the number of chirps per minute plus forty, or $T = N/4 + 40$).

Precisely because it was so empirical, Egyptian mathematics could also be mystifying. The formulas were useful, but many of them had no logical explanation. An Egyptian would believe in them because they appeared to work and not because of an understanding of *why* they worked.

In contrast, pure mathematics had its origins in ancient Greece. Unlike the Egyptians, the Greeks were disinclined to use formulas that had no apparent logic to them. Merely because a formula worked was insufficient reason for the Greeks to rely on it. The only mathematics they considered reliable was that which could be surmised from logical, not empirical, evidence.

Thales of Miletus (625?–?547 B.C.E.) is generally credited with having been the first person in history to introduce the concept of a logical proof into mathematics. But it was ARISTOTLE who fleshed out the concept some two centuries later by writing the

first book on deductive logic. Aristotle titled his classic work the *Organon* (Greek for "instrument of reason"). In it he spells out fourteen rules and several canons by which conclusions can be surmised logically from assumptions.

Aristotle's canons include the law of identity (everything is identical to itself), the law of contradiction (nothing can both be and not be), and the law of the excluded middle (something is either true or false; there is no third possibility). The canons were intended to express verities that most of us would call common sense, whereas the rules were a distillation of Aristotle's meticulous study of syllogisms.

A syllogism is a three-step exercise in deductive reasoning of the form

(If) all men are mortal
(and if) Socrates is a man
(then) Socrates is mortal.

The first two statements are assumptions; the third statement is the conclusion, which, as Aristotle put it, "follows of necessity" from the assumptions. We may doubt the credibility of the assumptions, Aristotle explained, but if the rules of deductive reasoning have been followed there is no doubting the conclusion.

Because it was so logical, Greek mathematics could be irrelevant or downright fanciful. For example, Aristotelian logic permits one to argue that

(If) three unicorns are worth one mermaid
(and) one mermaid is worth three elves
(then) one unicorn is worth one elf.

The argument is logical, but it is not useful or true in terms of what we know to be real. *See* SYMBOLIC LOGIC.

Applied Mathematics

True to their dissimilar origins, pure and applied mathematics today remain related but distinct subjects. Applied mathematicians are like scientists; pure mathematicians are like poets, constrained by the rules of reason and rhyme. Whereas applied mathematicians and scientists wish to describe the real

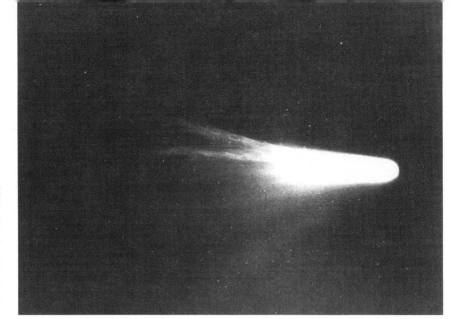

Figure 2. *(Mathematics)* Predicting the future. Photograph of Halley's comet taken from CT10, March 7, 1986. Using mathematics, astronomers can predict the exact itinerary of Halley's comet, the precise moment of a solar eclipse, and the particulars of many other celestial phenomena. The Bettmann Archive, Inc.

world, pure mathematicians and poets endeavor to describe the world of their own imagination.

Both pure and applied mathematics are basically quantitative disciplines, but the two rely on completely different standards of proof. In judging the validity of a formula or thesis, applied mathematicians ask: Is it relevant? Can it be used to describe something in the real world? Like scientists testing a hypothesis, applied mathematicians rely on their powers of observation to determine the answer.

Perhaps the quintessential example of applied mathematics is arithmetic, the study of numbers (*see* NUMBER). People who know nothing else about mathematics understand the relevance of arithmetic. Millions use it every day to balance checkbooks, follow recipes, compute mileage, and calculate the best deal when shopping for groceries.

Another outstanding although less widely known example of applied mathematics is the calculus, the study of infinity. It was first developed in the seventeenth century by Isaac Newton and Gottfried Leibniz, and it has become the mathematical basis of modern science, used by astronomers to compute the path of Halley's comet, by physicists to design a nuclear bomb, by chemists to estimate the efficacy of a new drug, and by biologists to describe fetal development.

Applied mathematics, to put it briefly, is the extremely precise language of science. When used properly it is virtually unambiguous. In contrast, social languages such as English are about 25 percent ambiguous.

Pure Mathematics

In judging the validity of a formula or thesis, pure mathematicians ask: Is it logical? Can it be surmised, following the rules of Aristotelian logic, from a set of explicitly stated assumptions? Unlike scientists,

pure mathematicians rely on their powers of pure reason to determine the answer.

Perhaps the most familiar example of pure mathematics is ordinary geometry, the study of shapes. Geometry originated in ancient Egypt as bits and pieces of practical knowledge about land surveying and ARCHITECTURE. The word *geometry* derives from the Greek for "to measure the earth."

The fundamental ideas about points, lines, planes, and solids were gleaned from everyday experiences with landmarks, footpaths, farmers' fields, and granite blocks. The important geometrical concept of parallel lines as lines that never meet was likely associated in Egyptian minds with such earthy phenomena as plow lines or the ruts dug into roads by two-wheeled carts.

By Euclid's time, around 300 B.C.E., there had been accumulated hundreds of geometrical rules of thumb. Euclid showed how they all could be deduced logically from just ten assumptions. These assumptions, moreover, were quite believable, including apparent truisms such as "A straight line can be drawn from any point to any other point," "All right angles are equal to each other," "If equals are added to equals, the sums are equal," and "The whole is equal to the sum of its parts."

There were mathematicians who challenged some of Euclid's assumptions, but, as Aristotle had shown, there was no doubting the conclusions. Euclid's theorems were all if-then arguments derived strictly according to the rules of logic. As a result Euclidean geometry was a model of pure mathematics.

Theoretical Implications

Twentieth-century mathematicians in both the pure and the applied traditions have made startling discoveries about the two most important questions: Is mathematics as a whole logical, and is mathematics as a whole relevant? The first surprise is that despite their impressive efforts, pure mathematicians have not been able to prove that mathematics as a whole is logical. In fact, they have come to the unsettling conclusion that it is actually *impossible* to prove such a thing.

The first to recognize this was Viennese logician Kurt Gödel. In 1931 he proved that there will always be mathematical truths that cannot be established as being true, using the rules of Aristotelian logic. Gödel reached that conclusion by considering a statement akin to "This statement cannot be proved true, using the rules of Aristotelian logic." What Gödel soon realized was that this statement leads inescapably to a logical contradiction. Suppose, on the one hand, we prove it to be true, using the rules of Aristotelian logic. Then by its own assertion it is false. Now suppose, on the other hand, we prove it to be false. Then by its own assertion it is true. Either way there is a logical contradiction. And yet in a rather bizarre way, precisely because of our inability to establish it as being true or false, the statement *is* true: "This statement cannot be proved true, using the rules of Aristotelian logic."

Gödel proved that mathematics is and always will be riddled with an indefinite number of these unprovable truths. If mathematical knowledge is thought of as a body of laws, then Gödel proved that there will always be loopholes in the laws. Try to eliminate the ambiguities by passing new laws, he demonstrated, and new loopholes will inevitably be created. Is mathematics logical? The answer is permanently ambiguous.

Applied mathematicians also have arrived at a surprising answer to their own age-old question, Is mathematics relevant? The answer appears to be yes, but the reasons for it are not very clear. Mathematics is relevant in the sense that it can be used to represent physical reality exceedingly well. Only with mathematics are we able to account for the movement of planets around the sun, the shapes of molecules, and the color of the sky. "The book of Nature," as Galileo once asserted, "is written in the language of mathematics."

Puzzlingly, pure mathematics has proved to be every bit as relevant as applied mathematics. That is unexpected considering that pure mathematics is created to be logical, not necessarily realistic. Abstract mathematical creations such as negative numbers, imaginary numbers, and matrices were invented by pure mathematicians and had no purpose other than to help make mathematics more logical. Yet each one of these ideas has since been found to describe some real phenomenon. Negative numbers, for example, can be used to describe a novel form of matter called antimatter. Imaginary numbers can be used to describe the fourth dimension of time. And matrices

can be used to describe the world of the atom, centerpiece of modern quantum physics.

If only a few pure mathematical ideas had turned out to have some relevance in describing the natural world, then the coincidence might be considered nothing more than chance. But in fact the coincidence is great enough to have compelled the German mathematician, physicist, and Nobel laureate Eugene Wigner to speak of it as the "unreasonable effectiveness of mathematics" in describing reality. Mathematics does not merely invent ideas that just happen to describe physical reality; rather, the mathematical imagination seems to be an extra sense with which we literally perceive the natural world (*see* MODE). If thought of in this way, the coincidence between the natural world and the mathematical world is not any more mysterious than the coincidence between the natural world and the world revealed to us through the five senses.

If a mathematical sixth sense does exist, modern biology suggests that it probably evolved, just as did all the animal senses, in order to enhance our survivability as a species. "Perceiving . . . reality," as the French biologist and Nobel laureate François Jacob put it, "is a biological necessity." In this view, therefore, abstractions like negative numbers, imaginary numbers, and matrices are not merely figments of a mathematician's imagination; by virtue of helping us to perceive more accurately the world around us, they are instruments of our survival.

Bibliography. David Bergamini et al., *Mathematics*, New York, 1963; Michael Guillen, *Bridges to Infinity: The Human Side of Mathematics*, New York, 1983; Morris Kline, *Mathematics and the Search for Knowledge*, New York, 1985; Lynn M. Osen, *Women in Mathematics*, Cambridge, Mass., 1974, reprint 1982; Dan Pedoe, *The Gentle Art of Mathematics*, New York, 1958, reprint 1972; Jagjit Singh, *Great Ideas of Modern Mathematics: Their Nature and Use*, New York, 1959.

MICHAEL A. GUILLEN

MAXWELL, JAMES (1831–1879)

Scottish physicist whose electromagnetic equations helped provide the theoretical basis for later advances in communications technology, including RADIO and television broadcasting. James Clerk Maxwell was born into a well-to-do family in Edinburgh, Scotland. His mother died when he was eight years old, and he was raised by a father who encouraged his interest in science. After attending the University of Edinburgh for three years, he studied MATHEMATICS at Trinity College, Cambridge University, graduating in 1854.

Maxwell's academic career included two more years at Cambridge as a bachelor-scholar and a fellow, and professorships at Marischal College (Aberdeen) and King's College (London). From 1865 to 1871 he devoted himself solely to his research; in 1871 he reluctantly gave up his independent study to become the first professor of experimental physics at the Cavendish Laboratory of Cambridge University.

Maxwell sought to pull together the many discrete experimental results in a given area—or, as he put it, "to deduce the most general conclusions from the data at our disposal." He made advances in such fields as color vision, the kinetic theory of gases, and statistical mechanics.

But Maxwell's greatest achievement—and the one with the most important implications for communications—was his unification of the fields of electricity and magnetism. Maxwell's advancements in this area built on the work of MICHAEL FARADAY, who rejected the predominant view that electricity and magnetism could be explained in terms of action at a distance (i.e., that they act on distant objects directly, with nothing intervening). He postulated the existence of "lines of force" extending in every direction from a magnetic pole or an electric charge. Together all the lines of force associated with a particular magnetic pole or electric charge constitute a field of force, he believed. Faraday, however, was an experimenter, not a mathematician, and his field ideas were not widely accepted. Maxwell, on the other hand, was a skillful mathematician. After reading Faraday's *Experimental Researches in Electricity*, he spent years consolidating and expanding Faraday's work and developing his own electromagnetic theory. Eventually Maxwell was able to express this synthesis in mathematical notation—his groundbreaking equations, in which the idea of fields was central.

The term *Maxwell's Equations* means almost universally to physicists and engineers a certain set of four tensor equations connecting electric and magnetic flux densities and electric and magnetic field strengths with the electric charge density. If mathematical results are translated into physical facts, the equations account for all the experimental results known at Maxwell's time and, within certain limitations, today.

Wavelike characteristics had previously been noted. However, Maxwell's electromagnetic theory, as expressed by his equations, maintained that any change in electric and magnetic fields will result in the propagation of electromagnetic waves. Furthermore, the equations predicted not only that light consists of electromagnetic waves but also that electromagnetic radiation exists at wavelengths longer and shorter than light. Thus the theoretical foundations of telephony, radio, television, and radar and the use of

Figure 1. *(Maxwell, James)* James Maxwell. The Bettmann Archive, Inc.

X rays, infrared rays, and ultraviolet rays owe much to Maxwell (*see also* SPECTRUM).

Maxwell's Equations have had a great practical impact and a philosophical impact of nearly equal importance. The significance of the replacement of the widely held belief in action at a distance with the field theory implicit in Maxwell's Equations was summed up by the physicist Albert Einstein: "This change in the conception of Reality is the most profound and the most fruitful that physics has experienced since the time of Newton."

JOHN G. BRAINERD

MEAD, GEORGE HERBERT (1863–1931)

U.S. philosopher and social psychologist, one of the founders of the school of thought that came to be called symbolic interactionism. The son of a Congregational minister, George Herbert Mead eventually turned away from his religious upbringing. While attending Oberlin College he met Henry Castle, with whom he established a close relationship and whose sister Helen he married in 1891. Castle persuaded Mead to join him in graduate studies at Harvard. There Mead was influenced by Josiah Royce, in whose philosophical idealism he found liberation from theology and Puritan ethics.

After studying physiological psychology in Berlin, Mead in 1891 joined the University of Michigan's philosophy department, which was chaired by JOHN DEWEY. Dewey and Mead formed a lifelong friendship, and when Dewey was appointed head of the University of Chicago's philosophy department in 1894, Mead followed him, remaining at Chicago until his death in 1931.

Along with Dewey and CHARLES HORTON COOLEY, Mead laid the foundations of symbolic interactionism. Besides Dewey, several influences played a major role in the development of Mead's thought. Hegelian idealism initially provided him with a broad context for inquiries into the nature of human experience, though in later years Mead turned to more empirical approaches. WILLIAM JAMES's *Principles of Psychology*, particularly its treatment of the human mind, presented, Mead believed, more scientific explanations of human nature. Another great influence was CHARLES DARWIN's theory of evolution, which inspired Mead to view the emergence of human nature and consciousness not in terms of immutable essences but as a process.

According to Mead, consciousness is responsible for the emergence of human beings as a distinct species. The individual's consciousness, in turn, emerges from a process of social interaction—from communication with other organisms—and requires reflexivity (the ability to reflect upon oneself, to become an object to oneself).

Mead begins his analysis of self-consciousness (which, he says, is what distinguishes a human being from a mere organism) by addressing the question of how an individual can get outside himself or herself experientially in such a way as to become an object to himself or herself (a process he calls self-indication). The answer lies in the ability to view oneself from the perspective of another—as the subject of another's reflections. In group settings the individual must internalize the generalized viewpoint of the social group to which he or she belongs—that is, he or she must take the position of the "generalized other" vis-à-vis himself or herself. Self-indication, Mead feels, is thus possible only when one perceives oneself as part of a social group; self-consciousness is impossible in isolation. Discussing mind and self, Mead said:

A self can arise only where there is a social process within which this self has had its initiation. It arises within that process. For that process, the communication and participation to which I have referred is essential. That is the way in which selves have arisen. That is where the individual is in a social process in which he is a part, where he does influence himself as he does others. . . . And there he turns back upon himself, directs himself. He takes

over those experiences which belong to his own organism. He identifies them with himself. What constitutes the particular structure of his experience is what we call his "thought." It is the conversation which goes on within the self. This is what constitutes his mind. For it is within this so-called "thought," of course, that he interprets his experience.

Human communication is made possible by the capacity of people to be objects to themselves. Human communication differs from other species' processes of communication because it uses significant symbols, which are gestures (including verbal gestures) that have identical meanings to ourselves and to others (*see* GESTURE). Communication with significant symbols—that is, human communication—occurs when a message affects not only others but also the individual who initiated it. Only humans can incorporate as part of their behavior the impact that a communication directed to others has had on themselves. Communication among humans is thus determined, according to Mead, by the reflexive capacity of people—by their self-consciousness. As Mead maintained: "Through the use of language, through the use of the significant symbol, then, the individual does take the attitude of others, especially these common attitudes, so that he finds himself taking the same attitude toward himself that the community takes."

Mead himself published only a few papers and no books. His work became known to sociologists and social psychologists at the University of Chicago through the graduate students who took his courses, disseminated his ideas and his notes and unpublished writings, and collected their own lecture notes from his classes for what became the book *Mind, Self, and Society*. Recognition by philosophers came later, as Mead's notes and writings were published posthumously. Mead's work has been very influential in social psychology, sociology, and the field of human communication. In communications it has been a foundation upon which the symbolic interaction perspective has been built.

Bibliography. Don F. Faules and Dennis C. Alexander, *Communication and Social Behavior: A Symbolic Interaction Perspective*, Reading, Mass., 1978; B. Aubrey Fisher, *Perspectives on Human Communication*, New York, 1978; George Herbert Mead, *The Individual and the Social Self*, ed. with an intro. by David L. Miller, Chicago, 1982; idem, *Mind, Self, and Society*, ed. with an intro. by Charles Morris, Chicago, 1934, reprint 1962; idem, *Movements of Thought in the Nineteenth Century*, ed. by Merritt H. Moore, Chicago, 1936; idem, *The Philosophy of the Act*, ed. with an intro. by Charles Morris, Chicago, 1938; idem, *The Philosophy of the Present*, ed. by Arthur E. Murphy, Chicago and London, 1932.

ABRAHAM NOSNIK

MEAD, MARGARET (1901–1978)

U.S. anthropologist. Margaret Mead's pioneering work in cultural anthropology contributed significantly to the evolving discipline of communications. She made extensive use of PHOTOGRAPHY and CINEMATOGRAPHY for documentation and analysis and in so doing was an important catalyst in the rise of the ETHNOGRAPHIC FILM and an influence on the DOCUMENTARY film field in general. Her work in Samoa made her a leader and inspiration to women who sought but because of their GENDER were denied opportunities for similar work in exotic places. Together with her teacher FRANZ BOAS and her close associate Ruth Benedict she made the notion of cultural patterns, developed by Benedict in her *Patterns of Culture* (1934), scientifically respectable.

Born in Philadelphia, Pennsylvania, Mead attended DePauw University for one year, transferred to Barnard College, where she received her B.A., and completed her graduate work at Columbia University, where she received her Ph.D. in 1929. When she was not away doing fieldwork her home base was New York—at the American Museum of Natural History,

where she was a curator of ethnology, and at Columbia University, where she was a member of the Department of Anthropology.

Mead learned to be an observer early in life. Her grandmother encouraged her to observe and keep notes on the behavior of her younger sisters, and this early training was invaluable for work in a field in which systematic observation and recording was one of the major methodologies. Mead contributed to many areas in anthropology—CULTURE and personality studies, research on child-rearing practices and sex roles, culture change, cultural patterns, NONVERBAL COMMUNICATION—and knew that one methodology was not suitable for work on all research problems. She was not afraid to borrow methodologies from other disciplines and to apply them to problems in anthropology. Her use of cross-cultural data to explore theoretical issues, as evidenced in *Sex and Temperament in Three Primitive Societies* (1935), presaged the development and expansion of area files and the exploitation of comparative techniques previously used by biologists but largely neglected by anthropologists. She was among the earliest users of the right-angle prism for studies of human commu-

Figure 1. *(Mead, Margaret)*   Margaret Mead visiting families in Byun Gede, Bali, in 1959. Twenty years previously, she had lived in and observed this same village community. Copyright Ken Heyman.

nicative behavior (although some contemporary ethologists unfortunately neglected her work and had to rediscover this important technique). A most elegant example of this approach is provided in *Balinese Character: A Photographic Analysis* (1942), a study done with her third husband, GREGORY BATESON. Mead and Bateson made many films together. She felt that photographic or film data were valuable checks against errors in observation and gave the researcher the freedom to study and reinterpret what had been observed away from the activity itself. One of Mead and Bateson's best-known films, *Bathing Babies in Three Cultures,* reflected her interest in mother-child interaction and nonverbal communication. Mead also did seminal work in the dynamics of conferences and workshops (*The Small Conference: An Innovation in Communication,* with Paul Byers, 1969). Finally, she succeeded to a scarcely equaled degree in making the popularization of difficult scientific issues a respectable activity for academics.

Mead's interests were wide ranging, and she believed in the value of interdisciplinary research. She "adopted" young women and men in various cognate disciplines—sociology, psychology, zoology—and explored with them issues of common interest. Thus she pursued questions on the importance of early maternal attachments with clinicians as well as discussing imprinting in geese with students of Konrad Lorenz. She did more than compel these surrogate offspring to review their ideas from new perspectives; she also brought them together and thus forced them to conduct their discourse in a jargon-free fashion. It was not a coincidence that a common thread in all their work was an interest in functional and structural features of communication. This effect was reinforced by Bateson, with whom many also had contact.

Mead's image has often been viewed as controversial, but that could be taken as a tribute to her willingness to allow herself to reflect publicly on issues of popular concern. The hundreds of popular articles she wrote or generated defy cataloging, addressing as they do virtually every contemporary problem. Her ability to express ideas in the idiom of her audience, another evidence of her communication skills, and her studious avoidance of ad hominem attacks on presumed adversaries contributed to her becoming the best-known and among the most-admired figures in twentieth-century anthropology. In 1979 she was posthumously awarded the U.S. presidential Medal of Freedom.

Bibliography. Mary Catherine Bateson, *With a Daughter's Eye: A Memoir of Margaret Mead and Gregory Bateson,* New York, 1984; Joan Gordon, ed., *Margaret Mead: The Complete Bibliography, 1925–1973,* The Hague, 1976; Jane Howard, *Margaret Mead: A Life,* New York, 1984; Margaret Mead, *An Anthropologist at Work: Writings of Ruth Benedict,* Boston, 1959, reprint Westport, Conn., 1977; idem, *Blackberry Winter: My Earlier Years,* New York, 1972, reprint 1985.

PETER H. KLOPFER

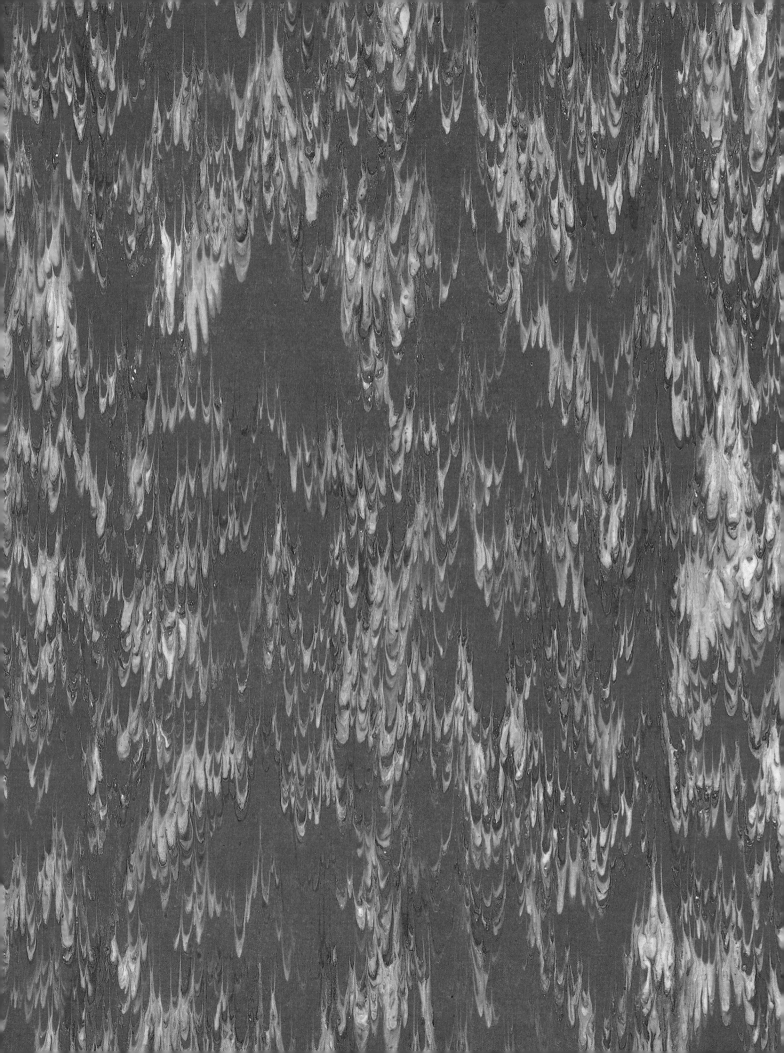